Index of American
Periodical Verse
1995

Rafael Catalá
and
James D. Anderson

The Scarecrow Press, Inc.
Lanham, Md., & London
1997

SCARECROW PRESS, INC.

Published in the United States of America
by Scarecrow Press, Inc.
4720 Boston Way
Lanham, Maryland 20706

4 Pleydell Gardens, Folkestone
Kent CT20 2DN, England

British Library Cataloguing in Publication Information Available

Library of Congress Cataloging-in-Publication Data

ISSN 0090-9130

ISBN 0–8108–3391-3 (cloth : alk. paper)

Contents

Preface

This twenty-fifth annual volume of the *Index* was produced with the cooperation of 300 participating periodicals from Canada, the United States, and the Caribbean. Nearly 7,000 entries (6,963) for individual poets and translators are included, with 19,698 entries for individual poems. A separate index provides access by title or first line.

The importance of the *Index* grows as its necessity becomes more apparent in circles of contemporary poetry research. The increasing demand for inclusion corroborates this fact. The *Index* constitutes an objective measure of poetry in North America, recording not only the publication of our own poets in Canada, the United States, and the Caribbean, but also those from other lands and cultures and from other times. Of course, the *Index*'s primary purpose is to show what poems have been published by particular poets, what poems have been translated by particular translators, and who wrote poems with particular titles or first lines. But taken together, the *Index* reveals trends and influences: the ebb and flow of particular poets, as well as the influence of cultures of other lands and times as represented by their poets published in North American journals.

James D. Anderson has made a major contribution to the *Index* by designing and refining computer programs that greatly facilitate the indexing process, proof-reading and error-checking, control of cross-references and consistency in names, sorting, formatting, and typesetting. To him also goes credit for managing relations with participating journals and for seeing that indexing gets done in a timely and accurate manner.

I dedicate this volume to Martha Park Sollberger, librarian *emerita*, for her valuable assistance over many years. She passed away on February 15, 1997.

Rafael Catalá
Co-Editor

Introduction

The *Index of American Periodical Verse* indexes poems published in a broad cross-section of poetry, literary, scholarly, popular, general, and "little" magazines, journals, and reviews published in the United States, Canada, and the Caribbean. These periodicals are listed in the "Periodicals Indexed" section, together with names of editors, addresses, issues indexed in this volume, and subscription information. Selection of periodicals to index is the responsibility of the editors, based on recommendations of poets, librarians, literary scholars, and publishers. Publishers participate by supplying copies of all issues to the editors. Criteria for inclusion include the quality of poems, their presentation, and the status or reputation of poets. Within these very broad and subjective guidelines, the editors attempt to include a cross-section of periodicals by type of publisher and publication, place of publication, language, and type of poetry. Periodicals published outside of North America are included only if they have North American editors.

Compilation

Citation data are compiled using the WordStar™ word-processing program, version 4, on an MS/DOS™ computer. "Shorthand" macro programs are used to repeat author headings for multiple poems by the same poet, create translator entries from author entries for translated poems, and transform complex author names into cross-reference entries. Sorting is done by "ARISsort," a fast program for sorting very large files written by Fred A. Rowley. Title entries are extracted from the original author entries. Sorted and formatted entries are transferred to a Macintosh computer with laser printer for typesetting and page formatting using Microsoft Word and PageMaker programs.

Persons interested in the precise details of compilation, including the computer programs used for error-checking, sorting, and formatting, should write to the editors at P.O. Box 38, New Brunswick, NJ 08903-0038. The *Index* data for 1982 through 1995 are available from the editors on microcomputer disks.

Names and Cross-References

Because many poets have compound surnames and surnames containing various prefixes, we recognize the need for systematic provision of cross-references from alternative forms of surname to the form chosen for entry in the *Index*. We have included cross-references whenever the form used for entry does not fall under the last part or element of the name. In addition, many poets pub-lish under different forms of the same name, for example, with or without a middle initial.   When poets are known to use different forms of the same name, alternative forms may be indicated using the format authorized by the *Anglo-American Cataloguing Rules*, Second Edition.   For example:

WHEATLEY, Pat (Patience)

This heading indicates that this poet has poems published under two forms of name: Pat Wheatley and Patience Wheatley.

When two or more different names refer to the same poet, one name will be chosen, with "see" references to the chosen name from other names.   When it is not possible to determine with assurance whether a single poet is using variant forms of name or different poets have similar names, both names will be used.   In such cases, "see also" references may be added to headings to remind users to check the variant name forms that might possibly refer to the same poet.

Format and Arrangement of Entries

The basic format and style of the *Index* remain unchanged.   Poets are arranged alphabetically first by surname, then by forenames.   In creating this alphabetical sequence, we have adopted principles of alphanumeric arrangement adopted in 1980 by the American Library Association and the Library of Congress.   Names are arranged on the basis of their spelling, rather than their pronunciation, so that, for example, names beginning with "Mac" and "Mc" are placed in separate sections.   Similarly, a space has a consistent arrangement value, coming before all numerals or letters.   Therefore, similar compound and prefixed surnames are often separated by some distance, as illustrated in the following examples.   Note that "De BOLT" precedes "DeBEVOISE" by a considerable number of entries.

De ANGELIS	Van BRUNT
De BOLT	Van DUYN
De GRAVELLES	Van HALTEREN
De LOACH	Van TOORN
De PALCHI	Van TROYER
De RONSARD	Van WERT
De VAUL	Van WINCKEL
DEAL	VANCE
DeBEVOISE	Vander DOES
DeFOE	VANDERBEEK
DEGUY	VanDEVENTER
Del VECCHIO	
DeLISLE	
DeMOTT	
DENNISON	
DER-HOVANESSIAN	
DESY	
DeYOUNG	

Abbreviations are also arranged on the basis of spelling, rather than pronunciation or meaning, so that "ST. JOHN" is *not* arranged as "SAINT JOHN," but as "S+T+space+JOHN."   Punctuation (including apostrophes and accents), signs, and symbols (other than alphabetic letters and numerals) are not considered,

viii

but a hyphen is arranged as if it were a space. Initial articles ("a," "an," "the" and their equivalents in other languages) are ignored in titles of poems and in names of corporate bodies, but they are considered in the arrangement of names of persons and places (e.g., La RUE, El Paso). Numerals, including Roman numerals, are arranged in numerical order preceding alphabetical letters rather than as if they were spelled out. Family names are arranged before considering forenames, so that "AN, Yue" comes before "AN TSAOI, Máire Mhac."

Under each poet's name, poems are arranged alphanumerically by title or, if there is no title, by first line. Poems with only "Untitled" printed as if it were the title are entered as "Untitled" plus the first line of the poem. Poems whose titles consist only of "Poem" are treated in the same way: the first line is added to this title. In the title index, two entries are provided, one under "Untitled" or "Poem" plus the first line, and one directly under the first line. Numbered poems are handled in the same way. Under poets, initial numbers are treated as the first part of titles, and they are so entered. In the title index, they are entered both under their initial numbers and under the part following the number, if any.

Poem titles and first lines are placed within quotation marks. All significant words of titles are capitalized, but in first lines, only the first word and proper nouns are capitalized. Incomplete excerpts from larger works are followed by the note "Excerpt" or "Excerpts," or, if they are presented as complete sections, by "Selection" or "Selections." The title, first line, or number of excerpts or selections may follow if given in the publication. For example:

WALCOTT, Derek
"Midsummer" (Selections: XXXIV-XXXVI). [Agni] (18) 83, p. 5-7.

WEBB, Phyllis
"The Vision Tree" (Selection: "I Daniel"). [PoetryCR] (5:2) Wint 83-84, p. 11.

WAINWRIGHT, Jeffrey
"Heart's Desire" (Excerpt: "Some Propositions and Part of a Narrative"). [Agni] (18) 83, p. 37.

WATTEN, Barret
"One Half" (Excerpts). [ParisR] (24:86) Wint 82, p. 112-113.

If an excerpt is treated as a complete "sub-work," it receives an independent entry, with reference to the larger work in a note. For example:

ANDERSON, Jack
"Magnets" (from "The Clouds of That Country"). [PoNow] (7:2, #38) 83, p. 23.

Notes about dedications, joint authors, translators, and sources follow the title, enclosed in parentheses. A poem with more than one author is entered under each author. Likewise, a translated poem is entered under each translator, as well as its author(s). Each entry includes the names of all authors and all translators. Multiple authors or translators are indicated by the abbreviation "w.," standing for "with." Translators are indicated by the abbreviation "tr. by," standing for "translated by," and original authors are indicated by the abbreviation "tr. of," standing for "translation of." For example:

ix

AGGESTAM, Rolf
"Old Basho" (tr. by Erland Anderson and Lars Nordström). [NewRena] (16) Spr
83, p. 25.

ANDERSON, Erland
"Old Basho" (tr. of Rolf Aggestam, w. Lars Nordström). [NewRena] (16) Spr 83,
p. 25.

NORDSTRÖM, Lars
"Old Basho" (tr. of Rolf Aggestam, w. Erland Anderson). [NewRena] (16) Spr 83,
p. 25.

The periodical citation includes an abbreviation standing for the periodical title, followed by volume and issue numbers, date, and page number(s). The periodical abbreviation is enclosed in square brackets. An alphabetical list of these periodical abbreviations is included at the front of the volume, followed by the full periodical titles, names of editors, addresses, the numbers of the issues indexed for this volume of the *Index*, and subscription information. A separate list of indexed periodicals is arranged by full periodical title, with a reference to the abbreviated title. Volume and issue numbers are included within parentheses. For example, (16:5) stands for volume 16, number 5; (21) refers to issue or volume 21 for a periodical that uses only one numerical sequence. Dates are given using abbreviations for months and seasons. Year of publication is indicated by the last two digits of the year, for example, 95. Please see the separate list of abbreviations at the front of the volume.

Compiling this year's *Index* has been an adventure into the wealth and variety of poetry published in U.S., Caribbean, and Canadian periodicals as well as the intricacies of bringing this richness together and organizing it into a consistent index. The world of poetry publication is a dynamic one, with new periodicals appearing, older periodicals declining, dying, reviving, and thriving. This year saw the loss of fourteen periodicals and the addition of fifteen new ones. One periodical that had been dropped in 1993 was reinstated. Both deleted and newly added periodicals are listed at the front of the volume. Keeping up with these changes is a big job, and we solicit our readers' suggestions as to periodicals that should be included in future volumes of the *Index*, and also, periodicals that could be dropped. Editors who would like their periodicals considered for inclusion in future volumes should send sample issues to:

Rafael Catalá, Editor
Index of American Periodical Verse
P.O. Box 38
New Brunswick, NJ 08903-0038

Although indexing is indispensable for the organization of any literature, so that particular works can be found when needed and scholarship and research facilitated, it is a tedious business. I know that we have made mistakes. We solicit your corrections and suggestions, which you may send to me at the above address.

James D. Anderson
Co-Editor

Abbreviations

dir., dirs.	director, directors
Dept.	Department
ed., eds.	editor, editors
(for.)	price for foreign countries
(ind.)	price for individuals
(inst.)	price for institutions
(lib.)	price for libraries
NS	new series
p.	page, pages
po. ed.	poetry editor
pub.	publisher
(stud.)	price for students
tr. by	translated by
tr. of	translation of
U.	University
w.	with
yr,	year

Months

Ja	January	Jl	July
F	February	Ag	August
Mr	March	S	September
Ap	April	O	October
My	May	N	November
Je	June	D	December

Seasons

Aut	Autumn	Spr	Spring
Wint	Winter	Sum	Summer

Years

91	1991	94	1994
92	1992	95	1995
93	1993	96	1996

Periodicals Added

Periodical acronyms are followed by titles. Full information may be found in the list of periodicals indexed.

AxeF: AXE FACTORY

Conduit: CONDUIT: the only magazine that risks annihilation

CrabOR: CRAB ORCHARD REVIEW: A Journal of Creative Works

DefinedP: DEFINED PROVIDENCE

Flyway: FLYWAY: A Literary Review

Gerbil: GERBIL: a queer culture zine

GreenHLL: THE GREEN HILLS LITERARY LANTERN: The Journal of the North Central Missouri Writer's Guild

Ledge: THE LEDGE: Poetry and Fiction Magazine

LiteralL: LITERAL LATTÉ: A Journal of Prose, Poetry & Art

LowellR: THE LOWELL REVIEW

ManyMM: MANY MOUNTAINS MOVING: a literary journal of diverse contemporary voices

NewMyths: NEW MYTHS / MSS,

NortheastCor: NORTHEAST CORRIDOR

Orion: ORION: People and Nature

Phoebe: PHOEBE: A Journal of Literary Arts

SpinningJ: SPINNING JENNY

Periodicals Deleted

Antaeus: ANTAEUS, Daniel Halpern, ed., The Ecco Press, 100 W. Broad St., Hopewell, NJ 08525. Nos. 75/76 (1993) was "The Final Issue."

Asylum: ASYLUM, Greg Boyd, ed., P.O. Box 6203, Santa Maria, CA 93456. No 1994 or 1995 issues received; letters not answered.

BlackBread: BLACK BREAD, Jessica Lowenthal, Sianne Ngai, eds., 46 Preston St., #2, Providence, RI 02906. No 1994 or 1995 issues received; letters not answered.

CoalC: COAL CITY REVIEW, Brian Daldorph, Sandra Tompson, eds., 1324 Connecticut, Lawrence, KS 66044. No 1995 issues received; letter returned by postal service.

Gypsy: GYPSY, Belinda Subraman, S. Ramnath, eds., 10708 Gay Brewer Dr., El Paso, TX 79935. No 1994 or 1995 issues received; letters not answered.

Lactuca: LACTUCA, Mike Selender, ed., P.O. Box 621, Suffern, NY 10901. No 1994 or 1995 issues received; letters not answered.

Mester: MESTER, Yuzhuo Qiu, ed., Dept. of Spanish and Portuguese, U. of California, Los Angeles, CA 90024-1532. No longer publishes poetry: "It publishes critical articles, interviews and book reviews."

MoodySI: MOODY STREET IRREGULARS: A Jack Kerouac Newsletter, Joy Walsh, Mike Basinski, eds., P.O. Box 157, Clarence Center, NY 14032. No longer published. No. 28 (1993) was: "The Last Word: Final Issue."

Nuez: LA NUEZ: Revista Internacional de Arte y Literatura, Rafael Bordao, ed., P.O. Box 023617, Brooklyn, NY 11202. Vol. 5, No. 15 (1994) was last issue.

PoetryUSA: POETRY USA, Jack Foley, ed., 2569 Maxwell Ave., Oakland, CA 94601. No 1994 or 1995 issues received; letters not answered.

RedBass: RED BASS, Jay Murphy, ed., 105 W. 28th St., 3rd floor, New York, NY 10001. No 1994 or 1995 issues received; letters not answered.

Shiny: SHINY: The Magazine of the Future, Michael Friedman, ed., pub., 3188 - 10th St., Boulder, CO 80304. No issues published 1993 or 1994; next issue had been expected Summer 1995, but not received; final letter of inquiry not answered.

Sparrow: SPARROW, Felix Stefanile, Selma Stefanile, eds., pubs., 103 Waldron St., West Lafayette, IN 47906. No 1994 or 1995 issues received; letters not answered.

Trasimagen: TRASIMAGEN: Revista Latinoamericana de Literatura y Arte, Lillian Haddock, directora; Lillian Haddock, Jose Luis Colon-Santiago, eds., P.O. Box 2581, Stuyvesant Station, New York, NY 10009. No 1994 or 1995 issues received; letter of inquiry returned by postal service.

Periodicals Indexed

Arranged by acronym, with names of editors, addresses, issues indexed, and subscription information. New titles added to the *Index* in 1995 are marked with an asterisk (*).

13thMoon: 13TH MOON : A Feminist Literary Magazine, Judith Emlyn Johnson, ed., Nancy Dunlop, Joanne Tangorra, po. eds., Dept. of English, State U. of NY, Albany, NY 12222. Issues indexed: (13:1/2). Subscriptions: $10/1 vol., $18/2 vols., $26/3 vols; Back issues: $6.50-$10/vol.

Abraxas: ABRAXAS, Ingrid Swanberg, ed., 2518 Gregory St., Madison, WI 53711. Issues indexed: No issues published 1992-1995 — No. 42 expected in 1996. Subscriptions: $12/4 issues; Single issue: $3; Double issues: $6.

AfAmRev: AFRICAN AMERICAN REVIEW, Division on Black American Literature and Culture, Modern Language Association, Joe Weixlmann, ed., Dept. of English, Indiana State U., Terre Haute, IN 47809. Issues indexed: (29:1-4). Subscriptions: $24/yr. (ind.), $48/yr. (inst.), $31/yr. (for.), $55/yr. (for. inst.). Single issue: $10, $12 (inst., for. ind.), $14 (for. inst.).

Agni: AGNI, Askold Melnyczuk, ed., Creative Writing Program, Boston U., 236 Bay State Rd., Boston, MA 02115. Issues indexed: (41-42). Subscriptions: $14.95/yr. (2 issues); $34.95/yr. (inst.), plus $4/yr. (for.); Single issue: $8.95.

AlabamaLR: ALABAMA LITERARY REVIEW, Theron Montgomery, ed., Ed Hicks, po. ed., Smith 253, Troy State U., Troy, AL 36082. Issues indexed: (9:1). Subscriptions: $5/yr. (1 issues); Single issue: $5; Back issues: $4.50.

Amelia: AMELIA, Frederick A. Raborg, Jr., ed., 329 "E" St., Bakersfield, CA 93304. Issues indexed: No 1995 issues received. Subscriptions: $25/yr. (4 issues), $48/2 yrs., $70/3 yrs.; $27/yr., $52/2 yrs., $76/3 yrs. (Canada, Mexico); $41/yr., $80/2 yrs., $118/3 yrs. (for. air mail); Single issue: $7.95, $8.50 (Canada & Mexico), $12 (for. air mail).

Americas: THE AMERICAS REVIEW, A Review of Hispanic Literature and Art of the USA, Lauro H. Flores, ed., U. of Houston, Houston, TX 77204-2090. Issues indexed: (23:1/2-3/4); p. 1 of 23:1/2 (Spr-Sum 95) states, in error: "vol. 22, Fall-Winter 1994, Nos. 3-4." Subscriptions: $15/yr. (ind.), $20/yr. (inst.); Single and back issues: $5; Double issues: $10.

AmerLC: AMERICAN LETTERS & COMMENTARY, Jeanne Beaumont, Anna Rabinowitz, eds., 850 Park Ave, Suite 5-B, New York, NY 10021. Issues indexed: (7). Subscriptions: $6/yr. (1 issue), $10/2 yrs., $15/3 yrs.

AmerPoR: THE AMERICAN POETRY REVIEW, Stephen Berg, David Bonanno, Arthur Vogelsang, eds., 1721 Walnut St., Philadelphia, PA 19103. Issues indexed: (24:1-6). Subscriptions: $16/yr., $29/2 yrs., $41/3 yrs.; $19/yr., $35/2 yrs., $50/3 yrs. (for.); classroom rate $8/yr. per student; Single issue: $3.50.

AmerS: THE AMERICAN SCHOLAR; Joseph Epstein, ed., The Phi Beta Kappa Society, 1811 Q St. NW, Washington, DC 20009. Issues indexed: (64:1-4). Subscriptions: $25/yr., $48/2 yrs., $69/3 yrs. (ind.); $30/yr., $58/2 yrs., $84/3 yrs. (inst.), plus $3/yr. (for.); Single issue: $6.95; $8 (inst.).

AmerV: THE AMERICAN VOICE, Frederick Smock, ed., The Kentucky Foundation for Women, Inc., 332 West Broadway, Suite 1215, Louisville, KY 40202. Issues indexed: (36-38). Subscriptions: $15/yr. (3 issues), $25/2 yrs., $35/3 yrs.; Back and single issues: $5.

AnotherCM: ANOTHER CHICAGO MAGAZINE, Barry Silesky, ed., pub., 3709 N. Kenmore, Chicago, IL 60613. Issues indexed: (29). Subscriptions: $15/yr., $60/5 yrs., $199.95/lifetime; Single issue: $8.

AnthNEW: THE ANTHOLOGY OF NEW ENGLAND WRITERS, Frank Anthony, ed., New England Writers/Vermont Poets Association, P.O. Box 483, Windsor, VT 05089. Issues indexed: (7). Single issue: $3.50.

AntigR: THE ANTIGONISH REVIEW, George Sanderson, ed., Box 5000, St. Francis Xavier U., Antigonish, Nova Scotia B2G 2W5 Canada. Issues indexed: (100-102/103); No. 101 is labeled "1995" on the spine, but "Spring, 1996" on the title-page verso. Subscriptions: $20/4 issues; Single issue: $6.

AntR: THE ANTIOCH REVIEW, Robert S. Fogarty, ed., David St. John, po. ed., P.O. Box 148, Yellow Springs, OH 45387-9910. Issues indexed: (53:1-4). Subscriptions: $35/yr. (4 issues); $48/yr. (inst.); $58/yr. (for.); Single issue: $6, $7.80 (Canada). Subscription address: P.O. Box 626, Dayton, OH 45459-0626.

ApalQ: APALACHEE QUARTERLY, Barbara Hamby, Mary Jane Ryals, Kim MacQueen, Lara Moody, Rikki Clark, Beth Meekins, eds., P.O. Box 10469, Tallahassee, FL 32302. Issues indexed: (43, 44/45). Subscriptions: $15/yr. (2 single issues & 1 double issue, ind.), $30/2 yrs.; $20/yr. (inst.); $30/yr., $50/2 yrs. (for.); Single issue: $5; Double issues: $10.

Arc: ARC: Canada's National Poetry Magazine, John Barton, Rita Donovan, eds., P.O. Box 7368, Ottawa, Ont. K1L 8E4 Canada. Issues indexed: (34-35). Subscriptions: $20/4 issues (2 years, Canada); $25/yr. (USA); $28/yr. (for.); Single issue: $8.50 (Canada), $8 (USA & for.).

Archae: ARCHAE, Alan Drake, Mikhail Horowitz, eds., Bridgewater, NJ 08807. Issues indexed: (5). Subscriptions: $7.32/yr. (1 issue); $8.88/yr. (for.).

Areíto: AREITO, Andrés Gómez, Director, P.O. Box 44-1803, Miami, FL 33144. Issues indexed: No 1995 issues received. Subscriptions: $12/yr. (ind.), $20/yr. (inst.), $18/yr. (for. ind.), $30/yr. (for. inst.).

Arion: ARION: A Journal of Humanities and the Classics, Herbert Golder, ed., 10 Lenox St., Brookline, MA 02146. Issues indexed: (3:2/3). Subscriptions: $19/yr. (3 issues, ind.), $35/yr. (inst.), $12/yr. (students), plus $3/yr. (for.); Single issue, $7; Double issue: $15; Back issues, $8. Subscription address: Arion, c/o Office of Scholarly Publications, Boston U., 985 Commonwealth Ave., Boston, MA 02215.

Arshile: ARSHILE: A Magazine of the Arts, Mark Salerno, ed., P.O. Box 3749, Los Angeles, CA 90078. Issues indexed: (4). Subscriptions: $18/2 issues, $36/4 issues (ind.); $25/2 issues, $50/4 issues (inst.); Single issue: $8-$10.

Art&Und: ART & UNDERSTANDING: The International Magazine of Literature and Art About AIDS, David Waggoner, ed., 25 Monroe St., Suite 205, Albany, NY 12210. Issues indexed: (4:1-5, #14-18). Subscriptions: $24.95/yr. (10 issues), $34.95/2 yrs.; Back issues: $10; Single issue: $3.95, $4.95 (Canada).

ArtfulD: ARTFUL DODGE, Daniel Bourne, ed., Dept. of English, College of Wooster, Wooster, OH 44691. Issues indexed: (28/29). Subscriptions: $10/4 issues (ind.), $16/4 issues (inst.); Single issue: $5.

Arts Indiana Literary Supplement —See HopewellR: HOPEWELL REVIEW (title change)

Ascent: ASCENT, W. Scott Olsen, ed., Dept. of English, Concordia College, 901 8th St. S., Moorhead, MN 56562. Issues indexed: (19:2-3, 20:1). Subscriptions: $9/yr. (3 issues), $18/2 yrs.; $5 (for.); Single issue: $3 (bookstore), $3.50 (mail).

Atlantic: THE ATLANTIC, William Whitworth, ed., Peter Davison, po. ed., 745 Boylston St., Boston, MA 02116-2603. Issues indexed: (275:1-6, 276:1-6). Subscriptions: $17.94/yr., $29.95/2 yrs., $39.95/3 yrs., plus $8/yr. (Canada), $15/yr. (for.); Single issue: $2.95, $3.50 (Canada); Back issues: $5 (Atlantic, Back Issues, 200 N. 12th St., Newark, NJ 07107). Subscription address: Atlantic Subscription Processing Center, Box 52661, Boulder, CO 80322.

Avec: AVEC, Cydney Chadwick, ed., P.O. Box 1059, Penngrove, CA 94951. Issues indexed: (9-10). Subscriptions: $12/2 issues; Single issue: $8.50.

*AxeF: AXE FACTORY, Joseph Farley, ed., P.O. Box 40691, Philadelphia, PA 19107. Issues indexed: (3-4); No. 4 is chapbook "Framework" by Jeff Vetock — ed. Subscriptions: $15/4 issues; Single issue: $5.

BambooR: BAMBOO RIDGE: The Hawaii Writers' Quarterly, Eric Chock, Darrell H. Y. Lum, eds., P.O. Box 61781, Honolulu, HI 96839-1781. Issues indexed: (65/66, 67/68). Subscriptions: $16/yr. (2 issues); Single issue, $5; Double issues: $5-8.

BellArk: BELLOWING ARK, Robert R. Ward, ed., P.O. Box 45637, Seattle, WA 98145. Issues indexed: (11:1-6). Subscriptions: $15/yr. (6 issues), $24/2 yrs.; Single issue, back issues: $3.

BellR: THE BELLINGHAM REVIEW, Knute Skinner, ed., Maureen Ott Trainor, po. ed., MS-9053, Western Washington U., Bellingham, WA 98225. Issues indexed: (18:1-2, #37-38). Subscriptions: $10/yr. (2 issues), $19/2 yrs., $25/3 yrs., plus $1/yr. (for.); through agencies, $12/yr.; Single issue: $2.50; Double issue: $5.

BelPoJ: THE BELOIT POETRY JOURNAL, Marion K. Stocking, ed., RR 2, Box 154, Ellsworth, ME 04605. Issues indexed: (45:3-4, 46:1-2). Subscriptions: $12/yr. (4 issues, ind.), $33/3 yrs.; $18/yr., $49.50/3 yrs. (inst.), plus $3.20/yr. (Canada), $3.70/yr. (for.); Single issue: $4.

BilingR: THE BILINGUAL REVIEW / LA REVISTA BILINGÜE, Gary D. Keller, ed., Hispanic Research Center, Arizona State U., Box 872702, Tempe, AZ 85287-2702. Issues indexed: (20:1-3). Subscriptions: $18/yr., $34/2 yrs., $48/3 yrs. (ind.); $32/yr. (inst.).

BlackALF: BLACK AMERICAN LITERATURE FORUM — See: AfAmRev: AFRICAN AMERICAN REVIEW (title change).

BlackBR: BLACK BEAR REVIEW, Ave Jeanne, po. ed., 1916 Lincoln St., Croydon, PA 19021-8026. Issues indexed: (20-21). Subscriptions: $10/yr. (2 issues); $12/yr. (lib.), plus $3 per copy (for.); Single issue: $5.

BlackMoon: BLACK MOON: Poetry of Imagination, Alan Britt, ed., pub., 233 Northway Rd, Reisterstown, MD 21136. Issues indexed: No 1995 published; No. 2 published in 1996. Single issue: $5 (No. 1), $8.95 (No. 2), plus $1.75 for postage and handling.

BlackWR: BLACK WARRIOR REVIEW, Mindy Wilson, ed., Madeline Marcotte, po. ed., U. of Alabama, P.O. Box 2936, Tuscaloosa, AL 35486-2936. Issues indexed: (21:2, 22:1). Subscriptions: $11/yr. (ind.), $17/yr. (inst.), plus $5/yr. (for.); Single issue: $6, plus $3 (for.).

Blueline: BLUELINE, Anthony O. Tyler, ed., Stephanie Coyne DeGhett, po. ed., English Dept., Potsdam College, SUNY, Potsdam, NY 13676. Issues indexed: 16. Single issue: $6.

Bogg: BOGG: An Anglo-American Journal, John Elsberg, ed., pub., 422 N. Cleveland St., Arlington, VA 22201. Issues indexed: (67). Subscriptions: $12/3 issues; Single issue: $4.50.

Bomb: BOMB MAGAZINE, Betsy Sussler, ed., pub., Roland Legiardi-Laura, po. ed., New Art Publications, P.O. Box 2003, Canal St. Station, New York, NY 10013. Issues indexed: (51-53). Subscriptions: $18/yr. (4 issues), $32/2 yrs.; $28/yr. (for.); Single issue: $4.

Border: BORDERLANDS: Texas Poetry Review, Dorothy Barnett, Pamela Cook, Liz Garton, D'Arcy Randall, Polly Robertus, Hazel Ward, dirs., P.O. Box 49818, Austin, TX 78765. Issues indexed: (6-7). Subscriptions: $17/yr. (2 issues, ind.), $33/2 yrs.; $19/yr. (inst.); Single issue: $10.

BostonR: BOSTON REVIEW, Joshua Cohen, ed., Kim Cooper, po. ed., Dept. of Political Science, E53-407, Massachusetts Institute of Technology, 30 Wadsworth St., Cambridge, MA 02139. Issues indexed: (20:1-4, 6); vol. 20, no. 5 not published (numbering error: no. 3 should have been no. 3/4; no. 4 should have been no. 5). Subscriptions: $15/yr., $30/2 yrs. (ind.); $18/yr., $36/2 yrs. (inst.), plus $6/yr. (Canada, Mexico), plus $12/yr. (other for.); Single issue: $4.50.

Boulevard: BOULEVARD, Richard Burgin, ed., Drexel U., P.O. Box 30386, Philadelphia, PA 19103. Issues indexed: (10:1/2, 10:3, #28/29, 30). Subscriptions: $12/3 issues, $20/6 issues, $25/9 issues; Single issue: $6; make checks payable to Opojaz, Inc.

BrooklynR: BROOKLYN REVIEW, Tim Gerken, Michael Gates, Giles Scott, Robert Zverina, po. eds., Lou Asekoff, faculty advisor, English Dept., Brooklyn College, Brooklyn, NY 11210. Issues indexed: No 1995 issues received. Single issue: $5.

Caliban: CALIBAN, Lawrence R. Smith, ed., P.O. Box 561, Laguna Beach, CA 92652. Issues indexed: No 1995 issues received. Subscriptions: $14/yr. (2 issues), $26/2 yrs. (ind.); $24/yr. (inst.), plus $2/yr. (for.); Single issue: $8.

Callaloo: CALLALOO: A Journal of African-American and African Arts and Letters, Charles H. Rowell, ed., Dept. of English, 322 Bryan Hall, U. of Virginia, Charlottesville, VA 22903. Issues indexed: (18:1-4). Subscriptions: $32/yr. (ind.), $65/yr. (inst.), plus $7 (Canada, Mexico), plus $17 (outside North America, air freight); Subscription address: The Johns Hopkins U. Press, Journals Publishing Division, 2715 N. Charles St., Baltimore, MD 21218-4319.

Calyx: CALYX: A Journal of Art and Literature by Women, Margarita Donnelly, managing ed., P.O. Box B, Corvallis, OR 97339-0539. Issues indexed: (16:1-2). Subscriptions: $18/vol. (3 issues), $32/2 vols., $42/3 vols.; $22.50/vol. (inst.), plus $10/vol. (Canada), plus $18/vol. (for.); $15/vol. (ind. low income); Single issue: $8 plus $1.25 postage.

CanLit: CANADIAN LITERATURE / LITTÉRATURE CANADIENNE, Eva-Marie Kröller, ed., U. of British Columbia, #167 - 1855 West Mall, Vancouver, BC Canada V6T 1Z2. Issues indexed: (144-147). Subscriptions: $40/yr. (ind.), $55/yr. (inst.) plus $10/yr. outside Canada; Single issue: $15; Double issue: $25.

CapeR: THE CAPE ROCK: A Gathering of Poets, Harvey Hecht, ed., Southeast Missouri State U., Cape Girardeau, MO 63701. Issues indexed: (30:1-2). Subscriptions: $7/yr. (2 issues, USA, Canada, Mexico); $8/yr. (other for.); Single issue: $5.

CapilR: THE CAPILANO REVIEW, Robert Sherrin, ed., 2055 Purcell Way, North Vancouver, BC V7J 3H5 Canada. Issues indexed: (Series 2:15-16). Subscriptions: $25/yr., $45/2 yrs. (ind.); $30/yr. (inst.); Single issue: $9.

CaribbeanW: THE CARIBBEAN WRITER, Erika J. Waters, ed., Research Publications Center, U. of the Virgin Islands, RR 2, Box 10,000, Kingshill, St. Croix, VI 00850. Issues indexed: (9). Subscriptions: $18/2 yrs. (2 issues); Single issue: $9 plus $1.50 postage & handling; Some back issues: $5 plus postage.

CarolQ: CAROLINA QUARTERLY, Amber Vogel, ed., Carrie Blackstock, po. ed., Greenlaw Hall CB#3520, U. of North Carolina, Chapel Hill, NC 27599-3520. Issues indexed: (47:2-3, 48:1). Subscriptions: $10/yr. (3 issues, ind.), $12/yr. (inst.); Single issue: $5.

CentR: THE CENTENNIAL REVIEW, R. K. Meiners, ed., College of Arts and Letters, 312 Linton Hall, Michigan State U., East Lansing, MI 48824-1044. Issues indexed: (39:1-3). Subscriptions: $12/yr. (3 issues), $18/2 yrs., plus $4.50/yr. (for.); Single issue: $6.

CentralP: CENTRAL PARK, Stephen-Paul Martin, Eve Ensler, Stacey Schrader, eds., Box 1446, New York, NY 10023. Issues indexed: (24). Subscriptions: $15/yr., 2 issues (ind.), $20/yr. (inst.); Single issue: $7.50 (ind.), $9 (inst).

Chain: CHAIN, Jena Osman, Juliana Spahr, eds., State U. of New York at Buffalo, 107 14th St., Buffalo, NY 14213. Issues indexed: (2). Subscriptions: $10/yr. (1 issue); $18/2 issues. Make checks payable to UB Foundation.

ChamLR: CHAMINADE LITERARY REVIEW, Loretta Petrie, ed., Jim Kraus, po. ed., Chaminade U. of Honolulu, 3140 Waialae Ave., Honolulu, HI 96816. Issues indexed: No 1995 issues received. Subscriptions: $10/yr. (2 issues); $18/2 yrs., plus $2 (for.); Single issue: $5; Double issue: $10.

ChangingM: CHANGING MEN: Issues in Gender, Sex and Politics, Michael Biernbaum, Rick Cote, eds., P.O. Box 639, Durham, NH 03825-0639; Bob Vance, po. ed., 1024 Emmet St., Petosky, MI 49770. Issues indexed: No 1995 issues received. Subscriptions: $24/4 issues, $40/4 issues (inst.); $16/4 issues (limited income); $27/4 issues (Canada & Mexico); $40/4 issues (for., air mail); Single issue: $6; Back issues: $5.50.

CharR: THE CHARITON REVIEW, Jim Barnes, ed., Northeast Missouri State U., Kirksville, MO 63501. Issues indexed: (21:1-2). Subscriptions: $9/2 issues (1 yr.), $15/4 issues; Single issue: $5.

ChatR: THE CHATTAHOOCHEE REVIEW: The DeKalb College Literary Quarterly, Lamar York, ed., Collie Owens, po. ed., 2101 Womack Road, Dunwoody, GA 30338-4497. Issues indexed: No 1995 issues received. Subscriptions: $15/yr. (4 issues), $25/2 yrs.; Single issue: $4.

Chelsea: CHELSEA, Richard Foerster, ed., P.O. Box 773, Cooper Station, New York, NY 10276-0773. Issues indexed: (58-59). Subscriptions: $13/yr. (2 issues or 1 double issue), $24/2 yrs.; $16/yr., $30/2 yrs. (for.); $18/yr., $34/2 yrs. (agencies); $21/yr., $40/2 yrs. (for. agencies); Single issue: $8.

ChiR: CHICAGO REVIEW, David Nicholls, ed., Devin Johnston & Angela Sorby, po. ed., Division of Humanities, U. of Chicago, 5801 S. Kenwood Ave., Chicago, IL 60637-1794. Issues indexed: (41:1, 2/3, 4). Subscriptions: $18/yr. (ind.); $35/yr. (inst.), plus $5/yr. (for.); Single issue: $6; Double issue: $8; Sample issue: $5.

ChironR: CHIRON REVIEW, Michael Hathaway, ed., 522 E. South Ave., St. John, KS 67576-2212. Issues indexed: (42-44/45). Subscriptions: $12/yr. (4 issues); $24/yr. (for.); $28/yr. (inst.); Single issue: $4; $8 (for.).

ChrC: THE CHRISTIAN CENTURY: An Ecumenical Weekly, James M. Wall, ed., 407 S. Dearborn St., Chicago, IL 60605-1150. Issues indexed: (112:1-37). Subscriptions: $38/yr.; $50/yr. (for.); Single issue: $2.

CimR: CIMARRON REVIEW, E. P. Walkiewicz, ed., Thomas Reiter, Sharon Gerald, Lisa Lewis, Doug Martin, Sally Shigley, po. eds., 205 Morrill Hall, Oklahoma State U., Stillwater, OK 74078-0135. Issues indexed: (110-113). Subscriptions: $12/yr., $15 (Canada); $30/3 yrs., $40 (Canada), plus $2.50/yr. (other for.); Single issue: $3.

CinPR: CINCINNATI POETRY REVIEW, Jeff Hillard, ed., Cincinnati Writers' Project, College of Mt. St. Joseph, 5701 Delhi Rd., Cincinnati, OH 45233. Issues indexed: No 1995 issues received. Subscriptions: $9/4 issues; Single issue: $3; Sample copies: $2.

ClockR: CLOCKWATCH REVIEW: A Journal of the Arts, James Plath, ed., Dept. of English, Illinois Wesleyan U., Bloomington, IL 61702-2900. Issues indexed: (10:1/2). Subscriptions: $8/yr. (2 issues); Single issue: $4; Double issue: $8.

ColEng: COLLEGE ENGLISH, National Council of Teachers of English, Louise Z. Smith, ed., Helene Davis, Lloyd Schwartz, po. eds., Dept. of English, UMass-Boston, Boston, MA 02125. Issues indexed: (57:1-8). Subscriptions: $40/yr. (ind.), $50/yr. (inst.), plus $6/yr. (for.); Single issue: $6.25; Subscription address: NCTE, 1111 W. Kenyon Rd., Urbana, IL 61801-1096.

ColR: COLORADO REVIEW, David Milofsky, ed., Jorie Graham, po. ed., Dept. of English, Colorado State U., Fort Collins, CO 80523. Issues indexed: (22:1-2); cover of 22:2 has "21:2" in error. Subscriptions: $15/yr. (2 issues), $28/2 yrs.; $25/yr. (inst.), plus $6/yr. (for.); Single issue: $8.

Colum: COLUMBIA: A Jounal of Literature and Art, Mike McGregor, ed., Jennifer Franklin, Elizabeth Stein, po. eds., Graduate Writing Division, School of the Arts, 404 Dodge Hall, Columbia U., New York, NY 10027. Issues indexed: (24/25); No. 23 "was never published." Subscriptions: $7/1 issue, $13/2 issues, $18/3 issues.

Comm: COMMONWEAL, Margaret O'Brien Steinfels, ed., Rosemary Deen, po. ed., 15 Dutch St., New York, NY 10038. Issues indexed: (122:1-22). Subscriptions: $39/yr., $41/yr. (Canada), $44/yr. (for.); $67/2 yrs., $71/2 yrs. (Canada), $77/2 yrs. (for.), plus $35-$44/yr for international air mail; Single issue: $2.

*Conduit: CONDUIT: the only magazine that risks annihilation, William D. Waltz, Brett Astor, eds., 3142 Lyndale Ave. S. #6, Minneapolis, MN 55408. Issues indexed: (3). Subscriptions: $10/yr. (4 issues, ind.); $15/yr. (inst.); Single issue: $2.50.

Confr: CONFRONTATION, Martin Tucker, ed., English Dept., C. W. Post Campus of Long Island U., Brookville, NY 11548. Issues indexed: (56/57). Subscriptions: $10/yr., $20/2 yrs., $30/3 yrs., plus $5/yr. (for.); Single issue: $7; Double issue: $10.

Conjunc: CONJUNCTIONS: Bi-Annual Volumes of New Writing, Bard College, Bradford Morrow, ed., 33 W. 9th St., New York, NY 10011. Issues indexed: (24-25). Subscriptions: Bard College, Annandale-on-Hudson, NY 12504; $18/yr. (2 issues), $32/2 yrs. (ind.); $25/yr., $45/2 yrs. (inst., for.); Back and single issues: $12.

ConnPR: THE CONNECTICUT POETRY REVIEW, Harley More, J. Claire White, eds., P.O. Box 818, Stonington, CT 06378. Issues indexed: (14:1). Single issue: $3 (including postage).

Conscience: CONSCIENCE: A Newsjournal of Prochoice Catholic Opinion, Maggie Hume, ed., Andrew Merton, po. ed., Catholics for a Free Choice, 1436 U St. NW, Washington, DC 20009-3997. Issues indexed: (16:1/2-4). Subscriptions: $10/yr., free to libraries; Single issue: $3.50; Back issues: $1-3.

ContextS: CONTEXT SOUTH, David Breeden, po. ed., pub., Box 4504, Schreiner College, 2100 Memorial Blvd., Kerrville, TX 78028-5697. Issues indexed: (4:2). Subscriptions: $10/3 issues.

CrabCR: CRAB CREEK REVIEW, Linda Clifton, Carol Orlock, eds., 4462 Whitman Ave. N., Seattle WA 98103. Issues indexed: No 1995 issues received. Subscriptions: $8/3 issues (1 volume), $15/2 volumes, plus $5/volume (for.); Back issues: $3; Anniversary Anthology: $10.

*CrabOR: CRAB ORCHARD REVIEW: A Journal of Creative Works, Richard Peterson, ed., Allison Joseph, po. ed., Dept. of English, Southern Illinois U., Carbondale, IL 62901-4503. Issues indexed: (1:1). Subscriptions: $10/yr. (2 issues, ind.), $20/2 yrs., $30/3 yrs.; $14/hr., $28/2 yrs., $42/3 yrs. (for. ind.); $12/yr., $24/2 yrs., $36/3 yrs. (inst.); $16/yr., $32/2 yrs., $48/3 yrs. (for. inst.); Single issue: $6.

Crazy: CRAZYHORSE, Ralph Burns, ed., Dept. of English, U. of Arkansas, 2801 S. University, Little Rock, AR 72204. Issues indexed: (48-49). Subscriptions: $10/yr. (2 issues), $18/2 yrs., $27/3 yrs. Single issue: $5.

CreamCR: CREAM CITY REVIEW, Mark Drechsler, Andrew Rivera, ed., Cynthia Belmont, Kristin Terwelp, po. eds., English Dept., U. of Wisconsin, P.O. Box 413, Milwaukee, WI 53201. Issues indexed: (19:1). Subscriptions: $12/yr. (2 issues), $21/2 yrs.; Single issue: $7; Sample and back issues: $5.

CrossCur: CROSSCURRENTS, Linda Brown Michelson, ed., 2200 Glastonbury Road, Westlake Village, CA 91361. Issues indexed: No 1995 issues received. Subscriptions: $18/yr. (4 issues), $25/2 yrs., $30/3 yrs.; Single issue: $6.

Crucible: CRUCIBLE, Terrence L. Grimes, ed., Barton College, College Station, Wilson, NC 27893. Issues indexed: (30-31). Subscriptions: $6/yr. (1 issue), $12/2 yrs; Back issues: $5.

CuadP: CUADERNOS DE POÉTICA, Diógenes Céspedes, Director, Apartado Postal 1736, Santo Domingo, Dominican Republic; US Editor: Rafael Catalá, P.O. Box 38, New Brunswick, NJ 08903. Issues indexed: No 1995 issues received. Subscriptions: America & Europe, $25/yr. (ind.), $30/yr. (inst.); Africa, Asia & Oceania, $30/yr. (ind.), $40/yr. (inst).

CumbPR: CUMBERLAND POETRY REVIEW, Bob Darrell, Sherry Bevins Darrell, John Gibson, Jeanne Gore, Elizabeth Hahn, Laurence Lerner, Joyce Sommer, Alison Touster-Reed, Eva Touster, Bard Young, eds., Poetics, Inc., P.O. Box 120128, Acklen Station, Nashville, TN 37212. Issues indexed: (14:2, 15:1). Subscriptions: $14/yr, $26/2 yrs. (ind.); $17/yr., $31/2 yrs. (inst.); $23/yr., $37/2 yrs. (for.); Single issue: $7; $10 (for.).

CutB: CUTBANK, Alex Speyer, Mary Park, eds., Karin Schalm, po. ed., Jocelyn Siler, faculty advisor, Dept. of English, U. of Montana, Missoula, MT 59812. Issues indexed: (42-44). Subscriptions: $12/yr., $22/2 yrs.; Single issue: $6.95-9.95; Sample copies: $4.

Dandel: DANDELION, Bonnie Benoit, managing ed., Janeen Werner-King, Gordon Pengilly, po. eds., Room 310, 223 - 12th Ave. S.W., Calgary, Alberta T2R 0G9 Canada. Issues indexed: (22:1). Subscriptions: $12/yr. (2 issues), $20/2 yrs.; $17/yr. (inst.); Single issue: $7.

*DefinedP: DEFINED PROVIDENCE, Gary J. Whitehead, ed., 26 E. Fort Lee Rd. #2-B, Bogota, NJ 07603. Issues indexed: (1:1-2, 2:1-2, 3). Subscriptions: $4/yr., $7/2 yrs. (ind); $5/yr., $9/2 yrs. (inst.).

DenQ: DENVER QUARTERLY, Bin Ramke, ed., U. of Denver, Denver, CO 80208. Issues indexed: (29:3-4, 30:1-2). Subscriptions: $15/yr., $28/2 yrs.; $18/yr. (inst.), plus $1/yr. (for.); Single issue: $5.

Descant: DESCANT, Karen Mulhallen, ed., P.O. Box 314, Station P, Toronto, Ontario M5S 2S8 Canada. Issues indexed: (26:1-4, #88-91). Subscriptions: $20/yr., $35/2 yrs. (ind.); $35/yr., $70/2 yrs. (inst.), plus $6/yr. (for.); Single issue: $10.

DogRR: DOG RIVER REVIEW, Laurence F. Hawkins, ed., Trout Creek Press, 5976 Billings Road, Parkdale, OR 97041-9610. Issues indexed: (14:1, #27). Subscriptions: $8/yr. (2 issues); Single issue: $4; Sample copy: $3, plus $2.50 (for.).

Drumvoices: DRUMVOICES REVUE: A Confluence of Literary, Cultural & Vision Arts, Eugene B. Redmond, ed., English Dept., Southern Illinois U. at Edwardsville in collaboration with the Eugene B. Redmond Writers Club of East St. Louis, Dept. of English, Box 1431, SIUE, Edwardsville, IL 62026-1431. Issues indexed: (4:1/2, 5:1/2). Subscriptions: $10/yr. (2 issues); Single issue: $6.

Elf: ELF: Eclectic Literary Forum, C. K. Erbes, ed., P. O. Box 392, Tonawanda, NY 14150. Issues indexed: (5:1-4). Subscriptions: $16/yr. (4 issues), $32/yr. (inst.), plus $8/yr. (for.); Single issue: $5.50.

EngJ: ENGLISH JOURNAL, National Council of Teachers of English, Leila Christenbury, ed., School of Education, Virginia Commonwealth U., P.O. Box 842020, Richmond, VA 23284-2020; David Black, po. ed., RR 1, Box 396, Louisa, VA 23093. Issues indexed: (84:1-8). Subscriptions: $40/yr. (ind.), $50/yr. (inst.), plus $6/yr. (for.); Single issue: $6.25; Subscription address: 1111 W. Kenyon Rd., Urbana, IL 61801-1096.

Epiphany: EPIPHANY: A Journal of Literature — *See:* OgalalaR: THE OGALALA REVIEW *(title change).*

Epoch: EPOCH, Michael Koch, ed., Burlin Barr, po., ed., 251 Goldwin Smith Hall, Cornell U., Ithaca, NY 14853-3201. Issues indexed: (44:1-3). Subscriptions: $11/yr.; $15/yr. (for.); Single issue: $5.

Event: EVENT: The Douglas College Review: New and Established Writers, Dale Zieroth, ed., Gillian Harding-Russell, po. ed., Douglas College, P.O. Box 2503, New Westminster, BC V3L 5B2 Canada. Issues indexed: (24:1-3). Subscriptions: $15/yr. + $1.05 GST, $25/2 yrs. + $1.75 GST; Single issue: $6.

EvergreenC: THE EVERGREEN CHRONICLES: A Journal of Gay and Lesbian Literature, Jim Berg, senior ed., Susan Raffo, managing ed., P.O. Box 8939, Minneapolis, MN 55408-0936. Issues indexed: (10:1-2); an additional "Special issue" in vol. 10 consisted of two novellas, which fell outside the scope of this index. Subscriptions: $15/yr. (2 issues), $28/2 yrs.; $18/yr. (for.); $20/yr. (inst.); Single issue: $7.95.

Eyeball: EYEBALL, Jabari Asim, ed., First Civilizations Inc., P.O. Box 8135, St. Louis, MO 63108. Issues indexed: No 1995 issues received. Subscriptions: $7/yr. (2 issues), $14/2 yrs., $21/3 yrs; $28/yr., $56/2 yrs., $82/3 yrs. (for.); Single issue: $3.50.

Farm: FARMER'S MARKET, Joanne Lowery, ed., Rachael Tecza, po. ed., Midwest Farmer's Market, Inc., Elgin Community College, 1700 Spartan Dr., Elgin, Il 60123-7193. Issues indexed: (12:1-2); Note: Fall-Wint 95 was numbered vol. 13, no. 2 in error; it should be vol. 12, no. 2, and is so numbered in this index. A correction note is included in vol. 13, no. 1 (Spr-Sum 96), p. 4. Subscriptions: $10/yr. (2 issues); Single issue: $6.

Field: FIELD: Contemporary Poetry and Poetics, Stuart Friebert, Alberta Turner, David Walker, David Young, eds., Rice Hall, Oberlin College, Oberlin, OH 44074. Issues indexed: (52-53). Subscriptions: $14/yr., $24/2 yrs.; Single issue: $7; Back issues: $12.

FloridaR: THE FLORIDA REVIEW, Russell Kesler, ed., Dept. of English, U. of Central Florida, Orlando, FL 32816. Issues indexed: (20:2, 21:1). Subscriptions: $7/yr., $11/2 yrs.; Single issue: $4.50.

*Flyway: FLYWAY: A Literary Review, Stephen Pett, ed., Gary Whitehead, po. ed., 203 Ross Hall, Iowa State U., Ames, IA 50011. Issues indexed: (1:1-3). Subscriptions: $18/yr. (3 issues), $32/2 yrs., plus $3 yr. (for.); Single issue: $6.

Footwork: FOOTWORK: Paterson Literary Review, Maria Mazziotti Gillan, ed., Passaic County Community College, 1 College Blvd., Paterson, NJ 07505-1179. Issues indexed: (24/25). Subscriptions: $10/issue.

FourQ: FOUR QUARTERS, John J. Keenan, ed., La Salle U., 1900 W. Olney, Philadelphia, PA 19141. Issues indexed: (9:1/2) Second Series. Subscriptions: $8/yr. (2 issues), $13/2 yrs.; Single issue: $4.

FreeL: FREE LUNCH: A Poetry Journal, Free Lunch Arts Alliance, Ron Offen, ed., P.O. Box 7647, Laguna Niguel, CA 92607-7647. Issues indexed: (14-15). Subscriptions: Free to all serious poets in the U.S.A.; $12/3 issues; $15/3 issues (for.); Single issue: $5, $6 (for.).

Gaia: GAIA: A Journal of Literature & Environmental Arts, Robert S. King, ed., Charles Fishman, po. ed., Whistle Press, Inc., P.O. Box 709, Winterville, GA 30683. Issues indexed: No 1995 issues received. Subscriptions: $9/2 issues, $16/4 issues, plus $4/2 issues (for.); Single issue: $6; Double issue: $8.

GeoR: GEORGIA REVIEW, Stanley W. Lindberg, ed., U. of Georgia, Athens, GA 30602. Issues indexed: (49:1-4). Subscriptions: $18/yr., $30/2 yrs., plus $5/yr. (for.); Single issue: $7-$10; Back issues: $7.

*Gerbil: GERBIL: a queer culture zine, Brad Pease, Tony Leuzzi, eds./pubs., P.O. Box 10692, Rochester, NY 14610. Issues indexed: (3-4). Subscriptions: $10/yr. (4 issues); $12/yr. (for.); Single issue: $3, $3.50 (for.).

GettyR: GETTYSBURG REVIEW, Peter Stitt, ed., Gettysburg College, Gettysburg, PA 17325-1491. Issues indexed: (8:1-4). Subscriptions: $18/yr., $32/2 yrs., $45/3 yrs.; $26/yr., $48/2 yrs., $69/3 yrs. (for.); Single issue: $7.

GlobalCR: GLOBAL CITY REVIEW, Linsey Abrams, E. M. Broner, eds., Simon H. Rifkind Center for the Humanities, City College of New York, 138th & Convent Ave., New York, NY 10031. Issues indexed: (5-6). Subscriptions: $12/yr. (2 issues); $20/2 yrs.; $15/yr., $25/2 yrs. (inst.); $17/yr., $30/2 yrs. (for.); Single and back issues: $6 plus $1 mailing charge.

GrahamHR: GRAHAM HOUSE REVIEW, Peter Balakian, Bruce Smith, eds., Colgate U. Press, Box 5000, Colgate U., Hamilton, NY 13346; Issues indexed: (19). Subscriptions: $15/2 yrs. (2 issues), $25/4 yrs.; Single issue: $7.50.

Grain: GRAIN, Saskatchewan Writers Guild, J. Jill Robinson, ed., Elizabeth Philips, po. ed., Box 1154, Regina, Saskatchewan S4P 3B4 Canada. Issues indexed: (22:3-4, 23:1-2). Subscriptions: $19.95+$1.40 GST/yr., $34.95+$2.45 GST/2 yrs., plus $4/yr. (U.S.), plus $6/yr. (for.); Single issue: $6.95.

GrandS: GRAND STREET, Jean Stein, ed., 131 Varick St. Rm. 906, New York, NY 10013. Issues indexed: (13:3-4, 14:1-2, #51-54). Subscriptions: $40/yr. (4 issues), $70/2 yrs.; $55/yr. (for.); Single issue: $12.95, $15 (Canada); Subscription address: Grand Street Subscription Service, Dept. GRS, P.O. Box 3000, Denville, NJ 07834.

*GreenHLL: THE GREEN HILLS LITERARY LANTERN: The Journal of the North Central Missouri Writer's Guild, Jack Smith, Ken Reger, eds., Joe Benevento, po. ed., Box 375, Trenton, MO 64683. Issues indexed: (5-6). Subscriptions: $5.95/yr. (1 issue).

GreenMR: GREEN MOUNTAINS REVIEW, Neil Shepard, ed. & po. ed., Johnson State College, Johnson, VT 05656. Issues indexed: (NS 8:1-2). Subscriptions: $12/yr. (2 issues), $18/2 yrs.; Single issue: $7.

GreensboroR: THE GREENSBORO REVIEW, Jim Clark, ed., Leigh Anne Couch, po. ed., Dept. of English, U. of North Carolina, Greensboro, NC 27412. Issues indexed: (57-59). Subscriptions: $8/yr. (2 issues), $20/3 yrs.; Single issue: $4.

HampSPR: THE HAMPDEN-SYDNEY POETRY REVIEW, Tom O'Grady, ed., P.O. Box 126, Hampden-Sydney, VA 23943. Issues indexed: (Winter, 1995). Subscriptions: $5/yr. (1 issue).

HangL: HANGING LOOSE, Robert Hershon, Dick Lourie, Mark Pawlak, Ron Schreiber, eds., 231 Wyckoff St., Brooklyn, NY 11217. Issues indexed: (66-67). Subscriptions: $17.50/3 issues, $33/6 issues, $50/9 issues (ind.); $21/3 issues, $42/6 issues, $63/9 issues (inst.); $28/3 issues, $50/6 issues, $70/9 issues (for.); Sample issue: $7 plus $1.50 postage and handling.

Harp: HARPER'S MAGAZINE, Lewis H. Lapham, ed., 666 Broadway, New York, NY 10012. Issues indexed: (290:1736-1741, 291:1742-1747). Subscriptions: $21/yr., plus $2/yr. (USA possessions, Canada), plus $20/yr. (for.); Single issue: $3.95; Subscription address: P.O. Box 7511, Red Oak, IA 51591-0511.

HarvardA: THE HARVARD ADVOCATE, Fay Lin, managing ed., Nadia Nurhussein, po. ed., 21 South St., Cambridge, MA 02138. Issues indexed: (129:3, 130:[1-2]); the Spring 95 issue is not numbered; the Fall 95 issue is numbered simply vol. CCXXX. Subscriptions: $15/yr. (ind.), $17/yr. (inst.), $20/yr. (for.); Single issue: $4.

HarvardR: HARVARD REVIEW, Stratis Haviaras, ed., Frederick Marchant, po. ed., Poetry Room, Harvard College Library, Cambridge, MA 02138. Issues indexed: (8-9). Subscriptions: $12/yr. (2 issues); $16/yr. (for. surface), $24/yr. (for. air mail); Single issue: $8.

HawaiiR: HR [Hawai'i Review], Robert Sean MacBeth, S. Gonzalez, eds., U. of Hawai'i at Manoa, 1733 Donaghho Rd., Dept. of English, Honolulu, HI 96822. Issues indexed: (19:2); 18:2-3 and 19:1 not received. Subscriptions: $25/yr. (3 issues), $45/2 yrs. (ind.); $30/yr., $50/2 yrs. (inst.); Single issue: $10.

HayF: HAYDEN'S FERRY REVIEW, Salima Keegan, Managing ed., Radu Hadrian Hotinceanu, Patricia Murphy, po. eds., Box 871502, Arizona State U., Tempe, AZ 85287-1502. Issues indexed: (16-17). Subscriptions: $10/yr. (2 issues), $18/2 yrs.; $13/yr., $26/2 yrs. (inst.); Single and back issues: $5 plus $1 postage.

HeavenB: HEAVEN BONE, Steven Hirsch, ed., pub., P.O. Box 486, Chester, NY 10918. Issues indexed: (12). Subscriptions: $16.95/4 issues; Single issue: $6.

Hellas: HELLAS: A Journal of Poetry and the Humanities, Gerald Harnett, ed., The Aldine Press, Ltd., 304 S. Tyson Ave., Glenside, PA 19038. Issues indexed: (6:1-2). Subscriptions: $14/yr. (2 issues), $24/2 yrs., plus $4/yr. (for.); Single issue: $7.50.

HighP: HIGH PLAINS LITERARY REVIEW, Robert O. Greer, Jr., ed., Joy Harjo, po. ed., 180 Adams St., Suite 250, Denver, CO 80206. Issues indexed: (10:1-3). Subscriptions: $20/yr. (3 issues), $38/2 yrs., plus $5/yr. (for.); Single issue: $7.

HiramPoR: HIRAM POETRY REVIEW, English Dept., Hiram College, Hale Chatfield, ed., P.O. Box 162, Hiram, OH 44234. Issues indexed: (58/59). Subscriptions: $8/yr. (2 issues); Single issue: $4.

HolCrit: THE HOLLINS CRITIC, John Rees Moore, ed., Hollins College, VA 24020. Issues indexed: (32:1-5). Subscriptions: $6/yr. (5 issues); $7.50/yr. (for.).

HopewellR: HOPEWELL REVIEW: New Work by Indiana's Best Writers, Joseph F. Trimmer, ed., Arts Indiana, Inc., The Majestic Building, 47 S. Pennsylvania St., Suite 701, Indianapolis, IN 46204-3622. Issues indexed: (7). Single issue: $6.95; Back issues: $1.95-$6.95 plus $2.50 shipping.

Hudson: THE HUDSON REVIEW, Paula Deitz, Frederick Morgan, eds., 684 Park Ave., New York, NY 10021. Issues indexed: (47:4, 48:1-3). Subscriptions: $24/yr., $46/2 yrs., $68/3 yrs., plus $4/yr. (for.); Single issue: $7, $9 (Canada).

IllinoisR: THE ILLINOIS REVIEW, Illinois Writers, Inc., Jim Elledge, ed., Dept. of English, Illinois State U., Campus Box 4240, Normal, IL 61790-4240. Issues indexed: (2:2, 3:1/2). Subscriptions: $10/yr. (2 issues), $18/yr. (inst.), $15/yr. (prepaid inst.); Single issue: $6.

Image: IMAGE: A Journal of the Arts & Religion, Gregory Wolfe, ed. and pub., Andrew Hudgins, Denise Levertov, Paul Mariani, po. eds., Richard Wilkinson, managing ed., P.O. Box 674, Kennett Square, PA 19348. Issues indexed: (9-12). Subscriptions: $30/yr. (4 issues), $60/2 yrs., $40/yr. (for.); Single issue: $10; Subscription address: P.O. Box 3000, Denville, NJ 07834-9351.

IndR: INDIANA REVIEW, Shirley Stephenson, ed., Christopher Green, Jennifer Grotz, Jeffrey McKenzie, Adam Sol, po. eds., Indiana U., 316 N. Jordan Ave., Bloomington, IN 47405. Issues indexed: (18:1-2). Subscriptions: $12/2 issues, $15/2 issues (inst.); $22/4 issues (ind.), $25/4 issues (inst.), plus $5/2 issues (for.); Single issue: $7.

Interim: INTERIM, A. Wilber Stevens, ed., Dept. of English, U. of Nevada, 4505 Maryland Parkway, Box 455011, Las Vegas, NV 89154-5011. Issues indexed: (14:1-2). Subscriptions: $8/yr. (2 issues), $13/2 yrs., $16/3 yrs. (ind.); $14/yr. (lib.), $16/yr. (for.); Single issue: $5, $8 (for.).

InterPR: INTERNATIONAL POETRY REVIEW, Mark Smith-Soto, ed., Dept. of Romance Languages, U. of North Carolina, Greensboro, NC 27412-5001. Issues indexed: (21:1-2). Subscriptions: $10/yr. (2 issues, ind.), $15/yr. (inst.), plus $2/yr. (for.); Single issue: $5.

InterQ: INTERNATIONAL QUARTERLY, Van K. Brock, ed., pub., Geoffrey Brock, Andrea Kelly, po. eds., P.O. Box 10521, Tallahassee, FL 32302-0521. Issues indexed: (2:1/2-3). Subscriptions: $30/yr. (4 issues), $55/2 yrs., $75/3 yrs. (ind.); $40/yr., $75/2 yrs., $100/3 yrs. (inst.), plus $5/issue (for.); Single issue: $8; Double issue: $10.

Inti: INTI: Revista de Literatura Hispánica, Roger B. Carmosino, ed., P.O. Box 20657, Cranston, RI 02920. Issues indexed: (42). Subscriptions: $30/yr. (2 issues, ind.), $20/yr. (students), $50/yr. (inst.); Single issue: $15.

Iowa: IOWA REVIEW, David Hamilton, ed., 308 EPB, U. of Iowa, Iowa City, IA 52242-1492. Issues indexed: (25:1-3). Subscriptions: $18/yr. (3 issues, ind.), $20/yr. (inst.), plus $3/yr. (for.); Single issue: $6.95.

Jacaranda: JACARANDA, Cornel Bonca, Bruce Kijewski, Laurence Roth, eds., English Dept., California State U., Fullerton, CA 92634. Issues indexed: (11). Subscriptions: $10/yr. (2 issues, ind.), $15/yr. (inst.); Sample issues: $6 (ind.), $8 (inst.).

JamesWR: THE JAMES WHITE REVIEW, A Gay Men's Literary Journal, Phil Willkie, pub., Clif Mayhood, po. ed., P.O. Box 3356, Butler Quarter Station, Minneapolis, MN 55403. Issues indexed: (12:1-3). Subscriptions: $14/yr., $24/2 yrs.; $16/yr., $30/2 yrs. (Canada); $20/yr. (other for.); Single issue: $5, $5 (Canada); Back issues: $1 (for minimum order of $10).

JlNJPo: THE JOURNAL OF NEW JERSEY POETS, Sander Zulauf, ed., Center for Teaching Excellence, County College of Morris, 214 Center Grove Rd., Randolph, NJ 07869-2086. Issues indexed: (17:1-2). Subscriptions: $7/yr. (2 issues), $12/2 yrs.; Single issue: $4.

Journal: THE JOURNAL, Kathy Fagan, Michelle Herman, eds., The Ohio State U., Dept. of English, 164 W. 17th Ave., Columbus, OH 43210. Issues indexed: (19:1-2). Subscriptions: $8/yr. (2 issues), $16/2 yrs., $24/3 yrs.; Single issue: $5.

Kaleid: KALEIDOSCOPE, International Magazine of Literature, Fine Arts, and Disability, Darshan Perusek, ed., Chris Hewitt, po. ed. (51 W. 86th St., #404, New York, NY 10024), United Disability Services, 326 Locust St., Akron, OH 44302-1876. Issues indexed: (30-31). Subscriptions: $9/yr. (2 issues, ind.), $14/yr. (inst.), plus $5/yr. (Canada), plus $8/yr. (other for.); Single issue: $5, $7 (for.); Sample issue: $4. Also available on audio cassette.

Kalliope: KALLIOPE: A Journal of Women's Art, Mary Sue Koeppel, ed., Florida Community College at Jacksonville, 3939 Roosevelt Blvd., Jacksonville, FL 32205. Issues indexed: (17:1-3). Subscriptions: $12.50/1 yr. (3 issues), $22/2 yrs. (ind.); $21/yr. (inst.), plus $6/yr. (for.); free to women in prison; Single issue: $7, plus $2 (for., single issue), $3 (for., double issue); Back issues: $4-8.

KenR: KENYON REVIEW, David H. Lynn, ed., Kenyon College, Gambier, OH 43022. Issues indexed: (NS 17:1-3/4). Subscriptions: $22/yr., $40/2 yrs., $60/3 yrs. (ind.); $30/yr. (inst.), plus $8 (for.); Single issue: $8, including postage; Double issue: $11; Back issues: $10.

LaurelR: LAUREL REVIEW, William Trowbridge, David Slater, Beth Richards, eds., GreenTower Press, Dept. of English, Northwest Missouri State U., Maryville, MO 64468. Issues indexed: (29:1-2). Subscriptions: $8/yr. (2 issues), $14/2 yrs.; $11/yr., $20/2 yrs. (for.); Single issue: $5; Back issues: $4.50.

*Ledge: THE LEDGE: Poetry and Fiction Magazine, Timothy Monaghan, ed, pub., 64-65 Cooper Ave., Glendale, NY 11385. Issues indexed: (18-19); No. 17 was indexed in the 1994 volume, but this listing for THE LEDGE was omitted from the list of periodicals indexed. Subscriptions: $9/1 yr. (2 issues), $15/2 yrs., $20/3 yrs.; Single issue: $5.

Light: LIGHT: A Quarterly of Light Verse, John Mella, ed., Box 7500, Chicago, IL 60680. Issues indexed: (13-15/16). Subscriptions: $16/yr. (4 issues), $28/2 yrs.; $24/yr. (for.); Single issue: $5; Double issue: $9; Back issues: $4.

LindLM: LINDEN LANE MAGAZINE, Belkis Cuza Malé, ed., P.O. Box 331964, Fort Worth, TX 76163. Issues indexed: (14:1); volume 13, numbers 2-4 not received. Subscriptions: $12/yr. (ind., 4 issues), $22/yr. (for., inst.); Single issue: $2.

*LiteralL: LITERAL LATTÉ: A Journal of Prose, Poetry & Art, Jenine Gordon, ed., pub., WordSCI, Inc., 61 E. 8th St., Ste 240, New York, NY 10003. Issues indexed: (1:1-6, 2:1-3). Subscriptions: $15/yr. (ind., 6 issues), $25/yr. (inst.), $30/yr. (for.); Single issue: $5.

LitR: THE LITERARY REVIEW: An International Journal of Contemporary Writing, Walter Cummins, ed., Fairleigh Dickinson U., 285 Madison Ave., Madison, NJ 07940. Issues indexed: (38:2-4, 39:1). Subscriptions: $18/yr., $21/yr. (for.); $30/2 yrs., $36/2 yrs. (for.); Single issue: $5, $6 (for.).

LouisL: LOUISIANA LITERATURE: A Review of Literature and Humanities, David C. Hanson, ed., Dept. of English, SLU-792, Southeastern Louisiana U., Box 792, Hammond, LA 70402. Issues indexed: (12:1-2). Subscriptions: $10/yr. (2 issues, ind.); $12.50/yr. (inst.), plus $5/yr. (Canada), plus $10/yr. (other for.).

*LowellR: THE LOWELL REVIEW, Judith Dickerman-Nelson, ed., Instant Karma Press, Inc., P.O. Box 184, Struthers, OH 44471. Issues indexed: ([1]-2); first issue, Summer 1994, is not numbered. Subscriptions: $7/yr. (1 issues); Back issues: $5.

LullwaterR: LULLWATER REVIEW, Marci C. Eggers, ed., Eric Brignac, po. ed., Box 22036, Emory U., Atlanta, GA 30322. Issues indexed: (5:1-2, 6:1-2). Subscriptions: $10/yr. (2 issues), plus $4 (for.); Single issue: $5.

Luz: LUZ: En Arte y Literatura, Verónica Miranda, Directora/Editora, Luz Bilingual Publishing, P.O. Box 571062, Tarzana, CA 91357-1062. Issues indexed: (8). Subscriptions: $25/yr. (3 issues), $45/2 yrs., $65/3 yrs.; $35/yr. (for.); Single issue: $8, plus $3 (for.).

MalR: THE MALAHAT REVIEW, U. of Victoria, Derk Wynand, ed., P.O. Box 1700, Victoria, BC, Canada V8W 2Y2. Issues indexed: (110-113). Subscriptions: $25/yr. (4 issues), $40/2 yrs.; Single issue: $7.

ManhatR: THE MANHATTAN REVIEW, Philip Fried, ed., 440 Riverside Dr., #45, New York, NY 10027. Issues indexed: (7:2, 8:1). Subscriptions: $10/2 issues (ind.), $14/2 issues (inst.), plus $3/issue (outside USA & Canada); Back issues: $5 (ind.), $7 (inst); include 6" x 9" envelope and $1.60 for postage.

Manoa: MANOA: A Pacific Journal of International Writing, Frank Stewart, ed., English Dept., U. of Hawai'i, Honolulu, HI 96822. Issues indexed: (7:1-2). Subscriptions: $20/yr. (2 issues), $36/2 yrs. (ind.); $26/yr., $46/2 yrs. (inst.); $23/yr., $41/2 yrs. (for. ind.); $31/yr., $56/2 yrs. (for. inst.), plus $12/yr. (for. air mail); Single issue: $15. Subscription address: U. of Hawaii Press, 2840 Kolowalu St., Honolulu, HI 96822.

*ManyMM: MANY MOUNTAINS MOVING: a literary journal of diverse contemporary voices, Naomi Horii, ed., 420 22nd St., Boulder, CO 80302. Issues indexed: (1:1-3, 2:1); "Inaugural issue" [1:1] not numbered. Subscriptions: $18/yr. (3 issues, ind.), $15/yr. (students, teachers), $14/yr. (gift subscriptions), plus $7.50/yr. (Canada), plus $15/yr. (other for.); Samples copies: $6.50; plus $2.50 (Canada), plus $5 (other for.).

MassR: THE MASSACHUSETTS REVIEW, Jules Chametzky, Mary Heath, Paul Jenkins, eds., Martín Espada, Anne Halley, Paul Jenkins, po. eds., Memorial Hall, U. of Massachusetts, Amherst, MA 01003. Issues indexed: (36:1-4). Subscriptions: $15/yr. (4 issues, ind.), $20/yr. (lib.), $25/yr. (for.); Single issue: $6.

MichQR: MICHIGAN QUARTERLY REVIEW, Laurence Goldstein, ed., 3032 Rackham Bldg., U. of Michigan, Ann Arbor, MI 48109. Issues indexed: (34:1-4). Subscriptions: $18/yr., $36/2 yrs. (ind.), $20/yr. (inst.); Single issue: $5; Back issues: $2.50.

MidAR: MID-AMERICAN REVIEW, Robert Early, George Looney, eds., Tony Gardner, po. ed., Dept. of English, Bowling Green State U., Bowling Green, OH 43403. Issues indexed: (15:1/2, 16:1). Subscriptions: $12/yr. (2 issues), $20/2 yrs., $28/3 yrs; Single issue: $7; Sample issue: $5.

MidwQ: THE MIDWEST QUARTERLY: A Journal of Contemporary Thought, James B. M. Schick, ed., Stephen E. Meats, po. ed., Pittsburg State U., Pittsburg, KS 66762-5889. Issues indexed: (36:2-4, 37:1). Subscriptions: $12/yr. plus $4 (for.); Single issue: $4.

MinnR: THE MINNESOTA REVIEW: a journal of committed writing, Jeffrey Williams, ed., pub., Rebecca Wee, po. ed., Dept. of English, East Carolina U., Greenville, NC 27858-4353. Issues indexed: (NS 43/44); NS 41/42 indexed in 1994 vol., but not listed. Subscriptions: $12/yr. (2 issues); $32/yr. (inst., for.), plus $5/yr. (for.); Single and back issues: $7.50; Double issue: $12.50.

MissouriR: THE MISSOURI REVIEW, Speer Morgan, ed., College of Arts & Science, 1507 Hillcrest Hall, U. of Missouri, Columbia, MO 65211. Issues indexed: (18:1-3). Subscriptions: $19/yr. (3 issues), $35/2 yrs., $45/3 yrs.; Single issue: $6.95.

MissR: MISSISSIPPI REVIEW, Frederick Barthelme, ed., The Center for Writers, U. of Southern Mississippi, Box 5144, Hattiesburg, MS 39406-5144. Issues indexed: (23:3, 24:1/2). Subscriptions: $15/yr. (2 issues), $28/2 yrs., $40/3 yrs., plus $2/yr. (for.); Single issue: usually $12.

ModernW : MODERN WORDS: a thoroughly queer international literary journal, Garland
Richard Kyle, ed., pub., 350 Bay St., No. 100, Box 325, San Francisco, CA 94133.
Issues indexed: (3). Subscriptions: $25/3 issues, $100/lifetime; Single issue: $10.

Nat: THE NATION, Katrina vanden Heuvel, ed., Grace Schulman, po. ed., 72 Fifth Ave., New
York, NY 10011. Issues indexed: (258: 1-16; 260:1-25, 261:1-22). 258:17-25 indexed
in 1994 volume. Subscriptions: $48/yr., $80/2 yrs., plus $18/yr. (for.); Single issue:
$2.50, $3.50 (Canada); Back issues: $4, $5 (for.). Send subscription correspondence to:
P.O. Box 10763, Des Moines, IA 50340-0763.

NegC: NEGATIVE CAPABILITY, Sue Brannan Walker, ed., 62 Ridgelawn Dr. East, Mobile,
AL 36608. Issues indexed: (14:3). Subscriptions: $18/yr. (3 issues, ind.), $22/yr. (inst.,
for.); Single issue: $6.

NewAW: NEW AMERICAN WRITING, Paul Hoover, Maxine Chernoff, eds., OINK! Press,
369 Molino Ave., Mill Valley, CA 94941. Issues indexed: (13). Subscriptions: $18/3
issues; $24/3 issues (inst.), plus $7/3 issues (for.); Single issue: $7.

NewDeltaR: NEW DELTA REVIEW, Joseph Cole, Chad Rohrbacher, po. eds., Rodger
Kamenetz, faculty advisor, Creative Writing Program, English Dept., Louisiana State
U., Baton Rouge, LA 70803-5001. Issues indexed: (12:1-2, 13:1). Subscriptions: $7/yr.
(2 issues); Single issue: $4.

NewEngR: NEW ENGLAND REVIEW, Middlebury Series, Stephen Donadio, ed., C. Dale
Young, po. consultant, Middlebury College, Middlebury, VT 05753. Issues indexed:
(17:1-4). Subscriptions: $23/yr. (4 issues), $43/2 yrs., $62/3 yrs. (ind.); $40/yr., $75/2
yrs., $108/3 yrs. (lib., inst.), plus $10/yr. (for. surface) or $20/yr. (for. air mail); Single
issue: $7, $9 (for. surface), $10 (for. air mail); subscription address: U. Press of New
England, 23 S. Main St., Hanover, NH 03755-2048.

NewL: NEW LETTERS, James McKinley, ed., U. of Missouri-Kansas City, 5100 Rockhill Rd.,
Kansas City, MO 64110. Issues indexed: (61:2-4, 62:1). Subscriptions: $17/yr. (4
issues), $28/2 yrs., $55/5 yrs. (ind.); $20/yr., $34/2 yrs., $65/5 yrs. (lib.); Single issue:
$5, $8 (Canada).

*NewMyths: NEW MYTHS / MSS, Robert Mooney, ed., Philip Brady, po. ed., Binghamton
U., P.O. Box 6000, Binghamton, NY 13902-6000. Issues indexed: (2:2/3:1). Single
copy: $12. "This is the last issue...."

NewOR: NEW ORLEANS REVIEW, Ralph Adamo, ed., Box 195, Loyola U., New Orleans,
LA 70118. Issues indexed: (21:1-3/4). Subscriptions: $18/yr. (4 issues, ind.), $21/yr.
(inst.), $32/yr. (for.); Back issues: $9.

NewRena: THE NEW RENAISSANCE: An international magazine of ideas and opinions,
emphasizing literature and the arts, Louise T. Reynolds, ed., James E. A. Woodbury, po.
ed., 9 Heath Road, Arlington, MA 02174-3614. Issues indexed: (9:2, #28).
Subscriptions: $21/3 issues, $39.50/6 issues; $22/3 issues, $41.50/6 issues (Canada);
$24/3 issues, $44/6 issues (other for.); Single issue: $9, $9.50 (for.).

NewRep: THE NEW REPUBLIC, Andrew Sullivan, ed., Mark Strand, po. ed., 1220 19th St.
NW, Washington, DC 20036. Issues indexed: (212:1-26, 213:1-26). Subscriptions:
$69.97/yr., $84.97/yr. (Canada), $99.97/yr. (elsewhere). Back issues: $3.50. Single
issue: $2.95. Subscription Service Dept., The New Republic, P.O. Box 602, Mount
Morris, IL 61054.

NewYorker: THE NEW YORKER, Pamela Maffei McCarthy, deputy ed., 20 W. 43rd St., New
York, NY 10036. Issues indexed: (70:43 [i.e. 44]-49, 71:1-42). Subscriptions: $36/yr.,
$60/2 yrs.; $77/yr. (Canada); $85/yr. (other for.); Single issue: $2.95; Subscription
correspondence to: Box 56447, Boulder, CO 80322.

NewYorkQ: THE NEW YORK QUARTERLY, William Packard, ed., P.O. Box 693, Old
Chelsea Station, New York, NY 10113. Issues indexed: (54-55). Subscriptions:
$15/yr., $30/2 yrs., $45/3 yrs.; $25/yr. (lib.), plus $5/yr. (for.); Single issue: $6.

NewYRB: THE NEW YORK REVIEW OF BOOKS, Robert B. Silvers, Barbara Epstein, eds., 250 W. 57th St., New York, NY 10107. Issues indexed: (42:1-20). Subscriptions: $49.50/yr., 93.50/2 yrs., 137.50/3 yrs.; Single issue: $3.25, $4.60 (Canada); NY Review of Books, P.O. Box 420384, Palm Coast, FL 32142-0384.

Nimrod: NIMROD, Francine Ringold, ed., Manly Johnson, po. ed., Arts and Humanities Council of Tulsa, 2210 S. Main St., Tulsa, OK 74114. Issues indexed: (38:2, 39:1); Vol. 39, No. 1 is labeled "Vol. 38, No. 1" in error on spine. Subscriptions: $15/yr. (2 issues), $25/2 yrs., plus $4/yr. (for.); Single issue: $8.

NoAmR: THE NORTH AMERICAN REVIEW, Robley Wilson, ed., Peter Cooley, po. ed., U. of Northern Iowa, Cedar Falls, IA 50614-0516. Issues indexed: (280:5-6); vol. 280, nos. 1-4 not received. Subscriptions: $18/yr., $25/yr. (Canada), $28/yr. (elsewhere); Single issue: $4, $5.25 (Canada).

NoCarLR: NORTH CAROLINA LITERARY REVIEW, Alex Albright, ed., English Dept., East Carolina U., Greenville, NC 27858-4353. Issues indexed: (2:2). Subscriptions: $17/2 issues, $31/4 issues, plus $3/issue (for.); Single issue: 12.

Noctiluca: NOCTILUCA: An International Magazine of Poetry, Judy Katz-Levine, ed., 10 Hillshire Ln., Norwood, MA 02062-3009. Issues indexed: (2:1, #4). Subscriptions: $10/3 issues.

NoDaQ: NORTH DAKOTA QUARTERLY, Robert W. Lewis, ed., Jay Meek, po. ed., U. of North Dakota, Grand Forks, ND 58202-7209. Issues indexed: None; next volume, 63, published in 1996. Subscriptions: $20/yr., $24/yr. (inst.); $23/yr. (for. ind.), $28/yr. (for. inst.); Single issue: $5 (ind.), $7 (for.); Special issues: $10, $12 (for.).

Northeast: NORTHEAST, John Judson, ed., Juniper Press, 1310 Shorewood Dr., La Crosse, WI 54601. Issues indexed: (Ser. 5:12-13). Subscriptions: $33 (2 issues, including books and gifts of the press, ind.), $38 (inst.); Single issue: $4.

*NortheastCor: NORTHEAST CORRIDOR, Susan Balée, Jeffrey Loo, Janna King, po. eds., English Dept., Beaver College, 450 S. Easton Rd., Glenside, PA 19038-3295. Issues indexed: (3). Subscriptions: $10/yr. (2 issues, ind.), $20/yr. (inst.); Single issue: $5.

NorthStoneR: THE NORTH STONE REVIEW, James Naiden, ed., D Station, Box 14098, Minneapolis, MN 55414. Issues indexed: (12). Subscriptions: $20/2 issues; Single issue: $10.

NowestR: NORTHWEST REVIEW, John Witte, ed. & po. ed., 369 PLC, U. of Oregon, Eugene, OR 97403. Issues indexed: (33:1-3). Subscriptions: $20/yr. (3 issues), $38/2 yrs., $53/3 yrs.; $17/yr., $31/2 yrs. (stud.), plus $4/yr. (for.); Single issue: $7.

Obs: OBSIDIAN II: Black Literature in Review, Gerald Barrax, ed. & po. ed., Dept. of English, Box 8105, North Carolina State U., Raleigh, NC 27695-8105. Issues indexed: No 1995 issues received. Subscriptions: $12/yr. (2 issues), $20/2 yrs.; $13/yr. (Canada), $15/yr. (other for.); Single issue: $5; Double issues: $10.

OgalalaR: THE OGALALA REVIEW, Gordon Grice, Tracy Hiatt Grice, eds., P.O. Box 2699, U. of Arkansas, Fayetteville, AR 72701. Issues indexed: No 1995 issues received. Subscriptions: $10/yr. (2 issues), $18/2 yrs; Single issue: $5.

OhioR: THE OHIO REVIEW, Wayne Dodd, ed., Ellis Hall, Ohio U., Athens, OH 45701-2979. Issues indexed: (53-54). Subscriptions: $16/yr. (2 issues), $40/3 yrs.; Single issue: $6.

Ometeca: OMETECA: Ciencia y Literatura, Science & Literature, Ciência e literatura, Rafael Catalá, ed., P.O. Box 38, New Brunswick, NJ 08903-0038. Issues indexed: No 1995 issues published. Subscriptions: $40/2 vols. (4 issues, ind., USA, Canada), $70/2 vols. (inst., USA, Canada); $60/2 vols. (ind., European Community, Australia, Japan), $80/2 vols. (inst., European Community, Australia, Japan); $44/2 vols. (ind., other countries), $56/2 vols. (inst., other countries).

OnTheBus: ONTHEBUS: A New Literary Magazine, Jack Grapes, ed., P.O. Box 481266, Bicentennial Station, Los Angeles, CA 90048. Issues indexed: No 1994 or 1995 issues received; next issue, #14 due in March 1997. Subscriptions: $28/3 issues (ind.), $33/3 issues (inst.); Single issue: $11, plus $1 postage; Double issue: $13.50 plus $1.50 postage; Subscription address: Bombshelter Press, 6684 Colgate Ave., Los Angeles, CA 90048.

OntR: ONTARIO REVIEW, Raymond J. Smith, ed., 9 Honey Brook Dr., Princeton, NJ 08540. Issues indexed: (42-43). Subscriptions: $12/yr. (2 issues), $22/2 yrs., $30/3 yrs., plus $2/yr. (for.); Single issue: $6.

*Orion: ORION: People and Nature, George K. Russell, ed., Emily Hiestand, Christopher Merrill, po eds., The Orion Society, The Myrin Institute, 136 E. 64th St., New York, NY 10021. Issues indexed: (14:1-4). Subscriptions: $20/yr. (4 issues), plus $5/yr. (for., surface mail), or plus $25/yr. (for., air mail); Single issue: $5.

Os: OSIRIS, Andrea Moorhead, ed., P.O. Box 297, Deerfield, MA 01342. Issues indexed: (40-41). Subscriptions: $12/2 issues; Single issue: $6.

Outbr: OUTERBRIDGE, Charlotte Alexander, ed., English Dept., College of Staten Island (CUNY), 2800 Victory Blvd., Staten Island, NY 10314. Issues indexed: No issues published in 1995; No. 26 published in 1996. Subscriptions: $6/issue. Published every 2 years.

OxfordM: OXFORD MAGAZINE, Constance Pierce, editorial advisor, Dept. of English, Bachelor Hall, Miami U., Oxford, OH 45056. Issues indexed:(9:2, 10:1). Single issue: $5.

Paint: PAINTBRUSH: A Journal of Contemporary Multicultural Literature, Ben Bennani, ed., Truman State U., Kirksville, MO 63501. Issues indexed: (22). Subscriptions: $15/yr. (1 issue, ind.), $20/yr. (inst.).

PaintedB: PAINTED BRIDE QUARTERLY, Kathy Volk Miller, Brian Brown, Marion Wrenn, eds., Painted Bride Arts Center, 230 Vine St., Philadelphia, PA 19106. Issues indexed: (55/56, 57). Subscriptions: $16/yr. (4 issues), $28/2 yrs., $20/yr. (lib., inst.); Single issue: $5. Distributed free to inmates.

PaintedHR: PAINTED HILLS REVIEW, Michael Ishii, Kara D. Kosmatka, eds., 2950 Portage Bay West #411, Davis, CA 95616. Issues indexed: No 1995 issues received. Subscriptions: $10/3 issues, $18/6 issues (USA & Canada); $14/3 issues, $24/6 issues (other for.); Single issue: $3.50.

ParisR: THE PARIS REVIEW, George A. Plimpton, Peter Matthiessen, Donald Hall, Robert Silvers, Blair Fuller, Maxine Groffsky, Jeanne McCulloch, James Linville, eds., Richard Howard, po. ed., Box S, 541 East 72nd St., New York, NY 10021. Issues indexed: (37:134-137). Subscriptions: $34/4 issues, plus $8/4 issues (for.); Single issue: $10, $14 (Canada); Subscription address: 45-39 171st Place, Flushing, NY 11358.

Parting: PARTING GIFTS, Robert Bixby, ed., pub., March Street Press, 3413 Wilshire Dr., Greensboro, NC 27408-2923. Issues indexed: (8:1-2). Subscriptions: $12/yr. (2 issues); Single issue: $6.

PartR: PARTISAN REVIEW, William Phillips, ed., Boston U., 236 Bay State Rd., Boston, MA 02215. Issues indexed: (62:1-4). Subscriptions: $22/yr. (4 issues), $40/2 yrs., $56/3 yrs.; $28/2 yrs. (for.); $32/yr. (inst.); Single issue: $6, plus $1.50 per issue postage and handling.

PassN: PASSAGES NORTH, Michael Barrett, ed., Kalamazoo College, 1200 Academy St., Kalamazoo, MI 49006-3295. Issues indexed: (16:1-2). Subscriptions: $10/yr., $18/2 yrs., plus $9/yr. (for.); Single issue: $6.

Pearl: PEARL, Joan Jobe Smith, Marilyn Johnson, Barbara Hauk, eds., 3030 E. 2nd St., Long Beach, CA 90803. Issues indexed: (22); No. 21 not received. Subscriptions: $15/yr. (3 issues, ind.); $20/yr. (lib.); $30/yr. (patrons); Single issue: $6.

Pembroke: PEMBROKE MAGAZINE, Shelby Stephenson, ed., Box 60, Pembroke State U., Pembroke, NC 28372. Issues indexed: (27). Subscriptions: $5/issue (USA, Canada, Mexico), $5.50/issue (other for.).

PennR: THE PENNSYLVANIA REVIEW, Ed Ochester, executive ed., Maria McLeod, po. ed., 526 Cathedral of Learning, U. of Pittsburgh, Pittsburgh, PA 15260. Issues indexed: (6:2); vol. 6, no. 1 not received. Subscriptions: $7/yr. (2 issues), $14/2 yrs.; Single issue: $4.

Pequod: PEQUOD, Mark Rudman, ed., Dept. of English, Room 200, New York U., 19 University Place, New York, NY 10003. Issues indexed: (39). Subscriptions: $12/yr. (2 issues), $20/2 yrs. (ind.); $18/yr., $34/2 yrs. (inst.), plus $3/yr. (for.); Single issue: $7.50-$10.

*Phoebe: PHOEBE: A Journal of Literary Arts, Jean Donnelly, ed., Graham Foust, po. ed., George Mason U., 4400 University Dr., Fairfax, VA 22030-4444. Issues indexed: (24:1-2). Subscriptions: $10/yr. (2 issues), $15/2 yrs.; Single issue: $6.

PikeF: THE PIKESTAFF FORUM, Robert D. Sutherland, James R. Scrimgeour, eds./pubs., P.O. Box 127, Normal, IL 61761. Issues indexed: No 1994 or 1995 issues published; No. 12 published in 1996; No. 13 "will be the magazine's final issue." Subscriptions: $12/6 issues; Single issue: $3.

Pivot: PIVOT, Martin Mitchell, ed., Sibyl Barsky Grucci, pub., 221 S. Barnard St., State College PA 16801. Issues indexed: No 1995 issues received. Subscriptions: $14/3 yrs. (3 issues), $15/3 yrs. (for.); Single issue: $5, $6 (for.).

Plain: PLAINSONGS, Dwight Marsh, ed., Dept. of English, Hastings College, Hastings, NE 68902-0269. Issues indexed: (15:2-3, 16:1). Subscriptions: $9/yr. (3 issues).

Ploughs: PLOUGHSHARES, Don Lee, ed., David Daniel, po. ed., Emerson College, 100 Beacon St., Boston, MA 02116-1596. Issues indexed: (21:1, 2/3, 4). Subscriptions: $19/yr., $36/2 yrs. (ind.); $24/yr. (for. ind.); $22/yr. (inst.), $27/yr. (for. inst.). Single issue: $8.95.

PlumR: THE PLUM REVIEW, Mike Hammer, Christina Daub, eds., P.O. Box 1347, Philadephia, PA 19105. Issues indexed: (8-9). Subscriptions: $14/yr. (2 issues), $28/2 yrs., $40/3 yrs. Subscription address: P.O. Box 1347, Philadelphia, PA 19105-1347.

Poem: POEM, Huntsville Literary Association, Nancy Frey Dillard, ed., c/o English Dept., U. of Alabama, Huntsville, AL 35899. Issues indexed: (73-74). Subscriptions: $10/yr.; Back issues: $5; Subscription address: Huntsville Literary Association, P.O. Box 919, Huntsville, AL 35804.

PoetC: POET AND CRITIC. No longer published. Succeeded by Flyway.

PoetL: POET LORE, Philip K. Jason, Geraldine Connolly, executive eds., The Writer's Center, 4508 Walsh St., Bethesda, MD 20815. Issues indexed: (90:1-4). Subscriptions: $10/yr. (Writer's Center members); $15/yr. (ind.); $24/yr. (inst.), plus $5/yr. (for.); Single issue: $4.50, plus $1 postage and handling; Samples: $4.

Poetry: POETRY, Joseph Parisi, ed., 60 W. Walton St., Chicago, IL 60610. Issues indexed: (165:4-6, 166:1-6, 167:1/2-3). Subscriptions: $25/yr. (ind.); $31/yr. (for.); $27/yr. (inst.); $33/yr. (for. inst.); Single issue: $2.50 plus $1.50 postage; Back issues: $3 plus $1.50 postage.

PoetryC: POETRY CANADA, Barry Dempster, po. ed., P.O. Box 1061, Kingston, Ont. K7L 4Y5 Canada. Issues indexed: (15:2-3). Subscriptions: $17.12/4 issues (ind.); $34.24/4 issues (inst.); Back issues: $5; Single issue: $4.95; Double issue: $7.95.

PoetryE: POETRY EAST, Richard Jones, ed., Dept. of English, 802 W. Belden Ave., DePaul U., Chicago, IL 60614. Issues indexed: (39-41). Subscriptions: $15/yr.; Single issue: $8.

PoetryNW: POETRY NORTHWEST, David Wagoner, ed., U. of Washington, 4045 Brooklyn Ave. NE, Seattle, WA 98105-6261. Issues indexed: (36:1-4). Subscriptions: $15/yr., $17/yr. (for.); Single issue: $5, $5.50 (for.).

PottPort: THE POTTERSFIELD PORTFOLIO, Ian Colford, ed., Collette Saunders, po. ed., The Gatsby Press, 5280 Green St., P.O. Box 27094, Halifax, Nova Scotia B3H 4M8 Canada. Issues indexed: (16:1); vol. 15, nos. 2-3 not published. Subscriptions: $18/yr. (3 issues), $32/2 yrs. Canada); $24/yr. (U.S. & for.); Single issue: $7.

Poz: POZ, Sean O'Brien Strub, exec. ed., Richard Pérez-Feria, ed., P.O. Box 1279 Old Chelsea Station, New York, NY 10113-1279. Issues indexed: (6-7); no. 5 not received. Subscriptions: $19.95/yr. (6 issues), $31.95/2 yrs.; $29.95/yr. (Canada); $49.95 (other for.); $79.95/yr. (inst.); available without cost to low-income HIV positive persons; Single copy: $3.95, $4.95 (Canada). Subscription address: POZ, Subscription Dept., P.O. Box 1965, Danbury, CT 06813-1965.

PraF: PRAIRIE FIRE: A Canadian Magazine of New Writing, Andris Taskans, ed., Méira Cook, Catherine Hunter, po. eds., 423-100 Arthur St., Winnipeg, Manitoba R3B 9Z9 Canada. Issues indexed: (16:1-4, #70-73). Subscriptions: $24/yr., $44/2 yrs. (ind.); $32/yr. (inst.), plus $4 (USA), plus $6 (other for.); Single issue: $10.95-11.95.

PraS: PRAIRIE SCHOONER, Hilda Raz, ed., 201 Andrews Hall, U. of Nebraska, Lincoln, NE 68588-0334. Issues indexed: (69:1-4). Subscriptions: $20/yr., $35/2 yrs., $46/3 yrs. (ind.); $22/yr. (lib.); Single issue: $6.45.

Prima: PRIMAVERA, Lisa Grayson, Kathleen Kuiper, Anneliese Lindeman, Martha Ann Selby, Ruth Young, eds., Box 37-7547, Chicago, IL 60637. Issues indexed: (18/19). Double issue: $10; Back issues: $5-$9.

ProseP: THE PROSE POEM: An International Journal, Peter Johnson, ed., English Dept., Providence College, Providence, RI 02918. Issues indexed: (3). Subscriptions: $8/annual issue, $12/2 yrs.; Back issues: $4.

Quarry: QUARRY, Mary Cameron, ed., P.O. Box 1061, Kingston, Ontario K7L 4Y5 Canada. Issues indexed: (43:4, 44:1-3). Subscriptions: $22.47/yr. (4 issues), $39.85/2 yrs. (8 issues); Single issue: $7.95.

QRL: QUARTERLY REVIEW OF LITERATURE, T. & R. Weiss, eds., 26 Haslet Ave., Princeton, NJ 08540. Issues indexed: (34). Subscriptions: $20/2 volumes (paper), $20/volume (cloth, inst.).

QW: QUARTERLY WEST, Lawrence Coates, M. L. Williams, ed., Margot Schilpp, po. ed., 317 Olpin Union, U. of Utah, Salt Lake City, UT 84112. Issues indexed: (40-41). Subscriptions: $11/yr. (2 issues), $20/2 yrs.; $14/yr., $26/2 yrs. (for.); Single issue: $6.50; Back issues: $5.

RagMag: RAG MAG, Beverly Voldseth, ed., pub., Black Hat Press, Box 12, 508 2nd Ave., Goodhue, MN 55027. Issues indexed: (12:2). Subscriptions: $10/yr. (2 issues), $15/2 yrs., plus $5/yr. (for.); Single issue: $6; Back issues: $4.

Raritan: RARITAN: A Quarterly Review, Richard Poirier, ed., Rutgers U., 31 Mine St., New Brunswick, NJ 08903. Issues indexed: (14:3-4, 15:1-2). Subscriptions: $16/yr., $26/2 yrs. (ind.); $20/yr., $30/2 yrs. (inst.), plus $5.50/yr. (for.); Single issue: $5; Back issues: $6.

RiverC: RIVER CITY: A Journal of Contemporary Culture, Paul Naylor, ed., Dept. of English, U. of Memphis, Memphis, TN 38152. Issues indexed: (15:2). Subscriptions: $12/yr. (ind., 2 issues), $24/3 yrs.; $18/yr. (inst.); Single issue: $7; subscription address: U. of Memphis, P.O. Box 1000, Dept. 313, Memphis, TN 38148, Memphis, TN 38148-0313.

RiverS: RIVER STYX: Multicultural Literary Explorers Since 1975, Jennifer Tabin, Richard Newman, eds., 3207 Washington Ave., St. Louis, MO 63103. Issues indexed: (41, 42/43, 44-45). Subscriptions: $20/3 issues, $35/6 issues; $48/9 issues; Single issue: $7.

Rosebud: ROSEBUD: For People Who Enjoy Writing, Roderick Clark, ed., P.O. Box 459, Cambridge, WI 53523. Issues indexed: (2:1-3). Subscriptions: $18/4 issues, $30/8 issues, plus $12/4 issues (for.); Single copy: $5.50, $6.50 (Canada); Subscription address: Beth Swan, 4218 Barnett St., Madison, WI 53704.

Salm: SALMAGUNDI: A Quarterly of the Humanities and Social Sciences, Robert Boyers, ed., Skidmore College, Saratoga Springs, NY 12866. Issues indexed: (106/107, 108). Subscriptions: $15/yr., $25/2 yrs. (ind.); $22/yr., $37/2 yrs. (inst.), plus $10/yr. (for.); Sample issues: $6; Single issue: $6; Double issue: $8.

SantaBR: SANTA BARBARA REVIEW, Patricia Stockton Leddy, ed., 104 La Vereda Ln., Santa Barbara, CA 93108. Issues indexed: (3:1-3). Subscriptions: $16/yr. (3 issues), plus $7.50/yr. (for.) or $24/yr. (for. air mail); Single issue: $7, plus $2.50 postage and handling.

SenR: SENECA REVIEW, Deborah Tall, ed., Hobart and William Smith Colleges, Geneva, NY 14456. Issues indexed: (25:1-2). Subscriptions: $8/yr. (2 issues), $15/2 yrs.; Single issue: $5.; Back issues: $5.

Sequoia: SEQUOIA: Stanford Literary Magazine, Carlos Rodríguez, managing ed., Susan Vanderborg, po. ed., Storke Publications Building, Stanford U., Stanford, CA 94305. Issues indexed: (36). Subscriptions: $10/yr. (1 issue), $12/yr. (for.).

SewanR: THE SEWANEE REVIEW, George Core, ed., U. of the South, Sewanee, TN 37383-1000. Issues indexed: (103:1-4). Subscriptions: $16/yr., $28/2 yrs., $40/3 yrs. (ind.); $20/yr., $38/2 yrs., $55/3 yrs. (inst.), plus $5/yr. (for.); Single issue: $5.75; Back issues: $8.

ShadowP: SHADOW PLAY, Jan Bender, ed., 99 Reynolds Rd., Grand Isle, VT 05458. Issues indexed: No 1994 issues received. Single issue: $4.

Shen: SHENANDOAH: The Washington and Lee University Review, R. T. Smith, ed., Troubadour Theater, 2nd Floor, Lexington, VA 24450. Issues indexed: (45:1-4). Subscriptions: $11/yr., $18/2 yrs., $25/3 yrs.; $14/yr., $24/2 yrs., $33/3 yrs. (for.); Single issue: $3.50; Back issues: $6.

SilverFR: SILVERFISH REVIEW, Rodger Moody, ed., P.O. Box 3541, Eugene, OR 97403. Issues indexed: (25-26). Subscriptions: $8/2 issues (ind.), $12/2 issues (inst.); Single issue: $4.

SingHM: SING HEAVENLY MUSE!: Women's Poetry and Prose, Ruth Berman, Karen Karsten, D. Perry Kidder, Sue Ann Martinson, Carol Master, Linda Webster, Carrie Wicks, eds., P.O. Box 13320, Minneapolis, MN 55414. Issues indexed: No 1995 issues published; No. 22 published in 1996. Subscriptions: $15/2 issues, $20/3 issues, $38/6 issues (ind.); $22/3 issues, $41/6 issues (inst.); $16/3 issues (low income); Single issue: $8 plus $2 postage and handling.

SinW: SINISTER WISDOM: A Journal for Lesbians, Akiba Onada-Sikwoia, ed., Ekua Omosupe, po. ed., P.O. Box 3252, Berkeley, CA 94703. Issues indexed: (55-56). Subscriptions: $17/yr. (4 issues), $30/2 yrs. (ind.); $30/yr. (inst.); $22/yr. (for.); $8-15/yr. (hardship); Free on request to women in prisons and mental institutions; Single issue: $5.

SlipS: SLIPSTREAM, Robert Borgatti, Livio Farallo, Dan Sicoli, eds., P.O. Box 2071, Niagara Falls, NY 14301. Issues indexed: (15). Subscriptions: $15/2 issues plus 2-3 chapbooks; Single issue: $5.

SmPd: THE SMALL POND MAGAZINE OF LITERATURE, Napoleon St. Cyr, ed., pub., P.O. Box 664, Stratford, CT 06497. Issues indexed: (32:1-3, #93-95). Subscriptions: $9/yr. (3 issues), $17/2 yrs., $25/3 yrs., plus $1.50/yr. (for.); Single issue: $3.25; Random back issues: $2.50.

SnailPR: THE SNAIL'S PACE REVIEW: A Biannual Little Magazine of Contemporary Poetry, Ken Denberg, Darby Penney, eds., RR 2 Box 403 Darwin Rd., Cambridge, NY 12816. Issues indexed: (3:2). Subscriptions: $7/yr. (ind.), $12/yr. (inst.); Sample copy: $4.

Sonora: SONORA REVIEW, Julie Newman, Alicia Saposnik, eds., Chris Weidenbach, po. ed., Dept. of English, U. of Arizona, Tucson, AZ 85721. Issues indexed: (29-30). Subscriptions: $12/2 issues, $24/4 issues, $36/6 issues; Single, back and sample issues: $6.

SoCaR: SOUTH CAROLINA REVIEW, Frank Day, Carol Johnston, eds., Dept. of English, Clemson U., Strode Tower, Box 341503, Clemson, SC 29634-1503. Issues indexed: (28:1). Subscriptions: $10/yr., $18/2 yrs., $26/3 yrs. (USA, Canada), plus $3/yr. (other for.); Sample issue: $10.

SoCoast: SOUTH COAST POETRY JOURNAL, John J. Brugaletta, ed., English Dept., California State U., Fullerton, CA 92634. Issues indexed: (18-19); No. 18 "is the final issue."

SoDakR: SOUTH DAKOTA REVIEW, Brian Bedard, ed., Dept. of English, U. of South Dakota, Box 111, U. Exchange, Vermillion, SD 57069. Issues indexed: (33:1-3/4). Subscriptions: $15/yr., $25/2 yrs. (USA, Canada), plus $1/yr. elsewhere; Single issue: $5; Double issue: $9.

SouthernHR: SOUTHERN HUMANITIES REVIEW, Dan R. Latimer, Virginia M. Kouidis, eds., 9088 Haley Center, Auburn U., AL 36849. Issues indexed: (29:1-4). Subscriptions: $15/yr.; Single issue: $5.

SouthernPR: SOUTHERN POETRY REVIEW, Ken McLaurin, ed., English Dept., U. of North Carolina, Charlotte, NC 28223. Issues indexed: (35:1-2). Subscriptions: $8/yr.

SouthernR: SOUTHERN REVIEW, James Olney, Dave Smith, eds., Louisiana State U., 43 Allen Hall, Baton Rouge, LA 70803-5005. Issues indexed: (31:1-4). Subscriptions: $20/yr., $36/2 yrs., $50/3 yrs.; $40/yr., $65/2 yrs., $90/3 yrs. (inst.); Single issue: $6, $12 (inst.).

SouthwR: SOUTHWEST REVIEW, Willard Spiegelman, ed., Southern Methodist U., Dallas, TX 75275. Issues indexed: (80:1, 2/3, 4). Subscriptions: $20/yr., $35/2 yrs., $50/3 yrs. (ind.); $25/yr. (inst.); Single issue: $5.

*SpinningJ: SPINNING JENNY, C. E. Harrison, ed., Black Dress Press, P.O. Box 356, Cooper Station, New York, NY 10276. Issues indexed: (1). Subscriptions: $10/yr. (2 issues); Single issue: $5.

Spirit: THE SPIRIT THAT MOVES US, Morty Sklar, ed., pub., P.O. Box 720820, Jackson Heights, NY 11372-0820. Issues indexed: No issues published 1992-1995; #12 published in 1966.

SpiritSH: SPIRIT: A Magazine of Poetry, David Rogers, ed., Dept. of English, Seton Hall U., South Orange, NJ 07079. Issues indexed: (60). Subscriptions: $4/yr. (2 issues); Single issue: $2; Back issues: $3.

Spitball: SPITBALL: The Literary Baseball Magazine, Mike Shannon, ed., William J. McGill, po. ed., 5560 Fox Rd., Cincinnati, OH 45239. Issues indexed: (48-49). Subscriptions: $16/yr. (4 issues); $22/yr. (Canada, U.S. funds); Single issue: $5.

SpoonR: THE SPOON RIVER POETRY REVIEW, Lucia Cordell Getsi, ed., 4240 English Dept., Illinois State U., Normal, IL 61790-4240. Issues indexed: (20:1-2); vol. 19, no. 2 not received. Subscriptions: $12/yr. (2 issues); $15/yr. (inst.); Single issue: $8.

Stand: STAND MAGAZINE, Daniel Schenker, Amanda Kay, U.S. eds., 122 Morris Rd., Lacey's Spring, AL 35754. Issues indexed: (36:2-3). Subscriptions: $25/yr., $46/2 yrs.; $18/yr. (students, unswaged); Single issue: $6.50; U.S.A. distributor: Anton J. Mikovsky, 50 E. 42nd St. Ste. 1809, New York, NY 10017.

Sulfur: SULFUR: A Literary Bi-Annual of the Whole Art, Clayton Eshleman, ed., English Dept., Eastern Michigan U., Ypsilanti, MI 48197. Issues indexed: (15:1-2, #36-37). Subscriptions: $14/2 issues (ind.), $20/2 issues (inst.), plus $4 (for. book rate) or $10 (for. air mail postage); Single issue: $9.

Sun: SUN: A Magazine of Ideas, Sy Safransky, ed., 107 N. Roberson St., Chapel Hill, NC 27516. Issues indexed: (229-240). Subscriptions: $32/yr., $60/2 yrs., $150/5 yrs., $300/10 yrs., $1,000 lifetime, plus $10/yr. (for.); Single issue: $3.50. Subscription address: The Sun, Subscription Service, P.O. Box 6706, Syracuse, NY 13217.

SycamoreR: SYCAMORE REVIEW, Michael Manley, ed., Brent Goodman, po. ed., Dept. of English, Heavilon Hall, Purdue U., West Lafayette, IN 47907. Issues indexed: (7:1-2). Subscriptions: $10/yr. (2 issues), $12/yr. (for.); Sample copy: $7, $8 (for.).

Talisman: TALISMAN: A Journal of Contemporary Poetry and Poetics, Edward Foster, ed., Box 3157, Jersey City, NJ 07303-3157. Issues indexed: (14-15). Subscriptions: $11/yr. (2 issues); $15/yr. (inst.), plus $2/yr. (for.); Single issue: $6.

TampaR: TAMPA REVIEW: Literary Journal of the University of Tampa, Richard Mathews, ed., Donald Morrill, Kathryn Van Spanckeren, po. eds., U. of Tampa, 401 W. Kennedy Blvd., Tampa, FL 33606-1490. Issues indexed: (10-11). Subscriptions: $10/yr. (2 issues), plus $4/yr. (for.); Single issue: $5.95.

TarRP: TAR RIVER POETRY, Peter Makuck, ed., Dept. of English, General Classroom Bldg., East Carolina U., Greenville, NC 27858-4353. Issues indexed: (34:2, 35:1). Subscriptions: $10/yr (2 issues), $18/2 yrs.; Single issue: $5.50.

TexasR: TEXAS REVIEW, Paul Ruffin, ed., Division of English and Foreign Languages, Sam Houston State U., Huntsville, TX 77341. Issues indexed: (15:3/4, 16:1/4). Subscriptions: $10/yr., $18/2 yrs., $26/3 yrs.; $10.50/yr. (Canada), $11/yr. (for.); Single issue: $5; Combined issue: $10.

Thirteenth Moon — See 13thMoon *(at beginning of list).*

Thrpny: THE THREEPENNY REVIEW, Wendy Lesser, ed., pub., P.O. Box 9131, Berkeley, CA 94709. Issues indexed: (60-63). Subscriptions: $16/yr., $28/2 yrs., $30/yr. (for.); Single issue: $4.

TickleAce: TICKLEACE: A Journal of Literary and Visual Art, Susan Ingersoll, Lawrence Mathews, Bruce Porter, Michael Winter, eds., P.O. Box 5353, St. John's, NF, A1C 5W2 Canada. Issues indexed: (27); No. 28 was indexed in the 1994 volume; nos. 29-30 not received. Subscriptions: $14/yr. (2 issues), $17/yr. (inst.), plus $5/yr. (U.S.), plus $7/yr. (other for.); Single issue: $8.

Trans: TRANSLATION, The Journal of Literary Translation, Lori M. Carlson, Frank MacShane, eds., The Translation Center, 412 Dodge Hall, Columbia U., New York, NY 10027. Issues indexed: No 1995 issues received. The Translation Center's "activities were suspended during the summer, following the unanticipated retirement of the director of the Center for health reasons" — Peter Smith, Dean, School of the Arts, Columbia U., 12-22-94.

Tricycle: TRICYCLE: The Buddhist Review, Helen Tworkov, ed., The Buddhist Ray, Inc., 92 Vandam St., New York, NY 10013. Issues indexed: (4:3-4, 5:1-2); vol. 3, nos. 3-4, vol. 4, nos. 1-2 not received. Subscriptions: $24/yr. (4 issues), $40/2 yrs., $60/3 yrs.; $29/yr. (for. surface mail), $39/yr. (for. air mail); Single copy: $6.50. Subscription address: Subscription Dept., TRI Box 3000, Denville, NJ 07834.

TriQ: TRIQUARTERLY, Reginald Gibbons, Susan Hahn, eds., Northwestern U., 2020 Ridge Ave., Evanston, IL 60208. Issues indexed: (93-95). Subscriptions: $24/yr. (3 issues), $44/2 yrs., $600/life (ind.); $36/yr., $68/2 yrs. (inst.), plus $5/yr. (for.); Single issue: cost varies; Sample copy: $5.

Turnstile: TURNSTILE, Curt Alliaume, Alison Berry, Daniel Bial, Tom Cockbill, Lindsey Crittenden, Vira DeFilippo, Twisne Fan, Ann McKay Farrell, Kit Haines, Marian Lizzi, Maria Tahim, George Witte, eds., 175 Fifth Ave., Suite 2348, New York, NY 10010. Issues indexed: (5:1). Subscriptions: $12/2 issues, $22/4 issues; Single issue: $6.50.

US1: US 1 WORKSHEETS, Norma Voorhees Sheard, secretary, Rod Tulloss, treasurer, US 1 Poets' Cooperative, P.O. Box 1, Ringoes, NJ 08551-0001. Issues indexed: (30/31). Subscriptions: $10/2 double issues; Single (double) issue: $6.

Verse: VERSE, Nancy Schoenberger, Brian Henry eds., Dept. of English, College of William and Mary, Williamsburg, VA 23187-8795. Issues indexed: (11:3/12:1, 12:2-3). Subscriptions: $15/yr. (3 issues); Back issue: $5; Single issue: $6.

VirQR: THE VIRGINIA QUARTERLY REVIEW: A National Journal of Literature and Discussion, Staige D. Blackford, ed., Gregory Orr, po. consultant, One West Range, Charlottesville, VA 22903. Issues indexed: (71:1-4). Subscriptions: $18/yr., $25/2 yrs., $33/3 yrs. (ind.); $22/yr., $30/2 yrs., $50/3 yrs. (inst.), plus $6/yr. (for.); Single issue: $5.

Vis: VISIONS INTERNATIONAL, Bradley R. Strahan, po. ed., pub., Black Buzzard Press, 1110 Seaton Lane, Falls Church, VA 22046. Issues indexed: (47-49). Subscriptions: $15/yr. (3 issues), $28/2 yrs. (ind.); $45/3 yrs. (lib.); Single issue: $4.50-$5.50.

War: WAR, LITERATURE, & THE ARTS: An International Journal of the Humanities, Donald Anderson, ed., Dept. of English, 2354 Fairchild Dr., Ste. 6D35, U.S. Air Force Academy, CO 80840-6242. Will Hochman, po. ed., Dept. of English, U. of Southern Colorado, Pueblo, CO 81001. Issues indexed: (7:1-2). Subscriptions: $10/yr. (2 issues), $18/2 yrs., $24/3 yrs. (ind.); $20/yr., $36/2 yrs., $48/3 yrs. (inst.), plus $5/yr. (for.). Make checks payable to: Academic Support Fund (WLA).

WashR: WASHINGTON REVIEW, Clarissa K. Wittenberg, ed., P.O. Box 50132, Washington, DC 20091-0132. Issues indexed: (20:5-6; 21:1-4). Subscriptions: $15/yr. (6 issues), $25/2 yrs.; Single issue: $4.

WeberS: WEBER STUDIES: An Interdisciplinary Humanities Journal, Neila C. Seshachari, ed., Weber State U., Ogden, UT 84408-1214. Issues indexed: (12:1-3). Subscriptions: $10/yr. (3 issues), $20/yr. (inst.), plus actual extra postage costs per year (for.); Back amd single issues: $7.

WebR: WEBSTER REVIEW, Nancy Schapiro, Robert Boyd, Greg Marshall, eds., English Dept., SLCC-Meramec, 11333 Big Bend Rd., St. Louis, MO 63122. Issues indexed: No 1995 issues received. Subscriptions: $5/yr. (1 issue).

WestB: WEST BRANCH: a twice-yearly magazine of poetry and fiction, Karl Patten, Robert Love Taylor, eds., Bucknell Hall, Bucknell U., Lewisburg, PA 17837. Issues indexed: (36-37). Subscriptions: $7/yr. (2 issues), $11/2 yrs.; Single issue: $4; Double issue: $7.

WestCL: WEST COAST LINE: A Journal of Contemporary Writing and Criticism, Roy Miki, ed., 2027 East Academic Annex, Simon Fraser U., Burnaby, BC V5A 1S6 Canada. Issues indexed: (29:1-3, #16-18). Subscriptions: $20/yr. (ind., 3 issues), $30/yr. (inst.); $30/yr. (for. ind.), $45/yr. (for. inst.); Single issue: $10.

WestHR: WESTERN HUMANITIES REVIEW, Barry Weller, ed., Richard Howard, po. ed., U. of Utah, Salt Lake City, UT 84112. Issues indexed: (49:1-4). Subscriptions: $20/yr. (4 issues, ind.), $26/yr. (inst.); Single issue: $6.

WilliamMR: THE WILLIAM AND MARY REVIEW, Laura Sims, ed., Telisha Moore, Forrest Pritchard, po. eds., College of William and Mary, P.O. Box 8795, Williamsburg, VA 23187. Issues indexed: (33). Subscriptions: $5/single issue, plus $1.50 (for.); Single issue: $5.50.

WillowR: WILLOW REVIEW, Paulette Roeske, ed., College of Lake County, 19351 W. Washington St., Grayslake, IL 60030-1198. Issues indexed: (22). Subscriptions: $13/3 issues, $20/5 issues; Single issue: $5.

WillowS: WILLOW SPRINGS, Nance Van Winckel, ed., J. Cailin Oakes, po. ed., 526 5th St., MS-1, Eastern Washington U., Cheney, WA 99004. Issues indexed: (35-36); No. 36 has "35" on spine, in error. Subscriptions: $10.50/yr. (2 issues), $20/2 yrs.; Single issue: $5.50.

Wind: WIND, Steven R. Cope, Charlie G. Hughes, eds., P.O. Box 24548, Lexington, KY 40524. Issues indexed: (75-76). Subscriptions: $10/yr. (2 issues, ind.), $12/yr. (inst.), $14/yr. (for.); Single issue: $6.

WindO: THE WINDLESS ORCHARD, Robert Novak, ed., English Dept., Indiana-Purdue U., Fort Wayne, IN 46805. Issues indexed: (59-60). Subscriptions: $10/3 issues; Single issue: $4.

Witness: WITNESS, Peter Stine, ed., Oakland Community College, Orchard Ridge Campus, 27055 Orchard Lake Road, Farmington Hills, MI 48334. Issues indexed: (9:1-2). Subscriptions: $12/yr. (2 issues), $22/2 yrs.; $18/yr., $34/2 yrs. (inst.), plus $4/yr. (for.); Single issue: $7.

WorldL: WORLD LETTER, Jon Cone, ed., 2726 E. Court St., Iowa City, IA 52245. Issues indexed: (6). Subscriptions: "Subscriptions are no longer being offered; ... will be published only when funds become available."

WorldO: WORLD ORDER, Firuz Kazemzadeh, Betty J. Fisher, Howard Garey, Robert H. Stockman, James D. Stokes, eds., Herbert Woodward Martin, po. consultant, National Spiritual Assembly of the Bahá'ís of the United States, 415 Linden Ave., Wilmette, IL 60091. Issues indexed: (26:3-4, 27:1-2). Subscriptions: $15/yr. (4 issues), $28/2 yrs.; $15/yr., $28/2 yrs. (for.); $20/yr., $38/2 yrs. (for. air mail); Single issue: $3.75.

WormR: THE WORMWOOD REVIEW, Marvin Malone, ed., P.O. Box 4698, Stockton, CA 95204-0698. Issues indexed: (35:1-4; #137-140). Subscriptions: $12/yr. (4 issues); $24/yr. (patrons); Back and single issues: $4.

Writ: WRIT, Roger Greenwald, ed., Innis College, U. of Toronto, 2 Sussex Ave., Toronto, Canada M5S 1J5. Issues indexed: (27). "Final issue of the magazine." Back issues: $10-$20.

Writer: THE WRITER, Sylvia K. Burack, ed., pub., 120 Boylston St., Boston, MA 02116-4615. Issues indexed: (108:1-12). Subscriptions: $28/yr., $52/2 yrs., $75/3 yrs., plus $8/yr. (for.); $10/5 issues for new subscribers; Single issue: $2.50.

WritersF: WRITERS' FORUM, Alexander Blackburn, ed., Victoria McCabe, po. ed., P.O. Box 7150, U. of Colorado, Colorado Springs, CO 80933-7150. Issues indexed: (21). Subscriptions: $8.95/yr. (1 issue) plus $1.05 postage and handling; Back issue sample: $5.95 plus $1.05 postage and handling.

XavierR: XAVIER REVIEW, Thomas Bonner, Jr., ed., Box 110C, Xavier U., New Orleans, LA 70125. Issues indexed: (15:1-2). Subscriptions: $10/yr. (2 issues, ind.), $15/yr. (inst.).

YaleR: THE YALE REVIEW, J. D. McClatchy, ed., Yale U., P.O. Box 208243, New Haven, CT 06520-8243. Issues indexed: (83:1-4). Subscriptions: $23.50/yr., $42/2 yrs., $62/3 yrs. (ind.); $34/yr., $61.50/2 yrs., $90/3 yrs. (for. ind.); $50/yr. (inst.), $56/yr. (for. inst.); Single issue: $8 (ind.), $16.50 (inst.), $12 (for. ind.), $17.50 (for. inst.); Subscription address: Subscriber Services Coordinator, Blackwell Publishers, 238 Main St., Cambridge, MA 02142; make checks payable to Blackwell Publishers.

YellowS: YELLOW SILK, Journal of Erotic Arts, Lily Pond, ed., pub., P.O. Box 6374, Albany, CA 94706. Issues indexed: (12:4, #48). Subscriptions: $30/yr. (4 issues, ind.), $38/yr. (lib., inst.), plus $8/yr. (for. surface mail) or $22/yr. (for. air mail); Single issue: $7.50.

Zyzzyva: ZYZZYVA: the last word, west coast writers & artists, Howard Junker, ed., 41 Sutter St., Suite 1400, San Francisco, CA 94104-4903. Issues indexed: (11:1-3/4, #41-43/44); although neither are so labeled, issue 42 consists of "The Writer's Notebook," ed. by Howard Junker (HarperCollins West, c1995, 249 p.), and issue 43/44 consists of "Strange Attraction: The Best of Ten Years of ZYZZYVA," ed. by Howard Junker (Reno: U. of Nevada Press, 1995, 338 p.). Although there may be poems, or drafts of poems, in "The Writer's Notebook," no poems were indexed from this volume. All poems in "Strange Attraction" were indexed. Subscriptions: $28/yr. (4 issues), $48/2 yrs. (ind.); $36/yr. (inst.); $48/yr. (for.); Single issue: $10.

Alphabetical List of Journals Indexed, with Acronyms

13th Moon: A Feminist Literary Magazine : 13th Moon

Abraxas : Abraxas
African American Review : AfAmRev
Agni : Agni
Alabama Literary Review : AlabamaLR
Amelia : Amelia
American Letters & Commentary : AmerLC
The American Poetry Review : AmerPoR
The American Scholar : AmerS
The American Voice : AmerV
The Americas Review: A Review of Hispanic Literature and Art of the USA :
    Americas
Another Chicago Magazine : AnotherCM
The Anthology of New England Writers : AnthNEW
The Antigonish Review : AntigR
The Antioch Review : AntR
Apalachee Quarterly : ApalQ
Arc: Canada's National Poetry Magazine : Arc
Archae : Archae
Areíto : Areíto
Arion: A Journal of Humanities and the Classics : Arion
Arshile: A Magazine of the Arts : Arshile
Art & Understanding: The International Magazine of Literature and Art About
    AIDS : Art&Und
Artful Dodge : ArtfulD
Arts Indiana Literary Supplement: *See* Hopewell Review *(title change)*
Ascent : Ascent
The Atlantic : Atlantic
Avec : Avec
Axe Factory : AxeF

Bamboo Ridge: The Hawaii Writers' Quarterly : BambooR
The Bellingham Review : BellR
Bellowing Ark : BellArk
The Beloit Poetry Journal : BelPoJ
The Bilingual Review / La Revista Bilingüe : BilingR
Black American Literature Forum: *See* African American Review *(title change)*
Black Bear Review : BlackBR
Black Moon: Poetry of Imagination : BlackMoon
Black Warrior Review : BlackWR
Blueline : Blueline
Bogg: An Anglo-American Journal : Bogg
Bomb Magazine : Bomb
Borderlands: Texas Poetry Review : Border
Boston Review : BostonR
Boulevard : Boulevard
Brooklyn Review : BrooklynR

Caliban : Caliban
Callaloo: A Journal of African-American and African Arts and Letters :
    Callaloo
Calyx: A Journal of Art and Literature by Women : Calyx
Canadian Literature / Littérature Canadienne : CanLit

The Cape Rock: A Gathering of Poets : CapeR
The Capilano Review : CapilR
The Caribbean Writer : CaribbeanW
Carolina Quarterly : CarolQ
The Centennial Review : CentR
Central Park : CentralP
Chain : Chain
Chaminade Literary Review : ChamLR
Changing Men: Issues in Gender, Sex and Politics : ChangingM
The Chariton Review : CharR
The Chattahoochee Review: The DeKalb College Literary Quarterly : ChatR
Chelsea : Chelsea
Chicago Review : ChiR
Chiron Review : ChironR
The Christian Century: An Ecumenical Weekly : ChrC
Cimarron Review : CimR
Cincinnati Poetry Review : CinPR
Clockwatch Review: A Journal of the Arts : ClockR
College English : ColEng
Colorado Review : ColR
Columbia: A Journal of Literature and Art : Colum
Commonweal : Comm
Conduit: the only magazine that risks annihilation : Conduit
Confrontation : Confr
Conjunctions: Bi-Annual Volumes of New Writing : Conjunc
The Connecticut Poetry Review : ConnPR
Conscience: A Newsjournal of Prochoice Catholic Opinion : Conscience
Context South : ContextS
Crab Creek Review : CrabCR
Crab Orchard Review: A Journal of Creative Works : CrabOR
Crazyhorse : Crazy
Cream City Review : CreamCR
Crosscurrents : CrossCur
Crucible : Crucible
Cuadernos de Poética : CuadP
Cumberland Poetry Review : CumbPR
Cutbank : CutB

Dandelion : Dandel
Defined Providence : DefinedP
Denver Quarterly : DenQ
Descant : Descant
Dog River Review : DogRR
Drumvoices Revue: A Confluence of Literary, Cultural & Vision Arts :
    Drumvoices

Elf: Eclectic Literary Forum : Elf
English Journal : EngJ
Epiphany: A Journal of Literature : *See* The Ogalala Review *(title change)*
Epoch : Epoch
Event: The Douglas College Review: New and Established Writers : Event
The Evergreen Chronicles: A Journal of Gay and Lesbian Literature :
    EvergreenC
Eyeball : Eyeball

Farmer's Market : Farm
Field: Contemporary Poetry and Poetics : Field
The Florida Review : FloridaR
Flyway: A Literary Review : Flyway
Footwork: Paterson Literary Review : Footwork
Four Quarters : FourQ
Free Lunch: A Poetry Journal : FreeL

Gaia: A Journal of Literature & Environmental Arts : Gaia
Georgia Review : GeoR
Gerbil: a queer culture zine : Gerbil

Gettysburg Review : GettyR
Global City Review : GlobalCR
Graham House Review : GrahamHR
Grain : Grain
Grand Street : GrandS
The Green Hills Literary Lantern: The Journal of the North Central Missouri
     Writer's Guild : GreenHLL
Green Mountains Review : GreenMR
The Greensboro Review : GreensboroR

The Hampden-Sydney Poetry Review : HampSPR
Hanging Loose : HangL
Harper's Magazine : Harp
The Harvard Advocate : HarvardA
Harvard Review : HarvardR
Hawai'i Review: See HR [Hawai'i Review] (title change)
Hayden's Ferry Review : HayF
Heaven Bone : HeavenB
Hellas: A Journal of Poetry and the Humanities : Hellas
High Plains Literary Review : HighP
Hiram Poetry Review : HiramPoR
The Hollins Critic : HolCrit
Hopewell Review: New Work by Indiana's Best Writers : HopewellR
HR [Hawai'i Review] : HawaiiR
The Hudson Review : Hudson

The Illinois Review : IllinoisR
Image: A Journal of the Arts & Religion : Image
Indiana Review : IndR
Interim : Interim
International Poetry Review : InterPR
International Quarterly : InterQ
Inti: Revista de Literatura Hispánica : Inti
Iowa Review : Iowa

Jacaranda : Jacaranda
The James White Review: A Gay Men's Literary Journal : JamesWR
The Journal : Journal
The Journal of New Jersey Poets : JlNJPo

Kaleidoscope: International Magazine of Literature, Fine Arts, and Disability :
     Kaleid
Kalliope: A Journal of Women's Art : Kalliope
Kenyon Review : KenR

Laurel Review : LaurelR
The Ledge: Poetry and Fiction Magazine : Ledge
Light: A Quarterly of Light Verse : Light
Linden Lane Magazine : LindLM
Literal Latté: A Journal of Prose, Poetry & Art : LiteralL
The Literary Review: An International Journal of Contemporary Writing : LitR
Louisiana Literature: A Review of Literature and Humanities : LouisL
The Lowell Review : LowellR
Lullwater Review : LullwaterR
Luz: En Arte y Literatura : Luz

The Malahat Review : MalR
The Manhattan Review : ManhatR
Manoa: A Pacific Journal of International Writing : Manoa
Many Mountains Moving: a literary journal of diverse contemporary voices :
     ManyMM
The Massachusetts Review : MassR
Memphis State Review: See River City (title change)
Michigan Quarterly Review : MichQR
Mid-American Review : MidAR
The Midwest Quarterly: A Journal of Contemporary Thought : MidwQ

The Minnesota Review: a journal of committed writing : MinnR
Mississippi Review : MissR
The Missouri Review : MissouriR
Modern Words: a thoroughly queer international literary journal : ModernW

The Nation : Nat
Negative Capability : NegC
New American Writing : NewAW
New Delta Review : NewDeltaR
New England Review : NewEngR
New Letters : NewL
New Myths / MSS : NewMyths
New Orleans Review : NewOR
The New Renaissance: An international magazine of ideas and opinions :
    NewRena
The New Republic : NewRep
The New York Quarterly : NewYorkQ
The New York Review of Books : NewYRB
The New Yorker : NewYorker
Nimrod : Nimrod
Noctiluca: An International Magazine of Poetry : Noctiluca
The North American Review : NoAmR
North Carolina Literary Review : NoCarLR
North Dakota Quarterly : NoDaQ
The North Stone Review : NorthStoneR
Northeast : Northeast
Northeast Corridor : NortheastCor
Northwest Review : NowestR

Obsidian II: Black Literature in Review : Obs
The Ogalala Review : OgalalaR
The Ohio Review : OhioR
Ometeca: Ciencia y Literatura, Science & Literature, Ciência e literatura :
    Ometeca
Ontario Review : OntR
OnTheBus: A New Literary Magazine : OnTheBus
Orion: People and Nature : Orion
Osiris : Os
Outerbridge : Outbr
Oxford Magazine : OxfordM

Paintbrush: A Journal of Contemporary Multicultural Literature : Paint
Painted Bride Quarterly : PaintedB
Painted Hills Review : PaintedHR
The Paris Review : ParisR
Parting Gifts : Parting
Partisan Review : PartR
Passages North : PassN
Pearl : Pearl
Pembroke Magazine : Pembroke
The Pennsylvania Review : PennR
Pequod : Pequod
Phoebe: A Journal of Literary Arts : Phoebe
The Pikestaff Forum : PikeF
Pivot : Pivot
Plainsongs : Plain
Ploughshares : Ploughs
The Plum Review : PlumR
Poem : Poem
Poet And Critic: *No longer published. Succeeded by* Flyway.
Poet Lore : PoetL
Poetry : Poetry
Poetry Canada : PoetryC
Poetry East : PoetryE
Poetry Northwest : PoetryNW
The Pottersfield Portfolio : PottPort

Poz : Poz
Prairie Fire: A Canadian Magazine of New Writing : PraF
Prairie Schooner : PraS
Primavera : Prima
The Prose Poem: An International Journal : ProseP

Quarry : Quarry
Quarterly Review of Literature : QRL
Quarterly West : QW

Rag Mag : RagMag
Raritan: A Quarterly Review : Raritan
River City: A Journal of Contemporary Culture : RiverC
River Styx: Multicultural Literary Explorers Since 1975 : RiverS
Rosebud: For People Who Enjoy Writing : Rosebud

Salmagundi: A Quarterly of the Humanities and Social Sciences : Salm
Santa Barbara Review : SantaBR
Seneca Review : SenR
Sequoia: Stanford Literary Magazine : Sequoia
The Sewanee Review : SewanR
Shadow Play : ShadowP
Shenandoah: The Washington and Lee University Review : Shen
Silverfish Review : SilverFR
Sing Heavenly Muse!: Women's Poetry and Prose : SingHM
Sinister Wisdom: A Journal for Lesbians : SinW
Slipstream : SlipS
The Small Pond Magazine of Literature : SmPd
The Snail's Pace Review: A Biannual Little Magazine of Contemporary Poetry :
    SnailPR
Sonora Review : Sonora
South Carolina Review : SoCaR
South Coast Poetry Journal : SoCoast
South Dakota Review : SoDakR
Southern Humanities Review : SouthernHR
Southern Poetry Review : SouthernPR
Southern Review : SouthernR
Southwest Review : SouthwR
Spinning Jenny : SpinningJ
Spirit: A Magazine of Poetry : SpiritSH
The Spirit That Moves Us : Spirit
Spitball: The Literary Baseball Magazine : Spitball
The Spoon River Poetry Review (formerly The Spoon River Quarterly) :
    SpoonR
Stand Magazine : Stand
Sulfur: A Literary Bi-Annual of the Whole Art : Sulfur
Sun: A Magazine of Ideas : Sun
Sycamore Review : SycamoreR

Talisman: A Journal of Contemporary Poetry and Poetics : Talisman
Tampa Review: Literary Journal of the University of Tampa : TampaR
Tar River Poetry : TarRP
Texas Review : TexasR
Thirteenth Moon: See 13th Moon (at beginning of list)
The Threepenny Review : Thrpny
TickleAce: A Journal of Literary and Visual Art : TickleAce
Translation: The Journal of Literary Translation : Trans
Tricycle: The Buddhist Review : Tricycle
Triquarterly : TriQ
Turnstile : Turnstile

US 1 Worksheets : US1

Verse : Verse
The Virginia Quarterly Review: A National Journal of Literature and Discussion
    : VirQR

Visions International : Vis

War, Literature, & the Arts: An International Journal of the Humanities : War
Washington Review : WashR
Weber Studies: An Interdisciplinary Humanities Journal : WeberS
Webster Review : WebR
West Branch: A twice-yearly magazine of poetry and fiction : WestB
West Coast Line: A Journal of Contemporary Writing and Criticism (*formerly*
    West Coast Review) : WestCL
Western Humanities Review : WestHR
The William and Mary Review : WilliamMR
Willow Review : WillowR
Willow Springs : WillowS
Wind : Wind
The Windless Orchard : WindO
Witness : Witness
World Letter : WorldL
World Order : WorldO
The Wormwood Review : WormR
Writ : Writ
The Writer : Writer
Writers' Forum : WritersF

Xavier Review : XavierR

The Yale Review : YaleR
Yellow Silk: Journal of Erotic Arts : YellowS

Zyzzyva: the last word, west coast writers and artists : Zyzzyva

Author Index

A., BETTY
   See BETTY A.
AAL, Katharyn Machan
   See MACHAN, Katharyn Howd
1. AALFS, Janet E.
   "She Said the Meat Tasted Queer." [EvergreenC] (10:1) Wint-Spr 95, p. 37.
2. ABBATE, Francesca M.
   "April." [CutB] (43) Wint 95, p. 44-45.
   "Today is almost summer." [CutB] (43) Wint 95, p. 46-47.
3. ABBE, Kate
   "Closet." [13thMoon] (13:1/2) 95, p. 5.
4. ABBEY, L. M.
   "Portrait of the Poetess Anna de Noailles, 1926" (after the painting by Tsugouharu
      Foujita). [LitR] (38:2) Wint 95, p. 207-208.
   "Retarded Boy." [HayF] (16) Spr-Sum 95, p. 112-113.
5. ABBOTT, Anthony
   "Come Lord Jesus" (1994 Literary Contest: Second Prize). [Crucible] (30) Fall 94, p. 4 -
      5.
6. ABDELLA, Zahra
   "Spirits" (WritersCorps Program, Washington, DC). [WashR] (21:2) Ag-S 95, p. 10.
7. ABELL, M. J.
   "Searching the Cave" (For my father). [SantaBR] (3:1) Spr 95, p. 22.
8. ABMA, Annette
   "Lagoon." [AntigR] (101) Spr 95, p. 7.
   "Midnight Stroll in September." [AntigR] (101) Spr 95, p. 9-10.
   "Passing Through Waterless Places." [AntigR] (101) Spr 95, p. 8.
9. ABRAHAMSON, Richard F.
   "A Feminist Deconstruction" (Literary Festival: Poetry: Honorable Mention). [EngJ]
      (84:4) Ap 95, p. 38.
10. ABRAMS-MORLEY, Liz
   "Equinox." [LowellR] (2) c1996, p. 107-108.
11. ABSE, Dannie
   "My Neighbour, Itzig." [Iowa] (25:3) Fall 95, p. 96.
   "Raise High the Glass." [Iowa] (25:3) Fall 95, p. 97.
12. ABSHER, John Stanley
   "Eno January 1994" (1994 Literary Contest: Sam Ragan Prize). [Crucible] (30) Fall
      94, p. 6-9.
13. ACKER, Ally
   "The Laundromat." [Sun] (235) Jl 95, p. 19.
   "Menagerie." [AmerV] (36) 95, p. 73-74.
14. ACREE, Carolyn
   "A Lake in Georgia." [HayF] (17) Fall-Wint 95, p. 116-117.
15. ADAIR, Diana
   "If My Mother Ever Sewed." [PoetryE] (40) Spr 95, p. 7.
16. ADAIR, Tracy May
   "Vengeance." [Calyx] (16:1) Sum 95, p. 72-73.
17. ADAIR, Virginia Hamilton
   "The Dark Hole." [NewYorker] (71:22) 31 Jl 95, p. 48.
   "English Visit." [NewYorker] (71:32) 16 O 95, p. 163.
   "Fair Warning." [NewYorker] (71:35) 6 N 95, p. 114.
   "God to the Serpent." [NewYorker] (71:40) 11 D 95, p. 46.
18. ADAM, Helen
   "In and Out of the Horn-Beam Maze." [RiverS] (42/43) 95, p. 3-4.
19. ADAMS, Anna
   "Jack and Kate Talk to Themselves." [NewYorkQ] (55) 95, p. 67.
   "The Sailor's Woman." [NewYorkQ] (54) 95, p. 71.

20. ADAMS, B. B.
    "Unstitching." [ChironR] (43) Sum 95, p. 34.
21. ADAMS, Coralie
    "Story Progression." [Bogg] (67) 95, p. 48-49.
22. ADAMS, Elizabeth
    "Cedar Grove." [SoCaR] (28:1) Fall 95, p. 180-181.
    "Checkered Linen." [SoCaR] (28:1) Fall 95, p. 181-182.
23. ADAMS, Hannah B.
    "The Palouse Apocalypse on All Hallows Eve." [BellArk] (11:1) Ja-F 95, p. 7.
    "Season's End." [BellArk] (11:1) Ja-F 95, p. 24.
24. ADAMS, Jon
    "Art Lesson." [EvergreenC] (10:2) Sum-Fall 95, p. 22.
    "Drought." [JamesWR] (12:1) Wint 95, p. 8.
    "Flood." [JamesWR] (12:1) Wint 95, p. 8.
25. ADAMS, Judith M.
    "On Sharing Carvel with Aunt Roneta." [Footwork] (24/25) 95, p. 208.
26. ADAMS, Kate
    "Bag of Tricks." [Vis] (49) 95, p. 10-11.
    "Dead Center." [Kalliope] (17:3) 95, p. 10.
    "Lost Astronaut." [Vis] (49) 95, p. 12.
27. ADAMS, Lavonne J.
    "Returning to Asheville, 1977." [NewDeltaR] (13:1) Fall 95-Wint 96, p. 54.
28. ADAMS, Michael
    "The Shape My Love Takes." [MidwQ] (36:4) Sum 95, p. 345.
29. ADAMS, Pat
    "Sign on a Bridge." [Poem] (74) N 95, p. 2-3.
30. ADAMS, Tahirih
    "Sleep." [Gerbil] (3) Sum 95, p. 17.
31. ADAMS, Terry
    "The Childless Man" (Honorable Mention, 1995 Editors' Prize). [SpoonR] (20:2) Sum-
        Fall 95, p. 48-49.
32. ADAMSON, Eve
    "Beatitudes." [MidwQ] (36:3) Spr 95, p. 289.
    "Echo in Iowa." [PraS] (69:4) Wint 95, p. 114-115.
33. ADANG, Rick
    "Play the Calliope" (1993 Poetry Contest, Second Place Winner). [DefinedP] (1:2)
        Spr-Sum 93, p. 59-60.
34. ADCOCK, Betty
    "After Geology, After Biology." [Shen] (45:2) Sum 95, p. 48-49.
    "At the Age When You Get Bad News." [Shen] (45:2) Sum 95, p. 50-51.
    "The Bird Woman" (for Barbara Johnson). [SouthernHR] (29:2) Spr 95, p. 126.
    "Love Poem." [SouthernHR] (29:3) Sum 95, p. 262.
    "Poem to a Friend Explaining Why I Did Not Attend the Convention of Professional
        Poets." [SouthernHR] (29:3) Sum 95, p. 263.
    "Two Poems with One Epigraph." [Shen] (45:2) Sum 95, p. 52.
    "The Woman Hidden in This Painting." [Shen] (45:2) Sum 95, p. 46-47.
35. ADCOCK, Ginger
    "At the Edge of the Red-Checkered Cloth." [Journal] (19:1) Spr-Sum 95, p. 17.
    "Tampa Swamp, 1959." [Journal] (19:1) Spr-Sum 95, p. 18-19.
36. ADDERLEY, Carol
    "Fast Forward / Fast Creed." [WorldL] (6) 95, p. 16.
37. ADDINGTON, Rosa Lea
    "Breaking the Spell." [Poem] (73) My 95, p. 53.
    "Fall From Grace." [Poem] (73) My 95, p. 54.
38. ADDISON, Jon
    "For My Hands." [WestB] (37) 95, p. 15.
39. ADDISON, Lloyd
    "The Cake Is Donna." [Drumvoices] (5:1/2) Fall-Wint 95-96, p. 89.
    "Far As Are Stars." [Drumvoices] (4:1/2) Fall-Wint 94-95, p. 30.
    "From Umbra." [Drumvoices] (4:1/2) Fall-Wint 94-95, p. 29.
40. ADDONIZIO, Kim
    "Broken Sonnets" (Volunteer Worker, Family Shelter, for JS). [ManyMM] (2:1) 95, p.
        127-129.
    "The Chair." [GettyR] (8:3) Sum 95, p. 493.
    "Intimacy." [Thrpny] (60) Wint 95, p. 39.
    "Phantom Anniversary." [AmerPoR] (24:4) Jl-Ag 95, p. 6.

"Physics." [AmerPoR] (24:4) Jl-Ag 95, p. 6.
"September." [PoetryE] (39) Fall 94, p. 7.
"The Story." [ManyMM] (2:1) 95, p. 126.
"Survivors." [GettyR] (8:3) Sum 95, p. 492.
"Traveling East." [PraS] (69:1) Spr 95, p. 50-51.
41. ADERMAN, Ruth Pierstorff
"View from the San Joaquin Hills." [ChironR] (43) Sum 95, p. 34.
42. ADHIKARI, Dinesh
"Man From a Developing Country" (tr. by Wayne Amtzis). [SenR] (25:2) Fall 95, p. 70-71.
43. ADOLPH, Andrea
"Candle Child" (after Waco). [SantaBR] (3:1) Spr 95, p. 63-64.
"Carpentry" (for Cynthia Luna). [SantaBR] (3:1) Spr 95, p. 64.
"Man Resembling a Hexagram." [SpoonR] (20:1) Wint-Spr 95, p. 18.
"Once Upon a Time." [SantaBR] (3:1) Spr 95, p. 63.
ADORNO, Pedro López
See LOPEZ ADORNO, Pedro
44. AGATHIAS SCHOLASTICUS (ca. 531-580 CE)
"Beautiful Melite, in the throes of middle age" (tr. by Sam Hamill). [PoetryE] (41) Aut 95, p. 18.
AGHA SHAHID ALI
See ALI, Agha Shahid
45. AGOSIN, Marjorie
"Los Desaparecidos." [MassR] (36:4) Wint 95-96, p. 582, 584.
"The Disappeared" (tr. by Celeste Kostopulos-Cooperman). [MassR] (36:4) Wint 95-96, p. 583, 585.
46. AGOSTINO, Paul
"Barricade." [ChironR] (42) Spr 95, p. 9.
"Celebrity Spokesperson." [WormR] (35:2, #138) 95, p. 51.
"Contest." [NewYorkQ] (55) 95, p. 101.
"Mortality Toes." [WormR] (35:2, #138) 95, p. 49-50.
"Natural Selection." [ChironR] (42) Spr 95, p. 9.
"Science Fiction and Nostalgia." [WormR] (35:2, #138) 95, p. 50.
"Squandered." [WormR] (35:2, #138) 95, p. 50.
"Theorists at the Barbecue." [WormR] (35:2, #138) 95, p. 51-52.
"Uppercut." [ChironR] (42) Spr 95, p. 9.
47. AGRAN, Rick
"Cartwheels." [LowellR] (2) c1996, p. 109.
"Shivaree." [LowellR] (2) c1996, p. 110.
48. AGRICOLA, Sandra
"The Stock Broker's Transformation." [DenQ] (30:2) Fall 95, p. 5.
49. AGUDELO, Dario Jaramillo
"Arfos" (from "Field Guide," tr. by Don Share). [Noctiluca] (2:1, #4) Spr 95, p. 60-61.
"Dinecos" (from "Field Guide," tr. by Don Share). [Noctiluca] (2:1, #4) Spr 95, p. 61.
"Guzguces" (from "Field Guide," tr. by Don Share). [Noctiluca] (2:1, #4) Spr 95, p. 62.
50. AGÜEROS, Jack
"Psalm for Bacalao." [MassR] (36:4) Wint 95-96, p. 586-588.
AGYEMANG, Kwadwo Opoku
See OPOKU-AGYEMANG, Kwadwo
51. AHL, Liz
"On a Volume of Milton Inscribed by My Father." [SouthernPR] (35:2) Wint 95, p. 46-48.
52. AHLSCHWEDE, Margrethe
"At the Office." [PraS] (69:2) Sum 95, p. 139-140.
"In My House Is the Horse." [PraS] (69:2) Sum 95, p. 138-139.
53. AHO, Margaret
"Love at 50." [BelPoJ] (46:1) Fall 95, p. 44.
"October 1994." [BelPoJ] (46:1) Fall 95, p. 43.
"Two Dreams." [QW] (40) Spr-Sum 95, p. 72-73.
54. AI
"Passing Though." [AmerPoR] (24:3) My-Je 95, p. 40-41.
55. AIKEN, William
"As Ishmael Went Down to the Sea I Go to Virgin Air." [Manoa] (7:1) Sum 95, p. 76.
"The Baptism." [Manoa] (7:1) Sum 95, p. 77.
"Century 21." [SoCoast] (18) Ja 95, p. 24-25.
"Crossroads." [DefinedP] (3) 95, p. 22.

"Draper Mountain, Pulaski." [Poetry] (166:1) Ap 95, p. 8-10.
"Last Word." [SouthernPR] (35:2) Wint 95, p. 56-57.
"Matins." [Iowa] (25:1) Wint 95, p. 57-58.
"To Beg I Am Ashamed." [SouthernPR] (35:2) Wint 95, p. 57-58.
"Vienna Boys' Choir." [LullwaterR] (5:1) 93-94, p. 59.
56. AIMONE, Joseph
    "The Face Artist." [Hellas] (6:1) Spr-Sum 95, p. 43.
57. AINSWORTH, Alan
    "Butcher Paper Sea." [LullwaterR] (6:2) Fall-Wint 95, p. 97.
    "Of Alabaster White And Red Coral." [PoetL] (90:2) Sum 95, p. 36.
58. AIVAS, Jose
    "Who Am I" (WritersCorps Program, Washington, DC). [WashR] (21:2) Ag-S 95, p. 17.
59. AIZENBURG, Mikhail (Aizenberg, Mikhail)
    "Among those. Among those, who is it starts" (in Russian and English, tr. by J. Kates).
        [InterQ] (2:1/2) 95, p. 72.
    "And Like a Silly Burrowing Sectarian" (in Russian and English, tr. by J. Kates).
        [KenR] (17:3/4) Sum-Fall 95, p. 92-93.
    "Imperceptible falling away of days" (in Russian and English, tr. by J. Kates). [InterQ]
        (2:1/2) 95, p. 74.
    "Who of those who step into the stream" (in Russian and English, tr. by J. Kates).
        [InterQ] (2:1/2) 95, p. 73.
60. AJAY, Stephen
    "Bukit Lawang, Sumatra: The Orangutan Preserve." [NewYorkQ] (55) 95, p. 84.
    "Finding Ourselves in Banaras." [Chelsea] (58) 95, p. 87.
    "Waking Among the Tibetans in McLeod Ganj." [NewYorkQ] (54) 95, p. 72.
61. AJAYI, Will Nash (grade 4, Tubman Elementary, Washington, DC)
    "My Story" (Poetry on the Metro Project). [WashR] (21:2) Ag-S 95, p. 14.
62. AKHMATOVA, Anna
    "Ah! it is you again" (tr. by Frances Laird). [PlumR] (8) [95], p. 86.
63. AKUTAGAWA, Fusei
    "Silk Tree Renga" (w. Araki Yasusada and Ozaki Kusatao. Tr. by Tosa Motokiyu, Ojiu
        Norinaga and Okura Kyojin). [GrandS] (14:1, #53) Sum 95, p. 28-30.
64. ALAMARES, Jay
    "Intriguing Poem." [ChironR] (42) Spr 95, p. 27.
    "Untitled: Can you help me?" [ChironR] (42) Spr 95, p. 27.
65. ALARCON, Francisco X.
    "Mestizo." [Zyzzyva] (11:3/4, #43/44) 95, "The Best of Ten Years of ZYZZYVA," p. 91-92.
66. ALBARELLI, Dean
    "Farm Haiku" (13 poems). [Witness] (9:2) 95, p. 58-59.
67. ALBERT, Floyd
    "Private Bedrooms" (The 1994 Allen Ginsberg Poetry Awards: Honorable Mention).
        [Footwork] (24/25) 95, p. 185-186.
68. ALBERT, Toya
    "Villar del Olmo." [Border] (7) Fall-Wint 96, p. 1.
    "Woman and Town, Mujer y Pueblo." [Border] (7) Fall-Wint 96, p. 2.
69. ALBERTI, Rafael
    "To the Hand" (tr. by Carolyn Tipton). [PartR] (62:1) Wint 95, p. 110.
70. ALBERTS, Ulvis
    "The Famous." [WormR] (35:2, #138) 95, p. 52-53.
    "Style." [WormR] (35:2, #138) 95, p. 54-55.
    "To D. W. Griffith." [WormR] (35:2, #138) 95, p. 53-54.
71. ALBISTON, Jordie
    "Solitary Beach" (for Camilla). [DefinedP] (2:2) Spr-Sum 94, p. 19-21.
72. ALBON, George
    "Memory of Air Types." [WestCL] (29:3, #18) Wint 95-96, p. 23-25.
    "Parachute Series" (2 selections). [WashR] (21:4) D 95-Ja 96, p. 12.
    "A Passion Reading." [WestCL] (29:3, #18) Wint 95-96, p. 28-29.
    "A Sighting." [WestCL] (29:3, #18) Wint 95-96, p. 27.
    "Thousands Count Out Loud" (Selections: XXVI, XXVII). [Talisman] (15) Wint 95 -
        96, p. 99.
    "Tuff Gong." [WestCL] (29:3, #18) Wint 95-96, p. 26.

73. ALBRECHT, Laura
   "Petting Zoo." [CapeR] (30:2) Fall 95, p. 43.
   "Prayer." [Conduit] (3) Sum 95, p. 13.
74. ALBRECHT, Malaika King
   "A Dialogue." [Vis] (47) 95, p. 30-31.
75. ALBRIGHT, Mia
   "After Men Defined Love." [AmerV] (37) 95, p. 36.
76. ALCALA, Carlos
   "Hamlet." [Light] (14) Sum 95, p. 16.
77. ALEIXO, Ricardo
   "Ejo-Lorun" (in Portuguese). [Callaloo] (18:4) Fall 95, p. 968.
   "Ejo-Lorun" (tr. by Phyllis Peres, w. Reetika Vazirani and Chi Lam). [Callaloo] (18:4)
      Fall 95, p. 800.
   "Great Mother" (tr. by Phyllis Peres, w. Reetika Vazirani and Chi Lam). [Callaloo]
      (18:4) Fall 95, p. 799.
   "Mamãe Grande." [Callaloo] (18:4) Fall 95, p. 967.
   "Pedaços de Mulher." [Callaloo] (18:4) Fall 95, p. 969.
   "Pieces of a Woman" (tr. by Carolyn Richardson Durham, w. Reetika Vazirani and Chi
      Lam). [Callaloo] (18:4) Fall 95, p. 801.
78. ALESHIRE, Joan
   "Break of Day: After Colette." [SenR] (25:2) Fall 95, p. 10-11.
   "Dog Star." [CrabOR] (1:1) Fall-Wint 95, p. 25-26.
   "The Fern in the Well: Fruitlands." [GreenMR] (8:1) Spr-Sum 95, p. 86-87.
   "Imaginary Twin." [CrabOR] (1:1) Fall-Wint 95, p. 23-24.
   "Women in the Water." [GreenMR] (8:1) Spr-Sum 95, p. 84-85.
   "The Yellow Transparents." [SenR] (25:2) Fall 95, p. 12-13.
ALESSANDRO, Patricia d'
   See D'ALESSANDRO, Patricia
79. ALESSIO, Carolyn
   "Jane Austen in the House of Mirrors." [HayF] (16) Spr-Sum 95, p. 126.
   "Lipstick Prints." [Plain] (15:2) Wint 95, p. 27.
   "My Father as Hopper." [ChiR] (41:2/3) 95, p. 100-101.
   "Redeeming Coupons." [HayF] (16) Spr-Sum 95, p. 127.
   "Tiki Idol." [AntR] (53:2) Spr 95, p. 198.
80. ALEXANDER, Christopher
   "Instructions for Men Found under the Heading 'Argument'." [GreensboroR] (58) Sum
      95, p. 127.
81. ALEXANDER, Elizabeth
   "Alka-Seltzer." [ChiR] (41:2/3) 95, p. 9-11.
   "Blues." [ChiR] (41:2/3) 95, p. 7-8.
   "Body of Life" (for Eddie Spencer). [CrabOR] (1:1) Fall-Wint 95, p. 27-30.
82. ALEXANDER, Pamela
   "Lettered Olives." [Chelsea] (59) 95, p. 165.
   "Mt. Auburn Owl." [Chelsea] (59) 95, p. 166.
   "Origin." [BelPoJ] (46:1) Fall 95, p. 26.
83. ALEXANDER, Will
   "Alchemic Moray's Reversal." [Sulfur] (15:1, #36) Spr 95, p. 163.
   "Breaking Through Linguistic Reason." [Sulfur] (15:1, #36) Spr 95, p. 164-165.
   "Entropy as the Bone Queen." [ChiR] (41:4) 95, p. 1-3.
   "From Across the Vapor Gulf" (Excerpts). [ChiR] (41:4) 95, p. 4.
84. ALEXIE, Sherman
   "Airplane." [HangL] (66) 95, p. 8-9.
   "At the Trial of Hamlet, Chicago, 1994." [BelPoJ] (46:1) Fall 95, p. 29-31.
   "Bob's Coney Island." [HangL] (66) 95, p. 6-7.
   "Capital Punishment." [IndR] (18:2) Fall 95, p. 23-26.
   "Death of the Landlord." [ManyMM] (1:2) 95, p. 33-35.
   "Defending Walt Whitman." [BelPoJ] (46:1) Fall 95, p. 27-28.
   "Faith" (For R. J.). [IndR] (18:2) Fall 95, p. 20.
   "How to Write the Great American Indian Novel." [IndR] (18:2) Fall 95, p. 21-22.
   "James Dean." [ChironR] (44/45) Aut-Wint 95, p. 2.
   "Last Song." [ChironR] (44/45) Aut-Wint 95, p. 2.
   "The Lover of Maps" (For Diane). [FreeL] (15) Aut 95, p. 30.
   "Marilyn Monroe." [ChironR] (44/45) Aut-Wint 95, p. 2.
   "Water Flowing Home" (For Diane). [FreeL] (14) Wint 95, p. 9.
   "When I Was My Father I Sang Love Songs to My Son." [HangL] (66) 95, p. 7.

85. ALEXIOU, Nikos
   "The Green Prince" (tr. by Dean Kostos). [Talisman] (15) Wint 95-96, p. 131.
86. ALEXIS, Austin
   "Intimidation." [Writer] (108:12) D 95, p. 22.
87. ALFERI, Pierre
   "Kub Or" (Selections, tr. by Cole Swensen). [Avec] (10) 95, p. 115-120.
88. ALFORD, Peg
   "Families" (Literary Festival: Poetry: Honorable Mention). [EngJ] (84:4) Ap 95, p. 41.
89. ALFRED O. (John Howard Pavilion, St. Elizabeth's Hospital, Washington, DC)
   "Locked in a Prison Camp" (WritersCorps Program). [WashR] (21:2) Ag-S 95, p. 10.
90. ALGARIN, Miguel
   "Nuyorican One Wing Olive-Skin Angel." [MassR] (36:4) Wint 95-96, p. 589.
91. ALI, Agha Shahid
   "The Correspondent." [DenQ] (29:3) Wint 95, p. 42-43.
   "A Fate's Brief Memoir" (for William Wadsworth). [TriQ] (95) Wint 95-96, p. 176-179.
   "Muharram in Srinagar, 1992." [YaleR] (83:2) Ap 95, p. 93.
   "A Pastoral." (for Suvir Kaul). [QW] (41) Aut-Wint 95-96, p. 208-209.
92. ALKALAY-GUT, Karen
   "And Who Will Remember Those Who Remember" (tr. of Yehuda Amichai). [PraS] (69:4) Wint 95, p. 133-135.
   "Early Encounters with an Analyst." [LowellR] [1] Sum 94, p. 87-88.
   "Porno" (tr. of Mordechai Geldmann). [MichQR] (34:4) Fall 95, p. 676-677.
   "Taking Out the Trash." [LowellR] [1] Sum 94, p. 86.
   "Tel Aviv." [MassR] (36:3) Aut 95, p. 421.
93. ALLARDT, Linda
   "Ask Her." [BelPoJ] (45:3) Spr 95, p. 38.
   "Waked to Listen." [BelPoJ] (45:3) Spr 95, p. 36-37.
   "Web Trail." [WestB] (37) 95, p. 50.
94. ALLEMAN, Michael (Mike)
   "Downriver." [Gerbil] (3) Sum 95, p. 21.
   "Lovers' eyes turn to others' bodies." [Gerbil] (4) Fall 95, p. 3.
95. ALLEN, Annette
   "Across Distance: A Blessing." [PoetL] (90:1) Spr 95, p. 23.
96. ALLEN, Dick
   "The Neo-Transcendentalist." [Boulevard] (10:1/2, #28/29) Spr 95, p. 83-85.
   "Throwing Caution to the Winds." [Boulevard] (10:1/2, #28/29) Spr 95, p. 81-82.
97. ALLEN, Fergus
   "Interesting Times." [GrandS] (13:3, #51) Wint 95, p. 119-120.
   "Knight-Errant." [GrandS] (13:3, #51) Wint 95, p. 116.
   "On the Quay." [Epoch] (44:3) 95, p. 316.
   "Time After Time." [Epoch] (44:3) 95, p. 317.
   "Up and Down." [GrandS] (13:3, #51) Wint 95, p. 117-118.
   "Useful Transactions in Philosophy." [NewYorker] (71:33) 23 O 95, p. 104.
98. ALLEN, Gilbert
   "Answered Prayers" (Robert Penn Warren Poetry Prize: Third Prize). [CumbPR] (15:1) Fall 95, p. 2-3.
   "The Arbitrary Angel." [CumbPR] (15:1) Fall 95, p. 6.
   "The Lawn Rangers." [CumbPR] (15:1) Fall 95, p. 4-5.
   "Semi-Private (with Cable)." [FloridaR] (21:1) 95, p. 68.
99. ALLEN, Jed
   "Walking Song." [GreenMR] (8:2) Fall-Wint 95-96, p. 117.
100. ALLEN, Margerie Goggin
   "Song for a Deaf Child." [Kaleid] (31) Sum-Fall 95, p. 27.
101. ALLEN, Mary C.
   "Letter with Line Breaks." [SpoonR] (20:1) Wint-Spr 95, p. 99-100.
102. ALLEN, Noel Catharine
   "Of a House." [HarvardA] (vol. 130) Fall 95, p. 8.
   "Winter's Cistern." [HarvardA] (vol. 130) Fall 95, p. 18.
103. ALLEN, Paul
   "Come Home." [NewAW] (13) Fall-Wint 95, p. 138-139.
104. ALLEN, S. Munden
   "The County Hospital Group Hears the Lady Defend Her Drinking." [SpoonR] (20:2) Sum-Fall 95, p. 145.
   "Hunting Love on Crowley's Ridge." [SpoonR] (20:2) Sum-Fall 95, p. 144.
   "Thunder." [SpoonR] (20:2) Sum-Fall 95, p. 143.

105. ALLEN, William
    "Bones, Joints, Flat Feet." [PoetryE] (39) Fall 94, p. 11.
    "Getty Station Playground Beach." [DefinedP] (1:1) Fall-Wint 92, p. 9.
    "Heartbreak Hotel." [PoetryE] (39) Fall 94, p. 13.
    "Madrigal to the Nuns of Santiago." [AmerV] (36) 95, p. 20.
    "Portrait of an Italian Soldier." [PoetryE] (39) Fall 94, p. 9.
106. ALLEY, Rick
    "Bewildered Again on the Same Street." [PoetryE] (40) Spr 95, p. 8.
    "Dissecting Uncle Sorrow." [Conduit] (3) Sum 95, p. 19.
    "Only Three of the Bees'" [sic]. [PoetryE] (40) Spr 95, p. 9.
107. ALLRED, Joanne
    "Domestic Gods." [WeberS] (12:2) Spr-Sum 95, p. 95.
    "Driving Home Late on a Starry Night." [WeberS] (12:2) Spr-Sum 95, p. 96.
    "Every Story Rewrites Itself." [WeberS] (12:2) Spr-Sum 95, p. 96-97.
108. ALLRED, Lorie
    "Raping a Woman." [NewYorkQ] (54) 95, p. 74.
109. ALMANZA, E.
    "Ex Machina" (First Place, Poetry Award). [NewL] (62:1) 96 (c1995), p. 10.
    "Marriage to the Earth" (First Place, Poetry Award). [NewL] (62:1) 96 (c1995), p. 10.
    "The Middle Part" (First Place, Poetry Award). [NewL] (62:1) 96 (c1995), p. 12.
    "Plenty" (First Place, Poetry Award). [NewL] (62:1) 96 (c1995), p. 9.
    "There Is No Name for Our Wanting" (First Place, Poetry Award). [NewL] (62:1) 96
        (c1995), p. 11.
    "Visitations" (First Place, Poetry Award). [NewL] (62:1) 96 (c1995), p. 13-15.
110. ALMEIDA, Hermes Jose
    "Plosive." [GrahamHR] (19) Wint 95-96, p. 37-38.
111. ALMON, Bert
    "The Gold Standard." [PoetryC] (15:3) Ag 95, p. 27.
    "Roy's Taxis." [Border] (6) Spr-Sum 95, p. 15.
112. ALMON, Margaret
    "Hopscotch." [TarRP] (34:2) Spr 95, p. 21.
    "Responding to the Bereaved." [CreamCR] (19:1) Spr 95, p. 110-111.
    "Scent" (For Rachel Carson). [CreamCR] (19:1) Spr 95, p. 112-113.
113. ALSON-MILKMAN, Rebecca
    "Holocaust." [HangL] (66) 95, p. 80-81.
    "Sex." [HangL] (66) 95, p. 81.
114. ALTER, Michael
    "Voices in the Dark Say 'Go On, Go On'." [HiramPoR] (58/59) Spr 95-Wint 96, p. 5.
115. ALTIZER, Nell
    "Cape Farewell" (In memoriam Joseph Chadwick). [KenR] (17:2) Spr 95, p. 133-137.
116. ALVARADO, Tito
    "Condition" (tr. by Maria Freer). [Arc] (35) Aut 95, p. 19.
    "Joy" (tr. by Maria Freer). [Arc] (35) Aut 95, p. 18.
    "Little Girl" (tr. by Maria Freer). [Arc] (35) Aut 95, p. 17.
117. ALVAREZ, Julia
    "Audition." [NewYorker] (71:16) 12 Je 95, p. 75.
    "The Dashboard Virgencita." [MassR] (36:4) Wint 95-96, p. 590-591.
    "The Lost & Found Señoritas." [MassR] (36:4) Wint 95-96, p. 591-592.
    "Redwing Sonnets." [AmerPoR] (24:6) N-D 95, p. 7-8.
    "Wallpaper." [AmerPoR] (24:6) N-D 95, p. 7.
    "The Way It Sounds." [MassR] (36:4) Wint 95-96, p. 590.
ALVAREZ, Pansy Maurer
    See MAURER-ALVAREZ, Pansy
118. ALVAREZ BRAVO, Armando
    "Desayuno de Allen's." [LindLM] (14:1) Mr/Spr 95, p. 3.
    "Método de Escritura Poética." [LindLM] (14:1) Mr/Spr 95, p. 3.
    "La Oreja de Van Gogh." [LindLM] (14:1) Mr/Spr 95, p. 3.
119. AMABILE, George
    "The Sun Shower." [Event] (24:2) Sum 95, p. 7-8.
120. AMBROGGIO, Luis Albert
    "Angel de ilusiones." [LindLM] (14:1) Mr/Spr 95, p. 20.
    "Llamarte y perderte." [LindLM] (14:1) Mr/Spr 95, p. 20.
121. AMICHAI, Yehuda
    "And Who Will Remember Those Who Remember" (tr. by Karen Alkalay-Gut).
        [PraS] (69:4) Wint 95, p. 133-135.

122. AMMONS, A. R.
    "Candle Lit." [HarvardR] (9) Fall 95, p. 34.
    "December Starlings." [BelPoJ] (45:4) Chapbook 22, Sum 95, p. 7.
    "Picking up Equations." [ParisR] (37:134) Spr 95, p. 221.
    "Taking Place." [Verse] (12:2) 95, p. 9.
123. AMTZIS, Wayne
    "Blind Man on a Revolving Chair" (tr. of Bhoopi Sherchan). [SenR] (25:2) Fall 95, p.
        68-69.
    "Man From a Developing Country" (tr. of Dinesh Adhikari). [SenR] (25:2) Fall 95, p.
        70-71.
AN, Ching
    See CHING, An
AN, Yue
    See YUE, An
AN TSAOI, Máire Mhac
    See Mhac an tSAOI, Máire
124. ANANIA, Michael
    "After a Drawing on Papyrus" (for Reg Gibbons). [PoetryE] (40) Spr 95, p. 10.
    "What Are Islands to Me Now" (For Barbara Guest). [ChiR] (41:2/3) 95, p. 104-106.
125. ANCHEVSKI, Zoran
    "The Admiral" (Klee, tr. of Slavko Janevski). [Vis] (48) 95, p. 28-29.
    "The End of the Tales" (tr. of Vlada Urosevic). [Vis] (48) 95, p. 36.
    "Fortress" (tr. of Mateya Matevski). [Vis] (48) 95, p. 32-34.
    "The Great Wall of China" (tr. of Mateya Matevski). [Vis] (48) 95, p. 35-36.
    "The Magician" (Ernst, tr. of Slavko Janevski). [Vis] (48) 95, p. 27-28.
    "The Magus" (Bosch, tr. of Slavko Janevski). [Vis] (48) 95, p. 27.
    "Shivers" (Goya, tr. of Slavko Janevski). [Vis] (48) 95, p. 29-30.
    "Truths" (tr. of Vlada Urosevic). [Vis] (48) 95, p. 37.
126. ANCROM, Nancy
    "Hymn and Return" (tr. of Pablo Neruda). [WillowS] (36) Je 95, p. 98-99.
127. ANDE, Karen
    "Famine" (Baidoa, Somalia 1992). [OxfordM] (10:1) Wint 94-Spr 95, p. 9.
128. ANDERSEN, Astrid Hjertenaes
    "Concertino" (tr. by Aina Gerner-Mathisen and Suzanne Bachner). [Nimrod] (38:2)
        Spr-Sum 95, p. 80-81.
    "Melancholia I, 1514" (tr. by A. Gerner-Mathisen and S. Bachner). [TampaR] (11)
        Fall 95, p. 56.
    "Yellow Sky" (tr. by Aina Gerner-Mathisen and Suzanne Bachner). [Nimrod] (38:2)
        Spr-Sum 95, p. 79.
129. ANDERSON, Beth
    "Octave." [HangL] (67) 95, p. 5.
130. ANDERSON, Bobby
    "Benefit Performance" (for Mark). [JamesWR] (12:3) Fall 95, p. 11.
131. ANDERSON, Catherine
    "1967." [Journal] (19:1) Spr-Sum 95, p. 61.
    "In August." [Journal] (19:1) Spr-Sum 95, p. 60.
132. ANDERSON, Chester G.
    "American Expresso" (An *aisling* for Carolina, James Joyce and Gabriel Garcia
        Márquez). [NorthStoneR] (12) 95, p. 52-53.
    "Family Album." [NorthStoneR] (12) 95, p. 48-49.
    "Miracle of Love & Art." [NorthStoneR] (12) 95, p. 50-51.
133. ANDERSON, Curt
    "February." [RagMag] (12:2) Spr 95, p. 8.
    "Riding Home." [RagMag] (12:2) Spr 95, p. 9.
134. ANDERSON, Daniel
    "Executive Geochrone" (A map shop in December). [Poetry] (167:3) D 95, p. 130-
        131.
135. ANDERSON, Gary
    "Anablephobia" (fear of looking up at high places). [AntigR] (101) Spr 95, p. 11.
    "Haptephobia" (fear of being touched). [AntigR] (101) Spr 95, p. 12.
136. ANDERSON, Hope
    "Postscript" (for S. Harvey). [Pembroke] (27) 95, p. 60.
    "Tufino, the Edge of a Map." [Pembroke] (27) 95, p. 59.
137. ANDERSON, Jack
    "Recognition Scenes." [HangL] (66) 95, p. 11.
    "A Text Fragrant With Ideas." [HangL] (66) 95, p. 10-11.

138. ANDERSON, Jon
    "The Afterlife." [AntR] (53:4) Fall 95, p. 438.
    "Attention to Detail." [AntR] (53:4) Fall 95, p. 435.
    "O Cleveland." [AntR] (53:4) Fall 95, p. 434.
    "Plaint." [Sonora] (29) Spr 95, p. 107-109.
    "Rags." [AntR] (53:4) Fall 95, p. 432-433.
    "Travels of a Budding Monk." [AntR] (53:4) Fall 95, p. 436-437.
139. ANDERSON, Kath M.
    "Coyote Gulch." [Poetry] (166:4) Jl 95, p. 210-212.
140. ANDERSON, Kemmer
    "Sailing for Patmos." [ChrC] (112:2) 18 Ja 95, p. 48.
    "Shalom, Yitzhak Rabin." [ChrC] (112:34) 22-29 N 95, p. 1115.
141. ANDERSON, Kirk
    "This Street Owes Me Something" (To Maya Angelou). [XavierR] (15:1) Spr 95, p. 43.
142. ANDERSON, Lori
    "Reading Chora? (A Condensed Duet)." [13thMoon] (13:1/2) 95, p. 6-9.
143. ANDERSON, Mark
    "Amphibians Explore and Colonize the Soul." [DefinedP] (2:2) Spr-Sum 94, p. 11-12.
    "Mill Town Still Life." [DefinedP] (2:2) Spr-Sum 94, p. 13.
    "The Open." [DefinedP] (2:2) Spr-Sum 94, p. 12.
    "Souvenir." [DefinedP] (2:2) Spr-Sum 94, p. 14.
144. ANDERSON, Nan
    "The Right Auricle." [PraS] (69:1) Spr 95, p. 72-75.
    "Why We Pray." [NortheastCor] (3) 95, p. 81.
145. ANDERSON, Nathalie F.
    "Stick Shift." [SouthernPR] (35:2) Wint 95, p. 33-34.
146. ANDERSON, Paul
    "Spring Equinox." [CapeR] (30:1) Spr 95, p. 1.
147. ANDERSON, Scott Edward
    "Dead Red Wing." [Blueline] (16) 95, p. 38.
    "Fallow Field" (Ticonderoga, NY). [Blueline] (16) 95, p. 84-85.
148. ANDERSON-JONES, Teruko
    "Brilliant Grief, Silent Snow." [AntigR] (101) Spr 95, p. 52-54.
149. ANDERTON, A. Lucy
    "Bird Song." [NewYorkQ] (54) 95, p. 107.
150. ANDOH, Motoo
    "The Bridge" (tr. by Tomoyuki Iino and Jon Silkin). [Stand] (36:2) Spr 95, p. 28-29.
151. ANDRADE, Eugenio de
    "Absence" (tr. by Alexis Levitin). [QW] (41) Aut-Wint 95-96, p. 212.
    "Almost Haiku" (tr. by Alexis Levitin). [JamesWR] (12:1) Wint 95, p. 8.
    "Between Two Blades" (tr. by Alexis Levitin). [MidAR] (15:1/2) 95, p. 235.
    "Birthday Prose" (tr. by Alexis Levitin). [ConnPR] (14:1) 95, p. 16.
    "Breakfast in Maspalomas" (tr. by Alexis Levitin). [SnailPR] (3:2) 95, p. 8.
    "Close to the Earth" (tr. by Alexis Levitin). [MidAR] (15:1/2) 95, p. 236.
    "O corpo nu, quase estranho." [Os] (41) 95, p. 4.
    "Os dedos brincam com a luz de março." [Os] (41) 95, p. 4.
    "Encirclement" (tr. by Alexis Levitin). [ConnPR] (14:1) 95, p. 14.
    "Epitaph for a Sailor Dying Young" (tr. by Alexis Levitin). [OxfordM] (10:1) Wint 94-Spr 95, p. 10.
    "Fazer de uma palavra um barco." [Os] (41) 95, p. 2.
    "Fingers play with the March light" (tr. by Alexis Levitin). [Os] (41) 95, p. 5.
    "Flush with the Ground" (tr. by Alexis Levitin). [ConnPR] (14:1) 95, p. 17.
    "Homage to Hans Christian Andersen" (tr. by Alexis Levitin). [SnailPR] (3:2) 95, p. 9.
    "I work the frail and bitter" (tr. by Alexis Levitin). [Os] (41) 95, p. 3.
    "Maspalomas, Without Nostalgia" (tr. by Alexis Levitin). [ConnPR] (14:1) 95, p. 15.
    "Minor Sonnet on the Arrival of Summer" (tr. by Alexis Levitin). [Confr] (56/57) Sum-Fall 95, p. 309.
    "The naked body, almost strange" (tr. by Alexis Levitin). [Os] (41) 95, p. 5.
    "October: Wine" (tr. by Alexis Levitin). [InterQ] (2:1/2) 95, p. 155.
    "Outubro: O Vinho." [InterQ] (2:1/2) 95, p. 155.
    "Seven Swords for a Melancholia" (tr. by Alexis Levitin). [PoetL] (90:1) Spr 95, p. 39.
    "Tempo em Que Se Morre." [SycamoreR] (7:1) Wint 95, p. 40.

"A Time in Which One Dies" (tr. by Alexis Levitin). [SycamoreR] (7:1) Wint 95, p. 41.
"To make a boat from a word" (tr. by Alexis Levitin). [Os] (41) 95, p. 3.
"A Torre." [InterQ] (2:1/2) 95, p. 155.
"A Tower" (tr. by Alexis Levitin). [InterQ] (2:1/2) 95, p. 155.
"Trabalho com a frágil e amarga." [Os] (41) 95, p. 2.
"Until Tomorrow" (tr. by Alexis Levitin). [NowestR] (33:2) 95, p. 37.
"Urgently" (tr. by Alexis Levitin). [NowestR] (33:2) 95, p. 36.
"Youth" (tr. by Alexis Levitin). [NowestR] (33:2) 95, p. 35.
152. ANDREWS, Betsy
   "Pearland" (Excerpts). [Phoebe] (24:2) 95, p. 39-48.
153. ANDREWS, Bruce
   "Mercury 2" (from Lip Service). [CentralP] (24) Spr 95, p. 17-20.
154. ANDREWS, Claudia Emerson
   "Auction." [SouthernR] (31:1) Wint 95, p. 1.
   "Flood: Preacher's sounding." [Poetry] (166:4) Jl 95, p. 214.
   "Gossip." [SouthernHR] (29:4) Fall 95, p. 342-343.
   "The Way to Water." [Poetry] (166:4) Jl 95, p. 213.
   "The Way to Water: Preacher remembers calling up his cows." [Poetry] (166:4) Jl 95, p. 213.
155. ANDREWS, Jim
   "Customs." [Quarry] (43:4) 95, p. 45-46.
   "Safe Cracking." [Quarry] (43:4) 95, p. 47-49.
156. ANDREWS, Nin
   "The Right Kind." [Ploughs] (21:1) Spr 95, p. 132.
   "Secondhand Smoke." [Ploughs] (21:1) Spr 95, p. 131.
   "That Cold Summer." [Ploughs] (21:4) Wint 95-96, p. 22-23.
   "What Is It About the Past." [Ploughs] (21:1) Spr 95, p. 130.
   "When a Woman Loves a Man." [Ploughs] (21:4) Wint 95-96, p. 24-25.
157. ANDREWS, Shari
   "Bluebell road." [PoetryC] (15:2) Je 95, p. 16.
   "Exclamations." [PoetryC] (15:2) Je 95, p. 16.
158. ANDREWS, Tom
   "Cinèma Vérité: A Map Is Not a Territory" (in memoriam Paul Celan). [ParisR] (37:134) Spr 95, p. 273-274.
   "Cinema Vérité: Brooding Kilmer, a Documentary." [SycamoreR] (7:2) Sum 95, p. 39-40.
   "Cinema Vérité: Six One-Line Filmscripts." [SycamoreR] (7:2) Sum 95, p. 38.
   "Cinema Vérité: The Mysterious Disappearance of Laurence Sterne." [SycamoreR] (7:2) Sum 95, p. 41.
   "A Word or Two" (after Karl Krolow). [PlumR] (9) [95 or 96], p. 82.
159. ANDROLA, Ron
   "I Talked About Steve Richmond to My Daughter." [Bogg] (67) 95, p. 11.
   "Poetry As Cause." [Pearl] (22) Fall-Wint 95, p. 26.
160. ANGEL
   "Father." [HawaiiR] (19:2) Fall 95, p. 196-197.
161. ANGEL, Ralph
   "At Your Convenience." [AmerPoR] (24:6) N-D 95, p. 5.
   "The Blessed." [AmerPoR] (24:6) N-D 95, p. 5.
   "Breaking and Entering." [AmerPoR] (24:6) N-D 95, p. 5.
   "Evolving Similarities." [AmerPoR] (24:6) N-D 95, p. 3-4.
   "Love's That Simple." [AmerPoR] (24:6) N-D 95, p. 6.
   "The Nothing That Is." [AmerPoR] (24:6) N-D 95, p. 6.
   "Trance Music." [AmerPoR] (24:6) N-D 95, p. 3.
   "Twilight." [AmerPoR] (24:6) N-D 95, p. 6.
   "Untitled: Or as along the river buildings brighten and grow dim again." [AmerPoR] (24:6) N-D 95, p. 3.
   "Veils of Prayer." [AmerPoR] (24:6) N-D 95, p. 4.
   "The Vigil." [AmerPoR] (24:6) N-D 95, p. 4.
   "You Think It's a Secret, But It Never Was One." [AmerPoR] (24:6) N-D 95, p. 6.
162. ANGELERI, Lucy
   "Montage." [GreenHLL] (6) 95, p. 12-13.
163. ANGELINE, Mary
   "Spectrum" (for Mei Mei Berssenbrugge). [Arshile] (4) 95, p. 26-31.
ANGELO, Patricia d'
   See D'ANGELO, Patricia

39

164. ANGELOU, Maya
"From a Black Woman to a Black Man (Million Man March Poem)." [Drumvoices]
(5:1/2) Fall-Wint 95-96, p. 125-127.
ANNA, Lynnette d'
See D'ANNA, Lynnette
165. ANNSFIRE, Joan
"At Work." [SinW] (55) Spr-Sum 95, p. 75-76.
ANONYMOUS
*Anonymous entries are arranged and grouped by nationality, ethnicity, gender, age,
place and/or date*
166. ANONYMOUS (Adult, Circulating Library, St. Elizabeth's Hospital, Washington, DC)
"Advice from a Friend" (WritersCorps Program). [WashR] (21:2) Ag-S 95, p. 13.
"Leon Said" (WritersCorps Program). [WashR] (21:2) Ag-S 95, p. 13.
"Shape of a Telephone" (WritersCorps Program). [WashR] (21:2) Ag-S 95, p. 13.
"Sketch of a Poet's Interior" (WritersCorps Program). [WashR] (21:2) Ag-S 95, p. 13.
167. ANONYMOUS (Chinese)
"In the Wilds There Is a Dead Doe" (from *The Book of Songs*, tr. by David Lunde).
[ChiR] (41:1) 95, p. 16.
168. ANONYMOUS (Chinook, 1888)
"Song: I won't care if you desert me" (tr. by Sam Hamill, after Franz Boas). [PoetryE]
(41) Aut 95, p. 34.
169. ANONYMOUS (Egyptian, ca. 13th c. BCE, traditional)
"Love Song" (tr. by Sam Hamill). [PoetryE] (41) Aut 95, p. 10.
170. ANONYMOUS (Egyptian, ca. 15th c. BCE, traditional)
"Love Song" (tr. by Sam Hamill). [PoetryE] (41) Aut 95, p. 9.
171. ANONYMOUS (Ghana, traditional)
"The Motor Under Me Is Running Hot" (from *An African Prayer Book*, compiled by
Archbishop Desmond Tutu). [Harp] (291:1742) Jl 95, p. 19.
172. ANONYMOUS (Greenland)
"The Barren Woman's Lament" (tr. by Lawrence Millman). [Nimrod] (38:2) Spr-Sum
95, p. 114.
"Narwhal Song" (tr. by Lawrence Millman). [Nimrod] (38:2) Spr-Sum 95, p. 116.
"Song of the Ptarmigan" (tr. by Lawrence Millman). [Nimrod] (38:2) Spr-Sum 95, p.
114.
"Young Girl's Lament" (tr. by Lawrence Millman). [Nimrod] (38:2) Spr-Sum 95, p.
115.
173. ANONYMOUS (Hawaiian traditional chant)
"Ka Pule Koko." [Manoa] (7:1) Sum 95, p. 162-163.
"The Net Prayer." [Manoa] (7:1) Sum 95, p. 163.
"Prayer for Growth and Increase." [Manoa] (7:1) Sum 95, p. 162.
"Pule Ho'ouluulu 'Ai." [Manoa] (7:1) Sum 95, p. 161-162.
174. ANONYMOUS (Male, Clean & Sober Streets, Washington, DC).
"Last Straw" (WritersCorps Program). [WashR] (21:2) Ag-S 95, p. 18.
175. ANONYMOUS (Oak Hill Youth Detention Center, Washington, DC)
"Poverty World" (WritersCorps Program). [WashR] (21:2) Ag-S 95, p. 4.
"Strong Black Woman" (WritersCorps Program). [WashR] (21:2) Ag-S 95, p. 4.
"You and the sweet chocolate gorgeous girl" (WritersCorps Program). [WashR]
(21:2) Ag-S 95, p. 4.
176. ANONYMOUS (Vietnamese folk poem)
"I Married at Fifteen" (tr. by Linh Dinh). [Manoa] (7:2) Wint 95, p. 47.
"It Took a Newly Dug Canal" (tr. by Linh Dinh). [Manoa] (7:2) Wint 95, p. 47.
"The Morning Star Fades in the Night Sky" (tr. by Linh Dinh). [Manoa] (7:2) Wint
95, p. 48.
"My Body Is Not Inferior to Hers" (tr. by Linh Dinh). [Manoa] (7:2) Wint 95, p. 48.
"Nine Stars Line Up Vertically" (tr. by Linh Dinh). [Manoa] (7:2) Wint 95, p. 47.
"Three Years at This Outpost" (tr. by Linh Dinh). [Manoa] (7:2) Wint 95, p. 48.
"Wobbly, Like a Hat without a Strap" (tr. by Linh Dinh). [Manoa] (7:2) Wint 95, p.
46.
177. ANONYMOUS (/Xam)
"//Kabbo's Request for Thread" (tr. by W. H. Bleek, Lucy Lloyd and Stephen
Watson). [ColR] (22:1) Spr 95, p. 61.
"Our Blood Makes Smoke" (tr. by W. H. Bleek, Lucy Lloyd and Stephen Watson).
[ColR] (22:1) Spr 95, p. 57.
"Song of the Broken String" (tr. by W. H. Bleek, Lucy Lloyd and Stephen Watson).
[ColR] (22:1) Spr 95, p. 59-60.

ANONYMOUS (/Xam)

"The Story of Ruyter" (tr. by W. H. Bleek, Lucy Lloyd and Stephen Watson). [ColR]
  (22:1) Spr 95, p. 58.
"The Wind Is One with the Man" (tr. by W. H. Bleek, Lucy Lloyd and Stephen
  Watson). [ColR] (22:1) Spr 95, p. 56.
178. ANONYMOUS (Youth, Circulating Library, St. Elizabeth's Hospital, Washington, DC)
  "My Life" (WritersCorps Program). [WashR] (21:2) Ag-S 95, p. 13.
179. ANSAY, A. Manette
  "Doing the Fat Man Dance." [SilverFR] (25) Sum 95, p. 10.
  "Ending." [NowestR] (33:2) 95, p. 26.
  "Fingerings." [PraS] (69:3) Fall 95, p. 135-136.
  "Lydia at a Tapestry Loom" (from a painting by Mary Cassatt). [PraS] (69:3) Fall 95,
    p. 136.
  "Second Honeymoon." [SilverFR] (25) Sum 95, p. 11.
  "Sheboygan, 1974" (for Charlotte). [PraS] (69:3) Fall 95, p. 135.
  "Where Do You Go?" [NowestR] (33:2) 95, p. 27-28.
180. ANSEL, Talvikki
  "John Clare." [Shen] (45:3) Fall 95, p. 52.
  "My Shining Archipelago." [Journal] (19:2) Fall-Wint 95, p. 23-25.
  "Stories: Wolf-Children." [Journal] (19:2) Fall-Wint 95, p. 21.
  "Swallowing." [Journal] (19:2) Fall-Wint 95, p. 22.
  "You Don't Know What Happened When You Froze." [WillowS] (35) Ja 95, p. 48.
181. ANSTETT, Aaron
  "By the Bay Door." [TampaR] (11) Fall 95, p. 58.
  "A Possible Reprieve." [PoetryE] (39) Fall 94, p. 14.
  "Sustenance." [PoetryE] (39) Fall 94, p. 15.
  "Tell Me." [SycamoreR] (7:1) Wint 95, p. 29.
  "This Town." [OhioR] (54) 95, p. 119.
  "Tracks." [GreenMR] (8:2) Fall-Wint 95-96, p. 128-129.
  "Waxwing, Warbler, Scythebill." [SycamoreR] (7:1) Wint 95, p. 28.
182. ANTHONY, Frank
  "Moonlight Cocktail" (Robert Penn Warren, 1905-1989). [AnthNEW] (7) 95, p. 6.
183. ANTLER
  "Berrygathering vs. Semengathering." [ChironR] (43) Sum 95, p. 7.
  "Brains Bashed In By Sledgehammers." [ChironR] (43) Sum 95, p. 2.
  "Cockfighting vs. Cocksucking." [ChironR] (43) Sum 95, p. 6.
  "'Do You Mind If I Nurse My Baby' vs. 'Do You Mind If I Suck My Young Pal's
    Cock?'" [ChironR] (43) Sum 95, p. 7.
  "If God Had a Mouth." [ChironR] (43) Sum 95, p. 7.
  "Job Replacement for Loggers of Old Growth." [RiverS] (41) 95, p. 27-29.
  "Learning the Constellations." [Wind] (75) Spr 95, p. 1.
  "Moon Lips." [ChironR] (43) Sum 95, p. 3.
  "Oh-Oh." [Sun] (240) D 95, p. 25.
  "Pussy Feels Like." [NewYorkQ] (54) 95, p. 48-49.
  "Redressing the Balance." [ChironR] (43) Sum 95, p. 3.
  "A Second Before It Bursts." [SmPd] (32:1, #93) Wint 95, p. 15.
  "Star-Struck Utopias of 2000." [RiverS] (41) 95, p. 27.
  "Suddenly I Realized." [NewYorkQ] (55) 95, p. 65-66.
  "Sweetcorn vs. Sweetcome." [ChironR] (43) Sum 95, p. 7.
  "Titsuckers." [ChironR] (43) Sum 95, p. 6.
  "What Every Boy Knows." [Sun] (237) S 95, p. 35.
184. ANWAY, Karen Sexton
  "Abstract." [RagMag] (12:2) Spr 95, p. 101.
  "Are You Safe in Your Bed Now That Jesse James Has Been Defeated?" [RagMag]
    (12:2) Spr 95, p. 100.
185. AOKI, Elizabeth
  "Speaking Language." [PoetryNW] (36:1) Spr 95, p. 25.
  "Three Excuses." [PoetryE] (41) Aut 95, p. 118.
186. AOUEISS, Lody
  "Friend of the Dead One" (tr. by Victor Dalmas). [Pembroke] (27) 95, p. 105-107.
187. APOLLINAIRE, Guillaume
  "At the Santé" (tr. by Donald Revell). [MissR] (23:3) 95, p. 80-82.
  "Procession" (tr. by Donald Revell). [MissR] (23:3) 95, p. 83-85.
188. APONICK, Kathleen
  "Afterword: The Death of Relatives." [Jacaranda] (11) [95 or 96?], p. 138.
  "Falmouth Heights." [LowellR] (2) c1996, p. 79.
  "The Past." [LowellR] (2) c1996, p. 77-78.

189. APONTE, Rachel
    "Clarisse." [Zyzzyva] (11:1, #41) Spr 95, p. 53.
190. APOTHEKER, Alison
    "Monotony of Lovers: Night of the Full Lunar Eclipse" (Inadvertently published
        under the name of Janet Bernichon in CR #43. Apologies to both poets).
        [ChironR] (44/45) Aut-Wint 95, p. 15.
191. APPELBAUM, David
    "Herding Toward the Ark." [AmerPoR] (24:4) Jl-Ag 95, p. 5.
192. APPELL, David
    "Naming the Rain." [SmPd] (32:2, #94) Spr 95, p. 24.
193. APPLEMAN, Philip
    "Parable of the Cave." [PartR] (62:3) Sum 95, p. 455.
    "A Priest Forever." [ParisR] (37:137) Wint 95, p. 258-262.
194. APPLEWHITE, James
    "House Beside a Stream." [SouthernR] (31:1) Wint 95, p. 2-3.
    "Inheriting the Homeplace." [Shen] (45:2) Sum 95, p. 92-94.
    "Walking Through October." [Shen] (45:2) Sum 95, p. 95.
195. APPLIN, Stephen
    "The Amber Wood." [Blueline] (16) 95, p. 86-87.
196. APTER, Ronnie
    "Balladesque" (tr. of Richard Wagner, w. Mark Herman). [GrahamHR] (19) Wint 95-
        96, p. 68.
    "Lili Marlene" (tr. of Richard Wagner, w. Mark Herman). [GrahamHR] (19) Wint 95-
        96, p. 67.
    "Slices" (tr. of Richard Wagner, w. Mark Herman). [GrahamHR] (19) Wint 95-96, p.
        66.
197. ARAGON, Francisco
    "Fountain" (tr. of Gerardo Diego). [Chelsea] (59) 95, p. 129.
    "Snow" (tr. of Gerardo Diego). [Chelsea] (59) 95, p. 130.
198. ARAKI, Yasusada
    "Silk Tree Renga" (w. Ozaki Kusatao and Akutagawa Fusei. Tr. by Tosa Motokiyu,
        Ojiu Norinaga and Okura Kyojin). [GrandS] (14:1, #53) Sum 95. p. 28-30.
    "Untitled, August 12, 1964" (tr. by Tosa Motokiyu, Ojiu Norinaga and Okura
        Kyojin). [GrandS] (14:1, #53) Sum 95, p. 25.
199. ARANCIO, Lawrence
    "My Springtime." [PoetryE] (39) Fall 94, p. 16.
200. ARANGUIZ, Manuel
    "Cuerpo de Silencio" (Excerpt). [Arc] (35) Aut 95, p. 3.
ARBITER, Petronius (d. 66 CE)
    See PETRONIUS ARBITER (d. 66 CE)
201. ARCANA, Judith
    "Apple Juice." [Calyx] (16:2) Wint 95-96, p. 31.
202. ARCENEAUX, Therese
    "The Burning Bush." [BellArk] (11:3) My-Je 95, p. 12.
    "Dogwood Spring." [BellArk] (11:3) My-Je 95, p. 8.
    "Forgotten Burial Ground." [Poem] (73) My 95, p. 55.
    "From Another Town in Another War." [Poem] (73) My 95, p. 56.
203. ARDOIN, Adrien
    "A Letter from Dayton" (after Li Po, and Ezra Pound). [WilliamMR] (33) 95, p. 57.
204. ARENA, Ardi Anna
    "Chiaro Scuro." [NewRena] (9:2, #28) Spr 95, p. 132.
    "Vino Vecchio." [NewRena] (9:2, #28) Spr 95, p. 133.
205. ARGENTARIUS, Marcus (ca. 60 BCE)
    "Her perfect naked breast" (tr. by Sam Hamill). [PoetryE] (41) Aut 95, p. 13.
206. ARGON, Xenia
    "Charles' River." [DefinedP] (1:2) Spr-Sum 93, p. 50.
207. ARGÜELLES, Ivan
    "Great and Strange Is the Flowering Field of Heaven." [SilverFR] (26) Wint 95, p.
        18-19.
208. ARIDJIS, Homero
    "Fragments and Commentaries" (I-III, tr. by George McWhirter). [HarvardR] (8) Spr
        95, p. 86-89.
209. ARIWARA no NARIHIRA (825-880)
    "Is that the same moon?" (tr. by Sam Hamill). [PoetryE] (41) Aut 95, p. 21.
210. ARJAN
    "The Oil Minister." [Descant] (26:1, #88) Spr 95, p. 91-98.

211. ARJONILLA, Christian
"L'éclat du corps." [Os] (41) 95, p. 25.
"Impressions d'Afrique." [Os] (41) 95, p. 26.
212. ARMAND, Octavio
"2, rue Saint Suplice" (tr. by Carol Maier). [OhioR] (54) 95, p. 21.
"Baptismal Pyre" (tr. by Carol Maier). [OhioR] (54) 95, p. 17.
"Father Demo Square" (tr. by Carol Maier). [OhioR] (54) 95, p. 18.
"Get Away, Muses!" (tr. by Carol Maier). [OhioR] (54) 95, p. 12-14.
"October" (tr. by Carol Maier). [OhioR] (54) 95, p. 19.
"Test" (tr. by Carol Maier). [OhioR] (54) 95, p. 20.
"Viento" (In Italian and English: Exercise in the Translations of Desire: Three
    Versions tr. by Carol Maier). [OhioR] (54) 95, p. 23-24.
"Will You Tear Up This Page?" (tr. by Carol Maier). [OhioR] (54) 95, p. 15.
"Words for a Zen Garden" (Chapbook: 9 poems, tr. by Carol Maier). [OhioR] (54)
    95, p. 9-21.
"Words for a Zen Garden" (tr. by Carol Maier). [OhioR] (54) 95, p. 16.
"Written on Sand" (tr. by Carol Maier). [OhioR] (54) 95, p. 11.
213. ARMANTROUT, Rae
"All." [Avec] (9) 95, p. 9.
"Articulation." [NewAW] (13) Fall-Wint 95, p. 44-45.
"Between." [RiverC] (15:1) Wint 95, p. 19.
"Circuit." [Avec] (9) 95, p. 10.
"Greeting." [NewAW] (13) Fall-Wint 95, p. 46.
"The Past." [Avec] (9) 95, p. 8.
"Performers." [Avec] (9) 95, p. 7.
"Requirements." [Avec] (9) 95, p. 11.
"Thinking." [Avec] (9) 95, p. 6.
"The Turn." [RiverC] (15:1) Wint 95, p. 20.
214. ARMBRUST, Roger
"I am clipping the fingernails." [NewYorkQ] (54) 95, p. 100.
215. ARMITAGE, Simon
"Book of Matches" (Excerpts). [Verse] (12:2) 95, p. 10-18.
"Chapter and Verse." [GrandS] (14:1, #53) Sum 95, p. 123.
"A Week and a Fortnight." [GrandS] (14:1, #53) Sum 95, p. 124.
216. ARMSTRONG, Gene
"Early Tigers" (Selections: 8 poems). [BellArk] (11:4) Jl-Ag 95, p. 4.
217. ARMSTRONG, Mary
"The Men from the Mill." [Kalliope] (17:2) 95, p. 14-15.
"The Way We Measure." [Kalliope] (17:2) 95, p. 12-13.
218. ARNAY (D.C. Vision Program, Tyler Elementary School, Washington, DC).
"Arnay" (WritersCorps Program). [WashR] (21:2) Ag-S 95, p. 19.
219. ARNOLD, Craig
"Saffron." [YaleR] (83:3) Jl 95, p. 121-123.
220. ARNOLD, Philip
"The Border Life." [Flyway] (1:1) Spr 95, p. 102-104.
221. ARP, Hans
"Roses Stroll the Streets of Porcelain" (tr. by William Seaton). [Chelsea] (59) 95, p.
    126.
222. ARRIETA, Marcia
"Few Words." [Bogg] (67) 95, p. 32.
"I did not know you." [RagMag] (12:2) Spr 95, p. 91.
223. ARROYO, Rane
"The Adventures of Juan Angel." [Crucible] (31) Fall 95, p. 40-43.
"Backyard: Letter to the Dead." [Farm] (13:2 [i.e. 12:2]) Fall-Wint 95, p. 5.
"Dream." [ManyMM] (2:1) 95, p. 81.
"Dream Starring Andy Garcia." [Gerbil] (4) Fall 95, p. 24.
"Little Joe." [ManyMM] (2:1) 95, p. 82-83.
"Post Atomic Bombs Prayer." [ManyMM] (2:1) 95, p. 84.
"Prayer to and for John the Baptist." [ManyMM] (2:1) 95, p. 85.
224. ARTAUD, Antonin
"Fragmentations" (tr. by Clayton Eshleman, w. Bernard Bador). [Sulfur] (15:2, #37)
    Fall 95, p. 60-70.
225. ARTEAGA, Alfred
"English 143B: Writing Verse in Berkeley." [RiverS] (41) 95, p. 11-12.

226. ARTHUR, Chris
"Appearances Can Be Deceptive" (Seven Extracts from a Continuing Series). [CentR] (39:1) Wint 95, p. 90-92.
"Codicil." [CimR] (110) Ja 96, p. 74-75.
"Ochre." [CentR] (39:1) Wint 95, p. 93-94.
"Trying Saints." [CimR] (110) Ja 96, p. 74.
227. ARTHUR, Jenny
"Letter to Marlon Brando." [Conduit] (3) Sum 95, p. 26.
"No One Is Happy." [Conduit] (3) Sum 95, p. 25.
228. ASHBERY, John
"Allotted Spree." [HarvardR] (8) Spr 95, p. 13.
"Atonal Music." [ColR] (22:1) Spr 95, p. 37.
"The Blot People." [AmerPoR] (24:1) Ja-F 95, p. 4.
"By an Earthquake." [ParisR] (37:135) Sum 95, p. 193-196.
"By Guess and By Gosh." [NewYRB] (42:15) 5 O 95, p. 13.
"Cantilever." [YaleR] (83:4) O 95, p. 67.
"Chapter II, Book 35." [AmerPoR] (24:1) Ja-F 95, p. 4.
"Coming Down from New York." [DenQ] (30:1) Sum 95, p. 10.
"The Desolate Beauty Parlor on Beach Avenue." [NewYorker] (71:39) 4 D 95, p. 72.
"The Faint of Heart." [DenQ] (30:1) Sum 95, p. 8-9.
"Fascicle." [AmerPoR] (24:1) Ja-F 95, p. 6.
"Five O'Clock Shadow." [ColR] (22:1) Spr 95, p. 34-35.
"Getting Back In." [NewYorker] (71:29) 25 S 95, p. 79.
"The Green Mummies." [AmerPoR] (24:1) Ja-F 95, p. 4.
"Hegel." [AmerPoR] (24:1) Ja-F 95, p. 5.
"I, Too." [YaleR] (83:4) O 95, p. 68.
"In an Inchoate Place." [AmerPoR] (24:1) Ja-F 95, p. 5.
"The Latvian." [NewRep] (213:16) 16 O 95, p. 54.
"Limited Liabilities." [AmerPoR] (24:1) Ja-F 95, p. 7.
"Love in Boots." [AmerPoR] (24:1) Ja-F 95, p. 5.
"The Military Base." [AmerPoR] (24:1) Ja-F 95, p. 6.
"My Name Is Dimitri." [AmerPoR] (24:1) Ja-F 95, p. 5.
"No Earthly Reason." [DenQ] (30:1) Sum 95, p. 6-7.
"Obedience School." [AmerPoR] (24:1) Ja-F 95, p. 4.
"Ode to John Keats." [Arshile] (4) 95, p. 10.
"Of a Particular Stranger." [Arshile] (4) 95, p. 12.
"Operators Are Standing By." [AmerPoR] (24:1) Ja-F 95, p. 3.
"Palindrome." [Arshile] (4) 95, p. 11.
"The Penitent." [GrandS] (14:2, #54) Fall 95, p. 201-202.
"A Poem of Unrest." [Poetry] (166:4) Jl 95, p. 188.
"The Problem of Anxiety." [Arshile] (4) 95, p. 9.
"Sleepers Awake." [Poetry] (166:4) Jl 95, p. 190-191.
"Theme." [Poetry] (166:4) Jl 95, p. 189-190.
"Title Search" (from And the Stars Were Shining). [Harp] (291:1744) S 95, p. 28.
"Touching, the Similarities." [DenQ] (29:4) Spr 95, back cover.
"Tower of Darkness." [Poetry] (166:4) Jl 95, p. 188.
"The Waiting Ceremony." [AmerPoR] (24:1) Ja-F 95, p. 3.
"The Walkways." [AmerPoR] (24:1) Ja-F 95, p. 6.
"When All Her Neighbors Came." [ColR] (22:1) Spr 95, p. 36.
"Woman Leaning." [Verse] (12:3) 95, p. 107.
"You Dropped Something." [GrandS] (14:2, #54) Fall 95, p. 199-201.
"You Would Have Thought." [AmerPoR] (24:1) Ja-F 95, p. 3.
229. ASHCROFT, Cliff
"Not with Us." [Stand] (36:3) Sum 95, p. 77.
230. ASHIDA, Takako
"A crying girl" (in Japanese and English, tr. by Jiro Nakano). [BambooR] (67/68) Sum-Fall 95, p. 1.
231. ASHLEY, Renée
"Letter to a Husband." [Chelsea] (59) 95, p. 176-177.
"Penelope's Voice: The Weaving." [AmerV] (38) 95, p. 71-74.
"Where You Go When You Sleep." [Chelsea] (59) 95, p. 172-175.
232. ASHTON, Jennifer
"An Elegy Is a Man." [Ploughs] (21:4) Wint 95-96, p. 28-29.
"Still Life with Motion" (after Giorgio de Chirico). [Ploughs] (21:4) Wint 95-96, p. 26-27.

233. ASKLEPIADOS (ca. 320 BCE)
"Think how unspeakably sweet" (tr. by Sam Hamill). [PoetryE] (41) Aut 95, p. 12.
234. ASPENSTRÖM, Werner
"An Account of Dizziness" (from *Murmur*, 1983, tr. by Robin Fulton). [QRL] (34)
95, book 3, p. 30.
"After a Night of Frost" (from *Within*, 1969, tr. by Robin Fulton). [QRL] (34) 95,
book 3, p. 21.
"After Playing Mozart All Day" (from *The Stairway*, 1964, tr. by Robin Fulton).
[QRL] (34) 95, book 3, p. 20.
"After the Storm" (tr. by Robin Fulton). [QRL] (34) 95, book 3, p. 53.
"At the Opera I Remember Another Song" (from *The Red Cloud*, 1986, tr. by Robin
Fulton). [QRL] (34) 95, book 3, p. 41.
"At the Same Time as Chagall" (from *Murmur*, 1983, tr. by Robin Fulton). [QRL]
(34) 95, book 3, p. 37-38.
"The Bells" (from *The Stairway*, 1964, tr. by Robin Fulton). [QRL] (34) 95, book 3,
p. 16.
"Birds, 18th Century Style" (from *Snow-legend*, 1949, tr. by Robin Fulton). [QRL]
(34) 95, book 3, p. 8.
"Busy Creatures" (from *Creatures*, 1988, tr. by Robin Fulton). [QRL] (34) 95, book
3, p. 48.
"The Butterfly" (from *The Stairway*, 1964, tr. by Robin Fulton). [QRL] (34) 95, book
3, p. 15.
"The Cat Pricks Up Its Ears" (from *The Red Cloud*, 1986, tr. by Robin Fulton). [QRL]
(34) 95, book 3, p. 40.
"The Child Rises" (from *Creatures*, 1988, tr. by Robin Fulton). [QRL] (34) 95, book
3, p. 49.
"The Comet" (from *Creatures*, 1988, tr. by Robin Fulton). [QRL] (34) 95, book 3, p.
52.
"Economic Geography" (from *Creatures*, 1988, tr. by Robin Fulton). [QRL] (34) 95,
book 3, p. 46-47.
"The Elephant" (from *The Stairway*, 1964, tr. by Robin Fulton). [QRL] (34) 95, book
3, p. 17.
"Engravings" (from *Creatures*, 1988, tr. by Robin Fulton). [QRL] (34) 95, book 3, p.
45.
"Fever" (from *Private and Public*, 1991, tr. by Robin Fulton). [QRL] (34) 95, book 3,
p. 56.
"The Fist Doesn't Always Win" (from *Meanwhile*, 1972, tr. by Robin Fulton). [QRL]
(34) 95, book 3, p. 24.
"The Gatepost" (from *Early One Morning, Late on Earth*, 1980, tr. by Robin Fulton).
[QRL] (34) 95, book 3, p. 27.
"The Glow-Worm" (from *Murmur*, 1983, tr. by Robin Fulton). [QRL] (34) 95, book
3, p. 31.
"Hamlet Should Have Died in the First Act" (from *By Day by Night*, 1961, tr. by
Robin Fulton). [QRL] (34) 95, book 3, p. 13.
"Happiness" (from *The Dogs*, 1954, tr. by Robin Fulton). [QRL] (34) 95, book 3, p. 9.
"The Heart" (from *The Stairway*, 1964, tr. by Robin Fulton). [QRL] (34) 95, book 3,
p. 19.
"The Horse" (from *The Stairway*, 1964, tr. by Robin Fulton). [QRL] (34) 95, book 3,
p. 15.
"The House-Sparrow" (from *Dictionary*, 1976, tr. by Robin Fulton). [QRL] (34) 95,
book 3, p. 24.
"The Ice-Stack" (from *Litany*, 1952, tr. by Robin Fulton). [QRL] (34) 95, book 3, p.
9.
"If There Were Only Two Words" (from *Dictionary*, 1976, tr. by Robin Fulton).
[QRL] (34) 95, book 3, p. 25.
"Ikaros and Master Granite" (from *Poems beneath the Trees*, 1956, tr. by Robin
Fulton). [QRL] (34) 95, book 3, p. 10.
"Il Gran Cavallo, or A Brief History of Leonardo's Horse" (from *Murmur*, 1983, tr.
by Robin Fulton). [QRL] (34) 95, book 3, p. 35-36.
"Imposing Buildings" (from *Creatures*, 1988, tr. by Robin Fulton). [QRL] (34) 95,
book 3, p. 51.
"In the Age of the Long Exposures" (from *The Red Cloud*, 1986, tr. by Robin Fulton).
[QRL] (34) 95, book 3, p. 41.
"In the Regions of Dream" (from *Murmur*, 1983, tr. by Robin Fulton). [QRL] (34) 95,
book 3, p. 32.

"I've Been Thinking of Van Gogh Again" (from *Murmur*, 1983, tr. by Robin Fulton).
[QRL] (34) 95, book 3, p. 33-35.
"The Lamp" (from *Creatures*, 1988, tr. by Robin Fulton). [QRL] (34) 95, book 3, p.
47.
"Lapidary Report" (from *Creatures*, 1988, tr. by Robin Fulton). [QRL] (34) 95, book
3, p. 44.
"The Larks" (from *Early One Morning, Late on Earth*, 1980, tr. by Robin Fulton).
[QRL] (34) 95, book 3, p. 27.
"Looking Up from the Cradle of Earth" (from *Within*, 1969, tr. by Robin Fulton).
[QRL] (34) 95, book 3, p. 22.
"Memorial" (from *Dictionary*, 1976, tr. by Robin Fulton). [QRL] (34) 95, book 3, p.
24.
"The Mill" (from *Murmur*, 1983, tr. by Robin Fulton). [QRL] (34) 95, book 3, p. 29.
"The Moon" (from *Litany*, 1952, tr. by Robin Fulton). [QRL] (34) 95, book 3, p. 9.
"More I Don't Know" (from *By Day by Night*, 1961, tr. by Robin Fulton). [QRL] (34)
95, book 3, p. 12.
"The Music" (from *Creatures*, 1988, tr. by Robin Fulton). [QRL] (34) 95, book 3, p.
48.
"Non Plus Ultra" (from *Creatures*, 1988, tr. by Robin Fulton). [QRL] (34) 95, book 3,
p. 50.
"The Oars" (from *The Stairway*, 1964, tr. by Robin Fulton). [QRL] (34) 95, book 3, p.
16-17.
"On Behalf of Matter" (from *By Day by Night*, 1961, tr. by Robin Fulton). [QRL] (34)
95, book 3, p. 12.
"On the Djurgård Ferry" (from *Poems beneath the Trees*, 1956, tr. by Robin Fulton).
[QRL] (34) 95, book 3, p. 10.
"One of the Horse's Legs Was Missing" (from *The Red Cloud*, 1986, tr. by Robin
Fulton). [QRL] (34) 95, book 3, p. 40.
"Otherwise Among the Squirrels" (from *Private and Public*, 1991, tr. by Robin
Fulton). [QRL] (34) 95, book 3, p. 55.
"Outside the Circle of Light" (from *By Day by Night*, 1961, tr. by Robin Fulton).
[QRL] (34) 95, book 3, p. 14.
"Paradise, Almost Like an Illness" (from *Within*, 1969, tr. by Robin Fulton). [QRL]
(34) 95, book 3, p. 21.
"The Pleiades" (from *Private and Public*, 1991, tr. by Robin Fulton). [QRL] (34) 95,
book 3, p. 56.
"Portrait" (from *Dictionary*, 1976, tr. by Robin Fulton). [QRL] (34) 95, book 3, p. 26.
"Portrait in December" (from *Poems beneath the Trees*, 1956, tr. by Robin Fulton).
[QRL] (34) 95, book 3, p. 11.
"Post Festum" (from *Murmur*, 1983, tr. by Robin Fulton). [QRL] (34) 95, book 3, p.
28.
"Probable Changes in the Language" (from *Creatures*, 1988, tr. by Robin Fulton).
[QRL] (34) 95, book 3, p. 51.
"The Redeemer Liveth" (from *Meanwhile*, 1972, tr. by Robin Fulton). [QRL] (34) 95,
book 3, p. 23.
"Revisiting" (from *Creatures*, 1988, tr. by Robin Fulton). [QRL] (34) 95, book 3, p.
50.
"The Rower" (tr. by Robin Fulton). [QRL] (34) 95, book 3, p. 54.
"The Sandal" (from *Creatures*, 1988, tr. by Robin Fulton). [QRL] (34) 95, book 3, p.
47.
"The Sardine on the Subway" (from *Meanwhile*, 1972, tr. by Robin Fulton). [QRL]
(34) 95, book 3, p. 23.
"Scenario for a Small Angry Cock" (from *Murmur*, 1983, tr. by Robin Fulton). [QRL]
(34) 95, book 3, p. 30.
"Seen from the Balloon of Dreams" (from *The Red Cloud*, 1986, tr. by Robin Fulton).
[QRL] (34) 95, book 3, p. 42.
"She Who Paused on the Path and Breathed in Deeply" (from *The Red Cloud*, 1986,
tr. by Robin Fulton). [QRL] (34) 95, book 3, p. 42.
"Silver" (from *Creatures*, 1988, tr. by Robin Fulton). [QRL] (34) 95, book 3, p. 49.
"The Sloth" (from *Creatures*, 1988, tr. by Robin Fulton). [QRL] (34) 95, book 3, p.
46.
"The Snail" (from *Creatures*, 1988, tr. by Robin Fulton). [QRL] (34) 95, book 3, p.
43.
"The Snow Leopard" (from *Murmur*, 1983, tr. by Robin Fulton). [QRL] (34) 95, book
3, p. 32.

"The Snowflake" (from *By Day by Night*, 1961, tr. by Robin Fulton). [QRL] (34) 95,
   book 3, p. 14.
"So That Something Will Be Heard" (from *The Stairway*, 1964, tr. by Robin Fulton).
   [QRL] (34) 95, book 3, p. 20.
"The Song" (tr. by Robin Fulton). [QRL] (34) 95, book 3, p. 54.
"The Spider" (from *The Stairway*, 1964, tr. by Robin Fulton). [QRL] (34) 95, book 3,
   p. 18.
"This Year Too" (from *Early One Morning, Late on Earth*, 1980, tr. by Robin
   Fulton). [QRL] (34) 95, book 3, p. 26.
"The Tower" (from *Private and Public*, 1991, tr. by Robin Fulton). [QRL] (34) 95,
   book 3, p. 55.
"The Tree" (from *The Red Cloud*, 1986, tr. by Robin Fulton). [QRL] (34) 95, book 3,
   p. 39.
"An Unusually Warm Day" (from *Early One Morning, Late on Earth*, 1980, tr. by
   Robin Fulton). [QRL] (34) 95, book 3, p. 27.
"Village Lilacs" (from *Litany*, 1952, tr. by Robin Fulton). [QRL] (34) 95, book 3, p.
   8.
"We Too Are Laymen, Said the Waves" (from *The Red Cloud*, 1986, tr. by Robin
   Fulton). [QRL] (34) 95, book 3, p. 39.
"What I Noticed in London" (from *Creatures*, 1988, tr. by Robin Fulton). [QRL] (34)
   95, book 3, p. 44-45.
"What's Left of the Year 1930" (from *By Day by Night*, 1961, tr. by Robin Fulton).
   [QRL] (34) 95, book 3, p. 13.
"Who Is Not a Child" (from *Creatures*, 1988, tr. by Robin Fulton). [QRL] (34) 95,
   book 3, p. 52.
"You and Me and the World" (from *The Stairway*, 1964, tr. by Robin Fulton). [QRL]
   (34) 95, book 3, p. 18.
235. ASSIS, Louiza
   "Solitária." [LowellR] [1] Sum 94, p. 43-44.
   "Wild Horses Run Free." [LowellR] [1] Sum 94, p. 41-42.
236. ASTOR, M. C.
   "Afternoon under the Roses" (for Dana, my Mother). [Pearl] (22) Fall-Wint 95, p.
      149.
237. ATALLA, S. V.
   "Baba Ghanouj." [PraS] (69:2) Sum 95, p. 70-71.
   "Diaspora." [PraS] (69:2) Sum 95, p. 71-72.
238. ATHEY, David
   "All Soul's Day, St. Paul Civic Center." [CapeR] (30:2) Fall 95, p. 39.
   "Cafe, Woman, Koan." [Northeast] (5:12) Sum 95, p. 24.
   "He Is Tired of Self-Portraits of Artists, Pouting." [PaintedB] (55/56) 95, p. 32.
   "Sophia's Pub." [BellArk] (11:4) Jl-Ag 95, p. 14.
239. ATKINS, Marcus
   "Kwanfly (Kwansaba '95)." [Drumvoices] (5:1/2) Fall-Wint 95-96, p. 12.
240. ATKINS, Priscilla
   "Blue Jay." [CreamCR] (19:1) Spr 95, p. 117.
   "The Spanish Professor." [CreamCR] (19:1) Spr 95, p. 116.
   "Watching for Meteors on Nestucca Bay." [CreamCR] (19:1) Spr 95, p. 118.
241. ATKINSON, Charles
   "After the Earthquake: Dreaming of Candlestick" (runner up, 1994 Borderlands
      Poetry Contest). [Border] (6) Spr-Sum 95, p. 16-17.
242. ATKINSON, Jennifer
   "The Miraculous." [Poetry] (165:6) Mr 95, p. 311.
243. ATKINSON, Michael
   "A. Dostoyevskaya, 1920." [PraS] (69:3) Fall 95, p. 141-142.
   "Gladiators." [OntR] (42) Spr-Sum 95, p. 111-112.
   "Notes for My Mother." [LaurelR] (29:1) Wint 95, p. 20-21.
   "Painting Bedrooms." [OntR] (42) Spr-Sum 95, p. 112-113.
   "A Trip to the Moon." [HiramPoR] (58/59) Spr 95-Wint 96, p. 6-7.
   "Vigo" (Dead in 1934, at 29 years, three weeks after the premiere of his third film).
      [SouthernPR] (35:1) Sum 95, p. 16-17.
244. ATSUMI, Ikuko
   "The Day When Mountains Move" (tr. of Akiko (1878-1942) Yosano, w. Kenneth
      Rexroth). [ManyMM] reprinted in every issue p. 2.
245. ATWAN, Robert
   "Annunciation." [Image] (10) Sum 95, p. 40-42.
   "Good Friday, 1993: Heading East." [Image] (10) Sum 95, p. 39.

246. ATWOOD, Margaret
"Ava Gardner Reincarnated as a Magnolia." [MichQR] (34:4) Fall 95, p. 583-585.
"Before" (For John T.). [AntigR] (102/103) Sum-Aug 95, p. 219-220.
"Cave Series" (Excerpt). [RiverS] (42/43) 95, p. 58.
"Instructions for the Third Eye." [RiverS] (42/43) 95, p. 56-57.
"A Visit." [Atlantic] (275:5) My 95, p. 76.
"You Come Back." [NoAmR] (280:5) S-O 95, p. 52.
247. AUBERT, Alvin
"Long Hard Song" (For Eugene Redmond, who saw fit to raise a poem in my name).
[Drumvoices] (4:1/2) Fall-Wint 94-95, p. 141.
248. AUBREY, Keith
"Bamboo Boat" (Guilin, 1991). [HolCrit] (32:5) D 95, p. 17.
"Listening to Dong Tinglan Play His New Guitar Composition for Minister Fang" (tr.
of Li Qi, 690?-754, w. Deng Yan). [Chelsea] (59) 95, p. 132-133.
"An Old Soldier's March" (tr. of Li Qi, 690?-754, w. Deng Yan). [Chelsea] (59) 95, p.
134.
"The River-Merchant's Wife: A Second Letter" (tr. of Li Po, w. Deng Yan).
[GrahamHR] (19) Wint 95-96, p. 79.
"Sent North on a Rainy Night" (tr. of Li Shang-yin, w. Deng Yan). [GrahamHR] (19)
Wint 95-96, p. 81.
"Viewing the Waterfall on Mt. Lu" (tr. of Li Po, w. Deng Yan). [GrahamHR] (19)
Wint 95-96, p. 80.
249. AUGUSTO, Ronald
"Homem ao Rubro Apócrifo." [Callaloo] (18:4) Fall 95, p. 920-921.
"Man to the Apocryphal Power of Rouge: Part I of Puya" (tr. by Reetika Vazirani).
[Callaloo] (18:4) Fall 95, p. 748-750.
250. AUSLÄNDER, Rose
"Biographical Note" (tr. by Robin Fulton). [MalR] (110) Spr 95, p. 75.
"Immortality" (tr. by Gary Sea). [ProseP] (4) 95, p. 8.
"Parting" (tr. by Robin Fulton). [MalR] (110) Spr 95, p. 74.
"Progress I" (tr. by Gary Sea). [ProseP] (4) 95, p. 7.
251. AUSTIN, Bob
"At the Milagrosso Store." [ChironR] (42) Spr 95, p. 24.
252. AVENA, Thomas
"All the Submarines of the US Navy." [DenQ] (30:1) Sum 95, p. 14-15.
"Pursuit." [DenQ] (30:1) Sum 95, p. 11-13.
253. AVERY, Brian C.
"One Dog's Summer" (The first transcontinental crossing by automobile). [WeberS]
(12:1) Wint 95, p. 57-58.
AVILA, Inés Hernández
See HERNANDEZ AVILA, Inés
254. AXINN, Donald Everett
"About the Truth and the Silence of Fog." [WritersF] (21) 95, p. 34.
"This Is What You Get." [WritersF] (21) 95, p. 32.
"What Matters." [WritersF] (21) 95, p. 33.
255. AYALA, Naomi
"Amber Hands." [CaribbeanW] (9) 95, p. 25-27.
"It Was Late and She Was Climbing." [Kalliope] (17:3) 95, p. 21.
"A Man Will Rush From Behind Me." [CaribbeanW] (9) 95, p. 23-24.
"Papo, Who'd Wanted to Be an Artist." [MassR] (36:4) Wint 95-96, p. 593.
"Reform." [MassR] (36:4) Wint 95-96, p. 594.
256. AYHAN, Ece
"Elegy for a Handwrought God" (tr. by Murat Nemet-Nejat). [Talisman] (14) Fall 95,
p. 42.
"Geranium and the Child" (tr. by Murat Nemet-Nejat). [Talisman] (14) Fall 95, p. 44.
"The Nigger in a Photograph" (tr. by Murat Nemet-Nejat). [Talisman] (14) Fall 95, p.
43.
"Phaeton" (tr. by Murat Nemet-Nejat). [Talisman] (14) Fall 95, p. 42.
"To Trace from Hebrew" (tr. by Murat Nemet-Nejat). [Talisman] (14) Fall 95, p. 42 -
43.
257. AYTON, Michael
"They Might Be Lovers." [Stand] (36:2) Spr 95, p. 18.
"You Have Been" (tr. of Cristiana Maria Sebastiani). [Stand] (36:2) Spr 95, p. 75.
258. AZAD, Shamim
"Conjugal Prayer" (in Bengali and English, tr. by Syed Manzoorul Islam and
Carolyne Wright, w. the author). [MidAR] (15:1/2) 95, p. 92-93.

"I Want to Pierce with the Arrows of My Voice" (in Bengali and English, tr. by Syed Manzoorul Islam and Carolyne Wright, w. the author). [MidAR] (15:1/2) 95, p. 96-99.
"Out-of-Order Remote-Control" (in Bengali and English, tr. by Syed Manzoorul Islam and Carolyne Wright, w. the author). [MidAR] (15:1/2) 95, p. 94-95.

AZPARREN, José Antonio Yépes
See YÉPES AZPARREN, José Antonio

BAASTAD, Erling Friis
See FRIIS-BAASTAD, Erling
259. BAATZ, Ronald
"After a Night of Snow Continuously Falling." [WormR] (35:4, #140) 95, p. 171.
"All His Ugly Daughters." [WormR] (35:4, #140) 95, p. 166.
"Always." [WormR] (35:1, #137) 95, p. 20.
"Asparagus." [WormR] (35:1, #137) 95, p. 22.
"At the Sink." [WormR] (35:4, #140) 95, p. 172.
"At This Point in the Road." [WormR] (35:4, #140) 95, p. 163-164.
"Ate Bird." [WormR] (35:1, #137) 95, p. 22.
"Black Walnut Trees." [WormR] (35:4, #140) 95, p. 177-178.
"Confuse the Birds." [WormR] (35:4, #140) 95, p. 172.
"Dinner." [WormR] (35:4, #140) 95, p. 167.
"Downhill." [WormR] (35:4, #140) 95, p. 162.
"Faithfully." [WormR] (35:1, #137) 95, p. 21.
"The First Place." [WormR] (35:4, #140) 95, p. 160.
"God's Hobby." [WormR] (35:1, #137) 95, p. 20.
"Great Leftovers." [WormR] (35:4, #140) 95, p. 161.
"I wake exhausted." [WormR] (35:4, #140) 95, p. 161.
"I'm Telling You." [WormR] (35:1, #137) 95, p. 21.
"It Amazes Me." [WormR] (35:1, #137) 95, p. 23-24.
"Lasagna." [WormR] (35:4, #140) 95, p. 176-177.
"Late in the Season." [WormR] (35:4, #140) 95, p. 167.
"New Air." [WormR] (35:4, #140) 95, p. 168.
"The Oldest Songs." [WormR] (35:4, #140) 95, p. 173.
"On the Inside of the Hot House." [WormR] (35:4, #140) 95, p. 164-165.
"Only for the Old and the Fragile." [WormR] (35:4, #140) 95, p. 178.
"Out in the Late October Garden." [WormR] (35:4, #140) 95, p. 169.
"Out in the Late October Garden" (Special Section: 27 poems). [WormR] (35:4, #140) 95, p. 159-178.
"Over More Tea." [WormR] (35:4, #140) 95, p. 170.
"The Pear and the Earth." [WormR] (35:4, #140) 95, p. 175-176.
"A Poet." [WormR] (35:4, #140) 95, p. 168-169.
"Quail." [WormR] (35:1, #137) 95, p. 22.
"Quiet Potatoes." [WormR] (35:4, #140) 95, p. 173-174.
"A Rainy Night and I Dream of Her Feet Again." [YellowS] (12:4, #48) Sum 95, p. 9.
"The Same Orange." [WormR] (35:1, #137) 95, p. 20-21.
"She Loved Mozart." [WormR] (35:4, #140) 95, p. 174-175.
"So Near, So Faraway." [WormR] (35:4, #140) 95, p. 165.
"The Spider Plant." [WormR] (35:1, #137) 95, p. 21-22.
"Such small gold leaves." [WormR] (35:4, #140) 95, p. 159.
"Uncut and Crowded with Dandelions." [WormR] (35:4, #140) 95, p. 163.
"Where the stream overflowed." [WormR] (35:4, #140) 95, p. 159.
260. BABB, Julie
"Mirage." [EvergreenC] (10:1) Wint-Spr 95, p. 52.
261. BABCOCK, J. C.
"Runs in the Family, or The Price to Pay." [JINJPo] (17:1) Spr 95, p. 29.
262. BACH, Glenn
"Breaking In." [Pearl] (22) Fall-Wint 95, p. 33.
"Burned." [Pearl] (22) Fall-Wint 95, p. 32.
"How Many Poets Does It Take." [WormR] (35:1, #137) 95, p. 16-17.
"Immaculate Correction." [WormR] (35:1, #137) 95, p. 15.
"Riot Poem #10,000." [Pearl] (22) Fall-Wint 95, p. 33-34.
"Scorpions Are Quiet When They Strike." [Pearl] (22) Fall-Wint 95, p. 35.
"Tongue-Tied and Twisted." [SlipS] (15) 95, p. 63-64.
263. BACHAR, Greg
"Balthus Invented by Color." [HawaiiR] (19:2) Fall 95, p. 74.

"She Was Russian and Loved Snow." [HawaiiR] (19:2) Fall 95, p. 178.
264. BACHMAN, Merle Lyn
"Stupni Do" (the music that keeps repeating, from a book-length manuscript called *Suspect Retrievals*). [Chain] (2) Spr 95, p. 14-18.
265. BACHMANN, Ingeborg
"Autumn Maneuver" (tr. by Peter Filkins). [CharR] (21:1) Spr 95, p. 93.
"Bohemia Lies by the Sea" (tr. by Peter Filkins). [CharR] (21:1) Spr 95, p. 95.
"Borrowed Time" (tr. by Peter Filkins). [MassR] (36:3) Aut 95, p. 342.
"In the Twilight" (tr. by Aaron Kramer, w. Siegfried Mandel). [Vis] (47) 95, p. 28.
"Paris" (tr. by Thomas Dorsett). [WillowS] (36) Je 95, p. 95.
"Salt and Bread" (tr. by Peter Filkins). [CharR] (21:1) Spr 95, p. 94.
267. BACHNER, Suzanne
"Concertino" (tr. of Astrid Hjertenaes Andersen, w. Aina Gerner-Mathisen). [Nimrod] (38:2) Spr-Sum 95, p. 80-81.
"Melancholia I, 1514" (tr. of Astrid Hjertenaes Andersen, w. A. Gerner-Mathisen). [TampaR] (11) Fall 95, p. 56.
"Yellow Sky" (tr. of Astrid Hjertenaes Andersen, w. Aina Gerner-Mathisen). [Nimrod] (38:2) Spr-Sum 95, p. 79.
268. BACON, Crystal V.
"Recollections." [OntR] (42) Spr-Sum 95, p. 114-115.
"Waiting for Fever to Pass." [OntR] (42) Spr-Sum 95, p. 115-117.
269. BADDOUR, Margaret Boothe
"Locked in Oak" (For Winston Edward Dees). [Crucible] (30) Fall 94, p. 16.
270. BADEN, Ruth Kramer
"Antics." [Light] (13) Spr 95, p. 19.
271. BADOR, Bernard
"Fragmentations" (tr. of Antonin Artaud, w. Clayton Eshleman). [Sulfur] (15:2, #37) Fall 95, p. 60-70.
272. BAER, William
"The Cuban Girl." [Hudson] (48:1) Spr 95, p. 96.
273. BAEZ, Fernando
"[Lo Que Resta]." [Luz] (8) Spr 95, p. 60.
BAG, Red Plastic
See RED PLASTIC BAG
274. BAGCHEE, Shyamal
"Best (Woman) Mind." [CanLit] (147) Wint 95, p. 46-47.
"Hinderland Poems: 4. Medicine Wheel, Bassano, Alberta" [sic]. [SoDakR] (33:3/4) Fall-Wint 95, p. 192.
"Hinderland Poems: 11. Paintpots, Yellowstone Park" [sic]. [SoDakR] (33:3/4) Fall - Wint 95, p. 191.
275. BAGGETT, Rebecca
"Alone." [PoetryE] (40) Spr 95, p. 12.
"Catalogue of Mothers." [ApalQ] (44/45) Fall 95-Wint 96, p. 5960.
"The Children Ask about Death." [PoetryE] (40) Spr 95, p. 11.
"Death." [Confr] (56/57) Sum-Fall 95, p. 327.
"First Night at the Artists' Colony" (For Caren and Lil). [PoetryE] (40) Spr 95, p. 13.
"Icarus." [PoetryE] (41) Aut 95, p. 119.
"Insomnia." [LullwaterR] (6:1) Spr-Sum 95, p. 8.
"A Poem for Activist Insomniacs." [PaintedB] (55/56) 95, p. 47-48.
"Third Daughter." [LullwaterR] (6:1) Spr-Sum 95, p. 9.
276. BAHLER, Michael F.
"Alex's Grandma." [Parting] (8:1) Sum 95, p. 32.
"Me and Olives." [Parting] (8:1) Sum 95, p. 37.
277. BAHORSKY, Russell
"A Reason for Leaving." [GreenMR] (8:2) Fall-Wint 95-96, p. 118.
"The Siege of Richmond" (After an Account by Constance Cary Harrison). [GreenMR] (8:2) Fall-Wint 95-96, p. 119.
278. BAHTI, Karni Pal
"The Moon Wears a Crooked Smile" (tr. of Gajanan Madhav Muktibodh). [AnotherCM] (29) Spr 95, p. 97-109.
279. BAI, Juyi
"In the Cold Pavillion: Entertaining" (tr. by James M. Cryer). [LitR] (38:3) Spr 95, p. 324.
"Lung Ch'ang Temple: The Lotus Pond" (tr. by James M. Cryer). [LitR] (38:3) Spr 95, p. 323.

"The Pond in Autumn" (tr. by James M. Cryer). [LitR] (38:3) Spr 95, p. 323.
"Welcoming My Neighbor to the East" (tr. by James M. Cryer). [LitR] (38:3) Spr 95, p. 323.
280. BAIGENT, Beryl
"Mary Earth Bound." [PoetryC] (15:3) Ag 95, p. 29.
281. BAILES, Dale Alan
"Morning at Naxos." [SouthernPR] (35:1) Sum 95, p. 33-34.
282. BAILEY, Beth
"Everything Is." [Gerbil] (3) Sum 95, p. 9.
"Surrounded" (A poem in 3 parts). [Gerbil] (4) Fall 95, p. 15.
283. BAILEY, Clay
"Legal Action." [Pearl] (22) Fall-Wint 95, p. 80-81.
284. BAILEY, Frizell
"The Nausea in Shakespeare's Othello." [Drumvoices] (5:1/2) Fall-Wint 95-96, p. 107.
285. BAILEY, Herbert S., Jr.
"Lessons in Navigation." [AmerS] (64:4) Aut 95, p. 556-557.
286. BAILEY, Jane
"It Is Easy to Believe in the Love of Trees." [Calyx] (16:2) Wint 95-96, p. 34-35.
"Visionary." [Calyx] (16:2) Wint 95-96, p. 36.
287. BAILEY, M. E.
"Hands." [SouthernPR] (35:2) Wint 95, p. 18.
"New Skin." [SouthernPR] (35:2) Wint 95, p. 17-18.
288. BAILEY, Mary Elizabeth
"The Pickle Barrel." [PoetryE] (39) Fall 94, p. 17.
289. BAINE, Harvey
"2 Poems for Bess." [Poem] (74) N 95, p. 6-7.
"By Faith or Eye." [Poem] (74) N 95, p. 5.
290. BAIRD, Ansie
"Landscape." [DenQ] (30:2) Fall 95, p. 6.
"Stage Three." [DenQ] (30:2) Fall 95, p. 7.
291. BAITOV, Nikolai
"Landscape with Ideas from Dostoevsky" (tr. by J. Kates). [NewEngR] (17:4) Fall 95, p. 33.
292. BAKER, David
"The Affair." [OhioR] (53) 95, p. 124.
"Creek in Town." [SouthernR] (31:4) O/Aut 95, p. 821-822.
"Graveyard." [CutB] (43) Wint 95, p. 80.
"The Kiss." [MidAR] (15:1/2) 95, p. 219-220.
"Violence." [SouthernR] (31:4) O/Aut 95, p. 820-821.
293. BAKER, Diana
"Feeling Something." [Pearl] (22) Fall-Wint 95, p. 120.
"Green Lights." [Pearl] (22) Fall-Wint 95, p. 120.
294. BAKER, Donald W.
"No." [LaurelR] (29:2) Sum 95, p. 70.
295. BAKER, June Frankland
"After Your Twenty-First Birthday" (for our daughter). [Poem] (73) My 95, p. 51.
"September" (for my mother). [Poem] (73) My 95, p. 52.
296. BAKER, Patsy B.
"Be Brave, Take a Stand." [Pembroke] (27) 95, p. 12.
297. BAKER, T.
"Amtrak." [SantaBR] (3:1) Spr 95, p. 112.
"In Flight from Involvement." [SantaBR] (3:1) Spr 95, p. 112.
298. BAKER, Tony
"For the Month Beginning." [WestCL] (29:2, #17) Fall 95, p. 8-14.
299. BAKOWSKI, Peter
"Bath Plug." [Quarry] (44:3) 95, p. 38.
"Bee." [Quarry] (44:3) 95, p. 38.
"Commas on the Roast." [Quarry] (44:3) 95, p. 38.
"Conversation in the Gentlemen's Club." [Vis] (47) 95, p. 34-35.
"Dear John." [Pearl] (22) Fall-Wint 95, p. 23.
"The Fly." [Pearl] (22) Fall-Wint 95, p. 23.
"For Around $1.50." [Pearl] (22) Fall-Wint 95, p. 23.
"For Hart Crane." [Bogg] (67) 95, p. 44.
"Miles Davis, Trumpeter." [Pearl] (22) Fall-Wint 95, p. 23.
"Portrait of Aaron Choates." [Bogg] (67) 95, p. 45-46.

"Postcards from Ironic City (No. 1)." [WormR] (35:1, #137) 95, p. 11.
"Postcards from Ironic City (No. 2)." [WormR] (35:1, #137) 95, p. 11.
"Subtle." [WormR] (35:1, #137) 95, p. 12.
"Succour." [Pearl] (22) Fall-Wint 95, p. 23.
"Toothpick." [Quarry] (44:3) 95, p. 38.
"Walking Along Slate Creek Road, Wilderville, Oregon, 1991." [Bogg] (67) 95, p. 46.
"While We Sleep." [WormR] (35:1, #137) 95, p. 12.
300. BALABAN, John
    "Lullaby for My Mother" (tr. of Blaga Dimitrova, w. Elena Hristova). [WillowS] (36) Je 95, p. 90-91.
    "Who Takes Care of the Blind Stork?" (tr. of Blaga Dimitrova, w. Elena Hristova). [WillowS] (36) Je 95, p. 89.
301. BALAKIAN, Peter
    "Physicians." [Agni] (42) 95, p. 37-40.
    "With Dick Hugo on the Pike." [Verse] (12:3) 95, p. 69-70.
302. BALAZS, Mary
    "In a City Park." [Wind] (75) Spr 95, p. 2.
303. BALDRIDGE, Wilson
    "Aphrodite Colleague" (from "Recumbent Figures," tr. of Michel Deguy). [Sulfur] (15:1, #36) Spr 95, p. 46.
    "Cardiogram (May)" (from "Recumbent Figures," tr. of Michel Deguy). [Sulfur] (15:1, #36) Spr 95, p. 44-45.
    "The Narrations" (from "Recumbent Figures," tr. of Michel Deguy). [Sulfur] (15:1, #36) Spr 95, p. 45.
    "Recumbent Figures" (from "Recumbent Figures," tr. of Michel Deguy). [Sulfur] (15:1, #36) Spr 95, p. 49-50.
    "Recumbent Figures" (Selections, tr. of Michel Deguy). [Sulfur] (15:1, #36) Spr 95, p. 44-51.
    "Translation" (from "Recumbent Figures," tr. of Michel Deguy). [Sulfur] (15:1, #36) Spr 95, p. 48-49.
    "Use Covered Yard (March)" (from "Recumbent Figures," tr. of Michel Deguy). [Sulfur] (15:1, #36) Spr 95, p. 44.
304. BALDWIN, Barbara
    "The Wheeled Fish." [NorthStoneR] (12) 95, p. 230-231.
305. BALL, Angela
    "Hall of Lost Violins." [ApalQ] (44/45) Fall 95-Wint 96, p. 61-62.
306. BALL, Beverly
    "In Morning." [MassR] (36:2) Sum 95, p. 324.
    "We Take a Walk After Dinner and Drinks." [Calyx] (16:2) Wint 95-96, p. 86.
307. BALL, Joseph H.
    "Click and Bang." [Poem] (73) My 95, p. 36.
    "The Dead." [CumbPR] (15:1) Fall 95, p. 7-8.
    "Eileen." [Poem] (73) My 95, p. 35.
    "Goodbye, Jenny Baxter." [CapeR] (30:1) Spr 95, p. 18.
    "Just Now." [WindO] (60) Fall-Wint 95, p. 9.
    "Letter to Christine." [Poem] (73) My 95, p. 37.
    "Mary Woke." [CapeR] (30:1) Spr 95, p. 19.
    "Reading Dr. Seuss to the Beautiful Children of Laurel Gardens." [SoDakR] (33:2) Sum 95, p. 66-67.
    "Things I've Lost." [CumbPR] (15:1) Fall 95, p. 9.
    "What Gift Can I Give You?" [Poem] (73) My 95, p. 34.
308. BALL, Sally
    "Early Attic." [SouthernR] (31:4) O/Aut 95, p. 823.
    "Miracles." [Witness] (9:2) 95, p. 86.
    "To His Sister." [PassN] (16:1) Sum 95, p. 4-5.
    "Trinket." [SpoonR] (20:2) Sum-Fall 95, p. 26.
    "Trinket 2" (for Martina). [SpoonR] (20:2) Sum-Fall 95, p. 27.
    "Trinket 3." [SpoonR] (20:2) Sum-Fall 95, p. 28.
    "Trinket 4." [SpoonR] (20:2) Sum-Fall 95, p. 29.
    "Trinket 5." [SpoonR] (20:2) Sum-Fall 95, p. 30.
    "Trinket 6." [SpoonR] (20:2) Sum-Fall 95, p. 31.
309. BALLANTYNE, Anne
    "Once Upon a Time." [AntigR] (100) Wint 95, p. 14.
310. BALLIETT, Whitney
    "Back." [NewYorker] (71:16) 12 Je 95, p. 91.

311. BALOIAN
"The Storyteller." [MidwQ] (37:1) Aut 95, p. 34.
312. BAMBER, Linda
"Arrival." [MassR] (36:2) Sum 95, p. 302.
"Objects." [PassN] (16:2) Wint 95, p. 19.
313. BANERJEE, Paramita
"Astrologer's Prediction" (tr. of Anuradha Mahapatra, w. Carolyne Wright).
[ManyMM] (1:3) 95, p. 158.
"Broken Boat" (tr. of Rama Ghosh, w. Carolyne Wright). [PoetryE] (39) Fall 94, p.
108.
"I Go" (tr. of Rama Ghosh, w. Carolyne Wright). [PoetryE] (39) Fall 94, p. 109.
"It Goes Back with What Thoughts" (tr. of Vijaya Mukhopadhyay, w. Carolyne
Wright and the author). [MidAR] (15:1/2) 95, p. 65.
"Mahalaya" (tr. of Vijaya Mukhopadhyay, w. Carolyne Wright and the author).
[MidAR] (15:1/2) 95, p. 63.
"Sandhiprakash Raga" (tr. of Vijaya Mukhopadhyay, w. Carolyne Wright and the
author). [MidAR] (15:1/2) 95, p. 69.
"Twelve Fifty A.M." (tr. of Vijaya Mukhopadhyay, w. Carolyne Wright and the
author). [MidAR] (15:1/2) 95, p. 67.
"What Is There to Fear" (tr. of Rama Ghosh, w. Carolyne Wright). [PoetryE] (39)
Fall 94, p. 110.
"Wind" (tr. of Anuradha Mahapatra, w. Carolyne Wright). [ManyMM] (1:3) 95, p.
162.
314. BANFORD, Joe
"Street Song." [AxeF] (3) 90, p. 37.
315. BANG, Mary Jo
"From a New Place" (for Catherine Scherer). [Salm] (108) Fall 95, p. 97-98.
"Granite City, Montana." [SouthwR] (80:4) Aut 95, p. 493.
"How to Leave a Prairie." [IndR] (18:2) Fall 95, p. 92.
"Real Time." [Journal] (19:2) Fall-Wint 95, p. 8.
"Where Snow Falls." [Journal] (19:2) Fall-Wint 95, p. 7.
316. BANGGO, Kathy Dee Kaleokealoha Kaloloahilani
"Ammo." [QW] (41) Aut-Wint 95-96, p. 274-275.
317. BANKS, Loy
"Taking Turns." [Ledge] (18) Sum 95, p. 93.
318. BANKS, Robert (Robert James)
"How a Fire Starts." [JamesWR] (12:2) Spr-Sum 95, p. 7.
"Maya." [EvergreenC] (10:2) Sum-Fall 95, p. 50.
"Storyteller Wearing Rings" (dedicated to Kenny Fries). [JamesWR] (12:1) Wint 95,
p. 13.
"Vital Signs." [JamesWR] (12:2) Spr-Sum 95, p. 17.
319. BANKS, Stanley E.
"Momma's Serial Songs." [MidwQ] (36:4) Sum 95, p. 346-347.
320. BANKS-RICHARDSON, S.
"And So I Stop Moving to Walk." [ChironR] (42) Spr 95, p. 32.
BAOLIN, Cheng
See CHENG, Baolin
321. BARAKA, Amiri
"Ballad Air & Fire" (For Sylvia or Amina). [RiverS] (42/43) 95, p. 62.
"Buddha Asked Monk." [CutB] (43) Wint 95, p. 7.
"Fusion Recipe." [ManyMM] (2:1) 95, p. 167.
"Propaganda." [Drumvoices] (5:1/2) Fall-Wint 95-96, p. 95.
"Red Power." [ManyMM] (2:1) 95, p. 170-171.
"The Sayings of Mantan Moreland (continued)." [ManyMM] (2:1) 95, p. 169.
"Superstar." [CutB] (43) Wint 95, p. 8.
"Venereal Culture." [ManyMM] (2:1) 95, p. 168.
322. BARANCZAK, Stanislaw
"History" (tr. by Michael and Aleksandra Parker). [Verse] (12:2) 95, p. 19.
"Lament 1" (tr. of Jan Kochanowski, w. Seamus Heaney). [Thrpny] (63) Fall 95, p.
13.
"Lament 2" (tr. of Jan Kochanowski, 1530-1584, w. Seamus Heaney). [PartR] (62:3)
Sum 95, p. 444-445.
"Lament 16" (tr. of Jan Kochanowski, 1530-1584, w. Seamus Heaney). [PartR] (62:3)
Sum 95, p. 443-444.
"The Three Magi" (To Lech Dymarski. Tr. by the author). [SenR] (25:1) Spr 95, p.
105.

323. BARANOW, Joan
    "Watching the Laparoscopy." [WestHR] (49:4) Wint 95, p. 312-313.
325. BARATTA, Edward (Edward Bartók-Baratta)
    "Dear Carol." [SycamoreR] (7:1) Wint 95, p. 39.
    "Dear Thomas." [SycamoreR] (7:1) Wint 95, p. 38.
    "Determined Fists." [PoetryE] (40) Spr 95, p. 14.
    "Drive." [Image] (12) Wint 95-96, p. 70-72.
    "Father." [Ascent] (19:3) Spr 95, p. 46.
    "How Things Happen." [ArtfulD] (28/29) 95, p. 46.
    "The Knife." [JINJPo] (17:2) Aut 95, p. 5.
    "Life after Dark." [GreensboroR] (58) Sum 95, p. 66-67.
    "The Man with a Wooden Leg." [PoetL] (90:1) Spr 95, p. 16.
    "No, Edward." [MidAR] (16:1) 95, p. 53-54.
    "Of Bargain Hunters." [PoetL] (90:1) Spr 95, p. 17-18.
    "Passage." [InterPR] (21:2) Fall 95, p. 92.
    "Tuesday's News." [DefinedP] (3) 95, p. 39-40.
    "Witness." [Image] (12) Wint 95-96, p. 69-70.
326. BARBARESE, J. T.
    "Postcard: Family, Ca. 1950 (Photographer Unknown)." [SewanR] (103:4) Fall 95, p. 487-492.
327. BARBER, David
    "American Forest Scene — Maple Sugaring" (— Currier & Ives). [NewEngR] (17:3) Sum 95, p. 162.
    "An American Sampler." [GettyR] (8:1) Wint 95, p. 96.
    "Apocrypha After Dark." [SouthwR] (80:1) Wint 95, p. 101-102.
    "The Lather." [Atlantic] (276:3) S 95, p. 56.
    "The Threshers." [GettyR] (8:1) Wint 95, p. 94-95.
328. BARBER, Jennifer
    "Back Streets." [Noctiluca] (2:1, #4) Spr 95, p. 4.
329. BARBOUR, Douglas
    "Breath Ghazals" (Selections: 42, 66, 34). [AntigR] (102/103) Sum-Aug 95, p. 294-296.
330. BARCIA, José Rubia
    "There Exists a Man" (tr. of Cesar Vallejo, w. Clayton Eshleman). [RiverS] (42/43) 95, p. 6.
331. BARDEN, Louise
    "Providence." [Crucible] (30) Fall 94, p. 37.
332. BARDSLEY, Wendy
    "Mother-Hood." [Stand] (36:2) Spr 95, p. 10.
333. BARFORD, Wanda
    "Fridays Are Special." [Stand] (36:3) Sum 95, p. 75.
334. BARGEN, Walter
    "Act Two." [CimR] (111) Ap 95, p. 66.
    "The Croak of Obsession." [MidwQ] (36:4) Sum 95, p. 347-348.
    "Giant Dirty Trick." [InterQ] (2:1/2) 95, p. 41.
    "In the Best of Weather" (Russian Parliment [sic] 8/20/91). [CapeR] (30:1) Spr 95, p. 46.
    "Proposition Six." [CapeR] (30:1) Spr 95, p. 47.
    "Rain of Shoes." [SpoonR] (20:2) Sum-Fall 95, p. 132-133.
    "The Sickness of Buildings." [InterQ] (2:1/2) 95, p. 40.
    "The Terrible Details." [SycamoreR] (7:2) Sum 95, p. 20.
    "Those Things." [LaurelR] (29:1) Wint 95, p. 104-105.
    "To Keep Going." [Farm] (12:1) Spr-Sum 95, p. 62-63.
335. BARGOWSKI, John (John D., Sr.)
    "Breaking the Seventh Commandment" (The 1994 Allen Ginsberg Poetry Awards: Honorable Mention). [Footwork] (24/25) 95, p. 186.
    "Chewing the Host." [Footwork] (24/25) 95, p. 69-70.
    "Counting Sins." [SlipS] (15) 95, p. 68.
    "Dust and Sleep." [PoetL] (90:3) Fall 95, p. 49-50.
    "Holy Cards." [Footwork] (24/25) 95, p. 70.
    "Making a Good Confession." [Footwork] (24/25) 95, p. 69.
    "On Three Legs." [WestB] (37) 95, p. 68-69.
    "Preferring Old Chevies." [FloridaR] (20:2) 95, p. 64-65.
    "The Starlings Have It All to Themselves." [LullwaterR] (6:2) Fall-Wint 95, p. 98-99.

336. BARKAN, Stanley H.
      "Abe Gurevitz" (In Memoriam: 1905-1993). [Footwork] (24/25) 95, p. 173-174.
      "The Bus Stop" (tr. of Andres Gottlieb). [Footwork] (24/25) 95, p. 210.
      "Eternal Crawl." [Footwork] (24/25) 95, p. 174.
      "Latin America, I'm Leaving You" (tr. of Andres Gottlieb). [Footwork] (24/25) 95, p.
           210.
      "Manifesto" (tr. of Andres Gottlieb, w. Renato Cavour). [Footwork] (24/25) 95, p.
           210.
      "Silence." [Footwork] (24/25) 95, p. 173.
337. BARKER, Adele
      "Taugal'u?" (tr. of Zoya Nenlyumkina, w. A. Cherevchenko). [Nimrod] (38:2) Spr-
           Sum 95, p. 110.
338. BARKER, Ann S.
      "Grief." [CumbPR] (14:2) Spr 95, p. 34-35.
339. BARKER, Lucile
      "Never Shades of Gray." [Bogg] (67) 95, p. 15.
340. BARKER, Susan Sanborn
      "In the Pretty Bluebird Kitchen." [MassR] (36:2) Sum 95, p. 233.
341. BARKER, Wendy
      "The Animi." [PoetL] (90:2) Sum 95, p. 29-30.
      "Ithaca — On the Landing." [FourQ] (9:1/2) Spr 95, p. 11-12.
      "Way of Whiteness." [Journal] (19:2) Fall-Wint 95, p. 33-34.
342. BARKS, Coleman
      "Be helpless and dumbfounded" (Mathnawi, IV, 3748-3754, tr. of Jelaluddin Rumi).
           [InterPR] (21:1) Spr 95, p. 16.
      "Everything you do has a quality" (Mathnawi, IV, 418-434, tr. of Jelaluddin Rumi).
           [InterPR] (21:1) Spr 95, p. 17.
      "Looking for the ocean, I found" (622, tr. of Jelaluddin Rumi). [InterPR] (21:1) Spr
           95, p. 11.
      "No one knows what makes the soul" (423, tr. of Jelaluddin Rumi). [InterPR] (21:1)
           Spr 95, p. 10.
      "Not until a person dissolves" (604, tr. of Jelaluddin Rumi). [InterPR] (21:1) Spr 95,
           p. 11.
      "Personal intelligence is not capable" (Mathnawi, IV, 1294-1300, tr. of Jelaluddin
           Rumi). [InterPR] (21:1) Spr 95, p. 13.
      "Soul of this world" (183, tr. of Jelaluddin Rumi). [InterPR] (21:1) Spr 95, p. 8-9.
      "They say, 'This majestic love you sing of is not a faithful love'" (1299, tr. of
           Jelaluddin Rumi). [InterPR] (21:1) Spr 95, p. 12-13.
      "When I see Your Face, the stones start spinning!" (tr. of Jelaluddin Rumi, 1207-
           1273). [PoetryE] (41) Aut 95, p. 23.
      "You see flag-lions playing in the wind" (Mathnawi, IV, 3051-3054, 3059-3084, tr. of
           Jelaluddin Rumi). [InterPR] (21:1) Spr 95, p. 14-15.
      "You who long for powerful positions" (188, tr. of Jelaluddin Rumi). [InterPR] (21:1)
           Spr 95, p. 8-9.
      "Your eyes are the mystery" (632, tr. of Jelaluddin Rumi). [InterPR] (21:1) Spr 95, p.
           11.
343. BARLOW, John
      "Let Me Unwrap the Wire." [Quarry] (44:1) 95, p. 116-117.
344. BARNES, A. Miriasiem
      "The Voices." [SinW] (56) Sum-Fall 95, p. 76-77.
345. BARNES, Daniel
      "At the Riverview Hotel" (December 1957). [Callaloo] (18:2) Spr 95, p. 382-383.
      "A Seneca Boy." [Callaloo] (18:2) Spr 95, p. 384-385.
346. BARNES, Dick
      "Be With Me Beauty." [ChironR] (43) Sum 95, p. 31.
      "Lucky Lady Video." [ChironR] (44/45) Aut-Wint 95, p. 41.
      "Paradiso IX." [Poetry] (165:5) F 95, p. 280.
347. BARNES, Djuna
      "Discant" (tr. by Christine Koschel). [AmerV] (38) 95, p. 46.
      "When the Kissing Flesh Is Gone" (tr. by Christine Koschel). [AmerV] (38) 95, p. 47.
348. BARNES, G.
      "Between Two Points." [WeberS] (12:3) Fall 95, p. 94.
      "Drinking from a Hose." [WeberS] (12:3) Fall 95, p. 94.
349. BARNES, Jim
      "At the Médicis Fountain." [PraS] (69:2) Sum 95, p. 136.
      "At the Tomb of Baudelaire." [PraS] (69:2) Sum 95, p. 137.

"I Typed This One Naked." [NewYorkQ] (54) 95, p. 78.
"My New Home." [NewYorkQ] (55) 95, p. 85-86.
"One O'Clock in the Morning." [QW] (40) Spr-Sum 95, p. 66.
"Parc de la Turlure." [PraS] (69:2) Sum 95, p. 135.
"Passerelle Debilly." [MidwQ] (36:4) Sum 95, p. 349-350.
"The Sun on Trocadero" (for Julien Green). [OhioR] (53) 95, p. 55.
"Triolet for Papa." [SouthwR] (80:2/3) Spr-Sum 95, p. 315.
"Weather." [QW] (40) Spr-Sum 95, p. 64-65.
"Weather Vane." [PraS] (69:2) Sum 95, p. 133-134.
350. BARNES, Kate
"Riding Out." [CreamCR] (19:1) Spr 95, p. 131.
"A Silver Watch." [BelPoJ] (46:2) Wint 95-96, p. 9.
351. BARNES, Katherine Russell
"The Charge." [Pembroke] (27) 95, p. 84.
352. BARNES, Richard
"Adrogué" (tr. of Jorge Luis Borges, w. Robert Mezey). [CutB] (42) Sum 94, p. 71-
72.
353. BARNES, Ruth
"Full." [Kaleid] (31) Sum-Fall 95, p. 46.
354. BARNETT, Lisa
"Girls on a Train." [PoetL] (90:2) Sum 95, p. 5-6.
"That Song." [NortheastCor] (3) 95, p. 104.
355. BARNETT, Ruth Anderson
"Dixie Leafs through Her Scrapbook" (runner up, 1994 Borderlands Poetry Contest).
[Border] (6) Spr-Sum 95, p. 18.
356. BARNEY, William D.
"A Bullsnake under Belknap Bridge" (runner up, 1994 Borderlands Poetry Contest).
[Border] (6) Spr-Sum 95, p. 19.
"The Lady and the Calliope" (runner up, 1994 Borderlands Poetry Contest). [Border]
(6) Spr-Sum 95, p. 20.
"Otter Biography." [Light] (13) Spr 95, p. 8.
357. BARNSTEAD, John
"Acrobat" (Inscription for a silhouette, tr. of Vladislav Khodasevitch). [AntigR] (101)
Spr 95, p. 79.
"November 2" (tr. of Vladislav Khodasevitch). [AntigR] (101) Spr 95, p. 85-89.
"Rachel's Tears" (tr. of Vladislav Khodasevitch). [AntigR] (101) Spr 95, p. 93.
"Seek Me" (tr. of Vladislav Khodasevitch). [AntigR] (101) Spr 95, p. 91.
"The Way of Grain" (tr. of Vladislav Khodasevitch). [AntigR] (101) Spr 95, p. 83.
"You Cannot Tell It All" (tr. of Vladislav Khodasevitch). [AntigR] (101) Spr 95, p.
81.
358. BARNSTONE, Aliki
"On the Hottest San Francisco Day in Recorded History He Plays Piano and She
Listens." [AntR] (53:1) Wint 95, p. 76-77.
359. BARNSTONE, Tony
"Agape" (tr. of César Vallejo, w. Willis Barnstone). [Jacaranda] (11) [95 or 96?], p.
70.
"The Black Cup" (tr. of César Vallejo, w. Willis Barnstone). [Jacaranda] (11) [95 or
96?], p. 71.
"The Flowing Style" (tr. of Sikong Tu, w. Chou Ping). [LitR] (38:3) Spr 95, p. 327.
"The Graceful Style" (tr. of Sikong Tu, w. Chou Ping). [LitR] (38:3) Spr 95, p. 326.
"In That Corner Where We Slept Together" (tr. of César Vallejo, w. Willis
Barnstone). [Jacaranda] (11) [95 or 96?], p. 68.
"Masses" (tr. of César Vallejo, w. Willis Barnstone). [Jacaranda] (11) [95 or 96?], p.
67.
"Oh The Four Walls of The Cell" (tr. of César Vallejo, w. Willis Barnstone).
[Jacaranda] (11) [95 or 96?], p. 69.
"Poets' Jade Splinters" (Selections, tr. of the anthology edited by Wei Qingzhi, w.
Chou Ping). [AmerPoR] (24:6) N-D 95, p. 41-50.
"The Transcendent Style" (tr. of Sikong Tu, w. Chou Ping). [LitR] (38:3) Spr 95, p.
327.
"The Vital Spirit Style" (tr. of Sikong Tu, w. Chou Ping). [LitR] (38:3) Spr 95, p.
326.
360. BARNSTONE, Willis
"Agape" (tr. of César Vallejo, w. Tony Barnstone). [Jacaranda] (11) [95 or 96?], p.
70.

"The Black Cup" (tr. of César Vallejo, w. Tony Barnstone). [Jacaranda] (11) [95 or 96?], p. 71.
"In That Corner Where We Slept Together" (tr. of César Vallejo, w. Tony Barnstone). [Jacaranda] (11) [95 or 96?], p. 68.
"Masses" (tr. of César Vallejo, w. Tony Barnstone). [Jacaranda] (11) [95 or 96?], p. 67.
"Oh The Four Walls of The Cell" (tr. of César Vallejo, w. Tony Barnstone). [Jacaranda] (11) [95 or 96?], p. 69.
361. BAROT, Rick
   "Inventory." [Thrpny] (62) Sum 95, p. 9.
   "Phantasmal Cities" (Walter Benjamin, Paris, 1940). [ParisR] (37:134) Spr 95, p. 38-41.
   "Some Remarks on Color" (from Wittgenstein). [GettyR] (8:3) Sum 95, p. 542.
362. BARQUET, Jesús J.
   "Salvación por la Imagen" (para rei, testigo presencial). [LindLM] (14:1) Mr/Spr 95, p. 15.
363. BARR, Tina
   "Leaving the Library at Night." [AxeF] (3) 90, p. 7.
   "Night Walks at the Artists' Colony." [AxeF] (3) 90, p. 6-7.
364. BARRACK, Jack
   "Edison Talking Machine." [LitR] (38:3) Spr 95, p. 363.
365. BARRATT, Amy
   "The Driver." [Quarry] (43:4) 95, p. 50.
   "The Gentleman Bandit." [Quarry] (43:4) 95, p. 51-52.
366. BARRESI, Dorothy
   "The Jaws of Life." [GettyR] (8:1) Wint 95, p. 77-81.
   "My Anger in 1934." [HarvardR] (8) Spr 95, p. 28-31.
   "The Older Brothers of Girls I Grew Up With." [AntR] (53:4) Fall 95, p. 446-448.
   "The Prodigal Daughter." [GettyR] (8:1) Wint 95, p. 82-84.
367. BARRETT, J. D., Sr.
   "A Prayer for Fish." [LullwaterR] (6:1) Spr-Sum 95, p. 14-15.
   "Remembering Centralhatchee Creek." [LullwaterR] (6:1) Spr-Sum 95, p. 16.
   "An Unbeaten Path." [LullwaterR] (6:1) Spr-Sum 95, p. 12-13.
   "What Words." [LullwaterR] (6:1) Spr-Sum 95, p. 11.
368. BARRETT, Nick
   "A Reformed Irish-Catholic Speaks" (for John Geisel). [IndR] (18:2) Fall 95, p. 98-99.
   "That Other World." [NewOR] (21:2) Sum 95, p. 8-9.
   "Woman in a Black Dress Arrives Like Pity in a Late Ohio Bar." [NewOR] (21:2) Sum 95, p. 10.
369. BARRETT, Virginia
   "Seduced by the Sun." [SouthernPR] (35:2) Wint 95, p. 63-64.
370. BARRINGTON, Judith
   "Why Young Girls Like to Ride Bareback." [KenR] (17:3/4) Sum-Fall 95, p. 49.
371. BARTKOWECH, R.
   "Systematic Apology." [AnotherCM] (29) Spr 95, p. 5-9.
372. BARTLETT, Brian
   "Brimming" (from ten letters and landscapes). [MalR] (112) Fall 95, p. 56-67.
   "Flying Crooked" (for Don Domanski). [PottPort] (16:1) Fall 95, p. 7-8.
   "In the Last Act." [AntigR] (101) Spr 95, p. 135.
   "A Puffball Tale." [AntigR] (101) Spr 95, p. 133-134.
   "Skylight." [Arc] (34) Spr 95, p. 78.
   "The Stirring of Notes" (for Karen). [PottPort] (16:1) Fall 95, p. 9.
   "A Swimmer Tale" (for Liane Heller). [PottPort] (16:1) Fall 95, p. 10-11.
   "A Vacation Tale." [AntigR] (101) Spr 95, p. 131-132.
373. BARTLEY, Jackie
   "Death in the Twilight." [SoDakR] (33:2) Sum 95, p. 104.
   "Southering." [SoDakR] (33:2) Sum 95, p. 56.
   "Squash Blossoms." [SoDakR] (33:2) Sum 95, p. 57.
BARTOK-BARATTA, Edward
   See BARATTA, Edward (Edward Bartók-Baratta)
374. BARTON, David
   "The Last Judgment." [JamesWR] (12:1) Wint 95, p. 9.
375. BARTON, John
   "Moonscape, with Men and Women." [Dandel] (22:1) 95, p. 70-71.
   "This Side of the Border." [CanLit] (144) Spr 95, p. 41-42.

"Wolves." [JamesWR] (12:3) Fall 95, p. 7.
376. BARTOW, Stuart
"On Finding an Owl Perched on a Dead Tree One Morning." [Chelsea] (59) 95, p. 167.
377. BASCOM, Tim
"Memorial" (In memory of George Bascom, doctor and poet). [ChrC] (112:14) 26 Ap 95, p. 458.
378. BASILIADIS, Nic
"The Man with the Blue Neo-Traditionalist Guernica." [Pearl] (22) Fall-Wint 95, p. 77.
"Unwrapped." [Bogg] (67) 95, p. 29.
379. BASKETT, Franz K.
"VI. The wind riffles the pages." [Parting] (8:1) Sum 95, p. 36.
"Dancing." [TampaR] (11) Fall 95, p. 65.
"The Maenad." [Poem] (73) My 95, p. 38-39.
"On Seeing the Disney Version of The Little Mermaid." [Poem] (73) My 95, p. 40.
380. BASKIN, Martha A.
"Wind." [LitR] (38:3) Spr 95, p. 420.
381. BASS, Ellen
"How Do Parents Make Love." [Chelsea] (59) 95, p. 39.
"Talking to God." [Chelsea] (59) 95, p. 37-38.
382. BASSEIN, Beth Ann
"Just Being There" (from Slopes to the River). [AmerPoR] (24:5) S-O 95, p. 22.
383. BATCHELOR, Rhonda
"The Backbone of the Moon" (for Raymond Carver). [PoetryC] (15:3) Ag 95, p. 12.
"Glad Ghost." [MalR] (113) Wint 95, p. 17.
"Mercurial." [PoetryC] (15:3) Ag 95, p. 12.
"Up All Night with the Universe." [PoetryC] (15:3) Ag 95, p. 12.
"Watcher." [MalR] (113) Wint 95, p. 18-19.
384. BATES, Jennifer
"Ash Wednesday." [Plain] (15:3) Spr 95, p. 23-24.
"Getting It Back." [Plain] (16:1) Fall 95, p. 26-27.
"In This New Life." [HolCrit] (32:3) Je 95, p. 19.
385. BATES, Marilyn
"Garden Justice." [Plain] (15:3) Spr 95, p. 27.
386. BATES, Scott
"Pizza." [SewanR] (103:2) Spr 95, p. 183.
387. BATHANTI, Joseph
"Uncles." [GreensboroR] (57) Wint 94-95, p. 40-42.
388. BATISTA, Liony E.
"Faces: The Lily" (For Casey). [Footwork] (24/25) 95, p. 29.
389. BATTSON, Jill
"Ashes of a Loved One." [Callaloo] (18:2) Spr 95, p. 344-345.
"In Summer." [Callaloo] (18:2) Spr 95, p. 343.
"Yvette, Yvonne." [Arc] (34) Spr 95, p. 69-70.
390. BAUDELAIRE, Charles
"Je n'ai pas oublié" (tr. by Millicent Bell). [PartR] (62:3) Sum 95, p. 449.
391. BAUER, Grace
"Artemisia Paints the Blood on Judith's Hands" (after Artemisia Gentileschi). [NewOR] (21:2) Sum 95, p. 89-90.
392. BAUMGAERTNER, Jill Peláez
"Ave and Benedicta" (for Thomas Howard). [ChrC] (112:1) 4-11 Ja 95, p. 18.
"Bathsheba." [ChrC] (112:7) 1 Mr 95, p. 238.
393. BAUTISTA, Ramón C.
"The Inauguration." [Zyzzyva] (11:3/4, #43/44) 95, "The Best of Ten Years of ZYZZYVA," p. 93-94.
394. BAXTER, Bart E.
"Paranoia for the Twenty-First Century." [ContextS] (4:2) 95, p. 4.
395. BAYER, Alicia
"10 Things My Daughter Learned from Fairy Tales." [HawaiiR] (19:2) Fall 95, p. 118.
396. BAYER, Deanne
"The Border Beyond." [DefinedP] (3) 95, p. 46.
"The Daughter I Never Had Dreams of Me." [DefinedP] (2:2) Spr-Sum 94, p. 42-43.
"For Dorothy Parker." [GreenHLL] (6) 95, p. 35.
"It's Not Over Till the Fat Lady Sings." [SmPd] (32:1, #93) Wint 95, p. 12.

"Man in a Chinese Painting." [SmPd] (32:1, #93) Wint 95, p. 13.
"The Man Who Would Be Seer." [SoDakR] (33:2) Sum 95, p. 118.
"The Phoenix Flower." [GreenHLL] (6) 95, p. 36.
"Requiem for Richard." [Plain] (15:2) Wint 95, p. 39.
"Socrates." [SoDakR] (33:2) Sum 95, p. 119.
397. BEACH, Judi K.
   "Printing Practice." [JlNJPo] (17:1) Spr 95, p. 18-19.
398. BEAL, Stephen
   "Color 498 in the DMC Floss System." [HangL] (67) 95, p. 8-9.
   "The Emperor of China." [HangL] (67) 95, p. 6-7.
   "Hastings Street, 1944." [HangL] (67) 95, p. 10-11.
399. BEAM, Jeffery
   "Bobwhite." [Pembroke] (27) 95, p. 126.
   "The Cough." [NoCarLR] (2:2) 95, p. 248.
   "Dandelion." [NoCarLR] (2:2) 95, p. 248.
   "Dog-Violet." [NoCarLR] (2:2) 95, p. 248.
   "Drought." [NoCarLR] (2:2) 95, p. 248.
   "Mistletoe." [NoCarLR] (2:2) 95, p. 248.
   "A Spell for Poem-Making." [Pembroke] (27) 95, p. 127.
   "What I Know about Poetry." [NoCarLR] (2:2) 95, p. 248.
BEAR, Ray Young (Ray A. Young)
   See YOUNG BEAR, Ray (Ray A.)
400. BEASLEY, Bruce
   "After Words." [VirQR] (71:2) Spr 95, p. 312-313.
   "Before Thanksgiving." [VirQR] (71:2) Spr 95, p. 309-310.
   "By Bread Alone." [Field] (52) Spr 95, p. 21-25.
   "Figure." [SouthernR] (31:1) Wint 95, p. 4-6.
   "Primavera." [Field] (52) Spr 95, p. 19-20.
   "Ugly Ohio." [VirQR] (71:2) Spr 95, p. 310-312.
401. BEASLEY, Conger, Jr.
   "Thoreau Meets the Woodchuck, 1846." [Interim] (14:2) Fall-Wint 95-96, p. 13-15.
402. BEASLEY, Katherine
   "Fifth Letter to Frank Spencer Robertson." [SlipS] (15) 95, p. 20.
   "First Letter to Frank Spencer Robertson." [SlipS] (15) 95, p. 18.
   "Fourth Letter to Frank Spencer Robertson." [SlipS] (15) 95, p. 19.
   "Second Letter to Frank Spencer Robertson." [SlipS] (15) 95, p. 18.
   "Third Letter to Frank Spencer Robertson." [SlipS] (15) 95, p. 19.
403. BEASLEY, Sherry
   "The Gift" (For K.). [SouthernPR] (35:2) Wint 95, p. 19.
404. BEATTY, Daniel
   "Aspect, 4." [Nimrod] (39:1) Fall-Wint 95, p. 97.
405. BEATTY, Jan
   "Introducing You to My Dead Father" (for Don). [PoetryE] (41) Aut 95, p. 94.
406. BEATTY, Paul
   "The Zip Coon Blues." [Phoebe] (24:1) 95, p. 93-94.
407. BEAUMONT, Jeanne Marie
   "Placebo Effects." [Poetry] (166:5) Ag 95, p. 265-266.
408. BECHTEL, Kay Ferguson
   "Clair, Descending." [SouthernPR] (35:1) Sum 95, p. 18.
409. BECK, Art
   "Premature Chariot" (tr. of Luxorius, 6th century C.E.). [ArtfulD] (28/29) 95, p. 27.
   "Proverbs." [PaintedB] (55/56) 95, p. 68.
   "They say, that when the fierce bear gives birth" (tr. of Luxorius, 6th century C.E.).
      [ArtfulD] (28/29) 95, p. 27.
410. BECKER, Anne
   "Second Scroll: Chicago." [AntR] (53:2) Spr 95, p. 203-205.
411. BECKER, Robin
   "The New Year." [CrabOR] (1:1) Fall-Wint 95, p. 31.
   "Spiritual Morning." [CrabOR] (1:1) Fall-Wint 95, p. 32.
412. BECKER, Sharon
   "La Llorona." [HayF] (17) Fall-Wint 95, p. 114-115.
413. BECKER, Therese
   "Branches." [PoetryE] (40) Spr 95, p. 16.
   "On Awakening" (for Rebecca Roberts). [PoetryE] (40) Spr 95, p. 15.
414. BECKERMANN, Paul
   "Rounding Third." [Spitball] (49) 95, p. 8.

415. BECKETT, Jennifer
"We Order the Special at Hamby's." [QW] (40) Spr-Sum 95, p. 206-207.
416. BEDARD, Emily A.
"The Length of Teeth." [IndR] (18:2) Fall 95, p. 89-90.
417. BEDIENT, Calvin (Cal)
"Any Son of a Bitch." [BostonR] (20:6) D 95-Ja 96, p. 22.
"Baskets and Ashes." [ColR] (22:1) Spr 95, p. 96.
"Candy Necklace." [BostonR] (20:6) D 95-Ja 96, p. 22.
"The Gods Do Not Fear Because They Are Not Any Place Among." [ColR] (22:2)
Fall 95, p. 103-104.
"Love-in Mit Wittgenstein." [ColR] (22:2) Fall 95, p. 97-98.
"Possum." [BostonR] (20:6) D 95-Ja 96, p. 22.
"Unclean Poem." [ColR] (22:2) Fall 95, p. 99-102.
"The Wild Troops of Proportion." [BostonR] (20:6) D 95-Ja 96, p. 22.
418. BEDOYA, Roberto
"Banff Morning." [Zyzzyva] (11:1, #41) Spr 95, p. 78.
419. BEDREGAL, Yolanda
"Martyrdom" (tr. by Carolyne Wright). [MidAR] (15:1/2) 95, p. 146.
"Night, I Know All About You" (tr. by Carolyne Wright). [MidAR] (15:1/2) 95, p.
144-145.
"Nocturne of Hope" (tr. by Carolyne Wright). [MidAR] (15:1/2) 95, p. 143.
"Pointless Journey" (tr. by Carolyne Wright). [MidAR] (15:1/2) 95, p. 147-148.
420. BEECHHOLD, Henry F.
"Einstein on His Motorcycle, or spukhafte Fernwirkungen." [US1] (30/31) 95, p. 3.
421. BEEDER, Amy
"First Five Years." [Ledge] (19) Wint 95, p. 45.
"The Grave Mover." [Ledge] (19) Wint 95, p. 44.
"Last Photo." [Boulevard] (10:3, #30) Fall 95, p. 46.
BEEK, Edith van
See Van BEEK, Edith
422. BEGAMUDRÉ, Ven
"Itineraries." [Grain] (23:1) Sum 95, p. 37-43.
"Tafelmusik Performs the 'Other' Brandenburg Concertos." [TickleAce] (27) Spr-
Sum 94, p. 74-75.
423. BEGGS, Marck L.
"Our Tendency to Trust Strangers" (from *Godworm*). [AmerPoR] (24:6) N-D 95, p.
26.
"Our Tendency to Trust Strangers" (from *Godworm*). [DenQ] (30:2) Fall 95, p. 144.
424. BEGLEY, Mark
"Blue Veined." [ChironR] (43) Sum 95, p. 30.
"For Gerald and Dan." [WormR] (35:2, #138) 95, p. 87.
"I'm Trying Hard." [WormR] (35:2, #138) 95, p. 86.
"Sitting." [WormR] (35:2, #138) 95, p. 86.
425. BEHLEN, Charles
"Flying" (runner up, 1994 Borderlands Poetry Contest). [Border] (6) Spr-Sum 95, p.
21.
426. BEHM, Richard (Richard H.)
"Communion." [SewanR] (103:1) Wint 95, p. 6.
"A Dream for Winter." [SewanR] (103:1) Wint 95, p. 5.
"Hearing Red." [SewanR] (103:1) Wint 95, p. 6.
"Things I Know About a Woman." [SpoonR] (20:1) Wint-Spr 95, p. 60-61.
427. BEHRENDT, Stephen C.
"Broken Wheel." [TexasR] (15:3/4) Fall-Wint 94, p. 76-77.
"Bull Thistles." [LitR] (38:3) Spr 95, p. 417.
"For the Owl." [TexasR] (15:3/4) Fall-Wint 94, p. 78.
"Jaffrey Center Cemetery." [TexasR] (15:3/4) Fall-Wint 94, p. 79.
"Purple Coneflowers." [MidwQ] (36:4) Sum 95, p. 351-352.
"Wreckage." [TexasR] (15:3/4) Fall-Wint 94, p. 80.
428. BEHRENS, Eric
"Letter to a Gardener." [Interim] (14:2) Fall-Wint 95-96, p. 21.
BEI, Dao
See BEI DAO
429. BEI DAO
"As I Know It" (tr. by Yanbing Chen and John Rosenwald). [BelPoJ] (46:2) Wint 95-
96, p. 38-39.

"Untitled: People hurry, arrive" (tr. by Yanbing Chen and John Rosenwald). [BelPoJ] (46:2) Wint 95-96, p. 40.
430. BEICHMAN, Janine
    "Life Story" (tr. of Ooka Makoto). [Descant] (26:2, #89) Sum 95, p. 45.
    "Morning Prayer" (tr. of Ooka Makoto). [Descant] (26:2, #89) Sum 95, p. 46.
    "Saki's Numazu" (tr. of Ooka Makoto). [Descant] (26:2, #89) Sum 95, p. 47-48.
431. BEKER, Ruth
    "Desert Weather." [Interim] (14:1) Spr-Sum 95, p. 23.
432. BEKRI, Tahar
    "Entre Deux Langues" (à A.L.T.). [Os] (41) 95, p. 17-19.
BEL, Natasha le
    See Le BEL, Natasha
433. BELEV, Georgi
    "Hide and Seek" (tr. by Lisa Sapinkopf). [Vis] (48) 95, p. 15.
    "Night Train" (tr. by Lisa Sapinkopf). [Vis] (48) 95, p. 14.
    "Sled" (tr. by Lisa Sapinkopf). [Vis] (48) 95, p. 14.
    "Summer" (tr. by Lisa Sapinkopf). [Vis] (48) 95, p. 12-13.
434. BELIEU, Erin
    "For Catherine: Juana, Infanta of Navarre." [Agni] (41) 95, p. 217-218.
    "The Silver Tree." [GreensboroR] (58) Sum 95, p. 3-4.
    "Watching the Giraffes Run. [PraS] (69:1) Spr 95, p. 51-52.
435. BELIN, Mel
    "Shoe Shine Man." [CapeR] (30:2) Fall 95, p. 34.
436. BELL, Anthea
    "A Deep-Sea Explorer of the Mind" (tr. of Birger Sellin). [GrandS] (13:4, #52) Spr 95, p. 139-162.
437. BELL, Antonio
    "Don't Stop" (WritersCorps Program, Washington, DC). [WashR] (21:2) Ag-S 95, p. 11.
    "First Line" (WritersCorps Program, Washington, DC). [WashR] (21:2) Ag-S 95, p. 11.
438. BELL, John
    "Cupid." [CumbPR] (15:1) Fall 95, p. 10.
439. BELL, Marvin
    "The Book of the Dead Man (#34)." [Shen] (45:1) Spr 95, p. 76-78.
    "The Book of the Dead Man (#44)." [Poetry] (165:4) Ja 95, p. 197-198.
    "The Book of the Dead Man (#45)." [Shen] (45:1) Spr 95, p. 74-75.
    "The Book of the Dead Man (#46)." [ColR] (22:1) Spr 95, p. 99-100.
    "The Book of the Dead Man (#51)." [Poetry] (165:4) Ja 95, p. 198-200.
    "The Book of the Dead Man (#53)." [HayF] (16) Spr-Sum 95, p. 30.
    "The Book of the Dead Man (#54)." [Poetry] (165:4) Ja 95, p. 200-202.
    "The Book of the Dead Man (#56)." [HarvardR] (8) Spr 95, p. 112-113.
    "The Book of the Dead Man (#57)." [ColR] (22:1) Spr 95, p. 97-98.
    "The Book of the Dead Man (#59)." [HayF] (16) Spr-Sum 95, p. 31.
440. BELL, Millicent
    "Je n'ai pas oublié" (tr. of Charles Baudelaire). [PartR] (62:3) Sum 95, p. 449.
441. BELLAMY, Joe David
    "Light Years." [TarRP] (34:2) Spr 95, p. 37.
BELLAMY, Linda Bohannon
    See BOHANNON-BELLAMY, Linda
442. BELLEN, Martine
    "Calamity Jane." [Conjunc] (24) 95, p. 277-286.
    "Confessions." [Phoebe] (24:1) 95, p. 103-111.
    "Mirror Ride." [NewAW] (13) Fall-Wint 95, p. 125-126.
    "The Seam." [NewAW] (13) Fall-Wint 95, p. 127-128.
443. BELLETTO, Oreste
    "Charity." [LullwaterR] (6:1) Spr-Sum 95, p. 62-64.
444. BELLIN, Steven
    "Coy Sketch." [CapeR] (30:2) Fall 95, p. 50.
    "I Want to Talk about You." [WilliamMR] (33) 95, p. 86.
445. BELLINGER, John M.
    "Closed for Business." [SmPd] (32:3, #95) Fall 95, p. 30-31.
    "The Very Last First Christmas." [SmPd] (32:3, #95) Fall 95, p. 30.
446. BELLM, Dan
    "The Last Hour of the Night." [Manoa] (7:1) Sum 95, p. 200-201.
    "Not There (1963)." [PassN] (16:1) Sum 95, p. 24.

"Sonetos" (Nicaragua, 1985). [PassN] (16:1) Sum 95, p. 22-23.
"Spoken with the Hands." [Manoa] (7:1) Sum 95, p. 199-200.
447. BELLMAN, Karin
"Kom Inte Och Säg (Don't Come and Tell Me Don't Come and Say)" (Selections: 1-
6, tr. by Robin Fulton). [MalR] (111) Sum 95, p. 77.
448. BELLOWS, Timothy
"Late Fall Birds." [MidwQ] (36:3) Spr 95, p. 290.
449. BEN-LEV, Dina
"I Walk Out and Hear Who Cares." [PoetryNW] (36:2) Sum 95, p. 32-33.
"Letter to My Unmet Mother." [PoetryNW] (36:2) Sum 95, p. 31-32.
"What the Landlord Did Not Say" (for Ralph Gertz. From "Sober on a Small Plane,"
winner, The Quentin R. Howard Poetry Prize: 1994 Chapbook Competition).
[Wind] (75) Spr 95, p. 91.
450. BEN-TOV, S.
"Heredity." [MichQR] (34:3) Sum 95, p. 377-381.
"Jerusalem Sunset." [PlumR] (8) [95], p. 81.
"The Tank and the Fossil." [VirQR] (71:3) Sum 95, p. 498-499.
"Theodorakis' Ballad." [VirQR] (71:3) Sum 95, p. 499-500.
451. BEN-YEHUDA, Gil-Ohz
"Goose Steps" (runner up, 1994 Borderlands Poetry Contest). [Border] (6) Spr-Sum
95, p. 22.
452. BENDALL, Molly
"The Book of Sharp Silhouettes." [ParisR] (37:134) Spr 95, p. 122-123.
453. BENEDETTI, Ryan
"Blind Dogs." [CutB] (42) Sum 94, p. 7.
"Love Song." [CutB] (42) Sum 94, p. 8-9.
454. BENEDETTO, Judith
"Geminid Shower." [Crucible] (31) Fall 95, p. 30.
455. BENEDICT, Elinor
"Partings" (runner up, 1994 Borderlands Poetry Contest). [Border] (6) Spr-Sum 95, p.
23.
456. BENEDIKT, Michael
"All That Talk About 'High-Tech' in the Future Notwithstanding ...." [NewRep]
(213:3/4) 17-24 Jl 95, p. 50.
"Of an 'Only Child''s World." [Iowa] (25:2) Spr-Sum 95, p. 116-119.
"A Retiring 'Professor of Practicality'." [Agni] (42) 95, p. 151-154.
457. BENET, Maria M.
"Winter White." [Pearl] (22) Fall-Wint 95, p. 148.
458. BENEVENTO, Joe
"At Thomas Hill Lake." [GreenHLL] (5) 94, p. 77.
"Dream Class." [GreenHLL] (5) 94, p. 72-73.
"House Hunting." [GreenHLL] (5) 94, p. 70.
"How Don Quixote Is Not User Friendly." [GreenHLL] (5) 94, p. 74-75.
"Love, Death and Magic Realism." [Elf] (5:1) Spr 95, p. 24-25.
"Petunias." [CapeR] (30:2) Fall 95, p. 10.
"Reading Don Quixote Once More." [GreenHLL] (5) 94, p. 76.
"St. Joseph of Kirksville." [GreenHLL] (5) 94, p. 71.
"These Poems For You, Hellene." [GreenHLL] (5) 94, p. 68.
"Two Birthdays." [GreenHLL] (5) 94, p. 69.
459. BENFEY, Christopher
"Epitaph for Mariana Gryphius, His Brother Paul's Little Daughter" (tr. of Andreas
Gryphius, 1616-1664). [NewRep] (213:25) 18 D 95, p. 44.
"To the Virgin Mary" (tr. of Andreas Gryphius, 1616-1664). [NewRep] (213:25) 18
D 95, p. 44.
460. BENJAMIN, Michael
"Storm" (WritersCorps Project, Washington, DC). [WashR] (21:2) Ag-S 95, p. 19.
461. BENNETT, Bruce
"Betrayal." [LaurelR] (29:2) Sum 95, p. 43.
"Bottom Feeders." [Light] (15/16) Aut-Wint 95-96, p. 8.
"The Deserted Campus." [Light] (15/16) Aut-Wint 95-96, p. 10.
"Dramatis Personae." [Light] (15/16) Aut-Wint 95-96, p. 7.
"The Drunk." [Light] (15/16) Aut-Wint 95-96, p. 7.
"The Duke's Gallery." [Light] (15/16) Aut-Wint 95-96, p. 9.
"The Evidence." [Light] (15/16) Aut-Wint 95-96, p. 10.
"Flip Side." [Light] (15/16) Aut-Wint 95-96, p. 10.
"Frequent Contributor." [HarvardR] (9) Fall 95, p. 102.

"Gathering." [Light] (15/16) Aut-Wint 95-96, p. 7.
"Homage." [Light] (13) Spr 95, p. 22.
"The Horror." [Light] (15/16) Aut-Wint 95-96, p. 8.
"Idea Man." [Light] (15/16) Aut-Wint 95-96, p. 9.
"In the Pen." [Light] (15/16) Aut-Wint 95-96, p. 8.
"Involuntary Magic." [Light] (15/16) Aut-Wint 95-96, p. 7.
"Late Reckoning." [Light] (14) Sum 95, p. 10.
"Late Romantic." [Light] (13) Spr 95, p. 13.
"Literary Exchange." [Light] (15/16) Aut-Wint 95-96, p. 9.
"Living Well." [Light] (15/16) Aut-Wint 95-96, p. 8.
"The Message from the Metropolis." [Light] (15/16) Aut-Wint 95-96, p. 9.
"Moving to Music." [LaurelR] (29:2) Sum 95, p. 42.
"My World." [Light] (15/16) Aut-Wint 95-96, p. 7.
"Obstinate." [Light] (15/16) Aut-Wint 95-96, p. 9.
"Queens Man Shot to Death." [Hellas] (6:1) Spr-Sum 95, p. 25.
"West of the Hudson." [Light] (14) Sum 95, p. 20.
462. BENNETT, Deborah A.
"Gethsemane." [AfAmRev] (29:1) Spr 95, p. 87.
"In the Ruins." [AfAmRev] (29:1) Spr 95, p. 88-89.
"The Remember Yard." [AfAmRev] (29:1) Spr 95, p. 88.
"Sweet Water in the Rock." [AfAmRev] (29:1) Spr 95, p. 87.
"Under the Joshua Tree." [AfAmRev] (29:1) Spr 95, p. 89.
463. BENNETT, Guy
"Untitled: Loathing history you dip back." [WashR] (21:3) O-N 95, p. 22.
"Untitled: The future weight of words unthought." [WashR] (21:3) O-N 95, p. 22.
464. BENNETT, John (John M.)
"Sloshing." [Bogg] (67) 95, p. 20.
"Where We're Going." [ChironR] (43) Sum 95, p. 20.
465. BENNETT, Stefanie
"Passage — Moscow 1915." [Footwork] (24/25) 95, p. 51.
466. BENSE, Robert
"Afternoon Visit." [HiramPoR] (58/59) Spr 95-Wint 96, p. 8.
467. BENSON, Amy
"9th and Woodward." [WestB] (37) 95, p. 45-46.
468. BENSUSSEN, Henri
"Masbata Loate." [SinW] (56) Sum-Fall 95, p. 91.
469. BENTLEY, Beth
"Seaven Teares (for Broken Consorts)." [GettyR] (8:4) Aut 95, p. 601-602.
470. BENTLEY, Laura Treacy
"Camden Park." [SmPd] (32:2, #94) Spr 95, p. 10.
471. BENTLEY, Nelson
"Two Apocalypses." [BellArk] (11:1) Ja-F 95, p. 3-6.
472. BENTLEY, Roy
"Detail from the Bombing of a Thing Struck by Light." [ArtfulD] (28/29) 95, p. 110.
"History." [ArtfulD] (28/29) 95, p. 111.
"The Power of Intelligent Engineering: The P-38 Can Opener." [ArtfulD] (28/29) 95, p. 113.
"Shooting Water Buffalo near An Loc." [ArtfulD] (28/29) 95, p. 112.
473. BENTLEY, Sean
"Capture." [CapeR] (30:2) Fall 95, p. 26-27.
"Fencers." [WritersF] (21) 95, p. 89.
"Sleep in the Encantadas." [WritersF] (21) 95, p. 88.
474. BENTZMAN, Bruce Harris
"Condominiums You Would Own." [WindO] (59) Spr 95, p. 39-40.
475. BENZ, Stephen
"Third World Roads." [Border] (6) Spr-Sum 95, p. 24-26.
476. BERG, Charity
"The Wolf's Return" (tr. of Edgar O'Hara, collectively w. Rachel Breeden et al.).
[Americas] (23:3/4) Fall-Wint 95, p. 154-155.
477. BERG, Stephen
"Footnotes to an Unfinished Poem" (Selections: 1-30). [DenQ] (29:4) Spr 95, p. 5-10.
"Rimbaud" (6 selections, for Lou). [KenR] (17:1) Wint 95, p. 131-135.
"To My Son." [Jacaranda] (11) [95 or 96?], p. 134-135.
"To My Son." [NewYorker] (71:12) 15 My 95, p. 74.
478. BERGAMINO, Gina
"Communion in Venice." [NewYorkQ] (55) 95, p. 79.

"Kaleidoscope." [LouisL] (12:2) Fall 95, p. 86.
"Photograph." [LouisL] (12:2) Fall 95, p. 84-85.
"Promise." [NewYorkQ] (54) 95, p. 68.
"Sometimes." [LouisL] (12:2) Fall 95, p. 87.
"Speculation." [Footwork] (24/25) 95, p. 75.
"The Telephone, My Judgement." [Footwork] (24/25) 95, p. 75.
479. BERGER, Bruce
    "Late Sibelius." [DenQ] (30:1) Sum 95, p. 16.
    "Myoptics." [DenQ] (30:1) Sum 95, p. 17.
    "Relativity." [Light] (15/16) Aut-Wint 95-96, p. 15.
480. BERGER, Jacqueline
    "The Body's Gold Leaf." [GreensboroR] (58) Sum 95, p. 22.
    "Drawn to That Which Draws Away." [FloridaR] (20:2) 95, p. 62-63.
    "Still Life with Red Table." [SantaBR] (3:2) Sum 95, p. 106.
481. BERGER, L. R.
    "Dreaming of the Front Lines." [Descant] (26:1, #88) Spr 95, p. 68.
    "First Wars." [WestB] (37) 95, p. 25.
    "Hand to Mouth." [Descant] (26:1, #88) Spr 95, p. 66.
    "Mosaic." [Descant] (26:1, #88) Spr 95, p. 65.
    "Nightmares." [Descant] (26:1, #88) Spr 95, p. 69-70.
    "Sightings." [BelPoJ] (45:3) Spr 95, p. 23-26.
    "That Great Loneliness." [Descant] (26:1, #88) Spr 95, p. 67.
    "Window of Sixteen Panes." [Descant] (26:1, #88) Spr 95, p. 71-74.
482. BERGIE, Sigrid
    "Between Minneapolis & Albert Lea." [NorthStoneR] (12) 95, p. 61.
483. BERGMAN, David
    "Mapplethorpe's Lily." [MidAR] (15:1/2) 95, p. 155.
484. BERK, Ilhan
    "The Denizens of the Arcade Hristaki" (tr. by Murat Nemet-Nejat). [Talisman] (14)
        Fall 95, p. 47-49.
    "Fish Market, Backstage Street" (tr. by Murat Nemet-Nejat). [Talisman] (14) Fall 95,
        p. 45-46.
485. BERKE, Judith
    "Cave in the Ravine." [Ploughs] (21:4) Wint 95-96, p. 30.
    "Courtyard of the Hospital at Arles." [MassR] (36:1) Spr 95, p. 137.
    "Story" (after "Farmhouse in Auvers with Two Figures"). [Ploughs] (21:4) Wint 95-
        96, p. 31.
    "Street in Saintes-Maries." [DenQ] (30:2) Fall 95, p. 8-9.
    "Theory of the Waves" (after *Reminiscence of the North*). [AmerPoR] (24:6) N-D 95,
        p. 24.
    "Twelve Sunflowers in a Vase." [MassR] (36:1) Spr 95, p. 136.
486. BERKOWITZ, Jonathan M.
    "Alphabet City." [SantaBR] (3:1) Spr 95, p. 72.
    "The Oncologist." [ArtfulD] (28/29) 95, p. 104.
    "The Silver Moon." [SantaBR] (3:1) Spr 95, p. 72.
    "Visiting an Old Friend." [SantaBR] (3:1) Spr 95, p. 73.
487. BERLIND, Bruce
    "Ballad" (tr. of György Petri, w. Mária Körösy). [InterQ] (2:1/2) 95, p. 149.
    "Credos." [NewL] (62:1) 96 (c1995), p. 120.
    "The Degrees of Recognition" (tr. of György Petri, w. Mária Körösy). [InterQ]
        (2:1/2) 95, p. 151-153.
    "Hampstead Heath, October." [PoetL] (90:1) Spr 95, p. 28.
    "Snowfall in Boston" (tr. of Ottó Orbán, w. Mária Körösy). [LitR] (38:3) Spr 95, p.
        352-353.
    "Staircase" (tr. of György Petri, w. Mária Körösy). [PoetryE] (39) Fall 94, p. 119.
    "Such Important Conversations" (tr. of György Petri, w. Mária Körösy). [InterQ]
        (2:1/2) 95, p. 146-147.
    "To M.A." (tr. of György Petri, w. Mária Körösy). [InterQ] (2:1/2) 95, p. 150.
488. BERMAN, Ruth
    "Queen Colors." [TexasR] (15:3/4) Fall-Wint 94, p. 81.
    "Queen Dance." [TexasR] (15:3/4) Fall-Wint 94, p. 82.
489. BERN, Dan
    "The Ballad of Dave and Eddie." [Zyzzyva] (11:3/4, #43/44) 95, "The Best of Ten
        Years of ZYZZYVA," p. 95-103.
BERNAL, Mairym Cruz
    See CRUZ-BERNAL, Mairym

490. BERNARD, April
"See It Does Rise." [Colum] (24/25) 95, p. 145.
"The Wise Word, The Good Word." [Colum] (24/25) 95, p. 146.
491. BERNARD, Artis
"Beautiful Childhood." [WestHR] (49:4) Wint 95, p. 358.
"Calling Up the Swim Team." [Border] (7) Fall-Wint 96, p. 3.
"The Eastern Seaboard." [WestHR] (49:4) Wint 95, p. 359-360.
492. BERNARD, Pam
"Chiara Favarone." [PraS] (69:2) Sum 95, p. 132-133.
493. BERNHARD, Jim
"Earache" (for Marla Simpson, Mother, 10/27/94). [BellArk] (11:1) Ja-F 95, p. 16.
"Errand with Sasha at Eight." [BellArk] (11:4) Jl-Ag 95, p. 12.
"In the Light of the Moon." [BellArk] (11:2) Mr-Ap 95, p. 12.
"Old Radio." [BellArk] (11:2) Mr-Ap 95, p. 12.
"The Poet." [BellArk] (11:2) Mr-Ap 95, p. 12.
"A Small Sweet Moment at Breakfast." [BellArk] (11:1) Ja-F 95, p. 16.
"Wanda Jackson." [BellArk] (11:3) My-Je 95, p. 9.
494. BERNICHON, Janet
"Calvin." [Bogg] (67) 95, p. 33.
"The Last Detail." [ChironR] (43) Sum 95, p. 36.
495. BERNICHON, Janet [i.e. Alison Apotheker]
"Monotony of Lovers: Night of the Full Lunar Eclipse" (Inadvertently published
under the name of Janet Bernichon. Author is Alison Apotheker). [ChironR]
(43) Sum 95, p. 31.
496. BERNOFSKY, Susan
"A 21st-Century Hurdy-Gurdy: In the Evening Sky Looms a Ferris Wheel" (tr. of
Yoko Tawada). [YellowS] (12:4, #48) Sum 95, p. 38.
497. BERNOW, Stephen
"States of Matter" (1993 Poetry Contest, First Place Winner). [DefinedP] (1:2) Spr -
Sum 93, p. 56-58.
498. BERNSTEIN, Carole
"Against Hope" (Selections: Prelude, 1. Little Monster). [HangL] (67) 95, p. 13-14.
"Familiar." [Poetry] (165:6) Mr 95, p. 312-313.
"My Sister's Instrument." [Footwork] (24/25) 95, p. 21.
"The Tomb of Alexander VII by Bernini, 1678." [HangL] (67) 95, p. 15-17.
499. BERNSTEIN, Charles
"Are You Being Sarcastic?" [Avec] (10) 95, p. 162.
"The Influence of Kinship Patterns upon Perception of an Ambiguous Stimulus."
[Verse] (12:2) 95, p. 20-23.
"Max.Weber's Favorite Tylenol for Teething." [Sulfur] (15:1, #36) Spr 95, p. 161 -
162.
"Ms. Otis Regrets." [NewAW] (13) Fall-Wint 95, p. 5-12.
"Power Walking." [Avec] (10) 95, p. 164.
"Residual Rubbernecking." [Avec] (10) 95, p. 161.
"Revolutionary Poem." [Avec] (10) 95, p. 163.
500. BERNSTEIN, J. B.
"Bang." [IllinoisR] (3:1/2) Fall 95-Spr 96, p. 24.
"Perchance to Dream." [IllinoisR] (3:1/2) Fall 95-Spr 96, p. 47-48.
501. BERNSTEIN, Laura
"Fever." [CapeR] (30:2) Fall 95, p. 12.
502. BERRETT, Jean
"De Rerum Natura, Book II" (Excerpt, tr. of Lucretius, w. Jonathan Spiegel).
[WillowS] (36) Je 95, p. 110.
503. BERRIGAN, Edmund
"Desert Wreck." [HangL] (67) 95, p. 33.
504. BERRY, D. C.
"Basset Hound." [TarRP] (34:2) Spr 95, p. 6.
"Green and Blue." [Journal] (19:2) Fall-Wint 95, p. 31.
"Handbird." [Journal] (19:2) Fall-Wint 95, p. 32.
"Ho Chi Minh City Cemetery." [OhioR] (54) 95, p. 128.
"Marriage Wrestling." [TampaR] (11) Fall 95, p. 64.
"Roasting Marshmallows at the Beach." [SouthernPR] (35:2) Wint 95, p. 16.
"Zen Deck." [ChiR] (41:1) 95, p. 28.
505. BERRY, Eleanor
"Birthday." [Crazy] (48) Spr 95, p. 58-60.
"This Winter Place." [Crazy] (48) Spr 95, p. 55.

"What You Would Have Seen" (for D. H.). [Crazy] (48) Spr 95, p. 56-57.
506. BERRY, Jake
    "5:30." [HeavenB] (12) 95, p. 11.
    "Bambu Drezi: Book Two" [sic] (Excerpt). [HeavenB] (12) 95, p. 72.
    "Brambu Drezi, Book 2" [sic] (Selections: 2.15, 2.2A, 2.9A). [NewOR] (21:2) Sum
        95, p. 42-44.
    "Folktales #2." [HeavenB] (12) 95, p. 11.
    "Nod." [HeavenB] (12) 95, p. 11.
507. BERRY, James
    "Distant Faces Close." [Epoch] (44:3) 95, p. 286-287.
    "Duplication." [Epoch] (44:3) 95, p. 289.
    "Images." [Epoch] (44:3) 95, p. 288.
508. BERRY, Paul
    "Old New Year's Eve, Wells." [Bogg] (67) 95, p. 26.
509. BERRY, Simeon
    "California." [NewDeltaR] (12:2) Spr-Sum 95, p. 14-15.
    "Sketches of Spain" (1995 Poetry Competition: Honorable Mention). [Elf] (5:2) Sum
        95, p. 18.
510. BERRY, Wendell
    "Ye Must Be Born Again." [BelPoJ] (45:4) Chapbook 22, Sum 95, p. 8.
511. BERRYHILL, Lori
    "Full Moon" (Second Robert Penn Warren Poetry Award). [AnthNEW] (7) 95, p. 10.
512. BERSSENBRUGGE, Mei-mei
    "The Four Year Old Girl." [Conjunc] (24) 95, p. 271-276.
513. BERTHEAUD, Patricia
    "The Great Cement Leviathan." [AmerPoR] (24:1) Ja-F 95, p. 25.
    "I Lament the Cleansing of Dead Bodies." [AmerPoR] (24:1) Ja-F 95, p. 25.
514. BERTOLINO, James
    "Belief." [QRL] (34) 95, book 4, p. 29.
    "Bird." [QRL] (34) 95, book 4, p. 43.
    "The Body Holographic." [QRL] (34) 95, book 4, p. 18.
    "A Boy and His Dog." [QRL] (34) 95, book 4, p. 27.
    "Breath." [WritersF] (21) 95, p. 90.
    "Broken Things." [QRL] (34) 95, book 4, p. 26-27.
    "Call It Dawn." [QRL] (34) 95, book 4, p. 8.
    "Creation Dance." [QRL] (34) 95, book 4, p. 10.
    "A Crystal." [QRL] (34) 95, book 4, p. 44.
    "Dragonfly." [QRL] (34) 95, book 4, p. 9.
    "A Dream." [QRL] (34) 95, book 4, p. 42.
    "Everything Moistens with Love." [QRL] (34) 95, book 4, p. 15.
    "The Family Sedan." [QRL] (34) 95, book 4, p. 28.
    "The Flying Dwarf." [QRL] (34) 95, book 4, p. 25.
    "Gaia Spins." [QRL] (34) 95, book 4, p. 13.
    "The Game." [QRL] (34) 95, book 4, p. 34.
    "Ghazal: The Seduction." [RiverC] (15:2) Sum 95, p. 123.
    "Gratitude." [QRL] (34) 95, book 4, p. 23.
    "Island Meditation." [QRL] (34) 95, book 4, p. 48.
    "Juncos." [QRL] (34) 95, book 4, p. 46.
    "Kisses." [QRL] (34) 95, book 4, p. 21.
    "The Ladle." [QRL] (34) 95, book 4, p. 42.
    "Like a Planet." [QRL] (34) 95, book 4, p. 50.
    "Lines to Restore Van Gogh's Ear." [QRL] (34) 95, book 4, p. 32-33.
    "Log Entries." [QRL] (34) 95, book 4, p. 37.
    "Loons." [QRL] (34) 95, book 4, p. 45.
    "Mantis." [QRL] (34) 95, book 4, p. 24.
    "The Mending." [QRL] (34) 95, book 4, p. 45.
    "Metabolism." [QRL] (34) 95, book 4, p. 14.
    "Metabolism." [WritersF] (21) 95, p. 90.
    "Moon." [QRL] (34) 95, book 4, p. 43.
    "The Mosaic." [RiverC] (15:2) Sum 95, p. 125.
    "Mountain Lullaby." [QRL] (34) 95, book 4, p. 20.
    "My Youth Rises." [QRL] (34) 95, book 4, p. 28.
    "Near McCracken's Pond." [QRL] (34) 95, book 4, p. 48.
    "The New Order." [QRL] (34) 95, book 4, p. 47.
    "A Nudity of Loons." [QRL] (34) 95, book 4, p. 19.
    "Octopus." [QRL] (34) 95, book 4, p. 41.

"On the Futility of Resisting the New Paradigm." [QRL] (34) 95, book 4, p. 36.
"Osprey." [QRL] (34) 95, book 4, p. 12.
"Pacific Prayer." [QRL] (34) 95, book 4, p. 50.
"Paranormal Boot Camp." [QRL] (34) 95, book 4, p. 33.
"Pawnee Fog." [QRL] (34) 95, book 4, p. 23.
"Schisms." [QRL] (34) 95, book 4, p. 47.
"See Willow." [QRL] (34) 95, book 4, p. 17.
"Shivering." [QRL] (34) 95, book 4, p. 44.
"Snail Buddha." [QRL] (34) 95, book 4, p. 14.
"Snail River: Poems, 1985-1993" (For Lois, and for my Mother, Doris). [QRL] (34)
    95, book 4, p. 1-52.
"Something Sinuous." [QRL] (34) 95, book 4, p. 11.
"Space Hawk." [QRL] (34) 95, book 4, p. 39.
"A Species." [QRL] (34) 95, book 4, p. 29.
"Spirits." [QRL] (34) 95, book 4, p. 46.
"A Spring Crocus: For the Children of AIDS." [QRL] (34) 95, book 4, p. 30.
"The Swallow." [QRL] (34) 95, book 4, p. 16.
"Toast for an Insect Lover." [QRL] (34) 95, book 4, p. 21.
"Turnips." [QRL] (34) 95, book 4, p. 8.
"The Visitation." [QRL] (34) 95, book 4, p. 38.
"The Wave." [QRL] (34) 95, book 4, p. 49.
"Weasel Brow." [QRL] (34) 95, book 4, p. 41.
"A Wedding Toast." [QRL] (34) 95, book 4, p. 20.
"Whales." [QRL] (34) 95, book 4, p. 49.
"What Abides." [RiverC] (15:2) Sum 95, p. 124.
"When the World Was Right." [QRL] (34) 95, book 4, p. 35.
"Yellow Gates." [QRL] (34) 95, book 4, p. 11.
515. BERTRAND, Aloysius
    "Nesle Tower" (tr. by Gian Lombardo). [ProseP] (4) 95, p. 9.
    "Viol da Gamba" (tr. by Gian Lombardo). [ProseP] (4) 95, p. 10-11.
516. BESKIN, Lisa
    "Crazy." [CimR] (112) Jl 95, p. 108.
    "This Winter." [MidwQ] (37:1) Aut 95, p. 35.
517. BESLER, Carol
    "Keeping the Ground from Rising." [RiverS] (45) 95, p. 1-2.
518. BETHANIS, Peter
    "Fenceposting at the Allen Farm." [Farm] (13:2 [i.e. 12:2]) Fall-Wint 95, p. 69.
519. BETHEL, Gar
    "Exhilaration." [MidwQ] (36:4) Sum 95, p. 353.
520. BETTY A. (Rachael's Women's Center, Washington, DC).
    "Homelessness" (WritersCorps Program). [WashR] (21:2) Ag-S 95, p. 9.
521. BEURSKENS, Huub
    "Coda" (tr. by Deirdre Kovac). [CimR] (112) Jl 95, p. 15.
    "Holland's Pasture" (tr. by Deirdre Kovac). [CimR] (112) Jl 95, p. 15.
522. BEVERIDGE, Robert P.
    "Jeffrey Dahmer's Bedroom." [HawaiiR] (19:2) Fall 95, p. 155-156.
BEY, Veronica Lewis
    See LEWIS-BEY, Veronica
523. BIALOSKY, Jill
    "The Dawn of the End of Civilization." [SenR] (25:2) Fall 95, p. 89.
    "The End of Desire." [SenR] (25:2) Fall 95, p. 88.
524. BIARUJIA, Javant
    "The Masque (A Variation)." [IllinoisR] (3:1/2) Fall 95-Spr 96, p. 89.
    "Rehearsals of Gesture." [IllinoisR] (3:1/2) Fall 95-Spr 96, p. 55.
525. BIBBINS, Mark
    "The Last Week." [Art&Und] (4:2, #15) Ap 95, p. 45.
    "Test." [Art&Und] (4:2, #15) Ap 95, p. 44.
526. BICK, Susann
    "My Tarzan." [HolCrit] (32:3) Je 95, p. 18-19.
527. BICKERSTAFF, Patsy Anne
    "Evening of the First Dance" (Robert Penn Warren Poetry Prize: First Prize).
        [CumbPR] (15:1) Fall 95, p. 11.
    "The Professor's Garden." [CumbPR] (15:1) Fall 95, p. 12.
528. BIDART, Frank
    "Lady Bird." [ParisR] (37:134) Spr 95, p. 139.
    "Love Incarnate" (Dante, Vita Nuova). [ParisR] (37:134) Spr 95, p. 138.

"Overheard Through the Walls of the Invisible City." [ParisR] (37:134) Spr 95, p. 139.
529. BIDNEY, Martin
"Boaz" (tr. of Else Lasker-Schüler). [NewMyths] (2:2/3:1) 95, p. 149.
"Ruth" (tr. of Else Lasker-Schüler). [NewMyths] (2:2/3:1) 95, p. 150.
"Sabaoth" (tr. of Else Lasker-Schüler). [NewMyths] (2:2/3:1) 95, p. 151.
"Shulamith" (tr. of Else Lasker-Schüler). [NewMyths] (2:2/3:1) 95, p. 152.
"To God" (tr. of Else Lasker-Schüler). [NewMyths] (2:2/3:1) 95, p. 153.
530. BIEBER, Christina
"Letter: to the Man Who Could Keep Me from Becoming an Old Maid by Degrees." [LullwaterR] (6:1) Spr-Sum 95, p. 36-37.
531. BIEHL, Michael
"After the Corpus Christi Feast Day Procession." [Callaloo] (18:2) Spr 95, p. 339-340.
"The Solipsists." [Callaloo] (18:2) Spr 95, p. 341-342.
532. BIEN, Jeff
"And No One Drowns." [PoetryC] (15:3) Ag 95, p. 13.
"Parables." [PoetryC] (15:3) Ag 95, p. 13.
"The Particular Evasiveness of Grace and Beauty." [PoetryC] (15:3) Ag 95, p. 13.
533. BIENEN, Leslie
"Dreams of My Mother." [PraS] (69:4) Wint 95, p. 98.
"Transformations." [PraS] (69:4) Wint 95, p. 99.
534. BIENVENUE, Roberta
"Global Warming." [QW] (41) Aut-Wint 95-96, p. 169.
535. BIER, Jesse
"The Cook Islands Christian Church, Raratonga." [WestB] (36) 95, p. 98.
"The Last Horse and My Father." [WestB] (36) 95, p. 99.
536. BIERDS, Linda
"Van Leeuwenhoek, 1675." [Thrpny] (63) Fall 95, p. 6.
537. BIESPIEL, David
"Holy Water" (for Stanley Plumly). [PlumR] (8) [95], p. 28-38.
538. BIFFAR, Donna
"Cold Blue Sheets" (For Quentin, My Stepfather). [FreeL] (15) Aut 95, p. 24.
"Doing the Laundry." [FreeL] (15) Aut 95, p. 25.
"The Next Generation." [Farm] (13:2 [i.e. 12:2]) Fall-Wint 95, p. 14-15.
"Taking Lunch to Men in the Fields." [Farm] (13:2 [i.e. 12:2]) Fall-Wint 95, p. 13.
539. BIGGINS, Michael
"At the Bottom" (tr. of Ales Debeljak). [Verse] (12:2) 95, p. 39.
540. BILGERE, George
"At the Vietnam Memorial." [Poetry] (166:3) Je 95, p. 141.
"Driving Range." [PoetL] (90:2) Sum 95, p. 61.
"Focal Point." [PoetL] (90:2) Sum 95, p. 62.
"Oklahoma." [LitR] (38:2) Wint 95, p. 229.
541. BILL, Jim
"Midnight Kitchen." [HiramPoR] (58/59) Spr 95-Wint 96, p. 9.
542. BILLER, Elizabeth
"Ashland Mornings." [Plain] (15:3) Spr 95, p. 22-23.
"Autumn is." [SmPd] (32:3, #95) Fall 95, p. 14.
"Charisma, Climbing the Hill." [Writer] (108:3) Mr 95, p. 12.
543. BILLITER, William
"Depth Charge." [PoetryE] (40) Spr 95, p. 17.
544. BINDER, Amy Olson
"Medusa, to Herself." [Interim] (14:1) Spr-Sum 95, p. 21.
"Mutton." [SouthernHR] (29:4) Fall 95, p. 362.
"Pomegranates." [SouthernHR] (29:4) Fall 95, p. 363.
"The Well." [Interim] (14:1) Spr-Sum 95, p. 21.
545. BIRKS, Ian C.
"Letters to Frank Lynch" (Excerpt). [IllinoisR] (3:1/2) Fall 95-Spr 96, p. 50.
546. BIRNBAUM, Alfred
"House-Hunting" (tr. of Kobayashi Kyoji). [Descant] (26:2, #89) Sum 95, p. 121-132.
547. BIRNES, Anna
"Communion." [SmPd] (32:2, #94) Spr 95, p. 29-30.
"Maurice Asher 1880-1952 *My Grandfather*." [SmPd] (32:2, #94) Spr 95, p. 28.
548. BISHOP, Alan
"For John Thompson (1978)." [AntigR] (102/103) Sum-Aug 95, p. 271-272.

68

549. BISHOP, Ellen
  "American Goddess." [PraS] (69:4) Wint 95, p. 146-149.
550. BISHOP, James
  "Confession." [FreeL] (15) Aut 95, p. 3-6.
551. BISHOP, Wendy
  "Entropy in a Small Universe." [DefinedP] (1:2) Spr-Sum 93, p. 25-26.
  "Motorcycle Ghazals." [ColEng] (57:6) O 95, p. 710.
  "The Red Clearing" (after a line by Rimbaud). [DefinedP] (1:2) Spr-Sum 93, p. 27.
  "Remember Staying Awake All Night." [DefinedP] (3) 95, p. 36.
552. BITA, Lili
  "Excavations" (tr. by Robert Zaller). [Footwork] (24/25) 95, p. 78.
  "Theme with Shadows" (tr. by Robert Zaller). [Footwork] (24/25) 95, p. 78.
553. BJARTMARSSON, Sigfús
  "63" (from "Zombie," tr. by David McDuff). [Nimrod] (38:2) Spr-Sum 95, p. 71.
554. BJOSTAD, Doug
  "San Francisco" (Loft Inroads Program for Gay, Lesbian, and Bisexual Writers).
    [EvergreenC] (10:1) Wint-Spr 95, p. 97-98.
555. BLACK, David
  "Time Pieces." [EngJ] (84:4) Ap 95, p. 17.
556. BLACK, Elizabeth
  "The Green Man." [SouthernHR] (29:3) Sum 95, p. 220.
557. BLACK, Kevin
  "Vermilion Border." [PottPort] (16:1) Fall 95, p. 28-29.
558. BLACK, Ralph
  "Empire." [NortheastCor] (3) 95, p. 48-49.
  "Poem for the Sleeper." [NortheastCor] (3) 95, p. 31-32.
559. BLACK, Sophie Cabot
  "Beacon." [DenQ] (29:3) Wint 95, p. 5.
  "Easter." [DenQ] (29:4) Spr 95, p. 11.
  "Horse." [DenQ] (29:4) Spr 95, p. 12.
  "How the Soul Moves." [AmerPoR] (24:2) Mr-Ap 95, p. 41.
  "Nature, Who Misunderstands." [DenQ] (29:3) Wint 95, p. 6.
560. BLACKARD, John A.
  "Housepainting on Liberty Road." [Crucible] (31) Fall 95, p. 21-25.
561. BLACKBURN, Charles, Jr.
  "The Doves Fly at Dusk." [Pembroke] (27) 95, p. 125.
  "Nietzsche's Headaches" (In memory of Charlie Stanford). [Crucible] (30) Fall 94, p. 23.
562. BLACKSTON, Daniel
  "Moon." [HiramPoR] (58/59) Spr 95-Wint 96, p. 10-11.
563. BLACKWOOD, Margaret
  "The Palest of Shades." [PraF] (16:2, #71) Sum 95, p. 31.
564. BLAGG, Max
  "The Bump" (I-VIII). [Bomb] (52) Sum 95, p. 85-87.
565. BLAIR, David McLaughlin
  "County Mayo Carting Business, 1907." [GreensboroR] (57) Wint 94-95, p. 78-79.
566. BLAIR, John
  "Parting in the Rain" (tr. of Shu Ting, w. Zhaoming Qian). [PoetryE] (39) Fall 94, p. 122.
  "The Singing House." [LullwaterR] (6:1) Spr-Sum 95, p. 38-40.
  "This, Too, Is Everything" (In Response to a Young Friend's "Everything," tr. of Shu Ting, w. Zhaoming Qian). [PoetryE] (39) Fall 94, p. 123-124.
567. BLAIR, Morgan
  "Mother." [HawaiiR] (19:2) Fall 95, p. 121-122.
568. BLAIR, Peter
  "Discussing the Dream of Culture with Professor Kwaam." [Vis] (49) 95, p. 20.
569. BLAKE, Jonathan
  "Trying to Be Tender." [PoetryE] (41) Aut 95, p. 95.
570. BLAKE, Rosemary
  "At Three A.M." [AntigR] (102/103) Sum-Aug 95, p. 181.
  "Our Lady of Mount Carmel." [AntigR] (102/103) Sum-Aug 95, p. 180.
  "Piazza Navona 11." [AntigR] (102/103) Sum-Aug 95, p. 179.
571. BLAKE, William (1757-1827)
  "Visions" (Excerpt). [PoetryE] (41) Aut 95, p. 33.
BLANC, Diane Le
  See LeBLANC, Diane

BLANC, Jean le
   See LeBLANC, Jean
572. BLANCHARD, Len
   "A Christmas Peace." [JamesWR] (12:3) Fall 95, p. 19.
   "Flying Human." [BellArk] (11:4) Jl-Ag 95, p. 11.
   "Hanging With the Sea Oats." [JamesWR] (12:3) Fall 95, p. 18.
   "A Telling Light." [JamesWR] (12:3) Fall 95, p. 6.
   "World Without End." [BellArk] (11:4) Jl-Ag 95, p. 11.
573. BLANCHFIELD, Brian
   "Pied Spring" (tr. of Ou-Yang Hsiu). [LitR] (38:3) Spr 95, p. 331.
574. BLAND, Celia
   "Wisdom Teeth." [Chain] (2) Spr 95, p. 26-27.
575. BLANDIANA, Ana
   "As If" (tr. by Seamus Heaney). [SouthernR] (31:3) Jl/Sum 95, p. 469.
   "Hunt" (tr. by Seamus Heaney). [SouthernR] (31:3) Jl/Sum 95, p. 471.
   "Inhabited by a Song" (tr. by Seamus Heaney). [SouthernR] (31:3) Jl/Sum 95, p. 468.
   "Loneliness" (tr. by Seamus Heaney). [SouthernR] (31:3) Jl/Sum 95, p. 470-471.
   "Maybe There's Somebody Dreaming Me" (tr. by Seamus Heaney). [SouthernR]
      (31:3) Jl/Sum 95, p. 469-470.
576. BLANGO, Lashawn
   "The Blues" (WritersCorps Program, Washington, DC). [WashR] (21:2) Ag-S 95, p.
      12.
577. BLANKENBURG, Gary
   "At My Father's Viewing." [Parting] (8:1) Sum 95, p. 14.
   "Carl, a Tall Thin Black Man." [Parting] (8:1) Sum 95, p. 13-14.
   "Golfing." [GreenHLL] (6) 95, p. 56.
   "Her Name Was Billie Jean Larue." [Parting] (8:1) Sum 95, p. 7.
   "The Same Drum." [WindO] (60) Fall-Wint 95, p. 10-11.
578. BLANKENBURG, Jodie
   "Recital." [IndR] (18:2) Fall 95, p. 100-103.
579. BLASER, Robin
   "Nomad." [Sulfur] (15:2, #37) Fall 95, p. 117.
580. BLAZEK, Douglas
   "Composing for Strings." [Zyzzyva] (11:1, #41) Spr 95, p. 79.
581. BLAZEVIC, Neda Miranda
   "Van Gogh's Peasant-Woman" (tr. by Dasha Culic Nisula). [Vis] (48) 95, p. 16.
582. BLEDSOE, Tony
   "Always Alone." [ChironR] (43) Sum 95, p. 15.
   "Days and Nights of the Slow Death." [ChironR] (44/45) Aut-Wint 95, p. 33.
583. BLEEK, W. H.
   "//Kabbo's Request for Thread" (tr. of anonymous /Xam poem, w. Lucy Lloyd and
      Stephen Watson). [ColR] (22:1) Spr 95, p. 61.
   "Our Blood Makes Smoke" (tr. of anonymous /Xam poem, w. Lucy Lloyd and
      Stephen Watson). [ColR] (22:1) Spr 95, p. 57.
   "Song of the Broken String" (tr. of anonymous /Xam poem, w. Lucy Lloyd and
      Stephen Watson). [ColR] (22:1) Spr 95, p. 59-60.
   "The Story of Ruyter" (tr. of anonymous /Xam poem, w. Lucy Lloyd and Stephen
      Watson). [ColR] (22:1) Spr 95, p. 58.
   "The Wind Is One with the Man" (tr. of anonymous /Xam poem, w. Lucy Lloyd and
      Stephen Watson). [ColR] (22:1) Spr 95, p. 56.
584. BLEHERT, Dean
   "All Happy Endings Are the Same." [NewYorkQ] (55) 95, p. 92-93.
   "Hein?" [Light] (14) Sum 95, p. 9.
   "Is This the Voice." [Bogg] (67) 95, p. 30.
   "Not Goodbye, But Good Buy!" [Light] (15/16) Aut-Wint 95-96, p. 12.
   "T.S. Eliot." [Light] (14) Sum 95, p. 14.
585. BLEOCA, Liviu
   "A Dance in Masks" (tr. of Aurel Rau, w. Adam J. Sorkin). [Vis] (48) 95, p. 43.
586. BLESSING, Marlene
   "Say the Fathers." [PoetryNW] (36:4) Wint 95-96, p. 35.
587. BLITZ, Michael
   "English 101 Fishkill Correctional Facility 1983." [ColEng] (57:7) N 95, p. 842-843.
588. BLOCH, Benjamin
   "Letter to My Brother." [SantaBR] (3:2) Sum 95, p. 26.
   "Numbers." [SantaBR] (3:2) Sum 95, p. 25.
   "Under Treeline." [SantaBR] (3:2) Sum 95, p. 27.

589. BLOCK, Ron
"Mother." [PraS] (69:1) Spr 95, p. 61.
"Strip Joint." [Ploughs] (21:1) Spr 95, p. 24-25.
590. BLOMAIN, Karen
"Elvis Stamps" (runner up, 1994 Borderlands Poetry Contest). [Border] (7) Fall-Wint 96, p. 4.
591. BLOOM, Barbara
"Reading Your Poem on Miracles." [NorthStoneR] (12) 95, p. 225.
592. BLOOM, Ronna
"Marmalade." [Grain] (23:2) Aut 95, p. 58.
"To Fit the Absence." [Grain] (23:2) Aut 95, p. 57.
593. BLOOM, Sarah
"Catherine to Her Demon." [Phoebe] (24:1) 95, p. 17-23.
594. BLOOMFIELD, Maureen
"Charing Cross." [WestHR] (49:1) Spr 95, p. 42.
595. BLOTTENBERGER, Mike
"Priorities" (from Morsels of Manna). [AmerPoR] (24:4) Jl-Ag 95, p. 22.
596. BLUE SPRUCE, Paula
"Katsina" (To Jack. And, in memory, to Sandy). [QRL] (34) 95, book 5, p. 1-58.
597. BLUGER, Marianne
"Porchlight." [MalR] (112) Fall 95, p. 15.
598. BLUMENTHAL, Jay A.
"Breakfast: A War Poem." [SoCaR] (28:1) Fall 95, p. 70.
"Half-Baked Alaska." [SoCaR] (28:1) Fall 95, p. 72.
"The Last Great Age of Breakfast." [SoCaR] (28:1) Fall 95, p. 71.
"Poetry in the Arctic." [SoCaR] (28:1) Fall 95, p. 71-72.
599. BLUMENTHAL, Michael
"Hungarian Fall" (tr. of Peter Kantor, w. Eszter Füséki). [Agni] (42) 95, p. 16-17.
"Once I Thought" (tr. of Peter Kantor, w. Eszter Füséki). [Agni] (42) 95, p. 18.
"The Pleasures of Abstraction." [Verse] (12:2) 95, p. 24-25.
600. BLUNK, Jonathan
"East Allen Street." [JINJPo] (17:2) Aut 95, p. 33.
"Raritan Valley." [Nat] (261:12) 16 O 95, p. 444.
601. BLY, Robert
"After Dream." [ManyMM] [1:1] D 94, p. 48.
"Anger Against Children." [Stand] (36:3) Sum 95, p. 19-21.
"Bad People." [Atlantic] (275:3) Mr 95, p. 68.
"The Boy Looking for His Parents." [Hudson] (48:3) Aut 95, p. 426.
"Brooding on Justice." [ManhatR] (8:1) Fall 95, p. 13.
"A Dreaming That Is Like Reading." [Stand] (36:3) Sum 95, p. 19.
"A Family Picture." [Hudson] (48:3) Aut 95, p. 425.
"For Those Whom the Sea Takes." [HarvardR] (8) Spr 95, p. 109.
"The Giant Who Knew Aristotle." [BelPoJ] (45:4) Chapbook 22, Sum 95, p. 10.
"He Wanted to Live His Life Over." [ManhatR] (8:1) Fall 95, p. 11.
"If I were a poet of love" (tr. of Antonio Machado, 1875-1939). [PoetryE] (41) Aut 95, p. 37.
"Landscape Painters." [NorthStoneR] (12) 95, p. 196.
"The Man Who Wants to Save Your Life." [Boulevard] (10:3, #30) Fall 95, p. 94-95.
"Nudging a Poem." [Sun] (231) Mr 95, p. 30.
"The Old Woman Frying Perch" (For D. H.). [Boulevard] (10:3, #30) Fall 95, p. 94.
"On the Word Reality." [Pequod] (39) 95, p. 9.
"A Poem Is Some Remembering." [ManhatR] (8:1) Fall 95, p. 12.
"Reading Dr. Nuland's Book." [Pequod] (39) 95, p. 11.
"Reading Silence in the Snowy Fields." [Hudson] (48:3) Aut 95, p. 425-426.
"Seas" (tr. of Steinum Sigurthardotter). [HarvardR] (8) Spr 95, p. 91.
"A Story About the Train Trip." [PlumR] (8) [95], p. 91.
"Talking with Genghis Khan." [ManhatR] (8:1) Fall 95, p. 14.
"That Routine." [NorthStoneR] (12) 95, p. 197.
"The Thinker's Dog." [Pequod] (39) 95, p. 12.
"Waking on the Farm." [Poetry] (167:3) D 95, p. 154.
"The Waltz." [Pequod] (39) 95, p. 10.
"Ways We Could be Heroes." [Nat] (260:7) 20 F 95, p. 251.
"Winter Afternoon by the Lake" (For Owen). [BelPoJ] (45:4) Chapbook 22, Sum 95, p. 9.
602. BLYTHE, Randy
"The Contortionist." [BlackWR] (22:1) Fall-Wint 95, p. 85-86.

603. BOARDMAN, Barbara Lynn
"Two Snowflakes." [WorldO] (27:2) Wint 95-96, p. 33.
604. BOAS, Franz
"Song: I won't care if you desert me" (tr. of Chinook poem, 1888, adapted by Sam
Hamill). [PoetryE] (41) Aut 95, p. 34.
605. BOE, Marilyn J.
"The Son Without Children Asks." [PoetryE] (41) Aut 95, p. 96.
606. BOEHRER, Bruce Thomas
"To the Only Senior Colleague, in a Field of Twenty-Two, Who Voted to Deny Me
Tenure." [ApalQ] (43) Spr 95, p. 63-65.
607. BOEKE, Wanda
"70" (tr. of Elly de Waard). [CimR] (112) Jl 95, p. 13.
608. BOES, Don
"Altitude." [Farm] (13:2 [i.e. 12:2]) Fall-Wint 95, p. 70-71.
609. BOGAN, Kathleen
"Immune Means Memory." [WritersF] (21) 95, p. 60-62.
610. BOGEN, Don
"Card Catalog." [WestHR] (49:4) Wint 95, p. 330-331.
611. BOGIN, Nina
"Let's Share the Frugal Meal." [Hudson] (48:1) Spr 95, p. 61.
"The Orchards of Vandoncourt." [Hudson] (48:1) Spr 95, p. 59-60.
"Seven Hawks." [Hudson] (48:1) Spr 95, p. 57-59.
"Stockholm, Summer 1990" (for Madeleine Hatz). [Hudson] (48:1) Spr 95, p. 63.
"There's No Hour." [Hudson] (48:1) Spr 95, p. 62.
612. BOGREN, Jeanette Baker
"Chance Meeting." [WritersF] (21) 95, p. 163.
613. BOHAC, Janet
"Loss." [Vis] (49) 95, p. 22.
614. BOHANNON, J. P.
"On a Photograph of Jacquline Roque and Her Husband Picasso." [SantaBR] (3:1)
Spr 95, p. 85-86.
"Pegeen Mike." [SantaBR] (3:1) Spr 95, p. 86.
"Penelope." [SantaBR] (3:1) Spr 95, p. 87-88.
615. BOHANNON-BELLAMY, Linda
"Gestures of Idea" (Excerpts). [SpoonR] (20:2) Sum-Fall 95, p. 10-17.
616. BOHORQUEZ, Douglas
"El Vertice Fugitivo de la Luna." [Luz] (8) Spr 95, p. 52.
617. BOHRER, Ronny Ann
"Spruce Head Island, Maine." [NewDeltaR] (12:1) Fall-Wint 94, p. 52-53.
BOIS, Annette du
See DuBOIS, Annette
618. BOISSEAU, Michelle
"Fresh Is Air, Too." [Agni] (42) 95, p. 149-150.
"In Reserve." [Ploughs] (21:1) Spr 95, p. 146.
"The Next Child." [Ploughs] (21:1) Spr 95, p. 149-150.
"Pleiades." [OhioR] (54) 95, p. 131-132.
"Why You Said It" (for my sister Madeline). [Ploughs] (21:1) Spr 95, p. 147-148.
619. BOJORQUEZ, Mario
"Bitacora de Viaje de Fortúm Ximénez, Descubridor y Conquistador de la Isla de la
California." [Luz] (8) Spr 95, p. 10-18.
"Ship's Log of the Voyage of Fortum Ximenez, Discoverer and Conqueror of the
Island of California" (tr. by Angela McEwan). [Luz] (8) Spr 95, p. 11-19.
620. BÖK, Christian
"Silicon Tapestries" (Selections). [ChiR] (41:4) 95, p. 31-33.
"Virtual Realities" (Selections: VR-1 - VR-6). [ChiR] (41:4) 95, p. 27-30.
621. BOKUR, Debra
"Eulogy, June." [Kalliope] (17:2) 95, p. 16.
622. BOLAND, Eavan
"The Glass King." [SenR] (25:1) Spr 95, p. 67-68.
"The Harbor." [NewYorker] (71:10) 1 My 95, p. 92.
"In Exile." [TampaR] (10) Spr 95, p. 39.
"Mother Ireland." [Poetry] (167:1/2) O-N 95, p. 93.
623. BOLDEN, Louis
"Keep Me Out of the Rain" (WritersCorps Project, Washington, DC). [WashR] (21:2)
Ag-S 95, p. 20.

624. BOLDT, Christine
"Breathless." [WorldO] (26:3) Spr 95, p. 25.
"Completion of the Cycle" (III. Earth, IV. Fire). [WorldO] (26:4) Sum 95, p. 44-45.
625. BOLIEK, Robert
"Langley." [Hellas] (6:1) Spr-Sum 95, p. 27.
626. BOLLING, Madelon
"Things of This Magnitude" (for Marsha, sine qua nihil). [BellArk] (11:6) N-D 95, p. 25.
627. BOLLS, Imogene
"Barring the Unforeseen" (In Memory of John R. Milton, from his letter of March 21, 1994). [SoDakR] (33:3/4) Fall-Wint 95, p. 28-29.
"Dream Poem: Deer Dance." [WritersF] (21) 95, p. 112-113.
"Mountain Dawn." [WritersF] (21) 95, p. 113.
628. BOLSTER, Stephanie
"Alice, Dying, 1934." [AntigR] (102/103) Sum-Aug 95, p. 62.
"Alice's Hand." [TickleAce] (27) Spr-Sum 94, p. 56.
"Close Your Eyes and Think of England." [TickleAce] (27) Spr-Sum 94, p. 57.
"Come to the edge of the barn the property really begins there" (first line is one of John Ashbery's "37 Haiku"). [MalR] (110) Spr 95, p. 100.
"Egg-timer." [AntigR] (102/103) Sum-Aug 95, p. 60.
"Hydrangea." [CanLit] (146) Aut 95, p. 28.
"In Which Alice Spots, Across a Plate of Rolls, Her Future Husband's Back." [Grain] (22:3) Wint 95, p. 111.
"Iris." [CanLit] (146) Aut 95, p. 29.
"Life & Death in the Conservatory." [Dandel] (22:1) 95, p. 69.
"Portrait of Alice as an English Landscape." [AntigR] (102/103) Sum-Aug 95, p. 61.
"Portrait of Alice As Universe." [TickleAce] (27) Spr-Sum 94, p. 55.
"The Skin Beneath Fingernails." [PoetryC] (15:3) Ag 95, p. 28.
"Too low for nettles but it is exactly the way people think and feel" (first line is one of John Ashbery's "37 Haiku"). [MalR] (110) Spr 95, p. 101.
"Two Deaths in January 1898." [Grain] (22:3) Wint 95, p. 112.
"Virginia Woolf's Mother in the Blurred Garden." [Arc] (34) Spr 95, p. 33.
629. BOMBA, Bernard
"I Am Sure of This." [Footwork] (24/25) 95, p. 72.
"In First Leaf-Flowering." [Footwork] (24/25) 95, p. 73.
"Poetry in the Locked Ward" (For Peter Arakawa). [Footwork] (24/25) 95, p. 72-73.
"To a Young Artist." [WindO] (59) Spr 95, p. 31-32.
"Walking Home from a Bar Late at Night with an Old Friend, Feeling Our Age." [SoCoast] (18) Ja 95, p. 38-39.
BOMBARD, Joan La
See LaBOMBARD, Joan
630. BOMMARITO, Angela
"The Umpire Refutes the Apotheosis of Hype." [IndR] (18:2) Fall 95, p. 152-153.
631. BONA, Mary Jo
"Cool Grey Day." [Footwork] (24/25) 95, p. 52-53.
"May Poem, for Phillip." [Footwork] (24/25) 95, p. 52.
"Snoqualmie Falls, July." [Footwork] (24/25) 95, p. 53.
632. BONACCI, Michael
"Sorry Bread" (Loft Inroads Program for Gay, Lesbian, and Bisexual Writers). [EvergreenC] (10:1) Wint-Spr 95, p. 99.
633. BONAFFINI, Luigi
"Among People Laughing" (tr. of Albino Pierro). [NewRena] (9:2, #28) Spr 95, p. 78.
"And What Am I?" (tr. of Albino Pierro). [NewRena] (9:2, #28) Spr 95, p. 77.
634. BOND, Bruce
"All Saints' Eve." [LaurelR] (29:2) Sum 95, p. 103.
"The Confederate Dead." [SewanR] (103:3) Sum 95, p. 335-336.
"Feast of the Seven Sorrows." [WestHR] (49:4) Wint 95, p. 361.
"Isaac." [WestHR] (49:4) Wint 95, p. 360.
"Native Tongue." [YaleR] (83:4) O 95, p. 83.
"Photograph of the 5th Vermont at Camp Griffin, Virginia." [SewanR] (103:3) Sum 95, p. 337.
"Postcard from Cold Harbor." [SewanR] (103:3) Sum 95, p. 338.
"The Rowers." [SouthwR] (80:4) Aut 95, p. 444.
635. BOND, Joan
"Grey Black." [PottPort] (16:1) Fall 95, p. 74.
"Prairie Passion." [PottPort] (16:1) Fall 95, p. 73.

"Tea and Toast." [PottPort] (16:1) Fall 95, p. 75.
636. BONDS, Diane
"Sea Watchers" (a painting by Edward Hopper). [CimR] (110) Ja 96, p. 81.
"Western Motel" (a painting by Edward Hopper, 1957). [MichQR] (34:1) Wint 95, p.
90-91.
BONGIORNO, Marylou Tibaldo
See TIBALDO-BONGIORNO, Marylou
637. BONINA, Mary
"Healing Waters." [Noctiluca] (2:1, #4) Spr 95, p. 23.
638. BONNEFOY, Yves
"The Snow" (tr. by Hoyt Rogers). [Agni] (41) 95, p. 38.
"Summer Again" (tr. by Hoyt Rogers). [Agni] (41) 95, p. 37.
"A Voice" (tr. by Hoyt Rogers). [HarvardR] (9) Fall 95, p. 31.
639. BONOMO, Joe
"Afternoon to Bachelard." [Pequod] (39) 95, p. 95.
"Imagine a Bird's-eye View." [NewDeltaR] (12:1) Fall-Wint 94, p. 22-23.
"Sketch, With Four Walls." [OhioR] (54) 95, p. 70.
"Vanishings from That Neighborhood." [OhioR] (54) 95, p. 71.
640. BOOKER, Stephen Todd
"Charged Particulars." [AfAmRev] (29:3) Fall 95, p. 478.
641. BOOKEY, Ted
"Good News / Bad News." [LowellR] [1] Sum 94, p. 72.
642. BOOTH, Philip
"Ages." [Poetry] (167:3) D 95, p. 152-153.
"Looking." [RiverS] (41) 95, p. 50.
"Three Poets Near the 92nd Street Y." [BelPoJ] (46:2) Wint 95-96, p. 5.
"Views." [GeoR] (49:3) Fall 95, p. 631.
643. BORAN, Pat
"The Dead Man's Clothes." [Poetry] (167:1/2) O-N 95, p. 74.
"Ghosts." [SouthernR] (31:3) Jl/Sum 95, p. 525.
"Moon Street." [SouthernR] (31:3) Jl/Sum 95, p. 523-524.
644. BORG, Shannon
"Under the City, Under the Sea." [PoetryNW] (36:2) Sum 95, p. 12.
645. BORGES, Jorge Luis
"Adrogué" (tr. by Robert Mezey and Richard Barnes). [CutB] (42) Sum 94, p. 71-72.
"All Our Yesterdays" (tr. by Robert Mezey). [NewYRB] (42:20) 21 D 95, p. 16.
"The Causes" (tr. by Robert Mezey). [CutB] (42) Sum 94, p. 73-74.
"Heráclito." [RiverS] (42/43) 95, p. 17.
"Heraclitus" (tr. by Carlos Suarez). [RiverS] (42/43) 95, p. 16.
"Ricardo Güiraldes" (tr. by Robert Mezey). [CutB] (42) Sum 94, p. 70.
"Street with Pink Store" (tr. by Robert Mezey). [CutB] (42) Sum 94, p. 68-69.
646. BORGES, Millicent (Millicent C.)
"Birdfood for Charlie Parker" (For Ornette Coleman. The 1994 Allen Ginsberg
Poetry Awards: Honorable Mention). [Footwork] (24/25) 95, p. 187.
"In Prague." [TampaR] (11) Fall 95, p. 13.
"Like Nameless Skyscrapers." [NewDeltaR] (12:1) Fall-Wint 94, p. 56-57.
"Living Only with the Hands." [SmPd] (32:1, #93) Wint 95, p. 16.
"Sound Is a Circle" (for Miles Davis). [XavierR] (15:1) Spr 95, p. 51-52.
647. BORGES-ROSEN, Carole
"912 Toulouse." [CimR] (112) Jl 95, p. 97-98.
"Dreamseeker's Journey." [Poetry] (165:6) Mr 95, p. 338-339.
648. BORINSKY, Alicia
"Betrayal" (tr. by Cola Franzen). [MassR] (36:4) Wint 95-96, p. 595.
"The Critics' Trade" (to José Emilio Pacheco, tr. by Cola Franzen). [MassR] (36:4)
Wint 95-96, p. 596.
"Ocupaciones de la Crítica" (a José Emilio Pacheco). [MassR] (36:4) Wint 95-96, p.
596.
"Traición." [MassR] (36:4) Wint 95-96, p. 595.
"Welcome" (tr. by Cola Franzen). [AmerV] (36) 95, p. 113.
649. BORKHUIS, Charles
"Orpheus Dividing." [HeavenB] (12) 95, p. 36-37.
650. BORNSTEIN, Judith
"Addressing the Tree of Poetry" (tr. of Penelope Boutos). [Vis] (47) 95, p. 6.
"Cheese" (tr. of Penelope Boutos). [Vis] (48) 95, p. 25.
"The Greeks Have a Word for it" (tr. of Penelope Boutos). [Vis] (47) 95, p. 4.
"Gypsy Clothes" (tr. of Penelope Boutos). [Vis] (48) 95, p. 24.

"I Love to Eat" (tr. of Penelope Boutos). [Vis] (48) 95, p. 24.
"The Little Stranger" (tr. of Penelope Boutos). [Vis] (49) 95, p. 21.
"The Milkmen" (tr. of Penelope Boutos). [Vis] (48) 95, p. 26.
"Portrait of Mr. Dionysus" (tr. of Penelope Boutos). [Vis] (47) 95, p. 5.
651. BOROUGHS, Brooke
    "Sidestepping." [HopewellR] (7) 95, p. 86-87.
652. BORUCH, Marianne
    "The American Opera Company." [Iowa] (25:1) Wint 95, p. 151-152.
    "Aubade." [Iowa] (25:1) Wint 95, p. 150.
    "The Book of Hand Shadows." [DenQ] (30:2) Fall 95, p. 12.
    "Car Covered with Snow." [MassR] (36:2) Sum 95, p. 280.
    "Chinese Brushwork." [DenQ] (30:2) Fall 95, p. 10-11.
    "Exhaustion." [Iowa] (25:1) Wint 95, p. 149-150.
    "The Great Ape House." [SouthernR] (31:4) O/Aut 95, p. 824-825.
    "Happiness." [GeoR] (49:2) Sum 95, p. 386.
    "Library Stereopticon." [MassR] (36:2) Sum 95, p. 279.
    "Old Ball Field." [Iowa] (25:1) Wint 95, p. 149.
    "X-ray Vision." [DenQ] (30:2) Fall 95, p. 13-14.
653. BORUM, Poul
    "Short Waves" (tr. of Christian Bundegaard). [Pequod] (39) 95, p. 13-19.
BOSELAAR, Laure-Anne
    See BOSSELAAR, Laure-Anne
654. BOSMAN, Jane
    "The Laundry Pile." [Pembroke] (27) 95, p. 102.
655. BOSQUET, Alain
    "Another Era." [Poetry] (166:3) Je 95, p. 160.
    "The Chain." [Poetry] (166:3) Je 95, p. 162.
    "Everything Is Ready." [Poetry] (166:3) Je 95, p. 161.
    "A Film" (tr. by William Jay Smith). [NewYorker] (71:27) 11 S 95, p. 78.
    "Loose Leaves" (tr. by William Jay Smith). [AmerPoR] (24:4) Jl-Ag 95, p. 19.
    "Nothing At All" (tr. by James Laughlin). [Agni] (41) 95, p. 69.
    "An Old Gentleman." [Poetry] (166:3) Je 95, p. 159.
    "An Ordinary Day" (tr. by James Laughlin). [Agni] (41) 95, p. 68.
    "An Ordinary Day" (tr. by William Jay Smith). [AmerPoR] (24:4) Jl-Ag 95, p. 19.
    "When I'm No Longer Around" (tr. by William Jay Smith). [AmerPoR] (24:4) Jl-Ag
        95, p. 19.
656. BOSS, Laura
    "Blackbirds." [Footwork] (24/25) 95, p. 171.
    "Emily Dickinson Speaks to an Unpublished Poet." [Footwork] (24/25) 95, p. 171.
    "Honeymoon." [Footwork] (24/25) 95, p. 171.
    "On Not Believing in Astrology." [Footwork] (24/25) 95, p. 172.
    "When It Comes to Clothes." [Footwork] (24/25) 95, p. 172.
657. BOSSELAAR, Laure-Anne
    "Amen" (for Carol Houck Smith, from "Between Dog and Wolf"). [Nimrod] (39:1)
        Fall-Wint 95, p. 95-96.
    "At the Musée Rodin in Paris" (for Herman de Coninck). [DenQ] (29:4) Spr 95, p. 13.
    "The Cellar." [MassR] (36:1) Spr 95, p. 40-41.
    "From My Window I See Mountains." [ManyMM] (2:1) 95, p. 125.
    "The Hour Between Dog and Wolf" (for Maëlle). [InterQ] (2:3) 95, p. 102-104.
    "Letter from Jake's Place, Durango" (from "Between Dog and Wolf"). [Nimrod]
        (39:1) Fall-Wint 95, p. 94.
    "Loving You in Flemish" (for Kurt). [MassR] (36:1) Spr 95, p. 41-42.
    "The Pallor of Survival." [ManyMM] (2:1) 95, p. 124.
    "Sunday Drive through Eagle Country." [ManyMM] (2:1) 95, p. 123.
    "Unable to Find the Right Way." [SycamoreR] (7:1) Wint 95, p. 35.
BOSVEID, Jennifer
    See BOSVELD, Jennifer
658. BOSVELD, Jennifer
    "The Discovery." [BlackBR] (20) Spr-Sum 95, p. 22.
    "Duuuuh." [Wind] (76) Fall 95, p. 3-4.
    "Response to Guided Imagery Workshop in Which We Were to Find Great Solace in
        Going to the Sea." [ChironR] (43) Sum 95, p. 33.
659. BOTTKE, Amy
    "How to Approach Your Lover's Wife." [LouisL] (12:1) Spr 95, p. 43-44.
    "Sweetheart." [LouisL] (12:1) Spr 95, p. 41-42.

660. BOTTOMS, David
"The Blue Mountains." [NewRep] (212:2/3) 9-16 Ja 95, p. 44.
661. BOTTS, DeLois
"Turning Points in My Life" (WritersCorps Program, Washington, DC). [WashR]
(21:2) Ag-S 95, p. 4.
"Winter" (WritersCorps Program, Washington, DC). [WashR] (21:2) Ag-S 95, p. 4.
662. BOUCH, Lynda Lou
"Revelation No. 1." [BellArk] (11:4) Jl-Ag 95, p. 13.
"Try This, It Worked for Me." [BellArk] (11:4) Jl-Ag 95, p. 13.
663. BOUCHER, Alan
"The Fourth Wise Man from the East" (tr. of Hannes Pétursson). [Vis] (47) 95, p. 13.
BOUCHET, André du
    See Du BOUCHET, André
664. BOURNE, Daniel
"The Actor of Esperanto." [Salm] (106/107) Spr-Sum 95, p. 110-111.
"After the Cold War." [Ploughs] (21:1) Spr 95, p. 133-134.
"All the Philosophies in the World." [PraS] (69:3) Fall 95, p. 22.
"Chain" (tr. of Tomasz Jastrun). [SpoonR] (20:2) Sum-Fall 95, p. 75.
"Christmas Eve" (tr. of Tomasz Jastrun). [SpoonR] (20:2) Sum-Fall 95, p. 74.
"Flood Warning for Warsaw, Late Eighties, No Political Metaphors." [Ploughs]
(21:1) Spr 95, p. 135.
"Free" (tr. of Tomasz Jastrun). [SpoonR] (20:2) Sum-Fall 95, p. 75.
"Gotland" (tr. of Tomasz Jastrun). [Chelsea] (59) 95, p. 127.
"Human Interest Story." [PraS] (69:3) Fall 95, p. 21.
"Ladies and Gentlemen, the Prime Time Surreal." [LaurelR] (29:1) Wint 95, p. 45.
"Nativity." [GreensboroR] (59) Wint 95-96, p. 121.
"The Non-Linear as a Function of Regret" (Warsaw, late winter 1983). [PraS] (69:3)
Fall 95, p. 23.
"The Present Day" (tr. of Tomasz Jastrun). [SpoonR] (20:2) Sum-Fall 95, p. 74.
"Rat Gives You His Free Hand" (tr. of Stanislaw Esden-Tempski). [MidAR] (15:1/2)
95, p. 206.
"Underneath the Leaf" (tr. of Tomasz Jastrun). [Chelsea] (59) 95, p. 128.
665. BOURRASSA, Sylvie
"Unglued." [Dandel] (22:1) 95, p. 72.
666. BOUTOS, Penelope
"Addressing the Tree of Poetry" (tr. by Judith Bornstein). [Vis] (47) 95, p. 6.
"Cheese" (tr. by Judith Bornstein). [Vis] (48) 95, p. 25.
"The Greeks Have a Word for it" (tr. by Judith Bornstein). [Vis] (47) 95, p. 4.
"Gypsy Clothes" (tr. by Judith Bornstein). [Vis] (48) 95, p. 24.
"I Love to Eat" (tr. by Judith Bornstein). [Vis] (48) 95, p. 24.
"The Little Stranger" (tr. by Judith Bornstein). [Vis] (49) 95, p. 21.
"The Milkmen" (tr. by Judith Bornstein). [Vis] (48) 95, p. 26.
"Portrait of Mr. Dionysus" (tr. by Judith Bornstein). [Vis] (47) 95, p. 5.
667. BOUVARD, Marguerite (Marguerite Guzman)
"La Bora." [PraS] (69:4) Wint 95, p. 136.
"Fear." [Noctiluca] (2:1, #4) Spr 95, p. 42.
"Giving Testimony." [PraS] (69:4) Wint 95, p. 138.
"In Sarajevo." [PraS] (69:4) Wint 95, p. 139.
"Josefa's Dream." [Noctiluca] (2:1, #4) Spr 95, p. 43.
"Speaking to the Mountains." [PraS] (69:4) Wint 95, p. 137.
668. BOWDAN, Janet
"Esther's Requiem: What I Mean to Say Is." [DenQ] (30:2) Fall 95, p. 15-16.
669. BOWEN, Kevin
"The Bells" (tr. of Vu Cao, w. Nguyen Ba Chung). [Manoa] (7:2) Wint 95, p. 108.
"A Bridge" (tr. of Pham Tien Duat, w. Nguyen Quang Thieu). [Manoa] (7:2) Wint 95,
p. 167.
"Buying My Brother a Suit." [PoetL] (90:4) Wint 95-96, p. 13.
"Do Len" (Mother's Village, 9/83, tr. of Nguyen Duy, w. Nguyen Ba Chung).
[Manoa] (7:2) Wint 95, p. 95.
"Driving Home." [MassR] (36:4) Wint 95-96, p. 539-540.
"For Myles Who Communes with Planes." [PoetL] (90:2) Sum 95, p. 11-12.
"In Search of Maturin" (For Mick Neville). [SilverFR] (25) Sum 95, p. 26-28.
"In the Labor Market at Giang Vo" (tr. of Pham Tien Duat, w. Nguyen Ba Chung).
[Manoa] (7:2) Wint 95, p. 169.
"Lang Son, 1989" (10th anniversary of the border campaign, 2/79-2/89, tr. of Nguyen
Duy, w. Nguyen Ba Chung). [Manoa] (7:2) Wint 95, p. 96.

"A Little Fire: Mourning the Death of Mountbatten, Dublin, January 1978."
[SilverFR] (25) Sum 95, p. 29.
"The Moon in Circles of Flame" (tr. of Pham Tien Duat, w. Nguyen Quang Thieu).
[Manoa] (7:2) Wint 95, p. 168.
"Mutton." [PoetL] (90:4) Wint 95-96, p. 12.
"New Year's Fireworks" (Midnight, New Year's Day, 1992, tr. of Nguyen Duy, w.
Nguyen Ba Chung). [Manoa] (7:2) Wint 95, p. 94.
"Poem of a Garden" (tr. of Le Thi May, w. Nguyen Ba Chung). [Manoa] (7:2) Wint
95, p. 98.
"Red Earth, Blue Water" (tr. of Nguyen Duy, w. Nguyen Ba Chung). [Manoa] (7:2)
Wint 95, p. 96.
"White Circle" (tr. of Pham Tien Duat, w. Nguyen Quang Thieu). [Manoa] (7:2) Wint
95, p. 168.
670. BOWER, Aviva
"Anaglyph." [Sulfur] (15:1, #36) Spr 95, p. 14.
"At the Rodin Museum." [Sulfur] (15:1, #36) Spr 95, p. 15-17.
"Emulsions." [Sulfur] (15:1, #36) Spr 95, p. 15.
"Intoxication of Transgression." [Sulfur] (15:1, #36) Spr 95, p. 13.
"See." [Sulfur] (15:1, #36) Spr 95, p. 13-14.
671. BOWERING, George
"Shakespeare." [Pembroke] (27) 95, p. 53.
"Wolf Between the Trees." [Pembroke] (27) 95, p. 50-51.
"Work Socks." [Pembroke] (27) 95, p. 52.
672. BOWERS, Cathy Smith
"The Entry." [Atlantic] (275:4) Ap 95, p. 102.
673. BOWERS, Neal
"An Afterlife." [SewanR] (103:4) Fall 95, p. 495.
"The Age of Surrender" (for Nancy). [Hudson] (48:2) Sum 95, p. 274.
"Braille for the Body." [Flyway] (1:1) Spr 95, p. 72.
"Driving to Sleep." [DefinedP] (1:2) Spr-Sum 93, p. 35.
"Dusk." [TarRP] (35:1) Fall 95, p. 19.
"Faith at the Turn of the Century." [IndR] (18:1) Spr 95, p. 2.
"For the Ego." [Poetry] (166:1) Ap 95, p. 35.
"For the Record." [SewanR] (103:4) Fall 95, p. 494.
"Here." [Poetry] (166:1) Ap 95, p. 34.
"Home Cooking" (for Teri V.). [Flyway] (1:1) Spr 95, p. 73.
"Lilies." [DefinedP] (1:2) Spr-Sum 93, p. 33.
"Lost in the Vicinity." [SewanR] (103:4) Fall 95, p. 493.
"Migratory Patterns." [Shen] (45:2) Sum 95, p. 96.
"More Light!" (— Goethe). [Shen] (45:2) Sum 95, p. 97.
"The Muse Takes Off Her Gloves." [TarRP] (35:1) Fall 95, p. 18-19.
"Nothing." [SewanR] (103:1) Wint 95, p. 1-4.
"Outbound." [Shen] (45:2) Sum 95, p. 98.
"Peonies." [DefinedP] (1:2) Spr-Sum 93, p. 34.
"Persimmons." [TarRP] (35:1) Fall 95, p. 18.
"The Philosophy of Metaphor." [IndR] (18:1) Spr 95, p. 1.
"The Philosophy of Metaphor" (corrected reprint from 18:1). [IndR] (18:2) Fall 95, p.
183.
"Privileges." [Poetry] (166:1) Ap 95, p. 36.
"Training Camp." [FreeL] (15) Aut 95, p. 31.
674. BOWERS, Susanne R.
"The Dollhouse." [RagMag] (12:2) Spr 95, p. 22-23.
675. BOWLING, Tim
"Akhmatova." [MalR] (112) Fall 95, p. 39.
"Aprons." [Event] (24:2) Sum 95, p. 9.
"Midnight." [ClockR] (10:1/2) 95-96, p. 140.
"Neepawa." [Event] (24:2) Sum 95, p. 12.
"Nocturne." [Event] (24:2) Sum 95, p. 10-11.
"Snowy Owl After Midnight." [ClockR] (10:1/2) 95-96, p. 141-142.
"Two a.m." [MalR] (112) Fall 95, p. 38.
676. BOWMAN, Catherine
"No Sorry." [TriQ] (95) Wint 95-96, p. 200-201.
BOX, Annette le
See LeBOX, Annette
677. BOYD, Allison
"Corpus Delecti." [SmPd] (32:3, #95) Fall 95, p. 8.

77

"To Make a Flower." [SmPd] (32:3, #95) Fall 95, p. 7.
678. BOYD, Anthony
"Shantytown." [BlackBR] (20) Spr-Sum 95, back cover.
679. BOYD, Betsy McCorkle
"Crape Myrtle." [Crucible] (30) Fall 94, p. 18-19.
680. BOYER, Dale W.
"Weeds" (in memoriam). [EvergreenC] (10:2) Sum-Fall 95, p. 22.
681. BOYKIN, Janiesha
"My Grandmother" (WritersCorps Project, Washington, DC). [WashR] (21:2) Ag-S 95, p. 22.
682. BOYLE, Jennifer
"Messiah." [SoCoast] (19) 95, p. 9-10.
"Mozart Reincarnated as a Janitor Working Carnegie Hall." [SoCoast] (19) 95, p. 8.
"The Prostitute Speaks About Her Former Life." [SoCoast] (19) 95, p. 5-7.
683. BOYLE, Kevin
"The Lullaby of History." [PoetryE] (41) Aut 95, p. 68-69.
684. BRACKENBURY, Alison
"Count Orlov." [KenR] (17:3/4) Sum-Fall 95, p. 78.
"Katya." [KenR] (17:3/4) Sum-Fall 95, p. 77-78.
685. BRACKENBURY, Rosalind
"Thanksgiving." [Stand] (36:3) Sum 95, p. 4-5.
686. BRACKER, Jonathan
"On the Subway." [SoCoast] (18) Ja 95, p. 34-35.
"To a Very Unhappy Young Sailor." [SoCoast] (18) Ja 95, p. 41.
687. BRACUK, Diane
"Trust." [AntigR] (100) Wint 95, p. 124.
688. B'RACZ, Emoke
"Leaned into the frozen wind. Created a hole" (tr. of Katalin Ladik). [Vis] (47) 95, p. 8.
"White socks in his mouth" (tr. of Katalin Ladik). [Vis] (47) 95, p. 8.
689. BRADBURY, Steve
"Climbing in the Mountains After Being Released from Prison" (tr. of Chi Minh Ho). [Manoa] (7:2) Wint 95, p. 68.
"Cold Night" (tr. of Chi Minh Ho). [Manoa] (7:2) Wint 95, p. 68.
"Evening Tableau" (tr. of Chi Minh Ho). [Manoa] (7:2) Wint 95, p. 68.
"The Milestone" (tr. of Chi Minh Ho). [Manoa] (7:2) Wint 95, p. 69.
"On Reading of Wendell Willkie's Reception in China" (tr. of Chi Minh Ho). [Manoa] (7:2) Wint 95, p. 67.
"On the Fall of a Tooth" (tr. of Chi Minh Ho). [Manoa] (7:2) Wint 95, p. 68.
"Scabies" (tr. of Chi Minh Ho). [Manoa] (7:2) Wint 95, p. 68.
"Seven Prison Poems" (tr. of Chi Minh Ho). [Manoa] (7:2) Wint 95, p. 67-69.
"Two Ballets" (tr. of Yuan Ch'iung-ch'iung) [HawaiiR] (19:2) Fall 95, p. 94-95.
690. BRADEN, Allen
"In Between." [BlackBR] (21) Fall-Wint 95, p. 24-25.
691. BRADLEY, George
"The Greenhouse Effect." [NewRep] (212:16) 17 Ap 95, p. 46.
"New Age Night at the Nuyorican." [ParisR] (37:134) Spr 95, p. 119-120.
"Scumble." [QW] (41) Aut-Wint 95-96, p. 174.
"Tobias, or The Idea Whose Time Had Come." [ParisR] (37:134) Spr 95, p. 120-121.
692. BRADLEY, John
"Cocoon." [ColEng] (57:6) O 95, p. 712.
"Letter to T'ao Ch'ien." [Farm] (12:1) Spr-Sum 95, p. 64.
"Memo to Ariadne." [ProseP] (4) 95, p. 12.
"Where I Live" (For William Stafford). [ColEng] (57:1) Ja 95, p. 82.
693. BRADLEY, Larry
"The Lover Returns." [JamesWR] (12:1) Wint 95, p. 13.
"The Moon Sings a Full Aria" (for Rob). [HiramPoR] (58/59) Spr 95-Wint 96, p. 12-13.
694. BRADSTREET, Anne (1612-1672)
"To My Dear and Loving Husband." [PoetryE] (41) Aut 95, p. 30.
695. BRADY, Patrick
"Convergence." [PaintedB] (57) 95, p. 68.
696. BRADY, Philip
"The Cathedral of Guadalajara" (por Guillermo). [Interim] (14:1) Spr-Sum 95, p. 36-40.
"Dear Sir Roger" (Belgian Congo of 1904). [InterPR] (21:1) Spr 95, p. 90-91.

"First Born" (for Anne Brady). [WestB] (37) 95, p. 22-24.
"The Salesman" (For my mother). [Footwork] (24/25) 95, p. 44.
"Scald." [LaurelR] (29:1) Wint 95, p. 23-25.
"Touring Plague Country" (cholera epidemic, Ibiaku, Zaire). [Footwork] (24/25) 95,
     p. 43.
697. BRAGGS, Earl S.
     "Crisco Martinez (1950-1967)." [ApalQ] (43) Spr 95, p. 75-76.
698. BRAHIC, Beverly
     "René Char at La Maison de Petrarch, Fontaine de Vaucluse." [AntigR] (102/103)
        Sum-Aug 95, p. 86.
     "Roadwork." [AntigR] (102/103) Sum-Aug 95, p. 85.
699. BRAHMAN, Calico
     "Applecloud Mynd." [HeavenB] (12) 95, p. 12-13.
700. BRAITHWAITE, Kent
     "Hubble." [ChironR] (44/45) Aut-Wint 95, p. 7.
BRAKEMAN, Diane Seuss
     See SEUSS-BRAKEMAN, Diane
701. BRAND, Alice G.
     "Transcript." [Vis] (49) 95, p. 4.
702. BRAND, Ian
     "The Man Who Sold Space." [PoetL] (90:3) Fall 95, p. 37-38.
     "Work." [PoetL] (90:3) Fall 95, p. 36.
703. BRANDÃO, Fiama Hasse Pais
     "Authenticity" (tr. by Alexis Levitin). [PraS] (69:1) Spr 95, p. 151.
     "Close to the Aviary" (tr. by Alexis Levitin). [SenR] (25:2) Fall 95, p. 58.
     "Close to the Peasant" (tr. by Alexis Levitin). [SenR] (25:2) Fall 95, p. 56.
     "A Dog, the Sea" (tr. by Alexis Levitin). [GrahamHR] (19) Wint 95-96, p. 69.
     "Light and Shadow" (tr. by Alexis Levitin). [SenR] (25:2) Fall 95, p. 57.
     "The Shadow of Two Dogs" (tr. by Alexis Levitin). [PraS] (69:1) Spr 95, p. 152.
704. BRANDT, Di
     "Dream-Work" (with photography by Diana Thorneycroft, essay by Sigrid Dahle).
        [Quarry] (44:1) 95, p. 87-100.
705. BRANDT, Pamela
     "Bill's Place." [Confr] (56/57) Sum-Fall 95, p. 350-351.
706. BRANNON, Jack
     "At the Vietnam Memorial, Washington, November 11, 1990." [WillowS] (35) Ja 95,
        p. 76-77.
707. BRASCHI, Giannina
     "The wind and I would have to take off and fly" (tr. by Tess O'Dwyer). [Footwork]
        (24/25) 95, p. 38.
708. BRASFIELD, James
     "Coast Range." [WeberS] (12:2) Spr-Sum 95, p. 98-100.
709. BRASON, Maris
     "Calm" (for Michael). [AmerPoR] (24:4) Jl-Ag 95, p. 36.
     "Roof." [AmerPoR] (24:4) Jl-Ag 95, p. 37.
710. BRASS, Perry
     "Phoebus Apollo Anoints the Heads of Scott Ross, Andrew DeMasi, William Parker,
        Chris DeBlasio, and Paul Jacobs" (dedicted to Hugh Young). [Art&Und] (4:4,
        #17) S-O 95, p. 41.
711. BRAUCHER, Karen
     "Flint." [SpoonR] (20:1) Wint-Spr 95, p. 31.
     "Time." [SpoonR] (20:1) Wint-Spr 95, p. 32-33.
712. BRAUD, Janice L.
     "Medusa Lives." [BellArk] (11:3) My-Je 95, p. 25.
     "When He Grins." [BellArk] (11:3) My-Je 95, p. 25.
713. BRAUN, Henry
     "An Angel of the War Years" (early 1970s. For Father Dan). [PaintedB] (57) 95, p.
        22.
     "At a Pier of the Ben Franklin Bridge." [PaintedB] (57) 95, p. 19.
     "Carl Rakosi in Orono." [PaintedB] (57) 95, p. 24.
     "Creative Writing Class." [PaintedB] (57) 95, p. 28.
     "Description of a Solstice" (for my grandson, Natsuo). [PaintedB] (57) 95, p. 32-35.
     "A Fulbright Scholars Remembers His France" (1955). [PaintedB] (57) 95, p. 25.
     "The Gettysburg Epiphany, Like" (the President discovered in the blowup of an old
        photograph). [PaintedB] (57) 95, p. 21.
     "The Grackles." [PaintedB] (57) 95, p. 23.

"In the Chemistry Lecture Hall at Temple." [PaintedB] (57) 95, p. 29.
"Initiation Into Chaos" (for Mandelbrot and Mandelstam). [PaintedB] (57) 95, p. 18.
"Lament for the Metaphors." [PaintedB] (57) 95, p. 24.
"Late Mail in Mt. Airy." [AxeF] (3) 90, p. 8.
"Late Mail in Mt. Airy." [PaintedB] (57) 95, p. 30.
"Morning in America" (early 1980s). [PaintedB] (57) 95, p. 20.
"The Professor." [PaintedB] (57) 95, p. 28.
"The Thief of Permission." [PaintedB] (57) 95, p. 31.
"Why I Am Not a Scientist." [PaintedB] (57) 95, p. 26-27.
714. BRAVEBOY-LOCKLEAR, Barbara
"Generational Differences." [Pembroke] (27) 95, p. 16.
715. BRAVERMAN, Melanie
"Day." [AmerPoR] (24:3) My-Je 95, p. 34.
"A Horse." [AmerPoR] (24:3) My-Je 95, p. 34.
716. BRAVO, Alejandra
"Hypnosis for Submission." [Arc] (35) Aut 95, p. 49.
"The Waiting Room." [Arc] (35) Aut 95, p. 50.
BRAVO, Armando Alvarez
See ALVAREZ BRAVO, Armando
BRAVO, Brandel France de
See FRANCE de BRAVO, Brandel
717. BRAXTON, Charlie R.
"Fly Fly Black Bird." [CutB] (44) Sum 95, p. 74.
"Haiku." [Drumvoices] (4:1/2) Fall-Wint 94-95, p. 140.
"Torn between Two Worlds (Jesus at the Crossroads)." [CutB] (44) Sum 95, p. 72-73.
"Visions of the Second Coming." [Drumvoices] (4:1/2) Fall-Wint 94-95, p. 139.
718. BRAZIEL, James
"My Father's Work." [HayF] (17) Fall-Wint 95, p. 44-45.
719. BREEDEN, Rachel
"The Wolf's Return" (tr. of Edgar O'Hara, collectively w. Charity Berg et al.).
[Americas] (23:3/4) Fall-Wint 95, p. 154-155.
720. BREIDING, G. Sutton
"Message of Hope." [HeavenB] (12) 95, p. 96.
"Ninety-Five Degrees." [HeavenB] (12) 95, p. 96.
721. BRENDAN-BROWN, Sean
"The Candy Block." [Plain] (15:3) Spr 95, p. 9.
"Coyote Run." [BlackBR] (21) Fall-Wint 95, p. 27.
"Jacqueline." [Plain] (15:2) Wint 95, p. 14.
"Sailing." [Plain] (16:1) Fall 95, p. 9.
"Sailing." [WillowR] (22) Spr 95, p. 9.
722. BRENNA, Beverley
"The Old Farm." [Grain] (23:1) Sum 95, p. 123.
723. BRENNAN, Matthew
"Air." [Poem] (74) N 95, p. 12.
"Capture the Flag" (for my brother Mike). [Footwork] (24/25) 95, p. 16.
"The Divorcee's Revenge." [Footwork] (24/25) 95, p. 17.
"Preheating" (for Bev). [Poem] (74) N 95, p. 11.
724. BRENNAN, Scott
"The Murals." [OxfordM] (10:1) Wint 94-Spr 95, p. 11.
725. BRENNAN, Sherry
"Sleep" (after Warhol, thanks to Pascale-Anne). [Chain] (2) Spr 95, p. 31-34.
726. BRESKIN, David
"Bugs." [ParisR] (37:134) Spr 95, p. 171.
"The Day I Take Her to the Hospital." [TriQ] (95) Wint 95-96, p. 204-206.
"Evidence of Bear." [TriQ] (95) Wint 95-96, p. 202-203.
"The Factory." [SouthernPR] (35:2) Wint 95, p. 20-21.
"Poem for a Businessman (Me)." [ParisR] (37:134) Spr 95, p. 170-171.
"Rain for Nineteen Hours." [Salm] (108) Fall 95, p. 105-106.
"Throw It Down (with Authority)." [NewAW] (13) Fall-Wint 95, p. 122.
727. BRESLIN, Paul
"You Are Here." [Poetry] (166:3) Je 95, p. 130-135.
728. BRETON, André
"Free Union" (tr. by Louis Simpson). [HarvardR] (9) Fall 95, p. 59-60.
729. BRETT, Brian
"The Father Considers His Children." [PoetryC] (15:3) Ag 95, p. 26.
"Hornby Island." [PoetryC] (15:3) Ag 95, p. 26.

BRETT

"Living at the Tideline." [PoetryC] (15:3) Ag 95, p. 26.
730. BREWER, Gay
"Good-Bye William Stafford." [NewYorkQ] (54) 95, p. 47.
"Patchwork." [LowellR] (2) c1996, p. 56.
"Your First Day Back in the World." [CumbPR] (14:2) Spr 95, p. 49.
731. BREWER, Jack
"Beginnings." [Pearl] (22) Fall-Wint 95, p. 38.
"Cliffs." [Pearl] (22) Fall-Wint 95, p. 36.
"Consuelo in a Charbroil Burger Place." [Pearl] (22) Fall-Wint 95, p. 37.
"In This Sandbox." [Pearl] (22) Fall-Wint 95, p. 38.
"Long Beach 2 A.M. Weeknight." [Pearl] (22) Fall-Wint 95, p. 37.
"Segments from Diary." [Pearl] (22) Fall-Wint 95, p. 36.
732. BREWER, Kenneth
"The Man I Hate." [WeberS] (12:2) Spr-Sum 95, p. 16-18.
733. BRICKMAN, Harriet
"Care." [MassR] (36:2) Sum 95, p. 246.
734. BRICUTH, John
"Just Let Me Say This About That" (Excerpt). [Raritan] (15:2) Fall 95, p. 71-82.
735. BRIDGES, Constance Quarterman
"Daughters" (For the women who told me). [JINJPo] (17:2) Aut 95, p. 14.
736. BRIDGFORD, Kim
"Along the Edge of the Sea." [LaurelR] (29:1) Wint 95, p. 38-39.
"Apology" (For Pete). [WeberS] (12:1) Wint 95, p. 99.
"Bingo at Rosewood" (for Aunt Lola). [Pearl] (22) Fall-Wint 95, p. 117.
"The Bird-Maker" (after *Creation of the Birds* by Remedios Varo). [PoetL] (90:4)
    Wint 95-96, p. 28.
"The Chair" (after a photograph by Walker Evans). [HolCrit] (32:4) O 95, p. 19.
"Friends." [Wind] (76) Fall 95, p. 5.
"Hell" (after a painting by Hieronymous Bosch). [PoetL] (90:4) Wint 95-96, p. 29.
"Just As the Slightest Puff of Wind." [LaurelR] (29:1) Wint 95, p. 39-40.
"The Last Countable Kingdom." [WeberS] (12:1) Wint 95, p. 100-101.
"The Line." [Plain] (15:2) Wint 95, p. 26-27.
"A Photograph of Spring." [SoCaR] (28:1) Fall 95, p. 54.
"Pigeons." [WeberS] (12:1) Wint 95, p. 99-100.
"Thirty." [WeberS] (12:1) Wint 95, p. 101.
"When the Darkness Comes." [SoCaR] (28:1) Fall 95, p. 55.
737. BRINGHURST, Robert
"New World Suite No. 3" (Excerpt). [PoetryC] (15:2) Je 95, p. 14-15.
"Parsvanatha." [Verse] (12:2) 95, p. 26.
738. BRISTER, J. G.
"After Mass." [Chelsea] (59) 95, p. 43.
"A Nun on Her Wedding Day." [Chelsea] (59) 95, p. 41.
"Ruth Among the Grain." [Chelsea] (59) 95, p. 42.
"What I Was Taught About Modern Verse" (for Chet Corey). [NorthStoneR] (12) 95,
    p. 54.
739. BRITT, Alan
"Driving through Fredericksburg, Virginia." [SantaBR] (3:1) Spr 95, p. 48.
"Ghosts." [ContextS] (4:2) 95, p. 6.
"Having Breakfast with a Mockingbird near Kansas, Missouri." [SantaBR] (3:1) Spr
    95, p. 45.
"Melancholia." [Conduit] (3) Sum 95, p. 21.
"Near Stuart, Florida." [SantaBR] (3:1) Spr 95, p. 46.
"On a Foggy Morning." [SantaBR] (3:1) Spr 95, p. 46.
"To Chelsea: On Her Second Birthday." [SantaBR] (3:1) Spr 95, p. 47.
740. BRITT, Linda
"A Wrong Turn." [GreenHLL] (6) 95, p. 11.
741. BRITTINGHAM, Kimberly
"Distress Wears a Crimson Dress." [EvergreenC] (10:2) Sum-Fall 95, p. 90.
742. BRKIC, Courtney Angela
"Baltimore, 1925." [CapeR] (30:1) Spr 95, p. 30.
743. BROADHURST, Nicole
"Belated Gift to the Bahamas." [CaribbeanW] (9) 95, p. 37-38.
"Lerlene and the Trick." [CaribbeanW] (9) 95, p. 39-40.
744. BROCHU, André
"Laps de Terre." [Os] (40) 95, p. 30-31.

745. BROCK, Geoffrey
"Earth and Death" (tr. of Cesare Pavese). [InterQ] (2:1/2) 95, p. 57-62.
"The Telephone Is Ringing" (It's for you, Michael). [ApalQ] (43) Spr 95, p. 66-68.
BROCK, Wendy Wirth
See WIRTH-BROCK, Wendy
746. BROCK-BROIDO, Lucie
"Also, None Among Us Has Seen God." [DenQ] (30:1) Sum 95, p. 27.
"Am Moor." [HarvardR] (9) Fall 95, p. 16.
"And You Know That I Know Milord That You Know." [DenQ] (30:2) Fall 95, back cover.
"At the River Unshin's Edge." [Verse] (12:3) 95, p. 92-93.
"Desunt Non Nulla." [DenQ] (30:1) Sum 95, p. 24.
"Did Not Come Back." [HarvardR] (9) Fall 95, p. 14.
"Dull Weather." [IndR] (18:2) Fall 95, p. 187.
"Everything Husk to the Will." [DenQ] (30:1) Sum 95, p. 20-22.
"Fair Copy from a Fair World." [DenQ] (30:1) Sum 95, p. 18-19.
"A Glooming Peace This Morning with It Brings." [DenQ] (30:2) Fall 95, p. 17.
"Gratitude." [DenQ] (30:1) Sum 95, p. 23.
"Grimoire." [HarvardR] (9) Fall 95, p. 15.
"Housekeeping." [DenQ] (30:1) Sum 95, p. 26.
"How Can It Be I Am No Longer I." [ParisR] (37:135) Sum 95, p. 272-273.
"The October Horse." [DenQ] (30:2) Fall 95, p. 18-20.
"Pompeian." [IndR] (18:2) Fall 95, p. 186.
"Rampion." [DenQ] (30:1) Sum 95, p. 25.
"That Same Vagabond Sweetness." [Verse] (12:3) 95, p. 93.
"Toxic Gumbo." [IndR] (18:2) Fall 95, p. 185.
747. BROCKI, Anselm
"November." [GreenHLL] (6) 95, p. 49.
"Personal Property." [WindO] (60) Fall-Wint 95, p. 19.
"Vitamin Z." [WindO] (60) Fall-Wint 95, p. 20.
748. BRODKEY, Harold
"Victim Song." [NewYorker] (71:10) 1 My 95, p. 83.
749. BRODSKY, Joseph
"At a Lecture." [NewRep] (212:19) 8 My 95, p. 40.
"Foreword to Peter Viereck's New Book, *Tide and Continuities: Last and First Poems*." [Boulevard] (10:3, #30) Fall 95, p. 114-116.
"Homage to Chekhov" (tr. by the author). [NewYorker] (71:23) 7 Ag 95, p. 70-71.
"In Memory of Clifford Brown" (tr. by the author). [NewRep] (213:24) 11 D 95, p. 40.
"Kolo" (A Balkan folk dance). [NewYRB] (42:12) 13 Jl 95, p. 15.
"MCMXCIV. Lousy times: nothing to steal and no one to steal from." [NewYRB] (42:10) 8 Je 95, p. 18.
"MCMXCV. The clowns are demolishing the circus." [NewYRB] (42:10) 8 Je 95, p. 18.
"Once More by the Potomac." [NewRep] (213:6) 7 Ag 95, p. 11.
750. BRODSKY, Louis Daniel
"November Planting" (For Janie Goldberg). [PaintedB] (55/56) 95, p. 67.
"Pecan Grove." [HolCrit] (32:5) D 95, p. 17-18.
751. BROGNIET, Eric
"The bicycle abandoned and rusted" (tr. by the author). [Vis] (49) 95, p. 13.
BROIDO, Lucie Brock
See BROCK-BROIDO, Lucie
752. BROMIGE, David
"Deliberate." [Avec] (10) 95, p. 86-89.
"Symptomatic." [Avec] (10) 95, p. 81-85.
"Vulnerable Bundles" (Selections: 1, 10, 12, 17, 23, 39, 57, 63, 70, 81, 85). [RiverC] (15:1) Wint 95, p. 8-18.
753. BRONK, William
"The Annihilation of Matter." [Talisman] (14) Fall 95, p. 6.
"The Body." [Talisman] (14) Fall 95, p. 7.
"Hard Times." [Talisman] (14) Fall 95, p. 3.
"The Puzzle There." [Talisman] (14) Fall 95, p. 6-7.
"Terms and Appearances." [Talisman] (14) Fall 95, p. 4.
"That Something There Is Should Be." [Talisman] (14) Fall 95, p. 5.
"Visitors' Day at the World." [Talisman] (14) Fall 95, p. 3.
"The Wakeful." [Talisman] (14) Fall 95, p. 4.

754. BROOK, Donna
"Message to Mary Ferrari in Jo'Burg." [RiverS] (44) 95, p. 25-26.
755. BROOKE, Paul
"Unchí na Miyé, na Oóyake Ota Kin: Grandma and I, and the Many Stories."
[Flyway] (1:1) Spr 95, p. 56-61.
756. BROOKHOUSE, Christopher
"Ohio, Knox County, September." [GettyR] (8:4) Aut 95, p. 712.
757. BROOKS, Barbara A.
"Winter's Coming." [Crucible] (31) Fall 95, p. 7.
758. BROOKS, David
"Paleozoic Phone Call." [WestB] (36) 95, p. 11.
"Sunday Morning Samba." [WestB] (36) 95, p. 11.
759. BROOKS, Gwendolyn
"I Am a Black." [Drumvoices] (4:1/2) Fall-Wint 94-95, p. 126.
"Uncle Seagram." [Drumvoices] (4:1/2) Fall-Wint 94-95, p. 127.
760. BROOKS, Stan
"Black Coffee." [AnthNEW] (7) 95, p. 15.
761. BROSMAN, Catharine Savage
"Amanda." [SewanR] (103:4) Fall 95, p. 496-497.
"The Dance." [SewanR] (103:2) Spr 95, p. 184-186.
"Flying Straight." [SewanR] (103:3) Sum 95, p. 377-379.
"Mathilde." [SewanR] (103:4) Fall 95, p. 497-498.
"Sacrament." [SewanR] (103:3) Sum 95, p. 379-380.
762. BROSTROM, Kerri
"Bulemia." [CapeR] (30:2) Fall 95, p. 20.
"Field Day." [CapeR] (30:2) Fall 95, p. 21.
763. BROUGHTON, J. (James)
"My Tortoise." [NewYorkQ] (55) 95, p. 53.
"The Partner." [FreeL] (15) Aut 95, p. 11.
"Steamy Sophistry." [NewYorkQ] (54) 95, p. 50.
764. BROUGHTON, T. Alan
"The Flight Home." [GreenMR] (8:1) Spr-Sum 95, p. 73.
"Freeze." [SenR] (25:1) Spr 95, p. 79-80.
"Li Ho Won't Quit Writing." [GreenMR] (8:1) Spr-Sum 95, p. 75-76.
"Praise." [GreenMR] (8:1) Spr-Sum 95, p. 74.
"Ringing the Bells." [TarRP] (34:2) Spr 95, p. 20-21.
"Three Voices." [LitR] (38:2) Wint 95, p. 180-182.
765. BROUSSEAU, Blake
"The Hunter." [DogRR] (14:1, #27) Sum 95, p. 8-9.
766. BROUWER, Joel
"Across the Tracks." [GreenMR] (8:2) Fall-Wint 95-96, p. 124.
"Geology." [ArtfulD] (28/29) 95, p. 62.
"Houdini." [ArtfulD] (28/29) 95, p. 60.
"Kelly." [ArtfulD] (28/29) 95, p. 61.
"May Day, 1921, In the Town of Vitebsk." [WillowS] (36) Je 95, p. 26-27.
"Souvenir Stand." [GreenMR] (8:2) Fall-Wint 95-96, p. 122.
"Story." [GreenMR] (8:2) Fall-Wint 95-96, p. 123.
767. BROWN, Alan C.
"Hölderlin's Grave, Tübingen." [Stand] (36:2) Spr 95, p. 74.
768. BROWN, Allan
"Advice to Travellers" (for Ken Stange). [Quarry] (44:2) 95, p. 72.
"All Hallows, 1972" (for E. P.). [CanLit] (147) Wint 95, p. 45.
"Cold Pastoral." [PoetryC] (15:2) Je 95, p. 12.
"Directions." [Quarry] (44:2) 95, p. 71.
"Paul Klee." [MalR] (113) Wint 95, p. 36.
"St. John the Baptist." [MalR] (113) Wint 95, p. 38.
"Watteau." [MalR] (113) Wint 95, p. 37.
769. BROWN, Andrea Carter
"Our Lady of Prague" (runner up, 1994 Borderlands Poetry Contest). [Border] (6)
Spr-Sum 95, p. 27.
"Paradox." [Blueline] (16) 95, p. 88.
770. BROWN, Arthur
"A Trumpet in the Morning." [RiverS] (42/43) 95, p. 8-9.
771. BROWN, Bill
"Fungus" (for Mary Oliver). [Poem] (73) My 95, p. 30.
"Still Life." [Poem] (73) My 95, p. 29.

"Value." [SouthernPR] (35:1) Sum 95, p. 28-29.
772. BROWN, Christopher Nicholas
"Boston, 1966-68." [NewYorkQ] (55) 95, p. 89-90.
773. BROWN, Cory
"ABC's." [WestB] (36) 95, p. 105.
"Kneeling at the Edge" (1-15, of 23). [Bomb] (51) Spr 95, p. 85-87.
"Orion." [WestB] (37) 95, p. 28-29.
"Thin Line." [Farm] (12:1) Spr-Sum 95, p. 65.
774. BROWN, Dan
"In the Chapel in My Head." [PartR] (62:2) Spr 95, p. 304.
775. BROWN, Deborah
"The Bloody Peony." [AnthNEW] (7) 95, p. 31.
776. BROWN, Elizabeth
"Things I Have Learned." [MassR] (36:2) Sum 95, p. 255.
777. BROWN, George
"Manhattan." [EvergreenC] (10:2) Sum-Fall 95, p. 50.
778. BROWN, Glen
"Dillinger, Alias Jimmy Lawrence." [IllinoisR] (2:2) Spr 95, p. 14.
"Web of Memory." [IllinoisR] (2:2) Spr 95, p. 13.
779. BROWN, Harry
"The Lesson, or, Once Again, Seize the Day." [Wind] (75) Spr 95, p. 3-4.
780. BROWN, Kurt
"The First Commandment." [ManyMM] (2:1) 95, p. 114-115.
"Hunger." [ManyMM] (2:1) 95, p. 113.
"Return of the Prodigals." [ManyMM] (2:1) 95, p. 116-118.
"The Virginian." [DenQ] (30:2) Fall 95, p. 21.
781. BROWN, Mary M.
"Some Things I Cannot Part With." [HopewellR] (7) 95, p. 88-89.
782. BROWN, Michael
"All I Have" (WritersCorps Project, Washington, DC). [WashR] (21:2) Ag-S 95, p. 22.
783. BROWN, Michael R.
"Cleopatra." [DefinedP] (1:2) Spr-Sum 93, p. 21.
784. BROWN, Patria
"Three Poems" (for William Stafford). [BellArk] (11:3) My-Je 95, p. 11.
785. BROWN, Robert
"i Is the Square Root of -1." [LitR] (38:3) Spr 95, p. 358-359.
"Thanksgiving." [NewMyths] (2:2/3:1) 95, p. 181-182.
BROWN, Sean (Sean Brendan)
    See BRENDAN-BROWN, Sean
786. BROWN, Susan
"The Archaeopteryx." [HayF] (17) Fall-Wint 95, p. 118-119.
787. BROWN, Susan E.
"The Drive." [HolCrit] (32:1) F 95, p. 18.
788. BROWN, Tim W.
"Allegheny Storm." [SlipS] (15) 95, p. 57.
"Galena Rose." [Ledge] (18) Sum 95, p. 85.
789. BROWN-DAVIDSON, Terri
"In Cabin #9." [LitR] (38:2) Wint 95, p. 178-179.
790. BROWN-WHEELER, Karen E.
"On Looking Up at the Sistine Chapel Ceiling." [LullwaterR] (6:2) Fall-Wint 95, p. 100.
791. BROWNE, Laynie
"Behind the opening hill is foreheads' diameter etched in satin purse." [Chain] (2) Spr 95, p. 35-37.
"Rebecca Letters" (Excerpts). [Phoebe] (24:1) 95, p. 11-13.
"Rebecca Letters" (Selections). [Avec] (9) 95, p. 1-5.
792. BROWNE, Wales
"Master Craftsmen" (for S. Sontag, tr. of Sasa Skenderija). [Vis] (48) 95, p. 8.
"The Occupation in Ten Scenes" (tr. of Sasa Skenderija). [Vis] (48) 95, p. 8.
793. BROWNING, Preston
"1600" (for R. R.). [PoetryE] (41) Aut 95, p. 97.
794. BROWNING, Sarah
"The Future's What We're Really After." [SycamoreR] (7:2) Sum 95, p. 30.
795. BROWNJOHN, Alan
"Three Ways with Kites." [Epoch] (44:3) 95, p. 283.

796. BRUCE, Debra
    "Desire's Recovery." [PraS] (69:3) Fall 95, p. 77-78.
    "A Mother's Explanations" (for Kevin Lee). [CumbPR] (15:1) Fall 95, p. 13.
    "Roberta." [PraS] (69:3) Fall 95, p. 78-79.
    "Sobachka." [CumbPR] (15:1) Fall 95, p. 14-15.
797. BRUGALETTA, John J.
    "Answers to Five Important Questions Posed by the Smithsonian Institution."
    [SoCoast] (19) 95, p. 14-15.
    "The Fly." [SoCoast] (19) 95, p. 11-13.
798. BRUMARU, Emil
    "Elegy: Oh, old and familiar kitchens of summer" (tr. by Adam Sorkin and Ioana
    Ieronim). [PlumR] (9) [95 or 96], p. 22.
    "The Second Elegy of the Detective Arthur" (tr. by Adam Sorkin and Ioana Ieronim).
    [PlumR] (9) [95 or 96], p. 23.
799. BRUNNER, Jeff
    "The Flags Fly" (1942). [DefinedP] (2:2) Spr-Sum 94, p. 47.
    "Transformations." [DefinedP] (2:2) Spr-Sum 94, p. 45-46.
800. BRUSH, Thomas
    "Old Man." [PoetryNW] (36:4) Wint 95-96, p. 34-35.
801. BRUTUS, Dennis
    "Untitled: Yes, Mandela, some of us." [Drumvoices] (4:1/2) Fall-Wint 94-95, p. 18.
802. BRYAN, Helen
    "The Nomad" (WritersCorps Project, Washington, DC). [WashR] (21:2) Ag-S 95, p.
    23.
803. BRYAN, Sharon
    "Abracadabra" (for Richard Blessing). [TarRP] (35:1) Fall 95, p. 8-9.
    "Foreseeing." [TarRP] (35:1) Fall 95, p. 10-11.
    "Sweater Weather: A Love Song to Language." [TarRP] (35:1) Fall 95, p. 12.
    "This." [TarRP] (35:1) Fall 95, p. 11.
804. BUBRIN, Vladimir
    "Letter" (To Domin Ticarev & Jerko Ikin, tr. of Vinko Grubisic). [Vis] (48) 95, p. 18.
805. BUCHANAN, C. J.
    "A Hunchback's Work." [QW] (41) Aut-Wint 95-96, p. 195.
    "Ripper" (Selection: "The Prince." To W. R. Moses). [ChiR] (41:1) 95, p. 85.
806. BUCHMANN, E. Hank
    "Garden of Gethsemane" (for Mary with the Hair Down). [BellArk] (11:6) N-D 95, p.
    4.
    "Hoeing Weeds in the Garden." [BellArk] (11:5) S-O 95, p. 16.
    "Rosie and the Ragged Coast." [BellArk] (11:5) S-O 95, p. 7.
807. BUCK, Paula Closson
    "After Childbirth." [OhioR] (53) 95, p. 146-147.
808. BUCKHOLTS, Claudia
    "At the Crossroads." [ConnPR] (14:1) 95, p. 39.
    "The Bees." [ConnPR] (14:1) 95, p. 38.
809. BUCKLEY, Christopher
    "Astronomy Lesson: At Cafe Menorca." [QW] (41) Aut-Wint 95-96, p. 162.
    "Camino Cielo — Santa Barbara, California." [QW] (41) Aut-Wint 95-96, p. 160-
    161.
    "Dreaming the Clouds of 1956." [Hudson] (48:3) Aut 95, p. 431-432.
810. BUCKNER, Jill
    "Madre Dolce." [SmPd] (32:2, #94) Spr 95, p. 7.
811. BUCKNER, Sally
    "Amethyst." [Pembroke] (27) 95, p. 110.
812. BUEGE, Bill
    "The Gun." [NewYorkQ] (55) 95, p. 87-88.
813. BUFFAM, Suzanne
    "Astronomical Love" (21 Contest Winner, First). [Grain] (22:3) Wint 95, p. 34.
    "Do You Want to See the One on My Wrist?" [MalR] (111) Sum 95, p. 52.
    "I Never Looked Anything Like Farrah Fawcett." [MalR] (111) Sum 95, p. 54.
    "Imagining My Mother" (21 Contest Winner, First). [Grain] (22:3) Wint 95, p. 32-33.
    "Made-for-tv." [MalR] (111) Sum 95, p. 55.
    "Signed Poems" (21 Contest Winner, First). [Grain] (22:3) Wint 95, p. 31.
    "Wednesdays at the Kerrisdale Pool." [MalR] (111) Sum 95, p. 53.
814. BUGEJA, Michael J.
    "The Assassin of Assisi." [ClockR] (10:1/2) 95-96, p. 21.
    "Baby Talk." [PraS] (69:1) Spr 95, p. 158-159.

"Body Genetic." [SpoonR] (20:1) Wint-Spr 95, p. 16.
"Body Talk." [PraS] (69:1) Spr 95, p. 160.
"Cicadas in New Jersey." [ClockR] (10:1/2) 95-96, p. 19-20.
"Generations." [Ascent] (19:2) Wint 95, p. 46.
"I Say." [SpoonR] (20:1) Wint-Spr 95, p. 17.
"Love Talk." [PraS] (69:1) Spr 95, p. 159.
"The Revisionist: On Noah's Ark." [Harp] (289 [i.e. 290]:1736) Ja 95, p. 35.
"Sans Nature." [QW] (41) Aut-Wint 95-96, p. 202.
815. BUI-BURTON, Kim Ly
"Family." [Footwork] (24/25) 95, p. 41.
816. BUKOWSKI, Charles
"Belfast." [WorldL] (6) 95, p. 8.
"Coffee (1985)." [WormR] (35:4, #140) 95, p. 190.
"Crawl." [NewYorkQ] (54) 95, p. 35-36.
"D. April 9, 1953 (1983)." [WormR] (35:1, #137) 95, p. 45-46.
"Death Is a Good Thing." [NewYorkQ] (54) 95, p. 34.
"Fame." [NewYorkQ] (55) 95, p. 34-36.
"The Fool Dines Out (1990)." [WormR] (35:2, #138) 95, p. 94-95.
"The Good Old Days." [SlipS] (15) 95, p. 72.
"The Gym Co@ch" [sic]. [NewYorkQ] (55) 95, p. 23-24.
"Hunk of Rock." [NewYorkQ] (55) 95, p. 40-47.
"Hymn from the Hurricane of the Blinking Eye." [Bogg] (67) 95, p. 12-14.
"Interview (1983)." [WormR] (35:2, #138) 95, p. 92-93.
"The Lady in the Castle and the Lady Not in the Castle (1985)." [WormR] (35:4,
    #140) 95, p. 188-190.
"Living with the Living Dead." [NewYorkQ] (54) 95, p. 37-38.
"Lucinda." [NewYorkQ] (55) 95, p. 25-29.
"The Masses (1989." [WormR] (35:1, #137) 95, p. 47.
"Observations on Music by an Alcoholic (1984)." [WormR] (35:1, #137) 95, p. 44-
    45.
"The Replacements." [NewYorkQ] (54) 95, p. 40.
"Richard Nixon Shook My Hand." [NewYorkQ] (54) 95, p. 39.
"Rosy Ass." [SlipS] (15) 95, p. 73-74.
"Snapshot (1985)." [WormR] (35:2, #138) 95, p. 93-94.
"Strange (1990)." [WormR] (35:1, #137) 95, p. 46.
"Toenails." [WorldL] (6) 95, p. 7-8.
"The Way It Works? (1988)." [WormR] (35:4, #140) 95, p. 190.
"Working Out — Again." [NewYorkQ] (55) 95, p. 37-39.
"Writers." [NewYorkQ] (55) 95, p. 30-33.
817. BULL, Arthur
"Crest." [AntigR] (100) Wint 95, p. 120-121.
"Up in the Rockies." [AntigR] (100) Wint 95, p. 122-123.
818. BULLARD, Christopher
"Evolution." [Hellas] (6:1) Spr-Sum 95, p. 87.
819. BULLINGTON, Mary Boxley
"The Lady in the Black Mantilla." [InterPR] (21:1) Spr 95, p. 74.
820. BUMBLE, Emily
"Blue." [PoetryNW] (36:4) Wint 95-96, p. 17.
"The Turtle." [PoetryNW] (36:4) Wint 95-96, p. 16.
821. BUMSTEAD, Leslie
"Angle of the Sea" (for Rosario). [Phoebe] (24:1) 95, p. 88-89.
"A Group of People, Ambiguous and at a Gas Station." [Phoebe] (24:1) 95, p. 86-87.
"The Italian Pen" (2 poems). [Phoebe] (24:1) 95, p. 90-91.
"Red Remembering" (Excerpt). [WashR] (20:6) Ap-My 95, p. 23.
822. BUNCH, Richard Alan
"Starving Godward." [XavierR] (15:1) Spr 95, p. 63.
823. BUNDEGAARD, Christian
"Short Waves" (tr. by Poul Borum). [Pequod] (39) 95, p. 13-19.
824. BUNTING, Sarah
"The Last Cornflake." [US1] (30/31) 95, p. 27.
825. BUNZLI, James
"At My Suggestion We Leave the Highway Near Rapid City." [Pequod] (39) 95, p.
    97-98.
826. BURCH, F. F.
"Ars Pathetica." [Light] (15/16) Aut-Wint 95-96, p. 25.

827. BURGESS, Lynne
"Noah." [RagMag] (12:2) Spr 95, p. 6.
"Ophelia's Advice for the Lake." [RagMag] (12:2) Spr 95, p. 5.
"Twin." [RagMag] (12:2) Spr 95, p. 6.
"Writing Weather." [RagMag] (12:2) Spr 95, p. 7.
828. BURKARD, Michael
"The Key." [PlumR] (8) [95], p. 58-59.
"Love from a Clerk." [Sonora] (29) Spr 95, p. 110.
"The Shadow's Concept." [AmerV] (37) 95, p. 85.
"Your Sister Life." [PlumR] (8) [95], p. 56-57.
829. BURKE, Brian
"Cottonwood." [Bogg] (67) 95, p. 15.
830. BURKE, Rebecca
"Persécuteur Persécuté." [SpinningJ] (1) Fall 95-Wint 96, p. 26-27.
831. BURKHOLDER, Kristen
"4th Week." [PaintedB] (55/56) 95, p. 55.
832. BURNHAM, D. S.
"Bandstand." [VirQR] (71:2) Spr 95, p. 302-303.
"Making Sure of Arithmetic: Grades 1-6." [VirQR] (71:2) Spr 95, p. 301-302.
833. BURNHAM, Deborah
"Earrings." [Poem] (74) N 95, p. 42.
"Roadside Stand." [Poem] (74) N 95, p. 40.
"Rosa Luxemburg, Gardening." [Poem] (74) N 95, p. 41.
"The Woman Who Gave Birth to an Onion." [Poem] (74) N 95, p. 43.
834. BURNS, Elizabeth
"After All." [DenQ] (30:2) Fall 95, p. 22.
"Year of Meteors." [DenQ] (30:2) Fall 95, p. 23.
835. BURNS, Gerald
"A Church in Daylight." [AnotherCM] (29) Spr 95, p. 12-14.
"Pendant Eros." [NewAW] (13) Fall-Wint 95, p. 52-53.
836. BURNS, Michael
"Remembering a Friend at Middle Age Who Went to the Bars Alone and Danced."
[NewOR] (21:2) Sum 95, p. 96.
837. BURNS, Ralph
"The Happy Story." [GrahamHR] (19) Wint 95-96, p. 85.
"To My Father in Heaven." [GrahamHR] (19) Wint 95-96, p. 86-90.
838. BURNSIDE, John
"Agoraphobia." [NewYorker] (71:42) 25 D 95-1 Ja 96, p. 122.
"Hypothesis." [Poetry] (166:4) Jl 95, p. 198.
"A Miracle on Market Day." [Epoch] (44:3) 95, p. 269.
"The Rainbow." [Epoch] (44:3) 95, p. 275.
"The Sand Merchant's Wife." [NewYorker] (70:47) 30 Ja 95, p. 90.
"Schadenfreude." [Epoch] (44:3) 95, p. 271.
"Stockholm Syndrome." [Verse] (12:2) 95, p. 27-28.
"A Stolen Child." [Epoch] (44:3) 95, p. 270.
"Swimming in the Flood." [NewYorker] (71:35) 6 N 95, p. 128.
"A Swimming Lesson." [NewYorker] (71:25) 21-28 Ag 95, p. 108.
"The Tithe Barn." [Epoch] (44:3) 95, p. 274.
"Ukiyo-e." [NewYorker] (71:22) 31 Jl 95, p. 59.
"Washing Day, Antibes" (after James Gunn). [Agni] (42) 95, p. 15.
"Witch." [Epoch] (44:3) 95, p. 272-273.
839. BURR, Gray
"Theme." [Hellas] (6:2) Fall-Wint 95, p. 46.
840. BURRIS, Sidney
"Strong's Winter." [SouthernR] (31:1) Wint 95, p. 7-8.
841. BURROW, Christopher
"Fly-Trap." [SmPd] (32:1, #93) Wint 95, p. 30.
842. BURROWS, E. G.
"The Colly Birds." [PoetryNW] (36:4) Wint 95-96, p. 24.
"Skim Ice." [Ascent] (20:1) Fall 95, p. 54.
"Wild Dogs." [Ascent] (20:1) Fall 95, p. 55.
843. BURRS, Mick
"Reasons Why I Did Not Attend My Father's Funeral." [Grain] (23:1) Sum 95, p.
121-122.
844. BURRUS, Harry
"Migration." [RagMag] (12:2) Spr 95, p. 65.

845. BURSK, Christopher
"Annexation." [ManhatR] (8:1) Fall 95, p. 54-55.
"Does Poetry Matter?" [Poetry] (166:5) Ag 95, p. 279.
"Don't Let Go." [ManyMM] (1:3) 95, p. 57.
"Five-to-Seven Armed Robbery." [ManyMM] (1:3) 95, p. 50-51.
"Foster Child." [ManyMM] (1:3) 95, p. 54-56.
"Justice." [ManhatR] (8:1) Fall 95, p. 56-57.
"The Kingdom." [ManhatR] (7:2) Wint 95, p. 41-43.
"Light Polarized, Pored Over." [Chelsea] (59) 95, p. 44-48.
"The Missing Brother." [ManhatR] (8:1) Fall 95, p. 52-53.
"The Tramp Steamer." [ManhatR] (7:2) Wint 95, p. 40.
"The Unbreakable Chain." [ManyMM] (1:3) 95, p. 52-53.
"Usurper and Usurped." [ManhatR] (8:1) Fall 95, p. 58.
"A Way to Pass the Time." [ManhatR] (8:1) Fall 95, p. 59-60.
"Why You See So Many A's on My Class Roster" (Selections: 2, 7). [ColEng] (57:3)
    Mr 95, p. 338-340.
"You're Dead." [LullwaterR] (6:2) Fall-Wint 95, p. 56-58.
846. BURSKY, Rick
"Bone Factory Confessions." [OxfordM] (9:2) Fall-Wint 93, p. 39.
"Commandments." [IllinoisR] (3:1/2) Fall 95-Spr 96, p. 82.
"The Decisions." [IllinoisR] (3:1/2) Fall 95-Spr 96, p. 15.
"The Fall." [IllinoisR] (3:1/2) Fall 95-Spr 96, p. 23.
"Origins." [Verse] (12:2) 95, p. 29.
"Repentance." [SpoonR] (20:2) Sum-Fall 95, p. 89.
"The Splintered Voice of Wood." [SpoonR] (20:2) Sum-Fall 95, p. 90.
"They Found a Body in the Tall Milkweeds." [SpoonR] (20:2) Sum-Fall 95, p. 91.
"Three Men Sitting on the Front Steps of an Apartment House." [OxfordM] (9:2)
    Fall-Wint 93, p. 38.
847. BURT, John
"Barren Season." [WestHR] (49:4) Wint 95, p. 362-363.
"Charles Capers" (St. Helena Island, South Carolina, 1815). [ParisR] (37:134) Spr 95,
    p. 271.
"Ice Storm." [ParisR] (37:134) Spr 95, p. 272.
"Mary's Gift." [ParisR] (37:134) Spr 95, p. 272.
"Night on the *River Queen*" (Palm Sunday, 1865). [SouthernR] (31:2) Ap/Spr 95, p.
    256.
"The Phantom Arm" (for Ron Cox). [NewL] (61:3) 95, p. 78.
"What Ellen Said." [SouthernR] (31:2) Ap/Spr 95, p. 256-257.
848. BUSCH, Trent
"Treading Time" (for Kendall). [GreensboroR] (59) Wint 95-96, p. 66.
849. BUSH, Duncan
"Night. Midsummer." [Epoch] (44:3) 95, p. 302-303.
850. BUSH, Juvia
"Untitled: I went to a school full of knuckleheads" (WritersCorps Project,
    Washington, DC). [WashR] (21:2) Ag-S 95, p. 21.
851. BUSH, Lawrence
"On Sale This Week" (visual poem). [HeavenB] (12) 95, p. 84.
852. BUSHE, Paddy
"Field System, Church Island." [SouthernR] (31:3) Jl/Sum 95, p. 739-740.
853. BUSHKOWSKY, Aaron
"Halley's Comet, September 1986." [PoetryC] (15:2) Je 95, p. 13.
"Nightcap." [PoetryC] (15:2) Je 95, p. 13.
"Power Failure on the Third Planet." [PoetryC] (15:2) Je 95, p. 13.
BUSTILLO, Camilo Pérez
    See PÉREZ-BUSTILLO, Camilo
854. BUTCHER, Grace
"Announcement as if With Distant Drums." [PoetryE] (41) Aut 95, p. 108.
"Changing Gods." [PoetryE] (41) Aut 95, p. 109-110.
"The End." [PoetryE] (41) Aut 95, p. 107.
"The Wind Never Stops on the Prairie, They Say." [PoetryE] (41) Aut 95, p. 111-112.
855. BUTLER, Diana Hochstedt
"Dawn." [SantaBR] (3:1) Spr 95, p. 89.
856. BUTSON, Barry
"Long Steps." [Crucible] (30) Fall 94, p. 25.
"Sisters of the Afternoon." [Bogg] (67) 95, p. 18-19.
"Trucker's Side." [Plain] (15:2) Wint 95, p. 22.

857. BUTSON, Denver
"Some Minor Explosions." [MidAR] (16:1) 95, p. 19-20.
858. BUTTON, Margo
"Day of the Dead, Mexico." [AntigR] (102/103) Sum-Aug 95, p. 165.
"Freedom." [Dandel] (22:1) 95, p. 33.
"The Laundering." [PraF] (16:2, #71) Sum 95, p. 55.
"Passim" (Latin: here and there). [AntigR] (102/103) Sum-Aug 95, p. 166.
859. BUTTRESS, Derrick
"Traveler." [Bogg] (67) 95, p. 27.
860. BUTTS, W. E.
"In the Woods at Hills Acres." [AnthNEW] (7) 95, p. 16.
"Meditation on My Fiftieth Birthday." [DefinedP] (3) 95, p. 18.
"Sunday Evening at the Stardust Cafe." [MidAR] (15:1/2) 95, p. 224-225.
861. BYARS, Anne
"Triste" (druid sacrifice). [NorthStoneR] (12) 95, p. 30.
862. BYER, Kathryn Stripling
"Delphia." [EngJ] (84:7) N 95, p. 68.
"Full Moon." [EngJ] (84:7) N 95, p. 68.
"Snow Breath." [Shen] (45:3) Fall 95, p. 55.
"Tobacco." [Shen] (45:3) Fall 95, p. 54.
"Wild." [Shen] (45:3) Fall 95, p. 56-57.
863. BYRD, Gregory
"The Caller's Message" (For Shawna). [TampaR] (11) Fall 95, p. 32.
"Farewell to Lincoln Square." [ColEng] (57:3) Mr 95, p. 337.
864. BYRD, Sigman
"Diorama of Medieval Weather." [NewEngR] (17:4) Fall 95, p. 112.
"The Enigma of a Day" (Based on the painting by Giorgio de Chirico). [NewEngR]
(17:4) Fall 95, p. 113.
"Secrets of the Planetarium" (runner up, 1994 Borderlands Poetry Contest). [Border]
(6) Spr-Sum 95, p. 28.
"Waiting for Angels." [SouthwR] (80:4) Aut 95, p. 491-492.
865. BYRKIT, Becky
"Analogue." [Ploughs] (21:1) Spr 95, p. 35.
"Brunch at Alcatraz" (after Apollinaire). [AnotherCM] (29) Spr 95, p. 15-16.
"Narrative Suite." [BlackWR] (22:1) Fall-Wint 95, p. 136-140.
"Whoa." [Ploughs] (21:1) Spr 95, p. 34.
866. BYRNE, Edward
"Awaiting the Afternoon Rain." [SoCoast] (18) Ja 95, p. 32.
"Grace Notes" (for Alex). [CapeR] (30:2) Fall 95, p. 18-19.
"High-Ridge Road." [AlabamaLR] (9:1) 95, p. 8.
"Late Winter Lament." [TampaR] (11) Fall 95, p. 45.
"Triptych: Fly-By over the Wildlife Refuge." [FloridaR] (20:2) 95, p. 40-41.
867. BYRNE, Michelle
"Alchemy." [PoetryE] (41) Aut 95, p. 106.
"The Dead." [PoetryE] (41) Aut 95, p. 103.
"Dead Birds." [PoetryE] (41) Aut 95, p. 101-102.
"Lent." [PoetryE] (41) Aut 95, p. 104-105.
868. BYRNE, Nan
"Mothers." [CreamCR] (19:1) Spr 95, p. 126-127.
869. BYRNES, Barbara
"Perspective" (Literary Festival: Poetry: Honorable Mention). [EngJ] (84:4) Ap 95, p.
40.
870. BYRON, George Gordon, Lord
"Don Juan" (Excerpt). [Light] (13) Spr 95, p. 24.
BYRON, Lord
See BYRON, George Gordon, Lord

C., K.
See K. C.
C. RA
See RA, C.
871. CABALLERO-ROBB, Maria Elena
"Dear Homunculus." [NowestR] (33:2) 95, p. 30-31.

872. CABICO, Regie
   "Tribute: The Poet Is Shiva Isis Mothermary Neffertiti & Judy Garland." [PennR]
      (6:2) 95, p. 12.
   "You Are Not a Harry Connick Song." [PennR] (6:2) 95, p. 12.
   "You Bring Out the Writer in Me." [PennR] (6:2) 95, p. 12.
   "You Bring Out the Writer in Me: I broke up with this guy I was seeing." [PennR]
      (6:2) 95, p. 13.
873. CABIEDES-FINK, Alicia
   "XXVII. To blunt your edges" (tr. of María Fernanda Espinosa, w. Ted Maier).
      [InterPR] (21:1) Spr 95, p. 27.
   "XXX. Hopes are allowed" (tr. of María Fernanda Espinosa, w. Ted Maier). [InterPR]
      (21:1) Spr 95, p. 25.
874. CACOS, James
   "A Widow Swims from Shore." [HolCrit] (32:2) Ap 95, p. 15.
875. CADDEL, Richard
   "Hat of Darkness 'in the old manner'." [WestCL] (29:2, #17) Fall 95, p. 17.
   "Sketch for a Documentary on the Soundbite Generation." [WestCL] (29:2, #17) Fall
      95, p. 17.
   "A Struck Bell." [WestCL] (29:2, #17) Fall 95, p. 15-16.
876. CADER, Teresa
   "Empress Shotoku Invents Printing in 770." [Poetry] (166:2) My 95, p. 86-87.
   "A Legend of Paper Money." [BlackWR] (22:1) Fall-Wint 95, p. 1-2.
   "Wind, Horse, Snow." [Ploughs] (21:4) Wint 95-96, p. 32-33.
877. CADIOT, Oliver
   "Future, Ancient, Fugitive: The First Seven Pages of an Adventure Novel" (Selection:
      Part One: "The Shipwreck," tr. by Cole Swensen). [Avec] (9) 95, p. 112-118.
878. CADNUM, Michael
   "Gophers." [PoetryNW] (36:2) Sum 95, p. 26-27.
   "Homework." [PoetryNW] (36:2) Sum 95, p. 27.
   "Horizon." [SoDakR] (33:3/4) Fall-Wint 95, p. 165-166.
   "Rescue." [MidwQ] (36:3) Spr 95, p. 291.
   "Swimming Pool in the Desert." [WritersF] (21) 95, p. 74.
   "Wind." [PoetryNW] (36:2) Sum 95, p. 28.
879. CAFAGÑA, Marcus
   "The Broken World." [KenR] (17:2) Spr 95, p. 138-140.
   "Little Girl in Blue, 1918." [Ploughs] (21:1) Spr 95, p. 140.
   "Modigliani: Venus Naturalis." [HarvardR] (9) Fall 95, p. 58.
   "My Aunt Calls from Bellevue." [Thrpny] (63) Fall 95, p. 9.
880. CAI, Qijiao
   "Firefly" (tr. by Edward Morin and Chun-jian Xue). [InterQ] (2:3) 95, p. 115.
881. CAINE, Shulamith Wechter
   "Albumen Print of a Young Woman, 1890, Ogawa Isshin, Photographer." [BellR]
      (18:2, #38) Fall 95, p. 5-6.
   "Flea Market Fan." [Vis] (49) 95, p. 32.
882. CALBERT, Cathleen
   "Adam's Dream." [OhioR] (54) 95, p. 89-90.
   "After the Tragedy." [OhioR] (54) 95, p. 99-101.
   "Another Kind of Beauty" (Chapbook: 7 poems). [OhioR] (54) 95, p. 87-106.
   "Blackberry." [WestHR] (49:3) Fall 95, p. 276-278.
   "Dark Water." [WestHR] (49:3) Fall 95, p. 278-279.
   "A Lady with a Pomeranian." [PoetryNW] (36:1) Spr 95, p. 3-7.
   "The Last Angel Poem." [OhioR] (54) 95, p. 104-106.
   "Living with Monkeys." [Ploughs] (21:1) Spr 95, p. 128-129.
   "Lynda." [OhioR] (54) 95, p. 97-98.
   "A Man at the Chapel of Forgiveness." [OhioR] (54) 95, p. 95-96.
   "My Summer As a Bride." [PoetryNW] (36:1) Spr 95, p. 7-10.
   "Playhouse." [OhioR] (54) 95, p. 91-94.
   "The Vampire Cat." [OhioR] (54) 95, p. 102-103.
   "The Wonderfully Yellow Umbrella." [OhioR] (53) 95, p. 128-129.
883. CALDWELL, Beverly
   "My Soul Recognizes Its Kin." [Border] (6) Spr-Sum 95, p. 29.
884. CALDWELL, Linda
   "The Beast Without Name." [Wind] (76) Fall 95, p. 6.
885. CALL, Jennifer
   "Brood Farm." [Ascent] (19:3) Spr 95, p. 19.
   "Koroshi." [Rosebud] (2:3) Aut-Wint 95, p. 54-55.

"The Littles." [Ascent] (19:3) Spr 95, p. 18.
886. CALLAHAN, Gerald N.
    "The Whiteness of Birds." [SouthernPR] (35:2) Wint 95, p. 22-23.
    "Winter Solstice." [MidwQ] (36:4) Sum 95, p. 354-355.
    "A Winter's Solstice" (For my 46th birthday). [MidwQ] (36:3) Spr 95, p. 292-293.
887. CALLAN, Annie
    "Echo." [AntR] (53:4) Fall 95, p. 439.
    "Hope." [AntR] (53:4) Fall 95, p. 440.
888. CALLIN, Richard
    "Close to Where the Animals Gather." [MidwQ] (36:2) Wint 95, p. 151-152.
889. CALZADILLA, Juan
    "Poetics" (tr. by Mary Crow). [MidAR] (15:1/2) 95, p. 43.
890. CAMACHO, Jorge Luis
    "Body Thought." [TickleAce] (27) Spr-Sum 94, p. 11.
    "Fine Maps." [TickleAce] (27) Spr-Sum 94, p. 9.
    "Finos Mapas." [TickleAce] (27) Spr-Sum 94, p. 8.
    "I Have Spent My Life." [TickleAce] (27) Spr-Sum 94, p. 12.
    "Leaving the City." [TickleAce] (27) Spr-Sum 94, p. 13.
    "Mujer al Final de la Calle." [TickleAce] (27) Spr-Sum 94, p. 10.
    "A Paper Flying among Us." [TickleAce] (27) Spr-Sum 94, p. 7.
    "A Woman at the End of a Street." [TickleAce] (27) Spr-Sum 94, p. 10.
891. CAMBRIDGE, Richard
    "Blemish." [Footwork] (24/25) 95, p. 12.
    "Crazy Horse Malt Liquor." [DefinedP] (1:2) Spr-Sum 93, p. 28-30.
    "The Life of a Man" (For Rubin "Hurricane" Carter). [Footwork] (24/25) 95, p. 12.
    "Morning in America." [Footwork] (24/25) 95, p. 11-12.
    "Through the Window of a Train." [DefinedP] (2:2) Spr-Sum 94, p. 48-49.
892. CAMERON, Jonathan
    "The Bone." [AnthNEW] (7) 95, p. 24.
893. CAMERON, Juan
    "Cámera Oscura" (Selections: Canto 1-3, 7-8, tr. by Cola Franzen). [Noctiluca] (2:1,
        #4) Spr 95, p. 46-50.
894. CAMIRE, Dennis
    "After the Quest for Fire." [MidAR] (15:1/2) 95, p. 302.
895. CAMMER, Les
    "After i had the snake" [sic]. [WormR] (35:4, #140) 95, p. 158.
    "Becky Estrogen." [WormR] (35:4, #140) 95, p. 157.
    "Dropped my multicolor pen and." [WormR] (35:4, #140) 95, p. 157.
    "The Gang." [WormR] (35:4, #140) 95, p. 157.
    "Have big donothing plans going." [WormR] (35:4, #140) 95, p. 158.
    "He doesnt like me calling him by his last name but" [sic]. [WormR] (35:4, #140) 95,
        p. 157.
    "I had snipers on the rooftops." [WormR] (35:4, #140) 95, p. 158.
    "I put the body in reverse." [WormR] (35:4, #140) 95, p. 158.
    "I remember the most beautiful." [WormR] (35:4, #140) 95, p. 158.
    "Ive been sending you morning poems" [sic]. [WormR] (35:4, #140) 95, p. 157.
    "Miss Indecisive." [WormR] (35:4, #140) 95, p. 157.
    "Of the Door." [WormR] (35:4, #140) 95, p. 157.
    "People equate silence with something." [WormR] (35:4, #140) 95, p. 158.
    "The Waitress." [WormR] (35:4, #140) 95, p. 158.
896. CAMPBELL, Carolyn
    "The Facts of Life." [ManyMM] (2:1) 95, p. 130.
    "The Woman from the Barrio." [ManyMM] (2:1) 95, p. 131.
897. CAMPBELL, Carolyn E.
    "Las Momias." [Ledge] (19) Wint 95, p. 111-112.
    "Tattooed Woman." [Kalliope] (17:2) 95, p. 17-18.
    "Tattooed Woman." [Ledge] (19) Wint 95, p. 109-110.
898. CAMPBELL, David
    "Hirokoji Plaza, a Print by Hiroshige." [BelPoJ] (46:1) Fall 95, p. 5.
899. CAMPBELL, Mary Baine
    "The Kiss." [SouthwR] (80:4) Aut 95, p. 446.
    "The Shock." [SouthwR] (80:4) Aut 95, p. 446-447.
900. CAMPBELL, Mary Belle
    "Bill Stafford, a Man for All Regions (1914-1993)." [Pembroke] (27) 95, p. 103.
901. CAMPBELL, Rick
    "Quitting Time." [SouthernPR] (35:1) Sum 95, p. 9.

902. CAMPBELL, Robert
    "An Expected Guest." [Atlantic] (275:6) Je 95, p. 58.
903. CAMPBELL, Susan Maxwell
    "Filling the Icon." [ChrC] (112:12) 12 Ap 95, p. 389.
904. CAMPION, Dan
    "Admonitions." [Poetry] (167:3) D 95, p. 143.
    "Clean, Well-Lighted." [Light] (15/16) Aut-Wint 95-96, p. 22.
    "Engagement." [Light] (14) Sum 95, p. 16.
    "Going Home." [IllinoisR] (3:1/2) Fall 95-Spr 96, p. 34-36.
    "Interference." [Flyway] (1:1) Spr 95, p. 16.
    "The Poems Escape." [Ascent] (19:2) Wint 95, p. 47.
    "Tables." [Ascent] (19:2) Wint 95, p. 27.
905. CAMPO, Rafael
    "El Día de los Muertos." [Thrpny] (62) Sum 95, p. 11.
    "My Childhood in Another Part of the World." [AmerV] (38) 95, p. 63.
    "Nobody Knows I'm Queer." [Zyzzyva] (11:1, #41) Spr 95, p. 168.
    "Prescription." [Zyzzyva] (11:1, #41) Spr 95, p. 169.
CAMPOS, Alvaro de
    See PESSOA, Fernando
906. CANCINO, Jorge
    "436" (tr. by Luciano P. Díaz). [Arc] (35) Aut 95, p. 10.
    "Eyemetrics" (tr. by Luciano P. Díaz). [Arc] (35) Aut 95, p. 8.
    "Rambling of the Poet" (tr. by Luciano P. Díaz). [Arc] (35) Aut 95, p. 9.
907. CANDLAND, Lara
    "Apres Maman." [SantaBR] (3:1) Spr 95, p. 100.
    "One More Long Poem" (to Eva). [SantaBR] (3:1) Spr 95, p. 101.
908. CANFIELD, Elizabeth
    "Bereavement." [GreenHLL] (6) 95, p. 40.
909. CANNON, Harold (Harold C.)
    "On the banks of the fair Susquehannah." [Light] (14) Sum 95, p. 24.
    "The River Zambesi" (Honorable Mention, 3rd Annual River Rhyme Competition).
        [Light] (13) Spr 95, p. 24.
910. CANNON, Melissa
    "Coppertone Riviera." [Bogg] (67) 95, p. 54.
    "Grandma to Little Red." [KenR] (17:1) Wint 95, p. 22.
    "Imagine Danger." [KenR] (17:1) Wint 95, p. 23-24.
911. CANNON, Moya
    "Viol." [Poetry] (167:1/2) O-N 95, p. 26.
    "Viola d'Amore." [Poetry] (167:1/2) O-N 95, p. 26.
912. CANNON, William
    "Accepting Tribute." [CumbPR] (14:2) Spr 95, p. 51-52.
    "The Courthouse Square." [SilverFR] (25) Sum 95, p. 18-19.
    "Fences." [CumbPR] (14:2) Spr 95, p. 53-54.
    "In My Dream." [PoetL] (90:2) Sum 95, p. 15.
    "Loneliness: Some Variations" (for my mother). [CumbPR] (14:2) Spr 95, p. 50.
    "September." [PoetL] (90:2) Sum 95, p. 13-14.
    "Tending the Holy Bond of Matrimony." [SilverFR] (25) Sum 95, p. 17.
913. CANTALUPO, Charles
    "Fort of Grain." [Os] (41) 95, p. 32-33.
CANTO, Carol B. de
    See DeCANTO, Carol B.
914. CANTON, Dário
    "Domestic Animals" (from "Animales Domésticos V. Sus Límites," tr. by D. M.
        Stroud). [Noctiluca] (2:1, #4) Spr 95, p. 55.
    "Innocents" (from "Infantiles," tr. by D. M. Stroud). [Noctiluca] (2:1, #4) Spr 95, p.
        53.
    "A Stroll through the Park" (from "Parques y Paseos," tr. by D. M. Stroud).
        [Noctiluca] (2:1, #4) Spr 95, p. 54.
915. CANTWELL, Kevin
    "Adam and Eve." [ParisR] (37:134) Spr 95, p. 118.
    "Advent Day at Mumford Quarry Nursery." [ParisR] (37:134) Spr 95, p. 118.
    "History." [TarRP] (34:2) Spr 95, p. 31.
916. CAPELLO, Phyllis
    "Demeter's Undoing." [Footwork] (24/25) 95, p. 65.
    "The Habit of Nature" (For J.G.). [Footwork] (24/25) 95, p. 64.
    "How Women Get to Hell." [Footwork] (24/25) 95, p. 64-65.

917. CAPPELLO, Mary
    "To My Grandmother." [Footwork] (24/25) 95, p. 56.
918. CAPPELLO, Rosemary
    "My Mother's Insomnia." [Pearl] (22) Fall-Wint 95, p. 150.
    "My Mother's Scars and Pains." [Pearl] (22) Fall-Wint 95, p. 151.
919. CAPRON, Richard
    "At the End." [Footwork] (24/25) 95, p. 143.
CARBEAU, Mitchell Les
    See LesCARBEAU, Mitchell
920. CARCAMO, Luis Ernesto
    "Vejez de Heroina." [Americas] (23:3/4) Fall-Wint 95, p. 124.
    "La Voz de los 80" (a partir de "Los Prisioneros"). [Americas] (23:3/4) Fall-Wint 95,
        p. 126.
    "Ya No Es Tiempo de Héroes." [Americas] (23:3/4) Fall-Wint 95, p. 125.
921. CARDEA, Caryatis
    "Falling Trees." [SinW] (55) Spr-Sum 95, p. 85-93.
922. CARDENAL, Ernesto
    "Prayer for Marilyn Monroe" (tr. by Samuel Tieman). [RiverS] (42/43) 95, p. 172 -
        173.
923. CARDILLO, Joe
    "All of the Days and Nights Ahead." [BellArk] (11:2) Mr-Ap 95, p. 11.
    "Aloneness." [BellArk] (11:3) My-Je 95, p. 13.
    "Among Women." [BellArk] (11:2) Mr-Ap 95, p. 11.
    "Antidote." [BellArk] (11:2) Mr-Ap 95, p. 11.
    "At 2 P.M. or So." [BellArk] (11:3) My-Je 95, p. 8.
    "Cidery Kisses." [BellArk] (11:2) Mr-Ap 95, p. 11.
    "During the Fall, You'd Better Know." [BellArk] (11:2) Mr-Ap 95, p. 11.
    "Fleetingly Thin." [BellArk] (11:2) Mr-Ap 95, p. 11.
    "The Kingdom." [BellArk] (11:2) Mr-Ap 95, p. 11.
    "Making Love." [BellArk] (11:2) Mr-Ap 95, p. 11.
    "Stillness." [BellArk] (11:3) My-Je 95, p. 13.
924. CAREY, Michael
    "Ash." [LaurelR] (29:1) Wint 95, p. 36-37.
    "To a Blooming Blackberry." [ChrC] (112:24) 16-23 Ag 95, p. 764.
925. CAREY, Tom
    "Original Sin." [NewAW] (13) Fall-Wint 95, p. 123-124.
926. CARGILE, Jean
    "How Much Does It Take to Build a House?" (tr. of Fernando Operé). [InterPR]
        (21:1) Spr 95, p. 23.
927. CARIAGA, Catalina
    "His Civil Rights." [Chain] (2) Spr 95, p. 47-61.
928. CARIOU, Warren
    "Heartspoon" (For G.). [Grain] (23:1) Sum 95, p. 90.
929. CARLIN, Patricia
    "In the Shadow of the Parthenon." [AmerLC] (7) 95, p. 108-109.
930. CARLOS (D.C. Center for Alcohol and Drug Abuse, Washington, DC)
    "The Couch of Past, Present and Future" (WritersCorps Program). [WashR] (21:2)
        Ag-S 95, p. 5.
931. CARLSEN, Ioanna
    "Japanese Women and Rain." [Chelsea] (58) 95, p. 132-133.
    "Shoes." [Chelsea] (58) 95, p. 133-134.
932. CARLSON, Barbara Siegel
    "Angel Voices." [Flyway] (1:2) Fall 95, p. 52.
    "Applesauce." [PraS] (69:4) Wint 95, p. 105.
    "Between This Quivering." [PraS] (69:4) Wint 95, p. 106.
933. CARLSON, Michael
    "Blueberry Eyes" (Franz Kline). [GrandS] (14:2, #54) Fall 95, p. 64-65.
    "Torches Mauve" (Franz Kline). [GrandS] (14:2, #54) Fall 95, p. 63.
934. CARLSON, Nancy Naomi
    "At Curfew." [LullwaterR] (6:1) Spr-Sum 95, p. 60-61.
935. CARLSON, R. S.
    "Moel River Question." [BlackBR] (21) Fall-Wint 95, p. 28.
936. CARMEN, Marilyn Elain
    "Aunt Marge You Can Still Dream of Horses." [Parting] (8:2) Wint 95-96, p. 36.

"For My Grandmother Who Was Committed to the Harriburg State Hospital When She Was Ninety by Her Two Daughters Margaret and Myrtle, My Aunts." [13thMoon] (13:1/2) 95, p. 10.

"I Hung the First Medicine Wheel for You Grandmother." [Footwork] (24/25) 95, p. 38.

937. CARMI, T.
"Deep in Her Dream" (tr. by Tsipi Keller and the author). [SenR] (25:2) Fall 95, p. 75.

"An Explosion in Jerusalem" (tr. by Tsipi Keller and the author). [SenR] (25:2) Fall 95, p. 73.

"If It So Pleases" (tr. by Tsipi Keller). [GrahamHR] (19) Wint 95-96, p. 72.

"In Memory of Dan Pagis (1930-1986)" (tr. by Tsipi Keller and the author). [SenR] (25:2) Fall 95, p. 76-79.

"Monologue in the Twilight of His Life" (tr. by Tsipi Keller and the author). [SenR] (25:2) Fall 95, p. 72.

"Monologue to the Child of His Old Age" (for Michael, tr. by Tsipi Keller). [GrahamHR] (19) Wint 95-96, p. 74-75.

"Mortification of the Soul" (Ein Hod, 1990, tr. by Tsipi Keller). [GrahamHR] (19) Wint 95-96, p. 76.

"Mourner's Monologue" (tr. by Tsipi Keller and the author). [SenR] (25:2) Fall 95, p. 74.

"The Mouth" (tr. by Tsipi Keller). [GrahamHR] (19) Wint 95-96, p. 73.

"A Time for Everything" (tr. by Tsipi Keller). [GrahamHR] (19) Wint 95-96, p. 77-78.

938. CARNECI, Magda
"The Blood Which Comes" (tr. by Adam J. Sorkin, w. the author). [Vis] (48) 95, p. 38.

"Instancy" (tr. by Adam J. Sorkin, w. the author). [Vis] (48) 95, p. 38.

"Wheel, Ruby and Vortex" (tr. by Adam J. Sorkin, w. the author). [Vis] (48) 95, p. 39.

939. CARNEY, Rob
"Cain Guts the Fatted Calf." [QW] (40) Spr-Sum 95, p. 57.

"Now Hiring Sphinxes for Border Patrol. Must Be Willing to Relocate." [PoetryNW] (36:4) Wint 95-96, p. 37-38.

"Wanted: Scarecrows, Haystacks and Mannequins encouraged to Apply." [PoetryNW] (36:4) Wint 95-96, p. 36-37.

"We've Read Your Application. Please Sit Down." [PoetryNW] (36:3) Aut 95, p. 3-4.

940. CARPATHIOS, Neil
"Yia Yia." [Ledge] (18) Sum 95, p. 49.

941. CARPENTER, Carol
"The Shopping Bag Lady." [SantaBR] (3:2) Sum 95, p. 104.

"Tea Party." [SantaBR] (3:2) Sum 95, p. 103.

"Their Marriage Album." [LouisL] (12:1) Spr 95, p. 53-54.

942. CARPENTER, David
"February." [Grain] (23:1) Sum 95, p. 16-17.

943. CARPENTER, Linda
"The Therapist." [Event] (24:1) Spr 95, p. 20-21.

944. CARPENTER, Mary Elizabeth
"Agating." [NorthStoneR] (12) 95, p. 67.

945. CARR, John
"Waking Up on a Sheep Island." [TexasR] (16:1/4) 95, p. 109.

"We Will Sleep Together Again." [TexasR] (16:1/4) 95, p. 110.

946. CARR, Julie
"Andy's Accident." [GreensboroR] (58) Sum 95, p. 128-129.

947. CARRIES-LEMAIRE, Emmelyne
"Hymn" (tr. by Gina Dorcely). [CaribbeanW] (9) 95, p. 99.

"Ode to Bolivar" (tr. by Gina Dorcely). [CaribbeanW] (9) 95, p. 95-99.

"Without Peace" (tr. by Gina Dorcely). [CaribbeanW] (9) 95, p. 101.

"Your Song Is Immortal" (tr. by Gina Dorcely). [CaribbeanW] (9) 95, p. 100.

948. CARRILLO, Albino
"Downpour." [MidwQ] (36:2) Wint 95, p. 153-154.

949. CARRILLO, Laura
"For Antiquity." [MidAR] (15:1/2) 95, p. 303-304.

950. CARROLL, Amy
"Life." [Border] (7) Fall-Wint 96, p. 5.

951. CARROLL, Angelica
    "I'm Bad" (WritersCorps Project, Washington, DC). [WashR] (21:2) Ag-S 95, p. 22.
952. CARROLL, Lewis
    "Poeta Fit, Non Nascitur" (Excerpt). [Light] (14) Sum 95, p. 24.
953. CARRUTH, Hayden
    "Mort Aux Belges!" [GreenMR] (8:1) Spr-Sum 95, p. 50.
    "Old Man's Sleep" (for James Laughlin). [GrahamHR] (19) Wint 95-96, p. 11.
    "Prepare." [GrahamHR] (19) Wint 95-96, p. 9-10.
    "Renaissance." [SenR] (25:1) Spr 95, p. 100-101.
    "Saturday at the Border." [Atlantic] (275:6) Je 95, p. 90.
954. CARSON, Anne
    "Shoes: An Essay on How Plato's *Symposium* Begins." [Iowa] (25:2) Spr-Sum 95, p.
    47-51.
    "TV Men: Hektor." [Raritan] (15:2) Fall 95, p. 62-70.
955. CARSON, Ciaran
    "Eesti." [Poetry] (167:1/2) O-N 95, p. 18-19.
    "Jacta Est Alea." [Poetry] (167:1/2) O-N 95, p. 20.
    "The Riddle of the Sands." [SouthernR] (31:3) Jl/Sum 95, p. 531-535.
    "The Swing" (tr. of Liam O Muirthile). [Poetry] (167:1/2) O-N 95, p. 69.
    "Vox et Praeterea Nihil." [Poetry] (167:1/2) O-N 95, p. 21.
956. CARTER, Anne Babson
    "Greed in Potters Field." [Nat] (258:12) 28 Mr 94, p. 428.
957. CARTER, Jared
    "Buzzards." [Hellas] (6:1) Spr-Sum 95, p. 95.
    "Hawkmoth." [Poetry] (166:2) My 95, p. 85.
    "Summons." [LaurelR] (29:2) Sum 95, p. 18.
958. CARTER, Laton
    "Alone." [WormR] (35:4, #140) 95, p. 180.
    "The Geese." [WormR] (35:4, #140) 95, p. 179.
    "The Girlfriend." [WormR] (35:4, #140) 95, p. 179.
959. CARTER, Steve
    "Classic." [WindO] (59) Spr 95, p. 9.
    "Sheherazade." [HayF] (17) Fall-Wint 95, p. 87.
    "Summer Job." [Plain] (15:3) Spr 95, p. 15.
CARTERET, Mark de
    See DeCARTERET, Mark
960. CARTLEDGE, Phyllis
    "Alien Ducks." [SoCoast] (18) Ja 95, p. 33.
961. CARVALHO, Marie J.
    "Begin Again." [HighP] (10:1) Spr 95, p. 38-39.
    "Bone Chant." [HighP] (10:1) Spr 95, p. 40-43.
    "For Grandma." [HighP] (10:1) Spr 95, p. 47-49.
    "Loco." [HighP] (10:1) Spr 95, p. 52-53.
    "Mother." [HighP] (10:1) Spr 95, p. 44-46.
    "Sticks and Stones." [HighP] (10:1) Spr 95, p. 50-51.
962. CARVER, Raymond
    "The Gift" (for Tess). [SenR] (25:1) Spr 95, p. 59-60.
963. CASE, David Allen
    "Logic." [CarolQ] (47:2) Wint 95, p. 83-84.
964. CASEY, Crysta
    "6:01." [BellArk] (11:4) Jl-Ag 95, p. 23.
    "Ballard Locks." [BellArk] (11:4) Jl-Ag 95, p. 23.
    "Karen." [BellArk] (11:4) Jl-Ag 95, p. 23.
    "Thirst." [BellArk] (11:4) Jl-Ag 95, p. 23.
965. CASEY, Deb
    "Boat." [KenR] (17:1) Wint 95, p. 124-126.
966. CASEY, Michael
    "Terminator." [HarvardR] (8) Spr 95, p. 117.
967. CASEY, Susan
    "Meeting My Grandfather in Heaven." [ManyMM] (1:2) 95, p. 17.
968. CASH, Eric
    "An End to Things." [Plain] (15:2) Wint 95, p. 23.
969. CASPERSON, Mylee
    "Sharpened by the Cement." [LowellR] (1) Sum 94, p. 71.
970. CASSELMAN, Barry
    "Cities of Umbrellas." [NorthStoneR] (12) 95, p. 202-2-3.

"Why Ask Where the Basques Come From?" [NorthStoneR] (12) 95, p. 204.
971. CASSIAN, Nina
     "On an Old Theme" (tr. by Dana Gioia). [Verse] (12:2) 95, p. 30.
972. CASSITY, Turner
     "Across the River and into the Sleaze." [YaleR] (83:3) Jl 95, p. 124-125.
     "Astrology in the Sahara Zagora." [Shen] (45:3) Fall 95, p. 70.
     "Christ of the Andes." [Poetry] (166:2) My 95, p. 79.
     "Days of Labor." [GreensboroR] (57) Wint 94-95, p. 38-39.
     "Neckties." [LullwaterR] (5:2) Fall-Wint 94, p. 73.
     "Oued Draa." [Shen] (45:3) Fall 95, p. 71.
     "A Word from Isobel." [Poetry] (165:5) F 95, p. 281.
973. CASTELLANOS, Luis
     "Tribute" (WritersCorps Program, Washington, DC). [WashR] (21:2) Ag-S 95, p. 17.
974. CASTILLO, Ana
     "El Chicle." [MassR] (36:4) Wint 95-96, p. 597.
975. CASTILLO, Orestes del
     "Let's jump through the magic crystal hat." [TickleAce] (27) Spr-Sum 94, p. 58.
976. CASTLE, Joanne
     "Gnawing." [Bogg] (67) 95, p. 34.
977. CASTLEBURY, John
     "1500 Tabloids on 38# Electrobrite." [PottPort] (16:1) Fall 95, p. 57.
     "Fossiling." [PottPort] (16:1) Fall 95, p. 56.
978. CASTON, Anne
     "Anatomy." [NewYorkQ] (54) 95, p. 96-98.
979. CASTON, Shanta
     "Appear Disappear" (WritersCorps Project, Washington, DC). [WashR] (21:2) Ag-S
     95, p. 22.
980. CASTRO, Michael
     "Chemayo." [Noctiluca] (2:1, #4) Spr 95, p. 27-29.
     "Lizard's Tales" (Excerpt). [RiverS] (42/43) 95, p. 5.
981. CATACALOS, Rosemary
     "Borderline: Brownsville / Matamoros" (for Oscar Ramírez). [SouthwR] (80:4) Aut
     95, p. 445.
982. CATALANO, Gary
     "Calendar." [PoetryC] (15:3) Ag 95, p. 20.
     "Description." [PoetryC] (15:3) Ag 95, p. 20.
     "Silhouette." [PoetryC] (15:3) Ag 95, p. 20.
983. CATALFAMO, Antonio
     "Analogie." [Arshile] (4) 95, p. 64.
     "Analogy" (tr. by Mark Salerno). [Arshile] (4) 95, p. 65.
     "Chronicles" (tr. by Mark Salerno). [Arshile] (4) 95, p. 67.
     "Cronache." [Arshile] (4) 95, p. 66.
     "Genealogia." [Arshile] (4) 95, p. 60.
     "Genealogy" (tr. by Mark Salerno). [Arshile] (4) 95, p. 61.
     "Passato e Presente." [Arshile] (4) 95, p. 62.
     "Past and Present" (tr. by Mark Salerno). [Arshile] (4) 95, p. 63.
     "Secrets" (tr. by Mark Salerno). [Arshile] (4) 95, p. 59.
     "Segreti." [Arshile] (4) 95, p. 58.
984. CATES, Ed
     "Housework" (tr. of Julian Tuwim). [Noctiluca] (2:1, #4) Spr 95, p. 5.
     "Quiet Storm" (tr. of Julian Tuwim). [Noctiluca] (2:1, #4) Spr 95, p. 6.
985. CATHERWOOD, Michael
     "Divorced and Leaving on Interstate 80." [MidwQ] (36:4) Sum 95, p. 356.
     "Running the Bulldozer at the State Street Dump." [Border] (6) Spr-Sum 95, p. 30.
986. CATLIN, Alan
     "I've Got a Friend Who." [SlipS] (15) 95, p. 23-24.
987. CATULLUS (ca. 84-54 BCE)
     "My woman says she'd rather have me" (tr. by Sam Hamill). [PoetryE] (41) Aut 95, p.
     14.
988. CAUFIELD, Michael
     "A Straight Angle until You Leave the Plane." [SantaBR] (3:2) Sum 95, p. 74.
989. CAUFIELD, Tom
     "Chicago, April 1994." [WormR] (35:4, #140) 95, p. 182.
     "Easter Sunday, 1994." [WormR] (35:4, #140) 95, p. 181-182.
     "Smitty, 2." [WormR] (35:4, #140) 95, p. 182-183.

990. CAUGHEY, Mark
"The Fore River Bridge." [WestHR] (49:3) Fall 95, p. 225.
"Rebuilding the Hold" (The Old Ship Church, Hingham — erected 1681). [WestHR] (49:3) Fall 95, p. 226-227.

991. CAULFIELD, Carlota
"Letter from a Virgin of the Sun to Her Lover" (For Abraham). [TexasR] (16:1/4) 95, p. 111.

992. CAUTHEN, Randy
"Driving Through." [SpinningJ] (1) Fall 95-Wint 96, p. 42.
"Near Phoenix." [SpinningJ] (1) Fall 95-Wint 96, p. 43.

993. CAVANAUGH, Bill
"Ulysses in the Drug Store." [HopewellR] (7) 95, p. 89-90.

994. CAVANAUGH, Susan
"Migration" (Third Place, Second Annual Poetry Contest). [PaintedB] (55/56) 95, p. 39-40.
"What the Gypsy Won't Tell You" (Third Place, Second Annual Poetry Contest). [PaintedB] (55/56) 95, p. 41-42.

995. CAVOUR, Renato
"Manifesto" (tr. of Andres Gottlieb, w. Stanley H. Barkan). [Footwork] (24/25) 95, p. 210.

996. CAYER, J.
"Kyrie at Caldor." [SouthernPR] (35:2) Wint 95, p. 31-32.

997. CAYLE
"Returning Home" (The 1994 Allen Ginsberg Poetry Awards: Honorable Mention). [Footwork] (24/25) 95, p. 187-189.

998. CECIL, Richard
"Arrow." [Crazy] (49) Wint 95, p. 55-56.
"Caliban and Ariel." [AmerPoR] (24:6) N-D 95, p. 23.
"The Education of a Professor." [Crazy] (49) Wint 95, p. 59-62.
"In the Fall When Everything's Dying." [BellR] (18:1, #37) Spr 95, p. 31.
"Incident at Third and Woodlawn." [AmerS] (64:2) Spr 95, p. 204-205.
"Lines Written in a Subjunctive Mood." [PoetryE] (39) Fall 94, p. 18-20.
"Living in Obscurity." [HopewellR] (7) 95, p. 91-92.
"A Portrait of the Artist's Bedroom." [Crazy] (49) Wint 95, p. 57-58.
"The Thinkers." [NewEngR] (17:2) Spr 95, p. 122-123.

999. CEDERING, Siv
"Skimming the Surface." [CumbPR] (15:1) Fall 95, p. 16-17.
"Sunday Traveler" (For William Stafford, in 1968). [Elf] (5:4) Wint 95, p. 7.

1000. CEFOLA, Ann
"Rosary Beads the Size of Baseballs." [Vis] (47) 95, p. 21.

1001. CELAYA, Gabriel
"44. The moon passes like a chill between the marble statues" (tr. by Martin Paul and José Elgorriaga). [QW] (41) Aut-Wint 95-96, p. 204.

1002. CENTOLELLA, Thomas
"The Raptors." [Ploughs] (21:1) Spr 95, p. 136-137.

1003. CERVANTES, Lorna Dee
"Archeology." [ManyMM] [1:1] D 94, p. 85.
"First Beating." [ManyMM] [1:1] D 94, p. 86.

1004. CESARIC, Dobrisa
"Fruit Tree, After a Rain" (tr. by P. H. Liotta). [Vis] (48) 95, p. 16.

1005. CETRANO, Sal
"Behold, the Sad Mind Wanders." [Wind] (76) Fall 95, p. 7.

1006. CHACE, Joel
"Barbershop Dialectic." [SpinningJ] (1) Fall 95-Wint 96, p. 35.
"Barbershop Etiquette." [SpinningJ] (1) Fall 95-Wint 96, p. 33.
"Hair Greek." [SpinningJ] (1) Fall 95-Wint 96, p. 34.
"Politics." [SpinningJ] (1) Fall 95-Wint 96, p. 32.

1007. CHADWICK, Cydney
"Confessions of a Noun." [IllinoisR] (3:1/2) Fall 95-Spr 96, p. 107.
"Respite." [WashR] (21:3) O-N 95, p. 25.

1008. CHALLENDER, Craig
"Winter Inventory" (for William Stafford). [MidwQ] (37:1) Aut 95, p. 36.

1009. CHALMER, Judith
"Dolls and Rags." [Footwork] (24/25) 95, p. 141-142.
"Sammy the *Goniff*." [Footwork] (24/25) 95, p. 141.

97

1010. CHAMBERLAIN, Cara
"The Soul, If Such a Thing Exists." [Jacaranda] (11) [95 or 96?], p. 84-85.
1011. CHAMBERLAIN, Karen
"Ephedra." [Orion] (14:1) Wint 95, p. 13.
"Riding the Lion, Riding the Lamb." [DenQ] (29:3) Wint 95, p. 7.
1012. CHAMORRO, Margarita
"I'm a Flower" (WritersCorps Program, Washington, DC). [WashR] (21:2) Ag-S 95,
p. 12.
"Soy una Flor" (WritersCorps Program, Washington, DC). [WashR] (21:2) Ag-S 95,
p. 12.
1013. CHAMPION, Miles
"Finishing Touches." [WestCL] (29:2, #17) Fall 95, p. 18.
"Forensic Asperities Docking." [WestCL] (29:2, #17) Fall 95, p. 20.
"Overlay." [WestCL] (29:2, #17) Fall 95, p. 19.
1014. CHANDLER, Tom
"Average Masterpiece." [Poetry] (166:5) Ag 95, p. 257.
"Champagne." [Poetry] (166:5) Ag 95, p. 261.
"Florida." [BellR] (18:1, #37) Spr 95, p. 50.
"My Grandfather's Closet." [OxfordM] (10:1) Wint 94-Spr 95, p. 12.
"Night Hike on Ballston Beach." [FloridaR] (21:1) 95, p. 25.
"Selling Door to Door." [Poetry] (166:5) Ag 95, p. 258.
"Tales of the Temporary Dead." [LitR] (38:2) Wint 95, p. 209.
1015. CHANDRA, G. S. Sharat
"After the Earthquake in India" (30 September 1993). [WeberS] (12:2) Spr-Sum 95,
p. 53.
"Overland Park, KS." [MidwQ] (36:4) Sum 95, p. 357-358.
1016. CHANEY, Joseph
"The Eclipse." [Nat] (260:22) 5 Je 95, p. 807.
"The Ends of Indolence." [Poem] (74) N 95, p. 13.
"The Work of the Lover." [Poem] (74) N 95, p. 14.
1017. CHANG, Garam C. C.
"I bow down to all holy Gurus" (tr. of Milarepa, Tibetan yogi, 1025-1135).
[Tricycle] (4:3, #15) Spr 95, p. 71.
CHANG, Soo Ko
See KO, Chang Soo
1018. CHANSKY, Ricia Anne
"The Cafe Venus." [ManyMM] (1:3) 95, p. 74.
"Memories." [SpinningJ] (1) Fall 95-Wint 96, p. 30.
1019. CHAPIN, Earl W.
"January the Something." [MassR] (36:2) Sum 95, p. 239.
1020. CHAPMAN, Rita Rouvalis
"Rio." [BlackBR] (21) Fall-Wint 95, p. 26.
1021. CHAPMAN, Robin (Robin S.)
"Camp Emmaeus." [Nimrod] (39:1) Fall-Wint 95, p. 122.
"Flamingos Bathing." [GreenMR] (8:2) Fall-Wint 95-96, p. 69.
"Laps." [PoetryE] (41) Aut 95, p. 56.
"Late." [PassN] (16:1) Sum 95, p. 15.
"Surabaya." [Iowa] (25:1) Wint 95, p. 56.
1022. CHAPPELL, Fred
"Epilogue to *Spring Garden*." [Image] (10) Sum 95, p. 63-67.
"Ode: 'Ma Douce Jouvance Est Passée'" (tr. of Pierre de Ronsard). [DefinedP] (2:2)
Spr-Sum 94, p. 39.
1023. CHAR, René
"For a Saxifrage Prometheus on Touching the Aeolian Hand of Hölderlin" (to
Denise Naville, tr. by Susanne Dubroff). [Image] (11) Fall 95, p. 33-34.
"Just as" (tr. by Susanne Dubroff). [Image] (11) Fall 95, p. 33.
"To ...." (tr. by Susanne Dubroff). [HarvardR] (9) Fall 95, p. 66.
"Vertical Village" (tr. by Susanne Dubroff). [HampSPR] Wint 95, p. 38.
1024. CHARACH, Ron
"Last Night in Srebrinica." [PraF] (16:4, #73) Wint 95-96, p. 111.
1025. CHARARA, Hayan
"Ashes." [HangL] (67) 95, p. 21-22.
"Half Dead." [HangL] (67) 95, p. 19-20.
"Holy Water." [HangL] (67) 95, p. 18.

98

1026. CHAREN
"Alphonso through the Ages" (tr. by the author and Peter Michelson). [ManyMM]
(2:1) 95, p. 94.
"Dear Brother Vimaladas" (tr. by the author and Marilyn Krysl). [ManyMM] (2:1)
95, p. 91.
"In the Name of Buddha" (tr. by the author and Peter Michelson). [ManyMM] (2:1)
95, p. 95.
"Negation of the Negation" (tr. by the author and Peter Michelson). [ManyMM]
(2:1) 95, p. 96.
"Resurrection" (tr. by the author and Marilyn Krysl). [ManyMM] (2:1) 95, p. 92.
"What I Might Forget" (tr. by the author and Peter Michelson). [ManyMM] (2:1) 95,
p. 93.
CHARME, Mark du
See DuCHARME, Mark
1027. CHASE, Aleka
"Departure." [RiverC] (15:2) Sum 95, p. 120.
1028. CHASE, Karen
"Venison." [NewYorker] (71:38) 27 N 95, p. 49.
1029. CHASKEY, Scott
"Dyas." [NewMyths] (2:2/3:1) 95, p. 220.
"Ode 10." [NewMyths] (2:2/3:1) 95, p. 219.
1030. CHATMAN, Lawan
"Untitled: All alone in my room staring at the wall" (w. Natasha Norris and Tene'
Lewis. WritersCorps Program, Washington, DC). [WashR] (21:2) Ag-S 95, p.
16.
1031. CHATTIGRÉ, J. Blue
"The Labor of Stones." [HayF] (17) Fall-Wint 95, p. 86.
1032. CHEEK, Chris
"Fogs" (Excerpt). [WestCL] (29:2, #17) Fall 95, p. 21-25.
CHEN, Gu
See GU, Chen
1033. CHEN, Lisa
"A Body Standard." [CreamCR] (19:1) Spr 95, p. 129.
1034. CHEN, Yanbing
"As I Know It" (tr. of Bei Dao, w. John Rosenwald). [BelPoJ] (46:2) Wint 95-96, p.
38-39.
"Untitled: People hurry, arrive" (tr. of Bei Dao, w. John Rosenwald). [BelPoJ]
(46:2) Wint 95-96, p. 40.
1035. CHENG, Baolin
"Public Monologue" (In memoriam: Ezra Pound, tr. of O-Yiang Jianghe Chengdu,
w. Richard Terrill). [PassN] (16:1) Sum 95, p. 11.
1036. CHENG, Boey Kim
"A child is a house that parents inhabit" (tr. of Helena Sinervo, w. the author).
[InterPR] (21:2) Fall 95, p. 63.
1037. CHENG, Fu
"Freedom's Good" (tr. by J. P. Seaton). [LitR] (38:3) Spr 95, p. 325.
CHENGDU, O-Yiang Jianghe
See O-YIANG JIANGHE CHENGDU
1038. CHEREVCHENKO, A.
"Taugal'u?" (tr. of Zoya Nenlyumkina, w. Adele Barker). [Nimrod] (38:2) Spr-Sum
95, p. 110.
1039. CHERKOVSKI, Neeli
"Baja Journal." [HeavenB] (12) 95, p. 59-60.
"The Poor." [Talisman] (15) Wint 95-96, p. 154.
1040. CHERNOW, Ann
"Aurora." [GreenHLL] (6) 95, p. 50.
"Proselytes." [Blueline] (16) 95, p. 6.
1041. CHERRY, James E.
"Juice." [Drumvoices] (5:1/2) Fall-Wint 95-96, p. 111.
1042. CHERRY, Kelly
"Advice to a Young Poet." [EngJ] (84:8) D 95, p. 39.
"Narrative." [EngJ] (84:8) D 95, p. 39.
"Needle Park, Madison, Wisconsin." [TarRP] (34:2) Spr 95, p. 1.
"Petition on Behalf of My Parents" (Both of whom had emphysema). [TarRP] (34:2)
Spr 95, p. 3.
"Trip to Las Vegas." [TarRP] (34:2) Spr 95, p. 2.

1043. CHERRY, Laura
"Sadness." [Flyway] (1:2) Fall 95, p. 54.
1044. CHERRY, Nancy
"Hauling the Garden." [BellR] (18:2, #38) Fall 95, p. 12-13.
"Learning to Say Those Words" (for I.D.M.). [Pearl] (22) Fall-Wint 95, p. 135.
"The Stepsister Leaves Cinderella." [Pearl] (22) Fall-Wint 95, p. 146.
"What I Do for Everyone." [SycamoreR] (7:1) Wint 95, p. 36-37.
"While I Am Waiting for You." [GreenHLL] (6) 95, p. 53.
1045. CHESS, Richard
"Dissolve." [NewEngR] (17:4) Fall 95, p. 55.
"Rabbi qua Mystic." [PoetryE] (39) Fall 94, p. 21-22.
"Revelation." [TriQ] (95) Wint 95-96, p. 207-208.
"Way Down." [DenQ] (29:3) Wint 95, p. 8.
1046. CHESTER, David
"Line." [CapeR] (30:2) Fall 95, p. 28.
"Tracks." [CapeR] (30:2) Fall 95, p. 29.
CHI, Lam
   See LAM, Chi
1047. CHIANESE, Bob
"Hall Canyon / Configuration." [SantaBR] (3:2) Sum 95, p. 29.
"Hall Canyon / Plates." [SantaBR] (3:2) Sum 95, p. 28.
CHIH-PEN, Yun-kai
   See YUN-KAI CHIH-PEN
1048. CHILCOTE, S.
"Every Night" (tr. of Nara Pallav). [TickleAce] (27) Spr-Sum 94, p. 84-85.
1049. CHILD, E. S.
"Tucking Them In." [LitR] (39:1) Fall 95, p. 84.
1050. CHILDERS, Joanne
"Live Oak." [Kalliope] (17:3) 95, p. 30.
1051. CHILOYAN, Slavik
"Critics" (tr. by Diana Der-Hovanessian). [GrahamHR] (19) Wint 95-96, p. 49.
"Dogs" (tr. by Diana Der-Hovanessian). [GrahamHR] (19) Wint 95-96, p. 49.
"Forbidden" (tr. by Diana Der-Hovanessian). [GrahamHR] (19) Wint 95-96, p. 49.
"Run and Escape" (tr. by Diana Der-Hovanessian). [GrahamHR] (19) Wint 95-96, p.
   50.
CHIMAKO, Tada
   See TADA, Chimako
1052. CHIN, David
"Sterling Williams' Nosebleed." [NewMyths] (2:2/3:1) 95, p. 142-144.
1053. CHIN, Justin
"The Secret Life of Flowers." [Sonora] (29) Spr 95, p. 50-52.
1054. CHIN, Marilyn
"Cauldron." [KenR] (17:2) Spr 95, p. 12-14.
"The Colonial Language Is English." [KenR] (17:2) Spr 95, p. 14-15.
"A Portrait of the Self as Nation, 1990-1991." [Zyzzyva] (11:3/4, #43/44) 95, "The
   Best of Ten Years of ZYZZYVA," p. 104-109.
1055. CHING, An
"Making a Fool of Myself" (tr. by J. P. Seaton). [LitR] (38:3) Spr 95, p. 339.
1056. CHING, Yun
"Old Man of the Creek" (tr. by J. P. Seaton). [LitR] (38:3) Spr 95, p. 330.
1057. CHISHOLM, Colin
"Mostar Bridge — Bosnia, 1987." [Sun] (240) D 95, p. 17.
1058. CHITWOOD, Michael
"After the Missionaries." [Poetry] (166:2) My 95, p. 78.
"By Water, Again." [OhioR] (53) 95, p. 34-35.
"Easy Street, Continental Homes, Luck, the Destination of Southern Conversation,
   and Dust." [TarRP] (35:1) Fall 95, p. 28-29.
"Past Due." [Field] (53) Fall 95, p. 55.
"The Rain's Ability to Expose the Dual Nature of Existence." [Thrpny] (60) Wint
   95, p. 21.
"Saints in the Aisles of Route 40 Gro. and Feed." [PoetryE] (40) Spr 95, p. 18.
"The Seasons Come and the Seasons Keep Coming." [OhioR] (54) 95, p. 65.
"The Shop." [Field] (53) Fall 95, p. 53.
"What to Expect." [Field] (53) Fall 95, p. 54.
1059. CHIU, Jeffrey
"Considerations." [HangL] (67) 95, p. 90-91.

"Perfect Pitch." [HangL] (67) 95, p. 88.
"Three Notes on a Kitchen Table." [HangL] (67) 95, p. 89.
CH'IUNG-CH'IUNG, Yuan
    See YUAN, Ch'iung-ch'iung
1060. CHMIELARZ, Sharon
    "Pictures From an Extinction: The Motherland." [SouthernPR] (35:2) Wint 95, p. 36-37.
    "Two Members in the Community of St. Gilgen: Austria, 1786." [CumbPR] (15:1) Fall 95, p. 20.
    "Two Variations on a Theme by Papa, Leopold, Mozart." [CumbPR] (15:1) Fall 95, p. 18-19.
1061. CHOPEL, Gendun
    "Tibetan Arts of Love" (Excerpt, tr. by Jeffrey Hopkins). [Tricycle] (4:3, #15) Spr 95, p. 47.
1062. CHORLTON, David
    "The Barber." [DogRR] (14:1, #27) Sum 95, p. 24.
    "The Cinema." [DogRR] (14:1, #27) Sum 95, p. 24.
    "Laboratory Dreams." [HeavenB] (12) 95, p. 58.
    "Other People." [Parting] (8:1) Sum 95, p. 6.
    "The Roof, the Walls, the Doors" (tr. of Hans Raimund). [Os] (40) 95, p. 6.
    "The Scholars." [GreenHLL] (6) 95, p. 73.
    "The Sky, the Meadow, the Forest" (tr. of Hans Raimund). [Os] (40) 95, p. 4.
    "Storm." [Parting] (8:1) Sum 95, p. 31.
1063. CHOU, Ping
    "The Flowing Style" (tr. of Sikong Tu, w. Tony Barnstone). [LitR] (38:3) Spr 95, p. 327.
    "The Graceful Style" (tr. of Sikong Tu, w. Tony Barnstone). [LitR] (38:3) Spr 95, p. 326.
    "Poets' Jade Splinters" (Selections, tr. of the anthology edited by Wei Qingzhi, w. Tony Barnstone). [AmerPoR] (24:6) N-D 95, p. 41-50.
    "The Transcendent Style" (tr. of Sikong Tu, w. Tony Barnstone). [LitR] (38:3) Spr 95, p. 327.
    "The Vital Spirit Style" (tr. of Sikong Tu, w. Tony Barnstone). [LitR] (38:3) Spr 95, p. 326.
1064. CHOULIARAS, Yiorgos
    "Exile on Land" (in Greek and English, tr. by David Mason and the author). [InterPR] (21:1) Spr 95, p. 28-29.
    "I Am Working on My Greek" (in Greek and English, tr. by David Mason and the author). [InterQ] (2:1/2) 95, p. 89.
    "The Myth of the Plumber" (in Greek and English, tr. by David Mason and the author). [InterQ] (2:1/2) 95, p. 89.
    "When Experience Speaks" (in Greek and English, tr. by David Mason and the author). [InterQ] (2:1/2) 95, p. 89.
1065. CHOW, Edmond
    "Blind Date." [Arc] (34) Spr 95, p. 57.
    "Comfort." [Arc] (34) Spr 95, p. 59.
    "Imminence." [Arc] (34) Spr 95, p. 58.
    "Ripe Bananas." [Dandel] (22:1) 95, p. 66.
1066. CHOWDHUR, Kabir
    "Market Prices" (tr. of Abul Hussain). [Drumvoices] (4:1/2) Fall-Wint 94-95, p. 120.
1067. CHRISMAN, Robert
    "The Wiz." [Drumvoices] (4:1/2) Fall-Wint 94-95, p. 128-129.
1068. CHRISTENSEN, Helena
    "Apprentice." [ManyMM] (1:3) 95, p. 48-49.
    "Her Road to Burial." [ManyMM] (1:3) 95, p. 46-47.
1069. CHRISTENSEN, Inger
    "Alphabet" (Selections, tr. by Pierre Joris). [Sulfur] (15:1, #36) Spr 95, p. 4-9.
1070. CHRISTENSEN, Marc
    "Cacophony." [PennR] (6:2) 95, p. 18.
1071. CHRISTIANSE, Yvette
    "Desire" (For E). [Colum] (24/25) 95, p. 86.
1072. CHRISTIANSON, Kevin
    "Late for work again." [BlackBR] (20) Spr-Sum 95, p. 19.
1073. CHRISTIE, A. V.
    "Cylburn Gardens." [Flyway] (1:3) Wint 95, p. 66.

"Proserpina's Lament." [PlumR] (9) [95 or 96], p. 46.
"Suture." [PlumR] (9) [95 or 96], p. 47.
"Their Titanic" (for Zoe). [Sonora] (30) Fall 95, p. 74.
1074. CHRISTIE, Antony (Anthony)
"Tourist in Croatia" (Summer 1994: 5 poems). [AntigR] (102/103) Sum-Aug 95, p.
11-15.
1075. CHRISTIE, Ruth
"Our Cat's Tale" (tr. of Mehmet Yasin, by Alev Reid, edited by Ruth Christie).
[HarvardR] (8) Spr 95, p. 92.
1076. CHRISTINA, Martha
"Like Any Other Day." [DefinedP] (3) 95, p. 24.
"Newly-Weds at the Fair." [DefinedP] (3) 95, p. 25-26.
"Off Warren Avenue." [DefinedP] (3) 95, p. 27.
"Something About a River." [DefinedP] (3) 95, p. 23.
1077. CHRISTOPHER, G. B. (Georgia, 1932-1994)
"The Deaf Choir at Harmony Grove." [LullwaterR] (6:2) Fall-Wint 95, p. 23.
"How We Speak About Pain." [LullwaterR] (6:2) Fall-Wint 95, p. 26-27.
"Hypothesis." [Border] (6) Spr-Sum 95, p. 31.
"The Knot Garden." [LullwaterR] (6:2) Fall-Wint 95, p. 24-25.
"Lesson in Mixed Media" (for Robert Rauschenberg). [AnotherCM] (29) Spr 95, p.
17.
"The Purple Pheasant." [LullwaterR] (6:2) Fall-Wint 95, p. 28-29.
1078. CHRISTOPHER, Nicholas
"The State Hospital, Honolulu." [Nat] (260:8) 27 F 95, p. 287.
"A Storm." [Nat] (258:11) 21 Mr 94, p. 391.
"When the Hurricane Swerved Toward the Island." [Nat] (260:4) 30 Ja 95, p. 136.
CHU-CHIEN, Pei-chien
    See PEI-CHIEN CHU-CHIEN
CHU-I, Po
    See BAI, Juyi
1079. CH'U-SHIH
"Eight: The Buddhas provided the sutras" (by Shih-te, with Harmonies by Ch'u-shih
and Shih-shu, tr. by Jim Sanford and J. P. Seaton). [LitR] (38:3) Spr 95, p.
336.
"Forty: Clouded mountains, folded layer upon layer" (by Shih-te, with Harmonies
by Ch'u-shih and Shih-shu, tr. by Jim Sanford and J. P. Seaton). [LitR] (38:3)
Spr 95, p. 337.
"Two: Don't you see?" (by Shih-te, with Harmonies by Ch'u-shih and Shih-shu, tr.
by Jim Sanford and J. P. Seaton). [LitR] (38:3) Spr 95, p. 335.
CHU-YI, Po
    See BAI, Juyi
1080. CHUANG, Tsu
"Now I am Going to Tell" (excerpt from "The Secret of Nurturing Growth," an Inner
Chapter of Chuang Tsu, tr. by Ngawang Nyima). [Archae] (5) Spr 95, p. 62.
1081. CHUBBS, Boyd
"Rake the Half-Hearted Fire." [TickleAce] (27) Spr-Sum 94, p. 54.
CHUILLEANAIN, Eiléan Ní
    See Ní CHUILLEANAIN, Eiléan
CHUN-JIAN, Xue
    See XUE, Chun-jian
CHUNG, Nguyen Ba
    See NGUYEN, Ba Chung
1082. CHURA, David
"Climbing in Silence." [Blueline] (16) 95, p. 82-83.
1083. CHURCH, Todd
"Meditations on a Lost World." [QW] (40) Spr-Sum 95, p. 58-59.
1084. CHUTE, Robert M.
"Arcadian." [CapeR] (30:1) Spr 95, p. 45.
"Father Isaac Jacques." [HiramPoR] (58/59) Spr 95-Wint 96, p. 14.
"Stripping Landlocked Salmon, Panther Run, Raymond, ME (From a 1930s Home
Movie)." [LitR] (38:2) Wint 95, p. 230.
CIEN FUEGOS
    See FUEGOS, Cien
1085. CIGALE, Alex
"Carnal Knowledge" (for Paul Pomeroy, 1964-1991). [Talisman] (15) Wint 95-96,
p. 148-149.

1086. CIHLAR, Jim
"Bare Bones." [MidwQ] (36:4) Sum 95, p. 359.
1087. CILENTO, Cara
"Asbury Park." [JlNJPo] (17:1) Spr 95, p. 3.
1088. CINELLI, Joan E.
"Allhallows Eve." [ChrC] (112:31) 1 N 95, p. 1018.
1089. CIRINO, Leonard J.
"Albion in the Rain." [ProseP] (4) 95, p. 13.
1090. CISNEROS, Sandra
"It Occurs to Me I Am the Creative/Destructive Goddess Coatlicue." [MassR] (36:4)
Wint 95-96, p. 599.
"Tango for the Broom." [MassR] (36:4) Wint 95-96, p. 598.
1091. CITINO, David
"The Discipline of Brick, the Sexuality of Corn." [MidAR] (15:1/2) 95, p. 120-121.
"Gathering the Dear Sweet Dead." [PraS] (69:2) Sum 95, p. 143.
"The Land of Atrophy." [PraS] (69:2) Sum 95, p. 140-142.
"A Natural History of Shadows." [DefinedP] (1:2) Spr-Sum 93, p. 24.
"Prognosis." [BelPoJ] (45:4) Chapbook 22, Sum 95, p. 11-13.
"Quattrocento Angels over Cleveland." [CentR] (39:2) Spr 95, p. 311-312.
"Rescue 911." [LaurelR] (29:2) Sum 95, p. 87-88.
"Sister Mary Appassionata Chases the Wind." [OhioR] (53) 95, p. 102-103.
"Stregone." [CentR] (39:2) Spr 95, p. 309-310.
"Tarantella." [NewL] (61:4) 95, p. 72-73.
"To Robert." [BelPoJ] (45:4) Chapbook 22, Sum 95, p. 14-15.
1092. CITIZEN KANE, April
"Voices." [SinW] (56) Sum-Fall 95, p. 52-53.
1093. CLAMAN, Henry N.
"Doing Time." [HighP] (10:3) Wint 95, p. 84.
1094. CLAMPITT, Amy (1920-1994)
"Green." [Orion] (14:1) Wint 95, p. 50.
"Hispaniola." [Verse] (12:2) 95, p. 31-32.
"Nondescript." [Orion] (14:1) Wint 95, p. 51.
"Pot Nomads." [NewYorker] (71:13) 22 My 95, p. 72.
"Sea Mouse." [Orion] (14:1) Wint 95, p. 51.
"The Sun Underfoot Among the Sundews." [Orion] (14:1) Wint 95, p. 50.
1095. CLARE, Elizabeth
"Angels." [HangL] (66) 95, p. 40.
"Words and Breath." [EvergreenC] (10:2) Sum-Fall 95, p. 97.
1096. CLARK, Elizabeth B.
"How Are You Not Going to Like Me" (tr. of Jairo Aníbal Niño). [Rosebud] (2:3)
Aut-Wint 95, p. 29.
"It's a Pretty Day" (tr. of Jairo Aníbal Niño). [GrahamHR] (19) Wint 95-96, p. 62.
"She Came to the Classroom" (tr. of Jairo Aníbal Niño). [GrahamHR] (19) Wint 95-
96, p. 64.
"You Went By" (tr. of Jairo Aníbal Niño). [GrahamHR] (19) Wint 95-96, p. 63.
1097. CLARK, Hilary
"Angels." [CapilR] (2:15) Spr 95, p. 74-81.
"Ça." [MalR] (113) Wint 95, p. 24.
"HER." [Grain] (23:1) Sum 95, p. 91-92.
"A Message." [MalR] (113) Wint 95, p. 22-23.
"Riddle." [MalR] (113) Wint 95, p. 20.
"Speak." [MalR] (113) Wint 95, p. 21.
1098. CLARK, Jeanne E.
"The Day Lucy Electra Blamed for Everything." [QW] (41) Aut-Wint 95-96, p. 192.
"How Lucy Electra Fights." [QW] (41) Aut-Wint 95-96, p. 193.
"Lucy Electra & Quinn Margaret: Xenia, Ohio, 1979." [QW] (41) Aut-Wint 95-96,
p. 191.
"Sleep." [SnailPR] (3:2) 95, p. 26-27.
1099. CLARK, Jeff
"Blow-Notes" (Excerpt). [BlackWR] (22:1) Fall-Wint 95, p. 101-104.
1100. CLARK, Judith
"The Evening News" (Bedford Hills Correctional Facility, 1994). [GlobalCR] (5)
Spr 95, p. 96-98.
1101. CLARK, Kevin
"The End." [BlackWR] (22:1) Fall-Wint 95, p. 141-142.
"Twelve." [ColEng] (57:4) Ap 95, p. 466-468.

CLARK, Robyn Heisey
 See HEISEY-CLARK, Robyn
1102. CLARK, Tom
 "A une Jeune Fille." [AmerPoR] (24:6) N-D 95, p. 9.
 "The Allée d'Argenson." [NewAW] (13) Fall-Wint 95, p. 79.
 "Astrolabe." [NewAW] (13) Fall-Wint 95, p. 81.
 "The Case of Miss Twitch." [NewAW] (13) Fall-Wint 95, p. 80.
 "Club Sahara." [AmerPoR] (24:6) N-D 95, p. 9.
 "Greed." [AmerPoR] (24:6) N-D 95, p. 9.
 "Like Real People." [IndR] (18:2) Fall 95, p. 168.
 "Mnemosyne." [IndR] (18:2) Fall 95, p. 169.
 "On the Beach." [AmerPoR] (24:6) N-D 95, p. 9.
 "Wet Petals." [AmerPoR] (24:6) N-D 95, p. 9.
1103. CLARKE, Catherine
 "Babble" (for Morgan Powell). [GrahamHR] (19) Wint 95-96, p. 104-105.
1104. CLARKE, John
 "If That Hand." [PoetryE] (40) Spr 95, p. 19.
 "Little Marsh." [OhioR] (54) 95, p. 76.
 "Night in the Country." [Flyway] (1:1) Spr 95, p. 18.
 "Our Day." [TarRP] (34:2) Spr 95, p. 6.
 "A Walk at First Light." [NewDeltaR] (12:2) Spr-Sum 95, p. 29.
1105. CLARKE, K. C.
 "Tomorrow Is a Long Time." [PoetL] (90:4) Wint 95-96, p. 11.
 "Upland." [PoetL] (90:4) Wint 95-96, p. 10.
1106. CLARKE, Kalo
 "L'Empire de la Mort." [BellR] (18:2, #38) Fall 95, p. 10.
1107. CLARKE, Michael
 "Acappellascape" (5 selections). [WormR] (35:1, #137) 95, p. 9.
 "It's Getting Dark on Good Friday." [Wind] (75) Spr 95, p. 5.
 "Sonnet for Christine." [WormR] (35:1, #137) 95, p. 8.
1108. CLARVOE, Jennifer
 "2217 Platenstrasse." [PartR] (62:4) Fall 95, p. 680-681.
 "Ruth's Garden." [YaleR] (83:3) Jl 95, p. 126-127.
1109. CLARY, Killarney
 "Certainty Presses In." [Epoch] (44:1) 95, p. 82.
 "Cicadas sizzle in the trees beyond the hum of screens." [Field] (52) Spr 95, p. 32.
 "Clear of oak groves, sunrise stretched a thin reach deep into the chamber." [ProseP]
   (4) 95, p. 15.
 "Early radios talk about traffic and weather as if they vary." [ProseP] (4) 95, p. 14.
 "Given away. This is the end of the longest night." [Phoebe] (24:1) 95, p. 45.
 "I list in my mind what I have left to do." [Phoebe] (24:1) 95, p. 47.
 "Maybe they're all singing to themselves, alone in malls." [Phoebe] (24:1) 95, p. 44.
 "North Over One of the Bridges." [Epoch] (44:1) 95, p. 83.
 "Of a heavy butterfly, disproportionately large." [Field] (52) Spr 95, p. 33.
 "She's worried about the roll of the boat." [Phoebe] (24:1) 95, p. 46.
 "Untitled: He gives me a name, pronounces it clumsily." [ColR] (22:2) Fall 95, p.
   159.
 "Untitled: I had a home in the hill with rag-patchwork birds." [ColR] (22:2) Fall 95,
   p. 160.
 "Untitled: Only the size of a hand, a pounded gold boat was disrupted." [ColR]
   (22:2) Fall 95, p. 157.
 "Untitled: Tenderness. And a black heart looms behind two faces." [ColR] (22:2)
   Fall 95, p. 158.
 "The wild boy of Aveyron who drinks his cool water from a cup." [Field] (52) Spr
   95, p. 31.
1110. CLAUSEN, Jan
 "Moments of Departure." [KenR] (17:1) Wint 95, p. 120-123.
1111. CLAUSER, Grant
 "Rhonda Still in Oregon." [SilverFR] (25) Sum 95, p. 32-33.
 "To My Father After the Stroke." [SilverFR] (25) Sum 95, p. 30-31.
1112. CLEAR, T.
 "Cheap Motels." [SlipS] (15) 95, p. 65.
 "The Man in the Apartment Downstairs Who Breaks in and Eats My Food." [SlipS]
   (15) 95, p. 66.
1113. CLEARY, Michael
 "Paramount Theater: Solipsism in the '50s." [LouisL] (12:1) Spr 95, p. 55-56.

1114. CLEARY, Suzanne
"Girls' School." [OhioR] (53) 95, p. 92-93.
"This" (for David. First Place, Poetry Award). [NewL] (61:2) 95, p. 72-73.
"Though the Grass" (First Place, Poetry Award). [NewL] (61:2) 95, p. 68-69.
"Thrift Shop" (First Place, Poetry Award). [NewL] (61:2) 95, p. 70-71.
1115. CLEAVELAND, Ruzha
"City Spirit" (tr. of Josip Osti). [InterPR] (21:1) Spr 95, p. 67.
"Destiny Doesn't Want to Share with Death the Last Gulp of Water, the Last Bit of
Food" (tr. of Josip Osti). [InterPR] (21:1) Spr 95, p. 63.
"Earthly and Heavenly Roads" (tr. of Josip Osti). [InterPR] (21:1) Spr 95, p. 61.
"Finally They Fall Sweetly from the Sky, Though Children Behind Darkened
Windows Do Not See Them" (tr. of Josip Osti). [InterPR] (21:1) Spr 95, p.
57, 59.
"I Don't Recognize Anymore the Town in Which I Knew Every Corner" (tr. of Josip
Osti). [MinnR] (43/44) 95, p. 11.
"A Letter to Kavafy" (tr. of Josip Osti). [LitR] (38:3) Spr 95, p. 354-355.
"Letters I Write You Leave in the Wind, But Roses I Send You I Send in Death" (tr.
of Josip Osti). [MinnR] (43/44) 95, p. 9.
"That Year a Belgian Poet, Whose Name You Were Able to Write But Not
Pronounce ..." (tr. of Josip Osti). [MinnR] (43/44) 95, p. 9-11.
"Today the Aggressor Attacked in Every Way and in All Parts of Town" (tr. of Josip
Osti). [InterPR] (21:1) Spr 95, p. 65.
1116. CLEMENTS, Arthur L.
"A Beautiful Woman Walks Naked" (For Susan). [Footwork] (24/25) 95, p. 39.
"He Called Again and Said." [Footwork] (24/25) 95, p. 40.
1117. CLEMENTS, Brian
"Dead Electron Catalogue" (Selections: 3 poems). [Agni] (41) 95, p. 105-107.
"The Great Verités." [AnotherCM] (29) Spr 95, p. 18-19.
"A Kind of Death." [NewMyths] (2:2/3:1) 95, p. 5.
"The Practice of Water." [PlumR] (8) [95], p. 90.
1118. CLEMENTS, Susan
"Gray Fire." [ManyMM] (1:3) 95, p. 75-77.
1119. CLEWELL, David
"Traveller's Advisory." [RiverS] (42/43) 95, p. 59-60.
CLIFF DWELLER
See DWELLER, Cliff
1120. CLIFT, G. W.
"The Dog Lady." [IllinoisR] (3:1/2) Fall 95-Spr 96, p. 30-33.
1121. CLIFTON, Harry
"MacNeice's London" (For Derek Mahon). [Poetry] (167:1/2) O-N 95, p. 36-37.
"A Spider Dance on the Bahnhofstrasse." [Poetry] (167:1/2) O-N 95, p. 35-36.
1122. CLIFTON, Lucille
"Auction Street" (for Angela McDonald). [RiverC] (15:2) Sum 95, p. 31.
"Lorena." [ParisR] (37:136) Fall 95, p. 147.
"The Mississippi River Empties into the Gulf." [RiverC] (15:2) Sum 95, p. 33.
"Old Man River." [RiverC] (15:2) Sum 95, p. 32.
"Poem in Praise of Menstruation." [RiverS] (42/43) 95, p. 163.
"Shadows." [ParisR] (37:137) Wint 95, p. 253-254.
"Untitled: Evening and my dead once husband." [Colum] (24/25) 95, p. 171.
1123. CLINTON, James H.
"Amanda, 1961." [SpoonR] (20:1) Wint-Spr 95, p. 97.
"Particle Storm." [SpoonR] (20:1) Wint-Spr 95, p. 96.
1124. CLINTON, Michelle T.
"Rethink the Word." [Zyzzyva] (11:1, #41) Spr 95, p. 170-171.
"Traditional Postmodern Neo-HooDoo Afra-Centric Sister in a Purple Head Rag
Mourning Death and Cooking." [Zyzzyva] (11:3/4, #43/44) 95, "The Best of
Ten Years of ZYZZYVA," p. 110-113.
1125. CLOOS, Carol
"Soundings." [Blueline] (16) 95, p. 63.
1126. CLOUGH, Jeanette
"Cain." [13thMoon] (13:1/2) 95, p. 11.
"Eurydice's Song." [13thMoon] (13:1/2) 95, p. 12.
1127. CLOVER, Joshua
"Jack's Boat." [ColR] (22:2) Fall 95, p. 144.
"Remarks on the Word 'Lucrative'." [ColR] (22:2) Fall 95, p. 145-147.
"Social Studies." [ColR] (22:2) Fall 95, p. 148-149.

"Union Pacific." [ColR] (22:1) Spr 95, p. 91-92.
1128. COADY, Michael
"The Public Record." [Poetry] (167:1/2) O-N 95, p. 80-81.
"Sister Imelda Rising on the Last Day." [Poetry] (167:1/2) O-N 95, p. 82-83.
"Watching 'The Dead' in the Living Room." [Poetry] (167:1/2) O-N 95, p. 81.
1129. COAN, Catherine
"How We Sleep." [PoetryNW] (36:2) Sum 95, p. 13-15.
1130. COBB, Ann
"Water." [HarvardR] (8) Spr 95, p. 115.
COBIAN, Armando Suarez
See SUAREZ COBIAN, Armando
1131. COCCIMIGLIO, Vic
"Father and Friend." [Pearl] (22) Fall-Wint 95, p. 39.
1132. COCHRAN, Leonard
"The Collection" (for C.V.R.). [SpiritSH] (60) 95, p. 3.
"En Route." [SpiritSH] (60) 95, p. 4.
"The Names of a Squirrel" (after the manner of a 13th century poem, "The Names of a Hare in English"). [SpiritSH] (60) 95, p. 1.
"While Throwing Away Old Letters." [SpiritSH] (60) 95, p. 2.
1133. COCHRANE, Guy
"Empty." [WormR] (35:1, #137) 95, p. 12.
"Old Timer." [WormR] (35:1, #137) 95, p. 12.
"The Science of Blues." [WormR] (35:1, #137) 95, p. 12.
"Spring Forward." [WormR] (35:1, #137) 95, p. 12.
1134. COE, Dina
"Birthday Rites in Color." [PoetL] (90:1) Spr 95, p. 33.
"Poem for a Former Spouse." [PoetL] (90:1) Spr 95, p. 34.
COEUR, Jo Le
See LeCOEUR, Jo
1135. COFER, Judith Ortiz
"Found Poem: Charm for the Love of a Woman." [AmerV] (37) 95, p. 107-108.
"Noche Nueve." [BilingR] (20:1) Ja-Ap 95, p. 69.
"The Tip." [MassR] (36:4) Wint 95-96, p. 600.
1136. COFFEL, Scott
"Oscar Wilde." [AntR] (53:2) Spr 95, p. 197.
1137. COFFMAN, Lisa
"For Najeema, 6, Who Admitted to Hitting Renee." [PaintedB] (55/56) 95, p. 73.
"Romeo Collision." [BelPoJ] (45:3) Spr 95, p. 32-35.
1138. COGAN, Nancy Adams
"Sugar Jim." [HiramPoR] (58/59) Spr 95-Wint 96, p. 15-17.
1139. COHEE, Marcia
"Group Therapy." [Pearl] (22) Fall-Wint 95, p. 13.
"Like Screwing the Head Back On." [SlipS] (15) 95, p. 16.
"You Cannot Keep the Full Moon." [GreenHLL] (6) 95, p. 54.
1140. COHEN, Ben
"Unfrozen." [NewRep] (213:16) 16 O 95, p. 6.
1141. COHEN, Bruce
"Home Town Chemistry." [PassN] (16:2) Wint 95, p. 16-17.
"In Case of God." [PassN] (16:2) Wint 95, p. 18.
"Pranks & College Literature." [MidAR] (16:1) 95, p. 57-58.
"Privacy." [PassN] (16:2) Wint 95, p. 14-15.
1142. COHEN, Lewis Zachary
"Mother, There Is a Rhinoceros in the Garden." [GlobalCR] (6) Fall 95, p. 82.
"My Call Clangs Through an Unlit House." [GlobalCR] (6) Fall 95, p. 83.
"Revelation." [GlobalCR] (6) Fall 95, p. 80-81.
1143. COHEN, Marc
"Orchids in Dungeon." [NewAW] (13) Fall-Wint 95, p. 96.
1144. COHEN, Miriam
"While with Cannons in the Midst of Bosnia." [BlackBR] (21) Fall-Wint 95, p. 36.
1145. COHEN, Miriam A.
"Deceased Cow's Note." [DogRR] (14:1, #27) Sum 95, p. 48.
1146. COHEN, Nancy Lipson
"My Apple Trees." [Blueline] (16) 95, p. 97.
1147. COHEN, Stephanie Kaplan
"The Burying Ground." [Parting] (8:2) Wint 95-96, p. 16.

1148. COLASURDO, Christine
"Music in the Planetarium." [DenQ] (29:4) Spr 95, p. 14-15.
1149. COLBURN, Don
"Birds." [PraS] (69:4) Wint 95, p. 104.
"Cul-de-sac." [PraS] (69:4) Wint 95, p. 103.
"Differences" (in memory of William Stafford). [PraS] (69:4) Wint 95, p. 102-103.
"Pansies at the Modern." [PoetL] (90:4) Wint 95-96, p. 6.
1150. COLBURN, Jean
"Something Happens." [LitR] (38:3) Spr 95, p. 362.
1151. COLBY, Joan
"Art in the Streets." [NewRena] (9:2, #28) Spr 95, p. 93-94.
"Two Deaths." [NewRena] (9:2, #28) Spr 95, p. 90-92.
1152. COLE, Henri
"40 Days and 40 Nights." [HarvardR] (8) Spr 95, p. 16-17.
"Apostasy." [HarvardR] (8) Spr 95, p. 17.
"Apostasy." [YaleR] (83:1) Ja 95, p. 83.
"Immaculate Mary Breathes the Air We Breathe." [ColR] (22:1) Spr 95, p. 109-110.
"Paper Dolls." [NewYorker] (70:43 [i.e. 44]) 9 Ja 95, p. 74.
"Plastilina." [NewYorker] (70:46) 23 Ja 95, p. 82.
1153. COLE, James
"The Downtown Café." [Light] (15/16) Aut-Wint 95-96, p. 30.
1154. COLE, Kevin
"Baptism 1964." [HopewellR] (7) 95, p. 93.
1155. COLE, Norma
"Untitled (from *Nostalgia*)." [Chain] (2) Spr 95, p. 62-63.
"We Address" (w. Amy Trachtenberg). [Zyzzyva] (11:1, #41) Spr 95, p. 80-84.
1156. COLE, Peter
"Functional Through a Believing." [Sulfur] (15:2, #37) Fall 95, p. 129-131.
1157. COLE, Robert
"Blue Money." [Bogg] (67) 95, p. 53.
1158. COLE, William Rossa
"I queried my crew on Penobscot Bay." [Light] (15/16) Aut-Wint 95-96, p. 34.
1159. COLEMAN, Connie
"Active Poem" (WritersCorps Program, Washington, DC). [WashR] (21:2) Ag-S 95,
    p. 13.
"Snow" (WritersCorps Program, Washington, DC). [WashR] (21:2) Ag-S 95, p. 13.
1160. COLEMAN, Earl
"A Failed Cartographer." [CapeR] (30:2) Fall 95, p. 42.
1161. COLEMAN, Horace
"Urban Trapshoot." [AfAmRev] (29:3) Fall 95, p. 479.
1162. COLEMAN, Jen
"Injury: Potential For" (Excerpts). [Phoebe] (24:2) 95, p. 33-38.
1163. COLEMAN, Kathryn
"And the Winner Is." [Writer] (108:3) Mr 95, p. 11.
1164. COLEMAN, Mary Ann
"Cove Forest." [LullwaterR] (6:1) Spr-Sum 95, p. 34-35.
1165. COLEMAN, Wanda
"American Sonnet (26)" (for and after Michelle T. Clinton). [RiverC] (15:2) Sum
    95, p. 13.
"American Sonnet (34)" (after Jones / Baraka). [RiverC] (15:2) Sum 95, p. 14.
"American Sonnet (35)." [RiverC] (15:2) Sum 95, p. 15.
1166. COLES, Don
"Alcaic" (tr. of Tomas Tranströmer). [MalR] (113) Wint 95, p. 10.
"The Longforgotten Captain" (tr. of Tomas Tranströmer). [MalR] (113) Wint 95, p.
    6-7.
"Nightingale in Badelunda" (tr. of Tomas Tranströmer). [MalR] (113) Wint 95, p. 9.
"Six Winters" (tr. of Tomas Tranströmer). [MalR] (113) Wint 95, p. 8.
"Yellowjacket" (tr. of Tomas Tranströmer). [MalR] (113) Wint 95, p. 11-13.
1167. COLES, Katharine
"Pantoum in Which Time Equals Space" (for Jack Droitcourt and for Eugene
    Gudaitis, 1992). [ParisR] (37:135) Sum 95, p. 37-38.
"Stereopticon." [QW] (41) Aut-Wint 95-96, p. 180-182.
1168. COLGIN, Paul David
"Thirty Long Waits." [Pearl] (22) Fall-Wint 95, p. 84.
COLIBAN, Taina Dutescu
See DUTESCU-COLIBAN, Taina

1169. COLINA, Paulo
"Agosto." [Callaloo] (18:4) Fall 95, p. 906-907.
"Ao Jeito de Alvaro de Campos." [Callaloo] (18:4) Fall 95, p. 909-910.
"August" (tr. by Phyllis Peres, w. Reetika Vazirani and Chi Lam). [Callaloo] (18:4) Fall 95, p. 734-735.
"Carnaval." [Callaloo] (18:4) Fall 95, p. 908.
"Carnival" (tr. by Phyllis Peres and Jane Kamide, w. Reetika Vazirani and Chi Lam). [Callaloo] (18:4) Fall 95, p. 736.
"Foreboding" (tr. by Phyllis Peres and Jane Kamide). [Callaloo] (18:4) Fall 95, p. 733.
"In the Style of Alvaro de Campos" (tr. by Phyllis Peres and Jane Kamide). [Callaloo] (18:4) Fall 95, p. 737-738.
"Pressentimento." [Callaloo] (18:4) Fall 95, p. 905.
1170. COLLINS, Billy
"1824." [PoetryE] (41) Aut 95, p. 51.
"Aristotle." [ParisR] (37:134) Spr 95, p. 231-233.
"The Best Cigarette." [Poetry] (165:4) Ja 95, p. 216-217.
"The Biography of a Cloud." [Poetry] (165:4) Ja 95, p. 217-218.
"Canada." [GettyR] (8:2) Spr 95, p. 364-365.
"Dream." [Crazy] (48) Spr 95, p. 28.
"Forsythia." [Poetry] (166:1) Ap 95, p. 5-6.
"Great Moments in American Literature." [PoetryE] (41) Aut 95, p. 49.
"Guest House." [AmerV] (38) 95, p. 38.
"Hand." [PlumR] (8) [95], p. 84.
"In the Room of a Thousand Miles." [Poetry] (166:5) Ag 95, p. 249-250.
"Influence." [Poetry] (165:4) Ja 95, p. 215-216.
"Japan." [GeoR] (49:3) Fall 95, p. 695-696.
"Lines Written on a Bench in St. Stephen's Green." [Crazy] (48) Spr 95, p. 29-30.
"The List of Ancient Pastimes." [PlumR] (8) [95], p. 82-83.
"Looking West." [PoetryE] (41) Aut 95, p. 48.
"Metropolis." [NewYorker] (71:19) 10 Jl 95, p. 62-63.
"Monday Morning." [AmerS] (64:4) Aut 95, p. 540.
"My Heart." [ParisR] (37:134) Spr 95, p. 226.
"On the Death of Bukowski." [FreeL] (14) Wint 95, p. 3-4.
"Russia." [FreeL] (14) Wint 95, p. 4.
"The Sex." [TriQ] (95) Wint 95-96, p. 99-100.
"Shoveling Snow with Buddha." [AmerPoR] (24:5) S-O 95, p. 18.
"Some Final Words." [AmerPoR] (24:5) S-O 95, p. 19.
"Sunday Morning with the Sensational Nightingales." [ParisR] (37:134) Spr 95, p. 227-228.
"Sweet Talk." [AmerPoR] (24:5) S-O 95, p. 18.
"The Way You Lean Against Me While I Drive." [PoetryE] (41) Aut 95, p. 50.
"What I Learned Today." [Poetry] (166:5) Ag 95, p. 250-252.
"Workshop." [ParisR] (37:134) Spr 95, p. 229-231.
1171. COLLINS, Judy
"Car Hop." [BellR] (18:1, #37) Spr 95, p. 8-9.
"Double Play at Strawberry Field." [BellR] (18:1, #37) Spr 95, p. 12.
"I Left My Body." [BellR] (18:1, #37) Spr 95, p. 10-11.
"Lake Padden, June, 10 p.m." [BellR] (18:1, #37) Spr 95, p. 13.
1172. COLLINS, Leigh
"Through the Trap-Door, Down." [Vis] (47) 95, p. 20.
1173. COLLINS, Loretta
"Bonfire" (for Hugh). [QW] (40) Spr-Sum 95, p. 54-56.
1174. COLLINS, Martha
"Current Affairs." [NewAW] (13) Fall-Wint 95, p. 90.
"Floor Study." [Field] (52) Spr 95, p. 83.
"Later That Day." [Field] (52) Spr 95, p. 81-82.
"Lets." [KenR] (17:2) Spr 95, p. 145-146.
"Means." [KenR] (17:2) Spr 95, p. 146.
"New Students, Old Teacher" (for the American poets, on the occasion of their readings, tr. of Nguyen Quang Thieu, w. the author). [Manoa] (7:2) Wint 95, p. 161.
"October" (tr. of Nguyen Quang Thieu, w. the author). [Manoa] (7:2) Wint 95, p. 162.
"Okay So What." [Field] (52) Spr 95, p. 80.
"Pinks." [ParisR] (37:137) Wint 95, p. 263-267.

"Points." [KenR] (17:2) Spr 95, p. 145.
"Races." [PartR] (62:1) Wint 95, p. 114.
"Return" (tr. of Richard Exner). [HarvardR] (9) Fall 95, p. 30.
"Sleeping In" (For my friends: Hai, Vinh, Manh. Tr. of Nguyen Quang Thieu, w. the
   author). [HarvardR] (8) Spr 95, p. 94.
"A Song of My Native Village" (for Chua, my native village, tr. of Nguyen Quang
   Thieu, w. the author). [Manoa] (7:2) Wint 95, p. 162-163.
"Times." [PartR] (62:1) Wint 95, p. 114.
1175. COLLINS, Pat Lowery
   "Eating Figs." [Vis] (49) 95, p. 14.
1176. COLLINS, Richard
   "Song of Encouragement" (tr. of Nichita Stanescu). [SouthernHR] (29:4) Fall 95, p.
      341.
1177. COLLOM, Jack
   "Band of Paint Colors." [ManyMM] [1:1] D 94, p. 95-96.
1178. COLMAN, Cathy A.
   "Newton's Law." [SouthernPR] (35:1) Sum 95, p. 69.
1179. COLT, Lisa
   "Harry in the Garden." [Sun] (236) Ag 95, p. 12.
1180. COMNINOS, Susan
   "Upstate April" (Author's name corrected from Comnios to Comninos in no. 16, p.
      108). [Blueline] (15) 94, p. 38.
COMNIOS, Susan
   See COMNINOS, Susan
1181. COMPTON, Jean
   "A Virgin Twice." [Elf] (5:1) Spr 95, p. 25.
1182. COMPTON, Jennifer
   "Trees for the Wood." [Bogg] (67) 95, p. 10.
1183. CONANT, Jeff
   "Ice." [Phoebe] (24:1) 95, p. 76.
   "Moon." [Phoebe] (24:1) 95, p. 77.
1184. CONE, Jon
   "Notes Found in Pockets." [WorldL] (6) 95, p. 35-37.
1185. CONE, Temple
   "The Basket." [Poem] (73) My 95, p. 57-58.
   "Silent Prayer." [Poem] (73) My 95, p. 59.
1186. CONELLY, William
   "Moral Check." [Light] (15/16) Aut-Wint 95-96, p. 14.
1187. CONKLIN, Laura
   "Black." [Ploughs] (21:4) Wint 95-96, p. 34.
1188. CONKLING, Helen
   "The Oboe Teacher." [Hudson] (47:4) Wint 95, p. 605-606.
   "The Soul of a Dead Bat." [Hudson] (47:4) Wint 95, p. 606-607.
1189. CONLEY, Susan
   "Learning Not to Tell." [RiverS] (45) 95, p. 7-8.
   "Paige's Wedding." [AntR] (53:4) Fall 95, p. 431.
   "Strange Fruit." [SpoonR] (20:2) Sum-Fall 95, p. 147.
   "True Romance." [SpoonR] (20:2) Sum-Fall 95, p. 146.
1190. CONLON, Christopher
   "The Singing Rain" (Elegy for the Old World). [BellArk] (11:5) S-O 95, p. 10-11.
1191. CONNELLAN, Leo
   "Shooter." [NewYorkQ] (54) 95, p. 51.
1192. CONNELLY, Joseph F.
   "Riddle" (Answers will be given in Light / 17). [Light] (15/16) Aut-Wint 95-96, p.
      15.
1193. CONNELLY, Karen
   "Letter to My Father's Country: a Prose Poem." [Quarry] (44:3) 95, p. 65-68.
   "An Original Sea." [PoetryC] (15:2) Je 95, p. 4-5.
1194. CONNOLLY, Geraldine
   "Blue Bridge." [WestB] (37) 95, p. 66.
   "Dickinson in Winter." [Chelsea] (58) 95, p. 102.
   "Where the Wave Begins." [Chelsea] (58) 95, p. 103.
1195. CONNOLLY, J. F.
   "Last Summer." [LitR] (39:1) Fall 95, p. 34-35.
1196. CONNOR, Julia
   "The Aberrant." [NewAW] (13) Fall-Wint 95, p. 120.

1197. CONNORS, Colleen
   "Leaving Once Is Hard." [SoCaR] (28:1) Fall 95, p. 105.
1198. CONOLEY, Gillian
   "All Girlhood Receding." [CrabOR] (1:1) Fall-Wint 95, p. 33-34.
   "The Big Picture." [Phoebe] (24:1) 95, p. 128-129.
   "Doubt Sets In." [Phoebe] (24:1) 95, p. 130-131.
   "Fortune." [DefinedP] (3) 95, p. 12-13.
   "This Cafe Life." [CrabOR] (1:1) Fall-Wint 95, p. 35.
   "Unknown to You and Saved by You." [DenQ] (29:3) Wint 95, p. 9-10.
1199. CONOVER, Carl
   "Epilogue: Polonius to the Audience." [SoCaR] (28:1) Fall 95, p. 106-108.
   "Palimpsest." [SoCaR] (28:1) Fall 95, p. 106.
1200. CONRAD, C. A.
   "The Frank Poems." [JamesWR] (12:2) Spr-Sum 95, p. 16.
   "Leaving the Only Bed in America That Keeps Me Satisfied." [ModernW] (3) Sum
      95, p. 105.
   "The Night River Phoenix Died." [ModernW] (3) Sum 95, p. 106-107.
1201. CONSTANTIN, Laurentiu
   "Anima Mundi" (tr. of Lucian Vasiliu, w. Adam J. Sorkin). [Vis] (48) 95, p. 47-48.
   "Field Blankets" (tr. of Lucian Vasiliu, w. Adam J. Sorkin). [Vis] (48) 95, p. 48.
1202. CONTI, Edmund
   "Anthony Ant." [Light] (15/16) Aut-Wint 95-96, p. 32.
   "Clerihew." [Light] (15/16) Aut-Wint 95-96, p. 23.
   "I(r)onic." [JINJPo] (17:1) Spr 95, p. 24.
   "One of Those Poems That Work Better with a Catchy Title." [DogRR] (14:1, #27)
      Sum 95, p. 17.
   "Sailing on the River Thames" (First Prize, 3rd Annual River Rhyme Competition).
      [Light] (13) Spr 95, p. 24.
   "Sailing, sailing on the Dead Sea." [Light] (14) Sum 95, p. 24.
   "A Sense of Place." [DogRR] (14:1, #27) Sum 95, p. 17.
   "Two Clerihews." [Light] (13) Spr 95, p. 14.
1203. COOK, Devan
   "El Canela." [ColEng] (57:4) Ap 95, p. 463.
1204. COOK, Juliet
   "Articulation." [NewDeltaR] (12:1) Fall-Wint 94, p. 1.
1205. COOK, Laura
   "Forget This Town, It Has Already Forgotten You." [Journal] (19:2) Fall-Wint 95,
      p. 51-52.
1206. COOK, Méira
   "Legends of Tongue" (3 selections: "Slip of the Tongue" I-III). [MalR] (112) Fall
      95, p. 93-95.
   "String Quartet." [WestCL] (29:3, #18) Wint 95-96, p. 5-7.
1207. COOK, R. L.
   "The Old House: Lochside." [Hellas] (6:2) Fall-Wint 95, p. 35-40.
1208. COOK, Rebecca
   "Picking Corn." [Plain] (15:2) Wint 95, p. 15.
1209. COOKE, Robert (Robert P.)
   "Welding Electrode Holder." [ChironR] (42) Spr 95, p. 29.
   "Work Gloves." [SouthernPR] (35:1) Sum 95, p. 8-9.
1210. COOKSHAW, Marlene
   "Cheating Death." [Event] (24:1) Spr 95, p. 22-23.
   "Dear Ones." [Grain] (23:2) Aut 95, p. 32.
   "Everything Necessary." [Event] (24:1) Spr 95, p. 24-27.
   "I Make Noise With My Mouth." [Grain] (23:2) Aut 95, p. 33.
   "Whoever's Responsible." [Grain] (23:2) Aut 95, p. 30-31.
1211. COOLEY, Dennis
   "Can feel it coming." [PraF] (16:4, #73) Wint 95-96, p. 25-26.
   "Look at that, Kay points." [PraF] (16:4, #73) Wint 95-96, p. 27.
   "Rubs his eyes takes a deep breath &." [PraF] (16:4, #73) Wint 95-96, p. 22-23.
   "This is in fall." [PraF] (16:4, #73) Wint 95-96, p. 27.
   "Timid sound at the door." [PraF] (16:4, #73) Wint 95-96, p. 24-25.
   "When he sees my startled face." [PraF] (16:4, #73) Wint 95-96, p. 23-24.
   "Yes she said prairie." [PraF] (16:4, #73) Wint 95-96, p. 26.
1212. COOLEY, Nicole
   "Confession" (The Roosevelt Mineral Baths). [Ploughs] (21:1) Spr 95, p. 80-81.
   "Patty Hearst: A Love Poem." [QW] (41) Aut-Wint 95-96, p. 196-197.

"The Red Shoes." [NewEngR] (17:3) Sum 95, p. 155-156.
"Self-Portrait: Frida Kahlo." [Nat] (261:22) 25 D 95, p. 834.
1213. COOLEY, Peter
"Driving, Christmas Eve." [IndR] (18:1) Spr 95, p. 99.
"Eventides." [OhioR] (54) 95, p. 68.
"For Jay Gatsby." [SouthernR] (31:2) Ap/Spr 95, p. 258-259.
"For Lear." [SouthernR] (31:2) Ap/Spr 95, p. 259-260.
"For Tess of the D'Ubervilles." [Shen] (45:3) Fall 95, p. 69.
"Little Mad Song." [DefinedP] (3) 95, p. 7.
"Monuments." [PoetryNW] (36:3) Aut 95, p. 37.
"Morning After My Death." [Iowa] (25:3) Fall 95, p. 154.
"A Motel Room in Waukegan, Illinois. Early Afternoon." [Border] (6) Spr-Sum 95,
    p. 32.
"No Land of Counterpane." [IndR] (18:1) Spr 95, p. 100.
"Sacred Conversation: Poem on My Birthday." [Northeast] (5:13) Wint 95-96, p.
    21-22.
"To Christ the Lord." [QW] (41) Aut-Wint 95-96, p. 200.
"To My Infant Son." [CrabOR] (1:1) Fall-Wint 95, p. 36.
"To the Reader." [PraS] (69:1) Spr 95, p. 62.
"To the Sun." [PraS] (69:1) Spr 95, p. 63.
"Transcendentals." [Poetry] (166:2) My 95, p. 77.
"A Vision." [Border] (6) Spr-Sum 95, p. 33.
"Why I Despise Myself." [DenQ] (29:4) Spr 95, p. 16.
1214. COOLIDGE, Clark
"A Blues for the Midwest Starts." [RiverC] (15:2) Sum 95, p. 21-25.
1215. COOPER, Burns
"The Fat Keeper." [Nimrod] (38:2) Spr-Sum 95, p. 64-65.
"Figures of Desire" (November in Fairbanks, for Barbara). [Nimrod] (38:2) Spr -
    Sum 95, p. 59-60.
"Inarticulate Reeds." [Nimrod] (38:2) Spr-Sum 95, p. 61-62.
"Toward Circle Hot Springs." [Nimrod] (38:2) Spr-Sum 95, p. 63.
1216. COOPER, Charles
"Compline" (For Stuart Henry). [ChrC] (112:5) 15 F 95, p. 164.
1217. COOPER, G. Burns
"Public Transport." [Hellas] (6:1) Spr-Sum 95, p. 33.
1218. COOPER, Julie R.
"Cross Words" (for James Merrill, 1926-1995. First Prize). [HarvardA] Contest
    Issue, Spr 95, p. 13.
"Lesson." [HarvardA] (vol. 130) Fall 95, p. 21.
1219. COOPER, Lia
"Cockroaches." [GreenHLL] (6) 95, p. 72.
"Explanations." [GreenHLL] (6) 95, p. 69.
"Therapy." [GreenHLL] (6) 95, p. 71.
"Travel Plans." [GreenHLL] (6) 95, p. 70.
1220. COOPER, M. Truman
"Intimacy." [Confr] (56/57) Sum-Fall 95, p. 345.
1221. COOPER, Wyn
"The Life of the Mind." [Agni] (41) 95, p. 98-99.
"Talk." [Ploughs] (21:4) Wint 95-96, p. 35-36.
1222. COOPER-FRATRIK, Julie
"In Cordoba, a Man." [DefinedP] (1:2) Spr-Sum 93, p. 44.
1223. COOPER-STONE, Robin
"Dinner in the Fall." [Ploughs] (21:1) Spr 95, p. 85.
COOPERMAN, Celeste Kostopulos
    See KOSTOPULOS-COOPERMAN, C. (Celeste)
1224. COOPERMAN, Matthew
"What the World Said." [MidAR] (16:1) 95, p. 68-70.
1225. COOPERMAN, Robert
"Apartment House" (A Plainsongs Award Poem). [Plain] (15:3) Spr 95, p. 4-5.
"Benjamin Johnson Recalls Encounters with Indians Along the Oregon Trail."
    [Farm] (13:2 [i.e. 12:2]) Fall-Wint 95, p. 24.
"Captain Homer Atkins, a Year after the Murder of Jimmy Ray Seagraves." [SlipS]
    (15) 95, p. 34.
"A Christmas Carol." [SnailPR] (3:2) 95, p. 6-7.
"Civilian Life." [ChironR] (42) Spr 95, p. 10.

111

"Coach Talmadge Howard, after Cleaning Up Jimmy Seagraves' Mess with Mary
  Sue Riley." [SlipS] (15) 95, p. 33.
"The Commandant of the Garrison at Tomis, at the Death of the Exiled Roman Poet,
  Ovid." [Northeast] (5:12) Sum 95, p. 30-31.
"Evasive Action." [SlipS] (15) 95, p. 37.
"For Our Fifteenth Anniversary" (for Beth). [SantaBR] (3:1) Spr 95, p. 106.
"A Forced Confession." [Footwork] (24/25) 95, p. 58.
"The General Deals with the Separatists." [LullwaterR] (6:1) Spr-Sum 95, p. 84-85.
"George III, Upon the Publication of Volume III of *The Rise and Fall of the Roman
  Empire*, 1788." [Parting] (8:1) Sum 95, p. 22.
"The Gladiator Marcellus Considers His Paramour, Drusilla, Wife of the Exiled Poet
  Ovid." [BellR] (18:1, #37) Spr 95, p. 39-40.
"A Good Boy at Heart." [Ledge] (19) Wint 95, p. 93.
"Handler of the Dead." [Footwork] (24/25) 95, p. 58.
"Little Odessa." [Plain] (16:1) Fall 95, p. 7.
"Maria Gisborne Sits to Tea with Mrs. Hunt and Keats, 12 July 1820." [LitR] (38:2)
  Wint 95, p. 242.
"My Father and FDR." [Northeast] (5:13) Wint 95-96, p. 30-31.
"Nothing to Lose." [Northeast] (5:13) Wint 95-96, p. 28-29.
"Perilla, Step-Daughter of the Exiled Poet Ovid, Entertains a Patron." [BellR] (18:1,
  #37) Spr 95, p. 38.
"Peter Thackeray, on the Oregon Trail, Thinks of Indians." [Farm] (13:2 [i.e. 12:2])
  Fall-Wint 95, p. 25-26.
"Sarah Riley Remembers Her Daughter's Troubles with Jimmy Ray Seagraves."
  [SlipS] (15) 95, p. 32.
"Still He Smiled." [ChironR] (42) Spr 95, p. 10.
"A Story from 1946." [Pearl] (22) Fall-Wint 95, p. 120.
"Symmetries." [Plain] (15:3) Spr 95, p. 14.
"A Texas Miracle." [ChironR] (42) Spr 95, p. 10.
"Tommy Riley, after the Murder of Jimmy Ray Seagraves." [SlipS] (15) 95, p. 31.
"Travelers." [SantaBR] (3:1) Spr 95, p. 105.
"The Two Musketeers." [SlipS] (15) 95, p. 35.
"Views of the General — the Prime Minister." [AntigR] (101) Spr 95, p. 112.
"What I'm Trying to Say." [SlipS] (15) 95, p. 35-36.
1226. COPE, Steven (Steven R.)
  "In Killdeer's Field." [WillowS] (35) Ja 95, p. 46-47.
  "Lifeguard at Shallow Point." [LullwaterR] (5:1) 93-94, p. 14.
1227. CORAY, Anne
  "Alaskan Born." [Nimrod] (38:2) Spr-Sum 95, p. 15.
  "Joe." [Nimrod] (38:2) Spr-Sum 95, p. 16.
  "Rhythmics." [Nimrod] (38:2) Spr-Sum 95, p. 15.
1228. CORBETT, William
  "Family." [Jacaranda] (11) [95 or 96?], p. 135-136.
  "Haying." [SycamoreR] (7:1) Wint 95, p. 42.
  "Song." [SycamoreR] (7:1) Wint 95, p. 43.
1229. CORBUS, Patricia
  "In Circe's Courtyard." [ParisR] (37:137) Wint 95, p. 120.
  "Words to a Dying Star." [ParisR] (37:137) Wint 95, p. 120-121.
1230. CORDARY, J.
  "Beets." [BelPoJ] (45:3) Spr 95, p. 12.
  "March." [BelPoJ] (45:3) Spr 95, p. 11.
  "Something Shy." [BelPoJ] (45:3) Spr 95, p. 10.
1231. CORDARY, Judith
  "Vase." [PoetryE] (41) Aut 95, p. 59.
1232. CORDING, Robert
  "After the Funeral." [Image] (9) Spr 95, p. 94-95.
  "Touch-Me-Not." [Image] (9) Spr 95, p. 96.
1233. COREY, Chet
  "Hunter." [ChironR] (43) Sum 95, p. 36.
  "The Island of Anger." [ChironR] (43) Sum 95, p. 32.
  "The Names of Women" (A Plainsongs Award Poem). [Plain] (15:2) Wint 95, p. 4-
  5.
  "Weather Report." [Plain] (15:3) Spr 95, p. 38.
1234. COREY, Stephen
  "Anything." [SouthernHR] (29:2) Spr 95, p. 124-125.

1235. CORMAN, Cid
"Love's availability" (tr. of Walter Gaspari). [Noctiluca] (2:1, #4) Spr 95, p. 14.
"Magadi" (from "Distance de Fuite," 1993, tr. of Esther Tellerman, w. the author).
    [Noctiluca] (2:1, #4) Spr 95, p. 32-37.
"Recovered Poems" (Selections: 1-3, tr. of Walter Gaspari). [Noctiluca] (2:1, #4)
    Spr 95, p. 17.
"Susceptitudes: 15 Poems." [WorldL] (6) 95, p. 29-33.
"We hear these brilliant vulgarities" (tr. of Walter Gaspari). [Noctiluca] (2:1, #4) Spr
    95, p. 15.
"We remain good friends" (tr. of Walter Gaspari). [Noctiluca] (2:1, #4) Spr 95, p.
    16.
"We sit and watch the river" (tr. of Walter Gaspari). [Noctiluca] (2:1, #4) Spr 95, p.
    14.
"What beauty will you show me" (tr. of Walter Gaspari). [Noctiluca] (2:1, #4) Spr
    95, p. 15.
"What sorrowfulness" (tr. of Walter Gaspari). [Noctiluca] (2:1, #4) Spr 95, p. 16.
"Where are you now" (tr. of Walter Gaspari). [Noctiluca] (2:1, #4) Spr 95, p. 14.
1236. CORN, Alfred
"After Neruda." [Verse] (12:2) 95, p. 33.
"Aphorisms." [Salm] (108) Fall 95, p. 115-118.
"The Bonfire." [Raritan] (15:1) Sum 95, p. 29-33.
"A Conch from Sicily." [WestHR] (49:2) Sum 95, p. 153.
"Little Erie Railroad." [WestHR] (49:2) Sum 95, p. 154-155.
"Maui: Concerto for Island and Developer." [BostonR] (20:3) Sum 95, p. 33.
"Stepson Elegy" (Virginia Whitaker MacMillan Corn, 1924-1992). [Agni] (41) 95,
    p. 39-43.
"Water Like a Philosopher's Stone." [PartR] (62:3) Sum 95, p. 445-446.
"Wonder Bread." [Nat] (260:12) 27 Mr 95, p. 432.
1237. CORNFORD, Adam
"Interfaces" (from *The Cyborg's Path*). [Talisman] (15) Wint 95-96, p. 79-80.
1238. CORNISH, Sam
"The Beating." [LowellR] (2) c1996, p. 6.
"Our Mothers Saying Goodbye." [LowellR] (2) c1996, p. 7.
"Sporting Men." [LowellR] (2) c1996, p. 5.
1239. CORR, Michael
"War." [RiverS] (42/43) 95, p. 28.
1240. CORREIA, Lepê
"Fadas Negras Nordestinas." [Callaloo] (18:4) Fall 95, p. 988.
"Fairy Tales for a Black Northeast" (tr. by Steven F. White). [Callaloo] (18:4) Fall
    95, p. 820.
"Meta-Dentro e Fora" (A D'Jesus Correia). [Callaloo] (18:4) Fall 95, p. 987.
"Meta-Score" (To D'Jesus Correia, tr. by Steven F. White). [Callaloo] (18:4) Fall 95,
    p. 819.
1241. CORRIGAN, Dawn
"Demaree Farm" (Knoxville, Tennessee). [ParisR] (37:135) Sum 95, p. 198-199.
"Letter to Lt. Demaree." [ParisR] (37:135) Sum 95, p. 197.
"The Princess." [ParisR] (37:135) Sum 95, p. 197-198.
1242. CORY, Cynthia Jay
"To Tell a Story (Cleaning Fish)." [ApalQ] (44/45) Fall 95-Wint 96, p. 58.
1243. CORY, Jim
"An Admirer." [ModernW] (3) Sum 95, p. 99.
"Hmmmm." [ModernW] (3) Sum 95, p. 100-101.
1244. COSIER, Tony
"Pastels." [AntigR] (102/103) Sum-Aug 95, p. 110.
"Red Pike." [AntigR] (102/103) Sum-Aug 95, p. 109.
"Wild Apples." [Blueline] (16) 95, p. 98.
1245. COSTA, Catherine D.
"Earl n Me." [SpinningJ] (1) Fall 95-Wint 96, p. 41.
"Sister." [SpinningJ] (1) Fall 95-Wint 96, p. 40.
1246. COSTA, Horacio
"The Boy and the Pillow" (For Manuel, tr. by M. B. Jordan, Clayton Eshleman and
    the author). [Sulfur] (15:1, #36) Spr 95, p. 131-146.
1247. COSTA, Kevin
"December Rains." [DefinedP] (2:1) Fall-Wint 93, p. 31-32.
1248. COSTLEY, Bill
"Mossy Lions (Leone Muscosi)." [Noctiluca] (2:1, #4) Spr 95, p. 30.

1249. COTRAU, Liviu
"Winter Vision at the Mouth of the River" (tr. of Ion Mircea, w. Adam J. Sorkin).
[Vis] (48) 95, p. 40.
1250. COTTERILL, Sarah
"Susan in the Potter's Field." [PoetryNW] (36:2) Sum 95, p. 41-43.
1251. COTTLE, Katherine
"Cole Slaw" (For my great grandmother, Mamie Gretel Oxley). [WillowS] (35) Ja
95, p. 74-75.
"My Father's Dreams." [Footwork] (24/25) 95, p. 42.
1252. COTTLE, Thomas
"Daisy Day." [NoCarLR] (2:2) 95, p. 127.
"Resignation." [NoCarLR] (2:2) 95, p. 127.
1253. COTTRELL, Christiel
"The Bear As Buddha." [Sun] (234) Je 95, p. 6.
1254. COULTER, Page P.
"Protocol" (from The Cowbridge at Dawn). [AmerPoR] (24:1) Ja-F 95, p. 33.
1255. COUNSIL, Wendy
"Fortress." [WestHR] (49:3) Fall 95, p. 281.
COURCY, Lynne Hugo de
See DeCOURCY, Lynne Hugo
1256. COVEY, Patricia
"Camouflage." [NewYorkQ] (54) 95, p. 76-77.
"New York Tenants." [NewYorkQ] (55) 95, p. 94.
"Vanity." [LitR] (38:2) Wint 95, p. 256-257.
1257. COWEE, Bill
"Fear Behind the Curtain." [WeberS] (12:2) Spr-Sum 95, p. 70.
1258. COX, Joseph T.
"Miles Standish Forest, Plymouth, Mass, 1934." [War] (7:1) Spr-sum 95, p. 61.
"Shaman" (for John Wolfe, 2/327 Infantry). [War] (7:2) Fall-Wint 95, p. 55.
1259. COX, Mark
"Get Me Again." [Journal] (19:2) Fall-Wint 95, p. 26-28.
"The Moles." [Journal] (19:2) Fall-Wint 95, p. 29-30.
"The Pier." [AmerPoR] (24:6) N-D 95, p. 51.
"The River." [AmerPoR] (24:6) N-D 95, p. 51.
1260. COX, Mary W.
"The Naked Truth" (Inspired by Henry Oliver Walker's mural in the Library of
Congress). [Light] (14) Sum 95, p. 15.
1261. COX, Terrance
"Naming of Plants II: Recall" (for Arleen Bush). [MalR] (113) Wint 95, p. 72-73.
1262. COYKENDALL, Scott
"The Morgue." [HayF] (17) Fall-Wint 95, p. 120-121.
1263. COYNE, Kevin
"At the Nursing Home for Nuns." [BelPoJ] (46:2) Wint 95-96, p. 6-7.
CRABBE, Chris Wallace
See WALLACE-CRABBE, Chris
1264. CRAIG, Mike
"At the Aquarium." [CutB] (44) Sum 95, p. 44-46.
"Epigraph." [CutB] (44) Sum 95, p. 112.
1265. CRAIK, Roger
"Differences." [Poem] (74) N 95, p. 31.
"To W. B. Yeats's Poem, 'To a Squirrel at Kyle-Na-No'." [Poem] (74) N 95, p. 32.
1266. CRAIN, Rachel Channon
"Train Crossing." [CapeR] (30:2) Fall 95, p. 35.
1267. CRAMER, Barbara
"The Way the Day Begins." [BellR] (18:2, #38) Fall 95, p. 11.
1268. CRAMER, Steven
"Intensive Care." [CrabOR] (1:1) Fall-Wint 95, p. 39-40.
"The Obscure." [CrabOR] (1:1) Fall-Wint 95, p. 37-38.
1269. CRANDALL, Jeff
"Positive." [NewDeltaR] (12:2) Spr-Sum 95, p. 49-50.
1270. CRANE, George
"A Thousand Pieces of Snow" (22 selections, tr. of Fung Hae Suh and Zhou Lu Jing,
w. Tsung Tsai). [Archae] (5) Spr 95, p. 6-29.
1271. CRANE, Hart
"The Broken Tower." [AmerPoR] (24:5) S-O 95, p. 56.

1272. CRANSTON, Adwain A.
"Winter Lodgings: One Hundred Verses and One Verse" (in Japanese and English). [Archae] (5) Spr 95, p. 30-46.
1273. CRANSTON, E. A.
"In the Fort." [US1] (30/31) 95, p. 11.
1274. CRASNARU, Daniela
"The Burning" (tr. by Adam J. Sorkin and Ioana Ieronim). [Vis] (48) 95, p. 39.
1275. CRAWFORD, John
"French Quarter at Eight" (from *I Have Become Familiar with the Rain*). [AmerPoR] (24:4) Jl-Ag 95, p. 22.
"I Have Become Familiar with the Rain" (Excerpt). [AmerPoR] (24:5) S-O 95, p. 22.
1276. CREECH, Morri (Morris)
"The Book of Absences." [PlumR] (9) [95 or 96], p. 80.
"Childhood." [Vis] (47) 95, p. 15.
"An Old Story." [PlumR] (9) [95 or 96], p. 81.
1277. CREELEY, Robert
"Credo." [ColR] (22:1) Spr 95, p. 114-116.
"A Feeling." [ColR] (22:1) Spr 95, p. 117.
"Four Days in Vermont." [Conjunc] (24) 95, p. 267-270.
"Given." [ColR] (22:1) Spr 95, p. 121.
"Goodbye." [ColR] (22:1) Spr 95, p. 127-128.
"Help." [RiverS] (42/43) 95, p. 159.
"Loops." [ColR] (22:1) Spr 95, p. 124.
"The Mirror." [ColR] (22:1) Spr 95, p. 122.
"Old Story." [ColR] (22:1) Spr 95, p. 120.
"Pictures." [ColR] (22:1) Spr 95, p. 123.
"Silence." [ColR] (22:1) Spr 95, p. 118-119.
"So." [RiverS] (42/43) 95, p. 158.
"Thinking." [ColR] (22:1) Spr 95, p. 125-126.
1278. CRENNER, James
"Another Summer Morning." [SenR] (25:1) Spr 95, p. 34.
CREW, Louie
See LI, Min Hua
1279. CREWS, Judson
"We Found a Wrecked Security in Intrinsic." [FreeL] (14) Wint 95, p. 5.
1280. CREWS, Mary
"Origami Flight." [Crucible] (31) Fall 95, p. 34.
1281. CRICHTON, Juliet
"Leaving & Left." [HampSPR] Wint 95, p. 21.
1282. CRILL, Hildred
"Agatha Christie Disappears." [CreamCR] (19:1) Spr 95, p. 115.
"Women of Avignon." [CreamCR] (19:1) Spr 95, p. 114.
1283. CRINNIN, Gerard (Gerry)
"Held Over for Another Smashed Weekend." [NewMyths] (2:2/3:1) 95, p. 69.
"Matins" (1995 Poetry Competition: The Ruth Cable Memorial Prize). [Elf] (5:2) Sum 95, p. 17.
"Strange Attractor." [NewMyths] (2:2/3:1) 95, p. 68.
1284. CRISICK, Maureen
"Arriving in Balaton." [SilverFR] (25) Sum 95, p. 12.
1285. CRIST-EVANS, Craig
"Every Spring." [GreenMR] (8:2) Fall-Wint 95-96, p. 89.
"How Camp Dogs Talk." [GreenMR] (8:2) Fall-Wint 95-96, p. 85-87.
"The Language of Guns." [GreenMR] (8:2) Fall-Wint 95-96, p. 88.
1286. CRIVELLONE, Maryfrances
"Bigfoot." [HawaiiR] (19:2) Fall 95, p. 119.
"Persephone's Turn." [HawaiiR] (19:2) Fall 95, p. 120.
1287. CROCKER, Daniel
"I Believe Socrates." [ChironR] (44/45) Aut-Wint 95, p. 15.
1288. CROFT, Jason
"Along the Roads Still Graveled." [GreenHLL] (6) 95, p. 17.
1289. CROFT, Lee B.
"Romance" (tr. of Alexander S. Pushkin). [HayF] (17) Fall-Wint 95, p. 19, 21.
1290. CROMETT, Judy Henningsgaard
"Boy Leading a Horse: Visiting the Paley Exhibit." [SmPd] (32:1, #93) Wint 95, p. 31.

1291. CRONIN, Jenny
  "Missing." [PoetL] (90:3) Fall 95, p. 26.
  "Strip." [PoetL] (90:3) Fall 95, p. 25.
1292. CRONIN, Leslie Kurtzahn
  "Under the Rug." [PlumR] (8) [95], p. 54.
1293. CROSS, William Stephen
  "All Night, in the Flesh" (tr. of Richard Exner). [InterQ] (2:1/2) 95, p. 99.
  "Black Birth" (tr. of Richard Exner). [InterQ] (2:1/2) 95, p. 100.
  "Detected" (for Oskar Jan Tauschinski, tr. of Richard Exner). [InterQ] (2:1/2) 95, p. 101.
1294. CROSSMAN, Rae
  "Confluence" (For R. Murray Schafer). [Descant] (26:1, #88) Spr 95, p. 132.
  "The Drums of the Sky." [Descant] (26:1, #88) Spr 95, p. 127-128.
  "The Spirit Bear." [Descant] (26:1, #88) Spr 95, p. 129-131.
  "Who Howls in the Forest." [Descant] (26:1, #88) Spr 95, p. 121-126.
  "Word Shaker." [Descant] (26:1, #88) Spr 95, p. 119-120.
1295. CROTEAU, Jeffrey
  "The Velvet Elvis Sestina." [Conscience] (16:4) Wint 95-96, p. 37.
1296. CROTTY, Patrick
  "Era's End" (tr. of Mairtín Odireáin). [SouthernR] (31:3) Jl/Sum 95, p. 472.
  "Mary Hogan's Quatrains" (tr. of Máire Mhac an tSaoi). [SouthernR] (31:3) Jl/Sum 95, p. 476-479.
  "Memory of Sunday" (tr. of Mairtín Odireáin). [SouthernR] (31:3) Jl/Sum 95, p. 472-473.
  "My Mother's Burial" (tr. of Seán Oríordáin). [SouthernR] (31:3) Jl/Sum 95, p. 474-475.
  "The Shannon Estuary Welcomes the Fish" (tr. of Nuala Ní Dhomhnaill). [SouthernR] (31:3) Jl/Sum 95, p. 480.
1297. CROW, Mary
  "Crying Wolf." [Nimrod] (39:1) Fall-Wint 95, p. 102.
  "Knives and Scissors." [Nimrod] (39:1) Fall-Wint 95, p. 101.
  "Poetics" (tr. of Juan Calzadilla). [MidAR] (15:1/2) 95, p. 43.
  "Stained Glass Window of a Woman Alone" (tr. of Yolanda Pantin). [GrahamHR] (19) Wint 95-96, p. 59-61.
1298. CROYSTON, John
  "Reading." [Footwork] (24/25) 95, p. 81.
1299. CROZIER, Lorna
  "Crossing Willow Bridge." [Event] (24:1) Spr 95, p. 28-29.
  "Millstone." [MalR] (110) Spr 95, p. 72-73.
  "Names of Loss and Beauty." [Event] (24:1) Spr 95, p. 30.
  "Naming the Light." [CanLit] (147) Wint 95, p. 10.
  "The Night of Your Conception." [Event] (24:1) Spr 95, p. 31-32.
  "Thirteen Small Poems for Your Penis." [Quarry] (44:1) 95, p. 81-86.
1300. CRUMMEY, Michael
  "Accidents: A Love Story" (a thirtieth anniversary poem). [TickleAce] (27) Spr-Sum 94, p. 117-118.
  "Apprenticeships." [Quarry] (44:2) 95, p. 110.
  "Fire on the Labrador" (after an etching by David Blackwood). [TickleAce] (27) Spr-Sum 94, p. 114.
  "Forge." [MalR] (113) Wint 95, p. 94-95.
  "Mona Lisa." [AntigR] (102/103) Sum-Aug 95, p. 87.
  "Power Outage" (for Rose). [TickleAce] (27) Spr-Sum 94, p. 116.
  "Rainy Season / Whale Music." [TickleAce] (27) Spr-Sum 94, p. 115.
  "Salt." [AntigR] (102/103) Sum-Aug 95, p. 88.
  "Victor Jara's Hands." [Dandel] (22:1) 95, p. 65.
1301. CRUNK, T.
  "Blues for Home." [CutB] (44) Sum 95, p. 24.
CRUZ, Víctor Hernández
  See HERNANDEZ-CRUZ, Víctor
1302. CRUZ-BERNAL, Mairym
  "Ballad of the Blood" (Selections: 7 poems, tr. of María Elena Cruz Varela, w. Deborah Digges). [AmerPoR] (24:4) Jl-Ag 95, p. 23-25.
  "Cutting Pablo's Hair." [BostonR] (20:1) F-Mr 95, p. 9.
  "The Pain of Pleasure." [BostonR] (20:1) F-Mr 95, p. 9.
  "Playmates in the Bathtub." [BostonR] (20:1) F-Mr 95, p. 9.

1303. CRUZ VARELA, María Elena
"Ballad of the Blood" (Selections: 7 poems, tr. by Deborah Digges and Mairym Cruz-Bernal). [AmerPoR] (24:4) Jl-Ag 95, p. 23-25.
1304. CRYER, James M.
"In the Cold Pavillion: Entertaining" (tr. of Po Chu-I). [LitR] (38:3) Spr 95, p. 324.
"Lung Ch'ang Temple: The Lotus Pond" (tr. of Po Chu-I). [LitR] (38:3) Spr 95, p. 323.
"The Pond in Autumn" (tr. of Po Chu-I). [LitR] (38:3) Spr 95, p. 323.
"Welcoming My Neighbor to the East" (tr. of Po Chu-I). [LitR] (38:3) Spr 95, p. 323.
1305. CSAMER, Mary Ellen (Merry Ellen)
"Safehouses." [AntigR] (101) Spr 95, p. 108-109.
"True Shape of the Heart." [Dandel] (22:1) 95, p. 6-7.
"Yellow Bag." [AntigR] (101) Spr 95, p. 110-111.
1306. CSOORI, Sándor
"Among the Ferns of Finland" (tr. by Len Roberts). [LitR] (38:3) Spr 95, p. 453.
"Autumn" (tr. by Len Roberts). [LitR] (38:3) Spr 95, p. 451.
"Can You Still Hear It?" (tr. by Len Roberts). [LitR] (38:3) Spr 95, p. 452.
"I Lock Myself In" (tr. by Len Roberts and László Vértes). [LitR] (38:3) Spr 95, p. 450.
"If You Were God's Relative" (tr. by Len Roberts). [Chelsea] (58) 95, p. 30.
"May the Water Keep Vigil with Me" (tr. by Len Roberts and Anette Marta). [GrandS] (14:2, #54) Fall 95, p. 22.
"So You Won't Be a Witness Today Either" (tr. by Len Roberts and Anette Marta). [GrandS] (14:2, #54) Fall 95, p. 21.
"With a Hangover" (tr. by Len Roberts and László Vértes). [LitR] (38:3) Spr 95, p. 449.
"You Enter the Moment" (tr. by Len Roberts). [Chelsea] (58) 95, p. 29.
1307. CUBLEY, Lannie
"What Lies Between Us." [SouthernPR] (35:1) Sum 95, p. 55.
1308. CUDDEBACK, Nicole
"Celadon Water Dropper, 11th-Century Korea." [WestHR] (49:2) Sum 95, p. 150-151.
"Corleto." [LaurelR] (29:1) Wint 95, p. 85.
"Grapefruit." [PoetL] (90:2) Sum 95, p. 59.
"Petrarch on the Mountain." [WestHR] (49:2) Sum 95, p. 151-152.
1309. CULHANE, Brian
"The Last Canto." [SouthernHR] (29:2) Spr 95, p. 170-171.
"Monument" (L.B., 1955-1979). [NewRep] (212:25) 19 Je 95, p. 44.
1310. CULLAR, Carol
"Howie Wazatski." [Kalliope] (17:1) 95, p. 8-9.
"Out, Out." [RagMag] (12:2) Spr 95, p. 97.
"The Pathfinder." [RagMag] (12:2) Spr 95, p. 96-97.
1311. CULVER, Irene
"A Doublebed in the Garden of Mundane" (one of four Neva poems). [BellArk] (11:1) Ja-F 95, p. 31.
"Hagop and Goodlap Hapgood & Happiness" (one of four Neva poems). [BellArk] (11:1) Ja-F 95, p. 31.
"Living" (one of four Neva poems). [BellArk] (11:1) Ja-F 95, p. 31.
"School in Neva Land" (one of four Neva poems). [BellArk] (11:1) Ja-F 95, p. 31.
1312. CUMBERLAND, Sharon
"I Know I Am Capable of Great Love." [LaurelR] (29:2) Sum 95, p. 17.
"Postulant." [IndR] (18:1) Spr 95, p. 96.
"Smoke Offering." [IndR] (18:1) Spr 95, p. 95.
1313. CUMMINGS, Darcy
"Butterfly Tree." [JINJPo] (17:2) Aut 95, p. 35.
"How I Learned to Let Go." [Footwork] (24/25) 95, p. 86.
1314. CUMMINS, James
"Guide." [CharR] (21:2) Fall 95, p. 106.
"Romantic Love." [CharR] (21:2) Fall 95, p. 105-106.
1315. CUMMINS, Richard J.
"At the Next Table: Speaking Italian." [Hellas] (6:1) Spr-Sum 95, p. 86.
1316. CUMPIAN, Carlos
"Hermanas Guapas (Pretty Sisters)." [AnotherCM] (29) Spr 95, p. 20-21.

1317. CUNAGIN, Karen
"On Leaving the Old House in Fallbrook" (for Barbara. 3rd Place — 1995 CR
Poetry Contest). [ChironR] (44/45) Aut-Wint 95, p. 32.
1318. CUNNINGHAM, Don
"The Stenciled Room." [DefinedP] (3) 95, p. 38.
"Summa." [HiramPoR] (58/59) Spr 95-Wint 96, p. 18.
1319. CUNNINGHAM, La Gail A.
"Neighborhood" (WritersCorps Program, Washington, DC). [WashR] (21:2) Ag-S
95, p. 16.
1320. CUNNINGHAM, Mark
"The Pineal Gland." [ProseP] (4) 95, p. 16.
"Tura Satana." [HawaiiR] (19:2) Fall 95, p. 147.
1321. CURBELO, Silvia
"The Secret History of Water" (Excerpt, after a photograph by J. Tomás Lopez).
[MidAR] (15:1/2) 95, p. 207-208.
1322. CURDY, Averill
"Apricots." [Calyx] (16:2) Wint 95-96, p. 87.
1323. CURNOW, Allen
"A Busy Port." [Verse] (12:2) 95, p. 34-35.
1324. CURRIER, Douglas K.
"Bite." [GreenHLL] (6) 95, p. 87-88.
"Reading to My Daughter." [GreenHLL] (6) 95, p. 89.
1325. CURRY, Elizabeth R.
"A Woman's Life." [GreenHLL] (6) 95, p. 97.
1326. CURTIS, Tony
"California Burning." [Epoch] (44:3) 95, p. 306-307.
"The Miracle." [SouthernR] (31:3) Jl/Sum 95, p. 526-528.
"Penance." [SouthernR] (31:3) Jl/Sum 95, p. 526.
CUSHING, Gaye Simmons
See SIMMONS-CUSHING, Gaye
1327. CUSHING, James
"Histories of Great Men and Women." [OxfordM] (10:1) Wint 94-Spr 95, p. 15.
"Letter to a Painter (1)." [LullwaterR] (5:1) 93-94, p. 56.
"Letter to a Painter (2)." [LullwaterR] (5:1) 93-94, p. 57.
"Letter to a Painter (2)." [MidwQ] (36:2) Wint 95, p. 155.
"Lovers in a Landscape." [OxfordM] (10:1) Wint 94-Spr 95, p. 13.
"Systematic Romanticism." [OxfordM] (10:1) Wint 94-Spr 95, p. 14.
"Twins." [LullwaterR] (5:1) 93-94, p. 58.
1328. CUSHMAN, Stephen
"Farewell and Hail." [FloridaR] (21:1) 95, p. 66.
"Make the Bed." [TarRP] (35:1) Fall 95, p. 17.
1329. CUTLER, Bruce
"Walt Whitman, I Hear You Saying." [MidwQ] (36:4) Sum 95, p. 360-361.
1330. CYR, Gilles
"L'amandier sauvage." [Os] (40) 95, p. 20.
"Des flocons." [Os] (40) 95, p. 22.
"Je ne vois pas." [Os] (40) 95, p. 23.
"Poèmes" (4 poems). [Os] (40) 95, p. 20-23.
"Sur les pentes." [Os] (40) 95, p. 21.
1331. CZURY, Craig
"But These Boys Today." [ProseP] (4) 95, p. 17.
1332. CZYZEWSKI, Wes
"On Dutch Neck Road." [US1] (30/31) 95, p. 26.

D., David
See DAVID D.
D., Michelle
See MICHELLE D.
1333. DABNEY, Stuart
"Sources of the Flute" (Anasazi ruins, New Mexico). [GeoR] (49:4) Wint 95, p. 799-
801.
1334. DACEY, Philip
"Cadenza Cum Cuff Links." [SycamoreR] (7:1) Wint 95, p. 10-11.
"Disney: The Wall." [MidAR] (15:1/2) 95, p. 117-119.
"Equinox." [Journal] (19:2) Fall-Wint 95, p. 5-6.

"Florence Nightingale in Egypt." [TexasR] (16:1/4) 95, p. 112-114.
"Letting Go of Chocolate" (for Carl Lindner). [SnailPR] (3:2) 95, p. 28.
"Postcard Sonnet: The Wall" (Washington, D.C., Summer, 1994). [DenQ] (30:1)
    Sum 95, p. 28.
"Self-Portrait in Lynd." [PoetryNW] (36:4) Wint 95-96, p. 39.
"Sentry: The Wall" (Washington, D.C.). [TarRP] (35:1) Fall 95, p. 23-24.
"Silver" (in memory of Ben Ludwig). [ColEng] (57:1) Ja 95, p. 85.
"Trousers." [LitR] (38:2) Wint 95, p. 270-271.
"Walt Whitman Falls Asleep Over Florence Nightingale's *Notes on Nursing.*" [Shen]
    (45:2) Sum 95, p. 36-39.
"Whitman: The Wall." [SycamoreR] (7:2) Sum 95, p. 43.
1335. DACHSEL, Marita
    "Salinas" (Short Grain Contest Winners: Prose Poem, Honourable Mention). [Grain]
        (22:3) Wint 95, p. 67.
1336. DACUS, Rachel
    "A Dance." [BellArk] (11:3) My-Je 95, p. 12.
    "Earth Lessons." [BellArk] (11:3) My-Je 95, p. 12.
    "Poet in Labor." [PoetL] (90:3) Fall 95, p. 27.
1337. DAGOLD, Raphael
    "Season of Burning Leaves." [QW] (40) Spr-Sum 95, p. 90-91.
1338. DAHL, David
    "Kalypso." [HeavenB] (12) 95, p. 43.
    "Momentum." [HeavenB] (12) 95, p. 4.
1339. DAHLKEMPER, Frank
    "Grasses in My Dream." [SouthernPR] (35:2) Wint 95, p. 39-43.
1340. DAIGON, Ruth
    "Ecology Lesson." [ChironR] (44/45) Aut-Wint 95, p. 10.
    "Every Herring Hangs by Its Own Head" (— Thomas Carlyle). [ChironR] (44/45)
        Aut-Wint 95, p. 10.
    "In This Watching Place." [ChironR] (44/45) Aut-Wint 95, p. 10.
    "In This Watching Place." [Kalliope] (17:3) 95, p. 50.
    "Not Yet Visible." [DefinedP] (2:2) Spr-Sum 94, p. 31-32.
    "Sudden Chill." [PraF] (16:2, #71) Sum 95, p. 54.
    "Summertime." [DefinedP] (2:2) Spr-Sum 94, p. 30-31.
    "What Happens." [DefinedP] (2:2) Spr-Sum 94, p. 28-29.
1341. DAILEY, Joel
    "A Distant Muzak." [NewOR] (21:2) Sum 95, p. 67.
    "Nuevo Laredo." [NewOR] (21:2) Sum 95, p. 67.
1342. DAILY, Mike
    "Gagaku Dream." [WormR] (35:4, #140) 95, p. 152.
    "Helen Morton." [WormR] (35:4, #140) 95, p. 152-153.
    "Mysteries." [WormR] (35:4, #140) 95, p. 151-152.
    "She Said." [WormR] (35:4, #140) 95, p. 152.
1343. DAKSHINAMOORTHY
    "Passage to America" (tr. of Ayyappa Paniker, w. the author, J. O. Perry, K.
        Satchidanandan, and Esther Y. Smith). [ManyMM] (1:3) 95, p. 120-126.
1344. D'ALESSANDRO, Patricia
    "Epigraph" (The 1994 Allen Ginsberg Poetry Awards: Honorable Mention).
        [Footwork] (24/25) 95, p. 190-192.
1345. DALEY, Michael
    "Fallen." [GrahamHR] (19) Wint 95-96, p. 83-84.
1346. DALIBARD, Jill
    "The Catalogue of Small Acts." [AntigR] (102/103) Sum-Aug 95, p. 82-84.
1347. DALLAS, Jon
    "Some Children Are Afraid." [GreenMR] (8:2) Fall-Wint 95-96, p. 110.
    "Thermal." [Plain] (15:2) Wint 95, p. 9.
1348. DALLAT, C. L.
    "On the Island." [Verse] (12:2) 95, p. 36-37.
1349. DALMAS, Victor
    "Friend of the Dead One" (tr. of Lody Aoueiss). [Pembroke] (27) 95, p. 105-107.
1350. DALTON, Mary
    "Cleaving." [TickleAce] (27) Spr-Sum 94, p. 113.
    "Glass, Looking Out." [TickleAce] (27) Spr-Sum 94, p. 110.
    "Mother, Games of the Language Poets." [TickleAce] (27) Spr-Sum 94, p. 111-112.
1351. DALY, Catherine
    "The Snow Queen." [Ascent] (19:2) Wint 95, p. 29.

1352. DALY, Chris
"We Don't Do Drive-by." [RagMag] (12:2) Spr 95, p. 38-39.
1353. DAME, Enid
"Dina's Happy Ending." [NewYorkQ] (54) 95, p. 67-68.
"Miriam's Water." [ManyMM] (1:3) 95, p. 20-21.
"Petaluma." [ManyMM] (1:3) 95, p. 22-23.
1354. DAN, Jon
"Villa-Lobos Played on a Piano" (tr. by Hallberg Hallmundsson). [Vis] (49) 95, p. 32.
1355. DANA, Robert
"Hello, Stranger." [AntR] (53:1) Wint 95, p. 72.
"Loose Change." [PlumR] (8) [95], p. 13.
"Off Day on Estéro." [HighP] (10:3) Wint 95, p. 38-39.
"The Way Day Begins." [HighP] (10:3) Wint 95, p. 36-37.
1356. DANELY, John C.
"Brad Pitt Borrows Grandpa's Riding Mower." [Rosebud] (2:3) Aut-Wint 95, p. 64.
"Martin Sheen Takes the Place of My Father." [Rosebud] (2:3) Aut-Wint 95, p. 63.
"Milla and Donald Sutherland Get-It-On in the Back of My Camry." [Rosebud] (2:3) Aut-Wint 95, p. 65.
1357. DANEZ, Carlos
"La Doble Fuente de Narciso." [Luz] (8) Spr 95, p. 57.
1358. DANGEL, Leo
"A Father and Son Standing at the Ruins." [MidwQ] (36:4) Sum 95, p. 361-362.
"Living Alone." [NorthStoneR] (12) 95, p. 241.
1359. D'ANGELO, Patricia
"In the Compost." [BelPoJ] (46:2) Wint 95-96, p. 8.
1360. DANIEL, Hal J., III
"A Quasi-Poetic Experience." [Crucible] (30) Fall 94, p. 20.
1361. DANIEL, John
"After." [NorthStoneR] (12) 95, p. 242.
"Marie Celeste." [NorthStoneR] (12) 95, p. 243.
1362. DANIELS, Barbara
"This Is a Practice Planet." [MassR] (36:1) Spr 95, p. 119.
"The Woman Who Tries to Believe." [MassR] (36:1) Spr 95, p. 120.
1363. DANIELS, Carl M.
"The First of Many Very Long Meals." [SlipS] (15) 95, p. 28.
1364. DANIELS, Celia A.
"Walk in Beauty" (Navajo saying). [MidwQ] (36:4) Sum 95, p. 363.
1365. DANIELS, Jim
"Almost Choking." [HolCrit] (32:3) Je 95, p. 20.
"Ashes." [CrabOR] (1:1) Fall-Wint 95, p. 41-42.
"Cemetery, Torre Gentile." [CimR] (110) Ja 96, p. 82-83.
"Cricket." [Crazy] (48) Spr 95, p. 70-71.
"Digger's Leak." [PassN] (16:1) Sum 95, p. 30.
"Fennel." [Crazy] (48) Spr 95, p. 72-73.
"Getting Over." [TampaR] (11) Fall 95, p. 33.
"Getting There." [AntR] (53:3) Sum 95, p. 336-337.
"Hold-up at The Uni-Mart, 98 Degrees." [PassN] (16:1) Sum 95, p. 31-32.
"Lasting, March, 1994." [TampaR] (11) Fall 95, p. 34-35.
"Logging Silence" (Shark Valley, the Everglades). [LowellR] (1) Sum 94, p. 10-11.
"My Mother's See-Through Blouse." [Iowa] (25:1) Wint 95, p. 116-118.
"Proving Grounds" (for my grandfather). [LowellR] (1) Sum 94, p. 5-9.
"Remembering the Fight Song." [LowellR] (1) Sum 94, p. 12.
"Salsa." [PoetL] (90:4) Wint 95-96, p. 5.
"Spider Boy Killed after Massive Manhunt." [ChiR] (41:4) 95, p. 95-96.
"What's Wrong with America." [MidAR] (15:1/2) 95, p. 111-112.
1366. D'ANNA, Lynnette
"Cool Jazz Riff." [PraF] (16:2, #71) Sum 95, p. 47.
1367. DANSON, Elizabeth
"Flying Across the Continent in Winter." [US1] (30/31) 95, p. 14.
1368. DANTE (Dante Alighieri)
"Canto XVIII, from The Inferno" (tr. by Stanley Plumly). [OhioR] (54) 95, p. 32-35.
"*Inferno*, Canto XV" (tr. by Armand Schwerner). [AmerPoR] (24:5) S-O 95, p. 24-25.

1369. DANTICAT, Edwidge
"Alabama" (A Sea Animal's Journal, tr. of René Depestre). [CaribbeanW] (9) 95, p. 90-91.
"Eros and Revolution" (A montage for a society full of consumers, tr. of René Depestre). [CaribbeanW] (9) 95, p. 89-90.
"How the Angels Would Cry" (for Nelly, tr. of René Depestre). [CaribbeanW] (9) 95, p. 93-94.
"Is It True?" (tr. of René Depestre). [CaribbeanW] (9) 95, p. 91-93.
"My Definition of Poetry" (tr. of René Depestre). [CaribbeanW] (9) 95, p. 94.
"Nostalgia" (tr. of René Depestre). [CaribbeanW] (9) 95, p. 88.
1370. DANUSER, Lori
"Barracoon." [AmerLC] (7) 95, p. 28-29.
"Mourning." [AmerLC] (7) 95, p. 30-31.
DAO, Bei
See BEI DAO
1371. DARCEY, Philip
"Shower Sex on Sunday." [PoetryNW] (36:1) Spr 95, p. 40.
1372. DARLING, Robert
"A Journey into Winter." [CumbPR] (14:2) Spr 95, p. 58.
1373. DARLINGTON, Andrew
"Biting the Feeding Hand / Drugstore Rock 'n' Roll." [AxeF] (3) 90, p. 38.
"The Girl Whose Name Is Death / Beyond the Barrier of Space, Time, and Leeds." [Bogg] (67) 95, p. 43.
1374. DARMS, Greg
"Alsea Tidewater." [BellArk] (11:4) Jl-Ag 95, p. 12.
1375. DARNELL, Carter
"Saturday." [SoCoast] (18) Ja 95, p. 58.
1376. DARUWALLA, Keki N.
"At Quarter to Four." [AnotherCM] (29) Spr 95, p. 87-89.
"The Future Folding into Itself." [AnotherCM] (29) Spr 95, p. 90.
"In the Footsteps of the Sanskrit Poets." [AnotherCM] (29) Spr 95, p. 86.
1377. DASELER, Robert
"Wind Instruments." [CimR] (111) Ap 95, p. 75.
1378. DASGUPTA, Buddhadeb
"The Balcony" (tr. by Lila Ray). [AnotherCM] (29) Spr 95, p. 91.
"The Coming One." [ManyMM] (1:3) 95, p. 140.
"Ears" (tr. by Lila Ray). [AnotherCM] (29) Spr 95, p. 95.
"Fingers" (tr. by Lila Ray). [AnotherCM] (29) Spr 95, p. 92.
"Get Ready" (tr. by Lila Ray). [AnotherCM] (29) Spr 95, p. 94.
"A Little Earlier." [ManyMM] (1:3) 95, p. 146.
"The Man." [ManyMM] (1:3) 95, p. 142.
"Shirt Number Seven." [ManyMM] (1:3) 95, p. 141.
"Six Days or Six Months" (tr. by Lila Ray). [AnotherCM] (29) Spr 95, p. 96.
"Soap." [ManyMM] (1:3) 95, p. 144-145.
"Swallowing Up" (tr. by Lila Ray). [AnotherCM] (29) Spr 95, p. 93.
"Umbrellas." [ManyMM] (1:3) 95, p. 143.
1379. DASGUPTA, Manjush
"About Morning" (tr. of Tapas Roy, w. Peter Michelson). [AnotherCM] (29) Spr 95, p. 115.
"She My Pupil." [ManyMM] (1:3) 95, p. 157.
"Time Warp" (tr. of Tapas Roy, w. Peter Michelson). [AnotherCM] (29) Spr 95, p. 116.
1380. DATTA, Jyotirmoy
"Guiltful" (tr. of Anuradha Mahapatra, w. Carolyne Wright). [ManyMM] (1:3) 95, p. 159.
"Primeval" (tr. of Anuradha Mahapatra, w. Carolyne Wright). [ManyMM] (1:3) 95, p. 160.
"Sleep" (tr. of Anuradha Mahapatra, w. Carolyne Wright). [ManyMM] (1:3) 95, p. 161.
1381. DAUER, Lesley
"Frida Fat and Thin." [PoetryE] (40) Spr 95, p. 22-23.
"Lois at the Hair Salon." [PoetryE] (40) Spr 95, p. 21.
"Making Peach Melba." [PoetryE] (40) Spr 95, p. 20.
1382. DAUGHERTY, Michael
"Lines from No-Man's Land." [Dandel] (22:1) 95, p. 8-9.
"Loose Nots." [Bogg] (67) 95, p. 8.

1383. DAUMAL, René
"Loyalty Oath" (tr. by Jordan Jones). [HeavenB] (12) 95, p. 34-35.
"No More" (from: *The Anti-Heaven*, tr. by Jordan Jones). [HeavenB] (12) 95, p. 32-33.
1384. DAVENPORT, Guy
"A Private Talk Among Friends" (tr. of Herondas). [GrandS] (14:1, #53) Sum 95, p. 53-58.
1385. DAVID, Gary
"Envoi: Beyond All These Words." [BlackBR] (20) Spr-Sum 95, p. 20.
1386. DAVID D. (John Howard Pavilion, St. Elizabeth's Hospital, Washington, DC)
"Freedom of the Blues" (WritersCorps Program). [WashR] (21:2) Ag-S 95, p. 10.
1387. DAVIDSON, Daniel
"Collected Works." [Talisman] (15) Wint 95-96, p. 105-110.
1388. DAVIDSON, Phebe
"Before a Storm in Carolina." [SoCoast] (18) Ja 95, p. 31.
DAVIDSON, Terri Brown
See BROWN-DAVIDSON, Terri
1389. DAVIES, Hilary
"Interior" (after Bonnard, tr. of Jean Joubert). [Verse] (12:2) 95, p. 77-78.
1390. DAVIES, Robert A.
"It No Longer Should Matter." [Northeast] (5:13) Wint 95-96, p. 26.
1391. DAVIGNON, Richard
"Puerto Vallarta." [Parting] (8:2) Wint 95-96, p. 36.
1392. DAVIS, Andrea C.
"Looking for China." [Poem] (74) N 95, p. 15.
"The Siren." [Poem] (74) N 95, p. 16.
1393. DAVIS, Angela J.
"Easter Monday." [CreamCR] (19:1) Spr 95, p. 107.
1394. DAVIS, Carol Ann
"The Lizard Fence." [QW] (40) Spr-Sum 95, p. 203.
1395. DAVIS, Carol V.
"Cracking the Sky" (Honorable Mention, 1995 Literary Awards). [GreensboroR] (59) Wint 95-96, p. 92.
"Fire." [SoDakR] (33:2) Sum 95, p. 25.
"Thunderstorm." [SoDakR] (33:2) Sum 95, p. 26-27.
1396. DAVIS, Caroline (Caroline J.)
"Card Houses." [Nimrod] (38:2) Spr-Sum 95, p. 14.
"Fox." [Prima] (18/19) 95, p. 73.
"Grandma's Marriage Recipe." [Quarry] (44:1) 95, p. 136.
"Legos, on the Way to Alaska." [Quarry] (44:1) 95, p. 135.
"Riding the Coin-Op Elephant." [SilverFR] (25) Sum 95, p. 13.
"Sweeping Up Dog Hair." [NewDeltaR] (12:1) Fall-Wint 94, p. 55.
"Wintergreen Street in the Earthquake, 1964." [Nimrod] (38:2) Spr-Sum 95, p. 14.
1397. DAVIS, Christopher
"How Can I Turn Off This Engine Now?" [ColR] (22:2) Fall 95, p. 150-151.
"Lovesong to an Empty Room." [Journal] (19:2) Fall-Wint 95, p. 53-55.
"A Satisfied Consumer." [GreensboroR] (57) Wint 94-95, p. 89-90.
1398. DAVIS, Claire
"The Children's Progress." [QW] (40) Spr-Sum 95, p. 198-199.
1399. DAVIS, Cortney
"Breaking the News." [Crazy] (49) Wint 95, p. 51-52.
"Hemorrhage, 3 a.m." [Crazy] (49) Wint 95, p. 53-54.
"Masturbation." [Crazy] (49) Wint 95, p. 46.
"On the Wards." [Crazy] (49) Wint 95, p. 47-48.
"This Is How I Imagine It." [Crazy] (49) Wint 95, p. 49-50.
1400. DAVIS, Frederick
"DCCCLXIX." [DogRR] (14:1, #27) Sum 95, p. 32-33.
1401. DAVIS, Gray
"Living Alone: What I Left Behind." [Calyx] (16:2) Wint 95-96, p. 32-33.
1402. DAVIS, Heather
"In Red Light." [SlipS] (15) 95, p. 59.
1403. DAVIS, John
"Recitative." [PoetL] (90:4) Wint 95-96, p. 17-18.
"She Wore Jeans in Marker's Tavern Parking Lot." [LullwaterR] (6:1) Spr-Sum 95, p. 28-29.
"Why Are You Late?" [BellR] (18:1, #37) Spr 95, p. 52.

1404. DAVIS, Jon
"Before the Rains." [Nimrod] (39:1) Fall-Wint 95, p. 103.
"Gold Card." [Manoa] (7:1) Sum 95, p. 182.
"A Letter to the Future." [Manoa] (7:1) Sum 95, p. 183.
"The Ritualized Forms." [Manoa] (7:1) Sum 95, p. 184.
1405. DAVIS, Jordan
"No of the Couples." [HangL] (67) 95, p. 24-25.
"Wine in a tall narrow glass." [HangL] (67) 95, p. 25.
1406. DAVIS, Leslie
"Before the Gypsy Told Her" (w. Hoa Nguyen). [Chain] (2) Spr 95, p. 64-66.
1407. DAVIS, Lyn
"The Care and Feeding of Birds: A Retrospective." [SinW] (55) Spr-Sum 95, p. 22-
23.
1408. DAVIS, Michael C.
"Hrasno." [PoetL] (90:4) Wint 95-96, p. 21-22.
1409. DAVIS, Olena Kalytiak
"Angels and Moths." [NowestR] (33:1) 95, p. 7.
"It's Shaped Like a Fork." [NowestR] (33:1) 95, p. 6.
"Like Kerosene." [PoetryNW] (36:4) Wint 95-96, p. 14.
"Like Working at Wal-Mart." [NewEngR] (17:1) Wint 95, p. 133-134.
"Palimpsest." [NewEngR] (17:1) Wint 95, p. 132-133.
1410. DAVIS, Sarah
"From Here, the View." [AntR] (53:2) Spr 95, p. 192.
"Shoreline." [AntR] (53:2) Spr 95, p. 193.
1411. DAVIS, Susan
"Identifying the Body." [WestHR] (49:1) Spr 95, p. 84.
"Returning to My Father's Office." [WestHR] (49:1) Spr 95, p. 83-84.
"Self-Portrait as Elegy." [WestHR] (49:1) Spr 95, p. 41.
1412. DAVIS, Susan L.
"Halo Is Hung Around Them." [VirQR] (71:3) Sum 95, p. 489-490.
"Mockingbird." [VirQR] (71:3) Sum 95, p. 492.
"Orange." [VirQR] (71:3) Sum 95, p. 490-491.
1413. DAVIS, William Virgil
"Twilight." [Border] (6) Spr-Sum 95, p. 34.
1414. DAVISON, Peter
"I Hardly Dream of Anyone Who Is Still Alive" (for William Matthews). [Atlantic]
(275:1) Ja 95, p. 90.
"Under the Roof of Memory" (In Memory of Jane Davison). [PartR] (62:1) Wint 95,
p. 112-113.
1415. DAVITT, Michael
"3AG" (in Irish and English). [Poetry] (167:1/2) O-N 95, p. 50-51.
1416. DAWE, Gerald
"Almost Forty." [SouthernR] (31:3) Jl/Sum 95, p. 682.
"A Fire in My Head" (for Dorothea). [SouthernR] (31:3) Jl/Sum 95, p. 679-681.
"Heart of Hearts." [SouthernR] (31:3) Jl/Sum 95, p. 682.
"Speedboats, 1972." [Verse] (12:2) 95, p. 38.
1417. DAWSON, Hester
"Review." [Light] (13) Spr 95, p. 21.
1418. DAWSON, Mark
"Letter of Recommendation." [Flyway] (1:1) Spr 95, p. 41.
1419. DAY, Holly
"The Last Hobbit." [HolCrit] (32:1) F 95, p. 20.
"The Tree By My Door." [ContextS] (4:2) 95, p. 16.
1420. DAY, Lucille
"Here We Are in Blackhawk." [PoetL] (90:3) Fall 95, p. 55.
De ...
See also names beginning with "De" without the following space, filed below in
their alphabetic positions, e.g., DeFOE.
De ANDRADE, Eugenio
See ANDRADE, Eugenio de
De BRAVO, Brandel France
See FRANCE de BRAVO, Brandel
De CAMPOS, Alvaro
See PESSOA, Fernando
1421. De FILIPPO, Vira J.
"Diego Above Castle Nuevo." [Turnstile] (5:1) 95, p. 61.

123

1422. De FRANCE, Steve
"Dancing." [Sun] (233) My 95, p. 33.
1423. De GRUTTOLA, Raffael
"Haiku: On the salt marsh." [Noctiluca] (2:1, #4) Spr 95, p. 24.
1424. De KOK, Ingrid
"Keeper." [TriQ] (93) Spr-Sum 95, p. 93.
"The Resurrection Bush." [TriQ] (93) Spr-Sum 95, p. 94.
"Transfer." [TriQ] (93) Spr-Sum 95, p. 91-92.
De los SANTOS, Marisa
See SANTOS, Marisa de los
De LUBICZ MILOSZ, Oscar Vladislas
See MILOSZ, Oscar Vladislas de Lubicz
1425. De MARIS, Ron
"Elegy on the Passing of the Tobacco Age." [TampaR] (11) Fall 95, p. 23-24.
"Medusa's Husband." [SewanR] (103:4) Fall 95, p. 499.
"Metamorphosis." [LitR] (38:3) Spr 95, p. 360.
"The Severn." [TampaR] (11) Fall 95, p. 25.
1426. De MATTIA, Sally
"A Mouse Trap." [BellArk] (11:3) My-Je 95, p. 5-7.
De MEDEIROS, Selene
See MEDEIROS, Selene de
De MORAES, Vincius
See MORAES, Vincius de
De RONSARD, Pierre
See RONSARD, Pierre de
1427. De STEFANO, John
"Malibu Beach 1966." [NowestR] (33:3) 95, p. 7-8.
"Ode to Charles Darwin." [NowestR] (33:3) 95, p. 11-13.
"On the Rappahannock" (for Mary Fairfax Griffith). [NowestR] (33:3) 95, p. 9.
"The Secrets of Celebration." [NowestR] (33:3) 95, p. 6.
"Three-Body Problem." [NowestR] (33:3) 95, p. 10.
1428. De VITO, E. B.
"Roses." [FourQ] (9:1/2) Spr 95, p. 25.
De WAARD, Elly de
See WAARD, Elly de
1429. DEAGON, Andrea Webb
"The Child Woken by Moonlight." [SouthernHR] (29:4) Fall 95, p. 359.
1430. DEAL, Kathleen Gunton
"For Robert and Raymond." [Hellas] (6:1) Spr-Sum 95, p. 97.
1431. DEAN, Anne
"Vacation America." [LitR] (38:2) Wint 95, p. 228.
1432. DEAN, Debra Kang
"Back to Back." [TarRP] (34:2) Spr 95, p. 11.
"Islands: To Ohnesorge-Fick in Overland Park." [TarRP] (34:2) Spr 95, p. 11-12.
"The Weep Line" (for my son David on his 18th birthday). [TarRP] (34:2) Spr 95, p. 10.
1433. DEANE, John F.
"Father." [Poetry] (167:1/2) O-N 95, p. 89.
1434. DEANE, Seamus
"Late Afternoon Hotel." [Epoch] (44:3) 95, p. 318.
"The Siege of Derry." [SouthernR] (31:3) Jl/Sum 95, p. 626-627.
"Silence." [Epoch] (44:3) 95, p. 319.
"Stepping Westward." [Epoch] (44:3) 95, p. 320.
1435. DEANOVICH, Connie
"Addition to Hitchcock, Take 3." [AmerLC] (7) 95, p. 51-53.
"Addition to Hitchcock, Take Two." [NewAW] (13) Fall-Wint 95, p. 32-33.
"Breakfast Sea." [AmerLC] (7) 95, p. 55-56.
"Epehemera [sic] Today on 'All My Children'" (Selections). [IllinoisR] (3:1/2) Fall 95-Spr 96, p. 40-44.
"Leonardo da Vinci Ocean." [AmerLC] (7) 95, p. 54.
"Requirements for a Saint." [NewAW] (13) Fall-Wint 95, p. 35.
"Requirements for the Visionary Cyclist." [NewAW] (13) Fall-Wint 95, p. 34.
"The Spotted Moon" (Excerpt). [Chain] (2) Spr 95, p. 67-70.
"The Spotted Moon" (Selection: 11). [WashR] (21:3) O-N 95, p. 22.
"The Spotted Moon" (Selections: 1-3). [Phoebe] (24:2) 95, p. 5-14.
"What Happened to Them." [WashR] (21:3) O-N 95, p. 8-9.

1436. DEBELJAK, Ales
  "At the Bottom" (tr. by Michael Biggins). [Verse] (12:2) 95, p. 39.
  "On the south side of Malta, where steep cliffs fall into the sea" (tr. by Christopher Merrill). [PlumR] (8) [95], p. 1.
  "The port grows dark" (tr. by Christopher Merrill). [PlumR] (8) [95], p. 2.
  "The river rushes on" (tr. by Christopher Merrill). [PlumR] (8) [95], p. 3.
  "Things can't go on like this forever" (tr. by Christopher Merrill). [PlumR] (8) [95], p. 4.
1437. DEBORAH (D.C. Center for Alcohol and Drug Abuse, Washington, DC)
  "Bless the Devil" (WritersCorps Program). [WashR] (21:2) Ag-S 95, p. 5.
  "The Two Syndrome" (WritersCorps Program). [WashR] (21:2) Ag-S 95, p. 5.
1438. DEBROT, Jack
  "Braille." [PoetryE] (39) Fall 94, p. 23.
  "Morning Poem." [PoetryE] (39) Fall 94, p. 26.
  "Poem for Your Eyes." [PoetryE] (39) Fall 94, p. 25.
  "Poem: Late at night your bed waits for me." [PoetryE] (39) Fall 94, p. 24.
  "Solitude." [PoetryE] (39) Fall 94, p. 27.
1439. DeCANTO, Carol B.
  "You Who Are in Our Stories" (to Bill Downey, 1922-1994). [SantaBR] (3:1) Spr 95, p. 5.
1440. DeCARTERET, Mark
  "More Nana Poems." [LowellR] (2) c1996, p. 21.
  "My Aunt the Magnificent." [LowellR] (2) c1996, p. 22-23.
1441. DeCOURCY, Lynne Hugo
  "Insomnia." [Prima] (18/19) 95, p. 79.
  "The Use of Women." [Prima] (18/19) 95, p. 77-78.
1442. DEDAIC, Mima
  "Cockroach Karma" (tr. by the author and B. R. Strahan). [Vis] (48) 95, p. 17-18.
  "Mysterious Land" (tr. by the author and B. R. Strahan). [Vis] (48) 95, p. 17.
  "What Could We Say about God?" (tr. of Ivan Slamnig, w. B. R. Strahan). [Vis] (48) 95, p. 19.
1443. DEDDENS, Catherine M.
  "The Suburban Deer." [CapeR] (30:2) Fall 95, p. 8.
1444. DeDONATO, Colette
  "Landscape." [NewAW] (13) Fall-Wint 95, p. 136.
DeFILLIPPO, Vira J.
  See De FILLIPPO, Vira J.
1445. DeFOE, Mark
  "The Eye of the Rabbit." [DefinedP] (3) 95, p. 47.
  "Gewgaws and Gherkins." [LaurelR] (29:1) Wint 95, p. 16.
  "In My West Virginia Home Town Everyone Believes in Something." [CumbPR] (14:2) Spr 95, p. 20-21.
DeFRANCE, Steve
  See De FRANCE, Steve
1446. DeFREESE, Allison (Allison A.)
  "Affairs." [ChironR] (44/45) Aut-Wint 95, p. 7.
  "Met a Fiction Writer." [ManyMM] (2:1) 95, p. 164-165.
  "Mowing the Lawn in Kansas" (3rd Prize, 9th Annual Contest). [SoCoast] (18) Ja 95, p. 55.
  "One Night in August." [ManyMM] (2:1) 95, p. 166.
1447. DEGENTESH, Katie
  "Why the Man in the Moon Can't Be Seen Tonight." [PlumR] (9) [95 or 96], p. 73.
DeGRUTTOLA, Raffael
  See De GRUTTOLA, Raffael
1448. DEGUY, Michel
  "Aphrodite Colleague" (from "Recumbent Figures," tr. by Wilson Baldridge). [Sulfur] (15:1, #36) Spr 95, p. 46.
  "Cardiogram (May)" (from "Recumbent Figures," tr. by Wilson Baldridge). [Sulfur] (15:1, #36) Spr 95, p. 44-45.
  "The Narrations" (from "Recumbent Figures," tr. by Wilson Baldridge). [Sulfur] (15:1, #36) Spr 95, p. 45.
  "Recumbent Figures" (from "Recumbent Figures," tr. by Wilson Baldridge). [Sulfur] (15:1, #36) Spr 95, p. 49-50.
  "Recumbent Figures" (Selections, tr. by Wilson Baldridge). [Sulfur] (15:1, #36) Spr 95, p. 44-51.

"Translation" (from "Recumbent Figures," tr. by Wilson Baldridge). [Sulfur] (15:1, #36) Spr 95, p. 48-49.
"Use Covered Yard (March)" (from "Recumbent Figures," tr. by Wilson Baldridge). [Sulfur] (15:1, #36) Spr 95, p. 44.
1449. DEISLER, Julia M.
"Solar Plexus (Braided Lives)." [Elf] (5:1) Spr 95, p. 30-31.
DeKOK, Ingrid
See De KOK, Ingrid
1450. DEKORT, Trevor N.
"Token Sex Poem." [Dandel] (22:1) 95, p. 75.
Del CASTILLO, Orestes
See CASTILLO, Orestes del
Del PINO, José Manuel
See PINO, José Manuel del
1451. Del VALLE, Lynda
"Silent Willie." [ColEng] (57:7) N 95, p. 841.
1452. DELANTY, Greg
"After Viewing *The Bowling Match at Castlemary, Cloyne* (1847)." [Atlantic] (275:2) F 95, p. 73.
"The Compositor." [Atlantic] (276:2) Ag 95, p. 70.
"The Crossing." [NewMyths] (2:2/3:1) 95, p. 94.
"Economic Pressure" (for Joseph McLoughlin). [SouthernR] (31:3) Jl/Sum 95, p. 751-752.
"On Skellig Michael." [NewMyths] (2:2/3:1) 95, p. 95.
"The Shrinking World" (To Mary & Niall on Catherine's first summer). [PraS] (69:4) Wint 95, p. 96.
"Vermont Aisling." [SouthernR] (31:3) Jl/Sum 95, p. 752-753.
1453. DELEA, Christine
"Next Time." [Interim] (14:1) Spr-Sum 95, p. 35.
1454. DELISLE, Greg
"A Dozen Chickens." [Ascent] (19:3) Spr 95, p. 56.
"The Rats of Hamelin." [Ascent] (19:3) Spr 95, p. 56.
"The Story of Putting My Feet Up." [CimR] (112) Jl 95, p. 91-92.
1455. DELMAN, Robin
"Looking for Elizabeth" (for Elizabeth Bishop). [Zyzzyva] (11:3/4, #43/44) 95, "The Best of Ten Years of ZYZZYVA," p. 114.
1456. DeLUCA, Geri
"Goneril's Complaint." [Footwork] (24/25) 95, p. 36-38.
1457. DeLUNA, Blas Manuel
"Blood That Sings, Part IV." [AntR] (53:4) Fall 95, p. 442-443.
DeMARIS, Ron
See De MARIS, Ron
DeMATTIA, Sally
See De MATTIA, Sally
1458. DEMCAK, Andrew
"Nature Story." [Pearl] (22) Fall-Wint 95, p. 40.
"Oysters" (for B.). [Pearl] (22) Fall-Wint 95, p. 42.
"Spoons" (for W.S.). [Pearl] (22) Fall-Wint 95, p. 41.
1459. DEMING, Alison Hawthorne
"31. On the first few nights spent in Scotland." [Sonora] (29) Spr 95, p. 25.
"32. Women alone suffer two kinds of rigidity" (after Hayden Carruth). [Sonora] (29) Spr 95, p. 26.
1460. DEMKO, John
"Untitled: Say you find something." [PennR] (6:2) 95, p. 18.
DeMORAES, Vincius
See MORAES, Vincius de
1461. DEMORY, Sean
"Arkansas Traveller." [HangL] (67) 95, p. 26-27.
"Rapture." [HangL] (67) 95, p. 28-30.
1462. DeMOTT, Robert
"The Art of Travel: Venice, after Henry James." [SouthernHR] (29:1) Wint 95, p. 10.
"Dusk at Point Reyes." [Farm] (13:2 [i.e. 12:2]) Fall-Wint 95, p. 36.
"Not Like Joy Exactly." [Farm] (13:2 [i.e. 12:2]) Fall-Wint 95, p. 37.
1463. DEMPSKY, Ian
"Hilt." [SantaBR] (3:2) Sum 95, p. 68.

"Lunar." [SantaBR] (3:2) Sum 95, p. 69.
1464. DEMPSTER, Barry
    "Blind." [Quarry] (44:2) 95, p. 70.
    "The Darkest Hour." [AntigR] (100) Wint 95, p. 150.
    "Disappearing Grandmothers." [Grain] (23:2) Aut 95, p. 104.
    "Endless Prayers." [AntigR] (100) Wint 95, p. 151.
1465. DEMPSTER, Brian Komei
    "Leaf Diary." [QW] (41) Aut-Wint 95-96, p. 190.
1466. DENG, Yan
    "Listening to Dong Tinglan Play His New Guitar Composition for Minister Fang"
        (tr. of Li Qi, 690?-754, w. Keith Aubrey). [Chelsea] (59) 95, p. 132-133.
    "An Old Soldier's March" (tr. of Li Qi, 690?-754, w. Keith Aubrey). [Chelsea] (59)
        95, p. 134.
    "The River-Merchant's Wife: A Second Letter" (tr. of Li Po, w. Keith Aubrey).
        [GrahamHR] (19) Wint 95-96, p. 79.
    "Sent North on a Rainy Night" (tr. of Li Shang-yin, w. Keith Aubrey). [GrahamHR]
        (19) Wint 95-96, p. 81.
    "Viewing the Waterfall on Mt. Lu" (tr. of Li Po, w. Keith Aubrey). [GrahamHR]
        (19) Wint 95-96, p. 80.
1467. DENGLER, Mary
    "Sacrament of Grace." [Interim] (14:1) Spr-Sum 95, p. 19.
1468. DeNIRO, Alan
    "Crisis." [ArtfulD] (28/29) 95, p. 68.
    "Elegy." [ArtfulD] (28/29) 95, p. 69.
    "Shot Able, Shot Baker." [ArtfulD] (28/29) 95, p. 74.
    "Sonnet." [ArtfulD] (28/29) 95, p. 70-71.
    "Testing the Limits, 1954." [ArtfulD] (28/29) 95, p. 72-73.
1469. DENMAN, Peter
    "At the Pipers' Club" (tr. of Biddy Jenkinson). [Poetry] (167:1/2) O-N 95, p. 23, 25.
1470. DENNING, Susan
    "The Sense of An Ending" (Honorable Mention, First Annual Poetry Awards).
        [LiteralL] (2:2) Fall 95, p. 4.
1471. DENNIS, Carl
    "All I've Wanted." [Agni] (42) 95, p. 59-60.
    "Book Fair." [Poetry] (166:2) My 95, p. 75-76.
    "Consolation." [NewRep] (212:9) 27 F 95, p. 39.
    "Old Woman." [Poetry] (166:2) My 95, p. 73-75.
    "Orpheus." [Poetry] (166:2) My 95, p. 72-73.
1472. DENNIS, Rodney Gove
    "City Hospital: Carolyn and Theodora." [HarvardR] (8) Spr 95, p. 116.
    "The Dining Room Through a Doorway." [NewEngR] (17:2) Spr 95, p. 57.
    "Her Last Weeks." [BelPoJ] (46:2) Wint 95-96, p. 10-11.
1473. DENNISON, Matt
    "Who Among Us?" [ChironR] (43) Sum 95, p. 28.
1474. DENNISON, Michael
    "Michelle Remembers the Tornado." [ApalQ] (43) Spr 95, p. 69-70.
1475. DENNY, Alma
    "School Cheer" (Progressive style). [Light] (13) Spr 95, p. 16.
    "Tax Schmax" (Diamond Clips, $260,000, Tax Incl. — Advt.). [Light] (14) Sum 95,
        p. 11.
    "Try One for Size." [Light] (15/16) Aut-Wint 95-96, p. 25.
1476. DENNY, David
    "Zen Cat." [Sun] (234) Je 95, p. 10.
1477. DENT, Peter
    "Clarity." [Os] (40) 95, p. 25.
1478. DENT, Tory
    "The Crying Game" (written to the song by Geoff Stephens). [Colum] (24/25) 95, p.
        87-93.
    "From the Defeat of Linear Thinking." [Colum] (24/25) 95, p. 94-95.
    "A Two-Way Mirror" (Selections: XIX, XXXI, XXXV, XXXIX, XLIII). [Pequod]
        (39) 95, p. 58-61.
1479. DePAUW, Dennis
    "The Green Rambler." [EngJ] (84:1) Ja 95, p. 76.
1480. DEPESTRE, René
    "Alabama" (A Sea Animal's Journal, tr. by Edwidge Danticat). [CaribbeanW] (9) 95,
        p. 90-91.

"Eros and Revolution" (A montage for a society full of consumers, tr. by Edwidge
     Danticat). [CaribbeanW] (9) 95, p. 89-90.
"How the Angels Would Cry" (for Nelly, tr. by Edwidge Danticat). [CaribbeanW]
     (9) 95, p. 93-94.
"Is It True?" (tr. by Edwidge Danticat). [CaribbeanW] (9) 95, p. 91-93.
"My Definition of Poetry" (tr. by Edwidge Danticat). [CaribbeanW] (9) 95, p. 94.
"Nostalgia" (tr. by Edwidge Danticat). [CaribbeanW] (9) 95, p. 88.
1481. DEPPE, Theodore (Ted)
     "Admission, Children's Unit." [MassR] (36:1) Spr 95, p. 134-135.
     "Family Portrait." [PassN] (16:2) Wint 95, p. 28-29.
     "Funeral March of Adolf Wolfli" (From an oral history of Lisa Becker, taken in
          Bern, Switzerland, 1970). [Harp] (290:1741) Je 95, p. 30-31.
     "Gooseberries." [PoetryNW] (36:4) Wint 95-96, p. 12-13.
     "The Japanese Deer" (For Denny Lynn, who likes to know what's true in my poems
          and what's "made up"). [KenR] (17:3/4) Sum-Fall 95, p. 179-180.
     "Letter to Suvorin" (—Anton Chekhov, Sakhalin Island, off the coast of Siberia,
          July 11, 1890). [PoetryNW] (36:4) Wint 95-96, p. 10-12.
     "The Russian Greatcoat." [SouthernPR] (35:1) Sum 95, p. 36-37.
1482. DER-HOVANESSIAN, Diana
     "Blockade of Armenia" (tr. of Hovaness Grigorian). [HarvardR] (8) Spr 95, p. 95.
     "Critics" (tr. of Slavik Chiloyan). [GrahamHR] (19) Wint 95-96, p. 49.
     "A Day" (tr. of Hrachia Tamrazian). [GrahamHR] (19) Wint 95-96, p. 46.
     "Debt" (tr. of Henrik Edoyan). [GrahamHR] (19) Wint 95-96, p. 53.
     "Dogs" (tr. of Slavik Chiloyan). [GrahamHR] (19) Wint 95-96, p. 49.
     "For Men Only" (tr. of Medakse). [GrahamHR] (19) Wint 95-96, p. 41.
     "Forbidden" (tr. of Slavik Chiloyan). [GrahamHR] (19) Wint 95-96, p. 49.
     "Hagop Mendsouri" (tr. of Hagop Movses). [GrahamHR] (19) Wint 95-96, p. 54-55.
     "Hiroshima Study" (tr. of Hrachia Saroukhan). [GrahamHR] (19) Wint 95-96, p. 43.
     "Luciole" (tr. of Gevorg Emin). [GrahamHR] (19) Wint 95-96, p. 51.
     "New Era" (tr. of Hrachia Tamrazian). [GrahamHR] (19) Wint 95-96, p. 47.
     "Night Study" (tr. of Hrachia Saroukhan). [GrahamHR] (19) Wint 95-96, p. 44.
     "Perhaps" (tr. of Sylva Gaboudikian). [GrahamHR] (19) Wint 95-96, p. 48.
     "Run and Escape" (tr. of Slavik Chiloyan). [GrahamHR] (19) Wint 95-96, p. 50.
     "Unnamed Places" (tr. of Artem Haroutiunian). [GrahamHR] (19) Wint 95-96, p.
          52.
     "War" (tr. of Yuri Sahakian). [GrahamHR] (19) Wint 95-96, p. 42.
     "Where Do You Think You Are Going?" (tr. of Hrachia Saroukhan). [GrahamHR]
          (19) Wint 95-96, p. 45.
1483. DERBY, Cheryl
     "Ripening." [Colum] (24/25) 95, p. 27.
1484. DERGE, William
     "Second Chance / Thoughts." [ChironR] (42) Spr 95, p. 29.
1485. DeROUS, Peter
     "Time We Knew." [Bogg] (67) 95, p. 50.
1486. DESBANK, Shashi
     "Amrapali" (tr. of Mallika Sengupta, w. Peter Michelson and the author).
          [ManyMM] (1:3) 95, p. 130-131.
1487. DESMOND, Sean
     "Wellfleet, 1994." [HarvardA] (129:3) Wint 95, p. 20.
1488. DeSTEFANO, Darin
     "A Fountain Thinks the Ocean Is Laughing." [CentralP] (24) Spr 95, p. 292-293.
DeSTEFANO, John
     See De STEFANO, John
1489. DESY, Peter
     "Alcohol." [GreenHLL] (6) 95, p. 100-101.
     "Anxiety." [WeberS] (12:2) Spr-Sum 95, p. 108.
     "At 60." [GreenHLL] (6) 95, p. 102.
     "Dad's Home." [ProseP] (4) 95, p. 18-19.
     "Nostalgia." [WormR] (35:1, #137) 95, p. 4.
     "Taking Care." [WormR] (35:1, #137) 95, p. 4-5.
1490. DETRO, John
     "Bag of Wind." [Sun] (238) O 95, p. 15.
1491. DEUTSCH, Gitta
     "An so einem Tag." [NewOR] (21:3/4) Fall-Wint 95, p. 118.
     "And still I cannot come to terms" (tr. by the author). [NewOR] (21:3/4) Fall-Wint
          95, p. 120.

"Ich bin den langen Nächten." [NewOR] (21:3/4) Fall-Wint 95, p. 120.
"Das Jahr ist vergangen." [NewOR] (21:3/4) Fall-Wint 95, p. 119.
"On such a day" (tr. by the author). [NewOR] (21:3/4) Fall-Wint 95, p. 118.
"The year has passed" (tr. by the author). [NewOR] (21:3/4) Fall-Wint 95, p. 119.
DeVITO, E. B.
        See De VITO, E. B.
1492. DEW, C. Stephen
        "March 11, 1994" (after being struck by lightning). [KenR] (17:3/4) Sum-Fall 95, p. 50.
DeWAARD, Elly de
        See WAARD, Elly de
1493. DeWINTER, Corrine
        "Daughters of India." [Plain] (15:3) Spr 95, p. 26.
        "En Passant." [Crucible] (31) Fall 95, p. 16.
        "Learning." [Crucible] (30) Fall 94, p. 15.
        "Premature." [Writer] (108:12) D 95, p. 22.
        "Spirit and Flesh." [Plain] (15:2) Wint 95, p. 19.
1494. DEWITT, Susan
        "Nettles." [Conscience] (16:4) Wint 95-96, p. 18.
DeWITT, Susan Kelly
        See KELLY-DeWITT, Susan
1495. DeYOUNG, Colin
        "Planting." [HarvardA] (129:3) Wint 95, p. 34.
1496. DEZEMBER, Mary
        "It Will Be Different This Time." [Wind] (76) Fall 95, p. 10.
        "Something Like Church or When a Woman Tries to Change Her Life (A Love
            Poem)." [Wind] (76) Fall 95, p. 8-9.
        "When I Had the American Dream." [Ledge] (19) Wint 95, p. 108.
1497. DHARMARAJ, Ramola
        "Dissolution and Return." [IndR] (18:2) Fall 95, p. 38-39.
        "Fingertip and End." [LiteralL] (1:2) S-O 94, p. 14.
        "I Came Upon a Field Once." [LiteralL] (1:2) S-O 94, p. 14.
        "Mockingbird's Song." [IndR] (18:2) Fall 95, p. 40-42.
DHOMHNAILL, Nuala Ni
        See Ni DHOMHNAILL, Nuala
Di ...
        See also names beginning with "Di" without the following space, filed below in
            their alphabetical positions, e.g., DiPALMA
1498. Di MICHELE, A.
        "I. El Ink (font)." [NewOR] (21:2) Sum 95, p. 45.
        "II. Qua Sink, Rotorelief." [NewOR] (21:2) Sum 95, p. 45.
1499. Di MICHELE, Mary
        "Crown of Roses" (Selections: 21, 24-26, 94). [Arc] (34) Spr 95, p. 22-24.
1500. Di PASQUALE, Emanuel
        "Ulysses." [NewYorkQ] (55) 95, p. 96.
1501. Di PIERO, W. S.
        "UFO." [Thrpny] (63) Fall 95, p. 17.
1502. Di PRIMA, Diane
        "Goodbye to All That." [Footwork] (24/25) 95, p. 2-3.
        "Workshop" (Atlantic Center for the Arts, New Smyrna Beach, Florida). [Footwork]
            (24/25) 95, p. 2.
1503. Di VINCENZO, Jan
        "#80. Small habits." [PlumR] (8) [95], p. 69.
1504. DIAL, Bob
        "Avalanche Pass." [ChironR] (42) Spr 95, p. 11.
        "The First Word." [Plain] (15:2) Wint 95, p. 18.
        "Lost in Schenectady." [Ledge] (19) Wint 95, p. 42-43.
        "No More Grandmothers!" (Second Prize, 1995 Poetry Contest). [Ledge] (19) Wint
            95, p. 40-41.
        "A Prayer for Winter." [ChironR] (42) Spr 95, p. 11.
        "The Town." [ChironR] (42) Spr 95, p. 11.
1505. DIAL, Yvonne Barnes
        "Peach." [Pembroke] (27) 95, p. 30.
1506. DIAZ, Luciano P.
        "436" (tr. of Jorge Cancino). [Arc] (35) Aut 95, p. 10.
        "The Bird of Winter" (tr. of Alfredo Lavergne). [Arc] (35) Aut 95, p. 52.

129

"Breakfast" (tr. of Alfredo Lavergne). [Arc] (35) Aut 95, p. 53.
"By the Sea" (tr. of Arturo Lazo). [Arc] (35) Aut 95, p. 23.
"The Cat" (for Jorge Etcheverry). [Arc] (35) Aut 95, p. 41.
"Eyemetrics" (tr. of Jorge Cancino). [Arc] (35) Aut 95, p. 8.
"Fall" (tr. of Nelly Davis Vallejos). [Arc] (35) Aut 95, p. 38.
"For Sara." [Arc] (35) Aut 95, p. 43.
"The Fragments of the Clan" (Selections: 77-78, 80, 86, 91, 94, 104-105, tr. of
    Nieves Fuenzalida). [Arc] (35) Aut 95, p. 75-76.
"Light and I" (tr. of Arturo Lazo). [Arc] (35) Aut 95, p. 24.
"Ode to a Young Poet." [Arc] (35) Aut 95, p. 42.
"Rain" (tr. of Nelly Davis Vallejos). [Arc] (35) Aut 95, p. 39.
"Rambling of the Poet" (tr. of Jorge Cancino). [Arc] (35) Aut 95, p. 9.
"The Sad Grapes" (tr. of Nelly Davis Vallejos). [Arc] (35) Aut 95, p. 40.
"The Size of a Lie" (tr. of Alfredo Lavergne). [Arc] (35) Aut 95, p. 51.
1507. DIAZ, Paula
    "And the Weather Tells Us Nothing." [DenQ] (29:3) Wint 95, p. 12.
    "Heliotrope." [DenQ] (29:3) Wint 95, p. 11.
1508. DIBBERN, Doug
    "We Breathe." [HangL] (67) 95, p. 31.
1509. DICKERMAN, Judith
    "Sentry." [Ledge] (18) Sum 95, p. 91-92.
1510. DICKEY, James
    "Air." [Verse] (12:2) 95, p. 40.
1511. DICKEY, R. P.
    "True West." [SoDakR] (33:3/4) Fall-Wint 95, p. 109-111.
1512. DICKEY, William
    "Archaeopteryx." [HarvardR] (8) Spr 95, p. 32.
    "The Arrival of the Titanic." [Poetry] (167:3) D 95, p. 140.
    "The Bone Pit." [SouthernR] (31:2) Ap/Spr 95, p. 261-264.
    "Boxes." [HarvardR] (8) Spr 95, p. 33.
    "Coming of Television News and the National Guard." [Poetry] (166:5) Ag 95, p.
        272.
    "Hat." [Poetry] (166:5) Ag 95, p. 271.
    "The Metamorphoses" (3 selections). [JamesWR] (12:3) Fall 95, p. 17.
    "The Metamorphoses" (Selections). [IndR] (18:1) Spr 95, p. 80-82.
    "Roses." [DenQ] (30:2) Fall 95, p. 24-25.
    "Semi-Private." [Poetry] (166:3) Je 95, p. 145.
    "Theft." [GeoR] (49:2) Sum 95, p. 489.
    "Theory and Substance of the Night." [GeoR] (49:2) Sum 95, p. 490.
1513. DICKINSON, Emily (1830-1886)
    "Making a Prairie." [Writer] (108:1) Ja 95, p. 17.
    "Wild Nights — Wild Nights!" [PoetryE] (41) Aut 95, p. 36.
1514. DICKINSON, Stephanie
    "Big G." [Ledge] (18) Sum 95, p. 51.
    "Exotic Dancer." [GreenHLL] (6) 95, p. 14.
    "Gunfire." [Ledge] (18) Sum 95, p. 52.
    "Of Your Boyfriend's Rough Housing and St. Vincent's Hospital." [ApalQ] (43) Spr
        95, p. 45.
    "Oral Roberts." [NewYorkQ] (54) 95, p. 83.
    "Shooter." [NewYorkQ] (55) 95, p. 95.
    "The Silent Arm" (the shotgun victim speaks to her paralyzed hand). [GreenHLL]
        (6) 95, p. 15-16.
1515. DICKSON, John
    "First Indication of Changing Climate." [AnotherCM] (29) Spr 95, p. 22-23.
    "The Grapes of Wrath." [AmerS] (64:3) Sum 95, p. 369-370.
    "High School Reunion." [Elf] (5:3) Fall 95, p. 27.
    "Lucretia." [Elf] (5:2) Sum 95, p. 25.
1516. DIEGO, Gerardo
    "Fountain" (tr. by Francisco Aragon). [Chelsea] (59) 95, p. 129.
    "Snow" (tr. by Francisco Aragon). [Chelsea] (59) 95, p. 130.
1517. DIESEL, Eric
    "Nature's Patterns Are Etched in Ice." [EvergreenC] (10:1) Wint-Spr 95, p. 63.
1518. DIGGES, Deborah
    "Ballad of the Blood" (Selections: 7 poems, tr. of María Elena Cruz Varela, w.
        Mairym Cruz-Bernal). [AmerPoR] (24:4) Jl-Ag 95, p. 23-25.
    "Morning After a Blizzard." [NewYorker] (71:3) 13 Mr 95, p. 77.

1519. DILL, Emil (Emil P., E. P.)
"April Inmate." [NortheastCor] (3) 95, p. 102.
"Ars Longa, Vita Brevis." [Plain] (15:3) Spr 95, p. 35.
"Float." [BlackBR] (21) Fall-Wint 95, p. 31.
1520. DILLARD, Annie
"Signals at Sea" (found poem, from the text of Charles H.
Cugle's *Practical Navigation*, 1936). [Harp] (291:1743) Ag 95, p. 32.
1521. DILLARD, Gavin Geoffrey
"Death in Marin." [ModernW] (3) Sum 95, p. 28-30.
1522. DILLARD, R. H. W.
"A Discussion of the Poems of David R. Slavitt." [Light] (15/16) Aut-Wint 95-96, p. 35-37.
1523. DILLON, Andrew
"Alone One Night" (for Gwen Reichert). [Poem] (74) N 95, p. 30.
"Death's News" (for John R. Milton). [SoDakR] (33:3/4) Fall-Wint 95, p. 233.
"A Letter from My Father." [CumbPR] (14:2) Spr 95, p. 55.
"Still Dark." [Poem] (74) N 95, p. 29.
"Walking to the Car." [Poem] (74) N 95, p. 28.
"The Whale of the Whole Self." [Flyway] (1:1) Spr 95, p. 84.
1524. DILLON, Enoch
"The Month of the Ground Hog." [Light] (13) Spr 95, p. 8.
"Overhead." [Light] (14) Sum 95, p. 17.
1525. DiLORENZO, Gabrielle
"The Limbo Marriage." [CaribbeanW] (9) 95, p. 53-57.
1526. DILSAVER, Paul
"Art Critics." [SmPd] (32:3, #95) Fall 95, p. 29.
DiMICHELLE, Mary
See Di MICHELLE, Mary
1527. DIMITRI, Candace Love
"Blind Lead." [AnthNEW] (7) 95, p. 25.
1528. DIMITROVA, Blaga
"Lullaby for My Mother" (tr. by John Balaban and Elena Hristova). [WillowS] (36) Je 95, p. 90-91.
"Who Takes Care of the Blind Stork?" (tr. by John Balaban and Elena Hristova). [WillowS] (36) Je 95, p. 89.
1529. DINE, Carol
"Freestanding." [PraS] (69:3) Fall 95, p. 128.
"Genetics." [PraS] (69:3) Fall 95, p. 126-127.
"Third Floor / Oncology." [PraS] (69:3) Fall 95, p. 127-128.
1530. DINELTSOI, Mazii
"Language." [WeberS] (12:3) Fall 95, p. 33, 35.
"Saad." [WeberS] (12:3) Fall 95, p. 32, 34.
"Spring." [WeberS] (12:3) Fall 95, p. 35, 37.
"Tó Háálí." [WeberS] (12:3) Fall 95, p. 34, 36.
1531. DINGS, Fred
"The Evening After." [ParisR] (37:134) Spr 95, p. 124-125.
"The Fire." [Poetry] (166:2) My 95, p. 100.
"The Glowing Coal." [WestHR] (49:1) Spr 95, p. 16.
"In the Season of Memory." [PoetL] (90:3) Fall 95, p. 57.
"The Last Voyage." [WestHR] (49:1) Spr 95, p. 15.
"Migratory Flight." [Poetry] (166:2) My 95, p. 102.
"The Past." [Poetry] (166:2) My 95, p. 102.
"Revelations." [Poetry] (166:2) My 95, p. 101.
"Words for a Perfect Evening." [Poetry] (166:2) My 95, p. 99.
1532. DINH, Linh
"Ba Doi Gorge" (tr. of Ho Xuan Huong). [DenQ] (30:2) Fall 95, p. 32.
"I Married at Fifteen" (tr. of Vietnamese folk poem). [Manoa] (7:2) Wint 95, p. 47.
"I Refuse to Be Lambasted by Your Bloated I Ching." [Sulfur] (15:1, #36) Spr 95, p. 87-89.
"Impaled with a pitchfork Vincent Van Gogh." [Sulfur] (15:1, #36) Spr 95, p. 89.
"Inventory." [NortheastCor] (3) 95, p. 82.
"It Took a Newly Dug Canal" (tr. of Vietnamese folk poem). [Manoa] (7:2) Wint 95, p. 47.
"Letter to My Bed." [Sulfur] (15:1, #36) Spr 95, p. 89.
"The Morning Star Fades in the Night Sky" (tr. of Vietnamese folk poem). [Manoa] (7:2) Wint 95, p. 48.

"My Body Is Not Inferior to Hers" (tr. of Vietnamese folk poem). [Manoa] (7:2)
Wint 95, p. 48.
"My seminal life has been wasted through phony experiences." [Sulfur] (15:1, #36)
Spr 95, p. 88.
"Nine Stars Line Up Vertically" (tr. of Vietnamese folk poem). [Manoa] (7:2) Wint
95, p. 47.
"The Paper Fan" (tr. of Ho Xuan Huong). [DenQ] (30:2) Fall 95, p. 33.
"Three Years at This Outpost" (tr. of Vietnamese folk poem). [Manoa] (7:2) Wint
95, p. 48.
"Wobbly, Like a Hat without a Strap" (tr. of Vietnamese folk poem). [Manoa] (7:2)
Wint 95, p. 46.
1533. DiPALMA, Ray
"Hôtel des Ruines" (Selections: 8 poems). [AmerPoR] (24:2) Mr-Ap 95, p. 17-18.
DiPASQUALE, Emanuel di
See Di PASQUALE, Emanuel
DiPIERO, W. S.
See Di PIERO, W. S.
DiPRIMA, Diane
See Di PRIMA, Diane
1534. DISCH, Tom
"A Canine in Recovery" (for Michael Ryan). [Light] (15/16) Aut-Wint 95-96, p. 13.
"Capital Punishment" (For Elsa). [Poetry] (165:4) Ja 95, p. 189-191.
"Donna Reed in the Scary Old House." [ParisR] (37:136) Fall 95, p. 81-82.
"The Fireworks." [ParisR] (37:135) Sum 95, p. 274-275.
"In Praise of History" (For Norman). [Poetry] (165:4) Ja 95, p. 187-188.
"The Lipstick on the Mirror." [Poetry] (165:4) Ja 95, p. 192.
"The Moon on the Crest of the New-Fallen Snow." [ParisR] (37:135) Sum 95, p.
275-276.
1535. DISCHELL, Stuart
"An Account." [ColR] (22:2) Fall 95, p. 171-172.
"An Arrangement." [ColR] (22:2) Fall 95, p. 169-170.
"Ellipsis, Third or Fourth Dot, Depending." [Agni] (41) 95, p. 214-215.
"Evening III." [BostonR] (20:4) O-N 95, p. 29.
"The Girls in Their Summer Dresses, Take II." [HarvardR] (9) Fall 95, p. 92.
1536. DISKIN, Trayce
"And Then I Thought I Heard Him Speak" (Narcissus). [NewOR] (21:3/4) Fall-Wint
95, p. 108.
"The Frugal Repast" (Picasso, 1904). [PoetL] (90:3) Fall 95, p. 33.
1537. DITMARS, Margaret
"Trees of the New World." [YaleR] (83:2) Ap 95, p. 98-99.
1538. DITSKY, John
"Epigrammar." [BellR] (18:1, #37) Spr 95, p. 41.
1539. DITTA, Joseph M.
"Driving the Gravel Roads." [MidwQ] (36:4) Sum 95, p. 364-365.
"Remembering Ming" (to Sal, the bruised). [Footwork] (24/25) 95, p. 59.
"To My Daughter Living in England." [Footwork] (24/25) 95, p. 59.
"Worries In and Out of Proportion." [Footwork] (24/25) 95, p. 59.
1540. DIVAKARUNI, Chitra
"The Babies" (The 1994 Allen Ginsberg Poetry Awards: First Prize). [Footwork]
(24/25) 95, p. 182.
"The Owner of the Spice Bazaar Contemplates Evening" (The 1994 Allen Ginsberg
Poetry Awards: First Prize). [Footwork] (24/25) 95, p. 182.
1541. DIVANT, Kay
"A Hymn in Honor of the World." [DenQ] (30:2) Fall 95, p. 26.
DiVINCENZO, Jan
See Di VINCENZO, Jan
1542. DIXON, Alan
"Eastbourne and Charleston." [Poetry] (166:5) Ag 95, p. 253.
"Les Maîtres." [Poetry] (166:5) Ag 95, p. 254.
1543. DIXON, Betty L.
"Past to Present." [SoCoast] (18) Ja 95, p. 27.
1544. DIXON, K. Reynolds
"Night Refuge, Will Rogers Beach." [PoetL] (90:4) Wint 95-96, p. 19-20.
1545. DJEBAR, Assia
"A Country Without Memory" (tr. by Joanna Goodman). [SenR] (25:2) Fall 95, p.
59.

DJEBAR

"I Slit the Neck of the Rooster" (tr. by Joanna Goodman). [SenR] (25:2) Fall 95, p. 60.

1546. DJURIC, Dubrovka
"Proposals for Investigating Languages, Meanings, and Contexts of Conscious and Unconscious in Postmodern and Postcommunist Societies." [Chain] (2) Spr 95, p. 71-75.

1547. DOBBS, Kevin
"1st Rule of Poker." [PoetL] (90:1) Spr 95, p. 48.

1548. DOBYNS, Stephen
"Allegorical Matters." [AmerPoR] (24:2) Mr-Ap 95, p. 3.
"Art et al." [AmerPoR] (24:2) Mr-Ap 95, p. 4.
"Being Happy" (for Carol Houck Smith). [NewEngR] (17:1) Wint 95, p. 135-136.
"Best in the Business." [Agni] (41) 95, p. 216.
"The Big Difference." [GreenMR] (8:1) Spr-Sum 95, p. 11-12.
"Cold Marble." [NoAmR] (280:6) N-D 95, p. 18-19.
"Consequence." [AmerPoR] (24:2) Mr-Ap 95, p. 5-6.
"Crimson Invitation." [AmerPoR] (24:2) Mr-Ap 95, p. 7-8.
"Dead Curtain." [Salm] (108) Fall 95, p. 91-93.
"Dead Dreaming." [NortheastCor] (3) 95, p. 46.
"Digging the Knife Deeper." [AmerPoR] (24:2) Mr-Ap 95, p. 6.
"Education." [BlackWR] (21:2) Spr-Sum 95, p. 103-104.
"Garden Bouquet." [ParisR] (37:135) Sum 95, p. 80-82.
"Getting Together." [NewEngR] (17:1) Wint 95, p. 136-137.
"Golden Broilers." [AmerPoR] (24:2) Mr-Ap 95, p. 6-7.
"Gutter Trouble." [AmerPoR] (24:2) Mr-Ap 95, p. 5.
"Heaven." [BlackWR] (21:2) Spr-Sum 95, p. 105-106.
"His Decision." [Salm] (108) Fall 95, p. 96.
"Hopeless Tools." [AmerPoR] (24:2) Mr-Ap 95, p. 6.
"Lil' Darlin'." [GettyR] (8:3) Sum 95, p. 418-419.
"Middle-Aged Black Men" (for Hayden Carruth). [GettyR] (8:3) Sum 95, p. 415-417.
"No Hands." [Salm] (108) Fall 95, p. 94-95.
"Nocturnal Obstruction." [Boulevard] (10:1/2, #28/29) Spr 95, p. 197-198.
"Nouns of Assemblage." [AmerPoR] (24:2) Mr-Ap 95, p. 3-4.
"Pink Spot." [GreenMR] (8:1) Spr-Sum 95, p. 10.
"Pushing Ahead." [AmerPoR] (24:2) Mr-Ap 95, p. 7.
"Rattletrap." [Hudson] (48:3) Aut 95, p. 428-430.
"Second Skin." [HarvardR] (9) Fall 95, p. 102.
"Spiritual Chickens." [SenR] (25:1) Spr 95, p. 56-57.
"Street Racket." [GreenMR] (8:1) Spr-Sum 95, p. 8-9.
"Then What Is the Question." [ParisR] (37:135) Sum 95, p. 79-80.
"Trying Not to Be Cynical." [Iowa] (25:3) Fall 95, p. 83-84.
"When a Friend" (Ellis Settle, 1924-93). [Hudson] (48:3) Aut 95, p. 427-428.
"Who Is Mistaken?" [AmerPoR] (24:2) Mr-Ap 95, p. 7.
"Winter Nights." [AmerPoR] (24:2) Mr-Ap 95, p. 5.
"Wolves in the Street." [Verse] (12:2) 95, p. 41.
"The World as Textbook." [NortheastCor] (3) 95, p. 39.

1549. DOCHERTY, John
"Deconstructing Pregnancy." [TexasR] (15:3/4) Fall-Wint 94, p. 83.

1550. DOCKETT, Dionne
"Unspoken Words Finally Spoken" (WritersCorps Project, Washington, DC). [WashR] (21:2) Ag-S 95, p. 21.

1551. DODD, Elizabeth
"Bicycling in the Great Salt Marsh." [MidwQ] (36:4) Sum 95, p. 365-366.
"Blackjack." [CimR] (112) Jl 95, p. 110.
"Southerly." [TarRP] (35:1) Fall 95, p. 16.
"Taphonomy." [CharR] (21:1) Spr 95, p. 82.

1552. DODD, Wayne
"Paysage d'Hiver." [GeoR] (49:3) Fall 95, p. 653-655.
"Triptych for the Millennium." [DenQ] (29:4) Spr 95, p. 17-20.

1553. DODSON, Keith A.
"After School." [AxeF] (3) 90, p. 29.
"Paternal Fear." [AxeF] (3) 90, p. 29.

1554. DOHERTY, Dennis
"Out of the Sun." [Blueline] (16) 95, p. 22.
"Winter Critters." [Blueline] (16) 95, p. 62.

1555. DOLIN, Sharon
    "Floating Robert." [NewAW] (13) Fall-Wint 95, p. 135.
    "No Nose" (after Gronk). [NewAW] (13) Fall-Wint 95, p. 134.
1556. DOLLIS, John
    "Butterfly Effect." [NewOR] (21:3/4) Fall-Wint 95, p. 85-87.
    "The Four of July: Instructions (Made in China)." [NewOR] (21:3/4) Fall-Wint 95,
        p. 88.
    "Lecture." [NewOR] (21:3/4) Fall-Wint 95, p. 89.
1557. DOMEN, Ron
    "The Steel Pail." [SlipS] (15) 95, p. 11-12.
1558. DONAGHY, Daniel
    "What We Talked About." [Spitball] (48) 95, p. 19.
1559. DONAGHY, Michael
    "Acts of Contrition." [Verse] (12:2) 95, p. 42.
    "The Break." [Epoch] (44:3) 95, p. 258.
    "Our Life Stories." [Epoch] (44:3) 95, p. 259.
    "Reliquary." [Poetry] (165:6) Mr 95, p. 323.
    "Repair." [Epoch] (44:3) 95, p. 260.
1560. DONALD, Merlin
    "Airport Hotel." [AntigR] (100) Wint 95, p. 93.
    "Cavendish Moonrise." [AntigR] (100) Wint 95, p. 94.
    "The Electronic Tribe." [AntigR] (100) Wint 95, p. 97.
    "Gentle Moons Over Smokestacks." [AntigR] (100) Wint 95, p. 95.
    "Let the Laces Decide." [AntigR] (100) Wint 95, p. 96.
1561. DONALD (Clean & Sober Streets, Washington, DC).
    "Last Straw" (WritersCorps Program). [WashR] (21:2) Ag-S 95, p. 18.
1562. DONALDSON, Jeffery
    "Bird Bath." [AntigR] (100) Wint 95, p. 9.
    "A Lesson from the The Teaching Garden." [AntigR] (100) Wint 95, p. 10.
    "The Picture in the Window." [AntigR] (100) Wint 95, p. 12-13.
    "The Spoils of Patronage" (April 16, 1902). [ParisR] (37:137) Wint 95, p. 268-273.
    "A Wedding Cake." [AntigR] (100) Wint 95, p. 11.
DONATO, Colette de
    See DeDONATO, Colette
DONG-PO, Su
    See SU, Dong-Po
1563. DONLAN, John
    "Lions." [Event] (24:3) Wint 95-96, p. 43.
    "Witness." [Event] (24:3) Wint 95-96, p. 44.
1564. DONNELL, David
    "Communist Girls: Innocent Strangers." [Descant] (26:1, #88) Spr 95, p. 50-51.
    "Corn Fields" (Morning Light, Hanlan's Point). [Descant] (26:1, #88) Spr 95, p. 48-
        49.
1565. DONNELLY, Jean
    "Ettard." [Sulfur] (15:1, #36) Spr 95, p. 10-12.
1566. DONNELLY, Laura
    "Another Stafford County Curve Poem." [ChironR] (43) Sum 95, p. 15.
1567. DONNELLY, Marilyn P.
    "The Course of True Love." [Light] (15/16) Aut-Wint 95-96, p. 19.
1568. DONNELLY, P. N. W.
    "Otamatata Pa." [Vis] (49) 95, p. 37.
1569. DONNELLY, Susan
    "Man on The Subway." [PassN] (16:1) Sum 95, p. 29.
    "Night Stop." [PassN] (16:1) Sum 95, p. 28.
1570. DONOGHUE, John
    "Rage." [OxfordM] (10:1) Wint 94-Spr 95, p. 16.
    "Solo." [OxfordM] (10:1) Wint 94-Spr 95, p. 16-17.
1571. DONOHOE, Thomas
    "About the Need of Demarcation." [SoCoast] (18) Ja 95, p. 20.
1572. DONOHUE, Angelin Moran
    "In a Vacuum Gold Sublimes." [QW] (41) Aut-Wint 95-96, p. 175.
1573. DONOHUE, Sheila P.
    "Fishing." [PraS] (69:4) Wint 95, p. 128-129.
1574. DONOVAN, Gerard
    "Child of an Old Victory." [WilliamMR] (33) 95, p. 7.
    "On the Way to Southampton Town." [WilliamMR] (33) 95, p. 98.

1575. DONOVAN, Katie
"Entering the Mare." [SouthernR] (31:3) Jl/Sum 95, p. 519-520.
"Grooming" (for my mother). [SouthernR] (31:3) Jl/Sum 95, p. 520-522.
1576. DOOLIN, Lucas
"Araby." [BellArk] (11:6) N-D 95, p. 16.
"GTA." [BellArk] (11:6) N-D 95, p. 16.
"Pub." [BellArk] (11:6) N-D 95, p. 16.
"Shooter." [BellArk] (11:6) N-D 95, p. 16.
1577. DOPP, Jamie
"Mating Ritual." [PraF] (16:2, #71) Sum 95, p. 46-47.
1578. DOR, Moshë
"Flemish Painting" (tr. by Bernhard Frank). [PoetryE] (40) Spr 95, p. 25.
"Interpretations" (tr. by Bernhard Frank). [PoetryE] (40) Spr 95, p. 24.
"Parting" (tr. by the author). [Agni] (42) 95, p. 99.
1579. DORCELY, Gina
"Hymn" (tr. of Emmelyne Carriès-Lemaire). [CaribbeanW] (9) 95, p. 99.
"Ode to Bolivar" (tr. of Emmelyne Carriès-Lemaire). [CaribbeanW] (9) 95, p. 95-99.
"Without Peace" (tr. of Emmelyne Carriès-Lemaire). [CaribbeanW] (9) 95, p. 101.
"Your Song Is Immortal" (tr. of Emmelyne Carriès-Lemaire). [CaribbeanW] (9) 95, p. 100.
DOREN, John van
See Van DOREN, John
1580. DORESKI, William
"Black-Girdered Towers." [Wind] (75) Spr 95, p. 7-8.
"Gazebo on Spruce Point." [DefinedP] (1:2) Spr-Sum 93, p. 10-11.
"Jesus on the Radio." [WindO] (59) Spr 95, p. 42.
"A Meteor." [GreensboroR] (57) Wint 94-95, p. 3.
"Orange County." [Wind] (75) Spr 95, p. 6.
1581. DORGAN, Theo
"Seven Versions of Loss Eternal." [Poetry] (167:1/2) O-N 95, p. 70-71.
"Western." [SouthernR] (31:3) Jl/Sum 95, p. 628.
1582. DORIAN
"Other Means." [CapeR] (30:1) Spr 95, p. 34.
"Unveil." [CapeR] (30:1) Spr 95, p. 35.
1583. DORIAN, Marguerite
"Bas Relief of Heroes" (tr. of Nichita Stanescu, w. Elliott B. Urdang). [MidAR]
(15:1/2) 95, p. 222-223.
1584. DORIS, Stacy
"Cameo Appearance by a Talk Show Hostess" (Selections). [Phoebe] (24:1) 95, p.
49-54.
1585. DORN, Alfred
"Rondeau of a Host." [Light] (15/16) Aut-Wint 95-96, p. 31.
1586. DORPH, Doug
"Broken Cars." [Footwork] (24/25) 95, p. 71.
"The Discoverer." [BellR] (18:2, #38) Fall 95, p. 9.
"Family Whistle." [ChironR] (42) Spr 95, p. 29.
"The Lurch of Winter." [PlumR] (8) [95], p. 16.
"Nature Show Elephant Cock." [Sonora] (30) Fall 95, p. 73.
"Post-nasal Drip." [GreenMR] (8:2) Fall-Wint 95-96, p. 98.
"Solzhenitsyn Eating Ice Cream." [PlumR] (8) [95], p. 17.
"The Titan." [BellR] (18:2, #38) Fall 95, p. 8.
1587. DORSETT, Thomas
"Dead Cat Sonnet" (tr. of Vincius de Moraes, w. Moyses Purisch). [WillowS] (36)
Je 95, p. 94.
"The Drunkard." [WindO] (59) Spr 95, p. 14.
"Humbly, I Wish to Cultivate" (tr. of Ruth Rosenfeld). [InterPR] (21:1) Spr 95, p.
43.
"Paris" (tr. of Ingeborg Bachmann). [WillowS] (36) Je 95, p. 95.
"Sometimes You Grow from My Hand Like a Tree" (tr. of Ruth Rosenfeld).
[InterPR] (21:1) Spr 95, p. 45.
1588. DORY, Regina
"Jerome Jones" (WritersCorps Program, Washington, DC). [WashR] (21:2) Ag-S
95, p. 10.
1589. DOSS, Alan
"Mid November 1993." [SmPd] (32:2, #94) Spr 95, p. 14.

1590. DOSTAL, Cyril A.
   "I Like Doing Carpentry Because It Makes Me Feel Like Jesus." [LaurelR] (29:1)
      Wint 95, p. 22.
1591. DOTY, Mark
   "Atlantis." [Nat] (261:1) 3 Jl 95, p. 25.
   "Coastal." [NewYorker] (70:46) 23 Ja 95, p. 74.
   "Couture." [DefinedP] (2:2) Spr-Sum 94, p. 7-10.
   "A Display of Mackerel." [Atlantic] (276:3) S 95, p. 92.
   "A Green Crab's Shell." [NewYorker] (71:27) 11 S 95, p. 67.
   "Michael's Dream." [AmerV] (38) 95, p. 61-62.
   "Tunnel Music." [NewYorker] (71:29) 25 S 95, p. 48.
   "Wreck." [DefinedP] (2:2) Spr-Sum 94, p. 5-6.
1592. DOUCETTE, Concetta Ciccozzi
   "East of Rome." [Footwork] (24/25) 95, p. 138.
1593. DOUGHERTY, Edward A.
   "Aioi." [InterQ] (2:1/2) 95, p. 268.
   "Crossing Motoyasu Bridge." [InterQ] (2:1/2) 95, p. 269.
   "Delta." [InterQ] (2:1/2) 95, p. 271-272.
   "The Passion of Strontium." [InterQ] (2:1/2) 95, p. 270.
1594. DOUGHERTY, Sean Thomas
   "April Saturday" (for Patricia Smith). [DefinedP] (1:2) Spr-Sum 93, p. 47.
   "Channel Surfing on a Spring Afternoon the Crack of a Bat Brings Me Back to
      1977" (For Pop). [Footwork] (24/25) 95, p. 137.
   "Common Ground on an Asphalt Court." [Footwork] (24/25) 95, p. 136-137.
   "The Day I Fought Joe Louis." [Footwork] (24/25) 95, p. 136.
   "Eastern Pennsylvania" (for BB). [AxeF] (3) 90, p. 37.
   "Even the Stars Are Melting from the Moon." [ContextS] (4:2) 95, p. 5.
   "Far From the Adriatic Sun" (for SP). [BlackBR] (20) Spr-Sum 95, p. 24.
   "Far From the Banks of Jordan" (for Sherman Alexie). [LowellR] [1] Sum 94, p. 56-
      57.
   "Father." [DefinedP] (3) 95, p. 44.
   "Last Tuesday After Breakfast" (for S.P.). [DefinedP] (1:2) Spr-Sum 93, p. 48-49.
   "Like Wind Through Bare Branches." [Flyway] (1:3) Wint 95, p. 68.
   "Moon Grief Utterance." [DefinedP] (3) 95, p. 43.
   "Old Woman." [DefinedP] (1:2) Spr-Sum 93, p. 49.
   "On a Wet Day in Spring Washing Dishes." [Flyway] (1:3) Wint 95, p. 69-70.
   "Poem Made of Sun, Coal, Snow, and Sleep." [SpoonR] (20:1) Wint-Spr 95, p. 88-
      89.
   "The Puerto Rican Girls of French Hill." [AxeF] (3) 90, p. 36.
   "Snapshot." [Bogg] (67) 95, p. 15.
   "Snow." [DefinedP] (3) 95, p. 42.
1595. DOUGLAS, Kristen
   "Clocks." [WindO] (60) Fall-Wint 95, p. 21-22.
1596. DOUSKEY, Franz
   "Hitting the Bridge." [NewYorkQ] (55) 95, p. 68.
   "Tuberculosis" (Block 3, KL Auschwitz, April 10, 1943). [NewYorkQ] (54) 95, p.
      54.
1597. DOVE, Rita
   "Afield." [AmerPoR] (24:2) Mr-Ap 95, p. 10.
   "Blown Apart." [MissR] (23:3) 95, p. 46.
   "Canary" (for Michael S. Harper). [MissR] (23:3) 95, p. 29.
   "Demeter, Waiting." [AmerPoR] (24:2) Mr-Ap 95, p. 10.
   "Elevator Man, 1949." [MissR] (23:3) 95, p. 47-48.
   "Exit." [MissR] (23:3) 95, p. 36.
   "Flash Cards." [Writer] (108:1) Ja 95, p. 15.
   "Geometry." [Writer] (108:1) Ja 95, p. 15.
   "Golden Oldie." [MissR] (23:3) 95, p. 37.
   "The Gorge." [MissR] (23:3) 95, p. 20-21.
   "Her Island." [Poetry] (166:2) My 95, p. 63-68.
   "Heroes." [Callaloo] (18:2) Spr 95, p. 231.
   "History." [MissR] (23:3) 95, p. 50.
   "Lady Freedom Among Us." [MissR] (23:3) 95, p. 39-40.
   "Lullaby" (after Lorca's *Cancion Tonta*). [Colum] (24/25) 95, p. 65.
   "The Musician Talks About 'Process'." [MissR] (23:3) 95, p. 41-42.
   "Persephone, Falling." [MissR] (23:3) 95, p. 43.
   "Persephone in Hell." [GettyR] (8:2) Spr 95, p. 193-200.

"Persephone Underground." [MissR] (23:3) 95, p. 44.
"Sonnet in Primary Colors." [MissR] (23:3) 95, p. 49.
"Teotihuacan." [MissR] (23:3) 95, p. 45.
"Uncle Millet." [RiverS] (42/43) 95, p. 162.
"Wiederkehr." [AmerPoR] (24:2) Mr-Ap 95, p. 10.
"Wiring Home." [MissR] (23:3) 95, p. 38.
"Your Death." [SenR] (25:1) Spr 95, p. 76.
1598. DOW, Robert
      "How Should I Say This?" [MassR] (36:4) Wint 95-96, p. 524-525.
1599. DOWD, Juditha
      "Arresting the Heart." [JINJPo] (17:1) Spr 95, p. 42.
      "At Five O'Clock." [US1] (30/31) 95, p. 3.
1600. DOWD, Mandy Richmond
      "Stillwater" (Editors' Prize winner in poetry). [MissouriR] (18:1) 95, p. 36-40.
1601. DOWELL, Season Harper
      "Glass Catfish." [Prima] (18/19) 95, p. 76.
      "Past Pain (Breathless)." [CreamCR] (19:1) Spr 95, p. 102.
      "This Is the Year." [CreamCR] (19:1) Spr 95, p. 103.
1602. DOWLING, Jim
      "Revising the Future." [DefinedP] (2:1) Fall-Wint 93, p. 23.
1603. DOWNING, Ben
      "The Aged Phoenix" (after the drawing by Paul Klee). [SouthwR] (80:2/3) Spr-Sum
             95, p. 316.
1604. DOWNS, Buck
      "Avec Banjo." [Phoebe] (24:2) 95, p. 31.
      "Cafe Triste." [Phoebe] (24:2) 95, p. 32.
      "Dumb-Bucket." [Phoebe] (24:2) 95, p. 30.
1605. DOYLE, Gary
      "On Shooting a Snake in My Front Yard." [CapeR] (30:2) Fall 95, p. 48-49.
1606. DOYLE, Lynn
      "Intonation (Or an Explanation of the Poet)." [PlumR] (8) [95], p. 24-25.
1607. DOYLE, Margaret
      "Before You Go." [ChironR] (42) Spr 95, p. 25.
1608. DOYLE, Mike
      "Trout Spawning at Lardeau River" (for Rita, & for Ernie and Fay). [MalR] (110)
             Spr 95, p. 97-99.
1609. DOYLE, Sally
      "I'm Not That Kind of Brightness." [Chain] (2) Spr 95, p. 76-78.
1610. DRAKE, Jeannette
      "Cinderella Revisited." [SouthernR] (31:1) Wint 95, p. 9.
      "October Sabbatical." [SouthernR] (31:1) Wint 95, p. 9-10.
1611. DRAPER, Hal
      "Commemoration Service" (tr. of Heinrich Heine). [NewYRB] (42:13) 10 Ag 95, p.
             41.
1612. DRAWERT, Kurt
      "A Moment at the Window with the Black Frame" (tr. by Agnes Stein). [MidAR]
             (15:1/2) 95, p. 122.
1613. DRESMAN, Paul
      "Magpie Out of Abacus." [Vis] (49) 95, p. 9.
      "Marks on the Neck." [Vis] (49) 95, p. 8.
DRESSAY, Anne Le
      See Le DRESSAY, Anne
1614. DREW, Mark
      "My Father as Houdini." [GettyR] (8:3) Sum 95, p. 388-389.
1615. DREXEL, John
      "Archaeologist." [SantaBR] (3:3) Fall-Wint 95, p. 126.
      "At Chysauster." [SantaBR] (3:3) Fall-Wint 95, p. 127.
      "Between Now and Then." [OxfordM] (10:1) Wint 94-Spr 95, p. 18.
      "Chance Encounters." [ParisR] (37:136) Fall 95, p. 157.
      "Fantasia in Venice." [OxfordM] (10:1) Wint 94-Spr 95, p. 18.
1616. DRISCOLL, Frances
      "Difficult Word." [13thMoon] (13:1/2) 95, p. 13.
      "Here, Among Old Roses." [13thMoon] (13:1/2) 95, p. 14.
1617. DRISCOLL, Roz
      "Sculpture." [MassR] (36:2) Sum 95, p. 254.

1618. DRISKELL, Sue Terry
"Aerialists." [GreensboroR] (58) Sum 95, p. 95-96.
1619. DROST, Scott
"Casting the Oracle." [Elf] (5:3) Fall 95, p. 35.
1620. DRURY, John
"Cuttlefish." [SouthernR] (31:4) O/Aut 95, p. 826.
1621. DRUSKA, John
"Tuesday Afternoon at the Grand Art Institute." [HiramPoR] (58/59) Spr 95-Wint
96, p. 19-20.
1622. DRY, Paul
"At the End of the Hike." [AmerPoR] (24:1) Ja-F 95, p. 24.
1623. DRYANSKY, Amy
"The Lull Between Spokes." [MassR] (36:3) Aut 95, p. 474-476.
"A Short Message" (Third Robert Penn Warren Poetry Award). [AnthNEW] (7) 95,
p. 11.
Du ...
See also names beginning with "Du" without the following space, filed below in
their alphabetic positions, e.g., DuPLESSIS.
1624. Du BOUCHET, André
"A I R" (Selections, tr. by David Mus). [Sulfur] (15:1, #36) Spr 95, p. 196-197.
"Breath Log" (from A I R, tr. by David Mus). [Sulfur] (15:1, #36) Spr 95, p. 196-
197.
"Dictation" (from A I R, tr. by David Mus). [Sulfur] (15:1, #36) Spr 95, p. 199-202.
"I Can See Next to Nothing" (from A I R, tr. by David Mus). [Sulfur] (15:1, #36) Spr
95, p. 203.
"The Indwelling" (from OR ELSE THE SUN, OU LE SOLEIL, 1968, tr. by David
Mus). [DenQ] (30:1) Sum 95, p. 29-63.
"Morning" (from A I R, tr. by David Mus). [Sulfur] (15:1, #36) Spr 95, p. 198.
DUAT, Pham Tien
See PHAM, Tien Duat
1625. DUBIN, Ruth
"February" (tr. of Boris Pasternak). [DenQ] (29:4) Spr 95, p. 48.
"July Storm" (tr. of Boris Pasternak). [DenQ] (29:4) Spr 95, p. 46-47.
1626. DUBNOV, Eugene
"And in the Summer" (tr. by Anne Stevenson and the author). [Arc] (34) Spr 95, p.
35.
"A Great Wave Crashed" (tr. by Anne Stevenson and the author). [Arc] (34) Spr 95,
p. 34.
"March Morning" (to the memory of Ilya Rubin, tr. by Shirley Kaufman, w. the
author). [LitR] (38:2) Wint 95, p. 194.
"Outside by My Window" (tr. by Chris Newman, w. the author). [LitR] (38:2) Wint
95, p. 194.
1627. DuBOIS, Annette
"New Paths to Writer's Block (or, My Queendom for a Laser Printer)." [SinW] (55)
Spr-Sum 95, p. 35.
"Proof (Deborah)." [SinW] (55) Spr-Sum 95, p. 34.
DuBOUCHET, André
See Du BOUCHET, André
1628. DUBRIS, Maggie
"Willieworld" (Selection: IV). [Chain] (2) Spr 95, p. 79-91.
1629. DUBROFF, Susanne
"For a Saxifrage Prometheus on Touching the Aeolian Hand of Hölderlin" (to
Denise Naville, tr. of René Char). [Image] (11) Fall 95, p. 33-34.
"Just as" (tr. of René Char). [Image] (11) Fall 95, p. 33.
"To ...." (tr. of René Char). [HarvardR] (9) Fall 95, p. 66.
"Vertical Village" (tr. of René Char). [HampSPR] Wint 95, p. 38.
1630. DuCHARME, Mark
"Paradise" (Selection: 2). [NewAW] (13) Fall-Wint 95, p. 131.
1631. DUCKWORTH, David P.
"Roads." [Gerbil] (3) Sum 95, p. 20.
1632. DUDLEY, Ellen
"Ojo Caliente Suite." [ManyMM] (2:1) 95, p. 119-121.
"The Oranges." [AnthNEW] (7) 95, p. 30.
1633. DUEHR, Gary
"ii. What should I wear, today, today or the next day?" [SnailPR] (3:2) 95, p. 16.
"vi. On the train just before the doors open." [SnailPR] (3:2) 95, p. 17.

"The Dry Year: A Sequence" (2 selections). [Nimrod] (39:1) Fall-Wint 95, p. 106-107.
"Loop." [XavierR] (15:2) Fall 95, p. 66.
"The Other Side of the World" (Selections). [BellR] (18:2, #38) Fall 95, p. 12-13.
1634. DUEMER, Joseph
"Six Fragments From a Spring Journal." [TampaR] (10) Spr 95, p. 47-50.
1635. DUFAULT, Peter Kane
"Aleph." [NewRep] (212:23) 5 Je 95, p. 44.
"The Expanding Universe: Two Views." [NewYorker] (71:19) 10 Jl 95, p. 30.
1636. DUFF, Heather
"Bones in the Forest." [PottPort] (16:1) Fall 95, p. 65-66.
"Notes from the Paper Towel Dispenser." [PottPort] (16:1) Fall 95, p. 67-69.
1637. DUFF, S. K.
"Home Is Not Where I'm Headed" (The 1994 Allen Ginsberg Poetry Awards: Honorable Mention). [Footwork] (24/25) 95, p. 192.
"The Presence of Angels." [GreenMR] (8:2) Fall-Wint 95-96, p. 109.
1638. DUFFIN, K. E.
"Old Keys Highway." [HarvardR] (9) Fall 95, p. 96-97.
1639. DUGAN, Lawrence
"Half-a-Dozen Years Ago." [PoetryE] (39) Fall 94, p. 28.
"Out There." [PoetryE] (39) Fall 94, p. 29.
"When New York Was Irish." [PoetryE] (39) Fall 94, p. 30.
1640. DUGGAN, Devon Miller
"Williamsburg Fête Champetre: The Watteau Dress" (for Hannah, at ten, on a class trip to Williamsburg, in costume). [HolCrit] (32:2) Ap 95, p. 18.
1641. DUHAMEL, Denise
"Allergy." [SlipS] (15) 95, p. 30.
"And Whatever Happened to the Sea." [SilverFR] (25) Sum 95, p. 21.
"August." [PartR] (62:3) Sum 95, p. 454-455.
"Bangarang." [OxfordM] (10:1) Wint 94-Spr 95, p. 19-20.
"Boy Teacups and Girl Teacups." [Plain] (15:3) Spr 95, p. 19.
"Fairy Tale." [GlobalCR] (6) Fall 95, p. 68.
"How I First Became Aware of My Body Image Problem — And/or a Tribute to Russell Edson." [ArtfulD] (28/29) 95, p. 122-123.
"Let Me Explain" (w. Maureen Seaton). [PoetL] (90:2) Sum 95, p. 22-24.
"Loyalty." [LullwaterR] (5:1) 93-94, p. 28-29.
"May." [SilverFR] (25) Sum 95, p. 20.
"Religion." [Plain] (15:2) Wint 95, p. 28.
"Ricky with the Tuft and a Princess with a Small Brain." [WormR] (35:4, #140) 95, p. 183-184.
"Shoes." [SpinningJ] (1) Fall 95-Wint 96, p. 4-5.
"Summer." [Footwork] (24/25) 95, p. 170.
"The Threat." [Colum] (24/25) 95, p. 156-157.
"The Virtues of Little Husbands" (after the Inuit tale "The Man Who Used to Be Carried by His Wife" as told by Liivai Qumaaluk). [AmerV] (37) 95, p. 17.
1642. DUMARS, Denise
"Phoneme" (for Peggy Wheeler). [Prima] (18/19) 95, p. 71-72.
1643. DUMAS, Charles
"Bruce Died Today." [BlackBR] (20) Spr-Sum 95, p. 26-27.
1644. DUMAS, Henry
"America." [Drumvoices] (5:1/2) Fall-Wint 95-96, p. 112.
"Funk." [Drumvoices] (5:1/2) Fall-Wint 95-96, p. 112.
"Sweet Afterwards" (bettye, june 1967). [Drumvoices] (4:1/2) Fall-Wint 94-95, p. 33.
"Yams." [Drumvoices] (5:1/2) Fall-Wint 95-96, p. 112.
1645. DUMESNIL, Cheryl
"Cherry Blossoms" (for Phil). [LowellR] [1] Sum 94, p. 13.
1646. DUNATOV, Anne Marie
"Life Magazine: 1991 Photo of Clitoridectomy." [NewYorkQ] (55) 95, p. 99-100.
1647. DUNHAM, Rebecca
"Fish Chowder." [SycamoreR] (7:2) Sum 95, p. 31.
"Late Dinner, June" (First Place, Jacaranda Poetry Contest). [Jacaranda] (11) [95 or 96?], p. 20.
1648. DUNKELBERG, Kendall (Kendall A.)
"Concocted from the North for Joost de Wit" (tr. of Paul Snoek). [InterPR] (21:1) Spr 95, p. 39.

"In Space" (tr. of Paul Snoek). [SnailPR] (3:2) 95, p. 21.
"Welcome in My Underworld" (tr. of Paul Snoek). [SnailPR] (3:2) 95, p. 20.
"White-poem" (tr. of Paul Snoek). [LitR] (38:3) Spr 95, p. 351.
1649. DUNN, Stephen
"Fallacies." [Poetry] (166:1) Ap 95, p. 28.
"Heaven." [NewEngR] (17:3) Sum 95, p. 175.
"How to Write a Dream Poem." [GreenMR] (8:1) Spr-Sum 95, p. 6-7.
"The Last Hours." [SouthernR] (31:4) O/Aut 95, p. 828-829.
"Missing." [ParisR] (37:134) Spr 95, p. 131-132.
"Named." [GeoR] (49:3) Fall 95, p. 647-648.
"Poetry." [MidAR] (15:1/2) 95, p. 1.
"Responsibility." [GettyR] (8:3) Sum 95, p. 466-467.
"Slant." [GettyR] (8:3) Sum 95, p. 468.
"Solving the Puzzle." [BelPoJ] (45:4) Chapbook 22, Sum 95, p. 16.
"The Song." [NewEngR] (17:3) Sum 95, p. 176-177.
"The Substitute." [SenR] (25:1) Spr 95, p. 49-50.
"Terminal." [MidAR] (15:1/2) 95, p. 2-3.
"Why I Don't Win Arguments with You." [SouthernR] (31:4) O/Aut 95, p. 827-828.
"Wild." [MidAR] (15:1/2) 95, p. 4-5.
"Wind in a Jar." [Nat] (258:2) 17 Ja 94, p. 67.
1650. DUNN, T.
"Guided Tour of Bended Limb" (A found poem excerpted from "Mind Alive
Encyclopedia"). [SnailPR] (3:2) 95, p. 24-25.
1651. DUNNE, Seán
"One Sunday in the Gearagh." [Poetry] (167:1/2) O-N 95, p. 31-32.
"Russians in Paris." [Poetry] (167:1/2) O-N 95, p. 33-34.
"Simone Weil 1909-1940." [Shen] (45:4) Wint 95, p. 72.
1652. DUODUO
"Crossing the Sea." [PoetryC] (15:2) Je 95, p. 20.
"Dead, Ten Dead." [PoetryC] (15:2) Je 95, p. 20.
"In England." [PoetryC] (15:2) Je 95, p. 21.
"I've Always Delighted in a Shaft of Light in the Depth of Night." [PoetryC] (15:2)
Je 95, p. 21.
"Never Make Dreams." [PoetryC] (15:2) Je 95, p. 21.
"Reading Out Loud." [PoetryC] (15:2) Je 95, p. 21.
1653. DuPLESSIS, Rachel Blau
"Draft 23: Findings" (Selections: 11-13, 21). [Sulfur] (15:2, #37) Fall 95, p. 125-
128.
"Draft 24: Gap." [GrandS] (14:2, #54) Fall 95, p. 172-176.
"Draft 25: Segno." [WestCL] (29:2, #17) Fall 95, p. 122-125.
1654. DUPLIJ, Steven
"3 Cemeteries" (tr. by the author, w. Bradley R. Strahan). [Vis] (47) 95, p. 9.
1655. DuPONT, Lonnie Hull
"Swimming." [Poem] (74) N 95, p. 1.
1656. DUPUIS, Howard
"The Design." [LitR] (38:2) Wint 95, p. 273.
1657. DURAN, Claudio
"Frente a Gatineau River" (to Marcela, tr. by Margarita Feliciano). [Arc] (35) Aut
95, p. 21.
"Letter from Pichidangui to the Duran Vidal" (tr. by Margarita Feliciano). [Arc] (35)
Aut 95, p. 20.
1658. DURAN, Felipe H.
"Pito." [Footwork] (24/25) 95, p. 83.
1659. DURCAN, Paul
"My Belovèd Compares Herself to a Pint of Stout." [SouthernR] (31:3) Jl/Sum 95,
p. 691-692.
"A Snail in My Prime." [SouthernR] (31:3) Jl/Sum 95, p. 692-695.
1660. DURHAM, Carolyn Richardson
"Pieces of a Woman" (tr. of Ricardo Aleixo, w. Reetika Vazirani and Chi Lam).
[Callaloo] (18:4) Fall 95, p. 801.
1661. DURHAM, Diana
"Ante-Natal Circle." [DefinedP] (2:1) Fall-Wint 93, p. 12.
1662. DURKIN, Kevin
"Orphan in Her Ninety-Third Year." [Hellas] (6:2) Fall-Wint 95, p. 27.
"Test." [PoetL] (90:3) Fall 95, p. 52.

1663. DUTESCU, Dan
"Dog, My Brother" (tr. of Dona Rosu). [LitR] (38:2) Wint 95, p. 276.
1664. DUTESCU-COLIBAN, Taina
"Between Parallel Mirrors" (tr. of Cornelia Maria Savu, w. Adam J. Sorkin).
[13thMoon] (13:1/2) 95, p. 34.
"A Hazy Morning" (For Horia Bernea, tr. of Cornelia Maria Savu, w. Adam J.
Sorkin). [13thMoon] (13:1/2) 95, p. 35.
"A Locket" (tr. of Cornelia Maria Savu, w. Adam J. Sorkin). [13thMoon] (13:1/2)
95, p. 36.
"Love Poem at the Foot of the Deforested Hill" (tr. of Cornelia Maria Savu, w.
Adam J. Sorkin). [13thMoon] (13:1/2) 95, p. 37.
"Love Poem at the Mirror" (tr. of Cornelia Maria Savu, w. Adam J. Sorkin).
[13thMoon] (13:1/2) 95, p. 38.
"A Morning Fit for Writing Your Memoirs" (tr. of Cornelia Maria Savu, w. Adam J.
Sorkin). [13thMoon] (13:1/2) 95, p. 39.
DUY, Nguyen
See NGUYEN, Duy
DUYN, Mona van
See Van DUYN, Mona
1665. DWELLER, Cliff
"Rituals of Loss." [DefinedP] (1:1) Fall-Wint 92, p. 32.
1666. DWINELL, David
"Cross Country Skiing Spirit Mountain." [RagMag] (12:2) Spr 95, p. 34.
1667. DWYER, David
"Remembering John Milton." [SoDakR] (33:3/4) Fall-Wint 95, p. 164.
1668. DWYER, Deirdre
"1597 Larch." [Event] (24:2) Sum 95, p. 13-15.
"The Antique Scroll of the Body." [Arc] (34) Spr 95, p. 55.
"A Day at the Tate." [AntigR] (101) Spr 95, p. 136.
"Old Cabin Rain." [Dandel] (22:1) 95, p. 38.
"Paper, Scissors, Stone." [Arc] (34) Spr 95, p. 56.
1669. DYBEK, Stuart
"Fridge." [Boulevard] (10:3, #30) Fall 95, p. 135.
"Haibun." [CrabOR] (1:1) Fall-Wint 95, p. 43.
1670. DYCK, E. F.
"Mennomonk (or, Homunculus)." [Grain] (22:3) Wint 95, p. 130-137.
1671. DYE, Jeffrey L.
"Adèle." [Vis] (47) 95, p. 31.
"Dry Season Slaughter." [LitR] (39:1) Fall 95, p. 60.
"In Iowa, in August." [PoetL] (90:3) Fall 95, p. 48.
"Sunset Beach." [CapeR] (30:2) Fall 95, p. 22.
1672. DYER, Linda
"Nightfall." [Blueline] (16) 95, p. 51.
1673. DYER, Renee
"The View From Inside" (WritersCorps Program, Washington, DC). [WashR] (21:2)
Ag-S 95, p. 7.
1674. DZINA, Nancy
"Mandorla." [WestHR] (49:3) Fall 95, p. 275.
"Rosetta Talk." [WestHR] (49:3) Fall 95, p. 245.

1675. EACKNITZ, Susan
"Kedging." [NewOR] (21:2) Sum 95, p. 74.
1676. EADES, Gwilym
"Tornadoes." [Event] (24:2) Sum 95, p. 16-17.
1677. EADIE, Tom
"Anthropos Metros." [CanLit] (145) Sum 95, p. 120.
"Conductor." [AntigR] (100) Wint 95, p. 132.
"Youth Diffident." [AntigR] (100) Wint 95, p. 131.
1678. EADY, Cornelius
"Alabama, c. 1963: A Ballad by John Coltrane." [RiverS] (42/43) 95, p. 167.
"A Call of the Wild." [SenR] (25:2) Fall 95, p. 8.
"Conversation." [SenR] (25:2) Fall 95, p. 9.
"False Arrest." [SenR] (25:1) Spr 95, p. 97-98.
"Moth." [SenR] (25:2) Fall 95, p. 7.

1679. EARLY, Gerald
"Flamingo, or the Making of Salad" (a poem for parents who have lost young children). [SenR] (25:1) Spr 95, p. 84-86.
"With Linnet and Rosalin on the Evening of the Equinox (or an Exposition on the Big Bang Theory)." [AmerPoR] (24:5) S-O 95, p. 19.
1680. EATON, Charles Edward
"Blue Light." [Pembroke] (27) 95, p. 85.
"Chain of Events." [Poem] (74) N 95, p. 4.
"Foil." [ConnPR] (14:1) 95, p. 10-11.
"The Garden of Blood." [HiramPoR] (58/59) Spr 95-Wint 96, p. 21.
"Hammock Hyperbole." [LullwaterR] (6:2) Fall-Wint 95, p. 64-65.
"The Haystack in the Needle." [NewL] (62:1) 96 (c1995), p. 125.
"The Language Student." [Chelsea] (58) 95, p. 117.
"The Window Doctor." [LullwaterR] (5:2) Fall-Wint 94, p. 74-75.
1681. EATON, Tom
"Here and Now." [ChironR] (43) Sum 95, p. 21.
1682. EBERHART, Richard
"A Poem to You." [AnthNEW] (7) 95, p. 7.
1683. EBERTS, Max
"Bee in a Jar." [SouthernPR] (35:2) Wint 95, p. 27-28.
1684. EBNER, Shannon
"My Portuguese Desert Poem." [13thMoon] (13:1/2) 95, p. 15.
1685. ECHELBERGER, M. J.
"Pagan Sacrifice." [ChironR] (43) Sum 95, p. 15.
1686. ECHEVERRIA, Sophie Dominik
"Mirage por Arturo." [LitR] (38:3) Spr 95, p. 366.
1687. EDELBAUM, Donna
"Internal Motif." [Flyway] (1:1) Spr 95, p. 8.
"Memorial Day Parade" (For pilot Donald Patrick). [Flyway] (1:1) Spr 95, p. 9.
1688. EDELMANN, Carolyn Foote
"Listening." [US1] (30/31) 95, p. 12.
1689. EDENS, Walter
"Venders." [Border] (6) Spr-Sum 95, p. 35.
1690. EDGERLY, Leonard S.
"Give Me That Baby." [HighP] (10:1) Spr 95, p. 35-37.
"Imagining a Reader" (After Ted Kooser). [NewYorkQ] (54) 95, p. 102.
"The Secret History of Rock 'n' Roll." [BelPoJ] (46:2) Wint 95-96, p. 35.
1691. EDGINGTON, Amy
"What the Housemouse Knows." [SinW] (55) Spr-Sum 95, p. 12.
1692. EDKINS, Anthony
"A Big If." [SpiritSH] (60) 95, p. 8.
"Constructions." [SpiritSH] (60) 95, p. 7.
"Costa Brava." [SpiritSH] (60) 95, p. 7.
"Inarticulation." [SpiritSH] (60) 95, p. 7.
"Interrogating Piaf." [SpiritSH] (60) 95, p. 8.
"My Place in History." [SpiritSH] (60) 95, p. 9.
"A Trophy." [SpiritSH] (60) 95, p. 9.
1693. EDLIN, Ken
"A Little Twist of the Lips." [Verse] (12:2) 95, p. 43.
1694. EDMONDS, Amanda
"Trains." [NewMyths] (2:2/3:1) 95, p. 91-93.
1695. EDMONDSON, Gary
"Missionary." [TexasR] (15:3/4) Fall-Wint 94, p. 84.
1696. EDNEY, Julian
"Abandoned on the sunlit floor." [WilliamMR] (33) 95, p. 97.
"Cropduster." [SmPd] (32:2, #94) Spr 95, p. 14.
1697. EDOYAN, Henrik
"Debt" (tr. by Diana Der-Hovanessian). [GrahamHR] (19) Wint 95-96, p. 53.
1698. EDSON, Russell
"Accidents." [ProseP] (4) 95, p. 21.
"Balls." [ProseP] (4) 95, p. 26.
"Chickens." [BelPoJ] (45:4) Chapbook 22, Sum 95, p. 17.
"The Death of a Fly." [ProseP] (4) 95, p. 23.
"The Dinner Date." [CutB] (44) Sum 95, p. 63.
"The Good Old Days." [ProseP] (4) 95, p. 22.
"The Intuitive Journey." [SenR] (25:1) Spr 95, p. 26.

"The Laboratory." [Field] (52) Spr 95, p. 29.
"The Laws." [CutB] (44) Sum 95, p. 64.
"The Personal Garment." [CutB] (44) Sum 95, p. 65.
"The Portrait." [ProseP] (4) 95, p. 27.
"The Square Wheel." [Field] (52) Spr 95, p. 30.
"The Taste of the Horse." [ProseP] (4) 95, p. 24.
"The Weeping Farmer." [ProseP] (4) 95, p. 25.
1699. EDWARDS, Elizabeth
"Mise en Scene." [SycamoreR] (7:1) Wint 95, p. 25.
1700. EDWARDS, Ken
"Becoming" (from "Eight Plus Six"). [WestCL] (29:2, #17) Fall 95, p. 27.
"Eight Plus Six" (Selections: 4 poems). [WestCL] (29:2, #17) Fall 95, p. 26-27.
"Four" (from "Eight Plus Six"). [WestCL] (29:2, #17) Fall 95, p. 27.
"Interrogation Room Remix" (from "Eight Plus Six"). [WestCL] (29:2, #17) Fall 95, p. 26.
"Trembling in the Berserk Station" (from "Eight Plus Six"). [WestCL] (29:2, #17) Fall 95, p. 26.
1701. EDWARDS, Margaret
"Grief Dog." [Blueline] (16) 95, p. 34-35.
1702. EDWARDS, Mike J.
"New Hands." [PoetryE] (40) Spr 95, p. 26.
"Traveler." [PoetryE] (40) Spr 95, p. 27.
1703. EGAN, Moira
"Autumnal." [LaurelR] (29:1) Wint 95, p. 31-33.
"The Garden of Her Choosing." [LaurelR] (29:1) Wint 95, p. 30.
"Leda Gets Laid." [LaurelR] (29:1) Wint 95, p. 35.
"The Silk of the Tie." [LaurelR] (29:1) Wint 95, p. 33-34.
1704. EGEMO, Constance
"Resurrection." [MidwQ] (36:4) Sum 95, p. 366-367.
1705. EGER, Jeffrey
"Miriam No Longer Speaks Hungarian." [JlNJPo] (17:1) Spr 95, p. 16-17.
1706. EGERMEIER, Virginia
"Ambulatory with Radiating Chapels." [LitR] (38:2) Wint 95, p. 218.
1707. EHRET, Terry
"Aubade" (1942, from "The Thought She Might: Picasso Portraits. First Prize, The Pablo Neruda Prize for Poetry). [Nimrod] (39:1) Fall-Wint 95, p. 11-12.
"Bather" (1927, from "The Thought She Might: Picasso Portraits. First Prize, The Pablo Neruda Prize for Poetry). [Nimrod] (39:1) Fall-Wint 95, p. 3.
"Celestine" (1903, from "The Thought She Might: Picasso Portraits. First Prize, The Pablo Neruda Prize for Poetry). [Nimrod] (39:1) Fall-Wint 95, p. 1-2.
"Guernica I" (1937, from "The Thought She Might: Picasso Portraits. First Prize, The Pablo Neruda Prize for Poetry). [Nimrod] (39:1) Fall-Wint 95, p. 8.
"Guernica III" (1937, from "The Thought She Might: Picasso Portraits. First Prize, The Pablo Neruda Prize for Poetry). [Nimrod] (39:1) Fall-Wint 95, p. 8.
"Guernica IV" (1937, from "The Thought She Might: Picasso Portraits. First Prize, The Pablo Neruda Prize for Poetry). [Nimrod] (39:1) Fall-Wint 95, p. 9.
"Madonna of the Chickens" (after "Farmer's Wife on a Stepladder," 1933, from "The Thought She Might: Picasso Portraits. First Prize, The Pablo Neruda Prize for Poetry). [Nimrod] (39:1) Fall-Wint 95, p. 6.
"Nuclear Family." [Flyway] (1:2) Fall 95, p. 16-17.
"Nude Dressing Her Hair" (1940, from "The Thought She Might: Picasso Portraits. First Prize, The Pablo Neruda Prize for Poetry). [Nimrod] (39:1) Fall-Wint 95, p. 10.
"Two Women (La Muse)" (1935, from "The Thought She Might: Picasso Portraits. First Prize, The Pablo Neruda Prize for Poetry). [Nimrod] (39:1) Fall-Wint 95, p. 7.
"Woman in an Armchair" (1913, from "The Thought She Might: Picasso Portraits. First Prize, The Pablo Neruda Prize for Poetry). [Nimrod] (39:1) Fall-Wint 95, p. 2.
"Woman with Book" (1932, from "The Thought She Might: Picasso Portraits. First Prize, The Pablo Neruda Prize for Poetry). [Nimrod] (39:1) Fall-Wint 95, p. 4-5.
1708. EIFUKU, Empress (1271-1342)
"It's on-rushing time" (tr. by Sam Hamill). [RiverS] (44) 95, p. 34.
1709. EIGL, Gail M.
"For Wanting." [Pearl] (22) Fall-Wint 95, p. 110.

1710. EIKELBOOM, Jan
"Loves Me Like a Rock" (tr. by Greta Kilburn). [CimR] (112) Jl 95, p. 10.
1711. EIMERS, Nancy
"Autistic Twins at the Fireworks." [CrabOR] (1:1) Fall-Wint 95, p. 70-71.
1712. EINARSSON, Einar
"Above the Tree Lines." [Elf] (5:2) Sum 95, p. 32.
"Passing Poetry." [OxfordM] (10:1) Wint 94-Spr 95, p. 22.
"A Small, Mean Man." [OxfordM] (10:1) Wint 94-Spr 95, p. 21.
"When God Sings the Blues." [ChironR] (43) Sum 95, p. 36.
1713. EINHORN, Aliza
"Ceremony." [PoetL] (90:1) Spr 95, p. 42.
1714. EISDORFER, Sandra
"Meeting Place." [Border] (7) Fall-Wint 96, p. 6.
1715. EISELE, Thomas
"Rock n Roll's based on the beat." [PoetryE] (41) Aut 95, p. 113.
1716. EISEN, Christine
"Blank Screen." [BellArk] (11:3) My-Je 95, p. 14-15.
"Eve by the Pond." [BellArk] (11:6) N-D 95, p. 31.
"Roots." [BellArk] (11:3) My-Je 95, p. 15.
1717. EISENBERG, Susan
"Aliens." [ManyMM] (2:1) 95, p. 97.
"Partner #3." [PraS] (69:4) Wint 95, p. 125.
"The Summer She Decided to Quit" (for Sara D.). [PraS] (69:4) Wint 95, p. 126.
"UnWelcome Mats at the Construction Site" (for Cher, Donna and Cassandra).
[PraS] (69:4) Wint 95, p. 127-128.
1718. EKLUND, George
"63 Cents." [Wind] (76) Fall 95, p. 11.
"Dawn Dream." [Wind] (76) Fall 95, p. 13.
"Eschatological Serenade." [MidwQ] (36:3) Spr 95, p. 294.
"The Ox." [MidwQ] (36:3) Spr 95, p. 295.
"White Moths." [Wind] (76) Fall 95, p. 12.
EL, Otis Green
See GREEN EL, Otis
1719. ELDER, Dixon
"Contract." [RiverC] (15:2) Sum 95, p. 119.
1720. ELDER, Karl
"The Foreman and the Apprentice." [SycamoreR] (7:2) Sum 95, p. 32.
1721. ELGORRIAGA, José
"44. The moon passes like a chill between the marble statues" (tr. of Gabriel Celaya,
w. Martin Paul). [QW] (41) Aut-Wint 95-96, p. 204.
1722. ELIASSON, Gyrdir
"At the Foot of Mount Ararat" (tr. by Bernard Scudder). [Nimrod] (38:2) Spr-Sum
95, p. 73.
"Of the Last Descendant of Icarus" (tr. by Bernard Scudder). [Nimrod] (38:2) Spr-
Sum 95, p. 72.
1723. ELIZABETH, Martha
"Roberta Says the World Has Gone to Plastic." [NewEngR] (17:4) Fall 95, p. 128.
1724. ELKINS, Carolyn
"The Drowning Beach." [NewDeltaR] (12:1) Fall-Wint 94, p. 81-83.
1725. ELLEDGE, Jim
"The Man I Love and I Have a Typical Evening the Night Richard M. Nixon Dies."
[CimR] (111) Ap 95, p. 64-65.
1726. ELLEFSON, J. C.
"On the Brink of Leaving Holiday Town." [ColEng] (57:6) O 95, p. 709.
"Sadie's Last Love Letter to the Imperial Capital." [ColEng] (57:6) O 95, p. 708.
1727. ELLEN
"At My Throat." [Plain] (15:2) Wint 95, p. 16-17.
"The Drummer." [Plain] (15:3) Spr 95, p. 13.
1728. ELLIK, Charles
"The Attic." [Pearl] (22) Fall-Wint 95, p. 45.
"God picks uneasily." [Pearl] (22) Fall-Wint 95, p. 43.
"How Was the Hag to Know You'd Used the Trick Before?" [Pearl] (22) Fall-Wint
95, p. 44.
"It Only Works with Ruby Slippers." [Pearl] (22) Fall-Wint 95, p. 45.
"Sunday Solstice." [Pearl] (22) Fall-Wint 95, p. 43.

ELLINGSON, Alice Olds
    See OLDS-ELLINGSON, Alice
1729. ELLIOT, Alistair
    "Big Fish" (tr. of Juvenal IV). [Arion] (3:2/3) Fall 95-Wint 96, p. 185-190.
1730. ELLIOTT
    "Untitled: I ain't normal, not even close." [ChironR] (44/45) Aut-Wint 95, p. 15.
1731. ELLIS, Angela M.
    "Jacob at Peniel." [ChrC] (112:25) 30 Ag-6 S 95, p. 806.
    "On Occasion." [Plain] (15:3) Spr 95, p. 37.
1732. ELLIS, Elwyn
    "Crabs" (Selections). [AmerPoR] (24:2) Mr-Ap 95, p. 16.
1733. ELLIS, R. Virgil (Ron)
    "Fort Bliss." [Rosebud] (2:3) Aut-Wint 95, p. 82-84.
1734. ELLIS, Scott
    "Easter." [Quarry] (44:1) 95, p. 118-119.
    "Pindrop Contributes to the Information Economy." [Quarry] (44:1) 95, p. 120.
1735. ELLIS, Stephen
    "Eventually, At Once." [Talisman] (15) Wint 95-96, p. 76-77.
    "PAX." [Talisman] (15) Wint 95-96, p. 75.
1736. ELLIS, Thomas Sayers
    "Fatal April" (Thomas Leon Ellis, Sr., 1945-1991). [Callaloo] (18:2) Spr 95, p. 234-
        235.
    "The Market." [Callaloo] (18:2) Spr 95, p. 236.
    "A Psychoalphadiscobetabioaquadoloop." [Callaloo] (18:2) Spr 95, p. 237-238.
    "Tambourine Tommy." [Callaloo] (18:2) Spr 95, p. 232-233.
    "View-Master" (for my mother). [BostonR] (20:2) Ap-My 95, p. 27.
    "View of the Library of Congress from Paul Laurence Dunbar High School" (For
        Doris Craig and Michael Olshausen). [SouthernR] (31:2) Ap/Spr 95, p. 265-
        267.
1737. ELLISTON, Deborah A.
    "Morning" (for Linda). [SinW] (55) Spr-Sum 95, p. 13.
1738. ELLMAN, Kitsey
    "Proof." [BellR] (18:1, #37) Spr 95, p. 30.
1739. ELLSWORTH, Anne
    "Epilogue." [DogRR] (14:1, #27) Sum 95, p. 51.
    "Escape." [DogRR] (14:1, #27) Sum 95, p. 51.
1740. ELMENDORF, Bob
    "Somewhere Between the Stars and Snails." [SnailPR] (3:2) 95, p. 10.
1741. ELMIRA (D.C. Center for Alcohol and Drug Abuse)
    "If" (WritersCorps Program). [WashR] (21:2) Ag-S 95, p. 5.
1742. ELOVIC, Barbara
    "Anne Frank" (The 1994 Allen Ginsberg Poetry Awards: Honorable Mention).
        [Footwork] (24/25) 95, p. 193.
1743. ELSE, Victoria
    "Sabbath." [ParisR] (37:136) Fall 95, p. 80.
1744. ELSON, Christopher
    "On Benoît's Tomb." [TickleAce] (27) Spr-Sum 94, p. 53.
1745. ÉLUARD, Paul
    "The Lover" (tr. by Louis Simpson). [HarvardR] (9) Fall 95, p. 61.
1746. ELYSHEVITZ, Alan
    "First Aid" (Honorable Mention, First Annual Poetry Awards). [LiteralL] (2:2) Fall
        95, p. 4.
1747. EMANUEL, James A.
    "Bojangles and Jo." [AfAmRev] (29:1) Spr 95, p. 92.
    "The Haiku King." [AfAmRev] (29:1) Spr 95, p. 92.
    "Jazz on the Move (A Haiku Sequence)." [CharR] (21:1) Spr 95, p. 71.
    "Jazzanatomy." [AfAmRev] (29:1) Spr 95, p. 92.
1748. EMANUEL, Lynn
    "Film Noir Sex: All Those Hotel Rooms Lit Up at Night Mean." [MichQR] (34:4)
        Fall 95, p. 597.
1749. EMERSON, Jocelyn (Jocelyn L.)
    "Bridge." [ColR] (22:2) Fall 95, p. 195.
    "Ere Long." [DenQ] (29:3) Wint 95, p. 13-14.
    "The Lighthouse." [ColR] (22:2) Fall 95, p. 193-194.
    "Stasis." [ColR] (22:2) Fall 95, p. 196.

1750. EMERY, Thomas
"Pegasus in Vegas." [HopewellR] (7) 95, p. 94-95.
1751. EMIN, Gevorg
"Luciole" (tr. by Diana Der-Hovanessian). [GrahamHR] (19) Wint 95-96, p. 51.
1752. EMMETT, Elaine
"Like Vermeer." [Poem] (74) N 95, p. 33.
"Sleeping on Our Graves." [Poem] (74) N 95, p. 35.
"Swallowing Fire." [Poem] (74) N 95, p. 34.
1753. EMMONS, Dick
"Sinful Syntax." [Light] (14) Sum 95, p. 11.
1754. EMMONS, Jeanne
"Equilibrium of Lily Pads." [SoCoast] (18) Ja 95, p. 62.
"Poppies Opening." [CimR] (112) Jl 95, p. 105.
"Preservation." [SoCoast] (18) Ja 95, p. 16-17.
"These Baptizing Waters" (1st Prize, 9th Annual Contest). [SoCoast] (18) Ja 95, p.
    28-29.
"Vacuuming." [CimR] (112) Jl 95, p. 104.
1755. ENANI, M.
"Features" (tr. of Farooq Shooshah). [Vis] (47) 95, p. 26.
1756. ENGELS, John
"Blaze." [Shen] (45:3) Fall 95, p. 25-27.
"A Fly Box." [NewEngR] (17:2) Spr 95, p. 9-12.
"Green Bay Flies." [NewEngR] (17:2) Spr 95, p. 16-18.
"Hatch." [NewEngR] (17:2) Spr 95, p. 19-20.
"Letter." [NewEngR] (17:2) Spr 95, p. 13-16.
"A Painting of an Angler, Fishing the Source" (for Nick Lyons). [Shen] (45:3) Fall
    95, p. 28-29.
"White Miller." [NewEngR] (17:2) Spr 95, p. 20-21.
1757. ENGLAND, Amy
"Waiting Table" (For Lucy, Sarah, and Ben). [ChiR] (41:2/3) 95, p. 66-69.
1758. ENGLAND, Gerald
"Tanka 12." [Bogg] (67) 95, p. 52.
1759. ENGLE, Diane
"Recipe for Whale Stew, in Sapphic Stanza." [Pearl] (22) Fall-Wint 95, p. 85.
"Snowfall." [Elf] (5:3) Fall 95, p. 30.
1760. ENGLE, John D., Jr.
"Mower and Mower." [Light] (14) Sum 95, p. 8.
1761. ENGLEBERT, Michel
"Freefall." [NewDeltaR] (12:1) Fall-Wint 94, p. 58-59.
1762. ENGLER, Robert Klein
"Half Notes, Whole Notes." [Flyway] (1:1) Spr 95, p. 106.
"The Manderling Quartet at Spertus Institute." [LiteralL] (1:6) Spr 95, p. 13.
1763. ENGLISH, Zoë
"Aisha." [Talisman] (15) Wint 95-96, p. 180-183.
1764. ENNIS, John
"Hydroturbines." [Poetry] (167:1/2) O-N 95, p. 27-28.
1765. ENQUIST, Anna
"The Art of Poetry" (tr. by Manfred Wolf). [CimR] (112) Jl 95, p. 14.
"Harvest" (tr. by Manfred Wolf). [CimR] (112) Jl 95, p. 14.
1766. ENRIGHT, John
"Island Sight." [Manoa] (7:2) Wint 95, p. 129.
"Jungle." [Manoa] (7:2) Wint 95, p. 128.
"Pago-Buffalo." [Manoa] (7:2) Wint 95, p. 128.
"Virgin Frontiers." [Manoa] (7:2) Wint 95, p. 127.
1767. ENRIGHT, Sean
"Country Light." [Journal] (19:1) Spr-Sum 95, p. 20-21.
"Father Waking." [MidwQ] (36:3) Spr 95, p. 296.
1768. ENSING, Riemke
"From Picasso: Everytime it's a leap." [Descant] (26:1, #88) Spr 95, p. 82.
"From Picasso: Fish Hat." [Descant] (26:1, #88) Spr 95, p. 81.
"From Picasso: Simply." [Descant] (26:1, #88) Spr 95, p. 83.
"Meditations" (from Matisse). [Descant] (26:1, #88) Spr 95, p. 80.
1769. ENSLER, Eve
"Hair." [PennR] (6:2) 95, p. 8.
"My Vagina Was My Village." [PennR] (6:2) 95, p. 8.

1770. ENSLIN, Theodore
    "Modern Maturity." [BelPoJ] (45:4) Chapbook 22, Sum 95, p. 19.
    "My Maples in July." [BelPoJ] (45:4) Chapbook 22, Sum 95, p. 18.
    "Still Life — Abandoned House with Table." [BelPoJ] (45:4) Chapbook 22, Sum 95, p. 18.
1771. ENZENSBERGER, Hans Magnus
    "The Entombment" (tr. by the author). [HarvardR] (9) Fall 95, p. 113.
    "In Memory of Sir Hiram Maxim (1840-1916)" (tr. by the author). [HarvardR] (9) Fall 95, p. 113-114.
1772. EPPOLITO, Caterina
    "Bedlam Nursery Rhyme." [Nat] (258:1) 3-10 Ja 94, p. 32.
1773. EPPSTEIN, Maureen
    "Deer Dance at Tesuque Pueblo." [BellArk] (11:3) My-Je 95, p. 12.
    "Mallard Flight." [BellArk] (11:3) My-Je 95, p. 25.
    "The Quickening." [BellArk] (11:3) My-Je 95, p. 23.
1774. EPSTEIN, Daniel Mark
    "The Book of Matches." [NewRep] (212:11) 13 Mr 95, p. 40.
    "The Inheritance." [AmerS] (64:1) Wint 95, p. 66-67.
    "Phidias in Exile." [AmerS] (64:2) Spr 95, p. 236-239.
1775. EPSTEIN, Richard
    "The Botanic Garden." [Plain] (16:1) Fall 95, p. 27.
1776. EQUI, Elaine
    "Another Wall to Walk Through." [Phoebe] (24:1) 95, p. 26-27.
    "Femme-Maison" (after Louise Bourgeois). [AmerLC] (7) 95, p. 60.
    "The Heroine." [PlumR] (9) [95 or 96], p. 8-10.
    "Lesson." [AmerLC] (7) 95, p. 61.
    "Shield." [Phoebe] (24:1) 95, p. 28.
    "Starting to Rain" (for Joe Brainard). [PlumR] (9) [95 or 96], p. 6.
    "Where Is My Passport?" [PlumR] (9) [95 or 96], p. 7.
1777. ERB, Elke
    "Working Out" (tr. by Rosmarie Waldrop). [WorldL] (6) 95, p. 25.
1778. ERIC (D.C. Vision Program, Tyler Elementary School, Washington, DC).
    "Eric's Poem" (WritersCorps Program). [WashR] (21:2) Ag-S 95, p. 19.
1779. ERICKSON, Ann
    "Fish in Sea." [Bogg] (67) 95, p. 37.
    "Today the peace & war demonstrators." [Chain] (2) Spr 95, p. 94.
1780. ERIKSON, Jeffrey
    "The Things That Lie Within Our Bodies." [MidwQ] (36:2) Wint 95, p. 156.
1781. ERWIN, Cathy
    "Item: Ladies Timepiece (Old) Poor Condition." [Border] (7) Fall-Wint 96, p. 7.
1782. ESAREY, Debra
    "Present Perfect." [NewAW] (13) Fall-Wint 95, p. 119.
1783. ESAREY, Gary
    "Mr. Wang Goes to Washington: Americanizing the Wei" (Variations on Wang Wei's "Deer Park"). [Plain] (16:1) Fall 95, p. 22-23.
ESCAMILLA, Kleya Forté
    See FORTÉ-ESCAMILLA, Kleya
1784. ESDEN-TEMPSKI, Stanislaw
    "Rat Gives You His Free Hand" (tr. by Daniel Bourne). [MidAR] (15:1/2) 95, p. 206.
1785. ESHLEMAN, Clayton
    "The Boy and the Pillow" (For Manuel, tr. of Horacio Costa, w. M. B. Jordan and the author). [Sulfur] (15:1, #36) Spr 95, p. 131-146.
    "Fragmentations" (tr. of Antonin Artaud, w. Bernard Bador). [Sulfur] (15:2, #37) Fall 95, p. 60-70.
    "There Exists a Man" (tr. of Cesar Vallejo, w. José Rubia Barcia). [RiverS] (42/43) 95, p. 6.
1786. ESMAILIAN, Michelle
    "Cordelia's Executioner." [SoCoast] (18) Ja 95, p. 10.
    "Giant Sunflowers Only Bloom Once." [ManyMM] (2:1) 95, p. 140.
    "Man Stew." [ManyMM] (2:1) 95, p. 141.
    "Reciprocity." [ManyMM] (2:1) 95, p. 139.
    "Shopping." [TarRP] (34:2) Spr 95, p. 15.
1787. ESPADA, Martín
    "Beloved Spic" (Valley Stream, Long Island 1973). [HangL] (67) 95, p. 32.

"The Chair in the Dragon's Mouth" (Chelsea, Massachusetts). [Crazy] (49) Wint 95, p. 43-44.
"Do Not Put Dead Monkeys in the Freezer." [MassR] (36:4) Wint 95-96, p. 607-608.
"The Foreman's Wallet." [MidAR] (15:1/2) 95, p. 202-203.
"Governor Wilson of California Talks in His Sleep." [HangL] (67) 95, p. 33.
"Hands without Irons Become Dragonflies" (for Clemente Soto Vélez). [BilingR] (20:1) Ja-Ap 95, p. 59-65.
"The Hearse Driving." [Crazy] (49) Wint 95, p. 41-42.
"Huelga" (for César Chávez, 1927-1993). [BilingR] (20:2) My-Ag 95, p. 154.
"The Man Who Beat Hemingway" (for Kermit Forbes, Key West, Florida, 1994). [ClockR] (10:1/2) 95-96, p. 4-5.
"The Meaning of the Shovel" (Barrio René Cisneros, Managua, Nicaragua, 1982). [Nat] (261:1) 3 Jl 95, p. 33.
"My Native Costume." [BilingR] (20:1) Ja-Ap 95, p. 68.
"The Owl and the Lightning" (Brooklyn, New York). [MidAR] (15:1/2) 95, p. 200-201.
"The Piñata Painted with a Face Like Mine." [Crazy] (49) Wint 95, p. 37-38.
"Public School 190, Brooklyn 1963." [PartR] (62:3) Sum 95, p. 452.
"Rednecks" (Gaithersburg, Maryland). [Ploughs] (21:1) Spr 95, p. 16-17.
"The Saint Vincent de Paul Food Pantry Stomp" (Madison, Wisconsin, 1980). [RiverS] (42/43) 95, p. 166.
"Sing in the Voice of a God Even Atheists Can Hear" (for Demetria Martínez). [BilingR] (20:1) Ja-Ap 95, p. 66-67.
"Soliloquy at Gunpoint." [Crazy] (49) Wint 95, p. 45.
"These Trees" (tr. of Clemente Soto Vélez, w. Camilo Pérez-Bustillo). [MassR] (36:4) Wint 95-96, p. 641-649.
"Thieves of Light" (Chelsea, Massachusetts, 1991). [BilingR] (20:2) My-Ag 95, p. 155-157.
"The Trembling Puppet." [Crazy] (49) Wint 95, p. 39-40.

1788. ESPAILLAT, Rhina P.
"January." [Hellas] (6:2) Fall-Wint 95, p. 33.
"Last Day." [Poetry] (167:3) D 95, p. 155.
"Needlework." [AmerS] (64:2) Spr 95, p. 190.

1789. ESPENMILLER, Lisa
"Listening to Herbie." [BellArk] (11:6) N-D 95, p. 11.
"Open Spaces." [BellArk] (11:6) N-D 95, p. 7.
"With My Best Friend." [BellArk] (11:6) N-D 95, p. 5.

1790. ESPINAL, Raquel (grade 9, Ellington High School, Washington, DC)
"Nuevo Puerto Rico" (Poetry on the Metro Project). [WashR] (21:2) Ag-S 95, p. 15.

1791. ESPINOSA, María Fernanda
"XXVII. Romar tus filos." [InterPR] (21:1) Spr 95, p. 26.
"XXVII. To blunt your edges" (tr. by Ted Maier and Alicia Cabiedes-Fink). [InterPR] (21:1) Spr 95, p. 27.
"XXX. Hopes are allowed" (tr. by Ted Maier and Alicia Cabiedes-Fink). [InterPR] (21:1) Spr 95, p. 25.
"XXX. Las esperanzas están permitidas." [InterPR] (21:1) Spr 95, p. 24.

1792. ESPMARK, Kjell
"Prague Quartet" (tr. by Robin Fulton). [MalR] (110) Spr 95, p. 78-83.

1793. ESPOSITO, Carmine
"Circles." [Footwork] (24/25) 95, p. 207.

1794. ESQUINCA, Jorge
"Umbrella Suite" (tr. by D. M. Stroud). [Noctiluca] (2:1, #4) Spr 95, p. 56-57.

1795. ESTABROOK, Michael
"Because of the Encumbrance of Material Things." [Parting] (8:2) Wint 95-96, p. 42.
"Best Laid Plans (Or — When Dave Was 17)." [WindO] (60) Fall-Wint 95, p. 13.
"Bumper Sticker." [WindO] (60) Fall-Wint 95, p. 12.
"Don't Ask." [Parting] (8:2) Wint 95-96, p. 42.
"An Early Mythology." [Pearl] (22) Fall-Wint 95, p. 11.
"Patti." [Pearl] (22) Fall-Wint 95, p. 11.
"Shaking the Curls Back Off Her Face." [Bogg] (67) 95, p. 52.

1796. ESTES, Angie
"The Wintering of Geese." [LitR] (38:2) Wint 95, p. 210.

1797. ESTESS, Sybil Pittman
"What the Citizens of Texas Need." [Border] (7) Fall-Wint 96, p. 8-9.

1798. ESTEVA, Ananda
"Mama If You Only Knew Your Strength." [SinW] (56) Sum-Fall 95, p. 69-71.
1799. ESTEVE, Jean
"By the Fish." [Flyway] (1:2) Fall 95, p. 30.
"A Clear Sunday." [ChironR] (43) Sum 95, p. 33.
"If Then." [ChironR] (43) Sum 95, p. 24.
"Makeweight." [GreensboroR] (59) Wint 95-96, p. 120.
"Nourishment." [OxfordM] (10:1) Wint 94-Spr 95, p. 23.
"Sexual Intercourse." [NewYorkQ] (54) 95, p. 88.
1800. ESTEVES, Sandra María
"Puerto Rican Discovery #12: Token Views" (for the homeless, Penn Station, December 1990). [MassR] (36:4) Wint 95-96, p. 609.
1801. ESTROFF, Nadine
"A Healing in Room 1429." [SouthernPR] (35:2) Wint 95, p. 52-53.
1802. ETCHEVERRY, Jorge
"After years of burying myself in my own suffering" (from the unpublished volume Logbook, tr. by the author and Sharon Khan). [Arc] (35) Aut 95, p. 46.
"Consumerism & Guilt (the beginning of 1991)" (tr. by the author and Sharon Khan). [Arc] (35) Aut 95, p. 47-48.
"Where will I turn the serene birds of my pupils?" (from the unpublished volume Logbook, tr. by the author and Sharon Khan). [Arc] (35) Aut 95, p. 45.
1803. ETHELSDATTAR, Karen
"Middletown, Pennsylvania Nuclear Accident, 1979" (Three Mile Island). [InterQ] (2:1/2) 95, p. 282-283.
1804. ETSUCHI, Ayako
"Like a demon or ghost" (in Japanese and English, tr. by Jiro Nakano). [BambooR] (67/68) Sum-Fall 95, p. 2.
1805. ETTER, Carrie
"Making Love." [LitR] (38:2) Wint 95, p. 258.
"The Other Woman." [LaurelR] (29:1) Wint 95, p. 41.
"Reticence." [CimR] (111) Ap 95, p. 68.
"Visiting Illinois." [PoetL] (90:4) Wint 95-96, p. 49.
"Winter Equinox, Finland." [CimR] (111) Ap 95, p. 67.
"Your Son, My Son." [PoetL] (90:4) Wint 95-96, p. 48.
1806. ETTER, Dave
"By the Dawn's Early Light." [FreeL] (14) Wint 95, p. 13.
"Organ Music in Grain Valley, Missouri." [WestB] (36) 95, p. 43-45.
"Shoe in the Road." [WestB] (36) 95, p. 42-43.
"Singing in the Toyota." [FreeL] (14) Wint 95, p. 14.
1807. EUBANKS, Georgann
"The Neighbor Ladies Gather at a Safe Distance." [SouthernPR] (35:1) Sum 95, p. 23-24.
1808. EUGENE (D.C. Vision Program, Tyler Elementary School, Washington, DC).
"Eugene" (WritersCorps Program). [WashR] (21:2) Ag-S 95, p. 19.
1809. EURIPIDES
"Medea" (tr. by Mary-Kay Gamel). [QW] (40) Spr-Sum 95, p. 96-145.
1810. EVANS, David, Jr.
"A Tourist's Guide to Venomous Snakes in Australia." [SmPd] (32:1, #93) Wint 95, p. 10-11.
1811. EVANS, Lee
"10th Century Possession: Lady Rokujo Remembers the Night Her Spirit Flew From Her Body to Torment Princess Aoi" (After an episode from "The Tale of Genji"). [NowestR] (33:3) 95, p. 43-44.
"Making Love in My Mother's House." [NowestR] (33:3) 95, p. 42.
1812. EVANS, Michael
"At the Angle of Separation." [QW] (41) Aut-Wint 95-96, p. 178.
"Considerations in an Orange Grove." [QW] (41) Aut-Wint 95-96, p. 179.
"Leaving Fargo." [GreensboroR] (57) Wint 94-95, p. 75-76.
"Letter to Nat" (Shenandoah, Iowa). [WestB] (36) 95, p. 69.
"Poem for Where You Came From." [WestB] (36) 95, p. 68.
1813. EVETT, David
"Troll." [Light] (13) Spr 95, p. 21.
1814. EWART, Gavin (1916-1995)
"The Apostle to the Philistines." [Light] (13) Spr 95, p. 13.
"Late Auden." [Light] (14) Sum 95, p. 14.
"Sonnet: The Last Things." [Light] (15/16) Aut-Wint 95-96, inside back cover.

"TV Cookery." [Light] (13) Spr 95, p. 16.
1815. EXLER, Samuel
"Winter Thoughts." [PoetryE] (40) Spr 95, p. 28-32.
1816. EXNER, Richard
"All Night, in the Flesh" (tr. by William Stephen Cross). [InterQ] (2:1/2) 95, p. 99.
"Black Birth" (tr. by William Stephen Cross). [InterQ] (2:1/2) 95, p. 100.
"Detected" (for Oskar Jan Tauschinski, tr. by William Stephen Cross). [InterQ] (2:1/2) 95, p. 101.
"Entziffert" (für Oskar Jan Tauschinski). [InterQ] (2:1/2) 95, p. 101.
"Nachts, Leibhaftig." [InterQ] (2:1/2) 95, p. 99.
"Return" (tr. by Martha Collins). [HarvardR] (9) Fall 95, p. 30.
"Schwarzgeburt." [InterQ] (2:1/2) 95, p. 100.

1817. FABER, Louis (Louis S.)
"Enslaved." [Footwork] (24/25) 95, p. 170.
"Scribblings from the Gates of Hell." [BlackBR] (20) Spr-Sum 95, p. 37.
1818. FABIANI, Louise
"Animal Husbandry." [Event] (24:2) Sum 95, p. 18-20.
1819. FADER, Nava
"Apart." [SenR] (25:2) Fall 95, p. 42-43.
"My Achilles." [SenR] (25:2) Fall 95, p. 41.
"Ophelia." [SenR] (25:2) Fall 95, p. 44-45.
1820. FAGAN, Kathy
"Letter from the Garden." [Ploughs] (21:4) Wint 95-96, p. 56.
"She Attempts to Tell the Truth about True Romance." [MichQR] (34:2) Spr 95, p. 205-209.
"Two Tragedies, with Preface." [Ploughs] (21:4) Wint 95-96, p. 53-55.
1821. FAGAN, Robert
"The Invention of Printing." [Chelsea] (59) 95, p. 168-170.
1822. FAHNING, Sharon Rich
"The Collection." [Rosebud] (2:3) Aut-Wint 95, p. 118.
1823. FAHRLAND, Bridget
"Untitled: Not mustard, not ochre, not buttercup." [Agni] (41) 95, p. 70-71.
1824. FAIN, Sharon
"A Birth." [PoetryNW] (36:4) Wint 95-96, p. 3-4.
"Isla Mujeres: Weeks Before the Breakdown." [PoetryNW] (36:4) Wint 95-96, p. 4.
"On Seeing the Place Where I First Made Love." [PoetryNW] (36:4) Wint 95-96, p. 4-5.
1825. FAINLIGHT, Ruth
"Clinging Ivy." [Thrpny] (61) Spr 95, p. 18.
1826. FAIRCHILD, B. H.
"The Art of the Lathe" (from "C&W Machine Works." Finalist, The Nimrod / Hardman Awards). [Nimrod] (39:1) Fall-Wint 95, p. 62-63.
"The Himalayas." [PraS] (69:3) Fall 95, p. 103.
"The Invisible Man." [Thrpny] (61) Spr 95, p. 12.
1827. FAIRCHOK, Sherry
"Madeleine du Pin's Music Box." [Wind] (76) Fall 95, p. 14-15.
"Six Seeds." [Wind] (76) Fall 95, p. 16.
1828. FAITH, S.
"Puddinite." [Jacaranda] (11) [95 or 96?], p. 35.
1829. FALCO, Edward
"Winter Lake." [SpoonR] (20:2) Sum-Fall 95, p. 139.
1830. FALKENBERG, Marc
"Conversation with the Stone" (tr. of Yaak Karsunke). [TriQ] (93) Spr-Sum 95, p. 119.
1831. FALKNER, Gerhard
"Black / Red / Gold" (tr. by Rosmarie Waldrop). [ManhatR] (7:2) Wint 95, p. 64.
"The Ice Is Broken" (tr. by Rosmarie Waldrop). [ManhatR] (7:2) Wint 95, p. 65.
"The Split" (tr. by Rosmarie Waldrop). [ManhatR] (7:2) Wint 95, p. 66.
"Two to One" (tr. by Rosmarie Waldrop). [ManhatR] (7:2) Wint 95, p. 67.
"Vesuvius" (tr. by Rosmarie Waldrop). [ManhatR] (7:2) Wint 95, p. 68.
1832. FALLER, Bernard, Jr.
"Desert Funeral." [WritersF] (21) 95, p. 133.
"The Red Geranium." [ContextS] (4:2) 95, p. 7.

1833. FALLON, Peter
"Again." [Poetry] (167:1/2) O-N 95, p. 85.
"Carnaross 2." [Verse] (12:2) 95, p. 44.
"Easter." [Poetry] (167:1/2) O-N 95, p. 84.
1834. FAMA, Maria
"August Heat" (A variation on a Sestina). [Footwork] (24/25) 95, p. 32.
"Chambers." [Footwork] (24/25) 95, p. 32.
"Conversation." [Footwork] (24/25) 95, p. 33.
"The Ghost in My Bed." [Footwork] (24/25) 95, p. 32-33.
"Nonna Mattia" (The 1994 Allen Ginsberg Poetry Awards: Honorable Mention).
[Footwork] (24/25) 95, p. 194.
1835. FANNING, Roger
"One-Eyed Odin." [WestB] (37) 95, p. 43.
1836. FARALLO, Livio
"Base Sequences." [SlipS] (15) 95, p. 70.
1837. FAREWELL, Pat
"Back Then." [NewYorkQ] (55) 95, p. 69-70.
"Under Stars." [GreenMR] (8:2) Fall-Wint 95-96, p. 62.
1838. FARGAS, Laura
"An Animal of the Sixth Day." [GeoR] (49:4) Wint 95, p. 885-886.
"Doggy Doggerel." [GeoR] (49:3) Fall 95, p. 710.
"Living in Is." [GeoR] (49:4) Wint 95, p. 887.
1839. FARGNOLI, Patricia
"Breaking Silence — For My Son." [SpoonR] (20:2) Sum-Fall 95, p. 73.
"Frozen" (for my brother and in memory of R.D. 1941-47). [GreenMR] (8:2) Fall-
Wint 95-96, p. 63.
"Hardscrabble in Marlow, New Hampshire." [Flyway] (1:1) Spr 95, p. 108.
"In the City Without a Name." [PoetryNW] (36:4) Wint 95-96, p. 42-43.
"Location." [PoetryNW] (36:4) Wint 95-96, p. 41-42.
"My Brother Reads 'Old Soil'." [AnthNEW] (7) 95, p. 27.
"Vathana Tells of Her Hunger." [GreenMR] (8:2) Fall-Wint 95-96, p. 64-66.
1840. FARISS, Tina
"Gold." [Pearl] (22) Fall-Wint 95, p. 143.
1841. FARKAS, Endre
"For Those Who Deny the Holocaust." [PoetryC] (15:2) Je 95, p. 26.
1842. FARLEY, Joseph
"Eviction." [AxeF] (3) 90, p. 30.
"For Divine." [AxeF] (3) 90, p. 31.
1843. FARMER, Joy A.
"Penis Envy." [Poem] (74) N 95, p. 58.
1844. FARMER, Rod
"Metaphysics Footnote." [HampSPR] Wint 95, p. 27.
"Pigs." [Witness] (9:2) 95, p. 162.
1845. FARMER, Stephen
"Medieval, Part III" (Excerpts). [Avec] (9) 95, p. 146-161.
1846. FARNSWORTH, Robert
"Anniversary." [BelPoJ] (45:3) Spr 95, p. 40-41.
"Wave." [SouthernR] (31:4) O/Aut 95, p. 830-831.
1847. FARRAR, Kimberly K.
"Back Alley, Astoria." [Ledge] (18) Sum 95, p. 26.
"Inside." [Ledge] (18) Sum 95, p. 24-25.
"Inside." [LullwaterR] (5:1) 93-94, p. 62-63.
1848. FARRELL, Jody
"Poems of a Mother." [Art&Und] (4:5, #18) N 95, p. 16.
1849. FARRELL, Mia
"Eating Cuban Food." [AxeF] (3) 90, p. 38.
1850. FARWELL, Lauralyn
"Blue Shirt." [PennR] (6:2) 95, p. 15.
1851. FASEL, Ida
"Answers, Anyone?" [ChrC] (112:9) 15 Mr 95, p. 294.
"As If." [ChrC] (112:29) 18 O 95, p. 950.
"The Civil War." [ChrC] (112:10) 22-29 Mr 95, p. 320.
1852. FATTORI, Joanne
"Primigenius." [SmPd] (32:2, #94) Spr 95, p. 26.
1853. FAUCHEREAU, Serge
"L'Enfer N'Est Pas" (tr. by Ron Padgett). [Agni] (42) 95, p. 35.

"Les Gestes Qu'On Peut Faire" (tr. by Ron Padgett). [Agni] (42) 95, p. 36.
1854. FAUDREE, Paja
"Approaching Winter Solstice." [SouthernPR] (35:1) Sum 95, p. 47-48.
1855. FEALEY, Patrick
"60 Minutes w/ the Savages." [WormR] (35:1, #137) 95, p. 6.
"Jaywalking the Airwaves." [WormR] (35:1, #137) 95, p. 5.
"Late Favors Smell." [WormR] (35:1, #137) 95, p. 7.
"A Nice Vietnam War Story." [WormR] (35:1, #137) 95, p. 8.
"Sonofabook!" [WormR] (35:1, #137) 95, p. 7-8.
1856. FEATHERDANCING, Kyos
"In Remembrance." [SinW] (56) Sum-Fall 95, p. 60-61.
1857. FEATHERSTON, Dan
"Place of No Smoke Hole" (for Gerrit Lansing). [Talisman] (15) Wint 95-96, p. 39-
40.
"Sugar Skulls." [Talisman] (15) Wint 95-96, p. 81-82.
1858. FEAVER, Vicki
"Horned Poppy." [NewYorker] (71:14) 29 My 95, p. 70.
1859. FEDERMAN, Raymond
"A Dialogue Concerning the Nose" (Freely adapted from *Cyrano de Bergerac*).
[Iowa] (25:3) Fall 95, p. 1.
"The Right of Life." [Sulfur] (15:1, #36) Spr 95, p. 179-180.
"Survival." [Sulfur] (15:1, #36) Spr 95, p. 178-179.
1860. FEDO, David
"The Carousel on the Croisette." [ManyMM] (2:1) 95, p. 28-29.
"The Marriage Museum" (to Susan). [Pearl] (22) Fall-Wint 95, p. 14.
1861. FEIGENBAUM, Erika
"Untrue." [SinW] (55) Spr-Sum 95, p. 59.
1862. FEIN, Richard J.
"Conception." [Light] (14) Sum 95, p. 18.
1863. FEINSTEIN, Robert N.
"Do-Do to Order." [Light] (15/16) Aut-Wint 95-96, p. 18.
"The Open Mind." [Light] (15/16) Aut-Wint 95-96, p. 29.
1864. FEINSTEIN, Sascha
"Christmas Eve." [NewEngR] (17:3) Sum 95, p. 83-84.
"Coltrane, Coltrane." [NewEngR] (17:3) Sum 95, p. 85-87.
"December Blues." [NewEngR] (17:3) Sum 95, p. 87-88.
1865. FEIRSTEIN, Frederick
"Bert Wooley." [QRL] (34) 95, book 2, p. 29-30.
"Celebrating" (to Dick Allen). [QRL] (34) 95, book 2, p. 16-20.
"The Coup." [QRL] (34) 95, book 2, p. 41-43.
"Creature of History." [QRL] (34) 95, book 2, p. 48.
"Creature of History: A Sequence." [QRL] (34) 95, book 2, p. 33-51.
"Daydreaming." [QRL] (34) 95, book 2, p. 35.
"Earth Angel." [QRL] (34) 95, book 2, p. 26-27.
"Ending the Twentieth Century" (For Linda and David — ATNC). [QRL] (34) 95,
book 2, p. 1-54.
"Fin de Siècle." [QRL] (34) 95, book 2, p. 31-32.
"Gravedona." [QRL] (34) 95, book 2, p. 36-37.
"Hawaii — Drifting to the Volcano." [QRL] (34) 95, book 2, p. 50-51.
"Journal of the Plague Years." [QRL] (34) 95, book 2, p. 28.
"The Lake." [QRL] (34) 95, book 2, p. 28.
"A Letter to Friends." [QRL] (34) 95, book 2, p. 30-31.
"The Magic Kingdom." [QRL] (34) 95, book 2, p. 9.
"Manhattan Elegy." [QRL] (34) 95, book 2, p. 7.
"Manhattan Elegy & Other Goodbyes: A Sequence." [QRL] (34) 95, book 2, p. 6-
32.
"Middle Age." [QRL] (34) 95, book 2, p. 34-35.
"New Year's Eve." [QRL] (34) 95, book 2, p. 23.
"New York Spontaneous." [QRL] (34) 95, book 2, p. 22-23.
"Parade." [QRL] (34) 95, book 2, p. 11.
"Peasant Carts" (for Roger Hecht). [QRL] (34) 95, book 2, p. 46.
"The Poet to His Younger Self." [QRL] (34) 95, book 2, p. 27.
"Ramponio." [QRL] (34) 95, book 2, p. 40-41.
"The Seduction at Villa Carlotta." [QRL] (34) 95, book 2, p. 38.
"Song of the Suburbs." [QRL] (34) 95, book 2, p. 25.
"Spectacle." [QRL] (34) 95, book 2, p. 10.

"Spring." [QRL] (34) 95, book 2, p. 8.
"Stresa — The Borromeo Islands." [QRL] (34) 95, book 2, p. 38-39.
"The Sundial." [QRL] (34) 95, book 2, p. 24.
"Survivor." [QRL] (34) 95, book 2, p. 49.
"Tell Me a Story." [QRL] (34) 95, book 2, p. 14-15.
"Trümmelbach." [QRL] (34) 95, book 2, p. 47.
"Underground Song." [QRL] (34) 95, book 2, p. 20-21.
"Venice Spontaneous." [QRL] (34) 95, book 2, p. 44-45.
"War Zone." [QRL] (34) 95, book 2, p. 12-13.
1866. FEKETY, Robert
"Genesis II: A Parable for the 21st Century About Gene Transfer Therapy."
[MichQR] (34:3) Sum 95, p. 372-376.
1867. FELDMAN, Alan
"A Letter." [HarvardR] (9) Fall 95, p. 89.
1868. FELDMAN, Irving
"The Lowdown." [SouthwR] (80:4) Aut 95, p. 492.
"Malke Toyb" (Deaf Malke). [Nat] (258:8) 28 F 94, p. 282.
1869. FELDMAN, Laura
"Atonia." [Avec] (10) 95, p. 75-80.
"Forty Miners, The" (Excerpt). [Avec] (9) 95, p. 33-43.
"Revelatory: Images of Their Homelife." [Avec] (9) 95, p. 44-49.
1870. FELICIANO, Margarita
"Frente a Gatineau River" (to Marcela, tr. of Claudio Durán). [Arc] (35) Aut 95, p. 21.
"Letter from Pichidangui to the Duran Vidal" (tr. of Claudio Durán). [Arc] (35) Aut 95, p. 20.
1871. FELL, Mary
"Confessional." [SycamoreR] (7:2) Sum 95, p. 13.
"Prayer in Bad Weather." [SycamoreR] (7:2) Sum 95, p. 10.
"Slugs." [SycamoreR] (7:2) Sum 95, p. 11-12.
1872. FELTON, Donna
"Little Girl" (WritersCorps Program, Washington, DC). [WashR] (21:2) Ag-S 95, p. 7.
FEMINA, Gerry La
See LaFEMINA, Gerry
1873. FENDT, Gene
"Dark." [SpoonR] (20:2) Sum-Fall 95, p. 148.
"The Longest Jump Shot Ever." [Plain] (15:3) Spr 95, p. 34.
1874. FENG, Anita N.
"Adolescents Assigned to Stalk Fire in Manchuria." [PraS] (69:1) Spr 95, p. 20.
"The Day Tiananmen Square Filled with Shoes." [PraS] (69:1) Spr 95, p. 19.
"Explaining Fountains to a Child." [Prima] (18/19) 95, p. 39-40.
"Growing Up on the Sly." [PraS] (69:1) Spr 95, p. 18.
"Humid Isn't It." [Prima] (18/19) 95, p. 37-38.
"Premonition" (Honorable Mention, 1995 Editors' Prize). [SpoonR] (20:2) Sum-Fall 95, p. 45.
"The Son of Heaven." [PraS] (69:1) Spr 95, p. 17.
1875. FENLON, Tara M.
"Elegy" (Caravaggio, 1607, and his painting *Death of the Virgin*). [AntR] (53:1) Wint 95, p. 62.
1876. FENNELLY, Beth Ann
"Asked for a Happy Memory of Her Father, a Daughter Remembers Wrigley Field." [PoetryNW] (36:3) Aut 95, p. 27.
"Deaths" (after Pedro Salinas). [PoetryNW] (36:3) Aut 95, p. 26-27.
"Mousetrap." [ProseP] (4) 95, p. 28.
"Poem Not to Be Read at Your Wedding." [Farm] (12:1) Spr-Sum 95, p. 84.
1877. FERGUS, Howard A.
"For Mandela." [CaribbeanW] (9) 95, p. 30.
"Virgin Gorda (1993)." [CaribbeanW] (9) 95, p. 31-32.
1878. FERNANDEZ, Guillermo
"The Avaricious Flower" (tr. by Bond Snodgrass). [PlumR] (9) [95 or 96], p. 75.
"Here Again" (tr. by Bond Snodgrass). [PlumR] (9) [95 or 96], p. 76-77.
1879. FERRANTE, Lou
"The Metaphysical Consideration of Smoking." [ChironR] (43) Sum 95, p. 30.
1880. FERRARELLI, Rina
"October." [LaurelR] (29:1) Wint 95, p. 46-47.

1881. FERRÉ, Rosario
    "Requiem" (in Spanish and English, tr. by the author). [MassR] (36:4) Wint 95-96,
        p. 612-613.
    "The Shadow of Guilt" (tr. by the author). [MassR] (36:4) Wint 95-96, p. 611.
    "La Sombra de la Culpa." [MassR] (36:4) Wint 95-96, p. 610.
1882. FERRO, Jéanpaul
    "Song Sheets." [HawaiiR] (19:2) Fall 95, p. 195.
1883. FERRY, David
    "I.v. To Pyrrha" (tr. of Horace). [Raritan] (14:3) Wint 95, p. 20.
    "I.10. To Mercury" (tr. of Horace). [Pequod] (39) 95, p. 146.
    "I.xv. The Prophecy of Nereus" (tr. of Horace). [Raritan] (14:3) Wint 95, p. 20-22.
    "1.34. Of the God's Power" (tr. of Horace). [TriQ] (93) Spr-Sum 95, p. 153.
    "II.4. To Xanthias" (tr. of Horace). [Pequod] (39) 95, p. 147.
    "II.vii. To an Old Comrade in the Army of Brutus" (tr. of Horace). [Raritan] (14:3)
        Wint 95, p. 22.
    "II.11. To Quinctius Hirpinus" (tr. of Horace). [Thrpny] (62) Sum 95, p. 13.
    "III.i. Of Ostentation" (tr. of Horace). [Raritan] (14:3) Wint 95, p. 23-24.
    "III.5. The Example of Regulus" (tr. of Horace). [SouthernHR] (29:2) Spr 95, p.
        146-147.
    "III.6. To the Romans" (tr. of Horace). [Pequod] (39) 95, p. 148-150.
    "III.18. To Faunus" (tr. of Horace). [Pequod] (39) 95, p. 151.
    "III.22. To Diana" (tr. of Horace). [Pequod] (39) 95, p. 152.
    "IV.x. To Ligurinus" (tr. of Horace). [Raritan] (14:3) Wint 95, p. 24-25.
    "IV.xiii. To Lycia" (tr. of Horace). [Raritan] (14:3) Wint 95, p. 25-26.
    "111.26. To Venus" (tr. of Horace). [TriQ] (93) Spr-Sum 95, p. 151.
    "She Speaks Across the Years" (tr. and adaptation of Friedrich Hölderlin). [TriQ]
        (95) Wint 95-96, p. 170-171.
    "To Dellius" (tr. of Horace II.3). [Arion] (3:2/3) Fall 95-Wint 96, p. 169-170.
    "To Lydia" (tr. of Horace, I.8). [Arion] (42) 95, p. 77-78.
    "To Maecenas" (tr. of Horace I.1). [Arion] (3:2/3) Fall 95-Wint 96, p. 167-168.
    "To Melpomene" (tr. of Horace IV.3). [Arion] (3:2/3) Fall 95-Wint 96, p. 171-172.
    "To Phyllis" (tr. of Horace IV.11). [Arion] (3:2/3) Fall 95-Wint 96, p. 173-174.
    "To Praise Aelius Lamia" (tr. of Horace, I.26). [Agni] (42) 95, p. 82.
    "To Pyrrhus" (tr. of Horace, III.20). [Agni] (42) 95, p. 79.
    "To Virgil" (tr. of Horace, I.24). [Agni] (42) 95, p. 80-81.
    "What's Playing Tonight." [Raritan] (15:1) Sum 95, p. 34.
1884. FESSLER, Michael
    "The Spirit of the Letter." [WormR] (35:4, #140) 95, p. 147.
    "Unfashionable Admission." [WormR] (35:4, #140) 95, p. 147-149.
1885. FETTERS, Clifford Paul
    "After Seeing the Kress Collection." [WritersF] (21) 95, p. 30.
    "Dawn Screen." [SantaBR] (3:3) Fall-Wint 95, p. 62.
    "Ripped Quilt." [SantaBR] (3:3) Fall-Wint 95, p. 62.
    "Watoto." [SantaBR] (3:3) Fall-Wint 95, p. 61.
    "Well Then, Walk With Me." [Plain] (15:2) Wint 95, p. 31.
1886. FIACC, Padraic
    "Initial Deception." [Poetry] (167:1/2) O-N 95, p. 72-73.
FICK, Marlon Ohnesorge
    See OHNESORGE-FICK, Marlon
1887. FICKERT, Kurt
    "The Anatomy of Pain." [Wind] (75) Spr 95, p. 9.
1888. FIELD, Edward
    "A Man and His Penis, or the Lover's Complaint." [ChironR] (44/45) Aut-Wint 95,
        p. 42-43.
    "St. Petersburg, 1918" (In memory of the USSR). [BelPoJ] (45:4) Chapbook 22,
        Sum 95, p. 20.
1889. FIELD, Simon
    "After Words." [Bogg] (67) 95, p. 40.
1890. FIELD, Susan
    "Believer." [US1] (30/31) 95, p. 19.
1891. FIELD, Thalia
    "The Compass Room, or Tripping (up) on True North." [Avec] (10) 95, p. 121-137.
    "Ululu (A Page & Peephole Opera)" (Selections). [Conjunc] (24) 95, p. 96-115.
1892. FIELDEN, Jay
    "Casting Lots." [NewYorker] (70:49) 13 F 95, p. 57.

FILES

1893. FILES, James L.
  "Birthday Morning with Coffee." [DefinedP] (1:2) Spr-Sum 93, p. 7.
FILIPPO, Vira J. de
  See De FILIPPO, Vira J.
1894. FILKINS, Peter
  "Autumn Maneuver" (tr. of Ingeborg Bachmann). [CharR] (21:1) Spr 95, p. 93.
  "Bohemia Lies by the Sea" (tr. of Ingeborg Bachmann). [CharR] (21:1) Spr 95, p. 95.
  "Borrowed Time" (tr. of Ingeborg Bachmann). [MassR] (36:3) Aut 95, p. 342.
  "Driving the Cattle Home" (after Bruegel). [CharR] (21:1) Spr 95, p. 91.
  "The New Year." [CharR] (21:1) Spr 95, p. 92.
  "Salt and Bread" (tr. of Ingeborg Bachmann). [CharR] (21:1) Spr 95, p. 94.
1895. FINALE, Frank
  "Before Bed." [Elf] (5:1) Spr 95, p. 29.
  "Check Out." [Footwork] (24/25) 95, p. 133.
  "Elementary." [Footwork] (24/25) 95, p. 133.
  "Reaching Bottom." [Footwork] (24/25) 95, p. 133.
  "Station Hill." [Elf] (5:1) Spr 95, p. 28.
1896. FINCH, Annie
  "Being a Constellation." [Agni] (41) 95, p. 133.
  "Hostage Wildflowers." [ManyMM] (2:1) 95, p. 48.
  "In the Great Reading Room." [ParisR] (37:137) Wint 95, p. 252.
  "Running in Church" (for Marie). [Agni] (41) 95, p. 134.
  "Whirling." [ManyMM] (2:1) 95, p. 49.
1897. FINCKE, Gary
  "The Almanac for Desire." [DefinedP] (3) 95, p. 14.
  "The Autonomic Curse." [NortheastCor] (3) 95, p. 8-9.
  "The Cabinet of Wonders." [MidAR] (15:1/2) 95, p. 33-34.
  "The Close Anniversary." [DefinedP] (3) 95, p. 15.
  "The Edison Bottle." [OhioR] (53) 95, p. 101.
  "The Era of the Vari-Vue." [OxfordM] (9:2) Fall-Wint 93, p. 77-78.
  "The Face of Christ." [ProseP] (4) 95, p. 29.
  "The First Report in Person." [PraS] (69:3) Fall 95, p. 107.
  "The Fury Which Follows Small Disappointments." [PraS] (69:3) Fall 95, p. 108-109.
  "The History of Passion Will Tumble This Week." [ProseP] (4) 95, p. 30.
  "Johnny Weismuller Learns the Tarzan Yell." [ParisR] (37:136) Fall 95, p. 154.
  "The Judgment Hair." [OxfordM] (10:1) Wint 94-Spr 95, p. 24-25.
  "Light Enough to Be Lifted." [MidAR] (15:1/2) 95, p. 31-32.
  "The Rain After Sunrise." [WillowS] (35) Ja 95, p. 25.
  "Say It." [PoetryNW] (36:1) Spr 95, p. 29.
  "The Startling Language of Shriveling Leaves." [PraS] (69:3) Fall 95, p. 106-107.
  "Sugar and Water." [NewDeltaR] (13:1) Fall 95-Wint 96, p. 51.
  "The Technology of Paradise." [GettyR] (8:3) Sum 95, p. 488-489.
  "Twenty-Five Inches per Week." [WestB] (37) 95, p. 10-11.
  "Writing Basics." [CapeR] (30:2) Fall 95, p. 9.
1898. FINDLAY, Seaton
  "Vermont." [Arc] (34) Spr 95, p. 72.
FINK, Alicia Cabiedes
  See CABIEDES-FINK, Alicia
1899. FINK, Robert A. (Bob)
  "Baseball, First Love." [Spitball] (48) 95, p. 30.
  "Crossing the Brazos." [TexasR] (15:3/4) Fall-Wint 94, p. 85.
  "Mary and John Clack Reach the Taylor Community Plateau." [TexasR] (15:3/4) Fall-Wint 94, p. 86.
  "What the .352 Batting Champ Does Not Tell Reporters." [Spitball] (48) 95, p. 31.
1900. FINKEL, Donald
  "On the Shingle." [SouthwR] (80:4) Aut 95, p. 438-442.
1901. FINKELSTEIN, Caroline
  "Garden in the Field." [Poetry] (166:2) My 95, p. 94.
1902. FINKELSTEIN, Miriam
  "Kidnapped." [HangL] (67) 95, p. 35.
  "Moving." [HangL] (67) 95, p. 36.
1903. FINKELSTEIN, Norman
  "Passing Over" (Excerpt). [Pequod] (39) 95, p. 41.
  "Track." [Pequod] (39) 95, p. 35-40.

155

FITTERMAN

1904. FINLEY, Michael
"The Sugar Trap." [MidwQ] (36:4) Sum 95, p. 368.
1905. FINNEGAN, Brenda Brown
"The Asmat Comes to Town." [TexasR] (16:1/4) 95, p. 115-117.
"Spring Break." [TexasR] (16:1/4) 95, p. 118.
1906. FINNEGAN, James
"Driving the Dead Man's Car." [Witness] (9:1) 95, p. 113.
"Figure-Ground." [ProseP] (4) 95, p. 31.
"From Sparta." [Witness] (9:1) 95, p. 112.
"Muldoon Monument Co." [VirQR] (71:4) Aut 95, p. 704-705.
"Running Lights." [Ploughs] (21:4) Wint 95-96, p. 57.
"Timorous Bells." [VirQR] (71:4) Aut 95, p. 705.
"Velvet." [VirQR] (71:4) Aut 95, p. 705-706.
1907. FINNELL, Dennis
"Cornucopia." [CharR] (21:1) Spr 95, p. 65.
"Misterioso." [CharR] (21:1) Spr 95, p. 68.
"Tongue. The End of the World Is Roadless. *Exile.*" [CharR] (21:1) Spr 95, p. 65-
67.
1908. FIRER, Susan
"The Beautiful Pain of Too Much." [SouthernPR] (35:2) Wint 95, p. 69-70.
"Married Women Wore Hats with Veils That Rolled. Unmarried Women Had
Feathered Hats." [CreamCR] (19:1) Spr 95, p. 136-137.
"My Coat of Flowers." [Iowa] (25:1) Wint 95, p. 59-60.
1909. FISCHER, Henry G.
"Adam's Rib." [Light] (15/16) Aut-Wint 95-96, p. 19.
"Feet." [Light] (13) Spr 95, p. 8.
"Gibbons." [Light] (15/16) Aut-Wint 95-96, p. 13.
"Le Malheur du Mallarméen." [Light] (15/16) Aut-Wint 95-96, p. 26.
"Mallarmé Inspires Some Alarm." [Light] (15/16) Aut-Wint 95-96, p. 26.
1910. FISCHER, Neil
"The Gift." [Agni] (42) 95, p. 45-46.
"Wounded." [Agni] (42) 95, p. 43-44.
1911. FISCHEROVA, Sylvia
"Untitled: Not that we didn't expect it" (tr. by Stuart Friebert. w. the author).
[LullwaterR] (5:2) Fall-Wint 94, p. 34-35.
"The Worst Is Being Conscious" (tr. by Stuart Friebert. w. the author). [LullwaterR]
(5:2) Fall-Wint 94, p. 33.
1912. FISHER, Allen
"Mummers' Strut." [WestCL] (29:2, #17) Fall 95, p. 28-37.
1913. FISHER, Eileen
"Standing at the Pond" (to ken when he is wanting to understand). [JINJPo] (17:1)
Spr 95, p. 41.
1914. FISHER, M. F. K.
"Why Again." [ParisR] (37:134) Spr 95, p. 296.
1915. FISHMAN, Charles
"The Boys Have Guns." [GeoR] (49:3) Fall 95, p. 708.
"Our Generation." [GeoR] (49:3) Fall 95, p. 709.
"A True History of Food" (for Judy Guheen). [LouisL] (12:1) Spr 95, p. 63-64.
1916. FISHMAN, Lisa
"The Equation of Motion." [PraS] (69:2) Sum 95, p. 74-75.
"Fidelity." [PraS] (69:2) Sum 95, p. 72-73.
1917. FISK, Molly
"Ford F150." [HarvardR] (9) Fall 95, p. 93.
"The Good-Bye." [Manoa] (7:2) Wint 95, p. 21-22.
"In the Morning." [PoetryE] (39) Fall 94, p. 34-35.
"Longing." [Manoa] (7:2) Wint 95, p. 22-23.
"Neighbor." [PoetryE] (39) Fall 94, p. 36.
"A Question About the World." [PoetryE] (39) Fall 94, p. 31-32.
"Walking Down Franklin Street." [PoetryE] (39) Fall 94, p. 33.
1918. FISTER, Mary
"Dreaming Her Sea-worthy" (in memory of Aunt Eleanor). [SouthernHR] (29:4)
Fall 95, p. 322-324.
"Freshening." [LaurelR] (29:1) Wint 95, p. 106-107.
1919. FITTERMAN, Robert
"Metropolis" (Selection: 5). [Phoebe] (24:1) 95, p. 79-84.

1920. FITZGERALD, Matt
"Goodness." [Light] (14) Sum 95, p. 19.
1921. FITZPATRICK, Kevin
"Breaking Point." [NorthStoneR] (12) 95, p. 75.
"Neighbors" (at the Big Top Liquor Store). [NorthStoneR] (12) 95, p. 76.
"Remembrances." [NorthStoneR] (12) 95, p. 74.
"Rush Hour." [NorthStoneR] (12) 95, p. 73.
1922. FITZPATRICK, Mark
"Wannabe, Age 14." [BlackBR] (20) Spr-Sum 95, p. 18-19.
1923. FIX, Charlene
"Sunday Ducks." [PaintedB] (55/56) 95, p. 71.
1924. FLAGG, Edward
"Piss Chip." [SlipS] (15) 95, p. 7.
1925. FLAHERTY, Kate
"On the Empty Shores of a Manmade Lake" (Ogallala, Nebraska). [Blueline] (16)
    95, p. 67.
FLAMME, Gladys la
    See LaFLAMME, Gladys
1926. FLANAGAN, Donnella
"The Wild Poem" (WritersCorps Program, Washington, DC). [WashR] (21:2) Ag-S
    95, p. 11.
1927. FLANAGAN, T. S.
"Blue Boots." [PoetryE] (41) Aut 95, p. 57.
1928. FLANDERS, Jane
"The Gift Clock." [SycamoreR] (7:1) Wint 95, p. 30.
"Ma Goose: The Interrogation." [ParisR] (37:134) Spr 95, p. 137.
"Stop Look Listen." [SycamoreR] (7:1) Wint 95, p. 31.
1929. FLANNERY, Matthew
"To the Tune: 'Yü Chia Ao'" (tr. of Ou-yang Hsiu, 1007-1072). [Chelsea] (58) 95, p.
    98.
1930. FLAVIN, Jack
"After the Ice Storm" (For Varsen). [CimR] (112) Jl 95, p. 96.
1931. FLECK, Ann
"Sympatica." [AntR] (53:1) Wint 95, p. 63.
1932. FLEETWOOD, Leah
"One of the Unemployed." [Stand] (36:2) Spr 95, p. 2-3.
1933. FLEISCHMAN, E.
"Michelle" (3 poems, with discussion questions). [Pearl] (22) Fall-Wint 95, p. 95-
    96.
1934. FLEMING, Bruce
"Cold Snap, Edmonds." [BellArk] (11:2) Mr-Ap 95, p. 13.
1935. FLEMING, Carrol B.
"Poet Not Taken." [CaribbeanW] (9) 95, p. 58-59.
1936. FLEMING, Gerald
"Subsurface Tension." [LowellR] (2) c1996, p. 72-73.
1937. FLEMING, Robert
"Nutty." [AfAmRev] (29:3) Fall 95, p. 475.
"Thirst." [AfAmRev] (29:3) Fall 95, p. 476.
"Totem." [AfAmRev] (29:3) Fall 95, p. 476-477.
1938. FLENNIKEN, Kathleen
"In London at Seventeen." [BellArk] (11:2) Mr-Ap 95, p. 27.
"In the Ten Seconds Before Sleep." [Vis] (49) 95, p. 5.
"Lady's Slipper" (for Mother). [BellArk] (11:2) Mr-Ap 95, p. 26.
"The Perfect Dress." [BellArk] (11:4) Jl-Ag 95, p. 5.
"Rika, in the Breeze." [BellArk] (11:2) Mr-Ap 95, p. 26.
"Science to a Wolf." [BellArk] (11:2) Mr-Ap 95, p. 26.
"Way Stations." [PoetL] (90:2) Sum 95, p. 56.
1939. FLICK, Sherrie
"Kicking the Dog." [SilverFR] (25) Sum 95, p. 40.
"Las Vegas Women." [SilverFR] (25) Sum 95, p. 39.
1940. FLINTOFF, Eddie
"Walking with Margaret." [Bogg] (67) 95, p. 47.
1941. FLOOD, Colleen
"Cartwheels." [PoetryC] (15:3) Ag 95, p. 29.
FLORE, Shirley Le
    See LeFLORE, Shirley

1942. FLOREA, Ted
"Cleaning Up." [Plain] (15:2) Wint 95, p. 10.
"On Two Gallon Men." [Plain] (16:1) Fall 95, p. 23.
1943. FLORY, Suzy
"Limosine Sex (My Detroit)" [sic]. [AxeF] (3) 90, p. 12-13.
"Tits & Innocence." [AxeF] (3) 90, p. 10-11.
1944. FLYNN, Jenny
"Echolalia." [CutB] (44) Sum 95, p. 20-21.
1945. FLYNN, Nicholas
"Almost Rodin." [PassN] (16:2) Wint 95, p. 6-7.
"Flood." [PassN] (16:2) Wint 95, p. 3-4.
"Worthless." [PassN] (16:2) Wint 95, p. 5.
1946. FODASKI, Liz
"The Anatomy of Associative Thought" (Excerpts). [Chain] (2) Spr 95, p. 95-98.
FOE, Mark de
See DeFOE, Mark
1947. FOERSTER, Richard
"Barberry." [PoetL] (90:3) Fall 95, p. 21.
"Butterfly Farm." [SouthernR] (31:4) O/Aut 95, p. 832.
"Icebound" (In memoriam J M). [Poetry] (167:3) D 95, p. 139.
"Little Homages." [PoetL] (90:3) Fall 95, p. 23-24.
"Nettle." [PoetL] (90:3) Fall 95, p. 22.
"Northern Lights." [PoetL] (90:3) Fall 95, p. 20.
"Valentines." [Poetry] (165:5) F 95, p. 249.
1948. FOGARTY, Brian
"Fisher." [AnthNEW] (7) 95, p. 32.
1949. FOGDALL, Kristin
"Intersection." [Agni] (41) 95, p. 109.
"The Salmon House." [Agni] (41) 95, p. 110-111.
1950. FOGEL, Alice B.
"Barbed Wire." [Witness] (9:2) 95, p. 23.
"Permission." [GreensboroR] (58) Sum 95, p. 111.
"Which Way the Winds Blow." [BelPoJ] (45:3) Spr 95, p. 42.
1951. FOGELIN, Florence
"The Art Lesson" (Honorable Mention, 1994 Narrative Poetry Context). [PoetL]
(90:2) Sum 95, p. 7-10.
"Famous Poet Returns to Read in Her Home Town." [CumbPR] (15:1) Fall 95, p.
21.
1952. FOGGO, Cheryl
"Touch." [CanLit] (145) Sum 95, p. 121.
1953. FOGLE, Andy
"Gloria." [Parting] (8:1) Sum 95, p. 40.
"Need." [Parting] (8:2) Wint 95-96, p. 24.
1954. FOGO, Peter
"Dying Man Asserts Himself." [BlackBR] (20) Spr-Sum 95, p. 31.
"In Lieu of Silence." [BlackBR] (20) Spr-Sum 95, p. 30.
1955. FOLEY, Jack
"Sample." [HeavenB] (12) 95, p. 5.
1956. FOLKART, Barbara
"Deux Déjeuners sur l'Herbe." [MalR] (112) Fall 95, p. 82-83.
"Dreaming Drowning." [Arc] (34) Spr 95, p. 38-39.
"Flight into Egypt" (Miniature from Les Très Belles Heures de Bruxelles, Brussels,
Bibliothèque Royale, ms. 11060-61). [MalR] (112) Fall 95, p. 80.
"Love Song from a Medieval Songbook (1511)" (Miniature from manuscript IV.90,
Bibliothèque Royale, Brussels). [MalR] (112) Fall 95, p. 81.
"The Martyrdom of Saint Sebastian" (after Odilon Redon). [PoetryC] (15:2) Je 95,
p. 26.
"Tear Water Pooling." [Arc] (34) Spr 95, p. 36-37.
1957. FOLLETT, C. B.
"Arms." [BellR] (18:1, #37) Spr 95, p. 53.
"Bloomfield Cemetery" (est. 1860). [Blueline] (16) 95, p. 58-59.
"Bush League." [Spitball] (48) 95, p. 76.
"Hovering." [DogRR] (14:1, #27) Sum 95, p. 20.
"How Straight Is Straight, How Long the Inch (Consider)." [NewL] (62:1) 96
(c1995), p. 80-81.
"Lake Winnipesaukee." [Blueline] (16) 95, p. 100.

1958. FOLTZ-GRAY, Dorothy
"The Best of Mothers." [CumbPR] (15:1) Fall 95, p. 22.
FOND, Carolyn Street la
See LaFOND, Carolyn Street
1959. FONTENOT, Ken
"Late November." [NewOR] (21:2) Sum 95, p. 21.
1960. FOO, Josie
"Childhood." [NorthStoneR] (12) 95, p. 108.
"Empty House." [NorthStoneR] (12) 95, p. 109.
"My City." [Kalliope] (17:1) 95, p. 15.
"A Poem: I've brought out a sheet of paper, smooth as the white of my eye."
[AmerV] (37) 95, p. 4.
"Workday." [NorthStoneR] (12) 95, p. 109.
1961. FORBES, Calvin
"Two Children's Songs." [ChiR] (41:2/3) 95, p. 12.
1962. FORBES, Latham
"Sestina for Donald." [AntigR] (102/103) Sum-Aug 95, p. 130-131.
1963. FORD, Adrian Robert
"Late Effect Snow" (Finalist, 1995 Greg Grummer Award in Poetry). [Phoebe]
(24:2) 95, p. 147.
"Phone First" (Finalist, 1995 Greg Grummer Award in Poetry). [Phoebe] (24:2) 95,
p. 146.
1964. FORD, Cathy
"The Lacquer Box, the Raku Vase." [PoetryC] (15:2) Je 95, p. 27.
"Queen of the Night, or Guaranteed to Bloom." [PoetryC] (15:2) Je 95, p. 27.
1965. FORD, Michael C.
"French Valentine to the Girl on Avenue Les Gobelins." [ChironR] (43) Sum 95, p.
19.
"How to Score Women at Discos." [ChironR] (43) Sum 95, p. 10.
"Skyscraper Pumps on the Staircase." [ChironR] (43) Sum 95, p. 10.
"Washington Park." [Pearl] (22) Fall-Wint 95, p. 136.
1966. FORD, William
"Adam & Eve in the Attic." [Iowa] (25:1) Wint 95, p. 155.
1967. FORD, William H.
"Fireflies." [Hellas] (6:1) Spr-Sum 95, p. 65.
FORGE, P. V. Le
See LeFORGE, P. V.
1968. FORHAN, Chris
"A Father's Advice to His Son." [WestB] (36) 95, p. 84-85.
"The Seattle Mariners on the Radio Near Sequim, Washington." [PraS] (69:1) Spr
95, p. 165-166.
1969. FORRESTER, Mark
"Later Reflections." [Plain] (16:1) Fall 95, p. 8.
1970. FORSTER, Stephen
"Sentence." [Noctiluca] (2:1, #4) Spr 95, p. 18.
1971. FORT, Charles
"Black Cat." [AmerPoR] (24:4) Jl-Ag 95, p. 28.
"Honey Child." [AmerPoR] (24:4) Jl-Ag 95, p. 28.
"How Had They Lived." [AmerPoR] (24:4) Jl-Ag 95, p. 27.
"Poe's Daughter." [AmerPoR] (24:4) Jl-Ag 95, p. 27.
"Understudy" (For Wendy). [AmerPoR] (24:4) Jl-Ag 95, p. 28.
"Work for Life in the City" (for Ben Cocoa). [AmerPoR] (24:4) Jl-Ag 95, p. 27.
1972. FORTÉ-ESCAMILLA, Kleya
"Coyotes." [SinW] (55) Spr-Sum 95, p. 49.
1973. FORTI, Eve
"Can't Wait for Perigee." [LowellR] [1] Sum 94, p. 75-76.
1974. FOSS, Phillip
"Ideate: A Grammar of the Catoptric Flesh." [Sulfur] (15:2, #37) Fall 95, p. 136-
139.
"Ideate: The Cartography of Woo." [NewAW] (13) Fall-Wint 95, p. 61-66.
1975. FOSTER, Jeanne
"Fencing." [NortheastCor] (3) 95, p. 108.
1976. FOSTER, Leslie
"For Miss Manners in a Blind Home." [ChrC] (112:13) 19 Ap 95, p. 424.
"Oracle for Today." [Northeast] (5:13) Wint 95-96, p. 3.

1977. FOSTER, Linda Nemec
    "Dancing with My Sister" (for Deborah). [Witness] (9:1) 95, p. 172.
    "The Earth from Space." [ArtfulD] (28/29) 95, p. 160.
    "Jupiter and His Moons." [ArtfulD] (28/29) 95, p. 162.
    "Mars." [ArtfulD] (28/29) 95, p. 161.
    "Mercury." [ArtfulD] (28/29) 95, p. 158.
    "Neptune." [ArtfulD] (28/29) 95, p. 165.
    "Planet X." [ArtfulD] (28/29) 95, p. 167.
    "Pluto." [ArtfulD] (28/29) 95, p. 166.
    "Ritual." [MidAR] (15:1/2) 95, p. 210-211.
    "Saturn and His Rings." [ArtfulD] (28/29) 95, p. 163.
    "Uranus." [ArtfulD] (28/29) 95, p. 164.
    "Venus." [ArtfulD] (28/29) 95, p. 159.
1978. FOSTER, Michael
    "A Vision of God." [InterPR] (21:1) Spr 95, p. 85.
1979. FOSTER, Sesshu
    "Floating World." [IllinoisR] (3:1/2) Fall 95-Spr 96, p. 62.
    "Like a wind out on the alkali flats." [DefinedP] (2:1) Fall-Wint 93, p. 22.
1980. FOSTER, Shirley
    "Looking Back." [PoetryE] (39) Fall 94, p. 37.
    "On Sunday Morning." [PoetryE] (39) Fall 94, p. 38.
1981. FOSTER, Stephen
    "Peter Waits Outside." [Bogg] (67) 95, p. 39.
1982. FOTIADE, Ramona
    "Cronophagy" (tr. by the author). [Noctiluca] (2:1, #4) Spr 95, p. 12.
1983. FOUST, Graham
    "Beloit." [SpinningJ] (1) Fall 95-Wint 96, p. 51.
1984. FOWLER, Anne C.
    "The Honey Bees." [LitR] (38:2) Wint 95, p. 211-212.
1985. FOWLER, Sherman L.
    "Universal Glue." [Drumvoices] (5:1/2) Fall-Wint 95-96, p. 13.
    "Writers Are Rights-Warriors." [Drumvoices] (5:1/2) Fall-Wint 95-96, p. 14.
1986. FOX, Faulkner
    "Cup of Caution." [PaintedB] (55/56) 95, p. 54.
    "Learning from the Gun." [Border] (7) Fall-Wint 96, p. 10.
    "Swing Low." [Border] (7) Fall-Wint 96, p. 11.
1987. FOX, Hugh
    "Dream Poem Written on World Map." [GreenHLL] (6) 95, p. 31-32.
    "Hopi." [WormR] (35:2, #138) 95, p. 61.
    "Rip Van Winkle in Chicago." [PoetryE] (39) Fall 94, p. 39.
    "Sex Talk to Boys." [ChironR] (43) Sum 95, p. 28.
1988. FOX, Skip
    "Wallet" (6 selections). [NewOR] (21:2) Sum 95, p. 48-49.
1989. FOX, Susan
    "Cro-Magnon." [ParisR] (37:134) Spr 95, p. 275-276.
1990. FOXCROFT, Bill
    "Henry's Muddy Shoes." [MalR] (113) Wint 95, p. 78-79.
    "Thin Man Wait for Spring." [MalR] (113) Wint 95, p. 80.
1991. FOY, John
    "Rue des Martyrs" (Selection: 12). [Poetry] (166:3) Je 95, p. 142.
1992. FOYE, Brian
    "Noah's Son Depressed." [Conduit] (3) Sum 95, p. 10.
    "Salt Lake City." [Conduit] (3) Sum 95, p. 11.
1993. FRAIND, Lori
    "Massacre, Ahmici, 1993" (A photograph by Gilles Peress). [AnthNEW] (7) 95, p. 13.
1994. FRAKE, Priscilla
    "Argument for Starting a Journal on the 3rd Page." [Vis] (49) 95, p. 6.
1995. FRANCE, Dara
    "Birthday." [Pearl] (22) Fall-Wint 95, p. 131.
    "Incident." [Pearl] (22) Fall-Wint 95, p. 131.
FRANCE, Steve de
    See De FRANCE, Steve
1996. FRANCE de BRAVO, Brandel
    "Calla Lily." [BlackWR] (21:2) Spr-Sum 95, p. 45-46.

1997. FRANCINE (D.C. Center for Alcohol and Drug Abuse, Washington, DC)
    "The Road Between Here and There" (WritersCorps Program). [WashR] (21:2) Ag -
    S 95, p. 5.
1998. FRANK, Bernhard
    "Buddha" (tr. of Rainer Maria Rilke). [HeavenB] (12) 95, p. 88.
    "Evening" (tr. of Rainer Maria Rilke). [HeavenB] (12) 95, p. 88.
    "Flemish Painting" (tr. of Moshë Dor). [PoetryE] (40) Spr 95, p. 25.
    "Interpretations" (tr. of Moshë Dor). [PoetryE] (40) Spr 95, p. 24.
    "The Minaret" (tr. of M. Winkler). [PoetryE] (40) Spr 95, p. 130.
    "Orpheus, Narcissus at the Baths." [IllinoisR] (3:1/2) Fall 95-Spr 96, p. 108.
1999. FRANKEL, David
    "For the Tenth Anniversary of John Gardner's Death." [NewMyths] (2:2/3:1) 95, p.
    346.
2000. FRANKEL-KESSLER, June
    "News Item. Updated." [Light] (13) Spr 95, p. 12.
2001. FRANZEN, Cola
    "Anchors." [Noctiluca] (2:1, #4) Spr 95, p. 3.
    "Apple Orchard in Winter." [Noctiluca] (2:1, #4) Spr 95, p. 1.
    "Betrayal" (tr. of Alicia Borinsky). [MassR] (36:4) Wint 95-96, p. 595.
    "Cámera Oscura" (Selections: Canto 1-3, 7-8, tr. of Juan Cameron). [Noctiluca]
    (2:1, #4) Spr 95, p. 46-50.
    "Circles." [Noctiluca] (2:1, #4) Spr 95, p. 2.
    "The Critics' Trade" (to José Emilio Pacheco, tr. of Alicia Borinsky). [MassR] (36:4)
    Wint 95-96, p. 596.
    "Deeps." [Noctiluca] (2:1, #4) Spr 95, p. 2.
    "Invasion" (tr. of Jorge Guillén). [HarvardR] (8) Spr 95, p. 93.
    "Welcome" (tr. of Alicia Borinsky). [AmerV] (36) 95, p. 113.
2002. FRASER, Caroline
    "Cain." [NewYorker] (71:8) 17 Ap 95, p. 89.
2003. FRASER, Gregory
    "How It Happened." [WestHR] (49:4) Wint 95, p. 366.
2004. FRASER, John George
    "Grassfires in High Winds." [AntigR] (101) Spr 95, p. 94.
2005. FRASER, Kathleen
    "Wing." [Conjunc] (24) 95, p. 74-80.
2006. FRASER, Sanford
    "Amtrak Limited." [NewYorkQ] (54) 95, p. 66.
    "Blue Hair." [NewYorkQ] (55) 95, p. 77.
2007. FRASIER, Carrie
    "After the Pesto Pasta." [LitR] (39:1) Fall 95, p. 85.
    "Guitars in Aruba." [Plain] (15:3) Spr 95, p. 8.
FRATRIK, Julie Cooper
    See COOPER-FRATRIK, Julie
2008. FRAZIER, Hood
    "Morning in the Blue Ridge." [ColEng] (57:3) Mr 95, p. 336-337.
2009. FRAZIER, Jan
    "The Raccoon." [HighP] (10:1) Spr 95, p. 90-91.
    "The Tree." [PlumR] (9) [95 or 96], p. 5.
2010. FRECH, Stephen
    "At the Center of a Garden Maze" (Governor's Palace, Williamsburg, Virginia).
    [LowellR] (2) c1996, p. 92.
    "Christ at the Column." [Ascent] (20:1) Fall 95, p. 22.
    "The Ninth Hour." [Ascent] (20:1) Fall 95, p. 23.
    "Two Men Playing Cards." [LowellR] (2) c1996, p. 91.
2011. FREDERICK, Mary Esther
    "The Tillamook Burn" (runner up, 1994 Borderlands Poetry Contest). [Border] (6)
    Spr-Sum 95, p. 36.
2012. FREDERIKSEN, Nancy
    "Emergence." [NorthStoneR] (12) 95, p. 192.
    "Facial Expression." [NorthStoneR] (12) 95, p. 193.
    "Gladiolus." [NorthStoneR] (12) 95, p. 194.
2013. FREELAND, Charles
    "Concerning Auto-Erotic Asphyxiation." [TarRP] (34:2) Spr 95, p. 34.
    "Concerning Life on the Island." [LullwaterR] (5:2) Fall-Wint 94, p. 36.
    "The Death of Irony." [PaintedB] (55/56) 95, p. 10-13.
    "Gothic Episodes." [NewOR] (21:2) Sum 95, p. 22-24.

2014. FREEMAN, Glenn (Glenn J.)
"Good Friday." [LullwaterR] (6:1) Spr-Sum 95, p. 80-82.
"The Leveling." [PoetL] (90:3) Fall 95, p. 53-54.
"Something Like a Poet." [ChironR] (43) Sum 95, p. 29.
2015. FREEMAN, Wendy K.
"Writing You." [Plain] (15:2) Wint 95, p. 34.
2016. FREEPERSON, Kathy
"Dr. White" (The 1994 Allen Ginsberg Poetry Awards: Honorable Mention).
[Footwork] (24/25) 95, p. 194.
2017. FREER, Maria
"Condition" (tr. of Tito Alvarado). [Arc] (35) Aut 95, p. 19.
"Joy" (tr. of Tito Alvarado). [Arc] (35) Aut 95, p. 18.
"Little Girl" (tr. of Tito Alvarado). [Arc] (35) Aut 95, p. 17.
2018. FREERICKS, Charles Avakian
"Archaeologist at Age Six." [LiteralL] (1:4) Ja-F 95, p. 12.
FREESE, Allison de (Allison A. de)
See DeFREESE, Allison (Allison A.)
FREIBERT, Stuart
See FRIEBERT, Stuart
2019. FREIRE-LIZAMA, Tatiana
"The Biter of Fingernails." [Descant] (26:1, #88) Spr 95, p. 21-22.
"Other Poets." [Descant] (26:1, #88) Spr 95, p. 19-20.
2020. FRENCH, Wendy
"Home" (21 Contest Winner, Second). [Grain] (22:3) Wint 95, p. 35.
"Kate" (21 Contest Winner, Second). [Grain] (22:3) Wint 95, p. 36-37.
"Scar" (21 Contest Winner, Second). [Grain] (22:3) Wint 95, p. 38.
"Spooning Blue" (21 Contest Winner, Second). [Grain] (22:3) Wint 95, p. 35.
2021. FRIEBERT, Stuart
"Almost Nothing" (tr. of Karl Krolow). [Field] (53) Fall 95, p. 85.
"Cockroach." [PraS] (69:1) Spr 95, p. 53.
"Cownose Ray." [Iowa] (25:1) Wint 95, p. 156.
"Dimpling." [PraS] (69:1) Spr 95, p. 54.
"Dune Willow" (for S. T. B.). [CentR] (39:2) Spr 95, p. 313-314.
"Earing Down." [PraF] (16:2, #71) Sum 95, p. 83.
"Gray Weakfish." [Footwork] (24/25) 95, p. 29.
"Heartweed." [ColR] (22:2) Fall 95, p. 193.
"Hook-and-Eye." [WritersF] (21) 95, p. 161.
"Hot Cod." [WritersF] (21) 95, p. 160.
"Hundred Fathom Curve." [PraS] (69:1) Spr 95, p. 52-53.
"July" (tr. of Karl Krolow). [Field] (53) Fall 95, p. 84.
"Roller Skates." [Bogg] (67) 95, p. 58.
"Shibboleth." [PraF] (16:2, #71) Sum 95, p. 83.
"String Figures." [SenR] (25:1) Spr 95, p. 13.
"Tail Walking." [PraS] (69:1) Spr 95, p. 54.
"Under a Spell" (tr. of Karl Krolow). [Field] (53) Fall 95, p. 83.
"Untitled: Not that we didn't expect it" (tr. of Sylvia Fischerová, w. the author).
[LullwaterR] (5:2) Fall-Wint 94, p. 34-35.
"View From the Window" (tr. of Karl Krolow). [OhioR] (54) 95, p. 25.
"What Remains" (tr. of Karl Krolow). [DefinedP] (2:2) Spr-Sum 94, p. 38.
"Whoever Could Still Say" (tr. of Karl Krolow). [OhioR] (54) 95, p. 26.
"The Worst Is Being Conscious" (tr. of Sylvia Fischerová, w. the author).
[LullwaterR] (5:2) Fall-Wint 94, p. 33.
2022. FRIED, Elliot
"Gas Stations." [Jacaranda] (11) [95 or 96?], p. 62-63.
2023. FRIED, Erich
"Courtship" (tr. by Lane Jennings). [Vis] (47) 95, p. 29.
"Growing Older" (tr. by Lane Jennings). [Vis] (47) 95, p. 29.
2024. FRIED, Steve
"Atheist Prayers." [HangL] (66) 95, p. 17-19.
2025. FRIEDERICH, Joel
"Pickled Pig's Feet." [PoetryNW] (36:4) Wint 95-96, p. 40.
2026. FRIEDLANDER, Benjamin
"The Job" (For Tinker Greene). [ChiR] (41:4) 95, p. 34.
"Skulker." [ChiR] (41:4) 95, p. 36.
"Walk a Mile in My Shoes." [ChiR] (41:4) 95, p. 35.

2027. FRIEDMAN, Dorothy
"Vietnam." [Writer] (108:8) Ag 95, p. 25.
2028. FRIEDMAN, Gerald
"Heroism in Los Alamos Canyon." [Plain] (15:2) Wint 95, p. 32-33.
2029. FRIEDMAN, Jeanne
"Fertility." [HiramPoR] (58/59) Spr 95-Wint 96, p. 22-23.
2030. FRIEDMAN, Jeff
"Jacob." [GrahamHR] (19) Wint 95-96, p. 34-35.
"Night Wind." [GrahamHR] (19) Wint 95-96, p. 32-33.
2031. FRIEDMAN, Michael
"Cloud." [AmerPoR] (24:5) S-O 95, p. 50.
"Music." [AmerPoR] (24:5) S-O 95, p. 50.
2032. FRIEDMAN, Sam
"Worms." [BlackBR] (20) Spr-Sum 95, p. 14.
2033. FRIEDMAN, Stanford
"An Appointment to Color." [ArtfulD] (28/29) 95, p. 67.
2034. FRIEDRICH, Paul
"In Everything I Want to Reach" (tr. of Boris Pasternak). [LitR] (39:1) Fall 95, p.
62-63.
"Winter Night" (tr. of Boris Pasternak). [LitR] (39:1) Fall 95, p. 61.
2035. FRIEND, Joshua
"Eyewitness, or Monopoly Victory." [HiramPoR] (58/59) Spr 95-Wint 96, p. 24.
"A Postmodern Displacement." [HiramPoR] (58/59) Spr 95-Wint 96, p. 25.
2036. FRIES, Kenny
"Instruments of Desire." [JamesWR] (12:1) Wint 95, p. 6.
"The Sacrifice of Desire." [JamesWR] (12:1) Wint 95, p. 6.
2037. FRIESEN, Patrick
"At the Sill." [CapilR] (2:15) Spr 95, p. 33-34.
"A Dog at the Door." [CapilR] (2:15) Spr 95, p. 37-38.
"Empty Coat." [MalR] (110) Spr 95, p. 77.
"Let Me Roll You." [CapilR] (2:15) Spr 95, p. 40.
"Our Hands." [CapilR] (2:15) Spr 95, p. 39.
"A Small Tenderness." [CapilR] (2:15) Spr 95, p. 35-36.
"The Wheels." [MalR] (110) Spr 95, p. 76.
2038. FRIIS-BAASTAD, Erling
"Filialis." [PoetryC] (15:3) Ag 95, p. 15.
"The Gods Are Changing Face." [PoetryC] (15:3) Ag 95, p. 15.
"The Strait" (for Raymond Carver). [PoetryC] (15:3) Ag 95, p. 15.
2039. FRIMAN, Alice
"The Chicken Flag." [LaurelR] (29:2) Sum 95, p. 66.
"Confession." [PraS] (69:3) Fall 95, p. 134.
"The Drawstring" (Award of Excellence). [HopewellR] (7) 95, p. 96.
"Flying Home" (after a visit to my mother). [Manoa] (7:1) Sum 95, p. 46.
"From the Looking Glass." [LaurelR] (29:2) Sum 95, p. 67.
"Honeymoon" (Ngorongoro, Tanzania). [NewL] (62:1) 96 (c1995), p. 111.
"Romance." [Chelsea] (59) 95, p. 160-161.
"Sunday Morning at the Beach, I Think of Mountains." [PraS] (69:3) Fall 95, p.
132-133.
"White River." [Manoa] (7:1) Sum 95, p. 45.
2040. FRISARDI, Andrew
"Yes and No." [PoetryE] (39) Fall 94, p. 40.
2041. FROMER, Kevin M.
"There Are Still Beautiful Things in the World." [BellArk] (11:5) S-O 95, p. 25.
2042. FROST, Carol
"Adultery." [IndR] (18:2) Fall 95, p. 170.
"Consent." [Crazy] (48) Spr 95, p. 74.
"Constancy." [PraS] (69:1) Spr 95, p. 57.
"Custom." [SouthernR] (31:4) O/Aut 95, p. 846.
"Fatherhood." [PraS] (69:1) Spr 95, p. 56.
"Hypocrisy." [PraS] (69:1) Spr 95, p. 55.
"In Common Places." [SenR] (25:1) Spr 95, p. 29.
"Lies." [IndR] (18:2) Fall 95, p. 171.
"Marriage." [ManyMM] (2:1) 95, p. 104.
"Nettles." [ManyMM] (2:1) 95, p. 105.
"Scorn." [SouthernR] (31:4) O/Aut 95, p. 845.
"Sex." [SouthernR] (31:4) O/Aut 95, p. 847.

"To Kill a Deer." [Jacaranda] (11) [95 or 96?], p. 137.
2043. FROST, Celestine
"Day Clean." [SoCaR] (28:1) Fall 95, p. 183.
2044. FROST, Elisabeth
"Cathedral." [Shen] (45:4) Wint 95, p. 47-48.
2045. FROST, Richard
"The Hawk." [SenR] (25:1) Spr 95, p. 99.
FU, Cheng
   See CHENG, Fu
2046. FUCHS, Greg
"Half Fast" (3 selections). [WashR] (20:5) F-Mr 95, p. 6.
"Sabbath, Mon Dias." [WashR] (20:5) F-Mr 95, p. 6.
"Size Medium." [WashR] (20:5) F-Mr 95, p. 6.
"Sonic Etude." [WashR] (20:5) F-Mr 95, p. 6.
2047. FUEGOS, Cien
"Jen Nuration Ex (An open letter to my comrades)." [Pearl] (22) Fall-Wint 95, p. 101.
2048. FUENZALIDA, Nieves
"The Fragments of the Clan" (Selections: 77-78, 80, 86, 91, 94, 104-105, tr. by Luciano P. Díaz). [Arc] (35) Aut 95, p. 75-76.
2049. FUGII, Itsuma
"Your souls that have fallen" (in Japanese and English, tr. by Jiro Nakano). [BambooR] (67/68) Sum-Fall 95, p. 3.
2050. FUHAKU (1714-1807)
"Such complete stillness" (Haiku, tr. by Sam Hamill). [WillowS] (36) Je 95, p. 96.
2051. FUHRMAN, Joanna
"Domestic Comforts." [HangL] (66) 95, p. 20-21.
"Geese." [HangL] (66) 95, p. 22-23.
"Why Love Is a Better Antidote to Music Than the Color Blue." [HangL] (66) 95, p. 21.
2052. FUJII, Fumiko
"Tonight again, the only light to aid me" (in Japanese and English, tr. by Jiro Nakano). [BambooR] (67/68) Sum-Fall 95, p. 4.
2053. FUJIOKA, Toshiko
"Calling 'Fish' in the Evening" (tr. by Kazuya Honda and Jon Silkin). [Stand] (36:3) Sum 95, p. 35.
2054. FUKUSHIMA, Ichio
"Keloids! Unbearably grotesque" (in Japanese and English, tr. by Jiro Nakano). [BambooR] (67/68) Sum-Fall 95, p. 5.
FUKUYABU, Kiyowara no
   See KIYOWARA no FUKUYABU
2055. FULLER, Heather
"Between Here and Else, the City" (Winner, 1995 Greg Grummer Award in Poetry). [Phoebe] (24:2) 95, p. 136.
"The Delicate Art of the Rifle." [WashR] (21:1) Je-Jl 95, p. 12.
"Earlier and Urban." [WashR] (21:1) Je-Jl 95, p. 12.
"Fission" (Winner, 1995 Greg Grummer Award in Poetry). [Phoebe] (24:2) 95, p. 134.
"Hotel of Miracles" (from "Between Here and Else"). [WashR] (21:1) Je-Jl 95, p. 13.
"Mantras" (Winner, 1995 Greg Grummer Award in Poetry). [Phoebe] (24:2) 95, p. 135.
"Perhaps This Is a Recue Fantasy." [Phoebe] (24:1) 95, p. 124-125.
"Sudden Clutter" (Winner, 1995 Greg Grummer Award in Poetry). [Phoebe] (24:2) 95, p. 132-133.
"Telegram." [Phoebe] (24:1) 95, p. 122-123.
2056. FULLER, John
"Sunflowers." [Epoch] (44:3) 95, p. 308-309.
2057. FULTON, Alice
"Drills." [KenR] (17:2) Spr 95, p. 97-98.
"Echo Location." [KenR] (17:2) Spr 95, p. 99-100.
"World Wrap." [TriQ] (95) Wint 95-96, p. 172-175.
2058. FULTON, Robin
"About Her Love" (tr. of Lennart Sjögren). [MalR] (111) Sum 95, p. 33.
"An Account of Dizziness" (from *Murmur*, 1983, tr. of Werner Aspenström). [QRL] (34) 95, book 3, p. 30.

"After a Night of Frost" (from *Within*, 1969, tr. of Werner Aspenström). [QRL] (34) 95, book 3, p. 21.
"After Playing Mozart All Day" (from *The Stairway*, 1964, tr. of Werner Aspenström). [QRL] (34) 95, book 3, p. 20.
"After the Storm" (tr. of Werner Aspenström). [QRL] (34) 95, book 3, p. 53.
"At the Opera I Remember Another Song" (from *The Red Cloud*,1986, tr. of Werner Aspenström). [QRL] (34) 95, book 3, p. 41.
"At the Same Time as Chagall" (from *Murmur*, 1983, tr. of Werner Aspenström). [QRL] (34) 95, book 3, p. 37-38.
"The Bells" (from *The Stairway*, 1964, tr. of Werner Aspenström). [QRL] (34) 95, book 3, p. 16.
"Biographical Note" (tr. of Rose Ausländer). [MalR] (110) Spr 95, p. 75.
"Birds, 18th Century Style" (from *Snow-legend*, 1949, tr. of Werner Aspenström). [QRL] (34) 95, book 3, p. 8.
"Busy Creatures" (from *Creatures*, 1988, tr. of Werner Aspenström). [QRL] (34) 95, book 3, p. 48.
"The Butterfly" (from *The Stairway*, 1964, tr. of Werner Aspenström). [QRL] (34) 95, book 3, p. 15.
"The Cat Pricks Up Its Ears" (from *The Red Cloud*,1986, tr. of Werner Aspenström). [QRL] (34) 95, book 3, p. 40.
"The Child Rises" (from *Creatures*, 1988, tr. of Werner Aspenström). [QRL] (34) 95, book 3, p. 49.
"The Comet" (from *Creatures*, 1988, tr. of Werner Aspenström). [QRL] (34) 95, book 3, p. 52.
"Den Döde Andas (The Dead Man Breathes)" (Selections: 3 poems, tr. of Staffan Söderblom). [MalR] (111) Sum 95, p. 93-95.
"Economic Geography" (from *Creatures*, 1988, tr. of Werner Aspenström). [QRL] (34) 95, book 3, p. 46-47.
"The Elephant" (from *The Stairway*, 1964, tr. of Werner Aspenström). [QRL] (34) 95, book 3, p. 17.
"Engravings" (from *Creatures*, 1988, tr. of Werner Aspenström). [QRL] (34) 95, book 3, p. 45.
"Fever" (from *Private and Public*, 1991, tr. of Werner Aspenström). [QRL] (34) 95, book 3, p. 56.
"The Fist Doesn't Always Win" (from *Meanwhile*, 1972, tr. of Werner Aspenström). [QRL] (34) 95, book 3, p. 24.
"The forest has many stairways, few doors" (from "Den Döde Andas (The Dead Man Breathes)," tr. of Staffan Söderblom). [MalR] (111) Sum 95, p. 95.
"The Gatepost" (from *Early One Morning, Late on Earth*, 1980, tr. of Werner Aspenström). [QRL] (34) 95, book 3, p. 27.
"The Glow-Worm" (from *Murmur*, 1983, tr. of Werner Aspenström). [QRL] (34) 95, book 3, p. 31.
"Hamlet Should Have Died in the First Act" (from *By Day by Night*, 1961, tr. of Werner Aspenström). [QRL] (34) 95, book 3, p. 13.
"Happiness" (from *The Dogs*, 1954, tr. of Werner Aspenström). [QRL] (34) 95, book 3, p. 9.
"The Heart" (from *The Stairway*, 1964, tr. of Werner Aspenström). [QRL] (34) 95, book 3, p. 19.
"The Horse" (from *The Stairway*, 1964, tr. of Werner Aspenström). [QRL] (34) 95, book 3, p. 15.
"The House-Sparrow" (from *Dictionary*, 1976, tr. of Werner Aspenström). [QRL] (34) 95, book 3, p. 24.
"I call the animals home" (from "Den Döde Andas (The Dead Man Breathes)," tr. of Staffan Söderblom). [MalR] (111) Sum 95, p. 93.
"The Ice-Stack" (from *Litany*, 1952, tr. of Werner Aspenström). [QRL] (34) 95, book 3, p. 9.
"If There Were Only Two Words" (from *Dictionary*, 1976, tr. of Werner Aspenström). [QRL] (34) 95, book 3, p. 25.
"Ikaros and Master Granite" (from *Poems beneath the Trees*, 1956, tr. of Werner Aspenström). [QRL] (34) 95, book 3, p. 10.
"Il Gran Cavallo, or A Brief History of Leonardo's Horse" (from *Murmur*, 1983, tr. of Werner Aspenström). [QRL] (34) 95, book 3, p. 35-36.
"Imposing Buildings" (from *Creatures*, 1988, tr. of Werner Aspenström). [QRL] (34) 95, book 3, p. 51.
"In the Age of the Long Exposures" (from *The Red Cloud*,1986, tr. of Werner Aspenström). [QRL] (34) 95, book 3, p. 41.

"In the Regions of Dream" (from *Murmur*, 1983, tr. of Werner Aspenström). [QRL]
   (34) 95, book 3, p. 32.
"In Winter" (tr. of Sarah Kirsch). [MalR] (110) Spr 95, p. 71.
"I've Been Thinking of Van Gogh Again" (from *Murmur*, 1983, tr. of Werner
   Aspenström). [QRL] (34) 95, book 3, p. 33-35.
"Kom Inte Och Säg (Don't Come and Tell Me Don't Come and Say)" (Selections: 1-
   6, tr. of Karin Bellman). [MalR] (111) Sum 95, p. 77.
"The Lamp" (from *Creatures*, 1988, tr. of Werner Aspenström). [QRL] (34) 95,
   book 3, p. 47.
"Lapidary Report" (from *Creatures*, 1988, tr. of Werner Aspenström). [QRL] (34)
   95, book 3, p. 44.
"The Larks" (from *Early One Morning, Late on Earth*, 1980, tr. of Werner
   Aspenström). [QRL] (34) 95, book 3, p. 27.
"Looking Up from the Cradle of Earth" (from *Within*, 1969, tr. of Werner
   Aspenström). [QRL] (34) 95, book 3, p. 22.
"Memorial" (from *Dictionary*, 1976, tr. of Werner Aspenström). [QRL] (34) 95,
   book 3, p. 24.
"The Mill" (from *Murmur*, 1983, tr. of Werner Aspenström). [QRL] (34) 95, book 3,
   p. 29.
"The Moon" (from *Litany*, 1952, tr. of Werner Aspenström). [QRL] (34) 95, book 3,
   p. 9.
"More I Don't Know" (from *By Day by Night*, 1961, tr. of Werner Aspenström).
   [QRL] (34) 95, book 3, p. 12.
"The Music" (from *Creatures*, 1988, tr. of Werner Aspenström). [QRL] (34) 95,
   book 3, p. 48.
"The Nightingale in Badelunda" (tr. of Tomas Tranströmer). [Verse] (12:2) 95, p.
   137.
"Non Plus Ultra" (from *Creatures*, 1988, tr. of Werner Aspenström). [QRL] (34) 95,
   book 3, p. 50.
"The Oars" (from *The Stairway*, 1964, tr. of Werner Aspenström). [QRL] (34) 95,
   book 3, p. 16-17.
"On Behalf of Matter" (from *By Day by Night*, 1961, tr. of Werner Aspenström).
   [QRL] (34) 95, book 3, p. 12.
"On the Djurgård Ferry" (from *Poems beneath the Trees*, 1956, tr. of Werner
   Aspenström). [QRL] (34) 95, book 3, p. 10.
"One of the Horse's Legs Was Missing" (from *The Red Cloud*,1986, tr. of Werner
   Aspenström). [QRL] (34) 95, book 3, p. 40.
"Otherwise Among the Squirrels" (from *Private and Public*, 1991, tr. of Werner
   Aspenström). [QRL] (34) 95, book 3, p. 55.
"Outside the Circle of Light" (from *By Day by Night*, 1961, tr. of Werner
   Aspenström). [QRL] (34) 95, book 3, p. 14.
"Paradise, Almost Like an Illness" (from *Within*, 1969, tr. of Werner Aspenström).
   [QRL] (34) 95, book 3, p. 21.
"Parting" (tr. of Rose Ausländer). [MalR] (110) Spr 95, p. 74.
"The Pleiades" (from *Private and Public*, 1991, tr. of Werner Aspenström). [QRL]
   (34) 95, book 3, p. 56.
"Portrait" (from *Dictionary*, 1976, tr. of Werner Aspenström). [QRL] (34) 95, book
   3, p. 26.
"Portrait in December" (from *Poems beneath the Trees*, 1956, tr. of Werner
   Aspenström). [QRL] (34) 95, book 3, p. 11.
"Post Festum" (from *Murmur*, 1983, tr. of Werner Aspenström). [QRL] (34) 95,
   book 3, p. 28.
"Prague Quartet" (tr. of Kjell Espmark). [MalR] (110) Spr 95, p. 78-83.
"Probable Changes in the Language" (from *Creatures*, 1988, tr. of Werner
   Aspenström). [QRL] (34) 95, book 3, p. 51.
"The Redeemer Liveth" (from *Meanwhile*, 1972, tr. of Werner Aspenström). [QRL]
   (34) 95, book 3, p. 23.
"Revisiting" (from *Creatures*, 1988, tr. of Werner Aspenström). [QRL] (34) 95,
   book 3, p. 50.
"The Rower" (tr. of Werner Aspenström). [QRL] (34) 95, book 3, p. 54.
"The Sandal" (from *Creatures*, 1988, tr. of Werner Aspenström). [QRL] (34) 95,
   book 3, p. 47.
"The Sardine on the Subway" (from *Meanwhile*, 1972, tr. of Werner Aspenström).
   [QRL] (34) 95, book 3, p. 23.
"Scenario for a Small Angry Cock" (from *Murmur*, 1983, tr. of Werner
   Aspenström). [QRL] (34) 95, book 3, p. 30.

"Seen from the Balloon of Dreams" (from *The Red Cloud,*1986, tr. of Werner Aspenström). [QRL] (34) 95, book 3, p. 42.
"She Who Paused on the Path and Breathed in Deeply" (from *The Red Cloud,*1986, tr. of Werner Aspenström). [QRL] (34) 95, book 3, p. 42.
"Silver" (from *Creatures,* 1988, tr. of Werner Aspenström). [QRL] (34) 95, book 3, p. 49.
"The Sloth" (from *Creatures,* 1988, tr. of Werner Aspenström). [QRL] (34) 95, book 3, p. 46.
"The Snail" (from *Creatures,* 1988, tr. of Werner Aspenström). [QRL] (34) 95, book 3, p. 43.
"The Snow Leopard" (from *Murmur,* 1983, tr. of Werner Aspenström). [QRL] (34) 95, book 3, p. 32.
"The Snowflake" (from *By Day by Night,* 1961, tr. of Werner Aspenström). [QRL] (34) 95, book 3, p. 14.
"So That Something Will Be Heard" (from *The Stairway,* 1964, tr. of Werner Aspenström). [QRL] (34) 95, book 3, p. 20.
"The Song" (tr. of Werner Aspenström). [QRL] (34) 95, book 3, p. 54.
"The Spider" (from *The Stairway,* 1964, tr. of Werner Aspenström). [QRL] (34) 95, book 3, p. 18.
"This Year Too" (from *Early One Morning, Late on Earth,* 1980, tr. of Werner Aspenström). [QRL] (34) 95, book 3, p. 26.
"The Tower" (from *Private and Public,* 1991, tr. of Werner Aspenström). [QRL] (34) 95, book 3, p. 55.
"The Tree" (from *The Red Cloud,*1986, tr. of Werner Aspenström). [QRL] (34) 95, book 3, p. 39.
"The unpainted buildings, the places" (from "Den Döde Andas (The Dead Man Breathes)," tr. of Staffan Söderblom). [MalR] (111) Sum 95, p. 94.
"An Unusually Warm Day" (from *Early One Morning, Late on Earth,* 1980, tr. of Werner Aspenström). [QRL] (34) 95, book 3, p. 27.
"Village Lilacs" (from *Litany,* 1952, tr. of Werner Aspenström). [QRL] (34) 95, book 3, p. 8.
"We Too Are Laymen, Said the Waves" (from *The Red Cloud,*1986, tr. of Werner Aspenström). [QRL] (34) 95, book 3, p. 39.
"What I Noticed in London" (from *Creatures,* 1988, tr. of Werner Aspenström). [QRL] (34) 95, book 3, p. 44-45.
"What's Left of the Year 1930" (from *By Day by Night,* 1961, tr. of Werner Aspenström). [QRL] (34) 95, book 3, p. 13.
"Who Is Not a Child" (from *Creatures,* 1988, tr. of Werner Aspenström). [QRL] (34) 95, book 3, p. 52.
"You and Me and the World" (from *The Stairway,* 1964, tr. of Werner Aspenström). [QRL] (34) 95, book 3, p. 18.
2059. FULTON, Tracy
"The Myth of Origins" (Finalist, 1995 Allen Tate Memorial Competition). [Wind] (76) Fall 95, p. 28-29.
2060. FUNDERBURK, Julie
"Sleepwalkers." [GreensboroR] (58) Sum 95, p. 85-86.
2061. FUNG, Hae Suh
"A thousand Pieces of Snow" (w. Zhou Lu Jing, 22 selections, tr. by Tsung Tsai and George Crane). [Archae] (5) Spr 95, p. 6-29.
2062. FUNGE, Robert
"A 36¢ Poem." [SpoonR] (20:1) Wint-Spr 95, p. 28.
"A Birthday Poem" (for Jennifer). [HiramPoR] (58/59) Spr 95-Wint 96, p. 26.
"Devils." [BlackBR] (21) Fall-Wint 95, p. 22-23.
"Empty Places." [SpoonR] (20:1) Wint-Spr 95, p. 29.
"Expectations." [MidwQ] (37:1) Aut 95, p. 37.
"The FU-Man Meets an Old Flame." [SpoonR] (20:1) Wint-Spr 95, p. 27.
"The Red Pepper Song." [SpoonR] (20:1) Wint-Spr 95, p. 30.
2063. FUNK, Allison
"Assateague Island." [Drumvoices] (4:1/2) Fall-Wint 94-95, p. 31.
"Midnight." [Drumvoices] (4:1/2) Fall-Wint 94-95, p. 32.
"Sea Change." [Poetry] (166:4) Jl 95, p. 215-216.
"Wandering Prayer." [Journal] (19:1) Spr-Sum 95, p. 5-6.
"When the Light Changes." [Journal] (19:1) Spr-Sum 95, p. 7-8.
2064. FUNKHOUSER, D. P.
"Tiramisu Dreams" (Honorable Mention, 9th Annual Contest). [SoCoast] (18) Ja 95, p. 22-23.

2065. FUNKHOUSER, Erica
"The Accident." [Atlantic] (276:6) D 95, p. 114.
2066. FURBISH, Dean
"The Church of Cyril and Methodius in Burgas." [XavierR] (15:1) Spr 95, p. 64.
2067. FURMANSKI, Lisa
"Bed-Ridden." [SpoonR] (20:2) Sum-Fall 95, p. 69.
"The Diagnosis." [SpoonR] (20:2) Sum-Fall 95, p. 67-68.
2068. FURR, Derek
"Everything Being As It Should Be." [CumbPR] (15:1) Fall 95, p. 23.
2069. FURUYOSHI, Yoshihiko
"To die for your country" (in Japanese and English, tr. by Jiro Nakano). [BambooR]
(67/68) Sum-Fall 95, p. 6.
FUSEI, Akutagawa
See AKUTAGAWA, Fusei
2070. FÜSÉKI, Eszter
"Hungarian Fall" (tr. of Peter Kantor, w. Michael Blumenthal). [Agni] (42) 95, p.
16-17.
"Once I Thought" (tr. of Peter Kantor, w. Michael Blumenthal). [Agni] (42) 95, p.
18.
2071. FUSHIMA, Emperor (1265-1317)
"Come back, love, tonight" (tr. by Sam Hamill). [RiverS] (44) 95, p. 34.
2072. FUSSELMAN, Amy
"Going Off the Pill." [NewYorkQ] (55) 95, p. 76.
2073. FUTORANSKY, Luisa
"Crema Catalana" (tr. by Jason Weiss). [Sulfur] (15:2, #37) Fall 95, p. 132.
"She, the Fisherwoman" (tr. by Jason Weiss). [Sulfur] (15:2, #37) Fall 95, p. 133.

2074. GABBARD, G. N.
"A Knotty Musick." [Light] (14) Sum 95, p. 8.
"Matriculation" (A Candlemas Carol). [Light] (15/16) Aut-Wint 95-96, p. 11.
"Nelson's Last Words, or, The Ballad of the Pair-Royal." [Light] (13) Spr 95, p. 10.
2075. GABOUDIKIAN, Sylva
"Perhaps" (tr. by Diana Der-Hovanessian). [GrahamHR] (19) Wint 95-96, p. 48.
2076. GABRIEL, Margaret
"Johnny Light" (in memory of my brother). [TickleAce] (27) Spr-Sum 94, p. 86-87.
2077. GADD, Bernard
"Teacher Admonishes." [Bogg] (67) 95, p. 4.
2078. GADE, Lisa
"History of the Highways" (with thanks to RP). [VirQR] (71:2) Spr 95, p. 303-305.
"Seven Riddles of the Dead." [SouthernPR] (35:1) Sum 95, p. 56-57.
2079. GAGE, Jennifer
"13 December." [MissouriR] (18:3) 95, p. 76.
"Milagros." [MissouriR] (18:3) 95, p. 78.
"Pilgrimage, Louisiana." [MissouriR] (18:3) 95, p. 77.
"Sta. Lucia." [MissouriR] (18:3) 95, p. 69.
"Sta. Lucia Critiques Her Childhood." [MissouriR] (18:3) 95, p. 70.
"Sta. Lucia Encounters Mechanical Difficulties." [MissouriR] (18:3) 95, p. 75.
"Sta. Lucia Sheds Light on the Art of Buon Fresco." [MissouriR] (18:3) 95, p. 71-
74.
2080. GAGNON, Madeleine
"C'était la nuit des étoiles filantes." [Os] (41) 95, p. 6.
"Chair de lune déroulée jusqu'au drap." [Os] (41) 95, p. 7.
"La nuit tous les êtres sont mous." [Os] (41) 95, p. 8.
2081. GAINES, Reg E.
"A Lake Called Kim" (Dedicated to Kim Horne). [Footwork] (24/25) 95, p. 62.
"Motherless Child." [Footwork] (24/25) 95, p. 62-63.
2082. GALASSI, Jonathan
"News from Mount Amiata" (tr. of Eugenio Montale). [HarvardR] (8) Spr 95, p. 90-
91.
2083. GALE, Edward A.
"Murder by Scansion." [LiteralL] (1:4) Ja-F 95, p. 7.
2084. GALEANO, Laura
"HIV Positive." [ApalQ] (44/45) Fall 95-Wint 96, p. 70.
2085. GALEF, David
"Greener Grass." [Hellas] (6:1) Spr-Sum 95, p. 32.

"Newborns." [Light] (15/16) Aut-Wint 95-96, p. 17.
"Possibilities." [Light] (13) Spr 95, p. 20.
2086. GALLAGHER, Ann Maureen
"One More Try." [FourQ] (9:1/2) Spr 95, p. 38.
2087. GALLAGHER, Ashley
"Somewhere in Georgia." [QW] (40) Spr-Sum 95, p. 204-205.
2088. GALLAGHER, Jean
"Particular Annunciation" (Or, We Discuss Having a Child). [Comm] (122:6) 24 Mr
95, p. 17.
2089. GALLAGHER, Tess
"Above the Bridge" (tr. of Liliana Ursu, w. Adam Sorkin). [Kalliope] (17:3) 95, p.
19.
"Because the Dream Is My Tenderest Arm." [VirQR] (71:4) Aut 95, p. 706-707.
"Harmless." [AmerPoR] (24:1) Ja-F 95, p. 42.
"Hybrid." [SenR] (25:1) Spr 95, p. 32.
"The Kiss of the Voyeur." [Jacaranda] (11) [95 or 96?], p. 153.
"Laughter and Stars." [VirQR] (71:4) Aut 95, p. 707-709.
"No, Not Paradise." [AmerPoR] (24:1) Ja-F 95, p. 42.
"Stand In." [Kalliope] (17:1) 95, p. 26.
"Tawny Equilibrium." [Kalliope] (17:1) 95, p. 25.
"Worth It Or Not?" [Kalliope] (17:1) 95, p. 27.
2090. GALLAHER, Edwin
"The Bureau." [WestHR] (49:2) Sum 95, p. 160.
"I Might Be at a Winery, Turning Out Bottles of Thunderbird, Which Everybody
Loves" (— William Glass). [WestHR] (49:2) Sum 95, p. 167.
"Marvell's World." [ParisR] (37:137) Wint 95, p. 115.
"Masked Ball" (attributed to Ensor). [WestHR] (49:2) Sum 95, p. 161.
"Negative Handprints at Gargas" (c. 15,000-10,000 B.C., Hautes-Pyrénées, France).
[ParisR] (37:137) Wint 95, p. 116.
2091. GALLAHER, John
"Breathing Lesson." [Border] (6) Spr-Sum 95, p. 37.
2092. GALLAWAY, Scott
"Painting with My Father." [DefinedP] (3) 95, p. 45.
2093. GALLER, David
"For Billie." [TriQ] (93) Spr-Sum 95, p. 124.
"Male Trio." [TriQ] (93) Spr-Sum 95, p. 125.
"Watching Pool." [SouthernR] (31:4) O/Aut 95, p. 848.
2094. GALLIK, Daniel
"3 days of rain, the morning clears, the river rises." [Nimrod] (39:1) Fall-Wint 95, p.
105.
2095. GALLOWAY, Will
"Abrasions." [WestHR] (49:3) Fall 95, p. 280.
2096. GALVIN, Brendan
"At Ellen Doyle's Brook." [NewRep] (212:6) 6 F 95, p. 38.
"Captain Teabag and the Wellfleet Witches." [TarRP] (35:1) Fall 95, p. 25-27.
"Crossing Pentland Firth." [PraS] (69:3) Fall 95, p. 130-131.
"An Illuminated Page from the Celtic Manuscript of Lough Glen." [GettyR] (8:3)
Sum 95, p. 490-491.
"Pondycherry." [Atlantic] (275:4) Ap 95, p. 90.
"Quilt Song." [Shen] (45:2) Sum 95, p. 88.
"Single Malt." [BlackWR] (21:2) Spr-Sum 95, p. 66-67.
"Sky and Island Light." [PraS] (69:3) Fall 95, p. 131-132.
"Uncle Patrick and the Doppelgangers." [Shen] (45:2) Sum 95, p. 86-87.
"West Cork: The Road Bowlers." [PraS] (69:3) Fall 95, p. 129-130.
2097. GALVIN, James
"Christmas, 1960." [ColR] (22:1) Spr 95, p. 93-94.
"The Other Reason It Rains, etc." (for Ray Worster, 1918-1984, and Lyle Van
Waning, 1922-1988). [Orion] (14:3) Sum 95, p. 57.
"Real Wonder." [Orion] (14:3) Sum 95, p. 57.
"Speaking Terms." [Orion] (14:3) Sum 95, p. 57.
2098. GALVIN, Martin
"Gardener." [Bogg] (67) 95, p. 25.
"School Nurse." [TexasR] (16:1/4) 95, p. 119-121.
2099. GAMBILL, Peggy
"Folklore, Dying." [Pembroke] (27) 95, p. 46-47.
"A View from the Milky Way." [CapeR] (30:2) Fall 95, p. 47.

2100. GAMEL, Mary-Kay
"Medea" (tr. of Euripides). [QW] (40) Spr-Sum 95, p. 96-145.
2101. GANASSI, Ian (Ian Leonidis)
"Mercedes Lourdes Irina Herrera" (for Emiddo Rinaldo Ganassi). [DenQ] (29:4) Spr 95, p. 21-26.
"Virgil's *Aeneid,* Book II, Lines 268-297." [NewEngR] (17:4) Fall 95, p. 100-103.
"White Christmas." [PlumR] (9) [95 or 96], p. 114-115.
2102. GANDER, Forrest
"All About Technique." [HarvardR] (9) Fall 95, p. 27.
"The First Ballad" (after St. John of the Cross). [Manoa] (7:1) Sum 95, p. 99-100.
"The Second Ballad" (after St. John of the Cross). [Manoa] (7:1) Sum 95, p. 100.
"Voyager." [ColR] (22:1) Spr 95, p. 19-22.
2103. GANDLEVSKY, Sergey
"Untitled: There's our street, let's say —" (tr. by Philip Metres). [WillowS] (36) Je 95, p. 92-93.
2104. GANSWORTH, Eric L.
"My Sister's Back Yard." [SlipS] (15) 95, p. 45-46.
"Stinkpot." [SlipS] (15) 95, p. 44-5.
"Wine and Cheese." [SlipS] (15) 95, p. 47-48.
2105. GANZEL, Barbara
"I Would Miss" (after "I Go Back to May 1937," by Sharon Olds). [SouthernPR] (35:1) Sum 95, p. 53-54.
2106. GARCIA, Carlos Ernesto
"A Ciento Cincuenta Mil Grados Bajo Cero." [Luz] (8) Spr 95, p. 30.
"Hasta la Cólera Se Pudre (Even Rage Will Rot)" (3 selections in Spanish and English, tr. by Elizabeth Gamble Miller). [Luz] (8) Spr 95, p. 27-31.
"A Hundred Fifty Thousand Degrees Below Zero" (tr. by Elizabeth Gamble Miller). [Luz] (8) Spr 95, p. 31.
"Son Como el Rocio." [Luz] (8) Spr 95, p. 27.
"The Summer of 80 and Five" (tr. by Elizabeth Gamble Miller). [Luz] (8) Spr 95, p. 29.
"They Are Like the Dew" (tr. by Elizabeth Gamble Miller). [Luz] (8) Spr 95, p. 27.
"Verano del 80 y Cinco." [Luz] (8) Spr 95, p. 28.
2107. GARCIA, Joey
"Feeding the Ancestors." [Calyx] (16:1) Sum 95, p. 50-51.
2108. GARCIA, Richard
"Certain Images, Excluded from My Poems, Form a Parade." [Ploughs] (21:1) Spr 95, p. 26-27.
"Chickenhead." [ProseP] (4) 95, p. 32.
"Note Folded Thirteen Ways" (Literary Award Poem). [GreensboroR] (57) Wint 94-95, p. 102.
2109. GARCIA LORCA, Federico
"Casida of the Branches" (tr. by Joel Zeltzer). [DefinedP] (1:2) Spr-Sum 93, p. 19.
"In a Different Style" (tr. by Joel Zeltzer). [DefinedP] (1:2) Spr-Sum 93, p. 20.
"Interrupted Concert" (tr. by Joel Zeltzer). [DefinedP] (1:2) Spr-Sum 93, p. 18.
2110. GARCIA PABON, Leonardo
"La Abuela Rosa." [Americas] (23:3/4) Fall-Wint 95, p. 128-130.
2111. GARCIA VACA, Gustavo Alberto
"Above It All, a Tear." [SantaBR] (3:1) Spr 95, p. 103.
"Al Irte de Me Vista." [SantaBR] (3:1) Spr 95, p. 102.
"On Your Leaving from My Sight." [SantaBR] (3:1) Spr 95, p. 102.
"Río." [SantaBR] (3:1) Spr 95, p. 104.
"River." [SantaBR] (3:1) Spr 95, p. 104.
"Sobre Todo, una Lágrima." [SantaBR] (3:1) Spr 95, p. 103.
2112. GARDIEN, Kent
"Johnny." [IllinoisR] (3:1/2) Fall 95-Spr 96, p. 60-61.
2113. GARDINIER, Suzanne
"Two Girls." [AmerV] (38) 95, p. 36-37.
2114. GARDNER, Charles A.
"Chiapas, Mexico" (for Sym). [NewEngR] (17:2) Spr 95, p. 84.
"Dick the Fish." [NewEngR] (17:2) Spr 95, p. 85.
2115. GARDNER, Geoffrey
"At My Place 'The Little Orchard' I" (tr. of Robert Melançon). [SenR] (25:2) Fall 95, p. 65.
"At My Place 'The Little Orchard' VII" (tr. of Robert Melançon). [SenR] (25:2) Fall 95, p. 66.

"At My Place 'The Little Orchard' VIII" (tr. of Robert Melançon). [SenR] (25:2) Fall
    95, p. 67.
"Blind Painting III" (tr. of Robert Melançon). [SenR] (25:2) Fall 95, p. 61.
"Blind Painting IV" (tr. of Robert Melançon). [SenR] (25:2) Fall 95, p. 62.
"Blind Painting V" (tr. of Robert Melançon). [SenR] (25:2) Fall 95, p. 63.
"Blind Painting VI" (tr. of Robert Melançon). [SenR] (25:2) Fall 95, p. 64.
"Blind Painting VII" (tr. of Robert Melançon). [PlumR] (9) [95 or 96], p. 24.
"Blind Painting VIII" (tr. of Robert Melançon). [PlumR] (9) [95 or 96], p. 25.
"In a Foreign Land" (tr. of Jules Supervielle). [PlumR] (8) [95], p. 85.
"Untitled: And then my objects began to smile" (tr. of Jules Supervielle).
    [Jacaranda] (11) [95 or 96?], p. 111.
"Untitled: For thirty years I've been searching" (tr. of Jules Supervielle). [WillowS]
    (36) Je 95, p. 106.
"Untitled: Since I know nothing of our life except" (tr. of Jules Supervielle).
    [Jacaranda] (11) [95 or 96?], p. 110.
"The Wake" (tr. of Jules Supervielle). [Jacaranda] (11) [95 or 96?], p. 112.
2116. GARDNER, John
    "The African Violet." [NewMyths] (2:2/3:1) 95, p. 379.
    "The Beeophrys." [NewMyths] (2:2/3:1) 95, p. 380.
    "The Gentian." [NewMyths] (2:2/3:1) 95, p. 381.
    "The Helleborus." [NewMyths] (2:2/3:1) 95, p. 382.
    "The Nasturtium." [NewMyths] (2:2/3:1) 95, p. 383.
    "The Phlox." [NewMyths] (2:2/3:1) 95, p. 384.
    "Rose Madder." [NewMyths] (2:2/3:1) 95, p. 385.
    "The Water Lily." [NewMyths] (2:2/3:1) 95, p. 386.
    "The Yucca." [NewMyths] (2:2/3:1) 95, p. 387.
2117. GARDNER, Mary
    "Maria." [PoetL] (90:2) Sum 95, p. 28.
2118. GARDNER, Stephen
    "Drinking Toward Sleep." [TexasR] (16:1/4) 95, p. 122.
    "Large Hands." [NewDeltaR] (12:2) Spr-Sum 95, p. 53.
    "The Litany of Foods Gone Bad." [CharR] (21:2) Fall 95, p. 87.
    "Pastoral in the Shadow of a City." [TexasR] (16:1/4) 95, p. 123.
2119. GAREY, Terry A.
    "Bank Jobs" (The 1994 Allen Ginsberg Poetry Awards: Honorable Mention).
    [Footwork] (24/25) 95, p. 195-196.
2120. GARMON, John
    "Conway." [MidwQ] (36:4) Sum 95, p. 369-370.
2121. GARREN, Christine
    "Vacation." [SouthwR] (80:2/3) Spr-Sum 95, p. 333.
    "Vestibule." [SouthwR] (80:2/3) Spr-Sum 95, p. 333.
2122. GARRETT, Nola
    "Game 5." [PoetL] (90:4) Wint 95-96, p. 7-8.
    "Game 10." [PoetL] (90:4) Wint 95-96, p. 9.
    "Names of Curtains" (after Donald Hall). [PoetL] (90:3) Fall 95, p. 56.
    "The Pastor's Wife Considers Pinball, Game 7." [Flyway] (1:1) Spr 95, p. 46.
    "The Pastor's Wife Considers Pinball, Game 9." [Flyway] (1:1) Spr 95, p. 48-50.
2123. GARRISON, David
    "Carolina Backroad, 1968." [NowestR] (33:1) 95, p. 45.
    "Dominion" (tr. of Pedro Salinas). [PoetryE] (39) Fall 94, p. 120.
    "Guidelines." [CutB] (42) Sum 94, p. 42.
    "Man with Brown Face and Monkey." [SouthernHR] (29:1) Wint 95, p. 73.
    "Matrix, 1952-53." [NowestR] (33:1) 95, p. 46-47.
    "More" (tr. of Pedro Salinas). [PoetryE] (39) Fall 94, p. 121.
2124. GARRISON, Deborah
    "Worked Late on a Tuesday Night." [NewYorker] (71:1) 20-27 F 95, p. 235.
2125. GARRISON, Peggy
    "To My Husband in Jail." [GlobalCR] (5) Spr 95, p. 114-116.
2126. GARRISON, Randall
    "Pretty Young Girl in the Charleston Market." [CapeR] (30:2) Fall 95, p. 24.
2127. GARRON, Jacqueline
    "Birthdays." [NewYorkQ] (54) 95, p. 81.
2128. GARSON, Robert (Robert J.)
    "Head Start." [InterPR] (21:2) Fall 95, p. 94.
    "Dilemma." [SpoonR] (20:2) Sum-Fall 95, p. 70.
    "The Drive." [SpoonR] (20:2) Sum-Fall 95, p. 71.

"Nine-Fingered Men." [SpoonR] (20:2) Sum-Fall 95, p. 72.
2129. GARTEN, Bill
"Frame 3000." [Crucible] (31) Fall 95, p. 15.
2130. GARTHE, Karen
"Rebecca's Vase." [NewAW] (13) Fall-Wint 95, p. 110-111.
"There's a Place All Minty." [NewAW] (13) Fall-Wint 95, p. 109.
2131. GARTON, Victoria
"Hope and Despair, the Couple." [Poem] (74) N 95, p. 54.
"Lost Dreams." [Poem] (74) N 95, p. 53.
2132. GARVEY, Pamela
"At Night." [SantaBR] (3:2) Sum 95, p. 109.
"Burning Giraffe" (a painting by Salvador Dali). [SantaBR] (3:2) Sum 95, p. 107.
"Jason." [SantaBR] (3:2) Sum 95, p. 109.
"Love Poem" (for John). [SantaBR] (3:2) Sum 95, p. 108.
2133. GARZA, San Juanita
"Speaking in Tongues." [NewAW] (13) Fall-Wint 95, p. 143-144.
2134. GASH, Sondra
"Dyeing Indigo." [US1] (30/31) 95, p. 23.
2135. GASKI, Harald
"The Sun My Father" (21 selections, tr. of Nils-Aslak Valkeapaa, w. Lars
    Nordstrom and Ralph Salisbury). [CharR] (21:1) Spr 95, p. 55-64.
2136. GASPAR, Frank (Frank X.)
"Kapital." [KenR] (17:2) Spr 95, p. 111-112.
"Let Him Be Only a Thought." [TampaR] (10) Spr 95, p. 28-29.
"Mass for the Grace of a Happy Death." [Pearl] (22) Fall-Wint 95, p. 46.
"Small Prayer for the World without Mercy on Us." [KenR] (17:2) Spr 95, p. 110-
    111.
"South." [Pearl] (22) Fall-Wint 95, p. 47.
"Whiskey." [KenR] (17:2) Spr 95, p. 109-110.
"A Witness Gives His Version." [TampaR] (10) Spr 95, p. 30-31.
2137. GASPARI, Walter
"Love's availability" (tr. by Cid Corman). [Noctiluca] (2:1, #4) Spr 95, p. 14.
"Recovered Poems" (Selections: 1-3, tr. by Cid Corman). [Noctiluca] (2:1, #4) Spr
    95, p. 17.
"We hear these brilliant vulgarities" (tr. by Cid Corman). [Noctiluca] (2:1, #4) Spr
    95, p. 15.
"We remain good friends" (tr. by Cid Corman). [Noctiluca] (2:1, #4) Spr 95, p. 16.
"We sit and watch the river" (tr. by Cid Corman). [Noctiluca] (2:1, #4) Spr 95, p. 14.
"What beauty will you show me" (tr. by Cid Corman). [Noctiluca] (2:1, #4) Spr 95,
    p. 15.
"What sorrowfulness" (tr. by Cid Corman). [Noctiluca] (2:1, #4) Spr 95, p. 16.
"Where are you now" (tr. by Cid Corman). [Noctiluca] (2:1, #4) Spr 95, p. 14.
2138. GASS, William H.
"Erection." [RiverS] (42/43) 95, p. 45.
"Single Sentence Poem #1." [RiverS] (42/43) 95, p. 45.
2139. GASTIGER, Joseph
"Doctor's Orders." [SpinningJ] (1) Fall 95-Wint 96, p. 44-45.
GAUNTLETT, Delores McAnuff
    See McANUFF-GAUNTLETT, Delores
2140. GAVIN, Larry M.
"Falling Star: Winter" (Literary Festival: Poetry: Honorable Mention). [EngJ] (84:4)
    Ap 95, p. 42.
2141. GAVIN, Tim
"On the Teaching of Prescriptive Grammar to a Young Inner City Boy." [BlackBR]
    (20) Spr-Sum 95, p. 36.
2142. GAVRONSKY, Serge
"Translations" (tr. of Michelle Grangaud). [TriQ] (94) Fall 95, p. 79-93.
2143. GAZOLLA, Ana Lúcia A.
"Solstice" (tr. of Leda Martins, w. Kevin John Keys). [Callaloo] (18:4) Fall 95, p.
    871.
2144. GEBHARDT, Susan
"French Rolled Hems." [NewOR] (21:3/4) Fall-Wint 95, p. 110.
"Movie Music." [NewOR] (21:3/4) Fall-Wint 95, p. 109.
2145. GEDDES, Gary
"An Eye for the Ladies" (from "Flying Blind." Honorable Mention, The Pablo
    Neruda Prize for Poetry). [Nimrod] (39:1) Fall-Wint 95, p. 33-34.

"Flying Blind" (from "Flying Blind." Honorable Mention, The Pablo Neruda Prize
for Poetry). [Nimrod] (39:1) Fall-Wint 95, p. 38-39.
"Luck of the Irish" (from "Flying Blind." Honorable Mention, The Pablo Neruda
Prize for Poetry). [Nimrod] (39:1) Fall-Wint 95, p. 35-37.
2146. GEIGER, Timothy
"1. Submerging" (for my father). [SantaBR] (3:2) Sum 95, p. 123.
"2. Neon Tetras." [SantaBR] (3:2) Sum 95, p. 124.
"3. The Other Side." [SantaBR] (3:2) Sum 95, p. 125.
"4. A Wedding." [SantaBR] (3:2) Sum 95, p. 126.
"5. Flight." [SantaBR] (3:2) Sum 95, p. 127.
"Another Atmosphere" (5 poems). [SantaBR] (3:2) Sum 95, p. 123-127.
"Building a New Home." [DefinedP] (1:2) Spr-Sum 93, p. 38-39.
"Debts and Balances." [QW] (40) Spr-Sum 95, p. 76.
"In the Light Factory." [GreensboroR] (59) Wint 95-96, p. 141.
"A Ritual." [SantaBR] (3:2) Sum 95, p. 128.
2147. GELDMANN, Mordechai
"Porno" (tr. by Karen Alkalay-Gut). [MichQR] (34:4) Fall 95, p. 676-677.
2148. GELETA, Greg
"Libertina Patre Natus." [Pearl] (22) Fall-Wint 95, p. 138.
"Plotting Between Movements of a Mozart Concerto" (for William J. Harris).
[AxeF] (3) 90, p. 19-20.
"Sleeping Hydra" (tr. of Silvina Ocampo). [SnailPR] (3:2) 95, p. 29.
"A Tiger Speaks" (tr. of Silvina Ocampo). [ArtfulD] (28/29) 95, p. 100-101.
"Where I Was Born." [AxeF] (3) 90, p. 20.
2149. GELMAN, Juan
"Truths" (tr. by Bond Snodgrass). [PlumR] (8) [95], p. 8-11.
"Truths" (tr. by Bond Snodgrass). [PlumR] (9) [95 or 96], p. 110-113.
2150. GEMIN, Pamela
"4th of July." [Prima] (18/19) 95, p. 124.
"18/38." [BellArk] (11:4) Jl-Ag 95, p. 10.
"Aurora, July Downhill." [BellArk] (11:5) S-O 95, p. 13.
"Bombshelter." [NewDeltaR] (13:1) Fall 95-Wint 96, p. 60-62.
"Enemy Mine." [SpoonR] (20:2) Sum-Fall 95, p. 85-86.
"Flashback, 1973." [SpoonR] (20:2) Sum-Fall 95, p. 83-84.
"Knots and Untyings." [BellArk] (11:4) Jl-Ag 95, p. 10.
"The Last Bad Habit." [Prima] (18/19) 95, p. 122-123.
"Reasons to Remain" (for Janet Norton). [BellArk] (11:5) S-O 95, p. 13.
"That Woman." [SpoonR] (20:2) Sum-Fall 95, p. 81-82.
2151. GENCARELLI, Lucia
"Running My Mouth." [Footwork] (24/25) 95, p. 60.
2152. GENEGA, Paul
"The Monk." [FreeL] (14) Wint 95, p. 30.
"Reconsidering the Cat" (For Helen Adam). [FreeL] (14) Wint 95, p. 31.
2153. GENOVESE, Barbara
"Gypsy Tide." [SantaBR] (3:3) Fall-Wint 95, p. 27.
2154. GENOWAYS, Ted
"Pietà." [MidwQ] (36:3) Spr 95, p. 297.
2155. GENT, Andrew
"Bad Dog." [PoetryE] (39) Fall 94, p. 41.
"The Box." [PoetryE] (39) Fall 94, p. 43.
"Not Writing Political Poems." [PoetryE] (39) Fall 94, p. 45.
"We Want Everything We Do." [PoetryE] (39) Fall 94, p. 46.
"What Inches Down." [PoetryE] (39) Fall 94, p. 44.
"Who Writes Poems." [PoetryE] (39) Fall 94, p. 42.
2156. GEORGE (Clean & Sober Streets, Washington, DC).
"Last Straw" (WritersCorps Program). [WashR] (21:2) Ag-S 95, p. 18.
2157. GEORGE, Diana Hume
"I Pushed Her and She Fell Down." [TriQ] (95) Wint 95-96, p. 153-155.
2158. GEORGE, Faye
"Only the Words." [Poetry] (166:3) Je 95, p. 163.
2159. GEORGES, Danielle Legros
"Another Ode to Salt." [CaribbeanW] (9) 95, p. 61.
2160. GEORGIA
"Dogscape." [Nimrod] (38:2) Spr-Sum 95, p. 23.
"Promenade in May." [Nimrod] (38:2) Spr-Sum 95, p. 26.
"Walking Home in Igloolik." [Nimrod] (38:2) Spr-Sum 95, p. 25.

2161. GERALD, Sharon
"Attendance." [MidAR] (16:1) 95, p. 71-73.
2162. GERANIS, Stelios
"Clothes of the Naked" (tr. by Dean Kostos). [Talisman] (15) Wint 95-96, p. 117.
2163. GERNER-MATHISEN, A. (Aina)
"Concertino" (tr. of Astrid Hjertenaes Andersen, w. Suzanne Bachner). [Nimrod]
(38:2) Spr-Sum 95, p. 80-81.
"Melancholia I, 1514" (tr. of Astrid Hjertenaes Andersen, w. S. Bachner). [TampaR]
(11) Fall 95, p. 56.
"Yellow Sky" (tr. of Astrid Hjertenaes Andersen, w. Suzanne Bachner). [Nimrod]
(38:2) Spr-Sum 95, p. 79.
2164. GERNES, Sonia
"The Bank." [HopewellR] (7) 95, p. 97.
"Traps." [HopewellR] (7) 95, p. 98.
2165. GERSTLER, Amy
"Crown of Weeds" (after John Ruskin). [ColR] (22:2) Fall 95, p. 139-140.
"The Underworld." [ColR] (22:2) Fall 95, p. 141.
GERVEN, Claudia van
See Van GERVEN, Claudia
2166. GERVITZ, Gloria
"Pythia: the Prophetess of Apollo at Delphi" (for Eduardo. Chapbook with an
introduction by Mark Schafer, tr. by Deborah Owen and Burton Raffel).
[LitR] (38:3) Spr 95, p. 383-416.
2167. GERY, John
"Giving Up the Ghost." [LouisL] (12:2) Fall 95, p. 82.
"Night Glimpse." [LouisL] (12:2) Fall 95, p. 83.
2168. GESSNER, Michael
"Lines on a Dog's Face." [OxfordM] (9:2) Fall-Wint 93, p. 52.
2169. GETTY, Sarah
"Channel 2: Horowitz Playing Mozart." [WestHR] (49:2) Sum 95, p. 171-172.
"Deer, 6:00 A.M." [WestHR] (49:2) Sum 95, p. 170-171.
2170. GHAZZAWI, Izzat
"The Songs." [InterQ] (2:1/2) 95, p. 156-157.
2171. GHIGNA, Charles
"Freudian Slips Hung Out to Dry." [Light] (15/16) Aut-Wint 95-96, p. 21.
"A Moving Sermon." [Light] (15/16) Aut-Wint 95-96, p. 31.
2172. GHIMOSOULIS, Kostis
"The Purpose of Sleep Perhaps" (tr. by Yannis Goumas). [Vis] (48) 95, p. 19.
2173. GHOLSON, Christien
"The Deal (Woodcuts Floating in a Pool of Burning Oil)." [HawaiiR] (19:2) Fall 95,
p. 44.
"End of the Loading Dock: Collage on Canvas Made with Garbage." [Parting] (8:2)
Wint 95-96, p. 44.
"The First Shall Be Last, the Last Shall Be First." [BellArk] (11:4) Jl-Ag 95, p. 11.
"I Discover My First Name: Water" (Looking out over Lake Michigan after reading
Antler's "The Discovery of Lake Michigan"). [BellArk] (11:1) Ja-F 95, p. 10-
11.
"Longing: Pen and Ink of a Figure in a Window." [BellArk] (11:4) Jl-Ag 95, p. 11.
"Nets Thrown into the Sea." [BellArk] (11:5) S-O 95, p. 8-9.
"Thinking of Iowa Summer Grass, Listening to the Oregon Rain Beat the Tent."
[Bogg] (67) 95, p. 46.
"The Veils of the Muslim Women as Tiles in a Fluid Mosque." [Parting] (8:2) Wint
95-96, p. 45.
"You Can Tell a Lot About People by the Way They Hand Out leaflets During Rush
Hour." [BellArk] (11:3) My-Je 95, p. 10.
2174. GHOSH, Rama
"Broken Boat" (tr. by Paramita Banerjee and Carolyne Wright). [PoetryE] (39) Fall
94, p. 108.
"I Go" (tr. by Paramita Banerjee and Carolyne Wright). [PoetryE] (39) Fall 94, p.
109.
"What Is There to Fear" (tr. by Paramita Banerjee and Carolyne Wright). [PoetryE]
(39) Fall 94, p. 110.
2175. GIANAKOPOULOS, Thomas
"Afterwards." [WormR] (35:4, #140) 95, p. 180.
"Barbara." [WormR] (35:4, #140) 95, p. 180-181.

2176. GIANNINI, David
"Care of the Soul (In Minnesota)." [SpiritSH] (60) 95, p. 5-6.

2177. GIBB, Robert
"After the Reunion." [PoetryE] (40) Spr 95, p. 39-40.
"Brain Coral." [PoetryE] (40) Spr 95, p. 33-34.
"Climbing the Slope." [MidAR] (16:1) 95, p. 55-56.
"Enough." [PoetryE] (40) Spr 95, p. 41-42.
"Flash Bulbs." [NewEngR] (17:1) Wint 95, p. 9.
"The Frog Pond." [Manoa] (7:2) Wint 95, p. 29-30.
"Horses." [PraS] (69:3) Fall 95, p. 81-82.
"In the Emergency Room." [PoetryE] (40) Spr 95, p. 35-36.
"Late Night Listening to The Band." [Manoa] (7:2) Wint 95, p. 31-32.
"Making the Lake." [Manoa] (7:2) Wint 95, p. 30-31.
"Mr. Qualters Teaches Drawing to the Students of Woodlawn Junior High School,
       1961." [WestB] (36) 95, p. 102-103.
"Salvation Army." [PoetryE] (40) Spr 95, p. 37-38.
"To the First Bees of Spring." [PraS] (69:3) Fall 95, p. 80-81.
"The Wind Devil." [SouthernR] (31:2) Ap/Spr 95, p. 268-269.
"Wood Work." [TarRP] (34:2) Spr 95, p. 8-9.

2178. GIBBONS, Reginald
"Homage to Longshot O'Leary" (Excerpt. For Tom McGrath). [ManyMM] [1:1] D
       94, p. 87-88.
"Summer Night." [PoetryE] (41) Aut 95, p. 70.
"White Beach" (for D.Y.). [SouthernR] (31:1) Wint 95, p. 11-14.

2179. GIBSON, Amy
"Cunnilingus." [OhioR] (53) 95, p. 145.
"Three Poems for My Cousin Rena." [OhioR] (53) 95, p. 143-144.

2180. GIBSON, Becky Gould
"Laying Out the Dead." [SouthernPR] (35:2) Wint 95, p. 23-24.
"A Woman's Shroud: Ocracoke, North Carolina, circa 1890." [Pembroke] (27) 95, p.
       95-98.

2181. GIBSON, Grace L.
"Not Coming Back." [Pembroke] (27) 95, p. 104.

2182. GIBSON, Margaret
"In the Retreat House of the Virgin Guadalupe." [Shen] (45:4) Wint 95, p. 26-29.
"Indian Graves." [CrabOR] (1:1) Fall-Wint 95, p. 75-76.
"The Sweet Grass Hills." [CrabOR] (1:1) Fall-Wint 95, p. 72-74.

2183. GIBSON, Morgan
"In Mind of Moths." [Noctiluca] (2:1, #4) Spr 95, p. 30.

2184. GIBSON, Shirley Mann
"Tantramar Poems" (14 poems. In Memory of John Thompson, 1938-1976).
       [AntigR] (102/103) Sum-Aug 95, p. 250-264.

2185. GIBSON, Stephen Robert
"Disappearing by the Cape Fear." [PoetryNW] (36:1) Spr 95, p. 11.
"The Erotic Dreams of the Poor." [PoetryNW] (36:2) Sum 95, p. 38.
"Lions" (for JKH). [Ledge] (18) Sum 95, p. 107-108.
"The Waiting." [PoetryNW] (36:1) Spr 95, p. 10-11.

2186. GIEG, Harry
"This Little Piggy" (Third Place, Jacaranda Poetry Contest). [Jacaranda] (11) [95 or
       96?], p. 22-23.

2187. GIELLA, Alfonso
"Books." [Footwork] (24/25) 95, p. 61.
"Dream House." [Footwork] (24/25) 95, p. 61.
"Point of View." [Footwork] (24/25) 95, p. 60.
"Portrait of Allen Ginsberg." [Footwork] (24/25) 95, p. 61.
"The Sea." [Footwork] (24/25) 95, p. 60.
"That Day." [Footwork] (24/25) 95, p. 61.
"That Old Cemetery." [Footwork] (24/25) 95, p. 61.

2188. GIGANTE, Denise
"The Bloomingdale House of Music." [OxfordM] (10:1) Wint 94-Spr 95, p. 26-27.
"The Bloomingdale House of Music." [PoetL] (90:3) Fall 95, p. 15-16.
"The Blue Surrounding Everything." [OxfordM] (10:1) Wint 94-Spr 95, p. 27-28.
"Cynthia Arriving with Five Suitcases." [PoetL] (90:3) Fall 95, p. 17.
"The Song of Linen Chrysanthemums." [ApalQ] (44/45) Fall 95-Wint 96, p. 56-57.

2189. GIGUERE, Roland
"Apparition." [Os] (41) 95, p. 28.

"Images Perdues." [Os] (41) 95, p. 27.
2190. GILBERT, Celia
"Translated." [NewYorker] (70:48) 6 F 95, p. 64.
2191. GILBERT, Cheryl
"What Great-Grandma Said." [HiramPoR] (58/59) Spr 95-Wint 96, p. 27.
2192. GILBERT, Christopher
"Pleasant Street: The Republic of Particulars." [MassR] (36:2) Sum 95, p. 203-204.
2193. GILBERT, Margaret
"Bell Jar." [SilverFR] (26) Wint 95, p. 41.
"Black Magic." [SilverFR] (26) Wint 95, p. 40.
"Cut." [SilverFR] (26) Wint 95, p. 44.
"Eating Oatmeal." [NewYorkQ] (54) 95, p. 80.
"Man in Black" (February 11, 1963). [SilverFR] (26) Wint 95, p. 42.
"Sylvia & Ted." [SilverFR] (26) Wint 95, p. 43.
"Thanksgiving Dinner." [PoetryE] (39) Fall 94, p. 47.
2194. GILBERT, Marie
"Morning Canvas." [Crucible] (31) Fall 95, p. 14.
2195. GILBERT, Sandra M.
"Doing Laundry." [SenR] (25:1) Spr 95, p. 22.
"Going to Connecticut" (for J.R.). [BelPoJ] (45:4) Chapbook 22, Sum 95, p. 24-25.
"The Mall." [BelPoJ] (45:4) Chapbook 22, Sum 95, p. 23.
"Thirty Years Later I Meet Your 17-Year-Old Daughter the Poet" (for R.I.S.).
[BelPoJ] (45:4) Chapbook 22, Sum 95, p. 21-22.
2196. GILDNER, Gary
"Collecting Cowpies." [PoetryNW] (36:2) Sum 95, p. 34-35.
"A Gift." [PoetryNW] (36:2) Sum 95, p. 33-34.
"In the Garden with Margaret." [NewL] (61:4) 95, p. 89.
2197. GILDROY, Doreen
"Myth and Mathematics." [AntR] (53:1) Wint 95, p. 60-61.
2198. GILGUN, John
"Great Yellow Hawk" (for Hans Bremer). [Elf] (5:1) Spr 95, p. 21.
"Horror in Ringold Alley." [JamesWR] (12:1) Wint 95, p. 12.
2199. GILL, Evalyn Pierpoint
"Martha" (For a friend who chose to end her life). [Crucible] (30) Fall 94, p. 40-41.
2200. GILL, James Vladimir
"Words Found above a Swinging Gate." [ProseP] (4) 95, p. 6.
2201. GILL, John
"6/16/94." [HangL] (66) 95, p. 24.
"Elegy." [HangL] (66) 95, p. 26-27.
"Little Sweets." [HangL] (66) 95, p. 25.
GILLAN, Maria Mazziotti
See MAZZIOTTI GILLAN, Maria
2202. GILLESPIE, Sandra
"Native Tongue." [Calyx] (16:1) Sum 95, p. 68.
"What We Call Love Is Seldom What We Fall Into." [Calyx] (16:1) Sum 95, p. 70-
71.
"Without Turning." [Calyx] (16:1) Sum 95, p. 69.
2203. GILLETT, Mary Jo Firth
"Chicken Tile." [SycamoreR] (7:1) Wint 95, p. 17.
2204. GILLIE, Paul
"Sounds Without Echoes." [HolCrit] (32:2) Ap 95, p. 20.
2205. GILLISPIE, Charles
"Ernie's Ladder." [AnotherCM] (29) Spr 95, p. 48.
2206. GILLMAN, Richard
"When Cows Stare Back." [SewanR] (103:2) Spr 95, p. 187-189.
2207. GILMORE, Harold
"One More Time." [SantaBR] (3:3) Fall-Wint 95, p. 77.
2208. GILONIS, Harry
"For Michael Finnissy." [WestCL] (29:2, #17) Fall 95, p. 39.
"A Poem for Colin, Judy and Southease." [WestCL] (29:2, #17) Fall 95, p. 38-39.
2209. GILSDORF, Ethan
"Grammar Lesson." [NewYorkQ] (54) 95, p. 65.
2210. GIMÉNEZ-ROSELLO, Carmen
"The Practicality of Hands." [Kalliope] (17:1) 95, p. 4.

2211. GINSBERG, Allen
"C'mon Pigs of Western Civilization, Eat More Grease." [LiteralL] (1:3) N-D 94, p. 7.
"Journal Dream." [ManyMM] (1:3) 95, p. 78-79.
"Now and Forever." [Nat] (258:16) 25 Ap 94, p. 572.
"Ode to Failure." [RiverS] (42/43) 95, p. 38.
"Peace in Bosnia-Herzegovina." [Nat] (258:14) 11 Ap 94, p. 498.
"Sakyamuni Coming Out from the Mountain" (Liang Kai, Southern Sung). [Tricycle] (5:1, #17) Fall 95, p. 71.
"Small Satori." [ManyMM] (1:3) 95, p. 80-81.

2212. GINZO, Mark, Jr.
"Possession." [SpiritSH] (60) 95, p. 16.
"Tio Roberto." [SpiritSH] (60) 95, p. 17.

2213. GIOIA, Dana
"Cleared Away." [Verse] (12:2) 95, p. 45.
"Long Distance." [Elf] (5:2) Sum 95, p. 38.
"On an Old Theme" (tr. of Nina Cassian). [Verse] (12:2) 95, p. 30.

2214. GIOSEFFI, Daniela
"On Top of the Empire State." [Footwork] (24/25) 95, p. 33-34.
"The Ruby Throated Hummingbirds Are Gone." [JINJPo] (17:1) Spr 95, p. 5.

2215. GIRAULT, Norton
"A Mother's Message to Her Son the Astronaut." [Light] (14) Sum 95, p. 11.

2216. GIRONDA, Belle
"Smoke burbles below the ladder." [13thMoon] (13:1/2) 95, p. 16.

2217. GISCOMBE, C. S.
"All (Facts, Stories, Chance)" (to Ken McClane). [RiverS] (41) 95, p. 6-10.
"Dayton, O. — the 50s & 60s." [SenR] (25:1) Spr 95, p. 91-95.

2218. GIZZI, Michael
"I ll Repose Never" [sic]. [Avec] (10) 95, p. 69.
"The Incumbents in Her Garden." [Avec] (10) 95, p. 73.
"Interferon" (For MG). [Avec] (10) 95, p. 70-71.
"The Rejected Perfume." [Avec] (10) 95, p. 72.
"The Seller of Still Lives." [Avec] (10) 95, p. 74.

2219. GIZZI, Peter
"Caption." [Sulfur] (15:1, #36) Spr 95, p. 160.
"Fear of Music." [Conjunc] (24) 95, p. 192-193.
"From a Field Glass." [Conjunc] (24) 95, p. 194.
"Knuckle Ball." [Phoebe] (24:2) 95, p. 20-21.
"Ledger Domain." [NewAW] (13) Fall-Wint 95, p. 57-60.
"Several Vistas." [Phoebe] (24:2) 95, p. 22.
"A Textbook of Chivalry" (11 selections). [Avec] (10) 95, p. 12-22.
"A World Entire." [ParisR] (37:134) Spr 95, p. 224-225.

2220. GJUZEL, Bogomil
"A Flight" (tr. by P. H. Liotta). [Vis] (48) 95, p. 31.
"Survival" (tr. by P. H. Liotta). [Vis] (48) 95, p. 30.
"Vita Nuova" (tr. by P. H. Liotta). [Vis] (48) 95, p. 31.

2221. GLAD, John
"While the Boys Are Sleeping" (tr. of Krassin Himmirsky, w. the author). [Vis] (48) 95, p. 9.

2222. GLADDING, Jody
"Eclipse." [ParisR] (37:134) Spr 95, p. 177.
"New Moon." [ParisR] (37:134) Spr 95, p. 177-178.
"Phase." [Epoch] (44:2) 95, p. 217.
"Raspberry." [Epoch] (44:2) 95, p. 216.
"Same Foot." [Epoch] (44:2) 95, p. 219.
"So." [Epoch] (44:2) 95, p. 218.
"Stitches." [GreenMR] (8:1) Spr-Sum 95, p. 98.

2223. GLADE, Jon Forrest
"True Love." [Bogg] (67) 95, p. 41.
"True Love (Bernie's Bar, 1975)." [Pearl] (22) Fall-Wint 95, p. 119.

2224. GLADHART, Amalia
"Detour." [SouthernPR] (35:1) Sum 95, p. 49-50.

2225. GLANCY, Diane
"1891, Claude Monet, 'Haystacks in the Snow' Coyote at the Metropolitan Museum, New York." [ManyMM] [1:1] D 94, p. 104.
"Boarding School for Indian Women." [SenR] (25:1) Spr 95, p. 108-110.

"Ghost Dance." [ManyMM] [1:1] D 94, p. 105.
"The Great American Bottom." [Field] (52) Spr 95, p. 78.
"The Laundress with the Yellowed Linens." [ManyMM] [1:1] D 94, p. 106.
"Monet's *Water Lilies*." [Field] (52) Spr 95, p. 79.
"Mostly It Was Arid Here Before the Windmill." [MidwQ] (36:4) Sum 95, p. 371-372.
"Swan's Life Span." [Footwork] (24/25) 95, p. 10.
2226. GLANCY, Gabrielle
    "An Exercise in Sadness." [NewYorker] (71:8) 17 Ap 95, p. 104.
2227. GLASER, Elton
    "Bedtime Legends Near Esplanade." [LouisL] (12:2) Fall 95, p. 75-76.
    "Bird Lady." [LaurelR] (29:1) Wint 95, p. 100-103.
    "Brain Damage in the Lunar Transitions." [PraS] (69:4) Wint 95, p. 93-94.
    "The Cove." [PraS] (69:4) Wint 95, p. 97-98.
    "Crab Festival in Henderson, Louisiana" (for Karen). [LouisL] (12:1) Spr 95, p. 49-50.
    "Early Love." [PraS] (69:4) Wint 95, p. 92.
    "Home for the Holidays." [SouthernR] (31:1) Wint 95, p. 15-17.
    "In Another Life" (For Gerald Stern). [Poetry] (166:1) Ap 95, p. 29-33.
    "Late Fifties on Front Street." [GettyR] (8:3) Sum 95, p. 539.
    "Oscillating Fan." [PoetryNW] (36:3) Aut 95, p. 22-23.
    "Prospecting on Abbey Island." [PraS] (69:4) Wint 95, p. 97.
    "Secrets." [PraS] (69:4) Wint 95, p. 95.
    "Smoking." [Shen] (45:4) Wint 95, p. 67.
    "Turning with the Animals." [PlumR] (9) [95 or 96], p. 48-49.
    "Under Glass in the Tropics of January." [LaurelR] (29:1) Wint 95, p. 99.
2228. GLASER, Michael S.
    "Fractals." [PoetL] (90:1) Spr 95, p. 40.
    "Translation." [PoetL] (90:4) Wint 95-96, p. 45-46.
2229. GLASS, Jesse
    "The Job." [LitR] (39:1) Fall 95, p. 40.
2230. GLASSER, Jane Ellen
    "Another Time." [PoetryNW] (36:4) Wint 95-96, p. 8.
    "Dog Days." [Light] (14) Sum 95, p. 8.
    "The Parrot-Ox." [HolCrit] (32:2) Ap 95, p. 16.
    "Six Ways to Hide." [PoetryNW] (36:4) Wint 95-96, p. 9.
2231. GLATT, Lisa
    "Maps." [Pearl] (22) Fall-Wint 95, p. 107-108.
2232. GLAZE, Andrew
    "Sword." [NewYorkQ] (55) 95, p. 54-55.
    "Thoreau Again." [NewYorkQ] (54) 95, p. 52.
2233. GLAZER, Michele
    "Tourist." [Field] (53) Fall 95, p. 88-89.
2234. GLAZIER, Loss Pequeño
    "The Essay." [Talisman] (15) Wint 95-96, p. 97.
2235. GLAZNER, Greg
    "Two Worlds." [QW] (41) Aut-Wint 95-96, p. 176-177.
2236. GLEASON, Kate
    "After a Painting by Wolfe Kahn." [GreenMR] (8:2) Fall-Wint 95-96, p. 55.
    "After Fighting for Hours." [GreenMR] (8:2) Fall-Wint 95-96, p. 56.
2237. GLENN, Laura
    "Early Darkness." [Boulevard] (10:1/2, #28/29) Spr 95, p. 211.
    "The Gift-Wrapped Present." [Ascent] (19:2) Wint 95, p. 58.
    "No Place for This Lifetime." [Ascent] (19:2) Wint 95, p. 59.
2238. GLICKMAN, Susan
    "Fish Are Jumping, and the Cotton Is High." [MalR] (112) Fall 95, p. 24.
    "You're Gonna Spread Your Wings, and Take to the Sky." [MalR] (112) Fall 95, p. 25.
2239. GLISSANT, Édouard
    "A Field of Islands" (Excerpts, tr. by Jefferson Humphries). [InterQ] (2:1/2) 95, p. 38-39.
    "Verses" (1-10. Excerpted from *La terre inquiete*, tr. by Jefferson Humphries). [NewOR] (21:2) Sum 95, p. 79-81.
2240. GLOEGGLER, Tony
    "Down's Syndrome." [Ledge] (18) Sum 95, p. 111.

2241. GLÜCK, Louise
"Circe's Grief." [Ploughs] (21:4) Wint 95-96, p. 58.
"Circe's Power." [NewYorker] (71:7) 10 Ap 95, p. 90.
"Ithaca." [NewYorker] (71:19) 10 Jl 95, p. 52.
"Penelope's Stubbornness." [Ploughs] (21:4) Wint 95-96, p. 59.
2242. GNUP-KRUIP, Valentina
"Definitions of Grace" (Winner, 1995 Allen Tate Memorial Competition). [Wind]
(76) Fall 95, p. 27.
2243. GOBA, Ronald J.
"Knocks." [DefinedP] (1:2) Spr-Sum 93, p. 12.
"Pregnant Pause." [DefinedP] (1:2) Spr-Sum 93, p. 13.
2244. GODFREY, Shahara
"Hot Comb." [SinW] (56) Sum-Fall 95, p. 66-67.
2245. GOEDICKE, Patricia
"Before Dawn." [BelPoJ] (45:4) Chapbook 22, Sum 95, p. 26-28.
"Birds Like Basketball Players." [PoetL] (90:2) Sum 95, p. 57-58.
"Chase Scene, Many Levels." [ManhatR] (8:1) Fall 95, p. 28-30.
"From the Cliffs." [ManhatR] (8:1) Fall 95, p. 42-44.
"The Gestures of Feeling." [ManhatR] (8:1) Fall 95, p. 25-27.
"Hero." [Hudson] (47:4) Wint 95, p. 599-601.
"Ideas." [CutB] (44) Sum 95, p. 42-43.
"In Bear Country." [BelPoJ] (45:4) Chapbook 22, Sum 95, p. 32-33.
"In the Skull's Tingling Auditorium." [ManhatR] (8:1) Fall 95, p. 31-34.
"In These Burning Stables." [BelPoJ] (45:4) Chapbook 22, Sum 95, p. 34-35.
"The Jelly Between the Ears." [BelPoJ] (45:4) Chapbook 22, Sum 95, p. 29-31.
"Lifeline." [ManhatR] (8:1) Fall 95, p. 35-38.
"O'Keeffe's Doorway." [LaurelR] (29:1) Wint 95, p. 72-73.
"Submarine." [SenR] (25:1) Spr 95, p. 23-24.
"Ten Billion Blackbirds." [BelPoJ] (45:4) Chapbook 22, Sum 95, p. 36-37.
"Treehouse." [PoetryNW] (36:4) Wint 95-96, p. 26-30.
"Under Cygnus." [ManhatR] (8:1) Fall 95, p. 39-41.
"The Word Float." [ManhatR] (8:1) Fall 95, p. 21-24.
2246. GOERNER, Leslie
"Grace." [BellArk] (11:6) N-D 95, p. 31.
"Lesson in Perspective." [BellArk] (11:6) N-D 95, p. 9.
"Memorial." [BellArk] (11:1) Ja-F 95, p. 27.
2247. GOETHE, Johann Wolfgang von
"Nocturne" (tr. by Keith Waldrop). [DefinedP] (2:1) Fall-Wint 93, p. 7.
2248. GOETSCH, Douglas
"Dark Morning." [Nimrod] (39:1) Fall-Wint 95, p. 108.
"Lawyer." [HangL] (67) 95, p. 39.
"November." [HangL] (67) 95, p. 38-39.
"Sleeping Next to My Grandfather." [HangL] (67) 95, p. 37.
2249. GOETT, Lise
"Lingerie." [WestHR] (49:2) Sum 95, p. 123-124.
"Medicine" (Finalist, 1995 Greg Grummer Award in Poetry). [Phoebe] (24:2) 95, p.
150.
"Threnody." [WestHR] (49:2) Sum 95, p. 126.
"White Nights." [WestHR] (49:2) Sum 95, p. 124-125.
2250. GOETZ, Melody
"Red Cross Poems" (6 poems). [AntigR] (101) Spr 95, p. 25-30.
2251. GOFF, Cindy
"I Feel Unattractive During Mating Season." [LullwaterR] (5:1) 93-94, p. 16.
"Staying Up Too Late for Sir." [LullwaterR] (5:1) 93-94, p. 17.
2252. GOFF, Madeline
"The Jewelry Maker." [Vis] (49) 95, p. 13.
2253. GOGGSHALL, G. E.
"His Hands Are Clean." [SmPd] (32:3, #95) Fall 95, p. 34.
2254. GOGOL, John M.
"Alpha" (tr. of Tadeusz Rösewicz). [NorthStoneR] (12) 95, p. 56.
"Knowledge" (tr. of Tadeusz Rösewicz). [NorthStoneR] (12) 95, p. 57.
2255. GOING, Jo
"Otter Woman." [Nimrod] (38:2) Spr-Sum 95, p. 11.
"Sacred Bones." [Nimrod] (38:2) Spr-Sum 95, p. 12.
"Saying Goodbye." [Nimrod] (38:2) Spr-Sum 95, p. 13.

2256. GÖKNAR, Erdag
"An Anatolian Phoenix." [InterQ] (2:1/2) 95, p. 88.
"Fragment: Crossing the Desert of Lop." [InterQ] (2:1/2) 95, p. 87.
"Second Generation in America." [InterQ] (2:1/2) 95, p. 86.
2257. GOLDBARTH, Albert
"Across Town." [PoetryE] (39) Fall 94, p. 49.
"Ancient Semitic Rituals for the Dead." [Boulevard] (10:3, #30) Fall 95, p. 15-27.
"As One." [Boulevard] (10:1/2, #28/29) Spr 95, p. 52-53.
"Background." [ChiR] (41:4) 95, p. 77-79.
"Bright Motes in the Corner of Your Eye." [PoetL] (90:2) Sum 95, p. 45.
"The Canary." [QW] (41) Aut-Wint 95-96, p. 156-157.
"Cognitive/Semantic." [OhioR] (54) 95, p. 77-86.
"Coinages: A Fairy Tale." [MidAR] (15:1/2) 95, p. 216-218.
"Comparative." [PoetryE] (39) Fall 94, p. 48.
"The Compasses." [GettyR] (8:1) Wint 95, p. 126-127.
"The Compasses." [Harp] (290:1739) Ap 95, p. 29.
"Complete with Starry Night and Bourbon Shots." [QW] (41) Aut-Wint 95-96, p. 151-153.
"Creatures of the Abyss." [BelPoJ] (45:4) Chapbook 22, Sum 95, p. 38-39.
"DNA." [PraS] (69:1) Spr 95, p. 77-80.
"Exorcism." [PoetL] (90:2) Sum 95, p. 46.
"An Explanation." [CreamCR] (19:1) Spr 95, p. 148-149.
"Flower." [Boulevard] (10:1/2, #28/29) Spr 95, p. 48-49.
"Giotto: Saint Francis Preaching to the Birds: About 1300." [SenR] (25:1) Spr 95, p. 77-78.
"The Girl Who Married a Wooden Pounder." [BelPoJ] (46:2) Wint 95-96, p. 14-15.
"The Gods of Info-Flow, and the Delivery of the Same." [ColR] (22:2) Fall 95, p. 127-133.
"Great Topics of the World." [GeoR] (49:3) Fall 95, p. 607-608.
"Hail." [QW] (41) Aut-Wint 95-96, p. 154-155.
"Heart on a Chain." [BelPoJ] (45:4) Chapbook 22, Sum 95, p. 40-44.
"Let's Visit a Toy Factory!" [SycamoreR] (7:1) Wint 95, p. 20.
"The Messenger." [PoetryNW] (36:3) Aut 95, p. 42-43.
"The Neighborhood, 1956" (for David Clewell). [WillowS] (35) Ja 95, p. 45.
"News from Home." [Agni] (42) 95, p. 13-14.
"The Nitrogen Cycle." [WestHR] (49:1) Spr 95, p. 52-53.
"Notes from the Desktop." [GettyR] (8:1) Wint 95, p. 124-125.
"The Other Way." [BelPoJ] (46:2) Wint 95-96, p. 16-17.
"Parallel." [Shen] (45:1) Spr 95, p. 47-48.
"Poem Beginning with Three Lines by Dr. Seuss." [Light] (13) Spr 95, p. 11.
"Preparation." [WillowS] (35) Ja 95, p. 44.
"Private Life." [IndR] (18:1) Spr 95, p. 84-85.
"The Red Shift." [PoetL] (90:2) Sum 95, p. 47.
"Remains Song." [WestHR] (49:1) Spr 95, p. 56-57.
"Repairwork." [CreamCR] (19:1) Spr 95, p. 150-151.
"Roses and Skulls." [OntR] (42) Spr-Sum 95, p. 51-52.
"San Antonio, TX: The 'Happy Jazz Band' versus Versus." [CreamCR] (19:1) Spr 95, p. 152-153.
"A Short Trip Full of Small Shame, Through the Place of the Blurring of Tenses." [IllinoisR] (2:2) Spr 95, p. 7-9.
"So much like a Renaissance figure of Death." [PoetL] (90:2) Sum 95, p. 44.
"A Solid Is Not Solid." [Boulevard] (10:1/2, #28/29) Spr 95, p. 50-51.
"Square eggs." [Light] (15/16) Aut-Wint 95-96, p. 29.
"Stop Me If You've Heard This One." [LaurelR] (29:1) Wint 95, p. 59-70.
"This Needle's Tip." [WestHR] (49:1) Spr 95, p. 54-55.
"This Space I Want to Consider Now." [QW] (41) Aut-Wint 95-96, p. 158.
"Thread Through History." [Poetry] (166:2) My 95, p. 90-91.
"Try As He Might, His Poem Reenacts the Play of Someone Who's Seven." [CreamCR] (19:1) Spr 95, p. 146-147.
"Two Cents." [ParisR] (37:136) Fall 95, p. 158-159.
"Units." [PoetryNW] (36:1) Spr 95, p. 19-21.
"Unthinkable." [DenQ] (29:3) Wint 95, p. 15-16.
"Us / Claudia / Talleyrand." [YaleR] (83:2) Ap 95, p. 96-97.
"Waiting." [IndR] (18:1) Spr 95, p. 83.
"What the Diva Told Me." [PraS] (69:1) Spr 95, p. 76.

"A Wooden Eye. An 1884 Silver Dollar. A Homemade Explosive. A Set of False
Teeth. And a 14-Karat Gold Ashtray." [Poetry] (166:2) My 95, p. 91-93.
"A Yield." [NewEngR] (17:4) Fall 95, p. 70-71.
2258. GOLDBERG, Beckian Fritz
"Amazon." [Field] (52) Spr 95, p. 13.
"Annunciation." [Jacaranda] (11) [95 or 96?], p. 116-117.
"The Book of Hens." [PoetryE] (41) Aut 95, p. 98.
"The First House Is Burning." [Field] (52) Spr 95, p. 14-16.
"Flowering Adam." [Field] (52) Spr 95, p. 17-18.
"I Have Lived Here All My Life." [Field] (52) Spr 95, p. 12.
"In the Badlands of Desire." [Jacaranda] (11) [95 or 96?], p. 117-118.
"Lucifer's Crown." [BlackWR] (21:2) Spr-Sum 95, p. 107-110.
"To a Girl Writing Her Father's Death." [Jacaranda] (11) [95 or 96?], p. 114-115.
"The Tongue of the Sphinx" (for Rick Noguchi). [PoetryE] (41) Aut 95, p. 99-100.
2259. GOLDEN, Renny
"Accompaniment." [InterQ] (2:1/2) 95, p. 19.
2260. GOLDENSOHN, Barry
"Thelonius Monk Dancing." [HarvardR] (8) Spr 95, p. 27.
2261. GOLDENSOHN, Lorrie
"Clearwater." [Salm] (106/107) Spr-Sum 95, p. 122-124.
"Night Window." [AntR] (53:1) Wint 95, p. 59.
"Timor Mortis." [Poetry] (167:3) D 95, p. 141-142.
2262. GOLDING, Mary
"Convertible." [PoetL] (90:2) Sum 95, p. 18.
2263. GOLDMAN, Diana Lee
"Madonna de Luna." [SoDakR] (33:2) Sum 95, p. 55.
2264. GOLDSWORTHY, Peter
"A Statistician to His Love." [Verse] (12:2) 95, p. 46.
2265. GOLUB, Deborah
"Pas de Deux." [MassR] (36:2) Sum 95, p. 248.
2266. GOLVIN, Sandra
"Witnessing" (For Michael C.). [SpoonR] (20:2) Sum-Fall 95, p. 64-66.
2267. GOMEZ, Magdalena
"La Terraza." [MassR] (36:4) Wint 95-96, p. 614-615.
2268. GOMEZ, Sonia
"Child Bride." [ManyMM] (2:1) 95, p. 102-103.
"Directions for Crab." [ManyMM] (2:1) 95, p. 100-101.
2269. GOMPERT, Chris
"Bluefish (Pomatomus saltatrix)." [BellArk] (11:4) Jl-Ag 95, p. 12.
"A Crew of One" (for Cecil Newcomb). [BellArk] (11:6) N-D 95, p. 11.
"From Beyond the Treeline." [BellArk] (11:5) S-O 95, p. 16.
"La Gente (The People)." [PoetL] (90:1) Spr 95, p. 47.
"Lilac Manifesto." [BellArk] (11:4) Jl-Ag 95, p. 14.
2270. GONÇALVES, Egito
"Adam and Eve" (tr. by Alexis Levitin). [InterPR] (21:1) Spr 95, p. 41.
"Adão e Eva." [InterPR] (21:1) Spr 95, p. 40.
"The Angel of the Clock / Chartres" (tr. by Alexis Levitin). [SilverFR] (25) Sum 95,
p. 42.
"Elisabeta" (tr. by Alexis Levitin). [SilverFR] (25) Sum 95, p. 45.
"La Havana" (tr. by Alexis Levitin). [SilverFR] (25) Sum 95, p. 43.
"Number 7 from Dedikation" (tr. by Alexis Levitin). [PoetryE] (39) Fall 94, p. 106.
"Number 10 from Dedikation" (tr. by Alexis Levitin). [PoetryE] (39) Fall 94, p. 107.
"La Picolla Madona" (tr. by Alexis Levitin). [SilverFR] (25) Sum 95, p. 44.
"The Power of Literature" (tr. by Alexis Levitin). [HarvardR] (9) Fall 95, p. 29.
"Untitled: A woman's face" (tr. by Alexis Levitin). [SilverFR] (25) Sum 95, p. 41.
2271. GONTAREK, Leonard
"Into March." [PoetryNW] (36:1) Spr 95, p. 41.
2272. GONZALEZ, Ray
"The Cost of Family." [MassR] (36:4) Wint 95-96, p. 617.
"Ése." [MassR] (36:4) Wint 95-96, p. 616-617.
"Explain." [KenR] (17:3/4) Sum-Fall 95, p. 177-178.
"The Heat of Arrivals." [KenR] (17:3/4) Sum-Fall 95, p. 176.
"How?" [KenR] (17:3/4) Sum-Fall 95, p. 175.
"These Days." [MassR] (36:4) Wint 95-96, p. 617-618.

181

GORHAM

2273. GONZALEZ, Rigoberto
  "Breakfast Ruined for Our Village" (Winner — 1994 Borderlands Poetry Contest).
    [Border] (6) Spr-Sum 95, p. 12-13.
  "Marías, Old Indian Mothers" (Winner — 1994 Borderlands Poetry Contest).
    [Border] (6) Spr-Sum 95, p. 6-7.
  "Penny Men" (for Emiliano, who came to live, and die, picking grapes. Winner —
    1994 Borderlands Poetry Contest). [Border] (6) Spr-Sum 95, p. 8-9.
  "Perla at the Mexican Border Assembly Line of Dolls" (Winner — 1994
    Borderlands Poetry Contest). [Border] (6) Spr-Sum 95, p. 2-3.
  "La Ruina del Almuerzo del Pueblo" (Winner — 1994 Borderlands Poetry Contest).
    [Border] (6) Spr-Sum 95, p. 10-11.
  "You and the Tijuana Mule" (Winner — 1994 Borderlands Poetry Contest).
    [Border] (6) Spr-Sum 95, p. 4-5.
2274. GOOBIE, Beth
  "The Ritual of Remembering" (Third Place, 1995 Poetry Contest). [PraF] (16:4,
    #73) Wint 95-96, p. 85-87.
2275. GOOD, David R. C.
  "Augury." [QW] (41) Aut-Wint 95-96, p. 194.
2276. GOOD, George
  "Change of Life." [Comm] (122:15) 8 S 95, p. 15.
2277. GOOD, Regan Maud
  "Rose Garden." [AntR] (53:1) Wint 95, p. 68-69.
2278. GOODLAND, Giles
  "The Sand." [CumbPR] (14:2) Spr 95, p. 45-46.
2279. GOODMAN, Brent
  "Casino." [Flyway] (1:2) Fall 95, p. 44.
  "Gravity: A Triptych." [Flyway] (1:2) Fall 95, p. 45.
2280. GOODMAN, Diane
  "Jewel's Hair." [AfAmRev] (29:1) Spr 95, p. 90-91.
  "The Way Jewel Prays." [AfAmRev] (29:1) Spr 95, p. 90.
2281. GOODMAN, Henrietta
  "Jakarta." [CutB] (43) Wint 95, p. 78.
  "Spring." [CutB] (43) Wint 95, p. 76-77.
2282. GOODMAN, Joanna
  "A Country Without Memory" (tr. of Assia Djebar). [SenR] (25:2) Fall 95, p. 59.
  "I Slit the Neck of the Rooster" (tr. of Assia Djebar). [SenR] (25:2) Fall 95, p. 60.
  "Watermark." [Sonora] (29) Spr 95, p. 53.
2283. GOODMAN, Loren
  "Remembering Werner Heisenberg." [SouthernPR] (35:2) Wint 95, p. 7-8.
2284. GOODMAN, Maria
  "Fishermen at Night." [PaintedB] (55/56) 95, p. 86.
  "Icicle Tempting the Children." [OxfordM] (10:1) Wint 94-Spr 95, p. 29.
  "If Fog." [PaintedB] (55/56) 95, p. 85.
2285. GOODMAN, Miriam
  "A Zigzag Course." [Footwork] (24/25) 95, p. 27.
2286. GOODRICH, Patricia
  "Defining the Dark." [Footwork] (24/25) 95, p. 180.
2287. GOODTIMES, Art
  "Ninth Inning." [Sun] (230) F 95, p. 35.
2288. GOODWIN, Rufus
  "Night Talk" (Selections: II-III). [Noctiluca] (2:1, #4) Spr 95, p. 22.
2289. GOOSENS, Ken
  "Memory." [Vis] (49) 95, p. 26.
2290. GORDON, Charlotte
  "Paradise Is the Release from the Worlds of Birth and Death" (— The Tibetan Book
    of the Dead). [Sun] (229) Ja 95, p. 37.
2291. GORDON, Kirpal
  "Putting in a Few Appearances." [HeavenB] (12) 95, p. 3.
2292. GORDON, Myles
  "Silence." [Parting] (8:2) Wint 95-96, p. 40.
2293. GORGAS, Carolle
  "Letter from the Farm." [AnthNEW] (7) 95, p. 18.
2294. GORHAM, Sarah
  "Man Drinking a Cup of Coffee." [KenR] (17:1) Wint 95, p. 26.
  "My Daughter Defaces the Life of Emily Dickinson." [KenR] (17:1) Wint 95, p. 25.
  "Poem Ending in Denial." [PoetryNW] (36:4) Wint 95-96, p. 43-45.

182

GORRICK

2295. GORRICK, Anne
"Additional Instances of Ground." [HeavenB] (12) 95, p. 56-57.
2296. GOTT, George
"To Cilene." [OxfordM] (10:1) Wint 94-Spr 95, p. 30.
2297. GOTTESMAN, Carl A.
"Don't Speak." [PoetryE] (40) Spr 95, p. 43-44.
2298. GOTTLIEB, Andres
"The Bus Stop" (tr. by Stanley H. Barkan). [Footwork] (24/25) 95, p. 210.
"Latin America, I'm Leaving You" (tr. by Stanley H. Barkan). [Footwork] (24/25) 95, p. 210.
"Manifesto" (tr. by Renato Cavour and Stanley H. Barkan). [Footwork] (24/25) 95, p. 210.
2299. GOTTLIEB, Arthur (Arthur G.)
"Houdini." [Ledge] (18) Sum 95, p. 29-30.
"Insubstantial People." [Northeast] (5:12) Sum 95, p. 25.
"Jesus in Jerusalem." [SmPd] (32:2, #94) Spr 95, p. 27.
"The Lost." [Ledge] (18) Sum 95, p. 27-28.
"Marriages Made in Heaven." [Crucible] (30) Fall 94, p. 21-22.
"Scarecrow." [WritersF] (21) 95, p. 29.
"The Sentry." [ChironR] (42) Spr 95, p. 14.
"The Way We Won the War." [ChironR] (43) Sum 95, p. 32.
2300. GOUDE, Gary
"Hello." [NewYorkQ] (54) 95, p. 93.
2301. GOULD, Janice
"Late Summer in the Sierra." [WeberS] (12:3) Fall 95, p. 64-65.
"Your Least Good Lover." [WeberS] (12:3) Fall 95, p. 65-66.
2302. GOULD, Kathleen
"Nomad's Song." [EngJ] (84:8) D 95, p. 51.
2303. GOULD, Owen
"Coyote and White-Tail Deer." [WeberS] (12:3) Fall 95, p. 88-89.
2304. GOULD, Roberta
"Larger." [Blueline] (16) 95, p. 85.
2305. GOUMAS, Yannis
"Death Cannot Be Photographed" (tr. of Maria Lagoureli). [Vis] (48) 95, p. 21.
"Don't Shoot the Piano Player" (tr. of Maria Lagoureli). [Vis] (48) 95, p. 20.
"The Dresser" (tr. of Maria Lagoureli). [Vis] (48) 95, p. 21.
"A Few Years Hence" (tr. of Alexandra Plastira). [Vis] (48) 95, p. 22.
"The Purpose of Sleep Perhaps" (tr. of Kostis Ghimosoulis). [Vis] (48) 95, p. 19.
"Recovery" (tr. of Alexandra Plastira). [Vis] (48) 95, p. 22.
2306. GOYETTE, Susan
"Guilt." [Arc] (34) Spr 95, p. 21.
"I Know Women." [Arc] (34) Spr 95, p. 19.
"Sisters." [Arc] (34) Spr 95, p. 18.
2307. GRABELLE, Samantha
"Winter." [DefinedP] (1:1) Fall-Wint 92, p. 30-31.
2308. GRABILL, James (Jim)
"In the Sanctuary of Forgetting." [SilverFR] (26) Wint 95, p. 21.
"Some of These Things." [SilverFR] (26) Wint 95, p. 20.
"Some Transmutation of Desire: A Momentum." [PoetryE] (39) Fall 94, p. 50-51.
"Some Transmutation of Desire: The Bridge Asks." [PoetryE] (39) Fall 94, p. 52.
2309. GRACE, D. G.
"Auto-Da-Fé." [Border] (7) Fall-Wint 96, p. 12.
2310. GRACE, Maggie Ann
"Holding Form." [Calyx] (16:2) Wint 95-96, p. 68-69.
2311. GRACE, Susan Andrews
"Ferry Woman Sleep" (Excerpt from *The Ferry Woman's History of the World,* 3rd v., chapter 3: Discovery). [Grain] (22:4) Spr 95, p. 76.
"Gilliosa Understands Romantic Love, at Last" (Excerpt from *The Ferry Woman's History of the World,* 3rd v., chapter 3: Discovery). [Grain] (22:4) Spr 95, p. 75.
"Her First Sacrament" (Excerpt from *The Ferry Woman's History of the World,* 3rd v., chapter 3: Discovery). [Grain] (22:4) Spr 95, p. 74.
2312. GRAF, Ted
"The Truth about Texas." [NewDeltaR] (12:2) Spr-Sum 95, p. 12-13.
2313. GRAHAM, Adelle
"Gold-Vermillion Fruits." [CutB] (42) Sum 94, p. 43-44.

2314. GRAHAM, David
"First Babies of the Universe." [TampaR] (11) Fall 95, p. 59.
"Long Overdue Note to My College Professor Who Broke Down and Cried One Morning in 1974 While Teaching Yeats." [SycamoreR] (7:2) Sum 95, p. 25-26.
"Observing Pi." [TampaR] (11) Fall 95, p. 26-27.
"Ode to a Supermarket" (for Eric Nelson). [SycamoreR] (7:2) Sum 95, p. 23-24.
2315. GRAHAM, Jorie
"The End of Progress" (Eurydice to Orpheus). [AmerPoR] (24:6) N-D 95, p. 30-31.
"The Errancy." [Ploughs] (21:4) Wint 95-96, p. 60-62.
"The Hurrying-Home." [AmerPoR] (24:6) N-D 95, p. 29.
"Little Requiem." [ParisR] (37:137) Wint 95, p. 141-143.
"Motive Elusive." [AmerPoR] (24:6) N-D 95, p. 31-32.
"Oblivion." [AmerPoR] (24:6) N-D 95, p. 28-29.
"Of the Ever-Changing Agitation in the Air." [NewYorker] (71:36) 13 N 95, p. 88.
"Recovered from the Storm." [AmerPoR] (24:6) N-D 95, p. 32.
"Red Umbrella." [AmerPoR] (24:6) N-D 95, p. 30.
"The Scanning." [AmerPoR] (24:6) N-D 95, p. 33-34.
"Sea-Blue Aubade." [NewRep] (212:26) 26 Je 95, p. 36.
"Spelled from the Shadows." [AmerPoR] (24:6) N-D 95, p. 28.
"The Strangers." [YaleR] (83:2) Ap 95, p. 31-32.
"Studies in Secrecy." [AmerPoR] (24:6) N-D 95, p. 31.
"Submitting." [YaleR] (83:2) Ap 95, p. 33-34.
"Untitled One." [AmerPoR] (24:6) N-D 95, p. 27-28.
2316. GRAHAM, Taylor
"Finding Water." [Border] (6) Spr-Sum 95, p. 38.
"Three and the Goldbug Mine." [OxfordM] (10:1) Wint 94-Spr 95, p. 31.
2317. GRAHAM, Vicki
"Tracks." [WillowS] (35) Ja 95, p. 24.
2318. GRAHN, Judy
"Descent to the Butch of the Realm." [Zyzzyva] (11:3/4, #43/44) 95, "The Best of Ten Years of ZYZZYVA," p. 35-41.
2319. GRANGAUD, Michelle
"Translations" (tr. by Serge Gavronsky). [TriQ] (94) Fall 95, p. 79-93.
2320. GRANGER, Gary
"Low Tide at Laguna." [Pearl] (22) Fall-Wint 95, p. 97.
2321. GRANT, Victoria Mary
"Landscaping." [ChrC] (112:4) 1-8 F 95, p. 102.
2322. GRAPES, Jack
"Here's a Poem." [BellR] (18:1, #37) Spr 95, p. 43.
"Suspect." [BellR] (18:1, #37) Spr 95, p. 42.
2323. GRASK, Julie Sandblom
"How to Go to Europe." [NewL] (62:1) 96 (c1995), p. 78-79.
2324. GRAVER, Elizabeth
"I Tell Myself." [Boulevard] (10:3, #30) Fall 95, p. 166-167.
2325. GRAVES, Michael
"You Reached Within." [HolCrit] (32:4) O 95, p. 20.
2326. GRAVES, Robert
"The Face in the Mirror" (January 12, 1957). [NewYorker] (71:26) 4 S 95, p. 80.
"The Lost Jewel" (December 25, 1954). [NewYorker] (71:26) 4 S 95, p. 74.
"My Name and I" (January 6, 1951). [NewYorker] (71:26) 4 S 95, p. 79.
2327. GRAY, Alison T.
"The Launching." [LouisL] (12:1) Spr 95, p. 6-7.
"Notre Dame" (winner, 9th annual Prize for Poetry). [LouisL] (12:1) Spr 95, p. 1-3.
"Within Nichols Canyon Road." [LouisL] (12:1) Spr 95, p. 4-5.
2328. GRAY, Andrew
"Leningrad." [MalR] (112) Fall 95, p. 40-42.
2329. GRAY, Elizabeth T., Jr.
"Ghazal 18" (For Eleanor Mitten. From the Díwán, tr. of Khwajah Shams Uddin Muhammad Háfiz-i Shirazi). [HarvardR] (8) Spr 95, p. 82.
"Ghazal 35" (From the Díwán, tr. of Khwajah Shams Uddin Muhammad Háfiz-i Shirazi). [HarvardR] (8) Spr 95, p. 82.
2330. GRAY, Jeffrey
"Among the Amak." [AmerPoR] (24:4) Jl-Ag 95, p. 17.
"Ancient Love." [AmerPoR] (24:4) Jl-Ag 95, p. 17.
"A Tunisian Story." [AmerPoR] (24:4) Jl-Ag 95, p. 17.

2331. GRAY, Kendra (grade 6, Shepherd Elementary, Washington, DC)
"Only to Know" (Poetry on the Metro Project). [WashR] (21:2) Ag-S 95, p. 14.
2332. GRAY, Pamela
"Christina." [Kalliope] (17:2) 95, p. 19-20.
2333. GRAY, Pat
"Sex and Breakfast" (1995 Poetry Competition: Honorable Mention). [Elf] (5:2)
Sum 95, p. 19.
2334. GRAY, Patrick Worth
"Climbing." [MidwQ] (36:4) Sum 95, p. 373-374.
2335. GRAY, Robert
"One Father's Summer." [JamesWR] (12:1) Wint 95, p. 13.
2336. GREAVES, Nicole
"Girl in a Darkroom" (Honorable Mention, Jacaranda Poetry Contest). [Jacaranda]
(11) [95 or 96?], p. 40.
2337. GREEN, Andrew
"Starlings." [NewEngR] (17:1) Wint 95, p. 124.
2338. GREEN, Benjamin
"The Beauty of Mountain and Water: Fishing" (after the Japanese and Chinese).
[BellArk] (11:6) N-D 95, p. 26.
"Faith: How You, Grandfather, Came to Believe in Fish." [BellArk] (11:6) N-D 95,
p. 26.
"Fooling the Fish." [BellArk] (11:1) Ja-F 95, p. 13.
"How Splendid (After Trakl)." [BellArk] (11:6) N-D 95, p. 27.
"The Incomplete Fisherman's Manifesto." [BellArk] (11:1) Ja-F 95, p. 12.
"The Miracle Voice." [BellArk] (11:6) N-D 95, p. 27.
"The Sound of Fish Dreaming." [BellArk] (11:1) Ja-F 95, p. 13.
"A Touch of the Wild." [BellArk] (11:1) Ja-F 95, p. 12.
"You Can't Fish the Same River Twice." [BellArk] (11:2) Mr-Ap 95, p. 13.
"You Can't Fish the Same River Twice." [BellArk] (11:3) My-Je 95, p. 9.
"You Can't Get There by Taxi." [BellArk] (11:6) N-D 95, p. 27.
GREEN, Carmen Rogers
See ROGERS-GREEN, Carmen
2339. GREEN, Daniel
"Kukri." [HolCrit] (32:1) F 95, p. 16.
"Olfactory 1915." [CapeR] (30:1) Spr 95, p. 6.
"Sans Plumage." [OxfordM] (10:1) Wint 94-Spr 95, p. 32-33.
2340. GREEN, Loweda B.
"As the Darkness Surrounds Us" (after William Stafford). [Crucible] (31) Fall 95, p.
9.
2341. GREEN, Samuel
"Bird Watching" (for Howard Aaron). [PraS] (69:1) Spr 95, p. 153-154.
"Communion." [PraS] (69:1) Spr 95, p. 154-155
2342. GREEN EL, Otis
"The Plot" (WritersCorps Project, Washington, DC). [WashR] (21:2) Ag-S 95, p.
20.
2343. GREENAWAY, William
"First House." [LowellR] (2) c1996, p. 96.
2344. GREENBAUM, Jessica
"The Sisyphus Report." [PraS] (69:1) Spr 95, p. 164-165.
2345. GREENBERG, Alvin
"City Life." [GreensboroR] (58) Sum 95, p. 68.
"Environmental Hazards." [ManyMM] [1:1] D 94, p. 107.
"It's Christmas again, the season of violence." [RiverS] (44) 95, p. 16.
"Street Scene." [RiverS] (44) 95, p. 17.
2346. GREENBERG, Barbara L.
"The Vase." [GlobalCR] (6) Fall 95, p. 13.
"The Visitation." [GettyR] (8:3) Sum 95, p. 464-465.
2347. GREENBERG, David
"Color Comes to Night." [Ploughs] (21:4) Wint 95-96, p. 68.
"Common Will." [Ploughs] (21:4) Wint 95-96, p. 66.
"The Hole in the Ocean." [Ploughs] (21:4) Wint 95-96, p. 67.
"Schoolyard with Boat." [Ploughs] (21:4) Wint 95-96, p. 63-65.
2348. GREENBERG, David Micah
"Poorer As Animals Talk." [NewRep] (213:8/9) 21-28 Ag 95, p. 40.

2349. GREENBERG, Uri Zvi
"Under the Tooth of Their Plow" (tr. by Milton Teichman). [AmerPoR] (24:4) Jl-Ag 95, p. 37.
2350. GREENE, Blandine
"It's My Day" (WritersCorps Program, Washington, DC). [WashR] (21:2) Ag-S 95, p. 12.
2351. GREENE, Jeffrey
"The Cherry Tree." [Colum] (24/25) 95, p. 155.
2352. GREENE, Marian S.
"Chairs." [US1] (30/31) 95, p. 21.
2353. GREENLAW, Lavinia
"The Heat of It." [Verse] (12:3) 95, p. 104.
"In a Dark Room." [Verse] (12:3) 95, p. 106.
"Iron Lung." [Verse] (12:3) 95, p. 104-105.
"Red Rackham's Treasure." [Verse] (12:3) 95, p. 105.
2354. GREENMUN, Linda
"Burls." [SouthernPR] (35:1) Sum 95, p. 28.
2355. GREENWALD, Martha
"1813" (After Thomas Love Peacock's *Memoirs of Percy Bysshe Shelley*). [Poetry] (166:1) Ap 95, p. 19-20.
"Kol Nidre, Iowa." [Flyway] (1:1) Spr 95, p. 10-11.
2356. GREENWAY, Betty
"Collecting Shells." [CapeR] (30:1) Spr 95, p. 4.
"Covers." [CreamCR] (19:1) Spr 95, p. 125.
"Oh My America." [Poem] (73) My 95, p. 42-43.
"Self-Portrait." [Poem] (73) My 95, p. 41.
2357. GREENWAY, William
"Bread of Heaven." [Poem] (74) N 95, p. 49.
"Dark Enough for You." [NewMyths] (2:2/3:1) 95, p. 250.
"Every Reason." [NewMyths] (2:2/3:1) 95, p. 251.
"Layers." [Poem] (74) N 95, p. 47.
"Others." [Poem] (74) N 95, p. 48.
"Yearn." [Poetry] (166:3) Je 95, p. 164.
2358. GREENWOOD, Catherine
"Black Labels." [Grain] (22:3) Wint 95, p. 91.
2359. GREER, Laurie
"Almanack: 21 July." [Poetry] (166:4) Jl 95, p. 225.
"Dark Matters." [Poetry] (167:3) D 95, p. 132-133.
2360. GREGER, Debora
"The Age of Reason." [Nat] (261:14) 30 O 95, p. 516.
"Bearings." [SenR] (25:1) Spr 95, p. 20.
"The Blessing of the Throats." [Poetry] (166:1) Ap 95, p. 23-24.
"The British Museum." [Poetry] (166:1) Ap 95, p. 21-23.
"British Rail." [GettyR] (8:3) Sum 95, p. 486-487.
"Early Rome." [Nat] (258:3) 24 Ja 94, p. 98.
"Much Too Late." [Nat] (258:8) 28 F 94, p. 276.
"Ovid at Land's End." [YaleR] (83:2) Ap 95, p. 91-92.
"Passiontide." [SouthwR] (80:4) Aut 95, p. 488-490.
"Subtropical Elegy" (in memory of Amy Clampitt). [GettyR] (8:2) Spr 95, p. 241-244.
"To Dido Later." [PartR] (62:2) Spr 95, p. 301.
"The Trompe l'Oeil of History" (after Tiepolo). [ParisR] (37:137) Wint 95, p. 103.
2361. GREGERSON, Linda
"Bad Blood." [PartR] (62:1) Wint 95, p. 107-109.
"Blazon." [SenR] (25:1) Spr 95, p. 51-52.
"Fish Dying on the Third Floor at Barney's." [Ploughs] (21:4) Wint 95-96, p. 69-71.
2362. GREGG, Linda
"Hephaestus Alone." [TriQ] (95) Wint 95-96, p. 151.
"In the Javanese Light." [GreenMR] (8:1) Spr-Sum 95, p. 13.
2363. GREGOIRE, A. William
"Minus Zero." [DefinedP] (1:1) Fall-Wint 92, p. 29.
"Sonnet: The intuitive cry seduced swift voices." [DefinedP] (1:1) Fall-Wint 92, p. 28.
"The World Where You Live." [DefinedP] (1:1) Fall-Wint 92, p. 27.
2364. GREGOR, Arthur
"A Bond." [Pembroke] (27) 95, p. 108-109.

"Une Journée à Paris." [Boulevard] (10:1/2, #28/29) Spr 95, p. 150-152.
2365. GREGORY, Robert
"Big Night-Animal Above the Trees" (Selections: 4th, 6th, 10th, 13th-14th, 16th).
[SilverFR] (26) Wint 95, p. 27-32.
"The Idea of a Fall." [PennR] (6:2) 95, p. 18-19.
"A Man in Black Shoes Walking Slowly Because His Case Is Heavy." [PaintedB]
(55/56) 95, p. 53.
"Reminder Too Long to Be a Sonnet." [AmerLC] (7) 95, p. 62.
2366. GRENIER, Arpine Konyalian
"Night Fares." [ChironR] (43) Sum 95, p. 36.
2367. GRENNAN, Eamon
"Alli Dying." [Poetry] (167:1/2) O-N 95, p. 6-7.
"Blossoming Elm." [Nat] (261:3) 17-24 Jl 95, p. 108.
"Border Crossing." [Shen] (45:4) Wint 95, p. 12.
"Breathing." [AmerPoR] (24:6) N-D 95, p. 20.
"Firefly." [SouthernR] (31:3) Jl/Sum 95, p. 746-748.
"Howth, January 1991." [Shen] (45:4) Wint 95, p. 10-11.
"Lake, Early Morning." [SouthernR] (31:3) Jl/Sum 95, p. 750.
"Leaving the Garden." [Poetry] (167:1/2) O-N 95, p. 6.
"Middle Age." [GettyR] (8:3) Sum 95, p. 440.
"On Fire." [AmerPoR] (24:6) N-D 95, p. 20.
"One Morning." [NewYorker] (71:24) 14 Ag 95, p. 37.
"Passing Cold Spring Station." [Nat] (261:11) 9 O 95, p. 400.
"Place." [NewRep] (213:17) 23 O 95, p. 42.
"Protection Racket." [Nat] (261:11) 9 O 95, p. 400.
"Setting Off." [GettyR] (8:3) Sum 95, p. 439.
"Shapes." [GettyR] (8:3) Sum 95, p. 436-438.
"Stone Flight." [YaleR] (83:2) Ap 95, p. 94-95.
"Streak of Light" (For Conor). [Poetry] (167:1/2) O-N 95, p. 8.
"Swan in Winter." [Verse] (12:2) 95, p. 47-50.
"Three Men Cleaning a Sewer." [NewMyths] (2:2/3:1) 95, p. 126.
"Through Glass." [NewMyths] (2:2/3:1) 95, p. 124-125.
"Village Funeral." [NewMyths] (2:2/3:1) 95, p. 123.
"Visit to Mount Jerome." [SouthernR] (31:3) Jl/Sum 95, p. 748-749.
"Wet Morning, Clareville Road." [NewYorker] (71:32) 16 O 95, p. 150-151.
2368. GRESSITT, Kit-Bacon
"Come of Age." [ChironR] (44/45) Aut-Wint 95, p. 31.
"Duplicity." [ChironR] (44/45) Aut-Wint 95, p. 31.
"Scheherazade" (for Kate). [ChironR] (44/45) Aut-Wint 95, p. 31.
2369. GREY, Charmaine Lava
"Lucy's Groceries." [CimR] (110) Ja 96, p. 72.
"Yo Yo." [Kaleid] (30) Wint-Spr 95, p. 62.
2370. GREY, John
"After Joey's Funeral." [Parting] (8:1) Sum 95, p. 17.
"Afternoon of the Philosopher." [DefinedP] (3) 95, p. 10-11.
"Airmen." [LiteralL] (1:3) N-D 94, p. 14.
"At the Station, Twenty Years Later." [InterPR] (21:2) Fall 95, p. 90-91.
"Chess." [DefinedP] (1:1) Fall-Wint 92, p. 18.
"Gale and I in the Gazebo." [Crucible] (31) Fall 95, p. 8.
"Get-Together." [Parting] (8:1) Sum 95, p. 18.
"Kicking Bear on the Q Street Bridge." [BlackBR] (20) Spr-Sum 95, p. 21.
"Lila." [LouisL] (12:1) Spr 95, p. 68.
"Mice Man." [Parting] (8:1) Sum 95, p. 15.
"Mrs Haynes Complains About Her Feet." [Parting] (8:2) Wint 95-96, p. 22.
"Respite." [BlackBR] (21) Fall-Wint 95, p. 5.
"Sins of the Fathers." [BlackBR] (21) Fall-Wint 95, p. 19-20.
"Some Wakes." [HiramPoR] (58/59) Spr 95-Wint 96, p. 28-29.
"This Sailing Game." [LiteralL] (2:3) N-D 95, p. 12.
"The View from Here." [HiramPoR] (58/59) Spr 95-Wint 96, p. 30-31.
"Waiting for the Boat." [DefinedP] (1:1) Fall-Wint 92, p. 19-20.
"The Walk for Hunger." [Wind] (75) Spr 95, p. 10.
"Words Deny Me." [NewRena] (9:2, #28) Spr 95, p. 127.
2371. GREY, Robert W.
"November 5." [Crucible] (30) Fall 94, p. 14.
"Yardwork." [Crucible] (31) Fall 95, p. 37-39.

2372. GRIBBLE, Thomas A.
"Sorry Dream" (A Plainsongs Award Poem). [Plain] (16:1) Fall 95, p. 20-21.
2373. GRIBBLE-NEAL, Iris
"Atomic Energy." [ChironR] (43) Sum 95, p. 26.
"Grandmothers." [ChironR] (43) Sum 95, p. 26.
"Like Red-Haired Stepchildren." [ChironR] (43) Sum 95, p. 26.
2374. GRIECO, Louise
"Gathering at Nightfall." [Blueline] (16) 95, p. 7.
2375. GRIFFIN, Brian
"Alone." [SouthernPR] (35:2) Wint 95, p. 19-20.
2376. GRIFFIN, Maureen Ryan
"Things We Think Will Stay." [Crucible] (31) Fall 95, p. 28-29.
2377. GRIFFIN, Walter
"At the All Night Cafeteria." [CapeR] (30:1) Spr 95, p. 43.
"At the All Night Cafeteria." [Poetry] (166:4) Jl 95, p. 196.
"Boardinghouse, Atlanta, 1959." [LullwaterR] (6:1) Spr-Sum 95, p. 32.
"Crazy Billy." [ChironR] (44/45) Aut-Wint 95, p. 9.
"Day Rooms." [Confr] (56/57) Sum-Fall 95, p. 315.
"First Bath" (for Nina-Maria Griffin). [TexasR] (16:1/4) 95, p. 124.
"Lesser Flamingos." [Border] (7) Fall-Wint 96, p. 14.
"My Stepfather's Eyebrows." [CapeR] (30:1) Spr 95, p. 42.
"My Stepfather's Eyebrows." [ChironR] (44/45) Aut-Wint 95, p. 9.
"My Stepfather's Eyebrows." [Confr] (56/57) Sum-Fall 95, p. 316.
"My Stepfather's Eyebrows." [MidAR] (15:1/2) 95, p. 221.
"Night Trains." [Border] (7) Fall-Wint 96, p. 13.
"The Season of the Falling Face." [GreensboroR] (58) Sum 95, p. 94.
"The Winged Leper." [ChironR] (44/45) Aut-Wint 95, p. 9.
2378. GRIFFITH, Cathy
"Psalms." [CapeR] (30:2) Fall 95, p. 33.
2379. GRIFFITH, Kevin
"Eating Poet" (Apologies to Mark Strand). [SouthernPR] (35:2) Wint 95, p. 11.
"The Ghost in Rilke's Wall" (Rilke's parents believed that a political prisoner had
    been buried alive in a wall). [Vis] (49) 95, p. 36.
"Neighbor." [ArtfulD] (28/29) 95, p. 124.
"Neighbor." [SouthernPR] (35:2) Wint 95, p. 60.
"Plagiarism." [LiteralL] (1:3) N-D 94, p. 14.
"Seven Creation Myths." [LullwaterR] (6:2) Fall-Wint 95, p. 12-13.
"The Severed Head Man." [LullwaterR] (6:2) Fall-Wint 95, p. 14-15.
2380. GRIGORIAN, Hovaness
"Blockade of Armenia" (tr. by Diana Der-Hovanessian). [HarvardR] (8) Spr 95, p.
    95.
2381. GRILLO, Paul
"The Blue Spark." [SlipS] (15) 95, p. 12.
2382. GRIMES, Linda Sue
"Couples in the Park." [Elf] (5:4) Wint 95, p. 24.
"The Man in the Poem 2." [BellR] (18:2, #38) Fall 95, p. 16.
"The Man in the Poem 7" (owed to Ron Smits' "Wolf Creek"). [BellR] (18:2, #38)
    Fall 95, p. 17.
2383. GRIMM, Susan
"Boiling It Down." [CimR] (110) Ja 96, p. 73.
"Dancing Backwards." [PoetryNW] (36:2) Sum 95, p. 44.
"Ravenous Flower." [PoetryNW] (36:2) Sum 95, p. 43.
"Thirteen." [GreenMR] (8:2) Fall-Wint 95-96, p. 58.
"Yellowstone." [GreenMR] (8:2) Fall-Wint 95-96, p. 59.
2384. GRINER, Lee
"Highway 72." [SouthernPR] (35:1) Sum 95, p. 44.
"Interstate 65." [SouthernPR] (35:1) Sum 95, p. 44.
2385. GRINNELL, Claudia
"End of the Year." [NewOR] (21:2) Sum 95, p. 62.
2386. GRISWOLD, Jay
"Deathwatch on the Potomac." [PaintedB] (55/56) 95, p. 87-88.
"The House on 33rd St." [WritersF] (21) 95, p. 43.
"El Pinguino's." [Plain] (16:1) Fall 95, p. 24-25.
"Searching for Scotellaro." [WritersF] (21) 95, p. 42-43.
2387. GROCHOCKI, Sheryl
"Quinceañera." [PoetL] (90:1) Spr 95, p. 41.

2388. GROOMS, Anthony
"Tsunami." [WeberS] (12:2) Spr-Sum 95, p. 48.
2389. GROSHOLZ, Emily
"Accident and Essence." [MichQR] (34:2) Spr 95, p. 211-212.
"Le Déjeuner sur l'Herbe." [TarRP] (35:1) Fall 95, p. 33-34.
"On the Corner of Campbell and Kennedy Streets." [TarRP] (35:1) Fall 95, p. 33.
"Through the Darkness Be Thou Near Me" (for Benjamin). [MichQR] (34:2) Spr 95, p. 210-211.
"Tour of the Flower Depot on Sanary." [Hudson] (48:3) Aut 95, p. 449.
2390. GROSS, David
"Woodhenge." [Elf] (5:1) Spr 95, p. 27.
2391. GROSS, Luray
"I Dream of Escaping with Wild Man." [US1] (30/31) 95, p. 1.
2392. GROSS, Pamela
"Associated Wing." [Journal] (19:2) Fall-Wint 95, p. 9-12.
"Matthew Paris Maps the Move of the Hive." [Poetry] (165:4) Ja 95, p. 206-208.
"Persephone's Daughter Addresses the Pomegranate." [OhioR] (54) 95, p. 122.
"Spread Wing / Red-Shafted Flicker." [PoetryNW] (36:3) Aut 95, p. 24.
2393. GROSS, Tina
"The Body Resents Ornament." [Flyway] (1:1) Spr 95, p. 82.
2394. GROSSBERG, Benjamin Scott
"A Brief Tour with Whitman." [WestHR] (49:1) Spr 95, p. 11-12.
"Coupling." [JamesWR] (12:3) Fall 95, p. 19.
2395. GROSSMAN, Allen
"June, June." [Ploughs] (21:4) Wint 95-96, p. 72.
2396. GROSSMAN, Edith
"Rest in Peace" (tr. of Nicanor Parra). [RiverS] (42/43) 95, p. 79.
2397. GROSSMAN, Rebekah
"The Rowan Tree." [US1] (30/31) 95, p. 16.
2398. GROTH, Patricia Celley
"The Deer Party." [US1] (30/31) 95, p. 22.
"Sheol." [BellArk] (11:5) S-O 95, p. 16.
2399. GROTZ, Jennifer
"First Glasses." [SycamoreR] (7:2) Sum 95, p. 16-17.
"The Pedicure." [NewOR] (21:2) Sum 95, p. 95.
2400. GROUEV, Ivaylo
"Aladdin's Lamp." [TickleAce] (27) Spr-Sum 94, p. 97-98.
"Along the Road." [TickleAce] (27) Spr-Sum 94, p. 95-97.
"Jungle Symphony." [TickleAce] (27) Spr-Sum 94, p. 93-94.
2401. GROW, M. E.
"Gulls" (runner up, 1994 Borderlands Poetry Contest). [Border] (6) Spr-Sum 95, p. 39.
"Three Years Old" (The 1994 Allen Ginsberg Poetry Awards: Honorable Mention). [Footwork] (24/25) 95, p. 196.
2402. GROWNEY, JoAnne
"Snowbound." [FourQ] (9:1/2) Spr 95, p. 44.
2403. GRUBB, David (David H. W.)
"Fear of Farms." [Stand] (36:2) Spr 95, p. 18.
"Stanley Spencer Arriving in Heaven" (for Nick and Mary Parry). [Verse] (12:2) 95, p. 51-54.
2404. GRUBISIC, Vinko
"Letter" (To Domin Ticarev & Jerko Ikin, tr. by Vladimir Bubrin). [Vis] (48) 95, p. 18.
2405. GRUMMAN, Bob
"Mathemaku No 4a" (revised version). [NewOR] (21:2) Sum 95, p. 63.
2406. GRUMMER, Greg
"Cain, During Therapy." [Wind] (75) Spr 95, p. 11.
"Cain, on the Verge of Relocation." [Wind] (75) Spr 95, p. 12.
"Eve, on the Stoop, Naming Things." [Wind] (75) Spr 95, p. 13.
2407. GRUNBERGER, Aimée
"Don't Touch That Dial." [AmerPoR] (24:3) My-Je 95, p. 42.
"The World Is a Dangerous Place." [AmerPoR] (24:3) My-Je 95, p. 42.
GRUTTOLA, Raffael de
See De GRUTTOLA, Raffael

2408. GRYPHIUS, Andreas (1616-1664)
"Epitaph for Mariana Gryphius, His Brother Paul's Little Daughter" (tr. by Christopher Benfey). [NewRep] (213:25) 18 D 95, p. 44.
"To the Virgin Mary" (tr. by Christopher Benfey). [NewRep] (213:25) 18 D 95, p. 44.

2409. GU, Chen
"Curves" (tr. by Xu Juan). [AxeF] (3) 90, p. 45.
"Far and Near" (tr. by Xu Juan). [AxeF] (3) 90, p. 45.

2410. GUDMUNDSSON, Einar Mar
"Homer the Singer of Tales" (tr. by Bernard Scudder). [Nimrod] (38:2) Spr-Sum 95, p. 76-77.

2411. GUENTHER, Charles
"World of Fun." [MidwQ] (36:4) Sum 95, p. 374-375.

2412. GUENTHER, Gabriele
"Ah! Les Beaux Jours de Bonheur Indicible" (for Iva). [MalR] (113) Wint 95, p. 39-41.
"Arterio-Circus." [Jacaranda] (11) [95 or 96?], p. 78.
"At the Bus Stop." [Event] (24:2) Sum 95, p. 22.
"Autism." [AntigR] (100) Wint 95, p. 133.
"Clear Monday." [Quarry] (44:2) 95, p. 52.
"The Grounding of Dora Maar." [MalR] (113) Wint 95, p. 42-43.
"January 18: A Face in the Mail." [Quarry] (44:2) 95, p. 46.
"Letter to a Father." [Jacaranda] (11) [95 or 96?], p. 73-76.
"Loitering." [Jacaranda] (11) [95 or 96?], p. 77.
"The Sea." [Event] (24:2) Sum 95, p. 23.
"Speaking As If the Heart Were an Animal." [Event] (24:2) Sum 95, p. 21.
"The Summer I Turned Nineteen." [AntigR] (100) Wint 95, p. 134.
"Talk to Me." [Quarry] (44:2) 95, p. 48-49.
"Vers la Flamme" (after a sonata by Alexander Scriabin). [Quarry] (44:2) 95, p. 50-51.
"Will You Sleep with Me?" [Quarry] (44:2) 95, p. 47.

2413. GUESS, Carol
"Answering Back." [HiramPoR] (58/59) Spr 95-Wint 96, p. 32.

2414. GUEST, Barbara
"Aspirancy." [Zyzzyva] (11:1, #41) Spr 95, p. 65-66.
"The Body Gate." [AmerLC] (7) 95, p. 14-15.
"Finally, to the Italian Girl." [AmerLC] (7) 95, p. 16-20.
"A Mistake the Size of an Eyelash." [Arshile] (4) 95, p. 20.
"Music History." [Conjunc] (24) 95, p. 72-73.
"Neiges Fondantes." [Arshile] (4) 95, p. 19.
"Others." [Avec] (9) 95, p. 21-32.
"Revolution and Lullaby." [NewAW] (13) Fall-Wint 95, p. 1-4.
"Summon Song" (from Others). [AmerLC] (7) 95, p. 21.
"This Is Illyria, Lady" (Twelfth Night). [Pembroke] (27) 95, p. 111.

GUEVARA, Maurice Kilwein
See KILWEIN GUEVARA, Maurice

2415. GUIGOU, Alberto
"Metrópoli." [LindLM] (14:1) Mr/Spr 95, p. 5.

2416. GUILD, Wendy
"Blind." [CutB] (43) Wint 95, p. 9-10.

2417. GUILLÉN, Jorge
"Invasion" (tr. by Cola Franzen). [HarvardR] (8) Spr 95, p. 93.

2418. GUISTA, Michael (Michael Blaine)
"Circling, and You Drive." [PraS] (69:4) Wint 95, p. 81.
"Learning to Read." [SpoonR] (20:1) Wint-Spr 95, p. 19-21.
"San Joaquin." [SpoonR] (20:2) Sum-Fall 95, p. 100-104.
"Vessel." [PraS] (69:4) Wint 95, p. 82.

2419. GULLANS, Charles
"A Meditative Pause by the Hero in a Long Narrative." [MichQR] (34:2) Spr 95, p. 251-252.

2420. GUMILEV, Nikolai S.
"She" (tr. by Frances Laird). [PlumR] (8) [95], p. 87.

2421. GUNDY, Jeff
"All This Talk Just Exasperates the Problem." [AntR] (53:1) Wint 95, p. 65.
"Crawl Space." [Crazy] (49) Wint 95, p. 76-77.
"Crumbs." [SpoonR] (20:1) Wint-Spr 95, p. 14-15.

"Ears." [Journal] (19:1) Spr-Sum 95, p. 15.
"For the New York City Poet Who Informed Me That Few People Live This Way."
    [Journal] (19:1) Spr-Sum 95, p. 13-14.
"The New Asceticism." [ArtfulD] (28/29) 95, p. 45.
"Right Here, or The Realist Aesthetic." [MidAR] (16:1) 95, p. 17-18.
"Tongues." [Farm] (12:1) Spr-Sum 95, p. 18.
"Winter Flowers." [SpoonR] (20:1) Wint-Spr 95, p. 13.
2422. GUNN, Mark
    "Missouri" (after Thomas Hart Benton). [SouthernHR] (29:1) Wint 95, p. 72-73.
2423. GUNN, Thom
    "1975." [Zyzzyva] (11:3/4, #43/44) 95, "The Best of Ten Years of ZYZZYVA," p.
        42.
    "Dancing David." [Thrpny] (60) Wint 95, p. 17.
    "The Missing." [Verse] (12:2) 95, p. 55-56.
    "A Wood Near Athens." [ParisR] (37:135) Sum 95, p. 190-192.
2424. GUNNARS, Kristjana
    "Exiles Among You" (35-36, 38). [Arc] (34) Spr 95, p. 40-42.
    "Exiles Among You 22." [Dandel] (22:1) 95, p. 10.
    "Exiles Among You 26." [Dandel] (22:1) 95, p. 11.
2425. GUNSTROM, Nickie J.
    "Alarm" (1993 Poetry Contest, Third Place Winner). [DefinedP] (1:2) Spr-Sum 93,
        p. 60.
    "Alchemy." [MidwQ] (36:3) Spr 95, p. 298.
    "Blue Lint." [MidwQ] (36:2) Wint 95, p. 157.
    "Taking Place." [MidwQ] (36:2) Wint 95, p. 158.
2426. GÜNTHER, Gabriele
    "Poem for Marie." [ChiR] (41:1) 95, p. 65-66.
2427. GUO, Wei
    "Autumn" (tr. of Ting Shu, w. Ginny MacKenzie). [InterQ] (2:1/2) 95, p. 123.
    "A Room for Two Girls" (tr. of Ting Shu, w. Ginny MacKenzie). [InterQ] (2:1/2)
        95, p. 121-122.
    "Sicily Sun" (tr. of Ting Shu, w. Ginny MacKenzie). [InterQ] (2:1/2) 95, p. 124.
    "This Place a Gift" (tr. of Ting Shu, w. Ginny MacKenzie). [InterQ] (2:1/2) 95, p.
        125.
2428. GUPPY, Stephen
    "Near the Grave of Amelia Earhart." [Quarry] (44:1) 95, p. 79-80.
2429. GURAN, Holly
    "Climbing." [Noctiluca] (2:1, #4) Spr 95, p. 8-9.
2430. GURKIN, Kathryn (Kathryn B., Kathryn Bright)
    "Enablers Have Their Own Agendas." [Crucible] (30) Fall 94, p. 27.
    "Necessary Magic." [Pembroke] (27) 95, p. 94.
    "Old Bones." [Crucible] (31) Fall 95, p. 11.
2431. GÜRPINAR, Melisa
    "The Bank Teller Tecelli Bey" (tr. by Murat Nemet-Nejat). [Talisman] (14) Fall 95,
        p. 56-59.
2432. GUSSLER, Phyllis Sanchez
    "Dispensation: My Father Paints the Golden Gate." [CarolQ] (47:3) Sum 95, p. 48-
        49.
2433. GUSTAFSON, Jim
    "Angels / Memory / Life: First Equation." [HangL] (66) 95, p. 30.
    "Maddening Joy." [HangL] (66) 95, p. 28-29.
    "Uncle Boyd." [HangL] (66) 95, p. 29.
2434. GUSTAFSON, Joseph
    "This Record's for You." [Pearl] (22) Fall-Wint 95, p. 11.
2435. GUSTAFSSON, Lars
    "Lines on March 28" (tr. by Robert Hedin). [Nimrod] (38:2) Spr-Sum 95, p. 84.
    "Virvlarna" (tr. by Robert Hedin). [Nimrod] (38:2) Spr-Sum 95, p. 82.
    "Whirls" (tr. by Robert Hedin). [Nimrod] (38:2) Spr-Sum 95, p. 83.
2436. GUSTAVSON, Jeffrey
    "Landscape." [PlumR] (9) [95 or 96], p. 58.
GUT, Karen Alkalay
    See ALKALAY-GUT, Karen
2437. GWIAZDA, P. K.
    "There Are Few Witnesses." [GreenHLL] (6) 95, p. 77.

2438. GWYNN, R. S.
"On the Threshold" (sonnet, tr. of Albrecht Haushofer). [SewanR] (103:3) Sum 95,
    p. 381.
"Sir Thomas More" (sonnet, tr. of Albrecht Haushofer). [SewanR] (103:3) Sum 95,
    p. 382.
"Time" (sonnet, tr. of Albrecht Haushofer). [SewanR] (103:3) Sum 95, p. 382.
2439. GYLYS, Beth
"Balloon Heart." [PoetryE] (41) Aut 95, p. 67.
"Narcissist #1-3." [Ploughs] (21:4) Wint 95-96, p. 91.
"Not an Affair a Sestina." [ParisR] (37:136) Fall 95, p. 155-156.
"Pursuit of Happiness." [Ploughs] (21:4) Wint 95-96, p. 90.
"Three Poems" (Narcissist #1-3). [Ploughs] (21:4) Wint 95-96, p. 91.
2440. GYÖRI, Ladislao P.
"Travel" (tr. by the author). [Luz] (8) Spr 95, p. 43.
"Viaje." [Luz] (8) Spr 95, p. 41.

H., L.
        See L. H.
2441. H. G. K.
"El Mundo Pobre." [BlackBR] (20) Spr-Sum 95, p. 16-17.
2442. H. T.
"The Milk Icon" (Selections). [Chain] (2) Spr 95, p. 222-225.
HA, Jin
        See JIN, Ha
2443. HABA, James
"My Only Life." [US1] (30/31) 95, p. 4.
2444. HABER, Leo
"Sonnet Allegro." [SouthernPR] (35:2) Wint 95, p. 30-31.
2445. HABOVA, Dana
"The Day of the Pollyanna" (tr. of Miroslav Holub, w. David Young). [GrandS]
    (13:4, #52) Spr 95, p. 58.
2446. HABRA, Hedy
"Encounters" (LLM English Language Poetry Prize). [LindLM] (14:1) Mr/Spr 95, p.
    8.
"I Haven't Written a Poem in a Long Time" (LLM English Language Poetry Prize).
    [LindLM] (14:1) Mr/Spr 95, p. 8.
"Vanishing Shadow" (LLM English Language Poetry Prize). [LindLM] (14:1)
    Mr/Spr 95, p. 8.
2447. HACKER, Marilyn
"The body is immobile, left behind" (tr. of Claire Malroux). [PoetryE] (41) Aut 95,
    p. 71.
"Cheek like a lamp on the pillow" (tr. of Claire Malroux). [AmerPoR] (24:1) Ja-F
    95, p. 35.
"Didn't Sappho say her guts clutched up like this?" (1 of 3 sonnets). [RiverS]
    (42/43) 95, p. 97.
"Every morning the curtain rises" (tr. of Claire Malroux). [AmerPoR] (24:1) Ja-F
    95, p. 35.
"The face Divides its space" (tr. of Claire Malroux). [AmerPoR] (24:1) Ja-F 95, p.
    34.
"The father's shadow" (tr. of Claire Malroux). [AmerPoR] (24:1) Ja-F 95, p. 35.
"Fingers probe" (tr. of Claire Malroux). [AmerPoR] (24:1) Ja-F 95, p. 34.
"Grief" (for Iva). [MissouriR] (18:3) 95, p. 44-46.
"In October" (tr. of Claire Malroux). [AmerPoR] (24:1) Ja-F 95, p. 35.
"The lipstick poised in the air and the feeling of having made up life" (tr. of Claire
    Malroux). [PoetryE] (41) Aut 95, p. 74.
"O little one, this longing is the pits" (1 of 3 sonnets). [RiverS] (42/43) 95, p. 96.
"Octet Before Winter" (4 selections, tr. of Claire Malroux). [PoetryE] (41) Aut 95,
    p. 71.
"Often, like anyone, I ask myself" (tr. of Claire Malroux). [PoetryE] (41) Aut 95, p.
    72.
"Passed" (tr. of Claire Malroux). [AmerPoR] (24:1) Ja-F 95, p. 34.
"Scars on Paper." [AmerPoR] (24:5) S-O 95, p. 46-47.
"She devours the walls" (tr. of Claire Malroux). [AmerPoR] (24:1) Ja-F 95, p. 35.
"The sky has grey hair" (tr. of Claire Malroux). [AmerPoR] (24:1) Ja-F 95, p. 34.
"Sonnets" (3 poems). [RiverS] (42/43) 95, p. 96-97.

"A star in distress" (tr. of Claire Malroux). [AmerPoR] (24:1) Ja-F 95, p. 35.
"Street Scenes III." [Nat] (261:21) 18 D 95, p. 800.
"Tentative Gardening" (for N.G.). [Nat] (260:18) 8 My 95, p. 648.
"Well, damn, it's a relief to be a slut" (1 of 3 sonnets). [RiverS] (42/43) 95, p. 96.
"When the birds disperse" (tr. of Claire Malroux). [AmerPoR] (24:1) Ja-F 95, p. 35.
"Wisteria on a wrought-iron door, mid-boulevard" (tr. of Claire Malroux). [PoetryE]
    (41) Aut 95, p. 73.
2448. HACKETT, Robert
    "Tanganyika." [CutB] (42) Sum 94, p. 11.
2449. HADARI, Atar
    "Anaesthetic." [SantaBR] (3:2) Sum 95, p. 23.
    "Barn." [Light] (15/16) Aut-Wint 95-96, p. 31.
    "Definitions." [PoetryE] (40) Spr 95, p. 45.
    "I would my heart were still inside." [PoetryE] (40) Spr 95, p. 46.
    "Memoirs of Los Angeles." [SantaBR] (3:2) Sum 95, p. 24.
    "On the Way Home, a Woman." [SantaBR] (3:2) Sum 95, p. 22.
2450. HADAS, Rachel
    "Aleatory III." [CumbPR] (14:2) Spr 95, p. 47-48.
    "Arguments of Silence" ("Silence is death"). [YaleR] (83:1) Ja 95, p. 80-82.
    "Black Wings." [Raritan] (14:3) Wint 95, p. 27-28.
    "Genealogies." [Verse] (12:2) 95, p. 57-59.
    "The Glass of Milk" (in memory of Paul Douglas). [WestHR] (49:4) Wint 95, p.
        297.
    "Green Lawn Crisscrossed." [WestHR] (49:4) Wint 95, p. 298-299.
    "The Lost House." [NewEngR] (17:4) Fall 95, p. 56.
    "Lullaby." [Raritan] (14:3) Wint 95, p. 28.
    "Mayday at the Frick." [Thrpny] (61) Spr 95, p. 31.
    "Paradigm Shift." [YaleR] (83:1) Ja 95, p. 78-79.
    "Peculiar Sanctity." [ParisR] (37:134) Spr 95, p. 161-162.
    "Performances, Assortments." [WestHR] (49:1) Spr 95, p. 13-14.
    "The Red Hat." [NewYorker] (70:45) 16 Ja 95, p. 55.
    "Refrains" (for Ann Lauterbach). [WestHR] (49:4) Wint 95, p. 296.
    "The Reunion." [NewEngR] (17:4) Fall 95, p. 58.
    "Riverside Park." [NewYorker] (71:34) 30 O 95, p. 91.
    "Samian Morning, 1971." [NewEngR] (17:4) Fall 95, p. 57-58.
    "Shells." [NewRep] (212:17) 24 Ap 95, p. 44.
    "Stances." [Raritan] (14:3) Wint 95, p. 29.
    "Still-Life in Garden." [NewYorker] (71:12) 15 My 95, p. 96.
    "Sunset." [BostonR] (20:2) Ap-My 95, p. 22.
2451. HADDUCK, Kevin
    "Antiphonal." [BellArk] (11:1) Ja-F 95, p. 26.
    "At the Same Time of Mind." [BellArk] (11:5) S-O 95, p. 12.
    "By April Moons." [BellArk] (11:1) Ja-F 95, p. 25.
    "Having Known This." [BellArk] (11:5) S-O 95, p. 12.
    "Toward Easter." [ChrC] (112:12) 12 Ap 95, p. 393.
2452. HADFIELD, Charles
    "The Watchmender." [Os] (40) 95, p. 36-38.
2453. HAEHL, Anne L.
    "You Don't Often Hear." [ChironR] (43) Sum 95, p. 28.
2454. HAFIZ-I SHIRAZI, Khwajah Shams Uddin Muhammad
    "Ghazal 18" (From the Díwán, tr. by Elizabeth T. Gray, Jr. For Eleanor Mitten).
        [HarvardR] (8) Spr 95, p. 82.
    "Ghazal 35" (From the Díwán, tr. by Elizabeth T. Gray, Jr.). [HarvardR] (8) Spr 95,
        p. 82.
2455. HAGEDORN, Jessica
    "The Mummy." [RiverS] (42/43) 95, p. 93-95.
2456. HAGELAND, Katherine
    "Three Wishes." [ChironR] (43) Sum 95, p. 25.
2457. HAGER, Stephanie
    "My First Rejection." [NewYorkQ] (55) 95, p. 83.
    "The Woman on the T.V." [Pearl] (22) Fall-Wint 95, p. 126.
2458. HAGUE, Richard
    "Trying to Unload" (Finalist, 1995 Allen Tate Memorial Competition). [Wind] (76)
        Fall 95, p. 30-31.
2459. HAHN, Elizabeth
    "Dream of the Demented." [Crucible] (30) Fall 94, p. 28.

2460. HAHN, Kimiko
"Another Use for Ice." [AmerV] (38) 95, p. 35.
2461. HAHN, Robert
"Angels." [WestHR] (49:3) Fall 95, p. 234-235.
"False Dawn" (Wellfleet Harbor). [BelPoJ] (45:4) Chapbook 22, Sum 95, p. 45-46.
"Heaven on Earth." [GreenMR] (8:1) Spr-Sum 95, p. 77-78.
"Memories of Texas Falls." [WestHR] (49:3) Fall 95, p. 230-233.
"Olmsted's Fens Corrected by Shircliff." [ParisR] (37:134) Spr 95, p. 175-176.
"Summer and Winter at the Mount" (1975 and 1985). [ParisR] (37:134) Spr 95, p. 172-174.
2462. HAHN, Susan
"The Devil's Legs." [PoetryE] (40) Spr 95, p. 48.
"Disorderly Conduct." [Poetry] (165:5) F 95, p. 268-269.
"Earthquake." [SouthwR] (80:1) Wint 95, p. 34.
"Felony." [PoetryE] (40) Spr 95, p. 47.
"He Who Whittled My Soul." [ChiR] (41:2/3) 95, p. 117.
"The Lovers." [Poetry] (165:5) F 95, p. 271.
"Music from a High-Strung Instrument." [ChiR] (41:2/3) 95, p. 118.
"Nerve." [PraS] (69:2) Sum 95, p. 166.
"Nijinsky's Dog." [AmerPoR] (24:3) My-Je 95, p. 39.
"Pneumonia." [Poetry] (165:5) F 95, p. 267-268.
"Poison." [Poetry] (165:5) F 95, p. 269-270.
2463. HAILES, Nettie
"The Farewell" (WritersCorps Project, Washington, DC). [WashR] (21:2) Ag-S 95, p. 23.
2464. HAINES, John
"The Ancestors." [Hudson] (48:1) Spr 95, p. 53.
"Another Country." [Manoa] (7:1) Sum 95, p. 74-75.
"Clouds at 30,000 Feet." [Hudson] (48:1) Spr 95, p. 55-56.
"If I Could Have All." [Nimrod] (38:2) Spr-Sum 95, p. 66.
"Nighthawks." [Manoa] (7:1) Sum 95, p. 75.
"Rodin: The Gates of Hell." [Hudson] (48:1) Spr 95, p. 54.
2465. HAINING, James
"Little Golden Aquariums." [GrandS] (13:3, #51) Wint 95, p. 192-193.
2466. HAKUSHIMA, Kiyo
"Once again summer has come" (in Japanese and English, tr. by Jiro Nakano). [BambooR] (67/68) Sum-Fall 95, p. 7.
2467. HALES, Corrinne
"Chosen." [PraS] (69:4) Wint 95, p. 60-63.
"Hunger." [NewMyths] (2:2/3:1) 95, p. 254-255.
"Reconciliation." [Ploughs] (21:1) Spr 95, p. 30-33.
"Sputnik: October 4, 1957." [PraS] (69:4) Wint 95, p. 58-60.
"Storm." [Ploughs] (21:1) Spr 95, p. 28-29.
"Unsolved." [PoetryE] (40) Spr 95, p. 49-50.
2468. HALEY, Jack
"I Fell in Love with a Woman of the Opposite Sex." [MassR] (36:2) Sum 95, p. 241.
2469. HALEY, Vanessa
"Blindness." [HampSPR] Wint 95, p. 7.
"The Body's Mystery." [HampSPR] Wint 95, p. 5-6.
"House of Wings." [HampSPR] Wint 95, p. 6.
2470. HALL, Barry
"October." [SilverFR] (25) Sum 95, p. 7.
2471. HALL, Christopher W.
"Commuters." [PaintedB] (57) 95, p. 65-66.
"Magenta." [PaintedB] (57) 95, p. 64.
2472. HALL, Daniel
"Salvage." [NewRep] (212:10) 6 Mr 95, p. 36.
2473. HALL, Donald
"1951." [NewEngR] (17:3) Sum 95, p. 7.
"The Advocate." [GreenMR] (8:1) Spr-Sum 95, p. 47.
"Antiquities." [Thrpny] (62) Sum 95, p. 20.
"B.Y.O." [SouthernHR] (29:4) Fall 95, p. 361.
"A Beard for a Blue Pantry" (Alice Mattison dreamed that I wrote a poem with this title). [Poetry] (165:5) F 95, p. 283-284.
"Bermuda, Bermuda." [Boulevard] (10:3, #30) Fall 95, p. 45.
"The Black Faced Sheep." [SenR] (25:1) Spr 95, p. 36-38.

"The Comfort" (1 of 6 poems in "Mortal Engines"). [SewanR] (103:1) Wint 95, p. 9.
"The Daughters of Edward D. Boit." [GettyR] (8:2) Spr 95, p. 289-296.
"The Embrace." [Nat] (260:6) 13 F 95, p. 216.
"Extended Care." [Poetry] (165:5) F 95, p. 285-286.
"The Face Over the Body." [Nat] (258:1) 3-10 Ja 94, p. 23.
"Four." [SewanR] (103:4) Fall 95, p. 500.
"Frank O'Hara." [NewEngR] (17:3) Sum 95, p. 9.
"Goggles and Helmet." [Poetry] (165:5) F 95, p. 284-285.
"Gordon of the Grolier Book Shop." [NewEngR] (17:3) Sum 95, p. 8.
"The Heart." [NewYorker] (71:9) 24 Ap 95, p. 70.
"The House." [SouthernHR] (29:4) Fall 95, p. 360.
"I Wanted to Live Here." [Nat] (260:6) 13 F 95, p. 216.
"Late Pleasures" (1 of 6 poems in "Mortal Engines"). [SewanR] (103:1) Wint 95, p.
    7.
"Literature." [NewEngR] (17:3) Sum 95, p. 9-10.
"Mortal Engines" (6 poems). [SewanR] (103:1) Wint 95, p. 6-9.
"Notes from China." [SouthwR] (80:2/3) Spr-Sum 95, p. 331-332.
"A Novel in Two Volumes." [Verse] (12:2) 95, p. 60.
"One Place." [Nat] (261:10) 2 O 95, p. 364.
"Prospero's Tune." [SewanR] (103:4) Fall 95, p. 501.
"The Reception." [GreenMR] (8:1) Spr-Sum 95, p. 48.
"Rings" (1 of 6 poems in "Mortal Engines"). [SewanR] (103:1) Wint 95, p. 8.
"Shame." [NewYorker] (71:36) 13 N 95, p. 72.
"Sighs" (1 of 6 poems in "Mortal Engines"). [SewanR] (103:1) Wint 95, p. 9.
"A Story." [NewEngR] (17:3) Sum 95, p. 10-11.
"Telephone" (1 of 6 poems in "Mortal Engines"). [SewanR] (103:1) Wint 95, p. 7.
"Watch" (1 of 6 poems in "Mortal Engines"). [SewanR] (103:1) Wint 95, p. 8-9.
"Without." [Poetry] (167:3) D 95, p. 144-145.
"The Words." [Poetry] (165:5) F 95, p. 286.
"The Worker." [Agni] (41) 95, p. 65-66.
2474. HALL, Irving C.
"Coral Sea." [NewL] (61:3) 95, p. 19.
"Prime." [NewL] (61:3) 95, p. 18.
2475. HALL, James Baker
"Dividing Ridge" (from "Stopping on the Edge to Wave"). [Wind] (75) Spr 95, p.
    71.
2476. HALL, Judith
"Bergman's Cancer." [ColR] (22:2) Fall 95, p. 165-166.
"Hats, a Chiaroscuro Madrigal." [ParisR] (37:134) Spr 95, p. 234.
"The Monarch Birthmark." [WestHR] (49:3) Fall 95, p. 220-221.
2477. HALL, Kathryn
"Café Quadri." [NewEngR] (17:4) Fall 95, p. 98-99.
2478. HALL, Michael
"Xcerpt #4: Ode to Langston Hughes (the return of the drum)." [Drumvoices]
    (5:1/2) Fall-Wint 95-96, p. 102.
2479. HALL, Phil
"To Invoke Amy Cosh." [WestCL] (29:1, #16) Spr-Sum 95, p. 95-97.
"Valuable Anger (Urson)." [WestCL] (29:1, #16) Spr-Sum 95, p. 98-101.
2480. HALL, S. J.
"Innocence." [Prima] (18/19) 95, p. 105.
2481. HALL, Sharonda M.
"Untitled: An afro to way out there" (WritersCorps Program, Washington, DC).
    [WashR] (21:2) Ag-S 95, p. 17.
2482. HALLEY, Anne
"In Poland" (tr. of Rolf Zimmermann). [MassR] (36:3) Aut 95, p. 412-413.
2483. HALLIDAY, Mark
"Barge." [OhioR] (53) 95, p. 79.
"Contemporary Fiction." [ChiR] (41:1) 95, p. 5-6.
"Detail." [ChiR] (41:4) 95, p. 67-68.
"Gatsby Quiz." [ChiR] (41:1) 95, p. 1-2.
"Meaning." [ChiR] (41:1) 95, p. 3-4.
"Narragansett Boulevard." [Chelsea] (59) 95, p. 171.
"Postcard From Thailand." [OhioR] (53) 95, p. 80-81.
"Yong Man on Sixth Avenue." [ChiR] (41:4) 95, p. 65-66.

2484. HALLMUNDSSON, Hallberg
"Christ on a Cold Stone" (Wood Carving in the Rijksmuseum, Amsterdam). [Vis] (49) 95, p. 24.
"Untitled 1: The room caught fire. We didn't see it" (tr. of Johann Hjalmarsson). [Vis] (49) 95, p. 24.
"Villa-Lobos Played on a Piano" (tr. of Jon Dan). [Vis] (49) 95, p. 32.
2485. HALME, Kathleen
"Diorama Notebook." [DenQ] (30:1) Sum 95, p. 64-65.
"The Eloquence of Objects, the Demise of Material Culture." [VirQR] (71:4) Aut 95, p. 701-703.
"In Silence Visible and Perpetual Calm." [Boulevard] (10:3, #30) Fall 95, p. 136.
"Incidents and Accidents." [DenQ] (30:1) Sum 95, p. 67.
"Nuptial Suite for Signe Saari." [Pembroke] (27) 95, p. 72.
"Poem with Ethnic Overtones." [VirQR] (71:4) Aut 95, p. 703-704.
"The Speaking Face of Earth." [DenQ] (30:1) Sum 95, p. 66.
"The Subjunctive of Pomegranate." [Pembroke] (27) 95, p. 71.
2486. HALPERIN, Mark
"On Consecrating the Flag" (tr. of Juri Talvet, w. the author). [Vis] (49) 95, p. 33-34.
2487. HALPERN, Daniel
"Her Body." [Ploughs] (21:4) Wint 95-96, p. 92-95.
"Monterchi." [Verse] (12:2) 95, p. 61-62.
"The New Road." [DenQ] (30:2) Fall 95, p. 27-28.
2488. HALSALL, Jalaine
"Don't Stop." [BlackWR] (21:2) Spr-Sum 95, p. 47-49.
"Liberace's Sister." [BlackWR] (21:2) Spr-Sum 95, p. 50-51.
2489. HAMADA, Yoko
"You raised that same hand." (in Japanese and English, tr. by Jiro Nakano). [BambooR] (67/68) Sum-Fall 95, p. 8.
2490. HAMANN, Shannon
"Hide." [FreeL] (14) Wint 95, p. 22-23.
"A Note on the Refrigerator." [FreeL] (14) Wint 95, p. 24.
2491. HAMBLIN, Robert
"Advice to a Young Poet" (for Kaleigh). [CapeR] (30:1) Spr 95, p. 14-15.
"Running: Cape Girardeau, November 1993." [CapeR] (30:1) Spr 95, p. 16-17.
2492. HAMBURGER, Michael
"Surgical Ward." [Stand] (36:3) Sum 95, p. 56-57.
2493. HAMBY, Barbara
"Deception." [WestHR] (49:3) Fall 95, p. 260-261.
"Delirium." [ParisR] (37:134) Spr 95, p. 135-136.
"Nose." [ParisR] (37:134) Spr 95, p. 133-134.
"St. Clare's Underwear." [WestHR] (49:3) Fall 95, p. 258-259.
2494. HAMER, Forrest
"The Calling." [BelPoJ] (45:3) Spr 95, p. 6-9.
"Getting Happy." [Zyzzyva] (11:3/4, #43/44) 95, "The Best of Ten Years of ZYZZYVA," p. 115-116.
"Goldsboro Narrative #24: Second Benediction" (for Mr. Holman). [KenR] (17:2) Spr 95, p. 132.
2495. HAMILL, P.
"The Cow-Nose Ray" (Isle of Palms, S.C.). [NewEngR] (17:2) Spr 95, p. 141-143.
2496. HAMILL, Sam
"I. Give up erotic games, Kabir" (tr. of Kabir, 15th c.). [PoetryE] (41) Aut 95, p. 25.
"II. Sometimes, everywhere I look" (tr. of Kabir, 15th c.). [PoetryE] (41) Aut 95, p. 25.
"Beautiful Melite, in the throes of middle age" (tr. of Agathias Scholasticus, ca. 531-580 CE). [PoetryE] (41) Aut 95, p. 18.
"Come back, love, tonight" (tr. of Emperor Fushima, 1265-1317). [RiverS] (44) 95, p. 34.
"Doing, a Filthy Pleasure Is, and Short" (tr. of Petronius Arbiter, d. 66 CE). [PoetryE] (41) Aut 95, p. 16.
"Elegy" (tr. of Sojun Ikkyu, 1394-1481). [Agni] (42) 95, p. 125.
"Elegy: It is almost dawn." [DefinedP] (1:2) Spr-Sum 93, p. 6.
"Elegy to His Mistress" (tr. of Ovid, 43 BCE-17 CE). [PoetryE] (41) Aut 95, p. 15.
"Face to Face with My Lover on Daito's Anniversary" (tr. of Ikkyu Sojun, 1394-1481). [PoetryE] (41) Aut 95, p. 26.

HAMILL

"Face to Face with My Lover on Daito's Anniversary" (tr. of Sojun Ikkyu, 1394-1481). [Agni] (42) 95, p. 121.
"First Love" (tr. of Vidyapati, 14th c.). [PoetryE] (41) Aut 95, p. 27.
"The garden insects" (tr. of Kyogoku Tamekane, 1254-1332). [RiverS] (44) 95, p. 345.
"Her perfect naked breast" (tr. of Marcus Argentarius, ca. 60 BCE). [PoetryE] (41) Aut 95, p. 13.
"I love love's delicacy" (tr. of Sappho, 6th c. BCE). [PoetryE] (41) Aut 95, p. 11.
"Is that the same moon?" (tr. of Ariwara no Narihira, 825-880). [PoetryE] (41) Aut 95, p. 21.
"It's on-rushing time" (tr. of Empress Eifuku, 1271-1342). [RiverS] (44) 95, p. 34.
"Late evening finally comes" (tr. of Otomo no Yakamochi, 718-785). [PoetryE] (41) Aut 95, p. 20.
"The long rope of spring" (tr. of Kiyowara no Fukuyabu, 10th Century). [RiverS] (44) 95, p. 34.
"Love delivers to me its sweetest thoughts" (tr. of Francesco Petrarch, 1304-1374). [PoetryE] (41) Aut 95, p. 24.
"Love Song" (tr. of traditional Egyptian poem, ca. 13th c. BCE). [PoetryE] (41) Aut 95, p. 10.
"Love Song" (tr. of traditional Egyptian poem, ca. 15th c. BCE). [PoetryE] (41) Aut 95, p. 9.
"My Hand Is Lady Mori's Hand" (tr. of Sojun Ikkyu, 1394-1481). [Agni] (42) 95, p. 122.
"My Love's Dark Place Is Fragrant Like Narcissus" (tr. of Sojun Ikkyu, 1394-1481). [Agni] (42) 95, p. 124.
"My woman says she'd rather have me" (tr. of Catullus, ca. 84-54 BCE). [PoetryE] (41) Aut 95, p. 14.
"Night Talk in a Dream Chamber" (tr. of Sojun Ikkyu, 1394-1481). [Agni] (42) 95, p. 123.
"On the temple bell" (Haiku, tr. of Kobayashi Issa, 1762-1826). [WillowS] (36) Je 95, p. 96.
"Only the moon" (Haiku, tr. of Kikusha-ni, 1752-1826). [WillowS] (36) Je 95, p. 96.
"Resentment Near the Jade Steps" (tr. of Li Po, 701-762). [PoetryE] (41) Aut 95, p. 19.
"Song: I won't care if you desert me" (tr. of Chinook poem, 1888, after Franz Boas). [PoetryE] (41) Aut 95, p. 34.
"Song: She lowers her fragrant curtain" (tr. of Liu Yung, 987-1053). [PoetryE] (41) Aut 95, p. 22.
"Song: Winter skies are cold and low" (tr. of Tzu Yeh, 4th c. CE). [PoetryE] (41) Aut 95, p. 17.
"Such complete stillness" (Haiku, tr. of Fuhaku, 1714-1807). [WillowS] (36) Je 95, p. 96.
"Ten Thousand Sutras" (after Hakuin). [PoetryE] (41) Aut 95, p. 38-39.
"Think how unspeakably sweet" (tr. of Asklepiados, ca. 320 BCE). [PoetryE] (41) Aut 95, p. 12.
"Thus spring begins: old" (Haiku, tr. of Kobayashi Issa, 1762-1826). [WillowS] (36) Je 95, p. 96.
"Time after time" (tr. of Kyogoku Tamekane, 1254-1332). [RiverS] (44) 95, p. 34.
"Untitled: Ø last, that lanced vocative." [Jacaranda] (11) [95 or 96?], p. 141-142.
"A world of dew" (Haiku, tr. of Kobayashi Issa, 1762-1826). [WillowS] (36) Je 95, p. 96.

2497. HAMILTON, Alfred Starr
"Beautiful." [JINJPo] (17:2) Aut 95, p. 2.
"Five Senses." [Footwork] (24/25) 95, p. 56.
"Mirrorland." [JINJPo] (17:2) Aut 95, p. 1.
"Mount Monadnock." [Footwork] (24/25) 95, p. 56.
"A Town Without a Soul." [JINJPo] (17:2) Aut 95, p. 3.

2498. HAMILTON, Carol
"A Backyard Without Psychic Roots." [ChironR] (43) Sum 95, p. 16.
"December." [ChironR] (43) Sum 95, p. 16.
"Forked Tongues." [CapeR] (30:2) Fall 95, p. 3.
"Monarch Journey." [CapeR] (30:2) Fall 95, p. 4-5.
"My Mother's Relish Plate." [ChironR] (43) Sum 95, p. 16.
"Pomegranate." [Bogg] (67) 95, p. 33.
"Translation." [WritersF] (21) 95, p. 31.

2499. HAMILTON, Fritz
"The Lord is my keeper I shall not weep." [Pearl] (22) Fall-Wint 95, p. 79.
"When I fall into the 3-liter plastic bottle." [Pearl] (22) Fall-Wint 95, p. 78.
2500. HAMMER, Mike
"I Am Not Going to Tell You the Truth." [PlumR] (9) [95 or 96], p. 21.
"In Lieu of a Long Dark." [PaintedB] (57) 95, p. 67.
2501. HAMMER, Patrick, Jr.
"Woman Commits Suicide by Jumping into Lake." [Footwork] (24/25) 95, p. 179.
HAMMIL, P.
See HAMILL, P.
2502. HAMMON, Shannon
"The Peony." [ColR] (22:2) Fall 95, p. 142-143.
2503. HAMMOND, Blaine
"The Lost Shepherd." [BlackBR] (21) Fall-Wint 95, p. 8.
2504. HAMOD, Sam
"The Beduoin Dress" [sic]. [Vis] (47) 95, p. 32.
2505. HAN-SHAN (circa 7th-9th c.)
"I came once to sit on Cold Mountain" (tr. by Burton Watson). [Tricycle] (4:3, #15)
    Spr 95, p. 60.
"I Considered Painting Two Flowers" (tr. by Peter Stambler). [SpoonR] (20:1) Wint-
    Spr 95, p. 82.
"Judging a Scroll by Its Ribbons" (tr. by Peter Stambler). [WillowS] (36) Je 95, p.
    100.
"What I Find I Name Cheerfully" (tr. by Peter Stambler). [SpoonR] (20:1) Wint-Spr
    95, p. 82.
2506. HANCOCK, Jennifer
"Driving Home." [AntR] (53:2) Spr 95, p. 191.
2507. HANCOCK, Kate
"Belonging." [GreenMR] (8:2) Fall-Wint 95-96, p. 60.
"The Nativity Glitter Dome." [GreenMR] (8:2) Fall-Wint 95-96, p. 61.
2508. HANDLER, Joan Cusack
"At the Beach." [JINJPo] (17:2) Aut 95, p. 18.
"The Break." [PaintedB] (55/56) 95, p. 29-30.
"Mess." [PaintedB] (55/56) 95, p. 31.
"Prayer Outside the Church." [JINJPo] (17:2) Aut 95, p. 19-20.
2509. HANDLIN, Jim
"After Visiting a Tang Tomb." [Footwork] (24/25) 95, p. 10.
"For Diane." [Footwork] (24/25) 95, p. 9-10.
"Saying Farewell to My Father." [Footwork] (24/25) 95, p. 9.
HANH, Thich Nhat
See THICH, Nhat Hanh
2510. HANIFAN, Jil
"Aha Now I See." [13thMoon] (13:1/2) 95, p. 17.
"Unfinished." [13thMoon] (13:1/2) 95, p. 18.
2511. HANKE, Peter
"Alexander Pope Lowers His Standards in the Admirals' Club at La Guardia
    Airport" (runner up, 1994 Borderlands Poetry Contest). [Border] (7) Fall-
    Wint 96, p. 15-16.
2512. HANLON, G. (Gail)
"Long, Quiet Highway." [PoetL] (90:4) Wint 95-96, p. 24.
"Nuclear Winter." [SnailPR] (3:2) 95, p. 30.
2513. HANNAH, Sarah
"Marble Hill." [PoetL] (90:3) Fall 95, p. 47.
2514. HANSEN, Jefferson
"Land Scrapes of a New Town" (For Elizabeth). [Avec] (9) 95, p. 119-134.
"The Moon   The Moon   The moon." [Sulfur] (15:2, #37) Fall 95, p. 134-135.
2515. HANSEN, Tom
"A Little Song That Doesn't Even Rhyme." [MidwQ] (36:4) Sum 95, p. 376.
"November." [MidwQ] (36:2) Wint 95, p. 159.
2516. HANSEN, Twyla
"Midwestern Autumn." [MidwQ] (36:4) Sum 95, p. 377-378.
"Platte River State Park, Late January." [LaurelR] (29:2) Sum 95, p. 89-90.
2517. HANSON, Julie Jordan
"Buttons." [WestB] (36) 95, p. 86.
2518. HANSON, Kenneth O.
"Table with Objects." [Interim] (14:1) Spr-Sum 95, p. 6-7.

2519. HANTMAN, Barbara
"The Vintners These Days" (from *Wistfulness and other Foibles*). [AmerPoR] (24:3)
My-Je 95, p. 20.
2520. HANTULA, Sari
"But the memory did not sleep, the time we killed did not stay" (tr. of Lauri
Otonkoski). [InterPR] (21:2) Fall 95, p. 59.
"Come home! yells the mute longing" (tr. of Arto Melleri). [InterPR] (21:2) Fall 95,
p. 45.
"Credo" (tr. of Lauri Otonkoski). [InterPR] (21:2) Fall 95, p. 54-55.
"Deep in the forest, a big moose is asleep" (tr. of Sirkka Turkka). [InterPR] (21:2)
Fall 95, p. 35.
"Despite all, only one footstep behind you has fallen too deep" (tr. of Jouni Inkala).
[InterPR] (21:2) Fall 95, p. 71.
"The Era When Letters Break Down" (tr. of Arto Melleri). [InterPR] (21:2) Fall 95,
p. 47.
"Even though I could call out after you I" (tr. by Sari Hantula). [InterPR] (21:2) Fall
95, p. 25.
"Even though I could call out after you I" (tr. of Sari Hantula). [InterPR] (21:2) Fall
95, p. 25.
"Four-Footed Us" (tr. of Arto Melleri). [InterPR] (21:2) Fall 95, p. 53.
"The girl is so healthy that fever" (tr. of Helena Sinervo). [InterPR] (21:2) Fall 95, p.
65.
"The Hanged" (tr. of Tomi Kontio). [InterPR] (21:2) Fall 95, p. 81.
"I have been right too many times" (tr. of Jouni Inkala). [InterPR] (21:2) Fall 95, p.
73.
"I know this decomposed form of time began in water" (tr. of Jouni Inkala).
[InterPR] (21:2) Fall 95, p. 75.
"Let Us Dance" (tr. of Tomi Kontio). [InterPR] (21:2) Fall 95, p. 77.
"Let's have a war, that's what the seed of hatred" (tr. of Arto Melleri). [InterPR]
(21:2) Fall 95, p. 49.
"A letter from Heaven: my eyes are watering" (tr. of Sirkka Turkka). [InterPR]
(21:2) Fall 95, p. 39.
"The night has come. As if a wing" (tr. of Sirkka Turkka). [InterPR] (21:2) Fall 95,
p. 33.
"Occultism" (tr. of Tomi Kontio). [InterPR] (21:2) Fall 95, p. 79.
"People talk about suffering a lot" (tr. of Sirkka Turkka). [InterPR] (21:2) Fall 95, p.
37.
"Plato" (tr. of Lauri Otonkoski). [InterPR] (21:2) Fall 95, p. 57.
"Please look after human beings, animals move around" (tr. by Sari Hantula).
[InterPR] (21:2) Fall 95, p. 25.
"Please look after human beings, animals move around" (tr. of Sari Hantula).
[InterPR] (21:2) Fall 95, p. 25.
"Queen Hysteria" (tr. of Arto Melleri). [InterPR] (21:2) Fall 95, p. 41, 43.
"The sea raises you to your feet. And dead calm" (tr. of Mirkka Rekola). [InterPR]
(21:2) Fall 95, p. 25.
"The Sirens" (tr. of Riina Katajavuori). [InterPR] (21:2) Fall 95, p. 83.
"Take the pole as it comes, take a man, it's tasty" (tr. of Helena Sinervo). [InterPR]
(21:2) Fall 95, p. 67.
"This city is a disease that eats thin routes through the head" (tr. of Riina
Katajavuori). [InterPR] (21:2) Fall 95, p. 85.
"This one, too, is an assigned task, in service" (tr. of Mirkka Rekola). [InterPR]
(21:2) Fall 95, p. 31.
"Those who talk lose lots of words" (tr. of Lauri Otonkoski). [InterPR] (21:2) Fall
95, p. 61.
"Vuorimiehenkatu. Helsinki" (tr. of Jouni Inkala). [InterPR] (21:2) Fall 95, p. 68-69.
"When I saw the face of John the Baptist in the water" (tr. of Mirkka Rekola).
[InterPR] (21:2) Fall 95, p. 27.
"When the world is full of agents of my memory" (tr. of Mirkka Rekola). [InterPR]
(21:2) Fall 95, p. 29.
"The Whole Kingdom" (tr. of Riina Katajavuori). [InterPR] (21:2) Fall 95, p. 87.
"You Can't See It with the Eye Alone" (tr. of Arto Melleri). [InterPR] (21:2) Fall 95,
p. 51.
2521. HARDER, Dan
"Form / Unformed / Perfect." [Witness] (9:1) 95, p. 16.
"The Poppy." [Witness] (9:1) 95, p. 17.
"The Santa Monica Zenway." [Witness] (9:1) 95, p. 17.

2522. HARDIN, Jeff
"On the Day of Your Death." [ConnPR] (14:1) 95, p. 25.
"Overtaken." [ConnPR] (14:1) 95, p. 26.
"Through a Field into Trees" (for W.R.). [Poem] (73) My 95, p. 20-21.
2523. HARDING, Rachel Elizabeth
"Charcoal." [Callaloo] (18:2) Spr 95, p. 335-336.
"Mercy." [Callaloo] (18:2) Spr 95, p. 337-338.
2524. HARDY, Carole Wood
"Garden Spider." [Orion] (14:4) Aut 95, p. 33.
2525. HARDY, Thomas
"Afterwards." [PartR] (62:3) Sum 95, p. 473.
"The Convergence of the Twain." [PartR] (62:3) Sum 95, p. 368-369.
"The Darkling Thrush." [PartR] (62:3) Sum 95, p. 355-356.
"Your Last Drive." [PartR] (62:3) Sum 95, p. 467.
2526. HARER, Katherine
"Remembering Music." [Calyx] (16:2) Wint 95-96, p. 70-71.
2527. HARJO, Joy
"The Creation Story." [Drumvoices] (4:1/2) Fall-Wint 94-95, p. 36.
"An Explosion of Horses." [RiverS] (42/43) 95, p. 39-40.
"Reconciliation, a Prayer" (for the Audre Lorde Memorial, January 18, 1993).
[IndR] (18:1) Spr 95, p. 26-27.
2528. HARLEY, Peter
"On a Cucumber Sandwich." [TickleAce] (27) Spr-Sum 94, p. 61-62.
2529. HARMES, James
"20th Century Boy." [MissouriR] (18:2) 95, p. 198.
"Copper Wire." [MissouriR] (18:2) 95, p. 196-197.
"Decadence: Newport Beach, California." [MissouriR] (18:2) 95, p. 192-193.
"Elegy As Evening, As Exodus" (North of Malibu). [MissouriR] (18:2) 95, p. 191.
"In Any Country" (an Epithalamium). [MissouriR] (18:2) 95, p. 194.
"Mother to Daughter." [MissouriR] (18:2) 95, p. 195.
2530. HARMON, Georganne
"The Concert" (to Eddie Kao). [Pearl] (22) Fall-Wint 95, p. 134.
2531. HARMON, William
"Air." [CarolQ] (47:3) Sum 95, p. 60.
"Plan for a Totem." [CarolQ] (47:3) Sum 95, p. 61-62.
2532. HARMS, James
"My Own Little Piece of Hollywood." [QW] (40) Spr-Sum 95, p. 78-79.
2533. HAROUTIUNIAN, Artem
"Unnamed Places" (tr. by Diana Der-Hovanessian). [GrahamHR] (19) Wint 95-96,
p. 52.
2534. HARP, Jerry
"The Millennium Turning." [Verse] (12:2) 95, p. 63.
2535. HARPER, L. L. (Linda Lee)
"I-II It Was perfectly True." [SpoonR] (20:2) Sum-Fall 95, p. 63.
"At the Other Grandfather's Door." [GeoR] (49:4) Wint 95, p. 904.
"Before the Crash" (Forence, Alabama, 1929). [AntigR] (101) Spr 95, p. 120.
"Between the Garage and the House" (Sandheger Place, 1959). [AntigR] (101) Spr
95, p. 118-119.
"Coming Up Empty." [LullwaterR] (6:2) Fall-Wint 95, p. 50-51.
"The Duet." [InterQ] (2:1/2) 95, p. 137.
"Fishing Alone." [InterQ] (2:1/2) 95, p. 138.
"In Augusta, Georgia." [SoCoast] (18) Ja 95, p. 57.
"Lucy." [AntigR] (101) Spr 95, p. 117.
"Of Bones." [HiramPoR] (58/59) Spr 95-Wint 96, p. 33.
"She Opens the Door." [BellR] (18:2, #38) Fall 95, p. 34.
2536. HARPER, Michael S.
"Changes on Coleman Hawkins' Birthday" (for Robert Burns Stepto and in memory
of his parents). [Crazy] (49) Wint 95, p. 7-8.
"Crypt" (In memoriam, Ralph Waldo Ellison, 1914-1994). [Callaloo] (18:2) Spr 95,
p. 319-320.
"The Ghost of Soulmaking: For Ruth Oppenheim" (Lynda Hull Memorial Poetry
Award). [Crazy] (49) Wint 95, p. 9-10.
"Manong, Angola." [CutB] (43) Wint 95, p. 79.
"Mule." [Crazy] (49) Wint 95, p. 11-12.
"Prologue of an Arkansas Traveler." [KenR] (17:3/4) Sum-Fall 95, p. 25-33.

2537. HARPER, Sue
"Gladstone Street." [AntigR] (102/103) Sum-Aug 95, p. 111-112.
2538. HARPER, Toni
"Shelf Life." [FreeL] (15) Aut 95, p. 9-10.
2539. HARRIGAN, Vince
"Autumn Meditating." [RagMag] (12:2) Spr 95, p. 55.
2540. HARRIS, Cheryl Irene
"From the War Journals" (January 16, 1991). [Drumvoices] (4:1/2) Fall-Wint 94-95,
p. 20-22.
"Home" (for themba, leonardo and willie, may 1991). [Drumvoices] (4:1/2) Fall-
Wint 94-95, p. 19.
2541. HARRIS, E.
"At the Public Baths in Kyoto." [Grain] (22:4) Spr 95, p. 47.
"I Asked the Stonemason." [Grain] (22:4) Spr 95, p. 46.
2542. HARRIS, F. Dianne
"Morphine." [Ledge] (19) Wint 95, p. 128.
2543. HARRIS, Henry Troy
"Waiting." [Pearl] (22) Fall-Wint 95, p. 109.
2544. HARRIS, James
"Deliverance." [PoetryE] (41) Aut 95, p. 66.
2545. HARRIS, Jana
"Dot" (Laura Soward, b. 1897). [Ploughs] (21:1) Spr 95, p. 151-153.
"Midday, Too Hot for Chores" (July 1878). [Ploughs] (21:1) Spr 95, p. 154-155.
"Mrs. Bishop's Pilot Rock Chapeaux and Notions Shop, 1882." [Ploughs] (21:1) Spr
95, p. 156-157.
2546. HARRIS, Jennifer
"A Certain Likeness." [NewYorkQ] (54) 95, p. 81.
2547. HARRIS, Joseph
"The Importance of Being Ogden." [Light] (13) Spr 95, p. 18.
"Town and Country." [Light] (15/16) Aut-Wint 95-96, p. 29.
2548. HARRIS, Kathleen
"Untitled: Large white arms in a sleeveless top, sweaty." [FreeL] (14) Wint 95, p.
15.
2549. HARRIS, Ken
"Tic." [NewOR] (21:2) Sum 95, p. 50.
"Vamp." [NewOR] (21:2) Sum 95, p. 50.
2550. HARRIS, Marie
"Louis Antoine de Bougainville, Who Circumnavigated the Globe (1766-1769) ...
Discovers Longboat Key in the Off-Season." [HangL] (66) 95, p. 31.
"Love Poem" (2-14-94). [HangL] (66) 95, p. 32.
"Sometimes the Wider World Can Only Be Apprehended Obliquely." [HangL] (66)
95, p. 32.
2551. HARRIS, Maureen
"Animal Dreams." [PottPort] (16:1) Fall 95, p. 54-55.
2552. HARRIS, Peggy
"Making Ourselves Bare." [Poem] (74) N 95, p. 55.
2553. HARRISON, Jeffrey
"Alexander Kinglake and the Giraffe of Paris." [ParisR] (37:137) Wint 95, p. 106-
107.
"Convenience Store." [Poetry] (166:3) Je 95, p. 156-157.
"Little Portrait." [Nat] (261:6) 28 Ag-4 S 95, p. 216.
"Two Salutations" (for James Merrill). [ParisR] (37:137) Wint 95, p. 107-109.
2554. HARRISON, Jim
"Time Suite." [NowestR] (33:2) 95, p. 100-105.
2555. HARRISON, Joseph
"Adam." [BostonR] (20:3) Sum 95, p. 23.
"Frost Heaves." [BostonR] (20:3) Sum 95, p. 23.
"Not Playing Possum." [ParisR] (37:134) Spr 95, p. 179.
"R. M. H." [BostonR] (20:3) Sum 95, p. 23.
"Scylla and Charybdis." [BostonR] (20:3) Sum 95, p. 23.
2556. HARRISON, Neil
"At Blue Hole." [MidwQ] (36:4) Sum 95, p. 379.
2557. HARRISON, Pamela
"Came the Rain." [GreenMR] (8:1) Spr-Sum 95, p. 97.
"What to Make of It." [CimR] (112) Jl 95, p. 106-107.

2558. HARRISON, Tony
  "The Kaisers of Carnuntum" (drama in verse). [Arion] (3:2/3) Fall 95-Wint 96, p. 191-235.
  "Two into One." [Epoch] (44:3) 95, p. 262-263.
  "Wordsworth's Stone." [Epoch] (44:3) 95, p. 261.
2559. HARROD, Lois Marie
  "Desire." [SpoonR] (20:1) Wint-Spr 95, p. 105.
  "Drought." [SpoonR] (20:1) Wint-Spr 95, p. 104.
  "Figurative Speech." [US1] (30/31) 95, p. 6.
  "A Light to Read By." [Vis] (49) 95, p. 21.
  "Sonnet of Salvation." [Vis] (47) 95, p. 10.
  "The Sonnet of the Big Screen." [SoCoast] (18) Ja 95, p. 36.
2560. HARSENT, David
  "After Rembrandt." [Epoch] (44:3) 95, p. 292-293.
  "The Double." [Epoch] (44:3) 95, p. 290-291.
  "Père Caboche." [Epoch] (44:3) 95, p. 294-295.
2561. HART, Henry
  "Dioramas of King Philip's War." [GettyR] (8:3) Sum 95, p. 500-501.
  "Directives." [NewYorker] (71:33) 23 O 95, p. 48.
  "Mountain Burial." [WilliamMR] (33) 95, p. 54-55.
  "Pocahontas in Jamestown." [SouthernHR] (29:1) Wint 95, p. 12-13.
  "The Prisoner of Camau." [BelPoJ] (46:1) Fall 95, p. 34-40.
2562. HART, Jack
  "More Than a Cupid's Bow." [Hellas] (6:1) Spr-Sum 95, p. 36.
2563. HART, James
  "The Function of Shock." [PoetryNW] (36:1) Spr 95, p. 22.
  "The Volunteer." [PoetryNW] (36:1) Spr 95, p. 22-23.
  "What Sins Matter." [PoetryNW] (36:1) Spr 95, p. 21.
2564. HART, Kenneth
  "In a Place Such as This." [BellR] (18:1, #37) Spr 95, p. 37.
2565. HART, Kevin
  "Approaching Sleep." [Verse] (12:2) 95, p. 64-65.
2566. HARTENBACH, Mark
  "Matter of Perception." [ChironR] (43) Sum 95, p. 28.
2567. HARTMARK, Laura
  "Azalea." [InterQ] (2:1/2) 95, p. 23.
2568. HARTNETT, Michael
  "IX. Do Neasa." [Poetry] (167:1/2) O-N 95, p. 60.
  "XVIII. In memoriam Sheila Hackett." [Poetry] (167:1/2) O-N 95, p. 60-61.
  "XXVI. Across the road, perhaps last week." [Poetry] (167:1/2) O-N 95, p. 61.
  "Parables for Clane" (For the staff of Clane General Hospital). [Poetry] (167:1/2) O-N 95, p. 62-63.
2569. HARTSELL, John
  "Bats" (21 Contest Winner, Third). [Grain] (22:3) Wint 95, p. 40.
  "Marlo and H2O" (21 Contest Winner, Third). [Grain] (22:3) Wint 95, p. 39.
2570. HARVEY, Francis
  "Fishermen." [Poetry] (167:1/2) O-N 95, p. 12.
  "Love Letters." [Poetry] (167:1/2) O-N 95, p. 13.
  "Sheepmen." [Poetry] (167:1/2) O-N 95, p. 14.
  "The Space Between." [Poetry] (167:1/2) O-N 95, p. 13.
  "The Wheelwright and the Boy." [Poetry] (167:1/2) O-N 95, p. 12.
2571. HARVEY, Gayle Elen
  "Everything in the World." [GreenHLL] (6) 95, p. 85.
  "Love Pantoum." [Poem] (73) My 95, p. 32.
  "Silver Anniversary." [Poem] (73) My 95, p. 33.
2572. HARVEY, John
  "Angelus Novus." [ParisR] (37:135) Sum 95, p. 85-88.
  "Epistle." [GettyR] (8:3) Sum 95, p. 524-525.
  "Walt Disney World." [GettyR] (8:3) Sum 95, p. 523.
2573. HARVEY, Shernika
  "The Bubble Angel" (WritersCorps Program, Washington, DC). [WashR] (21:2) Ag-S 95, p. 6.
2574. HARVOR, Elisabeth
  "August, Dipper Harbour." [Arc] (34) Spr 95, p. 13-15.
  "The Bad Air of the Century." [Quarry] (43:4) 95, p. 22-24.
  "Blowtorch Alchemy." [Arc] (34) Spr 95, p. 11-12.

2575. HASEGAWA, Seisaku
    "Alas — in the midst of sandbanks" (in Japanese and English, tr. by Jiro Nakano).
        [BambooR] (67/68) Sum-Fall 95, p. 9.
2576. HASKINS, Lola
    "Burrows." [LowellR] [1] Sum 94, p. 46.
    "Elegy on a Winter Morning." [LowellR] [1] Sum 94, p. 47.
    "From the Closet." [Flyway] (1:1) Spr 95, p. 7.
    "I want this poem to scream." [NewYorkQ] (54) 95, p. 14.
    "In the Gulf, with Balaji." [BelPoJ] (46:2) Wint 95-96, p. 25.
    "Night Walking." [Flyway] (1:1) Spr 95, p. 6.
    "On Passing Fifty." [SouthernR] (31:1) Wint 95, p. 18.
    "Pick-Up Dancing at the Cypress." [LowellR] [1] Sum 94, p. 45.
    "Spell for a Poet Getting On." [PraS] (69:3) Fall 95, p. 144.
2577. HASS, Robert
    "After Enduring" (tr. of Czeslaw Milosz, w. the author). [OhioR] (53) 95, p. 31.
    "An Appeal" (tr. of Czeslaw Milosz). [Verse] (12:2) 95, p. 96-98.
    "Body" (tr. of Czeslaw Milosz, w. the author). [NewYorker] (71:7) 10 Ap 95, p. 60.
    "Dawns" (tr. of Czeslaw Milosz). [RiverS] (42/43) 95, p. 140-141.
    "Faint Music." [Zyzzyva] (11:1, #41) Spr 95, p. 130-131.
    "The Garden of Earthly Delights: Hell" (tr. of Czeslaw Milosz, w. the author).
        [OhioR] (53) 95, p. 30.
    "A Hall" (tr. of Czeslaw Milosz, w. the author). [NewYorker] (71:8) 17 Ap 95, p.
        77.
    "House in Krasnogruda" (tr. of Czeslaw Milosz, w. the author). [AmerPoR] (24:2)
        Mr-Ap 95, p. 55.
    "In Szetejnie" (tr. of Czeslaw Milosz, w. the author). [AmerPoR] (24:2) Mr-Ap 95,
        p. 54.
    "In the Saliva / in the Paper" (tr. of Frida Kahlo). [TriQ] (95) Wint 95-96, p. 276.
    "Interrupted Meditation." [ColR] (22:2) Fall 95, p. 93-96.
    "Iowa City: Early April." [TriQ] (95) Wint 95-96, p. 46-48.
    "Lithuania, After Fifty-Two Years" (Selections, tr. of Czeslaw Milosz, w. the
        author). [AmerPoR] (24:2) Mr-Ap 95, p. 55.
    "One More Contradiction" (tr. of Czeslaw Milosz, w. the author). [GeoR] (49:1) Spr
        95, p. 129.
    "Pierson College" (tr. of Czeslaw Milosz, w. the author). [Thrpny] (61) Spr 95, p. 5.
    "Privilege of Being." [Verse] (12:2) 95, p. 66-67.
    "Retired" (tr. of Czeslaw Milosz, w. the author). [PartR] (62:2) Spr 95, p. 293-294.
    "Sonnet." [NewYorker] (70:43 [i.e. 44]) 9 Ja 95, p. 49.
    "Tahoe in August." [Zyzzyva] (11:3/4, #43/44) 95, "The Best of Ten Years of
        ZYZZYVA," p. 43-44.
    "To Mrs. Professor in Defense of My Cat's Honor and Not Only" (tr. of Czeslaw
        Milosz, w. the author). [NewYRB] (42:5) 23 Mr 95, p. 42.
    "To My Daimonion" (tr. of Czeslaw Milosz, w. the author). [PartR] (62:2) Spr 95, p.
        292-293.
    "The Wall of a Museum" (tr. of Czeslaw Milosz, w. the author). [Zyzzyva] (11:1,
        #41) Spr 95, p. 163.
    "You Whose Name" (tr. of Czeslaw Milosz, w. the author). [PartR] (62:2) Spr 95, p.
        295.
2578. HASSLER, David
    "Long Walk Home." [TarRP] (35:1) Fall 95, p. 36-37.
    "The Prayer Wheel." [TarRP] (35:1) Fall 95, p. 36.
    "Travel Can Be a Way of Mourning" (for Inge). [IndR] (18:2) Fall 95, p. 121-122.
2579. HATHAWAY, Michael
    "Angel Sitting on the Edge of My Bed at 5 A.M." [Pearl] (22) Fall-Wint 95, p. 137.
    "The Burning Bed." [Pearl] (22) Fall-Wint 95, p. 137.
2580. HATHAWAY, William
    "The Apologist for Love." [NewOR] (21:2) Sum 95, p. 93-94.
    "Country Girl." [GettyR] (8:2) Spr 95, p. 276-278.
    "The Natural Law of Culture." [Crazy] (48) Spr 95, p. 66-67.
    "Who Killed Keats." [GettyR] (8:2) Spr 95, p. 279-280.
2581. HATSUI, Shizue
    "A photo of a school boy" (in Japanese and English, tr. by Jiro Nakano). [BambooR]
        (67/68) Sum-Fall 95, p. 10.
2582. HAUSHOFER, Albrecht
    "On the Threshold" (sonnet, tr. by R. S. Gwynn). [SewanR] (103:3) Sum 95, p. 381.
    "Sir Thomas More" (sonnet, tr. by R. S. Gwynn). [SewanR] (103:3) Sum 95, p. 382.

"Time" (sonnet, tr. by R. S. Gwynn). [SewanR] (103:3) Sum 95, p. 382.
2583. HAVEN, Stephen
   "A Geography of Movement." [AmerPoR] (24:5) S-O 95, p. 48.
2584. HAVIRD, Ashley Mace
   "Jeté." [Vis] (49) 95, p. 17.
2585. HAWORTH-HOEPPNER, Edward
   "Boy at Ten." [Poem] (74) N 95, p. 63.
   "The Dead of Winter." [PraS] (69:1) Spr 95, p. 86-87.
   "History." [LullwaterR] (5:1) 93-94, p. 66.
   "Long Promise." [OxfordM] (9:2) Fall-Wint 93, p. 108-109.
   "Mid-Winter Thaw." [IndR] (18:2) Fall 95, p. 27-28.
   "Miscarriage." [OxfordM] (9:2) Fall-Wint 93, p. 106-107.
   "Mitochrondria." [Flyway] (1:3) Wint 95, p. 72-73.
   "Parts and Service." [MidwQ] (37:1) Aut 95, p. 38-39.
   "Restlessness." [PraS] (69:1) Spr 95, p. 88-89.
   "Shadowbox." [Poem] (74) N 95, p. 62.
   "Spirits of Place." [Poem] (74) N 95, p. 59-61.
   "Spring: The North Shore." [IndR] (18:2) Fall 95, p. 29-30.
   "Texts for Wednesday's Class." [PraS] (69:1) Spr 95, p. 85-86.
   "Variation on a Theme." [PraS] (69:1) Spr 95, p. 84-85.
   "Winona." [HayF] (16) Spr-Sum 95, p. 110-111.
2586. HAXTON, Brooks
   "The Black Raincoat." [TriQ] (93) Spr-Sum 95, p. 107-108.
   "Catalpa, Meaning Head with Wings." [SouthernR] (31:1) Wint 95, p. 19-20.
   "Century Flower." [TriQ] (93) Spr-Sum 95, p. 104-106.
   "Days." [TriQ] (93) Spr-Sum 95, p. 103.
   "Further Revelations on the Planet Wokka." [PoetryE] (40) Spr 95, p. 53.
   "Giotto's Angel over the Dead Christ Spread His Arms in Flight." [SouthernR]
      (31:1) Wint 95, p. 20-21.
   "It Comes to Me: Concision!" [ParisR] (37:136) Fall 95, p. 76-77.
   "Keepsake." [PoetryE] (40) Spr 95, p. 52.
   "The Last Confession of Roger Tory Peterson." [ParisR] (37:136) Fall 95, p. 75.
   "The Learned Hevelius When He Mapped the Moon Found Waters There As Kepler
      and Pythagoras Had Done." [VirQR] (71:1) Wint 95, p. 113-114.
   "Molybdenum." [Atlantic] (276:1) Jl 95, p. 44.
   "The Nature of the Beast." [TriQ] (93) Spr-Sum 95, p. 109.
   "On the Inundated First Site of the Town of Greenville." [VirQR] (71:1) Wint 95, p.
      114.
   "One More Thing." [GettyR] (8:2) Spr 95, p. 349-350.
   "Ray." [TriQ] (93) Spr-Sum 95, p. 110.
   "Repertory." [GettyR] (8:2) Spr 95, p. 347-348.
   "Sonnet at Forty." [PoetryE] (40) Spr 95, p. 51.
   "Two Ladies." [VirQR] (71:1) Wint 95, p. 115.
   "Wild Geraniums." [Boulevard] (10:1/2, #28/29) Spr 95, p. 210.
   "Wisdom." [ParisR] (37:136) Fall 95, p. 75-76.
2587. HAYASE, Yuzuru
   "Radiation concealed" (in Japanese and English, tr. by Jiro Nakano). [BambooR]
      (67/68) Sum-Fall 95, p. 11.
2588. HAYDEN, Chris
   "Little Las Vegas." [Drumvoices] (5:1/2) Fall-Wint 95-96, p. 15.
   "Triumph of Her Will" (for Jackie Joyner-Kersee). [Drumvoices] (5:1/2) Fall-Wint
      95-96, p. 16.
2589. HAYDEN, Dolores
   "Language of the Fan." [Hellas] (6:1) Spr-Sum 95, p. 40-41.
2590. HAYES, Carol (Carol Porter)
   "The Birth of Guilt." [Pembroke] (27) 95, p. 70.
   "What Can't Be Spoken Of." [AlabamaLR] (9:1) 95, p. 56-57.
2591. HAYES, Glenn
   "Anima." [PoetryC] (15:3) Ag 95, p. 11.
   "Fences." [PoetryC] (15:3) Ag 95, p. 11.
   "Suburban Post-Apocalypse Harvest Song." [PoetryC] (15:3) Ag 95, p. 11.
   "Summer New World Night." [PoetryC] (15:3) Ag 95, p. 11.
2592. HAYES, Jana
   "Dancing." [Os] (40) 95, p. 14-15.
2593. HAYES, John
   "Godsword." [Bogg] (67) 95, p. 24.

2594. HAYES, Terrance
"The Earth God." [PoetL] (90:4) Wint 95-96, p. 35-36.
2595. HAYHURST, Joanne
"Memorial Day Parade." [Blueline] (16) 95, p. 2-3.
2596. HAYMAN, Dick
"Condimenting Nash." [Light] (13) Spr 95, p. 18.
"Par-Cheesy." [Light] (13) Spr 95, p. 13.
"Words to Create By." [Light] (14) Sum 95, p. 21.
2597. HAYMON, Ava Leavell
"Waiting for Dark." [Prima] (18/19) 95, p. 12-13.
2598. HAYNES, Linda Collins
"The Night Dutch Murphy Died." [HopewellR] (7) 95, p. 99.
2599. HAYS, Angelyn
"One of the Cardinal Seasons." [ClockR] (10:1/2) 95-96, p. 139.
"Starlings." [ClockR] (10:1/2) 95-96, p. 138.
2600. HAZELDINE, Nigel
"Zuni Koar." [AnthNEW] (7) 95, p. 26.
2601. HAZNERS, Dainis
"3/17 PM Pills." [Parting] (8:2) Wint 95-96, p. 13.
"3/21." [Parting] (8:2) Wint 95-96, p. 14.
"3/25 Friday AM Rain." [Parting] (8:2) Wint 95-96, p. 15.
2602. HAZO, Samuel
"Lines at Sea on Love and Death." [AmerS] (64:1) Wint 95, p. 38-40.
"Matador." [Boulevard] (10:1/2, #28/29) Spr 95, p. 178-180.
"Once Against a Time." [GeoR] (49:2) Sum 95, p. 429-430.
"To Stop and Be Stopped in Lourmarin." [AmerS] (64:3) Sum 95, p. 436-437.
HE, Li
See LI, He
2603. HEAD, Gwen
"Shooting Stars." [SouthernR] (31:4) O/Aut 95, p. 849-850.
"Villanelle" (for A. R. N.). [SouthernR] (31:4) O/Aut 95, p. 850-851.
2604. HEALEY, Stephen
"Anatomy of Silence." [PoetryE] (39) Fall 94, p. 33-34.
"Why I Sing." [SouthernPR] (35:1) Sum 95, p. 14-16.
2605. HEALY, Randolph
"Frogs." [WestCL] (29:2, #17) Fall 95, p. 43-44.
"Heresiarch." [WestCL] (29:2, #17) Fall 95, p. 42-43.
"World War II." [WestCL] (29:2, #17) Fall 95, p. 45.
2606. HEANEY, Seamus
"As If" (tr. of Ana Blandiana). [SouthernR] (31:3) Jl/Sum 95, p. 469.
"Diptych." [CutB] (42) Sum 94, p. 47-48.
"A Dog Was Crying To-night in Wicklow Also" (In memory of Donatus Nwoga).
[Poetry] (167:1/2) O-N 95, p. 1-2.
"Hailstones." [SenR] (25:1) Spr 95, p. 73-74.
"The Haw Lantern." [Verse] (12:2) 95, p. 68.
"Hunt" (tr. of Ana Blandiana). [SouthernR] (31:3) Jl/Sum 95, p. 471.
"Inhabited by a Song" (tr. of Ana Blandiana). [SouthernR] (31:3) Jl/Sum 95, p. 468.
"Lament 1" (tr. of Jan Kochanowski, w. Stanislaw Baranczak). [Thrpny] (63) Fall
95, p. 13.
"Lament 2" (tr. of Jan Kochanowski, 1530-1584, w. Stanislaw Baranczak). [PartR]
(62:3) Sum 95, p. 444-445.
"Lament 16" (tr. of Jan Kochanowski, 1530-1584, w. Stanislaw Baranczak). [PartR]
(62:3) Sum 95, p. 443-444.
"Loneliness" (tr. of Ana Blandiana). [SouthernR] (31:3) Jl/Sum 95, p. 470-471.
"Maybe There's Somebody Dreaming Me" (tr. of Ana Blandiana). [SouthernR]
(31:3) Jl/Sum 95, p. 469-470.
"Mycenae Nightwatch." [Poetry] (167:1/2) O-N 95, p. 2-4.
"Remembered Columns." [Poetry] (167:1/2) O-N 95, p. 2.
"Resolutions." [NewMyths] (2:2/3:1) 95, p. 117-118.
"The Sharping Stone." [NewYorker] (71:33) 23 O 95, p. 62-63.
"The Swing." [SouthernR] (31:3) Jl/Sum 95, p. 676-678.
2607. HEATH-STUBBS, John
"Not All at Once." [Epoch] (44:3) 95, p. 315.
2608. HEBALD, Carol
"Catalonia in the Vestibule." [Confr] (56/57) Sum-Fall 95, p. 32-33.
"First Prayer." [Confr] (56/57) Sum-Fall 95, p. 33-34.

2609. HECHT, Anthony
"Death the Poet: A Ballade-Lament for the Makers." [SewanR] (103:1) Wint 95, p. 10.
"For James Merrill: An Adieu." [Poetry] (166:6) S 95, p. 316.
"Matisse — Blue Interior with Two Girls — 1947." [ColR] (22:1) Spr 95, p. 14-15.
2610. HECHT, Susan
"Workshopping with the Great Male Poets." [ChironR] (43) Sum 95, p. 30.
2611. HECK, April
"The Bridge." [GreensboroR] (57) Wint 94-95, p. 77.
2612. HEDDEREL, Vance Philip
"For Months I Waited Outside the Door." [JamesWR] (12:2) Spr-Sum 95, p. 8.
"The Uninhabited Angel." [JamesWR] (12:2) Spr-Sum 95, p. 8.
2613. HEDGES, David
"The Curious Stares and the Hungry Eyes." [Hellas] (6:1) Spr-Sum 95, p. 42.
2614. HEDIN, Robert
"Dies Illae" (from "Night Music," tr. of Rolf Jacobsen). [Nimrod] (38:2) Spr-Sum 95, p. 78.
"Lines on March 28" (tr. of Lars Gustafsson). [Nimrod] (38:2) Spr-Sum 95, p. 84.
"Play" (from "Night Music," tr. of Rolf Jacobsen). [Nimrod] (38:2) Spr-Sum 95, p. 78.
"Virvlarna" (tr. of Lars Gustafsson). [Nimrod] (38:2) Spr-Sum 95, p. 82.
"Whirls" (tr. of Lars Gustafsson). [Nimrod] (38:2) Spr-Sum 95, p. 83.
HEE-JIN, Park
See PARK, Hee-Jin
2615. HEFFERNAN, Michael
"Another Story." [Shen] (45:4) Wint 95, p. 40.
"Extracorporeal." [GettyR] (8:3) Sum 95, p. 527.
"The Muse." [TriQ] (95) Wint 95-96, p. 152.
"The Virgin's Revery" [sic]. [SouthernHR] (29:3) Sum 95, p. 246-248.
2616. HEFLIN, Jack
"How Sadness Enters the Gardener's Journal." [LouisL] (12:1) Spr 95, p. 45.
2617. HEIGHTON, Steven
"Poet with Sedna, Goddess of the Sea." [Nimrod] (38:2) Spr-Sum 95, p. 27.
2618. HEIM, Scott
"Apple-Head." [MidwQ] (36:3) Spr 95, p. 299-300.
"Donna Summer." [SilverFR] (25) Sum 95, p. 8-9.
"Emergencies." [ApalQ] (43) Spr 95, p. 77-79.
2619. HEIMAN, Jamie
"Snap Shot." [Confr] (56/57) Sum-Fall 95, p. 342.
2620. HEIN, Kurt
"Morning Anthem." [WorldO] (27:1) Fall 95, p. 7.
2621. HEINE, Heinrich
"Commemoration Service" (tr. by Hal Draper). [NewYRB] (42:13) 10 Ag 95, p. 41.
"Gedächtnisfeier." [NewYRB] (42:13) 10 Ag 95, p. 41.
2622. HEINLEIN, David A.
"Ki" (— the life-spirit in each person, also permeating the universe). [US1] (30/31) 95, p. 7.
2623. HEINY, Katherine
"The Barbie Doll Games" (for Jojo). [SycamoreR] (7:1) Wint 95, p. 19.
"Compliments." [SycamoreR] (7:1) Wint 95, p. 18.
2624. HEINZELMAN, Kurt
"Delivery of a Speech Whose Time Has Come." [Border] (6) Spr-Sum 95, p. 40.
2625. HEISE, Thomas
"Cycles." [Pearl] (22) Fall-Wint 95, p. 116.
"Dedication" (for Edward / Vivian Heise). [Blueline] (16) 95, p. 101.
"Migration." [Pearl] (22) Fall-Wint 95, p. 116.
2626. HEISEY-CLARK, Robyn
"On Palm Sunday." [MassR] (36:4) Wint 95-96, p. 564.
"Widow Sleep." [MassR] (36:4) Wint 95-96, p. 565.
2627. HEJINIAN, Lyn
"A Border Comedy." [Chain] (2) Spr 95, p. 110-113.
"Sight" (Excerpt, w. Leslie Scalapino). [Zyzzyva] (11:1, #41) Spr 95, p. 153-160.
2628. HELD, Dennis
"In Praise of Abandon." [WillowS] (35) Ja 95, p. 32.
2629. HELLER, Dorothy
"Food for Thought." [Light] (15/16) Aut-Wint 95-96, p. 20.

2630. HELLER, Michael
"Allotments" (by M., the subject of "The Study"). [AmerLC] (7) 95, p. 72-73.
"As If It Weren't" (by M., the subject of "The Study"). [AmerLC] (7) 95, p. 70-71.
"Failure" (by M., the subject of "The Study"). [AmerLC] (7) 95, p. 82-83.
"Funereal" (by M., the subject of "The Study"). [AmerLC] (7) 95, p. 74-75.
"Lost Longing" (by M., the subject of "The Study"). [AmerLC] (7) 95, p. 87.
"The Neighborhood" (by M., the subject of "The Study"). [AmerLC] (7) 95, p. 80.
"To Go Home" (by M., the subject of "The Study"). [AmerLC] (7) 95, p. 78.
"To Know of Counsel" (by M., the subject of "The Study"). [AmerLC] (7) 95, p. 88.
"To Say a Word" (by M., the subject of "The Study"). [AmerLC] (7) 95, p. 85.
2631. HELLUS, Al
"For Singles Only." [LullwaterR] (5:1) 93-94, p. 34-35.
"Vegetable." [PennR] (6:2) 95, p. 20.
2632. HELMER, Nika
"Heart-Stone." [BelPoJ] (46:1) Fall 95, p. 16.
2633. HELSTERN, Linda Lizut
"Trick or Treat" (runner up, 1994 Borderlands Poetry Contest). [Border] (7) Fall-Wint 96, p. 17-18.
2634. HELWIG, Maggie
"August 6, Novi Sad." [PoetryC] (15:3) Ag 95, p. 4.
"Manerplaw." [Quarry] (44:2) 95, p. 96-98.
"Paris — Hagiographies." [PoetryC] (15:3) Ag 95, p. 4.
"Variations on Spring." [PoetryC] (15:3) Ag 95, p. 5.
2635. HELWIG, Susan
"The Black Dogs in Rostock" (for Daniel Jones, 1959-1994). [PoetryC] (15:2) Je 95, p. 26.
2636. HEMAN, Bob
"True Adventure." [ProseP] (4) 95, p. 33.
2637. HEMPHILL, Caroline
"Between Women, Ashes Pass." [GrahamHR] (19) Wint 95-96, p. 29.
"The Long Armenian Winter." [GrahamHR] (19) Wint 95-96, p. 27-28.
"When I Come Again." [GrahamHR] (19) Wint 95-96, p. 31.
"While You Were Killing Us." [GrahamHR] (19) Wint 95-96, p. 30.
2638. HENDERSON, Archibald
"Death Will Not Come." [NorthStoneR] (12) 95, p. 226.
"Interstate." [GreenHLL] (6) 95, p. 105.
"Lone Wolf." [NorthStoneR] (12) 95, p. 227.
2639. HENDERSON, Charity
"Nickelville Road." [HiramPoR] (58/59) Spr 95-Wint 96, p. 34-35.
2640. HENDERSON, David W.
"The Fires Burned All Summer" (for H.C.). [CumbPR] (15:1) Fall 95, p. 26-28.
"Victory Garden." [CumbPR] (15:1) Fall 95, p. 24-25.
2641. HENDON, Judy
"Revisions" (for my father). [Pearl] (22) Fall-Wint 95, p. 147.
"Silverlake." [BellArk] (11:2) Mr-Ap 95, p. 26.
2642. HENDRICKS, Jeanette
"The Equinox." [BellArk] (11:3) My-Je 95, p. 25.
"Metal, Half Shiny." [BellArk] (11:4) Jl-Ag 95, p. 22.
"This Feeling between Us." [BellArk] (11:3) My-Je 95, p. 11.
2643. HENDRICKS, Keith Gabriel
"Mercury Pursues the Flurry and Opens Eyebrows of Snow to Receive Colin Rowe, Falling." [SpinningJ] (1) Fall 95-Wint 96, p. 36-37.
"My Shotgun Wedding to the Shape-Shifting Queen of the Hive." [SpinningJ] (1) Fall 95-Wint 96, p. 38.
"When You Went to Class with a Suntanned Soul." [HiramPoR] (58/59) Spr 95-Wint 96, p. 37.
"Words Spit From a Shadow." [HiramPoR] (58/59) Spr 95-Wint 96, p. 36.
2644. HENDRICKSON, John
"The Real Duty of Children." [Hellas] (6:1) Spr-Sum 95, p. 90.
"A Short View of Overpopulation." [Hellas] (6:1) Spr-Sum 95, p. 91.
"To the Lord of Amps Dying Young." [Hellas] (6:1) Spr-Sum 95, p. 92.
2645. HENDRYSON, Barbara (Barbara A.)
"Stars." [Kalliope] (17:2) 95, p. 21-22.
"Stars." [Plain] (15:2) Wint 95, p. 12-13.
"Tango, Tango." [Kalliope] (17:3) 95, p. 20.

207

"This Is How He Began to Show Me the Dark." [SouthernPR] (35:1) Sum 95, p. 63-64.
"The Violence." [BellR] (18:1, #37) Spr 95, p. 48.
2646. HENLEY, Jim
"Ozymandias III." [Hudson] (48:1) Spr 95, p. 100.
2647. HENN, Mary Ann
"You Cry." [ChironR] (42) Spr 95, p. 29.
2648. HENNEDY, Hugh
"In the Laundermat Again" [sic]. [DefinedP] (1:2) Spr-Sum 93, p. 46.
2649. HENNEN, Tom
"Country Latin." [NorthStoneR] (12) 95, p. 62.
"Picking a World." [NorthStoneR] (12) 95, p. 64.
"A Real Rain This Morning." [NorthStoneR] (12) 95, p. 63.
"Spring Follows Winter Once More." [NorthStoneR] (12) 95, p. 63.
"The Trees Have Bewitched Themselves." [NorthStoneR] (12) 95, p. 64.
"Working with Idleness." [NorthStoneR] (12) 95, p. 65.
2650. HENNING, Barbara
"Manual Typewriters Are Superior." [PoetryE] (40) Spr 95, p. 54.
"Tonight There Is a Dangerous Rip Tide." [Talisman] (15) Wint 95-96, p. 102-103.
2651. HENNING, Dianna
"Apprenticeship." [LullwaterR] (6:1) Spr-Sum 95, p. 56-57.
"Cautionary Glass." [LullwaterR] (6:2) Fall-Wint 95, p. 54-55.
"Kicking the Habit." [LullwaterR] (6:1) Spr-Sum 95, p. 58.
"Narrative Hung by the Sea" (runner up, 1994 Borderlands Poetry Contest). [Border] (7) Fall-Wint 96, p. 20.
2652. HENRIE, Carol
"The Cell." [PraS] (69:2) Sum 95, p. 107-108.
"Emily's Room." [PoetryNW] (36:1) Spr 95, p. 13.
"The Night I Drove to the Bridge." [PraS] (69:2) Sum 95, p. 105-106.
"Pond Snakes." [PoetryNW] (36:1) Spr 95, p. 12.
2653. HENRY, Brian (Brian T.)
"After Happy Hour." [HolCrit] (32:2) Ap 95, p. 19.
"Exhumation." [HangL] (67) 95, p. 40.
"Jasmine Tea." [HangL] (67) 95, p. 41.
2654. HENRY, Ronnica
"Don't fear the reaper." [Poz] (7) Ap-My 95, p. 28.
"Glad Cling Wrap, clear." [Poz] (7) Ap-My 95, p. 28.
"We stand like stringless puppets." [Poz] (7) Ap-My 95, p. 28.
2655. HENSON, Lance
"Concerto in Four Movements." [WeberS] (12:3) Fall 95, p. 149.
"Prayer for the Lenape." [WeberS] (12:3) Fall 95, p. 148.
HENSON, Sandra Meek
See MEEK-HENSON, Sandra
2656. HENTZ, Robert R.
"Of Worms and Fire." [CapeR] (30:1) Spr 95, p. 5.
2657. HEPWORTH, Robert
"Buffalo Wings." [NewDeltaR] (13:1) Fall 95-Wint 96, p. 30-31.
2658. HERBERT, W. N.
"What Graham Does." [Verse] (12:2) 95, p. 69-70.
2659. HERBERT, Wendy
"The Sewing Teacher." [Flyway] (1:3) Wint 95, p. 8-9.
2660. HERBST, Nikki
"The Charm Bracelet Personal Flotation Device" (Finalist, 1995 Greg Grummer Award in Poetry). [Phoebe] (24:2) 95, p. 152-153.
"Little Black Sambo Turned to Peanut Butter for Your Sins" (Finalist, 1995 Greg Grummer Award in Poetry). [Phoebe] (24:2) 95, p. 155.
"The Woman Who Gave Up Thinking" (Finalist, 1995 Greg Grummer Award in Poetry). [Phoebe] (24:2) 95, p. 154.
2661. HERMAN, Mark
"Balladesque" (tr. of Richard Wagner, w. Ronnie Apter). [GrahamHR] (19) Wint 95-96, p. 68.
"Lili Marlene" (tr. of Richard Wagner, w. Ronnie Apter). [GrahamHR] (19) Wint 95-96, p. 67.
"Slices" (tr. of Richard Wagner, w. Ronnie Apter). [GrahamHR] (19) Wint 95-96, p. 66.

2662. HERNANDEZ AVILA, Inés
    "Coyote Woman Finds Fox at the Street Fair in Port Townsend" (For Kathy Fox).
    [Americas] (23:3/4) Fall-Wint 95, p. 122-123.
    "For Itseyaya and the Spirit of Coyote Creek." [Americas] (23:3/4) Fall-Wint 95, p.
    119-121.
    "Luminous Serpent Songs" (For Beto from Port Townsend, September 13, 1993).
    [Americas] (23:3/4) Fall-Wint 95, p. 116-117.
    "Moving to the Sound's Waters" (Port Townsend, September 1993). [Americas]
    (23:3/4) Fall-Wint 95, p. 115.
    "Steps of Cleansing." [Americas] (23:3/4) Fall-Wint 95, p. 118.
2663. HERNANDEZ-CRUZ, Víctor
    "Islands." [MassR] (36:4) Wint 95-96, p. 601-602.
    "The Lower East Side of Manhattan." [MassR] (36:4) Wint 95-96, p. 602-606.
    "Mesa Blanca." [RiverS] (45) 95, p. 26-28.
    "Problems with Hurricanes." [RiverS] (42/43) 95, p. 168.
2664. HERNTON, Calvin
    "Victoria Williams." [Drumvoices] (4:1/2) Fall-Wint 94-95, p. 123.
2665. HERONDAS
    "A Private Talk Among Friends" (tr. by Guy Davenport). [GrandS] (14:1, #53) Sum
    95, p. 53-58.
2666. HEROUX, Jason
    "Spring." [Bogg] (67) 95, p. 32.
2667. HERRERA, Juan Felipe
    "The Anthropomorphic Cabinet." [MassR] (36:4) Wint 95-96, p. 620.
    "Aphrodisiacal Dinner Jacket." [MassR] (36:4) Wint 95-96, p. 619-620.
    "Giraffe on Fire" (Selections: 5 poems). [AmerPoR] (24:4) Jl-Ag 95, p. 3-5.
2668. HERRICK, Robert (1591-1674)
    "To His Mistress." [PoetryE] (41) Aut 95, p. 29.
2669. HERRMANN, Duane L.
    "Sun Magnificent." [WorldO] (27:1) Fall 95, p. 19.
2670. HERRSTROM, David (David Sten)
    "Between States." [US1] (30/31) 95, p. 11.
    "Cabot's Tune." [Colum] (24/25) 95, p. 63-64.
    "Forgiveness Among the Animals." [US1] (30/31) 95, p. 12.
    "The Reunion." [Footwork] (24/25) 95, p. 63.
2671. HERSHON, Robert
    "As Natural As Breathing." [PoetryNW] (36:1) Spr 95, p. 30.
    "But That's Not Poetry" (for Mark Pawlak). [PoetryNW] (36:1) Spr 95, p. 30-31.
    "F Train Questions This Morning." [PoetryNW] (36:1) Spr 95, p. 31.
2672. HERTZ, Howard
    "Stateroom Scene." [ApalQ] (43) Spr 95, p. 55-62.
2673. HESTER, Stephen
    "After the Shutdown." [PlumR] (9) [95 or 96], p. 74.
2674. HEYEN, William
    "After-Image." [OntR] (43) Fall-Wint 95-96, p. 18.
    "At Shoreham." [SenR] (25:1) Spr 95, p. 75.
    "The Bear." [TriQ] (93) Spr-Sum 95, p. 162.
    "Before." [TriQ] (93) Spr-Sum 95, p. 158.
    "Blood & Sage." [TriQ] (93) Spr-Sum 95, p. 171.
    "Breasts." [TriQ] (93) Spr-Sum 95, p. 153.
    "The Calves." [Witness] (9:2) 95, p. 148-149.
    "Disk Text." [Witness] (9:2) 95, p. 152.
    "Duration." [TriQ] (93) Spr-Sum 95, p. 156-157.
    "Flame." [TriQ] (93) Spr-Sum 95, p. 172.
    "Forces." [Witness] (9:2) 95, p. 151.
    "Government Protection." [TriQ] (93) Spr-Sum 95, p. 154.
    "Grasshopper Sperm." [TriQ] (93) Spr-Sum 95, p. 166.
    "The Grave." [TriQ] (93) Spr-Sum 95, p. 169.
    "The Herd." [TriQ] (93) Spr-Sum 95, p. 159.
    "The Leatherstocking Tales." [OntR] (43) Fall-Wint 95-96, p. 16.
    "Legend." [OntR] (43) Fall-Wint 95-96, p. 15.
    "Mushroom River." [TriQ] (93) Spr-Sum 95, p. 170.
    "An Officer's Story." [TriQ] (93) Spr-Sum 95, p. 155.
    "Placefulness." [TriQ] (93) Spr-Sum 95, p. 163.
    "Repossession." [TriQ] (93) Spr-Sum 95, p. 164.
    "Root Music." [Witness] (9:2) 95, p. 151.

"Scenarios." [TriQ] (93) Spr-Sum 95, p. 165.
"Semi-Colon Gene Calves: General Pool & Place Data." [Witness] (9:2) 95, p. 149-150.
"Sorrow Village." [TriQ] (93) Spr-Sum 95, p. 167.
"The Steadying." [TriQ] (93) Spr-Sum 95, p. 173.
"The Streams." [OntR] (43) Fall-Wint 95-96, p. 17.
"Texas Gulliver Malaria." [TriQ] (93) Spr-Sum 95, p. 168.
"The Tooth." [TriQ] (93) Spr-Sum 95, p. 160.
"Visitor (April 1978)." [TriQ] (93) Spr-Sum 95, p. 161.
"Wingdust." [Witness] (9:2) 95, p. 152.
2675. HIBBARD, Tom
"Little Daily Phantoms" (tr. of Philippe Soupault). [WillowS] (36) Je 95, p. 107.
2676. HICKEY, Sandra
"My Uncle." [Writer] (108:8) Ag 95, p. 26-27.
2677. HICKMAN, Trenton
"Siesta." [TarRP] (34:2) Spr 95, p. 9.
2678. HICKS, John V.
"Distortia" (For Gerry Shikatani). [Grain] (23:2) Aut 95, p. 34.
"I Pen a Frag Meant in Decipher." [Grain] (23:2) Aut 95, p. 35.
2679. HICOK, Bob
"Alzheimer's." [SouthernR] (31:2) Ap/Spr 95, p. 270.
"Clausewitz's Mail." [PoetryNW] (36:2) Sum 95, p. 18-19.
"Divorce." [PraS] (69:1) Spr 95, p. 58-59.
"Dogfish Mother" (from the Haida). [PraS] (69:1) Spr 95, p. 59-60.
"Duke." [Chelsea] (58) 95, p. 34-35.
"Eight." [Witness] (9:1) 95, p. 56-58.
"Extreme Measures." [Turnstile] (5:1) 95, p. 19-20.
"From the Woods." [TarRP] (34:2) Spr 95, p. 25-26.
"Ice Storm." [Chelsea] (58) 95, p. 37-39.
"Killing." [Ploughs] (21:1) Spr 95, p. 14-15.
"Memorial Day." [Witness] (9:2) 95, p. 139-140.
"Neighbor." [QW] (40) Spr-Sum 95, p. 70-71.
"Nurse." [IndR] (18:1) Spr 95, p. 86-87.
"Reunion." [TarRP] (34:2) Spr 95, p. 24-25.
"Rivera's Golden Gate Mural." [Boulevard] (10:3, #30) Fall 95, p. 160-162.
"Rothko's Last Meditation." [Poetry] (166:1) Ap 95, p. 37.
"Service." [Witness] (9:2) 95, p. 137-138.
"The Shrine." [PoetryE] (41) Aut 95, p. 63-64.
"Superstition." [PoetryNW] (36:2) Sum 95, p. 19-20.
"Voladores." [Chelsea] (58) 95, p. 35-36.
"Your Daughter." [KenR] (17:1) Wint 95, p. 148-149.
"Your Father Dead" (for J.F.). [Witness] (9:2) 95, p. 136-137.
2680. HIERRO, José
"The Hero" (tr. by Louis Bourne). [Stand] (36:2) Spr 95, p. 51-53.
2681. HIESTAND, Emily
"Bugs" (Peconic Bay, Long Island). [MichQR] (34:3) Sum 95, p. 331.
"Large, with Cheese, to Go." [PartR] (62:4) Fall 95, p. 678-679.
"Regional Airport" (Tuscaloosa, Alabama). [Atlantic] (276:4) O 95, p. 90.
"Souvenirs Entomologiques" (for Jean Henri Fabre). [MichQR] (34:3) Sum 95, p. 330.
"Travel Slides." [NewYorker] (71:25) 21-28 Ag 95, p. 91.
2682. HIGGINS, Andrew C.
"American Uniform Salesclerks's Creed." [Footwork] (24/25) 95, p. 82.
"French Ticklers Along the Mohawk Trail." [Footwork] (24/25) 95, p. 81-82.
2683. HIGGINS, Anne
"The Missing Children" (Literary Festival: Poetry: Honorable Mention). [EngJ] (84:4) Ap 95, p. 39.
2684. HIGGINS, Frank
"The Paperweight." [GreenHLL] (5) 94, p. 22.
"A Photo from Hiroshima." [GreenHLL] (5) 94, p. 23.
2685. HIGGINS, Rita Ann
"Prism." [Stand] (36:3) Sum 95, p. 49.
"The Temptation of Phillida." [SouthernR] (31:3) Jl/Sum 95, p. 624-625.
2686. HIGH, John
"Book of Mistranslations" (Selections: 29, 21, 13, 41, 25, 47, 9). [Talisman] (15) Wint 95-96, p. 120-123.

"The Book of Mistranslations" (Selections). [Avec] (10) 95, p. 145-155.
2687. HIGHFIELD, Arnold R.
"Regular Departures" (for Robert Nichols). [CaribbeanW] (9) 95, p. 70-71.
2688. HIGHTOWER, David
"Gettysburg." [Wind] (76) Fall 95, p. 17.
"My Nephew at Seven." [Wind] (76) Fall 95, p. 18.
2689. HIGHTOWER, Nancy
"Comedy of Errors." [NewYorkQ] (54) 95, p. 103.
2690. HIGHTOWER, Scott
"At Toledo." [Salm] (106/107) Spr-Sum 95, p. 112-113.
"For Maffeo Barberini" (Sacrifice of Abraham, 1603, Uffizi). [ParisR] (37:134) Spr
95, p. 128-129.
"In Passing." [WestHR] (49:2) Sum 95, p. 128-129.
"Physician's Heart." [ApalQ] (44/45) Fall 95-Wint 96, p. 65.
"Remainder." [Salm] (106/107) Spr-Sum 95, p. 114.
"Shadow Play" (Self-Portrait, George Platt Lynes, 1943). [WestHR] (49:2) Sum 95,
p. 127.
"A World Without Art." [ParisR] (37:134) Spr 95, p. 129-130.
2691. HIKINO, Osamu
"Anti-nuclear movement" (in Japanese and English, tr. by Jiro Nakano). [BambooR]
(67/68) Sum-Fall 95, p. 12.
2692. HILBERRY, Conrad
"Avenida Montejo." [Shen] (45:2) Sum 95, p. 44.
"Fork." [Shen] (45:2) Sum 95, p. 45.
"Responsibility." [Shen] (45:2) Sum 95, p. 40-41.
"Tepoztlan." [Shen] (45:2) Sum 95, p. 42-43.
2693. HILBERRY, Jane
"Dreaming of Where He Could Carry Them." [13thMoon] (13:1/2) 95, p. 19.
2694. HILBERT, Donna
"At Thirteen I Meet Holden." [Rosebud] (2:2) Sum 95, p. 14-15.
"February, Los Angeles." [Pearl] (22) Fall-Wint 95, p. 13.
2695. HILBERT, Ernie
"Two-part Invention No. 4." [PaintedB] (55/56) 95, p. 49-50.
2696. HILDEBIDLE, John
"The Inlet on Tuesday" (for Con Squires). [DefinedP] (2:2) Spr-Sum 94, p. 17-18.
2697. HILL, Henry F.
"Let Us Spray." [Light] (15/16) Aut-Wint 95-96, p. 14.
"Semper Paratus." [Light] (14) Sum 95, p. 14.
2698. HILL, Jennifer
"The Sigh." [DefinedP] (1:1) Fall-Wint 92, p. 21-22.
2699. HILL, Lindsay
"Car Lot Leaderboy." [Sulfur] (15:2, #37) Fall 95, p. 192-193.
"Dropped Series." [NewOR] (21:2) Sum 95, p. 66.
"Leaderboy." [Sulfur] (15:2, #37) Fall 95, p. 192.
"Leaderboy in Love." [Sulfur] (15:2, #37) Fall 95, p. 193.
"What My Father Said in the Underworld." [NewOR] (21:2) Sum 95, p. 66.
2700. HILL, Mary Crockett
"Tangles Not to Be Undone." [Comm] (122:4) 24 F 95, p. 11.
2701. HILL, Pamela Steed
"In Her Favorite Room." [Elf] (5:3) Fall 95, p. 36.
"Why We Are Here." [FourQ] (9:1/2) Spr 95, p. 26.
2702. HILL, Patricia
"Luminaria." [MassR] (36:2) Sum 95, p. 240.
2703. HILL, Peggy
"Gladys" (First Robert Penn Warren Poetry Award). [AnthNEW] (7) 95, p. 9.
2704. HILL, Selima
"Phoebe." [Epoch] (44:3) 95, p. 297.
2705. HILLES, Robert
"Answering the Phone." [Dandel] (22:1) 95, p. 32.
"Coat Hanger." [Dandel] (22:1) 95, p. 31.
"Quieted." [Dandel] (22:1) 95, p. 30-31.
2706. HILLMAN, Brenda
"Autumn Continued." [Colum] (24/25) 95, p. 148.
"The Cliffs." [ColR] (22:2) Fall 95, p. 108.
"Deep Noticing." [ColR] (22:2) Fall 95, p. 110.
"Doubting Chamber." [ColR] (22:2) Fall 95, p. 109.

"Mighty Forms." [Zyzzyva] (11:3/4, #43/44) 95, "The Best of Ten Years of
ZYZZYVA," p. 45-46.
"Proud Energy." [BostonR] (20:1) F-Mr 95, p. 20.
"Time Problem." [ColR] (22:1) Spr 95, p. 39-42.
"Very Moment." [Colum] (24/25) 95, p. 147.
2707. HILLRINGHOUSE, Mark
"New Jersey Outdoors." [Footwork] (24/25) 95, p. 140.
"Pancakes." [Footwork] (24/25) 95, p. 140.
"Route 46." [Footwork] (24/25) 95, p. 140.
"Submitting Around" (For Andy). [Footwork] (24/25) 95, p. 139.
"Thirteen Ways of Looking at an Essay" (For Andy Pawelczak). [ColEng] (57:3) Mr
95, p. 334-336.
"Trying to Stay Off Poems." [Footwork] (24/25) 95, p. 139.
2708. HILTON, David
"Halloween: An Oncology." [BelPoJ] (46:1) Fall 95, p. 23-25.
"Her Figure Defined by the Light" (for Joanne). [Bogg] (67) 95, p. 7.
"To Find the Standing Stones at Kenmare, Go." [BelPoJ] (46:1) Fall 95, p. 17-22.
2709. HILTON, Mary
"A Genealogy: a Borrowing" (Excerpts). [WashR] (20:5) F-Mr 95, p. 9.
2710. HIMELSBACH, James R.
"Her Moon." [LiteralL] (1:2) S-O 94, p. 15.
2711. HIMMIRSKY, Krassin
"A Portrait" (tr. by the author, w. Elisavietta Ritchie). [Vis] (48) 95, p. 9.
"While the Boys Are Sleeping" (tr. by the author, w. John Glad). [Vis] (48) 95, p. 9.
2712. HIND, Steven
"My Students, My Beneficiaries." [MidwQ] (36:4) Sum 95, p. 380.
2713. HINRICHSEN, Dennis
"On a Phone Call with Two Televisions." [BlackWR] (22:1) Fall-Wint 95, p. 122-
124.
2714. HINSEY, E. C. (Ellen C.)
"The Approach of War." [MissouriR] (18:3) 95, p. 165.
"The Art of Measuring Light" (From the Pont-Neuf, Paris. Runner-up, 1995 Editors'
Prize). [SpoonR] (20:2) Sum-Fall 95, p. 35-36.
"Death of the Tyrant." [MissouriR] (18:3) 95, p. 172-173.
"The Disasters of War, Spain, 1810" (After Goya). [MissouriR] (18:3) 95, p. 166.
"The Jumping Figure." [MissouriR] (18:3) 95, p. 174-175.
"Night in Clamart" (Marina Tsvetayeva, 1933). [MissouriR] (18:3) 95, p. 168-169.
"On a Visit to Budapest." [MissouriR] (18:3) 95, p. 167.
"Photograph, Off the Dry Salvages." [NewEngR] (17:3) Sum 95, p. 12.
"The Roman Arbor." [MissouriR] (18:3) 95, p. 170-171.
2715. HINSHELWOOD, Nigel
"Going Over It Alone." [ProseP] (4) 95, p. 34.
"A Little Celebration, by God a Feast." [PlumR] (9) [95 or 96], p. 106-108.
HIROAKI, Sato
See SATO, Hiroaki
HIROMI, Ito
See ITO, Hiromi
2716. HIRSCH, Edward
"Days of 1968." [Ploughs] (21:4) Wint 95-96, p. 97.
"Ethics of Twilight." [Ploughs] (21:4) Wint 95-96, p. 96.
"Orphic Rites" (Hart Crane, 1899-1933). [ChiR] (41:1) 95, p. 17-18.
"Resurrection Plant." [CrabOR] (1:1) Fall-Wint 95, p. 77.
2717. HIRSCH, Steve
"Ching Chi." [HeavenB] (12) 95, p. 78-79.
"Shoppin' List." [HeavenB] (12) 95, p. 89-91.
2718. HIRSCHHORN, Norbert
"He Sweeps the Kitchen Floor." [SouthernPR] (35:2) Wint 95, p. 38-39.
"Pupil Wei-Min Answers a Riddle." [PraS] (69:3) Fall 95, p. 46-47.
"Renewal Soup." [PraS] (69:3) Fall 95, p. 47-51.
"Self-Portrait." [PraS] (69:3) Fall 95, p. 52.
2719. HIRSCHMAN, Jack
"Indirectrevolution" (tr. of Anna Lombardo, w. Antonella Soldaini). [WorldL] (6)
95, p. 14-15.
"Let It Out, Fellas" (tr. of Anna Lombardo). [WorldL] (6) 95, p. 14.
"The Liberty Drum" (tr. of Pol Larak (Paul Laraque)). [Drumvoices] (4:1/2) Fall-
Wint 94-95, p. 121.

"Portrait of Nelson Peery." [Drumvoices] (4:1/2) Fall-Wint 94-95, p. 113.
"Russia." [WorldL] (6) 95, p. 34.
"Sleep with Certainty" (tr. of Anna Lombardo). [WorldL] (6) 95, p. 13.
2720. HIRSHFIELD, Jane
"Bees." [DenQ] (29:3) Wint 95, p. 17.
"Changing Everything." [DenQ] (29:3) Wint 95, p. 18.
"Hope and Love." [DenQ] (29:3) Wint 95, p. 19.
"Justice without Passion." [Zyzzyva] (11:3/4, #43/44) 95, "The Best of Ten Years of
    ZYZZYVA," p. 47.
"Narcissus: February 1991." [RiverS] (44) 95, p. 12.
2721. HIRSHKOWITZ, Lois
"Being Inside Me Inside My Study Inside Winter." [AmerLC] (7) 95, p. 117.
"Ladies Room at Mount Lebanon Cemetery." [Footwork] (24/25) 95, p. 46.
2722. HISAOKA, Katsuko
"College students obediently saluted to the command" (in Japanese and English, tr.
    by Jiro Nakano). [BambooR] (67/68) Sum-Fall 95, p. 13.
2723. HIX, H. L.
"As With the Skull, So With the Nose" (Darwin, *Descent of Man*). [GreenMR] (8:2)
    Fall-Wint 95-96, p. 121.
"From Santiago's Road" (After the Congress of the Spanish Association of
    Semiotics in A Coruña in December 1992, tr. of Jüri Talvet, w. the author).
    [NowestR] (33:1) 95, p. 87-89.
"The Last Crows Whose Cries Are Audible Here" (— Nietzsche, *On the Genealogy
    of Morals*). [NewEngR] (17:4) Fall 95, p. 18.
"A Number of Fragile and Brittle Things" (— Kierkegaard, *Johannes Climacus*).
    [GreenMR] (8:2) Fall-Wint 95-96, p. 120.
"On a Streetcorner or in a Restaurant's Revolving Door" (— Camus, The Myth of
    Sisyphus). [NewDeltaR] (12:1) Fall-Wint 94, p. 24.
2724. HJALMARSSON, Johann
"Untitled 1: The room caught fire. We didn't see it" (tr. by Hallberg Hallmundsson).
    [Vis] (49) 95, p. 24.
2725. HLHOPFFGARTEN
"In the Nave of Early Spring." [PlumR] (9) [95 or 96], p. 50-51.
"Letter from the Last War." [PlumR] (9) [95 or 96], p. 52.
2726. HO, Chi Minh
"Climbing in the Mountains After Being Released from Prison" (tr. by Steve
    Bradbury). [Manoa] (7:2) Wint 95, p. 68.
"Cold Night" (tr. by Steve Bradbury). [Manoa] (7:2) Wint 95, p. 68.
"Evening Tableau" (tr. by Steve Bradbury). [Manoa] (7:2) Wint 95, p. 68.
"The Milestone" (tr. by Steve Bradbury). [Manoa] (7:2) Wint 95, p. 69.
"On Reading of Wendell Willkie's Reception in China" (tr. by Steve Bradbury).
    [Manoa] (7:2) Wint 95, p. 67.
"On the Fall of a Tooth" (tr. by Steve Bradbury). [Manoa] (7:2) Wint 95, p. 68.
"Scabies" (tr. by Steve Bradbury). [Manoa] (7:2) Wint 95, p. 68.
"Seven Prison Poems" (tr. by Steve Bradbury). [Manoa] (7:2) Wint 95, p. 67-69.
HO, Xuan Huong
    See HUONG, Ho Xuan
2727. HOA, Nguyen
"Before the Gypsy Told Her" (w. Leslie Davis). [Chain] (2) Spr 95, p. 64-66.
2728. HOAG, Tara J.
"Desire's Architect." [Dandel] (22:1) 95, p. 37.
2729. HOAGLAND, Tony
"Candlelight." [Thrpny] (60) Wint 95, p. 37.
"Fred Had Watched a Lot of Kung Fu Episodes." [BlackWR] (22:1) Fall-Wint 95, p.
    16-17.
"Honda Pavarotti." [BlackWR] (22:1) Fall-Wint 95, p. 18-19.
"Item #3." [HarvardR] (9) Fall 95, p. 26.
"Medicine." [NewEngR] (17:1) Wint 95, p. 105-106.
"The Replacement." [NewEngR] (17:1) Wint 95, p. 104-105.
2730. HOAGLAND, William
"The Gate of Memory." [SenR] (25:2) Fall 95, p. 106.
"The Old Drum Dream." [WestB] (37) 95, p. 31-32.
"Rite of Passage." [WestB] (37) 95, p. 30.
HOAI, Van Tu
    See TU, Hoai Van

2731. HOBBS, James
"Blue River — Winter Keep." [BellArk] (11:2) Mr-Ap 95, p. 13.
"Life Rhythms." [BellArk] (11:5) S-O 95, p. 16.
"Midwest Storm." [BellArk] (11:5) S-O 95, p. 12.
"Midwest Storm." [BellArk] (11:6) N-D 95, p. 5.
"Restless in Paradise." [BellArk] (11:3) My-Je 95, p. 23.
"Traveling High and Dry" (Kansas I-70). [BellArk] (11:5) S-O 95, p. 12.
"Traveling High and Dry" (Kansas I-70). [BellArk] (11:5) S-O 95, p. 16.
2732. HOBEN, Sandra
"Dog" (for Laika, the first dog in space. 1995 Poetry Contest Winner). [Sonora] (30)
Fall 95, p. 59.
2733. HOCK, Gretchen
"The Women on the Porch" (West Texas, 1986). [TexasR] (15:3/4) Fall-Wint 94, p.
87-88.
2734. HODGE, Margaret
"Air with Air" (for the Marriage of Paula and Robert). [BellArk] (11:4) Jl-Ag 95, p.
15.
"Bethany Presbyterian, Built 1929" (to Kenneth Hay Strunk). [BellArk] (11:4) Jl-Ag
95, p. 15.
"For a 31st Birthday." [BellArk] (11:6) N-D 95, p. 7.
"For a Chance Friend" (to Mary Jo). [BellArk] (11:6) N-D 95, p. 7.
"From Point Hudson." [BellArk] (11:1) Ja-F 95, p. 26.
"Lady of the Mountain, Alaska." [BellArk] (11:6) N-D 95, p. 7.
"Letter I Could Have Sent to My Cousin at Nine." [BellArk] (11:2) Mr-Ap 95, p. 27.
"Phone Bill." [BellArk] (11:1) Ja-F 95, p. 27.
"Poems I Will Be Able to Write in Ten Years." [BellArk] (11:1) Ja-F 95, p. 25.
"Poems I Will Be Able to Write in Ten Years." [BellArk] (11:3) My-Je 95, p. 8.
"Seal Calling." [BellArk] (11:4) Jl-Ag 95, p. 15.
"Teakettle." [BellArk] (11:2) Mr-Ap 95, p. 27.
"Thoughts of Nelson." [BellArk] (11:6) N-D 95, p. 7.
"Writing through Music." [BellArk] (11:4) Jl-Ag 95, p. 15.
2735. HODGEN, John
"Stopping the Jesus." [MassR] (36:4) Wint 95-96, p. 526.
"This Day." [Sun] (232) Ap 95, p. 15.
2736. HODGES, Gregg
"Calling." [Shen] (45:1) Spr 95, p. 52.
2737. HOEFER, David
"The Barbers." [NewOR] (21:2) Sum 95, p. 71.
"Chinese Cigarettes." [HeavenB] (12) 95, p. 70.
"Gas Giants." [CentralP] (24) Spr 95, p. 139-140.
"Highways in the House." [NewOR] (21:2) Sum 95, p. 70.
2738. HOEHN, Jeanie
"As I Write This to You" (A Plainsongs Award Poem). [Plain] (16:1) Fall 95, p. 36-
37.
2739. HOEKSTRA, Misha
"Roustabout: Lines from Tom Miner" (Selection: XXIV, 11 July). [IllinoisR] (3:1/2)
Fall 95-Spr 96, p. 88.
2740. HOELLE, J. Nicole
"A Slip, a Shot, Askew." [NewAW] (13) Fall-Wint 95, p. 112-113.
HOEPPNER, Edward Haworth
See HAWORTH-HOEPPNER, Edward
2741. HOEY, Allen
"Clockworks at the British Museum." [TexasR] (16:1/4) 95, p. 125-126.
"The Eye on Fire." [SouthernHR] (29:1) Wint 95, p. 48.
"In the Precincts of Paradise." [CimR] (113) O 95, p. 62.
"Talking Their Way Toward Paradise." [CimR] (113) O 95, p. 65.
"The Tragedy of Matter." [SouthernHR] (29:3) Sum 95, p. 237.
"The Walk." [CimR] (113) O 95, p. 62-65.
2742. HOFER, Tony
"Grandfather Escapes Into a Sparrow." [WillowS] (36) Je 95, p. 16-17.
2743. HOFFER, Madeline
"Sewing the Sail." [Parting] (8:2) Wint 95-96, p. 46.
2744. HOFFMAN, Daniel
"Quandaries." [Boulevard] (10:3, #30) Fall 95, p. 47.
2745. HOFFMAN, Jeff
"Daily Prayer." [ArtfulD] (28/29) 95, p. 25.

"Second World War." [ArtfulD] (28/29) 95, p. 24.
2746. HOFFMANN, Roald
"Arctic Hegira." [GrandS] (13:4, #52) Spr 95, p. 110-111.
"Fact, Facet, Face." [Raritan] (15:1) Sum 95, p. 35.
"Natural History." [Chelsea] (59) 95, p. 7.
2747. HOFMANN, Michael
"Fairy Tale." [NewYorker] (70:46) 23 Ja 95, p. 56.
"Metempsychosis." [NewYorker] (71:32) 16 O 95, p. 116.
"Zirbelstrasse." [NewYorker] (71:17) 19 Je 95, p. 78-79.
2748. HOGAN, Judy
"This River 6" (January 6, 1991). [Crucible] (31) Fall 95, p. 17-18.
2749. HOGAN, Wayne
"Afghanistan, A Short Story." [DogRR] (14:1, #27) Sum 95, p. 30.
"Conspiracy Theory." [DogRR] (14:1, #27) Sum 95, p. 30.
"Leaves in the Second Act." [SpinningJ] (1) Fall 95-Wint 96, p. 47.
"A Miss Teen U.S.A. Contestant." [Parting] (8:1) Sum 95, p. 15.
"Musing Religiotly" [sic]. [SpinningJ] (1) Fall 95-Wint 96, p. 46.
"What California Means to Me, Part 24." [Parting] (8:1) Sum 95, p. 15.
2750. HOGGARD, James
"Dove Hunting Each Labor Day." [Manoa] (7:1) Sum 95, p. 71-72.
"I Only Know that Now" (tr. of Tino Villanueva). [MassR] (36:4) Wint 95-96, p.
653.
"In the Chiaroscuro of the Years" (tr. of Tino Villanueva). [MassR] (36:4) Wint 95-
96, p. 651.
"A Private Song on a Summer Afternoon" (Canto intimo de una tarde veraniega, tr.
of Raúl Mesa). [GrahamHR] (19) Wint 95-96, p. 70.
"Sand Bar on the Tigris" (Mosul, Iraq). [Manoa] (7:1) Sum 95, p. 72-73.
2751. HOGGE, Robert M.
"Incident at the Bridge." [WeberS] (12:1) Wint 95, p. 68-69.
2752. HOGUE, Cynthia
"On Independence." [SpoonR] (20:1) Wint-Spr 95, p. 65.
"Suppose These Houses Are Composed of Ourselves" (after a line by Wallace
Stevens, for Janice). [SpoonR] (20:1) Wint-Spr 95, p. 62-64.
2753. HOLAHAN, Susan
"A Blizzard: Guzzles As It Dazzles" (for Ruth Stone). [AmerLC] (7) 95, p. 115-116.
2754. HOLBROOK, Susan
"Misling the Laureate." [CapilR] (2:16) Sum 95, p. 17-24.
2755. HOLDEN, Elizabeth W.
"As the Cold Deepens." [VirQR] (71:2) Spr 95, p. 305-306.
"Red." [VirQR] (71:2) Spr 95, p. 306-307.
2756. HOLDEN, Jonathan
"Divorce." [RiverS] (45) 95, p. 4-5.
"Emptying the House." [TarRP] (34:2) Spr 95, p. 38-40.
"Faking." [SpoonR] (20:2) Sum-Fall 95, p. 131.
"Junk." [ManyMM] [1:1] D 94, p. 58-59.
"The Model Train." [TarRP] (34:2) Spr 95, p. 40-45.
"Quod Erat Demonstrandum." [RiverS] (45) 95, p. 3.
"Sea-World, San Diego, California." [ManyMM] (1:2) 95, p. 115-116.
2757. HÖLDERLIN, Friedrich
"She Speaks Across the Years" (tr. and adapted by David Ferry). [TriQ] (95) Wint
95-96, p. 170-171.
2758. HOLENDER, Barbara D.
"Bon Voyage, Mommy." [Light] (15/16) Aut-Wint 95-96, p. 18.
2759. HOLINGER, Richard
"Blown In." [SouthernPR] (35:2) Wint 95, p. 7.
"Ethnic Cleansing." [Ledge] (18) Sum 95, p. 86-87.
"White Voices." [WillowR] (22) Spr 95, p. 26-35.
2760. HOLLADAY, Hilary
"Snail." [Comm] (122:21) 1 D 95, p. 16.
"When Giants Walked the Earth." [Poem] (74) N 95, p. 22.
"Yonder" (for William Harmon). [LowellR] [1] Sum 94, p. 28-29.
2761. HOLLAHAN, Eugene
"Cicada in Circadia." [LullwaterR] (6:1) Spr-Sum 95, p. 74-75.
"Eschew Obfuscation." [LullwaterR] (6:1) Spr-Sum 95, p. 76-78.
"Incident at a Border." [SoDakR] (33:3/4) Fall-Wint 95, p. 193.
"The Pragmatist Enjoys an Earthquake." [LullwaterR] (5:1) 93-94, p. 30-31.

2762. HOLLAND, Andrea C.
"Bull Cuts Loose" (Finalist, 1995 Greg Grummer Award in Poetry). [Phoebe] (24:2) 95, p. 158.
"In a Shakespeare Bikini" (Finalist, 1995 Greg Grummer Award in Poetry). [Phoebe] (24:2) 95, p. 159.
2763. HOLLAND, Everett
"Mary Middling" (WritersCorps Project, Washington, DC). [WashR] (21:2) Ag-S 95, p. 19.
2764. HOLLAND, Lynn
"Coming of Age." [Plain] (16:1) Fall 95, p. 31.
2765. HOLLAND, Raymond
"Outside My Window" (WritersCorps Project, Washington, DC). [WashR] (21:2) Ag-S 95, p. 19.
2766. HOLLAND, Robin
"Getting Serious." [Poem] (74) N 95, p. 52.
"Maggie and the Gods." [Poem] (74) N 95, p. 50.
"Maggie's Washoe Hill." [Poem] (74) N 95, p. 51.
2767. HOLLAND, Trace
"The End" (WritersCorps Project, Washington, DC). [WashR] (21:2) Ag-S 95, p. 19.
2768. HOLLAND, Walter R.
"For Stan Leventhal." [JamesWR] (12:2) Spr-Sum 95, p. 17.
"Lisbon, Oct. 1994." [JamesWR] (12:2) Spr-Sum 95, p. 16.
2769. HOLLANDER, Jean
"The Locust Tree." [Parting] (8:2) Wint 95-96, p. 37.
"The Miracle of the Dogs." [US1] (30/31) 95, p. 4.
"Moondog." [Parting] (8:2) Wint 95-96, p. 8.
2770. HOLLANDER, John
"Across the Board, Parnassus Stakes." [PartR] (62:4) Fall 95, p. 675-676.
"After Blossoming." [Verse] (12:2) 95, p. 71-72.
"Arachne." [Poetry] (166:2) My 95, p. 87-89.
"From the Notes of a Traveller." [PartR] (62:4) Fall 95, p. 676-677.
"Oggi." [NewRep] (213:21) 20 N 95, p. 48.
"An Old Image (Alciati's Emblem #165)." [NewRep] (213:5) 31 Jl 95, p. 38.
"An Old Palindrome." [NewRep] (213:18) 30 O 95, p. 48.
"Variations on a Table-Top" (for Saul Steinberg, whose carved and painted Balsa table-tops were sculpted drawings of the table-tops they were drawn upon). [ParisR] (37:135) Sum 95, p. 277-280.
2771. HOLLEY, Margaret
"Cabbage Roses." [Shen] (45:4) Wint 95, p. 68-69.
"Fossil Flowers." [Flyway] (1:3) Wint 95, p. 64-65.
"Low Relief." [PraS] (69:2) Sum 95, p. 94-95.
"On the Beach." [Shen] (45:4) Wint 95, p. 70-71.
"The Sea of Tranquillity." [PraS] (69:2) Sum 95, p. 95.
2772. HOLLOW, Craig
" Απαθετα: Zen between Breaths." [SoCoast] (18) Ja 95, p. 6-7.
2773. HOLLOWAY, E. (Eachan)
"The Soldier." [PraS] (69:4) Wint 95, p. 144.
"Swimmers." [IndR] (18:2) Fall 95, p. 50.
2774. HOLLOWAY, Glenna
"Countenances." [SpoonR] (20:2) Sum-Fall 95, p. 87.
"Easy Grace." [ChrC] (112:21) 5-12 Jl 95, p. 679.
"Forgetting Sylvia Plath, 1932-1963." [Elf] (5:4) Wint 95, p. 30.
"Leaving Home." [SoCoast] (18) Ja 95, p. 14-15.
"Parvenu in a Stetson" (The 1994 Allen Ginsberg Poetry Awards: Honorable Mention). [Footwork] (24/25) 95, p. 197.
2775. HOLM, Bill
"Letting Go of What Cannot Be Held Back." [PraS] (69:4) Wint 95, p. 101.
"A Note on the Door." [PraS] (69:4) Wint 95, p. 100.
"Official Talk in Wuhan, 1992." [SenR] (25:1) Spr 95, p. 117.
2776. HOLMAN, Paul
"The Genii of a Secret State." [WestCL] (29:2, #17) Fall 95, p. 46-49.
2777. HOLMES, Darryl
"No Place for Us." [RiverS] (44) 95, p. 52-53.
2778. HOLMES, Elizabeth
"Belly." [Poetry] (165:6) Mr 95, p. 330.

"Doorstep." [Poetry] (165:6) Mr 95, p. 331.
"Franz Marc on the Piano." [CimR] (110) Ja 96, p. 84.
"Imperative." [PraS] (69:2) Sum 95, p. 63-65.
"Taking a History." [Poetry] (165:6) Mr 95, p. 329.
2779. HOLMES, Janet
"The Erotics of Detail." [Poetry] (165:5) F 95, p. 263-264.
"The Green Tuxedo." [CarolQ] (48:1) Fall 95, p. 38-40.
2780. HOLMES, Michael
"Semper Fi: A Love Story" (Excerpt). [Quarry] (43:4) 95, p. 62-65.
2781. HOLT, Sara L.
"Portrait of a Post-Modern Pair." [LullwaterR] (6:1) Spr-Sum 95, p. 33.
2782. HOLTHAUS, Gary
"Iowa Steel." [ManyMM] (1:3) 95, p. 43-45.
2783. HOLUB, Miroslav
"The Day of the Pollyanna" (tr. by Dana Hábova and David Young). [GrandS]
(13:4, #52) Spr 95, p. 58.
"Metaphysics" (tr. by David Young, w. the author). [GrandS] (13:4, #52) Spr 95, p.
60.
"Whale Songs" (tr. by David Young, w. the author). [GrandS] (13:4, #52) Spr 95, p.
59-60.
2784. HOLVEY, Christopher
"& ...." [Elf] (5:4) Wint 95, p. 25.
2785. HOLZER, Madeline Fuchs
"It Doesn't Get Any Better Than This." [Footwork] (24/25) 95, p. 148.
"Lunar Eclipse." [Footwork] (24/25) 95, p. 148.
"Predictions." [Footwork] (24/25) 95, p. 148.
2786. HOMER, Art
"County Road 142" (Appanoose). [MidwQ] (36:4) Sum 95, p. 381-382.
"Dream of Black Water." [Verse] (12:3) 95, p. 24-25.
2787. HOMER, Lawrence
"The Second September" (Honorable Mention, First Annual Poetry Awards).
[LiteralL] (2:2) Fall 95, p. 4.
2788. HONDA, Kazuya
"Calling 'Fish' in the Evening" (tr. of Toshiko Fujioka, w. Jon Silkin). [Stand] (36:3)
Sum 95, p. 35.
2789. HONES, Karen Lee
"Across the Border" (Honorable Mention, Poetry Award). [NewL] (61:2) 95, p. 66-
67.
2790. HONGO, Garrett
"Jigoku: On the Glamour of Self-Hate." [Zyzzyva] (11:3/4, #43/44) 95, "The Best of
Ten Years of ZYZZYVA," p. 48-53.
2791. HONIG, Edwin
"A Note to Bodega from the Miriam Hospital." [DefinedP] (3) 95, p. 58.
2792. HOOD, Charles
"In Praise of Ravens." [ColEng] (57:8) D 95, p. 942-943.
"The Note." [ColEng] (57:8) D 95, p. 943-944.
2793. HOOD, Marian R.
"Teaching Banana Slugs to Fly" (for M.J.). [Dandel] (22:1) 95, p. 67.
2794. HOOD, Thomas (1799-1845)
"Sea Song" (After Dibden). [Light] (15/16) Aut-Wint 95-96, p. 34.
2795. HOOGESTRAAT, Jane
"After the Moiseyev." [Poem] (73) My 95, p. 2-3.
"So This Blue." [Poem] (73) My 95, p. 1.
"Virginia-Tennessee Depot." [Poem] (73) My 95, p. 4.
2796. HOOKE, K. M.
"Physical Therapy, $79/Hr." [LowellR] (2) c1996, p. 76.
2797. HOOKINS, Clifford
"On the Way to the Meeting about Money at the Welfare Department."
[AnotherCM] (29) Spr 95, p. 53-56.
2798. HOOPER, Patricia
"The Best Hour" (On reading that morning is the best time for human procreation).
[Hudson] (48:3) Aut 95, p. 448.
"Buoyancy." [AmerPoR] (24:4) Jl-Ag 95, p. 28.
"In the Backyard." [Ploughs] (21:4) Wint 95-96, p. 98-99.
"November 6." [GreenMR] (8:2) Fall-Wint 95-96, p. 126.

2799. HOOPER, Virginia
"Garden Party Invention" (for Constance). [AmerLC] (7) 95, p. 63-65.
2800. HOOVER, Carmen
"Living with the Elk." [CutB] (44) Sum 95, p. 22-23.
2801. HOOVER, Paul
"American Heaven." [ChiR] (41:2/3) 95, p. 5-6.
"The Beautiful Cities." [AntR] (53:1) Wint 95, p. 75.
"Curtains in a Fire." [AntR] (53:1) Wint 95, p. 74.
"History Is Shy." [AmerLC] (7) 95, p. 107.
"Red Lilies." [ChiR] (41:2/3) 95, p. 3-4.
2802. HOPE, Akua Lezli
"Genny." [Chain] (2) Spr 95, p. 116-118.
2803. HOPE, Warren
"Nowhere Special." [Hellas] (6:1) Spr-Sum 95, p. 85.
HOPFFGARTEN, H. L.
See HLHOPFFGARTEN
2804. HOPKINS, Jeffrey
"Tibetan Arts of Love" (Excerpt, tr. of Gendun Chopel). [Tricycle] (4:3, #15) Spr
95, p. 47.
2805. HOPLER, Jay
"Brief Monologue Done in Heavy Shade" (after Blas de Otero). [PoetL] (90:1) Spr
95, p. 35.
"The Woman on Read Street." [PoetL] (90:4) Wint 95-96, p. 39.
2806. HOPPE, W. Joe
"Sanding Floors." [Border] (6) Spr-Sum 95, p. 41-42.
2807. HOPPEY, Tim
"Men of Rock." [ProseP] (4) 95, p. 35.
2808. HORACE
"I.v. To Pyrrha" (tr. by David Ferry). [Raritan] (14:3) Wint 95, p. 20.
"I.10. To Mercury" (tr. by David Ferry). [Pequod] (39) 95, p. 146.
"I.xv. The Prophecy of Nereus" (tr. by David Ferry). [Raritan] (14:3) Wint 95, p. 20-
22.
"1.34. Of the God's Power" (tr. by David Ferry). [TriQ] (93) Spr-Sum 95, p. 152.
"II.4. To Xanthias" (tr. by David Ferry). [Pequod] (39) 95, p. 147.
"II.vii. To an Old Comrade in the Army of Brutus" (tr. by David Ferry). [Raritan]
(14:3) Wint 95, p. 22.
"II.11. To Quinctius Hirpinus" (tr. by David Ferry). [Thrpny] (62) Sum 95, p. 13.
"III.i. Of Ostentation" (tr. by David Ferry). [Raritan] (14:3) Wint 95, p. 23-24.
"III.5. The Example of Regulus" (tr. by David Ferry). [SouthernHR] (29:2) Spr 95,
p. 146-147.
"III.6. To the Romans" (tr. by David Ferry). [Pequod] (39) 95, p. 148-150.
"III.18. To Faunus" (tr. by David Ferry). [Pequod] (39) 95, p. 151.
"III.22. To Diana" (tr. by David Ferry). [Pequod] (39) 95, p. 152.
"IV.x. To Ligurinus" (tr. by David Ferry). [Raritan] (14:3) Wint 95, p. 24-25.
"IV.xiii. To Lycia" (tr. by David Ferry). [Raritan] (14:3) Wint 95, p. 25-26.
"111.26. To Venus" (tr. by David Ferry). [TriQ] (93) Spr-Sum 95, p. 151.
"A Reversal" (I.5, tr. by Deborah H. Roberts). [Arion] (3:2/3) Fall 95-Wint 96, p.
177.
"Satires I, ix" (tr. by William Matthews). [OhioR] (54) 95, p. 27-30.
"To Dellius" (II.3, tr. by David Ferry). [Arion] (3:2/3) Fall 95-Wint 96, p. 169-170.
"To Lydia" (I.8, tr. by David Ferry). [Agni] (42) 95, p. 77-78.
"To Maecenas" (I.1, tr. by David Ferry). [Arion] (3:2/3) Fall 95-Wint 96, p. 167-
168.
"To Melpomene" (IV.3, tr. by David Ferry). [Arion] (3:2/3) Fall 95-Wint 96, p. 171-
172.
"To Phyllis" (IV.11, tr. by David Ferry). [Arion] (3:2/3) Fall 95-Wint 96, p. 173-
174.
"To Praise Aelius Lamia" (I.26, tr. by David Ferry). [Agni] (42) 95, p. 82.
"To Pyrrhus" (III.20, tr. by David Ferry). [Agni] (42) 95, p. 79.
"To Virgil" (I.24, tr. by David Ferry). [Agni] (42) 95, p. 80-81.
2809. HORI, Shozo
"We will never repeat this error again" (in Japanese and English, tr. by Jiro Nakano).
[BambooR] (67/68) Sum-Fall 95, p. 14.
2810. HORNIK, Jessica
"Cold Comfort." [YaleR] (83:4) O 95, p. 69.

2811. HORNOSTY, Cornelia C.
"Socks." [CanLit] (146) Aut 95, p. 67.
2812. HOROWITZ, Mikhail
"Chez Gersh II." [HeavenB] (12) 95, p. 17-18.
"Gardens for Carol." [Archae] (5) Spr 95, p. 56-61.
"To George Malkine." [HeavenB] (12) 95, p. 31.
2813. HORSTING, Eric
"Bulb Fields in Holland: Visiting My Cousins for the First Time." [LitR] (38:2)
Wint 95, p. 195.
"Iris." [Confr] (56/57) Sum-Fall 95, p. 337.
"Manifesto." [PoetryE] (39) Fall 94, p. 55.
2814. HORTON, Barbara Savadge
"Hair." [PoetryNW] (36:4) Wint 95-96, p. 25.
"Kalighut." [PassN] (16:1) Sum 95, p. 14.
2815. HORTON, Maclin
"Waco." [Image] (9) Spr 95, p. 73-74.
2816. HORVITZ, Lori
"Dreaming in Tongues." [13thMoon] (13:1/2) 95, p. 20.
"Life Inside a Dixie Cup." [13thMoon] (13:1/2) 95, p. 21-22.
2817. HOSPITAL, Carolina
"The clocks stop ticking" (Two Sonnets: I). [HighP] (10:1) Spr 95, p. 88.
"On the asphalt rests the bluejay" (Two Sonnets: II). [HighP] (10:1) Spr 95, p. 88-
89.
2818. HOST, R. M.
"Dreams of Bill Clinton: Beyond Hope: Patriot Fever." [BlackBR] (21) Fall-Wint
95, p. 32.
"Dreams of Bill Clinton: Straddling the Great Promise." [BlackBR] (21) Fall-Wint
95, p. 33.
"Fast Forward." [DogRR] (14:1, #27) Sum 95, p. 15.
"Jesse James: A Portrait." [BlackBR] (20) Spr-Sum 95, p. 7-9.
"Justice: for the Movement." [BlackBR] (20) Spr-Sum 95, p. 10-11.
2819. HOSTETLER, Sheri
"Drink Freely." [Footwork] (24/25) 95, p. 16.
"From Under the Shadow of Harvard: Vignettes." [Footwork] (24/25) 95, p. 16.
2820. HOSTOVSKY, Paul
"A A." [JINJPo] (17:2) Aut 95, p. 31-32.
2821. HOUCHIN, Ron
"Eating Fat." [LullwaterR] (6:2) Fall-Wint 95, p. 85.
"James Dickey Reading at Key West." [ClockR] (10:1/2) 95-96, p. 5.
"Seven Things You Can't Say about the Dead" (after Pat Boran). [SycamoreR] (7:2)
Sum 95, p. 44.
"The Unnaming, 1958" (for Claude Monet). [SouthernPR] (35:2) Wint 95, p. 29-30.
2822. HOUGH, Andreja Beth
"Crickets in the Hall." [Kalliope] (17:3) 95, p. 52.
"David Smith's 'Cubi X'" (1 of 4 poems in "Escape from The Sculpture Garden").
[SantaBR] (3:2) Sum 95, p. 49.
"Escape from The Sculpture Garden" (4 poems). [SantaBR] (3:2) Sum 95, p. 45-50.
"Lachaise's 'Standing Woman'" (1 of 4 poems in "Escape from The Sculpture
Garden"). [SantaBR] (3:2) Sum 95, p. 46.
"Oldenburg's 'Geometric Mouse'" (1 of 4 poems in "Escape from The Sculpture
Garden"). [SantaBR] (3:2) Sum 95, p. 49.
"Picasso's 'She Goat'" (1 of 4 poems in "Escape from The Sculpture Garden").
[SantaBR] (3:2) Sum 95, p. 51.
2823. HOUGH, Coleman
"Setting the Table." [SouthernPR] (35:2) Wint 95, p. 43-45.
2824. HOUGHTON, Timothy
"First Day of School." [ColEng] (57:5) S 95, p. 584-585.
"Iceman." [PoetL] (90:3) Fall 95, p. 12.
"Two Lives" (... the Russian-born mathematician Gregory Chudnovsky works on his
supercomputer ...). [Chelsea] (58) 95, p. 54-55.
2825. HOULE, Karen
"1620" (Short Grain Contest Winners: Prose Poem, First). [Grain] (22:3) Wint 95, p.
62-63.
2826. HOUSMAN, Naomi G.
"Childhood Fathers." [LullwaterR] (6:1) Spr-Sum 95, p. 83.

2827. HOUSTON, Beth
   "Back in Indiana." [GreensboroR] (59) Wint 95-96, p. 57-58.
   "Encounter." [LitR] (39:1) Fall 95, p. 32.
   "Family Reunion." [BellArk] (11:3) My-Je 95, p. 4.
   "A Few Old Photos." [BellArk] (11:2) Mr-Ap 95, p. 30-31.
   "Fragrance Garden, Golden Gate Park Arboretum." [NewMyths] (2:2/3:1) 95, p.
      252-253.
HOVANESSIAN, Diana Der
   See DER-HOVANESSIAN, Diana
2828. HOWARD, Ben
   "The Center of Attention" (Co. Monaghan, 1948). [Chelsea] (59) 95, p. 194-202.
   "Currencies." [Shen] (45:3) Fall 95, p. 30.
   "A Winter Fire." [SouthernHR] (29:3) Sum 95, p. 264-265.
2829. HOWARD, Eric
   "Shame." [Sun] (236) Ag 95, p. 19.
2830. HOWARD, Julie Kate
   "An Ex-Husband's New Address." [ChironR] (43) Sum 95, p. 33.
2831. HOWARD, Matthew
   "0." [AntR] (53:2) Spr 95, p. 206.
   "Coma" (for Lee Wichman). [ChiR] (41:2/3) 95, p. 90-91.
   "Shaving." [ChiR] (41:2/3) 95, p. 92-93.
2832. HOWARD, Richard
   "Further Triangulations" (after an initial three, some years back). [Verse] (12:2) 95,
      p. 73-74.
   "Nikolaus Mardruz to His Master Ferdinand, Count of Tyrol, 1565" (A tribute to
      Robert Browning and in celebration of the 65th birthday of Harold Bloom,
      who made such tribute only natural). [YaleR] (83:3) Jl 95, p. 20-27.
   "Like Most Revelations" (after Morris Louis). [KenR] (17:2) Spr 95, p. 162-163.
2833. HOWE, Bill
   "Disturbance is always an urban dance." [WashR] (21:1) Je-Jl 95, p. 7.
2834. HOWE, Fanny
   "Menace." [GrandS] (13:4, #52) Spr 95, p. 129.
   "Noted." [GrandS] (13:4, #52) Spr 95, p. 130.
2835. HOWE, Ken
   "Anton Bruckner: Fourth Symphony, First Movement." [MalR] (110) Spr 95, p. 85.
   "Free Translation of Mahler's 'Ging Heut' Morgen übers Feld'." [MalR] (110) Spr
      95, p. 84.
2836. HOWE, Marie
   "Watching Television." [PlumR] (9) [95 or 96], p. 56-57.
2837. HOWE, Susan Elizabeth
   "Feeding." [TarRP] (35:1) Fall 95, p. 20-21.
   "We Live in the Roadside Motel." [TarRP] (35:1) Fall 95, p. 21-22.
2838. HOWELL, Abigail
   "Boy in Fading Light Surrounded by Ice Trees" (First Runner-Up, Poetry Award).
      [NewL] (61:2) 95, p. 25.
   "The Husband Tries to Explain the Disappearance of His Wife." [13thMoon]
      (13:1/2) 95, p. 23-24.
   "The One Son" (First Runner-Up, Poetry Award). [NewL] (61:2) 95, p. 21.
   "Sunday Letter." [NoAmR] (280:5) S-O 95, p. 7.
   "The System Is Endless" (First Runner-Up, Poetry Award). [NewL] (61:2) 95, p. 23-
      25.
   "Tiny Cherries" (First Runner-Up, Poetry Award). [NewL] (61:2) 95, p. 26-27.
   "Why Be Depressed Here?" (First Runner-Up, Poetry Award). [NewL] (61:2) 95, p.
      22.
2839. HOWELL, Cameron
   "Back Home." [SouthernHR] (29:4) Fall 95, p. 343.
2840. HOWELL, Christopher
   "The Breakfast Table" (for Hanna Pauli). [CimR] (113) O 95, p. 58-59.
   "Family Values." [CimR] (113) O 95, p. 57.
   "The Getaway" (for Lew, 1944-1981). [WillowS] (35) Ja 95, p. 30-31.
   "The Record Player." [MissR] (23:3) 95, p. 97-98.
   "Sometimes at the Braille Calliope." [GreensboroR] (59) Wint 95-96, p. 3.
2841. HOWES, Patti
   "The Night the Cat Caught a Star." [AntigR] (102/103) Sum-Aug 95, p. 40.
2842. HOWES, Victor
   "Fable." [Light] (15/16) Aut-Wint 95-96, p. 30.

"The Thief." [Light] (15/16) Aut-Wint 95-96, p. 23.
2843. HOWLAND, Ron
"Elijah's Voice." [HawaiiR] (19:2) Fall 95, p. 34.
"In God We Thrust." [HawaiiR] (19:2) Fall 95, p. 35.
"Ophelia's Thoughts" (for Sue Walker). [Chelsea] (58) 95, p. 47.
"Self Help." [Chelsea] (58) 95, p. 44.
"Sunday Revisions." [Chelsea] (58) 95, p. 45-46.
2844. HOYT, Don A.
"Omens." [OxfordM] (10:1) Wint 94-Spr 95, p. 34.
2845. HOZUMI, Seishu
"The Americans have licked the core" (in Japanese and English, tr. by Jiro Nakano).
[BambooR] (67/68) Sum-Fall 95, p. 15.
2846. HRISTOVA, Elena
"Lullaby for My Mother" (tr. of Blaga Dimitrova, w. John Balaban). [WillowS] (36)
Je 95, p. 90-91.
"Who Takes Care of the Blind Stork?" (tr. of Blaga Dimitrova, w. John Balaban).
[WillowS] (36) Je 95, p. 89.
2847. HRU, Dakari
"The United Nations Afrikan Mothers' Luncheon." [Drumvoices] (4:1/2) Fall-Wint
94-95, p. 119.
2848. HSIU, Ou-yang (1007-1072)
"Pied Spring" (tr. by Brian Blanchfield). [LitR] (38:3) Spr 95, p. 331.
"To the Tune: 'Yü Chia Ao'" (tr. by Matthew Flannery). [Chelsea] (58) 95, p. 98.
HUA, Li Min
See LI, Min Hua
2849. HUBBELL, Brian
"Autobiography of an Egg." [BelPoJ] (45:3) Spr 95, p. 14-15.
"Certain Aspects of Descent." [BelPoJ] (45:3) Spr 95, p. 13.
"To a Woman of Many Houses." [BelPoJ] (45:3) Spr 95, p. 16-17.
2850. HUBELBANK, J. Sidney
"Vinton County, Ohio." [Elf] (5:4) Wint 95, p. 35.
2851. HUBKA, Ashley
"Skin" (after Adrienne Rich). [HarvardA] (129:3) Wint 95, p. 11.
2852. HUDA, Mohammad Nurul
"Body Theory" (tr. of Taslima Nasrin, w. Carolyne Wright). [GrandS] (14:1, #53)
Sum 95, p. 173-174.
"Things Cheaply Had" (tr. of Taslima Nasrin, w. Carolyne Wright and the author).
[NewYorker] (71:31) 9 O 95, p. 44.
2853. HUDGINS, Andrew
"Bryce Hospital: the Old Cemetery." [SenR] (25:1) Spr 95, p. 42.
2854. HUDSON, Carolyn
"Atsene and Fekirte." [BellArk] (11:5) S-O 95, p. 12.
"Crutches." [BellArk] (11:5) S-O 95, p. 12.
"Details." [BellArk] (11:5) S-O 95, p. 12.
"The Red Line." [BellArk] (11:5) S-O 95, p. 12.
2855. HUDSON, Frederick
"Woman on the Bus." [NewYorkQ] (54) 95, p. 73.
2856. HUDSON, June
"Being Saved." [Pearl] (22) Fall-Wint 95, p. 15.
2857. HUDSON, Marc
"After a Line by Antonio Machado." [PraS] (69:2) Sum 95, p. 27-28.
"Bathing Ian." [PoetryE] (40) Spr 95, p. 55-57.
"By Indian River, Baranof Island, Alaska." [PoetryE] (40) Spr 95, p. 58.
"A Familiar Song." [HopewellR] (7) 95, p. 100.
"This Is a Song." [PraS] (69:2) Sum 95, p. 26.
2858. HUDSON, Michael
"Comparative Anatomy." [Sulfur] (15:2, #37) Fall 95, p. 30-31.
"How Strolling Through a Public Park in August Can Intermittently Be an Egyptian
Experience." [PoetryE] (41) Aut 95, p. 78.
"Tragically, Beauty Is Only Ever Too Closely Considered." [PoetryE] (41) Aut 95,
p. 77.
2859. HUELSENBECK, Richard
"Schalaben — Schalabai — Schalamezomai" (tr. by William Seaton). [Chelsea] (59)
95, p. 122-123.
"Streams" (tr. by William Seaton). [Chelsea] (59) 95, p. 124.
"Tree" (tr. by William Seaton). [Chelsea] (59) 95, p. 125.

2860. HUEY, Amorak
"My Father's Home Run." [Spitball] (49) 95, p. 62.
2861. HUFFSTICKLER, Albert
"The Healing." [RagMag] (12:2) Spr 95, p. 80.
"Holidays, Holy Days." [RagMag] (12:2) Spr 95, p. 81.
"Inventory." [RagMag] (12:2) Spr 95, p. 82.
"Lines Looking Back." [RagMag] (12:2) Spr 95, p. 81.
"Threshold." [SlipS] (15) 95, p. 21.
2862. HUGGINS, Peter
"The Animals Noah Left Behind." [Farm] (13:2 [i.e. 12:2]) Fall-Wint 95, p. 73.
"The Death of Perry Mason." [SouthernPR] (35:1) Sum 95, p. 62-63.
"To Dante." [CapeR] (30:1) Spr 95, p. 36.
2863. HUGHES, Mary Gray
"What She Did." [Confr] (56/57) Sum-Fall 95, p. 338-340.
2864. HUGHES, Pamela
"Storm." [DefinedP] (3) 95, p. 32.
2865. HUGHES, Shannon
"A black hole in my head." [HangL] (67) 95, p. 93.
"In Memory of Mack Johnston 1977-1994." [HangL] (67) 95, p. 92.
"Kite." [HangL] (67) 95, p. 93.
2866. HUGHES, Sophie
"The Mind Thief." [WritersF] (21) 95, p. 140.
"Slitting the Dream Pillow." [LullwaterR] (6:1) Spr-Sum 95, p. 86.
2867. HUGHES, Ted
"Chaucer." [NewYorker] (70:45) 16 Ja 95, p. 48.
"The Error." [NewYorker] (71:18) 26 Je-3 Jl 95, p. 156-157.
2868. HUGHES, Winifred
"Field Notes for the Equinox." [US1] (30/31) 95, p. 27.
"Mortification of the Flesh." [JINJPo] (17:1) Spr 95, p. 22-23.
"Playthings." [JINJPo] (17:1) Spr 95, p. 21.
"Waking." [US1] (30/31) 95, p. 22.
2869. HUGO, Richard
"The Lady in Kicking Horse Reservoir" (holograph). [Verse] (12:3) 95, p. 5-6.
2870. HULL, J. M.
"Conrad Maas." [PottPort] (16:1) Fall 95, p. 41-42.
2871. HULL, Lynda
"Denouement." [Crazy] (48) Spr 95, p. 81-82.
"Rivers into Seas" (For Wally Roberts, 1951-1994). [Crazy] (48) Spr 95, p. 78-80.
"Street of Crocodiles." [IndR] (18:1) Spr 95, p. 3-6.
2872. HUME, Charity
"This Spring" (for Claire). [NortheastCor] (3) 95, p. 26-28.
2873. HUME, Christine
"Called up to Carpenter a New Tradition, I Make Use of a Standard Round Table." [DenQ] (30:2) Fall 95, p. 29-30.
"Helicopter Wrecked on a Hill." [DenQ] (30:2) Fall 95, p. 31.
"Hometown Piece." [PennR] (6:2) 95, p. 20.
"Out of the Album." [QW] (41) Aut-Wint 95-96, p. 198.
"Waiting for the Woodsman." [QW] (41) Aut-Wint 95-96, p. 199.
2874. HUMES, Harry
"The Comet." [Shen] (45:2) Sum 95, p. j84.
"Counting the Plants." [LaurelR] (29:2) Sum 95, p. 106.
"From the Apple Tree in Late October." [PoetryNW] (36:3) Aut 95, p. 19.
"The Leah Tree." [LaurelR] (29:2) Sum 95, p. 104.
"The New Dark." [LaurelR] (29:2) Sum 95, p. 105.
"The Other End." [GeoR] (49:2) Sum 95, p. 442.
"Poem with a Line from Wallace Stevens." [PoetryNW] (36:3) Aut 95, p. 18.
"The Snow Boat." [Shen] (45:2) Sum 95, p. 85.
"Tripe." [WestB] (37) 95, p. 67.
2875. HUMMELL, Austin
"Audible Ransom." [ColR] (22:1) Spr 95, p. 85.
"Premature Burial." [ColR] (22:1) Spr 95, p. 86.
"Salt Longing." [ColR] (22:1) Spr 95, p. 88.
"The Strapless Spider Ride." [ColR] (22:1) Spr 95, p. 87.
2876. HUMMER, T. R.
"The Dredges." [SouthernR] (31:1) Wint 95, p. 22-23.

2877. HUMPHREY, Paul
"Cracked Mirror." [Light] (15/16) Aut-Wint 95-96, p. 29.
"Dash." [Light] (13) Spr 95, p. 14.
"Nude Brood." [Light] (15/16) Aut-Wint 95-96, p. 14.
"Slip Trip." [Light] (14) Sum 95, p. 11.
2878. HUMPHREYS, Deborah L.
"Judges 4: 4." [US1] (30/31) 95, p. 13.
2879. HUMPHRIES, Jefferson
"A Field of Islands" (Excerpts, tr. of Édouard Glissant). [InterQ] (2:1/2) 95, p. 38-39.
"Verses" (1-10. Excerpted from *La terre inquiete*, tr. of Edouard Glissant).
[NewOR] (21:2) Sum 95, p. 79-81.
2880. HUNOLD, Rose Marie
"Bread Pudding." [CapeR] (30:1) Spr 95, p. 49.
2881. HUNT, Laird
"PIKA" (from *Snow Country*). [Talisman] (15) Wint 95-96, p. 114-116.
2882. HUNTER, Allison
"Life Near the Summit." [SouthernPR] (35:1) Sum 95, p. 36.
2883. HUNTER, Emmy
"Anywhere." [Talisman] (15) Wint 95-96, p. 155.
2884. HUONG, Ho Xuan
"Ba Doi Gorge" (tr. by Linh Dinh). [DenQ] (30:2) Fall 95, p. 32.
"The Paper Fan" (tr. by Linh Dinh). [DenQ] (30:2) Fall 95, p. 33.
2885. HURDLE, Crystal
"Enticescent." [Bogg] (67) 95, p. 54.
2886. HURLOW, Marcia (Marcia L.)
"André Breton." [PoetryE] (40) Spr 95, p. 59.
"Household Hazards." [ManyMM] [1:1] D 94, p. 97.
2887. HURSEY, Brett
"Duties." [Border] (7) Fall-Wint 96, p. 19.
"Evolution." [Ledge] (19) Wint 95, p. 92.
"The Girl Who Cuts Your Hair." [RagMag] (12:2) Spr 95, p. 24-25.
"Seeing-Eye Man." [OxfordM] (10:1) Wint 94-Spr 95, p. 35.
2888. HURWITZ, Anita
"The Telltale Noise of Dispensing Tissues." [PoetryC] (15:2) Je 95, p. 26.
2889. HUSSAIN, Abul
"Market Prices" (tr. by Kabir Chowdhur). [Drumvoices] (4:1/2) Fall-Wint 94-95, p. 120.
2890. HUSTON, River
"All my friends are dead." [Poz] (7) Ap-My 95, p. 28.
2891. HUTCHINS, Jessica
"The Defendant's Sister." [PennR] (6:2) 95, p. 21.
"Section 8." [LullwaterR] (5:2) Fall-Wint 94, p. 10.
2892. HUTCHISON, Joseph
"A Beach North of Depoe Bay." [Northeast] (5:13) Wint 95-96, p. 16.
"Reading Over My Reflection." [Northeast] (5:13) Wint 95-96, p. 17.
2893. HUYLER, Frank
"In Wartime." [PoetL] (90:1) Spr 95, p. 43-44.
"Moving the Hive." [Atlantic] (276:2) Ag 95, p. 80.
2894. HUYSER, Cindy
"Homenaje a José Guadalupe Posada. Homage to José Guadalupe Posada" (runner up, 1994 Borderlands Poetry Contest). [Border] (7) Fall-Wint 96, p. 21.
2895. HYATT, Jeff
"Success and Pasta Sauce." [PraF] (16:4, #73) Wint 95-96, p. 37.
2896. HYDE, Christine
"Wearing Your Blue Y-Fronts." [Bogg] (67) 95, p. 61.
HYE, Yung Park
See PARK, Hye Yung
2897. HYETT, Barbara Helfgott
"American Alligator." [PraS] (69:2) Sum 95, p. 144.
"His Wife." [Colum] (24/25) 95, p. 66.
"Houston Toad." [PraS] (69:2) Sum 95, p. 145.
"New Mexican Ridge-nosed Rattlesnake." [PraS] (69:2) Sum 95, p. 146.
"Two Snakes." [Hudson] (48:1) Spr 95, p. 99.
2898. HYLAND, Gary
"Lian Lian." [Grain] (23:1) Sum 95, p. 87-89.

223

2899. HYMANS, Don
"2000 Mile Stare." [ColR] (22:2) Fall 95, p. 119.
"Light-Housing." [DenQ] (30:2) Fall 95, p. 34.
"Passacaglia." [ColR] (22:2) Fall 95, p. 120.
2900. HYNES, Maureen
"Inedible." [AntigR] (101) Spr 95, p. 74-75.
"(It Just Stops, You Said" [sic]. [AntigR] (101) Spr 95, p. 76.
2901. HYSJULIEN, Jamie
"Visual Time." [SouthernPR] (35:1) Sum 95, p. 53.

2902. I, Seitai
"Where is the agony" (in Japanese and English, tr. by Jiro Nakano). [BambooR]
(67/68) Sum-Fall 95, p. 16.
2903. ICHIOKA, Masanori
"Another anti-nuclear petition?" (in Japanese and English, tr. by Jiro Nakano).
[BambooR] (67/68) Sum-Fall 95, p. 22.
2904. IERONIM, Ioana
"At the Bend of the Don" (tr. by the author, w. Adam J. Sorkin). [OxfordM] (10:1)
Wint 94-Spr 95, p. 36.
"At the Old Fortress" (tr. by the author, w. Adam J. Sorkin). [OxfordM] (10:1) Wint
94-Spr 95, p. 36-37.
"The Burning" (tr. of Daniela Crasnaru, w. Adam J. Sorkin). [Vis] (48) 95, p. 39.
"Car Graveyard" (tr. of Ion Stratan, w. Adam J. Sorkin). [LitR] (38:2) Wint 95, p.
185-190.
"Elegy: Oh, old and familiar kitchens of summer" (tr. of Emil Brumaru, w. Adam
Sorkin). [PlumR] (9) [95 or 96], p. 22.
"The Second Elegy of the Detective Arthur" (tr. of Emil Brumaru, w. Adam Sorkin).
[PlumR] (9) [95 or 96], p. 23.
"Summer Afternoon" (tr. by the author, w. Adam J. Sorkin). [OxfordM] (10:1) Wint
94-Spr 95, p. 37.
"You Must Prove Yourself a Peaceful Animal Now" (tr. of Domnita Petri, w. Adam
J. Sorkin). [Vis] (48) 95, p. 41-42.
"Your Life Will Be Like This" (tr. by the author, w. Adam J. Sorkin). [OxfordM]
(10:1) Wint 94-Spr 95, p. 38.
IERONIOM, Ioana
See IERONIM, Ioana
2905. IERULLI, Claudio
"Who You Are." [AntigR] (100) Wint 95, p. 108.
2906. IGEL, Jayne-Ann
"The Allmar" (tr. by Rosmarie Waldrop). [ManhatR] (7:2) Wint 95, p. 72.
"Nightly Round" (tr. by Rosmarie Waldrop). [ManhatR] (7:2) Wint 95, p. 69.
"The sex of houses gave birth to strange places" (tr. by Rosmarie Waldrop).
[ManhatR] (7:2) Wint 95, p. 70.
"Unvoiced Sounds" (tr. by Rosmarie Waldrop). [ManhatR] (7:2) Wint 95, p. 71.
2907. IGNATOW, David
"The Artist." [IllinoisR] (3:1/2) Fall 95-Spr 96, p. 59.
"As If." [Pequod] (39) 95, p. 62.
"A Bark." [NewEngR] (17:1) Wint 95, p. 103.
"Because." [OntR] (43) Fall-Wint 95-96, p. 19.
"Fanny's Calves." [IllinoisR] (3:1/2) Fall 95-Spr 96, p. 103.
"For Johannes Edfelt." [DefinedP] (2:1) Fall-Wint 93, p. 13.
"For Johannes Edfelt." [Nat] (261:17) 20 N 95, p. 645.
"It's Amazing." [IllinoisR] (3:1/2) Fall 95-Spr 96, p. 29.
"It's Amazing." [OhioR] (53) 95, p. 32.
"Light." [ProseP] (4) 95, p. 37.
"The Man Who Fell Apart in the Street As He Walked." [Elf] (5:2) Sum 95, p. 23.
"The Man Who Fell Apart in the Street As He Walked." [ProseP] (4) 95, p. 36.
"The Ride." [Elf] (5:2) Sum 95, p. 22.
"Sanguine." [NewEngR] (17:1) Wint 95, p. 103.
"Stars." [DefinedP] (2:1) Fall-Wint 93, p. 14.
"Untitled: Think of this." [Elf] (5:2) Sum 95, p. 24.
"We." [Poetry] (165:5) F 95, p. 282.
2908. IGUCHI, Shizuko
"Thirty years have gone" (in Japanese and English, tr. by Jiro Nakano). [BambooR]
(67/68) Sum-Fall 95, p. 17.

2909. IINO, Tomoyuki
"The Bridge" (tr. of Motoo Andoh, w. Jon Silkin). [Stand] (36:2) Spr 95, p. 28-29.
"Sleep Deeply in the Wilderness of Elegy" (tr. of Masato Inagawa, w. Jon Silkin).
[Stand] (36:2) Spr 95, p. 73.
2910. IKKYU, Sojun (1394-1481)
"Elegy" (tr. by Sam Hamill). [Agni] (42) 95, p. 125.
"Face to Face with My Lover on Daito's Anniversary" (tr. by Sam Hamill). [Agni]
(42) 95, p. 121.
"Face to Face with My Lover on Daito's Anniversary" (tr. by Sam Hamill).
[PoetryE] (41) Aut 95, p. 26.
"My Hand Is Lady Mori's Hand" (tr. by Sam Hamill). [Agni] (42) 95, p. 122.
"My Love's Dark Place Is Fragrant Like Narcissus" (tr. by Sam Hamill). [Agni] (42)
95, p. 124.
"Night Talk in a Dream Chamber" (tr. by Sam Hamill). [Agni] (42) 95, p. 123.
2911. IKONOMI, Ilir
"I Am Setting the Alarm" (tr. of Visar Zhiti). [Vis] (48) 95, p. 7.
"Saturday Disgouring the Week" (tr. of Arben Prendi). [Vis] (48) 95, p. 6.
IKUKO, Atsumi
See ATSUMI, Ikuko
2912. IMAI, Tokuzaburo
"The streets still smoldering" (in Japanese and English, tr. by Jiro Nakano).
[BambooR] (67/68) Sum-Fall 95, p. 23.
2913. IMAMOTO, Harue
"Run under the beam!" (in Japanese and English, tr. by Jiro Nakano). [BambooR]
(67/68) Sum-Fall 95, p. 24.
2914. IMSDAHL, Peter
"Intercourse." [PlumR] (9) [95 or 96], p. 1.
2915. INADA, Lawson Fusao
"Denver Union Station." [ManyMM] (2:1) 95, p. 142-143.
"Doin' a 'California'." [ManyMM] (1:2) 95, p. 72-73.
"Even If You're Not a Buddhist." [Tricycle] (4:3, #15) Spr 95, p. 78.
"Even If You're Not Buddhist." [ManyMM] (1:2) 95, p. 64-65.
"Exemplary Teachers." [ManyMM] (1:2) 95, p. 56-63.
"The Grand Silos of California." [ManyMM] [1:1] D 94, p. 68.
"Grandmother" (For Grandmother: Mijiu Inada, Yoshiko Saito). [ManyMM] [1:1] D
94, p. 67.
"Grandmother" (For Grandmother Mijiu Inada, Yoshiko Saito). [Tricycle] (4:3, #15)
Spr 95, p. 77.
"Making It Stick." [ManyMM] (1:2) 95, p. 68.
"Messing with the Sisters." [ManyMM] (1:2) 95, p. 66.
"A Nice Place." [ManyMM] (1:2) 95, p. 67.
"A Nice Place." [Tricycle] (4:3, #15) Spr 95, p. 76.
"Nobody, Nothing." [ManyMM] (1:2) 95, p. 69-71.
"A World of Passengers" (For David Kherdian). [ManyMM] [1:1] D 94, p. 65-66.
2916. INAGAWA, Masato
"Sleep Deeply in the Wilderness of Elegy" (tr. by Tomoyuki Iino and Jon Silkin).
[Stand] (36:2) Spr 95, p. 73.
2917. INCE, Özdemir
"Continuities" (tr. by Murat Nemet-Nejat). [Talisman] (14) Fall 95, p. 51.
"Stay With Me" (tr. by Murat Nemet-Nejat). [Talisman] (14) Fall 95, p. 52.
2918. INCHAÚSPE, Juan Manuel (1940-1991)
"How Comforting to Collapse in One's Room" (tr. by Joan Lindgren). [LitR] (39:1)
Fall 95, p. 27.
"I Cannot Sit Down to Wait" (tr. by Joan Lindgren). [LitR] (39:1) Fall 95, p. 29.
"I Go Out Early" (tr. by Joan Lindgren). [LitR] (39:1) Fall 95, p. 30.
"I Have Patiently Tried" (tr. by Joan Lindgren). [LitR] (39:1) Fall 95, p. 30.
"It Is True" (tr. by Joan Lindgren). [LitR] (39:1) Fall 95, p. 28-29.
"Once More April" (tr. by Joan Lindgren). [LitR] (39:1) Fall 95, p. 28.
"Once More You Are" (tr. by Joan Lindgren). [LitR] (39:1) Fall 95, p. 28.
"Seamless Thoughts" (tr. by Joan Lindgren). [LitR] (39:1) Fall 95, p. 30-31.
"This Morning on Awakening" (tr. by Joan Lindgren). [LitR] (39:1) Fall 95, p. 31.
"You Have Nothing But Words" (tr. by Joan Lindgren). [LitR] (39:1) Fall 95, p. 29.
"Yours" (tr. by Joan Lindgren). [LitR] (39:1) Fall 95, p. 27.
2919. INEZ, Colette
"Confounded Song." [OhioR] (53) 95, p. 54.
"Encounter at the Jardins Botaniques." [MassR] (36:2) Sum 95, p. 218.

"Found Child." [CimR] (111) Ap 95, p. 60.
"Imhotep Sweeps into My Dream of Wanting to Be Saved from Humdrumness." [LullwaterR] (5:1) 93-94, p. 8.
"Minnesotan in Paris." [CimR] (111) Ap 95, p. 59.
"Royal Coaches Taking the Queen." [LullwaterR] (5:1) 93-94, p. 9.
2920. INGERSON, Martin (Martin I.)
"Poems of the Winter Solstice, 1956-1966" (For Suzanne Rouse). [BellArk] (11:2) Mr-Ap 95, p. 7-10.
"Red" (for Christine). [BellArk] (11:3) My-Je 95, p. 7.
2921. INGRAHAM, Elizabeth
"The Expansion Room." [SouthernPR] (35:1) Sum 95, p. 19-22.
2922. INGRAM, Heather
"Identity (Post-Divorce)." [PottPort] (16:1) Fall 95, p. 36.
2923. INKALA, Jouni
"Despite all, only one footstep behind you has fallen too deep" (tr. by Sari Hantula). [InterPR] (21:2) Fall 95, p. 71.
"I have been right too many times" (tr. by Sari Hantula). [InterPR] (21:2) Fall 95, p. 73.
"I know this decomposed form of time began in water" (tr. by Sari Hantula). [InterPR] (21:2) Fall 95, p. 75.
"Olen ollut liian monta kertaa oikeassa." [InterPR] (21:2) Fall 95, p. 72.
"Silti takanasi on vain yksi liian syvälle maahan." [InterPR] (21:2) Fall 95, p. 70.
"Tiedän tämä maatunut ajan muoto alkoi vedestä." [InterPR] (21:2) Fall 95, p. 74.
"Vuorimiehenkatu. Helsinki" (in Finnish and English, tr. by Sari Hantula). [InterPR] (21:2) Fall 95, p. 68-69.
2924. INOUE, Seikan
"Half scorched pieces of brains and throats" (in Japanese and English, tr. by Jiro Nakano). [BambooR] (67/68) Sum-Fall 95, p. 25.
2925. IPELLIE, Alootook
"The Igloos Are Calm in the Camp." [Nimrod] (38:2) Spr-Sum 95, p. 44.
2926. IRIE, Kevin
"Sparrows on Ossington Avenue." [CanLit] (145) Sum 95, p. 106.
2927. IRONSPIKE, Bucky
"The Fountainhead." [Poem] (73) My 95, p. 5.
2928. IRVINE, Suey
"Charles Sykes: His Burial." [BellArk] (11:6) N-D 95, p. 5.
"Sacred Longing." [BellArk] (11:6) N-D 95, p. 5.
2929. IRWIN, Kip
"Conspiracies." [Sun] (236) Ag 95, p. 25.
2930. IRWIN, Mark
"Archbishop of Canterbury Ramsey and the Bishop of Southwick" (Photograph by Robert Mapplethorpe, 1975). [NewEngR] (17:2) Spr 95, p. 65-66.
"As We Wonder." [MidAR] (15:1/2) 95, p. 149.
"Buffalo Nickel." [AmerPoR] (24:4) Jl-Ag 95, p. 39.
"Discovery." [AmerPoR] (24:4) Jl-Ag 95, p. 40.
"History's Pause." [OhioR] (53) 95, p. 104-106.
"Quick, Now, Always" (for Reyes García). [AmerPoR] (24:4) Jl-Ag 95, p. 39.
"Serious Earth." [DenQ] (30:1) Sum 95, p. 68-69.
"Sparrow." [NewEngR] (17:3) Sum 95, p. 82.
"Vines." [WillowS] (36) Je 95, p. 9.
"Vista." [OhioR] (53) 95, p. 107.
"The Window." [WillowS] (36) Je 95, p. 8.
2931. ISAAC, Doug
"Past Present, Tense: A Mennonite Heritage" (An Excerpt). [PraF] (16:2, #71) Sum 95, p. 68-69.
2932. ISAKSSON, Folke
"Grandmother and the Tramps" (tr. by Stephen Klass). [CumbPR] (14:2) Spr 95, p. 26.
"Grandmother's Cat" (tr. by Stephen Klass). [CumbPR] (14:2) Spr 95, p. 24.
"I Mormors Hus." [CumbPR] (14:2) Spr 95, p. 23.
"In Grandmother's House" (tr. by Stephen Klass). [CumbPR] (14:2) Spr 95, p. 22.
"Mormor och Luffarna." [CumbPR] (14:2) Spr 95, p. 27.
"Mormors Katt." [CumbPR] (14:2) Spr 95, p. 25.
2933. ISHIBASHI, Teruko
"I sit down to halt the Atomic Bomb testing" (in Japanese and English, tr. by Jiro Nakano). [BambooR] (67/68) Sum-Fall 95, p. 21.

226

2934. ISHII, Momoyo
"Mothers, wives, sisters" (in Japanese and English, tr. by Jiro Nakano). [BambooR]
(67/68) Sum-Fall 95, p. 18.
2935. ISHII, Sadako
"One that lies down" (in Japanese and English, tr. by Jiro Nakano). [BambooR]
(67/68) Sum-Fall 95, p. 20.
2936. ISHIKAWA, Nobuko
"The exterior of the Hiroshima Dome" (in Japanese and English, tr. by Jiro Nakano).
[BambooR] (67/68) Sum-Fall 95, p. 19.
2937. ISKANDER, Natasha Nefertiti
"Sister" (Michael Jasper Gioia Award Winner for 1995). [Sequoia] (36) 94-95, p.
60-61.
2938. ISLAM, Syed Manzoorul
"Conjugal Prayer" (tr. of Shamim Azad, w. Carolyne Wright and the author).
[MidAR] (15:1/2) 95, p. 93.
"Fantasy" (tr. of Ruby Rahman, w. Carolyne Wright and the author). [MidAR]
(15:1/2) 95, p. 85-89.
"I Want to Pierce with the Arrows of My Voice" (tr. of Shamim Azad, w. Carolyne
Wright and the author). [MidAR] (15:1/2) 95, p. 97, 99.
"Journal" (tr. of Ruby Rahman, w. Carolyne Wright and the author). [MidAR]
(15:1/2) 95, p. 81, 83.
"Moon-Struck" (tr. of Ruby Rahman, w. Carolyne Wright and the author). [MidAR]
(15:1/2) 95, p. 77, 79.
"Out-of-Order Remote-Control" (tr. of Shamim Azad, w. Carolyne Wright and the
author). [MidAR] (15:1/2) 95, p. 95.
"This Afternoon Knows" (tr. of Ruby Rahman, w. Carolyne Wright and the author).
[MidAR] (15:1/2) 95, p. 73, 75.
2939. ISRAELI, Henry
"American Gothic." [Descant] (26:1, #88) Spr 95, p. 18.
"Kettles." [Descant] (26:1, #88) Spr 95, p. 17.
"Responsibility." [Descant] (26:1, #88) Spr 95, p. 13-16.
ISSA, Kobayashi
See KOBAYASHI, Issa (1762-1826)
2940. ITAMASU, Yukie
"Lonely rainy night" (in Japanese and English, tr. by Jiro Nakano). [BambooR]
(67/68) Sum-Fall 95, p. 26.
2941. ITO, Hiromi
"Moro Reflex." [RiverS] (45) 95, p. 53-54.
"Underground." [RiverS] (45) 95, p. 35.
2942. ITTERBEEK, Eugène van
"Nightbook: 60" (tr. by Adam J. Sorkin). [ConnPR] (14:1) 95, p. 37.
"Only in the fire" (from "Transparent Waiting," tr. of Annie Reniers, w. Adam J.
Sorkin). [MalR] (110) Spr 95, p. 106.
"Transparent Waiting" (Selections: 2 poems, tr. of Annie Reniers, w. Adam J.
Sorkin). [MalR] (110) Spr 95, p. 106-107.
"You stay all eternity" (from "Transparent Waiting," tr. of Annie Reniers, w. Adam
J. Sorkin). [MalR] (110) Spr 95, p. 107.
2943. IUPPA, M. J.
"Grief Is Milkweed." [ManyMM] (2:1) 95, p. 50.
"Something Left in the Basket." [ManyMM] (2:1) 95, p. 51.
2944. IVERSON, Teresa
"Here the Marsh." [Orion] (14:4) Aut 95, p. 64.
"Kaleidoscope" (for D. S. Carne-Ross, apologies to Sir Thomas Browne). [Orion]
(14:4) Aut 95, p. 64.
2945. IVES, Rich
"As Soon As You Know." [NewOR] (21:2) Sum 95, p. 91.
"A Gift." [ArtfulD] (28/29) 95, p. 105.
"Sofia Kovalevskaya at Palobino, 1857." [WillowS] (35) Ja 95, p. 29.
2946. IVO, Lêdo
"Hiding" (tr. by Kerry Shawn Keys). [PoetryE] (39) Fall 94, p. 111.
"The Literary Narcissus" (tr. by Kerry Shawn Keys). [PoetryE] (39) Fall 94, p. 114.
"Postcard from a Battle" (tr. by Kerry Shawn Keys). [PoetryE] (39) Fall 94, p. 113.
"Truth and Falsehood" (tr. by Kerry Shawn Keys). [PoetryE] (39) Fall 94, p. 112.
2947. IWAMOTO, Hiroshi
"The deployment of 'tomahawk' missiles can begin a nuclear crisis" (in Japanese and
English, tr. by Jiro Nakano). [BambooR] (67/68) Sum-Fall 95, p. 27.

2948. IZUMI, Asao
"On newspapers spread on depot platforms" (in Japanese and English, tr. by Jiro
Nakano). [BambooR] (67/68) Sum-Fall 95, p. 28.

J, T. M.
See T. M. J.
2949. JABES, Edmond
"Of Solitude as the Space of Writing" (tr. by Rosmarie Waldrop). [OhioR] (54) 95,
p. 41-44.
"Outside Time, the Dream of the Book" (tr. by Rosmarie Waldrop). [OhioR] (54)
95, p. 38-40.
"The Page as a Place to Subvert Both Whiteness and the Word" (tr. by Rosmarie
Waldrop). [OhioR] (54) 95, p. 36-37.
2950. JACKMAN, David
"To the Maid of the Eastern Eyes." [CaribbeanW] (9) 95, p. 42-43.
2951. JACKSON, Fleda Brown
"Bus Stop." [AmerPoR] (24:6) N-D 95, p. 25.
"Fishpond" (for Judith Calhoun). [Iowa] (25:1) Wint 95, p. 111-115.
"Ginny Dolls." [WestB] (37) 95, p. 41-42.
"Stones." [NewMyths] (2:2/3:1) 95, p. 16.
2952. JACKSON, Richard
"Buy One, Get One Free." [GettyR] (8:3) Sum 95, p. 528-530.
"Petrarchan Figures" (Selections: II, CCXII). [GreenMR] (8:2) Fall-Wint 95-96, p.
142.
2953. JACKSON, Robert A.
"Pop Culture: 2 Nov. 1994." [Drumvoices] (5:1/2) Fall-Wint 95-96, p. 108.
2954. JACKSON, Taj
"Dream of Burning." [SmPd] (32:1, #93) Wint 95, p. 34-35.
"Fugitive Chores, Stealth." [SmPd] (32:1, #93) Wint 95, p. 35.
"Signature." [SmPd] (32:1, #93) Wint 95, p. 33-34.
2955. JACOBIK, Gray
"Dust Storm." [Ploughs] (21:4) Wint 95-96, p. 100.
"First Marriage." [Ploughs] (21:4) Wint 95-96, p. 101.
"Matisse's Odalisques." [Interim] (14:2) Fall-Wint 95-96, p. 8-9.
"Skirts." [GeoR] (49:4) Wint 95, p. 905.
"Windows." [Interim] (14:2) Fall-Wint 95-96, p. 9.
2956. JACOBIK, Jane Gray
"The Crab." [LaurelR] (29:1) Wint 95, p. 79.
2957. JACOBOWITZ, Judah
"Refuge." [Plain] (16:1) Fall 95, p. 29.
2958. JACOBS, Bruce A.
"The Beer Joint." [ManyMM] (1:2) 95, p. 107.
"Church Lady." [AfAmRev] (29:1) Spr 95, p. 93-94.
"Friendly Skies." [AfAmRev] (29:1) Spr 95, p. 94.
"Masons." [ManyMM] (1:2) 95, p. 108.
"The Neighborhood." [AfAmRev] (29:1) Spr 95, p. 93.
2959. JACOBS, Dale
"Holding the Corner." [PoetL] (90:4) Wint 95-96, p. 43.
2960. JACOBS, Douglas
"Dog Days." [Border] (6) Spr-Sum 95, p. 43-44.
2961. JACOBS, J. L.
"Doorsteps." [AmerLC] (7) 95, p. 66.
2962. JACOBS, Peter
"September Frost." [IndR] (18:2) Fall 95, p. 141-147.
2963. JACOBSEN, Josephine
"Program." [NewYorker] (71:37) 20 N 95, p. 76.
"Voyage." [NewYorker] (71:21) 24 Jl 95, p. 39.
2964. JACOBSEN, Rolf
"Dies Illae" (from "Night Music," tr. by Robert Hedin). [Nimrod] (38:2) Spr-Sum
95, p. 78.
"Play" (from "Night Music," tr. by Robert Hedin). [Nimrod] (38:2) Spr-Sum 95, p.
78.
2965. JACOBY, Jay
"Apostrophizing the Lemon." [Light] (14) Sum 95, p. 8.

2966. JACQMIN, François
"After it had snowed" (tr. by Dick Schneider). [ManhatR] (7:2) Wint 95, p. 45.
"At twilight, when I look" (tr. by Dick Schneider). [ManhatR] (7:2) Wint 95, p. 57.
"The cold consumed the sparrows" (tr. by Dick Schneider). [ManhatR] (7:2) Wint 95, p. 50.
"Day's end had that perfection" (tr. by Dick Schneider). [ManhatR] (7:2) Wint 95, p. 55.
"I am not an author, but a confused passerby" (tr. by Dick Schneider). [ManhatR] (7:2) Wint 95, p. 49.
"I can't make it to the world, like" (tr. by Dick Schneider). [ManhatR] (7:2) Wint 95, p. 53.
"I had to gather up my own immensity" (tr. by Dick Schneider). [ManhatR] (7:2) Wint 95, p. 52.
"I make myself rare and taciturn so that my words" (tr. by Dick Schneider). [ManhatR] (7:2) Wint 95, p. 47.
"It is not enough to sleep" (tr. by Dick Schneider). [ManhatR] (7:2) Wint 95, p. 54.
"No forest, and no thought even" (tr. by Dick Schneider). [ManhatR] (7:2) Wint 95, p. 44.
"The noise snow makes renders barely perceptible" (tr. by Dick Schneider). [ManhatR] (7:2) Wint 95, p. 48.
"Since the frost settled in the orchard" (tr. by Dick Schneider). [ManhatR] (7:2) Wint 95, p. 51.
"There were some moments of sublime blindness" (tr. by Dick Schneider). [ManhatR] (7:2) Wint 95, p. 46.
"What would be the triumph spoken" (tr. by Dick Schneider). [ManhatR] (7:2) Wint 95, p. 56.
2967. JACQUES, Ben
"In Arizona." [WormR] (35:1, #137) 95, p. 11.
"Ritual of Preparation." [WormR] (35:1, #137) 95, p. 10.
"This Morning Out of the Corner of My Eye." [WormR] (35:1, #137) 95, p. 11.
2968. JAEGER, Lowell
"Working on My Words." [PraS] (69:1) Spr 95, p. 156-158.
2969. JAFFE, Maggie
"Nuke Porn: I-II." [InterQ] (2:1/2) 95, p. 284.
2970. JAGO, Carol
"Conjure Woman at a Desk" (Literary Festival: Poetry: Honorable Mention). [EngJ] (84:4) Ap 95, p. 38.
2971. JAGO, Michael
"The Frog and the Ozone." [Light] (15/16) Aut-Wint 95-96, p. 13.
"The Self-Adhesive Postage Stamp." [Light] (14) Sum 95, p. 17.
2972. JAMES, Cynthia
"Woman Descendant." [CaribbeanW] (9) 95, p. 28-29.
2973. JAMES, Darius H.
"Duchamp As Iron Lawn Jockey" (for David Hammons and the nights at Vazac's). [GrandS] (13:3, #51) Wint 95, p. 33.
2974. JAMES, David
"The Beginning of Another." [MidwQ] (36:2) Wint 95, p. 160.
"For Love or Money." [TarRP] (34:2) Spr 95, p. 14-15.
2975. JAMES, Lysa
"Autobiography." [Conscience] (16:1/2) Spr-Sum 95, p. 42.
"A Sense." [Conscience] (16:1/2) Spr-Sum 95, p. 36.
"Undoing the Misogynist." [ManyMM] (2:1) 95, p. 30-31.
"Wishbone." [ManyMM] (2:1) 95, p. 32.
2976. JAMES, Miguel
"Yo Creo en los Espiritus de Mis Antepasados." [Luz] (8) Spr 95, p. 54-56.
2977. JAMES, Sibyl
"Beyond Confessions." [ProseP] (4) 95, p. 38.
2978. JAMES "BUSTER" P. (John Howard Pavilion, St. Elizabeth's Hospital, Washington, DC)
"Thinking Back" (WritersCorps Program). [WashR] (21:2) Ag-S 95, p. 10.
2979. JANABI, Hatif
"The Abyss" (tr. by Khaled Mattawa). [IndR] (18:2) Fall 95, p. 49.
"The Chemistry of Knowledge" (tr. by Khaled Mattawa). [GrahamHR] (19) Wint 95-96, p. 56.
"An Initial Description" (tr. by Khaled Mattawa). [IndR] (18:2) Fall 95, p. 45.

229

"Poems of the New Regions" (tr. by Khaled Mattawa). [IndR] (18:2) Fall 95, p. 46-
48.
"Savage Continents" (tr. by Khaled Mattawa). [ArtfulD] (28/29) 95, p. 8-9.
"To Where?" (tr. by Khaled Mattawa). [ArtfulD] (28/29) 95, p. 10-11.
"A Window Small as a Palm Vast as Suffering" (tr. by Khaled Mattawa). [IndR]
(18:2) Fall 95, p. 43-44.
"The Yellow Face of Hunger" (tr. by Khaled Mattawa). [GrahamHR] (19) Wint 95-
96, p. 57-58.
2980. JANES, Percy
"The Wall." [TickleAce] (27) Spr-Sum 94, p. 82.
2981. JANEVSKI, Slavko
"The Admiral" (Klee, tr. by Zoran Anchevski). [Vis] (48) 95, p. 28-29.
"The Magician" (Ernst, tr. by Zoran Anchevski). [Vis] (48) 95, p. 27-28.
"The Magus" (Bosch, tr. by Zoran Anchevski). [Vis] (48) 95, p. 27.
"Shivers" (Goya, tr. by Zoran Anchevski). [Vis] (48) 95, p. 29-30.
2982. JANIK, Phyllis
"Cutting Corners." [NewRena] (9:2, #28) Spr 95, p. 57-58.
2983. JANOWITZ, Phyllis
"The Necessary Angel." [RiverS] (42/43) 95, p. 177.
"Rattle and Roll." [PraS] (69:4) Wint 95, p. 77-78.
"Some Dream." [FreeL] (14) Wint 95, p. 6-7.
2984. JANZEN, Jean
"Another Life." [GettyR] (8:3) Sum 95, p. 390.
"Claiming the Dust." [Poetry] (166:4) Jl 95, p. 201-202.
"Magnolia." [Poetry] (166:4) Jl 95, p. 200-201.
2985. JAQUISH, Karen I.
"Vermont Graveyard." [Plain] (15:3) Spr 95, p. 36.
"Vultures at Kellogg Bay." [SouthernPR] (35:2) Wint 95, p. 59.
2986. JARDINE, Gerri
"The Veteran." [CutB] (44) Sum 95, p. 82-83.
2987. JARMAN, Mark
"Psalm: First Forgive the Silence." [Image] (9) Spr 95, p. 26.
"Unholy Sonnet 1." [SouthernR] (31:4) O/Aut 95, p. 852.
"Unholy Sonnet 2." [SouthernR] (31:4) O/Aut 95, p. 852-853.
"Unholy Sonnets" (3 poems). [Image] (9) Spr 95, p. 25-26.
"The Worry Bird." [Thrpny] (62) Sum 95, p. 25.
2988. JASPER, Matt
"Divining." [GrandS] (13:4, #52) Spr 95, p. 79.
"Mathematician." [GrandS] (13:4, #52) Spr 95, p. 78.
"Sunlight Floods the Room. Three Are Drowned." [GrandS] (13:4, #52) Spr 95, p.
81.
"A Translation, Purdy Group Home." [GrandS] (13:4, #52) Spr 95, p. 80.
2989. JASPER, Pat
"Antebellum." [Arc] (34) Spr 95, p. 81-82.
"Easter Sunday, 1961, Corte del Contento." [Arc] (34) Spr 95, p. 79-80.
"St. Lucia: A Guided Tour" (for Derek Walcott). [Arc] (34) Spr 95, p. 83-85.
2990. JASTRUN, Tomasz
"Chain" (tr. by Daniel Bourne). [SpoonR] (20:2) Sum-Fall 95, p. 75.
"Christmas Eve" (tr. by Daniel Bourne). [SpoonR] (20:2) Sum-Fall 95, p. 74.
"Free" (tr. by Daniel Bourne). [SpoonR] (20:2) Sum-Fall 95, p. 75.
"Gotland" (tr. by Daniel Bourne). [Chelsea] (59) 95, p. 127.
"The Present Day" (tr. by Daniel Bourne). [SpoonR] (20:2) Sum-Fall 95, p. 74.
"Underneath the Leaf" (tr. by Daniel Bourne). [Chelsea] (59) 95, p. 128.
2991. JAUSS, David
"Cyrano." [Shen] (45:1) Spr 95, p. 22-23.
"Lemons" (Kierling Sanatorium, May 11, 1924). [ParisR] (37:135) Sum 95, p. 200-
201.
"The Year Nobody Died." [PaintedB] (55/56) 95, p. 51-52.
2992. JAY, Cellan
"August Fast." [MalR] (110) Spr 95, p. 102.
"Mohammed's Coat." [MalR] (110) Spr 95, p. 103.
2993. JAY, Criss
"Poem for the Dead Children." [SantaBR] (3:3) Fall-Wint 95, p. 72.
2994. JAY, Peter
"Statements" (tr. of Éva Tóth, w. Laura Schiff). [AmerPoR] (24:1) Ja-F 95, p. 36.

"Teiresias Wailing" (tr. of Éva Tóth, w. Laura Schiff). [AmerPoR] (24:1) Ja-F 95, p. 36.
"Van Gogh Gives Evidence" (tr. of Éva Tóth, w. Laura Schiff). [AmerPoR] (24:1) Ja-F 95, p. 36.
2995. JAYME, M.
"Company Property" (runner up, 1994 Borderlands Poetry Contest). [Border] (6) Spr-Sum 95, p. 45-46.
2996. JECH, Jon
"Real Men in America" (Excerpt). [BellArk] (11:1) Ja-F 95, p. 8-9.
2997. JEFFRIES, Alan
"Alphabet." [Poem] (73) My 95, p. 9.
"How It Ends" (for W. C.). [Poem] (73) My 95, p. 10.
"My Death" (after Vallejo and Justice). [WormR] (35:1, #137) 95, p. 2-3.
"Sweet Lies." [WormR] (35:1, #137) 95, p. 1-2.
"You Are." [PoetryE] (40) Spr 95, p. 60-61.
"Your Favorite Poem." [WormR] (35:1, #137) 95, p. 3.
2998. JELLEMA, Rod
"Civitas." [PlumR] (8) [95], p. 89.
"Getting Back in Time." [PlumR] (8) [95], p. 88.
"Herm Wyken to Himself." [Field] (52) Spr 95, p. 52.
"Young Man at the Laundromat, Watching the Spinning Dryers." [Field] (52) Spr 95, p. 53.
2999. JENKIN, Ann Timoney
"Furnished Rooms." [Footwork] (24/25) 95, p. 79.
"Wind Bells." [Footwork] (24/25) 95, p. 80.
3000. JENKINS, Louis
"Drinking Poem." [PoetryE] (40) Spr 95, p. 62.
3001. JENKINS, Rachel Ferris
"Upon His Death." [MassR] (36:2) Sum 95, p. 236-237.
3002. JENKINSON, Biddy
"At the Pipers' Club" (tr. by Peter Denman). [Poetry] (167:1/2) O-N 95, p. 23, 25.
"Cumann Na bPíobairí." [Poetry] (167:1/2) O-N 95, p. 22, 24.
3003. JENNERMANN, Donald
"Farewell Strains" (from *Bearing North*). [AmerPoR] (24:5) S-O 95, p. 22.
3004. JENNINGS, Edison
"Chestnuts" (Honorable Mention, First Annual Poetry Awards). [LiteralL] (2:1) Sum 95, p. 15.
3005. JENNINGS, Lane
"Courtship" (tr. of Erich Fried). [Vis] (47) 95, p. 29.
"Growing Older" (tr. of Erich Fried). [Vis] (47) 95, p. 29.
3006. JENSEN, Barbara
"Riding in a Car with No Inside Door Handles." [Kalliope] (17:2) 95, p. 23-24.
3007. JENSEN, Laura
"Happiness." [SenR] (25:1) Spr 95, p. 35.
3008. JENSI, Paul
"M'Lady." [WormR] (35:4, #140) 95, p. 149-150.
3009. JEROZAL, Gregory
"Essay Question." [HampSPR] Wint 95, p. 19.
"Someone, Somewhere." [HampSPR] Wint 95, p. 20.
3010. JETTPACE, Lynn A.
"Hawaii." [Wind] (75) Spr 95, p. 14.
3011. JEWELL, Andrew
"Coltrane's Sound." [Plain] (15:3) Spr 95, p. 12.
3012. JEWELL, David
"Recipe for a Shoe." [Border] (7) Fall-Wint 96, p. 22.
3013. JEWELL, Terri L.
"Sine Qua Non." [Kalliope] (17:3) 95, p. 76.
3014. JEWETT, Michelle
"My Mother Has Two Daughters." [Pearl] (22) Fall-Wint 95, p. 131.
3015. JILKA, Lucy
"In the Orrery." [AmerV] (38) 95, p. 39.
JIM, Rex Lee
See DINELTSOI, Mazii
3016. JIMÉNEZ URE, Alberto
"(Las Bogas Escriturales)." [Luz] (8) Spr 95, p. 53.

3017. JIN, Ha
"The Past." [NewEngR] (17:1) Wint 95, p. 7.
"Status." [NewEngR] (17:1) Wint 95, p. 8.
3018. JODEN, Toshie
"The Atomic Bomb destroyed Hiroshima" (in Japanese and English, tr. by Jiro
Nakano). [BambooR] (67/68) Sum-Fall 95, p. 29.
3019. JOE, J. B.
"Poem of 29 Lines, Series -01." [WestCL] (29:1, #16) Spr-Sum 95, p. 104.
"Poem of 29 Lines, Series 0." [WestCL] (29:1, #16) Spr-Sum 95, p. 102.
"Poem of 29 Lines, Series 1" (4 poems with same title). [WestCL] (29:1, #16) Spr-
Sum 95, p. 103, 110-112.
"Poem of 29 Lines, Series 2" (2 poems with same title). [WestCL] (29:1, #16) Spr-
Sum 95, p. 106-107.
"Poem of 29 Lines, Series 3." [WestCL] (29:1, #16) Spr-Sum 95, p. 105.
"Poem of 29 Lines, Series 4" (2 poems with same title). [WestCL] (29:1, #16) Spr-
Sum 95, p. 108-109.
3020. JOFRÉ, Manuel Alcides
"Axes of Spring." [Arc] (35) Aut 95, p. 73.
"The Conservation Game." [Arc] (35) Aut 95, p. 74.
"Grand Piano." [Arc] (35) Aut 95, p. 72.
3021. JOHANNES, Joan
"Jeffrey, Remember the Bag of Plums?" (Literary Festival: Poetry: Honorable
Mention). [EngJ] (84:4) Ap 95, p. 39.
3022. JOHNS, Larry W.
"Rodney." [JamesWR] (12:2) Spr-Sum 95, p. 8.
3023. JOHNSON, Allen, Jr.
"Bother and Oh Blow!" [Light] (13) Spr 95, p. 7.
3024. JOHNSON, Brian
"Self-Portrait (Kneeling)." [ProseP] (4) 95, p. 39.
3025. JOHNSON, Dave
"Dave Gibson Makes His Way Down." [NewDeltaR] (13:1) Fall 95-Wint 96, p. 52-
53.
3026. JOHNSON, David F.
"The Kikuyu Boy." [AlabamaLR] (9:1) 95, p. 25.
3027. JOHNSON, Greg
"Survivor Guilt." [OntR] (42) Spr-Sum 95, p. 93-94.
"With Death Comes." [OntR] (42) Spr-Sum 95, p. 94.
3028. JOHNSON, Guy
"The Inner Garden." [Drumvoices] (4:1/2) Fall-Wint 94-95, p. 106-107.
"Somalia." [Drumvoices] (4:1/2) Fall-Wint 94-95, p. 104-105.
"Third from the Son." [Drumvoices] (4:1/2) Fall-Wint 94-95, p. 109.
"The Wooden Sky." [Drumvoices] (4:1/2) Fall-Wint 94-95, p. 107-108.
3029. JOHNSON, James
"Lehighton Bound." [WestB] (36) 95, p. 70.
3030. JOHNSON, Jim
"What We Eat." [NorthStoneR] (12) 95, p. 222-223.
3031. JOHNSON, John W.
"The Laborer of the Deep" (WritersCorps Program, Washington, DC). [WashR]
(21:2) Ag-S 95, p. 7.
3032. JOHNSON, Jonathan
"Renewal." [CreamCR] (19:1) Spr 95, p. 168-169.
3033. JOHNSON, Kathy Allison
"The Rudiments of Rutabagas." [Rosebud] (2:2) Sum 95, p. 65.
3034. JOHNSON, Lemuel
"Hagar." [MichQR] (34:1) Wint 95, p. 75-76.
"Pompeii." [MichQR] (34:1) Wint 95, p. 73-74.
3035. JOHNSON, Linnea
"Ascension." [Nimrod] (39:1) Fall-Wint 95, p. 110.
"Joan of Arc Receiving Her Revelation" (oil on canvas, Jules Bastien-Lepage, 1879.
(Honorable Mention, 1995 Editors' Prize). [SpoonR] (20:2) Sum-Fall 95, p.
42-44.
"Our Red Hair." [Nimrod] (39:1) Fall-Wint 95, p. 111.
"Saying with Color and Shapes" (Selections: 1-2). [Nimrod] (39:1) Fall-Wint 95, p.
109.
3036. JOHNSON, Margot
"The Perks Are Too Many." [Pearl] (22) Fall-Wint 95, p. 133.

3037. JOHNSON, Mark Allan
"Northwest Passage" (Excerpt). [BellArk] (11:1) Ja-F 95, p. 22.

3038. JOHNSON, Melissa
"Guinevere Dreaming by the Fire." [Border] (7) Fall-Wint 96, p. 24.
"Odalisque." [Border] (7) Fall-Wint 96, p. 23.

3039. JOHNSON, Michael L.
"The Day William Stafford Died." [MidwQ] (36:4) Sum 95, p. 383-384.
"Dixie 'The Marilyn Monroe of Burlesque' Evans at the Strippers Hall of Fame."
[Pearl] (22) Fall-Wint 95, p. 123.

3040. JOHNSON, Nicholas
"Country Life." [Journal] (19:2) Fall-Wint 95, p. 49.
"Degrees of Freedom." [Journal] (19:2) Fall-Wint 95, p. 50.

3041. JOHNSON, Penny
"Cherry Blossoms." [BellArk] (11:4) Jl-Ag 95, p. 10.
"Midwest Thunder Storm." [BellArk] (11:4) Jl-Ag 95, p. 10.
"Mother Daughter Thunder." [BellArk] (11:4) Jl-Ag 95, p. 10.

3042. JOHNSON, Peter
"The Disconsolation of Philosophy." [IllinoisR] (3:1/2) Fall 95-Spr 96, p. 65.
"Einstein's Brain." [QW] (41) Aut-Wint 95-96, p. 187.
"Pretty Happy!" [Field] (53) Fall 95, p. 49.

3043. JOHNSON, Pyke, Jr.
"Bird Watching." [Light] (13) Spr 95, p. 7.

JOHNSON, Robin Smith
See SMITH-JOHNSON, Robin

3044. JOHNSON, Sarah Gail
"Pantoum for the Hungry Girl." [HayF] (17) Fall-Wint 95, p. 122.

3045. JOHNSON, Sheila Golburgh
"Come to Me at Ginger." [PoetryE] (40) Spr 95, p. 63.
"In China." [PoetryE] (40) Spr 95, p. 64.

3046. JOHNSON, Sherry
"And March Comes In." [PoetryC] (15:2) Je 95, p. 17.
"Traveling to Sleep." [PoetryC] (15:2) Je 95, p. 17.
"The Welkin's Drum." [PoetryC] (15:2) Je 95, p. 17.

3047. JOHNSON, Sheryl
"Ella in Paris" (for Ella Fitzgerald). [Drumvoices] (5:1/2) Fall-Wint 95-96, p. 17.
"Nativity Seen" (For Lady Day). [Drumvoices] (5:1/2) Fall-Wint 95-96, p. 18-19.

3048. JOHNSON, Soren
"Looking for Jane." [Plain] (16:1) Fall 95, p. 25.

3049. JOHNSON, Susan
"Gypsy." [MassR] (36:1) Spr 95, p. 58.
"Retreat." [PoetryNW] (36:4) Wint 95-96, p. 15-16.

3050. JOHNSON, Tom
"Antietam on a Spring Day." [ChrC] (112:17) 17 My 95, p. 533.
"The Cove City Bridge." [Pembroke] (27) 95, p. 80-81.
"When the Stoplight Changes." [Pembroke] (27) 95, p. 82.

3051. JOHNSON, William
"A Pulling" (for the Katiches). [PoetryNW] (36:1) Spr 95, p. 14-15.

3052. JOHNSON, Yolanda
"Can I Learn You?" (Loft Inroads Program for Gay, Lesbian, and Bisexual Writers).
[EvergreenC] (10:1) Wint-Spr 95, p. 95.

3053. JOHNSTON, Allan
"Flight" (for my father, d. 1990). [Vis] (47) 95, p. 24.

3054. JOHNSTON, Douglas
"Of Paramount Importance." [TickleAce] (27) Spr-Sum 94, p. 59-60.

3055. JOHNSTON, Fred
"Spiders." [SouthernR] (31:3) Jl/Sum 95, p. 687.
"Traditional Music." [SouthernR] (31:3) Jl/Sum 95, p. 687-688.

3056. JOHNSTON, Gail
"Good Fences." [CanLit] (146) Aut 95, p. 110.

3057. JOHNSTON, Marilyn
"This Lily Brooding on Its Stem" (For Ray). [SmPd] (32:2, #94) Spr 95, p. 31.

3058. JOHNSTON, Mark
"Vermeer: Young Lady Adorning Herself with a Pearl Necklace." [DefinedP] (3)
95, p. 51-52.

3059. JOINES, Rick
"Translation" (for Rupert and Michael). [QW] (40) Spr-Sum 95, p. 200-202.

3060. JOLLIFF, William
"Calling My Son from a Vision." [SpoonR] (20:2) Sum-Fall 95, p. 136.
"Cornpicker on the Liar's Bench." [CumbPR] (14:2) Spr 95, p. 19.
"The Duty of Crows." [Journal] (19:2) Fall-Wint 95, p. 35.
"Judgment." [Border] (6) Spr-Sum 95, p. 47.
"Merle Freeman's Auction." [CapeR] (30:2) Fall 95, p. 1.
"Pictures of Katie." [Border] (7) Fall-Wint 96, p. 25-26.
"Sunrise, the Thirty-Ninth Week." [Journal] (19:2) Fall-Wint 95, p. 36.
3061. JONAS, Ann Rae
"Structures." [ArtfulD] (28/29) 95, p. 168-171.
3062. JONASON, Myrr
"Winter Apples." [AmerV] (36) 95, p. 50.
3063. JONES, Alice
"The Biopsy." [Zyzzyva] (11:3/4, #43/44) 95, "The Best of Ten Years of
ZYZZYVA," p. 117-119.
"Boat." [QW] (40) Spr-Sum 95, p. 77.
"Form." [MassR] (36:2) Sum 95, p. 219.
"Hammerhead Shark." [Chelsea] (58) 95, p. 83.
"Inside." [MassR] (36:2) Sum 95, p. 219.
"Song." [DenQ] (29:4) Spr 95, p. 27.
"Will." [MassR] (36:2) Sum 95, p. 220.
3064. JONES, Benjamin
"Crusade." [LullwaterR] (6:2) Fall-Wint 95, p. 53.
3065. JONES, Billy
"3 More Runs to Make My Century." [WormR] (35:2, #138) 95, p. 65-66.
"#10. I had a grandfather I never met." [WormR] (35:2, #138) 95, p. 69-70.
"#12. Just enough rain." [WormR] (35:2, #138) 95, p. 76.
"#27. I've written a poem for a killer after watching him on the news." [WormR]
(35:2, #138) 95, p. 74-75.
"#28. Go easy mister." [WormR] (35:2, #138) 95, p. 81.
"#29. I found a honeyeater." [WormR] (35:2, #138) 95, p. 71-72.
"#32. When I was a boy." [WormR] (35:2, #138) 95, p. 76.
"#34. Mysterious mischievous min min lights." [WormR] (35:2, #138) 95, p. 77-78.
"#37. Trees swaying." [WormR] (35:2, #138) 95, p. 75.
"#38. Hokusai waves." [WormR] (35:2, #138) 95, p. 80.
"100 Years Later." [WormR] (35:2, #138) 95, p. 75.
"Almost 60." [WormR] (35:2, #138) 95, p. 80.
"Buddha Poem." [WormR] (35:2, #138) 95, p. 68.
"Cat House." [WormR] (35:2, #138) 95, p. 79.
"Cockroach Art." [WormR] (35:2, #138) 95, p. 71.
"Dada." [WormR] (35:2, #138) 95, p. 70-71.
"Dingo at the Door." [WormR] (35:2, #138) 95, p. 81.
"Dingo-Man." [WormR] (35:2, #138) 95, p. 74.
"For a Wasp." [WormR] (35:2, #138) 95, p. 75-76.
"Good Guy Poem." [WormR] (35:2, #138) 95, p. 73.
"Heroes 2." [WormR] (35:2, #138) 95, p. 82.
"His Casket Was Covered with Sunflowers." [WormR] (35:2, #138) 95, p. 64.
"How to Become an Expatriate." [WormR] (35:2, #138) 95, p. 66.
"It's All Part of Being a Poet." [WormR] (35:2, #138) 95, p. 68.
"Japan." [WormR] (35:2, #138) 95, p. 72-73.
"Keeping a Journal." [WormR] (35:2, #138) 95, p. 66-67.
"Lazy Poem." [WormR] (35:2, #138) 95, p. 79.
"Leap Year 1992." [Footwork] (24/25) 95, p. 68.
"Little Redhead." [WormR] (35:2, #138) 95, p. 67.
"The Muse." [WormR] (35:2, #138) 95, p. 65.
"My 1st Hero." [WormR] (35:2, #138) 95, p. 82.
"Rainy Night." [WormR] (35:2, #138) 95, p. 72.
"Rising Sun Beer." [WormR] (35:2, #138) 95, p. 68-19.
"Shale Poem." [WormR] (35:2, #138) 95, p. 73.
"Skink eyes." [WormR] (35:2, #138) 95, p. 82.
"Sleeping Bum." [WormR] (35:2, #138) 95, p. 77.
"Snake Eyes." [WormR] (35:2, #138) 95, p. 64.
"Splitting Up?" [WormR] (35:2, #138) 95, p. 78.
"Stir-Fry Poem." [WormR] (35:2, #138) 95, p. 80.
"Time Is the Biggest Trick of All" (Special Section: 42 poems). [WormR] (35:2,
#138) 95, p. 63-82.

"Torch Poem." [WormR] (35:2, #138) 95, p. 70.
"Universal Lovers." [WormR] (35:2, #138) 95, p. 78.
"Waiting on a Desperate Check." [WormR] (35:2, #138) 95, p. 80.
3066. JONES, Christopher
"Bad Mycophile." [ChironR] (44/45) Aut-Wint 95, p. 21.
"The Incomplete Road Kill Almanac." [ChironR] (43) Sum 95, p. 27.
"The Pigs All Cry for Circe." [ChironR] (43) Sum 95, p. 27.
3067. JONES, D. G.
"Imperfect Ghazals" (for John Thompson). [AntigR] (102/103) Sum-Aug 95, p. 221-223.
JONES, Deryn Rees
See REES-JONES, Deryn
3068. JONES, Hettie
"Birthday Presents 1989" (for Joyce Johnson). [HangL] (66) 95, p. 35.
"Civil War." [HangL] (66) 95, p. 36.
"Freddie, in Memoriam." [HangL] (66) 95, p. 37.
"Mother America" (for Chuck Wachtel). [HangL] (66) 95, p. 34.
"Three Little Love Songs." [HangL] (66) 95, p. 33.
3069. JONES, Ina
"Frenzy of Polishing." [WestB] (36) 95, p. 80-81.
"Shadbush." [WestB] (36) 95, p. 82-83.
"Winter Mourning Doves." [CapeR] (30:1) Spr 95, p. 44.
3070. JONES, Ira B.
"Blues 1: Hoochie Blues." [Drumvoices] (4:1/2) Fall-Wint 94-95, p. 132.
"Midnight Black 1." [Drumvoices] (4:1/2) Fall-Wint 94-95, p. 133.
3071. JONES, Jordan
"Loyalty Oath" (tr. of René Daumal). [HeavenB] (12) 95, p. 34-35.
"No More" (from: *The Anti-Heaven*, tr. of René Daumal). [HeavenB] (12) 95, p. 32-33.
3072. JONES, Pat
"The Art of Washing Clothes." [Pearl] (22) Fall-Wint 95, p. 16.
3073. JONES, Paul
"What Can Answer." [CarolQ] (48:1) Fall 95, p. 13.
3074. JONES, Robert C.
"If Dr. William Carlos Williams Instead of Mr. John Milton Had Written 'Paradise Lost'." [Comm] (122:11) 2 Je 95, p. 12.
3075. JONES, Robert Hunter
"Managed Care." [NowestR] (33:3) 95, p. 45.
3076. JONES, Rodney
"Dirty Blues." [Crazy] (49) Wint 95, p. 16-17.
"An Errand for My Grandmother." [Poetry] (166:3) Je 95, p. 127.
"Filling the Gully." [PoetryNW] (36:4) Wint 95-96, p. 20-21.
"First Fraudulent Muse." [PoetryNW] (36:4) Wint 95-96, p. 19-20.
"The First Space-Travelers." [Poetry] (166:3) Je 95, p. 128-129.
"Ground Sense." [Shen] (45:3) Fall 95, p. 87.
"Hunger." [NewOR] (21:3/4) Fall-Wint 95, p. 32-33.
"Mortal Sorrows." [Poetry] (166:3) Je 95, p. 125-126.
"On Censorship." [NewOR] (21:3/4) Fall-Wint 95, p. 29-31.
"A Prayer to the Goddess." [QW] (40) Spr-Sum 95, p. 80-81.
"Sentience" (Chapbook: 11 poems). [BlackWR] (21:2) Spr-Sum 95, p. 69-94.
"Sex." [QW] (41) Aut-Wint 95-96, p. 170-171.
"Things That Happen Once." [QW] (40) Spr-Sum 95, p. 82-83.
"Thy Rod and Thy Staff." [Shen] (45:3) Fall 95, p. 88-89.
"TV." [Atlantic] (275:1) Ja 95, p. 52.
"Waking Up." [GrandS] (14:2, #54) Fall 95, p. 106-108.
3077. JONES, Roger
"Arrivals." [TexasR] (16:1/4) 95, p. 127-128.
"A Door Ajar" (for HNS). [TexasR] (16:1/4) 95, p. 129.
"Eclipse." [TexasR] (16:1/4) 95, p. 130.
3078. JONES, Rolin
"Buttoning Your Dress." [NewYorkQ] (54) 95, p. 95.
JONES, Teruko Anderson
See ANDERSON-JONES, Teruko
3079. JOPEK, Krysia
"Masks and Visions." [PraS] (69:3) Fall 95, p. 139.
"Rhapsody." [PraS] (69:3) Fall 95, p. 141-142.

3080. JOPP, Jessica
"Imbrium Basin in the Sea of Rains." [PlumR] (8) [95], p. 60.
3081. JORDAN, Barbara
"Elegy for Fireflies." [Orion] (14:2) Spr 95, p. 14.
"Hammond Pond." [Orion] (14:2) Spr 95, p. 14.
"Meander." [Orion] (14:2) Spr 95, p. 15.
3082. JORDAN, June
"Des Moines Iowa Rap." [RiverS] (42/43) 95, p. 48.
"Leila's Song of the Wise Young Women" (part of the libretto for a new opera).
[Harp] (290:1740) My 95, p. 20-21.
3083. JORDAN, M. B.
"The Boy and the Pillow" (For Manuel, tr. of Horacio Costa, w. Clayton Eshleman
and the author). [Sulfur] (15:1, #36) Spr 95, p. 131-146.
3084. JORDAN, Ray
"Chemo" (in memory of Cindy Parker). [DefinedP] (1:1) Fall-Wint 92, p. 14-15.
"Gone Light." [DefinedP] (1:1) Fall-Wint 92, p. 13.
"Sappers." [DefinedP] (1:1) Fall-Wint 92, p. 12.
3085. JORIS, Pierre
"Alphabet" (Selections, tr. of Inger Christensen). [Sulfur] (15:1, #36) Spr 95, p. 4-9.
"Black & Blue." [Sulfur] (15:1, #36) Spr 95, p. 187.
"The Emptiness of Too Much Fullness." [Sulfur] (15:1, #36) Spr 95, p. 185-186.
3086. JORON, Andrew
"The Fast Secret." [NewAW] (13) Fall-Wint 95, p. 129-130.
"The Removes." [CentralP] (24) Spr 95, p. 53.
3087. JOSEPH, Alex
"Abandon" (K.). [JamesWR] (12:1) Wint 95, p. 6.
3088. JOSEPH, Allison
"The Black Santa." [ManyMM] (2:1) 95, p. 40-41.
"On Being Told I Don't Speak Like a Black Person." [ManyMM] (2:1) 95, p. 38-39.
"The Park Story." [Plain] (15:3) Spr 95, p. 7.
"Salt." [NewDeltaR] (13:1) Fall 95-Wint 96, p. 26-27.
"Traitor." [ManyMM] [1:1] D 94, p. 61-63.
3089. JOSEPH, Lawrence
"Before Our Eyes." [Verse] (12:2) 95, p. 75-76.
3090. JOUBERT, Jean
"Interior" (after Bonnard, tr. by Hilary Davies). [Verse] (12:2) 95, p. 77-78.
JUAN, Xu
    See XU, Juan
JUDEVINE MOUNTAIN
    See MOUNTAIN, Judevine
3091. JUDGE, Michael
"Crow Dream." [SouthernR] (31:2) Ap/Spr 95, p. 271.
"The Shape of Stone." [SycamoreR] (7:1) Wint 95, p. 12.
3092. JUDSON, John
"First Scar." [Poem] (73) My 95, p. 8.
"Fog Suite at Eastport" (#1, #2). [Poem] (73) My 95, p. 6-7.
"Our Past Is Prologue, But to What?" [NoAmR] (280:5) S-O 95, p. 9.
3093. JUHL, Timothy
"Saint." [EvergreenC] (10:2) Sum-Fall 95, p. 73.
JUN, Wang
    See WANG, Jun
3094. JUNKINS, Donald
"Bimini: From the Compleat Angler." [DefinedP] (2:2) Spr-Sum 94, p. 15.
"Bimini: Paradise Beach." [DefinedP] (2:2) Spr-Sum 94, p. 16.
"The Shoals Between Red Point and the Sister." [BelPoJ] (45:4) Chapbook 22, Sum
95, p. 47.
3095. JUSTER, A. M.
"Giftshop Blues." [Light] (14) Sum 95, p. 21.
3096. JUSTICE, Donald
"The Miami of Other Days" (An Improvisation). [NewYorker] (71:28) 18 S 95, p.
66.
"Twenty Questions." [SenR] (25:1) Spr 95, p. 11.
"Vague Memory from Childhood." [NewYorker] (71:21) 24 Jl 95, p. 77.
3097. JUSTINIANO, Eddie
"Records of Rhythms" (for my father). [CaribbeanW] (9) 95, p. 60.

3098. JUVENAL
"Big Fish" (Juvenal IV, tr. by Alistair Elliot). [Arion] (3:2/3) Fall 95-Wint 96, p. 185-190.

K., H. G.
See H. G. K.
K., W. T.
See W. T. K.
3099. K. C.
"Mary's Field." [IndR] (18:1) Spr 95, p. 67.
3100. KABIR (15th c.)
"I. Give up erotic games, Kabir" (tr. by Sam Hamill). [PoetryE] (41) Aut 95, p. 25.
"II. Sometimes, everywhere I look" (tr. by Sam Hamill). [PoetryE] (41) Aut 95, p. 25.
3101. KACIAN, Jim
"A Sonnet for Philip Glass." [Bogg] (67) 95, p. 5.
3102. KAGAWA, Tsugio
"This morning upon awakening" (in Japanese and English, tr. by Jiro Nakano). [BambooR] (67/68) Sum-Fall 95, p. 30.
3103. KAHAKALAU, Ku
"Kaho'olawe i Ka Malie." [Manoa] (7:1) Sum 95, p. 166.
"Kaho'olawe in the Calm." [Manoa] (7:1) Sum 95, p. 166.
3104. KAHL, Tim
"The Old Man and the Tree" (tr. of Stein Mehren). [Vis] (47) 95, p. 10.
"Shrivel Level." [Conduit] (3) Sum 95, p. 20.
3105. KAHLO, Frida
"In the Saliva / in the Paper" (tr. by Robert Hass). [TriQ] (95) Wint 95-96, p. 276.
3106. KALAMARAS, George
"At Midnight, the Angel of Death Fills the Trees." [MidwQ] (37:1) Aut 95, p. 40.
"Buddy Guy's Blues and the Discovery of Feedback." [RiverC] (15:2) Sum 95, p. 16-18.
"Hysteresis." [Iowa] (25:3) Fall 95, p. 80-81.
"Mud." [NewL] (61:4) 95, p. 69-71.
"The Opening." [Talisman] (15) Wint 95-96, p. 59-60.
"The Widow of Zakynthos." [TampaR] (11) Fall 95, p. 55.
3107. KALENDEK, Julie
"Destination." [Avec] (9) 95, p. 70-74.
"Leaf Season." [Avec] (9) 95, p. 67-69.
3108. KALINSKI, Todd
"Another love Letter to Dick Nixon." [ChironR] (43) Sum 95, p. 34.
"As the Baseball Strike Continues." [NewYorkQ] (54) 95, p. 91-92.
3109. KALISH, Susan Freis
"Like a New Mexico Roadmap." [PoetL] (90:2) Sum 95, p. 17.
3110. KALLEBERG, Garrett
"Hollow Chamber." [DenQ] (29:4) Spr 95, p. 28.
"The Instruments of Proof." [Talisman] (15) Wint 95-96, p. 72-74.
3111. KALLET, Marilyn
"Dear Orpheus." [HawaiiR] (19:2) Fall 95, p. 53-54.
"Forget the Silk." [Ledge] (18) Sum 95, p. 106.
"Passover." [InterQ] (2:3) 95, p. 107.
3112. KALOTRA, Sally
"The Rain" (Excerpt). [WashR] (21:2) Ag-S 95, p. 23.
3113. KAMAL, Daud (David)
"The Day Brightens Slowly." [Vis] (47) 95, p. 14.
"Ideogram" (for Margaret Harbottle, d. 5 April 1977). [Vis] (49) 95, p. 23.
"A Village Morning." [Vis] (47) 95, p. 15.
3114. KAMANDA, Kama
"Je me souviens du Dieu noir." [Os] (41) 95, p. 37.
"Je suis le feu né de la transe primordiale." [Os] (41) 95, p. 35.
"O Egypt, Ma Terre d'Origine." [Os] (41) 95, p. 38.
"Obélisques de mes Ancêtres, je vous réclame." [Os] (41) 95, p. 36.
3115. KAMIDE, Jane
"Carnival" (tr. of Paulo Colina, w. Phyllis Peres, Reetika Vazirani and Chi Lam). [Callaloo] (18:4) Fall 95, p. 736.

"Foreboding" (tr. of Paulo Colina, w. Phyllis Peres). [Callaloo] (18:4) Fall 95, p. 733.
"In the Style of Alvaro de Campos" (tr. of Paulo Colina, w. Phyllis Peres). [Callaloo] (18:4) Fall 95, p. 737-738.
"Types of Life" (tr. of Jônatas Conceição da Silva, w. Phyllis Peres). [Callaloo] (18:4) Fall 95, p. 773.

3116. KAMROWSKI, Julie
  "Sea Water." [Kalliope] (17:2) 95, p. 25.
3117. KANAGO, Andrew
  "New Poem." [Plain] (16:1) Fall 95, p. 18.
3118. KANAHELE, Pualani Kanaka'ole
  "Descendants of Lono, Prayer for 'Awa." [Manoa] (7:1) Sum 95, p. 165-166.
  "He Koihonua No Kanaloa, He Moku." [Manoa] (7:1) Sum 95, p. 20-22.
  "History for Kanaloa, an Island." [Manoa] (7:1) Sum 95, p. 22-24.
  "Mo'o Lono, Pule 'Awa." [Manoa] (7:1) Sum 95, p. 165.
3119. KANAKA'OLE, Edith
  "E Ho Mai Ka 'Ike." [Manoa] (7:1) Sum 95, p. 157.
  "Grant Me the Understanding." [Manoa] (7:1) Sum 95, p. 157.
3120. KANAKA'OLE, Nalani
  "Kihapai o Lono." [Manoa] (7:1) Sum 95, p. 160.
  "The Religious Duties of Lono." [Manoa] (7:1) Sum 95, p. 161.
3121. KANDA, Mikio
  "Overflowing the orbita, the maggots crawl on the senseless face" (in Japanese and English, tr. by Jiro Nakano). [BambooR] (67/68) Sum-Fall 95, p. 31.
KANE, April Citizen
  See CITIZEN KANE, April
3122. KANE, Jean
  "A Winter's Valentine." [CarolQ] (48:1) Fall 95, p. 82.
3123. KANE, Philip
  "Opera." [Bogg] (67) 95, p. 4.
3124. KANGAS, J. R.
  "Auld Lang Syne." [OxfordM] (10:1) Wint 94-Spr 95, p. 39-40.
  "Breath of Eden." [WindO] (59) Spr 95, p. 38.
  "Dazzleblitz Tutorial." [ChironR] (43) Sum 95, p. 33.
  "Rambling in the Garden." [WindO] (59) Spr 95, p. 37.
3125. KANTOR, Peter
  "Hungarian Fall" (tr. by Michael Blumenthal and Eszter Füséki). [Agni] (42) 95, p. 16-17.
  "Once I Thought" (tr. by Michael Blumenthal and Eszter Füséki). [Agni] (42) 95, p. 18.
3126. KAPLAN, Amanda L.
  "Begin." [MidAR] (15:1/2) 95, p. 305-306.
3127. KAPLAN, Carol Genyea
  "Photograph with Hats." [PraS] (69:2) Sum 95, p. 97-98.
  "Slaughtering Supper." [PraS] (69:2) Sum 95, p. 96.
3128. KARAFF, Kim
  "Sunburnt Reply to Summer's End, Lake Schaefer, Indiana" (Honorable Mention, 1995 Editors' Prize). [SpoonR] (20:2) Sum-Fall 95, p. 39.
3129. KARP, Vickie
  "The Juniper Bonsai." [ParisR] (37:134) Spr 95, p. 269-270.
  "One Hundred Well-Cut Leaves." [NewRep] (212:14) 3 Ap 95, p. 40.
3130. KARR, Muriel
  "Coming Closer." [BellArk] (11:2) Mr-Ap 95, p. 25.
  "Days Going By." [BellArk] (11:2) Mr-Ap 95, p. 25.
  "Going Home" (for Melinda). [BellArk] (11:3) My-Je 95, p. 8.
  "Have Another." [BellArk] (11:3) My-Je 95, p. 8.
  "Pricked with Light." [BellArk] (11:2) Mr-Ap 95, p. 25.
  "The Red Healing." [BellArk] (11:2) Mr-Ap 95, p. 25.
  "The Story Without a Pause But in the Wrong Order." [BellArk] (11:2) Mr-Ap 95, p. 25.
  "To Ride the Muscled Edge." [BellArk] (11:2) Mr-Ap 95, p. 25.
  "World Where Time Runs Out." [BellArk] (11:1) Ja-F 95, p. 24.
3131. KARSUNKE, Yaak
  "Conversation with the Stone" (tr. by Marc Falkenberg). [TriQ] (93) Spr-Sum 95, p. 119.
  "Light" (tr. by André Lefevre). [TriQ] (93) Spr-Sum 95, p. 121.

"Long Afterwards" (tr. by André Lefevre). [TriQ] (93) Spr-Sum 95, p. 120.
"Rather Free, after Brecht" (tr. by André Lefevre). [TriQ] (93) Spr-Sum 95, p. 123.
"To the Beloved Dead" (tr. by André Lefevre). [TriQ] (93) Spr-Sum 95, p. 122.
3132. KARTSONIS, Ariana-Sophia M.
"Tearing Away" (1995 Crossing Boundaries Poetry Runnerup). [InterQ] (2:3) 95, p. 99-101.
3133. KASDORF, Julia
"Brooklyn Bridge Showing Painters on Suspenders, 1914" (for Rudy Wiebe, 1994. After an anonymous photograph from the Municipal Archives of the City of NY). [IndR] (18:1) Spr 95, p. 179-180.
"The Coat of a Visiting Nurse." [PoetL] (90:2) Sum 95, p. 20.
"First Gestures." [Poetry] (165:5) F 95, p. 261-262.
"The Lesson of Hard-Shelled Creatures." [IndR] (18:1) Spr 95, p. 177-178.
"Lymphoma" (for Darcy Lynn). [PoetL] (90:2) Sum 95, p. 21.
"Wife of a Resident Alien." [PlumR] (9) [95 or 96], p. 79.
3134. KASISCHKE, Laura
"Andy's Lanes & Lounge: A Prologue." [Interim] (14:1) Spr-Sum 95, p. 9-11.
"Century." [IndR] (18:2) Fall 95, p. 56-58.
"Cocktail Waitress." [GeoR] (49:2) Sum 95, p. 426-428.
"Drink Me." [MichQR] (34:3) Sum 95, p. 332-333.
"Lady Luck." [Interim] (14:1) Spr-Sum 95, p. 12-14.
"My Heart." [SenR] (25:2) Fall 95, p. 18-20.
"Peace." [Interim] (14:1) Spr-Sum 95, p. 15-18.
"Second Wife." [SenR] (25:2) Fall 95, p. 14-17.
"The World's Largest Living Thing." [PlumR] (9) [95 or 96], p. 78.
3135. KASPER, Catherine
"From 'Lives of the Saints'." [MidAR] (16:1) 95, p. 74-76.
3136. KASPER, M.
"Lighter, Darker" (tr. of Piotr Sommer, w. the author). [Agni] (42) 95, p. 120.
3137. KASSELL, Nancy
"Klee Series." [SpoonR] (20:1) Wint-Spr 95, p. 86-87.
"The Poet As a Young Girl." [SpoonR] (20:1) Wint-Spr 95, p. 85.
3138. KATAJAVUORI, Riina
"Koko Valtakunta." [InterPR] (21:2) Fall 95, p. 86.
"Seireenit." [InterPR] (21:2) Fall 95, p. 82.
"The Sirens" (tr. by Sari Hantula). [InterPR] (21:2) Fall 95, p. 83.
"Tämä kaupunki on tauti, joka syö päähän ohuita reittejä." [InterPR] (21:2) Fall 95, p. 84.
"This city is a disease that eats thin routes through the head" (tr. by Sari Hantula). [InterPR] (21:2) Fall 95, p. 85.
"The Whole Kingdom" (tr. by Sari Hantula). [InterPR] (21:2) Fall 95, p. 87.
3139. KATAOKA, Sadao
"Suddenly the street is darkened" (in Japanese and English, tr. by Jiro Nakano). [BambooR] (67/68) Sum-Fall 95, p. 32.
3140. KATES, J.
"Among those. Among those, who is it starts" (tr. of Mikhail Aizenburg). [InterQ] (2:1/2) 95, p. 72.
"And Like a Silly Burrowing Sectarian" (tr. of Mikhail Aizenberg). [KenR] (17:3/4) Sum-Fall 95, p. 92-93.
"Imperceptible falling away of days" (tr. of Mikhail Aizenburg). [InterQ] (2:1/2) 95, p. 74.
"Landscape with Ideas from Dostoevsky" (tr. of Nikolai Baitov). [NewEngR] (17:4) Fall 95, p. 33.
"Noah's Raven." [CreamCR] (19:1) Spr 95, p. 130.
"Saint Petersburg, End of the 20th Century" (tr. of Alexandra Sozonova). [MidAR] (15:1/2) 95, p. 109-110.
"Untitled: from Munich, 1991" (tr. of Tatyana Shcherbina). [KenR] (17:3/4) Sum-Fall 95, p. 114-115.
"Untitled: Something for the branching nervous system" (tr. of Tatyana Shcherbina). [GrahamHR] (19) Wint 95-96, p. 65.
"Who of those who step into the stream" (tr. of Mikhail Aizenburg). [InterQ] (2:1/2) 95, p. 73.
3141. KATO, Teruko
"Blades of young grass" (in Japanese and English, tr. by Jiro Nakano). [BambooR] (67/68) Sum-Fall 95, p. 33.

3142. KATROVAS, Richard
"The Search Party." [NewOR] (21:3/4) Fall-Wint 95, p. 122-129.
3143. KATZ-LEVINE, Judy
"Carnival." [Noctiluca] (2:1, #4) Spr 95, p. 11.
"Ghazal of a Transference." [Noctiluca] (2:1, #4) Spr 95, p. 10.
3144. KAUFFMAN, Jane
"Angelo's a Hero Here." [13thMoon] (13:1/2) 95, p. 88.
"The High Romance of Four." [13thMoon] (13:1/2) 95, p. 89.
"The Privacy of a Global Thing." [13thMoon] (13:1/2) 95, p. 90.
"The Water Table, There It Is." [13thMoon] (13:1/2) 95, p. 91.
3145. KAUFMAN, Alan
"Across the Mississippi." [Witness] (9:2) 95, p. 168-171.
3146. KAUFMAN, Andrew
"The Cinnamon Bay Sonnets" (Selections: #1, 8, 3, 4. Honorable Mention, The
Pablo Neruda Prize for Poetry). [Nimrod] (39:1) Fall-Wint 95, p. 57-58.
3147. KAUFMAN, Margaret
"Fortunate in Death." [BelPoJ] (45:3) Spr 95, p. 39.
3148. KAUFMAN, Shirley
"The Fowl of the Air" (tr. of Meir Wieseltier). [Field] (53) Fall 95, p. 72.
"March Morning" (to the memory of Ilya Rubin, tr. of Eugene Dubnov, w. the
author). [LitR] (38:2) Wint 95, p. 194.
"Thin Livestock" (tr. of Meir Wieseltier). [Field] (53) Fall 95, p. 71.
"Window to the Future" (from "Windows near Mallarmé," tr. of Meir Wieseltier).
[Field] (53) Fall 95, p. 73.
3149. KAVEN, Bob
"Aubade." [Noctiluca] (2:1, #4) Spr 95, p. 20.
"I Am Getting Magazines in the Mail." [Noctiluca] (2:1, #4) Spr 95, p. 21.
"The Song Called Nothing." [Noctiluca] (2:1, #4) Spr 95, p. 19.
3150. KAY, Linda
"Antiope the Amazon" (Honorable Mention, Jacaranda Poetry Contest). [Jacaranda]
(11) [95 or 96?], p. 36-37.
3151. KAY, Margaret
"Cameo Brooch." [Vis] (49) 95, p. 29.
KAZUE, Shinkawa
See SHINKAWA, Kazue
KE, Mang
See MANG, Ke
3152. KEACH, Stanley
"The Tribe That Shares Its Dreams." [Parting] (8:2) Wint 95-96, p. 33.
3153. KEARNS, Ann
"Release." [Footwork] (24/25) 95, p. 41.
3154. KEARNS, Rick
"Aurelio's Vengeance, Puerto Rico, 1901." [MassR] (36:4) Wint 95-96, p. 621-623.
"The Columbus Big Ticket Theory." [Drumvoices] (4:1/2) Fall-Wint 94-95, p. 110-
111.
"Conga." [Drumvoices] (4:1/2) Fall-Wint 94-95, p. 112.
"Jíbaros." [MassR] (36:4) Wint 95-96, p. 623.
"Sixth Street, Coltrane, Full Moon." [Drumvoices] (5:1/2) Fall-Wint 95-96, p. 93-
94.
3155. KECKLER, W. B.
"Ten and Six Themes for a Painting" (after N. Engonopoulos). [Talisman] (15) Wint
95-96, p. 118-119.
3156. KEEFE, David
"Adulteries." [DefinedP] (3) 95, p. 49.
"Bosnia 1993 : So Far, So Near" (After William Stafford's "A Ritual to Read to
Each Other"). [ConnPR] (14:1) 95, p. 12.
"The Lights of Bray" (for Robert Bly). [ProseP] (4) 95, p. 40.
"Real People Who Know." [DefinedP] (3) 95, p. 50.
3157. KEEGAN, Linda
"Forecast." [MidwQ] (36:3) Spr 95, p. 301-302.
"My Own Small Hands." [Bogg] (67) 95, p. 40.
"Winnow Down." [PoetL] (90:3) Fall 95, p. 44.
3158. KEEL, Amelia
"Burglar." [OxfordM] (10:1) Wint 94-Spr 95, p. 41.
"Making Jam." [OxfordM] (10:1) Wint 94-Spr 95, p. 41-42.

3159. KEELAN, Claudia
"And Its Discontents." [AmerPoR] (24:5) S-O 95, p. 45.
"Parable 4." [BlackWR] (22:1) Fall-Wint 95, p. 21-22.
"Parable 4b (against the Objective Correlative)." [BlackWR] (22:1) Fall-Wint 95, p.
23-24.
"Parable 5." [RiverS] (41) 95, p. 37.
"Richter." [BlackWR] (22:1) Fall-Wint 95, p. 20.
"Spring." [BlackWR] (22:1) Fall-Wint 95, p. 25.
"Zone." [AmerPoR] (24:5) S-O 95, p. 45.
3160. KEELEY, Carol
"Favorite Truths." [NewAW] (13) Fall-Wint 95, p. 106-107.
3161. KEELING, Bret
"Jessie — Part II." [WillowS] (35) Ja 95, p. 66-67.
"One Night Stand." [WillowS] (35) Ja 95, p. 68.
3162. KEENE, John R.
"Eulogy." [AfAmRev] (29:3) Fall 95, p. 481.
"Heroic Figures" (for A.). [AfAmRev] (29:3) Fall 95, p. 481-482.
3163. KEENER, Earl R.
"Shadow Play." [WestB] (37) 95, p. 72-73.
3164. KEENER, LuAnn
"The Blood-Tie." [Kalliope] (17:1) 95, p. 64.
3165. KEHLEN, John Pavel
"Five Short Poems of Tabito in Praise of Wine" (tr. of Otomo no Tabito, 665-773).
[LowellR] [1] Sum 94, p. 83.
3166. KEILEY, Lizbeth
"Partial Waking." [CentralP] (24) Spr 95, p. 125-128.
3167. KEITH, Bill
"The Alchemy of Letters." [AfAmRev] (29:1) Spr 95, p. 95.
"Olde Myth" (for bryan mchugh). [AfAmRev] (29:1) Spr 95, p. 96.
3168. KEITH, David
"The Man Troubled by Authority." [ContextS] (4:2) 95, p. 8.
3169. KEITH, Greg
"Gone North." [SpoonR] (20:2) Sum-Fall 95, p. 94.
"Silly" (for Caz). [SpoonR] (20:2) Sum-Fall 95, p. 95.
3170. KEITH, W. J.
"The Birds of Brazil." [AntigR] (102/103) Sum-Aug 95, p. 205.
"David Jones." [AntigR] (102/103) Sum-Aug 95, p. 203.
"The Deathbed of Thomas Mann." [AntigR] (100) Wint 95, p. 31-35.
"Norman Cameron." [AntigR] (102/103) Sum-Aug 95, p. 202.
"Philip Larkin." [AntigR] (102/103) Sum-Aug 95, p. 201.
"T.S. Eliot." [AntigR] (102/103) Sum-Aug 95, p. 204.
3171. KEITHLEY, George
"Venice: The Morning Market Opens." [Hellas] (6:2) Fall-Wint 95, p. 74.
3172. KELLER, David
"The Forest of Delight." [US1] (30/31) 95, p. 11.
"Thinking What to Say." [US1] (30/31) 95, p. 1.
3173. KELLER, Emily
"Cayuga Island." [HolCrit] (32:2) Ap 95, p. 14.
3174. KELLER, Frankie (Age 9)
"Different" (from an anthology of poetry by young people about AIDS).
[NewYorker] (71:13) 22 My 95, p. 98.
3175. KELLER, Michael
"The Choice." [SouthernR] (31:1) Wint 95, p. 24-25.
"Snapper." [SouthernR] (31:1) Wint 95, p. 24-25.
3176. KELLER, Tsipi
"Deep in Her Dream" (tr. of T. Carmi, w. the author). [SenR] (25:2) Fall 95, p. 75.
"An Explosion in Jerusalem" (tr. of T. Carmi, w. the author). [SenR] (25:2) Fall 95,
p. 73.
"If It So Pleases" (tr. of T. Carmi). [GrahamHR] (19) Wint 95-96, p. 72.
"In Memory of Dan Pagis (1930-1986)" (tr. of T. Carmi, w. the author). [SenR]
(25:2) Fall 95, p. 76-79.
"Monologue in the Twilight of His Life" (tr. of T. Carmi, w. the author). [SenR]
(25:2) Fall 95, p. 72.
"Monologue to the Child of His Old Age" (for Michael, tr. of T. Carmi).
[GrahamHR] (19) Wint 95-96, p. 74-75.

"Mortification of the Soul" (Ein Hod, 1990, tr. of T. Carmi). [GrahamHR] (19) Wint
95-96, p. 76.
"Mourner's Monologue" (tr. of T. Carmi, w. the author). [SenR] (25:2) Fall 95, p.
74.
"The Mouth" (tr. of T. Carmi). [GrahamHR] (19) Wint 95-96, p. 73.
"A Time for Everything" (tr. of T. Carmi). [GrahamHR] (19) Wint 95-96, p. 77-78.
3177. KELLEY, Alita
"The Builder" (for Jaime Garcia Maffla, tr. of Armando Romero). [ProseP] (4) 95,
p. 64.
"Traveling Man" (tr. of Armando Romero). [ProseP] (4) 95, p. 63.
3178. KELLEY, Karen
"The Half-Finished Path." [Talisman] (15) Wint 95-96, p. 86-87.
"Venus Return." [Chain] (2) Spr 95, p. 119-122.
3179. KELLEY, Kathleen M.
"In Provincetown." [EvergreenC] (10:1) Wint-Spr 95, p. 16.
3180. KELLEY, Peggy
"Six of Discs, West — Success." [Border] (7) Fall-Wint 96, p. 27.
3181. KELLEY, Tina
"Explaining Easter" (Rayong, Thailand, 1992). [LitR] (39:1) Fall 95, p. 64-65.
3182. KELLY, Anne M.
"Echidna at the Blue River Cafe." [AntigR] (100) Wint 95, p. 24.
3183. KELLY, Carol White
"Out of Deep, Unordered Water" (For Ashley Gayle). [ChrC] (112:9) 15 Mr 95, p.
284.
3184. KELLY, J. Patrick
"Prayer." [Northeast] (5:13) Wint 95-96, p. 4.
"The Sky, the Water." [CapeR] (30:2) Fall 95, p. 13.
3185. KELLY, Michael
"Academic Salon." [HeavenB] (12) 95, p. 68.
"Poem: With the rains the sunsets are becoming." [HeavenB] (12) 95, p. 68.
3186. KELLY-DeWITT, Susan (See also DEWITT, Susan)
"Nu'uanu Falls." [LullwaterR] (6:2) Fall-Wint 95, p. 20-21.
3187. KELVIN, Norman
"Inanna." [SewanR] (103:3) Sum 95, p. 383.
3188. KEMMETT, Bill
"Final Poem." [PoetryE] (40) Spr 95, p. 65.
"Purgatory." [DefinedP] (3) 95, p. 33.
"Root Search." [DefinedP] (2:2) Spr-Sum 94, p. 44.
3189. KEMP, Arnold J.
"You Can't Run Away." [RiverS] (45) 95, p. 85.
3190. KEMPHER, Ruth Moon
"The James Dean Variations." [WormR] (35:2, #138) 95, p. 83-84.
"The Kohler Ad." [Kalliope] (17:3) 95, p. 6-7.
"Meeting Gerald Locklin at the Holiday Inn Bar in Great Bend, Kansas." [WormR]
(35:2, #138) 95, p. 84.
"Pole Beans and Fences." [ChironR] (44/45) Aut-Wint 95, p. 14.
"Sundays, at Home." [LullwaterR] (6:1) Spr-Sum 95, p. 59.
"Tough Audience" (Poetry Rendezvous 1994, Great Bend Public Library, Great
Bend, Ks.). [ChironR] (44/45) Aut-Wint 95, p. 14.
"Woodstock Reverie, At the Brookwood Inn" (Bushnells Basin, New York).
[ChironR] (44/45) Aut-Wint 95, p. 14.
3191. KENDALL, Robert
"We're Not Alone." [Footwork] (24/25) 95, p. 142.
"You're Waiting for It to Ring the Bell?" [Footwork] (24/25) 95, p. 142.
3192. KENISTON, Ann
"Criminal." [SpoonR] (20:2) Sum-Fall 95, p. 20-21.
"The Friend." [SpoonR] (20:2) Sum-Fall 95, p. 18-19.
"In a Dream, Two Years After." [Crazy] (49) Wint 95, p. 78.
"Punishment." [CreamCR] (19:1) Spr 95, p. 140-142.
3193. KENNEDY, Chris
"Childhood Variations." [DefinedP] (3) 95, p. 19-20.
"Chinese Umbrella" (San Francisco, 1978, after the assassinations of Mayor
Moscone and Supervisor Milk). [CreamCR] (19:1) Spr 95, p. 138-139.
"Grand Finale." [DefinedP] (3) 95, p. 21.

3194. KENNEDY, John
  "Great-Uncle Owen" (who wrote prose poems to his nephews serving in WW II, and drowned in his bathtub). [CimR] (113) O 95, p. 54-55.
  "An Hour Into Spring." [CimR] (113) O 95, p. 55-56.
  "Looking at Cells Under My Children's Microscope." [FloridaR] (20:2) 95, p. 60-61.
  "Matthew: Tax Collector." [BlackWR] (21:2) Spr-Sum 95, p. 101-102.
3195. KENNEDY, Laura H.
  "Mars in the Eastern Sky." [Elf] (5:1) Spr 95, p. 26.
3196. KENNEDY, Mick
  "Shoes." [WindO] (60) Fall-Wint 95, p. 3.
3197. KENNEDY, X. J.
  "Belated Alarm." [Light] (13) Spr 95, p. 12.
  "Blues for Oedipus." [Light] (13) Spr 95, p. 13.
  "Byron, who swam the Hellespont." [Light] (15/16) Aut-Wint 95-96, p. 34.
  "Hamlet in a Nutshell." [Light] (13) Spr 95, p. 15.
  "Maples in January" (for Edgar Bowers). [SoCoast] (19) 95, p. 17.
  "One day while steaming up the Amazon." [Light] (14) Sum 95, p. 24.
  "The Poetry Mafia." [SoCoast] (19) 95, p. 18.
  "Shriveled Meditation." [NorthStoneR] (12) 95, p. 77.
  "Street Moths." [DefinedP] (1:2) Spr-Sum 93, p. 55.
  "Then and Now." [SoCoast] (19) 95, p. 19.
  "Thinking While Writing." [NorthStoneR] (12) 95, p. 77.
  "To a friend a Literary Prize Passed Over." [SoCoast] (19) 95, p. 16.
  "To His Lover, That She Be Not Overdressed." [DefinedP] (3) 95, p. 53.
3198. KENNELLY, Brendan
  "The Hag of Beare" (from the Irish). [SouthernR] (31:3) Jl/Sum 95, p. 401-403.
  "I Wonder Now What Distance." [SouthernR] (31:3) Jl/Sum 95, p. 631-632.
  "Time for Breaking." [SouthernR] (31:3) Jl/Sum 95, p. 629-630.
  "Where Women Pray and Judge." [SouthernR] (31:3) Jl/Sum 95, p. 629.
3199. KENNELLY, Louise
  "To be Carried Away by Floating." [NowestR] (33:3) 95, p. 40-41.
  "To Carry Loose in the Hands." [GreensboroR] (59) Wint 95-96, p. 65.
3200. KENNEY, Richard
  "The Encantadas" (Selections: 9-12). [Verse] (12:2) 95, p. 79-84.
3201. KENNEY, Richard H.
  "Swinglesby." [Spitball] (49) 95, p. 36-37.
3202. KENNING, Janet
  "The Way of Trees" (for Jeannine Savard). [LaurelR] (29:1) Wint 95, p. 44.
3203. KENNY, Maurice
  "I Will Tell You a Story, Rakwaho." [RiverS] (42/43) 95, p. 32.
3204. KENNY, Richard
  "Graffiti." [Jacaranda] (11) [95 or 96?], p. 143-144.
3205. KENYON, Jane (1947-1995)
  "Afternoon at MacDowell." [Poetry] (167:3) D 95, p. 147.
  "The Call." [Poetry] (167:3) D 95, p. 146-147.
  "Cesarean." [NewYorker] (71:11) 8 My 95, p. 69.
  "Dutch Interiors" (For Caroline). [Poetry] (167:3) D 95, p. 148.
  "Fat." [NewYorker] (70:47) 30 Ja 95, p. 61.
  "Happiness." [Poetry] (165:5) F 95, p. 288.
  "How Like the Sound." [NewYorker] (71:11) 8 My 95, p. 40.
  "Man Sleeping." [Poetry] (167:3) D 95, p. 146.
  "Man Waking." [NewYorker] (71:11) 8 My 95, p. 59.
  "Mosaic of the Nativity: Serbia, Winter, 1993." [Poetry] (167:3) D 95, p. 149.
  "Reading Aloud to My Father." [Poetry] (165:5) F 95, p. 287.
  "Reading Late of the Death of Keats." [SenR] (25:1) Spr 95, p. 46.
  "The Way Things Are in Franklin." [NewYorker] (71:20) 17 Jl 95, p. 29.
3206. KEON, Wayne
  "The Apocalypse Will Begin." [CanLit] (144) Spr 95, p. 78-81.
  "It Ain't Exactly Heaven." [CanLit] (144) Spr 95, p. 8-9.
3207. KERBAUGH, Jim
  "P.S." [IllinoisR] (3:1/2) Fall 95-Spr 96, p. 51-52.
3208. KERCHEVAL, Jesse Lee
  "14 Metaphors for Sex (The Sex That We're Not Having)." [PoetryNW] (36:3) Aut 95, p. 34.
  "Another Life." [PraS] (69:3) Fall 95, p. 24-25.
  "Blue House, Red Door." [PraS] (69:3) Fall 95, p. 28-29.

"Daughter Nearly Two." [DenQ] (30:2) Fall 95, p. 35.
"Dreaming Against a Backdrop." [Iowa] (25:3) Fall 95, p. 158-159.
"Falling to the Sound of My Mother's Voice." [OhioR] (54) 95, p. 123-124.
"Glass House." [SouthernPR] (35:1) Sum 95, p. 22-23.
"Life on Other Planets." [PoetryNW] (36:3) Aut 95, p. 36-37.
"Picture with No Frame." [PoetryNW] (36:3) Aut 95, p. 33.
"There Are Secrets I Can't Keep." [PoetryNW] (36:3) Aut 95, p. 35-36.
"Things That Have Escaped Me." [PraS] (69:3) Fall 95, p. 25-28.
3209. KERLEY, Lisa R.
    "Little Souvenirs." [Pembroke] (27) 95, p. 83.
3210. KERLIKOWSKE, Elizabeth
    "Surrendering." [Parting] (8:2) Wint 95-96, p. 26.
3211. KERMAN, Judith
    "Bounded Sea" (tr. of Dulce María Loynaz). [Chelsea] (59) 95, p. 131.
    "In the Aquarium" (tr. of Dulce María Loynaz). [Chelsea] (59) 95, p. 131.
    "Summer House, a Fine Old Family." [HiramPoR] (58/59) Spr 95-Wint 96, p. 38.
3212. KERNAN, Nathan
    "April." [Agni] (42) 95, p. 61.
    "Dear Ghost" (for Darragh Park). [Agni] (42) 95, p. 62.
3213. KERR, Don
    "Am I Blue, Kieslowski, 1993." [Grain] (23:1) Sum 95, p. 21-22.
    "Edward Hopper." [CanLit] (145) Sum 95, p. 60-61.
3214. KERR, Katherine
    "The Cicada's Song" (Short Grain Contest Winners: Prose Poem, Second). [Grain]
        (22:3) Wint 95, p. 64.
3215. KERR, Lisa Drnec
    "The Pioneer." [OxfordM] (9:2) Fall-Wint 93, p. 51.
3216. KERRIGAN, T. S.
    "Strandhill." [SouthernR] (31:2) Ap/Spr 95, p. 272.
3217. KERWIN, Bill
    "You Took the Movies With You." [HiramPoR] (58/59) Spr 95-Wint 96, p. 39.
3218. KESSLER, Edward
    "Pain." [Poetry] (165:6) Mr 95, p. 327-328.
3219. KESSLER, Jascha
    "Arctic Journey" (tr. of Kirsti Simonsuuri, w. the author). [Nimrod] (38:2) Spr-Sum
        95, p. 85.
KESSLER, June Frankel
    See FRANKEL-KESSLER, June
3220. KESSLER, Milton
    "Aunt Minnie." [NewMyths] (2:2/3:1) 95, p. 78-79.
    "Scales." [Sulfur] (15:2, #37) Fall 95, p. 4-6.
3221. KESSLER, Rod
    "The Deaf Boy." [CharR] (21:2) Fall 95, p. 86.
    "The Elm Tree on Lafayette Street." [CharR] (21:2) Fall 95, p. 85.
3222. KESSLER, Sydney
    "And All of the Umbrellas Came Down in a Single Afternoon." [Parting] (8:2) Wint
        95-96, p. 44.
    "So What of War's Denouement." [Parting] (8:1) Sum 95, p. 27.
    "Their Returned." [Parting] (8:2) Wint 95-96, p. 1.
3223. KETCHEK, Michael
    "I got this army jacket." [SlipS] (15) 95, p. 27.
3224. KETONEN, Jussi
    "Exercises in Project Management." [NewAW] (13) Fall-Wint 95, p. 117-118.
3225. KETRYS, Joan Ellen
    "Apple Pie." [Poem] (73) My 95, p. 50.
    "Picking Parsley Under the Snow." [Poem] (73) My 95, p. 49.
3226. KEVORKIAN, Kyle
    "Inside the Arc." [SantaBR] (3:3) Fall-Wint 95, p. 74.
3227. KEWLEY, Dorothea
    "Seventeen in a Small Town." [WindO] (59) Spr 95, p. 8.
3228. KEY, Kathleen
    "The Holy Rollers of Faith Baptist Church." [CapeR] (30:2) Fall 95, p. 23.
3229. KEYISHIAN, Marjorie
    "As If His Father Would Never Get Feeble." [Footwork] (24/25) 95, p. 155-156.
    "Neighborhood." [Footwork] (24/25) 95, p. 155.

244

3230. KEYS, Kerry Shawn
"Hiding" (tr. of Lêdo Ivo). [PoetryE] (39) Fall 94, p. 111.
"The Literary Narcissus" (tr. of Lêdo Ivo). [PoetryE] (39) Fall 94, p. 114.
"Postcard from a Battle" (tr. of Lêdo Ivo). [PoetryE] (39) Fall 94, p. 113.
"Truth and Falsehood" (tr. of Lêdo Ivo). [PoetryE] (39) Fall 94, p. 112.
3231. KEYS, Kevin John
"Solstice" (tr. of Leda Martins, w. Ana Lúcia A. Gazolla). [Callaloo] (18:4) Fall 95, p. 871.
3232. KGOSITSILE, William Keorapetse
"Memorial." [Drumvoices] (4:1/2) Fall-Wint 94-95, p. 24.
"Where Her Eye Sits" (after reading Cheryl Harris' *From the War Journals*). [Drumvoices] (4:1/2) Fall-Wint 94-95, p. 23.
3233. KHAIYAT, Mahdy Y.
"Life's Voyage." [SantaBR] (3:1) Spr 95, p. 108.
"Linkages." [SantaBR] (3:1) Spr 95, p. 107.
"Risky Business." [SantaBR] (3:1) Spr 95, p. 108.
"Shangri-La." [SantaBR] (3:1) Spr 95, p. 107.
"Trounced." [Plain] (15:2) Wint 95, p. 15-16.
3234. KHAN, Sharon
"After years of burying myself in my own suffering" (from the unpublished volume *Logbook*, tr. of Jorge Etcheverry, w. the author). [Arc] (35) Aut 95, p. 46.
"Consumerism & Guilt (the beginning of 1991)" (tr. of Jorge Etcheverry, w. the author). [Arc] (35) Aut 95, p. 47-48.
"Where will I turn the serene birds of my pupils?" (from the unpublished volume *Logbook*, tr. of Jorge Etcheverry, w. the author). [Arc] (35) Aut 95, p. 45.
3235. KHODASEVITCH, Vladislav
"Acrobat" (Inscription for a silhouette, in Russian and English, tr. by John Barnstead). [AntigR] (101) Spr 95, p. 78-79.
"November 2" (in Russian and English, tr. by John Barnstead). [AntigR] (101) Spr 95, p. 84-89.
"Rachel's Tears" (in Russian and English, tr. by John Barnstead). [AntigR] (101) Spr 95, p. 92-93.
"Seek Me" (in Russian and English, tr. by John Barnstead). [AntigR] (101) Spr 95, p. 90-91.
"The Way of Grain" (in Russian and English, tr. by John Barnstead). [AntigR] (101) Spr 95, p. 82-83.
"You Cannot Tell It All" (in Russian and English, tr. by John Barnstead). [AntigR] (101) Spr 95, p. 80-81.
3236. KICH, Martin
"Eighth-Grade Basketball Tryouts." [Parting] (8:2) Wint 95-96, p. 25.
"From a High Ridge." [Parting] (8:2) Wint 95-96, p. 30.
"In a Country of Dirt Roads." [CapeR] (30:1) Spr 95, p. 22.
"The Sheeny." [SlipS] (15) 95, p. 40-41.
3237. KIDDE, Kay
"New England, Early March." [ContextS] (4:2) 95, p. 18.
3238. KIERNAN, Phyllis
"Unreasonable Doubts." [Prima] (18/19) 95, p. 62.
3239. KIKUSHA-NI (1752-1826)
"Only the moon" (Haiku, tr. by Sam Hamill). [WillowS] (36) Je 95, p. 96.
3240. KILBURN, Greta
"Loves Me Like a Rock" (tr. of Jan Eikelboom). [CimR] (112) Jl 95, p. 10.
3241. KILCHEK, Jewel
"Me." [ChironR] (44/45) Aut-Wint 95, p. 47.
3242. KILDEGAARD, Athena (Athena O.)
"A Lesson." [Vis] (47) 95, p. 25-26.
"On the Plaza Before the Basilica of the Virgin of Guadalupe." [MidAR] (16:1) 95, p. 15-16.
"Ripe Cherries." [PoetryE] (40) Spr 95, p. 67.
"Sisters Hiding." [PoetryE] (40) Spr 95, p. 66.
3243. KILGORE, Deborah
"Strange Temptation." [PoetL] (90:4) Wint 95-96, p. 23.
3244. KILWEIN GUEVARA, Maurice
"Spirit." [KenR] (17:3/4) Sum-Fall 95, p. 37.
"To the Dead Farmer." [KenR] (17:3/4) Sum-Fall 95, p. 38.
3245. KIM, Ike
"Mourning" (Excerpts). [Chain] (2) Spr 95, p. 123.

245

3246. KIM, Myung Mi
"Dura" (Excerpts). [Conjunc] (24) 95, p. 153-158.
"Hummingbird." [Sulfur] (15:1, #36) Spr 95, p. 72-80.
3247. KIM, Sue Kwock
"At the Palace of Shimcheong's Mother: a Tapestry." [PraS] (69:4) Wint 95, p. 33.
"On Pike Street" (For Isaac). [Poetry] (165:5) F 95, p. 274.
"The Robe-Maker" (Yi Dynasty court robe, Victoria and Albert Museum).
[NewRep] (212:20) 15 My 95, p. 42.
"Women Singing in the Deep Sea" (after an eighteenth-century Korean painting).
[ParisR] (37:134) Spr 95, p. 126-127.
3248. KIM, Y. U.
"After Soccer." [NewRena] (9:2, #28) Spr 95, p. 70.
3249. KIMATA, Osamu
"Let the voice of a girl" (in Japanese and English, tr. by Jiro Nakano). [BambooR]
(67/68) Sum-Fall 95, p. 34.
3250. KIMBRELL, James
"Empty House." [Poetry] (165:4) Ja 95, p. 209.
"Rooftop." [AntR] (53:1) Wint 95, p. 64.
"True Descenders" (After Luca Signorelli's The Damned Cast into Hell). [Poetry]
(165:5) F 95, p. 278-279.
3251. KIMURA, Fusako
"As clothes left from the burning fires" (in Japanese and English, tr. by Jiro
Nakano). [BambooR] (67/68) Sum-Fall 95, p. 35.
3252. KINCAID, Joan Payne
"Alternatives and Hokey Cowboy Hats." [ContextS] (4:2) 95, p. 15.
"Lou Owns the Candy Store." [Parting] (8:1) Sum 95, p. 39.
"She." [SlipS] (15) 95, p. 27.
"Something Out There in the Bushes." [Bogg] (67) 95, p. 16.
"Vernal Vortex." [ContextS] (4:2) 95, p. 14.
"Wedding Pic 5." [Parting] (8:2) Wint 95-96, p. 27.
"Wedding Pic 8." [Parting] (8:2) Wint 95-96, p. 26.
3253. KINERK, Robert
"Advice to a Daughter Going to College." [Light] (15/16) Aut-Wint 95-96, p. 18.
3254. KING, Basil
"Appetites" (Part III). [HeavenB] (12) 95, p. 66-67.
3255. KING, James S.
"Stranded." [HopewellR] (7) 95, p. 101.
3256. KING, Julie
"Daydreams of Summer." [Interim] (14:1) Spr-Sum 95, p. 5.
"Sunday at St. Josaphat's." [Interim] (14:1) Spr-Sum 95, p. 4.
3257. KING, June W.
"But We Are Not Potatoes." [Kalliope] (17:3) 95, p. 31.
3258. KING, Kevin
"The First Time They Made Love." [PlumR] (9) [95 or 96], p. 55.
3259. KING, R. D.
"Journal of Horns." [NowestR] (33:1) 95, p. 50.
3260. KING, Robert
"Quartet." [MidwQ] (36:4) Sum 95, p. 385.
3261. KING, Robert S.
"Graveside Pyre." [BlackBR] (20) Spr-Sum 95, p. 38.
"Progress." [GreenHLL] (6) 95, p. 86.
3262. KING, Rosamond S.
"Climbing to the Mountaintop." [PoetL] (90:2) Sum 95, p. 16.
3263. KING, Willie James
"Still Looking." [LullwaterR] (5:2) Fall-Wint 94, p. 54.
3264. KINGS, Robert
"Books." [BellArk] (11:5) S-O 95, p. 14-15.
3265. KINGSTON, Katie
"Professional." [Plain] (16:1) Fall 95, p. 28.
3266. KINNELL, Galway
"The Angel." [Verse] (12:2) 95, p. 85.
"Daybreak." [Orion] (14:1) Wint 95, back cover.
3267. KINNEY, Martha
"At the State Hospital." [FreeL] (15) Aut 95, p. 19.
"Back from Nam." [FreeL] (15) Aut 95, p. 18.
"Yesterday I Saw a Cow Running." [FreeL] (15) Aut 95, p. 16-17.

3268. KINSELLA, Thomas
"Dream." [Poetry] (167:1/2) O-N 95, p. 90-91.
"I Put My Hand in My Bosom." [Poetry] (167:1/2) O-N 95, p. 90.
"Natural Life." [Poetry] (167:1/2) O-N 95, p. 92.
3269. KINSEY, C. A.
"Suicide Written in Red Ink." [ChironR] (43) Sum 95, p. 15.
3270. KINSEY, Leland
"The Last Steel Pier Diving Horses." [GreenMR] (8:1) Spr-Sum 95, p. 102.
3271. KINSOLVING, Susan
"The Lotus Floats." [WestHR] (49:4) Wint 95, p. 316.
"Ne-m'oubliez-pas." [WestHR] (49:4) Wint 95, p. 316.
"Small Alchemies." [WestHR] (49:4) Wint 95, p. 314.
"Watercolor." [WestHR] (49:4) Wint 95, p. 314.
"Writing You from Wessex." [WestHR] (49:4) Wint 95, p. 315.
3272. KIPP, Karen
"Bascule." [GrahamHR] (19) Wint 95-96, p. 15-16.
"Blow." [GrahamHR] (19) Wint 95-96, p. 18-19.
"Wealth." [GrahamHR] (19) Wint 95-96, p. 17.
"Whistle Bones." [GrahamHR] (19) Wint 95-96, p. 14.
3273. KIRBY, Barney
"Driving North." [ProseP] (4) 95, p. 41.
3274. KIRBY, David
"The Afterlife." [ChiR] (41:1) 95, p. 29-34.
"The End of Poverty." [MidAR] (15:1/2) 95, p. 226-228.
"Listening to John Crowe Ransom Read His Poetry." [SouthernR] (31:4) O/Aut 95,
p. 854-857.
"The Money Changer." [SouthernR] (31:1) Wint 95, p. 26-31.
"Monte (Peace in Our Time)." [HangL] (66) 95, p. 38.
3275. KIRCHDORFER, Ulf
"The Pillsbury Doughboy." [CapeR] (30:1) Spr 95, p. 40.
3276. KIRCHWEY, Karl
"Leaf Season, Columbia County." [PartR] (62:1) Wint 95, p. 109.
"Provincetown, February." [Nat] (258:7) 21 F 94, p. 240.
"Tiber Island" (In memoriam Amy Clampitt). [NewRep] (213:23) 4 D 95, p. 44.
"Zoo Story." [NewYorker] (70:47) 30 Ja 95, p. 74.
3277. KIRK, Kathleen
"Barn Fire." [SpoonR] (20:1) Wint-Spr 95, p. 45-46.
"The Bird That Cries in a Human Voice." [SpoonR] (20:1) Wint-Spr 95, p. 55-56.
"Combine." [SpoonR] (20:1) Wint-Spr 95, p. 42.
"Dreaming of Houses." [SpoonR] (20:1) Wint-Spr 95, p. 58-59.
"Pieces Caracteristiques" [sic]. [SpoonR] (20:1) Wint-Spr 95, p. 52-54.
"The Silver Distance." [SpoonR] (20:1) Wint-Spr 95, p. 49-51.
"Sound Stage." [SpoonR] (20:1) Wint-Spr 95, p. 57.
"Walking Beans." [SpoonR] (20:1) Wint-Spr 95, p. 47-48.
"Willow Tree." [SpoonR] (20:1) Wint-Spr 95, p. 43-44.
3278. KIRKLAND, Lashonda
"Down the Street" (WritersCorps Program, Washington, DC). [WashR] (21:2) Ag-S
95, p. 10.
3279. KIRKPATRICK, Kathryn
"Crossing the Border." [SouthernPR] (35:2) Wint 95, p. 74-77.
"The Goose." [Poem] (73) My 95, p. 68-69.
"El Mercado." [WillowR] (22) Spr 95, p. 15.
"Shark's Teeth." [Poem] (73) My 95, p. 66-67.
"When the Bleeding Comes." [SouthernPR] (35:1) Sum 95, p. 35.
3280. KIRKUP, James
"Player Piano." [Light] (14) Sum 95, p. 9.
3281. KIRSCH, Sarah
"In Winter" (tr. by Robin Fulton). [MalR] (110) Spr 95, p. 71.
3282. KIRSCHBAUM, Roger
"Leaving November" (in memory of Tim G.). [MidwQ] (36:4) Sum 95, p. 386-387.
"When It Rained in Peace Park." [Plain] (15:2) Wint 95, p. 30.
3283. KIRSCHENBAUM, Blossom S.
"Crime and Punishment." [Light] (13) Spr 95, p. 12.
3284. KIRSTEN-MARTIN, Diane
"Back in Yonkers, Circa 1972." [BellR] (18:1, #37) Spr 95, p. 24.

3285. KIRTS, Terry
"Cartography of the One-Room Town." [GreenMR] (8:2) Fall-Wint 95-96, p. 111-
112.
"Volunteer for Experiment." [NewDeltaR] (13:1) Fall 95-Wint 96, p. 57-59.
3286. KISTLER, William
"Café of the Found." [Nimrod] (39:1) Fall-Wint 95, p. 113.
"The City of Ancient Voices." [AmerPoR] (24:5) S-O 95, p. 17.
"Face Seen Beside the St. James Marquee." [Nimrod] (39:1) Fall-Wint 95, p. 112.
3287. KISTNER, John
"Ghosting the Road." [Pequod] (39) 95, p. 112.
3288. KITCHEN, Judith
"Octet: Brazil." [GreenMR] (8:1) Spr-Sum 95, p. 88-89.
"Winter Landscape." [SenR] (25:1) Spr 95, p. 58.
3289. KITSON, Herb
"The Waltons Get Cable TV." [NewYorkQ] (55) 95, p. 78.
3290. KITUAI, Kathy
"Sunday Driving." [Footwork] (24/25) 95, p. 28.
3291. KIVI, K. Linda
"Tabaganne." [SinW] (56) Sum-Fall 95, p. 49.
3292. KIYOWARA no FUKUYABU (10th Century)
"The long rope of spring" (tr. by Sam Hamill). [RiverS] (44) 95, p. 34.
3293. KIZER, Carolyn
"Arthur's Party." [Poetry] (166:5) Ag 95, p. 256.
"Halation." [ParisR] (37:134) Spr 95, p. 34-35.
"Index, a Mountain" (Part of the Cascade range, Washington, for Richard Hugo).
[Verse] (12:3) 95, p. 66-68.
"Lost in Translation" (for Lu Xing'er." [SouthernR] (31:4) O/Aut 95, p. 858-859.
"Medicine." [Poetry] (166:3) Je 95, p. 144.
3294. KLAASSEN, Tonja Gunvaldsen
"After the Plum Trees Burnt." [PoetryC] (15:3) Ag 95, p. 16.
"Approaching What Was Peculiar to the Girl, Joan of Arc." [PoetryC] (15:3) Ag 95,
p. 16.
"August Waskesiu." [MalR] (113) Wint 95, p. 81.
"Plains Fever: a Letter Home." [Grain] (22:4) Spr 95, p. 135-136.
3295. KLANDER, Sharon
"In Due Season." [WestHR] (49:1) Spr 95, p. 85-86.
3296. KLARE, Judy
"10:30 a.m., December." [OhioR] (53) 95, p. 148-149.
3297. KLASS, Stephen
"Grandmother and the Tramps" (tr. of Folke Isaksson). [CumbPR] (14:2) Spr 95, p.
26.
"Grandmother's Cat" (tr. of Folke Isaksson). [CumbPR] (14:2) Spr 95, p. 24.
"In Grandmother's House" (tr. of Folke Isaksson). [CumbPR] (14:2) Spr 95, p. 22.
3298. KLASSEN, Sarah
"Dangerous Elements." [CanLit] (146) Aut 95, p. 84.
"Pelicans." [MalR] (113) Wint 95, p. 52.
"Tea Cosy." [CanLit] (146) Aut 95, p. 85.
"Tundra Swans." [MalR] (113) Wint 95, p. 50-51.
3299. KLAUKE, Amy
"With None Besides." [SenR] (25:2) Fall 95, p. 95.
3300. KLEIN, Rosemary
"Saturday Passes." [HampSPR] Wint 95, p. 31.
"Structural Composition." [HampSPR] Wint 95, p. 30.
3301. KLEINSCHMIDT, Edward
"Anodyne of the Self." [HayF] (16) Spr-Sum 95, p. 128.
"Après Débris." [NewAW] (13) Fall-Wint 95, p. 95.
"Cooking to Music." [YellowS] (12:4, #48) Sum 95, p. 41.
"De Die Natali." [AmerLC] (7) 95, p. 24-25.
"The Family at the Bottom of the Page." [DenQ] (29:3) Wint 95, p. 20-21.
"In Girum Imus Nocte et Consumimur Igni." [NewEngR] (17:1) Wint 95, p. 151.
"Kill or Be Killed." [NewEngR] (17:1) Wint 95, p. 150-151.
"Let Up." [Witness] (9:1) 95, p. 100.
"Motion (Picture)." [HayF] (16) Spr-Sum 95, p. 129.
"Opposite." [AmerLC] (7) 95, p. 26-27.
"Perennial." [QW] (40) Spr-Sum 95, p. 84-87.
"Sound Crop." [Journal] (19:1) Spr-Sum 95, p. 16.

"Sound Suite." [DenQ] (29:3) Wint 95, p. 22-23.
"Speed of Life." [Witness] (9:1) 95, p. 101.
"Stir Crazy." [TriQ] (95) Wint 95-96, p. 97-98.
"Storm of Sequence." [AmerLC] (7) 95, p. 25-26.
"Sudden." [ColR] (22:2) Fall 95, p. 173-174.
"Transmigration of Souls." [PartR] (62:2) Spr 95, p. 304-305.
"Water Writing." [WestB] (36) 95, p. 79.

3302. KLEINZAHLER, August
"Aubade on East 12th Street." [GrandS] (13:3, #51) Wint 95, p. 98.
"Disclosures." [Thrpny] (61) Spr 95, p. 19.
"A Glass of Claret on a Difficult Morning." [AmerPoR] (24:1) Ja-F 95, p. 24.
"Glossolalia All the Way to Buffalo." [ChiR] (41:4) 95, p. 61-62.
"Land's End." [Zyzzyva] (11:3/4, #43/44) 95, "The Best of Ten Years of
     ZYZZYVA," p. 120-121.
"The Old Schoolyard in August." [AmerPoR] (24:1) Ja-F 95, p. 24.
"Red Sauce, Whiskey and Snow: A Still Life on Two Moving Panels." [GrandS]
     (13:3, #51) Wint 95, p. 99.
"Sapphics in Traffic." [Thrpny] (61) Spr 95, p. 19.
"Sunday, Across the Tasman." [NewYorker] (71:9) 24 Ap 95, p. 82-83.
"Uttar Pradesh." [ChiR] (41:4) 95, p. 63-64.
"Visits." [Thrpny] (61) Spr 95, p. 19.
"West." [ChiR] (41:4) 95, p. 60.
"The Wind in March." [Thrpny] (61) Spr 95, p. 19.

3303. KLOEFKORN, William
"Eating the Apple." [LaurelR] (29:2) Sum 95, p. 35-36.
"Geese." [EngJ] (84:2) F 95, p. 56.
"Geese." [LaurelR] (29:2) Sum 95, p. 34-35.
"In Switzerland." [PraS] (69:3) Fall 95, p. 83-84.
"KTSW, Sunday Morning." [Witness] (9:2) 95, p. 120-121.
"Last Visit." [MidwQ] (36:4) Sum 95, p. 387-388.
"Separations." [EngJ] (84:2) F 95, p. 56.
"Shooting the Sparrows." [Witness] (9:2) 95, p. 122-123.
"Singing Hymns with Unitarians." [PraS] (69:3) Fall 95, p. 86.
"Stealing Melons." [PraS] (69:3) Fall 95, p. 84-85.

3304. KNAPP, Trevor West
"The Dead Respond at Last to Our Entreaties." [PoetryNW] (36:4) Wint 95-96, p.
     45-46.
"A Dear John Letter: To Regret." [PoetryNW] (36:4) Wint 95-96, p. 46-47.
"Jeanne." [GreenMR] (8:2) Fall-Wint 95-96, p. 115-116.
"Learning Gravity." [Confr] (56/57) Sum-Fall 95, p. 333.
"Lost." [PoetL] (90:2) Sum 95, p. 38.
"My Father's Tractor." [ClockR] (10:1/2) 95-96, p. 83.
"The Walk." [GreenMR] (8:2) Fall-Wint 95-96, p. 114.
"The Way the Rats Died." [ClockR] (10:1/2) 95-96, p. 82.

3305. KNAUTH, Stephen
"Hamilton's Gown." [Jacaranda] (11) [95 or 96?], p. 132-133.

3306. KNIGHT, Arthur Winfield
"Boston Corbett: Hatter." [Parting] (8:1) Sum 95, p. 25.
"Kit Carson: Boggsville." [Parting] (8:1) Sum 95, p. 24.
"Your Touch." [Parting] (8:1) Sum 95, p. 24.

3307. KNIGHT, John Cantey
"Opening Price." [NewDeltaR] (13:1) Fall 95-Wint 96, p. 5-6.

3308. KNIGHT, Kit
"Ann Wallace, 1862: The Brigadier General's Widow." [Parting] (8:1) Sum 95, p.
     26.
"Mollie Bell: a Necessity of War." [Parting] (8:1) Sum 95, p. 12.
"Sally Tompkins, the Only Woman Every Commissioned in the Confederate Army."
     [Parting] (8:1) Sum 95, p. 9.

3309. KNIGHT, Lynne
"Bedtime Fable." [BelPoJ] (46:2) Wint 95-96, p. 26-27.
"Border Wars." [PoetryNW] (36:3) Aut 95, p. 38-40.
"I don't Want All of You." [PoetryE] (40) Spr 95, p. 68.
"Meditation Interrupted by Bats." [PoetryNW] (36:3) Aut 95, p. 40-41.
"Not Even They Could Stop It, and They Were Myth." [Poetry] (165:5) F 95, p.
     251-252.
"The Older Student's Story." [PoetryNW] (36:3) Aut 95, p. 40.

"These Are the Conditions, Then." [OntR] (43) Fall-Wint 95-96, p. 95.
3310. KNIGHT, Marilyn
"The Wife's Poem." [SoCaR] (28:1) Fall 95, p. 184.
3311. KNIGHTEN, Merrell
"The Senator Meets Robert Mapplethorpe." [WindO] (59) Spr 95, p. 30.
3312. KNOELLER, Christian
"At Pistol River, Oregon." [Elf] (5:4) Wint 95, p. 27.
"Be a Weed" (for Y.T.). [ConnPR] (14:1) 95, p. 24.
"Benediction (Guatemala)." [Vis] (47) 95, p. 11-12.
"The Burning Barrel." [Elf] (5:4) Wint 95, p. 26.
"Creating Signs." [WestB] (36) 95, p. 10.
"Praising the Night." [HiramPoR] (58/59) Spr 95-Wint 96, p. 41.
"Steps (Guatemala)." [Vis] (47) 95, p. 12.
"Varieties of Flight" (For P.M.). [HiramPoR] (58/59) Spr 95-Wint 96, p. 40.
3313. KNOEPFLE, John
"After the Nuclear Assurances." [InterQ] (2:1/2) 95, p. 267.
"Green Snake Interview: 'Lost in East St. Louis'." [Drumvoices] (4:1/2) Fall-Wint
94-95, p. 98-102.
"A Green Snake Interview: 'Psalm Six'." [CentR] (39:2) Spr 95, p. 302-308.
"Humanities Lecture at the Governor's Mansion on the Feastday of the Venerable
Bede." [InterQ] (2:1/2) 95, p. 266.
"Meditation on February 23rd." [AnotherCM] (29) Spr 95, p. 65.
"Peace Store." [Border] (6) Spr-Sum 95, p. 48.
3314. KNOTT, Bill
"Weltende Variation #1" (homage Jacob van Hoddis). [SenR] (25:1) Spr 95, p. 61.
3315. KNOTT, Kip
"The Grave Digger's Stones" (for William Stafford). [CapeR] (30:1) Spr 95, p. 31.
"Rehearsal." [CapeR] (30:1) Spr 95, p. 32.
3316. KNOX, Ann B.
"Quinsy." [ApalQ] (44/45) Fall 95-Wint 96, p. 66.
3317. KNOX, Jennifer
"The Kind of Pretty That Makes Your Head Spin." [Border] (6) Spr-Sum 95, p. 49-
50.
3318. KNUTSON, Nancy Roxbury
"My Sister-in-Law Decides." [Calyx] (16:2) Wint 95-96, p. 74.
3319. KO, Chang Soo
"Flower Vendor" (tr. of Sul-Ju Lee). [Vis] (47) 95, p. 27.
"Image of Buddha" (tr. of Hee-Jin Park). [Vis] (47) 95, p. 13.
3320. KOBAYASHI, Issa (1762-1826)
"On the temple bell" (Haiku, tr. by Sam Hamill). [WillowS] (36) Je 95, p. 96.
"Thus spring begins: old" (Haiku, tr. by Sam Hamill). [WillowS] (36) Je 95, p. 96.
"A world of dew" (Haiku, tr. by Sam Hamill). [WillowS] (36) Je 95, p. 96.
3321. KOBAYASHI, Kyoji
"House-Hunting" (tr. by Alfred Birnbaum). [Descant] (26:2, #89) Sum 95, p. 121-
132.
3322. KOBYLARZ, Philip
"Books." [MichQR] (34:2) Spr 95, p. 271.
"The Great Wall." [Epoch] (44:1) 95, p. 90.
"Low Tide 1856" (tr. of Jude Stéfan, w. Monique Manopoulos). [Chelsea] (58) 95,
p. 135.
"On the Subject of Boots." [PlumR] (8) [95], p. 55.
"Portrait of a Hill." [ArtfulD] (28/29) 95, p. 44.
"A Room in Arles." [Epoch] (44:1) 95, p. 88-89.
"To Thomas Gray" (tr. of Jude Stéfan, w. Monique Manopoulos). [Chelsea] (58) 95,
p. 136.
3323. KOCHANOWSKI, Jan (1530-1584)
"Lament 1" (tr. by Stanislaw Baranczak and Seamus Heaney). [Thrpny] (63) Fall 95,
p. 13.
"Lament 2" (tr. by Stanislaw Baranczak and Seamus Heaney). [PartR] (62:3) Sum
95, p. 444-445.
"Lament 16" (tr. by Stanislaw Baranczak and Seamus Heaney). [PartR] (62:3) Sum
95, p. 443-444.
"Threnody 5" (tr. by Leonard Kress). [ArtfulD] (28/29) 95, p. 19.
"Threnody 6" (tr. by Leonard Kress). [ArtfulD] (28/29) 95, p. 20.
"Threnody 14" (tr. by Leonard Kress). [ArtfulD] (28/29) 95, p. 21.

3324. KOCHI, Itaru
"The rain is falling on the white bones" (in Japanese and English, tr. by Jiro Nakano). [BambooR] (67/68) Sum-Fall 95, p. 36.
3325. KOCK, Kenneth
"The Strangers from the Sea" (drama). [Arshile] (4) 95, p. 44-56.
3326. KOEHLER, Michael
"The Mad Farmer" (for Wendell Berry). [Poem] (74) N 95, p. 38-39.
3327. KOEHLER, Rob
"The Buffalo Massacre." [SpoonR] (20:2) Sum-Fall 95, p. 76-80.
3328. KOENIG, Brenda A.
"Anauta's Passage." [PraS] (69:4) Wint 95, p. 29-30.
"The First Muse." [PraS] (69:4) Wint 95, p. 31-32.
3329. KOENINGER, Kainoa
"Even Tho the Rainbow Disappeared on You." [OxfordM] (9:2) Fall-Wint 93, p. 94-95.
3330. KOERTGE, Ron
"Aphrodisiacs." [ChironR] (44/45) Aut-Wint 95, p. 15.
"Expulsion from the Isle of Forgetfulness." [AnotherCM] (29) Spr 95, p. 67.
"In search of." [AnotherCM] (29) Spr 95, p. 66.
3331. KOESTENBAUM, Phyllis
"In *Black Narcissus*." [MichQR] (34:4) Fall 95, p. 678-679.
3332. KOETHE, John
"Songs My Mother Taught Me." [YaleR] (83:4) O 95, p. 84-87.
3333. KOHL, Paul
"Chu Lai P.O.W. Camp." [RiverS] (44) 95, p. 19.
"Flying West." [RiverS] (44) 95, p. 20.
3334. KOHLER, Sandra
"Equestrian." [Flyway] (1:1) Spr 95, p. 20.
"Names." [WestB] (37) 95, p. 47.
"Shuttle." [WestB] (36) 95, p. 12-13.
"Small Composition in The Colors of the Sky." [Footwork] (24/25) 95, p. 31.
"Three About the Body." [Footwork] (24/25) 95, p. 31.
"Three Women and a Mountain" (Section IV of "Mountains"). [Calyx] (16:1) Sum 95, p. 65.
"Why a Woman Can't Be Pope." [Calyx] (16:1) Sum 95, p. 64.
KOK, Ingrid de
See De KOK, Ingrid
3335. KOLATKAR, Arun
"The Butterfly." [ManyMM] (1:3) 95, p. 128.
"An Old Woman." [ManyMM] (1:3) 95, p. 127.
"Water Supply." [ManyMM] (1:3) 95, p. 129.
3336. KOLODNY, Susan
"The Cell." [BellR] (18:2, #38) Fall 95, p. 18-19.
"Los Feliz Hills." [NewEngR] (17:3) Sum 95, p. 179-180.
"Prayer: Hoh Rainforest." [NewEngR] (17:3) Sum 95, p. 178-179.
3337. KOLUMBAN, Nicholas
"An Anonymous Note" (tr. of Katalin Mezey). [PoetryE] (39) Fall 94, p. 116.
"The Confessions of a Newlywed" (tr. of Katalin Mezey). [PoetryE] (39) Fall 94, p. 117.
"God" (tr. of Katalin Mezey). [PoetryE] (39) Fall 94, p. 115.
"Thoughts on One Theme" (tr. of Katalin Mezey). [PoetryE] (39) Fall 94, p. 118.
3338. KOMOTO, Hiroshi
"I walk aimlessly" (in Japanese and English, tr. by Jiro Nakano). [BambooR] (67/68) Sum-Fall 95, p. 37.
3339. KOMOTO, Yoshiko
"I know, as a man with good grace" (in Japanese and English, tr. by Jiro Nakano). [BambooR] (67/68) Sum-Fall 95, p. 38.
3340. KOMUNYAKAA, Yusef
"Antebellum Silhouettes." [KenR] (17:1) Wint 95, p. 16-18.
"Asking." [RiverS] (42/43) 95, p. 91.
"Before the Windows of Casa Guidi." [PoetryE] (39) Fall 94, p. 58-59.
"Double Exposure." [PoetryE] (39) Fall 94, p. 56-57.
"Foreign Land" (tr. of Nguyen Quang Thieu, w. the author). [Manoa] (7:2) Wint 95, p. 163-164.
"The House." [Field] (52) Spr 95, p. 10-11.
"Netherworlds." [KenR] (17:1) Wint 95, p. 19-21.

251

KORIYAMA

"Nude Study." [KenR] (17:1) Wint 95, p. 15.
"On the Highway" (tr. of Nguyen Quang Thieu, w. the author). [Manoa] (7:2) Wint
     95, p. 164.
"Utetheisa Ornatrix, the First Goddess." [Thrpny] (62) Sum 95, p. 15.
"Vigilante." [SenR] (25:1) Spr 95, p. 120-121.
"The Wheelbarrow" (tr. of Nguyen Quang Thieu, w. the author). [Manoa] (7:2)
     Wint 95, p. 164-165.
3341. KONCEL, Mary A.
     "Come Back, Elvis, Come Back to Holyoke." [IllinoisR] (3:1/2) Fall 95-Spr 96, p.
          16.
     "Dead Horse." [ProseP] (4) 95, p. 42.
     "Red Door." [IllinoisR] (3:1/2) Fall 95-Spr 96, p. 86.
     "Simple as This Night." [IllinoisR] (3:1/2) Fall 95-Spr 96, p. 100.
3342. KONDO, Yoshimi
     "The white mushroom cloud has risen" (in Japanese and English, tr. by Jiro
          Nakano). [BambooR] (67/68) Sum-Fall 95, p. 39.
3343. KONO, Juliet S.
     "Tsunami Years" (76 poems, special double issue). [BambooR] (65/66), 173 p.
3344. KONO, Yoshiko
     "Not knowing his mother is dead" (in Japanese and English, tr. by Jiro Nakano).
          [BambooR] (67/68) Sum-Fall 95, p. 40.
3345. KONTIO, Tomi
     "The Hanged" (tr. by Sari Hantula). [InterPR] (21:2) Fall 95, p. 81.
     "Hirtetty." [InterPR] (21:2) Fall 95, p. 80.
     "Let Us Dance" (tr. by Sari Hantula). [InterPR] (21:2) Fall 95, p. 77.
     "Occultism" (tr. by Sari Hantula). [InterPR] (21:2) Fall 95, p. 79.
     "Okkultismia." [InterPR] (21:2) Fall 95, p. 78.
     "Tanssikaamme." [InterPR] (21:2) Fall 95, p. 76.
3346. KOONS, Cedar
     "Fool." [Sun] (236) Ag 95, p. 35.
     "Hierophant." [Sun] (236) Ag 95, p. 35.
3347. KOONTZ, Haven
     "Purity of Heart." [HopewellR] (7) 95, p. 102.
3348. KOONTZ, Tom
     "Rhymes for a Master of Social Work Preparing for an Interview on Blind St."
          [HopewellR] (7) 95, p. 103-104.
3349. KOOSER, Ted
     "A Box of Pastels." [SouthernPR] (35:1) Sum 95, p. 44-45.
     "Lawn Chairs." [Hudson] (48:2) Sum 95, p. 272.
     "Lobocraspis Griseifusa." [Poetry] (166:2) My 95, p. 86.
     "Lunch Hour." [SycamoreR] (7:2) Sum 95, p. 36.
     "A Midwinter Letter." [Hudson] (48:2) Sum 95, p. 273.
     "New Moon." [Poetry] (166:4) Jl 95, p. 217.
     "Poet." [Hudson] (48:2) Sum 95, p. 271.
     "A Point of View." [SycamoreR] (7:2) Sum 95, p. 35.
     "Stump-Burning in Spring." [SycamoreR] (7:2) Sum 95, p. 37.
3350. KOPELKE, Kendra
     "To an Old Sucker Fish." [Agni] (41) 95, p. 114-115.
3351. KOPP, Karl
     "Burning." [CharR] (21:1) Spr 95, p. 69.
3352. KORIYAMA, Naoshi
     "Air Raid" (tr. of Yoshihara Sachiko, w. Edward Lueders). [WeberS] (12:1) Wint
          95, p. 52.
     "Calendar Poem" (tr. of Tada Chimako, w. Edward Lueders). [WeberS] (12:1) Wint
          95, p. 56.
     "Chess" (tr. of Shinkawa Kazue, w. Edward Lueders). [WeberS] (12:1) Wint 95, p.
          54-55.
     "Dead Sun" (tr. of Tada Chimako, w. Edward Lueders). [WeberS] (12:1) Wint 95, p.
          56.
     "A Distant Mirror" (tr. of Shinkawa Kazue, w. Edward Lueders). [WeberS] (12:1)
          Wint 95, p. 54.
     "An Epitaph" (tr. of Yoshihara Sachiko, w. Edward Lueders). [WeberS] (12:1) Wint
          95, p. 51-52.
     "In My Garden" (tr. of Shinkawa Kazue, w. Edward Lueders). [WeberS] (12:1)
          Wint 95, p. 52-53.

"Late Summer" (tr. of Tada Chimako, w. Edward Lueders). [WeberS] (12:1) Wint
95, p. 55.
"Low Tide" (tr. of Yoshihara Sachiko, w. Edward Lueders). [WeberS] (12:1) Wint
95, p. 50-51.
"Me" (tr. of Tada Chimako, w. Edward Lueders). [WeberS] (12:1) Wint 95, p. 55.
"Of Bread and Roses" (tr. of Yoshihara Sachiko, w. Edward Lueders). [WeberS]
(12:1) Wint 95, p. 50.
"The Palm" (From "Poems About the Human Body," tr. of Shinkawa Kazue, w.
Edward Lueders). [WeberS] (12:1) Wint 95, p. 53.
"Quite Suddenly" (tr. of Yoshihara Sachiko, w. Edward Lueders). [WeberS] (12:1)
Wint 95, p. 51.
"The Sole" (From "Poems About the Human Body," tr. of Shinkawa Kazue, w.
Edward Lueders). [WeberS] (12:1) Wint 95, p. 53-54.
3353. KÖRÖSY, Mária
"Ballad" (tr. of György Petri, w. Bruce Berlind). [InterQ] (2:1/2) 95, p. 149.
"The Degrees of Recognition" (tr. of György Petri, w. Bruce Berlind). [InterQ]
(2:1/2) 95, p. 151-153.
"Snowfall in Boston" (tr. of Ottó Orbán, w. Bruce Berlind). [LitR] (38:3) Spr 95, p.
352-353.
"Staircase" (tr. of György Petri, w. Bruce Berlind). [PoetryE] (39) Fall 94, p. 119.
"Such Important Conversations" (tr. of György Petri, w. Bruce Berlind). [InterQ]
(2:1/2) 95, p. 146-147.
"To M.A." (tr. of György Petri, w. Bruce Berlind). [InterQ] (2:1/2) 95, p. 150.
3354. KORT, Susanne
"As I Recollect the July You (Milledgeville, 1944)" (to my Mother, with apologies
to E. Bishop). [NowestR] (33:3) 95, p. 39.
"Crowning Glory." [NowestR] (33:3) 95, p. 38.
"Don Antonio, At the Beach, Hand Over Heart, Declares His Love." [AntigR] (100)
Wint 95, p. 72.
"Green Totem: '43." [MalR] (110) Spr 95, p. 89.
"Manila." [AntigR] (100) Wint 95, p. 71.
"Party." [PassN] (16:2) Wint 95, p. 30.
"Redux." [Plain] (15:2) Wint 95, p. 35.
"Ripening." [MalR] (110) Spr 95, p. 87-88.
"Rita & Georgia" (after watching *Dancing into the Dream*). [NowestR] (33:1) 95, p.
54.
"Rite of Passage." [MalR] (110) Spr 95, p. 86.
"Rome" (for Antonio). [SpoonR] (20:1) Wint-Spr 95, p. 98.
"Transposition." [SenR] (25:2) Fall 95, p. 101.
"Untitled: Days it lords above me like a coin, a scission." [PaintedB] (57) 95, p. 60.
3355. KOSCHEL, Christine
"Discant" (tr. of Djuna Barnes). [AmerV] (38) 95, p. 46.
"When the Kissing Flesh Is Gone" (tr. of Djuna Barnes). [AmerV] (38) 95, p. 47.
3356. KOSSMAN, Nina
"Dreamer." [ConnPR] (14:1) 95, p. 40.
"I said, and another heard" (tr. of Marina Tsvetaeva). [GreenMR] (8:2) Fall-Wint
95-96, p. 140.
"Nights Without a Loved One" (tr. of Marina Tsvetaeva). [ConnPR] (14:1) 95, p.
41.
"No! Love's Hunger" (tr. of Marina Tsvetaeva). [ConnPR] (14:1) 95, p. 43.
"Not wasting your words" (tr. of Marina Tsvetaeva). [GreenMR] (8:2) Fall-Wint 95-
96, p. 140.
"Singing Suns" (tr. by the author). [QW] (40) Spr-Sum 95, p. 75.
"This Highly Unstable Love" (tr. by the author). [QW] (40) Spr-Sum 95, p. 74.
"Where I dropped little tears" (tr. of Marina Tsvetaeva). [GreenMR] (8:2) Fall-Wint
95-96, p. 141.
"With the eyes of a spellbound witch" (tr. of Marina Tsvetaeva). [GreenMR] (8:2)
Fall-Wint 95-96, p. 141.
"With this hand, which seafarers" (tr. of Marina Tsvetaeva). [GreenMR] (8:2) Fall-
Wint 95-96, p. 140.
"Yes, the Mysterious, Improbable Friend" (tr. of Marina Tsvetaeva). [ConnPR]
(14:1) 95, p. 44.
3357. KOSTELANETZ, Richard
"1001 Film Scenarios" (Excerpts). [HawaiiR] (19:2) Fall 95, p. 1, 22, 143, 150.
"Boards, moors, pampas, lawns." [MidwQ] (37:1) Aut 95, p. 33.
"Every day I come to feel more and more secure." [WorldL] (6) 95, p. 46.

"I noticed a striaght [sic] line drawing itself across the floor." [HeavenB] (12) 95, p. 86.
"Letter Poem: A to Z." [RagMag] (12:2) Spr 95, p. 76.
"On the verge of death" (From: *1001 Stories*). [CentralP] (24) Spr 95, p. 202.
"Opening" (Design: Eun-Ha Paek). [HawaiiR] (19:2) Fall 95, p. 200-208.
"Pointillism, language, connotations, essence." [MidwQ] (37:1) Aut 95, p. 32.
"Spanglish Repartitions" (Layout by Erik J. Ringerud). [HiramPoR] (58/59) Spr 95-Wint 96, p. 42.
"Swimpressuit." [MidwQ] (37:1) Aut 95, p. 31.
3358. KOSTOPULOS-COOPERMAN, C. (Celeste)
"The Disappeared" (tr. of Marjorie Agosín). [MassR] (36:4) Wint 95-96, p. 583, 585.
3359. KOSTOS, Dean
"Clothes of the Naked" (tr. of Stelios Geranis). [Talisman] (15) Wint 95-96, p. 117.
"The Green Prince" (tr. of Nikos Alexiou). [Talisman] (15) Wint 95-96, p. 131.
KOTARO, Takamura
See TAKAMURA, Kotaro
3360. KOUROUS, Sharon
"The Locked Door." [FourQ] (9:1/2) Spr 95, p. 64.
3361. KOVAC, Deirdre
"Coda" (tr. of Huub Beurskens). [CimR] (112) Jl 95, p. 15.
"Holland's Pasture" (tr. of Huub Beurskens). [CimR] (112) Jl 95, p. 15.
"What I Am Looking at, Not What I Say." [AmerLC] (7) 95, p. 49-50.
3362. KOVACIK, Karen
"The Art of Love." [CapeR] (30:2) Fall 95, p. 16.
"As Barbara Cartland Would Say, 'I Love You'." [Kalliope] (17:3) 95, p. 8.
"Come As You Are." [CapeR] (30:2) Fall 95, p. 15.
3363. KOVACS, Edna
"Adagio." [BellArk] (11:1) Ja-F 95, p. 27.
"Aurora's Breath." [BellArk] (11:5) S-O 95, p. 25.
"Daybreak along the Deschutes." [BellArk] (11:6) N-D 95, p. 11.
"Idyl." [BellArk] (11:3) My-Je 95, p. 10.
"The Sleeping Woman Dreams of a Lover She Has Never Met." [BellArk] (11:3) My-Je 95, p. 9.
3364. KOVACS, Louise
"Daddy." [AnthNEW] (7) 95, p. 33.
3365. KOYAMA, Ayao
"Into the desolate scene" (in Japanese and English, tr. by Jiro Nakano). [BambooR] (67/68) Sum-Fall 95, p. 41.
3366. KOZAKAI, Yoshimitsu
"Late at night" (in Japanese and English, tr. by Jiro Nakano). [BambooR] (67/68) Sum-Fall 95, p. 42.
3367. KRAJAC, Susan
"History." [EvergreenC] (10:2) Sum-Fall 95, p. 73.
3368. KRAMAN, Cynthia
"King Solomon and Dame Julian in the Nut Garden." [ParisR] (37:135) Sum 95, p. 83.
"Semiramis." [ParisR] (37:135) Sum 95, p. 84.
3369. KRAMER, Aaron
"Disillusioned People" (tr. of Dora Teitleboim). [Vis] (47) 95, p. 8.
"Father-in-Law." [Confr] (56/57) Sum-Fall 95, p. 324.
"In the Twilight" (tr. of Ingeborg Bachmann, w. Siegfried Mandel). [Vis] (47) 95, p. 28.
3370. KRAPF, Norbert
"Freiburg im Breisgau" (for Maggie Mills). [Elf] (5:1) Spr 95, p. 18-19.
"A Jewish Cemetery in Franconia" (for Helmut Haberkamm). [Elf] (5:3) Fall 95, p. 21-22.
"St. Martin's Day." [Elf] (5:3) Fall 95, p. 20-21.
"Tannenbaum, 1940." [Elf] (5:3) Fall 95, p. 22-23.
3371. KRASSNER, April
"The Structures We build." [PoetL] (90:2) Sum 95, p. 39-40.
3372. KRAUS, Sharon
"At the Open Air Cafe a Friend." [LowellR] (2) c1996, p. 74.
"Hymn." [LowellR] (2) c1996, p. 75.
"The Scar." [TriQ] (93) Spr-Sum 95, p. 130-131.
"Transgressor." [TriQ] (93) Spr-Sum 95, p. 132-133.

3373. KRAUSE, Judith
"Cave Canem." [Grain] (23:1) Sum 95, p. 116.
"Watchdogs." [Grain] (23:1) Sum 95, p. 116.
3374. KRAUSHAAR, Mark
"Students Have Fun with Dead Body." [CimR] (112) Jl 95, p. 109.
"Les Waverly: Secrets in Conversation." [PoetryNW] (36:3) Aut 95, p. 12-13.
3375. KRAUSS, Janet
"Shifting Zones." [GreenHLL] (6) 95, p. 103-104.
3376. KRAWIEC, Richard (Krawiek?)
"The Other Pittsburgh." [ManyMM] (2:1) 95, p. 26.
3377. KREBS, Michael
"They Put in a Gravel Road." [WritersF] (21) 95, p. 73.
3378. KRESH, David
"Aubade." [InterQ] (2:1/2) 95, p. 136.
"The Hurt." [InterQ] (2:1/2) 95, p. 135.
3379. KRESS, Leonard
"After Horace" (for Stephen Sandy). [Ledge] (18) Sum 95, p. 104-105.
"Hide and Seek." [Ledge] (18) Sum 95, p. 103.
"Redhot." [ArtfulD] (28/29) 95, p. 15-16.
"Spiritual Exercises" (after Saint Ignatius). [ArtfulD] (28/29) 95, p. 13-14.
"Threnody 5" (tr. of Jan Kochanowski). [ArtfulD] (28/29) 95, p. 19.
"Threnody 6" (tr. of Jan Kochanowski). [ArtfulD] (28/29) 95, p. 20.
"Threnody 14" (tr. of Jan Kochanowski). [ArtfulD] (28/29) 95, p. 21.
3380. KRETZ, Thomas
"Risen to Change." [ChrC] (112:12) 12 Ap 95, p. 402.
"Stone on the Root." [Pearl] (22) Fall-Wint 95, p. 20.
3381. KRICH, A. M.
"On Hampstead Heath." [AmerV] (38) 95, p. 20.
3382. KRICORIAN, Nancy
"My Armenia." [AntR] (53:2) Spr 95, p. 199.
3383. KRISAK, Len
"Still Life." [CumbPR] (14:2) Spr 95, p. 12.
3384. KROEKER, G. W.
"Watching the Fall." [Pearl] (22) Fall-Wint 95, p. 19.
3385. KROLL, Ernest
"Cable Car." [Light] (14) Sum 95, p. 20.
"Epiphany." [Light] (15/16) Aut-Wint 95-96, p. 12.
"Ghost Town." [WindO] (60) Fall-Wint 95, p. 5.
"The Great Ashtabula River Train Wreck (1876)." [WindO] (60) Fall-Wint 95, p. 4.
"Tumbleweed Tune." [Light] (14) Sum 95, p. 19.
3386. KROLOW, Karl
"Almost Nothing" (tr. by Stuart Friebert). [Field] (53) Fall 95, p. 85.
"July" (tr. by Stuart Friebert). [Field] (53) Fall 95, p. 84.
"Under a Spell" (tr. by Stuart Friebert). [Field] (53) Fall 95, p. 83.
"View From the Window" (tr. by Stuart Friebert). [OhioR] (54) 95, p. 25.
"What Remains" (tr. by Stuart Friebert). [DefinedP] (2:2) Spr-Sum 94, p. 38.
"Whoever Could Still Say" (tr. by Stuart Friebert). [OhioR] (54) 95, p. 26.
3387. KROMAN, Deborah
"Alice." [Bogg] (67) 95, p. 48.
3388. KRONEN, Steve
"Earhart Ascending." [SouthernR] (31:1) Wint 95, p. 32.
"Flowers, Things Vital and Unvital" (after Akhmatova). [SouthernR] (31:1) Wint
95, p. 32-33.
"The Last Evening" (after Rilke). [SouthernR] (31:1) Wint 95, p. 33.
3389. KRUGER, Joan E.
"Sincerely Yours." [Footwork] (24/25) 95, p. 85.
3390. KRUGOVOY, Anya
"Florence, 1986." [PoetL] (90:2) Sum 95, p. 43.
"The Old Beggar-Woman." [PoetL] (90:2) Sum 95, p. 41-42.
KRUIP, Valentina Gnup
See GNUP-KRUIP, Valentina
3391. KRUSOE, Nancy
"Geosynclines" (Excerpts, w. Jan Ramjerdi). [13thMoon] (13:1/2) 95, p. 93-103.
3392. KRYSL, Marilyn
"Dear Brother Vimaladas" (tr. of Charen, w. the author). [ManyMM] (2:1) 95, p. 91.

"Ghazals for the Turn of the Century" (Selections: 8 poems). [AnotherCM] (29) Spr
95, p. 68-72.
"Homage to Pierre-Auguste Renoir." [DenQ] (29:4) Spr 95, p. 29-30.
"Jet Set Chronologist" (Winner, 1995 Editors' Prize). [SpoonR] (20:2) Sum-Fall 95,
p. 33-34.
"Resurrection" (tr. of Charen, w. the author). [ManyMM] (2:1) 95, p. 92.
3393. KRYSS, Tom
"How People Learn." [ChironR] (43) Sum 95, p. 20.
3394. KUAN, Hsiu
"Chung-nan Mountain Monk" (tr. by J. P. Seaton). [LitR] (38:3) Spr 95, p. 328.
"A Hundred Sorrows" (tr. by J. P. Seaton). [LitR] (38:3) Spr 95, p. 329.
"Leaving It to You" (tr. by J. P. Seaton). [LitR] (38:3) Spr 95, p. 329.
"Mean Alleyways" (tr. by J. P. Seaton). [LitR] (38:3) Spr 95, p. 328.
3395. KUBICEK, J. L.
"Verified." [HampSPR] Wint 95, p. 18.
3396. KUCHINSKY, Walter
"Earth." [ChironR] (43) Sum 95, p. 25.
3397. KUDERKO, Lynne
"Because You Once Asked If I Would Ever Write About You I Write You a
Sentimental Poem." [PoetryNW] (36:1) Spr 95, p. 45-46.
"Five Ways to Write About Journey." [PoetryNW] (36:1) Spr 95, p. 44-45.
"Wedlock." [PoetryNW] (36:1) Spr 95, p. 46-47.
3398. KUHL, Nancy
"In the Arbor." [PoetryNW] (36:2) Sum 95, p. 21-22.
3399. KUMAR, Mina
"Dinner with Melanie." [ProseP] (4) 95, p. 43.
"I Give You a Gift That Is Completely." [HangL] (66) 95, p. 39.
"Maya." [ProseP] (4) 95, p. 44.
"Trade." [HangL] (66) 95, p. 40.
3400. KUMIN, Maxine
"After the Heat Wave." [NewMyths] (2:2/3:1) 95, p. 44.
"Almost Spring, Driving Home, Reciting Hopkins." [Poetry] (166:1) Ap 95, p. 7.
"The Bridge Builder." [TriQ] (95) Wint 95-96, p. 162-166.
"Early Thoughts of Winter." [Witness] (9:2) 95, p. 9.
"From the 18th Floor." [Footwork] (24/25) 95, p. 3.
"Vignette." [GreenMR] (8:1) Spr-Sum 95, p. 49.
3401. KUMOVE, Shirley
"Among the Chinese Lanterns" (tr. of Anna Margolin). [Writ] (27) 95, p. 14-15.
"Brisk (Brest-Litovsk)" (tr. of Anna Margolin). [Writ] (27) 95, p. 9-11.
"Drunk from the Bitter Truth" (tr. of Anna Margolin). [Writ] (27) 95, p. 12.
"Full of Night and Weeping" (tr. of Anna Margolin). [Writ] (27) 95, p. 13.
"I Want, Angry and Tender One" (tr. of Anna Margolin). [Writ] (27) 95, p. 17.
"Mary Wants to Be a Beggar Woman" (tr. of Anna Margolin). [Writ] (27) 95, p. 16.
"My Ancestors Speak" (tr. of Anna Margolin). [Writ] (27) 95, p. 7-8.
3402. KUNERT, Gunter
"On Bridges" (tr. by Agnes Stein). [MidAR] (15:1/2) 95, p. 44.
3403. KUNITZ, Stanley
"Halley's Comet." [NewYorker] (71:31) 9 O 95, p. 88.
"Hornworm: Autumn Lamentation." [AmerPoR] (24:4) Jl-Ag 95, p. 48.
"Hornworm: Summer Reverie." [AmerPoR] (24:4) Jl-Ag 95, p. 48.
"Touch Me." [NewYorker] (71:29) 25 S 95, p. 110.
3404. KUNKLE, Robert
"I Will Succeed, But." [Boulevard] (10:1/2, #28/29) Spr 95, p. 18.
"Like Lovers" (For Nicole). [Boulevard] (10:1/2, #28/29) Spr 95, p. 19.
3405. KUNSTLER, William M.
"When the Cheering Stopped." [Harp] (289 [i.e. 290]:1737) F 95, p. 28.
3406. KUNTZ, Laurie
"Turning Seven in a Foreign Land" (Honorable Mention, First Annual Poetry
Awards). [LiteralL] (2:1) Sum 95, p. 15.
3407. KUNZ, Peter
"In the Province of Hitachi" (After the woodcut by Hokusai). [YellowS] (12:4, #48)
Sum 95, p. 29.
"The Osprey Nest." [LullwaterR] (6:2) Fall-Wint 95, p. 94-95.
"The Woman Who Lives in the Sun" (After a stonecut by Kenojuak, Kingnit
settlement, Canadian Eastern Arctic). [YellowS] (12:4, #48) Sum 95, p. 28.

3408. KURAPEL, Alberto
"Friday February 5th" (tr. by Liliam Lipsky). [Arc] (35) Aut 95, p. 56.
"Prism" (tr. by Liliam Lipsky). [Arc] (35) Aut 95, p. 57.
"Today My Heart Went Away" (tr. by Liliam Lipsky). [Arc] (35) Aut 95, p. 55.
3409. KURASCH, David
"Star of the Silver Screen Sequence" (3 selections). [Farm] (12:1) Spr-Sum 95, p.
19-20.
3410. KURIHARA, Sadako
"The Flag, 1" (tr. by Richard H. Minear). [InterQ] (2:1/2) 95, p. 254.
"Ground Zero" (tr. by Richard H. Minear). [InterQ] (2:1/2) 95, p. 255.
"Hiroshima" (tr. by Richard H. Minear). [InterQ] (2:1/2) 95, p. 256.
"Let Us Be Midwives!" (An untold story of the atomic bombing, tr. by Richard H.
Minear). [InterQ] (2:1/2) 95, p. 253.
"Nevada, 1" (the resumption of nuclear testing by the U.S. and the U.S.S.R., tr. by
Richard H. Minear). [InterQ] (2:1/2) 95, p. 257.
"Prayer for a Nuclear-Free Tomorrow" (For Kazuko, tr. by Richard H. Minear).
[InterQ] (2:1/2) 95, p. 260.
"Rain" (tr. by Richard H. Minear). [InterQ] (2:1/2) 95, p. 261.
"Shades: The Post-Doomsday World" (tr. by Richard H. Minear). [InterQ] (2:1/2)
95, p. 258.
"When We Say 'Hiroshima'" (tr. by Richard H. Minear). [InterQ] (2:1/2) 95, p. 259.
3411. KURZ, Egon
"Caesar — Desist." [Light] (13) Spr 95, p. 17.
KUSATAO, Ozaki
See OZAKI, Kusatao
3412. KUSHNER, Dale
"Her Mind on the Two." [PraS] (69:4) Wint 95, p. 145.
3413. KUSSEROW, Adrie S.
"The Gift." [BellR] (18:2, #38) Fall 95, p. 20.
3414. KUUSISTO, Stephen
"A Brief Explanation." [ProseP] (4) 95, p. 45.
"Deserto in Terra Solo." [ProseP] (4) 95, p. 46.
"Harvest." [PartR] (62:3) Sum 95, p. 453-454.
"Lying Still." [SenR] (25:1) Spr 95, p. 104.
"No Name for It." [ProseP] (4) 95, p. 47-48.
3415. KUYA (Buddhist priest, 903-972)
"This is a tale that comes not from this world." [Tricycle] (4:4, #16) Sum 95, p. 44.
3416. KUZMA, Greg
"Having My Asshole Cut" (Homage to Walt Gardner). [GreenMR] (8:2) Fall-Wint
95-96, p. 90-97.
"Reciting THE HIGHWAYMAN" (for Miriam Gladding). [MidwQ] (36:4) Sum 95,
p. 389-391.
"A Rising." [Witness] (9:1) 95, p. 143-149.
"The Spider on the Windowsill." [Iowa] (25:1) Wint 95, p. 61-66.
3417. KWASNY, Melissa
"Mountain Pool." [PoetryNW] (36:2) Sum 95, p. 36.
"Snow Melt." [PoetryNW] (36:4) Wint 95-96, p. 18.
"Spruce." [PoetryNW] (36:2) Sum 95, p. 37.
3418. KYLE, Carol (1939-1995)
"Digging at the Shrine of Demeter in Deya, Majorca." [SpoonR] (20:1) Wint-Spr 95,
p. 110-111.
"The Equinox Without You." [SpoonR] (20:1) Wint-Spr 95, p. 115.
"The Flowering of Deya." [SpoonR] (20:1) Wint-Spr 95, p. 124.
"Living in a Museum." [SpoonR] (20:1) Wint-Spr 95, p. 112-114.
"The Moon and the Olive Tree." [SpoonR] (20:1) Wint-Spr 95, p. 123-124.
"Persephone Decides to Rise by Herself" (for Zohreh). [SpoonR] (20:1) Wint-Spr
95, p. 125-126.
"Persephone Discovers Sappho's Poetry in an Egyptian Tomb." [SpoonR] (20:1)
Wint-Spr 95, p. 119-120.
"Persephone Hears the Guatemalan Earthquake Underground." [SpoonR] (20:1)
Wint-Spr 95, p. 121-122.
"Wintering in Majorca" (9 poems). [SpoonR] (20:1) Wint-Spr 95, p. 109-128.
"You Ask If I Would Like a Picture of the Twelfth-Century Moorish Stone Terraces
in Majorca." [SpoonR] (20:1) Wint-Spr 95, p. 116-118.

3419. KYLE, Christiane Jacox
"Message of a Birth for Chile" (tr. of Gabriela Mistral). [PraS] (69:1) Spr 95, p. 21-23.
"Thrushes" (tr. of Gabriela Mistral). [PraS] (69:1) Spr 95, p. 24-25.
3420. KYOGOKU, Tamekane (1254-1332)
"The garden insects" (tr. by Sam Hamill). [RiverS] (44) 95, p. 35.
"Time after time" (tr. by Sam Hamill). [RiverS] (44) 95, p. 34.
KYOJI, Kobayashi
See KOBAYASHI, Kyoji
KYOJIN, Okura
See OKURA, Kyojin
KYOKO, Mori
See MORI, Kyoko
KYOKO, Uchida
See UCHIDA, Kyoko
3421. KYRIAKOS, S. H.
"A Door Open" (From Weather Conditions, tr. of Dino Siotis). [HarvardR] (8) Spr 95, p. 92.

L., SHELTON
See SHELTON L.
3422. L. H. (Dinner Program for Homeless Women, Washington, DC)
"The Hot One" (w. A. B. Lester, WritersCorps Program). [WashR] (21:2) Ag-S 95, p. 8.
La ...
See also names beginning with "La" without the following space, filed below in their alphabetic positions, e.g., LaPIERRE.
3423. La MANTIA, Benito
"Más Allá" (tr. from Italian into Spanish by Carlos Vitale). [Luz] (8) Spr 95, p. 39-40.
3424. LaBOMBARD, Joan
"Georgia O'Keeffe." [TarRP] (35:1) Fall 95, p. 35.
"Good-Bye." [TarRP] (35:1) Fall 95, p. 34-35.
3425. LACINA, Melody
"Skating." [BellR] (18:1, #37) Spr 95, p. 28.
3426. LADIK, Katalin
"Leaned into the frozen wind. Created a hole" (tr. by Emoke B'Racz). [Vis] (47) 95, p. 8.
"White socks in his mouth" (tr. by Emoke B'Racz). [Vis] (47) 95, p. 8.
3427. LADIN, Jay
"Arkansas." [WillowS] (36) Je 95, p. 7.
3428. LaFEMINA, Gerry
"The Afternoon the Our Lady of Perpetual Health Parish Picnic Was Rained Out." [AxeF] (3) 90, p. 26.
"For the Road" (tr. of Ali Yuce, w. Sinan Toprak). [HayF] (16) Spr-Sum 95, p. 61.
"July 14, 1992." [WestB] (36) 95, p. 30.
"To Blow Away the Darkness" (tr. of Ali Yuce, w. Sinan Toprak). [HayF] (16) Spr-Sum 95, p. 60.
3429. LAFKY, Jim
"On Burying Jane." [RagMag] (12:2) Spr 95, p. 83.
3430. LaFLAMME, Gladys
"After Eighty." [Blueline] (16) 95, p. 52.
"Sunday Morning." [Blueline] (16) 95, p. 66-67.
3431. LaFOND, Carolyn Street
"The Woman on the Left Arm of God." [BellArk] (11:3) My-Je 95, p. 24.
3432. LAGIER, Jennifer
"Eating It: The Compulsory Feast" (The 1994 Allen Ginsberg Poetry Awards: Honorable Mention). [Footwork] (24/25) 95, p. 198.
"Requiem for Two Corpses Starring Mother and Dad." [SantaBR] (3:1) Spr 95, p. 24.
3433. LAGOURELI, Maria
"Death Cannot Be Photographed" (tr. by Yannis Goumas). [Vis] (48) 95, p. 21.
"Don't Shoot the Piano Player" (tr. by Yannis Goumas). [Vis] (48) 95, p. 20.
"The Dresser" (tr. by Yannis Goumas). [Vis] (48) 95, p. 21.

3434. LAHEY, Joy
"Census." [NewOR] (21:2) Sum 95, p. 47.
"Misisipi." [NewOR] (21:2) Sum 95, p. 46.
"Sunset Limited." [NewOR] (21:2) Sum 95, p. 47.
3435. LAINO, E. J. Miller
"Boiling Over." [TarRP] (34:2) Spr 95, p. 30.
"First Night." [PraS] (69:4) Wint 95, p. 34-35.
"First Pelican." [GreenMR] (8:2) Fall-Wint 95-96, p. 46.
"In So Many Words." [SnailPR] (3:2) 95, p. 22.
"May 17th." [PraS] (69:4) Wint 95, p. 36-37.
"Telling the Truth." [MassR] (36:2) Sum 95, p. 205-206.
"Words and Sex." [GreenMR] (8:2) Fall-Wint 95-96, p. 47.
3436. LAIRD, Frances
"Ah! it is you again" (tr. of Anna Akhmatova). [PlumR] (8) [95], p. 86.
"She" (tr. of Nikolai S. Gumilev). [PlumR] (8) [95], p. 87.
3437. LAKANEN, Shannon
"A Place Between Us." [IndR] (18:2) Fall 95, p. 130-131.
3438. LAKE, Whitney
"Delivery." [US1] (30/31) 95, p. 27.
3439. LALLEY, Jacqueline
"Harker's House." [CumbPR] (15:1) Fall 95, p. 29-30.
3440. LAM, Chi
"August" (tr. of Paulo Colina, w. Phyllis Peres and Reetika Vazirani). [Callaloo]
    (18:4) Fall 95, p. 734-735.
"Carnival" (tr. of Paulo Colina, w. Phyllis Peres, Jane Kamide and Reetika
    Vazirani). [Callaloo] (18:4) Fall 95, p. 736.
"Ejo-Lorun" (tr. of Ricardo Aleixo, w. Phyllis Peres and Reetika Vazirani).
    [Callaloo] (18:4) Fall 95, p. 800.
"Great Mother" (tr. of Ricardo Aleixo, w. Phyllis Peres and Reetika Vazirani).
    [Callaloo] (18:4) Fall 95, p. 799.
"I Am" (tr. of Oliveira Silveira, w. Phyllis Peres and Reetika Vazirani). [Callaloo]
    (18:4) Fall 95, p. 813-814.
"Induca, Maria do Rosário" (tr. of Edimilson de Almeida Pereira, w. Phyllis Peres
    and Reetika Vazirani). [Callaloo] (18:4) Fall 95, p. 873.
"Mariana and the Word, Another Name" (tr. of Éle Semog, w. Phyllis Peres and
    Reetika Vazirani). [Callaloo] (18:4) Fall 95, p. 755.
"Morning Prayer" (for Núbia Pereira, tr. of Edimilson de Almeida Pereira, w.
    Phyllis Peres and Reetika Vazirani). [Callaloo] (18:4) Fall 95, p. 872.
"Much to the Sea" (for a black woman, tr. of José Carlos Limeira, w. Phyllis Peres
    and Reetika Vazirani). [Callaloo] (18:4) Fall 95, p. 818.
"Ouro Preto: Interpretation Itinerary" (tr. of Edimilson de Almeida Pereira, w.
    Phyllis Peres and Reetika Vazirani). [Callaloo] (18:4) Fall 95, p. 874.
"Pieces of a Woman" (tr. of Ricardo Aleixo, w. Carolyn Richardson Durham and
    Reetika Vazirani). [Callaloo] (18:4) Fall 95, p. 801.
"This Is for You" (tr. of Éle Semog, w. Phyllis Peres and Reetika Vazirani).
    [Callaloo] (18:4) Fall 95, p. 753.
3441. LAMA, Luis
"The Crow" (tro Brandon Lee). [Arc] (35) Aut 95, p. 77.
"The Days of the Lion." [Arc] (35) Aut 95, p. 78.
LaMANTIA, Benito
    See La MANTIA, Benito
3442. LAMAR, Paul
"Ars Poetica." [PraS] (69:2) Sum 95, p. 59-60.
"My Luck." [PraS] (69:2) Sum 95, p. 57-58.
"A Shooting Star." [PraS] (69:2) Sum 95, p. 58-59.
"The Visitor." [HiramPoR] (58/59) Spr 95-Wint 96, p. 43-44.
3443. LAMB, Joe
"Untitled: God is not dead." [Sun] (237) S 95, p. 22.
3444. LaMERS, Joyce
"Blunt Remark." [Light] (14) Sum 95, p. 17.
"Penelope and Ulysses Settle a Domestic Dispute" (Tennyson Revisited). [Light]
    (14) Sum 95, p. 10.
"Point of Order" (Possible Origin of the National Debt). [Light] (15/16) Aut-Wint
    95-96, p. 31.
"Politician." [Light] (14) Sum 95, p. 14.
"Squelch That Belch!" [Light] (13) Spr 95, p. 16.

"The Uele River." [Light] (15/16) Aut-Wint 95-96, p. 34.
3445. LAMMON, Martin
    "The Kiss." [CharR] (21:1) Spr 95, p. 77.
    "The Secret of Saturday Morning." [CharR] (21:1) Spr 95, p. 77.
3446. LAMON, Laurie
    "The Poem: Watches the road for the house." [PoetryNW] (36:4) Wint 95-96, p. 38.
3447. LaMONDA, Mark
    "Hostage Set Free." [Vis] (49) 95, p. 7.
3448. LANCASTER, Robert S.
    "Odysseus Sleepless." [SewanR] (103:3) Sum 95, p. 368-369.
3449. LANDALE, Zoë
    "Oatmeal Cookies." [CanLit] (146) Aut 95, p. 95-96.
3450. LANDGRAF, Susan
    "Say You Heard the Dark." [Kalliope] (17:1) 95, p. 12.
3451. LANDON, Luann
    "La Femme au Soleil." [CumbPR] (15:1) Fall 95, p. 33-34.
    "Folding Laundry." [CumbPR] (14:2) Spr 95, p. 7.
    "In a Paris Apartment" (For Françoise and Paul). [CumbPR] (14:2) Spr 95, p. 5-6.
    "O My Mothers." [CumbPR] (15:1) Fall 95, p. 32.
    "Sally's Shoes" (Robert Penn Warren Poetry Prize: Honorable Mention). [CumbPR]
        (15:1) Fall 95, p. 31.
3452. LANDRUM, David W.
    "Cat and Mandolin." [Hellas] (6:1) Spr-Sum 95, p. 22.
    "We Three" (tr. of Li Po). [Hellas] (6:1) Spr-Sum 95, p. 21.
3453. LANDRY, John
    "A Few Haiku." [Border] (7) Fall-Wint 96, p. 28.
    "Minding My Ps & Qs." [DefinedP] (3) 95, p. 37.
3454. LANDSMAN, Peggy
    "The Readiness Is All, or The 1979 Death of Eula Love Is Still Unavailable on
        Videotape." [Calyx] (16:1) Sum 95, p. 61.
3455. LANE, M. Travis
    "A Reader's Deductions." [CanLit] (145) Sum 95, p. 19.
    "Too Late." [PoetryC] (15:3) Ag 95, p. 28.
    "What Can Be Named in Numbers Reassures." [CanLit] (145) Sum 95, p. 20.
3456. LANG, Leonard
    "By the Summer Cabin." [MidwQ] (36:4) Sum 95, p. 393.
    "Kitchen Scene." [Journal] (19:2) Fall-Wint 95, p. 47-48.
3457. LANGAN, Steve
    "Death of Randall Jarrell" (A Plainsongs Award Poem). [Plain] (16:1) Fall 95, p. 5.
3458. LANGE, Art
    "Maze." [NewAW] (13) Fall-Wint 95, p. 82-84.
3459. LANGE, Pamela
    "Dangerous Things." [SpinningJ] (1) Fall 95-Wint 96, p. 16-17.
3460. LANGFORD, Don
    "On Visiting a Friend in the Camarillo Mental Institution." [LowellR] [1] Sum 94, p.
        91.
    "Singing in the Key of Z." [LowellR] [1] Sum 94, p. 89-90.
3461. LANGILLE, Carole
    "George at 88." [MalR] (113) Wint 95, p. 101.
    "Scanning an Afternoon in Winter." [MalR] (113) Wint 95, p. 100.
3462. LANGLAS, James
    "Cities." [WillowR] (22) Spr 95, p. 21.
3463. LANGLOIS, Alma Hansen
    "Making the Bed." [AnthNEW] (7) 95, p. 21.
3464. LANGRALL, Liza
    "Jonquils." [SouthernHR] (29:2) Spr 95, p. 148.
3465. LANIER, David
    "This Far, in Snow." [Poetry] (167:3) D 95, p. 134-135.
LANILAU, Carolyn Lei
    See LEI-LANILAU, Carolyn
3466. LANSING, Gerrit
    "In Erasmus Darwin's Generous Light." [Talisman] (15) Wint 95-96, p. 4-7.
3467. LaPIERRE, Matthew S. (Matthew Scott)
    "The Jerk" (3rd Place — 1995 CR Poetry Contest). [ChironR] (44/45) Aut-Wint 95,
        p. 32.
    "Passenger Seat." [ChironR] (44/45) Aut-Wint 95, p. 15.

"Thirteenth Summer." [ChironR] (43) Sum 95, p. 30.
3468. LAPINSKY, Steve
"Thai Food" (For Kim and Pawn). [SouthernPR] (35:2) Wint 95, p. 13-14.
3469. LAPP, Claudia E.
"Prayer." [SilverFR] (25) Sum 95, p. 46.
3470. LARAK, Pol (Paul Laraque)
"The Liberty Drum" (tr. by Jack Hirschman). [Drumvoices] (4:1/2) Fall-Wint 94-95, p. 121.
3471. LARBAUD, Valery
"The Gift of Myself" (tr. by Louis Simpson). [Hudson] (47:4) Wint 95, p. 538-539.
"Images" (tr. by Louis Simpson). [Hudson] (47:4) Wint 95, p. 540-541.
"Indian Ocean" (tr. by Louis Simpson). [Hudson] (47:4) Wint 95, p. 535-536.
"Night in the Port" (tr. by Louis Simpson). [Hudson] (47:4) Wint 95, p. 534-535.
"Ode" (tr. by Louis Simpson). [Hudson] (47:4) Wint 95, p. 533-534.
"The Old Cahors Station" (tr. by Louis Simpson). [Hudson] (47:4) Wint 95, p. 536.
"Postscript" (tr. by Louis Simpson). [Hudson] (47:4) Wint 95, p. 541-542.
"Yaravi" (tr. by Louis Simpson). [Hudson] (47:4) Wint 95, p. 537-538.
3472. LARDAS, Konstantinos
"Akimbo." [HarvardR] (9) Fall 95, p. 31.
3473. LAREW, Hiram
"No One in Sight." [Footwork] (24/25) 95, p. 77.
3474. LARKIN, Mary Ann
"Certain Things." [NewL] (62:1) 96 (c1995), p. 118-119.
3475. LARRABEE, Hart
"Gathering Incense" (tr. of Yoriko Ogihara). [ArtfulD] (28/29) 95, p. 41.
3476. LARSEN, Douglas
"The Last Sandwich" (after Richard Pryor). [OxfordM] (10:1) Wint 94-Spr 95, p. 43-44.
3477. LARSEN, Lance
"Gift." [QW] (41) Aut-Wint 95-96, p. 203.
3478. LARSON, Greg
"Mine." [DefinedP] (3) 95, p. 63.
3479. LARSON, Michael (Mike)
"Behind My Lips Like Words." [ChrC] (112:32) 8 N 95, p. 1052.
"The Games." [Image] (10) Sum 95, p. 96.
"The Hunted Man." [Image] (10) Sum 95, p. 96.
"Love in the Off-Season." [Image] (10) Sum 95, p. 95.
"Raymond of Penyafort." [Image] (10) Sum 95, p. 97.
"Words." [RagMag] (12:2) Spr 95, p. 71.
3480. LASDUN, James
"Curator." [NewYorker] (71:20) 17 Jl 95, p. 50-51.
"Woman Police Officer in Elevator." [NewYorker] (71:14) 29 My 95, p. 48-49.
3481. LASHLEY, Michael A.
"Calling Your Attention." [Drumvoices] (4:1/2) Fall-Wint 94-95, p. 138.
3482. LASKER-SCHÜLER, Else
"Boaz" (tr. by Martin Bidney). [NewMyths] (2:2/3:1) 95, p. 149.
"Ruth" (tr. by Martin Bidney). [NewMyths] (2:2/3:1) 95, p. 150.
"Sabaoth" (tr. by Martin Bidney). [NewMyths] (2:2/3:1) 95, p. 151.
"Shulamith" (tr. by Martin Bidney). [NewMyths] (2:2/3:1) 95, p. 152.
"To God" (tr. by Martin Bidney). [NewMyths] (2:2/3:1) 95, p. 153.
3483. LASOEN, Patricia
"5. The Traveller (account of the separation)" (tr. by Scott Rollins). [Vis] (47) 95, p. 37.
"6. The Traveller (account of the murder)" (tr. by Scott Rollins). [Vis] (47) 95, p. 37.
3484. LASSEN, Sandra Lake
"Doldrums." [SoCoast] (18) Ja 95, p. 56.
"Elegy for the Slave Ned, 1850." [AnthNEW] (7) 95, p. 22.
3485. LATTA, John
"Reading Cicero's De Oratore." [ChiR] (41:4) 95, p. 113-115.
3486. LATTA, Ruth
"Hickery Pickery." [Conscience] (16:3) Aut 95, p. 16.
3487. LAU, Barbara
"Splitting in Two." [Border] (7) Fall-Wint 96, p. 29.
3488. LAU, Evelyn
"The Monks' Song." [Confr] (56/57) Sum-Fall 95, p. 336.

3489. LAUBER, Peg
"Dreamless Sleep." [Kalliope] (17:1) 95, p. 67.
"Holy Fools." [Kalliope] (17:1) 95, p. 65.
"Saved." [Kalliope] (17:1) 95, p. 66.
3490. LAUCHLAN, Michael
"Elephants." [VirQR] (71:1) Wint 95, p. 110.
"Hospital Cafeteria." [VirQR] (71:1) Wint 95, p. 109.
3491. LAUE, John
"Til Death Do Us Part" (To a new close friend). [ChironR] (43) Sum 95, p. 21.
"To My Daughter." [ChironR] (44/45) Aut-Wint 95, p. 7.
3492. LAUGHLIN, J. (James)
"Akhmatova's Muse." [NewYorkQ] (54) 95, p. 101.
"Anima Mea." [Poetry] (165:4) Ja 95, p. 210.
"The Calendar of Fame." [Poetry] (165:4) Ja 95, p. 210.
"Coprophilus" (after Martial). [GrandS] (14:1, #53) Sum 95, p. 114.
"De Contemptu Mortis." [Hudson] (47:4) Wint 95, p. 598.
"De Iuventute." [ParisR] (37:137) Wint 95, p. 228.
"A Florilegium." [ParisR] (37:137) Wint 95, p. 227-228.
"Lines Found in a Haiku." [Chelsea] (59) 95, p. 157.
"Lines Found in a Haiku (II)." [Chelsea] (59) 95, p. 158.
"A Loved Book." [CarolQ] (47:2) Wint 95, p. 28.
"My Shoelaces" (from "Byways"). [Iowa] (25:1) Wint 95, p. 124-126.
"Nothing At All" (tr. of Alain Bosquet). [Agni] (41) 95, p. 69.
"An Ordinary Day" (tr. of Alain Bosquet). [Agni] (41) 95, p. 68.
"The Search." [Hudson] (47:4) Wint 95, p. 597.
"Their Silence." [GettyR] (8:2) Spr 95, p. 218.
"Two Wills Contend." [NewYorkQ] (54) 95, p. 55.
"The Wandering Words." [AmerV] (36) 95, p. 131.
"A Winter's Night." [NewYorker] (71:4) 20 Mr 95, p. 67.
"The Woman in the Painting" (for Vanessa). [GettyR] (8:2) Spr 95, p. 219.
3493. LAUGHLIN, Rosemary
"Metaphor for Writers" (Literary Festival: Poetry: Honorable Mention). [EngJ]
(84:4) Ap 95, p. 43.
3494. LAUGHRUN, Chris
"The Spring of the Year" (tr. of Yun-kai Chih-pen). [LitR] (38:3) Spr 95, p. 332.
"Summer Day in the Mountain" (tr. of Ts'an-liao Tzu). [LitR] (38:3) Spr 95, p. 333.
"White Lotus" (tr. of Pei-chien Chu-chien). [LitR] (38:3) Spr 95, p. 334.
3495. LAUINGER, Ann
"Tabernacles." [Confr] (56/57) Sum-Fall 95, p. 311.
3496. LAUREL, Hya
"Rainbowy." [Bogg] (67) 95, p. 36.
3497. LAURENCE, Alexander
"Funeral Cantata" (tr. of Maurice Roche). [ApalQ] (43) Spr 95, p. 27-35.
3498. LAURENCE, Larry
"Beginning at Dinner, Beginning with the Kitchen Table." [ProseP] (4) 95, p. 49.
3499. LAUTERBACH, Ann
"Figure Without Ground" (to RD & JC). [DenQ] (30:2) Fall 95, p. 36-42.
"Narrow Margins." [SenR] (25:1) Spr 95, p. 45.
"Poem of the Landscape" (To Bin Ramke). [Avec] (10) 95, p. 46-53.
"Sequence with Dream Objects in Real Time." [Avec] (10) 95, p. 42-45.
3500. LAUX, Dorianne
"After Twelve Days of Rain." [Zyzzyva] (11:3/4, #43/44) 95, "The Best of Ten
Years of ZYZZYVA," p. 122-124.
"Kah Tai Purgatorio." [Jacaranda] (11) [95 or 96?], p. 144-145.
"Music in the Morning." [HarvardR] (9) Fall 95, p. 33.
3501. LAVERGNE, Alfredo
"The Bird of Winter" (tr. by Luciano P. Díaz). [Arc] (35) Aut 95, p. 52.
"Breakfast" (tr. by Luciano P. Díaz). [Arc] (35) Aut 95, p. 53.
"The Size of a Lie" (tr. by Luciano P. Díaz). [Arc] (35) Aut 95, p. 51.
3502. LAVIERI, Jeanne
"Magic Mountain." [Elf] (5:4) Wint 95, p. 35.
3503. LAVINE, Rebecca
"After the Bay of Pigs." [Footwork] (24/25) 95, p. 51.
3504. LAW, Richard
"Metaphors." [IndR] (18:2) Fall 95, p. 132.

LAWLER

3505. LAWLER, Patrick
"Aldo Leopold Thinking Like a Mountain Meets Andre Collard Living Like One"
(for Nicole). [SycamoreR] (7:1) Wint 95, p. 46.
"(Breath)." [LowellR] [1] Sum 94, p. 30-34.
"A Character of Dostoyevsky Meets a Character of Camus." [SycamoreR] (7:1)
Wint 95, p. 44.
"Egaz Moniz Meets Marshall McLuhan." [DefinedP] (3) 95, p. 64.
"Man Killed by Static Cling." [Flyway] (1:2) Fall 95, p. 20-21.
"Mengele Invites Pavlov to Look Through the Eyes of the Dead." [SycamoreR]
(7:1) Wint 95, p. 45.
"St. Dymphna, Carrying Her Crying Heart, Comes to Lacan Who Carries His Own."
[CreamCR] (19:1) Spr 95, p. 134-135.
"(Water)." [CentralP] (24) Spr 95, p. 283-291.
3506. LAWRENCE, Ron
"3 x 2 Sides." [SantaBR] (3:3) Fall-Wint 95, p. 75.
"Anthony Young" (Los Angeles Times July 11, 1993). [Spitball] (48) 95, p. 29.
3507. LAWS, Kyle
"Cemetery on the Banks of the Purgatoire." [ChironR] (42) Spr 95, p. 26.
"Debris." [ChironR] (42) Spr 95, p. 26.
3508. LAWTHER, James M.
"Poetic License." [Crucible] (30) Fall 94, p. 33.
3509. LAWTON, Harry
"My Stepfather at Eighty-Three." [LiteralL] (1:4) Ja-F 95, p. 21.
3510. LAX, Robert
"The stone." [WorldL] (6) 95, p. 43.
3511. LAY, Amy
"A Light Will Come On Without Warning." [LullwaterR] (5:1) 93-94, p. 40-41.
3512. LAYTON, Peter
"Forest." [JINJPo] (17:1) Spr 95, p. 39.
"Hand Gravel." [JINJPo] (17:2) Aut 95, p. 30.
3513. LAZAR, Hank
"Days" (Selections: 9-13). [Talisman] (15) Wint 95-96, p. 100-101.
3514. LAZER, Hank
"Displayspace 4." [NewOR] (21:2) Sum 95, p. 58-61.
3515. LAZO, Arturo
"By the Sea" (tr. by Luciano P. Díaz). [Arc] (35) Aut 95, p. 23.
"Light and I" (tr. by Luciano P. Díaz). [Arc] (35) Aut 95, p. 24.
Le ...
See also names beginning with "Le" without the following space, filed below in
their alphabetic positions, e.g., LeFEVRE.
3516. LE, Thi May
"Leaving" (tr. by Nguyen Ba Chung). [Manoa] (7:2) Wint 95, p. 99.
"Poem of a Garden" (tr. by Nguyen Ba Chung and Kevin Bowen). [Manoa] (7:2)
Wint 95, p. 98.
"Wind and Widow" (tr. by Nguyen Ba Chung). [Manoa] (7:2) Wint 95, p. 97.
3517. Le BEL, Natasha
"Blind Man Studying His Lover." [HangL] (66) 95, p. 82.
"Boxing the Female." [HangL] (66) 95, p. 84-85.
"Foot Fire Burn Dance." [HangL] (66) 95, p. 83.
3518. Le DRESSAY, Anne
"Born Again ... and Again ... and Again." [Event] (24:2) Sum 95, p. 25-26.
3519. Le ZOTTE, Ann Claremont
"Amanda." [BellArk] (11:2) Mr-Ap 95, p. 24.
"Annie Fischer." [PlumR] (9) [95 or 96], p. 103.
"The Beginning of Deaf Poetry in America." [BellArk] (11:2) Mr-Ap 95, p. 24.
"In that City." [BellArk] (11:1) Ja-F 95, p. 11.
"Minimal Language Skills." [PlumR] (9) [95 or 96], p. 102.
"My House." [BellArk] (11:2) Mr-Ap 95, p. 24.
"A Paper Crane for Sadako Sasaki." [BellArk] (11:2) Mr-Ap 95, p. 24.
3520. LEA, Sydney
"Fourth of July." [SouthernR] (31:4) O/Aut 95, p. 890-896.
"Mudtime in the County." [VirQR] (71:4) Aut 95, p. 695-696.
"Peaceable Kingdom." [Salm] (108) Fall 95, p. 85-86.
"R.N., Women's Ward." [Salm] (108) Fall 95, p. 87-88.
"The Right Words in April." [VirQR] (71:4) Aut 95, p. 693-695.
"To the Bone." [GeoR] (49:4) Wint 95, p. 918-930.

3521. LEAHY, Anna
"After the Challenger." [QW] (41) Aut-Wint 95-96, p. 268-269.
3522. LEASE, Joseph
"Creases." [ColR] (22:2) Fall 95, p. 134-136.
"For Ada Levin Dubovik." [GreensboroR] (57) Wint 94-95, p. 103-104.
"Slivovitz" (for David Shapiro). [Talisman] (15) Wint 95-96, p. 132-136.
3523. LEAVITT, Michele
"I've Been a Good Father." [AnthNEW] (7) 95, p. 19.
LeBEL, Natasha
See Le BEL, Natasha
3524. LeBLANC, Diane
"The Relatives." [CapeR] (30:1) Spr 95, p. 11.
"Touch." [AnthNEW] (7) 95, p. 34.
3525. LeBLANC, Jean
"One Day the World Was Flat." [LullwaterR] (6:2) Fall-Wint 95, p. 96.
3526. LeBOX, Annette
"A Perfectly Happy Woman." [Event] (24:2) Sum 95, p. 24.
3527. LEBRE, Jacques
"Décembre." [Os] (40) 95, p. 11-13.
3528. LEBRE, Marcia
"To a Bosnian Gunman." [CharR] (21:2) Fall 95, p. 102.
3529. LECHAY, Dan
"In Limelight." [SouthwR] (80:1) Wint 95, p. 99-100.
3530. LECKIE, Ross
"The Unity of Art and Experience" (for Eleanor Cook). [AntigR] (102/103) Sum-
Aug 95, p. 46-52.
3531. LECKNER, Carole H.
"For 'Reindeer Moon'" (for Elizabeth Marshall Thomas author of "Reindeer Moon").
[Descant] (26:1, #88) Spr 95, p. 27.
"The Hunt for Ideas" (for Robert Kroetsch). [Descant] (26:1, #88) Spr 95, p. 28-30.
"The Silence We Speak." [Descant] (26:1, #88) Spr 95, p. 23-26.
3532. LeCOEUR, Jo
"Dead Man in the Woods (Hungry Husband at the Table)." [LouisL] (12:2) Fall 95,
p. 79-80.
"Gifted." [LouisL] (12:2) Fall 95, p. 81.
"Red Hot Gone Blue." [LouisL] (12:2) Fall 95, p. 77-78.
"Sleeping with a LRRP Will Make You Crazy." [Border] (6) Spr-Sum 95, p. 51-52.
3533. LECUYER, Tess
"Crow Feather." [SnailPR] (3:2) 95, p. 18.
"The Woman Who Swallowed." [13thMoon] (13:1/2) 95, p. 25.
3534. LEDBETTER, Sarah Broyles
"Life Story." [InterPR] (21:1) Spr 95, p. 95.
"Snapshot of the River Arno." [InterPR] (21:1) Spr 95, p. 94.
3535. LEDERER, Ann Neuser
"La Belle Province." [Wind] (76) Fall 95, p. 20.
"Caves and Towers." [Wind] (76) Fall 95, p. 19.
3536. LEDERER, Katherine
"The Language of Flowers" (After Bataille). [MinnR] (43/44) 95, p. 73.
"The Musical Theorist." [MinnR] (43/44) 95, p. 73.
"Potlatch." [MinnR] (43/44) 95, p. 72.
"Public Square." [MinnR] (43/44) 95, p. 72.
"What she said it was important — it came up." [HarvardR] (9) Fall 95, p. 62.
LeDRESSAY, Anne
See Le DRESSAY, Anne
3537. LEDWELL, Wendy Moore
"The Country Store Politicians." [Pembroke] (27) 95, p. 17.
3538. LEE, Angel
"Untitled: I am here u r there they say" (WritersCorps Project, Washington, DC).
[WashR] (21:2) Ag-S 95, p. 21.
3539. LEE, David
"The Legend of the Monster in 2 Draw." [Witness] (9:2) 95, p. 90.
3540. LEE, David Dodd
"Shot by Boy, Hawkins and Lee Die in a Flooded Quarry." [CutB] (42) Sum 94, p.
45-46.
3541. LEE, James B.
"Aubade" (WritersCorps Project, Washington, DC). [WashR] (21:2) Ag-S 95, p. 22.

3542. LEE, John B.
"As Free as Farm Dogs Used to Be." [Dandel] (22:1) 95, p. 64.
3543. LEE, Linda Caldwell
"Of Permanence, Change and Purpose." [HopewellR] (7) 95, p. 105.
3544. LEE, Priscilla
"Midwife." [KenR] (17:2) Spr 95, p. 17.
"Prayers to Buddha." [KenR] (17:2) Spr 95, p. 16-17.
"What My Grandfather Sang." [CreamCR] (19:1) Spr 95, p. 133.
"Wishbone." [CreamCR] (19:1) Spr 95, p. 132.
3545. LEE, Richard E.
"Funeral for a Tooth." [Pearl] (22) Fall-Wint 95, p. 48.
"Lunch Stop in This Ghost Town." [Pearl] (22) Fall-Wint 95, p. 49.
"News Item: 'Most married people talk to each other about 7 1/2 minutes a day.'"
    [Pearl] (22) Fall-Wint 95, p. 49.
"Thin Hymns (Fat Haiku)" (4 poems). [Pearl] (22) Fall-Wint 95, p. 50.
"To the Student Who Wrote 'Udder Shock' When He Meant Utter Shock." [Pearl]
    (22) Fall-Wint 95, p. 50.
3546. LEE, Sul-Ju
"Flower Vendor" (tr. by Chang Soo Ko). [Vis] (47) 95, p. 27.
3547. LEE, Tina Yun
"Joan of Arc." [Kalliope] (17:2) 95, p. 26-27.
3548. LEEDAHL, Shelley A.
"Jackhammer Crew, Idylwyld Bridge, Summer 1994." [Grain] (23:1) Sum 95, p. 57.
3549. LEEN, Mary K.
"Blue Landscape Gardener." [IllinoisR] (3:1/2) Fall 95-Spr 96, p. 81.
"Women in the Kitchen." [IllinoisR] (3:1/2) Fall 95-Spr 96, p. 64.
3550. LEFCOWITZ, Barbara F.
"Sarabande." [PoetL] (90:3) Fall 95, p. 51.
3551. LEFEVRE, André
"Light" (tr. of Yaak Karsunke). [TriQ] (93) Spr-Sum 95, p. 121.
"Long Afterwards" (tr. of Yaak Karsunke). [TriQ] (93) Spr-Sum 95, p. 120.
"Rather Free, after Brecht" (tr. of Yaak Karsunke). [TriQ] (93) Spr-Sum 95, p. 123.
"To the Beloved Dead" (tr. of Yaak Karsunke). [TriQ] (93) Spr-Sum 95, p. 122.
3552. LeFLORE, Shirley
"Drum." [RiverS] (42/43) 95, p. 30.
3553. LeFORGE, P. V.
"Bearded." [Interim] (14:2) Fall-Wint 95-96, p. 3.
"Flames" (L.A. Riots, 1992). [SouthernPR] (35:1) Sum 95, p. 10-11.
"Food Rut." [Interim] (14:2) Fall-Wint 95-96, p. 4-5.
3554. LEFTWICH, Jim
"Alto Ossia" (4 selections). [NewOR] (21:2) Sum 95, p. 64-65.
3555. LEGGO, Carl
"How Boats Are Built" (Literary Festival: Poetry: Honorable Mention). [EngJ]
    (84:4) Ap 95, p. 44.
"Lessons from Childhood." [AntigR] (102/103) Sum-Aug 95, p. 103-104.
"My Mother's House." [AntigR] (102/103) Sum-Aug 95, p. 105-106.
3556. LEGGOTT, Michele
"Every Bravery Coming Stars Love's Heartfelt Red." [WestCL] (29:2, #17) Fall 95,
    p. 132-133.
3557. LEGRIS, Sylvia
"Deep Snow." [Grain] (23:1) Sum 95, p. 85.
"Fallout." [Event] (24:3) Wint 95-96, p. 46-47.
"My Mother's Hands." [Event] (24:3) Wint 95-96, p. 45.
3558. LEHMAN, David
"Boy with Red Hair." [ParisR] (37:137) Wint 95, p. 255-257.
"Breeze Marine." [AmerPoR] (24:4) Jl-Ag 95, p. 21.
"The Choice." [AmerPoR] (24:4) Jl-Ag 95, p. 20.
"Eleventh Hour." [Ploughs] (21:4) Wint 95-96, p. 105.
"Fifth Amendment." [Ploughs] (21:4) Wint 95-96, p. 102.
"Madison Avenue." [AmerPoR] (24:4) Jl-Ag 95, p. 20.
"The Magician." [AmerPoR] (24:4) Jl-Ag 95, p. 21.
"Ninth Inning." [Ploughs] (21:4) Wint 95-96, p. 103.
"The Shield of a Greeting" (for J.A.). [Verse] (12:2) 95, p. 86.
"Tenth Commandment." [Ploughs] (21:4) Wint 95-96, p. 104.
"Times Square." [AmerPoR] (24:4) Jl-Ag 95, p. 20.
"Toward a Definition of Love." [MichQR] (34:4) Fall 95, p. 595-596.

"Twelfth Night." [Ploughs] (21:4) Wint 95-96, p. 106.
"Wedding Song." [ParisR] (37:137) Wint 95, p. 257.
"The World Trade Center." [ParisR] (37:136) Fall 95, p. 74.
3559. LEHR, Genevieve
"Christmas, 1993." [TickleAce] (27) Spr-Sum 94, p. 39.
"How Solitude Entered." [TickleAce] (27) Spr-Sum 94, p. 37.
"Pilé Moy" (for my daughter). [TickleAce] (27) Spr-Sum 94, p. 38.
3560. LEI-LANILAU, Carolyn
"Reconciling Hawaiian and Chinese in English." [NewAW] (13) Fall-Wint 95, p.
102.
"Saa Shi Mee." [NewAW] (13) Fall-Wint 95, p. 101.
3561. LEIBOWITZ, Roz
"And This Is the Way We Bury Our Lizard Baby Still, Soft in the Night." [Kalliope]
(17:1) 95, p. 18-19.
3562. LEIBY, Jeanne M.
"The Hungry Self." [PassN] (16:1) Sum 95, p. 18.
"Kjerringa." [PassN] (16:1) Sum 95, p. 19.
3563. LEIGHTTY, David
"With a Field Guide to Trees" (Red River Gorge, Wolfe County, Kentucky).
[CumbPR] (14:2) Spr 95, p. 28.
3564. LEITHAUSER, Brad
"After the Detonation of the Moon." [NewYRB] (42:3) 16 F 95, p. 29.
"Plus the Fact of You." [NewYorker] (71:24) 14 Ag 95, p. 50-51.
3565. LELAND, Kurt
"Adagio for Strings" (music of Samuel Barber). [CumbPR] (14:2) Spr 95, p. 8-9.
"At the Matisse Retrospective" (improvisations on a theme of Wallace Stevens).
[CumbPR] (14:2) Spr 95, p. 10-11.
"Entrance." [BelPoJ] (45:3) Spr 95, p. 18-19.
"The Garden Sibyl." [BelPoJ] (45:3) Spr 95, p. 20-21.
3566. LeMOINE, Frances
"Requiem." [Vis] (49) 95, p. 23.
3567. LENHART, Michael
"After the Party." [FreeL] (14) Wint 95, p. 12.
3568. LENIER, Sue
"In Praise of the Death of a Child." [GrandS] (13:3, #51) Wint 95, p. 222.
"The Late Foxes." [GrandS] (13:3, #51) Wint 95, p. 223-224.
3569. LENIHAN, Dan
"Evelyn Gets a Coupe de Ville." [WormR] (35:2, #138) 95, p. 59-60.
"Four Days Sloppy Drunk." [WormR] (35:2, #138) 95, p. 60-61.
"Riparian Blues." [WormR] (35:2, #138) 95, p. 58-59.
3570. LENSON, David
"A Cold Morning in July." [SouthernPR] (35:1) Sum 95, p. 48-49.
3571. LENT, Ernest
"Will Power." [Vis] (49) 95, p. 38-39.
3572. LENZ, Erika
"Breath: A Definition" (1995 Guy Owen Poetry Prize, Diane Wakoski, judge).
[SouthernPR] (35:2) Wint 95, p. 5-6.
"Sotto Voce." [MidAR] (15:1/2) 95, p. 307-308.
3573. LEONHARDT, Kenneth
"The Aimless Headless Horseman." [Light] (15/16) Aut-Wint 95-96, p. 15.
"A great lake is Superior." [Light] (14) Sum 95, p. 24.
"Greetings from the White Cliffs." [Light] (15/16) Aut-Wint 95-96, p. 25.
"Mootant Ninja Poem." [Light] (13) Spr 95, p. 20.
"Poetic Lie Sense" (by ?). [Light] (13) Spr 95, p. 17.
"Seafaring the fair Bering Sea." [Light] (15/16) Aut-Wint 95-96, p. 34.
"What I Gave Up for Lint" [sic]. [Light] (13) Spr 95, p. 9.
"Wry Bred." [Bogg] (67) 95, p. 61.
3574. LEONIN, Mia
"Miss Sue." [Witness] (9:2) 95, p. 80-81.
3575. LEOPOLD, Nikia
"Morning." [AmerS] (64:2) Spr 95, p. 206.
3576. LePAN, Douglas
"Macalister, or Dying in the Dark" (a fiction based on what is known of his life and
fate. Excerpts: 1-2, 9-10). [Quarry] (44:1) 95, p. 15-40.
3577. LEPIONKA, Mary Ellen
"Glory Seekers." [DefinedP] (2:1) Fall-Wint 93, p. 5-6.

3578. LesCARBEAU, Mitchell
"Feeding the Flame." [WestB] (36) 95, p. 101-102.
"The Persistence of Polytheism in Everyday Life." [HawaiiR] (19:2) Fall 95, p. 50-51.
"Under the Apple Tree." [HawaiiR] (19:2) Fall 95, p. 47.
"A Visit to the Holy Land." [LitR] (38:2) Wint 95, p. 196.
"Waiting for Persephone." [HawaiiR] (19:2) Fall 95, p. 48-49.
3579. LESLIE, Naton
"By Eye." [CharR] (21:1) Spr 95, p. 87.
"Don't Be Too Quick to Judge Me" (after Hank Williams with Bud Shrecengost on fiddle). [WestB] (36) 95, p. 65-66.
"Flint-Knapping." [CharR] (21:1) Spr 95, p. 85.
"I Saw the Light" (after Hank Williams). [WestB] (36) 95, p. 64-65.
"Mind Your Own Business" (after Hank Williams). [WestB] (36) 95, p. 66-67.
"The Saint Alive." [MidAR] (16:1) 95, p. 14.
"Straight-Backed Chairs." [CharR] (21:1) Spr 95, p. 86.
3580. LESSEN, Laurie Suzanne
"Riding the Raven" (from *Dance of the Carbon-Atom*). [AmerPoR] (24:4) Jl-Ag 95, p. 22.
3581. LESSER, Rika
"A Death" (tr. of Birgitta Trotzig). [ManhatR] (7:2) Wint 95, p. 30.
"In a dark tree, a green caterpillar, creeping" (tr. of Birgitta Trotzig). [ManhatR] (7:2) Wint 95, p. 33.
"In Jerusalem's implacable bedrock Adam's bones are buried" (tr. of Birgitta Trotzig). [ManhatR] (7:2) Wint 95, p. 31.
"My Sister Life" (tr. of Birgitta Trotzig). [ManhatR] (7:2) Wint 95, p. 32.
"Snow: the old Jewish cemetery in Prague" (tr. of Birgitta Trotzig). [ManhatR] (7:2) Wint 95, p. 29.
3582. LESTER, A. B.
"The Hot One" (w. L.H., WritersCorps Program, Dinner Program for Homeless Women, Washington, DC). [WashR] (21:2) Ag-S 95, p. 8.
"Packing Up the Pieces" (WritersCorps Program, Washington, DC). [WashR] (21:2) Ag-S 95, p. 8.
3583. LETELIER-RUZ, Elías
"On Leave in Managua" (tr. by Ken Norris). [Arc] (35) Aut 95, p. 70.
"Theory of the Shoes" (tr. by Ken Norris). [Arc] (35) Aut 95, p. 68.
"The Winter Where I Live" (to Osvaldo Nuñez, the traitor MP, tr. by Ken Norris). [Arc] (35) Aut 95, p. 69.
3584. LETKEMANN, Susan Rempel
"The Absence of Seasons." [PoetryC] (15:2) Je 95, p. 27.
3585. LEUZZI, Tony
"On Tuesday" (Photo by Bao Dam). [Gerbil] (4) Fall 95, p. 25.
"Snake-Hip Waltz" (for Bob DeFelice, image by Brad Pease). [Gerbil] (4) Fall 95, p. 9.
LEV, Dina Ben
See BEN-LEV, Dina
3586. LEVENTHAL, Ann Z.
"During the White Hours." [Kalliope] (17:1) 95, p. 76.
3587. LEVERICH, Anita
"Rope." [Flyway] (1:2) Fall 95, p. 18.
3588. LEVERING, Donald
"The Church of Feet on Wheels." [OxfordM] (10:1) Wint 94-Spr 95, p. 45.
3589. LEVERING, Jason
"Denmark." [Plain] (16:1) Fall 95, p. 19.
3590. LEVERTOV, Denise
"Altars." [Image] (9) Spr 95, p. 43.
"The Beginning of Wisdom." [AmerPoR] (24:5) S-O 95, p. 3.
"The Change." [SenR] (25:2) Fall 95, p. 6.
"Complaint and Rejoinder." [AmerPoR] (24:5) S-O 95, p. 4.
"Crow Spring." [AmerPoR] (24:5) S-O 95, p. 4.
"The Danger Moments." [AmerPoR] (24:5) S-O 95, p. 3.
"Firmament" (From a photograph by Mary Randlett). [BelPoJ] (45:4) Chapbook 22, Sum 95, p. 48.
"For Steve Blevins." [AmerPoR] (24:5) S-O 95, p. 4.
"A Gift." [AmerPoR] (24:5) S-O 95, p. 4.
"In Question." [SycamoreR] (7:2) Sum 95, p. 29.

"In Whom We Live and Move and Have Our Being." [Image] (9) Spr 95, p. 42.
"Link." [SenR] (25:1) Spr 95, p. 106-107.
"Pentimento." [AmerPoR] (24:5) S-O 95, p. 5.
"The Prayer Plant (Maranta Leuconeura)." [Image] (9) Spr 95, p. 42.
"Sheep in the Weeds" (from a photo by Mary Randlett). [SycamoreR] (7:2) Sum 95,
    p. 27.
"Threat" (from a photo by Mary Randlett). [SycamoreR] (7:2) Sum 95, p. 28.
"Wall." [AmerPoR] (24:5) S-O 95, p. 5.
"Writer and Reader." [AmerPoR] (24:5) S-O 95, p. 4.
3591. LEVI, Jan Heller
    "Here at the Lip of the Generous." [GrahamHR] (19) Wint 95-96, p. 26.
    "The Second Movement of Anything." [GrahamHR] (19) Wint 95-96, p. 24-25.
3592. LEVIN, Dana
    "Ambulance." [LiteralL] (1:4) Ja-F 95, p. 22.
3593. LEVIN, David
    "Ralph Ellison." [Callaloo] (18:2) Spr 95, p. 272.
3594. LEVIN, John
    "4th Floor." [WormR] (35:1, #137) 95, p. 37.
    "Advice from a Father without Children." [WormR] (35:1, #137) 95, p. 36.
    "Borrow." [WormR] (35:1, #137) 95, p. 30-31.
    "Buster Keaton May Have Been a Comedian to Some." [WormR] (35:1, #137) 95,
        p. 28.
    "Cagney." [WormR] (35:1, #137) 95, p. 28.
    "Caught Offguard." [WormR] (35:1, #137) 95, p. 39-40.
    "A Couple of Welshmen." [WormR] (35:1, #137) 95, p. 37-38.
    "Don't Quite Know How She Swung It." [WormR] (35:1, #137) 95, p. 30.
    "A Fast Glance at Orson Welles." [WormR] (35:1, #137) 95, p. 33-34.
    "For You Ambrose." [WormR] (35:1, #137) 95, p. 32.
    "A Framed Color Photo Tells Him the Whole Story." [WormR] (35:1, #137) 95, p.
        29-30.
    "Good Advice Can Turn Up Just About Anywhere." [WormR] (35:1, #137) 95, p.
        33.
    "Guys & Dolls." [WormR] (35:1, #137) 95, p. 35.
    "Have You Seen the Misfits Lately?" [WormR] (35:1, #137) 95, p. 38-39.
    "I'll Blame It on the Hollywood Blockade." [WormR] (35:1, #137) 95, p. 32.
    "The Improbabilities." [WormR] (35:1, #137) 95, p. 31.
    "Jack Nicholson." [WormR] (35:1, #137) 95, p. 29.
    "Noiret." [WormR] (35:1, #137) 95, p. 38.
    "One for Transformation." [WormR] (35:1, #137) 95, p. 38.
    "One Night at the Colonial Theatre." [WormR] (35:1, #137) 95, p. 35-36.
    "One of the Big Five." [WormR] (35:1, #137) 95, p. 27.
    "One of Them Years." [WormR] (35:1, #137) 95, p. 36.
    "One Way to Get Through It." [WormR] (35:1, #137) 95, p. 25.
    "Oops." [WormR] (35:1, #137) 95, p. 25.
    "Pamplona, '67." [WormR] (35:1, #137) 95, p. 31-32.
    "Playback." [WormR] (35:1, #137) 95, p. 26-27.
    "Put to the Test." [WormR] (35:1, #137) 95, p. 40.
    "The Real Meaning of Rosebud." [WormR] (35:1, #137) 95, p. 34.
    "Something to That Effect." [WormR] (35:1, #137) 95, p. 33.
    "A Suitcase the Color of Dark Mustard." [WormR] (35:1, #137) 95, p. 26.
    "Those Long Gut-Busting Laughs." [WormR] (35:1, #137) 95, p. 36.
    "When You're Out There" (Special Section: 33 poems). [WormR] (35:1, #137) 95,
        p. 25-40.
    "You Have the Right to Remain Silent." [WormR] (35:1, #137) 95, p. 31.
    "Young Billy Young." [WormR] (35:1, #137) 95, p. 34-35.
3595. LEVIN, Philip Dane
    "Terminal Ward." [Flyway] (1:2) Fall 95, p. 50-51.
3596. LEVIN, Phillis
    "After Dinner." [PlumR] (8) [95], p. 23.
    "Aphorisms of Nature." [WestHR] (49:2) Sum 95, p. 143-144.
    "Brief Bio." [NewYorker] (71:7) 10 Ap 95, p. 80.
    "Moira." [NewYorker] (71:28) 18 S 95, p. 46.
    "The Peddler." [Nat] (258:3) 24 Ja 94, p. 104.
    "Possessions." [WestHR] (49:2) Sum 95, p. 145-146.
    "Prologue / Epilogue." [WestHR] (49:2) Sum 95, p. 144.

3597. LEVIN, Susan
"Mexico Blue, Azul." [NewAW] (13) Fall-Wint 95, p. 137.
LEVINE, Judy Katz
See KATZ-LEVINE, Judy
3598. LEVINE, Julia (Julia B.)
"At the Vernal Pools." [PraS] (69:2) Sum 95, p. 29.
"The Distance Apart from Her." [SouthernPR] (35:2) Wint 95, p. 48-51.
"Overdue." [PraS] (69:2) Sum 95, p. 30.
3599. LEVINE, Mark
"Program Music." [NewAW] (13) Fall-Wint 95, p. 93-94.
3600. LEVINE, Miriam
"Aaron's Retreat." [PoetL] (90:4) Wint 95-96, p. 26.
"Cannibal." [PoetL] (90:4) Wint 95-96, p. 25.
"Mother After Surgery." [Poem] (74) N 95, p. 56.
"Wheelchair Racer." [Poem] (74) N 95, p. 57.
3601. LEVINE, Philip
"1953." [Nat] (260:1) 2 Ja 95, p. 31.
"Ask the Snow." [Nat] (258:12) 28 Mr 94, p. 427.
"The Dead." [Ploughs] (21:4) Wint 95-96, p. 126-127.
"Dreaming in Swedish." [Nat] (258:4) 31 Ja 94, p. 139.
"Gin." [Zyzzyva] (11:3/4, #43/44) 95, "The Best of Ten Years of ZYZZYVA," p.
    54-56.
"The Harbor at Nevermind, 1915." [TriQ] (95) Wint 95-96, p. 83-84.
"On the Run." [TriQ] (95) Wint 95-96, p. 86-87.
"Out of Work and Out of Luck." [TriQ] (95) Wint 95-96, p. 88.
"The Return: Orihuela, 1965" (for Miguel Hernandez). [Nat] (258:6) 14 F 94, p.
    211.
"The Seven Doors." [TriQ] (95) Wint 95-96, p. 85.
3602. LEVINE, Suzanne Jill
"Beloved Friend" (tr. of Cecilia Vicuña). [AmerPoR] (24:3) My-Je 95, p. 18-19.
"Mother & Daughter" (tr. of Cecilia Vicuña). [AmerPoR] (24:3) My-Je 95, p. 19.
3603. LEVINSON, James Heller
"Birdsong." [SmPd] (32:2, #94) Spr 95, p. 23-24.
"In the Cimitiere de Montparnasse There Are No Dead." [DogRR] (14:1, #27) Sum
    95, p. 21-23.
"Reach." [SmPd] (32:2, #94) Spr 95, p. 22.
3604. LEVINSON, Zev
"The Last Valley of the Day." [InterPR] (21:1) Spr 95, p. 72.
"Resummer." [GreensboroR] (57) Wint 94-95, p. 63.
3605. LEVITIN, Alexis
"Absence" (tr. of Eugenio de Andrade). [QW] (41) Aut-Wint 95-96, p. 212.
"Adam and Eve" (tr. of Egito Gonçalves). [InterPR] (21:1) Spr 95, p. 41.
"Almost Haiku" (tr. of Eugenio de Andrade). [JamesWR] (12:1) Wint 95, p. 8.
"The Angel of the Clock / Chartres" (tr. of Egito Gonçalves). [SilverFR] (25) Sum
    95, p. 42.
"Authenticity" (tr. of Fiama Hasse Pais Brandão). [PraS] (69:1) Spr 95, p. 151.
"Between Two Blades" (tr. of Eugenio de Andrade). [MidAR] (15:1/2) 95, p. 235.
"Birthday Prose" (tr. of Eugenio de Andrade). [ConnPR] (14:1) 95, p. 16.
"Breakfast in Maspalomas" (tr. of Eugenio de Andrade). [SnailPR] (3:2) 95, p. 8.
"Close to the Aviary" (tr. of Fiama Hasse Pais Brandão). [SenR] (25:2) Fall 95, p.
    58.
"Close to the Earth" (tr. of Eugenio de Andrade). [MidAR] (15:1/2) 95, p. 236.
"Close to the Peasant" (tr. of Fiama Hasse Pais Brandão). [SenR] (25:2) Fall 95, p.
    56.
"A Dog, the Sea" (tr. of Fiama Hasse Pais Brandao). [GrahamHR] (19) Wint 95-96,
    p. 69.
"Elisabeta" (tr. of Egito Gonçalves). [SilverFR] (25) Sum 95, p. 45.
"Encirclement" (tr. of Eugenio de Andrade). [ConnPR] (14:1) 95, p. 14.
"Epitaph for a Sailor Dying Young" (tr. of Eugenio de Andrade). [OxfordM] (10:1)
    Wint 94-Spr 95, p. 10.
"Fingers play with the March light" (tr. of Eugenio Andrade). [Os] (41) 95, p. 5.
"Flush with the Ground" (tr. of Eugenio de Andrade). [ConnPR] (14:1) 95, p. 17.
"La Havana" (tr. of Egito Gonçalves). [SilverFR] (25) Sum 95, p. 43.
"Homage to Hans Christian Andersen" (tr. of Eugenio de Andrade). [SnailPR] (3:2)
    95, p. 9.
"I work the frail and bitter" (tr. of Eugenio Andrade). [Os] (41) 95, p. 3.

"Light and Shadow" (tr. of Fiama Hasse Pais Brandão). [SenR] (25:2) Fall 95, p. 57.
"Maspalomas, Without Nostalgia" (tr. of Eugenio de Andrade). [ConnPR] (14:1) 95,
p. 15.
"Minor Sonnet on the Arrival of Summer" (tr. of Eugenio de Andrade). [Confr]
(56/57) Sum-Fall 95, p. 309.
"The naked body, almost strange" (tr. of Eugenio Andrade). [Os] (41) 95, p. 5.
"Number 7 from *Dedikation*" (tr. of Egito Gonçalves). [PoetryE] (39) Fall 94, p.
106.
"Number 10 from *Dedikation*" (tr. of Egito Gonçalves). [PoetryE] (39) Fall 94, p.
107.
"October: Wine" (tr. of Eugenio de Andrade). [InterQ] (2:1/2) 95, p. 155.
"La Picolla Madona" (tr. of Egito Gonçalves). [SilverFR] (25) Sum 95, p. 44.
"The Power of Literature" (tr. of Egito Gonçalves). [HarvardR] (9) Fall 95, p. 29.
"Seven Swords for a Melancholia" (tr. of Eugenio de Andrade). [PoetL] (90:1) Spr
95, p. 39.
"The Shadow of Two Dogs" (tr. of Fiama Hasse Pais Brandão). [PraS] (69:1) Spr
95, p. 152.
"A Time in Which One Dies" (tr. of Eugenio de Andrade). [SycamoreR] (7:1) Wint
95, p. 41.
"To make a boat from a word" (tr. of Eugenio Andrade). [Os] (41) 95, p. 3.
"A Tower" (tr. of Eugenio de Andrade). [InterQ] (2:1/2) 95, p. 155.
"Until Tomorrow" (tr. of Eugenio de Andrade). [NowestR] (33:2) 95, p. 37.
"Untitled: A woman's face" (tr. of Egito Gonçalves). [SilverFR] (25) Sum 95, p. 41.
"Urgently" (tr. of Eugenio de Andrade). [NowestR] (33:2) 95, p. 36.
"Youth" (tr. of Eugenio de Andrade). [NowestR] (33:2) 95, p. 35.
3606. LEVY, Andrew
"Song From My Family" (Excerpt). [Chain] (2) Spr 95, p. 128-131.
3607. LEVY, Howard
"The Doctor." [PraS] (69:3) Fall 95, p. 53-54.
"Early Morning Song" (for Sam and Nathaniel). [PraS] (69:3) Fall 95, p. 54-55.
"A Poem about Furniture" (for Baron Wormser). [Thrpny] (60) Wint 95, p. 33.
3608. LEW, Walter K.
"Yusejang (CBS News in Seoul)." [Chain] (2) Spr 95, p. 132.
3609. LEWIS, Gwyneth
"Pentecost." [Jacaranda] (11) [95 or 96?], p. 146-147.
"Pentecost." [ParisR] (37:135) Sum 95, p. 39-40.
"The Telegraph Baby: 1916." [NewRep] (212:3 [i.e. 4]) 23 Ja 95, p. 44.
3610. LEWIS, J. Patrick
"Among the literati of the Thames" (Third Prize, 3rd Annual River Rhyme
Competition). [Light] (13) Spr 95, p. 24.
"And God Made the Animals." [Light] (14) Sum 95, p. 22.
"Beneath a Shady Tree." [Light] (13) Spr 95, p. 7.
"Home Poem" (Or, The Sad Dog Song). [Light] (13) Spr 95, p. 20.
"How My Father Flew." [NewRena] (9:2, #28) Spr 95, p. 47.
"Ngan Do in Grosse Pointe." [NewRena] (9:2, #28) Spr 95, p. 45-46.
3611. LEWIS, Lisa
"The Young." [Agni] (42) 95, p. 56-57.
3612. LEWIS, R.
"The Planting." [Blueline] (16) 95, p. 79.
3613. LEWIS, Tene'
"I am Tene' A sexy cat" (WritersCorps Program, Washington, DC). [WashR] (21:2)
Ag-S 95, p. 16.
"Neighborhood Poem" (WritersCorps Program, Washington, DC). [WashR] (21:2)
Ag-S 95, p. 16.
"Untitled: All alone in my room staring at the wall" (w. Natasha Norris and Lawan
Chatman. WritersCorps Program, Washington, DC). [WashR] (21:2) Ag-S
95, p. 16.
3614. LEWIS-BEY, Veronica
"Rise, Sister, Rise" (WritersCorps Project, Washington, DC). [WashR] (21:2) Ag-S
95, p. 21.
3615. LEWYN, Gloria
"Grandfather." [SantaBR] (3:3) Fall-Wint 95, p. 29.
"Pas de Shoes." [SantaBR] (3:3) Fall-Wint 95, p. 31.
"Summer's Lease." [SantaBR] (3:3) Fall-Wint 95, p. 30.
"Variations on a Wash Stick." [SantaBR] (3:3) Fall-Wint 95, p. 28.

LeZOTTE, Ann Claremont
 See Le ZOTTE, Ann Claremont
3616. LI, He
 "Love Song" (to the tune "Digging a Well in the Back Garden," tr. by Jodi Varon).
  [YellowS] (12:4, #48) Sum 95, p. 12.
 "Song: Sitting Through the Night" (tr. by Jodi Varon). [YellowS] (12:4, #48) Sum
  95, p. 13.
3617. LI, Min Hua
 "Windshield, Poem Left on Gwailo's." [Footwork] (24/25) 95, p. 45.
3618. LI, Po (701-762)
 "Resentment Near the Jade Steps" (tr. by Sam Hamill). [PoetryE] (41) Aut 95, p. 19.
 "The River-Merchant's Wife: A Second Letter" (tr. by Keith Aubrey and Deng Yan).
  [GrahamHR] (19) Wint 95-96, p. 79.
 "Viewing the Waterfall on Mt. Lu" (tr. by Keith Aubrey and Deng Yan).
  [GrahamHR] (19) Wint 95-96, p. 80.
 "We Three" (tr. by David W. Landrum). [Hellas] (6:1) Spr-Sum 95, p. 21.
3619. LI, Qi (690?-754)
 "Listening to Dong Tinglan Play His New Guitar Composition for Minister Fang"
  (tr. by Keith Aubrey and Deng Yan). [Chelsea] (59) 95, p. 132-133.
 "An Old Soldier's March" (tr. by Keith Aubrey and Deng Yan). [Chelsea] (59) 95, p.
  134.
3620. LI, Shang-yin
 "Sent North on a Rainy Night" (tr. by Keith Aubrey and Deng Yan). [GrahamHR]
  (19) Wint 95-96, p. 81.
3621. LIAO, Angela S.
 "Mystic Zither." [AmerS] (64:1) Wint 95, p. 68.
3622. LIARDET, Tim
 "A Gothic Screenplay." [CimR] (111) Ap 95, p. 61-62.
3623. LIBBY, Anthony
 "From the Lives of the Sweat Bee." [SantaBR] (3:2) Sum 95, p. 67.
3624. LICHTENSTEIN, Jesse
 "Summer Song of Puget Sound." [HarvardA] (vol. 130) Fall 95, p. 10.
3625. LIEBEGOTT, Ali
 "I Never Promised You an Opium Den" (Selections: IX, XI). [SinW] (55) Spr-Sum
  95, p. 28-29.
3626. LIEBENTHAL, Jean
 "Explorer." [Poetry] (166:3) Je 95, p. 143.
3627. LIEBERMAN, Laurence
 "Farewell to the Lost Music Scores." [DenQ] (29:4) Spr 95, p. 31-36.
 "Freedom Spurned." [CaribbeanW] (9) 95, p. 77-79.
 "The Legend of Rode Pan Well." [TarRP] (35:1) Fall 95, p. 4-6.
 "Names Scrawled on the Priests' Satin Robes." [CharR] (21:1) Spr 95, p. 78-81.
 "Romp of the Cave Healer." [Hudson] (48:3) Aut 95, p. 443-447.
 "Sleuths." [PartR] (62:1) Wint 95, p. 118-120.
 "Undying Loyalty" (Essequebo River, Guyana). [Nat] (260:4) 30 Ja 95, p. 141.
 "Urn Burial." [BelPoJ] (45:4) Chapbook 22, Sum 95, p. 49-51.
3628. LIEBERMAN, Michael
 "Bioenergetics." [ApalQ] (44/45) Fall 95-Wint 96, p. 64.
 "The Cure of Logic" (from *Goldin at Elmhurst*). [TexasR] (16:1/4) 95, p. 131.
 "The Examined Life" (from *Goldin at Elmhurst*). [TexasR] (16:1/4) 95, p. 132.
 "Glutathione Cycle" (runner up, 1994 Borderlands Poetry Contest). [Border] (6)
  Spr-Sum 95, p. 53.
 "Goldin Meditates on Providence" (from *Goldin at Elmhurst*). [TexasR] (16:1/4) 95,
  p. 133.
 "Hebrews" (from *Goldin at Elmhurst*). [TexasR] (16:1/4) 95, p. 134.
 "Homage in Kind" (for Weldon Kees, after an observation by Kenneth Rexroth).
  [TampaR] (11) Fall 95, p. 11.
 "Hudspeth's Patient" (from *Goldin at Elmhurst*). [TexasR] (16:1/4) 95, p. 135-6.
 "Lucky." [PraS] (69:4) Wint 95, p. 28.
 "The Phone Call" (from *Goldin at Elmhurst*). [TexasR] (16:1/4) 95, p. 137.
 "Regret." [PraS] (69:4) Wint 95, p. 28.
 "The Shape of Honshu." [ApalQ] (44/45) Fall 95-Wint 96, p. 63.
3629. LIEBERT, Daniel
 "The Pageant Consumes Its Materials." [BlackBR] (20) Spr-Sum 95, p. 25.
3630. LIEBMAN, Karen
 "In the Art Gallery." [CimR] (110) Ja 96, p. 71.

LIFSHIN

3631. LIES, Betty
"Moon Song." [US1] (30/31) 95, p. 2.
3632. LIETZ, Robert
"Kimberly, in Winter, Spring." [HiramPoR] (58/59) Spr 95-Wint 96, p. 45-47.
3633. LIFSHIN, Lyn
"All Is Vanity." [CreamCR] (19:1) Spr 95, p. 106.
"Annie." [ManyMM] (1:2) 95, p. 109.
"Bones Sticking Up Through Flesh." [Footwork] (24/25) 95, p. 15.
"Cezanne's Brunch." [InterPR] (21:2) Fall 95, p. 103.
"The Child We Will Not Have." [InterQ] (2:1/2) 95, p. 90.
"Cinder Mellow." [HiramPoR] (58/59) Spr 95-Wint 96, p. 48-49.
"Crystal Madonna." [Bogg] (67) 95, p. 9.
"D.P." [GreenHLL] (6) 95, p. 84.
"The Daughter I Don't Have." [HiramPoR] (58/59) Spr 95-Wint 96, p. 50.
"The Daughter I Don't Have." [WilliamMR] (33) 95, p. 87.
"The Doctor." [WindO] (59) Spr 95, p. 21.
"Dream of the Pink and Black Lace Scarf." [AntigR] (102/103) Sum-Aug 95, p. 132.
"Early." [NewYorkQ] (54) 95, p. 53.
"The Erotic Mirror" (from the Governor's Motor Inn). [CreamCR] (19:1) Spr 95, p. 104-105.
"Estelle, Star Stones." [DefinedP] (2:2) Spr-Sum 94, p. 26-27.
"Estelle, Star Stones." [ManyMM] (2:1) 95, p. 178-179.
"The First Atrocities." [NewYorkQ] (55) 95, p. 60.
"For Three Days Things Kept Changing." [CapeR] (30:1) Spr 95, p. 7.
"Ginger Ale." [BellR] (18:2, #38) Fall 95, p. 21.
"He Said He Was in the Men's Room at the Airport, a William Buckley Story." [NewYorkQ] (55) 95, p. 56-57.
"He Said in the Hospital It." [Sun] (238) O 95, p. 19.
"Hotel." [Footwork] (24/25) 95, p. 15.
"I Met Him on Death Row." [NewYorkQ] (55) 95, p. 61-63.
"I Take My Mother on a Stroll in D.C." [Border] (6) Spr-Sum 95, p. 54.
"In My Mother's Bedroom." [Sun] (230) F 95, p. 15.
"In My Mother's Suitcase, Unpacked Two Years After It Was Packed Before Her Ambulance Ride Down Here." [OxfordM] (9:2) Fall-Wint 93, p. 110-111.
"In Spite of the Expenses." [Footwork] (24/25) 95, p. 14-15.
"Juniper Smoke Still Scents the Canyon." [WormR] (35:1, #137) 95, p. 24.
"The Mad Girl Reads a Retired General's Account of Hiroshima the Day the Sky Was Bleached a Bright White." [HeavenB] (12) 95, p. 94.
"Madonna Who Picks Difficult Men." [WindO] (59) Spr 95, p. 20.
"Manoir Genest." [WormR] (35:1, #137) 95, p. 24.
"Marilyn Monroe Decides to Go Meet Elvis." [Pearl] (22) Fall-Wint 95, p. 125.
"Marilyn Monroe Reads How Hikers Find a Man Buried 5000 Years." [Pearl] (22) Fall-Wint 95, p. 125.
"The Messenger, a Disease Control Specialist with the Bureau of Sexually Transmitted Diseases." [WindO] (59) Spr 95, p. 21-22.
"Miss Holden." [Footwork] (24/25) 95, p. 14.
"Mother and Daughter Photos." [Witness] (9:1) 95, p. 31.
"My Father Leaves Vilnius." [InterQ] (2:1/2) 95, p. 91.
"My Mother and the Worms." [US1] (30/31) 95, p. 29.
"My Mother Says Goodby to the House." [Sun] (230) F 95, p. 15.
"My Mother's 70th Call This Month." [WindO] (59) Spr 95, p. 19.
"My Sister Says She Wants Me to Come and Read Through Thirty Years of Diaries." [DogRR] (14:1, #27) Sum 95, p. 28-29.
"Natasha with Her Bruised Toes." [ManyMM] (1:2) 95, p. 110.
"Other Septembers." [MidwQ] (37:1) Aut 95, p. 41.
"The Partner." [WindO] (59) Spr 95, p. 15-16.
"Picasso." [DogRR] (14:1, #27) Sum 95, p. 15.
"Pissaro." [WindO] (59) Spr 95, p. 19-20.
"Prayer Painting Dream Diaries." [HeavenB] (12) 95, p. 92-93.
"The Roses Startle." [DogRR] (14:1, #27) Sum 95, p. 29.
"She Waits Like Some Sharp Cheddar in the Pantry." [BellR] (18:2, #38) Fall 95, p. 22.
"So Many Bodies All Over." [NewYorkQ] (55) 95, p. 58-59.
"So Many Bodies All Over." [WindO] (60) Fall-Wint 95, p. 31-32.
"The Split Maple Buckles Near Porter Field." [PaintedB] (55/56) 95, p. 59-60.
"Thirty Miles West of Chicago." [SlipS] (15) 95, p. 65.

"Titianna and the Young Girls in Ballets with Names of Flowers and Smells."
[ManyMM] (1:2) 95, p. 111.
"What to Do the Third Day of Rain on Indian Mountain." [Border] (6) Spr-Sum 95,
p. 55.
"With You." [WilliamMR] (33) 95, p. 24.
"Zora Music" (Yugoslavian born painter imprisoned in Dachau for anti Nazi
activities). [WindO] (59) Spr 95, p. 16-18.
3634. LIGHT, Kate
"Mostly." [Hellas] (6:1) Spr-Sum 95, p. 67.
3635. LIGHT, Steve
"Anchises" (tr. of Jean Baptiste Para). [InterPR] (21:1) Spr 95, p. 33.
"Eros in Shadow's Mask" (tr. of Jean Baptiste Para). [InterPR] (21:1) Spr 95, p. 35.
"Front Lines" (tr. of Jean Baptiste Para). [InterPR] (21:1) Spr 95, p. 37.
"Parturition of Magia Polla or The Birth of Virgil" (tr. of Jean Baptiste Para).
[InterPR] (21:1) Spr 95, p. 31.
"Sibyl" (tr. of Jean Baptiste Para). [InterPR] (21:1) Spr 95, p. 35.
3636. LIGNELL, Kathleen
"The Flight of Quetzalcoatl" (For Toni de Gerez, Mexico, 1995). [NewEngR] (17:4)
Fall 95, p. 16-17.
3637. LIKE, Joseph
"The Late, Late Movie." [IllinoisR] (3:1/2) Fall 95-Spr 96, p. 25.
3638. LIKEN, Lisa
"Even Though They Were Both Ovo-Lacto Vegetarians." [Jacaranda] (11) [95 or
96?], p. 81-82.
3639. LILJEBLAD, Jonathan N.
"David." [SantaBR] (3:1) Spr 95, p. 59.
"The 'Other', or Thoughts Thinking About the Census." [SantaBR] (3:1) Spr 95, p.
58.
"Schooning (skipping stones)." [SantaBR] (3:1) Spr 95, p. 60-62.
3640. LILLY, Rebecca
"Castle Hill." [NewOR] (21:2) Sum 95, p. 36.
"The Corner Shop." [OxfordM] (10:1) Wint 94-Spr 95, p. 46.
"The Novel." [SycamoreR] (7:1) Wint 95, p. 50.
"Old Photographs." [IllinoisR] (3:1/2) Fall 95-Spr 96, p. 80.
"The Postcard." [SycamoreR] (7:1) Wint 95, p. 49.
"The Streetcorner." [SycamoreR] (7:1) Wint 95, p. 51.
LILLYWHITE, Eileen Silver
See SILVER-LILLYWHITE, Eileen
3641. LIM-WILSON, Fatima
"The Beginning of Things." [PraS] (69:3) Fall 95, p. 105.
"Prima Gravida." [Poetry] (165:6) Mr 95, p. 314-315.
"Ringmaster's Wife." [PraS] (69:3) Fall 95, p. 104.
3642. LIMEHOUSE, Capers
"Calamity Jane's Last Letter to Her Daughter." [GreensboroR] (58) Sum 95, p. 87-
88.
3643. LIMEIRA, José Carlos
"Daily" (tr. by Phyllis Peres). [Callaloo] (18:4) Fall 95, p. 817.
"Diariamente." [Callaloo] (18:4) Fall 95, p. 985.
"Much to the Sea" (for a black woman, tr. by Phyllis Peres, w. Reetika Vazirani and
Chi Lam). [Callaloo] (18:4) Fall 95, p. 818.
"Tanto ao Mar" (para uma mulher negra). [Callaloo] (18:4) Fall 95, p. 986.
3644. LIN, Jiann L.
"Love Letter to Li Zi-An" (tr. of Xuanji Yu, w. David Young). [Field] (52) Spr 95,
p. 57.
"Melancholy Thoughts" (tr. of Xuanji Yu, w. David Young). [Field] (52) Spr 95, p.
55.
"Selling the Last Peonies" (tr. of Xuanji Yu, w. David Young). [Field] (52) Spr 95,
p. 56.
"Sent to Secretary Liu" (tr. of Xuanji Yu, w. David Young). [Field] (52) Spr 95, p.
60.
"Tribute to a Master Alchemist" (tr. of Xuanji Yu, w. David Young). [Field] (52)
Spr 95, p. 59.
"Visiting Master Zhao and Not Finding Him" (tr. of Xuanji Yu, w. David Young).
[Field] (52) Spr 95, p. 58.
"Washing Yarn Temple" (tr. of Xuanji Yu, w. David Young). [Field] (52) Spr 95, p.
54.

3645. LIN, Tan
"Soft Sector A Hub Section B Topo-Moo." [Chain] (2) Spr 95, p. 133-137.
3646. LIND, Laurinda
"Network." [ChironR] (44/45) Aut-Wint 95, p. 33.
3647. LINDEMAN, Jack
"Eye Drops." [BellArk] (11:2) Mr-Ap 95, p. 13.
"Eye Drops." [BellArk] (11:3) My-Je 95, p. 8.
"Italia." [BellArk] (11:4) Jl-Ag 95, p. 14.
"Italian Hours." [HolCrit] (32:2) Ap 95, p. 19.
3648. LINDGREN, Joan
"How Comforting to Collapse in One's Room" (tr. of Juan Manuel Inchauspe, 1940-
1991). [LitR] (39:1) Fall 95, p. 27.
"I Cannot Sit Down to Wait" (tr. of Juan Manuel Inchauspe, 1940-1991). [LitR]
(39:1) Fall 95, p. 29.
"I Go Out Early" (tr. of Juan Manuel Inchauspe, 1940-1991). [LitR] (39:1) Fall 95,
p. 30.
"I Have Patiently Tried" (tr. of Juan Manuel Inchauspe, 1940-1991). [LitR] (39:1)
Fall 95, p. 30.
"The International Athletes" (runner up, 1994 Borderlands Poetry Contest). [Border]
(7) Fall-Wint 96, p. 30-31.
"It Is True" (tr. of Juan Manuel Inchauspe, 1940-1991). [LitR] (39:1) Fall 95, p. 28-
29.
"Once More April" (tr. of Juan Manuel Inchauspe, 1940-1991). [LitR] (39:1) Fall
95, p. 28.
"Once More You Are" (tr. of Juan Manuel Inchauspe, 1940-1991). [LitR] (39:1) Fall
95, p. 28.
"Seamless Thoughts" (tr. of Juan Manuel Inchauspe, 1940-1991). [LitR] (39:1) Fall
95, p. 30-31.
"This Morning on Awakening" (tr. of Juan Manuel Inchauspe, 1940-1991). [LitR]
(39:1) Fall 95, p. 31.
"You Have Nothing But Words" (tr. of Juan Manuel Inchauspe, 1940-1991). [LitR]
(39:1) Fall 95, p. 29.
"Yours" (tr. of Juan Manuel Inchauspe, 1940-1991). [LitR] (39:1) Fall 95, p. 27.
3649. LINDNER, April
"A Brief Primer of Worries." [PraS] (69:3) Fall 95, p. 35-36.
"Kokoschka's Doll." [PraS] (69:3) Fall 95, p. 37-39.
3650. LINDNER, Carl
"Losing Weight." [CapeR] (30:1) Spr 95, p. 48.
3651. LINDOW, Sandra J.
"After Omelas" (for Ursula K. LeGuin, whose journey from Omelas brought her to
Tehanu). [Kaleid] (31) Sum-Fall 95, p. 57.
"Burning the Sweatshirt." [Kaleid] (31) Sum-Fall 95, p. 62.
"Dracones et Omnes Abyssi." [Kaleid] (31) Sum-Fall 95, p. 57.
3652. LINDSAY, David
"Frequent Stones." [AntigR] (102/103) Sum-Aug 95, p. 107-108.
3653. LINEBERGER, James
"Tonsillectomy." [OxfordM] (10:1) Wint 94-Spr 95, p. 47.
3654. LINEHAN, Don
"Colmcille's Farewell" (translated). [AntigR] (102/103) Sum-Aug 95, p. 184.
3655. LINEHAN, Moira
"Vow of Stability." [Poetry] (165:6) Mr 95, p. 326.
3656. LINEHAN, Susan
"What Danish Children Know, and Then Forget." [Vis] (47) 95, p. 22.
3657. LING, Yi
"Drinking Tea with Hermit Yuan at Greenmount Pool" (tr. by J. P. Seaton). [LitR]
(38:3) Spr 95, p. 322.
LINH, Dinh
See DINH, Linh
3658. LINKON, Sherry Lee
"Demands." [HiramPoR] (58/59) Spr 95-Wint 96, p. 51.
3659. LINMARK, R. Zamora
"Love IV (The Love Story of Angela Putana de la Luna and Enamorado Soledad as
told by Whores & Co.)." [HawaiiR] (19:2) Fall 95, p. 184-194.
3660. LIOTTA, P. H.
"27. Here is the poem I found in the runes" (1995 Crossing Boundaries Poetry First
Place Award). [InterQ] (2:3) 95, p. 89-98.

"Chronicle" (tr. of Branko Miljkovic). [Vis] (48) 95, p. 49.
"A Flight" (tr. of Bogomil Gjuzel). [Vis] (48) 95, p. 31.
"Fruit Tree, After a Rain" (tr. of Dobrisa Cesaric). [Vis] (48) 95, p. 16.
"Orpheus in Hell" (tr. of Branko Miljkovic). [Vis] (48) 95, p. 50.
"Stealing Pomegranates on Lopud" (For V. T. and P. J.). [Vis] (49) 95, p. 19.
"Sun" (tr. of Branko Miljkovic). [Vis] (48) 95, p. 49.
"Survival" (tr. of Bogomil Gjuzel). [Vis] (48) 95, p. 30.
"Sveti Naum" (the monastery of Sveti Naum, Macedonia). [Vis] (49) 95, p. 18.
"Tower of Skulls" (tr. of Branko Miljkovic). [Vis] (48) 95, p. 50.
"Vita Nuova" (tr. of Bogomil Gjuzel). [Vis] (48) 95, p. 31.
3661. LIPMAN, Joel
"Crane's Ass (Taxco, Mexico, 1933)." [WorldL] (6) 95, p. 26.
"Regardless" (to Yasser). [NewAW] (13) Fall-Wint 95, p. 105.
"Scorpion Soup (Tangier, Spanish Morocco, 1955)." [WorldL] (6) 95, p. 26-27.
3662. LIPPMAN, Matthew
"Burning Making." [SpinningJ] (1) Fall 95-Wint 96, p. 19.
"Out of the Wires." [SpinningJ] (1) Fall 95-Wint 96, p. 20-21.
"Raising Ali." [IndR] (18:1) Spr 95, p. 143-144.
"Something Velvet." [IndR] (18:1) Spr 95, p. 141-142.
3663. LIPSITZ, Lou
"Dream: Initiation." [SouthernPR] (35:1) Sum 95, p. 37-38.
3664. LIPSKY, Liliam
"Friday February 5th" (tr. of Alberto Kurapel). [Arc] (35) Aut 95, p. 56.
"Prism" (tr. of Alberto Kurapel). [Arc] (35) Aut 95, p. 57.
"Today My Heart Went Away" (tr. of Alberto Kurapel). [Arc] (35) Aut 95, p. 55.
3665. LISH, Gordon
"I, Format." [Boulevard] (10:3, #30) Fall 95, p. 48-74.
3666. LISHAN, Stuart
"Eclogues of Two Women" (Excerpt). [TampaR] (10) Spr 95, p. 53.
"July." [SantaBR] (3:1) Spr 95, p. 70-71.
3667. LISICK, Beth
"Empress of Sighs." [ClockR] (10:1/2) 95-96, p. 95-96.
"Man Comes Up to Me in a Bar #6." [ClockR] (10:1/2) 95-96, p. 96-97.
3668. LISK, Thomas (Thomas David)
"Baby Jays." [SpiritSH] (60) 95, p. 11.
"The Beautiful Grasmere Churchyard." [SpiritSH] (60) 95, p. 10.
"Fourteen Spanish Corks" (For Richard and Cara-lin Getty). [Poem] (74) N 95, p. 26.
"Mistranslations" (Homage to Joseph Cornell). [ProseP] (4) 95, p. 50.
"Take Yourself with You." [ApalQ] (43) Spr 95, p. 43-44.
"Too Late." [Poem] (74) N 95, p. 27.
3669. LISOWSKI, Krzysztof
"All Souls' Day" (tr. by Ewa-Hryniewicz Yarbrough). [LitR] (38:3) Spr 95, p. 356-357.
3670. LITOVITZ, Malca
"Bad Days" (for Denys Arcand). [Writ] (27) 95, p. 33.
"Bleu Clair." [Writ] (27) 95, p. 32.
"Dali's Anthropomorphic Cabinet." [Writ] (27) 95, p. 31.
"Four Oranges." [PraF] (16:4, #73) Wint 95-96, p. 13.
"Little Fires." [Writ] (27) 95, p. 30.
"Wrigley's Queen." [Writ] (27) 95, p. 29.
3671. LITTLE, Billy
"Angels Eat Hand Grenades for Breakfast." [WestCL] (29:3, #18) Wint 95-96, p. 31.
"My Father, The Rain." [WestCL] (29:3, #18) Wint 95-96, p. 30.
3672. LITTLE, Geraldine C.
"First Time." [Comm] (122:8) 21 Ap 95, p. 16.
3673. LITTLE, Jack
"Dickens of a Sale." [Light] (13) Spr 95, p. 13.
"Jarring News." [Light] (13) Spr 95, p. 22.
3674. LIU, Ken
"The Copy of Autumn — A Picnic." [HarvardA] (vol. 130) Fall 95, p. 25.
3675. LIU, Timothy
"Apostasy." [PoetryE] (39) Fall 94, p. 61.
"A Farther View." [WillowS] (35) Ja 95, p. 59.
"First Day." [PoetryE] (41) Aut 95, p. 75.
"Forty Years." [Ploughs] (21:4) Wint 95-96, p. 128.

"Giacometti." [PoetryE] (41) Aut 95, p. 76.
"The Marriage." [WestHR] (49:4) Wint 95, p. 294.
"Naked." [KenR] (17:2) Spr 95, p. 47-50.
"North Truro." [WillowS] (35) Ja 95, p. 58.
"Off I-80." [Witness] (9:2) 95, p. 24.
"Pietà." [Journal] (19:1) Spr-Sum 95, p. 9.
"Ripened Fruit Pulled Earthward to the Ground." [Journal] (19:1) Spr-Sum 95, p.
    10.
"Say Good Night." [Journal] (19:1) Spr-Sum 95, p. 11.
"She Smashes Dishes." [PoetryE] (39) Fall 94, p. 60.
"The Sign." [Ploughs] (21:4) Wint 95-96, p. 129.
"Strange Music." [AmerV] (38) 95, p. 60.
"That Room in Which Disaster Played a Part." [HarvardR] (9) Fall 95, p. 63.
"White Moths." [WestHR] (49:4) Wint 95, p. 295.
3676. LIU, Yung (987-1053)
    "Song: She lowers her fragrant curtain" (tr. by Sam Hamill). [PoetryE] (41) Aut 95,
        p. 22.
3677. LIVINGSTON, Billie
    "Boston YWCA." [Quarry] (44:3) 95, p. 78-79.
    "The Children's Aid Is Coming." [Quarry] (44:3) 95, p. 80-81.
    "His Third Wife." [Quarry] (44:3) 95, p. 76-77.
    "Shedding." [SpoonR] (20:2) Sum-Fall 95, p. 140.
LIZAMA, Tatiana Freire
    See FREIRE-LIZAMA, Tatiana
3678. LJUNG, Anne-Marie
    "Harvest." [BelPoJ] (46:2) Wint 95-96, p. 13.
LLOSA, Ricardo Pau
    See PAU-LLOSA, Ricardo
3679. LLOYD, D. H.
    "Bird." [Pearl] (22) Fall-Wint 95, p. 51.
    "VA Eligible?" [Pearl] (22) Fall-Wint 95, p. 52.
    "Vacuum Cleaner." [Pearl] (22) Fall-Wint 95, p. 51.
3680. LLOYD, Lucy
    "//Kabbo's Request for Thread" (tr. of anonymous /Xam poem, w. W. H. Bleek and
        Stephen Watson). [ColR] (22:1) Spr 95, p. 61.
    "Our Blood Makes Smoke" (tr. of anonymous /Xam poem, w. W. H. Bleek and
        Stephen Watson). [ColR] (22:1) Spr 95, p. 57.
    "Song of the Broken String" (tr. of anonymous /Xam poem, w. W. H. Bleek and
        Stephen Watson). [ColR] (22:1) Spr 95, p. 59-60.
    "The Story of Ruyter" (tr. of anonymous /Xam poem, w. W. H. Bleek and Stephen
        Watson). [ColR] (22:1) Spr 95, p. 58.
    "The Wind Is One with the Man" (tr. of anonymous /Xam poem, w. W. H. Bleek
        and Stephen Watson). [ColR] (22:1) Spr 95, p. 56.
3681. LLOYD, Marie Myers
    "Penumbra." [Quarry] (44:2) 95, p. 137.
    "Visitation." [Quarry] (44:2) 95, p. 138.
3682. LOCHHEAD, Douglas
    "John Thompson." [AntigR] (102/103) Sum-Aug 95, p. 224.
    "Love Sequence of Sorts." [AntigR] (100) Wint 95, p. 20-23.
3683. LOCKE, Christopher
    "The Quiet Heart." [LowellR] (2) c1996, p. 11.
3684. LOCKE, Duane
    "The Abandoned Farm House." [Rosebud] (2:3) Aut-Wint 95, p. 94.
    "An Intense Autumn." [AmerPoR] (24:1) Ja-F 95, p. 41.
    "A Long Time Ago." [AmerPoR] (24:1) Ja-F 95, p. 41.
3685. LOCKE, Edward
    "Advancing Back." [GeoR] (49:2) Sum 95, p. 387.
    "Copy Kid." [TarRP] (34:2) Spr 95, p. 19.
    "Is There Anyone Who Hasn't Said the Eyes Become the Windows of the Soul?"
        [HawaiiR] (19:2) Fall 95, p. 38-39.
    "Marilyn Monroe." [HawaiiR] (19:2) Fall 95, p. 148-149.
    "My Bible." [HawaiiR] (19:2) Fall 95, p. 40-43.
    "Time Out." [ApalQ] (44/45) Fall 95-Wint 96, p. 51-52.
LOCKLEAR, Barbara Braveboy
    See BRAVEBOY-LOCKLEAR, Barbara

3686. LOCKLIN, Gerald
"America First." [WormR] (35:2, #138) 95, p. 88.
"Better Long Hair Than Short." [WormR] (35:2, #138) 95, p. 89.
"The Book Depository" (with Rafael Zepeda, from "The Yellow Ford of Texas").
    [Pearl] (22) Fall-Wint 95, p. 72-74.
"A Dashing Figure." [Pearl] (22) Fall-Wint 95, p. 54.
"Don't Blame Me." [WormR] (35:2, #138) 95, p. 88.
"The Embers Aren't Yet Ashes." [SlipS] (15) 95, p. 56.
"The Exhibition Season." [AxeF] (3) 90, p. 16.
"A Few Bad Men." [SlipS] (15) 95, p. 56.
"The Frying Pan and the Fire." [WormR] (35:2, #138) 95, p. 87-88.
"Great Expectations." [WormR] (35:2, #138) 95, p. 89.
"He Didn't Feel a Day Over Eighty-Nine." [WormR] (35:2, #138) 95, p. 88.
"How Much Is That Doggie in the Leotard?" [Pearl] (22) Fall-Wint 95, p. 56.
"It's Probably Why So Many Motels Are in the Surrounding Communities." [Pearl]
    (22) Fall-Wint 95, p. 55.
"Leaving Yourself Behind." [WormR] (35:1, #137) 95, p. 42.
"Magritte: The Domain of Arnheim." [DefinedP] (1:2) Spr-Sum 93, p. 17.
"Mark My Words." [WormR] (35:2, #138) 95, p. 87.
"May Be Taken with Your Favorite Beverage." [WormR] (35:2, #138) 95, p. 89.
"Maybe They Think All Poets Drive Them." [WormR] (35:2, #138) 95, p. 89.
"Mitigating Circumstances." [WormR] (35:2, #138) 95, p. 87.
"My Heart Leapt Up." [WormR] (35:4, #140) 95, p. 187.
"Never Make Unreasonable Demands." [WormR] (35:1, #137) 95, p. 42.
"No Wonder the Arabs Wear Robes." [WormR] (35:2, #138) 95, p. 88.
"Paul Cézanne: The Card Players." [WormR] (35:4, #140) 95, p. 186.
"La Pensée Sauvage." [Pearl] (22) Fall-Wint 95, p. 54.
"Personal Storage." [WormR] (35:1, #137) 95, p. 43.
"Putting His Foot Down." [WormR] (35:1, #137) 95, p. 43.
"Reflections While Watching John Fante's 'Wait until Spring, Bandini'." [WormR]
    (35:1, #137) 95, p. 41.
"René Magritte: Personal Values." [Pearl] (22) Fall-Wint 95, p. 53.
"Score One for the Old Hollywood." [Pearl] (22) Fall-Wint 95, p. 53.
"Solitaire." [AxeF] (3) 90, p. 17.
"Strong Women." [SlipS] (15) 95, p. 55.
"Their Poems Bear Epigraphs." [WormR] (35:1, #137) 95, p. 43.
"To Hope and Hope Not." [WormR] (35:4, #140) 95, p. 187.
"Tuesday's Hero." [WormR] (35:4, #140) 95, p. 185.
"Tying Tin Cans to Tails." [WormR] (35:4, #140) 95, p. 184-185.
"Watching Them Unwind the Double Helix." [WormR] (35:4, #140) 95, p. 185-186.
"The Witnesses Meet My Teenage Daughter." [WormR] (35:1, #137) 95, p. 41-42.
3687. LOCKWOOD, Betty
"To Our Bodies." [MassR] (36:2) Sum 95, p. 249.
3688. LOCKWOOD, Virginia C.
"In Amber" (for Wildwood). [US1] (30/31) 95, p. 27.
3689. LODEN, Rachel
"DCEASE" [sic]. [NewAW] (13) Fall-Wint 95, p. 37.
"The Death of Checkers." [NewAW] (13) Fall-Wint 95, p. 36.
"Lives of the Saints." [Boulevard] (10:3, #30) Fall 95, p. 96.
3690. LOGAN (Simon, Michael)
"Stone, Water and Breath." [SmPd] (32:1, #93) Wint 95, p. 14-15.
3691. LOGAN, Sally
"Alzheimer's." [Crucible] (30) Fall 94, p. 24.
"A Fine-Looking Woman." [Pembroke] (27) 95, p. 89-90.
"Learning to Live Alone." [Pembroke] (27) 95, p. 87.
"Perfect." [Pembroke] (27) 95, p. 86.
"Seasoned." [Pembroke] (27) 95, p. 88.
"Solarization." [Crucible] (31) Fall 95, p. 5.
3692. LOGAN, Theann
"Ebony." [WestB] (37) 95, p. 11.
3693. LOGAN, William
"Ashbryn." [Verse] (12:3) 95, p. 94-95.
"Beauty" (after Horace, Odes I.25). [Arion] (3:2/3) Fall 95-Wint 96, p. 176.
"Dharma in Santa Moncia." [Iowa] (25:3) Fall 95, p. 131-132.
"The Fates." [ParisR] (37:135) Sum 95, p. 282.
"The Holy Sea." [Verse] (12:2) 95, p. 87.

"Insects." [ParisR] (37:135) Sum 95, p. 282.
"Larkin." [Poetry] (166:3) Je 95, p. 151.
"Last Chance Saloon." [Nat] (261:15) 6 N 95, p. 553.
"Leaving Venice." [Nat] (258:9) 7 Mr 94, p. 316.
"The Livery of Byzantium." [Nat] (258:7) 21 F 94, p. 247.
"Living." [Iowa] (25:3) Fall 95, p. 130.
"Mother on the St. Johns." [ParisR] (37:135) Sum 95, p. 281.
"The Old College." [SouthwR] (80:2/3) Spr-Sum 95, p. 282.
3694. LOGUE, Christopher
  "The Husbands" (Selection: "An Account of Books 3 and 4 of Homer's *Iliad*").
    [Thrpny] (63) Fall 95, p. 25.
3695. LOHMANN, Jeanne
  "Living in the Desert." [SantaBR] (3:2) Sum 95, p. 71.
  "The Logicians." [PoetryNW] (36:4) Wint 95-96, p. 33.
  "Walking on the Beach." [SantaBR] (3:2) Sum 95, p. 70.
3696. LOMBARDO, Anna
  "Indirectrevolution" (tr. by Jack Hirschman and Antonella Soldaini). [WorldL] (6)
    95, p. 14-15.
  "Let It Out, Fellas" (tr. by Jack Hirschman). [WorldL] (6) 95, p. 14.
  "Sleep with Certainty" (tr. by Jack Hirschman). [WorldL] (6) 95, p. 13.
3697. LOMBARDO, Gian
  "Nesle Tower" (tr. of Aloysius Bertrand). [ProseP] (4) 95, p. 9.
  "On the Bias." [ProseP] (4) 95, p. 51.
  "Viol da Gamba" (tr. of Aloysius Bertrand). [ProseP] (4) 95, p. 10-11.
3698. LONCAR, Michael
  "Giving My Head to the Mississippi." [SpinningJ] (1) Fall 95-Wint 96, p. 12.
  "Insomnia." [SpinningJ] (1) Fall 95-Wint 96, p. 13.
  "On Hearing Jerzy Kosinski Has Killed Himself." [PoetryE] (40) Spr 95, p. 69.
  "Wallace P. Hipslit, Age Nine, Footloose and Fancy Free, Standing on a Swing,
    About to Break His Leg." [SpinningJ] (1) Fall 95-Wint 96, p. 14-15.
3699. LONDRY, Michael
  "Lines for Fortune Cookies" (After Frank O'Hara, Short Grain Contest Winners:
    Prose Poem, Honourable Mention). [Grain] (22:3) Wint 95, p. 69-70.
3700. LONG, Barbara Meetze
  "Burning." [SouthernPR] (35:1) Sum 95, p. 59.
3701. LONG, Cathleen A.
  "How the River Named Them." [MidwQ] (36:3) Spr 95, p. 303.
3702. LONG, Donna J.
  "Anniversary." [TampaR] (10) Spr 95, p. 10.
  "False Perspective." [TampaR] (10) Spr 95, p. 11.
3703. LONG, Joel
  "Common Evenings." [PraS] (69:2) Sum 95, p. 61.
  "Nostalgia." [PraS] (69:2) Sum 95, p. 62.
3704. LONG, Robert Hill
  "Diaspora." [Hudson] (47:4) Wint 95, p. 602-604.
  "The Guitar Showing My Age." [Sun] (239) N 95, p. 33.
  "Memory Pepper." [HighP] (10:2) Fall 95, p. 62-64.
  "Riderless Horses." [HighP] (10:2) Fall 95, p. 59-61.
  "Sarah, 4:30 A.M." [VirQR] (71:2) Spr 95, p. 298-299.
  "Slightly Closer to the Sea." [SenR] (25:2) Fall 95, p. 90-91.
  "Small Clinic at Kilometer 7." [ProseP] (4) 95, p. 52-53.
  "To Seth, Ten Years Later." [VirQR] (71:2) Spr 95, p. 299-301.
3705. LONG, Susan Grafeld
  "Position Wanted." [PlumR] (9) [95 or 96], p. 104-105.
3706. LONGENBACH, James
  "The Grace of the Witch." [ParisR] (37:134) Spr 95, p. 42-43.
  "Letting Go." [ParisR] (37:134) Spr 95, p. 44-45.
  "The Origin of Angels." [ParisR] (37:134) Spr 95, p. 43-44.
3707. LONGLEY, Judy
  "Unfinished Mural / Powder Room, Radio City Music Hall" (for Stieglitz).
    [WestHR] (49:4) Wint 95, p. 332.
3708. LONGLEY, Michael
  "Baucis & Philemon" (after Ovid). [NewMyths] (2:2/3:1) 95, p. 127-130.
  "A Bed of Leaves." [NewYorker] (71:8) 17 Ap 95, p. 56.
  "The Branch." [NewYorker] (71:30) 2 O 95, p. 82.
  "The Camp-Fires." [Shen] (45:4) Wint 95, p. 5.

"Ceasefire." [NewYorker] (71:12) 15 My 95, p. 48.
"Chinese Objects." [NewYorker] (71:15) 5 Je 95, p. 75.
"Chinese Occasions." [NewYorker] (71:15) 5 Je 95, p. 65.
"The Design." [Poetry] (167:1/2) O-N 95, p. 65.
"The Dry Cleaners" (Poem Beginning with a Line of Raymond Carver).
    [SouthernR] (31:3) Jl/Sum 95, p. 754.
"A Flowering." [NewYorker] (70:49) 13 F 95, p. 40.
"The Ghost Orchid." [Shen] (45:4) Wint 95, p. 8.
"A Grain of Rice." [Shen] (45:4) Wint 95, p. 9.
"A Grain of Rice." [Verse] (12:2) 95, p. 88.
"Ivory & Water." [SouthernR] (31:3) Jl/Sum 95, p. 754-755.
"Phoenix." [SouthernR] (31:3) Jl/Sum 95, p. 755-756.
"The Pleiades." [Shen] (45:4) Wint 95, p. 6.
"The Quilt" (For Peggy O'Brien). [Poetry] (167:1/2) O-N 95, p. 64.
"Snow Bunting" (for Sarah). [Shen] (45:4) Wint 95, p. 7.
3709. LONGO, Perie
    "Morning after Taking the Exam." [PraS] (69:2) Sum 95, p. 100-101.
    "Tepee at a Childhood Haunt." [PraS] (69:2) Sum 95, p. 98-99.
3710. LOOMIS, Jon
    "L'Angelo di Roma." [PoetL] (90:1) Spr 95, p. 20.
    "Midsummer Letter from Dupont Circle." [PoetL] (90:1) Spr 95, p. 19.
    "My Third World." [OhioR] (53) 95, p. 126-127.
3711. LOONEY, George
    "Acceptable Damage." [TarRP] (34:2) Spr 95, p. 22-23.
    "The Inevitable Beauty of Gravity." [DenQ] (30:2) Fall 95, p. 43-45.
    "The Possibility of Touch." [HayF] (16) Spr-Sum 95, p. 63-65.
    "The Tongues of Water Birds." [Flyway] (1:2) Fall 95, p. 34-35.
    "Where Rivers Come Together." [LitR] (38:2) Wint 95, p. 213-217.
3712. LOOTS, Barbara
    "The Naming of Boats." [Light] (15/16) Aut-Wint 95-96, p. 15.
3713. LOPEZ, Theresa
    "Apricots." [Border] (7) Fall-Wint 96, p. 32.
3714. LOPEZ ADORNO, Pedro
    "Liquid Matter." [MassR] (36:4) Wint 95-96, p. 580.
    "Talking to the Waves." [MassR] (36:4) Wint 95-96, p. 581.
LORCA, Federico García
    See GARCIA LORCA, Federico
LORENZO, Gabrielle di
    See DiLORENZO, Gabrielle
3715. LOSCHIAVO, LindaAnn
    "The Crust." [LullwaterR] (6:1) Spr-Sum 95, p. 7.
    "Gradatim." [Elf] (5:3) Fall 95, p. 25.
    "Secret Midtown Garden." [Elf] (5:3) Fall 95, p. 24.
3716. LOTT, Rick
    "Dove Season." [Crazy] (48) Spr 95, p. 68-69.
    "Invisible Men." [InterQ] (2:3) 95, p. 111.
3717. LOUGHLIN, John
    "The Heart Is a Blue Vegetable That Sings When You Bite It." [BlackWR] (21:2)
        Spr-Sum 95, p. 144-145.
3718. LOUIS, Adrian C.
    "Vortex of Indian Fevers." [KenR] (17:1) Wint 95, p. 27-31.
3719. LOVE, Raymond D.
    "What Is Three?" [Light] (13) Spr 95, p. 20.
3720. LOVELL, Barbara (Barbara M.)
    "Her Rituals." [SouthernPR] (35:2) Wint 95, p. 64-67.
    "The Language of Flowers." [Crucible] (31) Fall 95, p. 27.
3721. LOVELL, Thoreau
    "Constantly Escaping." [Talisman] (15) Wint 95-96, p. 104.
3722. LOVELOCK, Yann
    "All Day Its Intimate and Hissing Strength." [Os] (41) 95, p. 13.
    "Bridging Night." [Os] (41) 95, p. 12.
3723. LOW, Denise
    "Elegy for July 28, 1994." [MidwQ] (36:4) Sum 95, p. 394.
    "Postmodernism in Kansas." [ChironR] (44/45) Aut-Wint 95, p. 7.
    "War Crimes." [ChironR] (43) Sum 95, p. 32.

LOW, Jackson Mac
    See Mac LOW, Jackson
3724. LOWELL, James
    "Terminal Day." [CanLit] (147) Wint 95, p. 9.
3725. LOWENSTEIN, Robert
    "Hearing Things." [CapeR] (30:1) Spr 95, p. 12.
3726. LOWERY, Joanne
    "The Eight Thousand." [Poem] (74) N 95, p. 25.
    "Flight." [Poem] (74) N 95, p. 24.
    "Mary Maitland Sums It Up." [TexasR] (15:3/4) Fall-Wint 94, p. 89-90.
    "Still Life: Woman with Body." [SpoonR] (20:1) Wint-Spr 95, p. 10.
    "Still Life: Woman with Pear." [SpoonR] (20:1) Wint-Spr 95, p. 12.
    "Still Life: Woman with Vase." [SpoonR] (20:1) Wint-Spr 95, p. 11.
    "Traveling at the Speed of Light." [Poem] (74) N 95, p. 23.
3727. LOYNAZ, Dulce María
    "Bounded Sea" (tr. by Judith Kerman). [Chelsea] (59) 95, p. 131.
    "In the Aquarium" (tr. by Judith Kerman). [Chelsea] (59) 95, p. 131.
3728. LU, Pamela
    "Departures." [Chain] (2) Spr 95, p. 138-141.
3729. LUBESKI, Lori
    "Shady Lane" (Selections). [Chain] (2) Spr 95, p. 142-144.
    "Winter." [Talisman] (15) Wint 95-96, p. 56-58.
LUBICZ MILOSZ, Oscar Vladislas de
    See MILOSZ, Oscar Vladislas de Lubicz
LUCA, Geri de
    See DeLUCA, Geri
3730. LUCAS, Brian D.
    "The Circle Marked." [Sulfur] (15:2, #37) Fall 95, p. 120-124.
3731. LUCAS, Tony
    "Amateur." [SoCoast] (19) 95, p. 29-30.
    "Down to Earth." [SoCoast] (19) 95, p. 28.
    "El Camino Real." [SoCoast] (19) 95, p. 26-27.
3732. LUCIA, Joseph P.
    "Old Soil." [HolCrit] (32:3) Je 95, p. 16.
3733. LUCIANO, Elizabeth
    "Love's Acolyte." [SinW] (56) Sum-Fall 95, p. 94.
3734. LUCRETIUS
    "De Rerum Natura, Book II" (Excerpt, tr. by Jonathan Spiegel and Jean Berrett).
        [WillowS] (36) Je 95, p. 110.
3735. LUDVIGSON, Susan
    "After Gatsby." [GettyR] (8:3) Sum 95, p. 502.
    "The Brain Enjoys Its Secret Life." [GettyR] (8:3) Sum 95, p. 504.
    "A Day Like Any Other." [Poetry] (166:1) Ap 95, p. 11.
    "The Gospel According to Mary Magdalene." [GettyR] (8:4) Aut 95, p. 699-711.
    "Letters Back (God Writes to Emily Dickinson)." [AmerV] (37) 95, p. 115-119.
    "Someday Even the Wicker Chairs." [GettyR] (8:3) Sum 95, p. 503.
    "What You Meant." [OhioR] (53) 95, p. 100.
    "Where Snow Falls." [OhioR] (53) 95, p. 98-99.
    "You Have to Go." [SouthernHR] (29:3) Sum 95, p. 266.
3736. LUEDERS, Edward
    "Air Raid" (tr. of Yoshihara Sachiko, w. Naoshi Koriyama). [WeberS] (12:1) Wint
        95, p. 52.
    "Calendar Poem" (tr. of Tada Chimako, w. Naoshi Koriyama). [WeberS] (12:1)
        Wint 95, p. 56.
    "Chess" (tr. of Shinkawa Kazue, w. Naoshi Koriyama). [WeberS] (12:1) Wint 95, p.
        54-55.
    "Dead Sun" (tr. of Tada Chimako, w. Naoshi Koriyama). [WeberS] (12:1) Wint 95,
        p. 56.
    "A Distant Mirror" (tr. of Shinkawa Kazue, w. Naoshi Koriyama). [WeberS] (12:1)
        Wint 95, p. 54.
    "An Epitaph" (tr. of Yoshihara Sachiko, w. Naoshi Koriyama). [WeberS] (12:1)
        Wint 95, p. 51-52.
    "In My Garden" (tr. of Shinkawa Kazue, w. Naoshi Koriyama). [WeberS] (12:1)
        Wint 95, p. 52-53.
    "Late Summer" (tr. of Tada Chimako, w. Naoshi Koriyama). [WeberS] (12:1) Wint
        95, p. 55.

"Low Tide" (tr. of Yoshihara Sachiko, w. Naoshi Koriyama). [WeberS] (12:1) Wint 95, p. 50-51.
"Me" (tr. of Tada Chimako, w. Naoshi Koriyama). [WeberS] (12:1) Wint 95, p. 55.
"Of Bread and Roses" (tr. of Yoshihara Sachiko, w. Naoshi Koriyama). [WeberS] (12:1) Wint 95, p. 50.
"The Palm" (From "Poems About the Human Body," tr. of Shinkawa Kazue, w. Naoshi Koriyama). [WeberS] (12:1) Wint 95, p. 53.
"Quite Suddenly" (tr. of Yoshihara Sachiko, w. Naoshi Koriyama). [WeberS] (12:1) Wint 95, p. 51.
"The Sole" (From "Poems About the Human Body," tr. of Shinkawa Kazue, w. Naoshi Koriyama). [WeberS] (12:1) Wint 95, p. 53-54.
3737. LUFTIG, Richard
"The Comedians." [Plain] (16:1) Fall 95, p. 12-13.
"The Old Couple." [FourQ] (9:1/2) Spr 95, p. 36-37.
3738. LUMBRERAS, Ernesto
"Hermitage for a Family Tree" (tr. by Bond Snodgrass). [PlumR] (8) [95], p. 70-71.
3739. LUMMIS, Suzanne
"To the Man in the Parking Lot at Sunset and Normandie." [Pearl] (22) Fall-Wint 95, p. 105.
LUNA, Blas Manuel de
See DeLUNA, Blas Manuel
3740. LUNA, Joyce
"Essays on the Horizons of Trees." [WestCL] (29:3, #18) Wint 95-96, p. 32.
"How Does the Strangeness of Grass." [WestCL] (29:3, #18) Wint 95-96, p. 34.
"Night Talk While Travelling the Outer Hebrides." [WestCL] (29:3, #18) Wint 95-96, p. 33.
3741. LUND, Tessa
"He Was Ordinary." [Stand] (36:2) Spr 95, p. 27.
3742. LUNDAY, Robert
"In Praise of Babel." [NewMyths] (2:2/3:1) 95, p. 17-24.
3743. LUNDBERG, Carol Wade
"Moving Toward the Rim." [Kalliope] (17:2) 95, p. 28-29.
3744. LUNDE, David
"In the Wilds There Is a Dead Doe" (from *The Book of Songs,* tr. of anonymous Chinese poem). [ChiR] (41:1) 95, p. 16.
3745. LUNDIN, Deanne
"In This Direction." [AntR] (53:4) Fall 95, p. 441.
3746. LUNN, Jean
"Poem on Two Words Slant-Rhymed by W. D. Snodgrass." [HampSPR] Wint 95, p. 39.
3747. LUSCHEI, Glenna
"January." [FreeL] (14) Wint 95, p. 8.
"Silver Lake." [FreeL] (14) Wint 95, p. 8.
"Sunflower." [FreeL] (14) Wint 95, p. 8.
3748. LUSK, Daniel
"And Then One Day." [PaintedB] (55/56) 95, p. 66.
"More Lies about the Presidency." [SouthernPR] (35:2) Wint 95, p. 55-56.
3749. LUST, Herbert
"It Wish It Were." [Sulfur] (15:2, #37) Fall 95, p. 188-191.
3750. LUTERMAN, Alison
"Accidents." [Sun] (239) N 95, p. 19.
"Bangkok Story." [Sun] (232) Ap 95, p. 19.
"Fairy Tail." [PoetryE] (40) Spr 95, p. 70.
"Georgia O'Keefe Speaks From Earth and Sky" [sic]. [PoetryE] (40) Spr 95, p. 71.
"Grandmother Nose Poem." [Sun] (230) F 95, p. 24-25.
"Invisible Work." [Sun] (230) F 95, p. 25.
"One" (for Dana Anderson). [PoetryE] (40) Spr 95, p. 73.
"Sonnet: Not so much other poets, or not only." [PoetryE] (40) Spr 95, p. 72.
3751. LUTOVICH, Diane
"Food for the Dead and the Living." [GreenHLL] (6) 95, p. 74.
3752. LUTZ, Jeanne
"No One Cares About the Death of a Penis." [BellR] (18:2, #38) Fall 95, p. 52.
3753. LUX, Thomas
"Grave Goods." [BelPoJ] (45:4) Chapbook 22, Sum 95, p. 52.
"One Meat Ball." [BlackWR] (21:2) Spr-Sum 95, p. 124-125.

3754. LUXORIUS (6th century C.E.)
"Premature Chariot" (tr. by Art Beck). [ArtfulD] (28/29) 95, p. 27.
"They say, that when the fierce bear gives birth" (tr. by Art Beck). [ArtfulD] (28/29)
95, p. 27.
3755. LUZZARO, Susan
"Comrade" (Nicola Sacco & Bartolomeo Vanzetti ... Executed in 1927). [13thMoon]
(13:1/2) 95, p. 26.
"Lascivious Absolution." [Kalliope] (17:3) 95, p. 70.
"Love Letter to a Computer Geek." [Kalliope] (17:3) 95, p. 71.
3756. LYKIARD, Alexis
"The Location." [SoCoast] (18) Ja 95, p. 50-51.
3757. LYLES, Peggy Willis
"A black bear" (Haiku). [Northeast] (5:12) Sum 95, p. 22.
"Haiku" (6 poems). [Northeast] (5:12) Sum 95, p. 22-23.
"Old song" (Haiku). [Northeast] (5:12) Sum 95, p. 22.
"Paired crabs writhe" (Haiku). [Northeast] (5:12) Sum 95, p. 23.
"The rose bowl" (Haiku). [Northeast] (5:12) Sum 95, p. 23.
"Sunset" (Haiku). [Northeast] (5:12) Sum 95, p. 22.
"Yellow rose" (Haiku). [Northeast] (5:12) Sum 95, p. 22.
3758. LYNCH, Doris
"Still Life: Woman with a Bundle on Her Head." [Prima] (18/19) 95, p. 104.
3759. LYNCH, Kathleen
"Cyclist." [SpoonR] (20:1) Wint-Spr 95, p. 91.
"Finch." [Ascent] (19:2) Wint 95, p. 48.
"Love: The Basics." [MidwQ] (37:1) Aut 95, p. 42.
"Nightwatch." [Ascent] (19:2) Wint 95, p. 49.
"The Spirit of Things." [SpoonR] (20:1) Wint-Spr 95, p. 90.
3760. LYNCH, Thomas
"Heavenward." [GettyR] (8:4) Aut 95, p. 572.
"Kisses." [GettyR] (8:4) Aut 95, p. 576.
"No Prisoners." [GettyR] (8:4) Aut 95, p. 573-575.
3761. LYNES, Andrea
"A Bone Could Never Be a Verb." [MassR] (36:2) Sum 95, p. 238.
3762. LYNES, Jeanette
"Disorders." [PottPort] (16:1) Fall 95, p. 45.
"Morning and the Centre." [PottPort] (16:1) Fall 95, p. 43.
"This Yellow Hunger of Yours." [PottPort] (16:1) Fall 95, p. 44.
3763. LYNN, Catherine
"The Color Pink." [Pearl] (22) Fall-Wint 95, p. 142.
3764. LYNSKEY, Edward C.
"Alabama at Forty Fathoms." [DogRR] (14:1, #27) Sum 95, p. 14.
"The Death of Blind Lemon Jefferson" (1897-1929). [PoetL] (90:4) Wint 95-96, p.
44.
"Keats in Montana." [RiverS] (45) 95, p. 52.
"The Last Living Confederate Veteran" (after a photograph by Eudora Welty).
[SoCoast] (18) Ja 95, p. 11.
"Mr. Robinson's Milk Man" (after Weldon Kees). [PoetL] (90:1) Spr 95, p. 11.
"Mrs. Lincoln's Poison Pen." [Farm] (12:1) Spr-Sum 95, p. 33.
"Nelson Algren's Bartender." [HampSPR] Wint 95, p. 49.
"The Stem of Jesse Taliaferro." [Border] (7) Fall-Wint 96, p. 33.
"The Stucco House." [Elf] (5:3) Fall 95, p. 38.
"Ted Williams Goes to war Again." [CapeR] (30:1) Spr 95, p. 29.
"Thoreau's Cranky Angel at Chernobyl." [CapeR] (30:1) Spr 95, p. 28.
"Tree Surgeon on the High Wire." [Farm] (12:1) Spr-Sum 95, p. 34.
"The Tree Surgeon's Maypole." [HampSPR] Wint 95, p. 49.
"U. S. Grant in the Adirondacks" (from last-known photograph, 1885). [Parting]
(8:2) Wint 95-96, p. 7.
LYNSKY, Edward C.
See LYNSKEY, Edward C.
3765. LYNX, Marcia
"Learning Your Place." [EvergreenC] (10:1) Wint-Spr 95, p. 90.
3766. LYON, George Ella
"Strung." [AmerV] (37) 95, p. 8-9.
3767. LYON, Hillary
"On the Screened Porch." [MidwQ] (37:1) Aut 95, p. 43.
"Postcard." [Poem] (74) N 95, p. 64.

3768. LYON, Rick
"Crabapple." [MissouriR] (18:1) 95, p. 146.
"The Dance." [MissouriR] (18:1) 95, p. 148.
"The Devotions." [MissouriR] (18:1) 95, p. 149.
"The Garden." [MissouriR] (18:1) 95, p. 144.
"The Pond." [MissouriR] (18:1) 95, p. 147.
"Rue des Deux Ponts." [MissouriR] (18:1) 95, p. 145.
3769. LYONS, Kimberly
"Female Circumcision." [Chain] (2) Spr 95, p. 145-146.
3770. LYONS, Richard
"The Corpse Washing." [ParisR] (37:135) Sum 95, p. 289-290.
"A Gift Box Divided Exactly in Half for Ernst and Rilke." [WestHR] (49:2) Sum 95,
p. 147-148.
"Homage to Max Ernst." [XavierR] (15:2) Fall 95, p. 27.
"Symmetry." [ParisR] (37:135) Sum 95, p. 289.
"Two Deaths in San Bernardino." [WestHR] (49:2) Sum 95, p. 148-149.
3771. LYONS, Robert
"The Artists." [BellArk] (11:1) Ja-F 95, p. 23.
"A Letter to Bill." [BellArk] (11:1) Ja-F 95, p. 23.
"Passage to the Ruins." [BellArk] (11:4) Jl-Ag 95, p. 9.
3772. LYONS, Stephen
"Cliff Swallows, Hanford Project." [Poem] (74) N 95, p. 36.
"Every Other Weekend." [Witness] (9:1) 95, p. 86.
"Trumpeter Swans, Rock Lake." [Poem] (74) N 95, p. 37.
3773. LYTHGOE, Michael Hugh
"Haiti." [CaribbeanW] (9) 95, p. 47-49.

M., Margaret
See MARGARET M.
3774. MAC, Kathy
"Spot Stray, Esq., Cat about Town." [PottPort] (16:1) Fall 95, p. 70.
3775. Mac LOW, Jackson
"A Stable Person" (Forties 98). [Talisman] (15) Wint 95-96, p. 54-55.
"Telegrapher Dynamo Pederasty Teeters" (Forties 57). [Talisman] (15) Wint 95-96,
p. 52-53.
"Who Builds White-Clocked Billowing Walls?" [Sulfur] (15:2, #37) Fall 95, p. 118-
119.
Mac...
See also names beginning with Mc...
3776. MacDONALD, C. G.
"The Bell Curve." [HampSPR] Wint 95, p. 34-35.
3777. MacDONALD, Cynthia
"Frank Blank Whose Depression Was Banished." [TriQ] (95) Wint 95-96, p. 158.
"The Great 14th Street Costume Company Clarence Ernest Klister, Prop." [TriQ]
(95) Wint 95-96, p. 159-161.
"How William Solomon Invokes Free Will." [TriQ] (95) Wint 95-96, p. 156-157.
3778. MacDONALD, Kathryn
"Dream in the Desert." [BellArk] (11:1) Ja-F 95, p. 24.
"Falling Light." [BellArk] (11:1) Ja-F 95, p. 24.
3779. MacDONALD, Tanis
"Forgetting to Speak Softly" (for W.). [PraF] (16:3, #72) Aut 95, p. 102-110.
3780. MACEIRA, Karen
"Memory with Banana Trees in Background." [SpinningJ] (1) Fall 95-Wint 96, p.
23.
3781. MacFADYEN, Janet
"Hymn." [Poetry] (166:2) My 95, p. 82-84.
3782. MACHADO, Antonio (1875-1939)
"If I were a poet of love" (tr. by Robert Bly). [PoetryE] (41) Aut 95, p. 37.
3783. MACHAN, Katharyn Howd
"At Equinox" (Finalist, The Nimrod / Hardman Awards). [Nimrod] (39:1) Fall-Wint
95, p. 64.
"Hunger." [Footwork] (24/25) 95, p. 45.
"Night Prayer." [Footwork] (24/25) 95, p. 44.
"Sister Ann Marie Tells About Father Murray As the Bus Passes a Sign for
Courtland." [Footwork] (24/25) 95, p. 44-45.

"Still" (Finalist, The Nimrod / Hardman Awards). [Nimrod] (39:1) Fall-Wint 95, p. 64.
3784. MACIEL, Olivia
"Lemon Water." [Prima] (18/19) 95, p. 103.
3785. MacINNES, Mairi
"The Ghostwriter." [Hudson] (48:1) Spr 95, p. 64-66.
"Missing." [NewYorker] (71:31) 9 O 95, p. 59.
"November Digging." [SewanR] (103:1) Wint 95, p. 11-12.
"Traveling North." [YaleR] (83:3) Jl 95, p. 128-130.
3786. MACIOCI, R. Nikolas
"Wool Request." [LullwaterR] (5:2) Fall-Wint 94, p. 79.
3787. MACK, Dorothy Blackcrow
"Double-Face Woman" (1995 Poetry Competition: Honorable Mention). [Elf] (5:2) Sum 95, p. 20.
3788. MacKENZIE, Ginny
"Autumn" (tr. of Ting Shu, w. Guo Wei). [InterQ] (2:1/2) 95, p. 123.
"A Room for Two Girls" (tr. of Ting Shu, w. Guo Wei). [InterQ] (2:1/2) 95, p. 121-122.
"Sicily Sun" (tr. of Ting Shu, w. Guo Wei). [InterQ] (2:1/2) 95, p. 124.
"This Place a Gift" (tr. of Ting Shu, w. Guo Wei). [InterQ] (2:1/2) 95, p. 125.
3789. MACKEY, Nathaniel
"Song of the Andoumboulou" (Selections: 28-29). [Phoebe] (24:1) 95, p. 29-41.
"Song of the Andoumboulou: 31." [ChiR] (41:4) 95, p. 13-17.
3790. MacKINNON, Margaret
"Lament for the Room Upstairs." [TarRP] (34:2) Spr 95, p. 7.
3791. MACKLIN, Elizabeth
"Attraction Steps into the House." [Thrpny] (63) Fall 95, p. 31.
"Marriages." [NewYorker] (71:10) 1 My 95, p. 61.
"A Myth for the Girl at Bedtime." [ColR] (22:1) Spr 95, p. 77-80.
"Psalm 103 & Vanity." [NewYorker] (70:46) 23 Ja 95, p. 69.
3792. MACKOWSKI, Joanie
"Seattle to Boston." [YaleR] (83:4) O 95, p. 70-71.
3793. MacLEAN, Kenneth
"For Joyce in Peace." [NorthStoneR] (12) 95, p. 235.
"Meditation on a Recluse" (Palisades Retreat, 1992). [NorthStoneR] (12) 95, p. 236.
"Reading the New Anthology." [NorthStoneR] (12) 95, p. 234.
3794. MacLEOD, K. J.
"Liberty's Token." [BelPoJ] (46:2) Wint 95-96, p. 18-19.
"My Family, Dying." [BelPoJ] (46:2) Wint 95-96, p. 20.
"Red Bartletts Mid-Life." [BelPoJ] (46:2) Wint 95-96, p. 21.
3795. MacLEOD, Kathryn
"Egypt." [Avec] (9) 95, p. 65-66.
"One Hour Out of Twenty-Four." [Avec] (9) 95, p. 61-64.
3796. MacLEOD, Sue
"Betrayal." [PottPort] (16:1) Fall 95, p. 37-39.
"A Mother Flies Home from the Mountains" (for Mary Joyce). [PottPort] (16:1) Fall 95, p. 40.
MacLOW, Jackson
See Mac LOW, Jackson
3797. MacNAUGHTON, Lou
"The Lottery and the Eleventh-Hour Believer." [Border] (7) Fall-Wint 96, p. 35.
"Stepping into the Watermelon Slush" (indexed from table of contents — this page blank in our copy). [Border] (7) Fall-Wint 96, p. 34.
3798. MACOMBER, Megan
"Earthquake Lake" (To MSB). [Turnstile] (5:1) 95, p. 73-74.
3799. MADDOCKS, Jim
"Tweezers." [Bogg] (67) 95, p. 35.
3800. MADDOX, Marjorie
"Anniversary Poem Interrupted with a Fight." [NortheastCor] (3) 95, p. 105.
"Eucharist." [Image] (12) Wint 95-96, p. 52.
"Maple Seed: A Love Poem." [Blueline] (16) 95, p. 1.
"Mother Tongue." [ColEng] (57:4) Ap 95, p. 461.
"Receptionism." [Image] (12) Wint 95-96, p. 54.
"Skin Rising." [InterQ] (2:3) 95, p. 106.
"Substantiation." [Image] (12) Wint 95-96, p. 53.

3801. MADDOX, William S.
"Streetcar." [XavierR] (15:1) Spr 95, p. 54.
3802. MADDUX, Carolyn
"Dance of the Equinox." [BellArk] (11:6) N-D 95, p. 4.
"Dreambox." [BellArk] (11:4) Jl-Ag 95, p. 22.
"Matins." [BellArk] (11:3) My-Je 95, p. 24.
"My Friend, Do Not Trouble the Waters." [BellArk] (11:6) N-D 95, p. 4.
3803. MADIGAN, Rick
"Doing Jannie's Wash." [HayF] (16) Spr-Sum 95, p. 94-95.
"Hurricane." [HayF] (16) Spr-Sum 95, p. 92-93.
3804. MADRID, Anthony
"Bagatelle." [PaintedB] (55/56) 95, p. 28.
"Folded in Sixteen." [CarolQ] (47:2) Wint 95, p. 61.
"The Grandmother Poem." [NewEngR] (17:1) Wint 95, p. 21.
3805. MAGEE, Harriet
"Clearing Out the Barn." [DefinedP] (1:2) Spr-Sum 93, p. 14.
3806. MAGEE, Kevin
"Author." [Chain] (2) Spr 95, p. 147.
"Directive." [Chain] (2) Spr 95, p. 147-148.
"Stampede Effect" (for Charles Olson). [Chain] (2) Spr 95, p. 148.
3807. MAGEE, Michael, Jr.
"Mantis Religiosa." [SpoonR] (20:1) Wint-Spr 95, p. 35-36.
"To an Anorexic Woman." [SpoonR] (20:1) Wint-Spr 95, p. 37-38.
"The Uncertainty Principle." [SpoonR] (20:1) Wint-Spr 95, p. 34.
3808. MAGER, Don
"Change." [Interim] (14:2) Fall-Wint 95-96, p. 5.
"Last Star." [WestHR] (49:4) Wint 95, p. 313.
"Shakespeare at Dusk, Latta Park, Charlotte, NC." [CapeR] (30:2) Fall 95, p. 44-46.
"Song of the Native Land" (tr. of Jaroslav Seifert). [LullwaterR] (6:2) Fall-Wint 95,
    p. 82-84.
3809. MAGGI, Maria Theresa
"The Man in the Web." [SouthernPR] (35:1) Sum 95, p. 29-33.
3810. MAGINNES, Al
"After Intermission." [PraS] (69:1) Spr 95, p. 167.
"Annulment." [MidAR] (15:1/2) 95, p. 241-243.
"Conversations With Air." [MidAR] (15:1/2) 95, p. 244-245.
"A Litany of Survivors." [MidAR] (15:1/2) 95, p. 239-240.
"The Marriage of Clothes." [NewOR] (21:2) Sum 95, p. 98-99.
"Sealegs." [PraS] (69:1) Spr 95, p. 168-169.
"Seasonal." [LaurelR] (29:1) Wint 95, p. 83-84.
"The Stories Weather Brings." [SilverFR] (25) Sum 95, p. 22-23.
"Sugar Lake." [MidAR] (15:1/2) 95, p. 237-238.
"The Terrible Weight of Beauty." [ChironR] (43) Sum 95, p. 35.
3811. MAGNUSON, Neil
"Bitch." [Plain] (16:1) Fall 95, p. 34.
3812. MAGNUSSON, Sigurdur A.
"Louis Armstrong." [Nimrod] (38:2) Spr-Sum 95, p. 75.
"Mona Lisa — Third Mosaic" (tr. of Linda Vilhjálmsdóttir). [Nimrod] (38:2) Spr-
    Sum 95, p. 69.
"Nights" (tr. of Linda Vilhjálmsdóttir). [Nimrod] (38:2) Spr-Sum 95, p. 69.
3813. MAGORIAN, James
"The Creek That Flows Both Directions." [MidwQ] (36:4) Sum 95, p. 395-396.
"Depot." [SouthernPR] (35:1) Sum 95, p. 40-41.
3814. MAHAFFEY, Phillip
"The Leg." [WillowS] (35) Ja 95, p. 43.
3815. MAHAPATRA, Anuradha
"Astrologer's Prediction" (tr. by Carolyne Wright. w. Paramita Banerjee).
    [ManyMM] (1:3) 95, p. 158.
"Guiltful" (tr. by Carolyne Wright, w. Jyotirmoy Datta). [ManyMM] (1:3) 95, p.
    159.
"Primeval" (tr. by Carolyne Wright, w. Jyotirmoy Datta). [ManyMM] (1:3) 95, p.
    160.
"Sleep" (tr. by Carolyne Wright, w. Jyotirmoy Datta). [ManyMM] (1:3) 95, p. 161.
"Wind" (tr. by Carolyne Wright. w. Paramita Banerjee). [ManyMM] (1:3) 95, p.
    162.

3816. MAHAPATRA, Jayanta
"Bazaar Scene." [TriQ] (94) Fall 95, p. 230.
"Heroism." [Poetry] (166:5) Ag 95, p. 276-277.
"A Hint of Grief." [TriQ] (94) Fall 95, p. 229.
"Living in Orissa." [TriQ] (94) Fall 95, p. 231.
"The Stories in Poetry." [NewL] (61:3) 95, p. 131-133.
3817. MAHARAJ, Niala
"Across Continents" (for Kim Johnson). [CaribbeanW] (9) 95, p. 44-45.
3818. MAHER, Jennifer
"Photograph: for Eriks." [CreamCR] (19:1) Spr 95, p. 159.
"Saturday Afternoon at the Pink House." [CreamCR] (19:1) Spr 95, p. 160.
3819. MAHLE, Benj
"The Friday Poem." [RagMag] (12:2) Spr 95, p. 40-43.
3820. MAHON, Derek
"Albums: The Wild West" (After Laforgue). [NewYorker] (70:43 [i.e. 44]) 9 Ja 95,
    p. 63.
"Burbles" (after Beckett). [SouthernR] (31:3) Jl/Sum 95, p. 515-516.
"Chinatown." [Poetry] (167:1/2) O-N 95, p. 10-11.
"To Mrs. Moore at Inishannon." [NewYorker] (71:4) 20 Mr 95, p. 75.
3821. MAHON, Robert Lee
"Liberal Education." [WindO] (59) Spr 95, p. 41.
3822. MAHONEY, Lisa
"Lamb." [Confr] (56/57) Sum-Fall 95, p. 323.
"The Thaw." [Interim] (14:2) Fall-Wint 95-96, p. 20-21.
3823. MAIDEN, Nell
"Atticus Moore Remembers Purple Butterbeans." [LullwaterR] (6:1) Spr-Sum 95, p.
    66-67.
"Preservation Hall Concert." [HampSPR] Wint 95, p. 28-29.
"Something to Believe In." [HampSPR] Wint 95, p. 28.
"What James Beard Can't Explain." [HampSPR] Wint 95, p. 29.
3824. MAIER, Carol
"2, rue Saint Suplice" (tr. of Octavio Armand). [OhioR] (54) 95, p. 21.
"Baptismal Pyre" (tr. of Octavio Armand). [OhioR] (54) 95, p. 17.
"Exercise in the Translations of Desire: Three Versions of Octavio Armand's
    'Viento'." [OhioR] (54) 95, p. 23-24.
"Father Demo Square" (tr. of Octavio Armand). [OhioR] (54) 95, p. 18.
"Get Away, Muses!" (tr. of Octavio Armand). [OhioR] (54) 95, p. 12-14.
"October" (tr. of Octavio Armand). [OhioR] (54) 95, p. 19.
"Test" (tr. of Octavio Armand). [OhioR] (54) 95, p. 20.
"Will You Tear Up This Page?" (tr. of Octavio Armand). [OhioR] (54) 95, p. 15.
"Words for a Zen Garden" (Chapbook: 9 poems, tr. of Octavio Armand). [OhioR]
    (54) 95, p. 9-21.
"Words for a Zen Garden" (tr. of Octavio Armand). [OhioR] (54) 95, p. 16.
"Written on Sand" (tr. of Octavio Armand). [OhioR] (54) 95, p. 11.
3825. MAIER, J. (Jennifer)
"Hymn to St. Agnes." [MidwQ] (36:3) Spr 95, p. 304-305.
"Live Oaks, New Orleans." [Kalliope] (17:1) 95, p. 69.
3826. MAIER, Ted
"XXVII. To blunt your edges" (tr. of María Fernanda Espinosa, w. Alicia Cabiedes-
    Fink). [InterPR] (21:1) Spr 95, p. 27.
"XXX. Hopes are allowed" (tr. of María Fernanda Espinosa, w. Alicia Cabiedes-
    Fink). [InterPR] (21:1) Spr 95, p. 25.
3827. MAIO, Samuel
"Art History Survey: Vermeer." [CharR] (21:2) Fall 95, p. 94.
"Club Casanova." [CharR] (21:2) Fall 95, p. 98-99.
"Last Letter to John Milton: In Memoriam." [SoDakR] (33:3/4) Fall-Wint 95, p. 98-
    102.
"The Paintings of Arnesti Gaspári." [CharR] (21:2) Fall 95, p. 95.
"Protestors at Disneyland." [CharR] (21:2) Fall 95, p. 96-97.
"Whisky à Gogo." [CharR] (21:2) Fall 95, p. 100-101.
3828. MAIR, Catherine
"Don't Let the Cleaning Lady's Daughter Come to Daycare." [Bogg] (67) 95, p. 31.
3829. MAJOR, Clarence
"September Mendocino." [NewAW] (13) Fall-Wint 95, p. 97-100.
3830. MAKELA, JoAnne
"Bone Lion." [RagMag] (12:2) Spr 95, p. 86.

"On Saturday I Receive an Ad from Kmart." [RagMag] (12:2) Spr 95, p. 87.
MAKOTO, Ooka
    See OOKA, Makoto
3831. MAKUCK, Peter
    "After the Perfect Place." [LaurelR] (29:1) Wint 95, p. 48-49.
    "Egret." [NoCarLR] (2:2) 95, p. 200.
    "Lobsters." [CimR] (110) Ja 96, p. 67-68.
    "On the Blue Again." [NoCarLR] (2:2) 95, p. 201.
    "Valentine" (for Phyllis). [CimR] (110) Ja 96, p. 69-70.
3832. MALANGA, Gerard
    "Memorial Day." [HarvardR] (9) Fall 95, p. 36.
    "What Becomes a Duchamp Most" (for Zoe). [HeavenB] (12) 95, p. 54-55.
3833. MALCOLM, River
    "Looking for Milkweed" (for Virginia). [Calyx] (16:1) Sum 95, p. 54-57.
3834. MALDONADO, Jesús María (El Flaco)
    "Canto for Wounded Warrior: Raúl (Tapón) Salinas." [Americas] (23:3/4) Fall-Wint
        95, p. 138-140.
    "Gently Lead Me Home" (Written on Hwy. 24, about ten miles from Othello, WA.
        For my wife, the steadying force in my life). [Americas] (23:3/4) Fall-Wint
        95, p. 131.
    "Memorias de César Chávez." [Americas] (23:3/4) Fall-Wint 95, p. 141.
    "Mis Poemas Son Tortillas Calientitas." [Americas] (23:3/4) Fall-Wint 95, p. 132.
    "El Molote Bailarín." [Americas] (23:3/4) Fall-Wint 95, p. 142-143.
    "Ricardo Sánchez: With Tortillas in His Pocket" (In Memoriam, Ricardo Sánchez,
        1941-1995). [Americas] (23:3/4) Fall-Wint 95, p. 26-29.
    "Soy Esa Voz .../ Soy Ese Chicanito" (For Tino Villanueva and Abelardo Delgado).
        [Americas] (23:3/4) Fall-Wint 95, p. 137.
    "Stronger Each Flight" (For my son Esteban). [Americas] (23:3/4) Fall-Wint 95, p.
        135-136.
    "Warm, Brown Canela Dreams" (For my wife Leonor). [Americas] (23:3/4) Fall-
        Wint 95, p. 133-134.
3835. MALENFANT, Chuck
    "What We Pray For." [CimR] (111) Ap 95, p. 69.
3836. MALI, Taylor
    "The Birds, the Bees, and the Gravestones in the Chimney" (for my father).
        [DefinedP] (2:2) Spr-Sum 94, p. 36-37.
    "Cracking Up." [DefinedP] (2:2) Spr-Sum 94, p. 37.
    "Will Mourning Never Come." [DefinedP] (2:2) Spr-Sum 94, p. 35.
3837. MALONE, Eileen
    "Mary Magdalene." [DefinedP] (2:1) Fall-Wint 93, p. 11.
3838. MALONE, Erin
    "After Winter." [PoetryNW] (36:4) Wint 95-96, p. 32-33.
    "A Mathematician's Collision with the Natural World." [PoetryNW] (36:4) Wint 95-
        96, p. 30-31.
    "Visit." [PoetryNW] (36:4) Wint 95-96, p. 31-32.
3839. MALONE, Ida
    "Haikus" (6 poems, WritersCorps Program, Washington, DC). [WashR] (21:2) Ag-S
        95, p. 7.
    "Personification of Death" (WritersCorps Program, Washington, DC). [WashR]
        (21:2) Ag-S 95, p. 7.
    "Personification of Pain" (WritersCorps Program, Washington, DC). [WashR]
        (21:2) Ag-S 95, p. 7.
3840. MALONE, Jacquelyn
    "Another Story." [CumbPR] (14:2) Spr 95, p. 39-40.
    "Sidewinder." [LowellR] (2) c1996, p. 8-9.
    "Sunburst." [LowellR] (2) c1996, p. 10.
3841. MALONE, Paul Scott
    "Indifference" (runner up, 1994 Borderlands Poetry Contest). [Border] (7) Fall-Wint
        96, p. 36.
3842. MALOUF, Diana
    "Wind." [WorldO] (26:4) Sum 95, p. 24.
3843. MALROUX, Claire
    "The body is immobile, left behind" (tr. by Marilyn Hacker). [PoetryE] (41) Aut 95,
        p. 71.
    "Cheek like a lamp on the pillow" (tr. by Marilyn Hacker). [AmerPoR] (24:1) Ja-F
        95, p. 35.

"Citadel" (tr. by C. K. Williams). [TriQ] (94) Fall 95, p. 191.
"Every morning the curtain rises" (tr. by Marilyn Hacker). [AmerPoR] (24:1) Ja-F 95, p. 35.
"The face Divides its space" (tr. by Marilyn Hacker). [AmerPoR] (24:1) Ja-F 95, p. 34.
"The father's shadow" (tr. by Marilyn Hacker). [AmerPoR] (24:1) Ja-F 95, p. 35.
"Fingers probe" (tr. by Marilyn Hacker). [AmerPoR] (24:1) Ja-F 95, p. 34.
"Illumination" (tr. by C. K. Williams). [TriQ] (94) Fall 95, p. 193.
"In October" (tr. by Marilyn Hacker). [AmerPoR] (24:1) Ja-F 95, p. 35.
"The lipstick poised in the air and the feeling of having made up life" (tr. by Marilyn Hacker). [PoetryE] (41) Aut 95, p. 74.
"Octet Before Winter" (4 selections, tr. by Marilyn Hacker). [PoetryE] (41) Aut 95, p. 71.
"Often, like anyone, I ask myself" (tr. by Marilyn Hacker). [PoetryE] (41) Aut 95, p. 72.
"Passed" (tr. by Marilyn Hacker). [AmerPoR] (24:1) Ja-F 95, p. 34.
"Prison for Stars" (tr. by C. K. Williams). [TriQ] (94) Fall 95, p. 192.
"Rough Being" (tr. by C. K. Williams). [TriQ] (94) Fall 95, p. 194.
"She devours the walls" (tr. by Marilyn Hacker). [AmerPoR] (24:1) Ja-F 95, p. 35.
"The sky has grey hair" (tr. by Marilyn Hacker). [AmerPoR] (24:1) Ja-F 95, p. 34.
"A star in distress" (tr. by Marilyn Hacker). [AmerPoR] (24:1) Ja-F 95, p. 35.
"When the birds disperse" (tr. by Marilyn Hacker). [AmerPoR] (24:1) Ja-F 95, p. 35.
"Wisteria on a wrought-iron door, mid-boulevard" (tr. by Marilyn Hacker). [PoetryE] (41) Aut 95, p. 73.
3844. MANCHESTER, Susan A.
"A Child in Winter Loses the Hour of Innocence." [TickleAce] (27) Spr-Sum 94, p. 80.
"Eastern Standard." [FourQ] (9:1/2) Spr 95, p. 56.
"Father Built a Wall." [LullwaterR] (6:2) Fall-Wint 95, p. 60-61.
"Sisters." [TickleAce] (27) Spr-Sum 94, p. 78-79.
"Susan's Dolls." [AntigR] (102/103) Sum-Aug 95, p. 142.
3845. MANDEL, Charlotte
"Flood Tide." [US1] (30/31) 95, p. 12.
3846. MANDEL, Oscar
"Homeric Simile." [PraS] (69:2) Sum 95, p. 124.
"The Schoolyard." [PraS] (69:2) Sum 95, p. 125.
"Untitled: In moments of fear." [PraS] (69:2) Sum 95, p. 126.
3847. MANDEL, Siegfried
"In the Twilight" (tr. of Ingeborg Bachmann, w. Aaron Kramer). [Vis] (47) 95, p. 28.
3848. MANDELL, Arlene L.
"Catching the 7:20." [Rosebud] (2:2) Sum 95, p. 46-47.
"Estate Sale." [Footwork] (24/25) 95, p. 22.
"Flight." [Footwork] (24/25) 95, p. 22.
"The Frog Prince." [SantaBR] (3:2) Sum 95, p. 102.
"Reading List, 1950-1975." [Footwork] (24/25) 95, p. 22.
3849. MANFRED, Freya
"A Body Heals." [NorthStoneR] (12) 95, p. 31.
3850. MANFREDI, Noreen
"Fragments." [Kaleid] (31) Sum-Fall 95, p. 46.
"Sometimes." [Kaleid] (31) Sum-Fall 95, p. 46.
3851. MANG, Ke
"In the Morning, It Has Just Rained" (tr. by Xu Juan). [AxeF] (3) 90, p. 44.
3852. MANICOM, David
"Cover Their Faces." [Quarry] (44:2) 95, p. 81-90.
3853. MANKIEWICZ, Angela Consolo
"We." [SlipS] (15) 95, p. 62.
3854. MANN, Charles Edward
"At This Speed." [Border] (7) Fall-Wint 96, p. 39.
"Beyond Nantucket." [Farm] (12:1) Spr-Sum 95, p. 85.
"In the Thicket" (for Linda). [WillowR] (22) Spr 95, p. 22.
"Signs Keep Mounting." [NewDeltaR] (12:2) Spr-Sum 95, p. 27.
"Stephen Gimbel." [Border] (7) Fall-Wint 96, p. 40.
"What's Left." [DogRR] (14:1, #27) Sum 95, p. 49.
3855. MANN, Jeff
"Leaf Stains." [HampSPR] Wint 95, p. 44.

3856. MANN, John
"Fughetta." [IllinoisR] (2:2) Spr 95, p. 18.
"The Gardener." [IllinoisR] (2:2) Spr 95, p. 17.
3857. MANNER, Eeva-Liisa
"How the Seasons Change" (tr. by Ritva Poom). [LitR] (38:3) Spr 95, p. 349.
3858. MANOO-RAHMING, Lelawattee
"Incarnation at the Caroni." [CaribbeanW] (9) 95, p. 68-69.
3859. MANOPOULOS, Monique
"Low Tide 1856" (tr. of Jude Stéfan, w. Philip Kobylarz). [Chelsea] (58) 95, p. 135.
"To Thomas Gray" (tr. of Jude Stéfan, w. Philip Kobylarz). [Chelsea] (58) 95, p. 136.
3860. MANROE, Candace
"Unseasonal Ending." [TexasR] (16:1/4) 95, p. 139-140.
3861. MANSILLA TORRES, Sergio
"Apuntes sobre Pioneer Square." [Americas] (23:3/4) Fall-Wint 95, p. 144.
"Un Cantor en la University Way Avenue." [Americas] (23:3/4) Fall-Wint 95, p. 147.
"Lucidez Que Duele." [Americas] (23:3/4) Fall-Wint 95, p. 145.
"Trébol de Cuatro Hojas para las Extranjeras Manos." [Americas] (23:3/4) Fall-Wint 95, p. 146.
MANTIA, Benito la
See La MANTIA, Benito
3862. MARCELLO, Leo Luke
"Get-Together Dinner, at Sea, February 21, 1937." [LouisL] (12:1) Spr 95, p. 60-61.
3863. MARCH, Andy
"The Power of Myth." [PoetryE] (40) Spr 95, p. 79-81.
"Sarajevo." [PoetryE] (40) Spr 95, p. 78.
3864. MARCHAND, Blaine
"Linguistics." [ModernW] (3) Sum 95, p. 77-78.
3865. MARCHANT, Fred
"Family Life." [WeberS] (12:2) Spr-Sum 95, p. 27.
"Petroglyphs at Parawan Gap." [WeberS] (12:2) Spr-Sum 95, p. 27.
"Sunday." [WeberS] (12:2) Spr-Sum 95, p. 28.
3866. MARCHITTI, Elizabeth
"Johnny Mapleseed." [Footwork] (24/25) 95, p. 68.
3867. MARCOTTE, Madeline
"Moonsocket." [LullwaterR] (6:1) Spr-Sum 95, p. 54.
"Rattus Norvegicus." [QW] (41) Aut-Wint 95-96, p. 159.
3868. MARCUS, Jacqueline
"Absolution Through the Cello." [CimR] (113) O 95, p. 61.
"Absolution Through the Cello." [Journal] (19:2) Fall-Wint 95, p. 16.
"Day After Thanksgiving (Hiding)." [ColEng] (57:8) D 95, p. 938-939.
"The Drowning." [ColEng] (57:8) D 95, p. 940-942.
"No Other Heaven." [KenR] (17:1) Wint 95, p. 95-97.
"Old Peasant, 1903" (after Paula Modersohn-Becker). [HayF] (17) Fall-Wint 95, p. 47.
"Vincent Van Gogh's Mulberry Tree." [ColEng] (57:8) D 95, p. 939-940.
3869. MARCUS, Mordecai
"The Kuzma Beard." [LullwaterR] (5:1) 93-94, p. 10-11.
"Nourishments." [Elf] (5:2) Sum 95, p. 29.
3870. MARCUS, Morton
"Chekhov's Funeral." [AntR] (53:1) Wint 95, p. 73.
"Growing Old." [ProseP] (4) 95, p. 56.
"Guillotine." [ProseP] (4) 95, p. 54-55.
3871. MARCUS, Peter
"Apple Song." [PraS] (69:3) Fall 95, p. 19.
"Backseat." [HarvardR] (9) Fall 95, p. 94.
"Comeback" (for Mark Cohn and Lyle Lovett). [PraS] (69:3) Fall 95, p. 20.
"Dark Remedies" (Selections: II, IV-VI). [NewEngR] (17:1) Wint 95, p. 107-109.
"Phoenix." [Ploughs] (21:1) Spr 95, p. 86.
"Shoe Shine." [PoetryE] (39) Fall 94, p. 62.
"To the Pier" (for Bob Marcus). [PoetryE] (39) Fall 94, p. 63.
3872. MARCUS, Stanley
"Chrome Yellow." [LitR] (38:3) Spr 95, p. 369.
"College Boy." [VirQR] (71:4) Aut 95, p. 696-697.
"Surfaces." [VirQR] (71:4) Aut 95, p. 697-698.

3873. MARCUS, Victor
    "Goodbye, My Sweet." [Light] (15/16) Aut-Wint 95-96, p. 20.
3874. MARGARET M. (Dinner Program for Homeless Women, Washington, DC)
    "Bandaging the City" (WritersCorps Program). [WashR] (21:2) Ag-S 95, p. 8.
3875. MARGOLIN, Anna
    "Among the Chinese Lanterns" (tr. by Shirley Kumove). [Writ] (27) 95, p. 14-15.
    "Brisk (Brest-Litovsk)" (tr. by Shirley Kumove). [Writ] (27) 95, p. 9-11.
    "Drunk from the Bitter Truth" (tr. by Shirley Kumove). [Writ] (27) 95, p. 12.
    "Full of Night and Weeping" (tr. by Shirley Kumove). [Writ] (27) 95, p. 13.
    "I Want, Angry and Tender One" (tr. by Shirley Kumove). [Writ] (27) 95, p. 17.
    "Mary Wants to Be a Beggar Woman" (tr. by Shirley Kumove). [Writ] (27) 95, p.
    16.
    "My Ancestors Speak" (tr. by Shirley Kumove). [Writ] (27) 95, p. 7-8.
3876. MARGOLIS, Gary
    "Proof of the Possible." [PraS] (69:4) Wint 95, p. 112-113.
    "To a Student Swept Up." [PraS] (69:4) Wint 95, p. 111-112.
3877. MARGOLIS, Michelle
    "Near St. John's." [PoetL] (90:4) Wint 95-96, p. 34.
3878. MARGOSHES, Dave
    "Barium Moon." [Grain] (23:1) Sum 95, p. 117-120.
3879. MARIANI, Paul
    "Antiphon." [Image] (12) Wint 95-96, p. 37-38.
    "Harry." [GettyR] (8:3) Sum 95, p. 494-495.
    "Pilgrim." [Image] (12) Wint 95-96, p. 36-37.
    "The Republic" (for David Ignatow). [GettyR] (8:3) Sum 95, p. 496-497.
    "Then." [Poetry] (167:3) D 95, p. 151.
3880. MARIANI, Rob (Robert)
    "The Hive in Autumn." [DefinedP] (1:1) Fall-Wint 92, p. 11.
    "Rehoboth Autumn." [DefinedP] (2:1) Fall-Wint 93, p. 10.
    "Totem Pole." [DefinedP] (1:1) Fall-Wint 92, p. 10.
3881. MARINETTI, F. T.
    "Flying Over the Heart of Italy" (from *The Pope's Monoplane*). [NewEngR] (17:4)
    Fall 95, p. 22-29.
3882. MARINOVICH, Matt
    "Demolition." [QW] (41) Aut-Wint 95-96, p. 205.
    "Dinner at the Grecian Urn." [QW] (41) Aut-Wint 95-96, p. 206-207.
    "Embarcadero." [Sonora] (29) Spr 95, p. 105-106.
3883. MARION, Paul
    "Smelling like Childhood." [LowellR] [1] Sum 94, p. 16.
3884. MARIS, Kathryn
    "Schooling." [NewL] (62:1) 96 (c1995), p. 77.
MARIS, Ron de
    See De MARIS, Ron
3885. MARKHAM, Malinda
    "The Fortune Teller's Daughter." [IndR] (18:1) Spr 95, p. 131-132.
3886. MARKOTIC, Nicole
    "1: Because the Wood Remembers." [WestCL] (29:1, #16) Spr-Sum 95, p. 89.
    "2: A Lip, Tucked Under." [WestCL] (29:1, #16) Spr-Sum 95, p. 90.
3887. MARKS, Corey
    "Light." [IndR] (18:1) Spr 95, p. 7-8.
    "Portrait of a Child." [AntR] (53:1) Wint 95, p. 70-71.
3888. MARKS, Gigi
    "A Child's Birthday Party." [Farm] (13:2 [i.e. 12:2]) Fall-Wint 95, p. 22.
    "Disarray." [Crazy] (49) Wint 95, p. 15.
    "Feasts." [PraS] (69:3) Fall 95, p. 33.
    "Formations." [Crazy] (49) Wint 95, p. 14.
    "Lost." [Farm] (13:2 [i.e. 12:2]) Fall-Wint 95, p. 23.
    "Why Here." [NowestR] (33:1) 95, p. 51.
    "Winter Night." [Crazy] (49) Wint 95, p. 13.
3889. MARKUS, Peter
    "Light." [ProseP] (4) 95, p. 57.
3890. MARLIS, Stefanie
    "Another Morning." [DenQ] (29:3) Wint 95, p. 24.
    "Carnival." [DenQ] (29:3) Wint 95, p. 25.
    "Days." [Manoa] (7:1) Sum 95, p. 197.
    "Dominoes." [Sonora] (30) Fall 95, p. 1.

"Evening on Valencia." [Manoa] (7:1) Sum 95, p. 197.
"The World." [Manoa] (7:1) Sum 95, p. 198.
3891. MARMARA, Nilgün
"The Family of Acrobats" (tr. by Murat Nemet-Nejat). [Talisman] (14) Fall 95, p. 53.
"Pedestrian" (tr. by Murat Nemet-Nejat). [Talisman] (14) Fall 95, p. 54.
3892. MARQUART, Debra
"Finding the Words." [Kalliope] (17:2) 95, p. 30-31.
3893. MARSH, Alec
"Moon Goddess." [TriQ] (95) Wint 95-96, p. 180-181.
3894. MARSH, Irene Eberling
"Trina's Dream." [Parting] (8:2) Wint 95-96, p. 43.
"Vivian's Dream." [Parting] (8:2) Wint 95-96, p. 43.
3895. MARSH, Karla
"Half White." [Grain] (23:2) Aut 95, p. 56.
"A Whisper to Conceive." [Grain] (23:2) Aut 95, p. 56.
3896. MARSH, William
"Poem beginning with a Line Sung by an Open Mike Guitarist at the Arborvitae Cafe." [Arshile] (4) 95, p. 18.
3897. MARSHALL, Jack
"Climbing Vine." [Zyzzyva] (11:1, #41) Spr 95, p. 125-128.
"The Evolution of Memory." [Talisman] (15) Wint 95-96, p. 127-130.
"Sesame." [Zyzzyva] (11:3/4, #43/44) 95, "The Best of Ten Years of ZYZZYVA," p. 57-69.
3898. MARSHALL, John
"The Traveller" (for Douwe Stuurman). [CanLit] (145) Sum 95, p. 82-83.
3899. MARSHALL, Jon
"Soulard Market." [GreenHLL] (5) 94, p. 83-84.
3900. MARSHALL, Tod
"Autumn Song" (tr. of Oscar Vladislas de Lubicz Milosz). [WillowS] (36) Je 95, p. 108.
"Blood-Ties." [HighP] (10:3) Wint 95, p. 56-57.
"Botticelli." [DenQ] (29:4) Spr 95, p. 37-41.
"The Bridge" (tr. of Oscar Vladislas de Lubicz Milosz). [WillowS] (36) Je 95, p. 109.
"Brothers Fishing." [ClockR] (10:1/2) 95-96, p. 143.
"In Praise of the Belly." [PoetryE] (39) Fall 94, p. 64-66.
"A Minor Prophecy" (upstate N.Y., 1971). [ClockR] (10:1/2) 95-96, p. 144.
"Parenting." [CreamCR] (19:1) Spr 95, p. 119.
"Routine Maintenance." [HighP] (10:3) Wint 95, p. 60.
"Sculpting." [PoetryE] (40) Spr 95, p. 82.
3901. MARSOCCI, R. F.
"Confirmation." [Parting] (8:2) Wint 95-96, p. 39.
3902. MARSTON, Jane
"Earth Song" (title of a birthday card featuring "Sea Garden," by Leonard Bencken). [Poem] (73) My 95, p. 45.
"Japanese Maples" (on view at the State Botanical Garden of Georgia). [Poem] (73) My 95, p. 46.
"The Monument Maker." [Poem] (73) My 95, p. 47.
"One More Time to Venice." [Poem] (73) My 95, p. 44.
"The Tiller." [Poem] (73) My 95, p. 48.
3903. MARTA, Anette
"May the Water Keep Vigil with Me" (tr. of Sándor Csoóri, w. Len Roberts). [GrandS] (14:2, #54) Fall 95, p. 22.
"So You Won't Be a Witness Today Either" (tr. of Sándor Csoóri, w. Len Roberts). [GrandS] (14:2, #54) Fall 95, p. 21.
3904. MARTEAU, Robert
"23 VIII 1983" (in French, tr. of Peter Nim). [Os] (40) 95, p. 17.
"Migrateurs" (in French, tr. of Peter Nim). [Os] (40) 95, p. 33.
"Les Petites Choses" (in French, tr. of Peter Nim). [Os] (40) 95, p. 19.
3905. MARTENS, Jacinta Taitano
"Drunk, with the Fragrance of Eucalyptus." [Footwork] (24/25) 95, p. 136.
"I'm New to This House." [Footwork] (24/25) 95, p. 136.
"In Cabo San Lucas." [Footwork] (24/25) 95, p. 136.
MARTHA CHRISTINA
See CHRISTINA, Martha

MARTHA ELIZABETH
See ELIZABETH, Martha
3906. MARTIAL
"I, xxxii. I do not like you, Jesse Helms" (tr. by William Matthews). [Pequod] (39)
95, p. 153.
"I, xxxvii. You shit into a gold urn, Bassus" (tr. by William Matthews). [Pequod]
(39) 95, p. 153.
"V, lix. No silver plate for you, this year, nor any gold" (tr. by William Matthews).
[Pequod] (39) 95, p. 153.
"VI, xix. I've charged the lout next door" (tr. by William Matthews). [Pequod] (39)
95, p. 153.
"VII, xc. Matho calls my epigrams 'uneven'" (tr. by William Matthews). [Pequod]
(39) 95, p. 154.
"VII, xcii. Whatever you need, you don't have to ask" (tr. by William Matthews).
[Pequod] (39) 95, p. 154.
"VIII, xii. Why don't I yearn to wed a rich wife?" (tr. by William Matthews).
[Pequod] (39) 95, p. 154.
"VIII, xx. Two hundred lines a day the nitwit writes" (tr. by William Matthews).
[Pequod] (39) 95, p. 154.
"VIII, xxix. Brevity's sweet, the couplet-maker hopes" (tr. by William Matthews).
[Pequod] (39) 95, p. 155.
"IX, vii. You'd just got back from your travels" (tr. by William Matthews). [Pequod]
(39) 95, p. 155.
"IX, xlvii. When you swore on your head and then by your sacred rites" (tr. by
William Matthews). [ManhatR] (7:2) Wint 95, p. 21.
"X, xiv. Among my friends, you swear, you're second to none" (tr. by William
Matthews). [Pequod] (39) 95, p. 155.
"X, lxxxi. Two randy men come to fuck Phyllis" (tr. by William Matthews).
[Pequod] (39) 95, p. 155.
"XI, xviii. You have given me, Lupus, a small farm" (tr. by William Matthews).
[ManhatR] (7:2) Wint 95, p. 22.
"XI, lxxiii. You'll come when I ask?" (tr. by William Matthews). [ManhatR] (7:2)
Wint 95, p. 23.
"Because you send lavish gifts to widows" (IV, lvi, tr. by William Matthews).
[Crazy] (48) Spr 95, p. 34.
"Could I give up your neck, Chloe, your face" (III, liii, tr. by William Matthews).
[Crazy] (48) Spr 95, p. 36.
"How can Philins be a father" (X, cii, tr. by William Matthews). [DenQ] (29:3) Wint
95, p. 26.
"Sextus, do you like writing books none but" (X, xxi, tr. by William Matthews).
[DenQ] (29:3) Wint 95, p. 26.
"You ask what's that stench in Marius's ear?" (III, xxvii, tr. by William Matthews).
[Crazy] (48) Spr 95, p. 37.
"Young beauties slink past and your cock is flaccid" (III, lxxvi, tr. by William
Matthews). [Crazy] (48) Spr 95, p. 35.
3907. MARTIN, Camille
"Incognito Broadcast." [NewOR] (21:2) Sum 95, p. 69.
"Métro." [NewOR] (21:2) Sum 95, p. 68-69.
3908. MARTIN, Carl
"Jupiter Flower" (After the Mozart symphony nicknamed "Jupiter"). [Pembroke]
(27) 95, p. 120-121.
"Traveling Beauty." [Pembroke] (27) 95, p. 121.
3909. MARTIN, Charles
"Stanzas After *Endgame*." [Boulevard] (10:3, #30) Fall 95, p. 137-141.
MARTIN, Diane Kirsten
See KIRSTEN-MARTIN, Diane
3910. MARTIN, Herbert Woodward
"Momentary Observations." [ChironR] (43) Sum 95, p. 28.
"Passing Into Light" (for Betty Youngkin Celebrating Light). [ChironR] (44/45)
Aut-Wint 95, p. 21.
3911. MARTIN, Jill
"Profile." [WillowR] (22) Spr 95, p. 10.
3912. MARTIN, Lynn
"Dead Fish / Rockfish." [PoetryE] (41) Aut 95, p. 47.
"Harris Hollow." [PoetryE] (41) Aut 95, p. 43.

"Needing 20 Windows and Looking for a Break, I Went to the Factory in Rocky Mount." [PoetryE] (41) Aut 95, p. 44-45.
"Unexpected Places." [AnthNEW] (7) 95, p. 35.
"Yesterday I Went into the woods." [PoetryE] (41) Aut 95, p. 46.
3913. MARTIN, Patrick
"The Basement." [ParisR] (37:137) Wint 95, p. 218.
"The Climber." [ParisR] (37:137) Wint 95, p. 217.
"Divorce." [ParisR] (37:137) Wint 95, p. 216.
"False Alarm." [ParisR] (37:137) Wint 95, p. 215.
"In Dog-Years." [ParisR] (37:137) Wint 95, p. 218-219.
"The Nights on False Island." [ParisR] (37:137) Wint 95, p. 221-222.
"Roaches." [ParisR] (37:137) Wint 95, p. 221.
"Sands." [ParisR] (37:137) Wint 95, p. 219-220.
3914. MARTIN, Paul
"Milltown." [SmPd] (32:3, #95) Fall 95, p. 33.
3915. MARTIN, Richard
"The Bartender in 1968" (for my father). [NewMyths] (2:2/3:1) 95, p. 184-185.
"On the Border of a Chill." [NewMyths] (2:2/3:1) 95, p. 181-182.
3916. MARTINELLI, Jeanne E.
"Aphrodisiac." [Drumvoices] (4:1/2) Fall-Wint 94-95, p. 34.
"Poets' Souls" (For Sterling). [Drumvoices] (4:1/2) Fall-Wint 94-95, p. 35.
3917. MARTINEZ, Demetria
"Imperialism." [MassR] (36:4) Wint 95-96, p. 624.
"Milagros" (after a painting by Francisco LeFebre). [MassR] (36:4) Wint 95-96, p. 626.
"We Talk about Spanish." [MassR] (36:4) Wint 95-96, p. 625.
3918. MARTINEZ, Dionisio D.
"Belated Valentine for Alina." [VirQR] (71:1) Wint 95, p. 111-113.
"God Asked Adam." [IndR] (18:1) Spr 95, p. 136.
"In a Duplex Near the San Andreas Fault." [MidAR] (15:1/2) 95, p. 113.
"Looking for Frank O'Hara on Fire Island." [GettyR] (8:1) Wint 95, p. 174.
"Nocturnes." [SenR] (25:1) Spr 95, p. 118-119.
"The Prodigal Son Buys a New Car." [MassR] (36:4) Wint 95-96, p. 627.
"The Prodigal Son Loses His Wife." [MassR] (36:4) Wint 95-96, p. 627.
"Starfish" (for Jessica Marie Cason). [MassR] (36:4) Wint 95-96, p. 628.
"Thermoluminescence." [IndR] (18:1) Spr 95, p. 135.
"The Vernacular of the Eyes." [MidAR] (15:1/2) 95, p. 114-116.
3919. MARTINEZ, Erik
"Advice to My Enemies." [Arc] (35) Aut 95, p. 12.
"How Come Welfare Paid Me." [Arc] (35) Aut 95, p. 11.
3920. MARTINEZ, Rubén Gerard
"Silent Pleas." [BilingR] (20:2) My-Ag 95, p. 166.
"Under God's Sidelong Shadow" (Malibu Fires). [BilingR] (20:2) My-Ag 95, p. 167.
3921. MARTINEZ, Victor
"Drinking Too Much." [LowellR] [1] Sum 94, p. 84-85.
3922. MARTINS, Leda
"Solstice" (tr. by Ana Lúcia A. Gazolla and Kevin John Keys). [Callaloo] (18:4) Fall 95, p. 871.
"Solstício." [Callaloo] (18:4) Fall 95, p. 1031.
3923. MARTONE, John
"Fold clothes." [Northeast] (5:12) Sum 95, p. 28.
"Going thru the house." [Northeast] (5:12) Sum 95, p. 29.
"More." [Northeast] (5:12) Sum 95, p. 28.
"Speckled slug." [Northeast] (5:12) Sum 95, p. 28.
3924. MARTONE, Michael
"At a Loss." [Flyway] (1:2) Fall 95, p. 13.
3925. MARUYAMA, David
"Poem to You." [ChironR] (43) Sum 95, p. 32.
3926. MARVELL, Andrew (1621-1678)
"To His Coy Mistress." [PoetryE] (41) Aut 95, p. 31-32.
3927. MARVIN, Jay
"2. Laying there on that slab in Vallegrande." [BlackBR] (21) Fall-Wint 95, p. 38.
"As If Nothing Matters." [ContextS] (4:2) 95, p. 10.
"His Frustration." [Pearl] (22) Fall-Wint 95, p. 27.
3928. MARVIN, John
"The Room." [HiramPoR] (58/59) Spr 95-Wint 96, p. 52-53.

"The Shape of Space." [Elf] (5:3) Fall 95, p. 34-35.
"Triptych Tony Tries Amherst, New York." [HiramPoR] (58/59) Spr 95-Wint 96, p. 54-57.
3929. MARY (D.C. Vision Program, Tyler Elementary School, Washington, DC).
"Storm" (WritersCorps Program). [WashR] (21:2) Ag-S 95, p. 19.
3930. MARZAN, Julio
"Foreign Heart." [MassR] (36:4) Wint 95-96, p. 630.
"The Translator at the Reception for Latin American Writers." [MassR] (36:4) Wint 95-96, p. 629.
3931. MASARIK, Al
"Gift." [AxeF] (3) 90, p. 15.
"Late in August." [AxeF] (3) 90, p. 14.
"Really Hot Sex." [AxeF] (3) 90, p. 14.
MASATO, Inagawa
   See INAGAWA, Masato
3932. MASON, David
"The Country I Remember: A Narrative." [Hudson] (48:2) Sum 95, p. 187-228.
"A Disagreement with Maud." [Light] (15/16) Aut-Wint 95-96, p. 21.
"Exile on Land" (tr. of Yiorgos Chouliaras, w. the author). [InterPR] (21:1) Spr 95, p. 28-29.
"I Am Working on My Greek" (tr. of Yiorgos Chouliaras, w. the author). [InterQ] (2:1/2) 95, p. 89.
"The Myth of the Plumber" (tr. of Yiorgos Chouliaras, w. the author). [InterQ] (2:1/2) 95, p. 89.
"Questions at Christmas." [Poetry] (167:3) D 95, p. 150.
"This Is Your Gift." [MidwQ] (36:4) Sum 95, p. 397.
"When Experience Speaks" (tr. of Yiorgos Chouliaras, w. the author). [InterQ] (2:1/2) 95, p. 89.
3933. MASON, Janet
"Natural History." [ModernW] (3) Sum 95, p. 104.
"When I Was Straight." [ModernW] (3) Sum 95, p. 102-103.
3934. MASON, Keith Antar
"The Exact Place." [HolCrit] (32:1) F 95, p. 17.
3935. MASSEY, Marina Guadalupe
"Michael's Song." [RiverS] (41) 95, p. 30.
3936. MASTERSON, Dan
"Last Days in Missolonghi." [GettyR] (8:3) Sum 95, p. 498-499.
3937. MASUDA, Misako
"I look at each boy's corpse" (in Japanese and English, tr. by Jiro Nakano).
   [BambooR] (67/68) Sum-Fall 95, p. 43.
3938. MASUDA, Reisuke
"Without a word, my wife returns" (in Japanese and English, tr. by Jiro Nakano).
   [BambooR] (67/68) Sum-Fall 95, p. 44.
3939. MATEVSKI, Mateya
"Fortress" (tr. by Zoran Anchevski). [Vis] (48) 95, p. 32-34.
"The Great Wall of China" (tr. by Zoran Anchevski). [Vis] (48) 95, p. 35-36.
MATHAIS, John
   See MATTHIAS, John
3940. MATHEWS, Aidan Carl
"Handicap." [Poetry] (167:1/2) O-N 95, p. 55.
"Way Out." [Poetry] (167:1/2) O-N 95, p. 52-53.
"When." [Poetry] (167:1/2) O-N 95, p. 54.
3941. MATHEWS, Harry
"Marriage of Two Minds: Received Visions." [YaleR] (83:2) Ap 95, p. 56-61.
3942. MATHIS, Cleopatra
"After the Operation." [Agni] (42) 95, p. 41-42.
"Poem for Marriage." [OhioR] (53) 95, p. 48-49.
MATHISEN, Aina Gerner
   See GERNER-MATHISEN, A. (Aina)
3943. MATSON, Suzanne
"Milk / Love." [HarvardR] (9) Fall 95, p. 88.
3944. MATSUMOTO, Chiyoji
"The road to a nuclear free world" (in Japanese and English, tr. by Jiro Nakano).
   [BambooR] (67/68) Sum-Fall 95, p. 45.

3945. MATSUMURA, Shofu
"It is a living mess" (in Japanese and English, tr. by Jiro Nakano). [BambooR] (67/68) Sum-Fall 95, p. 46.
3946. MATTAWA, Khaled
"The Abyss" (tr. of Hatif Janabi). [IndR] (18:2) Fall 95, p. 49.
"Borrowed Tongue." [NewEngR] (17:4) Fall 95, p. 149.
"Bread & Butter." [BlackWR] (22:1) Fall-Wint 95, p. 91-92.
"The Chemistry of Knowledge" (tr. of Hatif Janabi). [GrahamHR] (19) Wint 95-96, p. 56.
"Corpus Christi." [Crazy] (48) Spr 95, p. 47-48.
"Crank Call From Tabriz." [CutB] (43) Wint 95, p. 35-36.
"Cricket Mountain." [ArtfulD] (28/29) 95, p. 4.
"Days of 1932." [ArtfulD] (28/29) 95, p. 6.
"Days of 1948." [ArtfulD] (28/29) 95, p. 7.
"Days of 1959." [CrabOR] (1:1) Fall-Wint 95, p. 78.
"Double Portrait with Trains." [CrabOR] (1:1) Fall-Wint 95, p. 79-82.
"Fifty April Years." [Crazy] (48) Spr 95, p. 42-44.
"The First House" (tr. of Hashim Shafiq). [WillowS] (36) Je 95, p. 105.
"For Jamal Juma'a" (tr. of Sa'adi Youssef). [ArtfulD] (28/29) 95, p. 12.
"An Initial Description" (tr. of Hatif Janabi). [IndR] (18:2) Fall 95, p. 45.
"Ismailia Eclipse." [Crazy] (48) Spr 95, p. 49-52.
"Lucinda at St. John's Church, Geneva." [LitR] (38:2) Wint 95, p. 183-184.
"On the Red Sea" (tr. of Sa'adi Youssef). [WillowS] (36) Je 95, p. 104.
"Poems of the New Regions" (tr. of Hatif Janabi). [IndR] (18:2) Fall 95, p. 46-48.
"Samovar Love Compendium." [CimR] (112) Jl 95, p. 102-103.
"Savage Continents" (tr. of Hatif Janabi). [ArtfulD] (28/29) 95, p. 8-9.
"Selima!" [ArtfulD] (28/29) 95, p. 5.
"Three Kitchens." [Crazy] (48) Spr 95, p. 53-54.
"To His Father: A Biography." [KenR] (17:2) Spr 95, p. 113-117.
"To Where?" (tr. of Hatif Janabi). [ArtfulD] (28/29) 95, p. 10-11.
"Two River Ledger." [Crazy] (48) Spr 95, p. 45-46.
"A Window Small as a Palm Vast as Suffering" (tr. of Hatif Janabi). [IndR] (18:2) Fall 95, p. 43-44.
"The Yellow Face of Hunger" (tr. of Hatif Janabi). [GrahamHR] (19) Wint 95-96, p. 57-58.
3947. MATTERN, Evelyn
"Mornings." [InterPR] (21:1) Spr 95, p. 83.
MATTHAIS, John
See MATTHIAS, John
3948. MATTHEWS, William
"I, xxxii. I do not like you, Jesse Helms" (tr. of Martial). [Pequod] (39) 95, p. 153.
"I, xxxvii. You shit into a gold urn, Bassus" (tr. of Martial). [Pequod] (39) 95, p. 153.
"V, lix. No silver plate for you, this year, nor any gold" (tr. of Martial). [Pequod] (39) 95, p. 153.
"VI, xix. I've charged the lout next door" (tr. of Martial). [Pequod] (39) 95, p. 153.
"VII, xc. Matho calls my epigrams 'uneven'" (tr. of Martial). [Pequod] (39) 95, p. 154.
"VII, xcii. Whatever you need, you don't have to ask" (tr. of Martial). [Pequod] (39) 95, p. 154.
"VIII, xii. Why don't I yearn to wed a rich wife?" (tr. of Martial). [Pequod] (39) 95, p. 154.
"VIII, xx. Two hundred lines a day the nitwit writes" (tr. of Martial). [Pequod] (39) 95, p. 154.
"VIII, xxix. Brevity's sweet, the couplet-maker hopes" (tr. of Martial). [Pequod] (39) 95, p. 155.
"IX, vii. You'd just got back from your travels" (tr. of Martial). [Pequod] (39) 95, p. 155.
"IX, xlvii. When you swore on your head and then by your sacred rites" (tr. of Martial). [ManhatR] (7:2) Wint 95, p. 21.
"X, xiv. Among my friends, you swear, you're second to none" (tr. of Martial). [Pequod] (39) 95, p. 155.
"X, lxxxi. Two randy men come to fuck Phyllis" (tr. of Martial). [Pequod] (39) 95, p. 155.
"XI, xviii. You have given me, Lupus, a small farm" (tr. of Martial). [ManhatR] (7:2) Wint 95, p. 22.

"XI, lxxiii. You'll come when I ask?" (tr. of Martial). [ManhatR] (7:2) Wint 95, p. 23.
"Because you send lavish gifts to widows" (tr. of Martial IV, lvi). [Crazy] (48) Spr 95, p. 34.
"Big Tongue." [BlackWR] (21:2) Spr-Sum 95, p. 141-143.
"Could I give up your neck, Chloe, your face" (tr. of Martial III, liii). [Crazy] (48) Spr 95, p. 36.
"The Generations." [Shen] (45:2) Sum 95, p. 90-91.
"High Life in Manhattan." [GreenMR] (8:1) Spr-Sum 95, p. 51.
"How can Philins be a father" (X, cii, tr. of Martial). [DenQ] (29:3) Wint 95, p. 26.
"Literary Biography." [Light] (14) Sum 95, p. 16.
"Lunch in Hell." [TarRP] (35:1) Fall 95, p. 15.
"Night Prayer." [Shen] (45:2) Sum 95, p. 89.
"Portrait of the Artist As a Young Clarinettist." [Poetry] (165:6) Mr 95, p. 333.
"Room Full of Used Baby Furniture for Sale." [Poetry] (165:6) Mr 95, p. 332.
"Satires I, ix" (tr. of Horace). [OhioR] (54) 95, p. 27-30.
"Sextus, do you like writing books none but" (X, xxi, tr. of Martial). [DenQ] (29:3) Wint 95, p. 26.
"The Socratic Method." [SenR] (25:1) Spr 95, p. 102-103.
"Sorrow." [TarRP] (35:1) Fall 95, p. 14-15.
"Truffle Pigs." [NewYorker] (71:26) 4 S 95, p. 46.
"You ask what's that stench in Marius's ear?" (tr. of Martial III, xxvii). [Crazy] (48) Spr 95, p. 37.
"Young beauties slink past and your cock is flaccid" (tr. of Martial III, lxxvi). [Crazy] (48) Spr 95, p. 35.
3949. MATTHIAS, John
"C.P.R." [Salm] (106/107) Spr-Sum 95, p. 121.
"Everything to Be Endured" (For Ernest Sandeen). [Salm] (106/107) Spr-Sum 95, p. 119-120.
"Into Cyrillic." [AnotherCM] (29) Spr 95, p. 84.
"Mozart Variation #7" (tr. of Goran Sonnevi, w. G. Printz-Pahlson). [Vis] (49) 95, p. 35.
"Mozart Variation #8" (tr. of Goran Sonnevi, w. G. Printz-Pahlson). [Vis] (49) 95, p. 35.
"Mozart Variation #12" (tr. of Goran Sonnevi, w. G. Printz-Pahlson). [Vis] (47) 95, p. 11.
MATTIA, Sally de
   See De MATTIA, Sally
3950. MATTINGLY, Tracy
"The Plain States." [OxfordM] (9:2) Fall-Wint 93, p. 27-29.
"Requiem." [OxfordM] (9:2) Fall-Wint 93, p. 24-26.
3951. MATTOX, Gretchen
"The Olive Tree." [Pequod] (39) 95, p. 65-66.
3952. MATTSON, Kim
"Premonition." [GrahamHR] (19) Wint 95-96, p. 39.
3953. MAURER, Bonnie
"Ironing the Pocket of My Child's Dress." [HopewellR] (7) 95, p. 106.
3954. MAURER-ALVAREZ, Pansy
"Angles in the Apline Mode." [HangL] (67) 95, p. 54.
"Darlene's." [HangL] (67) 95, p. 49-51.
"I Slept Through the Rush Hour Alone." [HangL] (66) 95, p. 41.
"Like Grand Central Station." [HangL] (66) 95, p. 42-43.
"Midday Paris Saturday." [HangL] (67) 95, p. 52-53.
"On Reading 'Days and Nights' by Kenneth Koch." [HangL] (66) 95, p. 44-45.
"On Saint Martinien's Day, July 2, 1993" (after Frank O'Hara). [HangL] (66) 95, p. 45.
"This Sure Isn't the Pennsylvania Turnpike." [HangL] (67) 95, p. 45-48.
3955. MAUTNER, Janice
"Wrath of a Daydream (the Funeral of James Baldwin)." [AfAmRev] (29:4) Wint 95, p. 626-627.
3956. MAVIGLIA, Joseph
"Anorexia." [Descant] (26:1, #88) Spr 95, p. 53.
"Dead Squirrel." [Descant] (26:1, #88) Spr 95, p. 54-55.
"Easter." [Descant] (26:1, #88) Spr 95, p. 56.
"Moment of the Heart." [Descant] (26:1, #88) Spr 95, p. 52.

3957. MAXSON, H. A.
"Curley Finds Solace in the Company of Men." [CimR] (113) O 95, p. 47.
"Curley Sees That Keeper Look in Manny's Eyes." [CimR] (113) O 95, p. 46.
"Lull." [CimR] (113) O 95, p. 45.
"The Walking Tour: Alexander Wilson in America" (3 selections). [JlNJPo] (17:2)
Aut 95, p. 8-12.
3958. MAXWELL, Glyn
"Car Game." [ManhatR] (7:2) Wint 95, p. 19.
"County Event." [Verse] (12:2) 95, p. 89-90.
"The Devil at War." [ManhatR] (7:2) Wint 95, p. 17-18.
"A Swing from Gotham Central." [ManhatR] (7:2) Wint 95, p. 20.
3959. MAXWELL, Marina Ama Omowale
"To My Love Still." [CaribbeanW] (9) 95, p. 41.
3960. MAXWELL, Mary
"The Stonewall Jackson Hotel." [SouthernR] (31:1) Wint 95, p. 34-35.
"Team Player." [Pequod] (39) 95, p. 63-64.
"Thin Men." [Grain] (23:1) Sum 95, p. 54.
3961. MAXWELL, Timothy
"La Calle San Francisco — San Miguel de Allende, Mexico." [SantaBR] (3:1) Spr
95, p. 66.
"Silver." [SantaBR] (3:1) Spr 95, p. 65.
"Thoughts Upon Life in California." [SantaBR] (3:1) Spr 95, p. 67.
3962. MAY, Eleanor Rodman
"Dream Baby." [Crucible] (30) Fall 94, p. 26.
3963. MAY, Kerry Paul
"A Blessing." [SilverFR] (26) Wint 95, p. 37.
"Universe." [SilverFR] (26) Wint 95, p. 38.
"Wheat Belt" (for Brad). [SilverFR] (26) Wint 95, p. 39.
MAY, Le Thi
See LE, Thi May
3964. MAYER, Barbara J.
"Brookgreen Gardens." [Crucible] (30) Fall 94, p. 42.
"Pennsylvania Dutch Country." [Crucible] (31) Fall 95, p. 31.
3965. MAYERS, Florence Cassen
"A Source of Light." [AmerLC] (7) 95, p. 32-33.
3966. MAYERS, T. R.
"The Lucid Dreamer's Christmas Poems." [JlNJPo] (17:1) Spr 95, p. 37-38.
"Thanksgiving Day, in Transit." [JlNJPo] (17:1) Spr 95, p. 36.
3967. MAYES, Frances
"At Either End of Memory." [VirQR] (71:3) Sum 95, p. 486-489.
"Lines for Massimo." [NewAW] (13) Fall-Wint 95, p. 91-92.
3968. MAYFIELD, Damia (grade 8, Backus Junior High School, Washington, DC)
"Colors" (Poetry on the Metro Project). [WashR] (21:2) Ag-S 95, p. 14.
3969. MAYHOOD, Clif
"Muse of the Plate" (after a painting by Paul Bibbo). [JamesWR] (12:2) Spr-Sum
95, p. 18.
3970. MAZUR, Gail
"Bluebonnets." [Atlantic] (275:3) Mr 95, p. 94.
"A Green Watering Can." [GreensboroR] (57) Wint 94-95, p. 14-15.
"Traces." [Jacaranda] (11) [95 or 96?], p. 139-140.
3971. MAZZIOTTI GILLAN, Maria
"How Transparent We Are." [NewMyths] (2:2/3:1) 95, p. 72.
3972. MAZZOCCO, Robert
"In an Enemy Country." [Nat] (260:24) 19 Je 95, p. 900.
"Verbum Caro Hic Factum Est." [Nat] (261:8) 18 S 95, p. 292.
3973. MAZZOTTI, José Antonio
"The Fable of P. and G." (tr. by G. J. Racz). [LitR] (39:1) Fall 95, p. 82-83.
"Francesca / Inferno, V" (tr. by G. J. Racz). [LitR] (39:1) Fall 95, p. 81.
"Words" (tr. by G. Racz). [Vis] (47) 95, p. 20.
Mc ...
See also names beginning with Mac ...
3974. McALLISTER, Michael
"Sarasota" (Loft Inroads Program for Gay, Lesbian, and Bisexual Writers).
[EvergreenC] (10:1) Wint-Spr 95, p. 95-96.
3975. McALPINE, Katherine
"Advice to President Clinton on Confronting Congress." [Light] (14) Sum 95, p. 4.

"The Gardener's Last Instructions." [Light] (14) Sum 95, p. 6.
"New England Spring." [Light] (14) Sum 95, p. 4.
"On Not Bothering to Apply to the Arts Council." [Light] (14) Sum 95, p. 6.
"Paradise Inn." [Light] (14) Sum 95, p. 3.
"A Politician Ascends into Heaven." [Light] (14) Sum 95, p. 6.
"Rx for Type A's." [Light] (14) Sum 95, p. 4.
"Sonnet Stew" (from *The Sonnet: An Anthology*, Index of First Lines, with grateful
      acknowledgement to 14 authors). [Light] (14) Sum 95, p. 5.
"Waiting for Winter in La Sardina Loca." [Light] (14) Sum 95, p. 4.
"Yellow Submarine Homesick Blues Revisited." [Light] (14) Sum 95, p. 5.
3976. McANUFF-GAUNTLETT, Delores
      "The Last Child, Sold." [CaribbeanW] (9) 95, p. 72-73.
3977. McARTHUR, Mac
      "And the Women Upstairs." [JamesWR] (12:2) Spr-Sum 95, p. 12.
      "Delicate Men" (For Assotto Saint and James Orbinski). [JamesWR] (12:3) Fall 95,
         p. 9.
3978. McBREEN, Joan
      "Fionnuala." [SouthernR] (31:3) Jl/Sum 95, p. 529-530.
      "The Silken Robe." [SouthernR] (31:3) Jl/Sum 95, p. 529.
3979. McBRIDE, Mekeel
      "Her Small Body Bright with the Memory of Trees." [Conscience] (16:3) Aut 95, p.
         10.
      "I Want to Be a Ferris Wheel." [ChiR] (41:4) 95, p. 93-94.
      "Love Poem to Pilgrim Avocado." [ManyMM] [1:1] D 94, p. 92-93.
      "Metropolis." [FreeL] (15) Aut 95, p. 7.
      "The Nest." [Chelsea] (58) 95, p. 97.
      "Setting the Story Straight." [SenR] (25:1) Spr 95, p. 31.
      "Someone Complaining about the Title *Tree of Life* — I Go Home and Write *Station
         Wagon of Death*, or *Where It Gets You*, Which Isn't Nearly as Far as Quentin
         Tarantino Would Like Us All to Believe." [FreeL] (15) Aut 95, p. 8.
      "A Thing or Two That Might Be True." [ManyMM] [1:1] D 94, p. 94.
      "Zero Gravity." [Nat] (260:10) 13 Mr 95, p. 360.
3980. McBRYDE, Ian
      "Satellite." [Bogg] (67) 95, p. 55.
3981. McCABE, Diann A.
      "Luminary." [LullwaterR] (6:2) Fall-Wint 95, p. 92.
3982. McCABE, Susan
      "That Homer Girl." [HayF] (17) Fall-Wint 95, p. 66.
3983. McCABE, Victoria
      "Corpus Sine Pectore." [Bogg] (67) 95, p. 53.
3984. McCAFFERTY, Ed
      "Mermaids of the Subway." [Bogg] (67) 95, p. 38.
3985. McCAFFERTY, Maureen
      "The Tighter You Hold." [ClockR] (10:1/2) 95-96, p. 106.
      "To Switch on the Lamp." [ClockR] (10:1/2) 95-96, p. 107.
3986. McCAFFERY, Steven
      "Teachable Texts" (Excerpt). [WestCL] (29:1, #16) Spr-Sum 95, p. 64-77.
3987. McCAIN, Gillian
      "Direction." [Arshile] (4) 95, p. 14.
      "Freedom." [Arshile] (4) 95, p. 16.
      "Journey." [Arshile] (4) 95, p. 13.
      "Newspaper." [Arshile] (4) 95, p. 17.
      "Revolution." [Arshile] (4) 95, p. 15.
3988. McCANN, Daniel
      "Ecology." [CutB] (44) Sum 95, p. 47.
3989. McCANN, Janet
      "Arriving Home Early Again." [Crucible] (30) Fall 94, p. 39.
      "Halloween Carnival, 1950." [ChrC] (112:30) 25 O 95, p. 988.
3990. McCANN, Richard
      "Night Letter." [GlobalCR] (5) Spr 95, p. 67.
3991. McCANN, Sarah
      "Concrete Mixing." [HangL] (66) 95, p. 86.
      "Robert Frost as Father." [HangL] (66) 95, p. 86.
3992. McCARRISTON, Linda
      "Grateful" (to my brother). [SenR] (25:1) Spr 95, p. 115-116.
      "Little River." [GreenMR] (8:1) Spr-Sum 95, p. 72.

3993. McCARTHY, J. X.
"The Faithful Men" (in memoriam Charles Purrelli). [XavierR] (15:1) Spr 95, p. 41.
3994. McCARTHY, Jack
"Kathleen, Sitting Up on the Couch, Looking at a Picture Book." [Light] (13) Spr 95, p. 11.
3995. McCARTHY, JoAnne
"Learning to Swim." [Calyx] (16:2) Wint 95-96, p. 28-29.
3996. McCARTHY, Patricia
"Kiss." [PoetL] (90:3) Fall 95, p. 31.
3997. McCARTHY, Thomas
"The Garden of Sempervirons." [Poetry] (167:1/2) O-N 95, p. 5.
"Snap Election." [SouthernR] (31:3) Jl/Sum 95, p. 744-745.
"The Waiting Deputies." [SouthernR] (31:3) Jl/Sum 95, p. 743-744.
3998. McCARTNEY, Sharon
"As If We Knew Each Other." [Event] (24:2) Sum 95, p. 28-29.
"Dying, My Mother." [Grain] (23:2) Aut 95, p. 37.
"Needle and Spine." [Event] (24:2) Sum 95, p. 27.
3999. McCASLIN, Susan
"Book Room Angel." [Descant] (26:1, #88) Spr 95, p. 57.
"Energy Angel." [Descant] (26:1, #88) Spr 95, p. 58.
"Polysemous Angel." [Descant] (26:1, #88) Spr 95, p. 60.
"Seraph Angel." [Descant] (26:1, #88) Spr 95, p. 59.
"Symmetry Angel." [Descant] (26:1, #88) Spr 95, p. 61.
4000. McCLANAHAN, Rebecca
"The Angel." [SouthernPR] (35:2) Wint 95, p. 67-69.
"A Definition." [SouthernR] (31:1) Wint 95, p. 56-57.
4001. McCLATCHY, J. D.
"Dervish" (In memory of James Merrill). [Poetry] (166:6) S 95, p. 314-315.
McCLEAN, J. A.
See McLEAN, J. A.
4002. McCLEERY, Nancy
"Girl Talk" (Selections: 1, 3, 5, 9). [ManyMM] (2:1) 95, p. 144-147.
4003. McCLELLAN, Jane
"Shipping Out." [Parting] (8:2) Wint 95-96, p. 24.
4004. McCLURE, Michael
"Dark Meat 2" (for Jerome Rothenberg). [Sulfur] (15:2, #37) Fall 95, p. 75-80.
"Haikus" (for Harry and Monika. 2 poems). [HeavenB] (12) 95, p. 14.
"My Unconscious Is My Body But It Is Not." [WestCL] (29:2, #17) Fall 95, p. 142-144.
"Senate Hearings." [HeavenB] (12) 95, p. 15.
4005. McCLURE, Pamela
"Eurydice's Garden." [RiverS] (45) 95, p. 53.
"Immortal, Invisible." [ColR] (22:2) Fall 95, p. 176.
"My Father Throws Coins for Native Children." [ColR] (22:2) Fall 95, p. 175.
"No Time for Virgil, for the Horses." [Poem] (73) My 95, p. 63.
"Teaching Faulkner, Teaching Shelley." [Poem] (73) My 95, p. 64.
"The Visitor." [SouthernHR] (29:1) Wint 95, p. 69.
4006. McCOLL, Michael
"Toward Christmas in a Nuclear Home." [NortheastCor] (3) 95, p. 79-80.
4007. McCONNEL, Frances Ruhlen
"At the Hotel Alfa, Florence, April 1990." [BellR] (18:1, #37) Spr 95, p. 45.
4008. McCORD, Andrew
"At an Exhibit of Mughal Painting." [ParisR] (37:137) Wint 95, p. 283.
"Blue Hills" (for Rupak Roy). [PartR] (62:2) Spr 95, p. 305-306.
"In a Taxi in Kashmir." [YaleR] (83:4) O 95, p. 72-73.
4009. McCORD, Sandy
"High Plains Eulogy." [SmPd] (32:1, #93) Wint 95, p. 18.
"Totem." [Plain] (16:1) Fall 95, p. 14.
4010. McCORKLE, James
"Ontario County, Before the First Snow." [GreenMR] (8:2) Fall-Wint 95-96, p. 107-108.
"The Prodigals' Return." [Boulevard] (10:3, #30) Fall 95, p. 171-172.
"The Promise." [Boulevard] (10:3, #30) Fall 95, p. 172-173.
"'The Storm Is Passing Over,' She Sang." [Verse] (12:2) 95, p. 91-92.
"Transit." [GrahamHR] (19) Wint 95-96, p. 40.

4011. McCORMICK, Patrick
"Album Scratches #7." [CutB] (44) Sum 95, p. 80-81.
4012. McCRACKEN, Cathryn
"Out." [Pequod] (39) 95, p. 96.
4013. McCRARY, Jim
"Untitled: Finally the spot hits." [MidwQ] (36:4) Sum 95, p. 398-399.
4014. McCRAY, Sjohnna
"How to Move." [WillowS] (35) Ja 95, p. 69-71.
4015. McCREA, Kent
"The Days When I Was Hopelessly Shy." [Pequod] (39) 95, p. 103.
4016. McCUE, Duncan
"Dazzling Headlights." [Dandel] (22:1) 95, p. 33.
4017. McCULLOUGH, Aaron
"Hey Cinderella, Roll On." [Ascent] (19:3) Spr 95, p. 57.
4018. McCULLOUGH, Ken
"Bung Kriel (The Lake Where Cranes Mate)" (for Ginny Duncan, tr. of U Sam
    Oeur). [Iowa] (25:3) Fall 95, p. 49-50.
"The Elves Conceal My Buffalo and My Son: Phtdowl Concentration Camp, June
    1977" (for Ken McCullough, tr. of U Sam Oeur). [Iowa] (25:3) Fall 95, p. 54-
    56.
"The Loss of My Twins" (tr. of U Sam Oeur). [Iowa] (25:3) Fall 95, p. 52-53.
"The Moaning Nature of Cambodia" (for Carolyn Forché, tr. of U Sam Oeur).
    [Iowa] (25:3) Fall 95, p. 56-57.
"Oath of Allegiance (1952)" (tr. of U Sam Oeur). [Iowa] (25:3) Fall 95, p. 50-52.
4019. McCURDY, Harold (Harold G.)
"On the Home Front, 1917-1918." [SewanR] (103:3) Sum 95, p. 373-374.
"Visitation." [ChrC] (112:24) 16-23 Ag 95, p. 784.
4020. McDADE, Thomas Michael
"Oklahoma Radio." [WindO] (60) Fall-Wint 95, p. 15-16.
4021. McDANIEL, Debra Bokur
"Deeping." [Kalliope] (17:1) 95, p. 68.
4022. McDANIEL, Jeffrey
"Day 29, Where the Self Divides." [ClockR] (10:1/2) 95-96, p. 22-23.
"Dead Twin." [WillowS] (35) Ja 95, p. 55.
"Disasterology." [Epoch] (44:1) 95, p. 86-87.
"First Person Omniscient." [ClockR] (10:1/2) 95-96, p. 22.
"Twentynothing." [PennR] (6:2) 95, p. 14.
4023. McDANIEL, Tom
"Raising the Mast." [TexasR] (16:1/4) 95, p. 138.
4024. McDANIEL, Wilma Elizabeth
"Abner Woodson — Critic." [ChironR] (44/45) Aut-Wint 95, p. 13.
"Advice of Atheist to an Arthritic." [ChironR] (44/45) Aut-Wint 95, p. 13.
"Bible Stories." [HangL] (66) 95, p. 51.
"Child Training." [HangL] (66) 95, p. 47.
"A Country Dream Maker." [HangL] (66) 95, p. 46.
"Dustbowl Woman Ponders Manifest Destiny." [ChironR] (44/45) Aut-Wint 95, p.
    13.
"Lunch in Skipper's." [HangL] (66) 95, p. 50.
"November Evening." [HangL] (66) 95, p. 48.
"Predators." [HangL] (66) 95, p. 53.
"Spiritual Direction." [HangL] (66) 95, p. 52.
"Uncle Garland." [ChironR] (44/45) Aut-Wint 95, p. 13.
"Union Dues — Dec. 22, 1993." [HangL] (66) 95, p. 49.
"Wanda Has Sunday Off." [ChironR] (44/45) Aut-Wint 95, p. 13.
4025. McDARIS, Steven
"Abdul's Blues." [ChironR] (43) Sum 95, p. 30.
"Air Dancers." [SlipS] (15) 95, p. 61.
"A Lone Star Law." [ChironR] (44/45) Aut-Wint 95, p. 39.
4026. McDERMOTT, John
"Haiku Set: Osaka Life." [US1] (30/31) 95, p. 5.
4027. McDERMOTT, Sharon
"Open Mike, Beehive." [WestB] (36) 95, p. 14.
"The Poem That Begins in Remembering." [SouthernPR] (35:1) Sum 95, p. 46-47.
4028. McDONALD, aGregorio
"C-H-A-N-C-E-S (A Kwansaba)." [Drumvoices] (5:1/2) Fall-Wint 95-96, p. 20.
"Theorem (An Imperfect Kwansaba)." [Drumvoices] (5:1/2) Fall-Wint 95-96, p. 21.

4029. McDONALD, Ian
"Burning." [CaribbeanW] (9) 95, p. 80.
4030. McDONALD, Walter
"After Saigon." [ManyMM] [1:1] D 94, p. 90.
"Against Halley's Comet." [ManyMM] [1:1] D 94, p. 91.
"Alone for a Week in the Rockies." [MidAR] (15:1/2) 95, p. 205.
"Before They Bombed Haiphong." [OxfordM] (10:1) Wint 94-Spr 95, p. 49-50.
"Cousin Eddie and the Weather." [SilverFR] (25) Sum 95, p. 14-15.
"A Father Faithful to His Tasks." [Flyway] (1:1) Spr 95, p. 110.
"Father's Pocket Watch." [ColEng] (57:7) N 95, p. 840.
"For All Friends Walking Avenues." [MidwQ] (36:2) Wint 95, p. 161.
"Hardscrabble Nights." [LitR] (39:1) Fall 95, p. 33.
"Leaving the Middle Years." [ColEng] (57:1) Ja 95, p. 93.
"The Middle Years." [AmerS] (64:2) Spr 95, p. 240.
"The Middle Years." [Footwork] (24/25) 95, p. 66.
"The Middle Years." [IllinoisR] (2:2) Spr 95, p. 10.
"Nearing the End of the Century." [TarRP] (35:1) Fall 95, p. 32.
"Out of a Hat." [Footwork] (24/25) 95, p. 67.
"Rattler." [HampSPR] Wint 95, p. 26.
"Seventh Grade." [OxfordM] (10:1) Wint 94-Spr 95, p. 48.
"The Splendid Galleria." [Footwork] (24/25) 95, p. 66.
"The Summer Before the War." [PoetryE] (39) Fall 94, p. 67.
"The Summer Before the War." [SilverFR] (25) Sum 95, p. 16.
"War in the Persian Gulf." [OxfordM] (10:1) Wint 94-Spr 95, p. 48-49.
4031. McDOUGALL, Christal
"Lot's Wife to Her New Lover." [Ledge] (19) Wint 95, p. 17-18.
"Sun / Moon." [Ledge] (19) Wint 95, p. 19-20.
"Watching Horses" (Third Prize, 1995 Poetry Contest). [Ledge] (19) Wint 95, p. 15-16.
4032. McDOUGALL, Jo
"Everything You Wanted." [MidwQ] (36:4) Sum 95, p. 400.
4033. McDUFF, David
"63" (from "Zombie," tr. of Sigfús Bjartmarsson). [Nimrod] (38:2) Spr-Sum 95, p. 71.
4034. McELROY, Colleen J.
"In the National Geographic." [SenR] (25:1) Spr 95, p. 27-28.
"Way Out Wardell Plays Belgrade." [RiverS] (42/43) 95, p. 164-165.
4035. McEWAN, Angela
"Ship's Log of the Voyage of Fortum Ximenez, Discoverer and Conqueror of the Island of California" (tr. of Mario Bojórquez). [Luz] (8) Spr 95, p. 11-19.
4036. McEWEN, R. F.
"Boyle's Rebuke." [PraS] (69:4) Wint 95, p. 73-74.
"For Agnes Maddy Conlin (1892-1953) on the Occasion of Her Funeral." [PraS] (69:4) Wint 95, p. 70-72.
"Snow Gazer." [PraS] (69:4) Wint 95, p. 69.
"Winter Panes." [PraS] (69:4) Wint 95, p. 73.
4037. McFADDEN, David
"Dreamland Cuba." [MalR] (112) Fall 95, p. 36-37.
"The Straits of Florida." [MalR] (112) Fall 95, p. 33-35.
4038. McFADDEN, Joyce
"Diana's Garden." [Pearl] (22) Fall-Wint 95, p. 18.
4039. McFADDEN, Mary Ann
"The Beautiful Victoria" (Selections: 6, 14, 21. Honorable Mention, The Pablo Neruda Prize for Poetry). [Nimrod] (39:1) Fall-Wint 95, p. 59-61.
4040. McFALL, Gardner
"Leaving Heaven." [WestHR] (49:2) Sum 95, p. 120-121.
"Meditation on a Child's Lost Sandals." [Nat] (261:18) 27 N 95, p. 685.
4041. McFARLAND, Ron
"The Dog Days of August." [Spitball] (48) 95, p. 77.
"Evangeline Visits the Palouse." [WeberS] (12:1) Wint 95, p. 123-124.
"The Night Owls of Elk River." [WeberS] (12:1) Wint 95, p. 122-123.
"Packing Up." [IllinoisR] (3:1/2) Fall 95-Spr 96, p. 11-12.
"Wheatspill." [MidwQ] (37:1) Aut 95, p. 44.
4042. McFEE, Michael
"The Bat." [Poetry] (166:5) Ag 95, p. 259-260.

4043. McGARRY, Pamela
"Nightride." [Kalliope] (17:3) 95, p. 9.
4044. McGEE, Lynn
"Friend." [Sun] (229) Ja 95, p. 25.
4045. McGILL, William J.
"The Sadness of Moe Berg." [Spitball] (49) 95, p. 54.
4046. McGIMPSEY, David
"Kentucky Fried Dublin." [ApalQ] (43) Spr 95, p. 80-81.
4047. McGINN, Florence
"Two Left Paradise." [Footwork] (24/25) 95, p. 49.
4048. McGOOKEY, Kathleen
"August." [PoetryE] (40) Spr 95, p. 83.
"Beldora Burrell." [MissouriR] (18:2) 95, p. 87.
"Class Picture, My Grandmother As Teacher, 1922." [MissouriR] (18:2) 95, p. 86.
"Esther S." [MissouriR] (18:2) 95, p. 90.
"Leda." [MissouriR] (18:2) 95, p. 88.
"Near Drowning, Ihla Comprida, Brazil." [Epoch] (44:1) 95, p. 91.
"No light, just a sense of satisfaction, something sweet on the tongue." [ProseP] (4) 95, p. 59.
"Purple Martins, 1970." [Epoch] (44:1) 95, p. 92-93.
"Simple Arithmetic." [MissouriR] (18:2) 95, p. 89.
"Ugly, smiling Agnes with eight pearl buttons on her blouse." [ProseP] (4) 95, p. 58.
4049. McGOVERN, Robert
"Adeste." [ChrC] (112:37) 20-27 D 95, p. 1248.
4050. McGRATH, Beth
"Waterlock." [AxeF] (3) 90, p. 24.
4051. McGRATH, Campbell
"The Bob Hope Poem" (Two Selections). [TriQ] (94) Fall 95, p. 170-190.
"Maizel at Shorty's in Kendall." [TriQ] (95) Wint 95-96, p. 169.
"Seashells, Manasota Key." [ParisR] (37:136) Fall 95, p. 78-79.
"The Secret Life of Capital" (from "The Bob Hope Poem"). [TriQ] (94) Fall 95, p. 170-181.
"The Triumph of Rationalism" (from "The Bob Hope Poem"). [TriQ] (94) Fall 95, p. 182-190.
4052. McGRATH, Thomas
"Letter to an Imaginary Friend" (Selections: Part One, Section III, 4-5, Part Two, Section IV, 4). [NewEngR] (17:4) Fall 95, p. 47-52.
"Love in a Bus" (Chicago, 1942). [NewEngR] (17:4) Fall 95, p. 53.
"Ode for the American Dead in Asia." [NewEngR] (17:4) Fall 95, p. 53-54.
4053. McGUCKIAN, Medbh
"Asking for the Alphabet Back." [Verse] (12:3) 95, p. 110.
"Black Virgin." [Epoch] (44:3) 95, p. 264-265.
"Cathal's Voice (On the Impossibility of Being Made Love to in Irish)." [Verse] (12:3) 95, p. 108.
"Dante's Own Day." [NewMyths] (2:2/3:1) 95, p. 122.
"Daphne and Apollo" (tr. of Nuala Ní Dhomhnaill). [SouthernR] (31:3) Jl/Sum 95, p. 433, 435.
"Dividing the Political Temperature." [Epoch] (44:3) 95, p. 266-267.
"Drawing in Red Chalk at a Death Sale." [NewMyths] (2:2/3:1) 95, p. 121.
"English as a Foreign Language." [NewMyths] (2:2/3:1) 95, p. 119-120.
"Feachtas Gharraían Mhargaidh" (tr. by Nuala Ní Dhomhnaill). [SouthernR] (31:3) Jl/Sum 95, p. 447, 449.
"The Feastday of Peace." [Verse] (12:3) 95, p. 109.
"Foliage Ceiling Rose." [SouthernR] (31:3) Jl/Sum 95, p. 444.
"The Marianne Faithfull Hairdo" (tr. of Nuala Ní Dhomhnaill). [SouthernR] (31:3) Jl/Sum 95, p. 435, 437.
"The Merfolk and the Written Word" (tr. of Nuala Ní Dhomhnaill). [SouthernR] (31:3) Jl/Sum 95, p. 441, 443.
"The Mermaid in the Labour Ward" (tr. of Nuala Ní Dhomhnaill). [SouthernR] (31:3) Jl/Sum 95, p. 439, 441.
"On Ballycastle Beach." [Verse] (12:2) 95, p. 93-94.
"Operation Market Garden." [SouthernR] (31:3) Jl/Sum 95, p. 446, 448.
"The Orange Island." [Verse] (12:3) 95, p. 111.
"Plague Song." [Verse] (12:3) 95, p. 112.
"Rós Síleála Duilleogach" (tr. by Nuala Ní Dhomhnaill). [SouthernR] (31:3) Jl/Sum 95, p. 445.

"Their Word for Harvest Suffering." [Verse] (12:3) 95, p. 110.
"White Windsor Soap." [Epoch] (44:3) 95, p. 268.
4054. McHUGH, Heather
"Joke Heart." [Zyzzyva] (11:1, #41) Spr 95, p. 86.
"Meaning To and Fro." [Zyzzyva] (11:1, #41) Spr 95, p. 87.
"Nihil Privativum in the Household of Ken." [ColR] (22:1) Spr 95, p. 103.
"Pupil." [SenR] (25:1) Spr 95, p. 25.
"Radio Waves." [QW] (41) Aut-Wint 95-96, p. 168.
"Three Poems After Paul Valery." [ColR] (22:1) Spr 95, p. 101-102.
"Torpedoed Ark." [HarvardR] (8) Spr 95, p. 7-13.
4055. McHUGH, Janet
"Altered Consciousness." [DefinedP] (1:1) Fall-Wint 92, p. 33-34.
4056. McINNIS, Nadine
"A Kind of Love." [Dandel] (22:1) 95, p. 73.
4057. McIRVIN, Michael
"Poetry in an Age of Empire." [Conduit] (3) Sum 95, p. 24.
"Something to Believe In." [DefinedP] (3) 95, p. 16-17.
4058. McKAY, Don
"Alibi." [MalR] (110) Spr 95, p. 95.
"By Any Other Name." [Grain] (23:2) Aut 95, p. 79.
"Cirque." [MalR] (110) Spr 95, p. 92.
"Early Instruments." [MalR] (110) Spr 95, p. 90.
"Fates Worse Than Death." [Quarry] (44:2) 95, p. 5-6.
"Saxophone Improv: Embraceable You." [Grain] (23:2) Aut 95, p. 78.
"To Danceland." [Grain] (23:2) Aut 95, p. 80.
"To Speak of Paths." [MalR] (110) Spr 95, p. 91.
"Twinflower." [MalR] (110) Spr 95, p. 93-94.
4059. McKAY, Linda Back
"The Day I Died." [Parting] (8:1) Sum 95, p. 8.
4060. McKAY, Matthew
"The Farm." [Interim] (14:1) Spr-Sum 95, p. 7.
"Your Father." [Interim] (14:1) Spr-Sum 95, p. 8.
4061. McKEAN, James
"Good 'D'" (after Edward Hirsh). [Iowa] (25:1) Wint 95, p. 153-154.
"Rider." [GettyR] (8:1) Wint 95, p. 52-53.
"Your Leaving." [GettyR] (8:1) Wint 95, p. 54.
4062. McKECHNIE, Beth
"Countertops" (Short Grain Contest Winners: Prose Poem, Honourable Mention).
[Grain] (22:3) Wint 95, p. 68.
4063. McKEE, Laura
"Last Poem about the Moon." [PoetryNW] (36:2) Sum 95, p. 45-46.
4064. McKEE, Louis
"Fights." [ChironR] (44/45) Aut-Wint 95, p. 8.
"For the Beautiful Woman Across the Room." [ChironR] (44/45) Aut-Wint 95, p. 8.
"The Nurturing." [LowellR] (2) c1996, p. 19.
"On Finding a Joint in the Pocket of a Suitcoat I haven't Had on in Years."
[LowellR] (2) c1996, p. 18.
"Something Else." [ChironR] (44/45) Aut-Wint 95, p. 8.
4065. McKENNA, J. J.
"Noah and Company." [CapeR] (30:2) Fall 95, p. 38.
"The Star." [MidwQ] (36:4) Sum 95, p. 401.
4066. McKENTY, Bob
"Riddle" (Answers will be given in *Light* / 17). [Light] (15/16) Aut-Wint 95-96, p.
15.
4067. McKENZIE, Jeffrey
"Apology." [PoetL] (90:1) Spr 95, p. 38.
"Box." [PoetL] (90:1) Spr 95, p. 37.
"The Next City." [PoetL] (90:1) Spr 95, p. 36.
"Poem: There is no father here, bellowing drunk." [WestB] (36) 95, p. 45.
"Snakebite Saloon" (Selections: 3 poems). [OxfordM] (9:2) Fall-Wint 93, p. 98-100.
4068. McKERNAN, John
"At the Grave of Philip Larkin." [HampSPR] Wint 95, p. 36.
"Death by Daily Newspapers." [PraS] (69:3) Fall 95, p. 109.
"The Highway Signs to the Great City." [PraS] (69:3) Fall 95, p. 113.
"I Abused My Father." [ParisR] (37:134) Spr 95, p. 268.
"The Moth's." [OhioR] (53) 95, p. 91.

"Omaha Nebraska." [PraS] (69:3) Fall 95, p. 110.
"On Vacation in Vermont." [MidwQ] (37:1) Aut 95, p. 45.
"Planting Red Maple Saplings." [Field] (53) Fall 95, p. 76.
"A Plate of Time." [Ledge] (18) Sum 95, p. 23.
"The Shadow Beneath My Corpse Is Always." [ParisR] (37:134) Spr 95, p. 266.
"The Silence." [PoetryE] (40) Spr 95, p. 84-85.
"Something Is Dreadfully Wrong and I Want." [PraS] (69:3) Fall 95, p. 110.
"There Wasn't Any Light in the Candle." [PraS] (69:3) Fall 95, p. 112.
"These Paltry Shadows." [PraS] (69:3) Fall 95, p. 111.
"Thwumph." [NewEngR] (17:2) Spr 95, p. 82.
"The Use and Abuse of History." [BellR] (18:2, #38) Fall 95, p. 36.
"Waiter, I Would Like a Dish of Feebly." [ParisR] (37:134) Spr 95, p. 267-268.
"Washing My Hands Covered with Garden Dust." [PraS] (69:3) Fall 95, p. 114.
"When the Ghost of Weldon Kees Visited." [ParisR] (37:134) Spr 95, p. 267.
"With." [NewEngR] (17:2) Spr 95, p. 83.
4069. McKERNAN, Llewellyn
"After Twenty Centuries." [Kalliope] (17:3) 95, p. 32.
"No Love Lost." [Kalliope] (17:3) 95, p. 33.
"Rain Falls in Love with a Stream." [Kalliope] (17:3) 95, p. 37.
"Wayfarer." [Kalliope] (17:2) 95, p. 32.
4070. McKERRY, Paul D.
"Concerning Sacrifices." [AntigR] (101) Spr 95, p. 59-60.
4071. McKIERNAN, Ethna
"The Lock Maker." [NorthStoneR] (12) 95, p. 47.
4072. McKIERNAN, Laurie
"Juliette" (Loft Inroads Program for Gay, Lesbian, and Bisexual Writers).
[EvergreenC] (10:1) Wint-Spr 95, p. 96.
4073. McKIM, Elizabeth Gordon
"El Paso" (for EK). [DefinedP] (2:1) Fall-Wint 93, p. 20-21.
4074. McKINNEY, James
"My Nigga" (WritersCorps Project, Washington, DC). [WashR] (21:2) Ag-S 95, p.
20.
4075. McKINNEY, Joshua
"Chicken Slaughter." [NewYorkQ] (55) 95, p. 82.
"No Further Terms." [IndR] (18:1) Spr 95, p. 97-98.
4076. McKINNON, Bruce
"Abracadabra." [PoetryE] (40) Spr 95, p. 76-77.
"Hands." [PoetryE] (40) Spr 95, p. 74-75.
4077. McKINNON, Patrick
"Poem for Gramma Lavis" (The 1994 Allen Ginsberg Poetry Awards: Honorable
Mention). [Footwork] (24/25) 95, p. 198-199.
4078. McKINSEY, Martin
"Another Summer" (tr. of Yannis Ritsos). [PartR] (62:2) Spr 95, p. 299.
"Bitter Knowledge" (tr. of Yannis Ritsos). [KenR] (17:1) Wint 95, p. 76.
"Closing Words" (tr. of Yannis Ritsos). [Field] (52) Spr 95, p. 51.
"Forgetfulness" (tr. of Yannis Ritsos). [KenR] (17:1) Wint 95, p. 75-76.
"Garden in Autumn" (tr. of Yannis Ritsos). [Field] (52) Spr 95, p. 47.
"Hypothermia" (tr. of Yannis Ritsos). [VirQR] (71:3) Sum 95, p. 500.
"Minimal Harvest" (tr. of Yannis Ritsos). [PartR] (62:2) Spr 95, p. 299.
"Not Quite" (tr. of Yannis Ritsos). [Field] (52) Spr 95, p. 49.
"Painting Stones" (tr. of Yannis Ritsos). [Field] (52) Spr 95, p. 46.
"People and Suitcases" (tr. of Yannis Ritsos). [Field] (52) Spr 95, p. 48.
"Perhaps" (tr. of Yannis Ritsos). [KenR] (17:1) Wint 95, p. 75.
"Pointless Lucidity" (tr. of Yannis Ritsos). [VirQR] (71:3) Sum 95, p. 501.
"Post Script" (tr. of Yannis Ritsos). [Field] (52) Spr 95, p. 45.
"Self-Knowledge" (tr. of Yannis Ritsos). [Field] (52) Spr 95, p. 50.
"Sitting Out the Rain" (tr. of Yannis Ritsos). [ArtfulD] (28/29) 95, p. 59.
"Sparse Leavings" (tr. of Yannis Ritsos). [VirQR] (71:3) Sum 95, p. 502.
"Ticks of the Clock" (14 selections, tr. of Yannis Ritsos). [WillowS] (36) Je 95, p.
101-103.
"Tokens" (tr. of Yannis Ritsos). [VirQR] (71:3) Sum 95, p. 500-501.
"Two in the Afternoon" (tr. of Yannis Ritsos). [VirQR] (71:3) Sum 95, p. 501-502.
"What Cannot Be Weighed" (tr. of Yannis Ritsos). [ArtfulD] (28/29) 95, p. 58.
4079. McLAUGHLIN, Dale
"Cartography." [CimR] (111) Ap 95, p. 70.
"A Spinster Considers Her Cat." [CimR] (111) Ap 95, p. 71.

4080. McLAUGHLIN, Dorothy
"First Parents." [Footwork] (24/25) 95, p. 57.
4081. McLAUGHLIN, Ellen
"Iphigenia in Aulis" (a play). [Conjunc] (25) 95, p. 150-154.
"Iphigenia in Tauris" (a play). [Conjunc] (25) 95, p. 155-164.
4082. McLAUGHLIN, Lissa
"The Body's Executioner" (9 selections). [Avec] (9) 95, p. 96-101.
4083. McLEAN, J. A.
"A Poem in Plain Speaking." [WorldO] (26:3) Spr 95, p. 55.
"The Runner" (Inspired by an incident in Tahirzadeh). [WorldO] (26:4) Sum 95, p. 25.
4084. McLEAN, Kristie
"Meditation." [BellR] (18:2, #38) Fall 95, p. 7.
4085. McLEAN, Sammy
"Trumpets" (tr. of Georg Trakl). [SnailPR] (3:2) 95, p. 19.
4086. McLENNAN, Rob
"Desire." [PoetryC] (15:3) Ag 95, p. 17.
"Observances." [PoetryC] (15:3) Ag 95, p. 17.
4087. McLEOD, Margaret
"Midway" (for Melanie). [PottPort] (16:1) Fall 95, p. 22-23.
4088. McMAHON, Lynne
"At the Courthouse." [CrabOR] (1:1) Fall-Wint 95, p. 84.
"In Summer." [Field] (53) Fall 95, p. 41-49.
"Not Solely Mourning." [CrabOR] (1:1) Fall-Wint 95, p. 83.
"One of the Mineral Elements." [Agni] (41) 95, p. 130-131.
"Raving Sonnet." [CrabOR] (1:1) Fall-Wint 95, p. 85.
"Reprise." [NewRep] (213:10) 4 S 95, p. 40.
"Rimbaud." [Agni] (41) 95, p. 132.
"Too Cool." [ManyMM] (1:3) 95, p. 42.
4089. McMAHON, Michael (Mike)
"Living in Brueghel." [RagMag] (12:2) Spr 95, p. 63.
"The Men Who Wore White Socks." [SmPd] (32:1, #93) Wint 95, p. 36-37.
"New Evidence of Love After Death" (for JDT). [RagMag] (12:2) Spr 95, p. 62.
"Public Radio." [WindO] (59) Spr 95, p. 34.
"Sunapee Poverty." [RagMag] (12:2) Spr 95, p. 64.
4090. McMAHON, Pame
"Weird Is Good." [Footwork] (24/25) 95, p. 57-58.
4091. McMAHON, William
"Neighbor." [AnthNEW] (7) 95, p. 36.
4092. McMANIS, Ed
"Visiting Day." [Writer] (108:12) D 95, p. 20.
4093. McMANUS, James
"Preludes." [ParisR] (37:135) Sum 95, p. 93-95.
4094. McMASTER, Susan
"The Function of Prayer." [Quarry] (43:4) 95, p. 96.
"How God Sees." [Grain] (23:2) Aut 95, p. 36.
4095. McMILLAN, Ian
"Ted Hughes Is Elvis Presley." [Jacaranda] (11) [95 or 96?], p. 149-151.
4096. McMILLAN, Joan
"Heirlooms: Los Angeles, 1965." [WestB] (37) 95, p. 14-15.
4097. McMORRIS, Mark
"The Black Reeds." [Conjunc] (24) 95, p. 58-64.
"Space Between Us." [DenQ] (30:2) Fall 95, p. 46-51.
4098. McMULLEN, Richard E.
"Pills and Tablets." [Comm] (122:4) 24 F 95, p. 12.
4099. McMULLINS, Hilda
"Somewhere in a Dark Alley" (from Story Book Time). [AmerPoR] (24:3) My-Je 95, p. 20.
4100. McNAIR, Wesley
"Francis Bound." [GreenMR] (8:2) Fall-Wint 95-96, p. 24-25.
"House in Spring." [GreenMR] (8:2) Fall-Wint 95-96, p. 23.
"The Last Time Shorty Towers Fetched the Cows." [GreenMR] (8:2) Fall-Wint 95-96, p. 16.
"Mute." [GreenMR] (8:2) Fall-Wint 95-96, p. 21-22.
"Old Cadillacs." [GreenMR] (8:2) Fall-Wint 95-96, p. 27.
"Where I Live." [GreenMR] (8:2) Fall-Wint 95-96, p. 20.

4101. McNALLY, Judith
  "Old Times." [US1] (30/31) 95, p. 14.
4102. McNAMEE, Todd
  "Grandfather." [DogRR] (14:1, #27) Sum 95, p. 26-27.
4103. McNAUGHT, Jennifer
  "Grandmother's Oregon Trail Diary, 1977." [MidwQ] (36:4) Sum 95, p. 402-403.
4104. McNEILLEY, Michael
  "Fuck You, My Sister Said." [ChironR] (43) Sum 95, p. 28.
4105. McNEW, Christopher
  "Grandma Meteor." [PlumR] (9) [95 or 96], p. 26.
  "Town." [PennR] (6:2) 95, p. 21.
4106. McPARLAND, Robert P.
  "I Bring My Winter Lament to W.C. Williams Doorstep." [Footwork] (24/25) 95, p. 73.
4107. McPHEE, Peter
  "Leaves Are Done the Bonfire on Daniel Hatchet's Grave." [Quarry] (43:4) 95, p. 112.
4108. McPHERSON, Michael
  "The Coastal Zone." [Manoa] (7:2) Wint 95, p. 18-20.
4109. McPHERSON, Sandra
  "Edge Effect" (Arcadia Beach, Oregon). [Poetry] (166:4) Jl 95, p. 203-205.
  "Images." [Field] (52) Spr 95, p. 67-68.
  "Lessons Learned from a Small Drawing by Victor Joseph Gatto, Self-Taught Artist." [ParisR] (37:135) Sum 95, p. 51.
  "My Theory of Mockingbirds." [Poetry] (165:4) Ja 95, p. 212-213.
  "Ocean Water Absorbs Red, Orange, and Yellow Light" (Marshall Gulch Beach, Sonoma Coast). [HarvardR] (8) Spr 95, p. 20-22.
  "Painting Self-Portraits with the Widsom Project Women." [AmerV] (38) 95, p. 75-76.
  "Poem for My Fifty-First Birthday." [Field] (52) Spr 95, p. 69.
  "Precious Metal" (for my daughter, Phoebe). [Field] (53) Fall 95, p. 77-79.
  "Research Trail, Cold Canyon, November" (Solano County). [Poetry] (166:4) Jl 95, p. 206-209.
  "The Spaces Between Birds." [Field] (52) Spr 95, p. 64-66.
4110. McQUILKIN, Rennie
  "The Collecting" (for Pablito Perras). [OntR] (43) Fall-Wint 95-96, p. 41-43.
  "Swamp Song." [HiramPoR] (58/59) Spr 95-Wint 96, p. 58.
  "Valentine" (for James Merrill, 2/13/95). [Chelsea] (59) 95, p. 203.
4111. McRAY, Paul
  "Earthly Delights." [IllinoisR] (2:2) Spr 95, p. 19-20.
4112. McROBBIE, Kenneth
  "Borders, Borders, Letter on a Poet's Funeral: László Kalnóky, Dead at 74, Budapest." [CanLit] (144) Spr 95, p. 43-48.
4113. McSWEEN, Harold B.
  "Lineage." [SewanR] (103:4) Fall 95, p. 503.
  "Nuptials." [SewanR] (103:4) Fall 95, p. 502-503.
  "The Parlor." [SewanR] (103:4) Fall 95, p. 504.
4114. McVAY, Gwyn
  "Petroglyph." [GreensboroR] (59) Wint 95-96, p. 20.
4115. McWHIRTER, George
  "The Book of Contradictions" (For Angela). [HarvardR] (9) Fall 95, p. 90-91.
  "Fragments and Commentaries" (I-III, tr. of Homero Aridjis). [HarvardR] (8) Spr 95, p. 86-89.
4116. MEAD, Jane
  "The Great Pond." [Pequod] (39) 95, p. 85-88.
  "A Note on the Present State of the Future." [Pequod] (39) 95, p. 83-84.
4117. MEADE, Erica Helm
  "Malaria." [Sun] (238) O 95, p. 11.
4118. MECHEM, James
  "The Lady or the Tiger." [ChironR] (44/45) Aut-Wint 95, p. 21.
4119. MEDAKSE
  "For Men Only" (tr. by Diana Der-Hovanessian). [GrahamHR] (19) Wint 95-96, p. 41.
4120. MEDEIROS, Selene de
  "Hiroshima." [Drumvoices] (4:1/2) Fall-Wint 94-95, p. 27-28.
  "This Is How I Love You." [Drumvoices] (4:1/2) Fall-Wint 94-95, p. 25-26.

4121. MEDENICA, Susan
"Turtle Clay." [DefinedP] (1:2) Spr-Sum 93, p. 22.
4122. MEDINA, Pablo
"The Love of Blondes." [NewL] (62:1) 96 (c1995), p. 121-123.
4123. MEDINSKY, Dave
"Sweepstakes." [NewYorkQ] (54) 95, p. 94.
4124. MEDLIN, L.
"Na ustvennom advige ushedshikh v sebya" (tr. of Yunna Morits, w. Daniel
Weissbort). [InterQ] (2:1/2) 95, p. 75.
4125. MEDLINSKY, Dave
"For Better or Worse." [Plain] (16:1) Fall 95, p. 17.
"Luncheonette" (runner up, 1994 Borderlands Poetry Contest). [Border] (7) Fall-
Wint 96, p. 41.
"Night Mission." [Northeast] (5:12) Sum 95, p. 7.
"Philosophy." [Flyway] (1:3) Wint 95, p. 48.
"Ralph and Alice." [Flyway] (1:3) Wint 95, p. 49.
"Swan Lake." [Northeast] (5:12) Sum 95, p. 6.
4126. MEEK, Ed
"Yellow Shell Gas Pumps." [AnthNEW] (7) 95, p. 28.
4127. MEEK, Jay
"Another Version." [ProseP] (4) 95, p. 61.
"Bohémien." [ProseP] (4) 95, p. 60.
"Instrumentation" (pastiche of four sonnets by Ernest Raynaud). [BelPoJ] (46:1) Fall
95, p. 41.
"Jars." [WillowS] (36) Je 95, p. 28.
"Lines." [BelPoJ] (46:1) Fall 95, p. 42.
"Winnipeg in the Rain." [MidwQ] (36:4) Sum 95, p. 404-405.
4128. MEEK-HENSON, Sandra
"Dune #7" (southern Africa). [Pequod] (39) 95, p. 104.
4129. MEEKER, David
"Too Late." [ColR] (22:2) Fall 95, p. 163-164.
4130. MEEKER, Jami
"And Now, the News." [Hellas] (6:1) Spr-Sum 95, p. 24.
4131. MEGAW, Neill
"All the Ways Not Taken." [Elf] (5:1) Spr 95, p. 31.
"Anasazi Cliff Dwellings." [CumbPR] (14:2) Spr 95, p. 17.
"Angels." [Hellas] (6:2) Fall-Wint 95, p. 77-78.
"Attorney's Office." [CumbPR] (14:2) Spr 95, p. 16.
"In Praise of Babel." [Hellas] (6:1) Spr-Sum 95, p. 64.
"Like Snail Unwillingly to School." [Light] (15/16) Aut-Wint 95-96, p. 22.
"Marooned." [CumbPR] (14:2) Spr 95, p. 15.
"A Middle-aged Man Turns Over a New Leaf." [CumbPR] (14:2) Spr 95, p. 18.
"Miss Mercury." [CapeR] (30:2) Fall 95, p. 32.
"Scene from Jane Austen." [Hellas] (6:1) Spr-Sum 95, p. 63.
"Three-Man Catch for Shakespeare's Twelfth Night (II.iii)." [Light] (14) Sum 95, p.
7.
4132. MEHIGAN, Joshua
"The Story of All the Noise." [IllinoisR] (3:1/2) Fall 95-Spr 96, p. 66.
"The Story of Progress." [Wind] (76) Fall 95, p. 21.
"The Story of the Bird." [IllinoisR] (3:1/2) Fall 95-Spr 96, p. 95.
"The Story of the Birthday Gift." [IllinoisR] (3:1/2) Fall 95-Spr 96, p. 63.
"The Story of the Carnival." [Wind] (76) Fall 95, p. 22.
"The Story of the Suicide." [IllinoisR] (3:1/2) Fall 95-Spr 96, p. 19.
4133. MEHREN, Stein
"The Old Man and the Tree" (tr. by Tim Kahl). [Vis] (47) 95, p. 10.
4134. MEHRHOFF, Charlie
"Pornography." [AxeF] (3) 90, p. 9.
MEI, Yuan
See YUAN, Mei
4135. MEIDAV, Edie
"Fish Tacos, or, The Three Most Important Lies." [KenR] (17:3/4) Sum-Fall 95, p.
163-164.
"Half-Light." [KenR] (17:3/4) Sum-Fall 95, p. 164-166.
4136. MEIER, Kay
"Marriage in Three Acts." [CumbPR] (14:2) Spr 95, p. 41-42.
"Roomers, 1940s." [SlipS] (15) 95, p. 5.

4137. MEIER, Richard
"The Acrobat." [Chelsea] (59) 95, p. 216.
"Chiaroscuro." [GrahamHR] (19) Wint 95-96, p. 101.
"Second Ignorance." [GrahamHR] (19) Wint 95-96, p. 100.
4138. MEINERS, R. K.
"Bird Shadows." [CentR] (39:2) Spr 95, p. 300.
"Easter in the Mountains." [CentR] (39:2) Spr 95, p. 291-293.
"Eikampf Singing at the End." [CentR] (39:2) Spr 95, p. 299-300.
"Eikampf's Ascesis." [CentR] (39:2) Spr 95, p. 297.
"Eikampf's Dialectic." [CentR] (39:2) Spr 95, p. 298-299.
"From a Bestiary" (for Katie and Sally). [CentR] (39:2) Spr 95, p. 294-296.
"Material History." [CentR] (39:2) Spr 95, p. 301.
4139. MEINKE, Peter
"Ant Hills." [GeoR] (49:3) Fall 95, p. 577-578.
"Apples." [Poetry] (165:5) F 95, p. 275.
"Apples." [Writer] (108:7) Jl 95, p. 16.
"Chinese Wish Poem" (for James Nolan). [ManyMM] [1:1] D 94, p. 101-102.
"Japanese Soldier." [ManyMM] [1:1] D 94, p. 103.
"Mazzaroli's Cannon." [Poetry] (165:5) F 95, p. 276.
"Noreen." [NewRep] (212:13) 27 Mr 95, p. 40.
"The Secret Code" (for Jeanne). [GeoR] (49:3) Fall 95, p. 578-579.
4140. MEISCHEN, David
"I Shall Not Want." [Border] (7) Fall-Wint 96, p. 42-43.
4141. MEISKEY, Elinor
"The Wooden Dancer." [DefinedP] (1:2) Spr-Sum 93, p. 45.
4142. MEISSNER, Bill
"Something About Certain Old Baseball Fields." [MidwQ] (36:4) Sum 95, p. 406-
407.
4143. MEITNER, Erika
"Commute." [GreenHLL] (5) 94, p. 43-44.
"For Opa." [GreenHLL] (5) 94, p. 41.
"Monstersunflower." [GreenHLL] (5) 94, p. 45.
"On the Death of a Friend." [GreenHLL] (5) 94, p. 42.
"Testimony to Autumn." [GreenHLL] (5) 94, p. 46.
4144. MELANÇON, Robert
"At My Place 'The Little Orchard' I" (tr. by Geoffrey Gardner). [SenR] (25:2) Fall
95, p. 65.
"At My Place 'The Little Orchard' VII" (tr. by Geoffrey Gardner). [SenR] (25:2) Fall
95, p. 66.
"At My Place 'The Little Orchard' VIII" (tr. by Geoffrey Gardner). [SenR] (25:2)
Fall 95, p. 67.
"Blind Painting III" (tr. by Geoffrey Gardner). [SenR] (25:2) Fall 95, p. 61.
"Blind Painting IV" (tr. by Geoffrey Gardner). [SenR] (25:2) Fall 95, p. 62.
"Blind Painting V" (tr. by Geoffrey Gardner). [SenR] (25:2) Fall 95, p. 63.
"Blind Painting VI" (tr. by Geoffrey Gardner). [SenR] (25:2) Fall 95, p. 64.
"Blind Painting VII" (tr. by Geoffrey Gardner). [PlumR] (9) [95 or 96], p. 24.
"Blind Painting VIII" (tr. by Geoffrey Gardner). [PlumR] (9) [95 or 96], p. 25.
4145. MELLERI, Arto
"Come home! yells the mute longing" (tr. by Sari Hantula). [InterPR] (21:2) Fall 95,
p. 45.
"The Era When Letters Break Down" (tr. by Sari Hantula). [InterPR] (21:2) Fall 95,
p. 47.
"Four-Footed Us" (tr. by Sari Hantula). [InterPR] (21:2) Fall 95, p. 53.
"Kirjaimien Murtumisen Aika." [InterPR] (21:2) Fall 95, p. 46.
"Kuningatar Hysteria." [InterPR] (21:2) Fall 95, p. 40, 42.
"Let's have a war, that's what the seed of hatred" (tr. by Sari Hantula). [InterPR]
(21:2) Fall 95, p. 49.
"Nelijalkainen Me." [InterPR] (21:2) Fall 95, p. 52.
"Paljaalla Silmällä Sitä ei Näe." [InterPR] (21:2) Fall 95, p. 50.
"Queen Hysteria" (tr. by Sari Hantula). [InterPR] (21:2) Fall 95, p. 41, 43.
"Sota tarvitaan, puhkeaa." [InterPR] (21:2) Fall 95, p. 48.
"Tule kotiin! huutaa mykkä kaipaus." [InterPR] (21:2) Fall 95, p. 44.
"You Can't See It with the Eye Alone" (tr. by Sari Hantula). [InterPR] (21:2) Fall
95, p. 51.
4146. MELLINGER, Maria
"The Bare Facts." [BellArk] (11:1) Ja-F 95, p. 27.

"Bedazzlement and Rebellion." [BellArk] (11:6) N-D 95, p. 13.
"Dorothy." [BellArk] (11:3) My-Je 95, p. 31.
"Journal (jur'n'l)." [BellArk] (11:2) Mr-Ap 95, p. 31.
"Meade Baltz Paints 928 Plainfield Road." [BellArk] (11:3) My-Je 95, p. 10.
"Must Be Something Inside." [BellArk] (11:2) Mr-Ap 95, p. 31.
"Never Underestimate the Power of Soup." [BellArk] (11:3) My-Je 95, p. 31.
"Prayer." [BellArk] (11:1) Ja-F 95, p. 27.
"Singing 'Peace Sells'." [BellArk] (11:6) N-D 95, p. 13.
"So Why Were You Holding Her Hand?" [BellArk] (11:3) My-Je 95, p. 10.
"Somebody Put Something in My Drink." [BellArk] (11:6) N-D 95, p. 13.
"Zydeco — Defined." [BellArk] (11:5) S-O 95, p. 24.
"Zydeco — Dreams." [BellArk] (11:5) S-O 95, p. 24.
"Zydeco — The End." [BellArk] (11:5) S-O 95, p. 24.
4147. MELNYCZUK, Askold
    "Head: A Fragment." [AmerPoR] (24:1) Ja-F 95, p. 51.
4148. MELTON, Steve
    "Grits." [Chelsea] (58) 95, p. 48.
    "I Have Never Dared to Dance." [Chelsea] (58) 95, p. 49.
4149. MENDELL, Olga Elena
    "Siesta." [Confr] (56/57) Sum-Fall 95, p. 347-349.
4150. MENDINSKY, Dave
    "'57 Volvo." [NewDeltaR] (12:2) Spr-Sum 95, p. 25.
4151. MENDOZA, Andy (grade 5, Bancroft Elementary, Washington, DC)
    "Trouble" (Poetry on the Metro Project). [WashR] (21:2) Ag-S 95, p. 15.
4152. MENEBROKER, Ann
    "Clear Lake." [AxeF] (3) 90, p. 5.
    "Mature Women" (for Mary Zeppa). [Bogg] (67) 95, p. 8.
    "Patrick's Turtle Gets Immortalized." [AxeF] (3) 90, p. 3.
    "Symmetry" (for Kathryn Hohlwein). [AxeF] (3) 90, p. 2-3.
    "Three Poems." [AxeF] (3) 90, p. 4.
4153. MENES, Orlando Ricardo
    "Portrait of García Lorca" (tr. of Alfonsina Storni). [InterPR] (21:1) Spr 95, p. 19, 21.
    "A Sixth-Grade Angel's Letter to God." [ApalQ] (43) Spr 95, p. 36-37.
4154. MENESES, Vidaluz
    "Instant Matrimony" (tr. by Kate Peters). [HarvardR] (9) Fall 95, p. 97.
MENOZZI, Wallis Wilde
    See WILDE-MENOZZI, Wallis
4155. MERCHANT, Preston
    "Demona, Daughter of the Lightning." [PoetryNW] (36:3) Aut 95, p. 25.
4156. MERCK, Bryan E.
    "Commingling." [HiramPoR] (58/59) Spr 95-Wint 96, p. 61.
    "Winter's Deconstruction: Bossier City, Louisiana." [HiramPoR] (58/59) Spr 95-Wint 96, p. 59-60.
4157. MERCURIO, Katherine M.
    "How My Brother Dealt with Mother's Dying." [CapeR] (30:1) Spr 95, p. 10.
    "Living in Lowell with a Modern Romantic." [SoCoast] (18) Ja 95, p. 37.
4158. MEREDITH, Christopher Todd
    "Safeguards." [FreeL] (15) Aut 95, p. 22.
4159. MERRILL, Christopher
    "On the south side of Malta, where steep cliffs fall into the sea" (tr. of Ales Debeljak). [PlumR] (8) [95], p. 1.
    "The port grows dark" (tr. of Ales Debeljak). [PlumR] (8) [95], p. 2.
    "The river rushes on" (tr. of Ales Debeljak). [PlumR] (8) [95], p. 3.
    "Sagebrush" (for Ales Debeljak). [Pequod] (39) 95, p. 113.
    "Scotch Broom: an Inventory." [SenR] (25:1) Spr 95, p. 87.
    "Things can't go on like this forever" (tr. of Ales Debeljak). [PlumR] (8) [95], p. 4.
4160. MERRILL, James (1926-1995)
    "The Charioteer of Delphi." [Poetry] (166:6) S 95, p. 337-338.
    "Christmas Tree." [Poetry] (166:6) S 95, p. 313.
    "Days of 1994." [NewYRB] (42:5) 23 Mr 95, p. 9.
    "In the Pink." [SouthwR] (80:2/3) Spr-Sum 95, p. 205-206.
    "Koi" (January, 1995). [NewYorker] (71:5) 27 Mr 95, p. 60.
    "Last Words." [Poetry] (166:6) S 95, p. 338.
    "Midsummer Evening on the Prinsengracht" (for Hans). [Verse] (12:2) 95, p. 95.
    "Mirror." [Poetry] (166:6) S 95, p. 348-349.

"On the Block." [NewYorker] (71:2) 6 Mr 95, p. 93.
"Pearl." [NewYRB] (42:5) 23 Mr 95, p. 9.
"Rhapsody on Czech Themes" (For Allan Gurganus). [YaleR] (83:4) O 95, p. 17.
"An Upward Look." [NewYRB] (42:8) 11 My 95, p. 51.
"The Victor Dog." [Poetry] (166:6) S 95, p. 340-341.
"Vol. XLIV, No. 3." [NewYRB] (42:5) 23 Mr 95, p. 9.
4161. MERRIN, Jeredith
"Depression." [SouthwR] (80:2/3) Spr-Sum 95, p. 283-284.
"Tulpenwoede (1634-1637)." [Salm] (106/107) Spr-Sum 95, p. 117-118.
MERS, Joyce la
   See LaMERS, Joyce
4162. MERSMANN, James
"How My Father Milked." [SouthernHR] (29:3) Sum 95, p. 240.
4163. MERTA, Angela
"By Wind, by Rain." [NorthStoneR] (12) 95, p. 224.
4164. MERTON, Andrew
"The Dogwood's Apprentice." [Conscience] (16:4) Wint 95-96, p. 4.
4165. MERWIN, W. S.
"After Fires." [GrandS] (14:2, #54) Fall 95, p. 143-144.
"Before a Departure in Spring." [Poetry] (166:1) Ap 95, p. 12.
"Bodies of Water." [Boulevard] (10:1/2, #28/29) Spr 95, p. 237.
"Ceremony After an Amputation." [Poetry] (166:1) Ap 95, p. 13-14.
"The Cisterns." [GrandS] (14:2, #54) Fall 95, p. 145.
"Distant Morning." [Poetry] (165:6) Mr 95, p. 336.
"Green Fields." [Atlantic] (275:2) F 95, p. 54.
"Lament for the Makers." [Poetry] (166:6) S 95, p. 317-323.
"A Night Fragrance." [Poetry] (166:1) Ap 95, p. 15.
"Old Sound." [Poetry] (165:6) Mr 95, p. 334.
"Peire Vidal." [NewYorker] (71:40) 11 D 95, p. 80.
"Portrait." [ColR] (22:2) Fall 95, p. 197.
"The Red." [Nat] (261:11) 9 O 95, p. 392.
"Ship." [SenR] (25:1) Spr 95, p. 16.
"The Shortest Night." [Poetry] (165:6) Mr 95, p. 335.
"Substance." [NewYorker] (70:48) 6 F 95, p. 73.
"A Taste." [ColR] (22:1) Spr 95, p. 51-52.
"Thread." [ColR] (22:1) Spr 95, p. 54.
"The Time Before." [ColR] (22:1) Spr 95, p. 53.
"The Time Before." [Poetry] (165:6) Mr 95, p. 337.
"Upland House." [ColR] (22:2) Fall 95, p. 198.
4166. MESA, Raúl
"A Private Song on a Summer Afternoon" (Canto intimo de una tarde veraniega, tr.
      by James Hoggard). [GrahamHR] (19) Wint 95-96, p. 70.
4167. MESSER, Sarah
"I Keep Thinking of San Francisco." [SpinningJ] (1) Fall 95-Wint 96, p. 50.
"Infinity Is Closing." [SpinningJ] (1) Fall 95-Wint 96, p. 48-49.
4168. MESSERLI, Douglas
"The Boughs Bent in to Hinder" (tr. by Joe Ross). [Phoebe] (24:2) 95, p. 49-53.
"A Drift." [Avec] (10) 95, p. 158-159.
"The Extremes" (After Rae Armantrout, as Translated from American into French
      and out of it again). [Avec] (10) 95, p. 160.
"I Confess" (After Baudelaire). [Avec] (10) 95, p. 156.
"Questions" (After Pablo Neruda). [Avec] (10) 95, p. 157.
"Seizure." [Chain] (2) Spr 95, p. 157.
"Shadows." [Conjunc] (24) 95, p. 151-152.
"The Volcano" (after Mallarmé). [Conjunc] (24) 95, p. 150.
4169. MESSO, George
"Departure" (tr. of Rainer Maria Rilke). [Pearl] (22) Fall-Wint 95, p. 111.
"Night Arrives" (tr. of Rainer Maria Rilke). [Pearl] (22) Fall-Wint 95, p. 111.
"Sketch" (tr. of Rainer Maria Rilke). [Pearl] (22) Fall-Wint 95, p. 111.
"A Vague Elsewhere" (tr. of Rainer Maria Rilke). [Pearl] (22) Fall-Wint 95, p. 111.
4170. METCALF, Paul
"Cease and Desist" (Extracts). [Sulfur] (15:2, #37) Fall 95, p. 53-59.
4171. METH, Theodore Sager
"After Expulsion." [ChrC] (112:9) 15 Mr 95, p. 286.
4172. METRAS, Gary
"Straight Lines." [AmerV] (38) 95, p. 77.

"The Treehouse." [Noctiluca] (2:1, #4) Spr 95, p. 13.
4173. METRES, Philip
"Field Hospital" (tr. of Arseny Tarkovsky). [ArtfulD] (28/29) 95, p. 28-29.
"Untitled: There's our street, let's say —" (tr. of Sergey Gandlevsky). [WillowS]
(36) Je 95, p. 92-93.
4174. MEUEL, David
"After You Left." [Pearl] (22) Fall-Wint 95, p. 104.
"Ten Years Together." [Pearl] (22) Fall-Wint 95, p. 104.
4175. MEYER, Amy
"Gaspé Homestead." [QW] (41) Aut-Wint 95-96, p. 272.
4176. MEYER, Bob
"Crush." [HangL] (67) 95, p. 96.
"Hitachi." [HangL] (67) 95, p. 95.
"Nothing." [HangL] (67) 95, p. 94.
4177. MEYER, David C.
"Leaf" (for Vikram Seth). [Elf] (5:3) Fall 95, p. 39.
"Response" (for William Stafford). [Elf] (5:1) Spr 95, p. 32.
4178. MEYER, William, Jr.
"A Pine Tree Full of Buzzards." [Bogg] (67) 95, p. 60.
4179. MEYERS, Brad
"Wells." [BellArk] (11:4) Jl-Ag 95, p. 12.
4180. MEYERS, Jean B.
"How Swift How Secretly" (Literary Festival: Poetry: Honorable Mention). [EngJ]
(84:4) Ap 95, p. 40.
4181. MEYERS, Susan
"Art 101: The Morning of the President's Funeral." [Crucible] (30) Fall 94, p. 30-31.
"Learning to Leave" (Pitt County, N.C. 1995 Literary Contest: Sam Ragan Prize).
[Crucible] (31) Fall 95, p. 4.
4182. MEZEY, Katalin
"An Anonymous Note" (tr. by Nicholas Kolumban). [PoetryE] (39) Fall 94, p. 116.
"The Confessions of a Newlywed" (tr. by Nicholas Kolumban). [PoetryE] (39) Fall
94, p. 117.
"God" (tr. by Nicholas Kolumban). [PoetryE] (39) Fall 94, p. 115.
"Thoughts on One Theme" (tr. by Nicholas Kolumban). [PoetryE] (39) Fall 94, p.
118.
4183. MEZEY, Robert
"Adrogué" (tr. of Jorge Luis Borges, w. Richard Barnes). [CutB] (42) Sum 94, p.
71-72.
"All Our Yesterdays" (tr. of Jorge Luis Borges). [NewYRB] (42:20) 21 D 95, p. 16.
"The Causes" (tr. of Jorge Luis Borges). [CutB] (42) Sum 94, p. 73-74.
"Ricardo Güiraldes" (tr. of Jorge Luis Borges). [CutB] (42) Sum 94, p. 70.
"Street with Pink Store" (tr. of Jorge Luis Borges). [CutB] (42) Sum 94, p. 68-69.
"Trying to Begin." [SenR] (25:1) Spr 95, p. 15.
4184. Mhac an tSAOI, Máire
"Mary Hogan's Quatrains" (tr. by Patrick Crotty). [SouthernR] (31:3) Jl/Sum 95, p.
476-479.
"Shoa" (in Irish and English). [Poetry] (167:1/2) O-N 95, p. 38-39.
4185. MICCICHE, Laura
"The Klan Member." [Pequod] (39) 95, p. 114.
"The Mall." [CimR] (113) O 95, p. 50.
"Meditation for the Body." [Flyway] (1:1) Spr 95, p. 80.
"My Generation." [Flyway] (1:1) Spr 95, p. 81.
4186. MICHAEL (D.C. Vision Program, Tyler Elementary School, Washington, DC).
"Untitled: I like myself" (WritersCorps Program). [WashR] (21:2) Ag-S 95, p. 19.
4187. MICHAELS, Judith
"November." [US1] (30/31) 95, p. 25.
4188. MICHAELS, S.
"5 REM *******'SOAP'*******." [SmPd] (32:2, #94) Spr 95, p. 15.
4189. MICHAUD, Jacqueline
"Metropole Cafe." [AmerLC] (7) 95, p. 105-106.
4190. MICHAUD, Michael Gregg
"Moribundo." [ModernW] (3) Sum 95, p. 7-8.
"The Problem with Fish Sticks." [BlackBR] (21) Fall-Wint 95, p. 40.
"The Root of All Anger." [BlackBR] (21) Fall-Wint 95, p. 41.
MICHELE, Mary di
See Di MICHELE, Mary

4191. MICHELLE D. (Rachael's Women's Center, Washington, DC).
"Today I have been aching" (WritersCorps Program). [WashR] (21:2) Ag-S 95, p. 9.
4192. MICHELSON, Peter
"About Morning" (tr. of Tapas Roy, w. Manjush Dasgupta). [AnotherCM] (29) Spr
95, p. 115.
"Alphonso through the Ages" (tr. of Charen, w. the author). [ManyMM] (2:1) 95, p.
94.
"Amrapali" (tr. of Mallika Sengupta, w. Shashi Desbank and the author).
[ManyMM] (1:3) 95, p. 130-131.
"In the Name of Buddha" (tr. of Charen, w. the author). [ManyMM] (2:1) 95, p. 95.
"Negation of the Negation" (tr. of Charen, w. the author). [ManyMM] (2:1) 95, p.
96.
"The Tale of the Tongue" (tr. of K. Satchidanandan, w. the author). [AnotherCM]
(29) Spr 95, p. 117.
"Time Warp" (tr. of Tapas Roy, w. Manjush Dasgupta). [AnotherCM] (29) Spr 95,
p. 116.
"Tukaram" (tr. of Subodh Sarkar, w. Sharmila Ray). [ManyMM] (1:3) 95, p. 138-
139.
"What I Might Forget" (tr. of Charen, w. the author). [ManyMM] (2:1) 95, p. 93.
4193. MICHELSON, Richard
"Head of a Man Beneath a Woman's Breast" (Second Runner-Up, Poetry Award).
[NewL] (61:2) 95, p. 28-29.
"Salome" (Second Runner-Up, Poetry Award). [NewL] (61:2) 95, p. 29.
4194. MIDDLETON, Christopher
"Cypress at the Window: A Letter to Lotten." [ParisR] (37:135) Sum 95, p. 48-49.
"On a Photograph of Chekhov" (for Katharina Wagenbach). [ParisR] (37:135) Sum
95, p. 49-50.
4195. MIDDLETON, David
"At Franklin." [SewanR] (103:3) Sum 95, p. 329-334.
"For an Artist with Parkinson's" (to my father). [SouthernR] (31:1) Wint 95, p. 38-
39.
"The Wargamer." [SewanR] (103:3) Sum 95, p. 375-376.
4196. MIDDLETON, Peter
"Here Is a Clue." [WestCL] (29:2, #17) Fall 95, p. 50.
"Unflagging Optimism." [WestCL] (29:2, #17) Fall 95, p. 51.
4197. MIDGE, Tiffany
"Promises of Winter." [WeberS] (12:3) Fall 95, p. 140.
"The Running Boy." [WeberS] (12:3) Fall 95, p. 139.
"The Woman Who Married a Bear." [PoetryNW] (36:3) Aut 95, p. 31-32.
4198. MIGALDI, Renaldo
"As the Amish." [NewAW] (13) Fall-Wint 95, p. 121.
4199. MIGNON, Taylor
"Dogmother of All Dogmas." [Noctiluca] (2:1, #4) Spr 95, p. 31.
4200. MIKE (Clean & Sober Streets, Washington, DC).
"Last Straw" (WritersCorps Program). [WashR] (21:2) Ag-S 95, p. 18.
4201. MIKESELL, Janice H.
"Concupiscent Season" (after a trip through Forestburg melon country). [MidwQ]
(36:4) Sum 95, p. 408.
4202. MIKOLEY, Jim
"Body Fading Like an Echo." [Nimrod] (39:1) Fall-Wint 95, p. 114.
"Phone Call to My Brother." [ChironR] (43) Sum 95, p. 29.
4203. MIKULEC, Patrick B.
"Babel." [HawaiiR] (19:2) Fall 95, p. 23.
"Holy Day." [WestB] (36) 95, p. 97.
"Yellow Jackets." [WestB] (36) 95, p. 96.
4204. MIKUNI, Reiko
"If you so wish, cry for the National Defense" (in Japanese and English, tr. by Jiro
Nakano). [BambooR] (67/68) Sum-Fall 95, p. 47.
4205. MILAREPA (Tibetan yogi, 1025-1135)
"I bow down to all holy Gurus" (edited and tr. by Garam C. C. Chang). [Tricycle]
(4:3, #15) Spr 95, p. 71.
4206. MILBURN, Michael
"Accompaniment." [HarvardR] (9) Fall 95, p. 98.
4207. MILDER, Ben
"The Suppository." [Light] (14) Sum 95, p. 18.

4208. MILES, John
"Honor Lelepa's Secret" (Efate Isle Vanuatu). [Vis] (47) 95, p. 33.
4209. MILES, Ron
"Before the Reunion." [Descant] (26:1, #88) Spr 95, p. 100.
"Parent Becoming." [Descant] (26:1, #88) Spr 95, p. 99.
4210. MILES, Steve
"The Price of a Movie." [WritersF] (21) 95, p. 28.
"Question for My Father." [WilliamMR] (33) 95, p. 70-71.
4211. MILEY, James D.
"Dry Spell." [MidwQ] (36:4) Sum 95, p. 409-410.
4212. MILICH, Jennifer
"Ana and the Anole." [LowellR] [1] Sum 94, p. 14-15.
4213. MILITELLO, Jennifer
"Sunlight in an Empty Room." [GreensboroR] (59) Wint 95-96, p. 43.
"Tent Camping." [GreensboroR] (59) Wint 95-96, p. 42.
4214. MILJKOVIC, Branko
"Chronicle" (tr. by P. H. Liotta). [Vis] (48) 95, p. 49.
"Orpheus in Hell" (tr. by P. H. Liotta). [Vis] (48) 95, p. 50.
"Sun" (tr. by P. H. Liotta). [Vis] (48) 95, p. 49.
"Tower of Skulls" (tr. by P. H. Liotta). [Vis] (48) 95, p. 50.
MILKMAN, Rebecca Alson
See ALSON-MILKMAN, Rebecca
4215. MILLAN, Gonzalo
"Antiquarian" (tr. by Annegret Nill). [Arc] (35) Aut 95, p. 66.
"Monument" (tr. by Annegret Nill). [Arc] (35) Aut 95, p. 67.
"Night" (tr. by Annegret Nill). [Arc] (35) Aut 95, p. 65.
"Winged Fish" (tr. by Annegret Nill). [Arc] (35) Aut 95, p. 64.
4216. MILLAR, Joseph
"Hansel and Gretel's Father" (Honorable Mention, Jacaranda Poetry Contest).
[Jacaranda] (11) [95 or 96?], p. 38-39.
"Poem for a New Girlfriend." [Manoa] (7:2) Wint 95, p. 130.
"Rain." [Manoa] (7:2) Wint 95, p. 131.
4217. MILLER, Ann
"Markers." [HampSPR] Wint 95, p. 45.
"Meadow Crossing." [HampSPR] Wint 95, p. 47.
"Night." [HampSPR] Wint 95, p. 46.
4218. MILLER, Ben
"The Office Did Not Fit Him." [Parting] (8:2) Wint 95-96, p. 46.
"She Wanted to Be a Teacher." [Parting] (8:2) Wint 95-96, p. 46.
4219. MILLER, Carol E.
"Bodies of Water." [CreamCR] (19:1) Spr 95, p. 100.
"Catharine MacKinnon's Cat." [CreamCR] (19:1) Spr 95, p. 101.
4220. MILLER, Carolyn
"Still Life with Tropical Flowers." [GeoR] (49:2) Sum 95, p. 441.
4221. MILLER, David
"The Soprano." [Noctiluca] (2:1, #4) Spr 95, p. 40.
4222. MILLER, David Carson
"Into Thin Air." [CarolQ] (47:3) Sum 95, p. 58-59.
4223. MILLER, E. A.
"Alef." [ApalQ] (43) Spr 95, p. 82-84.
"The Wedding." [Poem] (73) My 95, p. 31.
4224. MILLER, Elizabeth Gamble
"Beginning" (tr. of Nela Rio). [Luz] (8) Spr 95, p. 33.
"The Breeze" (tr. of Nela Rio). [Luz] (8) Spr 95, p. 37.
"The Contracting of Laborers" (tr. of Claudio Rodríguez). [MidAR] (15:1/2) 95, p.
175, 177.
"Elegy from Simancas (Toward History)" (tr. of Claudio Rodríguez). [MidAR]
(15:1/2) 95, p. 181-187.
"Hasta la Cólera Se Pudre (Even Rage Will Rot)" (3 selections, tr. of Carlos Ernesto
García). [Luz] (8) Spr 95, p. 27-31.
"A Hundred Fifty Thousand Degrees Below Zero" (tr. of Carlos Ernesto García).
[Luz] (8) Spr 95, p. 31.
"In the Threshold of Sunset" (3 selections from an unpublished work, tr. of Nela
Rio). [Luz] (8) Spr 95, p. 33-37.
"Love Is to Blame" (tr. of Claudio Rodríguez). [MidAR] (15:1/2) 95, p. 179.

"The Market of Light" (Translation Chapbook Series Number 23, tr. of Claudio
Rodríguez). [MidAR] (15:1/2) 95, p. 167-187.
"The Rose Garden" (tr. of Nela Rio). [Luz] (8) Spr 95, p. 35.
"Song of Awakening" (tr. of Claudio Rodríguez). [MidAR] (15:1/2) 95, p. 171, 173.
"The Summer of 80 and Five" (tr. of Carlos Ernesto García). [Luz] (8) Spr 95, p. 29.
"They Are Like the Dew" (tr. of Carlos Ernesto García). [Luz] (8) Spr 95, p. 27.
4225. MILLER, Eric
"Deduction of the Aesthetic Judgement." [CanLit] (145) Sum 95, p. 37-38.
4226. MILLER, Errol
"Another Masterpiece for Judith." [Ledge] (18) Sum 95, p. 50.
"At Billy Bob's." [Parting] (8:2) Wint 95-96, p. 42.
"At Control Point 0." [CentR] (39:1) Wint 95, p. 88-89.
"Dixie Courts." [HampSPR] Wint 95, p. 14.
"Elsewhere on the Delta." [CentR] (39:1) Wint 95, p. 87-88.
"Everywhere Blue." [Parting] (8:2) Wint 95-96, p. 41.
"Fall in Louisiana." [Plain] (15:2) Wint 95, p. 11.
"For Antioch and Mars Hill." [SmPd] (32:1, #93) Wint 95, p. 32.
"From the Book of Lost Souls." [Elf] (5:4) Wint 95, p. 28-29.
"Junction City." [WestB] (36) 95, p. 95.
"Living This Life." [PaintedB] (57) 95, p. 55-56.
"Man Overboard." [GreenHLL] (6) 95, p. 106.
"Proud Mary's." [HampSPR] Wint 95, p. 14.
"South from Twilight." [AxeF] (3) 90, p. 18.
"Surely Spring Will Come." [GreensboroR] (59) Wint 95-96, p. 80-81.
"Unfinished Business." [GlobalCR] (6) Fall 95, p. 109-112.
"Urbana." [Dandel] (22:1) 95, p. 5.
4227. MILLER, F. Wyatt
"Song of Delmore." [SnailPR] (3:2) 95, back cover.
"Song of the King." [ApalQ] (44/45) Fall 95-Wint 96, p. 55.
4228. MILLER, Heather Ross
"Bow and Arrow Season." [Shen] (45:2) Sum 95, p. 76-77.
"Miss Baby, a Southern Gothic." [LouisL] (12:1) Spr 95, p. 36-37.
"Old Girls & Other Terrors." [LouisL] (12:1) Spr 95, p. 38-39.
"Pastimes." [Shen] (45:2) Sum 95, p. 78-79.
"Wolf Howl." [LouisL] (12:1) Spr 95, p. 40.
4229. MILLER, Jane
"Adventures Aplenty Lay Before You." [Colum] (24/25) 95, p. 37.
"Las Diamonds Are Una Chica's Best Amiga." [ColR] (22:2) Fall 95, p. 189-190.
"Far Away." [ColR] (22:1) Spr 95, p. 43-44.
"Separation." [ColR] (22:2) Fall 95, p. 191.
"Though Not Admonished of Your Intentions in Words." [Colum] (24/25) 95, p. 36.
4230. MILLER, Jim Wayne
"Then, and Now." [EngJ] (84:4) Ap 95, p. 18.
"Traveling." [EngJ] (84:4) Ap 95, p. 18.
4231. MILLER, John N.
"Der Rosenkavalier" (May 15, 1945). [PassN] (16:1) Sum 95, p. 16-17.
4232. MILLER, Leslie Adrienne
"Die Aufklarung." [InterQ] (2:3) 95, p. 114.
"Babes in Toyland." [PraS] (69:1) Spr 95, p. 108-110.
"Berlin Hinterhofs." [InterQ] (2:3) 95, p. 112-113.
"Deutsch Kaffee." [NorthStoneR] (12) 95, p. 206-207.
"The Keening." [RiverS] (45) 95, p. 89-91.
"Lawn Ornaments." [CrabOR] (1:1) Fall-Wint 95, p. 86-88.
"Rite of Winter." [PraS] (69:1) Spr 95, p. 105-107.
"Valediction for an Itinerant Lover." [NorthStoneR] (12) 95, p. 208-209.
"Yesterday Had a Man in It." [CrabOR] (1:1) Fall-Wint 95, p. 89-90.
4233. MILLER, Mark
"Man on the River Flats." [PoetryC] (15:3) Ag 95, p. 21.
"Windsurfers." [PoetryC] (15:3) Ag 95, p. 21.
4234. MILLER, Marlene
"The Handkerchief" (to Eghishe Charents, Armenian poet, 1897-1937).
[GrahamHR] (19) Wint 95-96, p. 12-13.
4235. MILLER, Michael
"At the Alligator." [RiverC] (15:2) Sum 95, p. 28-30.
4236. MILLER, Peter
"Tsunami." [HayF] (17) Fall-Wint 95, p. 84-85.

4237. MILLER, Philip
"The Family, Circa 1950." [CapeR] (30:2) Fall 95, p. 6.
"Late September." [GreenHLL] (6) 95, p. 19.
"Like a Movie." [LitR] (38:2) Wint 95, p. 272.
"Raging." [Confr] (56/57) Sum-Fall 95, p. 317-318.
"Thanksgiving Sun." [Ledge] (18) Sum 95, p. 90.
"Turning in Early." [GreenHLL] (6) 95, p. 20.
"What Won't Die." [Chelsea] (58) 95, p. 52-53.
"Where They Are." [Ledge] (18) Sum 95, p. 88-89.
"You Can't Win for Losing." [Confr] (56/57) Sum-Fall 95, p. 319.
4238. MILLER, Raeburn
"Balances." [LouisL] (12:2) Fall 95, p. 88.
"The Black Angel." [LouisL] (12:2) Fall 95, p. 89.
"A Couple of Revisions." [LouisL] (12:2) Fall 95, p. 92.
"Epitaphs." [LouisL] (12:2) Fall 95, p. 96.
"Ex Uno Plures." [LouisL] (12:2) Fall 95, p. 93.
"(Exeunt.)" [LouisL] (12:2) Fall 95, p. 98.
"Homecoming." [LouisL] (12:2) Fall 95, p. 95.
"In Memory of an Actor." [LouisL] (12:2) Fall 95, p. 97.
"Madoc." [LouisL] (12:2) Fall 95, p. 91.
"A Resurrection." [LouisL] (12:2) Fall 95, p. 94.
"Two Dead." [LouisL] (12:2) Fall 95, p. 90.
4239. MILLER, Ray
"Baby Bird." [Parting] (8:2) Wint 95-96, p. 19.
"Fame Is Not All It's Cracked Up to Be." [Parting] (8:2) Wint 95-96, p. 19-20.
4240. MILLER, Sarah (Sarah J.)
"Discovery." [HopewellR] (7) 95, p. 107-108.
"Lunatic." [Crucible] (31) Fall 95, p. 20.
"The Waterlilies." [Poem] (73) My 95, p. 65.
4241. MILLER, Tonya
"Steer Clear That Coyote." [HawaiiR] (19:2) Fall 95, p. 125.
MILLER LAINO, E. J.
See LAINO, E. J. Miller
4242. MILLETT, John
"The Bombing of Darmstadt — WWII, 1944." [Footwork] (24/25) 95, p. 50.
"The Collector." [Footwork] (24/25) 95, p. 50.
"For a Daughter." [Vis] (49) 95, p. 12.
"My Wife Leaves to Visit Her Mother." [Bogg] (67) 95, p. 20.
4243. MILLIGAN, Paula
"Equinox." [BellArk] (11:4) Jl-Ag 95, p. 21.
"House Special." [BellArk] (11:1) Ja-F 95, p. 25.
"Invocation." [BellArk] (11:4) Jl-Ag 95, p. 21.
"The Man Underground." [BellArk] (11:4) Jl-Ag 95, p. 21.
"Quiet Can Speak Audibly." [BellArk] (11:4) Jl-Ag 95, p. 21.
"Reflections." [BellArk] (11:1) Ja-F 95, p. 25.
4244. MILLIS, Christopher
"Elegy." [SenR] (25:1) Spr 95, p. 96.
"A Memory" (tr. of Umberto Saba). [InterQ] (2:1/2) 95, p. 55.
4245. MILLMAN, Lawrence
"The Barren Woman's Lament" (tr. of anonymous East Greenland songs). [Nimrod] (38:2) Spr-Sum 95, p. 114.
"Hershel Drift Logs" (from "Northern Latitudes"). [Nimrod] (38:2) Spr-Sum 95, p. 17.
"The Last Angakok" (Angmagssalik, Greenland, 1984, from "Northern Latitudes"). [Nimrod] (38:2) Spr-Sum 95, p. 128.
"Lichen" (for Richard Smythe, from "Northern Latitudes"). [Nimrod] (38:2) Spr - Sum 95, p. 17.
"Narwhal Song" (tr. of anonymous East Greenland songs). [Nimrod] (38:2) Spr - Sum 95, p. 116.
"Song of the Ptarmigan" (tr. of anonymous East Greenland songs). [Nimrod] (38:2) Spr-Sum 95, p. 114.
"Tent Dwellers" (Okak, Labrador, from "Northern Latitudes"). [Nimrod] (38:2) Spr - Sum 95, p. 128.
"Young Girl's Lament" (tr. of anonymous East Greenland songs). [Nimrod] (38:2) Spr-Sum 95, p. 115.

315

4246. MILLS, Billy
"Alba: In the Park." [WestCL] (29:2, #17) Fall 95, p. 52-57.
4247. MILLS, George
"Progress Report." [Atlantic] (276:6) D 95, p. 104.
4248. MILLS, Jess
"Like Ginger Root." [BellR] (18:2, #38) Fall 95, p. 35.
4249. MILLS, Lambert
"Robert Frost's Horse." [SoCoast] (18) Ja 95, p. 54.
4250. MILLS, Ralph J., Jr.
"11/92." [AmerPoR] (24:1) Ja-F 95, p. 26.
"Daylong This." [ChiR] (41:4) 95, p. 19.
"Fog Inland." [AmerPoR] (24:1) Ja-F 95, p. 26.
"No / Edge." [ChiR] (41:4) 95, p. 18.
"One Level Of." [AnotherCM] (29) Spr 95, p. 138-139.
"Plum / Sticks." [AmerPoR] (24:1) Ja-F 95, p. 26.
"Shimmer of." [Northeast] (5:12) Sum 95, p. 27.
"Where the Ground" (After Philippe Jaccottet). [ChiR] (41:4) 95, p. 20.
4251. MILLS, Wilmer Hastings
"Ghost Story" (Eyster Prize, Winner in Poetry). [NewDeltaR] (12:2) Spr-Sum 95, p. 1-2.
"New Home." [NewDeltaR] (12:2) Spr-Sum 95, p. 11.
4252. MILNE, Drew
"Carte Blanche" (Excerpt). [Sulfur] (15:1, #36) Spr 95, p. 151-154.
4253. MILOSZ, Czeslaw
"After Enduring" (tr. by the author and Robert Hass). [OhioR] (53) 95, p. 31.
"An Appeal" (tr. by Robert Hass). [Verse] (12:2) 95, p. 96-98.
"Body" (tr. by the author and Robert Hass). [NewYorker] (71:7) 10 Ap 95, p. 60.
"Dawns" (tr. by Robert Hass). [RiverS] (42/43) 95, p. 140-141.
"The Garden of Earthly Delights: Hell" (tr. by the author and Robert Hass). [OhioR] (53) 95, p. 30.
"A Hall" (tr. by the author and Robert Hass). [NewYorker] (71:8) 17 Ap 95, p. 77.
"House in Krasnogruda" (tr. by the author and Robert Hass). [AmerPoR] (24:2) Mr-Ap 95, p. 55.
"In Szetejnie" (tr. by the author and Robert Hass). [AmerPoR] (24:2) Mr-Ap 95, p. 54.
"Lithuania, After Fifty-Two Years" (Selections, tr. by the author and Robert Hass). [AmerPoR] (24:2) Mr-Ap 95, p. 55.
"One More Contradiction" (tr. by the author and Robert Hass). [GeoR] (49:1) Spr 95, p. 129.
"Pierson College" (tr. by the author and Robert Hass). [Thrpny] (61) Spr 95, p. 5.
"Report." [AmerPoR] (24:2) Mr-Ap 95, p. 56.
"Retired" (tr. by the author and Robert Hass). [PartR] (62:2) Spr 95, p. 293-294.
"To Mrs. Professor in Defense of My Cat's Honor and Not Only" (tr. by the author and Robert Hass). [NewYRB] (42:5) 23 Mr 95, p. 42.
"To My Daimonion" (tr. by the author and Robert Hass). [PartR] (62:2) Spr 95, p. 292-293.
"The Wall of a Museum" (tr. by the author and Robert Hass). [Zyzzyva] (11:1, #41) Spr 95, p. 163.
"You Whose Name" (tr. by the author and Robert Hass). [PartR] (62:2) Spr 95, p. 295.
4254. MILOSZ, Oscar Vladislas de Lubicz
"Autumn Song" (tr. by Tod Marshall). [WillowS] (36) Je 95, p. 108.
"The Bridge" (tr. by Tod Marshall). [WillowS] (36) Je 95, p. 109.
4255. MILTON, John R.
"All Things Begin." [SoDakR] (33:3/4) Fall-Wint 95, p. 30.
"The Loving Hawk." [SoDakR] (33:3/4) Fall-Wint 95, p. 28.
"The Promise of a Place." [SoDakR] (33:3/4) Fall-Wint 95, p. 25.
"Totem." [SoDakR] (33:3/4) Fall-Wint 95, p. 26.
"The Tree of Bones." [SoDakR] (33:3/4) Fall-Wint 95, p. 29.
"Western Requiem." [SoDakR] (33:3/4) Fall-Wint 95, p. 27.
4256. MILTON, Michael
"The Wallop." [ChironR] (43) Sum 95, p. 31.
4257. MIMS, Kevin
"The Condemned Man." [AnotherCM] (29) Spr 95, p. 140.
"The Law of Malfunctioning Machinery." [Pearl] (22) Fall-Wint 95, p. 88.

4258. MINANEL, S.
   "Thoreauly Turned Off." [Light] (15/16) Aut-Wint 95-96, p. 30.
4259. MINARD, Nancy
   "The River" (Short Grain Contest Winners: Prose Poem, Third). [Grain] (22:3) Wint
      95, p. 65-66.
4260. MINARELLI, Enzo
   "Tancat Hispanidad" (Excerpt). [FreeL] (14) Wint 95, p. 20-21.
4261. MINCZESKI, John
   "The News" (for Carei Thomas). [SpoonR] (20:1) Wint-Spr 95, p. 101-102.
4262. MINEAR, Richard H.
   "Blind" (tr. of Toge Sankichi). [InterQ] (2:1/2) 95, p. 264-265.
   "Eyes" (tr. of Toge Sankichi). [InterQ] (2:1/2) 95, p. 262-263.
   "The Flag, 1" (tr. of Kurihara Sadako). [InterQ] (2:1/2) 95, p. 254.
   "Ground Zero" (tr. of Kurihara Sadako). [InterQ] (2:1/2) 95, p. 255.
   "Hiroshima" (tr. of Kurihara Sadako). [InterQ] (2:1/2) 95, p. 256.
   "Let Us Be Midwives!" (An untold story of the atomic bombing, tr. of Kurihara
      Sadako). [InterQ] (2:1/2) 95, p. 253.
   "Nevada, 1" (the resumption of nuclear testing by the U.S. and the U.S.S.R., tr. of
      Kurihara Sadako). [InterQ] (2:1/2) 95, p. 257.
   "Prayer for a Nuclear-Free Tomorrow" (For Kazuko, tr. of Kurihara Sadako).
      [InterQ] (2:1/2) 95, p. 260.
   "Rain" (tr. of Kurihara Sadako). [InterQ] (2:1/2) 95, p. 261.
   "Shades: The Post-Doomsday World" (tr. of Kurihara Sadako). [InterQ] (2:1/2) 95,
      p. 258.
   "When We Say 'Hiroshima'" (tr. of Kurihara Sadako). [InterQ] (2:1/2) 95, p. 259.
MINH, Ho Chi
   See HO, Chi Minh
4263. MINNIS, Chelsey
   "Bruise" (Honorable Mention, Jacaranda Poetry Contest). [Jacaranda] (11) [95 or
      96?], p. 31.
   "Quake." [Jacaranda] (11) [95 or 96?], p. 30.
4264. MINOR, William
   "From Our Peasant Love." [PaintedB] (55/56) 95, p. 113.
4265. MINUS, Ed
   "Fragment from 'Breathless' at Harvard" (The Common Room, so-called, Lowell
      House, 1968). [Jacaranda] (11) [95 or 96?], p. 64-65.
4266. MIRANDA, Deborah A.
   "Baskets." [WeberS] (12:3) Fall 95, p. 116.
   "Indian Cartography." [WeberS] (12:3) Fall 95, p. 115.
   "Stories I Tell My Daughter." [Calyx] (16:2) Wint 95-96, p. 48-49.
   "Stories I Tell My Daughter." [WeberS] (12:3) Fall 95, p. 114-115.
4267. MIRCEA, Ion
   "Winter Vision at the Mouth of the River" (tr. by Adam J. Sorkin and Liviu Cotrau).
      [Vis] (48) 95, p. 40.
4268. MIROLLO, Gabriella
   "Cellini's Saltcellar." [Poetry] (165:5) F 95, p. 250.
4269. MISCHE, Elizabeth
   "In Ottawa for the First Time." [Blueline] (16) 95, p. 4-5.
4270. MISECK, Lorie
   "Home." [Event] (24:2) Sum 95, p. 30-31.
   "A Missing Person." [Event] (24:2) Sum 95, p. 34.
   "Pronouncing the Dead." [Event] (24:2) Sum 95, p. 32-33.
4271. MISHKIN, Julia
   "Changes in the Environment." [ManhatR] (7:2) Wint 95, p. 36-37.
   "Long Distance." [ManhatR] (7:2) Wint 95, p. 34-35.
   "Shape-Shifter." [ManhatR] (7:2) Wint 95, p. 38-39.
4272. MISTRAL, Gabriela
   "Message of a Birth for Chile" (tr. by Christiane Jacox Kyle). [PraS] (69:1) Spr 95,
      p. 21-23.
   "Thrushes" (tr. by Christiane Jacox Kyle). [PraS] (69:1) Spr 95, p. 24-25.
4273. MITA, Kaichi
   "Are they still reflected in your misty eyes?" (in Japanese and English, tr. by Jiro
      Nakano). [BambooR] (67/68) Sum-Fall 95, p. 48.
4274. MITCHAM, Judson
   "Hard Laughter." [SouthernR] (31:1) Wint 95, p. 40-41.
   "In the Sweet By and By." [GettyR] (8:2) Spr 95, p. 327-329.

317

MIYATA

"Together." [GettyR] (8:2) Spr 95, p. 330.
4275. MITCHELL, Cynthia
"Cinders." [Pearl] (22) Fall-Wint 95, p. 109.
4276. MITCHELL, Hayley R.
"After Two Weeks in This New Bed." [SouthernPR] (35:2) Wint 95, p. 71-72.
"Always a Bridesmaid." [Pearl] (22) Fall-Wint 95, p. 102.
"Rain." [PoetryNW] (36:2) Sum 95, p. 25.
"What the Grimm Girl Looks Forward To" (winner, 1955 Winter Competition:
Poetry). [Colum] (24/25) 95, p. 69-70.
4277. MITCHELL, Homer
"Elementals." [Poem] (73) My 95, p. 13.
"Style Dizzy Said." [Poem] (73) My 95, p. 14.
4278. MITCHELL, John
"Easter Shots." [NorthStoneR] (12) 95, p. 198-199.
"The Life of Fernando Cruz" (Arranged from a newspaper account). [NorthStoneR]
(12) 95, p. 200-201.
4279. MITCHELL, Mark
"The Razor." [PoetryE] (39) Fall 94, p. 68.
4280. MITCHELL, Nora
"After I Quit Drinking." [ColEng] (57:4) Ap 95, p. 465.
4281. MITCHELL, Roger
"Bones of Small Children." [PoetryNW] (36:3) Aut 95, p. 13.
"Braid." [Crazy] (49) Wint 95, p. 25-36.
"Clang." [DenQ] (30:1) Sum 95, p. 70.
"I Don't Know Where My Students Are This Year." [PoetryNW] (36:3) Aut 95, p.
14.
"Laughter in the Next Booth." [HayF] (16) Spr-Sum 95, p. 29.
"Remember." [PassN] (16:1) Sum 95, p. 6-7.
"Retirements in the Neighborhood." [HayF] (16) Spr-Sum 95, p. 28.
"Scumble." [ArtfulD] (28/29) 95, p. 47-55.
4282. MITCHELL, Susan
"Girl Tearing up Her Face." [ParisR] (37:134) Spr 95, p. 50-53.
"Softer." [WestHR] (49:4) Wint 95, p. 292-293.
"Venice." [ParisR] (37:134) Spr 95, p. 48-50.
"Wind / Breath, Breath / Wind." [Ploughs] (21:4) Wint 95-96, p. 130-132.
4283. MITCHNER, Gary
"Athena, Tour Guide. Aphrodite, Nympho." [ParisR] (37:136) Fall 95, p. 151-152.
"Morgan's Delphic Purification." [ParisR] (37:136) Fall 95, p. 152-153.
4284. MITCHNER, Stuart
"Barrymore in India." [Raritan] (15:2) Fall 95, p. 59-60.
"The Bijou Hotel." [Poetry] (166:5) Ag 95, p. 275.
"For Those Who Know How to See It." [BellArk] (11:6) N-D 95, p. 14.
"Louise Brooks As Lulu." [Poetry] (166:5) Ag 95, p. 274.
"Melville's Crossing." [Raritan] (15:2) Fall 95, p. 60-61.
"Smiling in Camden." [BellArk] (11:6) N-D 95, p. 14.
"A Stranger's Light." [BellArk] (11:6) N-D 95, p. 14.
4285. MITTENTHAL, Robert
"Criticism As Therapy" (Selections: 6-17). [Avec] (9) 95, p. 135-145.
4286. MITZNER, Rita
"A Poem in Praise of Voluptuous Women, well endowed with thighs, hips and
breasts ...." [Pearl] (22) Fall-Wint 95, p. 98.
4287. MIYAGI, Ken'ichi
"I will overcome the shattering of my mind" (in Japanese and English, tr. by Jiro
Nakano). [BambooR] (67/68) Sum-Fall 95, p. 49.
4288. MIYAMAE, Hatsuko
"A crowd of ten thousand are standing in despair" (in Japanese and English, tr. by
Jiro Nakano). [BambooR] (67/68) Sum-Fall 95, p. 51.
4289. MIYAMOTO, Masayoshi
"A few survivors" (in Japanese and English, tr. by Jiro Nakano). [BambooR] (67/68)
Sum-Fall 95, p. 52.
4290. MIYAMOTO, Shizuka
"Exhausted, I sew" (in Japanese and English, tr. by Jiro Nakano). [BambooR]
(67/68) Sum-Fall 95, p. 53.
4291. MIYATA, Sadamu
"I see the procession of burnt sores" (in Japanese and English, tr. by Jiro Nakano).
[BambooR] (67/68) Sum-Fall 95, p. 50.

4292. MIZER, Ray
"Beach Bonds" (for William Everson). [BellArk] (11:6) N-D 95, p. 12.
"Diorama: Preparing for Invasion, Pre-VJ Day." [BellArk] (11:6) N-D 95, p. 12.
"Fearstrike." [BellArk] (11:6) N-D 95, p. 12.
"Petition." [BellArk] (11:6) N-D 95, p. 12.
4293. MLINKO, Ange
"My Children Don't Grow They Multiply." [Agni] (42) 95, p. 58.
4294. MOCK, Jeff
"Bloodberry Jam." [QW] (40) Spr-Sum 95, p. 68.
"Chewing Tobacco" (Ralph Waldo Mock, 1905-1990). [Crazy] (49) Wint 95, p. 74-75.
"Fig Leaves" (Erma Stanley Mock, 1907-1988). [LaurelR] (29:2) Sum 95, p. 68-69.
"On the Nature of International Terrorism." [GreenMR] (8:2) Fall-Wint 95-96, p. 127.
"Shriek Therapy." [SycamoreR] (7:1) Wint 95, p. 24.
"Tornado Warnings" (for Tim). [GreensboroR] (58) Sum 95, p. 54-55.
4295. MOCKLER, Kathryn
"I've Seen This." [AntigR] (100) Wint 95, p. 149.
"Mid February." [AntigR] (100) Wint 95, p. 148.
4296. MOE, Frederick
"Gardening at Night." [OxfordM] (10:1) Wint 94-Spr 95, p. 52.
"The Old House." [OxfordM] (10:1) Wint 94-Spr 95, p. 51-52.
4297. MOES, Christopher
"Listen." [JamesWR] (12:1) Wint 95, p. 8.
4298. MOFFEIT, Tony
"Blue Corn Tortillas and Mexican Beer." [ChironR] (42) Spr 95, p. 3.
"Crazy Coyote." [ChironR] (44/45) Aut-Wint 95, p. 16.
"Dancers in the Dark Rain." [ChironR] (44/45) Aut-Wint 95, p. 16.
"I Got the Blues." [ChironR] (44/45) Aut-Wint 95, p. 16.
"Luminous Animal." [ChironR] (42) Spr 95, p. 2.
"Marguerita." [ChironR] (44/45) Aut-Wint 95, p. 17.
"Poetry Is Dangerous, the Poet Is an Outlaw." [ChironR] (42) Spr 95, p. 3.
"Robert Johnson." [ChironR] (44/45) Aut-Wint 95, p. 16.
"Your Bluffing Eyes." [ChironR] (44/45) Aut-Wint 95, p. 16.
4299. MOFFI, Larry
"A Jew Takes Communion." [Crazy] (49) Wint 95, p. 73.
4300. MOHARTY, Niranjan
"Relationship." [InterPR] (21:1) Spr 95, p. 92-93.
4301. MOHRING, Ron
"Andy." [MinnR] (43/44) 95, p. 62.
"Arrival." [WestB] (37) 95, p. 29.
"Baptism." [CumbPR] (14:2) Spr 95, p. 32-33.
"His Family to Call." [ArtfulD] (28/29) 95, p. 107.
"Late Poem to My Sister." [EvergreenC] (10:1) Wint-Spr 95, p. 38.
"Primer." [MinnR] (43/44) 95, p. 63.
"The Real Story." [GettyR] (8:1) Wint 95, p. 156-157.
"This World and All It Holds." [GettyR] (8:1) Wint 95, p. 158-159.
"The Useful Machine." [GettyR] (8:4) Aut 95, p. 591-592.
"What We Carry Back." [Border] (7) Fall-Wint 96, p. 44.
MOINE, Frances le
See LeMOINE, Frances
4302. MOLDAW, Carol
"The Butterfly." [Orion] (14:2) Spr 95, p. 51.
"Relict." [Thrpny] (62) Sum 95, p. 30.
MOLEN, Robert vander
See VanderMOLEN, Robert
4303. MOMOI, Beverly Acuff
"About Love." [RiverS] (41) 95, p. 26.
4304. MONAGAN, George (George C.)
"Final Moorings." [Writer] (108:8) Ag 95, p. 24.
"Saturday Matinee." [Pearl] (22) Fall-Wint 95, p. 132.
"Saturday Matinee." [SlipS] (15) 95, p. 6.
4305. MONAGHAN, Timothy
"Emma." [RagMag] (12:2) Spr 95, p. 30-31.
"First Date." [NewYorkQ] (55) 95, p. 81.
"In the Dark." [RagMag] (12:2) Spr 95, p. 29.

"Stillborn." [RagMag] (12:2) Spr 95, p. 31.
"Storms." [NortheastCor] (3) 95, p. 64.
4306. MONAHAN, Dean W.
"A Poem for Dylan Thomas." [CapeR] (30:1) Spr 95, p. 38-39.
4307. MONAHAN, Jean
"One Hundred Days of a Hermit Crab." [Chelsea] (58) 95, p. 78-82.
"With the Flesh Remaining." [Chelsea] (58) 95, p. 77-78.
4308. MONCRIEFF, Karen
"Daddy's Magic." [SpoonR] (20:2) Sum-Fall 95, p. 129-130.
MONDA, Mark la
See LaMONDA, Mark
4309. MONEY, Peter
"Malua-Mele" (for Hanalei Tex). [HawaiiR] (19:2) Fall 95, p. 98-105.
4310. MONROE, Jonathan
"Disconnected." [Epoch] (44:2) 95, p. 204.
4311. MONSOUR, Leslie
"Middle Age." [PlumR] (9) [95 or 96], p. 53.
"Parking Lot." [PlumR] (9) [95 or 96], p. 54.
4312. MONTAG, Tom
"Ben's Confrontation" (from "The Complete Ben Zen"). [Northeast] (5:13) Wint 95-96, p. 18.
"The Complete Ben Zen" (Selections: 4 poems). [Northeast] (5:13) Wint 95-96, p. 18.
"More Good Advice" (from "The Complete Ben Zen"). [Northeast] (5:13) Wint 95-96, p. 18.
"On Deception" (from "The Complete Ben Zen"). [Northeast] (5:13) Wint 95-96, p. 18.
"Wrestling the Poem" (from "The Complete Ben Zen"). [Northeast] (5:13) Wint 95-96, p. 18.
4313. MONTAGUE, John
"Between." [Poetry] (167:1/2) O-N 95, p. 59.
"Border Sick-Call." [SouthernR] (31:3) Jl/Sum 95, p. 409-423.
"The Fault." [NewMyths] (2:2/3:1) 95, p. 112-116.
"Guardians." [NewYorker] (71:34) 30 O 95, p. 62.
"Lost Worlds" (For Elizabeth). [Poetry] (167:1/2) O-N 95, p. 58.
"Psychic Surgery." [Poetry] (167:1/2) O-N 95, p. 57.
"Remission." [Poetry] (167:1/2) O-N 95, p. 56.
"Wrath." [NewYorker] (71:38) 27 N 95, p. 65.
4314. MONTALBANO, Elizabeth
"Mother's Kitchen." [NewYorkQ] (55) 95, p. 80.
4315. MONTALE, Eugenio
"Little Testament" (tr. by Michael O'Brien). [Agni] (42) 95, p. 100-101.
"News from Mount Amiata" (tr. by Jonathan Galassi). [HarvardR] (8) Spr 95, p. 90-91.
4316. MONTAPERTO, Maria
"Navajo?" [Footwork] (24/25) 95, p. 28.
"While Watching a Rose." [Footwork] (24/25) 95, p. 28.
4317. MONTGOMERY, Missy-Marie
"Talking to Salvador Dali." [WestB] (37) 95, p. 34.
4318. MONTOYA, Andrés
"Again Tonight: Aztlándian Dream." [WillowS] (35) Ja 95, p. 78-79.
4319. MOOLTEN, David (David N.)
"At the Clinic." [NortheastCor] (3) 95, p. 33-34.
"Close." [NortheastCor] (3) 95, p. 62-63.
"Cornflakes." [AmerS] (64:3) Sum 95, p. 395-396.
"Housatonic." [RiverS] (41) 95, p. 5.
"Madame Butterfly." [NoAmR] (280:6) N-D 95, p. 6.
"Magic." [AmerS] (64:1) Wint 95, p. 90.
"The Miles." [NewEngR] (17:2) Spr 95, p. 89-90.
"The Sexton." [Chelsea] (58) 95, p. 42-43.
"Voyeur." [RiverS] (41) 95, p. 4.
"The White Vase." [BelPoJ] (46:1) Fall 95, p. 32-33.
4320. MOON, Janell
"The Deal." [SinW] (55) Spr-Sum 95, p. 77-78.
"Heritage." [EvergreenC] (10:2) Sum-Fall 95, p. 81.

4321. MOONEY, Christopher
"Bull." [Quarry] (43:4) 95, p. 109.
"Sawing Logs." [Quarry] (43:4) 95, p. 110.
"Slow Club." [Quarry] (43:4) 95, p. 108.
4322. MOONEY, Martin
"At a Boat Burning" (Portavogie, October 1993). [Field] (52) Spr 95, p. 70.
"Whites." [Field] (52) Spr 95, p. 71.
4323. MOORE, Berwyn J.
"The Deepness of Leaves and Light." [HiramPoR] (58/59) Spr 95-Wint 96, p. 63-64.
"Lighthouse" (Bald Head Island, North Carolina). [HiramPoR] (58/59) Spr 95-Wint
96, p. 62.
4324. MOORE, Carolyn
"Career Day at Union High: The Bryologist Speaks of Working with Mosses."
[Crucible] (30) Fall 94, p. 34-35.
4325. MOORE, Courtney
"Gone." [XavierR] (15:2) Fall 95, p. 54.
4326. MOORE, Jacqueline
"Putting the Sun Back in Father's Sky." [AnthNEW] (7) 95, p. 37.
4327. MOORE, Lenard D.
"Black and White" A Traditional Summer Kasen Renga, June 30, 1993 to July 25,
1994" (w. Jane Reichhold). [XavierR] (15:1) Spr 95, p. 29-31.
"Mother and Daughter." [Pembroke] (27) 95, p. 93.
"Seagulls at Waterside" (For Rita Dove). [Footwork] (24/25) 95, p. 137.
MOORE, Leonard D.
See MOORE, Lenard D.
4328. MOORE, Marijo
"Voices of Children." [Pembroke] (27) 95, p. 45.
4329. MOORE, Miles David
"Two Henrys." [Light] (14) Sum 95, p. 12.
4330. MOORE, Richard
"College Bound." [Light] (15/16) Aut-Wint 95-96, p. 19.
"Hitch." [Light] (14) Sum 95, p. 10.
"Man's Word to Woman." [Light] (13) Spr 95, p. 12.
"The Poet Laments the Decline of His Powers." [Light] (14) Sum 95, p. 15.
"There, But for the Grace of God." [Light] (15/16) Aut-Wint 95-96, p. 14.
"They're Cheaper Than You Think." [Light] (15/16) Aut-Wint 95-96, p. 23.
4331. MOORE, Sara S.
"End of the Rainbow." [SilverFR] (25) Sum 95, p. 24.
"The Russian Mafia." [SilverFR] (25) Sum 95, p. 25.
4332. MOORE, Todd
"Father Sank The." [Bogg] (67) 95, p. 16.
"Helping My." [Pearl] (22) Fall-Wint 95, p. 130.
"I Didn't Know." [WormR] (35:1, #137) 95, p. 10.
"The Night Hank." [FreeL] (15) Aut 95, p. 20.
"Playing w/." [WormR] (35:1, #137) 95, p. 10.
"Pretending to Fight." [Pearl] (22) Fall-Wint 95, p. 130.
4333. MOORHEAD, Andrea
"And It Was in Paris." [Os] (40) 95, p. 27.
"Dream Landscape." [Os] (41) 95, p. 21.
"Il Fut un Temps d'Attente" (tr. of Marie Uguay). [GrahamHR] (19) Wint 95-96, p.
71.
"Letter to the Wind." [Os] (40) 95, p. 29.
"The Light That Shines in Aachen." [Os] (41) 95, p. 24.
"Songs for the Soul: I." [IllinoisR] (3:1/2) Fall 95-Spr 96, p. 83-85.
"There Is No Sleep in Death." [Os] (40) 95, p. 28.
"We Have Walked Beyond Certainty." [Os] (41) 95, p. 22-23.
"We Live in the Glow of Steel." [Os] (40) 95, p. 26.
4334. MOOS, Michael
"End of the Year." [MidwQ] (36:4) Sum 95, p. 410.
4335. MOOSE, Ruth
"Findings." [Kalliope] (17:3) 95, p. 28.
"Ice." [HayF] (16) Spr-Sum 95, p. 98-99.
"The Potato Eaters" (after van Gogh). [HayF] (16) Spr-Sum 95, p. 96-97.
"Tea." [Kalliope] (17:3) 95, p. 29.
"Tea." [TarRP] (34:2) Spr 95, p. 36.
"What Happened." [HayF] (16) Spr-Sum 95, p. 100.

4336. MORA, Pat
"Honduran Ghosts." [MassR] (36:4) Wint 95-96, p. 631.
4337. MORAES, Vincius de
"Dead Cat Sonnet" (tr. by Thomas Dorsett and Moyses Purisch). [WillowS] (36) Je
95, p. 94.
4338. MORALES, Zulma (grade 6, Garrison Elementary, Washington, DC)
"Again and Again" (Poetry on the Metro Project). [WashR] (21:2) Ag-S 95, p. 15.
4339. MORAN, Daniel Thomas
"Melancholy." [Confr] (56/57) Sum-Fall 95, p. 326.
"With Ignatow at Whitman's Birthplace" (13 November 1994). [Confr] (56/57)
Sum-Fall 95, p. 325.
4340. MORAN, Laura
"Droppings." [DefinedP] (1:1) Fall-Wint 92, p. 16.
"Ornithology." [DefinedP] (1:1) Fall-Wint 92, p. 17.
4341. MORELAND, Jane
"After" (runner up, 1994 Borderlands Poetry Contest). [Border] (6) Spr-Sum 95, p.
56.
4342. MORGAN, Edwin
"Virtual and Other Realities - 6." [Verse] (12:2) 95, p. 99-100.
4343. MORGAN, Frederick
"In the Private Hospital." [NortheastCor] (3) 95, p. 35-36.
4344. MORGAN, Robert
"Electricity." [DefinedP] (1:2) Spr-Sum 93, p. 41.
"Fear of Height." [DefinedP] (1:2) Spr-Sum 93, p. 40.
"The Gift of Tongues." [Verse] (12:2) 95, p. 101.
"Madstone." [Shen] (45:3) Fall 95, p. 58.
"Mother Wit." [DefinedP] (1:1) Fall-Wint 92, p. 7.
"Spur." [DefinedP] (1:1) Fall-Wint 92, p. 8.
4345. MORGENSTERN, Christian
"Summons (Die Behorde)" (tr. by David R. Slavitt). [Light] (15/16) Aut-Wint 95-
96, p. 5.
4346. MORI, Kyoko
"Gathering Altar Flowers: For Jim Neilson, Fall, 1993." [Footwork] (24/25) 95, p.
88.
"Ghosts." [Footwork] (24/25) 95, p. 87-88.
"Weighing My Beliefs in New Mexico." [Footwork] (24/25) 95, p. 87.
4347. MORIARTY, Laura
"By and By." [Arshile] (4) 95, p. 38.
"The Case" (8 selections). [Avec] (10) 95, p. 34-41.
"Light." [Arshile] (4) 95, p. 36-37.
4348. MORIN, Edward
"Firefly" (tr. of Cai Qijiao, w. Chun-jian Xue). [InterQ] (2:3) 95, p. 115.
"Tinting Celery." [RiverS] (41) 95, p. 38-39.
4349. MORISHITA, Hiroshi
"A *kappa* is walking in front of my eyes" (in Japanese and English, tr. by Jiro
Nakano). [BambooR] (67/68) Sum-Fall 95, p. 54.
4350. MORITS, Yunna
"Between Scylla and Charybdis" (in Russian and English, tr. by Daniel Weissbort).
[InterQ] (2:1/2) 95, p. 77-78.
"Face" (in Russian and English, tr. by Daniel Weissbort). [InterQ] (2:1/2) 95, p. 79.
"Line" (in Russian and English, tr. by Daniel Weissbort). [InterQ] (2:1/2) 95, p. 76.
"Na ustvennom advige ushedshikh v sebya" (in Russian and English, tr. by Daniel
Weissbort and L. Medlin). [InterQ] (2:1/2) 95, p. 75.
4351. MORITZ, A. F.
"Beatrifying the Syllables of the Game" (tr. of Ludwig Zeller). [Arc] (35) Aut 95, p.
31.
"Body of Insomnia" (tr. of Ludwig Zeller). [Arc] (35) Aut 95, p. 33.
"From One Scribe to Another" (for the poet John Robert Colombo, tr. of Ludwig
Zeller). [Arc] (35) Aut 95, p. 32.
"The Little Walls Before China" (A courtier speaks to Ch'in Shih-huang-ti, ca. 210
BC). [Event] (24:2) Sum 95, p. 35-37.
"Ode to Apollo." [AntigR] (100) Wint 95, p. 58-60.
"On a Line by Catullus." [AntigR] (100) Wint 95, p. 57.
"On Distinction." [AntigR] (100) Wint 95, p. 46.
"Rest on the Flight into Egypt." [MalR] (111) Sum 95, p. 34-36.
"Woman Under the Lindens" (tr. of Ludwig Zeller). [Arc] (35) Aut 95, p. 34.

4352. MORLEY, Hilda
"For Carrington" (A Partly Found Poem). [AmerV] (37) 95, p. 120-130.
"Journey to Muzot." [NewAW] (13) Fall-Wint 95, p. 13-17.
"To Draw the Blinds." [GrandS] (13:3, #51) Wint 95, p. 176-177.
MORLEY, Liz Abrams
See ABRAMS-MORLEY, Liz
4353. MORLEY, Marjorie
"Downtown, P A." [BellArk] (11:5) S-O 95, p. 26.
"From My Front Window" (for Patrick). [BellArk] (11:5) S-O 95, p. 26.
"Idyl." [BellArk] (11:5) S-O 95, p. 26.
"Memories in Winter." [BellArk] (11:6) N-D 95, p. 23.
"Okanagan Idyl." [BellArk] (11:5) S-O 95, p. 26.
"South of Randle." [BellArk] (11:6) N-D 95, p. 23.
4354. MORLEY, Pamela
"Birddog." [WillowR] (22) Spr 95, p. 5.
4355. MORPHEW, Melissa
"The Missionary Writes to Her Fiancé Concerning Baptism." [Ascent] (19:2) Wint
95, p. 21.
"The Missionary Writes to Her Fiancé Concerning Desire." [PoetryE] (41) Aut 95,
p. 117.
"The Missionary Writes to Her Fiancé Concerning Hunger." [PoetryE] (41) Aut 95,
p. 116.
"The Missionary Writes to Her Fiancé Concerning Poetry." [Ascent] (19:2) Wint 95,
p. 20.
"The Missionary Writes to Her Fiancé Concerning the Living and the Dead."
[SouthernPR] (35:1) Sum 95, p. 60-61.
"Notes for a Lecture to the Art Students: Another Way to Hear." [PoetryE] (41) Aut
95, p. 114-115.
4356. MORRILL, Donald
"Everybody Wants to Nod 'Yes' to Something." [SycamoreR] (7:2) Sum 95, p. 42.
"Supplemental Adventures (A Narrative in Parts)" (Finalist, 1995 Greg Grummer
Award in Poetry). [Phoebe] (24:2) 95, p. 161-177.
"Thunder in Sunshine." [PoetL] (90:2) Sum 95, p. 31.
4357. MORRIS, Bernard E.
"Those Years of Waste." [Plain] (15:2) Wint 95, p. 29-30.
4358. MORRIS, Cecil
"The Cowboy in English" (for Rob Compton). [EngJ] (84:3) Mr 95, p. 61.
"For LB, 1943-1993." [EngJ] (84:3) Mr 95, p. 60.
"Indian Grounds." [EngJ] (84:3) Mr 95, p. 60-61.
"John Thompson." [EngJ] (84:3) Mr 95, p. 61.
"Subtext at the Conference." [EngJ] (84:7) N 95, p. 20.
4359. MORRIS, Herbert
"At the Morosco, Long Ago, Descending" (for Susan Strasberg, "attitude and
costume"). [Crazy] (48) Spr 95, p. 19-25.
"By Fire" (for Mark Doty). [DenQ] (30:1) Sum 95, p. 71-78.
"Certain Mysteries Flowing from the Gown" (for Stone Phillips). [Salm] (108) Fall
95, p. 99-104.
"The Hall, the Hall Grown Cold." [Boulevard] (10:1/2, #28/29) Spr 95, p. 20-28.
"Nighthawks" (Edward Hopper, oil on canvas, 1942). [Crazy] (48) Spr 95, p. 5-18.
"To Baden." [Boulevard] (10:3, #30) Fall 95, p. 75-81.
4360. MORRIS, Robin A.
"Gravity Stoop." [LowellR] (2) c1996, p. 106.
4361. MORRIS, Robin Amelia
"Container." [PaintedB] (57) 95, p. 40.
4362. MORRISON, John
"Kerouac Died." [ChironR] (42) Spr 95, p. 32.
4363. MORRISON, Kathi
"Hannah and the Artist." [SmPd] (32:2, #94) Spr 95, p. 25-26.
4364. MORRISON, Lillian
"Fish Fan." [Light] (13) Spr 95, p. 8.
4365. MORRISON, R. H.
"Confessions of an Aztec Chocolate-cup (Jícara)" (tr. of Joaquín Antonio Peñalosa).
[AntigR] (102/103) Sum-Aug 95, p. 129.
"Gray, Until ...." [Hellas] (6:2) Fall-Wint 95, p. 47.
"I Am Going to Bid You Farewell" (tr. of Joaquín Antonio Peñalosa). [AntigR]
(102/103) Sum-Aug 95, p. 127.

"Last Hope" (tr. of Paul Verlaine). [AntigR] (100) Wint 95, p. 107.
"Love Cast Down" (tr. of Paul Verlaine). [AntigR] (100) Wint 95, p. 103.
"On the Promenade" (tr. of Paul Verlaine). [AntigR] (100) Wint 95, p. 101.
"Parisian Sketch" (tr. of Paul Verlaine). [AntigR] (100) Wint 95, p. 99.
"The Sacred Secular." [SouthernR] (31:2) Ap/Spr 95, p. 273.
"The Winter's Past" (tr. of Paul Verlaine). [AntigR] (100) Wint 95, p. 105.
4366. MORRISON, Rusane
"They're Playing Our Song." [BellR] (18:1, #37) Spr 95, p. 44.
4367. MORRISSEY, Stephen
"Burning the Air with Love." [PoetryC] (15:2) Je 95, p. 6.
"Home." [AntigR] (101) Spr 95, p. 46-48.
"In the River." [Event] (24:1) Spr 95, p. 33-37.
"Magic." [AntigR] (101) Spr 95, p. 41-45.
4368. MORRO, Henry J.
"Chrissie's Shuffle" (San Francisco, 1969). [Pearl] (22) Fall-Wint 95, p. 128.
"Ode to Shit." [Pearl] (22) Fall-Wint 95, p. 127.
4369. MORROW, Edwin C.
"Walking with a Panther." [Drumvoices] (5:1/2) Fall-Wint 95-96, p. 24.
4370. MORSE, Michael
"Weather, Ersatz." [ColR] (22:1) Spr 95, p. 107-108.
4371. MORT, Graham
"Inheritance." [Stand] (36:3) Sum 95, p. 69.
4372. MORTENSON, Chris
"Hello, Mr. Packard." [NewYorkQ] (54) 95, p. 87.
4373. MORTON, Colleen
"Offspring." [HolCrit] (32:4) O 95, p. 18.
"Water Rising." [NewOR] (21:2) Sum 95, p. 97.
4374. MOSES, Emmanuel
"The Outer Land" (tr. by Agnes Stein). [MidAR] (15:1/2) 95, p. 204.
4375. MOSKUS, Charles D.
"At the Gun Shop." [Wind] (75) Spr 95, p. 15.
"Literary Life." [LullwaterR] (6:1) Spr-Sum 95, p. 65.
"Measurements." [SlipS] (15) 95, p. 26.
"Purpose." [Wind] (75) Spr 95, p. 16.
4376. MOSS, Catherine
"Riding the Palm Tree Stallions." [Dandel] (22:1) 95, p. 36-37.
4377. MOSS, Howard (1922-1987)
"Cardinal." [NewYorker] (71:35) 6 N 95, p. 88.
4378. MOSS, Jennifer
"Landscape." [Flyway] (1:1) Spr 95, p. 78-79.
"The Puppet." [PoetL] (90:2) Sum 95, p. 27.
4379. MOSS, Stanley
"Inheritance." [Nat] (260:5) 6 F 95, p. 179.
4380. MOSS, Thylias
"Accessible Heaven." [CrabOR] (1:1) Fall-Wint 95, p. 91.
"The Limitation of Beautiful Recipes" (for Hilda). [CrabOR] (1:1) Fall-Wint 95, p. 92.
4381. MOSSIN, Andrew
"The flame is an act of forgiveness." [Talisman] (15) Wint 95-96, p. 83.
MOTOKIYU, Tosa
See TOSA, Motokiyu
MOTOO, Andoh
See ANDOH, Motoo
4382. MOTT, Michael
"Gulland Rock." [Vis] (47) 95, p. 18.
"Here Is Elsewhere: The Dream of Descartes" (In Memory of Gregor Sebba). [SewanR] (103:2) Spr 95, p. 180-182.
"Hythe Ranges." [Vis] (47) 95, p. 19.
"The Only Human Voice" (tr. of Tolis Nikiforou, w. Donna Pastourmatzi). [Vis] (48) 95, p. 23.
"Pentecost." [Image] (11) Fall 95, p. 19-21.
"Piano at Midnight." [TarRP] (35:1) Fall 95, p. 39.
"Pyder Hundred" (Excerpt). [Verse] (12:2) 95, p. 102.
"Report from Rheims." [Image] (11) Fall 95, p. 21.
"Saenredam: Homage to the Seventeenth-Century Painter, Pieter Jansz Saenredam and to His Cat." [TarRP] (35:1) Fall 95, p. 37-38.

"Simple Directions." [Vis] (49) 95, p. 25.
"A Transfusion of Light into Words" (tr. of Tolis Nikiforou, w. Donna
    Pastourmatzi). [Vis] (48) 95, p. 23.
"Turner's 'Snow Storm: Hannibal and His Army Crossing the Alps'." [SewanR]
    (103:3) Sum 95, p. 371-372.
"The Vole." [Vis] (47) 95, p. 18.
"White Night." [TarRP] (35:1) Fall 95, p. 38-39.

MOTT, Robert de
    See DeMOTT, Robert

4383. MOUNTAIN, Judevine
    "All the Raucous Birds of Summer." [GreenMR] (8:1) Spr-Sum 95, p. 81.
    "Calling for Po Chu-Yi." [GreenMR] (8:1) Spr-Sum 95, p. 79.
    "Flawed Verse." [GreenMR] (8:1) Spr-Sum 95, p. 83.
    "In an Age of Academic Mandarins." [Sun] (238) O 95, p. 33.
    "My Old Woman." [WestB] (36) 95, p. 104.
    "Old Poet Refuses to Leave Home." [Sun] (238) O 95, p. 33.
    "Old Red Beard, My Friend." [Sun] (238) O 95, p. 32.
    "Thirty Years." [GreenMR] (8:1) Spr-Sum 95, p. 80.
    "What It Is Like to Read the Ancients." [WestB] (36) 95, p. 104-105.
    "When I Came to Judevine Mountain." [Sun] (238) O 95, p. 32.
    "When Nature Holds Its Breath." [GreenMR] (8:1) Spr-Sum 95, p. 82.

4384. MOURÉ, Erin
    "Brief & Fragile (A History of Reading)." [WestCL] (29:1, #16) Spr-Sum 95, p. 29-
        31.
    "Human Bearing." [WestCL] (29:1, #16) Spr-Sum 95, p. 32-35.
    "Measure for a Long Wound, for Robert's Grief, for Gail's (Wednesday Was Such a
        Bad Day)." [WestCL] (29:1, #16) Spr-Sum 95, p. 36.
    "Morphine, or The Cutting Stone." [WestCL] (29:1, #16) Spr-Sum 95, p. 3741.
    "Paris n Sleep." [ColR] (22:1) Spr 95, p. 67-72.

4385. MOVIUS, Geoffrey
    "Love in Their Language." [HarvardR] (9) Fall 95, p. 67.

4386. MOVSES, Hagop
    "Hagop Mendsouri" (tr. by Diana Der-Hovanessian). [GrahamHR] (19) Wint 95-96,
        p. 54-55.

4387. MOWAT, John
    "Beneath." [ChironR] (44/45) Aut-Wint 95, p. 41.

4388. MOXLEY, Jennifer
    "Enlightenment Evidence — Poems for Rosa Luxemburg" (Excerpts). [RiverC]
        (15:2) Sum 95, p. 121-122.
    "The Right to Counsel." [Phoebe] (24:1) 95, p. 119.
    "The Right to Remain Silent." [Phoebe] (24:1) 95, p. 118.

4389. MOYER, Emily
    "Six Forty-Five." [HangL] (66) 95, p. 87.

4390. MUCCI, John C.
    "Daybooks of the Dead." [Vis] (49) 95, p. 34.

4391. MUELLER, Jenny
    "Aquarium." [ChiR] (41:2/3) 95, p. 102-103.
    "Love Poem" (for T). [Atlantic] (275:6) Je 95, p. 78.

4392. MUELLER, Lisel
    "Gloves." [BlackWR] (21:2) Spr-Sum 95, p. 32.
    "In November." [BlackWR] (21:2) Spr-Sum 95, p. 31.
    "Things." [BlackWR] (21:2) Spr-Sum 95, p. 30.

4393. MUHAMMAD, Zitaqwa
    "Tell Me" (WritersCorps Program, Washington, DC). [WashR] (21:2) Ag-S 95, p.
        10.

4394. MUIR, John C.
    "Johnny T's Purple Heart." [EngJ] (84:6) O 95, p. 57.
    "Star Route Cafe, 2:00 A.M." [EngJ] (84:6) O 95, p. 56.

4395. MUKHOPADHYAY, Vijaya
    "It Goes Back with What Thoughts" (in Bengali and English, tr. by Paramita
        Banerjee and Carolyne Wright, w. the author). [MidAR] (15:1/2) 95, p. 64-65.
    "Mahalaya" (in Bengali and English, tr. by Paramita Banerjee and Carolyne Wright,
        w. the author). [MidAR] (15:1/2) 95, p. 62-63.
    "Sandhiprakash Raga" (in Bengali and English, tr. by Paramita Banerjee and
        Carolyne Wright, w. the author). [MidAR] (15:1/2) 95, p. 68-69.

"Twelve Fifty A.M." (in Bengali and English, tr. by Paramita Banerjee and Carolyne Wright, w. the author). [MidAR] (15:1/2) 95, p. 66-67.
4396. MUKTIBODH, Gajanan Madhav
"The Moon Wears a Crooked Smile" (tr. by Karni Pal Bahti). [AnotherCM] (29) Spr 95, p. 97-109.
4397. MULDER, Lucas
"Autumnal Poem" (for my mother). [CapilR] (2:16) Sum 95, p. 25-29.
"Awe Expressed through Fingers Tips (So Gently at First." [CapilR] (2:16) Sum 95, p. 30-31.
"Balance." [CapilR] (2:16) Sum 95, p. 35.
"For Roy Kiyooka." [CapilR] (2:16) Sum 95, p. 36-37.
"Three Polaroid Poems of Wales" (for Owen Jones). [CapilR] (2:16) Sum 95, p. 32-34.
"Untitled, or Impetus." [CapilR] (2:16) Sum 95, p. 38-41.
4398. MULDOON, Paul
"Angle" (tr. of Marin Sorescu). [SouthernR] (31:3) Jl/Sum 95, p. 484.
"Hay." [NewYorker] (71:24) 14 Ag 95, p. 42.
"My Dark Master" (tr. of Nuala Ní Dhomhnaill). [Poetry] (167:1/2) O-N 95, p. 77, 79.
"Shakespeare" (tr. of Marin Sorescu). [SouthernR] (31:3) Jl/Sum 95, p. 481-482.
"Symmetry" (tr. of Marin Sorescu). [SouthernR] (31:3) Jl/Sum 95, p. 482-484.
"Symposium." [NewYorker] (71:30) 2 O 95, p. 58.
"The Throwback." [Poetry] (167:1/2) O-N 95, p. 75.
"Wow and Flutter" (Selections: 1-10). [HarvardR] (8) Spr 95, p. 23-26.
4399. MULHERN, Maureen
"Investigators Are Measuring" (Finalist, 1995 Greg Grummer Award in Poetry). [Phoebe] (24:2) 95, p. 180.
"You Note the Heart in the Water" (Finalist, 1995 Greg Grummer Award in Poetry). [Phoebe] (24:2) 95, p. 181-182.
4400. MULLEN, Harryette
"Muse & Drudge" (Excerpts). [Chain] (2) Spr 95, p. 158-161.
4401. MULLEN, Kay
"Late October." [AntigR] (101) Spr 95, p. 57-58.
4402. MULLEN, Laura
"The Selected Letters." [DenQ] (30:1) Sum 95, p. 79-85.
4403. MULLER, Mario M.
"Bill Evans and the Birds of Appetite" (sonnets and images, w. Jeffrey Skinner). [Sonora] (29) Spr 95, p. 84-89.
4404. MULLINS, Brighde
"It Says Jesus." [ColR] (22:2) Fall 95, p. 180.
4405. MULLINS, Cecil J.
"Civilization." [Hellas] (6:1) Spr-Sum 95, p. 88.
4406. MULLINS, Keith A.
"The Coming Storm." [Rosebud] (2:3) Aut-Wint 95, p. 56.
4407. MULRANE, Scott
"At the Cave Named the Cat Hole." [DefinedP] (1:2) Spr-Sum 93, p. 23.
"Given Enough Rope." [DefinedP] (3) 95, p. 34.
MUNDELL, J. J. Reed
See REED-MUNDELL, J. J.
4408. MUNK, Jonathan
"Cutting Summer." [SenR] (25:2) Fall 95, p. 49-51.
"Ember Days." [SenR] (25:2) Fall 95, p. 52-55.
"Song of Quarantine." [SenR] (25:2) Fall 95, p. 46-48.
4409. MUÑOZ, Charles
"The Bull and the Angel." [BelPoJ] (46:1) Fall 95, p. 6-8.
"The Innocents." [BelPoJ] (46:1) Fall 95, p. 9-10.
4410. MUNRO, Jane Southwell
"Li — The Clinging, Fire." [MalR] (110) Spr 95, p. 108.
4411. MUNRO, Peter
"Balanced Lives." [SouthernPR] (35:1) Sum 95, p. 5-7.
"Ebb." [OntR] (42) Spr-Sum 95, p. 55.
"Letter to Myself, Bahia de los Muertes." [OntR] (42) Spr-Sum 95, p. 56.
"Loud Fish." [SantaBR] (3:3) Fall-Wint 95, p. 136.
"Open." [FourQ] (9:1/2) Spr 95, p. 45.
"Stealth." [SantaBR] (3:3) Fall-Wint 95, p. 137.
"Wooden Whales." [SantaBR] (3:3) Fall-Wint 95, p. 138-139.

4412. MUNSON, Peggy
"The Alchemist's Daughter." [SpoonR] (20:2) Sum-Fall 95, p. 114-115.
"Blot." [SpoonR] (20:2) Sum-Fall 95, p. 111.
"The Card Table." [SpoonR] (20:2) Sum-Fall 95, p. 110.
"The Cyst." [SpoonR] (20:2) Sum-Fall 95, p. 116-117.
"Divinity." [SpoonR] (20:2) Sum-Fall 95, p. 109.
"Floating." [SpoonR] (20:2) Sum-Fall 95, p. 108.
"My Sister and I Talk About the Divorce." [13thMoon] (13:1/2) 95, p. 27.
"Outside the City of Angels." [SpoonR] (20:2) Sum-Fall 95, p. 120-121.
"The Rise and Fall of Little Big Hair." [SpoonR] (20:2) Sum-Fall 95, p. 112.
"To the Girl Who Disappeared from My Old Neighborhood." [SpoonR] (20:2) Sum-Fall 95, p. 118-119.
"Weights and Measures." [SpoonR] (20:2) Sum-Fall 95, p. 113.
4413. MURA, David
"Issei Strawberry." [RiverS] (42/43) 95, p. 178.
4414. MURABITO, Stephen
"Lines for Your Second Birthday, Lines for My Thirty-Seventh" (For Angie and Stella). [Poem] (74) N 95, p. 65-66.
4415. MURATORI, Fred
"A Civilization" (Selection: XV). [FreeL] (15) Aut 95, p. 23.
4416. MURAWSKI, Elisabeth
"Brief." [PoetL] (90:2) Sum 95, p. 37.
"How I See You in Dreams Still." [PoetL] (90:4) Wint 95-96, p. 14.
"Mother and Daughter." [LitR] (39:1) Fall 95, p. 87.
"To Your Good Address." [PoetL] (90:4) Wint 95-96, p. 15.
4417. MURDZA, Thérèse
"Melora's Hips." [CumbPR] (15:1) Fall 95, p. 35-36.
"There Are Holes in the Walls Where." [EvergreenC] (10:2) Sum-Fall 95, p. 9.
4418. MURILLO, Diana
"The Man in the Train." [Footwork] (24/25) 95, p. 154.
4419. MURPHY, Peter E.
"The Exchange." [JINJPo] (17:1) Spr 95, p. 4.
4420. MURPHY, Richard
"Mangoes." [Poetry] (167:1/2) O-N 95, p. 88.
4421. MURPHY, Ryan
"18." [Gerbil] (3) Sum 95, p. 16.
4422. MURPHY, Sarah
"Ode to an Old Dress" (The 1994 Allen Ginsberg Poetry Awards: Honorable Mention). [Footwork] (24/25) 95, p. 200.
4423. MURPHY, Sheila (Sheila E.)
"Cracked Windshield." [WestCL] (29:3, #18) Wint 95-96, p. 14.
"Olive Leaves." [WestCL] (29:3, #18) Wint 95-96, p. 13.
"One Partial Aria." [HeavenB] (12) 95, p. 87.
"Parlors." [AmerLC] (7) 95, p. 99-100.
"Postcards Between the Sense of Soul and Sound (Harmonica)." [WestCL] (29:3, #18) Wint 95-96, p. 13.
"The Pretty Feather of a Happiness." [WestCL] (29:3, #18) Wint 95-96, p. 14.
"What one and beautiful more mind we are." [Bogg] (67) 95, p. 37.
4424. MURPHY, Timothy
"Feathers." [Light] (15/16) Aut-Wint 95-96, p. 12.
4425. MURPHY, Y. C.
"Brooklyn Tropicale." [PassN] (16:1) Sum 95, p. 9.
"Rest-Stop (Adrian, TX)" (Second Prize, First Annual Poetry Awards). [LiteralL] (2:1) Sum 95, p. 14.
4426. MURRAY, Aífe
"Margaret Maher, Emily Dickinson, and Kitchen Table Poetics" (2 selections). [Chain] (2) Spr 95, p. 162-164.
4427. MURRAY, Christopher
"In Your Bathing Suit." [CutB] (43) Wint 95, p. 37-38.
4428. MURRAY, G. E.
"Notes for the Interior Escape." [OxfordM] (9:2) Fall-Wint 93, p. 79.
"The Rainy Season Arrives in Southern Kyushu." [OxfordM] (9:2) Fall-Wint 93, p. 80.
4429. MURRAY, Joan
"Augustine Speaks." [ParisR] (37:134) Spr 95, p. 168-169.
"Queen of the Mist" (9 selections). [OntR] (42) Spr-Sum 95, p. 15-28.

"Telling Stories" (for Asia and Sheila). [PraS] (69:2) Sum 95, p. 20-23.
4430. MURRAY, Les A.
"The Sleepout." [Verse] (12:2) 95, p. 103.
4431. MURRAY, Marilyn
"Again and Again." [PoetL] (90:4) Wint 95-96, p. 47.
4432. MUS, David
"Breath Log" (from *A I R*, tr. of Andre du Bouchet). [Sulfur] (15:1, #36) Spr 95, p. 196-197.
"Dictation" (from *A I R*, tr. of Andre du Bouchet). [Sulfur] (15:1, #36) Spr 95, p. 199-202.
"I Can See Next to Nothing" (from *A I R*, tr. of Andre du Bouchet). [Sulfur] (15:1, #36) Spr 95, p. 203.
"A I R" (Selections, tr. of Andre du Bouchet). [Sulfur] (15:1, #36) Spr 95, p. 196-197.
"The Indwelling" (from OR ELSE THE SUN, OU LE SOLEIL, 1968, tr. of André du Bouchet). [DenQ] (30:1) Sum 95, p. 29-63.
"Morning" (from *A I R*, tr. of Andre du Bouchet). [Sulfur] (15:1, #36) Spr 95, p. 198.
4433. MUSE, Paul
"Flower Face" (at the Caribbean Christian Center for the Deaf). [CaribbeanW] (9) 95, p. 33-34.
4434. MUSGROVE, David
"Costs." [AlabamaLR] (9:1) 95, p. 34-35.
"Kingfisher." [AlabamaLR] (9:1) 95, p. 36.
"Tuxpan, March 1995." [AlabamaLR] (9:1) 95, p. 37-44.
4435. MUSIAL, Grzegorz
"All Souls' Day on the Bay" (tr. by Lia Purpura). [WillowS] (36) Je 95, p. 75.
"Charlottenburg — the Park Scenes" (tr. by Lia Purpura). [WillowS] (36) Je 95, p. 78-79.
"Death in Berlin" (tr. by Lia Purpura). [WillowS] (36) Je 95, p. 76-77.
"Untitled: In this house lived Stein the merchant" (tr. by Lia Purpura). [WillowS] (36) Je 95, p. 74.
"Untitled: Sweating the dark one" (tr. by Lia Purpura). [WillowS] (36) Je 95, p. 80.
4436. MUSINA, Alexandru
"Apocrypha the First" (tr. by Adam J. Sorkin and Radu Surdulescu). [Vis] (48) 95, p. 40.
"Experiments (A Chimera of the Real)" (The Sixth Experiment, Survival in Meaning, tr. by Adam J. Sorkin and Radu Surdulescu). [Vis] (48) 95, p. 41.
4437. MUSKAT, Timothy
"In My Thirty-Third Year." [PoetryE] (40) Spr 95, p. 86-87.
"Late at Night After a Visit from Friends" (Honorable Mention, 1995 Editors' Prize). [SpoonR] (20:2) Sum-Fall 95, p. 50-51.
"Numinosum." [Poem] (73) My 95, p. 15.
"Requiem." [Poem] (73) My 95, p. 16.
4438. MUSKE, Carol
"Having Fled the Cité Universitaire" (Paris, 1970). [ParisR] (37:137) Wint 95, p. 113-114.
"Ideal." [Verse] (12:2) 95, p. 104-105.
"Similes." [KenR] (17:2) Spr 95, p. 127-128.
4439. MUSSELMAN, Forrest
"Farmer's Rain." [RagMag] (12:2) Spr 95, p. 27.
"The Kite." [RagMag] (12:2) Spr 95, p. 26.
4440. MUSTON, Rex William
"Red-Tailed Quiescence." [CapeR] (30:1) Spr 95, p. 8-9.
MUTSUO, Takahashi
See TAKAHASHI, Mutsuo
4441. MUTTON, Paul
"That Someone Special." [CanLit] (144) Spr 95, p. 61.
4442. MYCUE, Edward
"Cross-Dressing." [CarolQ] (48:1) Fall 95, p. 57.
4443. MYERS, George, Jr.
"Sestina for Sleepers." [RiverS] (42/43) 95, p. 15.
4444. MYERS, J. William
"Cucumber Falls" (Fayette County, Pa. Nov. 11, 1967). [CentR] (39:1) Wint 95, p. 96.

"Like the Corner House" (The Downey House, Waynesburg, Pa.). [Blueline] (16) 95, p. 49.
"Precis of a Country Editor" (For Robert Eichenlaub). [Blueline] (16) 95, p. 48.
"Precis of a Country Editor" (For Robert Eichenlaub). [CentR] (39:1) Wint 95, p. 95.
4445. MYERS, Jack
"Backswing." [Ploughs] (21:1) Spr 95, p. 62-63.
"Blue Bayou Rooms." [DefinedP] (2:2) Spr-Sum 94, p. 22-23.
"The Butcher's Hand." [SenR] (25:1) Spr 95, p. 41.
"Happy Duende to Me." [SycamoreR] (7:1) Wint 95, p. 22-23.
"Keepers of the Pst." [WillowS] (36) Je 95, p. 24.
"Possessed." [WillowS] (36) Je 95, p. 23.
"The Second Hunger." [DefinedP] (1:2) Spr-Sum 93, p. 8-9.
"Self to Self." [WillowS] (36) Je 95, p. 22.
"Spoiled." [SycamoreR] (7:1) Wint 95, p. 21.
4446. MYERS, Joan Rohr
"Recycling." [ChrC] (112:21) 5-12 Jl 95, p. 668.
4447. MYERS, Madeleine
"Tense Images" (Literary Festival: Poetry: Second Place). [EngJ] (84:4) Ap 95, p. 37.
4448. MYERS, Madeleine Morningfire
"NewYorkMotherCade: 1939-1995. Toni Cade, Do Not Expect to Fade." [Drumvoices] (5:1/2) Fall-Wint 95-96, p. 22.
"Together in the Hoop in Thanks: In honor of Chief Elder Red Squirrel." [Drumvoices] (5:1/2) Fall-Wint 95-96, p. 22.
4449. MYERS, Neil
"Sesshin." [CharR] (21:2) Fall 95, p. 89.
4450. MYLES, Eileen
"Autumn Blues." [13thMoon] (13:1/2) 95, p. 28-29.
"Eileen's Vision." [AmerPoR] (24:3) My-Je 95, p. 52.
"An Explanation." [13thMoon] (13:1/2) 95, p. 30.
"The Open & the Close." [13thMoon] (13:1/2) 95, p. 31-32.
4451. MYLES, Naomi
"Windows." [Pembroke] (27) 95, p. 91-92.
MYUNG, Mi Kim
    See KIM, Myung Mi

4452. NACA, Kristin
"The Calling of a Seance." [PoetryNW] (36:1) Spr 95, p. 36-37.
"The First Time I Saw the Body." [PoetryNW] (36:1) Spr 95, p. 37-39.
4453. NADELMAN, Cynthia
"The Cathedral as Process." [PartR] (62:3) Sum 95, p. 456.
4454. NAGAI, Hiroko
"Millions of sons drafted by the Emperor are dead" (in Japanese and English, tr. by Jiro Nakano). [BambooR] (67/68) Sum-Fall 95, p. 55.
4455. NAGAI, Mariko
"Bathers." [Ledge] (19) Wint 95, p. 88-89.
"A Landscape of Want" (for my sister). [Ledge] (19) Wint 95, p. 90-91.
4456. NAGAI, Takashi
"In the middle of the flame" (in Japanese and English, tr. by Jiro Nakano). [BambooR] (67/68) Sum-Fall 95, p. 56.
4457. NAGY, Tricia
"Wishbone" (Runner-up, 1995 Editors' Prize). [SpoonR] (20:2) Sum-Fall 95, p. 37-38.
4458. NAIDEN, James
"A Triad with Red Poinsettias" (Nathan's 38th birthday eve poem, w. Nathan Viste-Ross and Louise Viste-Ross). [NorthStoneR] (12) 95, p. 205.
4459. NAKAMOTO, Masayo
"Ten thousands or more sank into this river" (in Japanese and English, tr. by Jiro Nakano). [BambooR] (67/68) Sum-Fall 95, p. 58.
4460. NAKAMURA, Kiyoto
"At the riverside" (in Japanese and English, tr. by Jiro Nakano). [BambooR] (67/68) Sum-Fall 95, p. 57.

4461. NAKANO, Jiro
"After robbing us of our sons and daughters" (tr. of Shigeo Sugino). [BambooR]
(67/68) Sum-Fall 95, p. 78.
"After the screaming, the scars, the scorched land" (tr. of Hakutei Yasuda).
[BambooR] (67/68) Sum-Fall 95, p. 99.
"Alas — in the midst of sandbanks" (tr. of Seisaku Hasegawa). [BambooR] (67/68)
Sum-Fall 95, p. 9.
"Although I live, I am given a funeral service" (tr. of Ichisaku Takeuchi).
[BambooR] (67/68) Sum-Fall 95, p. 84.
"The Americans have licked the core" (tr. of Seishu Hozumi). [BambooR] (67/68)
Sum-Fall 95, p. 15.
"Another anti-nuclear petition?" (tr. of Masanori Ichioka). [BambooR] (67/68) Sum-
Fall 95, p. 22.
"Anti-nuclear movement" (tr. of Osamu Hikino). [BambooR] (67/68) Sum-Fall 95,
p. 12.
"Are they still reflected in your misty eyes?" (tr. of Kaichi Mita). [BambooR]
(67/68) Sum-Fall 95, p. 48.
"As clothes left from the burning fires" (tr. of Fusako Kimura). [BambooR] (67/68)
Sum-Fall 95, p. 35.
"At broad daylight, a peony flower" (tr. of Hisako Osugi). [BambooR] (67/68) Sum-
Fall 95, p. 68.
"At high tide in this burnt city" (tr. of Yutaka Shiraki). [BambooR] (67/68) Sum-Fall
95, p. 77.
"At the riverside" (tr. of Kiyoto Nakamura). [BambooR] (67/68) Sum-Fall 95, p. 57.
"The Atomic Bomb destroyed Hiroshima" (tr. of Toshie Joden). [BambooR] (67/68)
Sum-Fall 95, p. 29.
"The Atomic Bomb killed indiscriminately" (tr. of Kaoru Yasui). [BambooR]
(67/68) Sum-Fall 95, p. 100.
"Blades of young grass" (tr. of Teruko Kato). [BambooR] (67/68) Sum-Fall 95, p.
33.
"Burnt and ulcerated, a blind infant" (tr. of Tomoo Ozawa). [BambooR] (67/68)
Sum-Fall 95, p. 70.
"Cicadas continuously sing" (tr. of Koichiro Tozawa). [BambooR] (67/68) Sum-Fall
95, p. 92.
"College students obediently saluted to the command" (tr. of Katsuko Hisaoka).
[BambooR] (67/68) Sum-Fall 95, p. 13.
"The constant search for a loved one" (tr. of Shizuko Ota). [BambooR] (67/68) Sum-
Fall 95, p. 69.
"The corpses of those who died of persecution" (tr. of Nobue Tashima). [BambooR]
(67/68) Sum-Fall 95, p. 88.
"The corpses of those who once met here" (tr. of Hiroshi Takeyama). [BambooR]
(67/68) Sum-Fall 95, p. 85.
"Crape myrtle — falls secretly" (tr. of Hisato Nogami). [BambooR] (67/68) Sum-
Fall 95, p. 65.
"A crowd of ten thousand are standing in despair" (tr. of Hatsuko Miyamae).
[BambooR] (67/68) Sum-Fall 95, p. 51.
"A crying girl" (tr. of Takako Ashida). [BambooR] (67/68) Sum-Fall 95, p. 1.
"The deployment of 'tomahawk' missiles can begin a nuclear crisis" (tr. of Hiroshi
Iwamoto). [BambooR] (67/68) Sum-Fall 95, p. 27.
"Each time I walk the valley road" (tr. of Midori Nitta). [BambooR] (67/68) Sum-
Fall 95, p. 63.
"Evening clouds dyed the color of blood" (tr. of Kuramoto Taniguchi). [BambooR]
(67/68) Sum-Fall 95, p. 86.
"Exhausted, I sew" (tr. of Shizuka Miyamoto). [BambooR] (67/68) Sum-Fall 95, p.
53.
"The exterior of the Hiroshima Dome" (tr. of Nobuko Ishikawa). [BambooR]
(67/68) Sum-Fall 95, p. 19.
"Facing a garden stone that never glistens" (tr. of Hachiro Shimauchi). [BambooR]
(67/68) Sum-Fall 95, p. 73.
"A few survivors" (tr. of Masayoshi Miyamoto). [BambooR] (67/68) Sum-Fall 95,
p. 52.
"Gone is everyone who I have relied upon" (tr. of Akira Shima). [BambooR] (67/68)
Sum-Fall 95, p. 72.
"Half scorched pieces of brains and throats" (tr. of Seikan Inoue). [BambooR]
(67/68) Sum-Fall 95, p. 25.

"He led the free life, never doubting the war cause" (tr. of Yoshiko Uchikoshi). [BambooR] (67/68) Sum-Fall 95, p. 95.

"He no longer lives, that man who once sang" (tr. of Kuniyo Takayasu). [BambooR] (67/68) Sum-Fall 95, p. 83.

"Her burnt face swollen, a naked girl" (tr. of Eizo Uchida). [BambooR] (67/68) Sum-Fall 95, p. 94.

"Her screams have ceased today" (tr. of Tomiko Yamaguchi). [BambooR] (67/68) Sum-Fall 95, p. 98.

"A *hibaku* woman, who refused my help" (tr. of Seishi Toyota). [BambooR] (67/68) Sum-Fall 95, p. 91.

"Human beings with gorged eyeballs" (tr. of Kimiko Nishioka). [BambooR] (67/68) Sum-Fall 95, p. 61.

"I have lost six children to the Atomic Bomb" (tr. of Kanae Takano). [BambooR] (67/68) Sum-Fall 95, p. 82.

"I know, as a man with good grace" (tr. of Yoshiko Komoto). [BambooR] (67/68) Sum-Fall 95, p. 38.

"I look at each boy's corpse" (tr. of Misako Masuda). [BambooR] (67/68) Sum-Fall 95, p. 43.

"I see the procession of burnt sores" (tr. of Sadamu Miyata). [BambooR] (67/68) Sum-Fall 95, p. 50.

"I sit down to halt the Atomic Bomb testing" (tr. of Teruko Ishibashi). [BambooR] (67/68) Sum-Fall 95, p. 21.

"I still hear their voices" (tr. of Chie Setoguchi). [BambooR] (67/68) Sum-Fall 95, p. 71.

"I walk aimlessly" (tr. of Hiroshi Komoto). [BambooR] (67/68) Sum-Fall 95, p. 37.

"I will overcome the shattering of my mind" (tr. of Ken'ichi Miyagi). [BambooR] (67/68) Sum-Fall 95, p. 49.

"If you are armed, stop your foolishness" (tr. of Kasu Ura). [BambooR] (67/68) Sum-Fall 95, p. 97.

"If you so wish, cry for the National Defense" (tr. of Reiko Mikuni). [BambooR] (67/68) Sum-Fall 95, p. 47.

"In the middle of the flame" (tr. of Takashi Nagai). [BambooR] (67/68) Sum-Fall 95, p. 56.

"In this river, the silent voices of ten thousand and more" (tr. of Kiyoko Uchimi). [BambooR] (67/68) Sum-Fall 95, p. 96.

"Into the desolate scene" (tr. of Ayao Koyama). [BambooR] (67/68) Sum-Fall 95, p. 41.

"It is a living mess" (tr. of Shofu Matsumura). [BambooR] (67/68) Sum-Fall 95, p. 46.

"A *kappa* is walking in front of my eyes" (tr. of Hiroshi Morishita). [BambooR] (67/68) Sum-Fall 95, p. 54.

"Keloids! Unbearably grotesque" (tr. of Ichio Fukushima). [BambooR] (67/68) Sum-Fall 95, p. 5.

"The large skull is the teacher's" (tr. of Shinoe Shoda). [BambooR] (67/68) Sum-Fall 95, p. 74.

"Late at night" (tr. of Yoshimitsu Kozakai). [BambooR] (67/68) Sum-Fall 95, p. 42.

"Let the voice of a girl" (tr. of Osamu Kimata). [BambooR] (67/68) Sum-Fall 95, p. 34.

"Like a demon or ghost" (tr. of Ayako Etsuchi). [BambooR] (67/68) Sum-Fall 95, p. 2.

"Like rotted wood" (tr. of Chihiro Nishimoto). [BambooR] (67/68) Sum-Fall 95, p. 60.

"Lonely rainy night" (tr. of Yukie Itamasu). [BambooR] (67/68) Sum-Fall 95, p. 26.

"A man's life is imprinted vividly" (tr. of Fumiko Shoji). [BambooR] (67/68) Sum-Fall 95, p. 75.

"Millions of sons drafted by the Emperor are dead" (tr. of Hiroko Nagai). [BambooR] (67/68) Sum-Fall 95, p. 55.

"Mothers, wives, sisters" (tr. of Momoyo Ishii). [BambooR] (67/68) Sum-Fall 95, p. 18.

"Not knowing his mother is dead" (tr. of Yoshiko Kono). [BambooR] (67/68) Sum-Fall 95, p. 40.

"On newspapers spread on depot platforms" (tr. of Asao Izumi). [BambooR] (67/68) Sum-Fall 95, p. 28.

"Once again summer has come" (tr. of Kiyo Hakushima). [BambooR] (67/68) Sum-Fall 95, p. 7.

"One that lies down" (tr. of Sadako Ishii). [BambooR] (67/68) Sum-Fall 95, p. 20.

"Outcry from the Inferno: Atomic Bomb Tanka Anthology" (edited and translated by Jiro Nakano). [BambooR] (67/68) Sum-Fall 95, 104 p.
"Overflowing the orbita, the maggots crawl on the senseless face" (tr. of Mikio Kanda). [BambooR] (67/68) Sum-Fall 95, p. 31.
"A photo of a school boy" (tr. of Shizue Hatsui). [BambooR] (67/68) Sum-Fall 95, p. 10.
"Politicians who deceive people" (tr. of Tsutomi Suzuki). [BambooR] (67/68) Sum - Fall 95, p. 80.
"Radiation concealed" (tr. of Yuzuru Hayase). [BambooR] (67/68) Sum-Fall 95, p. 11.
"The rain is falling on the white bones" (tr. of Itaru Kochi). [BambooR] (67/68) Sum-Fall 95, p. 36.
"The road to a nuclear free world" (tr. of Chiyoji Matsumoto). [BambooR] (67/68) Sum-Fall 95, p. 45.
"Run under the beam!" (tr. of Harue Imamoto). [BambooR] (67/68) Sum-Fall 95, p. 24.
"Severely charred by the Atomic Bomb" (tr. of Tadao Ogihata). [BambooR] (67/68) Sum-Fall 95, p. 67.
"Side-stepping the many corpses" (tr. of Toshie Nishioku). [BambooR] (67/68) Sum-Fall 95, p. 62.
"Sleeping each night alongside the neighboring nuclear weapons" (tr. of Sumiko Shinpu). [BambooR] (67/68) Sum-Fall 95, p. 76.
"The statue stands covered with shining dewdrops" (tr. of Takayoshi Nitta). [BambooR] (67/68) Sum-Fall 95, p. 64.
"The streets still smoldering" (tr. of tokuzaburo Imai). [BambooR] (67/68) Sum-Fall 95, p. 23.
"Suddenly the street is darkened" (tr. of Sadao Kataoka). [BambooR] (67/68) Sum - Fall 95, p. 32.
"Ten thousands or more sank into this river" (tr. of Masayo Nakamoto). [BambooR] (67/68) Sum-Fall 95, p. 58.
"'The Voices of Neptune' gradually die into a distance" (tr. of Masana Tsumura). [BambooR] (67/68) Sum-Fall 95, p. 93.
"Thirty years have gone" (tr. of Shizuko Iguchi). [BambooR] (67/68) Sum-Fall 95, p. 17.
"This morning upon awakening" (tr. of Tsugio Kagawa). [BambooR] (67/68) Sum - Fall 95, p. 30.
"To die for your country" (tr. of Yoshihiko Furuyoshi). [BambooR] (67/68) Sum - Fall 95, p. 6.
"Today I shall burn a little girl" (tr. of Hatsuyo Sugita). [BambooR] (67/68) Sum - Fall 95, p. 79.
"Together with my sister" (tr. of Aiko Nakazawa). [BambooR] (67/68) Sum-Fall 95, p. 59.
"Tonight again, the only light to aid me" (tr. of Fumiko Fujii). [BambooR] (67/68) Sum-Fall 95, p. 4.
"Two score and more lines drawn to study the epicenter" (tr. of Ei Taya). [BambooR] (67/68) Sum-Fall 95, p. 89.
"Under the summer sun" (tr. of Hayataro Numanaka). [BambooR] (67/68) Sum-Fall 95, p. 66.
"Undestroyed but beautified, the Genbaku Dome" (tr. of Kazue Tasaka). [BambooR] (67/68) Sum-Fall 95, p. 87.
"We will never repeat this error again" (tr. of Shozo Hori). [BambooR] (67/68) Sum-Fall 95, p. 14.
"Where is the agony" (tr. of Seitai I). [BambooR] (67/68) Sum-Fall 95, p. 16.
"The white mushroom cloud has risen" (tr. of Yoshimi Kondo). [BambooR] (67/68) Sum-Fall 95, p. 39.
"Wild birds silently eat the decayed flesh" (tr. of Kunio Toyohara). [BambooR] (67/68) Sum-Fall 95, p. 90.
"Without a word, my wife returns" (tr. of Reisuke Masuda). [BambooR] (67/68) Sum-Fall 95, p. 44.
"You raised that same hand." (tr. of Yoko Hamada). [BambooR] (67/68) Sum-Fall 95, p. 8.
"You should be satisfied if every living being" (tr. of Takeo Takahashi). [BambooR] (67/68) Sum-Fall 95, p. 81.
"Your souls that have fallen" (tr. of Itsuma Fugii). [BambooR] (67/68) Sum-Fall 95, p. 3.

4462. NAKANO, Aiko
"Together with my sister" (in Japanese and English, tr. by Jiro Nakano). [BambooR] (67/68) Sum-Fall 95, p. 59.
4463. NAKNI
"Dream-Catcher." [Elf] (5:3) Fall 95, p. 43.
"Early Forest Wolf." [Elf] (5:1) Spr 95, p. 43.
4464. NAMEROFF, Rochelle
"Channel Five." [ApalQ] (43) Spr 95, p. 53-54.
"Empties." [Iowa] (25:3) Fall 95, p. 2-3.
"Meditation at Chez Panisse" (with love and apologies to Robert Hass). [Iowa] (25:3) Fall 95, p. 5.
"Ricochet." [QW] (40) Spr-Sum 95, p. 88-89.
"Swamp Cooler" (for Tucson Joe). [Iowa] (25:3) Fall 95, p. 4.
4465. NANDINO, Elias
"Imprecation" (tr. by D. M. Stroud). [Noctiluca] (2:1, #4) Spr 95, p. 58.
"Personal Satisfaction" (tr. by D. M. Stroud). [Noctiluca] (2:1, #4) Spr 95, p. 58.
NAOSHI, Koriyama
  See KORIYAMA, Naoshi
NARIHIRA, Ariwara no (825-880)
  See ARIWARA no NARIHIRA (825-880)
4466. NASH, Roger
"Wedding in the Garden." [MalR] (112) Fall 95, p. 77-79.
"The Word-Umbrella." [Quarry] (43:4) 95, p. 128.
4467. NASH, Susan Smith
"Channel-Surfing the Apocalypse (A Day in the Life of the Fin-de-Millennium Mind)" (5 selections). [Avec] (10) 95, p. 1-11.
4468. NASRIN, Taslima
"Another Life" (tr. by Carolyne Wright, w. Farida Sarkar). [GrandS] (14:1, #53) Sum 95, p. 172.
"Body Theory" (tr. by Carolyne Wright, w. Mohammad Nurul Huda). [GrandS] (14:1, #53) Sum 95, p. 173-174.
"Things Cheaply Had" (tr. by Carolyne Wright, Mohammad Nurul Huda and the author). [NewYorker] (71:31) 9 O 95, p. 44.
4469. NATHAN, Leonard
"Ah." [Ploughs] (21:1) Spr 95, p. 68.
"Couple." [PoetL] (90:2) Sum 95, p. 25.
"For Those Who Wait." [NortheastCor] (3) 95, p. 30.
"From the Mountain." [NortheastCor] (3) 95, p. 29.
"In the Carpenter's Shop." [PoetL] (90:2) Sum 95, p. 26.
"A Man and His Dog." [EngJ] (84:2) F 95, p. 42.
"Snow Bound." [EngJ] (84:2) F 95, p. 42.
"A Winter Affair." [Ploughs] (21:1) Spr 95, p. 69.
NATON, Leslie
  See LESLIE, Naton
4470. NATT, Greg
"Endless Winter" (after Igor Chinnov). [Vis] (47) 95, p. 16.
"Memory" (after Sándor Csoóri). [Vis] (47) 95, p. 17.
4471. NAUEN, Elinor
"Asleep" (for Augusto Lori). [HangL] (66) 95, p. 57.
"Backyards, Brooklyn" (for Peggy DeCoursey). [HangL] (66) 95, p. 59.
"The Green Car." [HangL] (66) 95, p. 56.
"July Hay." [HangL] (66) 95, p. 54.
"Portrait." [HangL] (66) 95, p. 58.
"The Red Vine." [HangL] (66) 95, p. 55.
"Shall We Gather at the River." [HangL] (66) 95, p. 55.
"Storm Surpassing." [HangL] (66) 95, p. 54.
4472. NAUGHTON, Lara
"The Night Before." [Boulevard] (10:1/2, #28/29) Spr 95, p. 234.
4473. NAWROCKI, Jim
"Spoon." [JamesWR] (12:3) Fall 95, p. 7.
4474. NAYLOR, Paul
"The Federalist Papers." [NewOR] (21:2) Sum 95, p. 72-73.
4475. NAZMI, Nader
"Life Journey." [InterPR] (21:2) Fall 95, p. 97-98.
"Life Train." [InterPR] (21:2) Fall 95, p. 96.

NEAL, Iris Gribble
See GRIBBLE-NEAL, Iris
4476. NEALON, Chris (Christopher)
"Limited Prospect." [Jacaranda] (11) [95 or 96?], p. 83.
"Token Gesture." [JamesWR] (12:2) Spr-Sum 95, p. 11.
"Waltz." [PraS] (69:2) Sum 95, p. 147.
4477. NEALON, Joanna
"Why I Can't Write a Poem About Bosnia." [NortheastCor] (3) 95, p. 103.
4479. NECATIGIL, Behçet
"Extra Page" (tr. by Murat Nemet-Nejat). [Talisman] (14) Fall 95, p. 50.
"Unrequited" (tr. by Murat Nemet-Nejat). [Talisman] (14) Fall 95, p. 50.
4480. NEEDELL, Claire
"Salt Themes: An Autobiography" (Selections: 1-2, 4, 7, 21, 30, 33, 35). [Talisman]
(15) Wint 95-96, p. 111-113.
4481. NEELD, Judith
"Cat on Your Back." [OxfordM] (9:2) Fall-Wint 93, p. 40.
"Circling a Lion." [SnailPR] (3:2) 95, p. 23.
"The Climb: Hound Tor." [Bogg] (67) 95, p. 30.
"Hunters and Lovers II." [ClockR] (10:1/2) 95-96, p. 59.
"Van Gogh's Death." [ClockR] (10:1/2) 95-96, p. 58.
4482. NEELON, Ann
"Grandfather's Peonies." [Manoa] (7:2) Wint 95, p. 24-26.
"Night Owl." [Manoa] (7:2) Wint 95, p. 24.
"Pale Moon over Kigali." [Manoa] (7:2) Wint 95, p. 27-28.
4483. NEIDER, Mark
"Years Ahead." [CumbPR] (14:2) Spr 95, p. 44.
4484. NEILSON, W. D.
"This Old King" (inspired by "The old King," painting by Georges Rouault).
[Descant] (26:1, #88) Spr 95, p. 104.
"Wormsong." [Descant] (26:1, #88) Spr 95, p. 101-103.
NEJAT, Murat Nemet
See NEMET-NEJAT, Murat
4485. NELMS, Sheryl L.
"Dave's Ready." [Kaleid] (31) Sum-Fall 95, p. 18.
"Hang Gliding." [Kaleid] (30) Wint-Spr 95, p. 29.
"New Mexico Solstice." [Kaleid] (31) Sum-Fall 95, p. 18.
"South Dakota Dragonflies at Dusk." [Kaleid] (31) Sum-Fall 95, p. 19.
"Strippin Cotton." [Kaleid] (31) Sum-Fall 95, p. 19.
4486. NELSON, Bruce
"Good Poets Watch What They Do." [OxfordM] (10:1) Wint 94-Spr 95, p. 53.
4487. NELSON, James
"Fishing Coat." [Plain] (15:2) Wint 95, p. 8-9.
4488. NELSON, Jason
"Apple." [SantaBR] (3:2) Sum 95, p. 8.
"Basket." [SantaBR] (3:2) Sum 95, p. 8.
"Slip." [SantaBR] (3:2) Sum 95, p. 8.
"Tachometer." [SantaBR] (3:2) Sum 95, p. 8.
"Wrinkle." [SantaBR] (3:2) Sum 95, p. 8.
4489. NELSON, Michael
"Oranges and a Tangerine." [JamesWR] (12:2) Spr-Sum 95, p. 11.
4490. NELSON, Paul
"Tenigue." [OhioR] (53) 95, p. 120-121.
4491. NELSON, Ryan
"Autograph." [Plain] (15:3) Spr 95, p. 33.
4492. NELSON, Sandra
"A Is for Axe" (A Parody of Gertrude Stein's Alphabets and Birthdays). [RiverS]
(44) 95, p. 13.
"Beyond the Red Nose." [NewMyths] (2:2/3:1) 95, p. 89-90.
4493. NELSON, W. Dale
"Celebration of the Stone Bridges." [WestHR] (49:2) Sum 95, p. 189.
"Lot Too: For Willa Cather." [WestHR] (49:2) Sum 95, p. 190.
4494. NEMEROV, Howard
"Reading Pornography in Old Age." [RiverS] (42/43) 95, p. 44.

4495. NEMET-NEJAT, Murat
"The Bank Teller Tecelli Bey" (tr. of Melisa Gürpinar). [Talisman] (14) Fall 95, p. 56-59.
"Continuities" (tr. of Özdemir Ince). [Talisman] (14) Fall 95, p. 51.
"Days" (tr. of Mustafa Ziyalan). [Talisman] (14) Fall 95, p. 55.
"The Denizens of the Arcade Hristaki" (tr. of Ilhan Berk). [Talisman] (14) Fall 95, p. 47-49.
"Dying in a Turkish Bath" (tr. of Cemal Süreya). [Talisman] (14) Fall 95, p. 41.
"Elegy for a Handwrought God" (tr. of Ece Ayhan). [Talisman] (14) Fall 95, p. 42.
"Extra Page" (tr. of Behçet Necatigil). [Talisman] (14) Fall 95, p. 50.
"The Family of Acrobats" (tr. of Nilgün Marmara). [Talisman] (14) Fall 95, p. 53.
"Fish Market, Backstage Street" (tr. of Ilhan Berk). [Talisman] (14) Fall 95, p. 45 - 46.
"Geranium and the Child" (tr. of Ece Ayhan). [Talisman] (14) Fall 95, p. 44.
"Houri's Rose" (tr. of Cemal Süreya). [Talisman] (14) Fall 95, p. 41.
"In Your Country" (tr. of Cemal Süreya). [Talisman] (14) Fall 95, p. 39-40.
"The Nigger in a Photograph" (tr. of Ece Ayhan). [Talisman] (14) Fall 95, p. 43.
"Pedestrian" (tr. of Nilgün Marmara). [Talisman] (14) Fall 95, p. 54.
"Phaeton" (tr. of Ece Ayhan). [Talisman] (14) Fall 95, p. 42.
"Stay With Me" (tr. of Özdemir Ince). [Talisman] (14) Fall 95, p. 52.
"To Trace from Hebrew" (tr. of Ece Ayhan). [Talisman] (14) Fall 95, p. 42-43.
"Unrequited" (tr. of Behçet Necatigil). [Talisman] (14) Fall 95, p. 50.
4496. NENLYUMKINA, Zoya
"Taugal'u?" (tr. by A. Cherevchenko and Adele Barker). [Nimrod] (38:2) Spr-Sum 95, p. 110.
4497. NERUDA, Pablo
"Hymn and Return" (tr. by Nancy Ancrom). [WillowS] (36) Je 95, p. 98-99.
"Lyres Discourse" (from *Vuelta: Revista Mensual,* September 1993, tr. by Andrew L. Smith). [DenQ] (29:4) Spr 95, p. 133-134.
NESBITT, Julie Parson
See PARSON-NESBITT, Julie
4498. NESSET, Kirk
"France in Tahiti." [PoetL] (90:4) Wint 95-96, p. 50.
"Jeremiad." [PoetL] (90:4) Wint 95-96, p. 51-52.
"The Stinging and Saving." [NewOR] (21:2) Sum 95, p. 35.
"Thorn." [PoetL] (90:4) Wint 95-96, p. 53.
4499. NETH, Hubert
"She Knitted Him a Sweater." [ChrC] (112:35) 6 D 95, p. 1065.
4500. NEUFELDT, Leonard
"Lantern Procession From the Christkindlesmarkt." [LitR] (38:3) Spr 95, p. 361.
4501. NEVILL, Sue
"Lightly." [AnthNEW] (7) 95, p. 38.
4502. NEWCOMB, Rachel
"Black Wordsworth" (after V.S. Naipaul). [Interim] (14:2) Fall-Wint 95-96, p. 6.
"Everglades Legend." [Poem] (73) My 95, p. 61-62.
"In Zagora." [NewDeltaR] (12:1) Fall-Wint 94, p. 86-87.
"St. Anthony's Fire." [Poem] (73) My 95, p. 60.
"Territory." [InterPR] (21:1) Spr 95, p. 86.
"Trains." [Interim] (14:2) Fall-Wint 95-96, p. 7.
"Travel Etiquette." [NewDeltaR] (12:1) Fall-Wint 94, p. 84-85.
4503. NEWCOMB, Richard
"Avocado Sestina." [BellArk] (11:1) Ja-F 95, p. 26.
"Strange and Loveable." [BellArk] (11:1) Ja-F 95, p. 26.
"We've Sold the Gun." [BellArk] (11:3) My-Je 95, p. 24.
4504. NEWCOMBE, Karen L.
"A New Eve." [ParisR] (37:137) Wint 95, p. 126.
4505. NEWELL, Michael L.
"Annunciation." [BellArk] (11:5) S-O 95, p. 25.
"Consenting Adults." [BellArk] (11:1) Ja-F 95, p. 27.
"Day Dreaming." [BellArk] (11:4) Jl-Ag 95, p. 12.
"Nehemiah." [BellArk] (11:6) N-D 95, p. 11.
"Postcards from Abu Dhabi." [BellArk] (11:4) Jl-Ag 95, p. 14.
4506. NEWINGTON, Nina Crow
"A Name." [AmerV] (37) 95, p. 83-84.
4507. NEWLOVE, John
"An Examination." [CanLit] (144) Spr 95, p. 97.

4508. NEWMAN, Amy
"Doorway." [DenQ] (29:4) Spr 95, p. 42-43.
"Lilies." [DenQ] (29:4) Spr 95, p. 44-45.
4509. NEWMAN, Bill
"The Bird in 39 Main Street." [MassR] (36:2) Sum 95, p. 243-244.
4510. NEWMAN, Chris
"Outside by My Window" (tr. of Eugene Dubnov, w. the author). [LitR] (38:2) Wint 95, p. 194.
4511. NEWMAN, Lesléa
"Nutmeg." [Art&Und] (4:2, #15) Ap 95, p. 44.
4512. NEWMAN, Phoebe
"Ramadan." [SouthernPR] (35:2) Wint 95, p. 14-15.
4513. NEWMAN, Wade
"Creation Story." [OxfordM] (9:2) Fall-Wint 93, p. 75-76.
"Mary and Joseph." [OxfordM] (9:2) Fall-Wint 93, p. 74.
4514. NEWMANN, Franz J.
"Rails" (Köln-Hamburg / July 1993). [SlipS] (15) 95, p. 21-23.
4515. NEWMANN, Joan
"Rice" (For Bridget Anne Ryan). [Poetry] (167:1/2) O-N 95, p. 87.
"Rounders" (In memory of William Turner). [Poetry] (167:1/2) O-N 95, p. 86.
4516. NEWTON, John
"Mechanism." [Verse] (12:2) 95, p. 106-107.
4517. NEWTON, Lee
"Some Men Do." [LowellR] (2) c1996, p. 93.
"When the Planted Seed Grows Sad" (For Stu & Nancy). [LowellR] (2) c1996, p. 94-95.
4518. NGAI, Sianne
"Chrono / paradise." [Chain] (2) Spr 95, p. 167-171.
"Ex-Hume." [NewAW] (13) Fall-Wint 95, p. 132-133.
"The Hysterics Almanac" (Selections). [Avec] (10) 95, p. 100-106.
NGAWANG, Nyima
    See NYIMA, Ngawang
4519. NGUYEN, Ba Chung
"The Bells" (tr. of Vu Cao, w. Kevin Bowen). [Manoa] (7:2) Wint 95, p. 108.
"Color" (tr. of Nguyen Quyen, w. Bruce Weigl). [Manoa] (7:2) Wint 95, p. 160.
"Do Len" (Mother's Village, 9/83, tr. of Nguyen Duy, w. Kevin Bowen). [Manoa] (7:2) Wint 95, p. 95.
"In the Labor Market at Giang Vo" (tr. of Pham Tien Duat, w. Kevin Bowen). [Manoa] (7:2) Wint 95, p. 169.
"Lang Son, 1989" (10th anniversary of the border campaign, 2/79-2/89, tr. of Nguyen Duy, w. Kevin Bowen). [Manoa] (7:2) Wint 95, p. 96.
"Leaving" (tr. of Le Thi May). [Manoa] (7:2) Wint 95, p. 99.
"New Year's Fireworks" (Midnight, New Year's Day, 1992, tr. of Nguyen Duy, w. Kevin Bowen). [Manoa] (7:2) Wint 95, p. 94.
"Poem of a Garden" (tr. of Le Thi May, w. Kevin Bowen). [Manoa] (7:2) Wint 95, p. 98.
"Red Earth, Blue Water" (tr. of Nguyen Duy, w. Kevin Bowen). [Manoa] (7:2) Wint 95, p. 96.
"Wind and Widow" (tr. of Le Thi May). [Manoa] (7:2) Wint 95, p. 97.
4520. NGUYEN, Duy
"Do Len" (Mother's Village, 9/83, tr. by Nguyen Ba Chung and Kevin Bowen). [Manoa] (7:2) Wint 95, p. 95.
"Lang Son, 1989" (10th anniversary of the border campaign, 2/79-2/89, tr. by Nguyen Ba Chung and Kevin Bowen). [Manoa] (7:2) Wint 95, p. 96.
"New Year's Fireworks" (Midnight, New Year's Day, 1992, tr. by Nguyen Ba Chung and Kevin Bowen). [Manoa] (7:2) Wint 95, p. 94.
"Red Earth, Blue Water" (tr. by Nguyen Ba Chung and Kevin Bowen). [Manoa] (7:2) Wint 95, p. 96.
NGUYEN, Hoa
    See HOA, Nguyen
4521. NGUYEN, Quang Thieu
"A Bridge" (tr. of Pham Tien Duat, w. Kevin Bowen). [Manoa] (7:2) Wint 95, p. 167.
"Foreign Land" (tr. by Yusef Komunyakaa and the author). [Manoa] (7:2) Wint 95, p. 163-164.

"The Moon in Circles of Flame" (tr. of Pham Tien Duat, w. Kevin Bowen). [Manoa] (7:2) Wint 95, p. 168.
"New Students, Old Teacher" (for the American poets, on the occasion of their readings, tr. by Martha Collins and the author). [Manoa] (7:2) Wint 95, p. 161.
"October" (tr. by Martha Collins and the author). [Manoa] (7:2) Wint 95, p. 162.
"On the Highway" (tr. by Yusef Komunyakaa and the author). [Manoa] (7:2) Wint 95, p. 164.
"Sleeping In" (For my friends: Hai, Vinh, Manh. Tr. by the author and Martha Collins). [HarvardR] (8) Spr 95, p. 94.
"A Song of My Native Village" (for Chua, my native village, tr. by Martha Collins and the author). [Manoa] (7:2) Wint 95, p. 162-163.
"The Wheelbarrow" (tr. by Yusef Komunyakaa and the author). [Manoa] (7:2) Wint 95, p. 164-165.
"White Circle" (tr. of Pham Tien Duat, w. Kevin Bowen). [Manoa] (7:2) Wint 95, p. 168.
4522. NGUYEN, Quyen
"Color" (tr. by Nguyen Ba Chung and Bruce Weigl). [Manoa] (7:2) Wint 95, p. 160.
4523. Ní CHUILLEANAIN, Eiléan
"The Girl Who Married the Reindeer." [SouthernR] (31:3) Jl/Sum 95, p. 615-617.
"Recovery." [Verse] (12:2) 95, p. 108.
4524. Ní DHOMHNAILL, Nuala
"An Mhurúch san Ospidéal." [SouthernR] (31:3) Jl/Sum 95, p. 438, 440.
"Daphne agus Apollo." [SouthernR] (31:3) Jl/Sum 95, p. 432, 434.
"Daphne and Apollo" (tr. by Medbh McGuckian). [SouthernR] (31:3) Jl/Sum 95, p. 433, 435.
"Feachtas Gharraían Mhargaidh" (tr. of Medbh McGuckian). [SouthernR] (31:3) Jl/Sum 95, p. 447, 449.
"The Marianne Faithfull Hairdo" (tr. by Medbh McGuckian). [SouthernR] (31:3) Jl/Sum 95, p. 435, 437.
"The Merfolk and the Written Word" (tr. by Medbh McGuckian). [SouthernR] (31:3) Jl/Sum 95, p. 441, 443.
"The Mermaid in the Labour Ward" (tr. by Medbh McGuckian). [SouthernR] (31:3) Jl/Sum 95, p. 439, 441.
"Mo Mháistir Dorcha." [Poetry] (167:1/2) O-N 95, p. 76, 78.
"My Dark Master" (tr. by Paul Muldoon). [Poetry] (167:1/2) O-N 95, p. 77, 79.
"Na Murúcha ag Ní a gCeann." [SouthernR] (31:3) Jl/Sum 95, p. 434, 436.
"Na Murúcha agus an Litríocht." [SouthernR] (31:3) Jl/Sum 95, p. 440, 442.
"Rós Síleála Duilleogach" (tr. of Medbh McGuckian). [SouthernR] (31:3) Jl/Sum 95, p. 445.
"The Shannon Estuary Welcomes the Fish" (tr. by Patrick Crotty). [SouthernR] (31:3) Jl/Sum 95, p. 480.
4525. NIATUM, Duane
"Days We Need a Good Rain." [SoDakR] (33:3/4) Fall-Wint 95, p. 189-190.
"The Flower Merchant" (loosely based on Picasso's painting "Composition: The Peasants," cir. 1906). [WeberS] (12:3) Fall 95, p. 123-124.
"Wind Opens a Window on the Mind." [SoDakR] (33:3/4) Fall-Wint 95, p. 188.
4526. NIBBELINK, Herman
"By Late Afternoon." [RagMag] (12:2) Spr 95, p. 45.
"To Honor Our Fathers" (Upon hearing that a friend's father was dying in England). [RagMag] (12:2) Spr 95, p. 44.
4527. NICHOLS, Judith
"High Wire Kissing." [PoetL] (90:4) Wint 95-96, p. 59.
"Phone Sex Poem." [PoetL] (90:4) Wint 95-96, p. 60.
"The Unfolding, Coming Out." [PoetL] (90:4) Wint 95-96, p. 58.
4528. NICHOLSON, Wynne
"Suicide." [Grain] (23:1) Sum 95, p. 86.
4529. NICKEL, Barbara
"July, 1950, Auntie Marge." [Grain] (22:4) Spr 95, p. 31.
"Lines." [PraF] (16:2, #71) Sum 95, p. 114-119.
"The Rosary Sonatas" (After a cycle of 16 violin sonatas by Heinrich Biber, 1644-1704). [MalR] (111) Sum 95, p. 5-17.
4530. NICKERSON, Sheila
"Evensong." [WillowS] (36) Je 95, p. 29.
4531. NICKOL, Michelle
"Above the House." [SoCoast] (18) Ja 95, p. 8-9.

4532. NICOLETTI, Allan
"Green Fish Blue." [PoetryNW] (36:3) Aut 95, p. 8-9.

4533. NICOSIA, Gerald
"Fourth of July with the Buk in San Pedro." [NewYorkQ] (55) 95, p. 51-52.

4534. NICOSIA, Jim (James)
"Color-Blind Artist." [LiteralL] (1:2) S-O 94, p. 4.
"In Clover." [SpiritSH] (60) 95, p. 15.
"The Party." [SpiritSH] (60) 95, p. 14.
"Second Take on a Left Elbow." [SpiritSH] (60) 95, p. 14.
"She is there outside my window." [SpiritSH] (60) 95, p. 12.
"To Be an American." [SpiritSH] (60) 95, p. 13.

4535. NIDITCH, B. Z.
"Bosnia, 1995." [DogRR] (14:1, #27) Sum 95, p. 25.
"East River Cruise." [ChironR] (42) Spr 95, p. 30.
"In Memoriam Stephen Spender (1909-1995)." [HolCrit] (32:5) D 95, p. 19.
"Poet's Cruise." [ChironR] (42) Spr 95, p. 30.
"Tom Cat." [ChironR] (42) Spr 95, p. 30.

4536. NIEDELMAN, Hilda
"The Jade Plant." [Confr] (56/57) Sum-Fall 95, p. 346.

4537. NIELSEN, Daryl
"Aspen Burdened." [Parting] (8:1) Sum 95, p. 32.
"Poet's Agenda." [Parting] (8:1) Sum 95, p. 34.

4538. NIELSEN, Kristy
"Another Memory." [IllinoisR] (3:1/2) Fall 95-Spr 96, p. 79.
"Another Test." [IllinoisR] (3:1/2) Fall 95-Spr 96, p. 22.
"A Language with One Word." [Kalliope] (17:1) 95, p. 59-63.
"The Only Fire Man Will Ever Have: Daniel Speaks." [IllinoisR] (3:1/2) Fall 95-Spr 96, p. 67-70.

4539. NIELSEN, Pamela
"Dearest Bobo Pedophile Clown." [Pearl] (22) Fall-Wint 95, p. 129.

4540. NIJMEIJER, Peter
"Talent" (tr. of Kees Ouwens, w. Scott Rollins). [CimR] (112) Jl 95, p. 11.

4541. NIKIFOROU, Tolis
"The Only Human Voice" (tr. by Michael Mott and Donna Pastourmatzi). [Vis] (48) 95, p. 23.
"A Transfusion of Light into Words" (tr. by Michael Mott and Donna Pastourmatzi). [Vis] (48) 95, p. 23.

4542. NILL, Annegret
"Antiquarian" (tr. of Gonzalo Millán). [Arc] (35) Aut 95, p. 66.
"Monument" (tr. of Gonzalo Millán). [Arc] (35) Aut 95, p. 67.
"Night" (tr. of Gonzalo Millán). [Arc] (35) Aut 95, p. 65.
"Winged Fish" (tr. of Gonzalo Millán). [Arc] (35) Aut 95, p. 64.

4543. NILOOBAN, Rina
"Sage." [HangL] (67) 95, p. 98-99.
"Why I Didn't Visit the Doctor's Office." [HangL] (67) 95, p. 97.

4544. NIM, Peter
"23 VIII 1983" (in French, tr. by Robert Marteau). [Os] (40) 95, p. 17.
"23 VIII 1983" (in German). [Os] (40) 95, p. 16.
"Die Kleinen Dinge." [Os] (40) 95, p. 18.
"Kommt wer nicht da." [Os] (41) 95, p. 10-11.
"Migrateurs" (in French, tr. by Robert Marteau). [Os] (40) 95, p. 33.
"Les Petites Choses" (in French, tr. by Robert Marteau). [Os] (40) 95, p. 19.
"Die Zugvögel." [Os] (40) 95, p. 32.

NIMINO, Kurt
See NIMMO, Kurt

4545. NIMMO, Kurt
"Grave Robbers." [NewYorkQ] (54) 95, p. 44-45.
"Hit List." [ChironR] (44/45) Aut-Wint 95, p. 26.
"New Neighbor." [SlipS] (15) 95, p. 54.
"Theory." [ChironR] (44/45) Aut-Wint 95, p. 26.

4546. NIMNICHT, Nona
"Confinement." [Ploughs] (21:1) Spr 95, p. 83.
"Reenactment." [Ploughs] (21:1) Spr 95, p. 82.
"Sighting the Whale." [Ploughs] (21:1) Spr 95, p. 84.

4547. NIÑO, Jairo Aníbal
"Como No Me Vas a Querer." [Rosebud] (2:3) Aut-Wint 95, p. 28.

"How Are You Not Going to Like Me" (tr. by Elizabeth B. Clark). [Rosebud] (2:3) Aut-Wint 95, p. 29.
"It's a Pretty Day" (tr. by Elizabeth B. Clark). [GrahamHR] (19) Wint 95-96, p. 62.
"She Came to the Classroom" (tr. by Elizabeth B. Clark). [GrahamHR] (19) Wint 95-96, p. 64.
"You Went By" (tr. by Elizabeth B. Clark). [GrahamHR] (19) Wint 95-96, p. 63.
NIRO, Alan de
    See DeNIRO, Alan
4548. NISHIMOTO, Chihiro
    "Like rotted wood" (in Japanese and English, tr. by Jiro Nakano). [BambooR] (67/68) Sum-Fall 95, p. 60.
4549. NISHIOKA, Kimiko
    "Human beings with gorged eyeballs" (in Japanese and English, tr. by Jiro Nakano). [BambooR] (67/68) Sum-Fall 95, p. 61.
4550. NISHIOKU, Toshie
    "Side-stepping the many corpses" (in Japanese and English, tr. by Jiro Nakano). [BambooR] (67/68) Sum-Fall 95, p. 62.
4551. NISULA, Dasha Culic
    "Family (II)" (tr. of Sasa Vegri). [Vis] (48) 95, p. 51.
    "Van Gogh's Peasant-Woman" (tr. of Neda Miranda Blazevic). [Vis] (48) 95, p. 16.
4552. NITCHMANN, Karla
    "Bubbe's Reflections." [SinW] (56) Sum-Fall 95, p. 29-33.
4553. NITTA, Midori
    "Each time I walk the valley road" (in Japanese and English, tr. by Jiro Nakano). [BambooR] (67/68) Sum-Fall 95, p. 63.
4554. NITTA, Takayoshi
    "The statue stands covered with shining dewdrops" (in Japanese and English, tr. by Jiro Nakano). [BambooR] (67/68) Sum-Fall 95, p. 64.
4555. NIXON, John, Jr.
    "Dinosaur." [Light] (13) Spr 95, p. 21.
    "The Precisionist." [Comm] (122:19) 3 N 95, p. 15.
4556. NOBLE, Pam
    "Abishag." [Poem] (74) N 95, p. 45.
    "Achsah" (1995 Literary Contest: Second Prize). [Crucible] (31) Fall 95, p. 3.
    "Belshazzar's Mother." [GreensboroR] (58) Sum 95, p. 112-113.
    "Days on End." [LullwaterR] (6:2) Fall-Wint 95, p. 10-11.
    "Dreamcatcher." [Poem] (74) N 95, p. 44.
    "Hagar." [Poem] (74) N 95, p. 46.
4557. NOBLES, Edward
    "After the Fight." [PoetL] (90:4) Wint 95-96, p. 54.
4558. NOGAMI, Hisato
    "Crape myrtle — falls secretly" (in Japanese and English, tr. by Jiro Nakano). [BambooR] (67/68) Sum-Fall 95, p. 65.
4559. NOLAN, Pat
    "Home Alone." [HangL] (66) 95, p. 60.
    "Three Laments." [HangL] (66) 95, p. 61.
4560. NOMEZ, Naín
    "Incognita" (tr. by Christina Shantz). [Arc] (35) Aut 95, p. 35.
    "Never the Same Waters" (tr. by Christina Shantz). [Arc] (35) Aut 95, p. 36.
NOONAN, Mary-Beth O'Shea
    See O'SHEA-NOONAN, Mary-Beth
4561. NORDBRANDT, Henrik
    "A" (in Danish). [InterPR] (21:1) Spr 95, p. 52.
    "A" (tr. by Thom Satterlee). [InterPR] (21:1) Spr 95, p. 53.
    "Memory of Denizli" (tr. by Alex Taylor). [Vis] (47) 95, p. 32.
    "Ordet." [InterPR] (21:1) Spr 95, p. 54.
    "Thaw" (tr. by Thom Satterlee). [InterPR] (21:1) Spr 95, p. 55.
    "Tøbrud." [InterPR] (21:1) Spr 95, p. 54.
    "When We Leave Each Other." [Vis] (49) 95, p. 29.
    "The Word" (tr. by Thom Satterlee). [InterPR] (21:1) Spr 95, p. 55.
4562. NORDHAUS, Jean
    "Death Has Knocked at My Door." [WashR] (21:1) Je-Jl 95, p. 13.
    "I Am Dyeing My Clothes the Color of Mud" (for Elaine Magarrell). [PraS] (69:1) Spr 95, p. 163.
    "Illustrations." [NewRep] (212:21) 22 My 95, p. 38.
    "Yiddish." [Poetry] (165:6) Mr 95, p. 322.

4563. NORDSTROM, Alan
"Condensed Alphabet Soup (Literary Flavor)." [Light] (13) Spr 95, p. 23.
4564. NORDSTROM, Lars
"The Sun My Father" (21 selections, tr. of Nils-Aslak Valkeapaa, w.
Harald Gaski and Ralph Salisbury). [CharR] (21:1) Spr 95, p. 55-64.
NORINAGA, Ojiu
See OJIU, Norinaga
4565. NORMAN, Chad
"Five Islands" (for Sherry). [Quarry] (44:3) 95, p. 120.
"The Password is 'Drum'." [CanLit] (144) Spr 95, p. 112.
4566. NORMAN, Leslie
"Opening Doors." [SlipS] (15) 95, p. 11.
4567. NORMAN, Theresa
"Blessed." [ChironR] (43) Sum 95, p. 29.
4568. NORRIS, Kathleen
"Kitchen Trinity." [VirQR] (71:2) Spr 95, p. 313-314.
"Point Vierge." [Image] (9) Spr 95, p. 9-10.
"She Said Yeah." [VirQR] (71:2) Spr 95, p. 314.
"La Vierge Romane." [Image] (9) Spr 95, p. 8.
4569. NORRIS, Ken
"On Leave in Managua" (tr. of Elías Letelier-Ruz). [Arc] (35) Aut 95, p. 70.
"Theory of the Shoes" (tr. of Elías Letelier-Ruz). [Arc] (35) Aut 95, p. 68.
"The Winter Where I Live" (to Osvaldo Nuñez, the traitor MP, tr. of Elías Letelier-
Ruz). [Arc] (35) Aut 95, p. 69.
4570. NORRIS, Leslie
"His Father, Singing." [Epoch] (44:3) 95, p. 312-314.
"Peaches." [SewanR] (103:2) Spr 95, p. 190-191.
4571. NORRIS, Lisa
"Amusement Park." [PoetL] (90:4) Wint 95-96, p. 30.
"The Headhunter's Wife" (With gratitude to R.F. Barton and Ngídulu). [PoetL]
(90:4) Wint 95-96, p. 31-33.
4572. NORRIS, Natasha
"Untitled: All alone in my room staring at the wall" (w. Tene' Lewis and Lawan
Chatman. WritersCorps Program, Washington, DC). [WashR] (21:2) Ag-S
95, p. 16.
4573. NORTH, Charles
"Vetoed" (for Paul Violi). [NewAW] (13) Fall-Wint 95, p. 77-78.
4574. NORTHROP, Kate
"Two Stories." [BlackWR] (22:1) Fall-Wint 95, p. 120-121.
4575. NORTHUP, Harry E.
"The Sidewalk." [Pearl] (22) Fall-Wint 95, p. 124.
4576. NORTON, Michele
"Available Seeing." [PoetryE] (40) Spr 95, p. 88.
"Contained in an Earthly Garden." [PoetryE] (40) Spr 95, p. 90.
"Thinking." [PoetryE] (40) Spr 95, p. 89.
4577. NORTON, Sheila
"Edward Hopper Paints a Woman." [WillowR] (22) Spr 95, p. 3-4.
4578. NOTLEY, Alice
"Flowers." [NewAW] (13) Fall-Wint 95, p. 47-49.
4579. NOTO, John
"I. Ignition. Hyperlyric: The Expulsion from Childhood's Garden of Verse."
[Talisman] (14) Fall 95, p. 101.
"II. Conflagration. Hyperlyric Gambol: A Post-Poetic Oracular Bloodletting."
[Talisman] (14) Fall 95, p. 102-107.
"Root-Canal." [CentralP] (24) Spr 95, p. 109-110.
4580. NOVACK, Barbara
"Prelude." [CapeR] (30:2) Fall 95, p. 41.
4581. NOVAK, Katherine Bush
"White River Ferry, Sylamore, Arkansas, Saturday Night, 1940." [SmPd] (32:1,
#93) Wint 95, p. 7-8.
4582. NOVAKOVICH, Josip
"Before the Balkan Wars." [QW] (41) Aut-Wint 95-96, p. 201.
4583. NOVICK, Laurie
"Sideshow." [Art&Und] (4:3, #16) Je-Jl 95, p. 17.
4584. NOWAK, Mark (Mark A.)
"Custom." [CharR] (21:2) Fall 95, p. 103.

"Solitaire." [CharR] (21:2) Fall 95, p. 104.
"Zboze." [MidwQ] (36:4) Sum 95, p. 412.
4585. NOWICKI, Michael E.
"College Level." [Parting] (8:2) Wint 95-96, p. 16.
4586. NOWLAN, Alden
"Afterword to Genesis." [Kaleid] (31) Sum-Fall 95, p. 36.
"Escape from Eden." [Kaleid] (30) Wint-Spr 95, p. 47.
"In the Operating Room." [Kaleid] (30) Wint-Spr 95, p. 47.
"Postcard to a Ghost." [AntigR] (102/103) Sum-Aug 95, p. 225.
"Sunday Afternoon." [Kaleid] (31) Sum-Fall 95, p. 36.
4587. NOYES, Steve
"Khorosan." [Arc] (34) Spr 95, p. 54.
"Tent-Maker." [Arc] (34) Spr 95, p. 53.
4588. NUMANAKA, Hayataro
"Under the summer sun" (in Japanese and English, tr. by Jiro Nakano). [BambooR]
(67/68) Sum-Fall 95, p. 66.
NUÑEZ, Víctor Rodríguez
See RODRÍGUEZ NUÑEZ, Víctor
4589. NURKSE, D.
"Anvira." [ManhatR] (8:1) Fall 95, p. 19.
"At Fulton Mall." [PoetryNW] (36:2) Sum 95, p. 16-17.
"The Book of Loneliness." [ManhatR] (8:1) Fall 95, p. 18.
"Childhood and the Great Cities." [ManhatR] (7:2) Wint 95, p. 61-62.
"Childhood and the Great War." [ManhatR] (8:1) Fall 95, p. 16-17.
"The Coming Crash." [WestB] (37) 95, p. 69.
"Crossing the Ark Mountains." [Hudson] (48:1) Spr 95, p. 94-95.
"Excelsior Fashion Products, Easter." [KenR] (17:2) Spr 95, p. 142.
"Fever in a Rented Room." [WillowS] (35) Ja 95, p. 26.
"Final Separation." [Poetry] (165:6) Mr 95, p. 325.
"Immense Fires and Not Yet Summer." [AmerPoR] (24:4) Jl-Ag 95, p. 18.
"Lake Huron." [ManhatR] (8:1) Fall 95, p. 15.
"The Last Month of My Father's Life." [ManhatR] (7:2) Wint 95, p. 59.
"Neptune Avenue." [WillowS] (35) Ja 95, p. 27.
"Olmos." [ManhatR] (7:2) Wint 95, p. 58.
"Only Child." [Poetry] (165:6) Mr 95, p. 324-325.
"Peace after Long Sickness." [Hudson] (48:1) Spr 95, p. 93-94.
"Returning to the Capital." [WillowS] (35) Ja 95, p. 28.
"San Isidro." [AmerPoR] (24:4) Jl-Ag 95, p. 18.
"Scattering the March." [KenR] (17:2) Spr 95, p. 141.
"Snow Lake Island." [ManhatR] (7:2) Wint 95, p. 60.
"These Are Your Rights." [PoetryNW] (36:2) Sum 95, p. 15-16.
"Threshold of Liberty." [KenR] (17:2) Spr 95, p. 142-143.
"The Train to Manitoba." [ManhatR] (8:1) Fall 95, p. 20.
4590. NURMI, Earl
"Advice to a Son I Will Never Have." [AxeF] (3) 90, p. 27.
4591. NUTTER, Jude
"Hawkmoths." [NowestR] (33:2) 95, p. 33.
4592. NWABUEZE, Chim
"Flowers for the Inferno" (Excerpt). [Chelsea] (58) 95, p. 112-116.
4593. NYE, Naomi Shihab
"Darling." [Atlantic] (275:3) Mr 95, p. 104.
"Marie." [MidAR] (15:1/2) 95, p. 209.
"The Small Vases from Hebron." [ManyMM] [1:1] D 94, p. 69-70.
4594. NYHART, Nina
"The Beach Ball." [TampaR] (10) Spr 95, p. 67.
"Genus Genius." [SnailPR] (3:2) 95, p. 14.
"Once." [TampaR] (10) Spr 95, p. 67.
"The Parrot." [Shen] (45:1) Spr 95, p. 50-51.
"School." [TampaR] (10) Spr 95, p. 67.
"The Sewing Project." [Shen] (45:1) Spr 95, p. 49.
"The Wall." [GettyR] (8:3) Sum 95, p. 526.
4595. NYIMA, Ngawang
"Drake-Stoning Wang Wei" (pre-translations). [Archae] (5) Spr 95, p. 47-55.
"Now I am Going to Tell" (excerpt from "The Secret of Nurturing Growth," an Inner
Chapter of Chuang Tsu, tr. of Chuang Tsu). [Archae] (5) Spr 95, p. 62.

4596. NYSTROM, Keith
"Fall in New England." [DefinedP] (2:1) Fall-Wint 93, p. 18.

O., Alfred
     See ALFRED O.
4597. O MUIRTHILE, Liam
"An Luascán." [Poetry] (167:1/2) O-N 95, p. 68.
"The Swing" (tr. by Ciaran Carson). [Poetry] (167:1/2) O-N 95, p. 69.
4598. O SEARCAIGH, Cathal
"Night" (tr. by Frankie Sewell). [Poetry] (167:1/2) O-N 95, p. 67.
"Oíche." [Poetry] (167:1/2) O-N 95, p. 66.
4599. O-YIANG JIANGHE CHENGDU
"Public Monologue" (In memoriam: Ezra Pound, tr. by Cheng Baolin and Richard
     Terrill). [PassN] (16:1) Sum 95, p. 11.
4600. OAKES, Elizabeth (Beth)
"Because It Is Good to Be Afraid." [Manoa] (7:1) Sum 95, p. 49.
"Sleeper and Kite." [SouthernPR] (35:2) Wint 95, p. 45-46.
"Twice Born." [Manoa] (7:1) Sum 95, p. 47-48.
4601. OAKES, J. Cailin
"The Dance." [MidAR] (16:1) 95, p. 77-78.
"Running the Bulls." [PoetryNW] (36:3) Aut 95, p. 17-18.
4602. OAKS, Jeff
"The Building." [SouthernPR] (35:2) Wint 95, p. 20.
4603. OAKS, Lynne Butler
"One, Two, Many Times." [PaintedB] (55/56) 95, p. 108.
4604. OATES, Joyce Carol
"Ballad of Ashfield Avenue." [TriQ] (95) Wint 95-96, p. 167-168.
"Dakota Mystery, 10 May 1994." [Salm] (106/107) Spr-Sum 95, p. 116.
"Elegy: The Ancestors." [Salm] (106/107) Spr-Sum 95, p. 115.
"Falling Asleep at the Wheel, Route 98 North" (in memory of John Gardner).
     [NewMyths] (2:2/3:1) 95, p. 321-322.
"Recollection, in Tranquillity." [NewYorker] (71:18) 26 Je-3 Jl 95, p. 137.
"Sexy." [YaleR] (83:3) Jl 95, p. 95-101.
4605. OBRADOVIC, Biljana D.
"Where Does One Body End, Another Begin?" (for Meta Adamic). [MidwQ] (36:3)
     Spr 95, p. 306.
4606. O'BRIAN, Catherine
"Nail Polish." [LowellR] [1] Sum 94, p. 35-36.
"Sagrada!" [LowellR] [1] Sum 94, p. 37-40.
4607. O'BRIAN, Patrick
"The Deep Gold of a Pomegranate-Tree." [ParisR] (37:135) Sum 95, p. 134.
"A T'ang Landscape Remembered." [ParisR] (37:135) Sum 95, p. 134.
4608. O'BRIEN, Judith Tate
"Grandmother Blueshoe's New Name" (for Weckeah Bradley, oral historian of the
     Comanche Tribe). [Plain] (15:3) Spr 95, p. 29.
"Peacocks for an Absent Husband" (First Place, The 1995 Defined Providence
     Poetry Contest, Judged by Sean Thomas Dougherty). [DefinedP] (3) 95, p.
     65-66.
"Revelations" (for Gene). [Flyway] (1:2) Fall 95, p. 46-47.
4609. O'BRIEN, Laurie
"The 14-Year-Old Goethe Hears the Mozart Children in Court" (Frankfurt, August
     1763). [MissR] (23:3) 95, p. 86-87.
"Christina of St. Trond" (Brabant, 1150-1225). [MissR] (23:3) 95, p. 88-89.
"Inventing the Piano." [Poetry] (165:4) Ja 95, p. 211.
4610. O'BRIEN, Michael
"In or Out?" [GlobalCR] (6) Fall 95, p. 32-34.
"Little Testament" (tr. of Eugenio Montale). [Agni] (42) 95, p. 100-101.
"Marcel Duchamp." [Agni] (42) 95, p. 102.
4611. O'BRIEN, Sean
"Essay on Snow." [SouthernR] (31:4) O/Aut 95, p. 897-898.
"A Provincial Station." [SouthernR] (31:4) O/Aut 95, p. 897.
"Rain." [SouthernR] (31:4) O/Aut 95, p. 898-899.
4612. O'CALLAGHAN, Peter
"The Frenchman from Off the Hill." [RagMag] (12:2) Spr 95, p. 21.
"The Unemployment Office." [RagMag] (12:2) Spr 95, p. 20.

4613. OCAMPO, Silvina
"Sleeping Hydra" (tr. by Greg Geleta). [SnailPR] (3:2) 95, p. 29.
"A Tiger Speaks" (tr. by Greg Geleta). [ArtfulD] (28/29) 95, p. 100-101.
4614. OCHESTER, Ed
"The Barn." [PoetryE] (41) Aut 95, p. 88-89.
"Cooking in Key West." [ManyMM] (2:1) 95, p. 172-173.
"How to Read It." [LaurelR] (29:2) Sum 95, p. 16.
"Oct. 27, 1989." [PoetryE] (41) Aut 95, p. 90-91.
"Saying Goodbye to the Old Airport." [LaurelR] (29:2) Sum 95, p. 14-15.
"What He Did in Birmingham in April" (for Mike Srba). [ManyMM] (2:1) 95, p. 175.
4615. O'CONNELL, Bill
"Heat Wave." [PoetryE] (41) Aut 95, p. 58.
4616. O'CONNELL, Richard
"Rough A.M." [Light] (15/16) Aut-Wint 95-96, p. 31.
"Sir Richard Hawkins: His Observations" (From his *Observations* on his Voyage
into the South Sea, 1593). [ApalQ] (44/45) Fall 95-Wint 96, p. 47-50.
4617. O'CONNOR, Deirdre
"Farewell Thirty." [GrahamHR] (19) Wint 95-96, p. 98.
"Irish Cousins." [GrahamHR] (19) Wint 95-96, p. 99.
"Liminal." [Poetry] (166:4) Jl 95, p. 194-195.
"My Mother Sells Her Mother's House at 8 Edith Place." [Poetry] (166:4) Jl 95, p. 195.
4618. ODAM, Joyce
"Decidual." [Pearl] (22) Fall-Wint 95, p. 18.
"Densities." [Parting] (8:2) Wint 95-96, p. 21.
"Lumps." [Parting] (8:1) Sum 95, p. 39.
"Terrain." [Parting] (8:1) Sum 95, p. 38.
4619. O'DELL, John
"Through a Paper Screen." [Blueline] (16) 95, p. 3.
4620. ODHIAMBO, David Nandi
"Acid Jazz n'Nicotine." [TickleAce] (27) Spr-Sum 94, p. 108-109.
4621. ODIREAIN, Mairtín
"Era's End" (tr. by Patrick Crotty). [SouthernR] (31:3) Jl/Sum 95, p. 472.
"Memory of Sunday" (tr. by Patrick Crotty). [SouthernR] (31:3) Jl/Sum 95, p. 472-473.
4622. ODLIN, Reno
"Another Letter to James Laughlin." [AntigR] (100) Wint 95, p. 125-126.
4623. O'DONOGHUE, Bernard
"Child Language Acquisition." [Poetry] (167:1/2) O-N 95, p. 16.
"Kilmacow." [Poetry] (167:1/2) O-N 95, p. 17.
"Passive Smoking." [SouthernR] (31:3) Jl/Sum 95, p. 518.
"Reassurance." [Poetry] (167:1/2) O-N 95, p. 15.
"Second Class Relics." [SouthernR] (31:3) Jl/Sum 95, p. 517-518.
4624. O'DRISCOLL, Dennis
"The Next Poem." [NewEngR] (17:4) Fall 95, p. 141.
"You." [NewEngR] (17:4) Fall 95, p. 142.
4625. O'DWYER, Tess
"The wind and I would have to take off and fly" (tr. of Giannina Braschi).
[Footwork] (24/25) 95, p. 38.
OEUR, U Sam
See U, Sam Oeur
4626. OFFEN, Ron
"Answers, Questions" (for Rosine). [Pearl] (22) Fall-Wint 95, p. 21.
4627. OGDEN, Hugh
"Coming Back to the Garden." [SoDakR] (33:2) Sum 95, p. 65.
"In the Air." [Blueline] (16) 95, p. 64-65.
4628. OGIHARA, Yoriko
"Gathering Incense" (tr. by Hart Larrabee). [ArtfulD] (28/29) 95, p. 41.
4629. OGIHATA, Tadao
"Severely charred by the Atomic Bomb" (in Japanese and English, tr. by Jiro
Nakano). [BambooR] (67/68) Sum-Fall 95, p. 67.
4630. O'GRADY, Desmond
"Mustanbih" (For Peter Van de Kamp, tr. of Gabriel Rosenstock). [Poetry] (167:1/2)
O-N 95, p. 46-49.

4631. O'GRADY, Jennifer
"Composition." [PoetryE] (40) Spr 95, p. 91-92.
"One Explanation" (from *Singular Constructions*). [Harp] (290:1738) Mr 95, p. 29.
"Small Window." [ColR] (22:2) Fall 95, p. 186.
4632. O'GRADY, Thomas B.
"Exile." [PoetL] (90:2) Sum 95, p. 60.
"Land and Sea" (after Theógnis of Mégara). [Poem] (73) My 95, p. 22.
4633. O'GRADY, Tom
"Calligraphy." [PoetL] (90:3) Fall 95, p. 34.
"Cosmogram." [HampSPR] Wint 95, p. 53.
"He Troubles the Woods." [HampSPR] Wint 95, p. 55.
"Phosphorus." [HampSPR] Wint 95, p. 54.
"The Song of the Turtle." [PoetL] (90:3) Fall 95, p. 35.
"Such Beauty Tears You to Pieces" (for Roald Hoffman). [HampSPR] Wint 95, p. 54-55.
4634. O'HALLORAN, Jamie
"Last Summer" (in memoriam, Donna D'Agostino, 1957-1994). [CreamCR] (19:1) Spr 95, p. 128.
4635. O'HARA, Edgar
"Marinera del Este (con Andina Resbalosa)." [Americas] (23:3/4) Fall-Wint 95, p. 149-153.
"The Wolf's Return" (tr. collectively by Charity Berg, Rachel Breeden, et al.). [Americas] (23:3/4) Fall-Wint 95, p. 154-155.
4636. O'HARA, Ione S.
"Kite Over the Capitol." [Crucible] (31) Fall 95, p. 33.
4637. O'HARA, Mark
"Photo of My Grandfather, 1944." [CapeR] (30:2) Fall 95, p. 14.
"September 29, 1742: Bach." [WindO] (59) Spr 95, p. 43-44.
"Workplaces." [GreenHLL] (6) 95, p. 51-52.
4638. O'HAY
"The Luck of the Irish." [NewYorkQ] (54) 95, p. 89.
4639. O'HAY, Charles
"Tattoo." [Pearl] (22) Fall-Wint 95, p. 103.
"Uncle Drunk." [Pearl] (22) Fall-Wint 95, p. 103.
4640. O'HEHIR, Diana
"Spell for Protecting the Heart After Death." [AmerV] (36) 95, p. 92.
4641. OHMART, Ben
"Penitential." [BlackBR] (21) Fall-Wint 95, p. 37.
4642. OHNESORGE-FICK, Marlon
"Fate." [BelPoJ] (46:2) Wint 95-96, p. 28-31.
4643. OJAIDE, Tanure
"The Crow's Gift." [Pembroke] (27) 95, p. 128-129.
4644. OJIU, Norinaga
"Silk Tree Renga" (tr. of Araki Yasusada, Ozaki Kusatao and Akutagawa Fusei. Tr. w. Tosa Motokiyu and Okura Kyojin). [GrandS] (14:1, #53) Sum 95, p. 28-30.
"Untitled, August 12, 1964" (tr. of Araki Yasusada, w. Tosa Motokiyu and Okura Kyojin). [GrandS] (14:1, #53) Sum 95, p. 25.
4645. OKANTAH, Mwatabu S.
"Homeboy" (The 1994 Allen Ginsberg Poetry Awards: Honorable Mention). [Footwork] (24/25) 95, p. 200-201.
4646. O'KEEFE, Kerry
"Small Errands." [MassR] (36:2) Sum 95, p. 253.
4647. OKURA, Kyojin
"Silk Tree Renga" (tr. of Araki Yasusada, Ozaki Kusatao and Akutagawa Fusei. Tr. w. Tosa Motokiyu and Ojiu Norinaga). [GrandS] (14:1, #53) Sum 95, p. 28-30.
"Untitled, August 12, 1964" (tr. of Araki Yasusada, w. Tosa Motokiyu and Ojiu Norinaga). [GrandS] (14:1, #53) Sum 95, p. 25.
4648. OLAFSSON, Bragi
"Balm" (tr. by Bernard Scudder). [Nimrod] (38:2) Spr-Sum 95, p. 74.
"A Remarkable Occupation" (tr. by Bernard Scudder). [Nimrod] (38:2) Spr-Sum 95, p. 74.
4649. OLDEN, Megan
"Conversation among Witches" (from Macbeth). [Prima] (18/19) 95, p. 19-20.
"The Golden Children." [Prima] (18/19) 95, p. 16-18.

"Threading the Body." [Prima] (18/19) 95, p. 14-15.
4650. OLDER, Julia
    "If Poets Weren't So Stupid" (tr. of Boris Vian). [ApalQ] (44/45) Fall 95-Wint 96, p.
        45-46.
4651. OLDS, Sharon
    "The Animals." [RiverS] (42/43) 95, p. 120.
    "April, New Hampshire" (For Jane Kenyon and Donald Hall). [AmerPoR] (24:6) N-
        D 95, p. 21.
    "The Camp Bus, with My Son on It, Pulls Away from the Curb." [RiverS] (42/43)
        95, p. 121.
    "A Chair by the Fire." [Field] (53) Fall 95, p. 60-61.
    "The Day They Tied Me Up." [Verse] (12:2) 95, p. 109-110.
    "The Defense." [OntR] (43) Fall-Wint 95-96, p. 73-74.
    "Dirty Memories." [AmerPoR] (24:6) N-D 95, p. 22.
    "First." [AmerPoR] (24:6) N-D 95, p. 21.
    "First Formal." [Nat] (260:15) 17 Ap 95, p. 540.
    "The Foetus in the Voting Booth." [Field] (53) Fall 95, p. 63.
    "Grey Girl" (for Yusef Komunyakaa and Toi Derricotte). [AmerPoR] (24:6) N-D
        95, p. 22.
    "The Hand." [OntR] (43) Fall-Wint 95-96, p. 75-76.
    "Her First Week." [TriQ] (95) Wint 95-96, p. 89-90.
    "His Father's Cadaver." [TriQ] (95) Wint 95-96, p. 91-92.
    "January, Daughter." [NewYorker] (71:13) 22 My 95, p. 49.
    "Lifelong." [Field] (53) Fall 95, p. 62.
    "The Lonely Job" (newspaper headline — Executioner's Work: A Lonely Job).
        [BelPoJ] (45:4) Chapbook 22, Sum 95, p. 53.
    "My Son the Man." [NewYorker] (71:18) 26 Je-3 Jl 95, p. 116.
    "The Ordeal." [BelPoJ] (45:4) Chapbook 22, Sum 95, p. 54.
    "The Pediatrician Retires." [OntR] (43) Fall-Wint 95-96, p. 77.
    "Physics." [AmerPoR] (24:6) N-D 95, p. 22.
    "West." [TriQ] (95) Wint 95-96, p. 93.
4652. OLDS-ELLINGSON, Alice
    "Ordinary Interrogation" (for Norman Manea who wrote "The Interrogation" for
        APR). [SmPd] (32:1, #93) Wint 95, p. 17.
    "Tornado of Brilliance." [SmPd] (32:1, #93) Wint 95, p. 19.
4653. OLENSCHINSKI, Brigitte
    "Abrieb der Zehen, zum Beispiel." [InterPR] (21:1) Spr 95, p. 50.
    "Always So Fatigued in" (tr. by Gary Sea). [InterPR] (21:1) Spr 95, p. 51.
    "Immer So Müde Inmitten." [InterPR] (21:1) Spr 95, p. 50.
    "Klang Ohne Licht." [InterPR] (21:1) Spr 95, p. 48.
    "Over the Numb" (tr. by Gary Sea). [InterPR] (21:1) Spr 95, p. 51.
    "Die Räume." [InterPR] (21:1) Spr 95, p. 48.
    "Scraping the Knuckles, for Example" (tr. by Gary Sea). [InterPR] (21:1) Spr 95, p.
        51.
    "Sie Haben Nicht Bretter Genommen." [InterPR] (21:1) Spr 95, p. 46.
    "Sound without Light" (tr. by Gary Sea). [InterPR] (21:1) Spr 95, p. 49.
    "The Spaces" (tr. by Gary Sea). [InterPR] (21:1) Spr 95, p. 49.
    "They Did Not Use Boards" (tr. by Gary Sea). [InterPR] (21:1) Spr 95, p. 47.
    "Über der Tauben." [InterPR] (21:1) Spr 95, p. 50.
4654. OLES, Carole Simmons
    "Job Description: Clerk, Immigration and Naturalization Service, Federal Building."
        [SenR] (25:2) Fall 95, p. 31.
    "Summer, Stargazing" (with a line from Afanasy Fet). [SenR] (25:2) Fall 95, p. 32.
    "Travel: A Welcome" (for Annalisa). [BelPoJ] (45:4) Chapbook 22, Sum 95, p. 55-
        58.
    "Voices: Mother and Daughter." [KenR] (17:3/4) Sum-Fall 95, p. 143-145.
4655. OLINKA, Sharon
    "Elegy for Bob Bolles." [ChironR] (44/45) Aut-Wint 95, p. 40.
    "I Showed My Mother How to Make a Bed." [ChironR] (43) Sum 95, p. 25.
    "The Once Radical Professor." [ChironR] (44/45) Aut-Wint 95, p. 40.
4656. OLIVE, Harry
    "Routes Through the Difficult World." [Plain] (16:1) Fall 95, p. 11.
4657. OLIVE, Jason
    "The Mythic Hipster (Or Kerouac On Kerouac)." [HawaiiR] (19:2) Fall 95, p. 2-4.
4658. OLIVER, Douglas
    "The Childhood Map." [NewAW] (13) Fall-Wint 95, p. 50-51.

4659. OLIVER, Mary
"March." [VirQR] (71:1) Wint 95, p. 102.
"Seven White Butterflies." [Shen] (45:3) Fall 95, p. 21.
"Three Songs." [Shen] (45:3) Fall 95, p. 22-24.
"White Pine." [VirQR] (71:1) Wint 95, p. 101-102.
4660. OLLIVIER, L. L.
"The Itinerant Philosopher's Confession." [BellArk] (11:6) N-D 95, p. 9.
"Narrow Is the Way" (for Bill Chrystal). [BellArk] (11:6) N-D 95, p. 9.
"The Voice of All Things, Singing" (For Sandy). [BellArk] (11:5) S-O 95, p. 3-6.
4661. O'LOUGHLIN, Michael
"At the Grave of Father Hopkins." [Poetry] (167:1/2) O-N 95, p. 41.
"Birth Certificate: Amsterdam, 22 June 1988." [Poetry] (167:1/2) O-N 95, p. 40.
"Displacements." [Poetry] (167:1/2) O-N 95, p. 41-43.
4662. OLSEN, Lance
"Accidents." [BellR] (18:2, #38) Fall 95, p. 48-49.
"Losing Things." [SpinningJ] (1) Fall 95-Wint 96, p. 9.
"Moose." [BellR] (18:2, #38) Fall 95, p. 50-51.
4663. OLSEN, William
"After the Vision of a Storm Cloud, 31 July, 593 B.C." (Ezekiel). [Crazy] (48) Spr
95, p. 75-77.
"Deer Traffic." [ColR] (22:2) Fall 95, p. 167-168.
"Electric Church." [Crazy] (49) Wint 95, p. 68-69.
"Ghost Forest." [Boulevard] (10:1/2, #28/29) Spr 95, p. 181-182.
"How We Are Enlarged." [Crazy] (49) Wint 95, p. 70-71.
"The Human Heart." [Crazy] (49) Wint 95, p. 63-67.
"Kresges, 1963." [ParisR] (37:137) Wint 95, p. 122-125.
"Prophecy." [Crazy] (49) Wint 95, p. 72.
4664. OLSON, David
"East." [GreensboroR] (59) Wint 95-96, p. 56.
4665. OLSON, John
"Reelism" [sic]. [NewAW] (13) Fall-Wint 95, p. 28-29.
"The Secret Life of Utilities." [NewAW] (13) Fall-Wint 95, p. 30-31.
4666. OLSON, Sharon
"The Two Women." [Kalliope] (17:1) 95, p. 20.
4667. OLSSON, Kurt
"The Body." [LullwaterR] (5:1) 93-94, p. 76.
"Ear." [LullwaterR] (5:1) 93-94, p. 77.
4668. O'MALLEY, Mary
"The Otter Woman." [SouthernR] (31:3) Jl/Sum 95, p. 689-690.
4669. OMANSON, Bradley
"Class." [Hudson] (48:2) Sum 95, p. 278.
4670. OMARSDOTTIR, Kristin
"The Flowers on Women's Skirts" (tr. by Bernard Scudder). [Nimrod] (38:2) Spr-
Sum 95, p. 70.
4671. OMOSUPE, Ekua Rashidah
"My Name Is a Song." [SinW] (55) Spr-Sum 95, p. 21.
4672. ONADA-SIKWOIA, Akiba
"Giants." [SinW] (56) Sum-Fall 95, p. 11-12.
"The Language That Hates." [SinW] (56) Sum-Fall 95, p. 88-89.
4673. ONCINA, Lori
"My Favorite Pair of Socks." [BellArk] (11:4) Jl-Ag 95, p. 5.
4674. ONDAATJE, Michael
"From 'Claude Glass'." [AntigR] (102/103) Sum-Aug 95, p. 226.
"A Gentleman Compares His Virtue to a Jade." [Salm] (108) Fall 95, p. 30-32.
4675. ONESS, Chad
"Even at Ten." [Journal] (19:1) Spr-Sum 95, p. 67.
"Next Dream." [Journal] (19:1) Spr-Sum 95, p. 65-66.
"This Thick Paper." [Journal] (19:1) Spr-Sum 95, p. 68.
4676. ONESS, Elizabeth
"Ash Wednesday." [SantaBR] (3:1) Spr 95, p. 23.
4677. ONOPA, Paul
"Smoke House." [PoetL] (90:3) Fall 95, p. 11.
4678. OOKA, Makoto
"Life Story" (tr. by Janine Beichman). [Descant] (26:2, #89) Sum 95, p. 45.
"Morning Prayer" (tr. by Janine Beichman). [Descant] (26:2, #89) Sum 95, p. 46.
"Saki's Numazu" (tr. by Janine Beichman). [Descant] (26:2, #89) Sum 95, p. 47-48.

4679. OOSTERHOFF, Tonnus
"Fairy Tale" (tr. by Paul Vincent). [CimR] (112) Jl 95, p. 12.
4680. OPERÉ, Fernando
"¿Cuanto Lleva a un Hombre Construir Su Casa?" [InterPR] (21:1) Spr 95, p. 22.
"How Much Does It Take to Build a House?" (tr. by Jean Cargile). [InterPR] (21:1) Spr 95, p. 23.
4681. OPOKU-AGYEMANG, Kwadwo
"Dancing with Dizzy (or Manteca, by Mr. Birks)." [AfAmRev] (29:2) Sum 95, p. 257-258.
4682. OPPENHEIMER, Joel
"Animals." [NoCarLR] (2:2) 95, p. 71.
"Elephant Blues." [NoCarLR] (2:2) 95, p. 73.
"For Hoyt Wilhelm." [NoCarLR] (2:2) 95, p. 74-75.
"Ghosts." [NoCarLR] (2:2) 95, p. 80-81.
"Letters for MC" (her seventieth birthday, 1986). [NoCarLR] (2:2) 95, p. 78.
"The News." [NoCarLR] (2:2) 95, p. 76.
4683. ORBAN, Ottó
"Snowfall in Boston" (tr. by Bruce Berlind and Mária Körösy). [LitR] (38:3) Spr 95, p. 352-353.
4684. ORFANELLA, Lou
"Charcoal Drawings in the Park" (Literary Festival: Poetry: First Place). [EngJ] (84:4) Ap 95, p. 36.
4685. ORIORDAIN, Seán
"My Mother's Burial" (tr. by Patrick Crotty). [SouthernR] (31:3) Jl/Sum 95, p. 474-475.
ORITZ, Simon J.
See ORTIZ, Simon J.
4686. ORLEN, Steve
"Authority." [Agni] (41) 95, p. 128.
"Imagination." [Atlantic] (275:4) Ap 95, p. 102.
"Mr. & Mrs. Death." [Agni] (41) 95, p. 125-127.
"The Poets." [Agni] (41) 95, p. 129.
4687. ORMOND, Margaret
"Cape Bald" (First Place, 1995 Poetry Contest). [PraF] (16:4, #73) Wint 95-96, p. 68-70.
4688. ORMSBY, Eric
"Crows." [Blueline] (16) 95, p. 17.
"An Oak Skinned by Lightning." [Blueline] (16) 95, p. 36.
"Los Paramos." [Blueline] (16) 95, p. 80-81.
"The Suitors of My Grandmother's Youth." [NewRep] (212:15) 10 Ap 95, p. 44.
4689. O'ROURKE, Jim
"Hey, Robert!" [Footwork] (24/25) 95, p. 209.
"Mother's License." [Footwork] (24/25) 95, p. 209.
"What Love Is Doing." [Footwork] (24/25) 95, p. 209.
4690. ORR, Gregory
"Annunciation." [CarolQ] (47:2) Wint 95, p. 62.
"An Emissary From the Barbarians." [Jacaranda] (11) [95 or 96?], p. 57.
"The Fire Hydrant." [Boulevard] (10:1/2, #28/29) Spr 95, p. 123.
"Lament." [SycamoreR] (7:1) Wint 95, p. 15-16.
"Muse of Midnight." [SycamoreR] (7:1) Wint 95, p. 14.
"On a Highway East of Selma, Alabama, July, 1965." [SenR] (25:1) Spr 95, p. 81-83.
"Seljuk." [Jacaranda] (11) [95 or 96?], p. 58.
"Suspicions." [Boulevard] (10:1/2, #28/29) Spr 95, p. 122.
"Three For My Oldest Daughter." [Jacaranda] (11) [95 or 96?], p. 60-61.
"Untitled: Let historians puzzle it out." [Jacaranda] (11) [95 or 96?], p. 59.
4691. ORR, Priscilla
"Denial." [Footwork] (24/25) 95, p. 54.
"Forgiveness." [Footwork] (24/25) 95, p. 54.
4692. ORR, Thomas Alan
"Seventh Summer." [HopewellR] (7) 95, p. 108-109.
4693. ORR, Verlena
"Leaning into Winter" (For Dad July 15, 1902-August 4, 1992). [Flyway] (1:2) Fall 95, p. 48-49.
4694. ORTIZ, Simon (Simon J.)
"From Sand Creek." [RiverS] (42/43) 95, p. 33-35.

"A Gift to Give and Receive: A Tribute for Indian Children." [Pembroke] (27) 95, p. 43-44.
"Headlands Journal Entries & Poems, 1994." [SoDakR] (33:3/4) Fall-Wint 95, p. 210-217.
ORTIZ COFER, Judith
   See COFER, Judith Ortiz
4695. ORTOLANI, Al
   "The Oxbow." [MidwQ] (36:4) Sum 95, p. 413.
   "Water Strider." [WindO] (59) Spr 95, p. 26.
4696. ORTON, Barbara J.
   "Beekeeper." [LitR] (38:2) Wint 95, p. 260-261.
   "Dipping." [LitR] (38:2) Wint 95, p. 259-260.
4697. OSBEY, Brenda Marie
   "The Business of Pursuit: San Malo's Prayer." [AmerV] (36) 95, p. 114-121.
   "Everything Happens to (Monk and) Me." [AmerPoR] (24:1) Ja-F 95, p. 10-11.
   "The Head of Luís Congo Speaks." [AmerPoR] (24:1) Ja-F 95, p. 8-10.
4698. OSBORN, Andrew
   "P-O-W-E-R W-A-G-." [Border] (7) Fall-Wint 96, p. 45-46.
4699. OSER, Lee
   "Mosaic Days." [Comm] (122:4) 24 F 95, p. 11.
4700. O'SHEA-NOONAN, Mary-Beth
   "Sparklers." [BellArk] (11:5) S-O 95, p. 15.
4701. OSHEROW, Jacqueline
   "Beijing Rids Itself of Sparrows." [NewRep] (213:6) 7 Ag 95, p. 44.
   "Breezeway, Circa 1964." [NewRep] (212:24) 12 Je 95, p. 44.
   "London, Before and After, the Middle Way." [SouthwR] (80:1) Wint 95, p. 74-80.
   "Moses in Paradise." [TriQ] (95) Wint 95-96, p. 182-188.
   "My Cousin Abe, Paul Antschel and Paul Celan." [ParisR] (37:134) Spr 95, p. 263-265.
   "Terza Rima for a Sudden Change in Seasons." [Ploughs] (21:4) Wint 95-96, p. 133-137.
4702. OSING, Gordon T.
   "The Waitress" (The Penisula Hotel [sic], Hong Kong). [XavierR] (15:2) Fall 95, p. 64.
4703. OSSMANN, April
   "Y." [SpoonR] (20:2) Sum-Fall 95, p. 141-142.
4704. OSTERHAUS, Joe
   "The Scale of Light." [Agni] (41) 95, p. 44-46.
   "Sweet Decision." [Agni] (41) 95, p. 47.
4705. OSTHEIMER, Martha
   "As It Is." [IndR] (18:2) Fall 95, p. 91.
4706. OSTI, Josip
   "City Spirit" (tr. by Ruzha Cleaveland). [InterPR] (21:1) Spr 95, p. 67.
   "Destiny Doesn't Want to Share with Death the Last Gulp of Water, the Last Bit of Food" (tr. by Ruzha Cleaveland). [InterPR] (21:1) Spr 95, p. 63.
   "Earthly and Heavenly Roads" (tr. by Ruzha Cleaveland). [InterPR] (21:1) Spr 95, p. 61.
   "Finally They Fall Sweetly from the Sky, Though Children Behind Darkened Windows Do Not See Them" (tr. by Ruzha Cleaveland). [InterPR] (21:1) Spr 95, p. 57, 59.
   "Gradski Duh." [InterPR] (21:1) Spr 95, p. 66.
   "I Danas je Agresor Napadao, Svim Sredstvima, Sve Dijelove Grada." [InterPR] (21:1) Spr 95, p. 64.
   "I Don't Recognize Anymore the Town in Which I Knew Every Corner" (tr. by Ruzha Cleaveland). [MinnR] (43/44) 95, p. 11.
   "Konacno s Neba Padaju Secerleme, Ali to Djeca, Iza Zamracenih Prozora, ne Vide." [InterPR] (21:1) Spr 95, p. 56, 58.
   "A Letter to Kavafy" (tr. by Ruzha Cleaveland). [LitR] (38:3) Spr 95, p. 354-355.
   "Letters I Write You Leave in the Wind, But Roses I Send You I Send in Death" (tr. by Ruzha Cleaveland). [MinnR] (43/44) 95, p. 9.
   "Putevima Zemaljskim i Putevima Nebeskim." [InterPR] (21:1) Spr 95, p. 60.
   "S Mrtvima, Srecom, ne Treba Dijeliti Posljedni Gutljaj Vode, Posljednji Zalogaj Hrane." [InterPR] (21:1) Spr 95, p. 62.
   "That Year a Belgian Poet, Whose Name You Were Able to Write But Not Pronounce ..." (tr. by Ruzha Cleaveland). [MinnR] (43/44) 95, p. 9-11.

"Today the Aggressor Attacked in Every Way and in All Parts of Town" (tr. by
Ruzha Cleaveland). [InterPR] (21:1) Spr 95, p. 65.
4707. OSTRIKER, Alicia
"After Illness." [NewEngR] (17:2) Spr 95, p. 124-126.
"Brooklyn Twilight." [TriQ] (93) Spr-Sum 95, p. 129.
"Chanson." [Iowa] (25:3) Fall 95, p. 127.
"Chocolate Babies." [ManyMM] (1:2) 95, p. 38.
"Civic Center Park, San Francisco." [ManyMM] (1:2) 95, p. 36-37.
"A Clean Plate (Hartford 1955)." [SenR] (25:2) Fall 95, p. 36.
"The death of the Poet." [US1] (30/31) 95, p. 1.
"First Conversation with Tess." [ManyMM] [1:1] D 94, p. 42-43.
"Globule" (for May Swenson). [OntR] (42) Spr-Sum 95, p. 53-54.
"Krishna Speaks to the Summer Carpenter." [TriQ] (95) Wint 95-96, p. 182.
"The Life of the Mind." [DenQ] (30:2) Fall 95, p. 54-55.
"Marie at Tea." [TriQ] (93) Spr-Sum 95, p. 126-128.
"Migrant." [Iowa] (25:3) Fall 95, p. 128.
"Nude Descending." [DenQ] (30:2) Fall 95, p. 52-53.
"The Russian Army Goes into Baku." [SenR] (25:2) Fall 95, p. 37-38.
"The Studio (Homage to Alice Neel)." [Boulevard] (10:3, #30) Fall 95, p. 142-143.
"Terminal: A Poem for Aphrodite." [ManyMM] [1:1] D 94, p. 41.
"Translation" (for Judith Hemschemeyer). [US1] (30/31) 95, p. 26.
4708. OSUGI, Hisako
"At broad daylight, a peony flower" (in Japanese and English, tr. by Jiro Nakano).
[BambooR] (67/68) Sum-Fall 95, p. 68.
4709. O'SULLIVAN, Maggie
"Riverrunning (Realisations" [sic] (for Charles Bernstein). [WestCL] (29:2, #17)
Fall 95, p. 62-71.
4710. OSVAT, Martha
"On the Last Day of This Year." [CreamCR] (19:1) Spr 95, p. 161-163.
"Transylvanian Princess at the Ball." [CreamCR] (19:1) Spr 95, p. 164-167.
4711. OTA, Shizuko
"The constant search for a loved one" (in Japanese and English, tr. by Jiro Nakano).
[BambooR] (67/68) Sum-Fall 95, p. 69.
4712. OTOMO no YAKAMOCHI (718-785)
"Late evening finally comes" (tr. by Sam Hamill). [PoetryE] (41) Aut 95, p. 20.
4713. OTONKOSKI, Lauri
"But the memory did not sleep, the time we killed did not stay" (tr. by Sari Hantula).
[InterPR] (21:2) Fall 95, p. 59.
"Credo" (in Finnish and English, tr. by Sari Hantula). [InterPR] (21:2) Fall 95, p. 54-
55.
"Ei nukkunut muisti, ei pysynyt tapetty aika haudassaan." [InterPR] (21:2) Fall 95,
p. 58.
"Ne jotka puhuvat, menettävät paljon sanoja." [InterPR] (21:2) Fall 95, p. 60.
"Plato" (tr. by Sari Hantula). [InterPR] (21:2) Fall 95, p. 57.
"Platon." [InterPR] (21:2) Fall 95, p. 56.
"Those who talk lose lots of words" (tr. by Sari Hantula). [InterPR] (21:2) Fall 95, p.
61.
4714. O'TOOLE, John M.
"Bird Watcher." [Ascent] (20:1) Fall 95, p. 44.
"Charlatan." [Ascent] (20:1) Fall 95, p. 45.
4715. OTT, Kelly Elizabeth
"Believing." [LullwaterR] (5:1) 93-94, p. 78.
"Little Hauntings." [Border] (6) Spr-Sum 95, p. 57.
"This Wind Tonight." [Border] (6) Spr-Sum 95, p. 58.
4716. OTT, Martin
"Eve Day." [MidwQ] (37:1) Aut 95, p. 46.
4717. OTT, Rita
"Traveling Highway 2." [BellArk] (11:1) Ja-F 95, p. 25.
4718. OTTEN, Charlotte F.
"Interstate." [ChrC] (112:15) 3 My 95, p. 476.
OU-YANG, Hsiu (1007-1072)
See HSIU, Ou-yang (1007-1072)
4719. OUWENS, Kees
"Talent" (tr. by Scott Rollins and Peter Nijmeijer). [CimR] (112) Jl 95, p. 11.
4720. OVERSON, Kristin
"Kin." [Parting] (8:1) Sum 95, p. 16-17.

4721. OVERTON, Ron
"Europe's Spring Collections" (found: New York, 11/89)." [HangL] (66) 95, p. 64.
"Old Money." [HangL] (66) 95, p. 62.
"Real Life." [HangL] (66) 95, p. 63-64.
"Two Stories." [HangL] (66) 95, p. 65.
4722. OVID (43 BCE-17 CE)
"Amores" (Book 1, #5, tr. by Catherine A. Salmons). [HarvardR] (9) Fall 95, p. 28.
"Elegy to His Mistress" (tr. by Sam Hamill). [PoetryE] (41) Aut 95, p. 15.
4723. OWEN, Deborah
"Pythia: the Prophetess of Apollo at Delphi" (for Eduardo. Chapbook with an
introduction by Mark Schafer, tr. of Gloria Gervitz, w. Burton Raffel). [LitR]
(38:3) Spr 95, p. 383-416.
4724. OWEN, John
"Sixty Latin Epigrams" (8 selections in Latin and English, tr. by David R. Slavitt).
[Light] (15/16) Aut-Wint 95-96, p. 4-5.
4725. OWEN, Stephanie Hong
"Human Nature." [PoetL] (90:3) Fall 95, p. 30.
4726. OWEN, Sue
"The Flaw in the Flue." [MassR] (36:3) Aut 95, p. 364.
"The Flea Bites." [LouisL] (12:1) Spr 95, p. 57.
"Name Your Poison." [LouisL] (12:1) Spr 95, p. 58-59.
4727. OWENS, David
"Translating Tongues." [HopewellR] (7) 95, p. 110-111.
4728. OWENS, June
"Answering the Manatee" (3rd Place — 1995 CR Poetry Contest). [ChironR]
(44/45) Aut-Wint 95, p. 32.
"Flashman / Switchman." [Crucible] (31) Fall 95, p. 35-36.
"In the Wilderness" (1994 Literary Contest: First Prize). [Crucible] (30) Fall 94, p.
1-3.
4729. OWENS, Scott
"From Here." [SoDakR] (33:2) Sum 95, p. 39.
"His Huge Hands." [InterPR] (21:1) Spr 95, p. 84.
"Stone, Petal, Flesh." [Crucible] (31) Fall 95, p. 13.
"The Storm's Gifts." [SoDakR] (33:2) Sum 95, p. 38.
"The Sun Was Like an Oxymoron." [PoetryE] (39) Fall 94, p. 69-70.
"To." [CreamCR] (19:1) Spr 95, p. 120-121.
4730. OWENS, Suzanne
"For the One Who Wants My Daughter." [LullwaterR] (6:2) Fall-Wint 95, p. 30-31.
4731. OWER, John (John Bernard)
"Resurrection" (For Buddy Tate). [Farm] (12:1) Spr-Sum 95, p. 35.
"The Saguaro Harvester" (For Richard Shelton). [HolCrit] (32:3) Je 95, p. 17.
4732. OWNBEY, Brian
"The Good Work." [SouthernPR] (35:1) Sum 95, p. 7-8.
4733. OXENDINE, Sally Mae
"Listen." [Pembroke] (27) 95, p. 13.
4734. OZAKI, Kusatao
"Silk Tree Renga" (w. Araki Yasusada and Akutagawa Fusei. Tr. by Tosa
Motokiyu, Ojiu Norinaga and Okura Kyojin). [GrandS] (14:1, #53) Sum 95,
p. 28-30.
4735. OZAWA, Tomoo
"Burnt and ulcerated, a blind infant" (in Japanese and English, tr. by Jiro Nakano).
[BambooR] (67/68) Sum-Fall 95, p. 70.
4736. OZUG, Chuck
"Brothers." [DefinedP] (2:1) Fall-Wint 93, p. 16-17.
"What Is Left." [DefinedP] (2:1) Fall-Wint 93, p. 15.

P., James "Buster"
See JAMES "BUSTER" P.
P., Thomasina
See THOMASINA P.
4737. PABLOS, Analuisa
"Lo Siento." [QW] (41) Aut-Wint 95-96, p. 273.
PABON, Leonardo García
See GARCIA PABON, Leonardo

4738. PACHECO, José Emilio
"Los Condenados de la Tierra." [TriQ] (94) Fall 95, p. 238.
"Couples" (tr. by Cynthia Steele). [TriQ] (94) Fall 95, p. 237.
"For You" (tr. by Cynthia Steele). [TriQ] (94) Fall 95, p. 241.
"Para Ti." [TriQ] (94) Fall 95, p. 240.
"Parejas." [TriQ] (94) Fall 95, p. 236.
"Walter Benjamin Leaves Paris (1940)" (tr. by Cynthia Steele). [TriQ] (94) Fall 95, p. 243.
"Walter Benjamin Se Va de París (1940)." [TriQ] (94) Fall 95, p. 242.
"The Wretched of the Earth" (tr. by Cynthia Steele). [TriQ] (94) Fall 95, p. 239.
4739. PACK, Robert
"Beyond Forgetting." [PraS] (69:1) Spr 95, p. 49.
"Circle." [NewRep] (213:19) 6 N 95, p. 44.
"Drowning." [SenR] (25:1) Spr 95, p. 112-114.
"Listening." [PraS] (69:1) Spr 95, p. 48.
4740. PACKARD, William
"3-11-93." [NewYorkQ] (54) 95, p. 41.
"Poem about Pain" (for Lynne Savitt). [NewYorkQ] (55) 95, p. 71.
4741. PADDOCK, Harold
"Noel Dinn." [TickleAce] (27) Spr-Sum 94, p. 35-36.
4742. PADDOCK, Joe
"Fists of Root." [NorthStoneR] (12) 95, p. 228-229.
4743. PADEL, Ruth
"Archie." [Verse] (12:2) 95, p. 111.
"Cold." [NewYorker] (70:49) 13 F 95, p. 62.
"Conn." [SouthernHR] (29:3) Sum 95, p. 272-273.
"Stroke City." [HarvardR] (9) Fall 95, p. 32.
"Telling." [SouthernHR] (29:3) Sum 95, p. 271.
4744. PADGETT, Ron
"L'Enfer N'Est Pas" (tr. of Serge Fauchereau). [Agni] (42) 95, p. 35.
"Les Gestes Qu'On Peut Faire" (tr. of Serge Fauchereau). [Agni] (42) 95, p. 36.
"The Rule of Three." [Agni] (41) 95, p. 100.
4745. PAGE, Carolyn
"By the Glenwood." [AxeF] (3) 90, p. 25.
4746. PAGE, Judith
"Leto in the Fountain." [Crucible] (30) Fall 94, p. 17.
"My Seventh Grade Science Teacher." [Footwork] (24/25) 95, p. 78.
4747. PAGE, Sharon
"Matthew 5:28." [SantaBR] (3:1) Spr 95, p. 43.
"Timing." [SantaBR] (3:1) Spr 95, p. 44.
4748. PAGE, William
"Expressions." [LitR] (39:1) Fall 95, p. 67.
"Flight of the Dead." [LitR] (39:1) Fall 95, p. 66.
"Memphis." [ColEng] (57:1) Ja 95, p. 84.
PAHLSON, Goran Printz
See PRINTZ-PAHLSON, Goran
4749. PAINO, Frankie
"Keats in Rome." [MidAR] (15:1/2) 95, p. 156-158.
"Leda." [CharR] (21:1) Spr 95, p. 96.
4750. PALADINO, Thomas
"At Mid-Day." [SenR] (25:2) Fall 95, p. 94.
"Blues for an Urban Master." [QW] (40) Spr-Sum 95, p. 63.
"Chagall in Season." [InterPR] (21:1) Spr 95, p. 87.
4751. PALAIMA, Thomas G.
"Monad Noir" (Dedicated to Douglass Parker with apologies to Colin Dexter, Morse, and Thaw). [Arion] (3:2/3) Fall 95-Wint 96, p. 178-179.
4752. PALEY, Grace
"Somewhere." [RiverS] (42/43) 95, p. 126.
4753. PALING, Stephen
"The Seven Deadly Sins Speak to the Miller in His Sleep" (A Plainsongs Award Poem). [Plain] (15:2) Wint 95, p. 36-38.
"William Tell Confronts the King." [Hellas] (6:1) Spr-Sum 95, p. 93-94.
4754. PALLAV, Nara
"Every Night" (tr. by S. Chilcote). [TickleAce] (27) Spr-Sum 94, p. 84-85.
4755. PALLONE, Jill Haber
"To Bob." [Footwork] (24/25) 95, p. 162.

4756. PALMA, Michael
"In the Afternoon." [Northeast] (5:13) Wint 95-96, p. 27.
PALMA, Ray di
    See DiPALMA, Ray
4757. PALMER, John
"Attachments." [CimR] (110) Ja 96, p. 79.
4758. PALMER, Kimberly Townsend
"Signs from God." [XavierR] (15:2) Fall 95, p. 25-26.
4759. PALMER, Michael
"Anode (20 XII 94)." [CutB] (44) Sum 95, p. 7.
"Deck" (Selections). [Zyzzyva] (11:3/4, #43/44) 95, "The Best of Ten Years of
    ZYZZYVA," p. 70-74.
"SB." [CutB] (44) Sum 95, p. 8-9.
"Stanza." [Phoebe] (24:2) 95, p. 16.
"Under the Perseids" (to Jerry Estrin). [DenQ] (29:3) Wint 95, p. 27-28.
"Well." [Phoebe] (24:2) 95, p. 17.
4760. PALMER, Ronald V.
"The Ice Lake." [PoetryE] (41) Aut 95, p. 93.
4761. PALMER, Thelma J.
"It's All in Knowing Where to Look." [BellR] (18:2, #38) Fall 95, p. 39.
"A Rat's Tale." [BellR] (18:2, #38) Fall 95, p. 38.
4762. PALMER, Todd
"We Teach School" (Literary Festival: Poetry: Honorable Mention). [EngJ] (84:4)
    Ap 95, p. 43.
4763. PALMER, William
"The Woman in the Tray." [BellR] (18:1, #37) Spr 95, p. 14.
PAN, Douglas le
    See LePAN, Douglas
4764. PANIKER, Ayyappa
"Khajuraho" (tr. by the author). [AnotherCM] (29) Spr 95, p. 110-112.
"A Pair of Glasses" (tr. of Savithri Rajeevan, w. Arlene Zide). [ManyMM] (1:3) 95,
    p. 152-153.
"Passage to America" (tr. by the author, w. J. O. Perry, Dakshinamoorthy, K.
    Satchidanandan, and Esther Y. Smith). [ManyMM] (1:3) 95, p. 120-126.
4765. PANKEY, Eric
"Betraying the Muse." [Iowa] (25:3) Fall 95, p. 103-104.
"Savant of Birdcalls" (Papageno, *The Magic Flute*). [Iowa] (25:3) Fall 95, p. 102.
"Sworn Deposition." [Agni] (41) 95, p. 112-113.
4766. PANKOWSKI, Elsie
"Vision." [MidwQ] (36:4) Sum 95, p. 414-415.
4767. PANOSIAN, Cheryl
"Cruz In." [AnotherCM] (29) Spr 95, p. 165-166.
4768. PANTER, Nicole
"1979 Fuck You Punk Rock." [ChironR] (44/45) Aut-Wint 95, p. 25.
"A Fragment of My Unfinished Hollywood Novel, Not Yet Started." [ChironR]
    (44/45) Aut-Wint 95, p. 25.
"Fuck You Punk Rock / 1977." [ChironR] (44/45) Aut-Wint 95, p. 25.
4769. PANTIN, Yolanda
"Stained Glass Window of a Woman Alone" (tr. by Mary Crow). [GrahamHR] (19)
    Wint 95-96, p. 59-61.
4770. PAOLA, Suzanne
"Anniversary" (for Bruce). [QRL] (34) 95, book 1, p. 32-35.
"Apothecary Jar." [QRL] (34) 95, book 1, p. 49.
"Ash Wednesday." [QRL] (34) 95, book 1, p. 16.
"Black Raspberries." [QRL] (34) 95, book 1, p. 23.
"Blackbirds." [QRL] (34) 95, book 1, p. 49-50.
"Calenture and Loom" (for my brother). [QRL] (34) 95, book 1, p. 27-29.
"Conception." [Ploughs] (21:1) Spr 95, p. 76-77.
"Daphne." [QRL] (34) 95, book 1, p. 52.
"Death Which Is Natural & Not to Be Lamented, Feared, Nor Longed For." [QRL]
    (34) 95, book 1, p. 37-39.
"December Solstice." [QRL] (34) 95, book 1, p. 30-32.
"Deus Absconditus." [SouthernHR] (29:1) Wint 95, p. 70-71.
"Driftwood Beach: Theme & Variations." [WillowS] (36) Je 95, p. 12-13.
"For Lily." [QRL] (34) 95, book 1, p. 9.
"Genesis." [QRL] (34) 95, book 1, p. 13.

"Glass." [QRL] (34) 95, book 1, p. 57-61.
"The Harrowing of Hell." [QRL] (34) 95, book 1, p. 10.
"In the Cathedral of the Company of Death." [QRL] (34) 95, book 1, p. 45-46.
"Intensive Care." [QRL] (34) 95, book 1, p. 39.
"June Prayer." [QRL] (34) 95, book 1, p. 24.
"Lazarus." [QRL] (34) 95, book 1, p. 40-41.
"The Lost Twin." [QRL] (34) 95, book 1, p. 20-22.
"Medicine." [QRL] (34) 95, book 1, p. 43-44.
"Narcissus: Variations." [Shen] (45:4) Wint 95, p. 79-81.
"Nocturne: Insomnia." [QRL] (34) 95, book 1, p. 55.
"Paraclete." [QRL] (34) 95, book 1, p. 17.
"Phantom Spring: For a Friend Doubting Her Faith" (for Mary May). [QRL] (34)
    95, book 1, p. 47.
"Plague: Letter to Raymond of Capua." [QRL] (34) 95, book 1, p. 14.
"Rain." [QRL] (34) 95, book 1, p. 25-26.
"Red Riding Hood: Variations." [QRL] (34) 95, book 1, p. 53-54.
"Sakti." [Ploughs] (21:1) Spr 95, p. 78-79.
"Significant Flaw." [QRL] (34) 95, book 1, p. 15.
"Still Life at Christmas with Snow and Sickness." [QRL] (34) 95, book 1, p. 12-13.
"Thinking of Mary Magdalene: A Seduction Poem." [QRL] (34) 95, book 1, p. 50-
    51.
"Three Deaths." [QRL] (34) 95, book 1, p. 41-42.
"The Two." [QRL] (34) 95, book 1, p. 7-8.
"The White." [QRL] (34) 95, book 1, p. 29-30.
"Willow." [QRL] (34) 95, book 1, p. 11.
"The World Rising As a Mirror." [QRL] (34) 95, book 1, p. 18.
4771. PAOLUCCI, Anne
    "New York Sketches (P.S. # # in Staten Island)." [Elf] (5:2) Sum 95, p. 26.
    "New York Sketches (Throgs Neck, Queens)." [Elf] (5:2) Sum 95, p. 27.
4772. PAPALEO, Joseph
    "Living Images." [Footwork] (24/25) 95, p. 13.
    "Messages from the Superego: One." [Footwork] (24/25) 95, p. 13-14.
4773. PAPE, Greg
    "Bitterroot Car-Body Riprap." [MidAR] (15:1/2) 95, p. 47-48.
    "The Flying Red Horse." [MidAR] (15:1/2) 95, p. 45-46.
PAPPAS, Rita Signorelli
    See SIGNORELLI-PAPPAS, Rita
4774. PARA, Jean Baptiste
    "Anchise." [InterPR] (21:1) Spr 95, p. 32.
    "Anchises" (tr. by Steve Light). [InterPR] (21:1) Spr 95, p. 33.
    "Eros au Masque d'Ombre." [InterPR] (21:1) Spr 95, p. 34.
    "Eros in Shadow's Mask" (tr. by Steve Light). [InterPR] (21:1) Spr 95, p. 35.
    "Front Lines" (tr. by Steve Light). [InterPR] (21:1) Spr 95, p. 37.
    "Lignes de Front." [InterPR] (21:1) Spr 95, p. 36.
    "Parturition de Magia Polla, or [sic] La Naissance de Virgile." [InterPR] (21:1) Spr
        95, p. 30.
    "Parturition of Magia Polla or The Birth of Virgil" (tr. by Steve Light). [InterPR]
        (21:1) Spr 95, p. 31.
    "Sibyl" (tr. by Steve Light). [InterPR] (21:1) Spr 95, p. 35.
    "La Sibylle." [InterPR] (21:1) Spr 95, p. 34.
4775. PARHAM, Robert
    "1959." [CharR] (21:1) Spr 95, p. 73.
    "Bent By Music." [FourQ] (9:1/2) Spr 95, p. 54.
    "From the Foyer." [LullwaterR] (6:2) Fall-Wint 95, p. 59.
    "My Grandfather's Office." [SouthernPR] (35:2) Wint 95, p. 28-29.
    "The Old Boy Who Walked the Road Away." [XavierR] (15:1) Spr 95, p. 42.
4776. PARINI, Jay
    "Street Boys." [BostonR] (20:3) Sum 95, p. 41.
4777. PARK, Alice
    "Moon" (after Paul Verlaine, 1844-1896). [Hellas] (6:1) Spr-Sum 95, p. 66.
4778. PARK, Anthony
    "Shadow of Wings." [SouthernHR] (29:2) Spr 95, p. 145.
    "Woodcraft." [LitR] (38:3) Spr 95, p. 418.
4779. PARK, Hee-Jin
    "Image of Buddha" (tr. by Chang Soo Ko). [Vis] (47) 95, p. 13.

4780. PARK, Hye Yung
"My Father's Hand" (The 1994 Allen Ginsberg Poetry Awards: Third Prize).
[Footwork] (24/25) 95, p. 185.
"A Photograph of My Mother" (The 1994 Allen Ginsberg Poetry Awards:
Honorable Mention). [Footwork] (24/25) 95, p. 201.
4781. PARKER, Alan Michael
"Up." [NewRep] (212:22) 29 My 95, p. 42.
"The Widow." [TriQ] (95) Wint 95-96, p. 215-218.
4782. PARKER, Aleksandra
"History" (tr. of Stanislaw Baranczak, w. Michael Parker). [Verse] (12:2) 95, p. 19.
4783. PARKER, Dorothy
"Bohemia" (September 17, 1927). [NewYorker] (71:1) 20-27 F 95, p. 185.
4784. PARKER, Emily
"Kandinsky Takes a Shower." [HangL] (66) 95, p. 90.
"Poised." [HangL] (66) 95, p. 89.
"Post-Winter Menu." [HangL] (66) 95, p. 88.
4785. PARKER, J. Roberts
"To the Romantic Writing Poetry in Hyde Park." [Dandel] (22:1) 95, p. 76-77.
4786. PARKER, Leslie
"Friday's." [CapeR] (30:1) Spr 95, p. 37.
4787. PARKER, Mary Elizabeth
"A Gargoyle Warns a Sculptor in His Loft" (Greensboro Review Literary Award
Poem). [GreensboroR] (59) Wint 95-96, p. 19.
"Mask" (from "Artists in Winter." 1995 Literary Contest: First Prize). [Crucible]
(31) Fall 95, p. 1-2.
4788. PARKER, Michael
"History" (tr. of Stanislaw Baranczak, w. Aleksandra Parker). [Verse] (12:2) 95, p.
19.
4789. PARKER, Pam A.
"Transgress, Transdress" (— Marjorie Garber, Vested Interests). [ParisR] (37:134)
Spr 95, p. 235.
4790. PARMAN, Susan
"The Poetry of Things (I)." [HiramPoR] (58/59) Spr 95-Wint 96, p. 65.
4791. PARMET, Harriet
"Hour of the Wolves" (tr. of Volker von Torne, w. Kathleen Szautner). [Vis] (47)
95, p. 14.
4792. PARRA, Nicanor
"Rest in Peace" (tr. by Edith Grossman). [RiverS] (42/43) 95, p. 79.
4793. PARRISH, Virginia
"Cousins." [WillowS] (35) Ja 95, p. 72-73.
4794. PARSON-NESBITT, Julie
"Poor Wolf." [ApalQ] (44/45) Fall 95-Wint 96, p. 68-69.
4795. PARSONS, Dave
"Comforter" (for Nancy). [TexasR] (16:1/4) 95, p. 141-142.
"Memories of Camp Mathews (1961) in Finnish Rhapsody." [TexasR] (16:1/4) 95,
p. 143.
4796. PARTRIDGE, Dixie
"After a Home Move from Kenya." [SouthernPR] (35:1) Sum 95, p. 26-27.
"Cattails." [SouthernPR] (35:1) Sum 95, p. 27-28.
"Early Memory" (Salt River Range, Wyoming). [Comm] (122:20) 17 N 95, p. 22.
"Pilgrimage." [Comm] (122:20) 17 N 95, p. 22.
"Through a Still October Air." [MidwQ] (37:1) Aut 95, p. 47.
4797. PASCHEN, Elise
"Angling." [Poetry] (165:5) F 95, p. 266.
"Home for Heart." [Nat] (258:2) 17 Ja 94, p. 60.
"My Father's Gun." [TriQ] (95) Wint 95-96, p. 94.
"Salvage." [Poetry] (165:5) F 95, p. 265-266.
"Stealing." [TriQ] (95) Wint 95-96, p. 95-96.
PASCHKE, Mona Toscano
See TOSCANO-PASCHKE, Mona
4798. PASOLD, Lisa
"Bone Biography." [Grain] (23:2) Aut 95, p. 55.
PASQUALE, Emanuel di
See Di PASQUALE, Emanuel
4799. PASS, John
"Catch and Release." [CapilR] (2:15) Spr 95, p. 12-13.

"Invocation to the Character of Water." [CapilR] (2:15) Spr 95, p. 5-7.
"Kleanza Creek." [CapilR] (2:15) Spr 95, p. 10-11.
"The Lost Rivers of London." [CapilR] (2:15) Spr 95, p. 8-9.
"Nozzle." [CapilR] (2:15) Spr 95, p. 16-17.
"Owl Clover" (for Solveigh Harrison). [CapilR] (2:15) Spr 95, p. 14-15.
"Reprieve for the Body." [CanLit] (145) Sum 95, p. 84-85.
"Sea Blush." [CapilR] (2:15) Spr 95, p. 18.
4800. PASSARELLA, Lee
"Beethoven's *Harp Quartet.*" [WindO] (60) Fall-Wint 95, p. 7.
"July Memorial." [LullwaterR] (6:1) Spr-Sum 95, p. 55.
"Magnetic North" (University of South Florida, St. Petersburg). [WindO] (60) Fall-Wint 95, p. 6-7.
"A Matter of Perspective." [ApalQ] (44/45) Fall 95-Wint 96, p. 67.
"Nachtstücke." [CreamCR] (19:1) Spr 95, p. 158.
"Restoring the Fairmount Waterworks" (Philadelphia, July 1990). [SmPd] (32:2, #94) Spr 95, p. 9.
4801. PASSAUZA-TEMPLETON, Ardis
"The Basement." [Footwork] (24/25) 95, p. 67.
"Funeral." [Footwork] (24/25) 95, p. 67.
4802. PASSIKOFF, Ben
"Black Burying Ground." [BlackBR] (21) Fall-Wint 95, p. 4.
"Black Burying Ground." [InterPR] (21:1) Spr 95, p. 71.
"Street Walker." [SmPd] (32:3, #95) Fall 95, p. 22.
"Windshield Washer." [BlackBR] (21) Fall-Wint 95, p. 35.
4803. PASTAN, Linda
"The Almanac of Last Things." [NewRep] (213:1) 3 Jl 95, p. 40.
"April Again." [PraS] (69:1) Spr 95, p. 81.
"Camping at the Headlands of the Rappahannock." [PlumR] (8) [95], p. 67.
"Cosmic Dust: For David." [VirQR] (71:1) Wint 95, p. 103.
"Dreaming of Rural America." [GeoR] (49:2) Sum 95, p. 399-400.
"Dreaming of Rural America." [Harp] (291:1745) O 95, p. 36.
"Meditation at 30,000 Feet." [PraS] (69:1) Spr 95, p. 82.
"Memory." [PlumR] (8) [95], p. 68.
"News of the World." [GeoR] (49:3) Fall 95, p. 580.
"Nocturnal." [Poetry] (166:4) Jl 95, p. 199.
"October Catechisms." [Image] (12) Wint 95-96, p. 21-22.
"On the Threshold of Silence." [PlumR] (8) [95], p. 66.
"The Recovery Zone." [PraS] (69:1) Spr 95, p. 82.
"The Rescue." [Witness] (9:2) 95, p. 180.
"Ruins." [VirQR] (71:1) Wint 95, p. 102-103.
"The Way Things Are." [PraS] (69:1) Spr 95, p. 83.
4804. PASTERNAK, Boris
"February" (tr. by Ruth Dubin). [DenQ] (29:4) Spr 95, p. 48.
"In Everything I Want to Reach" (tr. by Paul Friedrich). [LitR] (39:1) Fall 95, p. 62-63.
"July Storm" (tr. by Ruth Dubin). [DenQ] (29:4) Spr 95, p. 46-47.
"Winter Night" (tr. by Paul Friedrich). [LitR] (39:1) Fall 95, p. 61.
4805. PASTOR, Ned
"Distinguished But Indistinguishable." [Light] (13) Spr 95, p. 22.
4806. PASTOURMATZI, Donna
"The Only Human Voice" (tr. of Tolis Nikiforou, w. Michael Mott). [Vis] (48) 95, p. 23.
"A Transfusion of Light into Words" (tr. of Tolis Nikiforou, w. Michael Mott). [Vis] (48) 95, p. 23.
4807. PASTRONE, Nicolas
"Movies." [PoetryE] (40) Spr 95, p. 93.
4808. PATE, Alexs
"Great Plains African." [NorthStoneR] (12) 95, p. 232-233.
"Tan." [NorthStoneR] (12) 95, p. 233.
4809. PATERSON, Don
"19:00: Auchterhouse." [Verse] (12:2) 95, p. 112.
4810. PATT, Dave
"The Honeybee." [WestB] (37) 95, p. 44-45.
4811. PATTEN, Karl
"Tell Me What Testudo Means." [CharR] (21:1) Spr 95, p. 70.

4812. PATTEN, Leslie
"The Search." [ChironR] (43) Sum 95, p. 32.
4813. PATTERSON, Don
"Trains." [Footwork] (24/25) 95, p. 144.
4814. PATTERSON, Juliet
"Real Biography." [EvergreenC] (10:2) Sum-Fall 95, p. 84.
4815. PATTERSON, Raymond (Raymond R.)
"Harlem Suite." [Drumvoices] (4:1/2) Fall-Wint 94-95, p. 136-137.
"Law and Order: NYPD." [Drumvoices] (5:1/2) Fall-Wint 95-96, p. 109.
"Oklahoma City, April 19, 1995." [Drumvoices] (5:1/2) Fall-Wint 95-96, p. 110.
"Owning Up to Bill." [Elf] (5:4) Wint 95, p. 12.
4816. PATTON, Christopher
"Below the Skin the Planet Is Magnificent." [PoetryC] (15:3) Ag 95, p. 22.
"Freighters." [CanLit] (147) Wint 95, p. 23-24.
"October Explores the Forest." [PoetryC] (15:3) Ag 95, p. 22.
"Scratches on the Negative." [PoetryC] (15:3) Ag 95, p. 23.
4817. PATTON, Sarah
"After Listening to Segovia" (Second Place, The 1995 Defined Providence Poetry
Contest, Judged by Sean Thomas Dougherty). [DefinedP] (3) 95, p. 67-68.
"Conversations with Light." [DefinedP] (3) 95, p. 54-55.
"Hospital Nights." [DefinedP] (3) 95, p. 56-57.
"The Indigo Door." [DefinedP] (2:1) Fall-Wint 93, p. 8-9.
"Rain Trembles." [Conscience] (16:1/2) Spr-Sum 95, p. 17.
"The Unfinished Room." [DefinedP] (1:2) Spr-Sum 93, p. 36-37.
"Van Gogh's Trees Are Burning." [Conscience] (16:1/2) Spr-Sum 95, p. 9.
4818. PAU-LLOSA, Ricardo
"After Leaving Leroy Lashley's Surprise Birthday Party." [Crazy] (49) Wint 95, p.
22-23.
"The Hollow." [DenQ] (30:1) Sum 95, p. 86-87.
"Inner Ear." [DenQ] (30:1) Sum 95, back cover.
"Radio Man." [DenQ] (30:1) Sum 95, p. 88-89.
"Segovia" (for Sergio). [Journal] (19:2) Fall-Wint 95, p. 57-59.
"Self-Image." [Crazy] (49) Wint 95, p. 24.
4819. PAUL, Jay
"Tall House." [Shen] (45:1) Spr 95, p. 121-124.
4820. PAUL, Martin
"44. The moon passes like a chill between the marble statues" (tr. of Gabriel Celaya,
w. José Elgorriaga). [QW] (41) Aut-Wint 95-96, p. 204.
4821. PAULIN, Tom
"My Skelf." [Poetry] (167:1/2) O-N 95, p. 44-45.
4822. PAULSON, Elizabeth
"Mendocino Sister." [DogRR] (14:1, #27) Sum 95, p. 4.
PAUW, Dennis de
See DePAUW, Dennis
4823. PAVEL, Margaret M.
"A Seed." [SinW] (56) Sum-Fall 95, p. 28.
4824. PAVELICH, Joe
"White Humpback." [TarRP] (34:2) Spr 95, p. 32.
"Winter Hog." [TarRP] (34:2) Spr 95, p. 32-33.
4825. PAVESE, Cesare
"Earth and Death" (tr. by Geoffrey Brock). [InterQ] (2:1/2) 95, p. 57-62.
"La Terra e la Morte." [InterQ] (2:1/2) 95, p. 57-62.
4826. PAVLICH, Walter
"Almost Cold." [Manoa] (7:1) Sum 95, p. 27.
"Boy on a Cliff above the Sea." [PraS] (69:1) Spr 95, p. 119.
"Fragments from The Book of Conversions." [SouthernPR] (35:1) Sum 95, p. 13-14.
"Halos." [Witness] (9:1) 95, p. 130.
"Happy Days." [PraS] (69:1) Spr 95, p. 124-125.
"Incorrectness." [PraS] (69:1) Spr 95, p. 120-121.
"Minor Summer Revelations." [Witness] (9:1) 95, p. 131.
"Pulling Over the Car to Listen to Blackbirds." [Manoa] (7:1) Sum 95, p. 28.
"Readiness." [PraS] (69:1) Spr 95, p. 124.
"The Rose Unwatered." [PraS] (69:1) Spr 95, p. 121-122.
"Sitting Near Water from Onion Peak." [PraS] (69:1) Spr 95, p. 122-123.
"Under the Arbor." [Manoa] (7:1) Sum 95, p. 28.

4827. PAVLICK, Martha M.
"The House Grew Dark." [Rosebud] (2:3) Aut-Wint 95, p. 118.
4828. PAVLOV, Konstantin
"Cry of a Former Dog" (tr. by Ludmilla G. Popova-Wightman). [LitR] (39:1) Fall
95, p. 58-59.
"Souls Are Possessed by Angels" (tr. by Ludmilla G. Popova-Wightman). [LitR]
(39:1) Fall 95, p. 59.
"Sweet Agony" (tr. by Ludmilla G. Popova-Wightman). [LitR] (39:1) Fall 95, p. 57.
"Theatrical Appeal" (tr. by Ludmilla G. Popova-Wightman). [LitR] (39:1) Fall 95,
p. 58.
4829. PAWELCZAK, Andy
"Prayer to an Unknown God." [Footwork] (24/25) 95, p. 76.
"What I Want to Be in the Next Life." [Footwork] (24/25) 95, p. 76.
4830. PAWLAK, Mark
"Abuelito, Little Grandfather" (from "Chaletenango," 1980). [Noctiluca] (2:1, #4)
Spr 95, p. 39.
"Like Butterflies" (after Charles Reznikoff, for Donna Brook). [Noctiluca] (2:1, #4)
Spr 95, p. 38.
4831. PAYACK, Peter
"Darkness at Dawn." [Noctiluca] (2:1, #4) Spr 95, p. 25.
"Musing on a Poet's Life." [Noctiluca] (2:1, #4) Spr 95, p. 26.
4832. PAYNE, Gerrye
"Now." [GreenHLL] (6) 95, p. 107.
4833. PAZ, Octavio
"Last Night" (tr. by Jorge Travieso Ravelo). [RiverS] (42/43) 95, p. 7.
"Vertical Hour" (tr. by Jorge Travieso Ravelo). [RiverS] (42/43) 95, p. 7.
4834. PEABODY, Richard
"Guitar Player." [Bogg] (67) 95, p. 24.
"Stevie Crane." [Bogg] (67) 95, p. 24.
"Vinegar Poems." [BlackBR] (21) Fall-Wint 95, p. 6-7.
4835. PEACE, Barbara Colebrook
"Chinese Art Gallery, Victoria, B.C." (In memoriam Mr. Yu Wong Tam, 1905-
1992). [AntigR] (102/103) Sum-Aug 95, p. 145-146.
"Inuit Sculpture: Woman by Lucy Kanayok." [AntigR] (102/103) Sum-Aug 95, p.
147.
"Island." [AntigR] (102/103) Sum-Aug 95, p. 149.
"On Visiting an Exhibition of Antique Chinese Embroideries." [AntigR] (102/103)
Sum-Aug 95, p. 143-144.
"Trespasser." [AntigR] (102/103) Sum-Aug 95, p. 150.
"Visiting My Mother After Cancer Surgery." [AntigR] (102/103) Sum-Aug 95, p.
148.
"Wickaninnish." [MalR] (110) Spr 95, p. 104.
"You Are Here, the Sign Says." [MalR] (110) Spr 95, p. 105.
4836. PEACOCK, Molly
"Subway Vespers." [Verse] (12:2) 95, p. 113.
4837. PEACOCK, Thomas D.
"Places." [MidwQ] (36:4) Sum 95, p. 415-416.
4838. PEARCE, Dianne
"Longed For." [AnthNEW] (7) 95, p. 39.
4839. PEARLBERG, Gerry Gomez
"Botanical Gardens at Night" (After Pablo Neruda's "Ode with a Lament").
[GlobalCR] (6) Fall 95, p. 42-45.
"The Death of Superman." [ApalQ] (43) Spr 95, p. 40-41.
"Poison Arrow Tree Frogs." [Calyx] (16:1) Sum 95, p. 66-67.
4840. PEARN, Victor
"Mask Dance." [Parting] (8:2) Wint 95-96, p. 12.
4841. PEARSON, Miranda
"Another Day." [Dandel] (22:1) 95, p. 35.
"At the Pool." [MalR] (110) Spr 95, p. 114-115.
4842. PEASE, Peter
"Rostropovic in Red Square" (Excerpt). [AmerPoR] (24:6) N-D 95, p. 26.
4843. PECK, Gail J.
"Other Lives." [SouthernPR] (35:1) Sum 95, p. 42.
4844. PECK, John
"From the Headland at Cumae." [ParisR] (37:137) Wint 95, p. 110-112.

357

"Passage to the Islands" (in memoriam John Mattern). [Salm] (108) Fall 95, p. 89-90.
"Raina." [PartR] (62:3) Sum 95, p. 447-449.
"Trio Threaded on Lines from the Parthian Hymns." [Agni] (41) 95, p. 75-78.
4845. PECKHAM, Joel B. (Joel B., Jr.)
"Grackles — Waco, TX." [NewDeltaR] (12:2) Spr-Sum 95, p. 16-17.
"Painting the Garden." [TexasR] (15:3/4) Fall-Wint 94, p. 91.
4846. PECKHAM, Susan Atefat
"Stoning Soraya." [TexasR] (15:3/4) Fall-Wint 94, p. 92-93.
4847. PECOR, Amanda
"Dried Flowers and Dolls." [NewDeltaR] (12:1) Fall-Wint 94, p. 21.
"Life Story." [PassN] (16:2) Wint 95, p. 24-25.
"Mary Magdalene and Me." [Journal] (19:2) Fall-Wint 95, p. 17-20.
4848. PECQUET, James
"Across the Street." [ChrC] (112:27) 27 S-4 O 95, p. 876.
4849. PEDDLE, Marcus
"Your Country." [TickleAce] (27) Spr-Sum 94, p. 81.
4850. PEDERSON, Cynthia
"Through the High Plains" (for Kurt). [MidwQ] (36:4) Sum 95, p. 416-417.
4851. PEELER, Tim
"Late." [Bogg] (67) 95, p. 55.
PEENEN, H. J. van
See Van PEENEN, H. J.
4852. PEFFER, George
"Toaster." [NewMyths] (2:2/3:1) 95, p. 221-222.
4853. PEI-CHIEN CHU-CHIEN
"White Lotus" (tr. by Chris Laughrun). [LitR] (38:3) Spr 95, p. 334.
4854. PEIRCE, Kathleen
"Blessing the Throat." [Field] (53) Fall 95, p. 66.
"Dyke Breach." [ColR] (22:2) Fall 95, p. 114.
"Expulsion and Annunciation." [Field] (53) Fall 95, p. 65.
"His and Hers." [Field] (53) Fall 95, p. 64.
"Person, Place, Gesture, Thing." [Field] (53) Fall 95, p. 67-68.
"Round." [ColR] (22:1) Spr 95, p. 95.
"Wren." [Field] (53) Fall 95, p. 69.
4855. PELIZZON, V. Penelope
"Clever and Poor." [Ploughs] (21:1) Spr 95, p. 141-142.
"They Lived Here." [Ploughs] (21:1) Spr 95, p. 143-145.
4856. PELLETIERE, Marcia
"Hot." [Footwork] (24/25) 95, p. 23.
4857. PEMBER, John
"Aunt Haze: When It Was Summer." [Footwork] (24/25) 95, p. 176.
"The Two-Hole Caddy Stuck on a Eighteen-Hole Course." [Footwork] (24/25) 95, p. 176-177.
4858. PEÑALOSA, Joaquín Antonio
"Confesiones de Una Jícara Azteca." [AntigR] (102/103) Sum-Aug 95, p. 128.
"Confessions of an Aztec Chocolate-cup (Jícara)" (tr. by R. H. Morrison). [AntigR] (102/103) Sum-Aug 95, p. 129.
"I Am Going to Bid You Farewell" (tr. by R. H. Morrison). [AntigR] (102/103) Sum-Aug 95, p. 127.
"Voy a Decirte Adiós." [AntigR] (102/103) Sum-Aug 95, p. 126.
4859. PENDER, Bennetta
"Who Am I" (WritersCorps Program, Washington, DC). [WashR] (21:2) Ag-S 95, p. 17.
4860. PENDERGRAFT, Heather
"Daphne." [LullwaterR] (5:1) 93-94, p. 36-39.
"Rosa, Osijek Kolodvor." [SycamoreR] (7:1) Wint 95, p. 47-48.
4861. PENDERGRAST, Quintia
"Cinquain" (WritersCorps Program, Washington, DC). [WashR] (21:2) Ag-S 95, p. 11.
4862. PENICK, Robert L.
"Notes of a Drunken Writer." [ChironR] (44/45) Aut-Wint 95, p. 17.
4863. PENNA, Sandro
"And is there beauty still in this world?" (tr. by Blake Robinson). [Chelsea] (59) 95, p. 117.
"At noontime, can't you see" (tr. by Blake Robinson). [Chelsea] (59) 95, p. 118.

"The black train puffing smoke comes" (tr. by Blake Robinson). [Chelsea] (59) 95, p. 119.
"Filled with sun's scent, my testicles" (tr. by Blake Robinson). [Chelsea] (59) 95, p. 118.
"For Renzo Vespignani" (tr. by Blake Robinson). [Chelsea] (59) 95, p. 118-119.
"He brings a new boy" (tr. by Blake Robinson). [Chelsea] (59) 95, p. 117.
"It's a sunny land. Beneath it lies" (tr. by Blake Robinson). [Chelsea] (59) 95, p. 119.
"Just in this sweet jail I feel" (tr. by Blake Robinson). [Chelsea] (59) 95, p. 117.
"Lights beam on the riverside" (tr. by Blake Robinson). [Chelsea] (59) 95, p. 118.
"Love, that old love inclined to hardheadedness?" (tr. by Blake Robinson). [Chelsea] (59) 95, p. 119.
"September" (tr. by Blake Robinson). [Chelsea] (59) 95, p. 117.
"So many birthdays toasted at table" (tr. by Blake Robinson). [Chelsea] (59) 95, p. 119.
"Spring on my mind and happy" (tr. by Blake Robinson). [Chelsea] (59) 95, p. 118.
"They've severed the world" (tr. by Blake Robinson). [Chelsea] (59) 95, p. 119.
"This melody's of a sin" (tr. by Blake Robinson). [Chelsea] (59) 95, p. 119.
"Veiled with scent of crushed grapes" (tr. by Blake Robinson). [Chelsea] (59) 95, p. 117.
"You're in the train's voice way off" (tr. by Blake Robinson). [Chelsea] (59) 95, p. 117.

4864. PENNANT, Edmund
"Melpomene." [Confr] (56/57) Sum-Fall 95, p. 329.

4865. PENNINGTON, Debra
"Adam's Curse Revisited." [Hellas] (6:2) Fall-Wint 95, p. 72-73.

4866. PENNOYER, Victoria Parsons
"Wild Pear Trees in New York City." [Confr] (56/57) Sum-Fall 95, p. 341.

4867. PEOPLES, J.
"First the Spirit" (Honorable Mention, Jacaranda Poetry Contest). [Jacaranda] (11) [95 or 96?], p. 32-34.

4868. PEPPER, Patric
"Feeding the Ducks." [Hellas] (6:1) Spr-Sum 95, p. 44.

4869. PERCHAN, Robert
"Deconstruction." [ApalQ] (43) Spr 95, p. 42.
"Sin." [ProseP] (4) 95, p. 62.

PERCHICK, Simon
See PERCHIK, Simon

4870. PERCHIK, Simon
"#14. Listen to your tears: each river." [SoDakR] (33:3/4) Fall-Wint 95, p. 231-232.
"159. The tree still terrified, its veins." [HangL] (67) 95, p. 66.
"183. Knots stay put and travelers." [HangL] (67) 95, p. 65.
"193. That worn down metal frame, its propeller." [SilverFR] (25) Sum 95, p. 35.
"302. Just to put one hand on this table." [Parting] (8:1) Sum 95, p. 20.
"311. But no. That stare again: grinding down." [NewDeltaR] (12:2) Spr-Sum 95, p. 30.
"328. You must use shadows to build." [Parting] (8:2) Wint 95-96, p. 48.
"339. These cornerstones shrink and forget." [Parting] (8:2) Wint 95-96, p. 47.
"351. In this dark room two walls." [SantaBR] (3:1) Spr 95, p. 40.
"352. As if a comet unable to fly." [SantaBR] (3:1) Spr 95, p. 41.
"358. From this park bench." [SantaBR] (3:1) Spr 95, p. 42.
"466. So what the moon has no tides." [SilverFR] (25) Sum 95, p. 36-37.
"603. What you hear could be a mountain." [DefinedP] (1:1) Fall-Wint 92, p. 6.
"Always one will wipe your eyelids." [DefinedP] (1:2) Spr-Sum 93, p. 16.
"And this innocent lace curtain." [DefinedP] (2:1) Fall-Wint 93, p. 29-30.
"And though my lips are harmless now." [Quarry] (44:3) 95, p. 102.
"At least a dozen times." [ContextS] (4:2) 95, p. 11.
"Because there's only one East." [GreenMR] (8:2) Fall-Wint 95-96, p. 84.
"Because there's only one East." [PoetL] (90:1) Spr 95, p. 26.
"Cross-hairs, the slow calibrating turn." [AnotherCM] (29) Spr 95, p. 167.
"Don't even think about it!" [SouthernHR] (29:4) Fall 95, p. 344.
"The drowned remember this from stars." [SnailPR] (3:2) 95, p. 4.
"Each night these branches lift off." [Os] (40) 95, p. 34.
"Even in August its contrails." [Conduit] (3) Sum 95, p. 23.
"Even in the womb these leaves." [Quarry] (44:3) 95, p. 103.
"Even your stone is rotting." [PaintedB] (55/56) 95, p. 56.

"Inside this acorn the frozen call." [WilliamMR] (33) 95, p. 37.
"It's just a roof :the jacket." [Manoa] (7:1) Sum 95, p. 181.
"It's the limp, an invisible heel." [PoetL] (90:4) Wint 95-96, p. 42.
"M8. With the power that draws lips together." [SoDakR] (33:3/4) Fall-Wint 95, p. 230.
"Or paying off someone :each funeral" [sic]. [SnailPR] (3:2) 95, p. 5.
"The plank reaching down for waves." [PraS] (69:1) Spr 95, p. 117-118.
"The rain is slower at airports." [Farm] (13:2 [i.e. 12:2]) Fall-Wint 95, p. 72.
"Shameless! you rush one finger." [Quarry] (44:3) 95, p. 104-105.
"She uses only the generic, in time." [Manoa] (7:1) Sum 95, p. 180.
"That sugar too, should grieve." [DenQ] (30:2) Fall 95, p. 57.
"These two twigs can't move anymore." [PoetL] (90:1) Spr 95, p. 27.
"They must learn it from the sun." [PraS] (69:1) Spr 95, p. 116-117.
"They work these claims the way a hypnotist." [DogRR] (14:1, #27) Sum 95, p. 50.
"This flower pressing against my palms." [DefinedP] (2:1) Fall-Wint 93, p. 30.
"This shallow dish dead center." [Os] (41) 95, p. 15.
"The tree has no heat left." [PaintedB] (55/56) 95, p. 57.
"The tree has no heat left, and there." [NewL] (62:1) 96 (c1995), p. 116.
"The tree still terrified, its veins." [Conduit] (3) Sum 95, p. 22.
"Untitled: Even this phone, swollen the way all mothers." [PlumR] (9) [95 or 96], p. 20.
"W 50." [OhioR] (54) 95, p. 125.
"W29." [DenQ] (29:3) Wint 95, p. 29.
"You can read in this light :a face" [sic]. [DefinedP] (2:2) Spr-Sum 94, p. 41.
"You can read in this light :a face" [sic]. [OxfordM] (9:2) Fall-Wint 93, p. 10.
"You climb and these steps spread out." [Os] (41) 95, p. 14.
"You don't yell across a tree." [DenQ] (30:2) Fall 95, p. 56.
"You listen for a flower." [DefinedP] (2:2) Spr-Sum 94, p. 40.
"You shower the way a prisoner." [PaintedB] (55/56) 95, p. 58.
4871. PERDOMO, Willie
"The Making of a Harlem Love Poem." [Bomb] (52) Sum 95, p. 82.
"New Years Eve, 1990." [Bomb] (52) Sum 95, p. 82.
4872. PEREIRA, Edimilson de Almeida
"As Frutas." [Callaloo] (18:4) Fall 95, p. 887.
"Circle" (tr. by Steven F. White). [Callaloo] (18:4) Fall 95, p. 714.
"The Dancer" (tr. by Steven F. White). [Callaloo] (18:4) Fall 95, p. 716.
"Escola." [Callaloo] (18:4) Fall 95, p. 885.
"The Fruit" (tr. by Steven F. White). [Callaloo] (18:4) Fall 95, p. 715.
"Induca, Maria do Rosário" (in Portuguese). [Callaloo] (18:4) Fall 95, p. 1033.
"Induca, Maria do Rosário" (tr. by Phyllis Peres, w. Reetika Vazirani and Chi Lam). [Callaloo] (18:4) Fall 95, p. 873.
"Iron" (tr. by Steven F. White). [Callaloo] (18:4) Fall 95, p. 717.
"Matina" (A Núbia Pereira). [Callaloo] (18:4) Fall 95, p. 1032.
"Morning Prayer" (for Núbia Pereira, tr. by Phyllis Peres, w. Reetika Vazirani and Chi Lam). [Callaloo] (18:4) Fall 95, p. 872.
"O Ferro." [Callaloo] (18:4) Fall 95, p. 889.
"O Passista." [Callaloo] (18:4) Fall 95, p. 888.
"Ouro Preto" (in Portuguese). [Callaloo] (18:4) Fall 95, p. 1034.
"Ouro Preto: Interpretation Itinerary" (tr. by Phyllis Peres, w. Reetika Vazirani and Chi Lam). [Callaloo] (18:4) Fall 95, p. 874.
"Roda." [Callaloo] (18:4) Fall 95, p. 886.
"School" (tr. by Steven F. White). [Callaloo] (18:4) Fall 95, p. 713.
4873. PERES, Phyllis
"August" (tr. of Paulo Colina, w. Reetika Vazirani and Chi Lam). [Callaloo] (18:4) Fall 95, p. 734-735.
"Carnival" (tr. of Paulo Colina, w. Jane Kamide, Reetika Vazirani and Chi Lam). [Callaloo] (18:4) Fall 95, p. 736.
"Daily" (tr. of José Carlos Limeira). [Callaloo] (18:4) Fall 95, p. 817.
"Ejo-Lorun" (tr. of Ricardo Aleixo, w. Reetika Vazirani and Chi Lam). [Callaloo] (18:4) Fall 95, p. 800.
"Foreboding" (tr. of Paulo Colina, w. Jane Kamide). [Callaloo] (18:4) Fall 95, p. 733.
"Great Mother" (tr. of Ricardo Aleixo, w. Reetika Vazirani and Chi Lam). [Callaloo] (18:4) Fall 95, p. 799.
"Hallucinations" (tr. of Éle Semog). [Callaloo] (18:4) Fall 95, p. 754.

"I Am" (tr. of Oliveira Silveira, w. Reetika Vazirani and Chi Lam). [Callaloo] (18:4)
Fall 95, p. 813-814.
"In the Style of Alvaro de Campos" (tr. of Paulo Colina, w. Jane Kamide).
[Callaloo] (18:4) Fall 95, p. 737-738.
"Induca, Maria do Rosário" (tr. of Edimilson de Almeida Pereira, w. Reetika
Vazirani and Chi Lam). [Callaloo] (18:4) Fall 95, p. 873.
"Mariana and the Word, Another Name" (tr. of Éle Semog, w. Reetika Vazirani and
Chi Lam). [Callaloo] (18:4) Fall 95, p. 755.
"Morning Prayer" (for Núbia Pereira, tr. of Edimilson de Almeida Pereira, w.
Reetika Vazirani and Chi Lam). [Callaloo] (18:4) Fall 95, p. 872.
"Much to the Sea" (for a black woman, tr. of José Carlos Limeira, w. Reetika
Vazirani and Chi Lam). [Callaloo] (18:4) Fall 95, p. 818.
"Ouro Preto: Interpretation Itinerary" (tr. of Edimilson de Almeida Pereira, w.
Reetika Vazirani and Chi Lam). [Callaloo] (18:4) Fall 95, p. 874.
"This Is for You" (tr. of Éle Semog, w. Reetika Vazirani and Chi Lam). [Callaloo]
(18:4) Fall 95, p. 753.
"Types of Life" (tr. of Jônatas Conceição da Silva, w. Jane Kamide). [Callaloo]
(18:4) Fall 95, p. 773.
4874. PÉREZ, Ariel T.
"Americanais Marielito." [BilingR] (20:1) Ja-Ap 95, p. 70.
"Americanized Marielito." [BilingR] (20:1) Ja-Ap 95, p. 71.
PÉREZ, Francia Recalde
See RECALDE PÉREZ, Francia
4875. PÉREZ, Irene
"Closed Bodega." [BilingR] (20:2) My-Ag 95, p. 164-165.
4876. PEREZ, Michelle
"Poetry in Public Places" (3rd Place — 1995 CR Poetry Contest). [ChironR] (44/45)
Aut-Wint 95, p. 32.
4877. PÉREZ-BUSTILLO, Camilo
"These Trees" (tr. of Clemente Soto Vélez, w. Martín Espada). [MassR] (36:4) Wint
95-96, p. 641-649.
4878. PERILLO, Lucia Maria
"Inseminator Man" (Chapbook: 14 poems). [BlackWR] (22:1) Fall-Wint 95, p. 41-
71.
4879. PERKINS, James Ashbrook
"The Cold Is No Fiction." [US1] (30/31) 95, p. 7.
4880. PERKINS, Richard King, II
"Answering Winter." [InterPR] (21:1) Spr 95, p. 73.
4881. PERLMAN, John
"Most assuredly a human frailty." [Talisman] (15) Wint 95-96, p. 78.
"Poem: Among the worlds of yellow monarchs." [Noctiluca] (2:1, #4) Spr 95, p. 41.
4882. PERNICE, Joe
"Paper Country" (for Tim Liptak). [Agni] (41) 95, p. 104.
"Screws." [Agni] (41) 95, p. 103.
4883. PERONARD, Kai
"I Woke Up." [NewRena] (9:2, #28) Spr 95, p. 81.
"Nighttime." [NewRena] (9:2, #28) Spr 95, p. 80.
4884. PERRAULT, John
"Found Art." [SpinningJ] (1) Fall 95-Wint 96, p. 31.
4885. PERRINE, Laurence (1915-1995)
"The Dragon and the Dragoman" (Excerpt). [Light] (15/16) Aut-Wint 95-96, inside
back cover.
"Limerick." [Light] (15/16) Aut-Wint 95-96, p. 14.
"A Musing." [Light] (13) Spr 95, p. 18.
4886. PERRON, Lee
"Fall Arrives." [CharR] (21:2) Fall 95, p. 92.
"If God Is Love." [CharR] (21:2) Fall 95, p. 91.
"Karma." [CharR] (21:2) Fall 95, p. 90.
"Picasso's Women and the Dance of Shiva." [CharR] (21:2) Fall 95, p. 91.
"This Time with Fury." [CharR] (21:2) Fall 95, p. 93.
4887. PERRY, J. O.
"Passage to America" (tr. of Ayyappa Paniker, w. the author, Dakshinamoorthy, K.
Satchidanandan, and Esther Y. Smith). [ManyMM] (1:3) 95, p. 120-126.
4888. PERRY, Kirk Hamlin
"Tomato Soup." [PoetryE] (40) Spr 95, p. 94.

4889. PERRY, Mary Herrington
"Garden Verses." [Farm] (12:1) Spr-Sum 95, p. 21.
"The Good Man." [Farm] (12:1) Spr-Sum 95, p. 22-24.
4890. PERRY, Stephen
"Woodpecker." [PoetryE] (40) Spr 95, p. 95-96.
"You." [AntR] (53:2) Spr 95, p. 196.
4891. PERSAUD, Arlene
"My Name, Is Not Mary." [HangL] (66) 95, p. 91.
"Seventeen Years." [HangL] (66) 95, p. 92.
4892. PERSAUD, Sasenarine
"From Manhattan Meetings." [Arc] (34) Spr 95, p. 51-52.
"The Man Who Went over Niagara Falls in a Barrel." [Arc] (34) Spr 95, p. 49.
4893. PERSUN, Terry L.
"The Letter." [RagMag] (12:2) Spr 95, p. 85.
"Only So Far." [RagMag] (12:2) Spr 95, p. 84.
4894. PESSOA, Fernando
"The Gods Are Happy" (tr. by Richard Zenith). [PartR] (62:1) Wint 95, p. 107.
"I Got Off the Train" (as Alvaro de Campos, tr. by Richard Zenith). [PartR] (62:1)
Wint 95, p. 106.
4895. PESTANA, Emily
"Clearwater." [RagMag] (12:2) Spr 95, p. 94.
"Travel Size." [RagMag] (12:2) Spr 95, p. 95.
4896. PETERS, Erskine
"A Photographer Takes a Trip to Nicaragua." [XavierR] (15:2) Fall 95, p. 51-53.
4897. PETERS, John
"Bleak Homecoming" (tr. of Takamura Kotaro). [SpoonR] (20:1) Wint-Spr 95, p.
69.
"Chieko Playing Among the Plovers" (tr. of Takamura Kotaro). [TampaR] (10) Spr
95, p. 14.
"Chieko Riding on the Wind" (tr. of Takamura Kotaro). [TampaR] (10) Spr 95, p.
13.
"Invaluable Chieko" (tr. of Takamura Kotaro). [SpoonR] (20:1) Wint-Spr 95, p. 68.
"Lemon Dirge" (tr. of Takamura Kotaro). [TampaR] (10) Spr 95, p. 15.
"Record of One Day" (tr. of Takamura Kotaro). [TampaR] (10) Spr 95, p. 14.
"To One Who Has Died" (tr. of Takamura Kotaro). [SpoonR] (20:1) Wint-Spr 95, p.
70.
4898. PETERS, Kate
"Instant Matrimony" (tr. of Vidaluz Meneses). [HarvardR] (9) Fall 95, p. 97.
4899. PETERS, Michael
"The Moon's Hand." [SpinningJ] (1) Fall 95-Wint 96, p. 23.
"Poem for Lost Thoughts." [SpinningJ] (1) Fall 95-Wint 96, p. 24.
"Weekend Star, The Morning Edition." [SpinningJ] (1) Fall 95-Wint 96, p. 22.
4900. PETERS, Robert
"Another Poet Overnight Guest." [ChironR] (42) Spr 95, p. 25.
"Century." [JamesWR] (12:1) Wint 95, p. 1.
"Christmas Matters: For Charles Bukowski." [NewYorkQ] (55) 95, p. 49-50.
"Lines on an English Butcher Shop Window" (Christmas, 1966). [Bogg] (67) 95, p.
9.
"Mengele's Uterus: The Sex Life of J. Edgar Hoover: A Fairy Tale" (Excerpts).
[ConnPR] (14:1) 95, p. 18-20.
"On Stopping for Breakfast at the Mar-T Cafe, Great Bend Washington, of *Twin
Peaks* Fame." [Pearl] (22) Fall-Wint 95, p. 118-119.
4901. PETERSEN, Paulann
"The Day Jesus Became a Woman." [Pearl] (22) Fall-Wint 95, p. 9.
"Fabrication." [NewRep] (213:15) 9 O 95, p. 38.
4902. PETERSON, Allan
"500 Times." [OxfordM] (10:1) Wint 94-Spr 95, p. 54.
"Bird Houses by Mail." [IndR] (18:2) Fall 95, p. 154.
"Blessing the Fleet." [LullwaterR] (5:2) Fall-Wint 94, p. 8.
"Counting Backwards." [ManyMM] (2:1) 95, p. 27.
"Counting Daylights." [OxfordM] (10:1) Wint 94-Spr 95, p. 54.
"The Dark Related" (Finalist, 1995 Greg Grummer Award in Poetry). [Phoebe]
(24:2) 95, p. 186.
"Democracy." [RiverS] (45) 95, p. 25.
"Expecting the Momentous." [NewDeltaR] (13:1) Fall 95-Wint 96, p. 24.
"Foreign Affairs." [SouthernPR] (35:2) Wint 95, p. 12.

"Formal Is Helpless." [RiverS] (44) 95, p. 27.
"The Least of Our Worries" (Finalist, 1995 Greg Grummer Award in Poetry).
    [Phoebe] (24:2) 95, p. 185.
"LOGO" (Finalist, 1995 Greg Grummer Award in Poetry). [Phoebe] (24:2) 95, p.
    184.
"Pantheon." [LullwaterR] (5:2) Fall-Wint 94, p. 9.
"Streamlining." [NewDeltaR] (13:1) Fall 95-Wint 96, p. 25.
"Taking for Instance." [Sonora] (30) Fall 95, p. 72.
"Too Many to Remember." [PlumR] (8) [95], p. 5.
"Writing on Their Hands." [RiverS] (44) 95, p. 28.
4903. PETERSON, Jim
"Fish to Fry." [GeoR] (49:3) Fall 95, p. 684.
"The Part About Guns." [GeoR] (49:3) Fall 95, p. 685-686.
4904. PETERSON, Mark Fenlon
"A Day Away from Concrete." [SantaBR] (3:3) Fall-Wint 95, p. 70.
"The Orange Shark." [SantaBR] (3:3) Fall-Wint 95, p. 71.
"The Ride." [SantaBR] (3:3) Fall-Wint 95, p. 71.
4905. PETERSON, Robert
"Bean Hollow Beach, Starlight" (for Clem Starck). [HangL] (66) 95, p. 68.
"Iglesia de San Francisco (Oaxaca)." [HangL] (66) 95, p. 66.
"January 27." [HangL] (66) 95, p. 69.
"Nolo Contendere." [HangL] (66) 95, p. 70.
"Zócalo" (from Six Oaxaca Poems). [HangL] (66) 95, p. 67-68.
4906. PETRARCH, Francesco (1304-1374)
"Love delivers to me its sweetest thoughts" (tr. by Sam Hamill). [PoetryE] (41) Aut
    95, p. 24.
4907. PETRI, Domnita
"You Must Prove Yourself a Peaceful Animal Now" (tr. by Adam J. Sorkin and
    Ioana Ieronim). [Vis] (48) 95, p. 41-42.
4908. PETRI, György
"A Felismerés Fokozatai [The Degrees of Recognition]." [InterQ] (2:1/2) 95, p. 154.
"A M.-Nak." [InterQ] (2:1/2) 95, p. 150.
"Az Ilyen Fontos Beszélgetések [Such Important Conversations]." [InterQ] (2:1/2)
    95, p. 148.
"Ballad" (tr. by Bruce Berlind and Mária Körösy). [InterQ] (2:1/2) 95, p. 149.
"Ballada." [InterQ] (2:1/2) 95, p. 149.
"The Degrees of Recognition" (tr. by Bruce Berlind and Mária Körösy). [InterQ]
    (2:1/2) 95, p. 151-153.
"Staircase" (tr. by Bruce Berlind, w. Mária Körösy). [PoetryE] (39) Fall 94, p. 119.
"Such Important Conversations" (tr. by Bruce Berlind and Mária Körösy). [InterQ]
    (2:1/2) 95, p. 146-147.
"To M.A." (tr. by Bruce Berlind and Mária Körösy). [InterQ] (2:1/2) 95, p. 150.
4909. PETRIE, Marc
"Dust Clouds." [SantaBR] (3:2) Sum 95, p. 73.
"Walking Stick" (Ashville [sic], North Carolina, September 17, 1994). [SantaBR]
    (3:2) Sum 95, p. 72.
4910. PETRIE, Paul
"The Accounting." [Interim] (14:2) Fall-Wint 95-96, p. 10-12.
"The Bow of Ulysses." [SewanR] (103:3) Sum 95, p. 370.
"God on His Sleepless Nights." [LitR] (38:2) Wint 95, p. 205.
4911. PETRONIUS ARBITER (d. 66 CE)
"Doing, a Filthy Pleasure Is, and Short" (tr. by Sam Hamill). [PoetryE] (41) Aut 95,
    p. 16.
4912. PETROSKY, Anthony
"This was not in the dream, but in the wakening before the dream." [OhioR] (54) 95,
    p. 120-121.
4913. PETROUSKE, Rosalie Sanara
"Moon Through an Amber Glass." [SouthernPR] (35:1) Sum 95, p. 38-39.
4914. PETRUCCI, Marvyn
"Observing Life in the Nile from the Veranda of the Prince Albert Hotel at Abû-
    Hamed." [LouisL] (12:1) Spr 95, p. 62.
"The Woman Who Bumps Into Me." [SpinningJ] (1) Fall 95-Wint 96, p. 28.
4915. PETTIT, Michael
"Comus." [CharR] (21:1) Spr 95, p. 89-90.
"Fat Tuesday." [CharR] (21:1) Spr 95, p. 88.
"The Ides of July." [SouthernR] (31:1) Wint 95, p. 43.

"Rex." [CharR] (21:1) Spr 95, p. 89.
"River Road." [SouthernR] (31:1) Wint 95, p. 42-43.
"Wednesday." [CharR] (21:1) Spr 95, p. 90.
"Zulu." [CharR] (21:1) Spr 95, p. 88.
4916. PÉTURSSON, Hannes
"The Fourth Wise Man from the East" (tr. by Alan Boucher). [Vis] (47) 95, p. 13.
4917. PFEIFER, Teresa M.
"Moon Room." [PoetryE] (41) Aut 95, p. 92.
4918. PHAM, Tien Duat
"A Bridge" (tr. by Nguyen Quang Thieu and Kevin Bowen). [Manoa] (7:2) Wint 95, p. 167.
"In the Labor Market at Giang Vo" (tr. by Nguyen Ba Chung and Kevin Bowen). [Manoa] (7:2) Wint 95, p. 169.
"The Moon in Circles of Flame" (tr. by Nguyen Quang Thieu and Kevin Bowen). [Manoa] (7:2) Wint 95, p. 168.
"White Circle" (tr. by Nguyen Quang Thieu and Kevin Bowen). [Manoa] (7:2) Wint 95, p. 168.
4919. PHILIP, M. Nourbese
"Ignoring Poetry (a work in progress)." [Chain] (2) Spr 95, p. 184-187.
4920. PHILLIPPY, Patricia
"For Miryam" (décédée à son vingt-sexième anniversaire). [SpoonR] (20:2) Sum-Fall 95, p. 60.
"The Poet Downstairs." [SpoonR] (20:2) Sum-Fall 95, p. 61-62.
4921. PHILLIPS, Carl
"After Intercourse, PA." [RiverS] (45) 95, p. 65.
"Alba: Failure." [HarvardR] (9) Fall 95, p. 21.
"As From a Quiver of Arrows." [Atlantic] (276:4) O 95, p. 102.
"In the Borghese Gardens." [Boulevard] (10:1/2, #28/29) Spr 95, p. 137.
"Inset from the Night-Time Anatomy Lesson." [RiverS] (45) 95, p. 64.
"Meditation: The Veil Between." [Boulevard] (10:1/2, #28/29) Spr 95, p. 136.
"On Morals." [ParisR] (37:135) Sum 95, p. 208-209.
"The Sibyl." [TriQ] (95) Wint 95-96, p. 146-150.
"The Swain's Invention." [ParisR] (37:135) Sum 95, p. 207.
"Tunnel" (For Frank). [HarvardR] (9) Fall 95, p. 22-23.
"Where It Hurts." [Thrpny] (61) Spr 95, p. 26.
"Youth with Satyr, Both Resting." [ParisR] (37:135) Sum 95, p. 209-210.
4922. PHILLIPS, Jennifer M.
"Hernando: From the Diary of an AIDS Chaplain." [BlackBR] (20) Spr-Sum 95, p. 13.
4923. PHILLIPS, Louis
"5 Healthy Young Men Gather in a London Park and Labor Valiantly to Keep John Donne's Holy Sonnets from Falling Out of the Sky onto the Heads of Innocent Victims." [ChironR] (43) Sum 95, p. 17.
"11. The Krazy Kat Rag" (#29. To Be Continued in Light / 15). [Light] (14) Sum 95, p. 23.
"11. The Krazy Kat Rag" (#30-31. To Be Continued in Light / 17). [Light] (15/16) Aut-Wint 95-96, p. 33.
"12. The Krazy Kat Rag" (#28. To Be Continued in Light / 14). [Light] (13) Spr 95, p. 23.
"C.O.D." [Light] (15/16) Aut-Wint 95-96, p. 23.
"Even on Troubled Waters Someone Sails Out Too Far." [ChironR] (43) Sum 95, p. 17.
"If I'm Such a Legend Then Why Am I So Lonely?" (— Judy Garland). [SantaBR] (3:1) Spr 95, p. 68.
"Interim Report from the City of Certainties." [Footwork] (24/25) 95, p. 13.
"Johnny Inkslinger Attends the Grand Opening of a Giant Supermarket in Spokane." [Footwork] (24/25) 95, p. 13.
"Johnny Inkslinger Considers Himself in Relation to the Open Squares of Paris." [LiteralL] (1:5) Early Spr 95, p. 12.
"The Philosopher Pens His Love Letter." [SantaBR] (3:1) Spr 95, p. 69.
"Selling Wordsworth to the Modern Reader." [OxfordM] (10:1) Wint 94-Spr 95, p. 56.
"Three Clerihews." [Light] (13) Spr 95, p. 11.
"What Separates Fathers From Sons." [ChironR] (43) Sum 95, p. 17.
"What the Bat Thinks." [LiteralL] (1:5) Early Spr 95, p. 12.
"Whatever Is Behind Us." [SoCoast] (18) Ja 95, p. 3.

4924. PHILLIPS, Patrick
"Baptism." [QW] (41) Aut-Wint 95-96, p. 278.
4925. PHILLIPS, Robert
"Cherry Suite." [ParisR] (37:136) Fall 95, p. 148-149.
"A Pretty Mocking of the Life." [ParisR] (37:136) Fall 95, p. 150.
4926. PHILLIPS, Rod
"18 Below Zero: Jan. 19, 1994." [Farm] (13:2 [i.e. 12:2]) Fall-Wint 95, p. 38.
"Planting Asparagus." [Farm] (13:2 [i.e. 12:2]) Fall-Wint 95, p. 39.
4927. PHILLIPS, Walt
"Cacophony." [ChironR] (43) Sum 95, p. 30.
"Even More." [DogRR] (14:1, #27) Sum 95, p. 19.
"Good." [DogRR] (14:1, #27) Sum 95, p. 19.
"Language Arts." [Pearl] (22) Fall-Wint 95, p. 83.
"Perspectives." [WindO] (59) Spr 95, p. 6.
"Potting Soil Won't Touch Our Angst." [ChironR] (44/45) Aut-Wint 95, p. 39.
"Settling." [Bogg] (67) 95, p. 42.
"To Some Extent." [WindO] (59) Spr 95, p. 5.
"Year Seventeen As the Ongoing Went On." [WindO] (59) Spr 95, p. 5-6.
"The Years Flow and the People Cope." [Pearl] (22) Fall-Wint 95, p. 83.
4928. PHILODEMUS
"Nocturnal, two-horned Selene" (V. 123, tr. by Joseph S. Salemi). [CarolQ] (47:2)
Wint 95, p. 48.
4929. PHILPOT, Tracy
"A Victim in a Beautiful House" (for Jody). [DenQ] (29:3) Wint 95, p. 30-31.
4930. PHIPPS, Marilene
"The Bull at Nan Souvenance." [Callaloo] (18:2) Spr 95, p. 433-436.
"Haitian Masks." [Callaloo] (18:2) Spr 95, p. 431-432.
"My Life in Nerette." [Callaloo] (18:2) Spr 95, p. 437-438.
4931. PICANO, Felice
"His Secret" (after learning of R.F.'s diagnosis). [ConnPR] (14:1) 95, p. 31.
"Motet." [ConnPR] (14:1) 95, p. 32.
"My Mother's Life." [ConnPR] (14:1) 95, p. 33-35.
4932. PICARD, Meredith
"Bluebird." [HampSPR] Wint 95, p. 48.
4933. PICCIONE, Anthony
"Nightshift, Waiting for My Wife's Return." [AmerPoR] (24:3) My-Je 95, p. 6.
"Patching Little Things." [AmerPoR] (24:3) My-Je 95, p. 6.
"Poetry Reading: We Heard She Was Coming." [AmerPoR] (24:3) My-Je 95, p. 6.
"Standing Still." [AmerPoR] (24:3) My-Je 95, p. 6.
4934. PICKARD, Deanna
"Her Lips." [Poetry] (165:5) F 95, p. 272-273.
4935. PICKRELL, Lee Ann
"A History of Kisses." [SantaBR] (3:2) Sum 95, p. 75.
"Wood Rings." [SantaBR] (3:2) Sum 95, p. 76.
4936. PIERCY, Marge
"Body of Discontent." [ChironR] (42) Spr 95, p. 7.
"In the House of Three A.M." [Footwork] (24/25) 95, p. 1.
"One Bird, If There Is Only One, Dies in the Night." [Footwork] (24/25) 95, p. 1.
"Too Bad You Came in Late." [ManyMM] [1:1] D 94, p. 71-72.
"The Voice of the Grackle." [MassR] (36:2) Sum 95, p. 256-257.
"A Warm Place Becomes a Cold Place." [ChironR] (42) Spr 95, p. 7.
4937. PIERMAN, Carol J.
"Joy Rides." [SycamoreR] (7:2) Sum 95, p. 18-19.
"Perpetuum Mobile." [Iowa] (25:3) Fall 95, p. 155-157.
PIERO, W. S. di
   See Di PIERO, W. S.
4938. PIERRE, Charles
"A Feather for Gail." [SmPd] (32:3, #95) Fall 95, p. 24.
PIERRE, Matthew Scott la
   See LaPIERRE, Matthew S. (Matthew Scott)
4939. PIERRO, Albino
"Among People Laughing" (tr. by Luigi Bonaffini). [NewRena] (9:2, #28) Spr 95, p.
78.
"And What Am I?" (tr. by Luigi Bonaffini). [NewRena] (9:2, #28) Spr 95, p. 77.
"E Cché Sùu Ié?" [NewRena] (9:2, #28) Spr 95, p. 76.
"Nd' 'a' Gente Ca Rirìte." [NewRena] (9:2, #28) Spr 95, p. 78.

365

PITA

4940. PIGGFORD, George
"Eating Curry." [JamesWR] (12:2) Spr-Sum 95, p. 13.
"The First Coffin Returns to Elizabeth, PA." [JamesWR] (12:2) Spr-Sum 95, p. 13.
4941. PILKINGTON, Kevin
"On the Sidewalk." [SlipS] (15) 95, p. 15.
4942. PILKINTON, Mary Lou
"Cadillac Preacher" (runner up, 1994 Borderlands Poetry Contest). [Border] (6) Spr-
Sum 95, p. 59.
4943. PILLAT, Monica
"I Wish I Were the Earth" (tr. by Adam J. Sorkin and the author). [Vis] (48) 95, p.
42.
4944. PILLER, J. A.
"What Change Makes." [NortheastCor] (3) 95, p. 101.
4945. PILLING, Marilyn (Marilyn Gear)
"Father." [AntigR] (102/103) Sum-Aug 95, p. 16-17.
"Journey." [AntigR] (102/103) Sum-Aug 95, p. 18.
"Proof." [Dandel] (22:1) 95, p. 4.
4946. PINARD, Mary
"Dream Text." [PraS] (69:1) Spr 95, p. 131-132.
"The Permanence of Intimacy" (for Brian). [PraS] (69:1) Spr 95, p. 126-128.
"Still, the Circulation." [PraS] (69:1) Spr 95, p. 128-130.
"Thorn Abbesses, The Netherlands." [PoetryE] (40) Spr 95, p. 97-98.
4947. PINCKNEY, Diana
"Jordan." [Crucible] (30) Fall 94, p. 32-33.
"Lot's Wife Looks Back." [SouthernPR] (35:2) Wint 95, p. 60-61.
4948. PINE, John C.
"Night Game" (Third Prize, 1995 Poetry Contest). [Ledge] (19) Wint 95, p. 104-
105.
PING, Chou
See CHOU, Ping
4949. PING, Wang
"Song of Calling Souls (The Drowned voices from the *Golden Venture*)." [Sulfur]
(15:1, #36) Spr 95, p. 90-97.
4950. PINKER, Michael
"Leads." [Footwork] (24/25) 95, p. 167.
4951. PINO, José Manuel del
"Doré I" (tr. by G. J. Racz). [WorldL] (6) 95, p. 19.
"Elegy I" (tr. by G. J. Racz). [WorldL] (6) 95, p. 20-21.
"The Evening" (Pedra, auga, tr. by G. J. Racz). [WorldL] (6) 95, p. 19-20.
4952. PINSKER, Sanford
"Death Arrives As Flashback." [CharR] (21:1) Spr 95, p. 72.
4953. PINSKY, Robert
"The Ice-Storm" (In Memory of Bernie Fields). [NewRep] (213:26) 25 D 95, p. 40-
41.
"Impossible to Tell" (to Robert Hass and in memory of Elliot Gilbert). [Thrpny] (60)
Wint 95, p. 10-11.
"Round." [NewRep] (212:1) 2 Ja 95, p. 40.
"Serpent Knowledge." [War] (7:2) Fall-Wint 95, p. 45-49.
"The Tuning." [Atlantic] (275:4) Ap 95, p. 101.
"The Want Bone." [Verse] (12:2) 95, p. 114.
4954. PIOMBINO, Nick
"10 Forms of Distortion." [Avec] (10) 95, p. 140-142.
"Dust." [Avec] (10) 95, p. 144.
"The Mirror in the Eye." [Avec] (10) 95, p. 143.
"Sanctuary." [Avec] (10) 95, p. 138-139.
4955. PIPKIN, Marshall
"I." [BellArk] (11:6) N-D 95, p. 15.
"Night Sequence." [BellArk] (11:5) S-O 95, p. 16.
"Opening Evening Worship." [BellArk] (11:5) S-O 95, p. 25.
4956. PISCAL, Michael D.
"Discovering the Right Words." [BelPoJ] (45:3) Spr 95, p. 28-29.
4957. PITA, Juana Rosa
"Custodio de Juana Rosa." [LindLM] (14:1) Mr/Spr 95, p. 10.
"Una Estación en Tren." [Luz] (8) Spr 95, p. 20.
"Feliz Falta." [LindLM] (14:1) Mr/Spr 95, p. 10.
"Hasta Que el Destino." [Luz] (8) Spr 95, p. 22.

"Paradises of the Run" (tr. by Mario de Salvatierra). [Luz] (8) Spr 95, p. 25.
"Paraisos en Fuga." [Luz] (8) Spr 95, p. 24.
"Precaución." [LindLM] (14:1) Mr/Spr 95, p. 10.
"A Season in Train" (tr. by Mario de Salvatierra). [Luz] (8) Spr 95, p. 21.
"Umbral de lo Abierto." [LindLM] (14:1) Mr/Spr 95, p. 10.
"Until Destiny" (tr. by Mario de Salvatierra). [Luz] (8) Spr 95, p. 23.
4958. PITKIN, Anne
"Christmas, for the Daughter in Manhattan." [PraS] (69:3) Fall 95, p. 34-35.
4959. PITTENDRIGH, Nadya
"Dominique." [CutB] (42) Sum 94, p. 17-18.
"The Next General." [CutB] (42) Sum 94, p. 15-16.
4960. PITTS, David
"Red Shift." [WillowR] (22) Spr 95, p. 8.
"Red Touching Yellow Kill a Fellow." [WillowR] (22) Spr 95, p. 6-7.
4961. PLACE, M. J.
"Midnight." [Hellas] (6:1) Spr-Sum 95, p. 45.
"Postprandial." [Hellas] (6:1) Spr-Sum 95, p. 46.
"'The Mount' in October." [PoetL] (90:3) Fall 95, p. 32.
PLASSE, Kelly vande
    See Vande PLASSE, Kelly
4962. PLASTIRA, Alexandra
"A Few Years Hence" (tr. by Yannis Goumas). [Vis] (48) 95, p. 22.
"Recovery" (tr. by Yannis Goumas). [Vis] (48) 95, p. 22.
4963. PLATT, Donald
"Bow." [WestHR] (49:3) Fall 95, p. 217-218.
"Glass Breaking." [WestHR] (49:3) Fall 95, p. 212-213.
"Nassau, 1956." [WestHR] (49:3) Fall 95, p. 218-219.
"Night Janitors." [WestHR] (49:3) Fall 95, p. 214-215.
"Paperweight." [WestHR] (49:3) Fall 95, p. 215-216.
4964. PLAYER, William
"Apartment Building." [SlipS] (15) 95, p. 10.
4965. PLEIMANN, John
"Had Anyone Cared to Listen." [CimR] (111) Ap 95, p. 77.
"Still Moving." [DefinedP] (3) 95, p. 8-9.
PLESSIS, Rachel Blau du
    See DuPLESSIS, Rachel Blau
4966. PLIURA, Vytautas
"Thomas." [ChironR] (43) Sum 95, p. 8-9.
4967. PLUMB, David
"Yellow." [SantaBR] (3:3) Fall-Wint 95, p. 115-116.
4968. PLUMLY, Stanley
"Canto XVIII, from The Inferno" (tr. of Dante Alighieri). [OhioR] (54) 95, p. 32-35.
"Keats in Burns Country." [Field] (53) Fall 95, p. 86-87.
"Nobody Sleeps." [AmerPoR] (24:6) N-D 95, p. 60.
4969. PLUMMER, Deb
"Navigation." [CapeR] (30:2) Fall 95, p. 25.
4970. PLUMMER, Pamela
"Crazy Woman Blues (or Blue Gardenia Blues)." [Drumvoices] (4:1/2) Fall-Wint
    94-95, p. 131.
"Upsouth Sister Blues" (for some Buffalo girls). [Drumvoices] (4:1/2) Fall-Wint 94-
    95, p. 130.
4971. PLUMPP, Sterling
"Poet" (for Thebe Neruda). [TriQ] (94) Fall 95, p. 113-115.
"When the Spirit Spray-Paints the Sky" (for Moagi, 1994). [TriQ] (94) Fall 95, p.
    116-119.
PO, Chu-i
    See BAI, Juyi
PO, Chü-yi
    See BAI, Juyi
PO, Li
    See LI, Po
4972. POBO, Kenneth
"Apple Tree." [FreeL] (14) Wint 95, p. 11.
"At Greyfriar's Bobby's Pub, Edinburgh." [ModernW] (3) Sum 95, p. 31.
"Chrysanthemums Coming." [DefinedP] (2:1) Fall-Wint 93, p. 19.
"Ibises for Camille." [ModernW] (3) Sum 95, p. 32-33.

"Kitchen Silences." [WeberS] (12:2) Spr-Sum 95, p. 47-48.
"Me, Harry Milgarten." [IllinoisR] (3:1/2) Fall 95-Spr 96, p. 53-54.
"Pointed Toes." [FreeL] (14) Wint 95, p. 10.
4973. POCH, John
"Disturbance." [WillowS] (35) Ja 95, p. 41.
4974. POILE, Craig
"Accommodations." [MalR] (110) Spr 95, p. 96.
4975. POLA
"The Kitchen Sink." [SinW] (56) Sum-Fall 95, p. 39.
4976. POLINER, Elizabeth
"East Hampton, Connecticut, 1977." [SenR] (25:2) Fall 95, p. 102.
4977. POLITO, Robert
"Overheard in the Love Hotel." [Bomb] (53) Fall 95, p. 32.
4978. POLLACK, Neal
"Sorts Meltdown" (from "The Ultimate Sports Poem," a found poem, assembled out
of sentences culled from nearly a year's worth of columns by Chicago Sun-
Times sportswriter Jay Mariotti). [Harp] (290:1738) Mr 95, p. 22-23.
4979. POLLET, Sylvester
"Dandelion Sutra #5." [Light] (14) Sum 95, p. 16.
"Sixty, Oh Dear!" (for Charlotte Herbold). [Light] (13) Spr 95, p. 9.
4980. POLLOCK, Dennis
"Pulse." [Blueline] (16) 95, p. 31.
4981. POMPEY, Tim
"Ojai Schoolhouse, 1905." [SantaBR] (3:3) Fall-Wint 95, p. 69.
4982. POND, Judith
"Blastocyst." [MalR] (111) Sum 95, p. 92.
4983. PONOS, Roman S.
"City of Lions (Heroes)." [PoetL] (90:1) Spr 95, p. 15.
4984. PONSON, Alvin, Jr.
"Home Bitter Home" (WritersCorps Project, Washington, DC). [WashR] (21:2) Ag-
S 95, p. 20.
PONT, Lonnie Hull du
See DuPONT, Lonnie Hull
4985. POOL, Michael
"The Sweet Decay of Hitsville." [TampaR] (10) Spr 95, p. 51.
4986. POOLE, Francis
"Left Eye Moon." [PoetL] (90:1) Spr 95, p. 46.
4987. POOLE, Joan Lauri
"Hold on to my hair." [Bogg] (67) 95, p. 38.
"Transcendentalists." [LitR] (38:2) Wint 95, p. 206.
4988. POOLOS, James
"1945." [PoetryE] (40) Spr 95, p. 99.
"Balthus' Girls." [PoetryE] (40) Spr 95, p. 102.
"Pastoral." [PoetryE] (40) Spr 95, p. 100-101.
4989. POOM, Ritva
"How the Seasons Change" (tr. of Eeva-Liisa Manner). [LitR] (38:3) Spr 95, p. 349.
4990. POPE, Deborah
"The Call." [Calyx] (16:2) Wint 95-96, p. 72-73.
"Exotic Nights at the Savoy, or a Footnote to the History of British Imperialism."
[LitR] (38:3) Spr 95, p. 364-365.
"Getting Through." [Poetry] (165:5) F 95, p. 260.
"In Dark Weather." [Poetry] (165:5) F 95, p. 258-259.
"Killing the Copperheads." [SouthernHR] (29:3) Sum 95, p. 238-239.
"The Last Animal Dies in the Sarajevo Zoo." [SouthernR] (31:1) Wint 95, p. 44-45.
"On the Shore." [PraS] (69:1) Spr 95, p. 149-150.
"Resolution." [Poetry] (165:5) F 95, p. 257-258.
"Room of Shadows." [SouthernHR] (29:1) Wint 95, p. 54.
"Sunday, Villefranche." [PraS] (69:1) Spr 95, p. 150-151.
4991. POPE, Deidre
"Daughter's Laughter." [SpoonR] (20:2) Sum-Fall 95, p. 98-99.
"Good Woman." [PoetL] (90:2) Sum 95, p. 19.
"Pudding." [SpoonR] (20:2) Sum-Fall 95, p. 96-97.
4992. POPE, Jacquelyn
"Alchemy." [CreamCR] (19:1) Spr 95, p. 109.
"Escape Artist." [CreamCR] (19:1) Spr 95, p. 108.

4993. POPOVA-WIGHTMAN, Ludmilla G.
"Cry of a Former Dog" (tr. of Konstantin Pavlov). [LitR] (39:1) Fall 95, p. 58-59.
"Don't ask the dragon-fly" (tr. of Danila Stoianov). [Vis] (48) 95, p. 11.
"Memory of a Dream" (tr. of Danila Stoianova). [US1] (30/31) 95, p. 17.
"Memory of a Dream" (tr. of Danila Stoianova). [Vis] (48) 95, p. 11.
"Souls Are Possessed by Angels" (tr. of Konstantin Pavlov). [LitR] (39:1) Fall 95, p.
    59.
"Sweet Agony" (tr. of Konstantin Pavlov). [LitR] (39:1) Fall 95, p. 57.
"Theatrical Appeal" (tr. of Konstantin Pavlov). [LitR] (39:1) Fall 95, p. 58.
4994. PORCH, Lottie E.
"Bitch?" [Footwork] (24/25) 95, p. 19.
"Blanco." [Footwork] (24/25) 95, p. 19.
"Buggin'." [Footwork] (24/25) 95, p. 19-20.
"A Daughter's Prayer." [Footwork] (24/25) 95, p. 20.
"Roundabout Table Love." [Footwork] (24/25) 95, p. 18-19.
4995. POREÉ, Kerry
"New Orleans." [XavierR] (15:2) Fall 95, p. 67-68.
4996. PORTER, Anne
"Five Wishes." [Comm] (122:18) 20 O 95, p. 14.
"A Safe Neighborhood." [Comm] (122:13) 14 Jl 95, p. 16.
"Summer Cottage." [Comm] (122:12) 16 Je 95, p. 15.
4997. PORTER, Browning
"Geranium." [NewEngR] (17:1) Wint 95, p. 149.
"Poem to Whisper in the Ear of a New Acquaintance." [PoetryE] (39) Fall 94, p. 71.
"The Poet Flexes His Magnanimity." [PoetryE] (39) Fall 94, p. 72.
4998. PORTER, Caryl
"The Way It Was in Nebraska." [MidwQ] (36:4) Sum 95, p. 418-419.
4999. PORTER, Helen
"The Bewilderbeast." [SinW] (55) Spr-Sum 95, p. 84.
"Moonlight begins to dance on a carpet of verdant moss." [SinW] (55) Spr-Sum 95,
    p. 83.
"Pain begets pain." [SinW] (55) Spr-Sum 95, p. 83.
5000. PORTER, Peter
"The Chair of Babel." [Verse] (12:2) 95, p. 115-117.
"The Lion of Antonello Da Messina." [Epoch] (44:3) 95, p. 305.
"Men Die, Women Go Mad." [Epoch] (44:3) 95, p. 304.
5001. PORTERFIELD, Susan
"About Suffering" (Rwanda 1994). [Nimrod] (39:1) Fall-Wint 95, p. 115.
5002. PORTS, Kim
"Keeping House Like Hestia." [MidwQ] (36:4) Sum 95, p. 419-420.
"Summer Storms." [Blueline] (16) 95, p. 32-33.
5003. POSANKA, Elaine
"China Futures." [SouthernHR] (29:3) Sum 95, p. 249.
5004. POSTON, Beverly J.
"Crow." [OxfordM] (10:1) Wint 94-Spr 95, p. 55.
5005. POTOS, Andrea
"Bride of Christ." [CimR] (113) O 95, p. 60.
"Yaya's Sweets." [Calyx] (16:2) Wint 95-96, p. 30.
5006. POTTER, Carol
"My Father, Dressed Like Trees." [MassR] (36:4) Wint 95-96, p. 562-563.
"Waiting for Seven Birds to Fly in from Utica." [SouthernPR] (35:2) Wint 95, p. 24-
    26.
5007. POTTER, G. W.
"Portraits of England: Place Names." [NewL] (61:4) 95, p. 90.
5008. POTTER, Jacklyn W.
"Para Alguien" (tr. of Rebeccah Watson, grade 4, Key Elementary, Washington,
    DC, Poetry on the Metro Project). [WashR] (21:2) Ag-S 95, p. 15.
5009. POTTS, Randall
"Canzone." [ColR] (22:1) Spr 95, p. 104-106.
5010. POWELL, Dannye Romine
"She Never Thought of Vegetables." [Poetry] (166:2) My 95, p. 95.
5011. POWELL, David
"Those who Eat the Days in Order." [SpinningJ] (1) Fall 95-Wint 96, p. 18.
5012. POWELL, Lynn
"Manna." [GettyR] (8:3) Sum 95, p. 420-421.
"Preparation for an Elegy" (For Doug). [Poetry] (166:3) Je 95, p. 140.

"Promised Land." [GettyR] (8:3) Sum 95, p. 422.
5013. POWELL, R. J.
"The Beach." [Event] (24:1) Spr 95, p. 39.
"A Garden." [Event] (24:1) Spr 95, p. 38.
"The Room." [Event] (24:1) Spr 95, p. 40.
5014. POWER, Marjorie
"Bird House in Autumn." [Conscience] (16:3) Aut 95, p. 18.
"The Blonde and Tishku." [SpoonR] (20:2) Sum-Fall 95, p. 134-135.
"Chips of Oracle from a Red Landscape." [SouthernPR] (35:2) Wint 95, p. 70-71.
"Study in Brown." [Conscience] (16:1/2) Spr-Sum 95, p. 25.
5015. POZ (Magazine)
"The Board of Ed thought that haiku could stop HIV." [Poz] (7) Ap-My 95, p. 28.
5016. POZZI, Catherine
"Nyx" (tr. by Louis Simpson). [HarvardR] (9) Fall 95, p. 64.
5017. PRADO, Holly
"Euridice Talks About Her Choice of Contemplation." [ConnPR] (14:1) 95, p. 7.
"A Man Kneels in the Grass." [ConnPR] (14:1) 95, p. 8.
"No God Is Local" (for Harry Northup). [ConnPR] (14:1) 95, p. 6.
"Our Panic When the God Himself Is Slain." [DenQ] (30:1) Sum 95, p. 90-91.
"This God's Music Is My Lost Face." [ConnPR] (14:1) 95, p. 5.
"Van Gogh Recovers." [DenQ] (30:1) Sum 95, p. 92-93.
5018. PRAHLAD, Swami Anand
"Caravanserai" (for Osho). [ManyMM] (2:1) 95, p. 108-109.
"Saint Judas" (for Nick). [ManyMM] (2:1) 95, p. 106-107.
5019. PRAISNER, Wanda S.
"The Coal Man by the Cellar Chute." [Footwork] (24/25) 95, p. 166.
"How Are You?" [US1] (30/31) 95, p. 4.
"Sleeping at Aunt Helen's." [Footwork] (24/25) 95, p. 166.
5020. PRATHER, David B.
"Thin Leaves, Simple Blooms." [Border] (7) Fall-Wint 96, p. 48.
5021. PRATT, Charles W.
"Afterwards, in the Parish Hall." [ChrC] (112:6) 22 F 95, p. 206.
"Grapevine." [ChrC] (112:20) 21-28 Je 95, p. 641.
"The House by the Railroad Tracks." [Hellas] (6:2) Fall-Wint 95, p. 79.
"When in Dublin" (Second Prize, 3rd Annual River Rhyme Competition). [Light]
(13) Spr 95, p. 24.
5022. PRATT, Minnie Bruce
"At Deep Midnight." [NewEngR] (17:2) Spr 95, p. 144-146.
"The Road to Selma." [AmerV] (36) 95, p. 100-103.
5023. PRAY, Bethany
"In Dream, in the Eden." [VirQR] (71:1) Wint 95, p. 115-116.
5024. PREFONTAINE, Jay
"Kissing Gamma Jean." [AlabamaLR] (9:1) 95, p. 26-28.
5025. PREFONTAINE, Joan Wolf
"Listening to Wild Turkeys." [MidwQ] (36:4) Sum 95, p. 420-421.
5026. PRENDI, Arben
"Saturday Disgouring the Week" (tr. by Ilir Ikonomi). [Vis] (48) 95, p. 6.
5027. PRESCOTT, Howard
"Kui Lee." [WilliamMR] (33) 95, p. 68.
5028. PRESLEY, Frances
"The Deluge." [Os] (40) 95, p. 2.
"The Girl's Dress" (from an etching by Irma Irsara). [Os] (41) 95, p. 31.
"This March" (for Elaine Randall). [Os] (41) 95, p. 29.
5029. PRESNELL, Barbara
"New Moon." [Wind] (75) Spr 95, p. 17-19.
"Sea Turtle Hatching." [Wind] (75) Spr 95, p. 20.
5030. PRESS, Karen
"Greenhouse." [Dandel] (22:1) 95, p. 68.
5031. PREWITT, Leah J.
"Daddy's Time." [CumbPR] (15:1) Fall 95, p. 37-38.
5032. PRICE, Laurie
"The History of Cobalt Blue." [HeavenB] (12) 95, p. 63-64.
"Straightedge." [NewAW] (13) Fall-Wint 95, p. 116.
"To Dream All Night of What Is Watching Us and Say the Name Is an Invitation."
[HeavenB] (12) 95, p. 65.

5033. PRICE, Reynolds
"An Actual Temple" (For Douglas Paschall). [Poetry] (166:2) My 95, p. 69-71.
"F. H. Again." [Shen] (45:3) Fall 95, p. 103.
"Recumbent, Sleeping." [Shen] (45:3) Fall 95, p. 102.
"Twenty-One Years." [SouthernR] (31:1) Wint 95, p. 46-47.

5034. PRILLWITZ, Roxanne
"Ann Hedonia." [PassN] (16:1) Sum 95, p. 27.
"Ann Hedonia Remembers Her Childhood." [PassN] (16:1) Sum 95, p. 25.
"Ann on the Farm." [PassN] (16:1) Sum 95, p. 26.

PRIMA, Diane di
   See Di PRIMA, Diane

5035. PRIME, Patricia
"Woman Posing" (from a painting by Ingres). [Bogg] (67) 95, p. 58.

5036. PRINCE, Heather Browne
"After Wind, the Cessation" (inspired by "The Peninsula," Seamus Heaney).
   [PoetryC] (15:3) Ag 95, p. 28.
"The Man, the Woman, the Dog." [AntigR] (102/103) Sum-Aug 95, p. 163.
"Seeing the World." [AntigR] (102/103) Sum-Aug 95, p. 164.

5037. PRINTZ-PAHLSON, G.
"Mozart Variation #7" (tr. of Goran Sonnevi, w. John Mathais [sic]). [Vis] (49) 95,
   p. 35.
"Mozart Variation #8" (tr. of Goran Sonnevi, w. John Mathais [sic]). [Vis] (49) 95,
   p. 35.
"Mozart Variation #12" (tr. of Goran Sonnevi, w. John Matthais [sic]). [Vis] (47)
   95, p. 11.

5038. PRITCHARD, Selwyn
"Bloody Metaphors." [PartR] (62:1) Wint 95, p. 121.

5039. PRIVETT, Katharine
"Tumult." [FourQ] (9:1/2) Spr 95, p. 53.

5040. PRIVETT, Katherine
"Smiles of the Traveling Show." [SpoonR] (20:1) Wint-Spr 95, p. 66-67.

5041. PROFFITT, James S.
"Untitled: This is how she loves." [Plain] (16:1) Fall 95, p. 13.

5042. PROPER, Stan
"Taking Risks." [Pearl] (22) Fall-Wint 95, p. 88.

5043. PROSNITZ, Howard
"Payne Whitney" (After reading James Schuyler's Payne Whitney Poems). [JINJPo]
   (17:2) Aut 95, p. 36.

5044. PROTOPOPESCU, Orel
"Dream of Exile." [SpoonR] (20:1) Wint-Spr 95, p. 80-81.

5045. PRUFER, Kevin
"1979" (For Jason). [LitR] (39:1) Fall 95, p. 36-37.
"My Father Recounts a Story from His Youth." [SouthernR] (31:2) Ap/Spr 95, p.
   274-276.
"My Sister and the Mist." [SouthernPR] (35:2) Wint 95, p. 26-27.
"Returning to Friedrichskoog with Erika." [Chelsea] (58) 95, p. 56.
"The Underground Tunnel." [FourQ] (9:1/2) Spr 95, p. 46.
"Winter in Devessey." [TexasR] (16:1/4) 95, p. 144-145.
"You Are Talking to Another Man at the Party." [SouthernR] (31:2) Ap/Spr 95, p.
   276-277.

5046. PRUNTY, Wyatt
"A Box of Leaves." [Verse] (12:2) 95, p. 118.
"Dog, Dog, Object, Object." [SouthernR] (31:1) Wint 95, p. 49-50.
"Driving the Christmas Lights." [Image] (11) Fall 95, p. 12-14.
"The God Doll." [SouthernR] (31:1) Wint 95, p. 48-49.
"Recumbent Angels." [Image] (11) Fall 95, p. 14.
"To My Son." [Image] (11) Fall 95, p. 11-12.

5047. PUCCIANI, Donna
"Perpetual Motion." [CapeR] (30:1) Spr 95, p. 24-25.

5048. PUGH, Sheenagh
"The Frozen." [Epoch] (44:3) 95, p. 311.
"The Old Road." [Epoch] (44:3) 95, p. 310.

5049. PURDY, Al
"On Being Human." [SouthernR] (31:4) O/Aut 95, p. 901-902.
"Procne into Robin." [SouthernR] (31:4) O/Aut 95, p. 900-901.

5050. PURDY, Arthur
"Old Man with a Beach Ball." [AmerS] (64:3) Sum 95, p. 422.
5051. PURISCH, Moyses
"Dead Cat Sonnet" (tr. of Vincius de Moraes, w. Thomas Dorsett). [WillowS] (36)
Je 95, p. 94.
5052. PURPURA, Lia
"All Souls' Day on the Bay" (tr. of Grzegorz Musial). [WillowS] (36) Je 95, p. 75.
"Charlottenburg — the Park Scenes" (tr. of Grzegorz Musial). [WillowS] (36) Je 95,
p. 78-79.
"Death in Berlin" (tr. of Grzegorz Musial). [WillowS] (36) Je 95, p. 76-77.
"Untitled: In this house lived Stein the merchant" (tr. of Grzegorz Musial).
[WillowS] (36) Je 95, p. 74.
"Untitled: Sweating the dark one" (tr. of Grzegorz Musial). [WillowS] (36) Je 95, p.
80.
5053. PUSHKIN, Alexander S.
"Romanc" (in Russian). [HayF] (17) Fall-Wint 95, p. 18, 20.
"Romance" (tr. by Lee B. Croft). [HayF] (17) Fall-Wint 95, p. 19, 21.
5054. PUTNAM, C. E.
"2000 LOVE 2000." [Phoebe] (24:2) 95, p. 57.
"An Unknown Happening in Yugoslavia 1914." [Phoebe] (24:2) 95, p. 58.
"What Ever Happened to Uncle Wayne?" [Phoebe] (24:2) 95, p. 56.

QI, Li
See LI, Qi
QI-JIAO, Cai
See CAI, Qijiao
5055. QIAN, Zhaoming
"Parting in the Rain" (tr. of Shu Ting, w. John Blair). [PoetryE] (39) Fall 94, p. 122.
"This, Too, Is Everything" (In Response to a Young Friend's "Everything," tr. of
Shu Ting, w. John Blair). [PoetryE] (39) Fall 94, p. 123-124.
QINGZHI, Wei
See WEI, Qingzhi
5056. QIU, Xiaolong
"Lines in Another Land" (For Guangming). [PraS] (69:3) Fall 95, p. 43-45.
"Stamp." [PraS] (69:3) Fall 95, p. 40-41.
"To Xiangxiang." [PraS] (69:3) Fall 95, p. 39-40.
"When I Was Conceived." [PraS] (69:3) Fall 95, p. 41-42.
5057. QUAGLIANO, Tony
"Letter from Hawaii to David Ray." [SouthernPR] (35:1) Sum 95, p. 61-62.
"Post Op." [ArtfulD] (28/29) 95, p. 103.
5058. QUAN, Andy
"Condensation." [EvergreenC] (10:2) Sum-Fall 95, p. 85.
5059. QUASIMODO, Salvatore
"Tollbridge" (tr. by William Wells). [OhioR] (54) 95, p. 31.
5060. QUATRONE, Chriss-Spike
"Angst (Not)." [Plain] (16:1) Fall 95, p. 15.
5061. QUEEN, Karen
"Last Visit." [FreeL] (15) Aut 95, p. 14-15.
5062. QUESENBERRY, Mattie F.
"A Child, Grown Invisible Beneath Colors." [SouthernPR] (35:1) Sum 95, p. 43.
5063. QUEYRAS, Sina
"Night Road." [MalR] (110) Spr 95, p. 113.
"Walking on Fire." [MalR] (110) Spr 95, p. 112.
5064. QUICK, Dan
"Study for La Vie." [ParisR] (37:135) Sum 95, p. 91.
"La Vie." [ParisR] (37:135) Sum 95, p. 91-92.
5065. QUINLAN, Alexis
"This Is Glistening, This Is Bright, Follow It." [Border] (7) Fall-Wint 96, p. 49-50.
5066. QUINN, Ann
"Clothespin." [NewYorker] (71:24) 14 Ag 95, p. 86.
"Years Ahead." [MassR] (36:2) Sum 95, p. 242.
5067. QUINN, Bernetta
"In Memory of Isak Dinesen." [AntigR] (100) Wint 95, p. 36.
"Landscape of a Mountain Drive" (Denver, Colorado). [AntigR] (100) Wint 95, p.
37.

"Learn From the Wind." [AntigR] (100) Wint 95, p. 38.
5068. QUINN, John Robert
"Graves." [SpiritSH] (60) 95, p. 18.
5069. QUINN, Roseanne Lucia
"1994-1944." [Footwork] (24/25) 95, p. 35.
"To My Father, Long Since Dead." [Footwork] (24/25) 95, p. 35-36.
5070. QUINTANA, Leroy
"Hubcaps and Hi-Fi." [MassR] (36:4) Wint 95-96, p. 632.
"What It Was Like." [MassR] (36:4) Wint 95-96, p. 633.
"Zen — Where I'm From." [MassR] (36:4) Wint 95-96, p. 632.
QUYEN, Nguyen
   See NGUYEN, Quyen

5071. RA, C.
"God Is Dead." [Pearl] (22) Fall-Wint 95, p. 84.
"Just Another Wanna-Be." [Pearl] (22) Fall-Wint 95, p. 84.
5072. RAAB, Lawrence
"The Band Was Still Playing." [NewEngR] (17:3) Sum 95, p. 126.
"The Best Days" (for Judy and Jenny). [NewEngR] (17:3) Sum 95, p. 128-129.
"Envy." [NewEngR] (17:3) Sum 95, p. 125.
"Figuring It Out." [NewEngR] (17:3) Sum 95, p. 127-128.
"Probable Facts." [DenQ] (30:2) Fall 95, p. 58.
"A Small Lie." [KenR] (17:3/4) Sum-Fall 95, p. 181-182.
"Spiders." [SouthwR] (80:4) Aut 95, p. 495.
"Years Later." [NewEngR] (17:3) Sum 95, p. 122-124.
5073. RABB, Margaret
"At Chartres." [CarolQ] (47:3) Sum 95, p. 46-47.
"On Melancholy Again" (1995 Lullwater Prize for Poetry Winner). [LullwaterR] (6:2) Fall-Wint 95, p. 16-17.
5074. RABINOWITZ, Anna
"Glossary." [DenQ] (30:1) Sum 95, p. 94-97.
"To Tell the Matter." [DenQ] (30:2) Fall 95, p. 59-61.
5075. RABINOWITZ, Sima
"Alumni Circuit Volume Five Number One." [EvergreenC] (10:1) Wint-Spr 95, p. 39-41.
5076. RACHEL, Naomi
"The Flight of Aristotle's Butterfly." [HampSPR] Wint 95, p. 40.
"Light." [HampSPR] Wint 95, p. 40-41.
5077. RACHLIN, Ellen
"Aspiration." [Confr] (56/57) Sum-Fall 95, p. 322.
RACZ, Emoke B'
   See B'RACZ, Emoke
5078. RACZ, G. J.
"Doré I" (tr. of José Manuel del Pino). [WorldL] (6) 95, p. 19.
"Elegy I" (tr. of José Manuel del Pino). [WorldL] (6) 95, p. 20-21.
"The Evening" (Pedra, auga, tr. of José Manuel del Pino). [WorldL] (6) 95, p. 19-20.
"The Fable of P. and G." (tr. of José Antonio Mazzotti). [LitR] (39:1) Fall 95, p. 82-83.
"Francesca / *Inferno, V*" (tr. of José Antonio Mazzotti). [LitR] (39:1) Fall 95, p. 81.
"Words" (tr. of Jose Antonio Mazzotti). [Vis] (47) 95, p. 20.
5079. RADACSI, Geri
"Our Wedding Gift." [GreenHLL] (6) 95, p. 34.
"Ruins of a Schoolhouse, Two Dot, Montana." [Elf] (5:1) Spr 95, p. 23.
"Sonny on Clarinet in the Quarter." [Elf] (5:1) Spr 95, p. 22.
5080. RADAVICH, David
"Past Imperfect" (Strolling in Stuttgart, 1990)." [InterQ] (2:1/2) 95, p. 102.
5081. RADELL, Karen M.
"Chiaro/Scuro." [LouisL] (12:1) Spr 95, p. 46.
5082. RAFFEL, Burton
"Pythia: the Prophetess of Apollo at Delphi" (for Eduardo. Chapbook with an introduction by Mark Schafer, tr. of Gloria Gervitz, w. Deborah Owen). [LitR] (38:3) Spr 95, p. 383-416.
"Sonnet Against Descartes, Kant, Spinoza, and You Too." [LitR] (38:3) Spr 95, p. 423.
"The Writing Life." [DenQ] (29:4) Spr 95, p. 49.

5083. RAFFERTY, Charles
"The Man Whose Luck Is Changing." [PaintedB] (55/56) 95, p. 16.
"The Man Whose Tastes Were Too Refined." [PoetryE] (40) Spr 95, p. 103.
"The Man Without Passion Arrives at the Grand Canyon." [PaintedB] (55/56) 95, p. 15.
"Romance" (Second Place, Second Annual Poetry Contest). [PaintedB] (55/56) 95, p. 37-38.
5084. RAGAN, James
"Obscurity" (Jan Zajic, 1950-1969, the second human torch to protest the 1968 Soviet invasion of Prague). [Bomb] (53) Fall 95, p. 30.
"The Ossuary at Kutná Hora." [Bomb] (53) Fall 95, p. 30.
5085. RAHIM, Jennifer
"A Drive Through Green." [CaribbeanW] (9) 95, p. 15-16.
"La Vega." [CaribbeanW] (9) 95, p. 12-14.
5086. RAHMAN, Ruby
"Fantasy" (in Bengali and English, tr. by Syed Manzoorul Islam and Carolyne Wright, w. the author). [MidAR] (15:1/2) 95, p. 84-89.
"Journal" (in Bengali and English, tr. by Syed Manzoorul Islam and Carolyne Wright, w. the author). [MidAR] (15:1/2) 95, p. 80-83.
"Moon-Struck" (in Bengali and English, tr. by Syed Manzoorul Islam and Carolyne Wright, w. the author). [MidAR] (15:1/2) 95, p. 76-79.
"This Afternoon Knows" (in Bengali and English, tr. by Syed Manzoorul Islam and Carolyne Wright, w. the author). [MidAR] (15:1/2) 95, p. 72-75.
RAHMING, Lelawattee Manoo
    See MANOO-RAHMING, Lelawattee
5087. RAIMUND, Hans
"Das Dach, Die Mauern, Die Türe." [Os] (40) 95, p. 7.
"Der Himmel, Die Wiese, Der Wald." [Os] (40) 95, p. 5.
"The Roof, the Walls, the Doors" (tr. by David Chorlton). [Os] (40) 95, p. 6.
"The Sky, the Meadow, the Forest" (tr. by David Chorlton). [Os] (40) 95, p. 4.
5088. RAINE, Heidi Neufeld
"Naked Out There" (tr. of Carmen Rodríguez, w. the author). [Arc] (35) Aut 95, p. 14.
"Positions" (tr. of Carmen Rodríguez, w. the author). [Arc] (35) Aut 95, p. 15-16.
5089. RAJADATTA
"A recluse went to the burning ground" (tr. by Andrew Schelling). [Sulfur] (15:1, #36) Spr 95, p. 85-86.
5090. RAJEEVAN, Savithri
"A Pair of Glasses" (tr. by Ayyappa Paniker and Arlene Zide). [ManyMM] (1:3) 95, p. 152-153.
5091. RAKOSI, Carl
"America." [AmerPoR] (24:4) Jl-Ag 95, p. 7.
"Hello." [AmerPoR] (24:4) Jl-Ag 95, p. 7.
"Man." [AmerPoR] (24:4) Jl-Ag 95, p. 8.
"The Old Country." [AmerPoR] (24:4) Jl-Ag 95, p. 7.
"Theologian." [AmerPoR] (24:4) Jl-Ag 95, p. 7.
"To the Man Inside." [AmerPoR] (24:4) Jl-Ag 95, p. 7.
"Who." [AmerPoR] (24:4) Jl-Ag 95, p. 7.
5092. RALPH, Brett
"The Man." [Conduit] (3) Sum 95, p. 12.
5093. RAMJERDI, Jan
"Geosynclines" (Excerpts, w. Nancy Krusoe). [13thMoon] (13:1/2) 95, p. 93-103.
5094. RAMKE, Bin
"& the War in France." [MissouriR] (18:1) 95, p. 165.
"As You Like It." [MissouriR] (18:1) 95, p. 161.
"Enter Celia, with a Writing." [MissouriR] (18:1) 95, p. 162-163.
"A History of His Heart." [MissouriR] (18:1) 95, p. 166-169.
"More's the Pity." [Boulevard] (10:1/2, #28/29) Spr 95, p. 100-102.
"Pretty Words, Parabolas." [MissouriR] (18:1) 95, p. 160.
"The Weather." [MissouriR] (18:1) 95, p. 164.
5095. RAMSAY, John G.
"To My First Name Only Advisees." [GrahamHR] (19) Wint 95-96, p. 102-103.
5096. RAMSDELL, Heather
"Kuaneonga Lake Polaroid" (for A.L.). [AmerLC] (7) 95, p. 92.
"Mary Triptych." [AmerLC] (7) 95, p. 91.
"Where Things of a Kind." [Talisman] (15) Wint 95-96, p. 96.

5097. RAMSEY, Paul
"A Runner Runs Near the Tennessee River." [Pembroke] (27) 95, p. 124.
"Writing the World." [Elf] (5:1) Spr 95, p. 29.
5098. RAND, Harry
"Painter of moonlight, Watteau." [PlumR] (9) [95 or 96], p. 116.
5099. RANDALL, D'Arcy
"From the Old Manse I." [SouthernPR] (35:2) Wint 95, p. 53-55.
5100. RANDALL, Julie Malvase
"The '60's." [SmPd] (32:3, #95) Fall 95, p. 25.
"Loving Leaves No Fossils." [Plain] (15:2) Wint 95, p. 20.
"Remembering Boris Karloff." [Plain] (16:1) Fall 95, p. 15.
5101. RANDALL, Margaret
"Antonio's Rice." [NewL] (62:1) 96 (c1995), p. 116-117.
"This Happens When a Woman's Heart Breaks" (for Dionne Brand). [AmerV] (37)
95, p. 71-72.
5102. RANDOLPH, Amy
"Easter Sunday." [PaintedB] (57) 95, p. 39.
5103. RANDOLPH, Sarah
"Communion." [GlobalCR] (5) Spr 95, p. 47.
5104. RANKIN, Paula
"Down the Road." [PartR] (62:3) Sum 95, p. 457-458.
"Making Up." [SouthernR] (31:1) Wint 95, p. 52.
"The Perfect Life." [LaurelR] (29:2) Sum 95, p. 40-41.
"Tuberculosis." [SouthernR] (31:1) Wint 95, p. 51-52.
5105. RANKINE, Claudia
"Sunset Returning." [LiteralL] (1:1) Je 94, p. 13.
5106. RANNEY, Michael
"Tee-shot, Fifteen." [Elf] (5:4) Wint 95, p. 34.
5107. RANSLEY, Rich
"La Cueva." [InterPR] (21:1) Spr 95, p. 70.
5108. RANSOM, Lisa
"In Praise of Coats." [Nimrod] (39:1) Fall-Wint 95, p. 116.
"Whirling Disease." [Nimrod] (39:1) Fall-Wint 95, p. 117.
5109. RAPHAEL, Dan
"Poem: Denali painted on a sawblade." [HeavenB] (12) 95, p. 43.
"What I first think is rain are the hands reaching out of the soil." [HeavenB] (12) 95,
p. 71.
5110. RAPPLEYE, Greg
"The Assistant Prosecutor's Story." [ArtfulD] (28/29) 95, p. 114-115.
"Separation." [NewDeltaR] (12:2) Spr-Sum 95, p. 28.
5111. RAPPOPORT, Lisa
"Insects in Amber" (Honorable Mention, First Annual Poetry Awards). [LiteralL]
(2:2) Fall 95, p. 4.
5112. RAS, Barbara
"Girl in the Widow's Walk" (Honorable Mention, 1995 Editors' Prize). [SpoonR]
(20:2) Sum-Fall 95, p. 40-41.
"Where the Sky Opens at the Very Top." [SouthernPR] (35:2) Wint 95, p. 15-16.
5113. RASH, Ron
"Among the Believers." [SouthernR] (31:2) Ap/Spr 95, p. 278.
"At an Abandoned Homestead in Watauga County." [TexasR] (15:3/4) Fall-Wint
94, p. 94.
"Cabbage." [TexasR] (15:3/4) Fall-Wint 94, p. 95.
"The Fox." [NewEngR] (17:1) Wint 95, p. 126.
"Harvest." [SouthernR] (31:2) Ap/Spr 95, p. 278-279.
"Kephart in the Smokies." [GreensboroR] (59) Wint 95-96, p. 82.
"On Broad River Bridge." [TexasR] (15:3/4) Fall-Wint 94, p. 96.
"Tobacco Barn." [TexasR] (15:3/4) Fall-Wint 94, p. 97.
5114. RASHID, Ian Iqbal
"The Heat Yesterday." [WestCL] (29:3, #18) Wint 95-96, p. 35.
"Returning to Canada." [WestCL] (29:3, #18) Wint 95-96, p. 36.
5115. RASULA, Jed
"Stopping by Woods on a Snowy Evening." [WestCL] (29:2, #17) Fall 95, p. 147.
5116. RATCLIFFE, Stephen
"Sculpture" (Selections: 19-21). [Chain] (2) Spr 95, p. 188-189.
"Sculpture" (Selections: 19-21). [NewAW] (13) Fall-Wint 95, p. 54-56.

5117. RATZLAFF, Keith
"Winterreise." [PoetryNW] (36:4) Wint 95-96, p. 22-23.
5118. RAU, Aurel
"A Dance in Masks" (tr. by Adam J. Sorkin and Liviu Bleoca). [Vis] (48) 95, p. 43.
5119. RAUSCHENBUSCH, Stephanie
"Descent from the Cross." [Footwork] (24/25) 95, p. 25-26.
"Georgetown Childhood." [Footwork] (24/25) 95, p. 25.
"Hunting Japanese Beetles." [Footwork] (24/25) 95, p. 25.
5120. RAVELO, Jorge Travieso
"Last Night" (tr. of Octavio Paz). [RiverS] (42/43) 95, p. 7.
"Vertical Hour" (tr. of Octavio Paz). [RiverS] (42/43) 95, p. 7.
5121. RAVIV, Miriam
"Never Did Nothing Bad." [Art&Und] (4:3, #16) Je-Jl 95, p. 14.
5122. RAVNDAL, Janeal Turnbull
"Easter Shift at the Safe-House." [ChrC] (112:12) 12 Ap 95, p. 389.
5123. RAWLINS, C. L.
"Hypolimnion." [QW] (41) Aut-Wint 95-96, p. 163.
"The Sage Café" (after misreading the words "safe cage" in a poem). [CumbPR]
       (14:2) Spr 95, p. 30-31.
5124. RAWORTH, Tom
"Silent Rows" (Excerpt). [Phoebe] (24:1) 95, p. 7-9.
5125. RAY, David
"Another Try." [Confr] (56/57) Sum-Fall 95, p. 314.
"A Bell Tower." [Confr] (56/57) Sum-Fall 95, p. 312-313.
"A Bird." [Footwork] (24/25) 95, p. 4-5.
"Freightloading Days." [Footwork] (24/25) 95, p. 5.
"Fundraising." [Footwork] (24/25) 95, p. 6-7.
"George." [Footwork] (24/25) 95, p. 6.
"Going to School." [Footwork] (24/25) 95, p. 5-6.
"Ice Cubes." [Footwork] (24/25) 95, p. 4.
"Italian Suite for Sam." [Footwork] (24/25) 95, p. 7-9.
"A Landscape." [Footwork] (24/25) 95, p. 6.
"Matins." [Footwork] (24/25) 95, p. 5.
"Orphanage." [Footwork] (24/25) 95, p. 7.
"A Statuette Raised from the Seafloor." [Footwork] (24/25) 95, p. 7.
"Warming the Hands." [WillowR] (22) Spr 95, p. 13.
5126. RAY, Lila
"The Balcony" (tr. of Buddhadep Dasgupta). [AnotherCM] (29) Spr 95, p. 91.
"Ears" (tr. of Buddhadep Dasgupta). [AnotherCM] (29) Spr 95, p. 95.
"Fingers" (tr. of Buddhadep Dasgupta). [AnotherCM] (29) Spr 95, p. 92.
"Get Ready" (tr. of Buddhadep Dasgupta). [AnotherCM] (29) Spr 95, p. 94.
"Six Days or Six Months" (tr. of Buddhadep Dasgupta). [AnotherCM] (29) Spr 95,
       p. 96.
"Swallowing Up" (tr. of Buddhadep Dasgupta). [AnotherCM] (29) Spr 95, p. 93.
5127. RAY, Sharmila
"Tukaram" (tr. of Subodh Sarkar, w. Peter Michelson). [ManyMM] (1:3) 95, p. 138 -
       139.
5128. RAYNETTA (D.C. Center for Alcohol and Drug Abuse, Washington, DC)
"Satan" (WritersCorps Program). [WashR] (21:2) Ag-S 95, p. 5.
5129. RAZAVI, Rebecca Hopkins
"Portrait of Dried Roses." [LullwaterR] (5:1) 93-94, p. 7.
"Snapping Ants in Half." [SmPd] (32:3, #95) Fall 95, p. 12.
5130. RAZEE, J. L. T.
"Salome at the Whispering Pines Care Center." [Jacaranda] (11) [95 or 96?], p. 108.
5131. REA, Susan
"February Thaw." [MidwQ] (36:3) Spr 95, p. 307.
"First Storm of Winter." [Plain] (16:1) Fall 95, p. 35.
5132. READER, Willie
"Home on the Range Is a Family Game." [MidwQ] (36:2) Wint 95, p. 162.
"It's Not What's Inside That Counts." [Border] (7) Fall-Wint 96, p. 51.
5133. READING, Peter
"Lucretian." [TriQ] (94) Fall 95, p. 109-112.
5134. REAGLER, Robin
"The Non-Confession." [ColR] (22:2) Fall 95, p. 187-188.
5135. REALUYO, Bino A.
"Glue Children." [BlackBR] (20) Spr-Sum 95, p. 12.

5136. REARDON, Alissa
"Sweets, Words, and Colors" (For Mae Thompson, April 17, 1892-April 17, 1987).
[Footwork] (24/25) 95, p. 26.
5137. RECALDE PÉREZ, Francia
"1533: La Coya." [Americas] (23:3/4) Fall-Wint 95, p. 157-158.
"Clouds." [Americas] (23:3/4) Fall-Wint 95, p. 159-160.
"Crossing the River." [Americas] (23:3/4) Fall-Wint 95, p. 156.
5138. RECHNITZ, Emily
"Wedding." [NewYorker] (71:21) 24 Jl 95, p. 61.
5139. RECTOR, Liam
"Father's Day." [HarvardR] (9) Fall 95, p. 101.
RED, Rockin'
See ROCKIN' RED
5140. RED PLASTIC BAG
"Ragga Ragga." [ClockR] (10:1/2) 95-96, p. 36.
5141. REDER, Claudia
"Study of Tree Shadows." [SycamoreR] (7:1) Wint 95, p. 13.
5142. REDGROVE, Peter
"Cornish Hills in the Black Mirror." [GrandS] (14:2, #54) Fall 95, p. 236-237.
"Eating Cannon." [ManhatR] (8:1) Fall 95, p. 78.
"Existing" (Chapbook: 6 poems). [CarolQ] (48:1) Fall 95, p. 41-56.
"Explanation of the Town's Unease." [ManhatR] (7:2) Wint 95, p. 84.
"Family Skin." [Verse] (12:3) 95, p. 90-91.
"Funeral Forest." [Epoch] (44:3) 95, p. 300-301.
"Griffonage." [Verse] (12:3) 95, p. 89.
"Heavy." [ManhatR] (8:1) Fall 95, p. 81.
"Hill Working." [ManhatR] (7:2) Wint 95, p. 85.
"In Malaga Cathedral." [ManhatR] (7:2) Wint 95, p. 80.
"The Laboratories." [GrandS] (13:4, #52) Spr 95, p. 18-19.
"Lair." [ManhatR] (8:1) Fall 95, p. 79.
"Llangattock Escarpment in the Black Mirror." [Verse] (12:2) 95, p. 119.
"Lugosi." [ManhatR] (8:1) Fall 95, p. 77.
"Manuduction." [GrandS] (14:2, #54) Fall 95, p. 238.
"Native Tongue." [ManhatR] (8:1) Fall 95, p. 72-74.
"Odious Poems: Good News for Bad." [ManhatR] (7:2) Wint 95, p. 78-79.
"Pistes." [ManhatR] (8:1) Fall 95, p. 75-76.
"Poems: I-XV." [GrandS] (14:2, #54) Fall 95, p. 234-236.
"Return." [Epoch] (44:3) 95, p. 298.
"Reveries." [GrandS] (13:4, #52) Spr 95, p. 21-22.
"Service." [Sulfur] (15:2, #37) Fall 95, p. 140-144.
"Shadows." [ManhatR] (8:1) Fall 95, p. 80.
"Superstition." [ManhatR] (7:2) Wint 95, p. 83.
"Two Poems of Accidental Pregnancy." [ManhatR] (7:2) Wint 95, p. 86.
"Underneathness." [Epoch] (44:3) 95, p. 299.
"Welsh Hills in the Black Mirror." [ManhatR] (7:2) Wint 95, p. 81-82.
"The Women Spin." [GrandS] (13:4, #52) Spr 95, p. 20.
5143. REDLIN, Josephine
"All the Carefully Measured Seconds." [Ploughs] (21:1) Spr 95, p. 20-21.
"Getting Used to It." [Sun] (238) O 95, p. 37.
"Giving Thanks" (for Angie and Darrell). [Ploughs] (21:1) Spr 95, p. 22-23.
"In-Law Ancestors." [Sun] (240) D 95, p. 11.
"Looking for You." [Sun] (237) S 95, p. 39.
5144. REDMOND, Eugene B.
"Ars Americana, 1996 (Haiku cum Tanka)" (Toni Cade Bambara, 1939-1995).
[Drumvoices] (5:1/2) Fall-Wint 95-96, p. 25.
5145. REDMOND, Kate
"Rand McNally Says 378 Miles to the Coast." [EvergreenC] (10:1) Wint-Spr 95, p.
90.
5146. REECE, Spencer
"Eclogue." [RagMag] (12:2) Spr 95, p. 90.
"Eurydice." [HawaiiR] (19:2) Fall 95, p. 52.
"Key West." [Boulevard] (10:1/2, #28/29) Spr 95, p. 153.
"Now." [SantaBR] (3:1) Spr 95, p. 55.
"Past One O'clock." [PaintedB] (55/56) 95, p. 8.
"Pentimento" (in memory of Mary Sue Agee). [RagMag] (12:2) Spr 95, p. 88-89.
"That Summer." [SantaBR] (3:1) Spr 95, p. 56.

"What Happened." [SantaBR] (3:1) Spr 95, p. 54.
"Winter Scene" (in memory of Pat Taylor). [PaintedB] (55/56) 95, p. 7.
5147. REED, Ishmael
    "Letter from Queen Elizabeth." [RiverS] (42/43) 95, p. 65-66.
    "The Pope Replies to the Ayatollah Khomeini." [RiverS] (42/43) 95, p. 63-64.
5148. REED, John R.
    "Feeding." [Confr] (56/57) Sum-Fall 95, p. 321.
    "Walking to Treatment." [Confr] (56/57) Sum-Fall 95, p. 320.
5149. REED, John Richard
    "Dresden Altarpiece." [WestHR] (49:4) Wint 95, p. 356.
    "The Other Shoe." [WestHR] (49:4) Wint 95, p. 357.
    "Secondary Education." [WestHR] (49:4) Wint 95, p. 356.
5150. REED, Marthe
    "Night lifts out of the almond orchard." [SmPd] (32:3, #95) Fall 95, p. 9.
    "Seasons fold over one another, and she sifts through them, through memory."
        [SmPd] (32:3, #95) Fall 95, p. 8-9.
    "Yet what has abandoned Orion remains, the autonomous memory." [SmPd] (32:3,
        #95) Fall 95, p. 9.
5151. REED, Stephen
    "Wasted Warrior." [Writer] (108:8) Ag 95, p. 26.
5152. REED-MUNDELL, J. J.
    "The Door." [AnthNEW] (7) 95, p. 40.
5153. REES, Elizabeth
    "Facing In." [SenR] (25:2) Fall 95, p. 96.
    "Returning from Egypt." [MidAR] (16:1) 95, p. 59.
5154. REES-JONES, Deryn
    "The Memory Tray." [Jacaranda] (11) [95 or 96?], p. 152.
5155. REESE, Steven
    "The Bread-Truck Hour." [PlumR] (9) [95 or 96], p. 19.
    "The Dish and the Spoon Come Home." [WestB] (37) 95, p. 48-49.
    "The Obvious Goods" (for Kelly). [PoetryNW] (36:3) Aut 95, p. 15.
    "Of Ills and Injury." [NewMyths] (2:2/3:1) 95, p. 87-88.
    "That Blue." [PlumR] (9) [95 or 96], p. 18.
    "Waiting, and Things." [NewMyths] (2:2/3:1) 95, p. 85-86.
    "Your Town." [PoetryNW] (36:3) Aut 95, p. 16.
5156. REEVE, David
    "The Import of Bukowski." [NewYorkQ] (54) 95, p. 42-43.
5157. REEVE, F. D.
    "Coasting." [AmerPoR] (24:4) Jl-Ag 95, p. 38.
    "The Death of Achilles." [SewanR] (103:3) Sum 95, p. 367.
    "The Geese." [NewL] (61:4) 95, p. 93.
    "Silence." [SewanR] (103:2) Spr 95, p. 169-170.
5158. REEVES, Trish
    "Goldeneye Duck." [MidwQ] (36:4) Sum 95, p. 422.
5159. REEVES, Troy
    "Old Pharaoh." [Crucible] (30) Fall 94, p. 11-12.
5160. REFFE, Candice
    "Crazy 4 U." [Agni] (42) 95, p. 23-24.
    "Everybody Loves the Spring." [Agni] (42) 95, p. 21-22.
5161. REHAK, Melanie
    "Adonis All Male Revue, November 24." [NewRep] (213:14) 2 O 95, p. 52.
5162. REHM, Pam
    "Serving Two Masters." [ChiR] (41:4) 95, p. 110-112.
5163. REIBETANZ, John
    "The Ark." [Quarry] (44:1) 95, p. 60-62.
    "A Chest of Angels." [ParisR] (37:137) Wint 95, p. 117-119.
    "Clark Kent Leaves His Clothes at Midland." [Quarry] (44:1) 95, p. 57-59.
5164. REICHARD, William
    "Long Winter Letter" (for Joshua Koestenbaum). [JamesWR] (12:3) Fall 95, p. 6.
    "Two Songs For My Brother." [JamesWR] (12:1) Wint 95, p. 13.
5165. REICHHOLD, Jane
    "Black and White" A Traditional Summer Kasen Renga, June 30, 1993 to July 25,
        1994" (w. Lenard D. Moore). [XavierR] (15:1) Spr 95, p. 29-31.
5166. REID, Alev
    "Our Cat's Tale" (tr. of Mehmet Yasin, edited by Ruth Christie). [HarvardR] (8) Spr
        95, p. 92.

5167. REID, Christopher
"Fetish." [GrandS] (14:1, #53) Sum 95, p. 74.
5168. REID, Monty
"Cabin" (for Deirdre Virgo). [Grain] (22:4) Spr 95, p. 125.
"Learning to Play 'Blackberry Blossom'." [Quarry] (44:1) 95, p. 76-77.
"Perseids" (for Garth & Susan Ward). [Grain] (22:4) Spr 95, p. 126.
REILLY, Edward J.
See RIELLY, Edward J.
5169. REINER, Christopher
"Fan and Sickle." [Avec] (10) 95, p. 61-68.
5170. REIS, Donna
"Apartment on 81st Street." [Ledge] (18) Sum 95, p. 109-110.
"Three Views from a Bronx Window." [HeavenB] (12) 95, p. 69.
5171. REISZ, Martina
"In the Mood." [WillowR] (22) Spr 95, p. 18.
5172. REITER, Thomas
"The Cassava Women (Grenada, West Indies, ca. 1700)." [CaribbeanW] (9) 95, p.
62-63.
5173. REKOLA, Mirkka
"Kun maailma on täynnä muistini agentteja." [InterPR] (21:2) Fall 95, p. 28.
"Kun näin Johannes Kastajan kasvot vedessä." [InterPR] (21:2) Fall 95, p. 26.
"Meri nostaa sinut pystyyn. Ja ihan tyyni." [InterPR] (21:2) Fall 95, p. 24.
"Myös tämä tehtävä on annettu, palveluksessa." [InterPR] (21:2) Fall 95, p. 30.
"Pidä huolta ihmisistä, eläimet liikkuvat." [InterPR] (21:2) Fall 95, p. 24.
"The sea raises you to your feet. And dead calm" (tr. by Sari Hantula). [InterPR]
(21:2) Fall 95, p. 25.
"This one, too, is an assigned task, in service" (tr. by Sari Hantula). [InterPR] (21:2)
Fall 95, p. 31.
"Vaikka voisin huutaa sinua minä." [InterPR] (21:2) Fall 95, p. 24.
"When I saw the face of John the Baptist in the water" (tr. by Sari Hantula).
[InterPR] (21:2) Fall 95, p. 27.
"When the world is full of agents of my memory" (tr. by Sari Hantula). [InterPR]
(21:2) Fall 95, p. 29.
5174. RELLER, Monica
"Evolutionary Creation." [WorldO] (27:1) Fall 95, p. 7.
5175. RENALDO (D.C. Vision Program, Tyler Elementary School, Washington, DC).
"Renaldo's Rap" (WritersCorps Program). [WashR] (21:2) Ag-S 95, p. 19.
5176. RENDLEMAN, Danny
"Mom & Pop Beer & Wine." [WeberS] (12:2) Spr-Sum 95, p. 80-81.
"Ten Drawings." [WeberS] (12:2) Spr-Sum 95, p. 81-82.
5177. RENDRICK, Bernice
"Black Beans." [SantaBR] (3:1) Spr 95, p. 19.
"Contour of the Herb Garden." [SantaBR] (3:1) Spr 95, p. 20.
"Tim's Place." [SantaBR] (3:1) Spr 95, p. 21.
5178. RENÉE, Robin
"New Brunswick Station." [NortheastCor] (3) 95, p. 78.
5179. RENIERS, Annie
"Only in the fire" (from "Transparent Waiting," tr. by Adam J. Sorkin and Eugène
Van Itterbeek). [MalR] (110) Spr 95, p. 106.
"Transparent Waiting" (Selections: 2 poems, tr. by Adam J. Sorkin and Eugène Van
Itterbeek). [MalR] (110) Spr 95, p. 106-107.
"Untitled: Ask the stones." [Iowa] (25:3) Fall 95, p. 82.
"You stay all eternity" (from "Transparent Waiting," tr. by Adam J. Sorkin and
Eugène Van Itterbeek). [MalR] (110) Spr 95, p. 107.
5180. RENKL, Margaret
"The Lost Queens." [SouthernHR] (29:4) Fall 95, p. 364.
"Rat." [BelPoJ] (45:3) Spr 95, p. 22.
5181. RENNER, Cooper Esteban
"The Elohim." [Chelsea] (59) 95, p. 36.
"From Lazarus in Torment." [Chelsea] (59) 95, p. 35.
5182. REPETTO, Vittoria
"The Choosing" (The 1994 Allen Ginsberg Poetry Awards: Honorable Mention).
[Footwork] (24/25) 95, p. 202.
5183. RESNICK, Rachel M.
"Happiness." [ChironR] (43) Sum 95, p. 36.
"Wilshire Boulevard Birthday Wish." [ChironR] (42) Spr 95, p. 32.

5184. RETSOV, Samuel
"Repetition Does Not Count." [Talisman] (15) Wint 95-96, p. 84-85.
5185. REVELL, Donald
"At the Santé" (tr. of Guillaume Apollinaire). [MissR] (23:3) 95, p. 80-82.
"A Branch of the Discipline." [ColR] (22:1) Spr 95, p. 83-84.
"City More Than I Suspected." [Verse] (12:2) 95, p. 120-121.
"Homage to Mrs. Jane Lead." [NewAW] (13) Fall-Wint 95, p. 85.
"Missal." [Colum] (24/25) 95, p. 38.
"The Other Case." [ColR] (22:1) Spr 95, p. 81.
"Pride." [ColR] (22:1) Spr 95, p. 82.
"Procession" (tr. of Guillaume Apollinaire). [MissR] (23:3) 95, p. 83-85.
"Psalter." [Colum] (24/25) 95, p. 39.
"To the Lord Protector." [Conjunc] (24) 95, p. 160-163.
"Upon Diagnosis." [PartR] (62:2) Spr 95, p. 300.
5186. REVERDY, Pierre
"Bruits de Nuit." [AntigR] (102/103) Sum-Aug 95, p. 32.
"Champ Clos." [AntigR] (102/103) Sum-Aug 95, p. 34.
"Enclosed Field" (tr. by R. W. Stedingh). [AntigR] (102/103) Sum-Aug 95, p. 35.
"Face a Face." [AntigR] (102/103) Sum-Aug 95, p. 36.
"Face to Face" (tr. by R. W. Stedingh). [AntigR] (102/103) Sum-Aug 95, p. 37.
"Night Noises" (tr. by R. W. Stedingh). [AntigR] (102/103) Sum-Aug 95, p. 33.
"Old Port" (tr. by R. W. Stedingh). [AntigR] (102/103) Sum-Aug 95, p. 39.
"Vieux Port." [AntigR] (102/103) Sum-Aug 95, p. 38.
REX LEE JIM
See DINELTSOI, Mazii
5187. REXROTH, Kenneth
"The Day When Mountains Move" (tr. of Akiko (1878-1942) Yosano, w. Ikuko
Atsumi). [ManyMM] reprinted in every issue p. 2.
5188. REYES, Verónica
"Con Cariño." [Pearl] (22) Fall-Wint 95, p. 143.
5189. REYNOLDS, Kate Fox
"Best Western." [PoetryE] (39) Fall 94, p. 73.
5190. RHATIGAN, Joe
"Bad Haircut." [AmerLC] (7) 95, p. 93-94.
5191. RHAU, Daisy
"Prayer" (For my father). [NewL] (62:1) 96 (c1995), p. 112-113.
5192. RHENISCH, Harold
"The Black Birds." [Event] (24:3) Wint 95-96, p. 50.
"The Brothers." [CanLit] (147) Wint 95, p. 125-126.
"But Then." [PoetryC] (15:3) Ag 95, p. 18.
"The Cold." [Event] (24:3) Wint 95-96, p. 48-49.
"The Dance." [PoetryC] (15:3) Ag 95, p. 19.
"A Million Grass Blades Blaze in a Meadow." [PoetryC] (15:3) Ag 95, p. 19.
"The Mind of the Earth." [PoetryC] (15:3) Ag 95, p. 18.
"Rivers Pouring into the Sea." [PoetryC] (15:3) Ag 95, p. 19.
"The Singing Birds." [Event] (24:3) Wint 95-96, p. 52-53.
"The Sphere." [Event] (24:3) Wint 95-96, p. 51.
5193. RHETT, Kathryn
"Wedding." [OhioR] (53) 95, p. 50-51.
"Winter in France." [GettyR] (8:4) Aut 95, p. 638.
5194. RHOADES, Lisa
"Connections." [Chelsea] (58) 95, p. 100-101.
"Flight." [Chelsea] (58) 95, p. 99-100.
"Strange Gravity." [Chelsea] (58) 95, p. 101.
"The Week I Thought I Was." [ArtfulD] (28/29) 95, p. 140.
5195. RHODENBAUGH, Suzanne
"At Quaker Meeting, The Spirit Dog." [CimR] (111) Ap 95, p. 63.
"Preparing for Immortality" (to Wendell Berry). [Hudson] (48:1) Spr 95, p. 97-98.
"Swallowing." [GreenMR] (8:2) Fall-Wint 95-96, p. 67-68.
5196. RHODES, Martha
"Why She Hurries Out, Then Home." [BostonR] (20:3) Sum 95, p. 39.
5197. RHODES, Shane
"The Moth Journals" (Excerpts: I-III). [Grain] (23:2) Aut 95, p. 77.
5198. RICE, Bruce
"Beresford Notes." [Grain] (23:1) Sum 95, p. 19-20.
"Prayer." [Grain] (23:1) Sum 95, p. 18-19.

5199. RICE, Oliver
"The Drunken Sailor." [Sonora] (30) Fall 95, p. 44.
5200. RICH, Adrienne
"Calle Visión." [Agni] (41) 95, p. 219-229.
"Dreams Before Waking." [RiverS] (42/43) 95, p. 67-68.
"Inscriptions" (3 selections). [ManyMM] (1:2) 95, p. 29-32.
"Inscriptions" (Selections: 3 poems). [AmerPoR] (24:3) My-Je 95, p. 3-5.
"Sending Love." [ParisR] (37:135) Sum 95, p. 76-78.
"Six Narratives." [CreamCR] (19:1) Spr 95, p. 154-156.
"Take." [Agni] (41) 95, p. 230-231.
"Then or Now." [Field] (52) Spr 95, p. 5-9.
5201. RICH, Susanna
"Taking Photographs." [SoCoast] (18) Ja 95, p. 44-45.
5202. RICHARDS, Marilee
"The Recent Dead." [LaurelR] (29:1) Wint 95, p. 18-19.
"Third Month." [Journal] (19:1) Spr-Sum 95, p. 62.
5203. RICHARDS, Melanie
"White Owl." [NorthStoneR] (12) 95, p. 237.
"White Tigers" (Grand Award Winner, Second National Sue Saniel Elkind Poetry
Contest). [Kalliope] (17:2) 95, p. 10-11.
5204. RICHARDS, Peter
"The Blue Nest." [ColR] (22:2) Fall 95, p. 125-126.
"Boy for Sale." [MassR] (36:2) Sum 95, p. 258.
"Circled Square Drawn to Scale." [MassR] (36:1) Spr 95, p. 56-57.
"Not Taking Place." [ColR] (22:2) Fall 95, p. 123-124.
"On the Conditions *Presently* Needed." [ColR] (22:2) Fall 95, p. 121-122.
"The Sea Looking On." [Agni] (42) 95, p. 98.
5205. RICHARDSON, Alex
"How My Life Revolves Around Blackberries." [Poem] (73) My 95, p. 11.
"Thaw." [Poem] (73) My 95, p. 12.
5206. RICHARDSON, Betzi
"Promise without a Name." [AntR] (53:3) Sum 95, p. 324-325.
5207. RICHARDSON, Fred
"Bloody Mary." [Pearl] (22) Fall-Wint 95, p. 122.
5208. RICHARDSON, Leslie E.
"Diminishment." [HampSPR] Wint 95, p. 50.
5209. RICHARDSON, Norma M.
"Potpourri." [HiramPoR] (58/59) Spr 95-Wint 96, p. 66.
RICHARDSON, S. Banks
See BANKS-RICHARDSON, S.
5210. RICHARDSON, Shirley A.
"Me." [Pembroke] (27) 95, p. 27.
5211. RICHMAN, Elliot
"The Death of Picasso." [BlackBR] (20) Spr-Sum 95, p. 35.
"The Fifty-Eight Thousand Samurai." [WindO] (59) Spr 95, p. 11.
"Five Plums Beside a Dead Woman in Hue." [WindO] (59) Spr 95, p. 12-13.
"How Christ Ripped My Eyes Out So I Could See" (The True Story of the First
Communion). [Ledge] (19) Wint 95, p. 129-131.
"Just Another Holocaust Poem." [BlackBR] (20) Spr-Sum 95, p. 35.
"Late at Night." [BlackBR] (21) Fall-Wint 95, p. 9.
"The Nighthawk." [Bogg] (67) 95, p. 41.
"The Tongues of Ten Thousand Snow Geese." [HiramPoR] (58/59) Spr 95-Wint 96,
p. 67.
"A Truck Full of Sharks." [WindO] (59) Spr 95, p. 10.
"Upon the Fiftieth Anniversary of the Liberation of the Concentration Camps."
[BlackBR] (21) Fall-Wint 95, p. 18.
5212. RICHMOND, Steve
"Gagaku: He envies his demons." [WormR] (35:4, #140) 95, p. 156.
"Gagaku: No need to hear the words first." [WormR] (35:4, #140) 95, p. 153-154.
"Gagaku: Now my girl in the kitchen hums to this gagaku music." [WormR] (35:4,
#140) 95, p. 154.
"Gagaku: O I feel good." [WormR] (35:4, #140) 95, p. 155.
"Gagaku: Reading an old gagaku." [WormR] (35:4, #140) 95, p. 154.
"Gagaku: This just this." [WormR] (35:4, #140) 95, p. 156.
"Gagaku: While I boast here of my great love and happiness." [WormR] (35:4,
#140) 95, p. 155.

5213. RICHSTONE, May
"Carpe Diem." [Light] (15/16) Aut-Wint 95-96, p. 22.
"Fashion Statement." [Light] (14) Sum 95, p. 17.
"Handwriting on the Wall." [Light] (15/16) Aut-Wint 95-96, p. 30.
"Strictly Speaking." [Light] (14) Sum 95, p. 19.
"Such Is Fate." [Light] (15/16) Aut-Wint 95-96, p. 21.
5214. RICHTER, Harvena
"The Pacing." [SoDakR] (33:2) Sum 95, p. 79-81.
5215. RICKEL, Boyer
"Exactly." [PraS] (69:2) Sum 95, p. 31.
"Nedwina Plough." [PraS] (69:2) Sum 95, p. 32-34.
"This." [PraS] (69:2) Sum 95, p. 34-35.
"Two Dreams of a Son in Middle Age." [PraS] (69:2) Sum 95, p. 36-39.
5216. RICKS, David
"Cycladic." [SouthernHR] (29:2) Spr 95, p. 144.
"Incident." [SouthwR] (80:2/3) Spr-Sum 95, p. 357.
"Somewhere." [SouthwR] (80:2/3) Spr-Sum 95, p. 357-358.
5217. RIDA, Shirley
"Morning Snowfall." [AnthNEW] (7) 95, p. 20.
5218. RIDGE, Lola
"Adelaide Crapsey." [FreeL] (15) Aut 95, p. 28.
"The Ghetto (Part II)" (Excerpt). [FreeL] (15) Aut 95, p. 26-27.
"Via Ignis" (Selection: IX). [FreeL] (15) Aut 95, p. 29.
5219. RIDL, Jack R.
"At Fifty." [PoetryE] (39) Fall 94, p. 74.
5220. RIELLY, Edward J.
"Nellie Fox Swings a Bat." [Spitball] (48) 95, p. 8-9.
5221. RIFENBURGH, Daniel
"Hawthorne." [ParisR] (37:135) Sum 95, p. 46-47.
"Melville / Ishmael." [ParisR] (37:135) Sum 95, p. 45-46.
5222. RIGGAN, Nancy
"Warning Ticket." [FourQ] (9:1/2) Spr 95, p. 35.
5223. RIGGS, Lynette A.
"3 Frames." [WeberS] (12:2) Spr-Sum 95, p. 117-118.
"Now and Then." [WeberS] (12:2) Spr-Sum 95, p. 118-119.
"Spring Bouquets." [WeberS] (12:2) Spr-Sum 95, p. 119.
5224. RIGSBEE, David
"The Dissolving Island." [CimR] (113) O 95, p. 52-53.
"Four Last Songs" (after Strauss, Vier Letzte Lieder, in memory of my brother,
1954-1992, a suicide). [SouthernR] (31:2) Ap/Spr 95, p. 280-295.
"High Summer" (for Gerald Stern). [CimR] (113) O 95, p. 51.
"Linking Light." [OhioR] (54) 95, p. 130.
"Wild Strawberries." [GreensboroR] (58) Sum 95, p. 51-53.
RIGSBY, David
See RIGSBEE, David
5225. RILEY, Michael D.
"Chalice and Madonna." [Interim] (14:1) Spr-Sum 95, p. 44-45.
"Kissing the Dead in Sleep." [Interim] (14:1) Spr-Sum 95, p. 43.
"Medusa." [Interim] (14:1) Spr-Sum 95, p. 46.
5226. RILEY, Peter
"Author" (Excerpt and selections from a sequence). [WestCL] (29:2, #17) Fall 95, p.
76-79.
"Delphine" (from the sequence "Author"). [WestCL] (29:2, #17) Fall 95, p. 79.
"E Questa Vita un Lampo" (from the sequence "Author"). [WestCL] (29:2, #17) Fall
95, p. 78.
"Hans Leo Hassler" (from the sequence "Author"). [WestCL] (29:2, #17) Fall 95, p.
77.
5227. RILEY, Tom
"Cranial Capacity." [Light] (14) Sum 95, p. 11.
"Fr. Bestseller." [Light] (13) Spr 95, p. 13.
"Self-Employment Blues." [Light] (13) Spr 95, p. 16.
"That Kind of Day." [Light] (15/16) Aut-Wint 95-96, p. 22.
5228. RILKE, Rainer Maria
"Buddha" (tr. by Bernhard Frank). [HeavenB] (12) 95, p. 88.
"Departure" (tr. by George Messo). [Pearl] (22) Fall-Wint 95, p. 111.
"Evening" (tr. by Bernhard Frank). [HeavenB] (12) 95, p. 88.

"Night Arrives" (tr. by George Messo). [Pearl] (22) Fall-Wint 95, p. 111.
"Sketch" (tr. by George Messo). [Pearl] (22) Fall-Wint 95, p. 111.
"A Vague Elsewhere" (tr. by George Messo). [Pearl] (22) Fall-Wint 95, p. 111.
5229. RIMA, Sean
"Heavy Machinery." [Interim] (14:1) Spr-Sum 95, p. 26.
5230. RIMBEY, Anne Giles
"Counting Points." [Kalliope] (17:1) 95, p. 16-17.
5231. RINGLER, Thor
"Personal Poem." [PoetryE] (40) Spr 95, p. 104.
5232. RINGOLD, Francine
"Annie's Place" (runner up, 1994 Borderlands Poetry Contest). [Border] (7) Fall-
Wint 96, p. 52-53.
5233. RIO, Nela
"Beginning" (tr. by Elizabeth Gamble Miller). [Luz] (8) Spr 95, p. 33.
"The Breeze" (tr. by Elizabeth Gamble Miller). [Luz] (8) Spr 95, p. 37.
"La Brisa." [Luz] (8) Spr 95, p. 36.
"Comienzo." [Luz] (8) Spr 95, p. 32.
"En el Umbral del Atardecer" (3 selections from an unpublished work). [Luz] (8)
Spr 95, p. 32-36.
"In the Threshold of Sunset" (3 selections from an unpublished work, tr. by
Elizabeth Gamble Miller). [Luz] (8) Spr 95, p. 33-37.
"The Rose Garden" (tr. by Elizabeth Gamble Miller). [Luz] (8) Spr 95, p. 35.
"El Rosedal." [Luz] (8) Spr 95, p. 34.
5234. RIORDAN, Maurice
"Chair." [SouthernR] (31:3) Jl/Sum 95, p. 618-619.
"Milk." [SouthernR] (31:3) Jl/Sum 95, p. 619-620.
5235. RIOS, Alberto Alvaro
"Aunt Matilde's Story of the Big Day." [IndR] (18:1) Spr 95, p. 48-49.
"Good Manners." [IndR] (18:1) Spr 95, p. 42.
"Lisandro's Wife." [IndR] (18:1) Spr 95, p. 43-44.
"My Chili." [IndR] (18:1) Spr 95, p. 50-54.
"What Abides." [IndR] (18:1) Spr 95, p. 45-47.
5236. RISDEN, E. L.
"Playing Tchaikovsky on Summer Vacation" (from Through a Glass Darkly).
[AmerPoR] (24:4) Jl-Ag 95, p. 22.
5237. RISTAU, Harland
"So." [Pearl] (22) Fall-Wint 95, p. 120.
5238. RITCHIE, Elisavietta
"Advice to a Daughter." [NewYorkQ] (54) 95, p. 63.
"Hokusai in Southern Maryland." [Vis] (47) 95, p. 25.
"Not Just about a Squirrel, of Course" (First Prize, 1995 Poetry Contest). [Ledge]
(19) Wint 95, p. 7-10.
"A Portrait" (tr. of Krassin Himmirsky, w. the author). [Vis] (48) 95, p. 9.
5239. RITSOS, Yannis
"Another Summer" (tr. by Martin McKinsey). [PartR] (62:2) Spr 95, p. 299.
"Bitter Knowledge" (tr. by Martin McKinsey). [KenR] (17:1) Wint 95, p. 76.
"Closing Words" (tr. by Martin McKinsey). [Field] (52) Spr 95, p. 51.
"Forgetfulness" (tr. by Martin McKinsey). [KenR] (17:1) Wint 95, p. 75-76.
"Garden in Autumn" (tr. by Martin McKinsey). [Field] (52) Spr 95, p. 47.
"Hypothermia" (tr. by Martin McKinsey). [VirQR] (71:3) Sum 95, p. 500.
"Minimal Harvest" (tr. by Martin McKinsey). [PartR] (62:2) Spr 95, p. 299.
"Not Quite" (tr. by Martin McKinsey). [Field] (52) Spr 95, p. 49.
"Painting Stones" (tr. by Martin McKinsey). [Field] (52) Spr 95, p. 46.
"People and Suitcases" (tr. by Martin McKinsey). [Field] (52) Spr 95, p. 48.
"Perhaps" (tr. by Martin McKinsey). [KenR] (17:1) Wint 95, p. 75.
"Pointless Lucidity" (tr. by Martin McKinsey). [VirQR] (71:3) Sum 95, p. 501.
"Post Script" (tr. by Martin McKinsey). [Field] (52) Spr 95, p. 45.
"Self-Knowledge" (tr. by Martin McKinsey). [Field] (52) Spr 95, p. 50.
"Sitting Out the Rain" (tr. by Martin McKinsey). [ArtfulD] (28/29) 95, p. 59.
"Sparse Leavings" (tr. by Martin McKinsey). [VirQR] (71:3) Sum 95, p. 502.
"Ticks of the Clock" (14 selections, tr. by Martin McKinsey). [WillowS] (36) Je 95,
p. 101-103.
"Tokens" (tr. by Martin McKinsey). [VirQR] (71:3) Sum 95, p. 500-501.
"Two in the Afternoon" (tr. by Martin McKinsey). [VirQR] (71:3) Sum 95, p. 501-
502.
"What Cannot Be Weighed" (tr. by Martin McKinsey). [ArtfulD] (28/29) 95, p. 58.

5240. RITTY, Joan
"What She Knew." [WestB] (37) 95, p. 16.
5241. RIVARD, David
"Against Gravity." [GreensboroR] (57) Wint 94-95, p. 60-62.
"Document Processing." [GreensboroR] (57) Wint 94-95, p. 57-59.
"Emergency Exit." [IndR] (18:1) Spr 95, p. 182-183.
"Fado." [IndR] (18:1) Spr 95, p. 181.
"Good." [HarvardR] (8) Spr 95, p. 108-109.
"Message to the Bride." [BostonR] (20:4) O-N 95, p. 23.
"Real Thing Strange." [Agni] (42) 95, p. 19-20.
5242. RIVARD, Ken
"Nat King Cole." [CanLit] (146) Aut 95, p. 49.
"Notes of Mother Song." [CanLit] (146) Aut 95, p. 50.
5243. RIVERA, Gina
"Divisions." [LullwaterR] (6:2) Fall-Wint 95, p. 19.
5244. RIXEN, Gail
"The Famous." [NorthStoneR] (12) 95, p. 55.
5245. ROACH, Tregenza A.
"The Times of Sunday." [CaribbeanW] (9) 95, p. 64-67.
ROBB, Maria Elena Caballero
See CABALLERO-ROBB, Maria Elena
5246. ROBBINS, Anthony
"Coordinates." [AnotherCM] (29) Spr 95, p. 168-170.
"Dim Backwater." [GettyR] (8:4) Aut 95, p. 621.
"What Are You Going Through?" [GettyR] (8:4) Aut 95, p. 622.
5247. ROBBINS, Doren
"The Injury in My Mouth Tells Me." [Sulfur] (15:2, #37) Fall 95, p. 186-187.
5248. ROBBINS, Michael
"15th St." (A Plainsongs Award Poem). [Plain] (15:2) Wint 95, p. 21.
"The Blueprint of Music." [SouthernPR] (35:1) Sum 95, p. 51.
"Letter to Jay Griswold (Never Mailed)." [Plain] (15:3) Spr 95, p. 11.
"Untitled: Tonight my father is crying because he has no word for winter."
[SouthernPR] (35:1) Sum 95, p. 52.
5249. ROBBINS, Richard
"The End of the World." [PoetryNW] (36:2) Sum 95, p. 46-47.
"Great Basin National Park." [Verse] (12:3) 95, p. 59-60.
"Spell." [MidwQ] (36:4) Sum 95, p. 423.
5250. ROBERSON, Katherine A.
"Thoughts While Braiding My Daughter's Hair" (The 1994 Allen Ginsberg Poetry
Awards: Honorable Mention). [Footwork] (24/25) 95, p. 202-203.
5251. ROBERT (D.C. Center for Alcohol and Drug Abuse, Washington, DC)
"First Kiss" (WritersCorps Program). [WashR] (21:2) Ag-S 95, p. 5.
5252. ROBERTS, Beth
"The Narrow Escape." [NewEngR] (17:4) Fall 95, p. 127.
5253. ROBERTS, David Thomas
"I Mandate Ridges Raving." [NewOR] (21:2) Sum 95, p. 57.
"Tiff Belt Parley." [NewOR] (21:2) Sum 95, p. 56.
"Toward Mena." [NewOR] (21:2) Sum 95, p. 56.
5254. ROBERTS, Deborah H.
"A Reversal" (tr. of Horace I.5). [Arion] (3:2/3) Fall 95-Wint 96, p. 177.
5255. ROBERTS, Jo
"I'd like to kiss your belly, sail." [13thMoon] (13:1/2) 95, p. 33.
5256. ROBERTS, Katrina
"The Ruffled Edge." [PaintedB] (55/56) 95, p. 25-26.
"The Ruffled Edge." [PaintedB] (57) 95, p. 5-8.
"Sestina About Reciprocity" (First Place, Second Annual Poetry Contest).
[PaintedB] (55/56) 95, p. 34-36.
5257. ROBERTS, Len
"Among the Ferns of Finland" (tr. of Sándor Csoóri). [LitR] (38:3) Spr 95, p. 453.
"Angels in the Experimental Catechism / Math Class." [PoetryNW] (36:2) Sum 95,
p. 9-10.
"Autumn" (tr. of Sándor Csoóri). [LitR] (38:3) Spr 95, p. 451.
"Can You Still Hear It?" (tr. of Sándor Csoóri). [LitR] (38:3) Spr 95, p. 452.
"Christmas, 1952." [WestB] (36) 95, p. 24-26.
"Contemplating Again the Jade Chrysanthemum, or Why the Ancient Chinese Poets
Remained Unmarried." [QW] (40) Spr-Sum 95, p. 92-93.

"Gathering." [WestB] (36) 95, p. 26-27.
"I Lock Myself In" (tr. of Sándor Csoóri, w. László Vértes). [LitR] (38:3) Spr 95, p. 450.
"If You Were God's Relative" (tr. of Sándor Csoóri). [Chelsea] (58) 95, p. 30.
"Last Night, Between Dusk and." [PoetryNW] (36:2) Sum 95, p. 10-11.
"May the Water Keep Vigil with Me" (tr. of Sándor Csoóri, w. Anette Marta). [GrandS] (14:2, #54) Fall 95, p. 22.
"Obedient." [NewEngR] (17:2) Spr 95, p. 108-109.
"Search for the Perfect Christmas Tree, Wassergass, Pennsylvania, 1993, After a Sleepless Night of Reading Poetry." [SenR] (25:2) Fall 95, p. 83-85.
"So You Won't Be a Witness Today Either" (tr. of Sándor Csoóri, w. Anette Marta). [GrandS] (14:2, #54) Fall 95, p. 21.
"The Statues." [WestB] (36) 95, p. 23-24.
"Survey, Autumn, Wassergass." [SenR] (25:2) Fall 95, p. 86-87.
"With a Hangover" (tr. of Sándor Csoóri, w. László Vértes). [LitR] (38:3) Spr 95, p. 449.
"You Enter the Moment" (tr. of Sándor Csoóri). [Chelsea] (58) 95, p. 29.
5258. ROBERTS, Phil
"Coyotes." [PottPort] (16:1) Fall 95, p. 58.
"Looking Back." [PottPort] (16:1) Fall 95, p. 59.
5259. ROBERTS, Stephen R.
"Barn Dream." [Border] (7) Fall-Wint 96, p. 54.
"Doves." [BellArk] (11:6) N-D 95, p. 9.
"Quaker Chainsaw." [Blueline] (16) 95, p. 37.
"Something for Julie." [Border] (7) Fall-Wint 96, p. 55-56.
"Spring Counterpoint." [BellArk] (11:6) N-D 95, p. 9.
5260. ROBERTS, Teresa Noelle
"A Capella, 'Danny Boy'." [BellArk] (11:4) Jl-Ag 95, p. 13.
"Banshee Sight" (Brooklyn, New York, 1882). [BellArk] (11:6) N-D 95, p. 8.
"Following the Dog Route." [BellArk] (11:6) N-D 95, p. 8.
"Pond." [BellArk] (11:4) Jl-Ag 95, p. 10.
"Samhain." [BellArk] (11:3) My-Je 95, p. 11.
5261. ROBERTSON, Brian
"Defective." [Pearl] (22) Fall-Wint 95, p. 121.
"One Night." [Pearl] (22) Fall-Wint 95, p. 121.
5262. ROBERTSON, David
"Country Legacy." [Witness] (9:2) 95, p. 44-45.
"Keeping Watch." [Witness] (9:2) 95, p. 43-44.
"What Is Left of the Sweetness." [Witness] (9:2) 95, p. 42.
5263. ROBERTSON, Robin
"Advent in Co. Fermanagh." [Agni] (41) 95, p. 72-74.
"At Dusk." [NewYorker] (71:10) 1 My 95, p. 40.
"The Cry of Cinyras." [Pequod] (39) 95, p. 21-22.
"A Decomposition." [GrandS] (14:1, #53) Sum 95, p. 64.
"Escapology." [GrandS] (14:1, #53) Sum 95, p. 63.
"The Flowers of the Forest." [NewYorker] (71:17) 19 Je 95, p. 57.
"The Immoralist." [Pequod] (39) 95, p. 24.
"A Show of Signs" (i.m. B.J.R. 1929-1990). [Pequod] (39) 95, p. 20.
"A Show of Signs" (i.m. B.J.R. 1929-1990). [Stand] (36:2) Spr 95, p. 50.
5264. ROBERTSON, William
"Death and Sex." [Grain] (23:1) Sum 95, p. 58.
"Farm Wife." [CanLit] (144) Spr 95, p. 125.
5265. ROBIN, Marilyn
"Mother to Son" (WritersCorps Program, Washington, DC). [WashR] (21:2) Ag-S 95, p. 12.
5266. ROBIN, Mark
"When Dexter Ran Away." [ContextS] (4:2) 95, p. 17.
5267. ROBINS, Corinne
"On the Vatican Steps." [NewAW] (13) Fall-Wint 95, p. 108.
5268. ROBINSON, Blake
"And is there beauty still in this world?" (tr. of Sandro Penna). [Chelsea] (59) 95, p. 117.
"At noontime, can't you see" (tr. of Sandro Penna). [Chelsea] (59) 95, p. 118.
"The black train puffing smoke comes" (tr. of Sandro Penna). [Chelsea] (59) 95, p. 119.

"Filled with sun's scent, my testicles" (tr. of Sandro Penna). [Chelsea] (59) 95, p. 118.
"For Renzo Vespignani" (tr. of Sandro Penna). [Chelsea] (59) 95, p. 118-119.
"He brings a new boy" (tr. of Sandro Penna). [Chelsea] (59) 95, p. 117.
"It's a sunny land. Beneath it lies" (tr. of Sandro Penna). [Chelsea] (59) 95, p. 119.
"Just in this sweet jail I feel" (tr. of Sandro Penna). [Chelsea] (59) 95, p. 117.
"Lights beam on the riverside" (tr. of Sandro Penna). [Chelsea] (59) 95, p. 118.
"Love, that old love inclined to hardheadedness?" (tr. of Sandro Penna). [Chelsea] (59) 95, p. 119.
"September" (tr. of Sandro Penna). [Chelsea] (59) 95, p. 117.
"So many birthdays toasted at table" (tr. of Sandro Penna). [Chelsea] (59) 95, p. 119.
"Spring on my mind and happy" (tr. of Sandro Penna). [Chelsea] (59) 95, p. 118.
"They've severed the world" (tr. of Sandro Penna). [Chelsea] (59) 95, p. 119.
"This melody's of a sin" (tr. of Sandro Penna). [Chelsea] (59) 95, p. 119.
"Veiled with scent of crushed grapes" (tr. of Sandro Penna). [Chelsea] (59) 95, p. 117.
"You're in the train's voice way off" (tr. of Sandro Penna). [Chelsea] (59) 95, p. 117.
5269. ROBINSON, Elizabeth
"Properties." [NewAW] (13) Fall-Wint 95, p. 42.
"Site Legend." [WashR] (20:6) Ap-My 95, p. 11.
"Sleeptalk." [NewAW] (13) Fall-Wint 95, p. 43.
5270. ROBINSON, Kim
"Ladies of Dim Time." [MalR] (111) Sum 95, p. 48-49.
"Red." [MalR] (111) Sum 95, p. 51.
"She-lagh: Blue." [MalR] (111) Sum 95, p. 50.
5271. ROBINSON, M. Christian
"The Difference Between Dark and Hard." [PennR] (6:2) 95, p. 17.
5272. ROBINSON, Martha
"A Sketch." [Light] (15/16) Aut-Wint 95-96, p. 29.
5273. ROBINSON, Peter
"A Burning Head." [Stand] (36:3) Sum 95, p. 62-67.
5274. ROBINSON, Yolanda
"Untitled: Throughout the day and the wildness of the Night" (WritersCorps Project, Washington, DC). [WashR] (21:2) Ag-S 95, p. 21.
5275. ROBISON, Margaret
"Loony Bin Trip." [Kaleid] (31) Sum-Fall 95, p. 45.
"Stigma." [Kaleid] (30) Wint-Spr 95, p. 38.
5276. ROBNOLT, J'Laine
"Gospel." [LouisL] (12:1) Spr 95, p. 65.
"The Lid." [LouisL] (12:1) Spr 95, p. 66-67.
"Twenty Thousand Days" (For Jim Whitehead). [CharR] (21:2) Fall 95, p. 88.
5277. ROBY, Gayle
"The Carpenter." [PraS] (69:1) Spr 95, p. 162.
"The Gamekeeper." [PraS] (69:1) Spr 95, p. 161.
ROBYN SARAH
See SARAH, Robyn
5278. ROCCHI, Maureen
"The Men in Their Suits." [Writer] (108:3) Mr 95, p. 12-13.
5279. ROCCO, Richard M.
"Died 1947, Age 47." [ChironR] (42) Spr 95, p. 19.
"It's Time to Move." [ChironR] (42) Spr 95, p. 19.
"Rebel at the Art Museum, 1960." [ChironR] (42) Spr 95, p. 19.
5280. ROCHE, Maurice
"Funeral Cantata" (tr. by Alexander Laurence). [ApalQ] (43) Spr 95, p. 27-35.
5281. ROCHELLE, Warren
"My Father's Heart." [Crucible] (31) Fall 95, p. 10.
5282. ROCK, David
"Give Me a Token." [OxfordM] (10:1) Wint 94-Spr 95, p. 57.
5283. ROCKIN' RED
"Dealing with Grief." [Light] (14) Sum 95, p. 18.
"His Future Ex-Wife." [Light] (15/16) Aut-Wint 95-96, p. 20.
5284. ROCKWELL, Tom
"Laurel As a Boy's Name." [NewYorkQ] (55) 95, p. 72-73.
"Licorice Tongued." [NewYorkQ] (54) 95, p. 64.
5285. RODERMAN, Juliet
"Winter." [ManyMM] (2:1) 95, p. 52.

5286. RODIA, Becky
"After the Funeral." [WeberS] (12:1) Wint 95, p. 111-112.
"Believer at the Ice Cream Parlor." [CreamCR] (19:1) Spr 95, p. 157.
"Hunger Pains." [WeberS] (12:1) Wint 95, p. 112.
"Mandolin." [WeberS] (12:1) Wint 95, p. 111.
5287. RODIER, Katharine
"After a Death" (for Evelyn and May Wright). [PoetryE] (40) Spr 95, p. 105.
5288. RODLEY, Laura
"Acupuncture Love." [MassR] (36:2) Sum 95, p. 247.
5289. RODRIGUES, Santan
"Inquisition." [AnotherCM] (29) Spr 95, p. 113.
"Notes from a Frontier Town." [AnotherCM] (29) Spr 95, p. 114.
5290. RODRIGUEZ, Carmen
"Home." [Arc] (35) Aut 95, p. 13.
"Naked Out There" (tr. by Heidi Neufeld Raine and the author). [Arc] (35) Aut 95,
p. 14.
"Positions" (tr. by Heidi Neufeld Raine and the author). [Arc] (35) Aut 95, p. 15-16.
5291. RODRIGUEZ, Claudio
"Canto del Despertar." [MidAR] (15:1/2) 95, p. 170, 172.
"The Contracting of Laborers" (tr. by Elizabeth Gamble Miller). [MidAR] (15:1/2)
95, p. 175, 177.
"La Contrata de Mozos." [MidAR] (15:1/2) 95, p. 174, 176.
"De Amor Ha Sido la Falta." [MidAR] (15:1/2) 95, p. 178.
"Elegía desde Simancas (Hacia la Historia)." [MidAR] (15:1/2) 95, p. 180-186.
"Elegy from Simancas (Toward History)" (tr. by Elizabeth Gamble Miller).
[MidAR] (15:1/2) 95, p. 181-187.
"Love Is to Blame" (tr. by Elizabeth Gamble Miller). [MidAR] (15:1/2) 95, p. 179.
"The Market of Light" (Translation Chapbook Series Number 23, tr. by Elizabeth
Gamble Miller). [MidAR] (15:1/2) 95, p. 167-187.
"Song of Awakening" (tr. by Elizabeth Gamble Miller). [MidAR] (15:1/2) 95, p.
171, 173.
5292. RODRIGUEZ, Luis
"To the Police Officer Who Refused to Sit in the Same Room as My Son Because
He's a 'Gang Banger'." [WillowR] (22) Spr 95, p. 14.
5293. RODRIGUEZ NUÑEZ, Víctor
"Número Equivocado." [Americas] (23:3/4) Fall-Wint 95, p. 162.
"Poema de los Nuncas." [Americas] (23:3/4) Fall-Wint 95, p. 163.
"World — An English Lesson." [Americas] (23:3/4) Fall-Wint 95, p. 161.
5294. ROE, Margie McCreless
"Late in Summer." [ChrC] (112:24) 16-23 Ag 95, p. 775.
5295. ROEDER, Jessica
"Dissolving a Book by Ernest Hemingway." [DenQ] (29:4) Spr 95, p. 50-51.
"Out." [AmerPoR] (24:5) S-O 95, p. 33-34.
5296. ROETHKE, Theodore
"The Chums." [Field] (53) Fall 95, p. 28.
"Frau Bauman, Frau Schmidt, and Frau Schwartze." [Field] (53) Fall 95, p. 10.
"The Lost Son." [Field] (53) Fall 95, p. 14-15.
"The Tree, the Bird." [Field] (53) Fall 95, p. 32.
"The Waking." [Field] (53) Fall 95, p. 20.
5297. ROGAL, Stan
"Personations, 21." [PoetryC] (15:3) Ag 95, p. 14.
"Personations, 30" (for Pam). [PottPort] (16:1) Fall 95, p. 24.
"Personations, 31." [PoetryC] (15:3) Ag 95, p. 14.
5298. ROGERS, Bruce Holland
"Listening, Listening." [IllinoisR] (3:1/2) Fall 95-Spr 96, p. 71-72.
"One Thing After Another." [IllinoisR] (3:1/2) Fall 95-Spr 96, p. 45-46.
5299. ROGERS, Denise M.
"Dreaming of Immortality in a Thatched Cottage" (based on a scroll painting
attributed to Tang Yin, 1470-1523). [GreenHLL] (5) 94, p. 27.
"The River Goddess." [GreenHLL] (5) 94, p. 29.
"The Scholar Dreams of His Entrance Into Heaven." [GreenHLL] (5) 94, p. 24.
"The Sleeping Dragon." [GreenHLL] (5) 94, p. 28.
"Transactions With the World." [GreenHLL] (5) 94, p. 25-26.
5300. ROGERS, Garnet
"Reintroduction" (for Sarah Rutledge Birnbaum who jumped from the Golden Gate
Bridge). [AxeF] (3) 90, p. 33.

"Thoughts While Driving." [AxeF] (3) 90, p. 32.
5301. ROGERS, Hoyt
    "The Snow" (tr. of Yves Bonnefoy). [Agni] (41) 95, p. 38.
    "Summer Again" (tr. of Yves Bonnefoy). [Agni] (41) 95, p. 37.
    "A Voice" (tr. of Yves Bonnefoy). [HarvardR] (9) Fall 95, p. 31.
5302. ROGERS, Linda
    "Bush Babies at the Boehme." [PoetryC] (15:2) Je 95, p. 18.
    "Civil Misunderstanding." [PoetryC] (15:2) Je 95, p. 19.
    "Days of the Inforiata." [PoetryC] (15:2) Je 95, p. 18.
    "Lay Down on Me." [PoetryC] (15:2) Je 95, p. 19.
    "Thursday Beatitude." [PoetryC] (15:2) Je 95, p. 18.
    "You Hear Them." [PoetryC] (15:2) Je 95, p. 19.
5303. ROGERS, Pattiann
    "Abundance and Satisfaction." [Iowa] (25:1) Wint 95, p. 157-159.
    "Against the Ethereal." [PraS] (69:3) Fall 95, p. 148-149.
    "Being Known: Goldfinches at Sea." [CrabOR] (1:1) Fall-Wint 95, p. 93-94.
    "Calling to Measure" (from The Journals of a Lost Believer). [Poetry] (166:2) My
        95, p. 97-98.
    "The Center of the Known Universe." [PraS] (69:3) Fall 95, p. 146-148.
    "The China Cabinet Festival: 21st Century." [CrabOR] (1:1) Fall-Wint 95, p. 95-96.
    "Design of Gongs." [Poetry] (166:2) My 95, p. 96-97.
    "Fractal: Repetition of Form Over a Variety of Scales." [QW] (41) Aut-Wint 95-96,
        p. 183.
    "'God Is in the Details,' Says Mathematician Freeman J. Dyson." [GettyR] (8:1)
        Wint 95, p. 69-70.
    "Inside the Universe Inside the Act." [QW] (41) Aut-Wint 95-96, p. 184-185.
    "Kaleidoscope: Free Will and the Nature of the Holy Spirit." [GettyR] (8:1) Wint
        95, p. 71-72.
    "Kissing a Kit Fox." [PlumR] (9) [95 or 96], p. 42-43.
    "The Long Marriage: A Translation." [PraS] (69:3) Fall 95, p. 145-146.
    "Mousefeet" (from a lecture on Muridae cosmology). [KenR] (17:3/4) Sum-Fall 95,
        p. 1-3.
    "Orange Thicket: To Speak in Tongues." [PlumR] (9) [95 or 96], p. 44-45.
    "Place and Proximity." [QW] (41) Aut-Wint 95-96, p. 186.
    "Where Do Your People Come From?" [KenR] (17:3/4) Sum-Fall 95, p. 3-4.
5304. ROGERS-GREEN, Carmen
    "Sarah Seh." [CaribbeanW] (9) 95, p. 50-52.
5305. ROGOFF, Jay
    "The Bride" (from "Venera"). [ParisR] (37:137) Wint 95, p. 223-223.
    "Only Child." [Salm] (106/107) Spr-Sum 95, p. 125-126.
    "The Queen" (from "Venera"). [ParisR] (37:137) Wint 95, p. 223.
    "The Slide." [Chelsea] (58) 95, p. 50-51.
    "Venera" (Selections: 3 poems). [ParisR] (37:137) Wint 95, p. 223-224.
    "The Virgin" (from "Venera"). [ParisR] (37:137) Wint 95, p. 224.
5306. ROHRER, Matt (Matthew)
    "After the Performance." [Iowa] (25:1) Wint 95, p. 54.
    "Found in the Museum of Old Science." [Iowa] (25:1) Wint 95, p. 52-53.
    "A Hummock in the Malookas" (for Jennifer Kitchell). [SouthernPR] (35:1) Sum
        95, p. 68-69.
    "Hymn to Be Sung on Good Friday." [Iowa] (25:1) Wint 95, p. 54-55.
    "Quick Sell the Pig." [CutB] (42) Sum 94, p. 10.
    "The Toads 1975." [Iowa] (25:1) Wint 95, p. 53.
5307. ROLLINGS, Alane
    "In Touching Distance." [TriQ] (93) Spr-Sum 95, p. 145-146.
    "The Life." [SenR] (25:1) Spr 95, p. 39-40.
    "The Logic of Opposites." [TriQ] (93) Spr-Sum 95, p. 149-150.
    "The Outback." [ChiR] (41:2/3) 95, p. 64-65.
    "The Substance of Evanescent Things." [TriQ] (93) Spr-Sum 95, p. 147-148.
5308. ROLLINS, Scott
    "5. The Traveller (account of the separation)" (tr. of Patricia Lasoen). [Vis] (47) 95,
        p. 37.
    "6. The Traveller (account of the murder)" (tr. of Patricia Lasoen). [Vis] (47) 95, p.
        37.
    "Talent" (tr. of Kees Ouwens, w. Peter Nijmeijer). [CimR] (112) Jl 95, p. 11.
5309. ROMANO, Rose
    "Beyond That." [SlipS] (15) 95, p. 53.

"Sending Out for Pizza." [SlipS] (15) 95, p. 31-32.
5310. ROMERO, Armando
"The Builder" (for Jaime Garcia Maffla, tr. by Alita Kelley). [ProseP] (4) 95, p. 64.
"Traveling Man" (tr. by Alita Kelley). [ProseP] (4) 95, p. 63.
5311. ROMERO, Danny
"Identification." [Drumvoices] (4:1/2) Fall-Wint 94-95, p. 122.
5312. ROMERO, Elaine
"Duende." [BilingR] (20:2) My-Ag 95, p. 158.
"Eclipse." [BilingR] (20:2) My-Ag 95, p. 159.
5313. ROMERO, Levi
"Easynights and a Pack of Frajos." [RiverS] (45) 95, p. 58-60.
5314. ROMOND, Edwin
"Macaroons" (for my mother). [Sun] (233) My 95, p. 7.
"To My Neighbor." [PoetL] (90:3) Fall 95, p. 58.
5315. ROMOSAN, Petru
"Spring Tale" (tr. by Adam J. Sorkin and Radu Surdulescu). [Vis] (48) 95, p. 43.
"Yorick, Yorick, Yorick, or How About You, Reader, Would You Hold My Skull in Your Hand?" (tr. by Adam J. Sorkin and Radu Surdulescu). [Vis] (49) 95, p. 7.
5316. ROMSTEDT, Nadine
"Sweet plum." [Bogg] (67) 95, p. 32.
5317. ROMTVEDT, David
"An English Country Cottage." [Event] (24:1) Spr 95, p. 41.
"My Death." [Sun] (235) Jl 95, p. 13.
"My Winter Wood." [Sun] (229) Ja 95, p. 33.
5318. RONK, Martha
"Accidents Will Happen." [Crazy] (49) Wint 95, p. 21.
"The Great Blue." [Crazy] (49) Wint 95, p. 20.
"My mind at cross-purposes, asking." [Jacaranda] (11) [95 or 96?], p. 154.
"Night and Day." [Crazy] (49) Wint 95, p. 19.
"No Tomorrow." [Crazy] (49) Wint 95, p. 18.
5319. RONSARD, Pierre de
"Ode: 'Ma Douce Jouvance Est Passée'" (tr. by Fred Chappell). [DefinedP] (2:2) Spr-Sum 94, p. 39.
5320. ROONEY, Padraig
"Home." [SouthernR] (31:3) Jl/Sum 95, p. 741-742.
5321. ROOT, William Pitt
"Courage: Revising the Text." [Comm] (122:1) 13 Ja 95, p. 13.
"In the House of Denial." [Comm] (122:6) 24 Mr 95, p. 14.
"The Old Racket Goes On." [Manoa] (7:1) Sum 95, p. 29-30.
5322. ROQUEPLAN, Fernand
"Big Women." [Vis] (47) 95, p. 36.
"Imagine the Bird Bathing, Cat Creeping, Man Sleeping." [LaurelR] (29:1) Wint 95, p. 81.
"The Posture of Hate." [LaurelR] (29:1) Wint 95, p. 82.
"Social Standards, Three Myths." [LaurelR] (29:1) Wint 95, p. 80-81.
5323. RORIPAUGH, Lee Ann
"Hiroshima Maiden." [SenR] (25:2) Fall 95, p. 103-105.
"The Woman Who Loves Insects." [CreamCR] (19:1) Spr 95, p. 123-124.
5324. RORIPAUGH, Robert
"Sleeping Out on Sulphur Creek in Autumn: For John." [SoDakR] (33:3/4) Fall-Wint 95, p. 107-108.
5325. ROSCOE, Jerry
"Cigarets" [sic]. [OhioR] (53) 95, p. 123.
5326. ROSE, Carol
"Elijah." [PraF] (16:4, #73) Wint 95-96, p. 54.
5327. ROSE, Jennifer
"A Morning Walk" (Sweet Briar, Virginia). [Chelsea] (59) 95, p. 204.
"Valedictory." [Poetry] (166:3) Je 95, p. 165.
5328. ROSE, Rachel
"Forgiving the River." [Arc] (34) Spr 95, p. 47.
"Of This More Is Yet to Come." [Arc] (34) Spr 95, p. 48.
"Return to Your Skin." [Calyx] (16:2) Wint 95-96, p. 85.
"Settlement." [Calyx] (16:2) Wint 95-96, p. 84.
5329. ROSE, Shawna
"Wait." [SpinningJ] (1) Fall 95-Wint 96, p. 29.

389

5330. ROSE, Wendy
    "Calling Home the Scientists." [RiverS] (42/43) 95, p. 29.
ROSELLO, Carmen Giménez
    See GIMÉNEZ-ROSELLO, Carmen
ROSEN, Carole Borges
    See BORGES-ROSEN, Carole
5331. ROSEN, Kenneth
    "Alice, Australia." [Ploughs] (21:1) Spr 95, p. 125-126.
    "Bog Girl." [NewEngR] (17:2) Spr 95, p. 86-87.
    "The Gulls." [BelPoJ] (45:4) Chapbook 22, Sum 95, p. 59.
    "Invisible City." [Ploughs] (21:1) Spr 95, p. 127.
    "Paradise Lost." [BelPoJ] (45:4) Chapbook 22, Sum 95, p. 60.
    "Red Letter." [MassR] (36:2) Sum 95, p. 281-282.
    "Salmonelle." [BelPoJ] (45:4) Chapbook 22, Sum 95, p. 61-62.
    "Skowhegan Owl." [Ascent] (20:1) Fall 95, p. 52.
    "The Squirrel." [NewEngR] (17:2) Spr 95, p. 87-88.
    "Storm." [Ascent] (20:1) Fall 95, p. 53.
5332. ROSEN, Michael J.
    "Make Your Own Zoo." [Witness] (9:1) 95, p. 78-80.
5333. ROSENBERG, Lisa
    "The Satellite Sky." [Thrpny] (60) Wint 95, p. 23.
5334. ROSENBERG, Liz
    "Hand of God." [AmerPoR] (24:1) Ja-F 95, p. 12.
    "The Kiss." [AmerPoR] (24:1) Ja-F 95, p. 12.
    "The Little Red Shoe" (After Perle Hessing). [SenR] (25:1) Spr 95, p. 111.
    "The Mailman." [AmerPoR] (24:1) Ja-F 95, p. 12.
    "One Child." [AmerPoR] (24:1) Ja-F 95, p. 12.
    "Remembering June." [AmerPoR] (24:1) Ja-F 95, p. 12.
    "Safe." [AmerPoR] (24:1) Ja-F 95, p. 12.
    "September." [NewMyths] (2:2/3:1) 95, p. 388.
    "Things of the World." [AmerPoR] (24:1) Ja-F 95, p. 12.
    "Wild Mind." [NewYorker] (71:39) 4 D 95, p. 58.
    "The Window." [AmerPoR] (24:1) Ja-F 95, p. 12.
5335. ROSENBLATT, Joe
    "A Gustable Journey." [PoetryC] (15:3) Ag 95, p. 7.
    "Out in the Bay." [PoetryC] (15:3) Ag 95, p. 6.
    "She Who Loves Tabbies." [PoetryC] (15:3) Ag 95, p. 7.
    "A Stranger in the Flickering Light." [PoetryC] (15:3) Ag 95, p. 7.
    "That Holy Ink." [PoetryC] (15:3) Ag 95, p. 6.
5336. ROSENFELD, Ruth
    "Humbly, I Wish to Cultivate" (tr. by Thomas Dorsett). [InterPR] (21:1) Spr 95, p. 43.
    "Ich Möchte Dich Mir Zaghaft Bauen." [InterPR] (21:1) Spr 95, p. 42.
    "Manchmal Wächst Du aus Meiner Hand Wie ein Baum." [InterPR] (21:1) Spr 95, p. 44.
    "Sometimes You Grow from My Hand Like a Tree" (tr. by Thomas Dorsett). [InterPR] (21:1) Spr 95, p. 45.
5337. ROSENSTOCK, Gabriel
    "Mustanbih" (For Peter Van de Kamp, in Irish and English, tr. by Desmond O'Grady). [Poetry] (167:1/2) O-N 95, p. 46-49.
5338. ROSENSTOCK, S. X.
    "Aubrey Beardsley on the Subject of His Own Willful Ignorance of the *Caprichos* of Francisco Goya." [ParisR] (37:134) Spr 95, p. 46-47.
5339. ROSENTHAL, M. L.
    "Shadow-Runners." [SouthernR] (31:2) Ap/Spr 95, p. 296-297.
5340. ROSENWALD, John
    "As I Know It" (tr. of Bei Dao, w. Yanbing Chen). [BelPoJ] (46:2) Wint 95-96, p. 38-39.
    "Untitled: People hurry, arrive" (tr. of Bei Dao, w. Yanbing Chen). [BelPoJ] (46:2) Wint 95-96, p. 40.
5341. ROSENZWEIG, Geri
    "October." [Parting] (8:1) Sum 95, p. 29.
    "Patches of Summer." [Confr] (56/57) Sum-Fall 95, p. 310.
    "Skeleton of a Young Pike Lough Ree, Ireland." [Parting] (8:1) Sum 95, p. 28.
    "West of Ireland." [NewDeltaR] (13:1) Fall 95-Wint 96, p. 29.

5342. RÖSEWICZ, Tadeusz
"Alpha" (tr. by John M. Gogol). [NorthStoneR] (12) 95, p. 56.
"Knowledge" (tr. by John M. Gogol). [NorthStoneR] (12) 95, p. 57.
5343. ROSS, David
"Algebra." [BellArk] (11:6) N-D 95, p. 31.
"Portraiture." [BellArk] (11:6) N-D 95, p. 31.
"Symbol." [BellArk] (11:2) Mr-Ap 95, p. 14.
"Willow." [BellArk] (11:2) Mr-Ap 95, p. 15.
"Wood Nymph." [YellowS] (12:4, #48) Sum 95, p. 18-19.
5344. ROSS, Joe
"The Fuzzy Logic Series" (Selections: 9 poems). [Avec] (9) 95, p. 12-20.
5345. ROSS, Linwood M.
"For Malcolm, with Gratitude." [AfAmRev] (29:4) Wint 95, p. 628-629.
ROSS, Louise Viste
See VISTE-ROSS, Louise
ROSS, Nathan Viste
See VISTE-ROSS, Nathan
5346. ROSSER, J. Allyn
"Before the Sickness Is Official." [Poetry] (166:3) Je 95, p. 148-149.
"The Cry." [GeoR] (49:3) Fall 95, p. 665-666.
"North Jersey Farmland, Vile Mood." [OhioR] (53) 95, p. 118-119.
"Realism." [NewEngR] (17:1) Wint 95, p. 23.
5347. ROSSI, Lee
"The Beauty Operator's Son." [ApalQ] (43) Spr 95, p. 72-73.
"My Father's Gun." [Chelsea] (58) 95, p. 40-41.
5348. ROSSMANN, Ed
"Eighth Period." [PoetryE] (39) Fall 94, p. 75.
5349. ROSTOVICH, Victoria
"Folk Tales." [CutB] (42) Sum 94, p. 75-77.
"Wash Duty." [CutB] (42) Sum 94, p. 78-79.
5350. ROSU, Dona
"As If Blind" (tr. by Ann Woodward). [Confr] (56/57) Sum-Fall 95, p. 335.
"Dog, My Brother" (tr. by Dan Dutescu). [LitR] (38:2) Wint 95, p. 276.
"Your Name" (tr. by Ann Woodward). [Confr] (56/57) Sum-Fall 95, p. 335.
5351. ROTH, Laurence
"You I." [AntR] (53:1) Wint 95, p. 66-67.
5352. ROTH, Linda
"What I Remember of the Fight I Stopped." [EngJ] (84:5) S 95, p. 50.
5353. ROTH, Ron
"Anniversary." [Plain] (15:3) Spr 95, p. 30.
"Country Music." [Plain] (15:3) Spr 95, p. 31.
5354. ROTH, Susan Harned
"His Country" (The 1994 Allen Ginsberg Poetry Awards: Honorable Mention).
[Footwork] (24/25) 95, p. 203.
5355. ROTHENBERG, Jerome
"Pain." [Sulfur] (15:2, #37) Fall 95, p. 71.
"Prologomena to a Poetics" (for Michael McClure). [Sulfur] (15:2, #37) Fall 95, p.
72-74.
"The Structural Study of Myth" (for Barbara Kirshenblatt-Gimblett). [RiverS]
(42/43) 95, p. 2.
5356. ROUFF, R.
"Minor Ideas." [InterQ] (2:1/2) 95, p. 281.
5357. ROUNDY, Richard
"The Corrugated Notebooks" (Excerpts). [WashR] (21:4) D 95-Ja 96, p. 11.
ROUS, Peter de
See DeROUS, Peter
5358. ROUSSEAU, Nancy
"J. Ford in the Water Hyacinths." [SoCoast] (18) Ja 95, p. 13.
5359. ROUZIER, Agnès
"Non, Rien" (Excerpts, tr. by Chet Wiener). [Avec] (9) 95, p. 173-180.
5360. ROWAN, Quentin
"Autumn in Three Colors." [HangL] (66) 95, p. 95-96.
"Prometheus at Coney Island." [HangL] (66) 95, p. 93-94.
5361. ROWE, Ronald
"Francavilla à Mare." [WritersF] (21) 95, p. 132-133.

391

RUDMAN

5362. ROXAS, Savina
    "Bread and Water" (Southern Italy, 1883). [Footwork] (24/25) 95, p. 55.
    "Sheep and Wolves" (Southern Italy, 1900). [Footwork] (24/25) 95, p. 55.
    "SS Lamerica" (Southern Italy, 1904). [Footwork] (24/25) 95, p. 55.
5363. ROXMAN, Susanna
    "In the Lapland Mountains." [WritersF] (21) 95, p. 45.
5364. ROY, Darlene
    "Cross / Overs" (For Toni Brown). [Drumvoices] (5:1/2) Fall-Wint 95-96, p. 26.
    "Transformed" (For Girvies Davis, executed on May 17, 1995). [Drumvòices]
        (5:1/2) Fall-Wint 95-96, p. 27.
5365. ROY, Lucinda
    "The Bread Man." [Shen] (45:1) Spr 95, p. 26.
    "The Man Who Played the Trumpet." [RiverS] (45) 95, p. 29-30.
    "Talking to a Writer." [RiverS] (45) 95, p. 31.
5366. ROY, Tapas
    "About Morning" (tr. by Peter Michelson and Manjush Dasgupta). [AnotherCM]
        (29) Spr 95, p. 115.
    "Time Warp" (tr. by Peter Michelson and Manjush Dasgupta). [AnotherCM] (29)
        Spr 95, p. 116.
5367. ROZDILSKY, Kristi
    "Chakra." [BellArk] (11:3) My-Je 95, p. 24.
    "Snapshot." [BellArk] (11:2) Mr-Ap 95, p. 26.
    "Taxonomy." [BellArk] (11:2) Mr-Ap 95, p. 26.
    "Thirst." [BellArk] (11:2) Mr-Ap 95, p. 27.
    "A Visit to Our Lady of Perpetual Incarnation." [BellArk] (11:3) My-Je 95, p. 7.
    "Visitor." [BellArk] (11:3) My-Je 95, p. 10.
5368. RUARK, Gibbons
    "Blue Shades for a Daughter." [Shen] (45:1) Spr 95, p. 120.
5369. RUBENSTEIN, Eliza
    "The Lake Isle of Innisfree." [LitR] (38:3) Spr 95, p. 425.
5370. RUBENSTEIN, Meridel
    "Critical Mass" (w. Ellen Zweig). [Conjunc] (24) 95, p. 165-187.
RUBIA BARCIA, José
    See BARCIA, José Rubia
5371. RUBIN, Anele
    "An Attempt at Explanation." [Footwork] (24/25) 95, p. 74.
    "Cold Ocean Moments." [Footwork] (24/25) 95, p. 74.
    "His Death." [SpoonR] (20:2) Sum-Fall 95, p. 58.
    "Listening to the Public Station." [SpoonR] (20:2) Sum-Fall 95, p. 59.
    "No One Knew." [Footwork] (24/25) 95, p. 74.
    "Sundays." [Footwork] (24/25) 95, p. 74.
5372. RUBIN, Larry
    "Backpacking in the Tyrol: Hazards and Escalations." [ColEng] (57:5) S 95, p. 585.
    "Lines for an Aunt in Intensive Care, Who Gave Piano Lessons." [SouthernHR]
        (29:3) Sum 95, p. 270.
5373. RUBIN, Louis D., Jr.
    "On a Ferryboat" (for M. J. R., 1893-1967). [SouthernR] (31:1) Wint 95, p. 53-57.
5374. RUBIN, Mark
    "Adjustment." [OhioR] (53) 95, p. 52.
    "Fishing: Montana Zen" (for Richard Hugo). [Verse] (12:3) 95, p. 48.
    "Readjustment." [OhioR] (53) 95, p. 53.
5375. RUBIN, Stan Sanvel
    "Partial List of the Saved." [VirQR] (71:4) Aut 95, p. 699-700.
5376. RUBINSTEIN, Raphael
    "In the Meantime." [AmerPoR] (24:4) Jl-Ag 95, p. 38.
    "Summer Reading." [Talisman] (15) Wint 95-96, p. 94-95.
5377. RUCKS, Carol
    "Soup." [WestB] (37) 95, p. 24.
5378. RUDERMAN, Ian
    "Untitled: She says that gorillas sometimes attack." [LiteralL] (1:5) Early Spr 95, p.
        21.
5379. RUDERMAN, Renée
    "Paper Shade." [BellR] (18:1, #37) Spr 95, p. 7.
5380. RUDMAN, Mark
    "Aesacus Risen." [Arion] (3:2/3) Fall 95-Wint 96, p. 183-184.
    "The Diver" (after Ovid). [Arion] (3:2/3) Fall 95-Wint 96, p. 179-182.

"Easter Weekend in Denver." [DenQ] (30:2) Fall 95, p. 62-70.
"On the Wheel of." [CrabOR] (1:1) Fall-Wint 95, p. 120-130.
"Pool Hall." [CrabOR] (1:1) Fall-Wint 95, p. 118-119.

5381. RUEFLE, Mary
"The Brooch." [AmerPoR] (24:5) S-O 95, p. 21.
"Nice Hands." [AmerPoR] (24:5) S-O 95, p. 21.
"School of Denial." [AmerPoR] (24:5) S-O 95, p. 21.
"Talking to Strangers." [AmerPoR] (24:1) Ja-F 95, p. 56.
"Topophilia." [AmerPoR] (24:5) S-O 95, p. 21.

5382. RUESCHER, Scott
"Sarge Beam" (Finalist, 1995 Greg Grummer Award in Poetry). [Phoebe] (24:2) 95, p. 187-189.

5383. RUETENIK, Sharon A.
"The Refugee" (from a painting by Marjorie Gibbons). [SmPd] (32:3, #95) Fall 95, p. 13-14.
"Seven Sees" [sic]. [SmPd] (32:3, #95) Fall 95, p. 13.

5384. RUGGIERI, Helen
"In the Dead End of November." [SlipS] (15) 95, p. 14.

5385. RUGO, Mariève
"Diane Arbus: to the Reader." [QW] (40) Spr-Sum 95, p. 62.
"Guilt." [ColEng] (57:5) S 95, p. 586.

5386. RUIZ, Jean Marie
"In Barcelona." [Jacaranda] (11) [95 or 96?], p. 104-105.

5387. RUIZ, Olivia
"Saul's Dream." [Zyzzyva] (11:1, #41) Spr 95, p. 139.

5388. RUMI, Jelaluddin (1207-1273)
"Be helpless and dumbfounded" (Mathnawi, IV, 3748-3754, tr. by Coleman Barks). [InterPR] (21:1) Spr 95, p. 16.
"Everything you do has a quality" (Mathnawi, IV, 418-434, tr. by Coleman Barks). [InterPR] (21:1) Spr 95, p. 17.
"Looking for the ocean, I found" (622, tr. by Coleman Barks). [InterPR] (21:1) Spr 95, p. 11.
"No one knows what makes the soul" (423, tr. by Coleman Barks). [InterPR] (21:1) Spr 95, p. 10.
"Not until a person dissolves" (604, tr. by Coleman Barks). [InterPR] (21:1) Spr 95, p. 11.
"Personal intelligence is not capable" (Mathnawi, IV, 1294-1300, tr. by Coleman Barks). [InterPR] (21:1) Spr 95, p. 13.
"Soul of this world" (183, in Persian and English, tr. by Coleman Barks). [InterPR] (21:1) Spr 95, p. 8-9.
"They say, 'This majestic love you sing of is not a faithful love'" (1299, tr. by Coleman Barks). [InterPR] (21:1) Spr 95, p. 12-13.
"When I see Your Face, the stones start spinning!" (tr. by Coleman Barks). [PoetryE] (41) Aut 95, p. 23.
"You see flag-lions playing in the wind" (Mathnawi, IV, 3051-3054, 3059-3084, tr. by Coleman Barks). [InterPR] (21:1) Spr 95, p. 14-15.
"You who long for powerful positions" (188, in Persian and English, tr. by Coleman Barks). [InterPR] (21:1) Spr 95, p. 8-9.
"Your eyes are the mystery" (632, tr. by Coleman Barks). [InterPR] (21:1) Spr 95, p. 11.

5389. RUMMEL, Mary Kay
"Cloister" (from "Heron Moon: The Wing's Shadow." Finalist, The Nimrod / Hardman Awards). [Nimrod] (39:1) Fall-Wint 95, p. 65-66.
"Tongues of Women / Tongues of Angels" (from "Heron Moon: The Wing's Shadow." Finalist, The Nimrod / Hardman Awards). [Nimrod] (39:1) Fall-Wint 95, p. 67.

5390. RUMSEY, Tessa
"Big Rig the Baroque Sky." [BlackWR] (21:2) Spr-Sum 95, p. 28-29.
"Big Rig the Baroque Sky" (Honorable Mention, 1995 Greg Grummer Award in Poetry). [Phoebe] (24:2) 95, p. 142-143.
"Bluebells" (Honorable Mention, 1995 Greg Grummer Award in Poetry). [Phoebe] (24:2) 95, p. 140-141.
"The Sundial." [ColR] (22:1) Spr 95, p. 48-50.
"Three Trees for a New World Economy" (Honorable Mention, 1995 Greg Grummer Award in Poetry). [Phoebe] (24:2) 95, p. 138-139.

5391. RUNCIMAN, Lex
"Applause." [PoetryE] (39) Fall 94, p. 76-77.
"Violence." [QW] (41) Aut-Wint 95-96, p. 188.
5392. RUNGREN, Lawrence
"Return." [LowellR] [1] Sum 94, p. 69.
"Roots." [LowellR] [1] Sum 94, p. 70.
5393. RUNYAN, Tana
"Driving to a Separate Heaven with My Aunt Jackie." [Event] (24:2) Sum 95, p. 38-39.
"RAF Manoeuvre." [Event] (24:2) Sum 95, p. 40.
5394. RUPPEL, Amy
"Living in Our Ant Farm." [Prima] (18/19) 95, p. 120-121.
5395. RUSS, Biff
"The Book of the Dead" (for H.R.). [PraS] (69:2) Sum 95, p. 76-77.
"True Story" (for Anna C., my student in the Frankford Library Creative Writing Workshop for Senior Citizens). [PraS] (69:2) Sum 95, p. 75-76.
5396. RUSS, Don
"The Cicadas at the Lake." [PoetryNW] (36:2) Sum 95, p. 24.
5397. RUSS, Lawrence
"Diversions." [Image] (12) Wint 95-96, p. 91.
"Stream near the Saugatuck Reservoir, Good Friday" (St. Matthew 26:52-53). [Image] (12) Wint 95-96, p. 92-94.
5398. RUSSAKOFF, Molly
"La Cosa Nostra." [AmerPoR] (24:1) Ja-F 95, p. 52-53.
"Harry." [AmerPoR] (24:1) Ja-F 95, p. 53.
"The Rescue Mission." [AmerPoR] (24:1) Ja-F 95, p. 53.
"A Shard of Night." [AmerPoR] (24:1) Ja-F 95, p. 52.
5399. RUSSELL, C. C.
"Photograph — Georgette, April 1993." [Pearl] (22) Fall-Wint 95, p. 82.
5400. RUSSELL, CarolAnn
"Mardi Gras." [Verse] (12:3) 95, p. 72-74.
"Tarkio" (in the spirit of James Wright). [MidwQ] (36:4) Sum 95, p. 425.
5401. RUSSELL, Julia L.
"Blue Blues." [Pembroke] (27) 95, p. 9.
"Chocolate." [Pembroke] (27) 95, p. 9.
"A New Metamorphose." [Pembroke] (27) 95, p. 8.
5402. RUSSELL, Peter
"A Child's Song" (for Kathleen Raine). [BellArk] (11:6) N-D 95, p. 27.
"Fable." [Elf] (5:4) Wint 95, p. 22.
"For Ezra Pound's Eightieth Birthday." [Elf] (5:4) Wint 95, p. 20.
"I like these drinking places full of men" (Six sonnets: XX). [BellArk] (11:3) My-Je 95, p. 16.
"I've Planned My Life" (one of three sonnets). [BellArk] (11:1) Ja-F 95, p. 16.
"Madrigal." [Elf] (5:4) Wint 95, p. 21.
"Muwashshah." [BellArk] (11:5) S-O 95, p. 25.
"Non Enses at Ex Norico Carmen" (for Q, tr. from a Galilean targum attributed to Albius Cittinus Stultus). [BellArk] (11:2) Mr-Ap 95, p. 16.
"An Old Man's Song" (for Stacy Kors). [BellArk] (11:6) N-D 95, p. 27.
"Old men should be explorers: so should the young" (Six sonnets: XLIII). [BellArk] (11:3) My-Je 95, p. 16.
"Paris 1967." [Elf] (5:4) Wint 95, p. 21.
"Sara Elizabeth Christina Born This Morning." [BellArk] (11:4) Jl-Ag 95, p. 16.
"A Small Thing" (one of three sonnets). [BellArk] (11:1) Ja-F 95, p. 16.
"A Solemnity" (Requiem Mass for Ezra Pound in St. Giorgio Maggiore, Venice, November 1972). [BellArk] (11:4) Jl-Ag 95, p. 16.
"Spring in Autumn." [Elf] (5:4) Wint 95, p. 22.
"These dunes are rounded like a woman's body" (Six sonnets: IV). [BellArk] (11:3) My-Je 95, p. 16.
"What is this life? What goad dictates what aim?" (Six sonnets: XXXVII). [BellArk] (11:3) My-Je 95, p. 16.
"What shall my days be for, if not to write" (Six sonnets: XXXIV). [BellArk] (11:3) My-Je 95, p. 16.
"Who is this woman always in my mind" (Six sonnets: III). [BellArk] (11:3) My-Je 95, p. 16.
"Wonder Reborn" (one of three sonnets). [BellArk] (11:1) Ja-F 95, p. 16.

5403. RUSSELL, Ran Diego
"Lunar Physics." [HolCrit] (32:2) Ap 95, p. 17.
"Mysteries of Childhood #1: Elephant Storm." [ChironR] (42) Spr 95, p. 24.
"October Irrigation." [ChironR] (43) Sum 95, p. 20.
5404. RUSSELL, Thomas
"Karnak's Revenge." [GreensboroR] (58) Sum 95, p. 126.
5405. RUSSELL, Timothy
"In Mobile Perpetuum." [WestB] (37) 95, p. 65.
"In Ohio." [WestB] (37) 95, p. 64.
"Say Something." [FreeL] (14) Wint 95, p. 4.
5406. RUSSO, Gianna
"18 Degrees Inside a Cliché." [TampaR] (11) Fall 95, p. 66.
5407. RUTH, Deborah Dashow
"A Hell of a Cocktail Party." [Hellas] (6:2) Fall-Wint 95, p. 28-29.
5408. RUTSALA, Vern
"The Protocol of Shadows." [TarRP] (35:1) Fall 95, p. 13-14.
"Reading: A Memoir." [PoetryNW] (36:1) Spr 95, p. 42-43.
"Run Sheep Run." [TarRP] (35:1) Fall 95, p. 13.
5409. RUTTAN, Rob
"Conductor" (for Sandra). [MalR] (112) Fall 95, p. 84-85.
"Sink to Stove." [MalR] (112) Fall 95, p. 86.
5410. RUWE, Donelle
"Darkling I Listen" (— J. Keats). [PoetryE] (39) Fall 94, p. 78-79.
5411. RYALS, Mary Jane
"Blessings." [CimR] (110) Ja 96, p. 76.
"Daughter." [SpinningJ] (1) Fall 95-Wint 96, p. 10-11.
"The Sestina of an Unmarried Mother." [CimR] (110) Ja 96, p. 77-78.
5412. RYAN, Catherine
"Leash Laws." [IllinoisR] (3:1/2) Fall 95-Spr 96, p. 26-28.
5413. RYAN, Kay
"Bestiary." [ParisR] (37:137) Wint 95, p. 225-226.
"A Cat / A Future." [NewYorker] (71:38) 27 N 95, p. 54.
"Crib." [ParisR] (37:137) Wint 95, p. 225.
"Crustacean Island." [NewYorker] (71:18) 26 Je-3 Jl 95, p. 186.
"Full Measure." [GeoR] (49:4) Wint 95, p. 802.
"Mirage Oases." [NewYorker] (71:27) 11 S 95, p. 48.
"A Plain Ordinary Steel Needle Can Float on Pure Water" (Ripley's "Believe It or
Not!"). [NewYorker] (71:23) 7 Ag 95, p. 33.
"Poetry in Translation." [ParisR] (37:137) Wint 95, p. 226.
"Relief." [NewYorker] (70:46) 23 Ja 95, p. 89.
5414. RYAN, Margaret
"Bernini: Bacchanal: Faun Teased by Children." [Poetry] (165:5) F 95, p. 277.
5415. RYAN, Martin
"Love Letter." [AmerS] (64:2) Spr 95, p. 284.
5416. RYAN, Michael
"Bunny." [NewYorker] (71:25) 21-28 Ag 95, p. 82.
"Diner Car." [Pearl] (22) Fall-Wint 95, p. 97.
"Tina." [Pearl] (22) Fall-Wint 95, p. 97.
5417. RYAN, R. M.
"The Accordionist." [NewRep] (213:22) 27 N 95, p. 40.
"Atomist." [Light] (14) Sum 95, p. 8.
5418. RYAN, Richard
"Deafness" (For my sister). [Poetry] (167:1/2) O-N 95, p. 30.
"Helix" (In memory of S. W. Hayter). [Poetry] (167:1/2) O-N 95, p. 29.
5419. RYBAK, Charles
"Hip Hop Ballad." [QW] (40) Spr-Sum 95, p. 208-209.
5420. RYOKAN (Zen monk-poet, c. 1758-1831)
"At Entsu-ji so long ago" (tr. by John Stevens). [Tricycle] (4:3, #15) Spr 95, p. 60.
"The Rabbit in the Moon" (tr. by Burton Watson). [Tricycle] (4:4, #16) Sum 95, p.
56-57.

5421. SABA, Umberto
"A Memory" (tr. by Christopher Millis). [InterQ] (2:1/2) 95, p. 55.
"Un Ricordo." [InterQ] (2:1/2) 95, p. 55.

SACHIKO, Yoshihara
    See YOSHIHARA, Sachiko
5422. SACKS, Peter
    "Aubade." [YaleR] (83:1) Ja 95, p. 77.
    "Dedication." [YaleR] (83:1) Ja 95, p. 77.
    "Halo for Marianne Moore." [ParisR] (37:135) Sum 95, p. 41-42.
    "The Words" (In memory of T. Carmi). [NewRep] (212:7) 13 F 95, p. 40.
SADAKO, Kurihara
    See KURIHARA, Sadako
5423. SADIN, Marjorie
    "Lenses." [ChironR] (43) Sum 95, p. 15.
5424. SADLER, Janet Longe
    "Handing the River Over." [MassR] (36:2) Sum 95, p. 245.
5425. SADOFF, Ira
    "At the Movies." [MichQR] (34:4) Fall 95, p. 586-587.
    "Biographical Sketch." [NewRep] (213:11) 11 S 95, p. 42.
    "Childish." [PraS] (69:1) Spr 95, p. 171.
    "An Errant Branch." [RiverS] (44) 95, p. 42.
    "February." [DenQ] (30:2) Fall 95, p. 72.
    "The Horse Wanted Sugar." [PraS] (69:1) Spr 95, p. 172.
    "Lament at Point Reyes." [PraS] (69:1) Spr 95, p. 170-171.
    "On the Use of Myth as Nostalgia for Universal Truth." [RiverS] (44) 95, p. 41.
    "Overheard." [ColR] (22:1) Spr 95, p. 73-74.
    "Solitude Etude." [ColR] (22:1) Spr 95, p. 75-76.
    "Standard Time." [AmerPoR] (24:5) S-O 95, p. 50.
    "Time and Space." [AmerPoR] (24:5) S-O 95, p. 50.
SADOWSKI, Jennifer Young
    See YOUNG-SADOWSKI, Jennifer
5426. SAENZ, Benjamin Alire
    "Fragments from Home." [SouthwR] (80:2/3) Spr-Sum 95, p. 334-356.
5427. SAFARIK, Allan
    "Moonlight Dogs." [Grain] (23:1) Sum 95, p. 55-56.
5428. SAFION, Lis
    "Fulfilled." [BellArk] (11:1) Ja-F 95, p. 24.
    "The Lost Umbrella." [BellArk] (11:3) My-Je 95, p. 25.
    "Night Vision." [BellArk] (11:6) N-D 95, p. 5.
    "The Order of the Universe." [BellArk] (11:3) My-Je 95, p. 10.
    "Protection Spell." [BellArk] (11:4) Jl-Ag 95, p. 13.
    "Union." [BellArk] (11:6) N-D 95, p. 5.
    "Zen Koan." [BellArk] (11:4) Jl-Ag 95, p. 13.
5429. SAHAKIAN, Yuri
    "War" (tr. by Diana Der-Hovanessian). [GrahamHR] (19) Wint 95-96, p. 42.
5430. SAIL, Lawrence
    "Father to Son." [Stand] (36:2) Spr 95, p. 61.
5431. SAISER, Marjorie
    "Calling Cardinals." [MidwQ] (36:4) Sum 95, p. 426-427.
    "The Child in the Checkered Dress." [LaurelR] (29:1) Wint 95, p. 71.
    "Everything's Been Written." [CimR] (113) O 95, p. 48-49.
    "I Very Nearly Wrote You." [Crazy] (48) Spr 95, p. 40-41.
    "Shopping." [CumbPR] (15:1) Fall 95, p. 41-42.
    "When I Sleep, I Go Far Away." [WestB] (37) 95, p. 71.
    "When I Think of My Mother." [CumbPR] (15:1) Fall 95, p. 39-40.
5432. SAJÉ, Natasha
    "Fable." [HarvardR] (9) Fall 95, p. 65.
5433. SALAS, Alejandro
    "Que hermoso quien se sienta frente a ti." [Luz] (8) Spr 95, p. 59.
5434. SALAZAR, Dixie
    "Celebration Cake" (for Zelma Toney). [LowellR] (1) Sum 94, p. 52-54.
    "Home Alone — Saturday Night." [LowellR] (1) Sum 94, p. 50-51.
    "The Lost Underwear of Central Park." [Ploughs] (21:1) Spr 95, p. 18-19.
5435. SALE, Terry
    "Swinging" (Literary Festival: Poetry: Honorable Mention). [EngJ] (84:4) Ap 95, p. 44.
5436. SALEH, Dennis
    "Atomizer." [SantaBR] (3:2) Sum 95, p. 112.
    "De Chirico. Noon of the Angels." [SantaBR] (3:2) Sum 95, p. 111.

"Egyptian Pastorals." [SantaBR] (3:3) Fall-Wint 95, p. 103.
"Rimmon." [SantaBR] (3:3) Fall-Wint 95, p. 104.
"Schwitters. White Collage." [SantaBR] (3:2) Sum 95, p. 110.
"The Traveling Egyptian and the New Deity." [SantaBR] (3:3) Fall-Wint 95, p. 100-102.
5437. SALEMI, Joseph S.
"Nocturnal, two-horned Selene" (tr. of Philodemus, V. 123). [CarolQ] (47:2) Wint 95, p. 48.
5438. SALERNO, Joe
"For My Daughter, After Our Walk During Which Nothing Special Happened." [Footwork] (24/25) 95, p. 177-178.
"For My Wife, After Twenty Years: An Allegory." [Footwork] (24/25) 95, p. 178.
"The Man with a Beer in His Hand." [Footwork] (24/25) 95, p. 177.
"No Wife, No Kids, No Work." [Footwork] (24/25) 95, p. 178.
5439. SALERNO, Mark
"Analogy" (tr. of Antonio Catalfamo). [Arshile] (4) 95, p. 65.
"Chronicles" (tr. of Antonio Catalfamo). [Arshile] (4) 95, p. 67.
"Content with Surfaces, or Anthony Campisi's 1949 Plymouth Special Deluxe." [Arshile] (4) 95, p. 21.
"Genealogy" (tr. of Antonio Catalfamo). [Arshile] (4) 95, p. 61.
"Past and Present" (tr. of Antonio Catalfamo). [Arshile] (4) 95, p. 63.
"Secrets" (tr. of Antonio Catalfamo). [Arshile] (4) 95, p. 59.
"Summer Resorts." [Arshile] (4) 95, p. 22.
5440. SALINAS, Pedro
"Dominion" (tr. by David Garrison). [PoetryE] (39) Fall 94, p. 120.
"More" (tr. by David Garrison). [PoetryE] (39) Fall 94, p. 121.
5441. SALISBURY, Ralph
"Christ Jesus among the Yunwiya." [ManyMM] (1:2) 95, p. 118.
"The Sun My Father" (21 selections, tr. of Nils-Aslak Valkeapaa, w. Harald Gaski and Lars Nordstrom). [CharR] (21:1) Spr 95, p. 55-64.
5442. SALKEY, Andrew
"A House of Exile." [MassR] (36:3) Aut 95, p. 341.
"Like Karlena, Like Us." [MassR] (36:3) Aut 95, p. 339-341.
5443. SALLIS, James
"Boston." [NewOR] (21:3/4) Fall-Wint 95, p. 35.
"Dawn" (à Yves Bonnefoy). [NewOR] (21:3/4) Fall-Wint 95, p. 34.
"Happy Endings." [NewOR] (21:3/4) Fall-Wint 95, p. 36.
"History of Philosophy." [WestB] (36) 95, p. 29.
"Other Conclusions." [HighP] (10:2) Fall 95, p. 58.
"Recovery." [NewOR] (21:3/4) Fall-Wint 95, p. 38.
"What Pavese Said." [NewOR] (21:3/4) Fall-Wint 95, p. 37.
5444. SALMONS, Catherine A.
"Amores" (Book 1, #5, tr. of Ovid). [HarvardR] (9) Fall 95, p. 28.
5445. SALTER, Mary Jo
"Young Girl Peeling Apples" (Nicholas Maes). [Verse] (12:2) 95, p. 122-123.
5446. SALTMAN, Bethany
"Portraits: A Series in Progress." [NewYorkQ] (54) 95, p. 84-86.
5447. SALVATIERRA, Mario de
"Paradises of the Run" (tr. of Juana Rosa Pita). [Luz] (8) Spr 95, p. 25.
"A Season in Train" (tr. of Juana Rosa Pita). [Luz] (8) Spr 95, p. 21.
"Until Destiny" (tr. of Juana Rosa Pita). [Luz] (8) Spr 95, p. 23.
5448. SAMARAS, Nicholas
"Episode in Stasis." [HarvardR] (9) Fall 95, p. 63.
"The Far Away: Georgia O'Keeffe." [Pequod] (39) 95, p. 124-125.
"A Weekend in Greece." [SouthwR] (80:1) Wint 95, p. 136.
5449. SAMPSON, Dennis
"In Hell." [OhioR] (54) 95, p. 126-127.
5450. SAMUELS, Lisa
"Grace." [NewOR] (21:2) Sum 95, p. 55.
"Terminus." [Talisman] (15) Wint 95-96, p. 126.
5451. SAMYN, Mary Ann
"Gone." [WestB] (36) 95, p. 46.
"Northbound." [WestB] (36) 95, p. 47-48.
"October Breakdown." [LullwaterR] (5:2) Fall-Wint 94, p. 7.
"Omitting the Heart." [WillowS] (36) Je 95, p. 14.
"Synchronization." [WestB] (36) 95, p. 46.

5452. SAN MIGUEL, Claudio
"Dar a Luz." [BilingR] (20:2) My-Ag 95, p. 162-163.
"Hombre Jaguar y Hombre Aguila." [BilingR] (20:2) My-Ag 95, p. 160-161.
5453. SANAZARO, Leonard
"New Year Triptych." [LowellR] (2) c1996, p. 104-105.
5454. SANBORN, Robert
"Sweeny at the K-Mart." [WillowR] (22) Spr 95, p. 17.
5455. SANBORNE, Jon
"Battery." [PaintedB] (57) 95, p. 9-10.
"Denim." [PaintedB] (57) 95, p. 11-12.
5456. SANCHEZ, Trinidad, Jr.
"Food Is Not Illegal." [BellR] (18:1, #37) Spr 95, p. 22-23.
5457. SANDERS, Bonnie Barry (Bonny Barry)
"Notes Held Lightly." [MidwQ] (36:4) Sum 95, p. 427-428.
"The Swing." [Kalliope] (17:1) 95, p. 7.
5458. SANDERS, Kristine
"He Doesn't Remember Anything." [Pearl] (22) Fall-Wint 95, p. 106.
"It Didn't Take Long." [ChironR] (44/45) Aut-Wint 95, p. 17.
5459. SANDERS, Mark
"Night Song, New Town." [OxfordM] (10:1) Wint 94-Spr 95, p. 58.
5460. SANDERS, Tony
"Psalm." [OhioR] (54) 95, p. 129.
5461. SANDRU, Mircea Florin
"Season" (tr. by Adam J. Sorkin and Lidia Vianu). [Vis] (48) 95, p. 44.
5462. SANDY, Stephen
"Air Power Suite." [PartR] (62:3) Sum 95, p. 450-451.
"But Then." [YaleR] (83:2) Ap 95, p. 62.
"Character as Fate." [Ploughs] (21:4) Wint 95-96, p. 138-140.
"Hogback Lookout." [SouthernR] (31:4) O/Aut 95, p. 903-904.
"A Measure of Things." [YaleR] (83:2) Ap 95, p. 63.
"Mogadishu, Mon Amour." [PartR] (62:3) Sum 95, p. 450.
5463. SANFORD, Christy Sheffield
"Library of Congress." [IllinoisR] (3:1/2) Fall 95-Spr 96, p. 101-102.
"Sopa (The Temptation of St. Anthony)." [IllinoisR] (3:1/2) Fall 95-Spr 96, p. 91-
94.
"Thirty-One Days in July." [HeavenB] (12) 95, p. 39-42.
5464. SANFORD, Jim
"Eight: The Buddhas provided the sutras" (with Harmonies by Ch'u-shih and Shih-
shu, tr. of Shih-te, w. J. P. Seaton). [LitR] (38:3) Spr 95, p. 336.
"Fifty-Four: In a hidden lair in these clouded woods" (tr. of Shih Te). [LitR] (38:3)
Spr 95, p. 321.
"Fifty-Two: Why worry about the commotions of life?" (tr. of Shih Te). [LitR]
(38:3) Spr 95, p. 321.
"Forty: Clouded mountains, folded layer upon layer" (with Harmonies by Ch'u-shih
and Shih-shu, tr. of Shih-te, w. J. P. Seaton). [LitR] (38:3) Spr 95, p. 337.
"Two: Don't you see?" (with Harmonies by Ch'u-shih and Shih-shu, tr. of Shih-te,
w. J. P. Seaton). [LitR] (38:3) Spr 95, p. 335.
5465. SANGER, Peter
"After Monteverdi." [AntigR] (100) Wint 95, p. 77.
"The Fountain." [AntigR] (100) Wint 95, p. 78.
"Medicine Bundle." [AntigR] (100) Wint 95, p. 79.
"To Clytie." [AntigR] (100) Wint 95, p. 80.
5466. SANGER, Richard
"Among Other Things." [Descant] (26:1, #88) Spr 95, p. 47.
"In the Museum." [Descant] (26:1, #88) Spr 95, p. 43-45.
"Odysseus and Calypso" (After Bax Beckmann's painting). [Descant] (26:1, #88)
Spr 95, p. 46.
SANKICHI, Toge
See TOGE, Sankichi
5467. SANNELLA, A.
"Harassment." [Bogg] (67) 95, p. 7.
5468. SANTAMARIA, Michele
"Daughter to Mother to Daughter." [LullwaterR] (6:2) Fall-Wint 95, p. 90-91.
"Laundry." [LullwaterR] (5:2) Fall-Wint 94, p. 101.

5469. SANT'ANNA, Affonso Romano de
"The Building" (from "The Body-Object & Other Examples, tr. by Lloyd Schwartz.
w. Rogério Zola Santiago). [PartR] (62:1) Wint 95, p. 110-111.
5470. SANTATERESA, Matt
"Sonnetina." [TickleAce] (27) Spr-Sum 94, p. 83.
5471. SantaVICCA, Ed
"Unearthed Gratitude." [Art&Und] (4:1, #14) Ja-F 95, p. 17.
5472. SANTIAGO, Rogério Zola
"The Building" (from "The Body-Object & Other Examples, tr. of Affonso Romano
de Sant'anna, w. Lloyd Schwartz). [PartR] (62:1) Wint 95, p. 110-111.
5473. SANTILLANES, Ismael G.
"On a Sweaty Saturday Afternoon." [Interim] (14:2) Fall-Wint 95-96, p. 16.
"Some Days Are Too Hot to Remember." [Interim] (14:2) Fall-Wint 95-96, p. 19.
"Waltzing with a Red Head" (For Charlie Buck). [Interim] (14:2) Fall-Wint 95-96,
p. 17-18.
5474. SANTILLI, Kristine Szamreta
"Still Life: A Room with Flowers." [JINJPo] (17:2) Aut 95, p. 21-23.
5475. SANTOS, Marisa de los
"Big Bend." [SouthwR] (80:1) Wint 95, p. 33.
"Housework." [PraS] (69:3) Fall 95, p. 137.
"Oil." [Flyway] (1:3) Wint 95, p. 26-27.
"Remission." [PraS] (69:3) Fall 95, p. 137-138.
5476. SANTOS, Sherod
"Elegy for My Sister." [NewYorker] (71:26) 4 S 95, p. 39.
5477. SAPIA, Yvonne V.
"Pond in Moonlight, in Sunlight." [Witness] (9:2) 95, p. 34.
5478. SAPINKOPF, Lisa
"As in a Rear-View Mirror" (tr. of Oksana Zabuzhko, w. the author). [MassR] (36:3)
Aut 95, p. 424.
"Conductor of Candles" (tr. of Oksana Zabuzhko, w. the author). [Ploughs] (21:4)
Wint 95-96, p. 180-181.
"Hide and Seek" (tr. of Georgi Belev). [Vis] (48) 95, p. 15.
"Night Train" (tr. of Georgi Belev). [Vis] (48) 95, p. 14.
"Prypiat — Still Life" (tr. of Oksana Zabuzhko, w. the author). [Ploughs] (21:4)
Wint 95-96, p. 179.
"Sled" (tr. of Georgi Belev). [Vis] (48) 95, p. 14.
"Summer" (tr. of Georgi Belev). [Vis] (48) 95, p. 12-13.
"Turn of the Century" (tr. of Oksana Zabuzhko, w. the author). [MassR] (36:3) Aut
95, p. 422-423.
5479. SAPPHO (6th c. BCE)
"I love love's delicacy" (tr. by Sam Hamill). [PoetryE] (41) Aut 95, p. 11.
5480. SARAH, Robyn
"April's Fools." [MalR] (112) Fall 95, p. 99.
"The Boys in August." [NewEngR] (17:4) Fall 95, p. 119.
"Lapse." [MalR] (112) Fall 95, p. 102-103.
"Letter to M, Montreal, 1992." [Grain] (22:4) Spr 95, p. 96-100.
"Plateau Mont Royal: A Few Particulars, 8th of August." [MalR] (112) Fall 95, p.
100-101.
"Redoing the Entrance." [Thrpny] (63) Fall 95, p. 21.
5481. SARANG, Vilas
"The Call." [ManyMM] (1:3) 95, p. 134.
"Cockroaches." [ManyMM] (1:3) 95, p. 132-133.
5482. SARAVIA, Reina I.
"I Wish I Had Two Wings" (WritersCorps Program, Washington, DC). [WashR]
(21:2) Ag-S 95, p. 12.
5483. SARGEANT, Charlotte W.
"Reality." [Pearl] (22) Fall-Wint 95, p. 87.
5484. SARGENT, Robert
"James P. Johnson." [Pembroke] (27) 95, p. 69.
"The Seriousness of Poetry"." [PoetryE] (40) Spr 95, p. 107.
"Sidney." [Pembroke] (27) 95, p. 69.
"Socrates." [Pembroke] (27) 95, p. 68.
"Trimeters" (Exodus 20:11). [PoetryE] (40) Spr 95, p. 106.
5485. SARKAR, Farida
"Another Life" (tr. of Taslima Nasrin, w. Carolyne Wright). [GrandS] (14:1, #53)
Sum 95, p. 172.

5486. SARKAR, Subodh
"Impure Vessel." [ManyMM] (1:3) 95, p. 135.
"Tukaram" (tr. by Peter Michelson, w. Sharmila Ray). [ManyMM] (1:3) 95, p. 138-139.
"What a Wife Is Like." [ManyMM] (1:3) 95, p. 136-137.
5487. SAROUKHAN, Hrachia
"Hiroshima Study" (tr. by Diana Der-Hovanessian). [GrahamHR] (19) Wint 95-96, p. 43.
"Night Study" (tr. by Diana Der-Hovanessian). [GrahamHR] (19) Wint 95-96, p. 44.
"Where Do You Think You Are Going?" (tr. by Diana Der-Hovanessian). [GrahamHR] (19) Wint 95-96, p. 45.
5488. SASANOV, Catherine
"Among the Disintegrating Angels: Mexico City Earthquake, 1985." [MidAR] (15:1/2) 95, p. 37-38.
"Opening the Border." [MidAR] (15:1/2) 95, p. 39-42.
5489. SASSI, Shannon
"Standing Horse." [AnthNEW] (7) 95, p. 17.
5490. SATCHIDANANDAN, K.
"Gandhi and Poetry" (tr. by the author). [ManyMM] (1:3) 95, p. 148-149.
"How Spring Arrived This Year" (tr. by the author). [ManyMM] (1:3) 95, p. 147.
"My Body, a City" (tr. by the author). [ManyMM] (1:3) 95, p. 150-151.
"Passage to America" (tr. of Ayyappa Paniker, w. the author, J. O. Perry, Dakshinamoorthy, and Esther Y. Smith). [ManyMM] (1:3) 95, p. 120-126.
"The Tale of the Tongue" (tr. by Peter Michelson and the author). [AnotherCM] (29) Spr 95, p. 117.
5491. SATO, Hiroaki
"The Architect's Nephew" (tr. of Mutsuo Takahashi). [RiverS] (45) 95, p. 86.
"The Eyes" (tr. of Mutsuo Takahashi). [RiverS] (45) 95, p. 87.
"Philosophical Garden-Making" (tr. of Mutsuo Takahashi). [RiverS] (45) 95, p. 88.
5492. SATTERLEE, Thom
"A" (tr. of Henrik Nordbrandt). [InterPR] (21:1) Spr 95, p. 53.
"Courtship." [Poem] (73) My 95, p. 27.
"Kathy's Photograph as a Girl." [Poem] (73) My 95, p. 28.
"Thaw" (tr. of Henrik Nordbrandt). [InterPR] (21:1) Spr 95, p. 55.
"The Word" (tr. of Henrik Nordbrandt). [InterPR] (21:1) Spr 95, p. 55.
5493. SATYAMURTI, Carole
"Birthmark." [Epoch] (44:3) 95, p. 281.
"The Snail Battalions." [Epoch] (44:3) 95, p. 280.
5494. SAUERMANN, Bernd
"The Addresses of Erie." [PoetL] (90:4) Wint 95-96, p. 41.
"The Odds on Cleveland." [PoetL] (90:4) Wint 95-96, p. 40.
5495. SAUM, Lon M.
"Offices, Garages." [OxfordM] (10:1) Wint 94-Spr 95, p. 59-60.
5496. SAVAGE, Tom
"Messages 1990 - 1994." [HangL] (67) 95, p. 78-79.
5497. SAVARESE, Ralph
"Snow Lamentation: Poznan, 1990-1991." [GrahamHR] (19) Wint 95-96, p. 20-23.
"Two for Jarrell." [Flyway] (1:3) Wint 95, p. 44-46.
5498. SAVITT, Lynne
"Dream-October's Beginning." [AxeF] (3) 90, p. 21.
"Michael's Memory Dream." [AxeF] (3) 90, p. 22.
"A Secret." [ChironR] (43) Sum 95, p. 36.
"Your Lover Is Too Young for You If." [NewYorkQ] (54) 95, p. 62.
5499. SAVOIE, Terry
"Imaginary Lives." [MidwQ] (36:4) Sum 95, p. 429.
5500. SAVORY, Elaine
"The First Stone." [CaribbeanW] (9) 95, p. 74-76.
5501. SAVU, Cornelia Maria
"Between Parallel Mirrors" (tr. by Adam J. Sorkin and Taina Dutescu-Coliban). [13thMoon] (13:1/2) 95, p. 34.
"A Hazy Morning" (For Horia Bernea, tr. by Adam J. Sorkin and Taina Dutescu-Coliban). [13thMoon] (13:1/2) 95, p. 35.
"A Locket" (tr. by Adam J. Sorkin and Taina Dutescu-Coliban). [13thMoon] (13:1/2) 95, p. 36.
"Love Poem at the Foot of the Deforested Hill" (tr. by Adam J. Sorkin and Taina Dutescu-Coliban). [13thMoon] (13:1/2) 95, p. 37.

"Love Poem at the Mirror" (tr. by Adam J. Sorkin and Taina Dutescu-Coliban).
[13thMoon] (13:1/2) 95, p. 38.
"A Morning Fit for Writing Your Memoirs" (tr. by Adam J. Sorkin and Taina
Dutescu-Coliban). [13thMoon] (13:1/2) 95, p. 39.
5502. SAYA, Tom
"Cockatoo." [SoDakR] (33:2) Sum 95, p. 88-90.
"The Grave." [ArtfulD] (28/29) 95, p. 102.
5503. SCAFIDI, Steve
"The Cow." [PraS] (69:2) Sum 95, p. 102-103.
"Drinking Gift Whiskey." [SouthernR] (31:1) Wint 95, p. 58-59.
"Enigma." [PraS] (69:2) Sum 95, p. 101-102.
5504. SCALAPINO, Leslie
"The Front Matter, Dead Souls" (Selection: "Now"). [Chain] (2) Spr 95, p. 195-202.
"The Front Matter, Dead Souls" (Selections). [Phoebe] (24:1) 95, p. 55-62.
"I'm on rim that's base" (From a new poem sequence). [WestCL] (29:2, #17) Fall 95,
p. 134-135.
"New Time" (Excerpts). [Conjunc] (24) 95, p. 188-191.
"Sight" (Excerpt, w. Lyn Hejinian). [Zyzzyva] (11:1, #41) Spr 95, p. 153-160.
5505. SCARECROW
"Near Silent Rhythm." [Elf] (5:3) Fall 95, p. 37.
"Paradise / Continued." [HeavenB] (12) 95, p. 30.
5506. SCATES, Maxine
"Green Pool." [QW] (41) Aut-Wint 95-96, p. 164-165.
"Still Life." [NowestR] (33:1) 95, p. 52-53.
"Wildness." [Crazy] (48) Spr 95, p. 26-27.
5507. SCATTERGOOD, Amy
"Hagiography." [NewEngR] (17:1) Wint 95, p. 153.
"Hallucination Island" (Honorable Mention, 1995 Literary Awards). [GreensboroR]
(59) Wint 95-96, p. 26-28.
"Kolgrim's Saga." [PoetryNW] (36:3) Aut 95, p. 10-11.
"Landscape of Failed Farms in Minnesota." [Sonora] (30) Fall 95, p. 54-55.
"Latitude Sailing." [GrandS] (13:3, #51) Wint 95, p. 67-69.
"The Lighthouse Keeper." [PoetryNW] (36:3) Aut 95, p. 9-10.
"Marionette Theatre." [QW] (41) Aut-Wint 95-96, p. 210-211.
"Parnell's Wife." [NewEngR] (17:1) Wint 95, p. 152.
"The Three-Part Invention." [CimR] (112) Jl 95, p. 93.
"The Treaty of Tordesillas, 1494." [CimR] (112) Jl 95, p. 94-95.
5508. SCHAACK, F. J.
"Between the V." [SantaBR] (3:2) Sum 95, p. 21.
"When a Hummingbird's Still." [SantaBR] (3:2) Sum 95, p. 20.
5509. SCHAEDLER, Brad
"Elegy for a Weatherman." [ChironR] (42) Spr 95, p. 24.
5510. SCHAEFER, Ted
"Performance." [NewL] (62:1) 96 (c1995), p. 124.
5511. SCHAFER, R. Murray
"Wolf Chant." [Descant] (26:1, #88) Spr 95, p. 115.
5512. SCHAFFER, Amanda
"Genesis, Revised" (After Picasso). [HarvardA] Contest Issue, Spr 95, p. 21.
5513. SCHAFFER, Julia
"Driving Miss Daisy - PG 13." [HangL] (67) 95, p. 100.
"Nine Months Before September 4, 1977." [HangL] (67) 95, p. 101.
"Vivian is 77 and beginning to wilt." [HangL] (67) 95, p. 102.
5514. SCHAFFNER, M. A.
"Chopstick Holders." [HampSPR] Wint 95, p. 37.
"Presents." [Hellas] (6:2) Fall-Wint 95, p. 45.
"Sunrise on the Navy Yard." [Elf] (5:4) Wint 95, p. 31.
5515. SCHAVRIEN, Judy
"When from Her Thousand Arms." [Vis] (47) 95, p. 27.
5516. SCHEDLER, Gilbert
"Feliz Navidad." [WindO] (59) Spr 95, p. 36.
5517. SCHEELE, Roy
"Maple Gold." [MidwQ] (36:4) Sum 95, p. 430-431.
5518. SCHEIDERMAN, Rick
"A River Ran There" (from Flowing Like the Grass). [AmerPoR] (24:5) S-O 95, p.
22.

5519. SCHELLING, Andrew
"A recluse went to the burning ground" (tr. of Rajadatta). [Sulfur] (15:1, #36) Spr 95, p. 85-86.
5520. SCHENDLER, Revan
"Self-Portrait." [NewYorker] (71:15) 5 Je 95, p. 46.
5521. SCHIFF, Laura
"Statements" (tr. of Éva Tóth, w. Peter Jay). [AmerPoR] (24:1) Ja-F 95, p. 36.
"Teiresias Wailing" (tr. of Éva Tóth, w. Peter Jay). [AmerPoR] (24:1) Ja-F 95, p. 36.
"Van Gogh Gives Evidence" (tr. of Éva Tóth, w. Peter Jay). [AmerPoR] (24:1) Ja-F 95, p. 36.
5522. SCHIFFERNS, Terry Lee
"Shopping at Bob's Quick." [ManyMM] (2:1) 95, p. 44.
"Withdrawal." [ManyMM] (2:1) 95, p. 43.
5523. SCHILLING, Mia
"On Balzac and You." [SouthernPR] (35:1) Sum 95, p. 34.
5524. SCHILPP, Margot
"Careful What I Wish For." [HighP] (10:3) Wint 95, p. 82-83.
"Leaving." [HighP] (10:3) Wint 95, p. 80-81.
"Shaking Hands." [HighP] (10:3) Wint 95, p. 78-79.
5525. SCHLAGEL, Anthony
"Single Parrot." [CentralP] (24) Spr 95, p. 200-201.
"Your Profound and Real Innocence." [CentralP] (24) Spr 95, p. 242-243.
5526. SCHLICHTENMYER, Brian
"Just Turned Seventeen That May." [WindO] (59) Spr 95, p. 7.
5527. SCHMIDT, Jan Zlotnik
"After Seeing a Far Woman Selling Her Paintings on Ky 32" [sic]. [Wind] (75) Spr 95, p. 21-22.
5528. SCHMIDT, Laura Stangel
"Remedial Art." [HayF] (17) Fall-Wint 95, p. 98.
5529. SCHMIDT, Paulette
"Starfish" (For Marcel Harrand, tr. of Philippe Soupault). [LitR] (38:2) Wint 95, p. 286-287.
5530. SCHMITT, Betty
"Christmas 1984." [HiramPoR] (58/59) Spr 95-Wint 96, p. 68.
5531. SCHMITT, Peter
"Arlington, 1964." [SouthernR] (31:2) Ap/Spr 95, p. 298.
"Drive-By." [SouthernR] (31:2) Ap/Spr 95, p. 299-301.
"First Summer Away" (Ocala, 1970). [SouthernR] (31:2) Ap/Spr 95, p. 298-299.
"Thanksgiving Story." [SouthernR] (31:2) Ap/Spr 95, p. 301-304.
5532. SCHMITZ, Barbara
"Supper." [MidwQ] (36:4) Sum 95, p. 432.
5533. SCHMITZ, Dennis
"The Alien Corn." [HayF] (16) Spr-Sum 95, p. 67.
"Crabgrass." [Field] (53) Fall 95, p. 82.
"Dances." [Field] (53) Fall 95, p. 80-81.
"Egoist." [HayF] (16) Spr-Sum 95, p. 66.
5534. SCHNEBERG, Willa
"The Bells of St. Bravo Sing Scat" (Honorable Mention, Jacaranda Poetry Contest). [Jacaranda] (11) [95 or 96?], p. 29.
"Hawthorne Bridge." [SilverFR] (25) Sum 95, p. 38.
5535. SCHNEIDER, Annerose D.
"Writing Pornography for My Lover." [Pearl] (22) Fall-Wint 95, p. 22.
5536. SCHNEIDER, Dick
"After it had snowed" (tr. of François Jacqmin). [ManhatR] (7:2) Wint 95, p. 45.
"At twilight, when I look" (tr. of François Jacqmin). [ManhatR] (7:2) Wint 95, p. 57.
"The cold consumed the sparrows" (tr. of François Jacqmin). [ManhatR] (7:2) Wint 95, p. 50.
"Day's end had that perfection" (tr. of François Jacqmin). [ManhatR] (7:2) Wint 95, p. 55.
"I am not an author, but a confused passerby" (tr. of François Jacqmin). [ManhatR] (7:2) Wint 95, p. 49.
"I can't make it to the world, like" (tr. of François Jacqmin). [ManhatR] (7:2) Wint 95, p. 53.
"I had to gather up my own immensity" (tr. of François Jacqmin). [ManhatR] (7:2) Wint 95, p. 52.

"I make myself rare and taciturn so that my words" (tr. of François Jacqmin). [ManhatR] (7:2) Wint 95, p. 47.
"It is not enough to sleep" (tr. of François Jacqmin). [ManhatR] (7:2) Wint 95, p. 54.
"No forest, and no thought even" (tr. of François Jacqmin). [ManhatR] (7:2) Wint 95, p. 44.
"The noise snow makes renders barely perceptible" (tr. of François Jacqmin). [ManhatR] (7:2) Wint 95, p. 48.
"Since the frost settled in the orchard" (tr. of François Jacqmin). [ManhatR] (7:2) Wint 95, p. 51.
"There were some moments of sublime blindness" (tr. of François Jacqmin). [ManhatR] (7:2) Wint 95, p. 46.
"What would be the triumph spoken" (tr. of François Jacqmin). [ManhatR] (7:2) Wint 95, p. 56.
5537. SCHNEIDER, J. L.
"Our Eyes Dream." [DefinedP] (1:1) Fall-Wint 92, p. 25-26.
"Presage." [DefinedP] (1:1) Fall-Wint 92, p. 23-24.
5538. SCHNEIDER, Pat
"Some Days I Say." [BellR] (18:1, #37) Spr 95, p. 49.
5539. SCHNEIDER, Steven P.
"Dive-Bombing" (for A.R. Ammons). [Pembroke] (27) 95, p. 122.
"Return" (For Rivca). [LitR] (39:1) Fall 95, p. 86.
5540. SCHNEIDERS, Jay
"The Geometry of Christmas at the Children's Home" (for Patricia Sawyer). [TampaR] (11) Fall 95, p. 43.
"Means of Transport." [QW] (40) Spr-Sum 95, p. 94.
"Warmth." [Event] (24:2) Sum 95, p. 41-42.
5541. SCHNEIDRE, P.
"A Word." [ChironR] (43) Sum 95, p. 34.
5542. SCHNOEKER-SHORB, Yvette A.
"Birds and Atoms." [Blueline] (16) 95, p. 39.
5543. SCHOENHALS, Karen
"Origami." [LullwaterR] (6:2) Fall-Wint 95, p. 9.
5544. SCHOFIELD, Don
"Hitching." [Ledge] (19) Wint 95, p. 126-127.
"Hometown Junkyard." [RiverS] (45) 95, p. 6.
"Spring Cleaning." [Verse] (12:3) 95, p. 43-44.
SCHOLASTICUS, Agathias (ca. 531-580 CE)
See AGATHIAS SCHOLASTICUS (ca. 531-580 CE)
5545. SCHÖNMAIER, Eleonore
"The Rise and Fall." [PottPort] (16:1) Fall 95, p. 31.
"The Sorrows." [PottPort] (16:1) Fall 95, p. 30.
5546. SCHORB, E. M.
"Before the Sermon." [PaintedB] (55/56) 95, p. 9.
"Camden: Way Back When." [NewDeltaR] (13:1) Fall 95-Wint 96, p. 28.
"Flashbacks." [ContextS] (4:2) 95, p. 12-13.
"Singlewide." [MassR] (36:1) Spr 95, p. 121-122.
5547. SCHOTT, Barbara
"I have endless stains all over myself" (Second Place, 1995 Poetry Contest). [PraF] (16:4, #73) Wint 95-96, p. 77-78.
"Memoirs of an Almost Expedition." [CanLit] (146) Aut 95, p. 65-66.
"Watermusic." [Vis] (49) 95, p. 30.
5548. SCHOTT, Penelope Scambly
"Motherlove / Hooked at the Nerves." [Footwork] (24/25) 95, p. 158.
"Our Mother Who Art in Art." [AmerV] (38) 95, p. 34.
"A Town Called LOST." [US1] (30/31) 95, p. 19.
5549. SCHRAF, Mark
"Cal's Son Cal Learned." [Spitball] (49) 95, p. 3.
5550. SCHRAMM, Darrell G. H.
"Rain." [Pearl] (22) Fall-Wint 95, p. 10.
5551. SCHREINER, Steven
"Convicts." [RiverS] (44) 95, p. 14.
"Failed Attempt." [Image] (11) Fall 95, p. 74.
"News From the Lab." [RiverS] (44) 95, p. 15.
"Twice Lost to Pity." [Image] (11) Fall 95, p. 75-76.
SCHÜLER, Else Lasker
See LASKER-SCHÜLER, Else

5552. SCHULMAN, Grace
"American Solitude." [ParisR] (37:135) Sum 95, p. 283-284.
"The Button Box." [WestHR] (49:1) Spr 95, p. 10.
5553. SCHULTZ, David
"Notes from My Grammar School." [Footwork] (24/25) 95, p. 75.
"Paterson City Hall." [Footwork] (24/25) 95, p. 76.
5554. SCHULTZ, Susan M.
"Aleatory Allegory." [Phoebe] (24:1) 95, p. 96-97.
"All the News That Fits." [Phoebe] (24:1) 95, p. 98-101.
"Authentic Lies." [NewAW] (13) Fall-Wint 95, p. 40-41.
"Mothers and Dinosaurs, Inc." [NewAW] (13) Fall-Wint 95, p. 38-39.
"Prospero in Milan." [Verse] (12:2) 95, p. 124.
5555. SCHULZ, Bill
"Crickets (8/14/91)" (for Teresa). [SenR] (25:2) Fall 95, p. 82.
"In This Movie." [SenR] (25:2) Fall 95, p. 81.
"Stille Nacht." [SenR] (25:2) Fall 95, p. 80.
5556. SCHUMACHER, Elizabeth
"Four Seasons in Spirit." [Sonora] (30) Fall 95, p. 2-4.
5557. SCHUTTENBERG, E. M.
"Mingled Light." [JINJPo] (17:1) Spr 95, p. 30.
5558. SCHWAGER, Elaine
"Definition." [Writ] (27) 95, p. 26.
"A Myth Around Your Fingers." [LiteralL] (2:2) Fall 95, p. 23.
"The Rose Light." [Writ] (27) 95, p. 28.
"The Tunnel." [Writ] (27) 95, p. 23-25.
"TV Light." [Writ] (27) 95, p. 27.
"Winds Like in Your Dream Came into My Dream." [LiteralL] (2:2) Fall 95, p. 18.
5559. SCHWALBAUM, Martin
"Giant Mountain" (from POEMS For My Kids). [Blueline] (16) 95, p. 20-21.
"Trillium" (from POEMS For My Kids). [Blueline] (16) 95, p. 18-19.
5560. SCHWARTZ, Deborah
"Stone Soup." [ModernW] (3) Sum 95, p. 87.
5561. SCHWARTZ, Hillel
"Dorothy, All Grown Up, Returns to Oz." [BelPoJ] (46:1) Fall 95, p. 11-15.
"Leaving Cortes Island." [CentR] (39:1) Wint 95, p. 85-86.
"Owl." [HampSPR] Wint 95, p. 4.
5562. SCHWARTZ, Howard
"Mississippi John Hurt Buried in the Pepper." [RiverS] (42/43) 95, p. 160.
"Relearning the Alphabet." [RiverS] (45) 95, p. 24.
5563. SCHWARTZ, Jason
"The Balusters." [Conjunc] (24) 95, p. 202-205.
5564. SCHWARTZ, Leonard
"Feature." [DenQ] (30:2) Fall 95, p. 71.
"Slumber, Party, and Frisson." [Talisman] (15) Wint 95-96, p. 88-91.
5565. SCHWARTZ, Lloyd
"The Building" (from "The Body-Object & Other Examples, tr. of Affonso Romano de Sant'anna, w. Rogério Zola Santiago). [PartR] (62:1) Wint 95, p. 110-111.
"Nostalgia" (The Lake at Night). [NewYorker] (71:26) 4 S 95, p. 60-61.
"Proverbs from Purgatory." [ParisR] (37:136) Fall 95, p. 83-85.
5566. SCHWARTZ, Magi
"The Maiden's Tale." [Kalliope] (17:1) 95, p. 6.
5567. SCHWARTZ, Matt
"Tickle." [Vis] (49) 95, p. 33.
5568. SCHWARTZ, Mimi
"At the Kunstmuseum." [US1] (30/31) 95, p. 13.
5569. SCHWARTZ, Rachel
"In the Basement." [HangL] (66) 95, p. 97.
"Nothing." [HangL] (66) 95, p. 98.
5570. SCHWARTZ, Ruth L.
"Because Summer" (Winner of the Chelsea Award for Poetry). [Chelsea] (58) 95, p. 21.
"Flamenco Guitar" (Winner of the Chelsea Award for Poetry). [Chelsea] (58) 95, p. 18.
"Golden Gate" (for D. and G. Winner of the Chelsea Award for Poetry). [Chelsea] (58) 95, p. 20.

"The Greatest Show on Earth" (Winner of the Chelsea Award for Poetry). [Chelsea] (58) 95, p. 17.
"Hayward Shoreline" (Winner of the Chelsea Award for Poetry). [Chelsea] (58) 95, p. 19.
"Why I Forgive My Younger Self Her Transgressions" (Winner of the Chelsea Award for Poetry). [Chelsea] (58) 95, p. 22.
5571. SCHWERNER, Armand
"*Inferno,* Canto XV" (tr. of Dante). [AmerPoR] (24:5) S-O 95, p. 24-25.
"The Work" (for Phill Niblock). [AmerPoR] (24:5) S-O 95, p. 23.
5572. SCISM, Elizabeth
"A Blind Man Peels an Orange." [XavierR] (15:2) Fall 95, p. 65.
"Riddle." [SouthernHR] (29:2) Spr 95, p. 155.
5573. SCOTT, Herbert
"The Most Terrible and Beautiful Thing." [PoetryNW] (36:4) Wint 95-96, p. 6.
"The Song the Grocer Sings." [PoetryNW] (36:4) Wint 95-96, p. 7.
"To Death, for My Father." [PoetryNW] (36:4) Wint 95-96, p. 5.
5574. SCOTT, Mark
"Concord Palinode" (for Jon Adolph). [WestHR] (49:4) Wint 95, p. 310-311.
"Crush." [WestHR] (49:4) Wint 95, p. 311.
5575. SCOTT, Mary
"Squash Blossom." [Ledge] (19) Wint 95, p. 106-107.
5576. SCOTT, Peter Dale
"The Loon's Egg." [AntR] (53:4) Fall 95, p. 444-445.
5577. SCRIMGEOUR, J. D.
"Funny." [Border] (6) Spr-Sum 95, p. 60.
"The Last Game." [TarRP] (34:2) Spr 95, p. 27.
5578. SCRIMGEOUR, James R.
"Babson Farm Quarry." [IllinoisR] (3:1/2) Fall 95-Spr 96, p. 87.
"The Chess World." [ChironR] (43) Sum 95, p. 22.
"Crow Lake." [GreenMR] (8:2) Fall-Wint 95-96, p. 125.
"The Large Dead Oak." [ChironR] (43) Sum 95, p. 22.
"The Meadow Yet Again." [ChironR] (43) Sum 95, p. 22.
5579. SCRUTON, James
"After the Party." [PoetryE] (40) Spr 95, p. 109.
"The Apple Sellers." [TarRP] (34:2) Spr 95, p. 4.
"Deerwatch." [TarRP] (34:2) Spr 95, p. 5.
"The Diviner." [Poetry] (166:4) Jl 95, p. 219.
"Hoops." [PoetryE] (40) Spr 95, p. 110.
"A Map of the Known World." [Poetry] (166:4) Jl 95, p. 218.
"V for Victory." [PoetryE] (40) Spr 95, p. 108.
"Your Are Here." [PoetryE] (40) Spr 95, p. 111.
5580. SCRYGLEY, Carolyn
"Ludice: June 10, 1942." [SmPd] (32:2, #94) Spr 95, p. 8.
5581. SCUDDER, Bernard
"At the Foot of Mount Ararat" (tr. of Gyrdir Elíasson). [Nimrod] (38:2) Spr-Sum 95, p. 73.
"Balm" (tr. of Bragi Olafsson). [Nimrod] (38:2) Spr-Sum 95, p. 74.
"The Flowers on Women's Skirts" (tr. of Kristin Omarsdóttir). [Nimrod] (38:2) Spr-Sum 95, p. 70.
"Homer the Singer of Tales" (tr. of Einar Mar Gudmundsson). [Nimrod] (38:2) Spr-Sum 95, p. 76-77.
"Of the Last Descendant of Icarus" (tr. of Gyrdir Elíasson). [Nimrod] (38:2) Spr-Sum 95, p. 72.
"A Remarkable Occupation" (tr. of Bragi Olafsson). [Nimrod] (38:2) Spr-Sum 95, p. 74.
5582. SCULLY, Maurice
"Adherence" (Selection: "Ballad, the expletives"). [WestCL] (29:2, #17) Fall 95, p. 80-84.
5583. SEA, Gary
"Always So Fatigued in" (tr. of Brigitte Olenschinski). [InterPR] (21:1) Spr 95, p. 51.
"Immortality" (tr. of Rose Ausländer). [ProseP] (4) 95, p. 8.
"Over the Numb" (tr. of Brigitte Olenschinski). [InterPR] (21:1) Spr 95, p. 51.
"Progress I" (tr. of Rose Ausländer). [ProseP] (4) 95, p. 7.
"Scraping the Knuckles, for Example" (tr. of Brigitte Olenschinski). [InterPR] (21:1) Spr 95, p. 51.

"Sound without Light" (tr. of Brigitte Olenschinski). [InterPR] (21:1) Spr 95, p. 49.
"The Spaces" (tr. of Brigitte Olenschinski). [InterPR] (21:1) Spr 95, p. 49.
"They Did Not Use Boards" (tr. of Brigitte Olenschinski). [InterPR] (21:1) Spr 95,
    p. 47.
5584. SEALS, Ernie
    "The End of FMF." [NewDeltaR] (13:1) Fall 95-Wint 96, p. 63-65.
5585. SEAMAN, Barbara
    "Mother and Son, Kazakhstan." [Kaleid] (31) Sum-Fall 95, p. 7.
    "Needle / Plow." [SpoonR] (20:2) Sum-Fall 95, p. 8.
    "Overnight." [ChrC] (112:22) 19-26 Jl 95, p. 714.
    "The Star of Bethlehem Appears As a Quilt Pattern." [SpoonR] (20:2) Sum-Fall 95,
    p. 9.
    "Stick Figure, Mogadishu." [Kaleid] (31) Sum-Fall 95, p. 7.
SEARCAIGH, Cathal O
    See O SEARCAIGH, Cathal
5586. SEATON, J. P.
    "Chung-nan Mountain Monk" (tr. of Kuan Hsiu). [LitR] (38:3) Spr 95, p. 328.
    "Drinking Tea with Hermit Yuan at Greenmount Pool" (tr. of Ling Yi). [LitR] (38:3)
    Spr 95, p. 322.
    "Eight: The Buddhas provided the sutras" (with Harmonies by Ch'u-shih and Shih-
    shu, tr. of Shih-te, w. Jim Sanford). [LitR] (38:3) Spr 95, p. 336.
    "Forty: Clouded mountains, folded layer upon layer" (with Harmonies by Ch'u-shih
    and Shih-shu, tr. of Shih-te, w. Jim Sanford). [LitR] (38:3) Spr 95, p. 337.
    "Freedom's Good" (tr. of Cheng Fu). [LitR] (38:3) Spr 95, p. 325.
    "A Hundred Sorrows" (tr. of Kuan Hsiu). [LitR] (38:3) Spr 95, p. 329.
    "Leaving It to You" (tr. of Kuan Hsiu). [LitR] (38:3) Spr 95, p. 329.
    "Making a Fool of Myself" (tr. of Ching An). [LitR] (38:3) Spr 95, p. 339.
    "Mean Alleyways" (tr. of Kuan Hsiu). [LitR] (38:3) Spr 95, p. 328.
    "Old Man of the Creek" (tr. of Ching Yun). [LitR] (38:3) Spr 95, p. 330.
    "So Be It" (tr. of Yuan Mei). [LitR] (38:3) Spr 95, p. 338.
    "To everything there is a season" (tr. of Seng Yü). [LitR] (38:3) Spr 95, p. 320.
    "Two: Don't you see?" (with Harmonies by Ch'u-shih and Shih-shu, tr. of Shih-te,
    w. Jim Sanford). [LitR] (38:3) Spr 95, p. 335.
5587. SEATON, Maureen
    "Body Parts." [NewRep] (213:2) 10 Jl 95, p. 34.
    "A Brief History of Faith." [IndR] (18:1) Spr 95, p. 36-37.
    "A Chorus of Horizontals." [ChiR] (41:2/3) 95, p. 36.
    "A Constant Dissolution of Molecules." [Boulevard] (10:1/2, #28/29) Spr 95, p. 98-
    99.
    "Fiddleheads." [GreenMR] (8:2) Fall-Wint 95-96, p. 48-49.
    "Let Me Explain" (w. Denise Duhamel). [PoetL] (90:2) Sum 95, p. 22-24.
    "Malleus Maleficarum." [AmerV] (36) 95, p. 60-61.
    "Near Wild Heaven." [NewL] (61:4) 95, p. 88.
    "Revelation." [ChiR] (41:2/3) 95, p. 37-38.
    "The Sculpture Garden." [ParisR] (37:135) Sum 95, p. 43-44.
    "Secrets of Water." [Ploughs] (21:1) Spr 95, p. 64-67.
    "Sin." [Calyx] (16:2) Wint 95-96, p. 53.
    "A Single Subatomic Event." [Colum] (24/25) 95, p. 24-25.
    "Toy Car." [GreenMR] (8:2) Fall-Wint 95-96, p. 50.
    "Transliminal." [NewL] (61:4) 95, p. 86-87.
    "When I Was Straight." [GreenMR] (8:2) Fall-Wint 95-96, p. 51.
    "When I Wore a Garter Belt." [Colum] (24/25) 95, p. 26.
5588. SEATON, William
    "Roses Stroll the Streets of Porcelain" (tr. of Hans Arp). [Chelsea] (59) 95, p. 126.
    "Schalaben — Schalabai — Schalamezomai" (tr. of Richard Huelsenbeck).
    [Chelsea] (59) 95, p. 122-123.
    "Streams" (tr. of Richard Huelsenbeck). [Chelsea] (59) 95, p. 124.
    "Tree" (tr. of Richard Huelsenbeck). [Chelsea] (59) 95, p. 125.
5589. SEAWARD, Alexander
    "Retirement" (for Joan). [Light] (15/16) Aut-Wint 95-96, p. 18.
5590. SEBASTIAN, Robert M.
    "Alphabet Note." [Light] (13) Spr 95, p. 14.
    "Attila." [Light] (13) Spr 95, p. 11.
    "Edna St. Vincent Millay." [Light] (14) Sum 95, p. 16.
    "Indira Gandhi." [Light] (15/16) Aut-Wint 95-96, p. 29.
    "Parental Note." [Light] (15/16) Aut-Wint 95-96, p. 17.

"Percy Bysshe Shelley." [Light] (14) Sum 95, p. 14.
5591. SEBASTIANI, Cristiana Maria
"You Have Been" (tr. by Michael Ayton). [Stand] (36:2) Spr 95, p. 75.
5592. SEGAL, Alethea Gail
"Hunger Universal." [Chelsea] (58) 95, p. 85-86.
"Listen to Darkness." [Chelsea] (58) 95, p. 84-85.
"The Well." [Chelsea] (58) 95, p. 84.
5593. SEIBLES, Tim
"Check Outside." [KenR] (17:1) Wint 95, p. 38-39.
"Disappointed." [NewEngR] (17:2) Spr 95, p. 58-59.
"The Gust." [Ploughs] (21:1) Spr 95, p. 87.
"Hey." [ArtfulD] (28/29) 95, p. 119.
"Never Daytime." [ArtfulD] (28/29) 95, p. 120-121.
"Playing Catch" (for Hermann Michaeli). [Ploughs] (21:1) Spr 95, p. 92-93.
"Ten Miles an Hour." [Ploughs] (21:1) Spr 95, p. 88-91.
"What Bugs Bunny Said to Red Riding Hood." [ArtfulD] (28/29) 95, p. 116-117.
"What the Wind Says" (after David Swanger). [ArtfulD] (28/29) 95, p. 118.
5594. SEIDMAN, Hugh
"Did I Say Father?" [NewYorker] (71:7) 10 Ap 95, p. 68.
"Phone Call." [NewYorker] (71:7) 10 Ap 95, p. 69.
5595. SEIFERLE, Rebecca
"The Book Breaks Open." [GlobalCR] (5) Spr 95, p. 48-51.
"Death Rattle." [PraS] (69:4) Wint 95, p. 38.
"The Ditch." [PraS] (69:4) Wint 95, p. 39.
"Mother Tongue." [HarvardR] (9) Fall 95, p. 68.
"Singular Cherubim." [IndR] (18:1) Spr 95, p. 38.
5596. SEIFERT, Jaroslav
"Song of the Native Land" (tr. by Don Mager). [LullwaterR] (6:2) Fall-Wint 95, p. 82-84.
5597. SEILER, Barry
"Bread and Butter." [HangL] (67) 95, p. 80.
"An Evening with Sam Peckinpah." [JlNJPo] (17:2) Aut 95, p. 17.
"Proverbs." [JlNJPo] (17:2) Aut 95, p. 15-16.
"Salami on Rye." [HangL] (67) 95, p. 80.
"The Stroll." [HangL] (67) 95, p. 81.
5598. SELAWSKY, John T.
"1975." [Poem] (73) My 95, p. 17.
"Ashes." [Poem] (73) My 95, p. 18.
"Rainstorm, Coming Upon the Frogs." [CapeR] (30:2) Fall 95, p. 2.
"Solstice." [Poem] (73) My 95, p. 19.
5599. SELBY, Joan
"Climacteric." [PoetL] (90:2) Sum 95, p. 32.
5600. SELBY, Martha Ann
"I as Myself" (tr. of Tilakavati). [Prima] (18/19) 95, p. 65-70.
5601. SELBY, Spencer
"Bear-Baiting." [Talisman] (15) Wint 95-96, p. 63-64.
"Moira." [NewAW] (13) Fall-Wint 95, p. 114.
"My Influence." [Sulfur] (15:1, #36) Spr 95, p. 183-184.
"No Island." [NewAW] (13) Fall-Wint 95, p. 115.
5602. SELERIE, Gavin
"Roxy" (Selections: 24, 32, 36, 46). [Sulfur] (15:1, #36) Spr 95, p. 188-192.
5603. SELLERS, Deborah
"Rememberings." [HopewellR] (7) 95, p. 112.
5604. SELLERS, Heather (Heather Laurie)
"April Sunburn." [MidwQ] (36:2) Wint 95, p. 163.
"Near Avalon." [SoCaR] (28:1) Fall 95, p. 58.
5605. SELLEY, April
"Hemingway." [SlipS] (15) 95, p. 43.
5606. SELLIN, Birger
"A Deep-Sea Explorer of the Mind" (tr. by Anthea Bell). [GrandS] (13:4, #52) Spr 95, p. 139-162.
5607. SELMAN, Robyn
"Heroic Sonnet." [Nat] (261:13) 13 O 95, p. 481.
"Work Song." [KenR] (17:3/4) Sum-Fall 95, p. 139-142.
5608. SELVING, Jan
"The Projectionist's Letter." [ProseP] (4) 95, p. 65-66.

5609. SEMANSKY, Chris
"Among Them." [SouthernPR] (35:1) Sum 95, p. 24-25.
"From the Diary of a Closet Shadow." [LullwaterR] (5:1) 93-94, p. 60.
5610. SEMENOVICH, Joseph
"I remember my step-father shouting from the bathroom." [SlipS] (15) 95, p. 41.
"The slack on the clothesline." [RagMag] (12:2) Spr 95, p. 70.
"When I Was a Kid." [Footwork] (24/25) 95, p. 179.
5611. SEMOG, Éle
"Alucinações." [Callaloo] (18:4) Fall 95, p. 925.
"Essa É Pra Você." [Callaloo] (18:4) Fall 95, p. 924.
"Hallucinations" (tr. by Phyllis Peres). [Callaloo] (18:4) Fall 95, p. 754.
"Mariana and the Word, Another Name" (tr. by Phyllis Peres, w. Reetika Vazirani
and Chi Lam). [Callaloo] (18:4) Fall 95, p. 755.
"Mariana E o Verbo, Codinome." [Callaloo] (18:4) Fall 95, p. 926.
"This Is for You" (tr. by Phyllis Peres, w. Reetika Vazirani and Chi Lam). [Callaloo]
(18:4) Fall 95, p. 753.
5612. SEMONES, Charles
"The Wild Rose Horse Saloon, Sweetwater, Nebraska Territory." [Plain] (15:3) Spr
95, p. 18.
SENG, Yü
See YÜ, Seng
5613. SENGUPTA, Mallika
"Amrapali" (tr. by Peter Michelson, w. Shashi Desbank and the author). [ManyMM]
(1:3) 95, p. 130-131.
5614. SENGUPTA, Sagaree
"Soup." [Prima] (18/19) 95, p. 61.
"Winter, Going to Work in a Tall Building." [Border] (7) Fall-Wint 96, p. 57.
5615. SENS, Jean-Marc
"Lament of the Icecream Man in the Snow." [PaintedB] (55/56) 95, p. 110.
5616. SEPULVEDA, Jesús
"Departamento 112." [Americas] (23:3/4) Fall-Wint 95, p. 168.
"Ella Es Una Hembra." [Americas] (23:3/4) Fall-Wint 95, p. 166-167.
"Eugene, Oregon." [Americas] (23:3/4) Fall-Wint 95, p. 165.
"Hotel Marconi." [Americas] (23:3/4) Fall-Wint 95, p. 173.
"Interdicto." [Americas] (23:3/4) Fall-Wint 95, p. 169.
"Marlowe." [Americas] (23:3/4) Fall-Wint 95, p. 170-171.
"Sucia de Moscas." [Americas] (23:3/4) Fall-Wint 95, p. 172.
5617. SEROWINSKI, Daniela
"Four Months After Turning Thirty." [PoetL] (90:3) Fall 95, p. 41.
5618. SERRALHEIRO, Paul
"Lesson in Winter." [Event] (24:2) Sum 95, p. 43.
5619. SERVIN, Jacques
"'Entrance Is Harmless,' She Said." [IllinoisR] (3:1/2) Fall 95-Spr 96, p. 77-78.
"Greg Is Fairly Matchless." [IllinoisR] (3:1/2) Fall 95-Spr 96, p. 98-99.
"An Invocatory Jazz History of the Pitchfork" (Excerpt). [IllinoisR] (3:1/2) Fall 95-
Spr 96, p. 109.
5620. SESHADRI, Vijay
"Alien Nation." [NewYorker] (71:40) 11 D 95, p. 72.
"Lifeline." [ParisR] (37:137) Wint 95, p. 36-41.
"The Lump." [SouthwR] (80:2/3) Spr-Sum 95, p. 272-281.
5621. SETH, Vikram
"Soon." [Verse] (12:2) 95, p. 125-126.
5622. SETOGUCHI, Chie
"I still hear their voices" (in Japanese and English, tr. by Jiro Nakano). [BambooR]
(67/68) Sum-Fall 95, p. 71.
5623. SETTEL, Ann
"Caught." [WestHR] (49:1) Spr 95, p. 87.
"Doris." [WestHR] (49:1) Spr 95, p. 90.
"Happy Mother's Day." [WestHR] (49:1) Spr 95, p. 86.
"Meeting at the Meeting (of the Women's Political Action Group)." [WestHR]
(49:1) Spr 95, p. 89.
"The Second Wife." [WestHR] (49:1) Spr 95, p. 88.
5624. SETTLE, Judith (Judith Holmes)
"Lighthouse Landing #8: Bald Head Island, September, 1993." [Crucible] (30) Fall
94, p. 13.

"The Sun Itself" (In memory of Anna Akhmatova, 1889-1966). [Crucible] (31) Fall 95, p. 32.
5625. SEUSS-BRAKEMAN, Diane
"Dream of My Father's Tooth." [NowestR] (33:2) 95, p. 29.
"Hit." [IndR] (18:1) Spr 95, p. 112.
"Let Go." [Prima] (18/19) 95, p. 7-8.
"Monkey." [IndR] (18:1) Spr 95, p. 111.
"This Is the Poem Which Shouldn't Be Able to Be Written." [Prima] (18/19) 95, p. 9-10.
"What Is There." [Prima] (18/19) 95, p. 11.
5626. SEWELL, Frankie
"Night" (tr. of Cathal O Searcaigh). [Poetry] (167:1/2) O-N 95, p. 67.
5627. SEWELL, Lisa
"The Denied." [PassN] (16:2) Wint 95, p. 31.
"Famadihana." [PassN] (16:1) Sum 95, p. 12-13.
"Ornithology." [GreensboroR] (59) Wint 95-96, p. 95.
"Refuge" (for L. E.). [GreensboroR] (59) Wint 95-96, p. 93-94.
5628. SEXTON, Tom
"Towns." [Nimrod] (39:1) Fall-Wint 95, p. 118.
5629. SEYBURN, Patty
"Myopia in Canada." [PoetryE] (40) Spr 95, p. 113-114.
"One of Those Things." [PoetryE] (40) Spr 95, p. 112.
"Stairway at 48 Rue de Lille." [PassN] (16:1) Sum 95, p. 10.
"You & them." [AnotherCM] (29) Spr 95, p. 171-172.
5630. SHADOIAN, Jack
"Looney Tunes 15 (Look Hard, Think Hard)." [AmerLC] (7) 95, p. 103-104.
"Marcie and the Birds." [Plain] (15:3) Spr 95, p. 32.
"Nightmare Arnie." [Conduit] (3) Sum 95, p. 9.
"True Stories 9 (Brilliant Corners)." [AmerLC] (7) 95, p. 104.
"Wet Tuesday." [Flyway] (1:1) Spr 95, p. 44.
"Zeroes." [Parting] (8:2) Wint 95-96, p. 45.
5631. SHAFFER, C. Lynn
"Expecting." [MidAR] (16:1) 95, p. 79.
"Motherfriend." [Wind] (75) Spr 95, p. 23.
"Twelfth Summer" (for Tabitha). [MidAR] (16:1) 95, p. 80-82.
5632. SHAFFER, Craig
"Tobacco Farming, 1937." [CarolQ] (47:3) Sum 95, p. 25.
5633. SHAFIQ, Hashim
"The First House" (tr. by Khaled Mattawa). [WillowS] (36) Je 95, p. 105.
5634. SHAFRIR-STILLMAN, Moshe D.
"The Butterfly Hunter" (Excerpt, from *The Promise of Rain*). [AmerPoR] (24:2) Mr-Ap 95, p. 16.
SHAHID ALI, Agha
See ALI, Agha Shahid
5635. SHAKESPEARE, William (1564-1616)
"Sonnet CXXIX. The expense of spirit in a waste of shame." [PoetryE] (41) Aut 95, p. 28.
5636. SHALSKY, Askold
"Angels." [ApalQ] (43) Spr 95, p. 38-39.
SHAN, Han
See HAN-SHAN
5637. SHANAHAN, Deirdre
"Inner Cities." [SouthernR] (31:3) Jl/Sum 95, p. 622-623.
"Site." [SouthernR] (31:3) Jl/Sum 95, p. 621-622.
5638. SHANER, Richard C.
"Watching for Alligators, Darling Refuge, Sanibel Island" (for Tom & Gerri Branca). [ColEng] (57:4) Ap 95, p. 462-463.
"Weir River Bridge." [ColEng] (57:4) Ap 95, p. 462.
SHANG-YIN, Li
See LI, Shang-yin
5639. SHANGE, Ntozake
"Blood Rhythms — Blood Currents — Blue Black N Stylin'." [RiverS] (44) 95, p. 1-2.
"Nappy Edges." [RiverS] (42/43) 95, p. 18-19.
SHANGYIN, Li
See LI, Shang-yin

5640. SHANTZ, Christina
"Incognita" (tr. of Naín Nómez). [Arc] (35) Aut 95, p. 35.
"Never the Same Waters" (tr. of Naín Nómez). [Arc] (35) Aut 95, p. 36.
5641. SHAPIRO, Alan
"My Mother and a Few Friends." [WestHR] (49:3) Fall 95, p. 256-257.
"Night Terrors." [Atlantic] (276:6) D 95, p. 76.
5642. SHAPIRO, Harvey
"1949." [Boulevard] (10:1/2, #28/29) Spr 95, p. 138.
"Choices." [Boulevard] (10:1/2, #28/29) Spr 95, p. 139.
"Epitaph." [PoetryE] (41) Aut 95, p. 121.
"He." [Agni] (42) 95, p. 119.
"Remembering." [PoetryE] (41) Aut 95, p. 120.
5643. SHAPIRO, Myra
"Holiday Mornings" (The 1994 Allen Ginsberg Poetry Awards: Honorable
Mention). [Footwork] (24/25) 95, p. 204.
"How I Learned to Kiss." [Pearl] (22) Fall-Wint 95, p. 99.
"Marriage: February 1953." [Pearl] (22) Fall-Wint 95, p. 99.
5644. SHAPIRO, Susan
"From a Young Woman of Ambition." [PoetryE] (39) Fall 94, p. 80.
SHARAT CHANDRA, G. S.
See CHANDRA, G. S. Sharat
5645. SHARE, Don
"Arfos" (from "Field Guide," tr. of Dario Jaramillo Agudelo). [Noctiluca] (2:1, #4)
Spr 95, p. 60-61.
"Dinecos" (from "Field Guide," tr. of Dario Jaramillo Agudelo). [Noctiluca] (2:1,
#4) Spr 95, p. 61.
"Guzguces" (from "Field Guide," tr. of Dario Jaramillo Agudelo). [Noctiluca] (2:1,
#4) Spr 95, p. 62.
"To the Angels." [Journal] (19:2) Fall-Wint 95, p. 15.
5646. SHARP, Michael
"Delicate Hands." [CaribbeanW] (9) 95, p. 46.
5647. SHATTUCK, M. Lisa
"The Hand That Feeds You." [LowellR] (2) c1996, p. 58.
"Stuff Dreams Are Made On." [LowellR] (2) c1996, p. 57.
5648. SHAVER, Jessica
"A Skeptic at Communion" (after Robert Herrick's "The Amber Bead"). [SoCoast]
(18) Ja 95, p. 61.
5649. SHAW, Angela
"Crepuscule." [Poetry] (165:6) Mr 95, p. 317.
"Miscarriage." [Poetry] (165:6) Mr 95, p. 316.
"Small Pleasures." [IndR] (18:1) Spr 95, p. 113-114.
5650. SHAW, Beverley
"A November Visit." [PottPort] (16:1) Fall 95, p. 25-26.
5651. SHAW, Catherine Harnett
"The Informer Speaks." [Border] (7) Fall-Wint 96, p. 58.
5652. SHAW, Deirdre
"Guarantee." [Pearl] (22) Fall-Wint 95, p. 14.
5653. SHAW, Janet
"The Other Garden." [TarRP] (35:1) Fall 95, p. 30.
5654. SHAW, Nancy
"Dance" (2 poems, w. Catriona Strang). [Avec] (10) 95, p. 112-113.
"Dine" (w. Catriona Strang). [Avec] (10) 95, p. 109.
"Ditch" (2 poems, w. Catriona Strang). [Avec] (10) 95, p. 107-108.
"Dote" (w. Catriona Strang). [Avec] (10) 95, p. 114.
"Drink" (2 poems, w. Catriona Strang). [Avec] (10) 95, p. 110-111.
5655. SHAW, Robert B.
"Hide and Seek." [Shen] (45:2) Sum 95, p. 82-83.
"Time-Lapse Photography." [Shen] (45:2) Sum 95, p. 80-81.
5656. SHCHERBINA, Tatyana
"Untitled: from Munich, 1991" (in Russian and English, tr. by J. Kates). [KenR]
(17:3/4) Sum-Fall 95, p. 114-115.
"Untitled: Something for the branching nervous system" (tr. by J. Kates).
[GrahamHR] (19) Wint 95-96, p. 65.
5657. SHEA, Amy
"Gender 101." [RagMag] (12:2) Spr 95, p. 102-103.

5658. SHEARD, Norma Voorhees
"Clytemnestra Considers Her Husband's Old Aunts" (for Cora Jane and Lillie
Augusta Brokaw). [US1] (30/31) 95, p. 28.
"Hot Air Balloon" (for three friends who die in August). [JlNJPo] (17:2) Aut 95, p.
25.

5659. SHECK, Laurie
"The Book of Persephone." [SenR] (25:2) Fall 95, p. 33-34.
"Childlessness: Frida Kahlo to Her Doctor." [SenR] (25:1) Spr 95, p. 53-55.
"The Unfinished." [SenR] (25:2) Fall 95, p. 35.

5660. SHECTMAN, Robin
"The Condor." [CumbPR] (15:1) Fall 95, p. 43.
"Spring." [CumbPR] (14:2) Spr 95, p. 29.

5661. SHELDON, Anne
"Menstrual Migraine." [Bogg] (67) 95, p. 50.

5662. SHELDON, Bill
"Say Cheese." [Bogg] (67) 95, p. 47.

5663. SHELDON, Glenn
"When Someone Cold Comes Home" (images by Brad Pease). [Gerbil] (4) Fall 95,
p. 18.

5664. SHELLEY, Percy Bysshe
"Ode to the West Wind." [Hellas] (6:1) Spr-Sum 95, p. 9-12.

5665. SHELTON, Richard
"The Happy Farmer." [Crazy] (48) Spr 95, p. 33.
"Runaway." [Crazy] (48) Spr 95, p. 32.

5666. SHELTON L. (John Howard Pavilion, St. Elizabeth's Hospital, Washington, DC)
"We've Tried So Long to Find Our Way" (WritersCorps Program). [WashR] (21:2)
Ag-S 95, p. 10.

5667. SHENFELD, Karen
"Mosquito Net." [Writ] (27) 95, p. 21.
"Sahara." [Writ] (27) 95, p. 22.
"The Things I Carry." [Writ] (27) 95, p. 18-19.
"Tunis." [Writ] (27) 95, p. 20.

5668. SHEPARD, Neil
"The Light Leap of the Dead." [DefinedP] (3) 95, p. 59-60.
"Lush Life." [WestHR] (49:1) Spr 95, p. 36-37.
"Monkey Forest Road" (Ubud, Bali). [AnotherCM] (29) Spr 95, p. 173-175.
"Pecos Wilderness, Lake Katherine, NM." [Ascent] (20:1) Fall 95, p. 32.
"Pecos Wilderness, NM." [Ascent] (20:1) Fall 95, p. 33.

5669. SHEPARD, Robin Mark
"They've Predicted the End of the World Again." [NewYorkQ] (54) 95, p. 90.

5670. SHEPARD, Roy
"At the Summer Place." [PoetL] (90:4) Wint 95-96, p. 38.
"Marigolds." [PoetL] (90:4) Wint 95-96, p. 37.

5671. SHEPHERD, J. Barrie
"Advent Saturday with Catriona." [ChrC] (112:36) 13 D 95, p. 1216.
"Cautionary." [ChrC] (112:13) 19 Ap 95, p. 428.
"Initial Offer." [ChrC] (112:19) 7-14 Je 95, p. 606.
"Lighting the Advent Candles" (For Joyce and Judith). [ChrC] (112:34) 22-29 N 95,
p. 1100.
"Seeing Whole." [ChrC] (112:32) 8 N 95, p. 1036.

5672. SHEPHERD, Paul
"Heat." [WilliamMR] (33) 95, p. 22.

5673. SHEPHERD, Reginald
"The Angel of Interruptions." [NewAW] (13) Fall-Wint 95, p. 88-89.
"Another Movable Feast." [SenR] (25:2) Fall 95, p. 40.
"Aubade." [GrahamHR] (19) Wint 95-96, p. 95.
"Avail." [MichQR] (34:1) Wint 95, p. 123.
"Black Ice on Green Dolphin Street." [Chelsea] (59) 95, p. 109-110.
"The Dead Girl." [ChiR] (41:2/3) 95, p. 41-42.
"Deep Water." [IndR] (18:2) Fall 95, p. 1.
"Depth of Field." [IndR] (18:2) Fall 95, p. 2.
"Drawing from Life." [Shen] (45:4) Wint 95, p. 78.
"Eros in His Striped Blue Shirt." [Ploughs] (21:1) Spr 95, p. 75.
"Follow Me." [Chelsea] (59) 95, p. 111.
"Found in Translation." [GreensboroR] (57) Wint 94-95, p. 16.
"Johnny Minotaur." [MichQR] (34:1) Wint 95, p. 122.

"Jouissance." [NewEngR] (17:3) Sum 95, p. 140.
"The Light Sieves What Escapes from Me." [IllinoisR] (2:2) Spr 95, p. 15.
"A Little Knowledge." [Nat] (260:13) 3 Ap 95, p. 468.
"Loved" (For Christopher Cutrone). [Chelsea] (59) 95, p. 112.
"Monarchs and Swallowtails Late in March." [Journal] (19:1) Spr-Sum 95, p. 12.
"My Brother the Rain." [IndR] (18:2) Fall 95, p. 3.
"Narcissus as Gnostic." [TriQ] (94) Fall 95, p. 235.
"Narcissus at the Adonis Theater." [Chelsea] (59) 95, p. 113.
"Narcissus in Plato's Cave." [TriQ] (94) Fall 95, p. 232.
"Narcissus Learning the Words to This Song." [TriQ] (94) Fall 95, p. 233-234.
"Narcissus Was a Sad Boy, But a Heavenly" (for Michael Anania). [DenQ] (29:4)
    Spr 95, p. 52.
"Odysseus Becalmed." [Chelsea] (59) 95, p. 114.
"Orion." [PraS] (69:4) Wint 95, p. 75.
"'Orpheus and Eros' by George Platt Lynes." [PraS] (69:4) Wint 95, p. 76-77.
"The Other August." [ChiR] (41:2/3) 95, p. 39-40.
"Pages from My Winter, 1982." [SenR] (25:2) Fall 95, p. 39.
"Pericles, Prince of Tyre: A Commentary." [GrandS] (13:4, #52) Spr 95, p. 219-222.
"Phaedra Again." [GrahamHR] (19) Wint 95-96, p. 96.
"Placet Futile" (long after Mallarmé). [GrahamHR] (19) Wint 95-96, p. 97.
"September Tenth, Near Love Canal." [IllinoisR] (2:2) Spr 95, p. 16.
"Skin Trade." [Ploughs] (21:1) Spr 95, p. 73-74.
"Trick of the Light." [Epoch] (44:1) 95, p. 84-85.
"Vampires." [WillowS] (36) Je 95, p. 21.
"West Willow" (for Christopher Cutrone). [Shen] (45:4) Wint 95, p. 76-77.
"Where It Passes, Untouchable." [GreensboroR] (57) Wint 94-95, p. 17.
5674. SHEPPARD, Robert
    "The Lores" (Twentieth Century Blues 30. Selection: Book 8, Hundred 2).
        [WestCL] (29:2, #17) Fall 95, p. 85-87.
5675. SHEPPARD, Simon
    "Haiku for John." [Art&Und] (4:1, #14) Ja-F 95, p. 17.
    "Moby Dick." [Art&Und] (4:1, #14) Ja-F 95, p. 17.
5676. SHEPPARD, Susan
    "Here." [OhioR] (53) 95, p. 95.
    "Iris of Midnight." [OhioR] (53) 95, p. 94.
5677. SHERCHAN, Bhoopi
    "Blind Man on a Revolving Chair" (tr. by Wayne Amtzis). [SenR] (25:2) Fall 95, p.
        68-69.
5678. SHERLOCK, Karl
    "Echo." [SoCoast] (18) Ja 95, p. 52-53.
    "The Repository of Souls." [SoCoast] (18) Ja 95, p. 48-49.
5679. SHERMAN, Jory
    "Light." [MidwQ] (36:4) Sum 95, p. 433.
5680. SHERMAN, Nancy
    "Black Ice." [MassR] (36:3) Aut 95, p. 375-376.
5681. SHERRILL, Steven
    "Hey Faggot They Must've Said." [SlipS] (15) 95, p. 8.
    "The History of String." [ArtfulD] (28/29) 95, p. 42.
    "The History of String, 2." [ArtfulD] (28/29) 95, p. 43.
    "In FryCook's World." [SlipS] (15) 95, p. 9-10.
5682. SHERRY, Pearl Andelson
    "Black Holes." [Chelsea] (59) 95, p. 179.
    "Thinning." [Chelsea] (59) 95, p. 178.
5683. SHEVIN, David
    "Leaving the New Orphanage." [Light] (15/16) Aut-Wint 95-96, p. 31.
5684. SHIELDS, Andrew
    "Anniversary." [InterQ] (2:1/2) 95, p. 285.
5685. SHIELDS, Bill
    "Waiting on No Man." [NewYorkQ] (55) 95, p. 91.
5686. SHIH-SHU
    "Eight: The Buddhas provided the sutras" (by Shih-te, with Harmonies by Ch'u-shih
        and Shih-shu, tr. by Jim Sanford and J. P. Seaton). [LitR] (38:3) Spr 95, p.
        336.
    "Forty: Clouded mountains, folded layer upon layer" (by Shih-te, with Harmonies
        by Ch'u-shih and Shih-shu, tr. by Jim Sanford and J. P. Seaton). [LitR] (38:3)
        Spr 95, p. 337.

"Two: Don't you see?" (by Shih-te, with Harmonies by Ch'u-shih and Shih-shu, tr. by Jim Sanford and J. P. Seaton). [LitR] (38:3) Spr 95, p. 335.

5687. SHIH-TE
"Eight: The Buddhas provided the sutras" (with Harmonies by Ch'u-shih and Shih-shu, tr. by Jim Sanford and J. P. Seaton). [LitR] (38:3) Spr 95, p. 336.
"Fifty-Four: In a hidden lair in these clouded woods" (tr. by Jim Sanford). [LitR] (38:3) Spr 95, p. 321.
"Fifty-Two: Why worry about the commotions of life?" (tr. by Jim Sanford). [LitR] (38:3) Spr 95, p. 321.
"Forty: Clouded mountains, folded layer upon layer" (with Harmonies by Ch'u-shih and Shih-shu, tr. by Jim Sanford and J. P. Seaton). [LitR] (38:3) Spr 95, p. 337.
"Two: Don't you see?" (with Harmonies by Ch'u-shih and Shih-shu, tr. by Jim Sanford and J. P. Seaton). [LitR] (38:3) Spr 95, p. 335.

5688. SHIMA, Akira
"Gone is everyone who I have relied upon" (in Japanese and English, tr. by Jiro Nakano). [BambooR] (67/68) Sum-Fall 95, p. 72.

5689. SHIMAUCHI, Hachiro
"Facing a garden stone that never glistens" (in Japanese and English, tr. by Jiro Nakano). [BambooR] (67/68) Sum-Fall 95, p. 73.

5690. SHINKAWA, Kazue
"Chess" (tr. by Naoshi Koriyama and Edward Lueders). [WeberS] (12:1) Wint 95, p. 54-55.
"A Distant Mirror" (tr. by Naoshi Koriyama and Edward Lueders). [WeberS] (12:1) Wint 95, p. 54.
"In My Garden" (tr. by Naoshi Koriyama and Edward Lueders). [WeberS] (12:1) Wint 95, p. 52-53.
"The Palm" (From "Poems About the Human Body," tr. by Naoshi Koriyama and Edward Lueders). [WeberS] (12:1) Wint 95, p. 53.
"The Sole" (From "Poems About the Human Body," tr. by Naoshi Koriyama and Edward Lueders). [WeberS] (12:1) Wint 95, p. 53-54.

5691. SHINN, Christopher
"True or False." [Flyway] (1:1) Spr 95, p. 43.
"A Warning to Myself as a Child." [Flyway] (1:1) Spr 95, p. 42.

5692. SHINPU, Sumiko
"Sleeping each night alongside the neighboring nuclear weapons" (in Japanese and English, tr. by Jiro Nakano). [BambooR] (67/68) Sum-Fall 95, p. 76.

5693. SHIPLEY, Vivian
"Action News, Channel Eight." [Journal] (19:1) Spr-Sum 95, p. 63.
"Against That Night." [DefinedP] (3) 95, p. 28.
"Black Hole." [AmerS] (64:4) Aut 95, p. 598.
"Catfishing in Cumberland Lake." [Poem] (73) My 95, p. 26.
"Daphne and Apollo." [NewYorkQ] (54) 95, p. 60.
"Hard Luck" (— Buster Keaton). [Flyway] (1:3) Wint 95, p. 24.
"Horse Breath Winter." [Journal] (19:1) Spr-Sum 95, p. 64.
"Horse Breath Winter." [Poem] (73) My 95, p. 23.
"Horse Breath Winter." [XavierR] (15:1) Spr 95, p. 53.
"How It Felt the Old Way." [Poem] (73) My 95, p. 25.
"How Sweet the Sound." [TexasR] (15:3/4) Fall-Wint 94, p. 98.
"Ice Bites Inward." [NewL] (61:4) 95, p. 91.
"Imposter Wears Crown." [ApalQ] (43) Spr 95, p. 74.
"In Braille." [Blueline] (16) 95, p. 16.
"Instinct." [WritersF] (21) 95, p. 73.
"A Keeper." [SouthernPR] (35:1) Sum 95, p. 64-65.
"The Last Wild Horses in Kentucky." [Poem] (73) My 95, p. 24.
"The Last Wild Horses in Kentucky." [WritersF] (21) 95, p. 72-73.
"Moonshine." [QW] (41) Aut-Wint 95-96, p. 189.
"No Creel Limit." [FloridaR] (21:1) 95, p. 50-51.
"Praying You Are Asleep." [WindO] (59) Spr 95, p. 29.
"Results of the Blood Test." [ChironR] (44/45) Aut-Wint 95, p. 33.
"Soon, Soon." [OxfordM] (10:1) Wint 94-Spr 95, p. 61.
"Stoney Creek Granite." [HayF] (16) Spr-Sum 95, p. 130.
"Unnatural." [Kalliope] (17:3) 95, p. 48-49.
"Unnatural." [PaintedB] (55/56) 95, p. 111-112.
"Upon Receiving a Letter." [SpoonR] (20:1) Wint-Spr 95, p. 23-24.
"Voices like Pulleys Rust Unused." [NewDeltaR] (12:2) Spr-Sum 95, p. 31.

5694. SHIRAKI, Yutaka
"At high tide in this burnt city" (in Japanese and English, tr. by Jiro Nakano).
[BambooR] (67/68) Sum-Fall 95, p. 77.
5695. SHIVDASANI, Menka (Shivdasanni, Menka)
"Buttoned Up." [AnotherCM] (29) Spr 95, p. 120.
"Forever Amber." [ManyMM] (1:3) 95, p. 154.
"Lover, Loser, Addict." [AnotherCM] (29) Spr 95, p. 118-119.
"Pest Control." [ManyMM] (1:3) 95, p. 156.
"Schoolgirl No More." [ManyMM] (1:3) 95, p. 155.
5696. SHNEIDRE, P.
"Get Your Coat." [WestHR] (49:4) Wint 95, p. 300.
5697. SHOAF, Diann Blakely
"An Appalachian Love Story" (1994 Literary Awards, Honorable Mention).
[GreensboroR] (57) Wint 94-95, p. 88.
"The Expulsion." [SouthernR] (31:4) O/Aut 95, p. 905-906.
"Fireflies." [TarRP] (35:1) Fall 95, p. 3-4.
"Gaugin in Alaska." [Verse] (12:2) 95, p. 127-128.
"Greek Love." [SpoonR] (20:1) Wint-Spr 95, p. 83-84.
"Reunion Banquet, Class of '79." [MichQR] (34:4) Fall 95, p. 514-515.
"Yucatan, December." [DenQ] (30:2) Fall 95, p. 73-75.
5698. SHOCKLEY, Lisa
"Crooked Leg." [DogRR] (14:1, #27) Sum 95, p. 35.
5699. SHODA, Shinoe
"The large skull is the teacher's" (in Japanese and English, tr. by Jiro Nakano).
[BambooR] (67/68) Sum-Fall 95, p. 74.
5700. SHOEMAKER, John
"Your Time Will Come." [ProseP] (4) 95, p. 67.
5701. SHOJI, Fumiko
"A man's life is imprinted vividly" (in Japanese and English, tr. by Jiro Nakano).
[BambooR] (67/68) Sum-Fall 95, p. 75.
5702. SHOLL, Betsy
"The Stream." [Field] (52) Spr 95, p. 72-73.
"Test Patterns." [Field] (52) Spr 95, p. 74-75.
"The Tiny Gate." [Field] (52) Spr 95, p. 76-77.
5703. SHOMER, Enid
"Black Drum." [Poetry] (166:3) Je 95, p. 136-137.
"Luna" (After the fifth miscarriage). [InterQ] (2:3) 95, p. 105.
"Painter's Whites." [NewOR] (21:3/4) Fall-Wint 95, p. 90.
"Passive Resistance" (Nevada Desert Experience, 1993). [Poetry] (166:1) Ap 95, p.
25-27.
"Therese Dreaming by Balthus, 1939." [Boulevard] (10:1/2, #28/29) Spr 95, p. 196.
5704. SHOOSHAH, Farooq
"Features" (tr. by M. Enani). [Vis] (47) 95, p. 26.
SHORB, Yvette A. Schnoeker
See SCHNOEKER-SHORB, Yvette A.
5705. SHORT, Gary
"Birds." [WritersF] (21) 95, p. 109.
"Elegy for My Mother" (Aldora Joyce 1922-1973). [WritersF] (21) 95, p. 110-111.
"Gentle." [AntR] (53:3) Sum 95, p. 328-329.
"The Giant Ants of Texas" (Lafcadio Hearn, 1881). [AntR] (53:3) Sum 95, p. 334-
335.
"Herida de Amor." [AntR] (53:3) Sum 95, p. 332-333.
"Naming." [WritersF] (21) 95, p. 108.
"On Hearing of My Cousin Tom's Death." [LitR] (38:3) Spr 95, p. 424.
"Psalm." [AntR] (53:3) Sum 95, p. 330-331.
"White." [AntR] (53:3) Sum 95, p. 326-327.
5706. SHORT DOG, "95" (Turkey Thicket Recreation Center, Washington, DC)
"The Bomb" (WritersCorps Project). [WashR] (21:2) Ag-S 95, p. 22.
5707. SHREVE, Georgia
"Allen's Point." [NewRep] (212:18) 1 My 95, p. 38.
"Pitiless." [PlumR] (9) [95 or 96], p. 11.
"Time of Mourning." [PartR] (62:3) Sum 95, p. 451.
5708. SHREVE, Sandy
"Leonine." [Quarry] (44:3) 95, p. 82.
5709. SHRUM, Lynne
"The Electrician and the Breadman." [InterPR] (21:2) Fall 95, p. 95.

5710. SHU, Ting
"Autumn" (In Chinese and English, tr. by Ginny MacKenzie and Guo Wei). [InterQ] (2:1/2) 95, p. 123.
"Cover Girl" (tr. by Xu Juan). [AxeF] (3) 90, p. 46.
"Parting in the Rain" (tr. by Zhaoming Qian and John Blair). [PoetryE] (39) Fall 94, p. 122.
"A Room for Two Girls" (In Chinese and English, tr. by Ginny MacKenzie and Guo Wei). [InterQ] (2:1/2) 95, p. 121-122.
"Sicily Sun" (In Chinese and English, tr. by Ginny MacKenzie and Guo Wei). [InterQ] (2:1/2) 95, p. 124.
"This Place a Gift" (In Chinese and English, tr. by Ginny MacKenzie and Guo Wei). [InterQ] (2:1/2) 95, p. 125.
"This, Too, Is Everything" (In Response to a Young Friend's "Everything," tr. by Zhaoming Qian and John Blair). [PoetryE] (39) Fall 94, p. 123-124.

5711. SHUFORD, Kelly
"Enrobed in Chocolate." [Jacaranda] (11) [95 or 96?], p. 103.
"Genetics 101." [MinnR] (43/44) 95, p. 64.
"Visiting." [MinnR] (43/44) 95, p. 64.

5712. SHUGRUE, Jim
"Above a Mountain Valley." [PoetryE] (41) Aut 95, p. 62.
"Each Page." [QW] (40) Spr-Sum 95, p. 69.
"A Gathering Place: 10." [InterQ] (2:1/2) 95, p. 103-106.

5713. SHUMAKER, Peggy
"The Clumsy Girl." [Nimrod] (38:2) Spr-Sum 95, p. 67.
"Wingspan of Sand." [Nimrod] (38:2) Spr-Sum 95, p. 68.

5714. SHUMATE, Kathleen
"Edma Learns Not to Regret" (15 mars 1869, for Berthe Morisot. 2nd Prize, 9th Annual Contest). [SoCoast] (18) Ja 95, p. 42-43.
"Sonata" (Adagio, Accoppiamento). [SoCoast] (18) Ja 95, p. 30.
"Wishbones." [SoCoast] (18) Ja 95, p. 5.

5715. SHURIN, Aaron
"Little Madrigal." [Arshile] (4) 95, p. 32.
"To John" (3 poems). [Arshile] (4) 95, p. 33-35.
"The Wanderer's Necklace." [Talisman] (15) Wint 95-96, p. 49-51.

5716. SHUTTLE, Penelope
"Any Painting." [ManhatR] (7:2) Wint 95, p. 7-8.
"Baby." [Epoch] (44:3) 95, p. 276-277.
"Dust." [Epoch] (44:3) 95, p. 278-279.
"Eight Frog Dreams." [ManhatR] (8:1) Fall 95, p. 65-67.
"Flood." [ManhatR] (7:2) Wint 95, p. 14.
"Forgive." [ManhatR] (7:2) Wint 95, p. 12-13.
"From Blue to Red." [ManhatR] (7:2) Wint 95, p. 9-11.
"Gauguin's New Life." [ManhatR] (8:1) Fall 95, p. 61.
"Hope." [ManhatR] (8:1) Fall 95, p. 68.
"Kingdom of Tiny Shoes." [ManhatR] (7:2) Wint 95, p. 16.
"A Man Like You." [ManhatR] (8:1) Fall 95, p. 63-64.
"Mouth-Painter." [ManhatR] (8:1) Fall 95, p. 70.
"No Secret." [ManhatR] (8:1) Fall 95, p. 62.
"Rescuing the Buddha." [ManhatR] (7:2) Wint 95, p. 15.
"Things." [ManhatR] (8:1) Fall 95, p. 69.

5717. SICKLER, Michael
"The Concession Stand" (Third Place, The 1995 Defined Providence Poetry Contest, Judged by Sean Thomas Dougherty). [DefinedP] (3) 95, p. 69-70.
"Mushroom Farming." [DefinedP] (3) 95, p. 35.

SIDJACK, David
See SIDJAK, Dave

5718. SIDJAK, Dave
"Alms." [Arc] (34) Spr 95, p. 60.
"Prairie Storm." [Arc] (34) Spr 95, p. 61.
"Surveying the West." [Dandel] (22:1) 95, p. 34.

5719. SIEBERT, Maryann
"Dream Gesture." [Footwork] (24/25) 95, p. 48.
"Transgression." [Footwork] (24/25) 95, p. 48.

5720. SIEGEL, Joan I.
"Black Cat." [CimR] (111) Ap 95, p. 74.
"Brahms' Intermezzi." [Northeast] (5:12) Sum 95, p. 26.

"Dance of the Sanderlings." [Comm] (122:10) 19 My 95, p. 22.
"Hiroshima 1991." [Comm] (122:14) 18 Ag 95, p. 18.
"How Our Cat Died on the Winter Solstice." [CumbPR] (14:2) Spr 95, p. 4.
"Later." [Comm] (122:10) 19 My 95, p. 22.
"Memorial." [Comm] (122:10) 19 My 95, p. 22.
"My Mother at Eighty-One." [Comm] (122:10) 19 My 95, p. 22.
"Piano Lesson." [LitR] (38:2) Wint 95, p. 290.
5721. SIGHTO, Alan B.
"Dadirdydebil." [RiverS] (41) 95, p. 31-33.
5722. SIGNORELLI-PAPPAS, Rita
"Folktale." [SouthernPR] (35:1) Sum 95, p. 59-60.
"Memory of Florence." [ColEng] (57:3) Mr 95, p. 338.
"Questions about Rainer Maria Rilke." [PoetL] (90:2) Sum 95, p. 51.
"Snapshot" (for Lena Signorelli, 1924-1955). [SouthernHR] (29:1) Wint 95, p. 11.
"Tea with Franny Glass." [PoetL] (90:2) Sum 95, p. 49-50.
"Widow." [Footwork] (24/25) 95, p. 67.
5723. SIKÉLIANOS, Eléni
"'A' 'History'" (for Polly Klaas — selections: one-six). [Chain] (2) Spr 95, p. 205 -
209.
5724. SIKEN, Richard
"Remission." [JamesWR] (12:3) Fall 95, p. 18.
"The Scene of the Crime." [JamesWR] (12:3) Fall 95, p. 18.
"This Is What We Were Avoiding." [JamesWR] (12:3) Fall 95, p. 7.
SIKONG, Tu
    See TU, Sikong
SIKWOIA, Akiba Onada
    See ONADA-SIKWOIA, Akiba
5725. SILANO, Martha
"For a Friend Who Sends Me a Flyer on the Art of Ear Candling and News Her
    Book Has Arrived." [PoetryNW] (36:3) Aut 95, p. 20-21.
"Of Course Your Ears Are Burning!" [PoetryNW] (36:3) Aut 95, p. 21-22.
5726. SILBERT, Layle
"I Hate Books." [US1] (30/31) 95, p. 16.
5727. SILESKY, Barry
"Celebration." [ManyMM] (1:3) 95, p. 19.
"Continental Drift." [ProseP] (4) 95, p. 68.
"Mesquite Beans." [ManyMM] [1:1] D 94, p. 108-109.
"Still Money." [ManyMM] [1:1] D 94, p. 110.
5728. SILKIN, Jon
"The Bridge" (tr. of Motoo Andoh, w. Tomoyuki Iino). [Stand] (36:2) Spr 95, p. 28 -
    29.
"Calling 'Fish' in the Evening" (tr. of Toshiko Fujioka, w. Kazuya Honda). [Stand]
    (36:3) Sum 95, p. 35.
"Inside the Gentian" (For Rodney Pybus on his fiftieth birthday). [Bogg] (67) 95, p.
    17.
"Orion, Twice Blinded, Then Murdered. They, the Gods, Placed Him Amongst the
    Stars." [CentR] (39:2) Spr 95, p. 287.
"Permission to Weep." [CentR] (39:2) Spr 95, p. 285.
"Permission to Weep." [Quarry] (44:3) 95, p. 35-36.
"A Short Poem for Hiroshima." [CentR] (39:2) Spr 95, p. 284.
"Sleep Deeply in the Wilderness of Elegy" (tr. of Masato Inagawa, w. Tomoyuki
    Iino). [Stand] (36:2) Spr 95, p. 73.
"Suburbs." [CentR] (39:2) Spr 95, p. 286.
"Suburbs." [Quarry] (44:3) 95, p. 33-34.
"Tasogare" (Cousins of a lifetime quarrel over a wedding gift given to the parents of
    one of them). [CentR] (39:2) Spr 95, p. 288-290.
"This Is the Kingdom." [Quarry] (44:3) 95, p. 37.
"Watersmeet" (In Northumberland, by Hexham, where the North and South Tyne
    rivers meet on their way east). [CentR] (39:2) Spr 95, p. 279-284.
5729. SILOOK, Susie
"For Saavla." [Nimrod] (38:2) Spr-Sum 95, p. 42.
"The Hunter." [Nimrod] (38:2) Spr-Sum 95, p. 41.
"Restless Native." [Nimrod] (38:2) Spr-Sum 95, p. 43.
5730. SILVA, Jônatas Conceição da
"Tipos de Vida." [Callaloo] (18:4) Fall 95, p. 945.

"Types of Life" (tr. by Phyllis Peres and Jane Kamide). [Callaloo] (18:4) Fall 95, p. 773.

5731. SILVA, Sam
"For the Oaks of an Invisible Age" (from *The Night That Made New York Go Down* — unpublished manuscript). [DogRR] (14:1, #27) Sum 95, p. 7.
"Last Days in Lima." [DogRR] (14:1, #27) Sum 95, p. 36.
"Making a Sacrifice Like Art" (from *Making a Sacrifice Like Art* — to be published by Trout Creek Press, Fall, 1995). [DogRR] (14:1, #27) Sum 95, p. 7.
"That Head Which the Sun Inhabits." [DogRR] (14:1, #27) Sum 95, p. 36.

5732. SILVEIRA, Oliveira
"I Am" (tr. by Phyllis Peres, w. Reetika Vazirani and Chi Lam). [Callaloo] (18:4) Fall 95, p. 813-814.
"Sou." [Callaloo] (18:4) Fall 95, p. 981-982.

5733. SILVER-LILLYWHITE, Eileen
"Moon Coyote and the Pink Cat" (after the painting by Elly Simmons). [OhioR] (54) 95, p. 66-67.

5734. SILVERMARIE, Sue
"Mumma's Voice." [Rosebud] (2:2) Sum 95, p. 42-43.

5735. SIMAKOWICZ, Gene
"Jazz Impressions" (The 1994 Allen Ginsberg Poetry Awards: Second Prize). [Footwork] (24/25) 95, p. 183-184.

5736. SIMAS, Joseph
"Easy Lessons in Reading, or Our Son Was a Tree (A Reader) before Hour of Rumor." [Avec] (9) 95, p. 75-82.

5737. SIMCOX, Helen Earle
"Epiphany." [RagMag] (12:2) Spr 95, p. 108.
"Thoughts of a Winter Child." [RagMag] (12:2) Spr 95, p. 109.

5738. SIMIC, Charles
"Against Winter." [ParisR] (37:137) Wint 95, p. 211.
"The Anniversary." [NewYorker] (71:1) 20-27 F 95, p. 215.
"Cafe Paradiso." [Ploughs] (21:4) Wint 95-96, p. 142.
"Charm School." [ChiR] (41:1) 95, p. 56.
"Dark Corner." [Boulevard] (10:1/2, #28/29) Spr 95, p. 54.
"Don't Wake the Cards." [Ploughs] (21:4) Wint 95-96, p. 141.
"The Emperor." [GrandS] (13:3, #51) Wint 95, p. 19-21.
"Entertaining the Canary." [HarvardR] (9) Fall 95, p. 35.
"The Father of Lies." [PartR] (62:2) Spr 95, p. 298.
"The Forest Walk." [BelPoJ] (45:4) Chapbook 22, Sum 95, p. 63.
"Free the Goldfish." [Field] (53) Fall 95, p. 75.
"Lone Tree." [Ploughs] (21:4) Wint 95-96, p. 145.
"Matches." [Verse] (12:2) 95, p. 129-130.
"The Mice Have Their Hearts in Their Mouths." [Verse] (12:3) 95, p. 87.
"Mystics." [Boulevard] (10:1/2, #28/29) Spr 95, p. 55.
"Night in the House of Cards." [PartR] (62:2) Spr 95, p. 297.
"The Number of Fools." [Ploughs] (21:4) Wint 95-96, p. 144.
"On the Road to Somewhere Else." [Ploughs] (21:4) Wint 95-96, p. 143.
"On the Sagging Porch." [Verse] (12:3) 95, p. 86.
"Pastoral Harpsichord." [GrandS] (13:3, #51) Wint 95, p. 18.
"Poor Little Devil." [Field] (53) Fall 95, p. 74.
"Shadow Publishing Company." [ParisR] (37:137) Wint 95, p. 209-210.
"The Street Preacher." [IndR] (18:1) Spr 95, p. 23-25.
"Sunset's Coloring Book." [GrandS] (13:3, #51) Wint 95, p. 22.
"Toad's Poolhall." [Verse] (12:3) 95, p. 88.
"Travelling." [SenR] (25:1) Spr 95, p. 12.
"Winter Evening." [NewYorker] (70:43 [i.e. 44]) 9 Ja 95, p. 56.
"The World's Greatest Ventriloquist." [ParisR] (37:137) Wint 95, p. 210.

5739. SIMMERMAN, Jim
"The Baptist." [HayF] (17) Fall-Wint 95, p. 22-23.
"The Kingdom Come." [HayF] (17) Fall-Wint 95, p. 24-25.

5740. SIMMONS, Jimila
"Untitled: At night i dream" (WritersCorps Program, Washington, DC). [WashR] (21:2) Ag-S 95, p. 17.
"Untitled: Do you ever sit in a room with everything off" (WritersCorps Program, Washington, DC). [WashR] (21:2) Ag-S 95, p. 17.

5741. SIMMONS, Shan
"Geology." [Sonora] (30) Fall 95, p. 19.

"Nothing But Her Dance." [Sonora] (30) Fall 95, p. 18.
5742. SIMMONS-CUSHING, Gaye
"Beckoning Barn with an Attitude." [Pembroke] (27) 95, p. 20-21.
"Counting Pews." [Pembroke] (27) 95, p. 22.
"Patchwork Images." [Pembroke] (27) 95, p. 23-24.
"Struggle." [Pembroke] (27) 95, p. 25.
5743. SIMMS, Colin
"200th Anniversary of the Year of the Sheep, 1792." [WestCL] (29:2, #17) Fall 95,
p. 88-89.
"All Animals Speak to Us." [WestCL] (29:2, #17) Fall 95, p. 89.
"The Great Pattern Is Analagous to the Great Music (Pibroch)" [sic] (Scriabin, 5th
Sonata). [WestCL] (29:2, #17) Fall 95, p. 90.
"(Rain in the Wind)" (for M. Biggs '83). [WestCL] (29:2, #17) Fall 95, p. 89.
"Sidewinder." [WestCL] (29:2, #17) Fall 95, p. 88.
"Whalebone Churchgate." [WestCL] (29:2, #17) Fall 95, p. 90.
5744. SIMON, Barbara M.
"Real Life." [CapeR] (30:2) Fall 95, p. 40.
5745. SIMON, Beth
"Brinjal." [PottPort] (16:1) Fall 95, p. 13.
"Caribe." [Nimrod] (39:1) Fall-Wint 95, p. 121.
"Dry." [Arc] (34) Spr 95, p. 63.
"Dry." [Nimrod] (39:1) Fall-Wint 95, p. 120.
"Ground Level." [Arc] (34) Spr 95, p. 62.
"Milwaukee Road." [PottPort] (16:1) Fall 95, p. 12.
"Out of Nowhere, the Body's Shape." [Nimrod] (39:1) Fall-Wint 95, p. 119.
5746. SIMON, Greg
"Bread Lines." [Ploughs] (21:4) Wint 95-96, p. 167-168.
"The Interpreters of Dreams." [Ploughs] (21:4) Wint 95-96, p. 165-166.
5747. SIMON, John Oliver
"Guaymas." [HangL] (66) 95, p. 71-72.
"Incognito." [HangL] (66) 95, p. 72.
5748. SIMON, Maurya
"El Dia de los Muertos." [PoetryE] (39) Fall 94, p. 82.
"Elegy on His Birthday." [Footwork] (24/25) 95, p. 30.
"Enough." [Shen] (45:3) Fall 95, p. 53.
"On Turning Forty." [PoetryE] (39) Fall 94, p. 81.
"Villanelle." [Verse] (12:2) 95, p. 131.
SIMON, Michael
See LOGAN
5749. SIMONSON, Michael
"Late to the Office." [RagMag] (12:2) Spr 95, p. 19.
"An Old Shinto Woman." [RagMag] (12:2) Spr 95, p. 19.
"Saint." [RagMag] (12:2) Spr 95, p. 18.
5750. SIMONSUURI, Kirsti
"Arctic Journey" (tr. by Jascha Kessler and the author). [Nimrod] (38:2) Spr-Sum
95, p. 85.
"Nocturne." [Nimrod] (38:2) Spr-Sum 95, p. 85.
"Wannsee." [Nimrod] (38:2) Spr-Sum 95, p. 86.
5751. SIMPSON, Doug
"The Plot." [GreenHLL] (6) 95, p. 18.
5752. SIMPSON, Elizabeth
"Lost Daughter." [ChrC] (112:33) 15 N 95, p. 1068.
5753. SIMPSON, Grace
"White Sands." [ChrC] (112:24) 16-23 Ag 95, p. 776.
5754. SIMPSON, Louis
"Free Union" (tr. of André Breton). [HarvardR] (9) Fall 95, p. 59-60.
"The Gift of Myself" (tr. of Valery Larbaud). [Hudson] (47:4) Wint 95, p. 538-539.
"Images" (tr. of Valery Larbaud). [Hudson] (47:4) Wint 95, p. 540-541.
"Indian Ocean" (tr. of Valery Larbaud). [Hudson] (47:4) Wint 95, p. 535-536.
"The Lover" (tr. of Paul Éluard). [HarvardR] (9) Fall 95, p. 61.
"Night in the Port" (tr. of Valery Larbaud). [Hudson] (47:4) Wint 95, p. 534-535.
"Nyx" (tr. of Catherine Pozzi). [HarvardR] (9) Fall 95, p. 64.
"Ode" (tr. of Valery Larbaud). [Hudson] (47:4) Wint 95, p. 533-534.
"The Old Cahors Station" (tr. of Valery Larbaud). [Hudson] (47:4) Wint 95, p. 536.
"Postscript" (tr. of Valery Larbaud). [Hudson] (47:4) Wint 95, p. 541-542.
"There You Are." [TampaR] (10) Spr 95, p. 16-17.

"These Sounds and This Movement" (Translations from the French of Valery
    Larbaud). [Hudson] (47:4) Wint 95, p. 533-542.
"Yaravi" (tr. of Valery Larbaud). [Hudson] (47:4) Wint 95, p. 537-538.
5755. SIMPSON, Matt
    "Write Off." [Verse] (12:2) 95, p. 132.
5756. SIMS, Laura
    "Restless Night." [PaintedB] (55/56) 95, p. 72.
5757. SINCLAIR, John
    "Thelonious: a Book of Monk" (Selections: 3 poems). [AfAmRev] (29:2) Sum 95, p.
        269-273.
5758. SINCLAIR, Michael
    "Mimosas." [RiverS] (41) 95, p. 15-17.
5759. SINDALL, Susan
    "Under the Big Top, My Swing Waits." [13thMoon] (13:1/2) 95, p. 40-41.
5760. SINERVO, Helena
    "A child is a house that parents inhabit" (tr. by the author and Boey Kim Cheng).
        [InterPR] (21:2) Fall 95, p. 63.
    "The girl is so healthy that fever" (tr. by Sari Hantula). [InterPR] (21:2) Fall 95, p.
        65.
    "Lapsi on talo jota vanhemmat asuvat." [InterPR] (21:2) Fall 95, p. 62.
    "Ota sinä seipäästä kun saat, ota mies, se maistuu." [InterPR] (21:2) Fall 95, p. 66.
    "Take the pole as it comes, take a man, it's tasty" (tr. by Sari Hantula). [InterPR]
        (21:2) Fall 95, p. 67.
    "Tyttö on niin terve, että kuume." [InterPR] (21:2) Fall 95, p. 64.
5761. SINGER, George
    "A Prayer for Bosnia." [HampSPR] Wint 95, p. 12.
    "A Prayer to My Pills." [HampSPR] Wint 95, p. 13.
5762. SINGER, Matt
    "What With You." [PlumR] (9) [95 or 96], p. 109.
5763. SINNETT, Mark
    "Doubting Thomas." [Quarry] (44:2) 95, p. 127.
    "The Wading Pool." [Quarry] (44:2) 95, p. 128.
5764. SIOTIS, Dino
    "A Door Open" (From *Weather Conditions,* tr. by S. H. Kyriakos). [HarvardR] (8)
        Spr 95, p. 92.
5765. SIROWITZ, Hal
    "Angry Cats." [ChironR] (43) Sum 95, p. 11.
    "Behind the Door." [ChironR] (43) Sum 95, p. 11.
    "The Contest." [ChironR] (43) Sum 95, p. 11.
    "Relaxants." [ChironR] (43) Sum 95, p. 11.
    "Wanting Imperfection." [ChironR] (43) Sum 95, p. 11.
5766. SIRR, Peter
    "Arrivals." [Poetry] (167:1/2) O-N 95, p. 9.
5767. SISSON, Jonathan
    "Blue Moon" (26 September 1950). [NorthStoneR] (12) 95, p. 10.
    "Honeymoon on Naxos." [NorthStoneR] (12) 95, p. 11.
    "Orison." [NorthStoneR] (12) 95, p. 8.
    "The Pines of Bloomington." [NorthStoneR] (12) 95, p. 7.
    "Rainy-Day Ramble." [NorthStoneR] (12) 95, p. 9.
    "Silver Anniversary." [NorthStoneR] (12) 95, p. 12.
    "The West Windows." [NorthStoneR] (12) 95, p. 12.
5768. SJÖGREN, Lennart
    "About Her Love" (tr. by Robin Fulton). [MalR] (111) Sum 95, p. 33.
5769. SKALSKY, Askold
    "The Dahlias at Ternopil." [InterPR] (21:2) Fall 95, p. 99-100.
5770. SKAU, Michael
    "Claude Johnson Finally Speaks of His Wife." [MidwQ] (36:4) Sum 95, p. 434-435.
5771. SKEATE, Jeffery
    "Japanese Music." [RagMag] (12:2) Spr 95, p. 98.
    "Where Do We Come From, Why Are We Here?" [RagMag] (12:2) Spr 95, p. 99.
5772. SKEEN, Anita
    "Disappearing Acts" (from "The White Bell." Finalist, The Nimrod / Hardman
        Awards). [Nimrod] (39:1) Fall-Wint 95, p. 69.
    "Taking in the Elements" (from "The White Bell." Finalist, The Nimrod / Hardman
        Awards). [Nimrod] (39:1) Fall-Wint 95, p. 68.

5773. SKELLEY, Jack
"Having a Beer in Death Valley." [IllinoisR] (3:1/2) Fall 95-Spr 96, p. 49.
5774. SKENDERIJA, Sasa
"Master Craftsmen" (for S. Sontag, tr. by Wales Browne). [Vis] (48) 95, p. 8.
"The Occupation in Ten Scenes" (tr. by Wales Browne). [Vis] (48) 95, p. 8.
5775. SKENE, K. V.
"Appetizers." [Bogg] (67) 95, p. 35-36.
5776. SKILLMAN, Judith
"An Anarchy." [SilverFR] (25) Sum 95, p. 34.
"A Conceit." [NowestR] (33:2) 95, p. 32.
5777. SKINNER, Jeffrey
"Bill Evans and the Birds of Appetite" (sonnets and images, w. Mario M. Muller).
[Sonora] (29) Spr 95, p. 84-89.
"The Distance." [DefinedP] (3) 95, p. 31.
"Head of a Tongueless Poet." [Flyway] (1:1) Spr 95, p. 74-75.
"Thank You Note to the Body." [DefinedP] (3) 95, p. 30.
5778. SKINNER, Knute
"Attendance." [HolCrit] (32:4) O 95, p. 17.
"Contradictions." [WormR] (35:4, #140) 95, p. 146.
"Familiars." [WormR] (35:4, #140) 95, p. 145.
"The Fire." [Event] (24:3) Wint 95-96, p. 54.
"Mushrooms Berkeley." [NewYorkQ] (54) 95, p. 56-57.
"Quarrelling." [WormR] (35:4, #140) 95, p. 146-147.
5779. SKLAREW, Myra
"Scrim." [Confr] (56/57) Sum-Fall 95, p. 330.
5780. SKLOOT, Floyd
"Daybreak." [Atlantic] (275:4) Ap 95, p. 101.
"Eggs." [PraS] (69:2) Sum 95, p. 66.
"Hurricane Watch." [PraS] (69:2) Sum 95, p. 67-68.
"Ishmael in Pursuit." [SilverFR] (26) Wint 95, p. 36.
"Lime at the Edges." [SouthernPR] (35:1) Sum 95, p. 25-26.
"Morning in Amity." [PraS] (69:2) Sum 95, p. 68-69.
"Prodigy." [SilverFR] (26) Wint 95, p. 34.
"Sourwood Nocturne." [Hudson] (47:4) Wint 95, p. 608.
"Summer Afternoon, Near Keel." [SilverFR] (26) Wint 95, p. 33.
"Weber in London, Spring 1826." [PraS] (69:2) Sum 95, p. 66-67.
5781. SKOLER, Emily
"I'm Glad." [PassN] (16:2) Wint 95, p. 12-13.
"Llegamos Sin Nada en las Manos." [PassN] (16:2) Wint 95, p. 10.
"Stay." [PassN] (16:2) Wint 95, p. 11.
5782. SKOOG, Ed
"The Genuine Suffering of Lawyers." [Sonora] (30) Fall 95, p. 21-22.
"Variation on the Idea of Crowds." [CutB] (44) Sum 95, p. 39-41.
5783. SLADE, Leonard A., Jr.
"There Will Be Blacks in Heaven" (from Vintage: New and Selected Poems).
[AmerPoR] (24:6) N-D 95, p. 26.
5784. SLAMNIG, Ivan
"What Could We Say about God?" (tr. by Mima Dedaic, w. B. R. Strahan). [Vis]
(48) 95, p. 19.
5785. SLAPIKAS, Carolyn
"My number is 34-22-35." [NewYorkQ] (55) 95, p. 74.
5786. SLAPPY, Wayne
"Africa's Daughter." [Footwork] (24/25) 95, p. 23.
"Cool Is More Than a Walk." [Footwork] (24/25) 95, p. 25.
"Evidently Not Evident Yet." [Footwork] (24/25) 95, p. 24.
"The Ransom." [Footwork] (24/25) 95, p. 24.
5787. SLATER, Judith
"Male and Female Created He Them." [Elf] (5:2) Sum 95, p. 30.
"Souvenir de Florence, Opus 70" (for an old man). [Elf] (5:2) Sum 95, p. 31.
5788. SLATER, Robert
"The World of Common Day" (for Stacey Brown). [NewL] (61:3) 95, p. 45.
5789. SLAUGHTER, William
"Gulangyu." [ProseP] (4) 95, p. 69.
5790. SLAVITT, David (David R.)
"Feet: an Anniversary Nonet" (For Janet). [Light] (13) Spr 95, p. 12.
"Harlequin." [Shen] (45:1) Spr 95, p. 100-101.

"Pocket Watch." [Shen] (45:1) Spr 95, p. 102-104.
"PS3569L.3" [sic: the correct punctuation for a Library of Congress class notation would be PS3569.L3] (For a bookmark on the publication of my 50th book).
[Light] (15/16) Aut-Wint 95-96, p. 6.
"Sixty Latin Epigrams of John Owen" (8 selections with English translations).
[Light] (15/16) Aut-Wint 95-96, p. 4-5.
"Smart Remarks." [Light] (15/16) Aut-Wint 95-96, p. 6.
"Summons (Die Behorde)" (from the German of Christian Morgenstern). [Light] (15/16) Aut-Wint 95-96, p. 5.
"Tryma." [Light] (15/16) Aut-Wint 95-96, p. 3.
5792. SLECHTA, Mary McLaughlin
"In Times of War." [ManyMM] (1:2) 95, p. 105-106.
"Landmark." [ManyMM] (1:2) 95, p. 104.
5793. SLEDZIK, Steven T.
"Lot's Salt Lick." [Plain] (15:3) Spr 95, p. 28.
5794. SLEIGH, Tom
"The Chain" (for my mother). [SouthernR] (31:4) O/Aut 95, p. 935.
"Crossing the Border." [Agni] (41) 95, p. 30-31.
"The Denial." [Agni] (41) 95, p. 32-34.
"The Distance Between." [Agni] (41) 95, p. 35-36.
"Great Island." [PartR] (62:3) Sum 95, p. 446-447.
"The Octopus." [Thrpny] (60) Wint 95, p. 22.
"The Safety of Sunday." [BostonR] (20:6) D 95-Ja 96, p. 19.
5795. SLOAN, Kay
"In the Spice Market." [WestHR] (49:1) Spr 95, p. 80-81.
5796. SLOBODA, Gary
"Chalmers Street." [Interim] (14:1) Spr-Sum 95, p. 3.
5797. SLOMAN, Joel
"Burning." [Writ] (27) 95, p. 35.
"Every Land Is an Improvisation." [Writ] (27) 95, p. 36.
"I Am a Boulevardier in Paris." [Writ] (27) 95, p. 38.
"I Am a Tree or a Dog." [Writ] (27) 95, p. 34.
"In Olden Times, When It Was, Like, Wet, Even Cretaceous." [Writ] (27) 95, p. 37.
5798. SLOMKOWSKA, Lusia
"Only One Name" (for the women of Adobeland, Pima County, Arizona). [SpoonR] (20:2) Sum-Fall 95, p. 56-57.
5799. SLONIMSKY, Lee
"Arrows." [CapeR] (30:1) Spr 95, p. 50.
"Breath." [RagMag] (12:2) Spr 95, p. 35.
"In These Woods." [RagMag] (12:2) Spr 95, p. 36-37.
"Now." [HiramPoR] (58/59) Spr 95-Wint 96, p. 69.
"Physics at the Beach." [JINJPo] (17:1) Spr 95, p. 2.
5800. SLOSS, Henry
"Death by Beauty." [Hellas] (6:1) Spr-Sum 95, p. 89.
5801. SLYMAN, Ernest
"Ever After." [Light] (15/16) Aut-Wint 95-96, p. 20.
5802. SMAILS, William
"My Ex-Girlfriend." [BellArk] (11:2) Mr-Ap 95, p. 10.
5803. SMALL, Abbott
"Only a Homeless Beggar." [RagMag] (12:2) Spr 95, p. 79.
5804. SMALLS, Jean
"Lament" (for Edward Kamau Brathwaite). [CaribbeanW] (9) 95, p. 81-86.
5805. SMELCER, John (John E.)
"Changing Seasons." [Atlantic] (275:2) F 95, p. 68.
"Dadzaasi Luk' Ae: Spawning Sockeye." [LitR] (38:2) Wint 95, p. 219.
"Easter Sunday." [ArtfulD] (28/29) 95, p. 108.
"Late September on the Russian River." [Rosebud] (2:2) Sum 95, p. 72-73.
5806. SMITH, Andrew L.
"Lyres Discourse" (from *Vuelta: Revista Mensual*, September 1993, tr. of Pablo Neruda). [DenQ] (29:4) Spr 95, p. 133-134.
5807. SMITH, Anne K.
"Sunday We Rest." [Boulevard] (10:1/2, #28/29) Spr 95, p. 236.
5808. SMITH, Anthony
"Postcard from the Algarve." [Pearl] (22) Fall-Wint 95, p. 87.

5809. SMITH, Arthur
"Late Century Ode for the Common Dead." [CrabOR] (1:1) Fall-Wint 95, p. 131-136.
5810. SMITH, Barbara
"From the Margins." [EngJ] (84:1) Ja 95, p. 92.
5811. SMITH, Barbara F.
"Meeting Their Eyes." [SmPd] (32:1, #93) Wint 95, p. 31.
5812. SMITH, Beatrice
"He Heard Her All Right. So Who's Aggravated?" [US1] (30/31) 95, p. 12.
"I've Learned to Be Suspicious." [US1] (30/31) 95, p. 3.
5813. SMITH, Brent Wade
"Stationary Bicycle." [JamesWR] (12:3) Fall 95, p. 9.
5814. SMITH, Bruce
"The Clearing." [PartR] (62:1) Wint 95, p. 115-117.
"Crossover." [AmerPoR] (24:2) Mr-Ap 95, p. 20.
"In Santa Croce." [NewMyths] (2:2/3:1) 95, p. 84.
"Virtual Work." [NewMyths] (2:2/3:1) 95, p. 80-83.
5815. SMITH, Charlie
"Anticipation." [NewYorker] (71:16) 12 Je 95, p. 82.
"At Five in the Afternoon." [Pequod] (39) 95, p. 67-73.
"Every One of Them." [Boulevard] (10:1/2, #28/29) Spr 95, p. 86-87.
"Father Fish." [Boulevard] (10:1/2, #28/29) Spr 95, p. 88.
"Home Lessons." [GettyR] (8:3) Sum 95, p. 401.
"Outpatient." [GettyR] (8:3) Sum 95, p. 402.
5816. SMITH, Cheryl Denise
"For Branford Marsalis." [Drumvoices] (5:1/2) Fall-Wint 95-96, p. 28.
"Word Sister." [Drumvoices] (5:1/2) Fall-Wint 95-96, p. 29.
5817. SMITH, Curt
"The Sweep." [Parting] (8:2) Wint 95-96, p. 23-24.
5818. SMITH, D. J.
"A Country Romance." [PaintedB] (57) 95, p. 41.
"Czestochowa Gate." [ClockR] (10:1/2) 95-96, p. 120.
"Man With Woman in Red." [WillowS] (35) Ja 95, p. 54.
"On Loan." [ClockR] (10:1/2) 95-96, p. 119.
"What I See From a Distance." [QW] (40) Spr-Sum 95, p. 61.
5819. SMITH, Dave (David)
"About the Farmer's Daughter." [TriQ] (94) Fall 95, p. 77.
"Accounts." [DenQ] (29:4) Spr 95, p. 56.
"Allen Tate's Grave" (Sewanee, Tennessee). [YaleR] (83:2) Ap 95, p. 64-65.
"Another Nature Moment." [TriQ] (94) Fall 95, p. 76.
"Arising." [KenR] (17:3/4) Sum-Fall 95, p. 160.
"Being on the Job." [YaleR] (83:2) Ap 95, p. 66-67.
"Boys in the Square at Bologna." [NewYorker] (71:13) 22 My 95, p. 64.
"Burglar Alarm." [GeoR] (49:2) Sum 95, p. 468.
"Canary Weather." [VirQR] (71:4) Aut 95, p. 693.
"Compost Pile." [SpoonR] (20:1) Wint-Spr 95, p. 9.
"Cows Calling." [DenQ] (29:4) Spr 95, p. 53.
"Crying in the Streets." [PartR] (62:4) Fall 95, p. 677.
"Descending." [KenR] (17:3/4) Sum-Fall 95, p. 162.
"Doctor's Office." [SouthernHR] (29:3) Sum 95, p. 250-251.
"Elegy for My Friend's Suit." [SouthernR] (31:4) O/Aut 95, p. 936.
"Elizabeth River Water Skiers." [SpoonR] (20:1) Wint-Spr 95, p. 7.
"Fantastic Pelicans Arrive." [KenR] (17:3/4) Sum-Fall 95, p. 162.
"Farrakhan." [DenQ] (29:4) Spr 95, p. 54.
"Fiddlers." [DenQ] (29:4) Spr 95, p. 55.
"Field Dressing." [KenR] (17:3/4) Sum-Fall 95, p. 161.
"First Tournament Learning Experience." [NewOR] (21:2) Sum 95, p. 13.
"Gold Bird and the Age." [NewOR] (21:2) Sum 95, p. 12.
"Hammer and Sickle" (for Bob Morgan). [SpoonR] (20:1) Wint-Spr 95, p. 8.
"In the Nansemond River." [SouthwR] (80:2/3) Spr-Sum 95, p. 317.
"The Innerness of Churchland." [SpoonR] (20:1) Wint-Spr 95, p. 9.
"Irish Whiskey in the Backyard." [TriQ] (94) Fall 95, p. 78.
"Latin Lesson." [VirQR] (71:4) Aut 95, p. 692.
"A Lay of Spring." [NewOR] (21:2) Sum 95, p. 11.
"A Librarian's Gift." [TriQ] (94) Fall 95, p. 73.

"Louis Armstrong and the Astronauts Meet at the Langley AFB Pool." [TriQ] (94) Fall 95, p. 71.
"A Map of Your Small Town." [PartR] (62:4) Fall 95, p. 678.
"Mississippi River Bridge." [TriQ] (94) Fall 95, p. 74.
"Nature Moment." [TriQ] (94) Fall 95, p. 75.
"Nine Ball." [KenR] (17:3/4) Sum-Fall 95, p. 160-161.
"On His Son's New Blue Guitar." [SpoonR] (20:1) Wint-Spr 95, p. 8.
"Performing Fiction." [AmerPoR] (24:5) S-O 95, p. 5.
"Quail" (for Charles Wright). [KenR] (17:3/4) Sum-Fall 95, p. 161.
"Seafarer." [SpoonR] (20:1) Wint-Spr 95, p. 7.
"Stalled on the Ebb Tide." [SouthernR] (31:4) O/Aut 95, p. 936-937.
"A Supernatural Narrative." [TriQ] (94) Fall 95, p. 72.
"Train to St. Andrews, Scotland" (for Douglas Dunn). [AmerPoR] (24:5) S-O 95, p. 5.
"Watering the Dog." [AmerPoR] (24:5) S-O 95, p. 5.
"Where the Bullpasture and the Cowpasture Couple." [VirQR] (71:4) Aut 95, p. 692-693.
"Wreck in the Woods." [SouthwR] (80:2/3) Spr-Sum 95, p. 317.

5820. SMITH, Donny
"Epigram" (after Strato of Sardis). [EvergreenC] (10:2) Sum-Fall 95, p. 90.

5821. SMITH, E. Russell
"Shrove Tuesday." [Grain] (23:2) Aut 95, p. 76.
"Toronto Stopover." [Arc] (34) Spr 95, p. 73.

5822. SMITH, Ellen McGrath
"A Parable." [ArtfulD] (28/29) 95, p. 106.

5823. SMITH, Esther Y.
"Passage to America" (tr. of Ayyappa Paniker, w. the author, J. O. Perry, Dakshinamoorthy, and K. Satchidanandan). [ManyMM] (1:3) 95, p. 120-126.

5824. SMITH, Iain Crichton
"Emigrants." [Stand] (36:3) Sum 95, p. 34.
"Happiness." [Stand] (36:3) Sum 95, p. 33.
"Incident." [Stand] (36:3) Sum 95, p. 34.

5825. SMITH, J. D.
"The Professor Puts on Soft Contacts." [Light] (15/16) Aut-Wint 95-96, p. 30.
"Teeth." [Light] (15/16) Aut-Wint 95-96, p. 22.

5826. SMITH, James Malone
"Frequencies." [PassN] (16:1) Sum 95, p. 8.

5827. SMITH, Jim
"The Little Bird." [Arc] (34) Spr 95, p. 71.

5828. SMITH, Joan Jobe
"The Hippies Were Coming" (for Nicole Brown Simpson). [ChironR] (43) Sum 95, p. 14.
"Mopping Floors Naked." [ChironR] (43) Sum 95, p. 14.

5829. SMITH, John
"Bulbs." [JINJPo] (17:1) Spr 95, p. 1.
"The Right Turn." [US1] (30/31) 95, p. 7.
"This Poem Is Called 'Without Frames'." [LitR] (38:2) Wint 95, p. 291.

5830. SMITH, Jordan
"For Appearances" (for Jane Cooper). [YaleR] (83:1) Ja 95, p. 76.
"Local Color." [NewEngR] (17:2) Spr 95, p. 62-63.
"Paper Thin." [NewEngR] (17:2) Spr 95, p. 60-61.
"Poem Remembering Two Lines of Tsvetayeva." [NewEngR] (17:2) Spr 95, p. 61-62.

5831. SMITH, Katherine
"Earthbound." [Vis] (47) 95, p. 39.
"Flight." [ClockR] (10:1/2) 95-96, p. 104.
"Jealousy." [ClockR] (10:1/2) 95-96, p. 105.

5832. SMITH, Keith
"Back to Bach." [PoetryE] (39) Fall 94, p. 83-84.

5833. SMITH, Kirsten
"Environmental." [PraS] (69:2) Sum 95, p. 24.
"Powders." [PraS] (69:2) Sum 95, p. 25.
"Swimming Lesson." [MassR] (36:1) Spr 95, p. 68.

5834. SMITH, Linda Wasmer
"Plain Is Only Skin Deep." [DefinedP] (1:2) Spr-Sum 93, p. 32.

5835. SMITH, Maggie
"Anna's Susceptibility Begins." [Poem] (74) N 95, p. 69.
"Once Again." [Poem] (74) N 95, p. 68.
"Stone Baby." [Poem] (74) N 95, p. 67.
5836. SMITH, Mary Lonnberg
"Cypress." [NorthStoneR] (12) 95, p. 58.
"Japanese Paintings: Plum Tree in the Moonlight (Tani Buncho)." [NorthStoneR]
(12) 95, p. 59.
"Japanese Temple, 15th Century." [NorthStoneR] (12) 95, p. 59.
"Taking the Cure." [NorthStoneR] (12) 95, p. 60.
"You've Gone Away." [NorthStoneR] (12) 95, p. 60.
5837. SMITH, Michael C.
"My Mother's Cures for Hiccups." [Jacaranda] (11) [95 or 96?], p. 98-99.
"Night Settlers." [Jacaranda] (11) [95 or 96?], p. 102.
"Plans." [Jacaranda] (11) [95 or 96?], p. 97.
"Shopping for Shoes With My Brother." [Jacaranda] (11) [95 or 96?], p. 100-101.
5838. SMITH, Michael S.
"Dinner on the Couch." [ContextS] (4:2) 95, p. 9.
"In the Swim in Business Class" (Selections: 4, 6). [Plain] (15:3) Spr 95, p. 24-25.
"A Lesson for a Peace-Loving Man." [Plain] (16:1) Fall 95, p. 34.
"Looking Down on Us." [CapeR] (30:1) Spr 95, p. 41.
"Memorandum, for Chuck and Chet." [WindO] (59) Spr 95, p. 24.
"On the Road at Mandalay in Dallas." [GreenHLL] (6) 95, p. 90.
"Reunion." [Interim] (14:1) Spr-Sum 95, p. 20.
"Three Approaches to Late Summer." [Hellas] (6:1) Spr-Sum 95, p. 30.
5839. SMITH, Michael V.
"Take What You Need." [Quarry] (44:1) 95, p. 133-134.
5840. SMITH, Nathaniel
"Amish Gothic." [ProseP] (4) 95, p. 70.
5841. SMITH, Norman H. C.
"The Long Holiday." [DogRR] (14:1, #27) Sum 95, p. 34-35.
5842. SMITH, Patricia
"The First Day - 1/1/96." [Jacaranda] (11) [95 or 96?], p. 11-13.
"Inauguration Sneak." [Jacaranda] (11) [95 or 96?], p. 18.
"Meanwhile, In Rwanda." [Jacaranda] (11) [95 or 96?], p. 19.
"Missing You Still" (For Michael, a week later). [Jacaranda] (11) [95 or 96?], p. 16.
"What Peter Arnett Said" (Johannesburg bombing, 4/24/94). [Jacaranda] (11) [95 or
96?], p. 14-15.
"The Woman Who Died in Line" (Election Day, Soweto). [Jacaranda] (11) [95 or
96?], p. 17.
5843. SMITH, Pete
"Rita." [Vis] (49) 95, p. 27-28.
5844. SMITH, R. T.
"All Clear" (fragment of a letter from Charleston, August, 1864). [LullwaterR] (6:2)
Fall-Wint 95, p. 32-34.
"Bookcase." [CumbPR] (15:1) Fall 95, p. 44-46.
"Crickets." [DefinedP] (1:2) Spr-Sum 93, p. 51-52.
"Forbidden Stitch." [CarolQ] (47:3) Sum 95, p. 22-23.
"Gristle and Sheela-Na-Gig." [SouthernPR] (35:2) Wint 95, p. 71-72.
"Gristle Epitaph." [SouthernPR] (35:2) Wint 95, p. 74.
"Hard Times." [CarolQ] (47:3) Sum 95, p. 24.
"The Hard Word." [Crucible] (31) Fall 95, p. 6.
"Insomnia." [Elf] (5:4) Wint 95, p. 23.
"Nickel Ring." [CumbPR] (15:1) Fall 95, p. 47-48.
"Orchard." [GeoR] (49:2) Sum 95, p. 401-402.
"Shiftless." [CarolQ] (47:2) Wint 95, p. 49.
"Stolen Measures" (Variants on Lazarus and Dives). [Shen] (45:1) Spr 95, p. 69-70.
"Storyteller." [DefinedP] (1:2) Spr-Sum 93, p. 52-53.
"Tourist." [Shen] (45:1) Spr 95, p. 71-73.
"Watercolorist." [Crucible] (30) Fall 94, p. 10.
5845. SMITH, Ray
"The Beaches" (from "No Eclipse," 1945). [NorthStoneR] (12) 95, p. 154.
"The Brink" (from "No Eclipse," 1945). [NorthStoneR] (12) 95, p. 151.
"Brooks Bishop" (Captain, Medical Corps, 1944, from "Willapa," typescript).
[NorthStoneR] (12) 95, p. 180.
"A Child's History of Armament." [NorthStoneR] (12) 95, p. 191.

"A Coat" (from "Weathering," 1980). [NorthStoneR] (12) 95, p. 171.
"The Deer on the Freeway" (1973. Selections: 2 poems). [NorthStoneR] (12) 95, p. 164-165.
"The Deer on the Freeway" (from "The Deer on the Freeway," 1973). [NorthStoneR] (12) 95, p. 165.
"Driftwood Shore." [NorthStoneR] (12) 95, p. 190.
"Duel with Otto" (from "Weathering," 1980). [NorthStoneR] (12) 95, p. 172.
"The Greening Tree" (1965. Selections: 3 poems). [NorthStoneR] (12) 95, p. 159-161.
"The Greening Tree" (from "The Greening Tree," 1965). [NorthStoneR] (12) 95, p. 161.
"Gull Working" (from "Weathering," 1980). [NorthStoneR] (12) 95, p. 170.
"In a French Field" (from "No Eclipse," 1945). [NorthStoneR] (12) 95, p. 157.
"In Memory." [NorthStoneR] (12) 95, p. 185-186.
"Inuit Child Burial" (Five centuries' preservation, from "Willapa," typescript). [NorthStoneR] (12) 95, p. 174.
"Joy of Flesh" (from "The Greening Tree," 1965). [NorthStoneR] (12) 95, p. 159.
"The Landing" (from "No Eclipse," 1945). [NorthStoneR] (12) 95, p. 153.
"Lines in Florence" (from "Willapa," typescript). [NorthStoneR] (12) 95, p. 181.
"Listen, For I Have Kept a Fanatic Heart" (from "No Eclipse," 1945). [NorthStoneR] (12) 95, p. 158.
"Mountain Earthquake." [NorthStoneR] (12) 95, p. 190.
"No Eclipse" (1945. Selections: 8 poems). [NorthStoneR] (12) 95, p. 151-158.
"The North Pacific Coast" (from "Willapa," typescript). [NorthStoneR] (12) 95, p. 175.
"Now Edner Drives" (from "The Yellow Lamp," 1978). [NorthStoneR] (12) 95, p. 168.
"October Rain" (1969. Selections: 2 poems). [NorthStoneR] (12) 95, p. 162-163.
"October Rain" (from "October Rain," 1969). [NorthStoneR] (12) 95, p. 163.
"Poe." [NorthStoneR] (12) 95, p. 191.
"The Popcorn Man" (from "Willapa," typescript). [NorthStoneR] (12) 95, p. 177.
"Retrospect" (from "Willapa," typescript). [NorthStoneR] (12) 95, p. 183.
"Riding in the Black Hills" (with a Sioux companion, WW II, from "Willapa," typescript). [NorthStoneR] (12) 95, p. 178.
"Sea Fades from the Shell" (from "Willapa," typescript). [NorthStoneR] (12) 95, p. 179.
"The Sound of the Surf." [NorthStoneR] (12) 95, p. 187-189.
"Stonehenge" (2500 B.C.). [NorthStoneR] (12) 95, p. 156.
"Tanks in Winter." [NorthStoneR] (12) 95, p. 184.
"Tendril: Poem" (for Franklin Brainard, from "Weathering," 1980). [NorthStoneR] (12) 95, p. 171.
"This Is a Mortal Woman" (from "The Deer on the Freeway," 1973). [NorthStoneR] (12) 95, p. 164.
"Threshing" (On the home farm, from "The Yellow Lamp," 1978). [NorthStoneR] (12) 95, p. 166-167.
"Till Hope Creates: Poems of Protest" (1981. Selection: 1 poem). [NorthStoneR] (12) 95, p. 173.
"Tonight" (from "No Eclipse," 1945). [NorthStoneR] (12) 95, p. 155.
"Troops Waiting" (from "No Eclipse," 1945). [NorthStoneR] (12) 95, p. 152.
"Unpoem for M" (from "October Rain," 1969). [NorthStoneR] (12) 95, p. 162.
"Valentine to the Slums" (from "Till Hope Creates: Poems of Protest," 1981). [NorthStoneR] (12) 95, p. 173.
"Waiting for My Father" (from "Willapa," typescript). [NorthStoneR] (12) 95, p. 176.
"The War Dead" (from "The Greening Tree," 1965). [NorthStoneR] (12) 95, p. 160.
"Weathering" (1980. Selections: 4 poems). [NorthStoneR] (12) 95, p. 170-172.
"Willapa" (from "Willapa," typescript). [NorthStoneR] (12) 95, p. 182.
"Willapa" (typescript). [NorthStoneR] (12) 95, p. 174-183.
"The Yellow Lamp" (1978. Selections: 3 poems). [NorthStoneR] (12) 95, p. 166-169.
"The Yellow Lamp" (from "The Yellow Lamp," 1978). [NorthStoneR] (12) 95, p. 169.
5846. SMITH, Rod
"Aaron." [Phoebe] (24:1) 95, p. 74.
"Arthur." [Phoebe] (24:1) 95, p. 69.
"Bailey." [Phoebe] (24:1) 95, p. 67.

"The Boy Poems" (Selections: 7 poems). [Phoebe] (24:1) 95, p. 63-74.
"Edmond." [Phoebe] (24:1) 95, p. 68.
"Harold #2." [Phoebe] (24:1) 95, p. 65.
"John Fitzgerald." [Phoebe] (24:1) 95, p. 70-73.
"Mel." [Phoebe] (24:1) 95, p. 66.
"Your Group Insurance Benefits." [Chain] (2) Spr 95, p. 210-211.
5847. SMITH, Ron
   "The Southern Poet Is Pursued by Eliot." [SouthernR] (31:1) Wint 95, p. 60-62.
5848. SMITH, Sheila K.
   "Go / Giovanni / Fire" (for James Baldwin). [RiverS] (41) 95, p. 13-14.
5849. SMITH, Simon
   "Didactic Ode" (from "For Company"). [WestCL] (29:2, #17) Fall 95, p. 92-93.
   "For Company" (i.m. L.W. 11 xii 31—3 xi 91. Selections). [WestCL] (29:2, #17)
      Fall 95, p. 91-93.
5850. SMITH, Steven Ross
   "To Forget." [PraF] (16:2, #71) Sum 95, p. 17.
5851. SMITH, Thomas Milana
   "Flexibility." [Footwork] (24/25) 95, p. 70-71.
   "I'll Meet You, Monday." [Footwork] (24/25) 95, p. 70.
5852. SMITH, Thomas R.
   "812 Sycamore Street." [Image] (9) Spr 95, p. 63.
   "Anniversary Poem." [NorthStoneR] (12) 95, p. 13.
   "Driving through Custer National Park." [Image] (9) Spr 95, p. 62-63.
   "Snow Sticking to the Hood." [ProseP] (4) 95, p. 71.
   "A Truth." [Image] (9) Spr 95, p. 62.
5853. SMITH, Tom
   "Jack's Beans: A Five-Year Diary" (5 selections). [Iowa] (25:3) Fall 95, p. 122-126.
5854. SMITH, Wen
   "Tinkle, Tinkle." [Light] (13) Spr 95, p. 9.
5855. SMITH, William Jay
   "A Film" (tr. of Alain Bosquet). [NewYorker] (71:27) 11 S 95, p. 78.
   "Loose Leaves" (tr. of Alain Bosquet). [AmerPoR] (24:4) Jl-Ag 95, p. 19.
   "An Ordinary Day" (tr. of Alain Bosquet). [AmerPoR] (24:4) Jl-Ag 95, p. 19.
   "When I'm No Longer Around" (tr. of Alain Bosquet). [AmerPoR] (24:4) Jl-Ag 95,
      p. 19.
5856. SMITH-JOHNSON, Robin
   "Missing Person." [AnthNEW] (7) 95, p. 29.
5857. SMITH-SOTO, Mark
   "Latino." [PlumR] (9) [95 or 96], p. 17.
   "President in My Heart." [Sun] (232) Ap 95, p. 37.
   "See It on Video." [Sun] (233) My 95, p. 19.
5858. SMITHER, Elizabeth
   "From a Ha-ha to a Cemetery." [MalR] (113) Wint 95, p. 107.
   "A Man Walking in White Shoes." [MalR] (113) Wint 95, p. 108.
   "My Mother Looking at Stars." [MalR] (113) Wint 95, p. 109.
5859. SMITS, Ronald (Ronald F.)
   "The History of Flight." [PoetryE] (40) Spr 95, p. 115.
   "The Trestle Bridge at Mahoning Creek." [FreeL] (14) Wint 95, p. 32.
5860. SMOCK, Frederick
   "Exam." [PoetryE] (41) Aut 95, p. 61.
   "La Wally." [PoetryE] (40) Spr 95, p. 116.
5861. SMOKEWOOD, Elaine
   "My Grandmother Wrestles the Angel of Death." [SouthernPR] (35:2) Wint 95, p.
      34-36.
5862. SMUTS, Brooke
   "Halcyon Days." [SantaBR] (3:1) Spr 95, p. 25.
   "My Father's Nest." [SantaBR] (3:1) Spr 95, p. 27.
   "Red Ground Road." [SantaBR] (3:1) Spr 95, p. 26.
5863. SMYTH, Donna E.
   "Family Papers." [PraF] (16:3, #72) Aut 95, p. 16-23.
5864. SMYTH, Edward
   "Elegy and Fugue" (words to accompany the String Quartet #15 by Shostokovitch.
      First Honorable Mention, The Pablo Neruda Prize for Poetry). [Nimrod]
      (39:1) Fall-Wint 95, p. 32.
   "Lapsed Rhymes for a Requiem Mass" (First Honorable Mention, The Pablo Neruda
      Prize for Poetry). [Nimrod] (39:1) Fall-Wint 95, p. 22.

"Mourning and the Art of Masonry" (First Honorable Mention, The Pablo Neruda Prize for Poetry). [Nimrod] (39:1) Fall-Wint 95, p. 30.
"The Mystery of the Incarnation" (First Honorable Mention, The Pablo Neruda Prize for Poetry). [Nimrod] (39:1) Fall-Wint 95, p. 27-28.
"Unto Dust" (First Honorable Mention, The Pablo Neruda Prize for Poetry). [Nimrod] (39:1) Fall-Wint 95, p. 31.
5865. SNEEDEN, Ralph
"Early Spring." [HayF] (17) Fall-Wint 95, p. 32.
"Garage Meditation." [HayF] (17) Fall-Wint 95, p. 33-35.
5866. SNEYD, Steve
"Something to Discuss with Fellow Strangers." [Bogg] (67) 95, p. 59-60.
5867. SNIDER, Bruce
"The Basin" (runner up, 1994 Borderlands Poetry Contest). [Border] (6) Spr-Sum 95, p. 61-62.
5868. SNIDER, Clifton
"For Jackie O., 1929-1994." [Pearl] (22) Fall-Wint 95, p. 59.
"Healing the House." [Pearl] (22) Fall-Wint 95, p. 57.
"Ignis Fatuus." [Pearl] (22) Fall-Wint 95, p. 58.
"The Scream." [Pearl] (22) Fall-Wint 95, p. 58.
5869. SNIVELY, Susan
"Talk to the Wall." [PoetryE] (40) Spr 95, p. 117-118.
5870. SNODGRASS, Bond
"The Avaricious Flower" (tr. of Guillermo Fernández). [PlumR] (9) [95 or 96], p. 75.
"Here Again" (tr. of Guillermo Fernández). [PlumR] (9) [95 or 96], p. 76-77.
"Hermitage for a Family Tree" (tr. of Ernesto Lumbreras). [PlumR] (8) [95], p. 70-71.
"Truths" (tr. of Juan Gelman). [PlumR] (8) [95], p. 8-11.
"Truths" (tr. of Juan Gelman). [PlumR] (9) [95 or 96], p. 110-113.
5871. SNODGRASS, W. D.
"Informing on a Couple Unknown Guys" (tr. of Leszek Szaruga). [Colum] (24/25) 95, p. 23.
5872. SNOEK, Paul
"Concocted from the North for Joost de Wit" (tr. by Kendall A. Dunkelberg). [InterPR] (21:1) Spr 95, p. 39.
"In Space" (tr. by Kendall Dunkelberg). [SnailPR] (3:2) 95, p. 21.
"Vergedicht vit het Noorden voor Joost de Vit." [InterPR] (21:1) Spr 95, p. 38.
"Welcome in My Underworld" (tr. by Kendall Dunkelberg). [SnailPR] (3:2) 95, p. 20.
"White-poem" (tr. by Kendall Dunkelberg). [LitR] (38:3) Spr 95, p. 351.
5873. SNOTHERLY, Mary
"Testimony on Haymarket Street." [Crucible] (30) Fall 94, p. 29.
5874. SNOW, Carol
"By the Pond." [ColR] (22:2) Fall 95, p. 155-156.
"News of." [ColR] (22:2) Fall 95, p. 152-154.
5875. SNOW, Karen
"Reading." [BelPoJ] (45:4) Chapbook 22, Sum 95, p. 64-65.
5876. SNYDER, Gary
"At Tower Peak." [Zyzzyva] (11:3/4, #43/44) 95, "The Best of Ten Years of ZYZZYVA," p. 75-76.
"Breasts." [RiverS] (42/43) 95, p. 47.
"Endless Streams and Mountains" (opening section of "Mountains and Rivers Without End"). [Orion] (14:3) Sum 95, p. 38-39.
"An Offering for Târâ." [YaleR] (83:1) Ja 95, p. 19-25.
"Tedious, the Affairs of Office." [BelPoJ] (45:4) Chapbook 22, Sum 95, p. 66.
5877. SNYDER, Jennifer
"Accordion." [PoetryNW] (36:1) Spr 95, p. 39.
"Cafes at Night." [PassN] (16:2) Wint 95, p. 8-9.
"Fathers." [PassN] (16:1) Sum 95, p. 20-21.
"Palm Springs." [BlackWR] (21:2) Spr-Sum 95, p. 123.
"River." [MidAR] (15:1/2) 95, p. 153-154.
"What the Light Did." [MidAR] (15:1/2) 95, p. 150-152.
5878. SNYDER, William, Jr.
"The Horse That Died Eating Flowers." [InterQ] (2:1/2) 95, p. 22.
"Human Factors." [Parting] (8:1) Sum 95, p. 21.
"Pouring Out." [Parting] (8:1) Sum 95, p. 21.

5879. SOBELMAN, 'Annah
"The Different Smokes on Top of the Roof." [IndR] (18:1) Spr 95, p. 35.
"Jesus and the Gray Sacrament." [ColR] (22:2) Fall 95, p. 115-118.
"Spring at the Cafe Figaro." [BostonR] (20:4) O-N 95, p. 18.
5880. SOBELMAN, Ellen
"In Dreams Lies Fragmentation." [SantaBR] (3:3) Fall-Wint 95, p. 65.
"To Die — To Sleep." [SantaBR] (3:3) Fall-Wint 95, p. 64.
5881. SOBIN, Anthony
"Another Birthday: Sending the Angel Ahead." [WillowS] (36) Je 95, p. 15.
"The Shakespeare Seminar Terrorists." [BelPoJ] (45:4) Chapbook 22, Sum 95, p.
67-68.
"Tattoo." [BelPoJ] (45:4) Chapbook 22, Sum 95, p. 69-70.
"Translation." [SoDakR] (33:2) Sum 95, p. 103.
"Wichita." [BelPoJ] (45:3) Spr 95, p. 5.
5882. SOBIN, Gustaf
"Pastoral." [Talisman] (15) Wint 95-96, p. 65-66.
"Premises." [Talisman] (15) Wint 95-96, p. 67-69.
"Towards the Blanched Alphabets." [Talisman] (15) Wint 95-96, p. 70-71.
5883. SOBSEY, Cynthia
"This Is Our Address." [Kalliope] (17:3) 95, p. 13.
5884. SOCOLOW, Elizabeth Anne
"Rock in an Antique House." [US1] (30/31) 95, p. 2.
5885. SODEN, Christopher S.
"One Very Cold, Dry Perfect Martini" (for Peter). [JamesWR] (12:2) Spr-Sum 95, p.
13.
"The World in a Book of Matches." [JamesWR] (12:2) Spr-Sum 95, p. 14.
5886. SÖDERBLOM, Staffan
"Den Döde Andas (The Dead Man Breathes)" (Selections: 3 poems, tr. by Robin
Fulton). [MalR] (111) Sum 95, p. 93-95.
"The forest has many stairways, few doors" (from "Den Döde Andas (The Dead
Man Breathes)," tr. by Robin Fulton). [MalR] (111) Sum 95, p. 95.
"I call the animals home" (from "Den Döde Andas (The Dead Man Breathes)," tr. by
Robin Fulton). [MalR] (111) Sum 95, p. 93.
"The unpainted buildings, the places" (from "Den Döde Andas (The Dead Man
Breathes)," tr. by Robin Fulton). [MalR] (111) Sum 95, p. 94.
5887. SODERLING, Janice
"Free Fall." [Event] (24:1) Spr 95, p. 42.
"In Celebration of Your Tongue." [TarRP] (34:2) Spr 95, p. 23.
"On Watching a Cat Catch a Butterfly." [CumbPR] (14:2) Spr 95, p. 3.
5888. SODOWSKY, Roland
"Tramp Visit." [MidwQ] (36:4) Sum 95, p. 436-437.
SOJUN, Ikkyu
See IKKYU, Sojun
5889. SOKOL, John
"Airboating in the Everglades." [Elf] (5:2) Sum 95, p. 28.
"Apologia" (for Shelly). [SpoonR] (20:1) Wint-Spr 95, p. 103.
"Letter to a Sister I Don't Have." [NewDeltaR] (12:2) Spr-Sum 95, p. 47-48.
"Sestina for the Years That Are Numbered" (for J.). [Hellas] (6:2) Fall-Wint 95, p.
75-76.
"Tell Me Your Dreams." [SoCoast] (18) Ja 95, p. 60.
"Thoughts Near the Close of Millennium." [QW] (41) Aut-Wint 95-96, p. 166-167.
5890. SOL, Adam
"Spork." [HopewellR] (7) 95, p. 113.
"Vienna March." [KenR] (17:1) Wint 95, p. 49-52.
5891. SOLDAINI, Antonella
"Indirectrevolution" (tr. of Anna Lombardo, w. Jack Hirschman). [WorldL] (6) 95,
p. 14-15.
5892. SOLIE, Karen
"Staying Awake." [Dandel] (22:1) 95, p. 74-75.
5893. SOLIZ, Christine
"A Description of the Morning in Seattle, a Dythyrambic Ride on Rainier Avenue."
[BellArk] (11:6) N-D 95, p. 6.
"The Drawing Plan." [BellArk] (11:6) N-D 95, p. 6.
"Jamming." [BellArk] (11:6) N-D 95, p. 6.
"Strange Worlds." [BellArk] (11:6) N-D 95, p. 6.

5894. SOLLY, Richard
"Everyone Has a Poem They Don't Want to Write." [PoetryE] (39) Fall 94, p. 85.
"Incarnation." [PoetryE] (39) Fall 94, p. 86-87.
"Seeking Refuge." [PoetryE] (39) Fall 94, p. 88-89.
5895. SOLNICKI, Jill
"Paradise Lost, by John Milton's Daughter." [PraF] (16:2, #71) Sum 95, p. 75.
5896. SOLOMON, Mark
"Detective." [HangL] (67) 95, p. 82-83.
"The Pleasure of a Ride." [HangL] (67) 95, p. 83.
"Sarajevo Serenade, July 1992." [Wind] (76) Fall 95, p. 32-33.
"Sydney Understood." [LullwaterR] (6:2) Fall-Wint 95, p. 62-63.
"Visitation: Lower Manhattan." [BelPoJ] (45:3) Spr 95, p. 30-31.
"Wisconsin." [FloridaR] (20:2) 95, p. 39.
5897. SOLOMON, Marvin
"Apostasy." [Wind] (76) Fall 95, p. 23.
"The Razor." [Poetry] (165:4) Ja 95, p. 193.
5898. SOLOMON, Sandy
"Annual Game, Thrumpton Cricket Ground." [SouthernR] (31:1) Wint 95, p. 63-64.
"For Edmund Under a Tree in Summer." [NewRep] (212:8) 20 F 95, p. 42.
"Lizard and I." [NewYorker] (71:23) 7 Ag 95, p. 60.
"The Water Is Taking Back Its Old Places" (NY Times, 18 July 1993). [SenR] (25:2)
Fall 95, p. 92-93.
5899. SOLONCHE, J. R.
"The Past." [LitR] (38:2) Wint 95, p. 243.
5900. SOMERVILLE, Jane
"Fine and Empty." [SouthernPR] (35:1) Sum 95, p. 11.
5901. SOMMER, Jason
"Meyer Tsits and the Children." [RiverS] (42/43) 95, p. 174-176.
5902. SOMMER, Piotr
"Lighter, Darker" (tr. by the author and M. Kasper). [Agni] (42) 95, p. 120.
5903. SONDE, Susan
"It Was Unique and It Was Common and It Was Sad at the Same Time." [AmerLC]
(7) 95, p. 113-114.
5904. SONG, Cathy
"Pa-ke." [SouthernR] (31:4) O/Aut 95, p. 938-939.
"Riverbed." [SouthernR] (31:4) O/Aut 95, p. 941-942.
"Rust." [Shen] (45:2) Sum 95, p. 34-35.
"The Valley Boat." [SouthernR] (31:4) O/Aut 95, p. 940-941.
5905. SONG, Terry
"Grackle" (runner up, 1994 Borderlands Poetry Contest). [Border] (7) Fall-Wint 96,
p. 59-60.
5906. SONGHAI, H.
"Parole for the Soul (the Sun Unarmed) Million Man March a Day of Atonement."
[Drumvoices] (5:1/2) Fall-Wint 95-96, p. 128-129.
5907. SONIAT, Katherine
"Along the Way." [EngJ] (84:1) Ja 95, p. 28.
"Blame It on the Cows." [AmerV] (36) 95, p. 37.
"Gendered Parts." [RiverS] (45) 95, p. 51.
"Isle of Poetry" (after Jean de Fremont d'Abancour's L'Histoire Veritable de Lucien,
1654). [HampSPR] Wint 95, p. 16.
"Open House." [DenQ] (29:3) Wint 95, p. 32-33.
"Otherwise/ or Mrs. Herbert Jones, Tour Guide, Speaks of Mrs. John Rolf, 1878"
[sic]. [HampSPR] Wint 95, p. 15.
"T-Backed in Orlando." [SpoonR] (20:2) Sum-Fall 95, p. 123-124.
"Vespers." [SpoonR] (20:2) Sum-Fall 95, p. 122.
5908. SONNEVI, Goran
"Mozart Variation #7" (tr. by John Mathais [sic] and G. Printz-Pahlson). [Vis] (49)
95, p. 35.
"Mozart Variation #8" (tr. by John Mathais [sic] and G. Printz-Pahlson). [Vis] (49)
95, p. 35.
"Mozart Variation #12" (tr. by John Matthais [sic] and G. Printz-Pahlson). [Vis] (47)
95, p. 11.
5909. SOOPIKIAN, Touba
"Echo Is Our Planet Earth Round?" [Pearl] (22) Fall-Wint 95, p. 145.
5910. SORBIN, Anthony
"Real Time." [LitR] (38:3) Spr 95, p. 422.

5911. SORENSEN, Janice
"At Times." [MassR] (36:2) Sum 95, p. 235.
5912. SORESCU, Marin
"Angle" (tr. by Paul Muldoon). [SouthernR] (31:3) Jl/Sum 95, p. 484.
"The Great Blind Man" (tr. by Adam J. Sorkin and Lidia Vianu). [Vis] (48) 95, p.
44.
"Shakespeare" (tr. by Paul Muldoon). [SouthernR] (31:3) Jl/Sum 95, p. 481-482.
"Symmetry" (tr. by Paul Muldoon). [SouthernR] (31:3) Jl/Sum 95, p. 482-484.
"Synchronization" (tr. by Adam J. Sorkin and Lidia Vianu). [Vis] (48) 95, p. 45.
5913. SORKIN, Adam (Adam J.)
"Above the Bridge" (tr. of Liliana Ursu, w. Tess Gallagher). [Kalliope] (17:3) 95, p.
19.
"Anima Mundi" (tr. of Lucian Vasiliu, w. Laurentiu Constantin). [Vis] (48) 95, p.
47-48.
"Apocrypha the First" (tr. of Alexandra Musina, w. Radu Surdulescu). [Vis] (48) 95,
p. 40.
"At the Bend of the Don" (tr. of Ioana Ieronim, w. the author). [OxfordM] (10:1)
Wint 94-Spr 95, p. 36.
"At the Old Fortress" (tr. of Ioana Ieronim, w. the author). [OxfordM] (10:1) Wint
94-Spr 95, p. 36-37.
"Between Parallel Mirrors" (tr. of Cornelia Maria Savu, w. Taina Dutescu-Coliban).
[13thMoon] (13:1/2) 95, p. 34.
"The Blood Which Comes" (tr. of Magda Carneci, w. the author). [Vis] (48) 95, p.
38.
"The Burning" (tr. of Daniela Crasnaru, w. Ioana Ieronim). [Vis] (48) 95, p. 39.
"Car Graveyard" (tr. of Ion Stratan, w. Ioana Ieronim). [LitR] (38:2) Wint 95, p.
185-190.
"The Collector" (tr. of Grete Tartler, w. Liliana Ursu). [Vis] (48) 95, p. 46.
"A Dance in Masks" (tr. of Aurel Rau, w. Liviu Bleoca). [Vis] (48) 95, p. 43.
"Elegy: Oh, old and familiar kitchens of summer" (tr. of Emil Brumaru, w. Ioana
Ieronim). [PlumR] (9) [95 or 96], p. 22.
"Experiments (A Chimera of the Real)" (The Sixth Experiment, Survival in
Meaning, tr. of Alexandru Musina, w. Radu Surdulescu). [Vis] (48) 95, p. 41.
"Field Blankets" (tr. of Lucian Vasiliu, w. Laurentiu Constantin). [Vis] (48) 95, p.
48.
"The Great Blind Man" (tr. of Marin Sorescu, w. Lidia Vianu). [Vis] (48) 95, p. 44.
"A Hazy Morning" (For Horia Bernea, tr. of Cornelia Maria Savu, w. Taina
Dutescu-Coliban). [13thMoon] (13:1/2) 95, p. 35.
"I Wish I Were the Earth" (tr. of Monica Pillat, w. the author). [Vis] (48) 95, p. 42.
"Instancy" (tr. of Magda Carneci, w. the author). [Vis] (48) 95, p. 38.
"A Locket" (tr. of Cornelia Maria Savu, w. Taina Dutescu-Coliban). [13thMoon]
(13:1/2) 95, p. 36.
"Love Poem at the Foot of the Deforested Hill" (tr. of Cornelia Maria Savu, w.
Taina Dutescu-Coliban). [13thMoon] (13:1/2) 95, p. 37.
"Love Poem at the Mirror" (tr. of Cornelia Maria Savu, w. Taina Dutescu-Coliban).
[13thMoon] (13:1/2) 95, p. 38.
"A Morning Fit for Writing Your Memoirs" (tr. of Cornelia Maria Savu, w. Taina
Dutescu-Coliban). [13thMoon] (13:1/2) 95, p. 39.
"Nightbook: 60" (tr. of Eugene van Itterbeek). [ConnPR] (14:1) 95, p. 37.
"Only in the fire" (from "Transparent Waiting," tr. of Annie Reniers, w. Eugène Van
Itterbeek). [MalR] (110) Spr 95, p. 106.
"Really, Don't You Believe Me?" (tr. of Liliana Ursu, w. the author). [Vis] (48) 95,
p. 47.
"The Sacred and the Profane" (tr. of Liliana Ursu, w. the author). [Vis] (48) 95, p.
46.
"Season" (tr. of Mircea Florin Sandru, w. Lidia Vianu). [Vis] (48) 95, p. 44.
"Season's End" (for Mirela, tr. of Liliana Ursu, w. the poet). [SnailPR] (3:2) 95, p.
12-13.
"The Second Elegy of the Detective Arthur" (tr. of Emil Brumaru, w. Ioana
Ieronim). [PlumR] (9) [95 or 96], p. 23.
"Spring Tale" (tr. of Petru Romosan, w. Radu Surdulescu). [Vis] (48) 95, p. 43.
"Summer Afternoon" (tr. of Ioana Ieronim, w. the author). [OxfordM] (10:1) Wint
94-Spr 95, p. 37.
"Synchronization" (tr. of Marin Sorescu, w. Lidia Vianu). [Vis] (48) 95, p. 45.
"Transparent Waiting" (Selections: 2 poems, tr. of Annie Reniers, w. Eugène Van
Itterbeek). [MalR] (110) Spr 95, p. 106-107.

"Wheel, Ruby and Vortex" (tr. of Magda Carneci, w. the author). [Vis] (48) 95, p. 39.

"Winter Vision at the Mouth of the River" (tr. of Ion Mircea, w. Liviu Cotrau). [Vis] (48) 95, p. 40.

"Yorick, Yorick, Yorick, or How About You, Reader, Would You Hold My Skull in Your Hand?" (tr. of Petru Romosan, w. Radu Surdulescu). [Vis] (49) 95, p. 7.

"You Must Prove Yourself a Peaceful Animal Now" (tr. of Domnita Petri, w. Ioana Ieronim). [Vis] (48) 95, p. 41-42.

"You stay all eternity" (from "Transparent Waiting," tr. of Annie Reniers, w. Eugène Van Itterbeek). [MalR] (110) Spr 95, p. 107.

"Your Life Will Be Like This" (tr. of Ioana Ieronim, w. the author). [OxfordM] (10:1) Wint 94-Spr 95, p. 38.

5914. SORNBERGER, Judith
"She Comes in Dreams." [PraS] (69:2) Sum 95, p. 127-128.
"She Feels Old." [PraS] (69:2) Sum 95, p. 129-130.
"She Tries to Teach Me How to Pray." [PraS] (69:2) Sum 95, p. 131.

5915. SOSNOFF, Granate
"Hapa New Years" (1/22/93 1:00 a.m., Lunar New Years Eve, Before my mother died). [SinW] (56) Sum-Fall 95, p. 82-86.

5916. SOTO, Gary
"Dressing for the Occasion." [DefinedP] (1:2) Spr-Sum 93, p. 42-43.
"The Essay Examination for What You Have Read in the Course World Religions." [MassR] (36:4) Wint 95-96, p. 635-636.
"Getting Ahead." [Poetry] (166:5) Ag 95, p. 268-269.
"Hand Washing." [Harp] (290:1740) My 95, p. 29.
"Hand Washing." [MichQR] (34:1) Wint 95, p. 87-89.
"The History of Science." [Poetry] (165:4) Ja 95, p. 203-204.
"Inferior Dog." [NewEngR] (17:1) Wint 95, p. 129-130.
"Moving Our Misery." [MassR] (36:4) Wint 95-96, p. 636.
"Pagan Life." [Poetry] (166:5) Ag 95, p. 269-270.
"Pompeii and the Uses of Our Imagination." [MassR] (36:4) Wint 95-96, p. 634-635.
"Profile with Rain." [Iowa] (25:1) Wint 95, p. 123.
"The Skeptics." [Poetry] (166:5) Ag 95, p. 267.
"Some History." [Poetry] (165:4) Ja 95, p. 204-205.
"Western Civilization." [Crazy] (48) Spr 95, p. 38-39.
"What Is Your Major?" [NewEngR] (17:1) Wint 95, p. 130-131.

SOTO, Mark Smith
See SMITH-SOTO, Mark

5917. SOTO VÉLEZ, Clemente
"Estos Arboles." [MassR] (36:4) Wint 95-96, p. 640-648.
"These Trees" (tr. by Camilo Pérez-Bustillo and Martín Espada). [MassR] (36:4) Wint 95-96, p. 641-649.

5918. SOULLIARD, Mitchell
"Monsoon: Steelton, PA." [AxeF] (3) 90, p. 9.

5919. SOUPAULT, Philippe
"Little Daily Phantoms" (tr. by Tom Hibbard). [WillowS] (36) Je 95, p. 107.
"Starfish" (For Marcel Harrand, tr. by Paulette Schmidt). [LitR] (38:2) Wint 95, p. 286-287.

5920. SOVIERO, Marcelle M.
"For X." [Pearl] (22) Fall-Wint 95, p. 17.
"Paper Doll." [Pearl] (22) Fall-Wint 95, p. 17.

5921. SOWERS, Sydney
"Peacock River Child." [SpoonR] (20:1) Wint-Spr 95, p. 94-95.

5922. SOZONOVA, Alexandra
"Saint Petersburg, End of the 20th Century" (tr. by J. Kates). [MidAR] (15:1/2) 95, p. 109-110.

5923. SPACKS, Barry
"Dot." [FreeL] (14) Wint 95, p. 27.
"Walking Home." [FreeL] (14) Wint 95, p. 26.

5924. SPAHR, Juliana
"Choosing Rooms" (Excerpts). [CentralP] (24) Spr 95, p. 221-223.
"The Letter." (Selections). [Avec] (9) 95, p. 87-95.
"Thrashing Seems Crazy." [Avec] (9) 95, p. 83-86.

5925. SPALDING, Esta
"Aperture." [MalR] (111) Sum 95, p. 106-118.

SPANCKEREN, Kathryn van
See Van SPANCKEREN, Kathryn
5926. SPANGLE, Douglas
"Revise This Sonnet." [DogRR] (14:1, #27) Sum 95, p. 31.
5927. SPARKS, Christine
"Dyslexia." [Kaleid] (31) Sum-Fall 95, p. 42.
"Suppertime." [Kaleid] (31) Sum-Fall 95, p. 42.
5928. SPARLING, George
"Me the Impotent Man Among Imaginary Monsters." [ChironR] (44/45) Aut-Wint
95, p. 41.
5929. SPEAKES, Richard
"The Comfort of Old Pain." [PoetryE] (40) Spr 95, p. 119.
5930. SPEARS, Jeremy
"Billie's Song." [IllinoisR] (3:1/2) Fall 95-Spr 96, p. 13.
"Family Dance." [Interim] (14:1) Spr-Sum 95, p. 42-43.
"Feast." [Interim] (14:1) Spr-Sum 95, p. 41-42.
"Milk of Wish." [PlumR] (8) [95], p. 26-27.
"Self-Portrait: Nude, Swimming by Night" (after James Merrill). [GreenMR] (8:2)
Fall-Wint 95-96, p. 130-131.
"Sestina with Moon." [JamesWR] (12:3) Fall 95, p. 6.
"The Sulfur Beach." [IllinoisR] (3:1/2) Fall 95-Spr 96, p. 18.
5931. SPECHT, Jerry
"I Say There Is No Physical Beauty." [Writer] (108:12) D 95, p. 20.
5932. SPECTOR, Robert D.
"Depreciation." [Confr] (56/57) Sum-Fall 95, p. 343.
5933. SPEER, Laurel
"Caniche Found Smothered by Juifs." [MassR] (36:1) Spr 95, p. 38.
"The First Mrs. Einstein." [Kalliope] (17:1) 95, p. 13.
"Horses at the Front." [MassR] (36:1) Spr 95, p. 39.
"Horses at the Front." [SnailPR] (3:2) 95, p. 31.
"Love Poem for Ray C." [ChironR] (42) Spr 95, p. 24.
"Nietzsche & Pig." [PraS] (69:1) Spr 95, p. 116.
"A Number of People Killed My Sister." [WritersF] (21) 95, p. 114.
"Old Man in the Trees." [Border] (6) Spr-Sum 95, p. 63.
"Orange Nehi." [SantaBR] (3:2) Sum 95, p. 61.
"Poverty." [DogRR] (14:1, #27) Sum 95, p. 16.
"She Hears a Gunshot & Walks Down to the Dock in a Pink Cashmere Sweater &
High Heels." [WestB] (37) 95, p. 32-33.
"Simon & G. in the Garden of Love." [PraS] (69:1) Spr 95, p. 115.
5934. SPENCE, Michael
"Flag Burning." [CharR] (21:1) Spr 95, p. 97.
5935. SPENCER, Patricia
"The Blame Is the Summer's." [CimR] (110) Ja 96, p. 80.
"Connecting Cable." [WindO] (59) Spr 95, p. 23.
"I Don't Know the Title or the Painter." [ArtfulD] (28/29) 95, p. 23.
5936. SPENDER, Stephen
"The Mythical Life and Love of D.H. Lawrence." [NewYRB] (42:14) 21 S 95, p.
37.
5937. SPERA, Gabriel
"Vacation in Stone Harbor." [OntR] (43) Fall-Wint 95-96, p. 98.
"Work Boots." [OntR] (43) Fall-Wint 95-96, p. 96-97.
5938. SPHERES, Duane
"Loves Me, Loves Me Not." [BellArk] (11:6) N-D 95, p. 30.
5939. SPIEGEL, Jonathan
"De Rerum Natura, Book II" (Excerpt, tr. of Lucretius, w. Jean Berrett). [WillowS]
(36) Je 95, p. 110.
5940. SPINELLI, Eileen
"Phyllis Dancing." [Footwork] (24/25) 95, p. 65.
"Rehobeth." [Footwork] (24/25) 95, p. 65.
"Watercolor Lesson in Leslie's Studio." [Footwork] (24/25) 95, p. 66.
5941. SPIRENG, Matthew J.
"The Amputee." [HampSPR] Wint 95, p. 8.
"Creation." [SouthernPR] (35:2) Wint 95, p. 63.
"Diving for the Bottom." [WritersF] (21) 95, p. 31.
"Father's Appetite for Corn." [SouthernPR] (35:2) Wint 95, p. 62-63.
"Hay Mowed and Raked." [Blueline] (16) 95, p. 99.

"Horse Loose, 2 A.M." [WritersF] (21) 95, p. 32.
"Killdeer After a Late Planting in Corn." [CapeR] (30:2) Fall 95, p. 17.
"Killing Chickens." [Blueline] (16) 95, p. 99.
"Mathematics and Other Obscenities." [Plain] (16:1) Fall 95, p. 30-31.
"Skidding" (for Baron Wormser). [Confr] (56/57) Sum-Fall 95, p. 344.
"The Snake in Death." [TampaR] (11) Fall 95, p. 44.
"Your Death." [FourQ] (9:1/2) Spr 95, p. 55.
5942. SPIRES, Elizabeth
"1999." [AmerPoR] (24:6) N-D 95, p. 10.
"Childhood." [AmerV] (37) 95, p. 57-58.
"Clock." [Image] (10) Sum 95, p. 15-17.
"Easter Sunday, 1955." [NewYorker] (71:6) 3 Ap 95, p. 94.
"Ever-Changing Landscape" (Ladew topiary gardens: Monkton, Maryland). [Verse]
    (12:2) 95, p. 133-136.
"The Great Sea." [Image] (10) Sum 95, p. 13-14.
"Mansion Beach." [SouthwR] (80:1) Wint 95, p. 59-62.
"The Night and the Doll." [SouthernR] (31:4) O/Aut 95, p. 944-945.
"On the Island" (for Josephine Jacobsen). [Boulevard] (10:3, #30) Fall 95, p. 163-
    165.
"The Rock." [SouthwR] (80:1) Wint 95, p. 58-59.
"Roman Lachrymatory Bottles." [Image] (10) Sum 95, p. 14-15.
"Seven Gough Square." [NewRep] (213:7) 14 Ag 95, p. 40.
"Theatre of Pain." [NewYorker] (71:20) 17 Jl 95, p. 66.
"Two Watchers." [SouthernR] (31:4) O/Aut 95, p. 943-944.
5943. SPIRO, Jane
"Recovery" (A poem for South Africa). [NorthStoneR] (12) 95, p. 244-245.
"Return to the Fatherland." [NorthStoneR] (12) 95, p. 246-247.
5944. SPIRO, Peter
"Playing the Grape." [BellR] (18:1, #37) Spr 95, p. 46-47.
"Windshield Wipers." [NortheastCor] (3) 95, p. 65-66.
5945. SPIVACK, Kathleen
"The Fig Tree." [Kalliope] (17:1) 95, p. 50-51.
"The Moon Tide." [Kalliope] (17:1) 95, p. 48-49.
"Poets Great and Small." [Kalliope] (17:1) 95, p. 53.
"Trout." [InterPR] (21:2) Fall 95, p. 93.
"The White Voyage." [Kalliope] (17:1) 95, p. 52-53.
5946. SPIVACK, Susan Fantl
"Night Music." [YellowS] (12:4, #48) Sum 95, p. 21.
5947. SPLAKE, T. Kilgore
"Old Poet and the Motorcycle." [NewYorkQ] (55) 95, p. 75.
5948. SPRAGUE, Joe
"Remedy." [DefinedP] (1:1) Fall-Wint 92, p. 35.
"What Number Are You Trying to Reach?" [DefinedP] (1:1) Fall-Wint 92, p. 36.
5949. SPRING, Justin
"Naming Things" (Toktok Nem Bilong Samting, from "Tok Pisin," tr. of Eldred Van
    Ooy). [Vis] (47) 95, p. 38.
5950. SPRINGER, Christina
"Redecorating." [PennR] (6:2) 95, p. 16.
SPRUCE, Paula Blue
    See BLUE SPRUCE, Paula
5951. SPULER, Rick
"Back Then" (tr. of Richard Wagner). [PlumR] (9) [95 or 96], p. 3.
"Moment at the Supermarket" (tr. of Richard Wagner). [PlumR] (9) [95 or 96], p. 4.
"Remote Control" (tr. of Richard Wagner). [PlumR] (9) [95 or 96], p. 2.
5952. SQUIRES, Geoffrey
"This" (Excerpt). [WestCL] (29:2, #17) Fall 95, p. 94-97.
SSU-K'UNG, T'u
    See TU, Sikong
ST. ...
    See also Saint ...
5953. ST. ANDREWS, B. A.
"Dear Ms Capulet." [Confr] (56/57) Sum-Fall 95, p. 331-332.
5954. ST. GERMAIN, Kandie
"Against Blood and Bone." [CreamCR] (19:1) Spr 95, p. 99.
5955. ST. JOHN, David
"The Dragon in the Lake." [SenR] (25:1) Spr 95, p. 69-72.

433

5956. ST. LOUIS, Ralph
"Radio Adventures, 1949." [Plain] (15:3) Spr 95, p. 6.
5957. ST. ONGE, Marie Louise
"Primus Nubere." [LowellR] (2) c1996, p. 54-55.
"Similies pour Ma Tante Louise." [LowellR] (2) c1996, p. 53.
5958. STAFFORD, Kim
"A Story I Remember Hearing That No One Told." [SenR] (25:1) Spr 95, p. 33.
5959. STAFFORD, William (1914-1993)
"Ask Me." [Rosebud] (2:2) Sum 95, p. 123.
"An Author Calls and Says He Is Dying." [NewMyths] (2:2/3:1) 95, p. 258.
"Grandmother" (reprinted from Elf 3:3). [Elf] (5:4) Wint 95, p. 13.
"Passwords" (Holograph, courtesy of Vince Clemente, trustee of the Walt Whitman
Birthplace, West Hills, Long Island, New York). [Elf] (5:4) Wint 95, front
cover.
"Reading and Writing on the Farm." [SenR] (25:1) Spr 95, p. 21.
"Waiting at the Beach." [RiverS] (42/43) 95, p. 27.
"With Kit, Age 7, at the Beach." [Orion] (14:4) Aut 95, back cover.
5960. STAHL, Judythe
"Dory." [Blueline] (16) 95, p. 8.
5961. STAHLSCHMIDT, Hans J.
"Cranes Mate for Life." [CumbPR] (15:1) Fall 95, p. 49.
5962. STAINSBY, Martha
"All I Have for a Heart." [HampSPR] Wint 95, p. 9.
"Down, Down, into the Deep." [HampSPR] Wint 95, p. 9-10.
"A Girl with a Knife." [MassR] (36:3) Aut 95, p. 440.
"Not Knowing Love." [HampSPR] Wint 95, p. 10.
5963. STALLINGS, A. E.
"Aeaea (Circe's Island)." [BelPoJ] (45:3) Spr 95, p. 27.
"Arachne Gives Thanks to Athena." [BelPoJ] (46:2) Wint 95-96, p. 36.
"Eurydice's Footnote." [Poetry] (165:5) F 95, p. 253.
"Listening to the Monkeys / of the Nearby Yerkes Regional Primate Research
Center." [Hellas] (6:2) Fall-Wint 95, p. 30-31.
"Musings on Sound and Sense ('Death' and 'Dead')." [Hellas] (6:1) Spr-Sum 95, p.
34-35.
"Poetical Correctness." [Hellas] (6:2) Fall-Wint 95, p. 32.
5964. STAMBLER, Peter
"Clambering Down I Cannot Look Back." [SnailPR] (3:2) 95, p. 1.
"A Farmer's Cry Carries All This Distance." [SnailPR] (3:2) 95, p. 2.
"I Considered Painting Two Flowers" (tr. of Han Shan). [SpoonR] (20:1) Wint-Spr
95, p. 82.
"Judging a Scroll by Its Ribbons" (tr. of Shan Han). [WillowS] (36) Je 95, p. 100.
"What I Find I Name Cheerfully" (tr. of Han Shan). [SpoonR] (20:1) Wint-Spr 95,
p. 82.
"Winter." [SnailPR] (3:2) 95, p. 3.
5965. STANESCU, Nichita
"Bas Relief of Heroes" (tr. by Marguerite Dorian and Elliott B. Urdang). [MidAR]
(15:1/2) 95, p. 222-223.
"Cantec de Incurajare." [SouthernHR] (29:4) Fall 95, p. 341.
"Song of Encouragement" (tr. by Richard Collins). [SouthernHR] (29:4) Fall 95, p.
341.
5966. STANG, Thom
"The Duchess" (3rd Place — 1995 CR Poetry Contest). [ChironR] (44/45) Aut-Wint
95, p. 32.
5967. STANLEY, A. M.
"Buddha's Smile." [GrahamHR] (19) Wint 95-96, p. 36.
5968. STANLEY, George
"Another Monastery" (for Jay & Pete). [Pembroke] (27) 95, p. 55.
"London." [Pembroke] (27) 95, p. 56.
"The Puck." [Pembroke] (27) 95, p. 54-55.
"Upper Fraser Canyon." [Pembroke] (27) 95, p. 56.
5969. STANSBERGER, Rick
"Autopsy Girl." [EngJ] (84:5) S 95, p. 73.
5970. STANTON, Kay
"Back Room." [SoCoast] (18) Ja 95, p. 26.
"Two Little Girls." [SoCoast] (18) Ja 95, p. 40.

5971. STANTON, Maura
"Anne Hathaway's Cottage." [NewEngR] (17:1) Wint 95, p. 147-148.
"Chairman." [RiverS] (42/43) 95, p. 179-180.
"Labyrinth." [ChiR] (41:1) 95, p. 43-44.
5972. STAP, Don
"Bluejays." [TriQ] (94) Fall 95, p. 120-121.
5973. STAPLES, Catherine
"Out Your Window." [PoetL] (90:3) Fall 95, p. 39-40.
5974. STARCK, Clemens
"Tulips." [SilverFR] (26) Wint 95, p. 26.
"Why Buddhists Don't Kill Flies." [SilverFR] (26) Wint 95, p. 25.
5975. STARK, Ellen Kreger
"Entering Aunt Suze's Kitchen" [sic]. [OxfordM] (10:1) Wint 94-Spr 95, p. 62-63.
5976. STARK, Susan Verelon
"Tamber's Dream." [Blueline] (16) 95, p. 40.
5977. STARKEY, David
"Dinner Blessing for the Lower Middle Class." [WindO] (60) Fall-Wint 95, p. 8.
"I Decide Not to Give Up Smoking After All." [SlipS] (15) 95, p. 38.
"The Lady Le Gros Pub." [WormR] (35:2, #138) 95, p. 85.
"The Lyon Brothers." [PoetL] (90:3) Fall 95, p. 45-46.
"Meeting the Toad." [WormR] (35:2, #138) 95, p. 84-85.
"Native American Childhood." [IllinoisR] (3:1/2) Fall 95-Spr 96, p. 58.
"Ontogeny Repeats Phylogeny." [HolCrit] (32:1) F 95, p. 19.
"The Planets." [CumbPR] (14:2) Spr 95, p. 36.
"Scrabble." [IllinoisR] (3:1/2) Fall 95-Spr 96, p. 104.
"Seven Uncommon Ways to Die at Home." [IllinoisR] (3:1/2) Fall 95-Spr 96, p. 20-21.
"St. Francis in Ecstasy." [SpinningJ] (1) Fall 95-Wint 96, p. 39.
"Suggestions to the Almighty for Scoring a Rape." [Wind] (75) Spr 95, p. 24.
"The Toad's Wild Ride." [WormR] (35:2, #138) 95, p. 86.
"Watching the Full Moon Rise Above the Pines in My Backyard" (after Li Po).
[Wind] (75) Spr 95, p. 25.
5978. STARNINO, Carmine
"Caserta, Italy — 1945." [MalR] (113) Wint 95, p. 48-49.
5979. STARRETT, Virginia
"Cinderella's Ball — Ten Years Later." [SoCoast] (19) 95, p. 23.
"Ichabod." [SoCoast] (19) 95, p. 24.
"Library." [SoCoast] (19) 95, p. 25.
"Pruning the Rose." [SoCoast] (19) 95, p. 20-21.
"Wisteria Psalm." [SoCoast] (19) 95, p. 22.
5980. STARZEC, Larry
"Surviving." [CapeR] (30:1) Spr 95, p. 23.
5981. STASIOWSKI, Carole A.
"At Your Birth" (for Alexander). [SpoonR] (20:1) Wint-Spr 95, p. 74-75.
"Fillings." [SpoonR] (20:1) Wint-Spr 95, p. 77.
"First Kiss, Age Twelve." [SpoonR] (20:1) Wint-Spr 95, p. 78-79.
"Man, Hammer, August Night." [SpoonR] (20:1) Wint-Spr 95, p. 76.
5982. STAUDT, David
"3 Stars." [CarolQ] (48:1) Fall 95, p. 81.
"Running Ultra Quiet." [PaintedB] (55/56) 95, p. 14.
5983. STECKLING, Robert
"The Horse War" (Inspired by Timothy Findley's The Wars. In memory of Earth and
Air and Fire and Water, Robert R. Ross, 1896-1922). [CanLit] (147) Wint 95,
p. 93-97.
5984. STECOPOULOS, Eleni
"The Rescue." [HarvardR] (8) Spr 95, p. 118.
5985. STEDINGH, R. W.
"Acrostic Numbers of the Killer Whale" (Vancouver Aquarium). [Event] (24:3)
Wint 95-96, p. 58-60.
"Arctic Wolf" (Stanley Park Zoo). [Event] (24:3) Wint 95-96, p. 56-57.
"Enclosed Field" (tr. of Pierre Reverdy). [AntigR] (102/103) Sum-Aug 95, p. 35.
"Face to Face" (tr. of Pierre Reverdy). [AntigR] (102/103) Sum-Aug 95, p. 37.
"Night Noises" (tr. of Pierre Reverdy). [AntigR] (102/103) Sum-Aug 95, p. 33.
"Old Port" (tr. of Pierre Reverdy). [AntigR] (102/103) Sum-Aug 95, p. 39.
"Sleeping Polar Bear" (Stanley Park Zoo). [Event] (24:3) Wint 95-96, p. 55.

435

5986. STEDMAN, Judy
  "Flesh." [Bogg] (67) 95, p. 34.
5987. STEDRONSKY, Carole
  "Gryphons." [CapeR] (30:1) Spr 95, p. 26.
  "Reclining Nude Among the Crocodiles." [CapeR] (30:1) Spr 95, p. 27.
5988. STEELE, Cynthia
  "Couples" (tr. of José Emilio Pacheco). [TriQ] (94) Fall 95, p. 237.
  "For You" (tr. of José Emilio Pacheco). [TriQ] (94) Fall 95, p. 241.
  "Walter Benjamin Leaves Paris (1940)" (tr. of José Emilio Pacheco). [TriQ] (94)
    Fall 95, p. 243.
  "The Wretched of the Earth" (tr. of José Emilio Pacheco). [TriQ] (94) Fall 95, p.
    239.
5989. STEELE, Lenora Jean
  "The Clothes Line" (a poem for my mother). [AntigR] (100) Wint 95, p. 152.
5990. STEELE, Marian
  "Atavistic Song." [NewRena] (9:2, #28) Spr 95, p. 134.
  "Unseasonable." [SoDakR] (33:3/4) Fall-Wint 95, p. 171.
  "The Widening Light." [SoDakR] (33:3/4) Fall-Wint 95, p. 172.
5991. STEELE, Pat
  "Dusk in Historic Hamilton." [SlipS] (15) 95, p. 69.
5992. STÉFAN, Jude
  "Low Tide 1856" (tr. by Monique Manopoulos and Philip Kobylarz). [Chelsea] (58)
    95, p. 135.
  "To Thomas Gray" (tr. by Monique Manopoulos and Philip Kobylarz). [Chelsea]
    (58) 95, p. 136.
5993. STEFANILE, Felix
  "Answering Robert Frost" (For Spencer Brown). [SewanR] (103:2) Spr 95, p. 192.
  "At Random." [Footwork] (24/25) 95, p. 4.
  "Ballad of the War Bride." [SewanR] (103:3) Sum 95, p. 384.
STEFANO, Darin de
  See DeSTEFANO, Darin
STEFANO, John de
  See De STEFANO, John
5994. STEFENHAGENS, Lyn
  "Market Day." [SmPd] (32:3, #95) Fall 95, p. 17.
5995. STEICHEN, Anne
  "Undressing After a Funeral." [HopewellR] (7) 95, p. 114-115.
5996. STEIG, Jeanne
  "My Kind of Guy." [Light] (13) Spr 95, p. 10.
5997. STEIN, Agnes
  "A Moment at the Window with the Black Frame" (tr. of Kurt Drawert). [MidAR]
    (15:1/2) 95, p. 122.
  "On Bridges" (tr. of Gunter Kunert). [MidAR] (15:1/2) 95, p. 44.
  "The Outer Land" (tr. of Emmanuel Moses). [MidAR] (15:1/2) 95, p. 204.
5998. STEIN, Charles
  "Color's Being." [Sulfur] (15:1, #36) Spr 95, p. 81.
  "Something Immutable." [Sulfur] (15:1, #36) Spr 95, p. 81-84.
5999. STEIN, Deborah
  "Ellis Island." [HangL] (66) 95, p. 99.
  "Heat." [HangL] (66) 95, p. 100.
  "Unearned Chance." [HangL] (66) 95, p. 100.
6000. STEIN, Jessica
  "Chord." [SinW] (55) Spr-Sum 95, p. 74.
  "Well-Behaved (Not About Her)." [HangL] (66) 95, p. 101.
6001. STEIN, Jill
  "Initiation." [US1] (30/31) 95, p. 13.
6002. STEIN, Kevin
  "Broken Pines." [PoetryNW] (36:2) Sum 95, p. 29-30.
6003. STEIN, Michael
  "Autumn." [CimR] (112) Jl 95, p. 99.
  "Rite of Autumn." [CharR] (21:1) Spr 95, p. 83.
6004. STEIN, Michael P.
  "Machpelah (Hebron, 1994)." [SoCoast] (18) Ja 95, p. 46-47.
6005. STEINBERG, Hugh
  "Coastline." [GrandS] (14:2, #54) Fall 95, p. 81.
  "Four Erotic Poems." [WillowS] (35) Ja 95, p. 56-57.

"Old Poem" (for Al Ulan). [Epoch] (44:1) 95, p. 81.
6006. STEINGESSER, Martin
"A Bell" (for Alex, because she asked). [AmerV] (36) 95, p. 139.
6007. STEINMAN, Lisa
"How to Tell a Zoo from a Construction Site." [QW] (41) Aut-Wint 95-96, p. 173.
"Lemons, Graphite, and Common Sense." [QW] (41) Aut-Wint 95-96, p. 172.
6008. STEINUM SIGURTHARDOTTER
"Seas" (tr. by Robert Bly). [HarvardR] (8) Spr 95, p. 91.
6009. STELMACH, Marjorie
"The Tower." [MalR] (112) Fall 95, p. 16-23.
"Working the Reversal." [Kalliope] (17:2) 95, p. 33-34.
6010. STENLEY, Stella
"A Veteran Returns Home." [Writer] (108:8) Ag 95, p. 25.
6011. STEPANCHEV, Stephen
"The Church in the Desert." [Comm] (122:7) 7 Ap 95, p. 20.
"The Eyes of a Blind Woman." [NewYorkQ] (55) 95, p. 64.
"Rescue." [Interim] (14:1) Spr-Sum 95, p. 33.
"A Woman from Benin." [Interim] (14:1) Spr-Sum 95, p. 34.
"A Wood in the Rhineland: October, 1944." [NewYorker] (71:10) 1 My 95, p. 54.
STEPHANILE, Felix
    See STEFANILE, Felix
6012. STEPHEN, Ian
"Berneray and Stornoway" (from two drawings by David Connearn). [WestCL]
    (29:2, #17) Fall 95, p. 99-100.
"Equinoctial Springs." [WestCL] (29:2, #17) Fall 95, p. 101.
"Stronger Than Neatness." [WestCL] (29:2, #17) Fall 95, p. 98.
"The Wind That Ruffles." [WestCL] (29:2, #17) Fall 95, p. 98.
6013. STEPHENS, Genevieve
"Less Than a Whisper." [CapeR] (30:2) Fall 95, p. 7.
6014. STEPHENS, Michael
"The Bus Driver on Madison Avenue." [HangL] (66) 95, p. 74-75.
"The Wild Swans." [HangL] (66) 95, p. 73.
6015. STEPHENSON, David
"At Redeemer's Church." [Hellas] (6:1) Spr-Sum 95, p. 23.
6016. STERLING, Gary
"The Grandmothers of Acoma." [WeberS] (12:1) Wint 95, p. 132.
"Indian Silver." [WeberS] (12:1) Wint 95, p. 133.
"Sherman Institute." [WeberS] (12:1) Wint 95, p. 132.
"The Singing Waters" (Santa Clara Pueblo). [WeberS] (12:1) Wint 95, p. 133.
"White." [WeberS] (12:1) Wint 95, p. 132.
6017. STERLING, Phillip
"Astronomy." [WestHR] (49:4) Wint 95, p. 348-349.
"A Certain Slant." [WestHR] (49:4) Wint 95, p. 354-355.
"Color Tour." [WestHR] (49:4) Wint 95, p. 351-352.
"Duplicate Scenes of the Earthly Paradise" (Eighteenth-century fireplace insert,
    Musée de la Vie wallonne). [ParisR] (37:134) Spr 95, p. 166-167.
"First Monday in September." [WestHR] (49:4) Wint 95, p. 350-351.
"The Widower Tells Other Passengers Where He's From." [WestHR] (49:4) Wint
    95, p. 353.
6018. STERN, Cathy
"Desert Storm." [ParisR] (37:135) Sum 95, p. 90.
"Domestic Archeology." [ParisR] (37:135) Sum 95, p. 90.
"Generation." [ParisR] (37:135) Sum 95, p. 89.
6019. STERN, Daniel
"Excommunication." [ParisR] (37:134) Spr 95, p. 277.
6020. STERN, Gerald
"Above Fourteenth." [ColR] (22:1) Spr 95, p. 111-113.
"Essay on Rime." [CutB] (43) Wint 95, p. 86-87.
"Hot Dog." [AmerPoR] (24:3) My-Je 95, p. 21-32.
"Ida." [KenR] (17:2) Spr 95, p. 118-120.
"Most of My Life." [NewYorker] (71:28) 18 S 95, p. 97.
"Oracle." [CutB] (43) Wint 95, p. 85.
"St. Mark's." [NewYorker] (71:2) 6 Mr 95, p. 87.
6021. STERN, Herbert
"Drinking Their Wine." [SpoonR] (20:2) Sum-Fall 95, p. 22.
"Sailing the Canals." [SpoonR] (20:2) Sum-Fall 95, p. 24-25.

"Severed Heads." [SpoonR] (20:2) Sum-Fall 95, p. 23.
6022. STERN, Robert
"The Forgotten Kite String." [AntigR] (100) Wint 95, p. 159.
"How Often I See." [AntigR] (100) Wint 95, p. 160.
"Midnight Has Run Out of Angels." [AntigR] (100) Wint 95, p. 161.
"The More We Learn About the Moon." [AntigR] (100) Wint 95, p. 161.
6023. STERN, Sarah
"Making Jam." [Parting] (8:1) Sum 95, p. 19.
6024. STERNLIEB, Barry
"March Hare." [LitR] (38:2) Wint 95, p. 241.
"The Mother Tongue." [MidwQ] (36:2) Wint 95, p. 164.
"No Two Ways About It." [MidwQ] (36:2) Wint 95, p. 165.
6025. STEVE (Clean & Sober Streets, Washington, DC).
"Last Straw" (WritersCorps Program). [WashR] (21:2) Ag-S 95, p. 18.
6026. STEVEN (age 14, DC Public Schools)
"Rollin' In My BMW" (Poetry on the Metro Project). [WashR] (21:2) Ag-S 95, p. 14.
6027. STEVEN, Kenneth C.
"Enid." [Quarry] (44:3) 95, p. 106.
6028. STEVENS, A. Wilber
"How Love Begins." [DefinedP] (3) 95, p. 29.
6029. STEVENS, Geoff
"Breakfast Burns My Eyes." [Bogg] (67) 95, p. 56.
6030. STEVENS, John
"At Entsu-ji so long ago" (tr. of Ryokan, Zen monk-poet, c. 1758-1831). [Tricycle] (4:3, #15) Spr 95, p. 60.
6031. STEVENS, Peter
"Bird in the Hand." [CanLit] (144) Spr 95, p. 141.
6032. STEVENSON, Anne
"All There Was." [Epoch] (44:3) 95, p. 284.
"And in the Summer" (tr. of Eugene Dubnov, w. the author). [Arc] (34) Spr 95, p. 35.
"Going Back to Ann Arbor" (To Don and Helen Hill on Olivia Avenue). [MichQR] (34:1) Wint 95, p. 52-54.
"A Great Wave Crashed" (tr. of Eugene Dubnov, w. the author). [Arc] (34) Spr 95, p. 34.
"The Theologian's Confession." [Epoch] (44:3) 95, p. 285.
6033. STEVENSON, Megan
"Branch of the Locust Tree." [HangL] (67) 95, p. 91.
6034. STEVER, Ed
"A History of Long Island." [Pearl] (22) Fall-Wint 95, p. 25.
6035. STEWARD, D. E.
"Agost." [Conjunc] (24) 95, p. 212-219.
"Febbraio." [Epoch] (44:1) 95, p. 56-62.
"Flossy." [DogRR] (14:1, #27) Sum 95, p. 5.
"Juny." [ApalQ] (44/45) Fall 95-Wint 96, p. 71-77.
"Marzo." [Chelsea] (58) 95, p. 104-111.
"Octobre." [ApalQ] (43) Spr 95, p. 46-52.
"Toll." [JINJPo] (17:1) Spr 95, p. 13-14.
6036. STEWART, Dolores
"Guns and Butter." [Hellas] (6:1) Spr-Sum 95, p. 96.
"Ill Wind." [LitR] (38:2) Wint 95, p. 288.
6037. STEWART, Jack
"Anonymous Call." [SouthernHR] (29:1) Wint 95, p. 14.
"Complexion." [Poem] (74) N 95, p. 18.
"Man Cruising the Lingerie Department, Looking to Buy" (for my wife). [Poem] (74) N 95, p. 17.
"Sounding Out." [Poem] (74) N 95, p. 19.
6038. STEWART, Pamela
"DOGS, Her Dreaming" (for Sheba and Sue). [PraS] (69:1) Spr 95, p. 103-104.
"The Red Window." [LowellR] (1) Sum 94, p. 92-97.
6039. STEWART, Pat
"First Act at the Circus" (from *The Saturday Collection*). [AmerPoR] (24:2) Mr-Ap 95, p. 16.
6040. STEWART, Sheila
"The Ladies and the Bomb." [Writ] (27) 95, p. 41.

"Moving Furniture." [Writ] (27) 95, p. 40.
"Rituals." [Writ] (27) 95, p. 42.
"Summertime." [Writ] (27) 95, p. 39.
6041. STEWART, Shirley
"Mr. Cardinal." [Light] (15/16) Aut-Wint 95-96, p. 13.
6042. STEWART, Susan
"The Ellipse." [ColR] (22:1) Spr 95, p. 62-66.
"The Spell." [GettyR] (8:2) Spr 95, p. 210-212.
6043. STILES, Deborah
"The Rules for Elevators" (for Renée). [PottPort] (16:1) Fall 95, p. 71-72.
6044. STILES, Dennis Ward
"Mowing Hay." [SouthernPR] (35:2) Wint 95, p. 21-22.
"A Poet Has Some Good Angry Scotch One Monday Afternoon." [HiramPoR]
(58/59) Spr 95-Wint 96, p. 70.
6045. STILL, James
"At Year's End." [AmerV] (38) 95, p. 121.
6046. STILLPOINT, Horehound
"Stranded in Sub-Atomica." [JamesWR] (12:2) Spr-Sum 95, p. 18.
6047. STILLWELL, Mary
"The Circle Dance" (Honorable Mention, First Annual Poetry Awards). [LiteralL]
(2:1) Sum 95, p. 16.
6048. STINUS, Eric
"Remnants of a Landscape." [Drumvoices] (4:1/2) Fall-Wint 94-95, p. 110.
6049. STOCKS, Cape
"The Doves in the Room" (WritersCorps Program, Washington, DC). [WashR]
(21:2) Ag-S 95, p. 13.
"Snow Poem" (WritersCorps Program, Washington, DC). [WashR] (21:2) Ag-S 95,
p. 13.
6050. STOCKWELL, Samn
"April in the Village." [NewYorker] (71:6) 3 Ap 95, p. 59.
6051. STODDART, Dana
"A Winter's Tale." [RagMag] (12:2) Spr 95, p. 17.
6052. STOIANOVA, Danila
"Don't ask the dragon-fly" (tr. by Ludmilla Popova-Wightman). [Vis] (48) 95, p. 11.
"Memory of a Dream" (in Bulgarian and English, tr. by Ludmilla G. Popova-
Wightman). [US1] (30/31) 95, p. 17.
"Memory of a Dream" (tr. by Ludmilla Popova-Wightman). [Vis] (48) 95, p. 11.
6053. STOKES, Peter
"Judy Said." [DenQ] (29:4) Spr 95, p. 57-59.
6054. STOKESBURY, Leon
"Bottom's Dream." [GeoR] (49:2) Sum 95, p. 388-390.
"The Legacy" (for Erin). [NewOR] (21:2) Sum 95, p. 31-34.
"Ready to Satisfy All Your Bereavement Needs." [GreensboroR] (58) Sum 95, p.
56.
6055. STOLLER, Francy
"For Steve / The Pectin of My Soul / in Mexico City, a Bale of Love." [Drumvoices]
(4:1/2) Fall-Wint 94-95, p. 133-134.
"Squeeze the Ball / Then / Let Go" (From last lecture to Free Peoples Workshop by
Etheridge Knight). [Drumvoices] (4:1/2) Fall-Wint 94-95, p. 135.
6056. STOLOFF, Carolyn
"Afternoon by the Central Park Sailing Pond." [PoetL] (90:2) Sum 95, p. 55.
"Is There Another Fruit with This Aroma." [PoetL] (90:2) Sum 95, p. 53-54.
"Sketch of Tilli." [WestB] (37) 95, p. 62-63.
"Stopping the Arrow to Weigh Its Flight." [Talisman] (15) Wint 95-96, p. 124.
"Your Path to Perspective." [Talisman] (15) Wint 95-96, p. 125.
6057. STONE, Alison
"Animal Games." [ManyMM] (2:1) 95, p. 160-161.
"Great House." [ManyMM] (2:1) 95, p. 162.
"My Hunger." [ManyMM] (2:1) 95, p. 159.
"Not Cure, Not Denial." [Poetry] (166:3) Je 95, p. 146-147.
"What the Russians Taught Me." [NewYorkQ] (54) 95, p. 69-70.
6058. STONE, Jennifer
"The Examined Life." [Rosebud] (2:3) Aut-Wint 95, p. 20.
"Last List." [Rosebud] (2:3) Aut-Wint 95, p. 19.
6059. STONE, Lewis Hammond
"Carmina Fulmen (Songs of Thunder)." [LiteralL] (2:3) N-D 95, p. 23.

"I Saw Charles Bukowski Wear a Tie." [LiteralL] (2:3) N-D 95, p. 20.
6060. STONE, Myrna
"The Amazing Vanishing Grace." [TriQ] (93) Spr-Sum 95, p. 98.
"From the Kitchen." [Poetry] (165:6) Mr 95, p. 319.
"Hotel Orvieto." [TriQ] (93) Spr-Sum 95, p. 97.
"In Extremis." [TriQ] (93) Spr-Sum 95, p. 95-96.
"Penitential." [Poetry] (165:6) Mr 95, p. 318.
"Taraxacum Officinale." [Poetry] (165:6) Mr 95, p. 320.
STONE, Robin Cooper
   See COOPER-STONE, Robin
6061. STONE, Ruth
"Another Report." [NewMyths] (2:2/3:1) 95, p. 197-198.
6062. STORACE, Patricia
"Casablanca Villanelle." [NewYRB] (42:14) 21 S 95, p. 12.
"Hilarion to Echo" (Alexandria, First Century, based on papyrus text ...).
   [NewYRB] (42:11) 22 Je 95, p. 10.
6063. STORNI, Alfonsina
"Portrait of García Lorca" (tr. by Orlando Ricardo Menes). [InterPR] (21:1) Spr 95,
   p. 19, 21.
"Retrato de García Lorca." [InterPR] (21:1) Spr 95, p. 18, 20.
6064. STORY, Nancy
"Living with AIDS" (for Alex). [BlackBR] (21) Fall-Wint 95, p. 21.
6065. STOTHART, Robert
"Day's Last Work." [WillowS] (35) Ja 95, p. 49.
6066. STOTT, Libby
"Cynthia Grooms." [PoetryE] (40) Spr 95, p. 120.
"Hip-Wading." [CumbPR] (14:2) Spr 95, p. 43.
"Sleepwalking Alone." [PoetryE] (40) Spr 95, p. 121.
6067. STOUT, Joe
"Leaving a Political Rally." [ChrC] (112:6) 22 F 95, p. 212.
6068. STOUT, Robert Joe
"Mekong Delta, July 13, 1967" (runner up, 1994 Borderlands Poetry Contest).
   [Border] (7) Fall-Wint 96, p. 61-62.
STOWELL, Phyliss
   See STOWELL, Phyllis
6069. STOWELL, Phyllis
"Large Thunder" (after Jacques Roubaud). [NewOR] (21:2) Sum 95, p. 14.
"The Mare." [13thMoon] (13:1/2) 95, p. 42-43.
"Pivot." [Epoch] (44:2) 95, p. 213.
"Snowtown." [Colum] (24/25) 95, p. 115.
6070. STRAHAN, Bradley R.
"3 Cemeteries" (tr. of Steven Duplij, w. the author). [Vis] (47) 95, p. 9.
"Bad Dreams" (tr. of Vlada Urosevic, w. the author). [Vis] (48) 95, p. 37.
"Cockroach Karma" (tr. of Mima Dedaic, w. the author). [Vis] (48) 95, p. 17-18.
"Mysterious Land" (tr. of Mima Dedaic, w. the author). [Vis] (48) 95, p. 17.
"Plastic Planet" (tr. of Vlada Urosevic, w. the author). [Vis] (47) 95, p. 38.
"Ragpickers." [Footwork] (24/25) 95, p. 52.
"Tracks." [Footwork] (24/25) 95, p. 52.
"What Could We Say about God?" (tr. of Ivan Slamnig, w. Mima Dedaic). [Vis]
   (48) 95, p. 19.
6071. STRAND, Mark
"The Disquieting Muses." [QW] (41) Aut-Wint 95-96, p. 213.
"The Great Poet Returns." [NewYorker] (71:37) 20 N 95, p. 62.
"A Season Just Around the Bend." [ColR] (22:1) Spr 95, p. 129.
"Some Last Words." [NewYorker] (71:14) 29 My 95, p. 90.
6072. STRANDQUIST, Bob
"Blackburn Lake." [Event] (24:3) Wint 95-96, p. 61-62.
"Cab Driver." [MalR] (113) Wint 95, p. 82-83.
6073. STRANG, Catriona
"Dance" (2 poems, w. Nancy Shaw). [Avec] (10) 95, p. 112-113.
"Dine" (w. Nancy Shaw). [Avec] (10) 95, p. 109.
"Ditch" (2 poems, w. Nancy Shaw). [Avec] (10) 95, p. 107-108.
"Dote" (w. Nancy Shaw). [Avec] (10) 95, p. 114.
"Drink" (2 poems, w. Nancy Shaw). [Avec] (10) 95, p. 110-111.
6074. STRASSER, Judith
"How to Stay Alive." [PraS] (69:4) Wint 95, p. 64.

"Legacy" (for GK). [PraS] (69:4) Wint 95, p. 66-67.
"On Reading Descartes' Error." [Poetry] (166:3) Je 95, p. 152-153.
"When Life Interferes with Art." [PraS] (69:4) Wint 95, p. 65.
6075. STRATAN, Ion
  "Car Graveyard" (tr. by Adam J. Sorkin and Ioana Ieronim). [LitR] (38:2) Wint 95,
    p. 185-190.
6076. STRAUS, Marc
  "Not God." [PoetryE] (39) Fall 94, p. 91.
  "Pocket Calendar." [PoetryE] (39) Fall 94, p. 92.
  "Questions and Answers." [PoetryE] (39) Fall 94, p. 90.
6077. STRAUSS, Liane
  "Supernova." [Iowa] (25:3) Fall 95, p. 98-101.
6078. STRICKER, Meredith
  "Documented Maze." [Chain] (2) Spr 95, p. 212-215.
6079. STRICKLAND, Stephanie
  "American Speech." [PoetL] (90:3) Fall 95, p. 5-10.
  "Striving All My Life." [KenR] (17:1) Wint 95, p. 54.
  "Young Willard Gibbs Is a Physicist." [KenR] (17:1) Wint 95, p. 53.
6080. STRINGER, A. E.
  "Iron Mullions." [SycamoreR] (7:2) Sum 95, p. 33-34.
6081. STROFFOLINO, Chris
  "Anecdote." [AxeF] (3) 90, p. 34.
  "Brief Layover." [NewAW] (13) Fall-Wint 95, p. 103-104.
  "Stealer's Wheel" (Selections: 7-9, 11-12, 15). [Phoebe] (24:2) 95, p. 59-62.
  "View of the World from the Blue Line." [AxeF] (3) 90, p. 35.
6082. STRONG, Beret E.
  "Central de Abastos, Oaxaca." [InterPR] (21:1) Spr 95, p. 88.
  "Offerings." [InterPR] (21:1) Spr 95, p. 89.
6083. STRONGIN, Lynn
  "All Giving Things." [AmerV] (37) 95, p. 3.
  "Burn." [Shen] (45:3) Fall 95, p. 106.
  "Nerves." [Shen] (45:3) Fall 95, p. 106.
  "The Pentecostal Beggars." [Descant] (26:1, #88) Spr 95, p. 84.
  "Photographs of Albatrosses." [Descant] (26:1, #88) Spr 95, p. 85-86.
  "Pig." [Descant] (26:1, #88) Spr 95, p. 87.
  "What Flashes on the Eye Is a Bright Wheat Field." [Shen] (45:3) Fall 95, p. 104-
    105.
6084. STROUD, D. M.
  "Domestic Animals" (from "Animales Domésticos V. Sus Límites," tr. of Dário
    Canton). [Noctiluca] (2:1, #4) Spr 95, p. 55.
  "Imprecation" (tr. of Elias Nandino). [Noctiluca] (2:1, #4) Spr 95, p. 58.
  "Innocents" (from "Infantiles," tr. of Dário Canton). [Noctiluca] (2:1, #4) Spr 95, p.
    53.
  "Personal Satisfaction" (tr. of Elias Nandino). [Noctiluca] (2:1, #4) Spr 95, p. 58.
  "The Statue" (tr. of Xavier Villaurrutia, 1903-1950). [Noctiluca] (2:1, #4) Spr 95, p.
    59.
  "A Stroll through the Park" (from "Parques y Paseos," tr. of Dário Canton).
    [Noctiluca] (2:1, #4) Spr 95, p. 54.
  "Umbrella Suite" (tr. of Jorge Esquinca). [Noctiluca] (2:1, #4) Spr 95, p. 56-57.
6085. STROUS, Allen
  "At Nettle's Edge." [OhioR] (53) 95, p. 122.
6086. STRUCK, Rebecca A.
  "Lemon Heads and Red Hots Are Great in My Mouth a Mess in My Bed." [Pearl]
    (22) Fall-Wint 95, p. 22.
6087. STRUTHERS, Ann
  "Beulah's Pain." [SpoonR] (20:1) Wint-Spr 95, p. 22.
  "Dogs." [Flyway] (1:1) Spr 95, p. 34.
  "The Ghosts of Hannibal's Elephants." [NewRena] (9:2, #28) Spr 95, p. 108.
  "Old Tiger's Kittens Make Their Rounds." [Flyway] (1:1) Spr 95, p. 36.
  "Transfer of Attachment." [NewRena] (9:2, #28) Spr 95, p. 107.
6088. STRUTHERS, Betsy
  "In Sites Made Sacred." [CanLit] (147) Wint 95, p. 76.
  "Son Underground." [Arc] (34) Spr 95, p. 16.
  "Turned Turtle." [Arc] (34) Spr 95, p. 17.
6089. STUART, Caren
  "In Front of a Fan." [Bogg] (67) 95, p. 21.

6090. STUART, Dabney
"Cells." [SouthernHR] (29:1) Wint 95, p. 50-53.
"Gospel Singer." [TarRP] (34:2) Spr 95, p. 50-51.
"Janus." [SewanR] (103:1) Wint 95, p. 13.
"Kokopelli." [TarRP] (34:2) Spr 95, p. 16-17.
"Love's Body." [SewanR] (103:1) Wint 95, p. 13-14.
"The Million-Dollar Road" (Ouray to Silverton, Colorado). [LaurelR] (29:2) Sum
95, p. 38-39.
"Parade." [LaurelR] (29:2) Sum 95, p. 37.
"Vows." [TarRP] (34:2) Spr 95, p. 17-19.
6091. STUART, Katherine
"Aunt Sally's Socks" (printed title is: "Aubt Sally's Socks"). [HampSPR] Wint 95, p.
51.
6092. STULL, Richard
"Wetlands." [Boulevard] (10:3, #30) Fall 95, p. 113.
6093. STULTS, Cynthia
"For My Sister" (In memory of Roy Michael Rye, 1962-1993). [AnotherCM] (29)
Spr 95, p. 176.
6094. STULTUS, Albius Cittinus
"Non Enses at Ex Norico Carmen" (for Q, tr. by Peter Russell from a Galilean
targum attributed to Albius Cittinus Stultus). [BellArk] (11:2) Mr-Ap 95, p.
16.
6095. SU, Adrienne
"An Afternoon in the Park." [Epoch] (44:2) 95, p. 214-215.
"Savannah Crabs." [ClockR] (10:1/2) 95-96, p. 6.
"We Have Been Given Away." [ClockR] (10:1/2) 95-96, p. 7.
6096. SU, Dong-Po
"He Xin Lang (To the Bridegroom)" (tr. by Yun Wang). [WillowS] (36) Je 95, p.
97.
6097. SUAREZ, Carlos (Carlos V.)
"Heraclitus" (tr. of Jorge Luis Borges). [RiverS] (42/43) 95, p. 16.
"South Atlantic" (to Don Juan Sanchez). [RiverS] (45) 95, p. 66-68.
6098. SUAREZ, Lou
"A Familiar Tale." [Plain] (15:3) Spr 95, p. 10.
6099. SUAREZ, Virgil
"American Sidewalk." [ManyMM] [1:1] D 94, p. 44-45.
"Donatila's Unrequited-Love Remedy." [Border] (6) Spr-Sum 95, p. 64.
"Sapos / Bullfrogs." [ManyMM] [1:1] D 94, p. 47.
"Tito the Barber (?-1995)." [InterPR] (21:2) Fall 95, p. 101-102.
"Uncle Isidoro." [ManyMM] [1:1] D 94, p. 46.
"The Wood Sculptor." [MassR] (36:4) Wint 95-96, p. 637-638.
"Xagua Castle, Cienfuegos." [MassR] (36:4) Wint 95-96, p. 638-639.
6100. SUAREZ COBIAN, Armando
"Psicalgia." [LindLM] (14:1) Mr/Spr 95, p. 27.
6101. SUBACH, Karen
"Tattoo" (for Primo Levi). [CutB] (44) Sum 95, p. 84-85.
6102. SUBRAMAN, Belinda
"A Celibate Life." [Bogg] (67) 95, p. 43.
6103. SUDERMAN, Elmer
"Plowing to Reach Libraries: August, 1936." [WindO] (59) Spr 95, p. 4.
SUDULESCU, Radu
See SURDULESCU, Radu
6104. SUGINO, Shigeo
"After robbing us of our sons and daughters" (in Japanese and English, tr. by Jiro
Nakano). [BambooR] (67/68) Sum-Fall 95, p. 78.
6105. SUGITA, Hatsuyo
"Today I shall burn a little girl" (in Japanese and English, tr. by Jiro Nakano).
[BambooR] (67/68) Sum-Fall 95, p. 79.
SUH, Fung Hae
See ZHOU, Lu Jing
6106. SUK, Julie
"The Acres You Cross." [Poetry] (166:4) Jl 95, p. 220.
"Rounds." [Poetry] (166:4) Jl 95, p. 221-222.
"Today You Traverse the Mountain." [Poetry] (166:4) Jl 95, p. 222-223.
SUL-JU, Lee
See LEE, Sul-Ju

6107. SULLINS, Wayne
"Among the Few." [PoetryE] (39) Fall 94, p. 95.
"First Rate Methods." [PoetryE] (39) Fall 94, p. 94.
"Site." [PoetryE] (39) Fall 94, p. 93.
6108. SULLIVAN, Mark
"Vie Contemplative — Elle Ouvre Son Livre (Cathedrale de Chartres)." [ArtfulD]
(28/29) 95, p. 22.
6109. SULLIVAN, Myra Longstreet
"My First and Second Life." [RagMag] (12:2) Spr 95, p. 12-16.
6110. SULLIVAN, Noelle
"Herringbone Sky." [PoetryNW] (36:2) Sum 95, p. 39-40.
"Keno." [PoetryNW] (36:2) Sum 95, p. 40-41.
6111. SULZMAN, Susannah
"Harvesting the Skeptics." [Comm] (122:22) 15 D 95, p. 11.
6112. SUMMERHAYES, Don
"Home Truth." [Event] (24:1) Spr 95, p. 43-44.
6113. SUPERVIELLE, Jules
"Et les objets se mirent à sourire." [Jacaranda] (11) [95 or 96?], p. 111.
"In a Foreign Land" (tr. by Geoffrey Gardner). [PlumR] (8) [95], p. 85.
"Puisque je ne sais rien de notre vie." [Jacaranda] (11) [95 or 96?], p. 110.
"Le Sillage." [Jacaranda] (11) [95 or 96?], p. 112.
"Untitled: And then my objects began to smile" (tr. by Geoffrey Gardner).
[Jacaranda] (11) [95 or 96?], p. 111.
"Untitled: For thirty years I've been searching" (tr. by Geoffrey Gardner). [WillowS]
(36) Je 95, p. 106.
"Untitled: Since I know nothing of our life except" (tr. by Geoffrey Gardner).
[Jacaranda] (11) [95 or 96?], p. 110.
"The Wake" (tr. by Geoffrey Gardner). [Jacaranda] (11) [95 or 96?], p. 112.
6114. SURDULESCU, Radu
"Apocrypha the First" (tr. of Alexandru Musina, w. Adam J. Sorkin). [Vis] (48) 95,
p. 40.
"Experiments (A Chimera of the Real)" (The Sixth Experiment, Survival in
Meaning, tr. of Alexandru Musina, w. Adam J. Sorkin). [Vis] (48) 95, p. 41.
"Spring Tale" (tr. of Petru Romosan, w. Adam J. Sorkin). [Vis] (48) 95, p. 43.
"Yorick, Yorick, Yorick, or How About You, Reader, Would You Hold My Skull in
Your Hand?" (tr. of Petru Romosan, w. Adam J. Sorkin). [Vis] (49) 95, p. 7.
6115. SURETTE, Debra
"To John Thompson, While Reading Stilt Jack" (Selections: III-IV, VI-VII, IX,
XVI). [AntigR] (102/103) Sum-Aug 95, p. 291-293.
6116. SÜREYA, Cemal
"Dying in a Turkish Bath" (tr. by Murat Nemet-Nejat). [Talisman] (14) Fall 95, p.
41.
"Houri's Rose" (tr. by Murat Nemet-Nejat). [Talisman] (14) Fall 95, p. 41.
"In Your Country" (tr. by Murat Nemet-Nejat). [Talisman] (14) Fall 95, p. 39-40.
6117. SUROWIECKI, John
"For Diane, Who Enjoyed Reading Mystery Novels." [IndR] (18:1) Spr 95, p. 162.
"Yale-New Haven, Mon Amour" (Diane: In Memoriam). [IndR] (18:1) Spr 95, p.
160-161.
6118. SURVANT, Joe
"Alpheus Waters" (August 27, 1863, from "Anne & Alpheus 1842-1882." Finalist,
The Nimrod / Hardman Awards). [Nimrod] (39:1) Fall-Wint 95, p. 72.
"Anne Waters" (September 2, 1862, from "Anne & Alpheus 1842-1882." Finalist,
The Nimrod / Hardman Awards). [Nimrod] (39:1) Fall-Wint 95, p. 70-71.
6119. SUTPHEN, Joyce
"Feeding the New Calf." [AnthNEW] (7) 95, p. 23.
"The Temptation to Invent." [Poetry] (165:5) F 95, p. 254.
6120. SUTTON, Dorothy (Dorothy Moseley)
"Deductive Reasoning." [PraS] (69:3) Fall 95, p. 101.
"In the Twilight of the Gods." [VirQR] (71:1) Wint 95, p. 107-108.
"Looking Up from Down Below: Another Perspective" (for Richard Wilbur). [PraS]
(69:3) Fall 95, p. 102.
"Mother's Day Visit to the Pietà." [VirQR] (71:1) Wint 95, p. 108-109.
6121. SUTTON, James
"Sonnet 77" (from Prometheus). [AmerPoR] (24:1) Ja-F 95, p. 33.

6122. SUTTON, Kimberly
"Little Courtney" (WritersCorps Program, Washington, DC). [WashR] (21:2) Ag-S 95, p. 16.
"My Neighborhood" (WritersCorps Program, Washington, DC). [WashR] (21:2) Ag-S 95, p. 16.
6123. SUTTON, Pamela
"Last Flower." [PoetryE] (40) Spr 95, p. 122.
6124. SUTTON, Virginia Chase
"In the Fitting Room." [Interim] (14:1) Spr-Sum 95, p. 22-23.
"Night Terrors." [IllinoisR] (3:1/2) Fall 95-Spr 96, p. 56-57.
6125. SUZI
"After Rimbaud." [NewAW] (13) Fall-Wint 95, p. 140-142.
6126. SUZUKI, Tsutomi
"Politicians who deceive people" (in Japanese and English, tr. by Jiro Nakano). [BambooR] (67/68) Sum-Fall 95, p. 80.
6127. SVENVOLD, Mark
"Graveyard Shift." [Ploughs] (21:1) Spr 95, p. 70-71.
"Postcards and Joseph Cornell." [Ploughs] (21:1) Spr 95, p. 72.
6128. SVOBODA, Terese
"American Lake." [CarolQ] (48:1) Fall 95, p. 58.
"Cosmo Dog." [AmerPoR] (24:2) Mr-Ap 95, p. 21.
"Dog / God." [AmerPoR] (24:2) Mr-Ap 95, p. 21.
"Lithium." [AmerPoR] (24:2) Mr-Ap 95, p. 21.
"The Root of Father Is Fat." [NewYorker] (71:9) 24 Ap 95, p. 44.
6129. SWAIM, Gary
"Rider of Asses" (Excerpt). [AmerPoR] (24:6) N-D 95, p. 26.
6130. SWAN, Marc
"1945 8.9 11:02." [BlackBR] (21) Fall-Wint 95, p. 17.
"Another Case of Death or Dismemberment." [FreeL] (14) Wint 95, p. 19.
"Columbian Surrealism." [BlackBR] (20) Spr-Sum 95, p. 33.
"Maja." [NortheastCor] (3) 95, p. 76.
"Mutual Consent." [RagMag] (12:2) Spr 95, p. 58.
"Perfect Lover." [RagMag] (12:2) Spr 95, p. 61.
"Pride." [RagMag] (12:2) Spr 95, p. 59-60.
"Stone Soldier." [BlackBR] (21) Fall-Wint 95, p. 16.
"Time Master." [RagMag] (12:2) Spr 95, p. 60.
6131. SWANEY, George
"Fantasia on a Theme by Jules White." [Plain] (16:1) Fall 95, p. 32-33.
6132. SWANGER, David
"Languages I Don't Speak." [GeoR] (49:4) Wint 95, p. 825-826.
"Wayne's School of Beauty." [PoetryNW] (36:1) Spr 95, p. 23.
6133. SWANN, Brian
"HIV." [YaleR] (83:3) Jl 95, p. 16.
"The Method of Liberation." [ColEng] (57:2) F 95, p. 198.
"Morning." [IllinoisR] (3:1/2) Fall 95-Spr 96, p. 17.
"The Myth of the Cave." [ColEng] (57:2) F 95, p. 197.
"The Offering." [IllinoisR] (3:1/2) Fall 95-Spr 96, p. 90.
"Stars Stars Stars." [ColEng] (57:2) F 95, p. 196.
6134. SWANN, Roberta
"Ghost Ranch." [AmerV] (37) 95, p. 48.
"O.R." [Confr] (56/57) Sum-Fall 95, p. 352.
"O.R." [LiteralL] (1:3) N-D 94, p. 15.
6135. SWANSON, Nancy V.
"Sunday's Child" (Literary Festival: Poetry: Honorable Mention). [EngJ] (84:4) Ap 95, p. 42.
6136. SWANSON, Peter
"Alcohol." [SmPd] (32:2, #94) Spr 95, p. 17.
6137. SWARTWOUT, Susan
"Sideways Through a Looking Glass." [IllinoisR] (3:1/2) Fall 95-Spr 96, p. 14.
6138. SWARTZ, David
"Acapulco Gold." [JlNJPo] (17:1) Spr 95, p. 27.
"The Artist." [JlNJPo] (17:1) Spr 95, p. 26.
6139. SWAYZE, Kimberly
"Consolatio." [PoetryNW] (36:3) Aut 95, p. 47.
"Damage." [PoetryNW] (36:2) Sum 95, p. 4-5.
"Extant Figure." [PoetryNW] (36:2) Sum 95, p. 5-8.

"First Sight." [PoetryNW] (36:3) Aut 95, p. 46.
"The Geographers Have Lost Their Way." [PoetryNW] (36:3) Aut 95, p. 45.
"How We Spent Our Time on the Planet." [PoetryNW] (36:3) Aut 95, p. 44.
"Must." [PoetryNW] (36:2) Sum 95, p. 3-4.
6140. SWEENEY, Helen
"The Dairy Farmer." [SoCoast] (18) Ja 95, p. 12.
6141. SWEENEY, Matthew
"The Compromise." [SouthernR] (31:3) Jl/Sum 95, p. 685-686.
"Russian." [SouthernR] (31:3) Jl/Sum 95, p. 684-685.
"The Sea." [SouthernR] (31:3) Jl/Sum 95, p. 683-604.
"Writing to a Dead Man" (In memory of Raymond Tyner). [Poetry] (166:3) Je 95, p. 154-155.
6142. SWENSEN, Cole
"Future, Ancient, Fugitive: The First Seven Pages of an Adventure Novel" (Selection: Part One: "The Shipwreck," tr. of Oliver Cadiot). [Avec] (9) 95, p. 112-118.
"How Photography Has Changed the Human Face." [Avec] (10) 95, p. 31-33.
"Kub Or" (Selections, tr. of Pierre Alferi). [Avec] (10) 95, p. 115-120.
"The Landscape Around Viarmes" (for F.). [Zyzzyva] (11:1, #41) Spr 95, p. 174-176.
"Should Something Happen to the Heart" (for H. A.). [Conjunc] (24) 95, p. 206-208.
"Signature" (for J.-P. A.). [Conjunc] (24) 95, p. 209-211.
"To Choir." [Avec] (10) 95, p. 26.
"To November." [Avec] (10) 95, p. 25.
"To Too." [Avec] (10) 95, p. 28.
"To Unbound." [Avec] (10) 95, p. 27.
"To White" (for R.R.). [Avec] (10) 95, p. 29.
"To Wren." [Avec] (10) 95, p. 30.
"Water, Water." [Avec] (10) 95, p. 23-24.
6143. SWENSON, Karen
"Belief." [ManyMM] (1:2) 95, p. 101-102.
"Word Power." [ManyMM] (1:2) 95, p. 100.
6144. SWENSON, May
"The Fluffy Stuff." [Nat] (258:16) 25 Ap 94, p. 564.
"Once There Were Glaciers." [Nat] (258:13) 4 Ap 94, p. 462.
6145. SWERDLOW, David
"Half-Sleep with Rain." [WestB] (36) 95, p. 28-29.
"Morning Prayers." [PaintedB] (55/56) 95, p. 61.
6146. SWIFT, Doug
"My Mother's Body." [Journal] (19:2) Fall-Wint 95, p. 45-46.
"Stripping the Dead." [WestB] (36) 95, p. 100-101.
6147. SWIGGART, Katherine
"Chateau Bungalows" (for David Case). [Colum] (24/25) 95, p. 9.
6148. SWISS, Thomas
"Here from There" (Sheridan Harbor Island, San Diego). [GreensboroR] (58) Sum 95, p. 64-65.
"Hey Now." [Agni] (41) 95, p. 123-124.
"In the Woods." [CimR] (112) Jl 95, p. 112-113.
"Lucky One." [CimR] (112) Jl 95, p. 111.
"The River." [BostonR] (20:1) F-Mr 95, p. 19.
6149. SYLVESTER (Clean & Sober Streets, Washington, DC).
"Last Straw" (WritersCorps Program). [WashR] (21:2) Ag-S 95, p. 18.
6150. SYLVESTER, Janet
"The Marsh." [SouthwR] (80:4) Aut 95, p. 494.
"That Mulberry Wine." [SenR] (25:1) Spr 95, p. 43-44.
"Vernacular." [Boulevard] (10:1/2, #28/29) Spr 95, p. 118-121.
6151. SZARUGA, Leszek
"Informing on a Couple Unknown Guys" [sic] (tr. by W. D. Snodgrass). [Colum] (24/25) 95, p. 23.
6152. SZAUTNER, Kathleen
"Hour of the Wolves" (tr. of Volker von Torne, w. Harriet Parmet). [Vis] (47) 95, p. 14.
6153. SZCZEPANSKI, Marian
"Building the Trail." [BellArk] (11:1) Ja-F 95, p. 24.
"Building the Trail." [BellArk] (11:6) N-D 95, p. 5.
"What the Blind Bird Knows" (for Bonnie). [BellArk] (11:1) Ja-F 95, p. 24.

"What the Blind Bird Knows" (for Bonnie). [BellArk] (11:6) N-D 95, p. 5.
6154. SZE, Arthur
"Rattlesnake Glyph." [RiverS] (45) 95, p. 57.
"The Redshifting Web." [AmerPoR] (24:3) My-Je 95, p. 8-10.
"Spring Snow." [HangL] (66) 95, p. 76.
6155. SZEMAN, Sherri
"Speaking for the Dead." [Border] (7) Fall-Wint 96, p. 63-65.
6156. SZIRTES, George
"Whispers." [Epoch] (44:3) 95, p. 282.
6157. SZPORLUK, Larissa
"Agnosia." [PoetL] (90:1) Spr 95, p. 9.
"Allegro of the Earth." [HarvardR] (8) Spr 95, p. 22.
"Downtrodden." [NewMyths] (2:2/3:1) 95, p. 145-146.
"Envoy of the Boat." [HarvardR] (9) Fall 95, p. 62.
"Ghost Continent." [Agni] (41) 95, p. 48.
"Ignis Fatuus." [IndR] (18:1) Spr 95, p. 68.
"Koan." [IndR] (18:1) Spr 95, p. 70-71.
"Libido." [LullwaterR] (6:2) Fall-Wint 95, p. 88-89.
"Mauvaises Terres." [HayF] (17) Fall-Wint 95, p. 36.
"Radiolaria." [IndR] (18:1) Spr 95, p. 72-73.
"Solar Wind." [IndR] (18:1) Spr 95, p. 69.
"Swordfish Season." [PoetL] (90:1) Spr 95, p. 10.

T., H.
See H. T.
6158. T. M. J. (Dinner Program for Homeless Women, Washington, DC)
"6 April 1995" (WritersCorps Program). [WashR] (21:2) Ag-S 95, p. 8.
6159. TABAKOW, Phil
"The First Time." [DenQ] (30:2) Fall 95, p. 76.
6160. TABITO, Otomo no (665-773)
"Five Short Poems of Tabito in Praise of Wine" (tr. by John Pavel Kehlen).
[LowellR] [1] Sum 94, p. 83.
6161. TADA, Chimako
"Calendar Poem" (tr. by Naoshi Koriyama and Edward Lueders). [WeberS] (12:1)
Wint 95, p. 56.
"Dead Sun" (tr. by Naoshi Koriyama and Edward Lueders). [WeberS] (12:1) Wint
95, p. 56.
"Late Summer" (tr. by Naoshi Koriyama and Edward Lueders). [WeberS] (12:1)
Wint 95, p. 55.
"Me" (tr. by Naoshi Koriyama and Edward Lueders). [WeberS] (12:1) Wint 95, p.
55.
6162. TAGGART, John
"Crosses." [Conjunc] (24) 95, p. 81-95.
"In Croce." [Sulfur] (15:1, #36) Spr 95, p. 155-159.
6163. TAGLIABUE, John
"Aristotle: 'God Moves the Universe by Being Desired'." [NewYorkQ] (54) 95, p.
58.
"At a Center of a Floating World." [Elf] (5:1) Spr 95, p. 16.
"Autobiographies Blossom, or Renoir Paints Monet Working in His Garden in
Argenteuil, 1873." [NewYorkQ] (54) 95, p. 58-59.
"Ceremony: the Greenness of Tea." [Elf] (5:1) Spr 95, p. 17.
"Hope as Tribal Totem." [Chelsea] (58) 95, p. 96.
"Magic Sounds, Magic Stories, That Will Cure Deafness." [CarolQ] (47:2) Wint 95,
p. 32.
"Notes While at an Exhibit of Many Japanese Umbrellas" (2 poems?). [Elf] (5:1)
Spr 95, p. 14-15.
"Notes While in a Tokyo Museum 1994" (4 poems). [Elf] (5:3) Fall 95, p. 28-29.
"With Internal-and-External Influences." [Elf] (5:1) Spr 95, p. 17.
6164. TAKACS, Nancy
"Pontiac." [WeberS] (12:1) Wint 95, p. 89.
6165. TAKAHASHI, Mutsuo
"The Architect's Nephew" (tr. by Hiroaki Sato). [RiverS] (45) 95, p. 86.
"The Eyes" (tr. by Hiroaki Sato). [RiverS] (45) 95, p. 87.
"Philosophical Garden-Making" (tr. by Hiroaki Sato). [RiverS] (45) 95, p. 88.

6166. TAKAHASHI, Takeo
"You should be satisfied if every living being" (in Japanese and English, tr. by Jiro Nakano). [BambooR] (67/68) Sum-Fall 95, p. 81.
6167. TAKAMURA, Kotaro
"Bleak Homecoming" (tr. by John Peters). [SpoonR] (20:1) Wint-Spr 95, p. 69.
"Chieko Playing Among the Plovers" (tr. by John Peters). [TampaR] (10) Spr 95, p. 14.
"Chieko Riding on the Wind" (tr. by John Peters). [TampaR] (10) Spr 95, p. 13.
"Invaluable Chieko" (tr. by John Peters). [SpoonR] (20:1) Wint-Spr 95, p. 68.
"Lemon Dirge" (tr. by John Peters). [TampaR] (10) Spr 95, p. 15.
"Record of One Day" (tr. by John Peters). [TampaR] (10) Spr 95, p. 14.
"To One Who Has Died" (tr. by John Peters). [SpoonR] (20:1) Wint-Spr 95, p. 70.
6168. TAKANO, Kanae
"I have lost six children to the Atomic Bomb" (in Japanese and English, tr. by Jiro Nakano). [BambooR] (67/68) Sum-Fall 95, p. 82.
6169. TAKAYASU, Kuniyo
"He no longer lives, that man who once sang" (in Japanese and English, tr. by Jiro Nakano). [BambooR] (67/68) Sum-Fall 95, p. 83.
6170. TAKEUCHI, Ichisaku
"Although I live, I am given a funeral service" (in Japanese and English, tr. by Jiro Nakano). [BambooR] (67/68) Sum-Fall 95, p. 84.
6171. TAKEYAMA, Hiroshi
"The corpses of those who once met here" (in Japanese and English, tr. by Jiro Nakano). [BambooR] (67/68) Sum-Fall 95, p. 85.
6172. TAKSA, Mark
"Lifting." [ColEng] (57:4) Ap 95, p. 464.
6173. TALBOT, John
"The Reader's Plaint" (intoned sotto voce). [Light] (15/16) Aut-Wint 95-96, p. 24.
6174. TALENTINO, A. (Arnold)
"Holy Water." [DefinedP] (2:2) Spr-Sum 94, p. 24-25.
"Lightning Bugs." [DefinedP] (1:2) Spr-Sum 93, p. 54.
"Old Barn." [DefinedP] (3) 95, p. 48.
6175. TALL, Deborah
"Children's Beach Museum." [PartR] (62:2) Spr 95, p. 302-303.
"Search" (for Sara Ann Wood, missing). [ColR] (22:2) Fall 95, p. 177-179.
6176. TALLEY, Doug
"The Day Star Risen." [AmerS] (64:4) Aut 95, p. 558.
6177. TALVET, Jüri
"From Santiago's Road" (After the Congress of the Spanish Association of Semiotics in A Coruña in December 1992, tr. by the author and H. L. Hix). [NowestR] (33:1) 95, p. 87-89.
"On Consecrating the Flag" (tr. by the author, w. Mark Halperin). [Vis] (49) 95, p. 33-34.
6178. TAMARKIN, Molly
"The Colonists" (runner up, 1994 Borderlands Poetry Contest). [Border] (6) Spr-Sum 95, p. 65-66.
"The Common Robusta." [Poetry] (166:5) Ag 95, p. 262-263.
"Pastry." [Poetry] (166:5) Ag 95, p. 263.
TAMEKANE, Kyogoku
See KYOGOKU, Tamekane (1254-1332)
6179. TAMEZ, Margo
"The Ceremony of Peyote." [HayF] (17) Fall-Wint 95, p. 64-65.
6180. TAMMEUS, Bill
"Harry." [NewL] (61:3) 95, p. 133.
6181. TAMRAZIAN, Hrachia
"A Day" (tr. by Diana Der-Hovanessian). [GrahamHR] (19) Wint 95-96, p. 46.
"New Era" (tr. by Diana Der-Hovanessian). [GrahamHR] (19) Wint 95-96, p. 47.
6182. TAN, Amy
"Biting Mother Tongue" (indexer's note: This poem is unattributed, but the entire issue is dedicated to Amy Tan's work). [Paint] (22) Aut 95, p. 67.
TAN, Lin
See LIN, Tan
6183. TANAKA, Gayle
"About Face, Without Face." [Zyzzyva] (11:1, #41) Spr 95, p. 177.
"Behind Face, Beyond Blood." [Zyzzyva] (11:1, #41) Spr 95, p. 179.
"Cut the Cord. A Bloodless Sacrifice." [Zyzzyva] (11:1, #41) Spr 95, p. 178.

447

TAYLOR

6184. TANIGUCHI, Chris
"His Hat (César Vallejo)." [Manoa] (7:2) Wint 95, p. 133-134.
"In Southeast Asia" (for W. S. T., who returned). [Manoa] (7:2) Wint 95, p. 132-133.
6185. TANIGUCHI, Kuramoto
"Evening clouds dyed the color of blood" (in Japanese and English, tr. by Jiro
Nakano). [BambooR] (67/68) Sum-Fall 95, p. 86.
6186. TANNY, Marlaina (Marlaina B.)
"A Man on His Bicycle Goes to Work." [CaribbeanW] (9) 95, p. 35-36.
"Small Death." [GrahamHR] (19) Wint 95-96, p. 82.
6187. TAORMINA, Albert Sgambati
"Due North." [HeavenB] (12) 95, p. 16.
"La Soledad." [HeavenB] (12) 95, p. 16.
6188. TAPPOUNI, Terry
"Old Woman in the Street." [Kalliope] (17:1) 95, p. 14.
6189. TAPSCOTT, Stephen
"Morelle." [Epoch] (44:2) 95, p. 211-212.
"Ours." [Atlantic] (276:5) N 95, p. 76.
"Partita Near Appomattox, Fading." [Epoch] (44:2) 95, p. 209-210.
6190. TARKOVSKY, Arseny
"Field Hospital" (tr. by Philip Metres). [ArtfulD] (28/29) 95, p. 28-29.
6191. TARN, Nathaniel
"ARC69.94." [Talisman] (15) Wint 95-96, p. 61.
"ARC70.94." [Talisman] (15) Wint 95-96, p. 62.
6192. TARTLER, Grete
"The Collector" (tr. by Adam J. Sorkin and Liliana Ursu). [Vis] (48) 95, p. 46.
6193. TARWOOD, J.
"Amazon Bus." [WillowR] (22) Spr 95, p. 19-20.
6194. TASAKA, Kazue
"Undestroyed but beautified, the Genbaku Dome" (in Japanese and English, tr. by
Jiro Nakano). [BambooR] (67/68) Sum-Fall 95, p. 87.
6195. TASHIMA, Nobue
"The corpses of those who died of persecution" (in Japanese and English, tr. by Jiro
Nakano). [BambooR] (67/68) Sum-Fall 95, p. 88.
6196. TATE, Haines Sprunt
"Car Trouble." [WestB] (37) 95, p. 40-41.
"Three Walks in Late Winter, Lake Michigan." [SpoonR] (20:1) Wint-Spr 95, p. 25-26.
6197. TATE, James
"At the Days End Motel." [Field] (52) Spr 95, p. 26.
"In a London Fog." [SenR] (25:1) Spr 95, p. 14.
"My Burden." [IllinoisR] (3:1/2) Fall 95-Spr 96, p. 73-75.
"Pie." [IllinoisR] (3:1/2) Fall 95-Spr 96, p. 96-97.
"Where Were You?" [Nat] (258:9) 7 Mr 94, p. 310.
6198. TAWADA, Yoko
"A 21st-Century Hurdy-Gurdy: In the Evening Sky Looms a Ferris Wheel" (tr. by
Susan Bernofsky). [YellowS] (12:4, #48) Sum 95, p. 38.
6199. TAYA, Ei
"Two score and more lines drawn to study the epicenter" (in Japanese and English,
tr. by Jiro Nakano). [BambooR] (67/68) Sum-Fall 95, p. 89.
6200. TAYLOR, Alex
"Memory of Denizli" (tr. of Henrik Nordbrandt). [Vis] (47) 95, p. 32.
6201. TAYLOR, Brian
"Darkling, I Listen." [MissouriR] (18:2) 95, p. 44-45.
"Heat Lightning." [MissouriR] (18:2) 95, p. 42.
"Home Thoughts." [MissouriR] (18:2) 95, p. 48.
"Rapunzel in Thebes." [MissouriR] (18:2) 95, p. 46-47.
"Rhapsody" (for Andrea Brownstein). [MissouriR] (18:2) 95, p. 43.
"Sirius Rising" (for Linda Horsley). [MissouriR] (18:2) 95, p. 40-41.
6202. TAYLOR, Bruce
"Firewatch." [CumbPR] (15:1) Fall 95, p. 57-59.
"The Long Straight" (the nullabor, W.A. Australia). [CumbPR] (15:1) Fall 95, p. 50-52.
"Taylor's Encyclopedia of Gardening" (Excerpt). [CumbPR] (15:1) Fall 95, p. 53-56.

6203. TAYLOR, Cheryl Boyce
"DeKalb Avenue Next." [Footwork] (24/25) 95, p. 64.
"For Noid Age 6." [Footwork] (24/25) 95, p. 64.
6204. TAYLOR, Dannyka
"The Blade, the Garnet, and Shades Deep as Madder." [Nimrod] (39:1) Fall-Wint
95, p. 126-127.
"How She Has Killed the Thing Beneath Them." [Nimrod] (39:1) Fall-Wint 95, p.
124-125.
"Mère." [Nimrod] (39:1) Fall-Wint 95, p. 123.
6205. TAYLOR, Eleanor Ross
"Harvest, 1925." [SenR] (25:1) Spr 95, p. 88-89.
6206. TAYLOR, Henry
"For Char Gardner, Preparing Her Art." [PlumR] (8) [95], p. 6-7.
"For William Stafford" (30 August 1993). [Poetry] (166:3) Je 95, p. 150.
"A Horseshoe to Hang Over the Door" (for Walt McDonald). [TexasR] (16:1/4) 95,
p. 146.
"In Memory of Dave Gardner." [TexasR] (16:1/4) 95, p. 147.
"Rawhide." [Witness] (9:2) 95, p. 67.
"Unfolded Maps." [BelPoJ] (45:4) Chapbook 22, Sum 95, p. 71-72.
6207. TAYLOR, Jane
"Witnessing." [Flyway] (1:3) Wint 95, p. 10-11.
6208. TAYLOR, John
"The Penis." [IllinoisR] (3:1/2) Fall 95-Spr 96, p. 76.
"The Rented House." [IllinoisR] (3:1/2) Fall 95-Spr 96, p. 105-106.
6209. TAYLOR, Judith
"Persephone." [Poetry] (165:6) Mr 95, p. 321.
"A Sneeze." [Jacaranda] (11) [95 or 96?], p. 106-107.
6210. TAYLOR, Kymberly
"The Hunter." [HawaiiR] (19:2) Fall 95, p. 123-124.
6211. TAYLOR, Linda
"Night Roads" (for Anne Bonney, 1947-1983). [WilliamMR] (33) 95, p. 85.
6212. TAYLOR, Reta
"I'm a Virgin He Said." [Pearl] (22) Fall-Wint 95, p. 100.
6213. TAYLOR, Scott
"The Dog's Prayer." [DogRR] (14:1, #27) Sum 95, p. 6.
6214. TAYLOR, William R.
"Lipstick." [JamesWR] (12:1) Wint 95, p. 8.
6215. TAYSON, Richard
"The Ascension." [HangL] (67) 95, p. 84-85.
"First Sex." [PraS] (69:3) Fall 95, p. 73-74.
"The Ice Cube." [Chelsea] (59) 95, p. 99-100.
"James Dean as Eurydice." [PraS] (69:3) Fall 95, p. 70-72.
"The Massage." [Chelsea] (59) 95, p. 101-102.
"Peschanka." [ParisR] (37:137) Wint 95, p. 280-281.
"Phone Sex." [ParisR] (37:137) Wint 95, p. 274-280.
"Skin." [PraS] (69:3) Fall 95, p. 76-77.
"What Stops Me Sometimes Doctor." [Chelsea] (59) 95, p. 98-99.
"Where Youth Grows Pale, and Spectre-Thin, and Dies." [PraS] (69:3) Fall 95, p.
74-76.
"Your Feet." [ParisR] (37:137) Wint 95, p. 281-282.
TE, Shih
See SHIH-TE
6216. TEICHMAN, Milton
"Under the Tooth of Their Plow" (tr. of Uri Zvi Greenberg). [AmerPoR] (24:4) Jl -
Ag 95, p. 37.
6217. TEITLEBOIM, Dora
"Disillusioned People" (tr. by Aaron Kramer). [Vis] (47) 95, p. 8.
6218. TEJADA, Roberto
"Honeycomb perfection of this form before me." [Sulfur] (15:2, #37) Fall 95, p. 28 -
29.
6219. TELLERMAN, Esther
"Magadi" (from "Distance de Fuite," 1993, tr. by Cid Corman, w. the author).
[Noctiluca] (2:1, #4) Spr 95, p. 32-37.
6220. TEMESVARI, Agnes
"The Bitteroot Rose" [sic]. [Os] (40) 95, p. 3.

TEMPLETON, Ardis Passauza
    See PASSAUZA-TEMPLETON, Ardis
TEMPSKI, Stanislaw Esden
    See ESDEN-TEMPSKI, Stanislaw
6221. TENENBAUM, Molly
    "As the Bright Chips Seek Their Places." [PraS] (69:4) Wint 95, p. 107-109.
    "Farmer's Market Visitation." [PoetryNW] (36:3) Aut 95, p. 5-6.
    "The Garden Walk." [PraS] (69:4) Wint 95, p. 110.
    "My Lost Apostrophes." [PoetryNW] (36:1) Spr 95, p. 15-17.
    "Teabag Ballad." [PoetryNW] (36:3) Aut 95, p. 6-7.
6222. TERMAN, Philip
    "For Ganya" (Finalist, The Nimrod / Hardman Awards). [Nimrod] (39:1) Fall-Wint
        95, p. 73-77.
    "For Irina Ratushinskaya." [PraS] (69:4) Wint 95, p. 131.
    "Some Days." [PraS] (69:4) Wint 95, p. 130.
    "The Wounds." [PraS] (69:4) Wint 95, p. 132.
6223. TERRANOVA, Elaine
    "Badgers." [RiverS] (41) 95, p. 2.
    "Night-Blooming Cereus." [AntR] (53:3) Sum 95, p. 321.
    "Saving the Art Teacher." [RiverS] (41) 95, p. 3.
    "The Spell." [RiverS] (41) 95, p. 1.
6224. TERRILL, Richard
    "Public Monologue" (In memoriam: Ezra Pound, tr. of O-Yiang Jianghe Chengdu,
        w. Cheng Baolin). [PassN] (16:1) Sum 95, p. 11.
6225. TERRIS, Susan
    "Luck." [SoCoast] (18) Ja 95, p. 18-19.
    "Self-Sufficiency." [PoetL] (90:2) Sum 95, p. 52.
    "Snake." [AntR] (53:2) Spr 95, p. 194.
    "The Thread." [13thMoon] (13:1/2) 95, p. 44.
    "An Unlovely Story." [ChironR] (43) Sum 95, p. 35.
    "What Margaret Knew" (Howard's End). [AntR] (53:2) Spr 95, p. 195.
6226. TEST, Becky
    "When Woman Speaks." [Kalliope] (17:2) 95, p. 35.
6227. TETER, Vivian
    "After the Fire Experiments" (Francis Bacon, *Novum Organum*). [GettyR] (8:2) Spr
        95, p. 255-256.
6228. TETI, Zona
    "Going Public." [Iowa] (25:3) Fall 95, p. 129.
6229. THATCHER, Timothy E.
    "The Wrestle Home." [AmerS] (64:3) Sum 95, p. 350-352.
6230. THESEN, Sharon
    "Gala Roses." [Sulfur] (15:1, #36) Spr 95, p. 18-24.
    "I Drive the Car" (for Robin, Renee, Melanie). [Pembroke] (27) 95, p. 57-58.
6231. THICH, Nhat Hanh
    "Oneness." [PoetryE] (40) Spr 95, back cover.
6232. THIELEN, Gregory
    "Chatechism" [sic]. [SouthernPR] (35:2) Wint 95, p. 32-33.
    "Shiloh." [SouthernPR] (35:1) Sum 95, p. 45.
THIEU, Nguyen Quang
    See NGUYEN, Quang Thieu
6233. THOMAS, Beth
    "Standstill in New York." [BellR] (18:1, #37) Spr 95, p. 26-27.
6234. THOMAS, Christopher
    "Going Among the Names" (for Randy Gillenwater). [Art&Und] (4:2, #15) Ap 95,
        p. 45.
    "Learning to Grow Old Together." [ChironR] (42) Spr 95, p. 15.
    "Letter Never Sent." [ChironR] (42) Spr 95, p. 15.
    "Living with the Uncommitted." [ChironR] (42) Spr 95, p. 15.
6235. THOMAS, Denise
    "A Reason for the Western Sky." [GettyR] (8:3) Sum 95, p. 540-541.
6236. THOMAS, Dylan
    "Do Not Go Gentle into That Good Night." [Flyway] (1:2) Fall 95, p. 7.
6237. THOMAS, G. Murray
    "Coast Highway Contradiction Addictions." [Pearl] (22) Fall-Wint 95, p. 60.
    "Refinery." [Pearl] (22) Fall-Wint 95, p. 62.
    "Wrong Numbers." [Pearl] (22) Fall-Wint 95, p. 61.

6238. THOMAS, Gail
"Barbara's Dying." [EvergreenC] (10:2) Sum-Fall 95, p. 29.
"Fairy Tale." [EvergreenC] (10:2) Sum-Fall 95, p. 39.
"Fruition." [EvergreenC] (10:2) Sum-Fall 95, p. 28.
"What Matters." [EvergreenC] (10:2) Sum-Fall 95, p. 38.
6239. THOMAS, Jim
"Being Close." [GreenHLL] (5) 94, p. 50.
"Concert in the Park." [GreenHLL] (5) 94, p. 52.
"Guest of the Colonel" (for Carolyn Forche). [GreenHLL] (5) 94, p. 48-49.
"Gypsy Robber." [GreenHLL] (5) 94, p. 51.
"Morning Doves." [GreenHLL] (6) 95, p. 37.
"Morning Dragons." [GreenHLL] (6) 95, p. 38-39.
"A Spring above Bistritca." [GreenHLL] (5) 94, p. 53.
"Temple of the Winds." [GreenHLL] (5) 94, p. 47.
6240. THOMAS, Joyce
"The Last Bulb." [Blueline] (16) 95, p. 60-61.
6241. THOMAS, Lamar
"Afternoon Meadow." [Nimrod] (39:1) Fall-Wint 95, p. 130.
"In a Cemetery off Wolfskin Road." [Nimrod] (39:1) Fall-Wint 95, p. 128-129.
6242. THOMAS, Larry D.
"Fox Fire." [TexasR] (16:1/4) 95, p. 148.
"Of Eyes Wondrously Wild" (for Lisa). [TexasR] (16:1/4) 95, p. 149.
"The Stringer" (For Roy L. Thomas and Samuel E. Thomas). [CapeR] (30:1) Spr 95,
    p. 13.
6243. THOMAS, Laurence W.
"Rift." [Light] (13) Spr 95, p. 12.
6244. THOMAS, Lew
"Suite: Art and the Emptiness of Language." [NewOR] (21:2) Sum 95, p. 75-78.
6245. THOMAS, Linda
"Confession." [ColEng] (57:6) O 95, p. 711.
6246. THOMAS, Randolph
"Migration." [SouthernPR] (35:2) Wint 95, p. 61-62.
"The Poltergeist." [LitR] (38:2) Wint 95, p. 269.
6247. THOMAS, Scott (Scott E.)
"Observatory for Sale." [RiverS] (45) 95, p. 69-70.
"The Revealing." [PoetryE] (40) Spr 95, p. 123.
"The Terminus." [PoetryE] (40) Spr 95, p. 124.
6248. THOMAS, Stanley J.
"Poetry Reading." [Bogg] (67) 95, p. 10.
6249. THOMAS, Terry
"Arse Poetica" [sic]. [HampSPR] Wint 95, p. 22.
"In Defense of Little Bo-Peep." [Plain] (15:2) Wint 95, p. 13.
"Ozzie Mantis." [HampSPR] Wint 95, p. 23.
6250. THOMASINA P. (Rachael's Women's Center, Washington, DC).
"The Anniversary" (WritersCorps Program). [WashR] (21:2) Ag-S 95, p. 9.
6251. THOMPSON, Jeanie
"Slave Gag." [SouthernHR] (29:3) Sum 95, p. 218.
"Thinking of a Young Jazz Trumpet Player." [Crucible] (30) Fall 94, p. 36.
"Winter Aspect." [SouthernHR] (29:3) Sum 95, p. 219.
"Zodiac." [SouthernPR] (35:1) Sum 95, p. 39-40.
THOMPSON, Juanita Torrence
    See TORRENCE-THOMPSON, Juanita
6252. THOMPSON, Kathleen
"Beauty and Distance." [BellArk] (11:4) Jl-Ag 95, p. 10.
6253. THOMPSON, Norma J.
"Public Housing" (WritersCorps Program, Washington, DC). [WashR] (21:2) Ag-S
    95, p. 7.
6254. THOMPSON, Ralph
"Mister Son." [CaribbeanW] (9) 95, p. 11.
6255. THOMPSON, Ricki
"On Water." [ChrC] (112:30) 25 O 95, p. 980.
6256. THOMPSON, Simon
"How Solitary Lies the City." [Event] (24:3) Wint 95-96, p. 63-65.
6257. THOMPSON, Spenser
"I'd Rather Not Discuss." [Pearl] (22) Fall-Wint 95, p. 24.

6258. THOMPSON, Stanley
"Albert King Sold at Auction." [RiverC] (15:2) Sum 95, p. 26-27.
6259. THOMPSON, Sue Ellen
"In the Apartments of the Divorced Men." [Rosebud] (2:1) Spr 95, p. 103.
6260. THOMPSON, Tom
"Honeymoon: Ostia Antica." [IndR] (18:2) Fall 95, p. 184.
6261. THOMPSON, William M., Jr.
"60. Not even a teacher of the worst sort." [Poetry] (166:3) Je 95, p. 158.
6262. THOMPSON-RUMPLE, Cindy
"Window Booth, Friday Morning." [CumbPR] (14:2) Spr 95, p. 37-38.
6263. THOMSON, David
"6 P.M." [BellArk] (11:6) N-D 95, p. 25.
"I Corinthians 13." [BellArk] (11:6) N-D 95, p. 24.
6264. THOMSON, Jeff
"Shadows in the Rain." [ManyMM] (2:1) 95, p. 176.
"South Chicago: an Ode" (Horace III.18). [ManyMM] (2:1) 95, p. 177.
6265. THORBURN, Alexander
"The City Hall." [PoetryNW] (36:1) Spr 95, p. 32-33.
"The Grain Elevator." [PoetryNW] (36:1) Spr 95, p. 33-34.
"The Hemp Warehouse." [Journal] (19:1) Spr-Sum 95, p. 22-23.
"The Opera House." [Journal] (19:1) Spr-Sum 95, p. 24-25.
"The Railroad Roundhouse." [Journal] (19:1) Spr-Sum 95, p. 26-27.
6266. THORBURN, Russell
"Apollinaire at a Baseball Game." [Northeast] (5:13) Wint 95-96, p. 14-15.
"Desire at the Quarry." [Parting] (8:1) Sum 95, p. 35.
"The Jean Cocteau Fan Club." [Parting] (8:1) Sum 95, p. 33-34.
6267. THORN, David
"The Crimson and Vermillion Sea." [SantaBR] (3:2) Sum 95, p. 90.
"Deep Parts." [SantaBR] (3:1) Spr 95, p. 110.
"The Hummingbird in Our Garden." [SantaBR] (3:1) Spr 95, p. 109.
"You Are the Beekeeper" (in memory of James Wright). [SantaBR] (3:1) Spr 95, p.
111.
6268. THORNTON, Russell
"Night Near Trikala." [MalR] (111) Sum 95, p. 58.
"Oriste." [CanLit] (147) Wint 95, p. 75.
"Thessaloniki Train Station." [MalR] (111) Sum 95, p. 56-57.
6269. THRASHER, T.
"Allen Ginsberg Had Taken Art Hostage." [Pearl] (22) Fall-Wint 95, p. 63-64.
"For H. R. M." [Pearl] (22) Fall-Wint 95, p. 64.
"I Want to Be Her Bra." [Pearl] (22) Fall-Wint 95, p. 64.
"Nothing Could Have Prepared Her for This." [Pearl] (22) Fall-Wint 95, p. 65.
"Speed." [Pearl] (22) Fall-Wint 95, p. 65.
"What My Father Says When I Tell Him that Yet Another One of My Poems Is
Going to Be Published." [Pearl] (22) Fall-Wint 95, p. 64.
6270. TIBALDO-BONGIORNO, Marylou
"The Woman Next Door." [Footwork] (24/25) 95, p. 167.
6271. TIBBETTS, Elizabeth
"Full as Pie." [Calyx] (16:2) Wint 95-96, p. 25.
"Ordering Hens." [Calyx] (16:2) Wint 95-96, p. 26-27.
6272. TIBBETTS, Frederick
"Calendrical Animals." [US1] (30/31) 95, p. 2.
"The Engulfed Cathedral." [Field] (52) Spr 95, p. 61-62.
"For a Friend Flying Home." [Raritan] (14:3) Wint 95, p. 31.
"From a Lost Year." [US1] (30/31) 95, p. 1.
"On the Death Mask of Whitman." [Raritan] (14:3) Wint 95, p. 30.
"Pagan Mysteries of the Renaissance." [Field] (52) Spr 95, p. 63.
"The Presence of Forces." [OntR] (43) Fall-Wint 95-96, p. 44.
6273. TIBERGHIEN, Susan M.
"Pear Tree." [ProseP] (4) 95, p. 72.
6274. TIEBER, Linda
"We're strolling on the outskirts of the forest." [NewYorkQ] (54) 95, p. 61.
6275. TIEMAN, John Samuel
"At My War's Wall, a Vietnam Requiem, in Which the Veteran Accepts the Dead."
[Drumvoices] (5:1/2) Fall-Wint 95-96, p. 92.
"Aubade." [Drumvoices] (5:1/2) Fall-Wint 95-96, p. 90.
"The Parables of the Truth Wife." [Drumvoices] (5:1/2) Fall-Wint 95-96, p. 91.

"Prayer for Marilyn Monroe" (tr. of Ernesto Cardenal). [RiverS] (42/43) 95, p. 172-173.
6276. TIERNEY, Karl
"Clone Nouveau." [ModernW] (3) Sum 95, p. 41-43.
"Patient Zero" (The 1994 Allen Ginsberg Poetry Awards: Honorable Mention).
[Footwork] (24/25) 95, p. 204-205.
"White Trash." [ModernW] (3) Sum 95, p. 40.
6277. TIGER, Madeline (Madeline J.)
"Scolding." [US1] (30/31) 95, p. 23.
"Snowman." [Footwork] (24/25) 95, p. 156.
6278. TIHANYI, Eva
"A Windfall Light." [CanLit] (146) Aut 95, p. 7-8.
6279. TILAKAVATI
"I as Myself" (tr. by Martha Ann Selby). [Prima] (18/19) 95, p. 65-70.
6280. TILLINGHAST, Richard
"Convergence." [SewanR] (103:2) Spr 95, p. 193.
"Father in October" (For Brownie and Kate). [NewRep] (212:12) 20 Mr 95, p. 40.
"Rhymes on the Feast of Stephen." [SewanR] (103:2) Spr 95, p. 194.
"A Visit." [PartR] (62:2) Spr 95, p. 307.
6281. TILLMAN, James
"Brother's Rage." [Spitball] (49) 95, p. 9.
6282. TILLMAN, Michael
"Untitled: I have a dream" (WritersCorps Project, Washington, DC). [WashR] (21:2)
Ag-S 95, p. 22.
6283. TILLONA, Carl
"The Poem of the Dress." [SpinningJ] (1) Fall 95-Wint 96, p. 3.
TING, Shu
See SHU, Ting
6284. TIPTON, Carolyn
"To the Hand" (tr. of Rafael Alberti). [PartR] (62:1) Wint 95, p. 110.
6285. TIPTON, James
"In This Solitude Which Is Never Really Solitude." [SoDakR] (33:2) Sum 95, p.
101-102.
6286. TITTEL, Cherie
"No Mail Today." [AxeF] (3) 90, p. 33.
6287. TIUS, Mary M.
"The Jellyfish." [Light] (14) Sum 95, p. 22.
"Ouch!" [Light] (15/16) Aut-Wint 95-96, p. 19.
6288. TOBIAS, John
"Reflections on a Gift of Watermelon Pickle Received from a Friend Called
Felicity." [LiteralL] (1:5) Early Spr 95, p. 13.
"Winter Amour." [LiteralL] (1:5) Early Spr 95, p. 13.
6289. TOBIN, Daniel
"Adult Love." [TampaR] (11) Fall 95, p. 67.
"A Centenary" (Maplewood Graveyard, Charlottesville). [War] (7:2) Fall-Wint 95,
p. 53-54.
"Pantoum." [CumbPR] (15:1) Fall 95, p. 60-61.
"Rooms." [CimR] (111) Ap 95, p. 72-73.
6290. TODD, David Y.
"Grandfather's Mockingbird Returns." [HiramPoR] (58/59) Spr 95-Wint 96, p. 71-73.
6291. TODD, J. C.
"Talking to Myself in Maryland" (Finalist, 1995 Allen Tate Memorial Competition).
[Wind] (76) Fall 95, p. 34-35.
6292. TODD, Theodora
"We Are on the Ferry Again." [WillowS] (36) Je 95, p. 18-20.
6293. TOGE, Sankichi
"Blind" (tr. by Richard H. Minear). [InterQ] (2:1/2) 95, p. 264-265.
"Eyes" (tr. by Richard H. Minear). [InterQ] (2:1/2) 95, p. 262-263.
6294. TOLAN, James
"Genius Loci." [InterQ] (2:1/2) 95, p. 24.
"Inheritance." [InterQ] (2:1/2) 95, p. 25.
6295. TOLEK
"Breathing." [Pearl] (22) Fall-Wint 95, p. 86.
"/ Laterally /" [RagMag] (12:2) Spr 95, p. 77.
"Lonely." [Pearl] (22) Fall-Wint 95, p. 86.

"/ Sprung /" [ChironR] (44/45) Aut-Wint 95, p. 41.
6296. TOMCIC, Goran
    "Moratorium" (tr. by the author). [PlumR] (8) [95], p. 12.
6297. TOMLINSON, Charles
    "Against Travel." [AmerPoR] (24:6) N-D 95, p. 40.
    "Gutenberg and the Grapes" (for Bill Murphy). [AmerPoR] (24:6) N-D 95, p. 39.
    "Improvement." [AmerPoR] (24:6) N-D 95, p. 40.
    "Interior." [AmerPoR] (24:6) N-D 95, p. 39.
    "Snapshot" (for Yoshikazu Uehata). [AmerPoR] (24:6) N-D 95, p. 39.
    "To Robert Creeley in the Judaean Desert." [AmerPoR] (24:6) N-D 95, p. 39.
    "Walks." [AmerPoR] (24:6) N-D 95, p. 39.
6298. TOMLINSON, Rawdon
    "Funeral Before My Dead Son's Third Birthday." [HiramPoR] (58/59) Spr 95-Wint
        96, p. 74-75.
    "Funeral Before My Dead son's Third Birthday." [HampSPR] Wint 95, p. 24-25.
    "Only Son" (Geronimo). [MidwQ] (36:4) Sum 95, p. 438-439.
TOMOYUKI, Iino
    See IINO, Tomoyuki
6299. TOMPKINS, Leslie Crutchfield
    "Chasing the Wild Rabbit." [Northeast] (5:13) Wint 95-96, p. 24-25.
    "Covering the Burn." [SouthernPR] (35:1) Sum 95, p. 58-59.
    "Hello, World" (for Bo). [Northeast] (5:13) Wint 95-96, p. 25.
    "Something Small, Solid, with Straight Lines." [Northeast] (5:13) Wint 95-96, p. 23.
6300. TOPRAK, Sinan
    "For the Road" (tr. of Ali Yuce, w. Gerry LaFemina). [HayF] (16) Spr-Sum 95, p.
        61.
    "To Blow Away the Darkness" (tr. of Ali Yuce, w. Gerry LaFemina). [HayF] (16)
        Spr-Sum 95, p. 60.
6301. TORGERSEN, Eric
    "After Rilke." [RiverS] (44) 95, p. 23.
    "Autographed Team Baseball." [RiverS] (44) 95, p. 24.
    "Even Things Die." [RiverS] (44) 95, p. 22.
6302. TORNE, Volker von
    "Hour of the Wolves" (tr. by Harriet Parmet and Kathleen Szautner). [Vis] (47) 95,
        p. 14.
6303. TORNEO, Dave
    "Memory and Desire." [SilverFR] (26) Wint 95, p. 16-17.
6304. TORRENCE-THOMPSON, Juanita
    "Little Tales." [GreenHLL] (6) 95, p. 55.
6305. TORRENS, Jackie
    "On Natural Death" (for P.). [PottPort] (16:1) Fall 95, p. 76-77.
6306. TORRES, Lisette (grade 9, Ellington High School, Washington, DC)
    "Orchestra" (Poetry on the Metro Project). [WashR] (21:2) Ag-S 95, p. 14-15.
TORRES, Sergio Mansilla
    See MANSILLA TORRES, Sergio
6307. TOSA, Motokiyu
    "Silk Tree Renga" (tr. of Araki Yasusada, Ozaki Kusatao and Akutagawa Fusei. Tr.
        w. Ojiu Norinaga and Okura Kyojin). [GrandS] (14:1, #53) Sum 95, p. 28-30.
    "Untitled, August 12, 1964" (tr. of Araki Yasusada, w. Ojiu Norinaga and Okura
        Kyojin). [GrandS] (14:1, #53) Sum 95, p. 25.
6308. TOSCANO, Rodrigo
    "The Disparities" (Selection: "Circular No. 7"). [WashR] (20:6) Ap-My 95, p. 11.
    "Prologue to a City Poem." [Chain] (2) Spr 95, p. 226-228.
6309. TOSCANO-PASCHKE, Mona
    "Before the Butcher's Wooden Altar." [Footwork] (24/25) 95, p. 18.
    "The Duke of Illyria." [Footwork] (24/25) 95, p. 18.
TOSHIKO, Fujioka
    See FUJIOKA, Toshiko
6310. TOTH, Éva
    "Statements" (tr. by Peter Jay and Laura Schiff). [AmerPoR] (24:1) Ja-F 95, p. 36.
    "Teiresias Wailing" (tr. by Peter Jay and Laura Schiff). [AmerPoR] (24:1) Ja-F 95,
        p. 36.
    "Van Gogh Gives Evidence" (tr. by Peter Jay and Laura Schiff). [AmerPoR] (24:1)
        Ja-F 95, p. 36.
6311. TOURBIN, Dennis
    "About Memory." [Arc] (34) Spr 95, p. 74-75.

"The Ocean Out the Window." [Arc] (34) Spr 95, p. 76-77.
6312. TOURÉ, Askia M.
"Milestones: September 28, 1991." [AfAmRev] (29:2) Sum 95, p. 247.
"Mirage / 1 (Doretha: A Profile)." [Drumvoices] (5:1/2) Fall-Wint 95-96, p. 87-88.
"A Song of Life / I: Earth" (for Bilal). [Drumvoices] (5:1/2) Fall-Wint 95-96, p. 86.
"Sun Ra's Utopian Chant." [AfAmRev] (29:2) Sum 95, p. 247-248.
6313. TOURTIDIS, Ilya
"I Saw Her." [PoetryC] (15:2) Je 95, p. 7.
"Night Thoughts." [PoetryC] (15:2) Je 95, p. 7.
TOV, S. Ben
See BEN-TOV, S.
6314. TOWNLEY, Roderick
"Mapmaking." [WestHR] (49:2) Sum 95, p. 155.
"Mozart's Pigtail." [WestHR] (49:2) Sum 95, p. 157.
"New Word Order." [WestHR] (49:2) Sum 95, p. 158.
"Sharing the Mirror." [WestHR] (49:2) Sum 95, p. 156.
"Wave." [ParisR] (37:135) Sum 95, p. 205-206.
6315. TOWNLEY, Wyatt
"Baby by Day." [WestHR] (49:1) Spr 95, p. 37-38.
"The Elms." [WestHR] (49:1) Spr 95, p. 39-40.
"In the Backyard." [WestHR] (49:4) Wint 95, p. 364-365.
"The Road" (for Brian Payer). [WestHR] (49:1) Spr 95, p. 40.
"The Storm in the Body." [MidwQ] (36:4) Sum 95, p. 440.
"The View." [NewL] (61:4) 95, p. 92.
6316. TOWNSEND, Ann
"Around the World." [TriQ] (95) Wint 95-96, p. 213.
"The Breathing Treatment." [KenR] (17:3/4) Sum-Fall 95, p. 52-53.
"First Death." [TriQ] (95) Wint 95-96, p. 211-212.
"First Language." [TriQ] (95) Wint 95-96, p. 214.
"In a Moment." [KenR] (17:3/4) Sum-Fall 95, p. 51-52.
6317. TOWNSEND, Cheryl A.
"Mending." [ChironR] (44/45) Aut-Wint 95, p. 33.
"When I Opened." [Pearl] (22) Fall-Wint 95, p. 22.
6318. TOWNSEND, Joanne
"Reckoning" (for Suzanne). [Elf] (5:1) Spr 95, p. 20.
6319. TOWNSEND, Raeven
"Raeven" (WritersCorps Project, Washington, DC). [WashR] (21:2) Ag-S 95, p. 19.
6320. TOYOHARA, Kunio
"Wild birds silently eat the decayed flesh" (in Japanese and English, tr. by Jiro
Nakano). [BambooR] (67/68) Sum-Fall 95, p. 90.
6321. TOYOTA, Seishi
"A *hibaku* woman, who refused my help" (in Japanese and English, tr. by Jiro
Nakano). [BambooR] (67/68) Sum-Fall 95, p. 91.
6322. TOZAWA, Koichiro
"Cicadas continuously sing" (in Japanese and English, tr. by Jiro Nakano).
[BambooR] (67/68) Sum-Fall 95, p. 92.
6323. TOZIER, Chris
"Regeneration." [CreamCR] (19:1) Spr 95, p. 123.
6324. TRACHTENBERG, Amy
"We Address" (w. Norma Cole). [Zyzzyva] (11:1, #41) Spr 95, p. 80-84.
6325. TRACHTENBERG, Paul
"A Buk Elegy." [NewYorkQ] (55) 95, p. 8.
"Ode to Marilyn." [ChironR] (42) Spr 95, p. 32.
6326. TRAINER, Yvonne
"12 Hours in Emergency in Galveston Texas." [Arc] (34) Spr 95, p. 65.
"And the Cow Jumped over the Moon." [Arc] (34) Spr 95, p. 66-68.
"Vincent." [Arc] (34) Spr 95, p. 64.
6327. TRAKL, Georg
"Trumpets" (tr. by Sammy McLean). [SnailPR] (3:2) 95, p. 19.
6328. TRAN, Truong
"Between Thumb and Index Finger." [PraS] (69:4) Wint 95, p. 141.
"Recipe #5." [PoetryE] (41) Aut 95, p. 60.
"Rituals." [PraS] (69:4) Wint 95, p. 140.
"Seeds." [PraS] (69:4) Wint 95, p. 142.
"Tongues." [AmerV] (38) 95, p. 21.

6329. TRANSTRÖMER, Tomas
"Alcaic" (tr. by Don Coles). [MalR] (113) Wint 95, p. 10.
"The Longforgotten Captain" (tr. by Don Coles). [MalR] (113) Wint 95, p. 6-7.
"Nightingale in Badelunda" (tr. by Don Coles). [MalR] (113) Wint 95, p. 9.
"The Nightingale in Badelunda" (tr. by Robin Fulton). [Verse] (12:2) 95, p. 137.
"Six Winters" (tr. by Don Coles). [MalR] (113) Wint 95, p. 8.
"Yellowjacket" (tr. by Don Coles). [MalR] (113) Wint 95, p. 11-13.
6330. TRANTER, John
"Rimbaud in Sydney." [Verse] (12:2) 95, p. 138-139.
6331. TRAPP, Tim
"Last House Before the Nursing Home." [MidwQ] (36:4) Sum 95, p. 441-442.
6332. TRAPPIO, Vera
"Personification of Death" (WritersCorps Program, Washington, DC). [WashR] (21:2) Ag-S 95, p. 4.
6333. TRAVERSIE, Ricky
"Ghost Dance." [WeberS] (12:3) Fall 95, p. 47.
"Stranger on Franklin Avenue." [WeberS] (12:3) Fall 95, p. 48.
TRAVIESO RAVELO, Jorge
  See RAVELO, Jorge Travieso
6334. TRAXLER, Patricia
"Night Bloom." [BostonR] (20:6) D 95-Ja 96, p. 34.
"The Red Skirt." [MidwQ] (36:4) Sum 95, p. 443.
6335. TREBOR
"Esta Noche." [EvergreenC] (10:1) Wint-Spr 95, p. 53-54.
"Hustler." [EvergreenC] (10:1) Wint-Spr 95, p. 55.
6336. TREBY, Ivor C.
"So Often." [HawaiiR] (19:2) Fall 95, p. 216.
"Translations from the Human." [BellR] (18:2, #38) Fall 95, p. 37.
6337. TREFETHEN, Tracy
"Authentic." [Phoebe] (24:1) 95, p. 115.
"Mirror Mirror." [Phoebe] (24:1) 95, p. 114.
6338. TREITEL, Renata
"Geranium." [CimR] (112) Jl 95, p. 100-101.
6339. TREMBLAY, Bill
"Walking Toward Round Butte." [MidwQ] (36:4) Sum 95, p. 445-446.
6340. TREMMEL, Robert
"Ars Poetica" (Wading for Walleyes in the Tailwater, Saylorville, Iowa). [MidwQ] (36:4) Sum 95, p. 448-449.
"Your First Time at Tootsie's Orchid Lounge" (Nashville, Tennessee). [MidwQ] (36:4) Sum 95, p. 447-448.
6341. TRENT, Christina
"Late Poem." [LullwaterR] (6:2) Fall-Wint 95, p. 44.
6342. TRENT, Tina
"Frederick Leaving." [LullwaterR] (5:2) Fall-Wint 94, p. 55.
"Waking to a Stranger." [LullwaterR] (5:1) 93-94, p. 15.
6343. TRENTHAM, Edwina
"Care Instructions" (for Liz on her forty-second birthday). [Sun] (229) Ja 95, p. 30.
"My Father's Gift." [MassR] (36:4) Wint 95-96, p. 687-688.
6344. TRETHEWEY, Eric
"Evening Walk." [DefinedP] (2:1) Fall-Wint 93, p. 24.
"Proper Reserve." [DefinedP] (2:1) Fall-Wint 93, p. 25.
6345. TRETHEWEY, Natasha
"At the Owl Club, North Gulfport, Mississippi 1950." [AfAmRev] (29:1) Spr 95, p. 83.
"At the Station." [SouthernR] (31:2) Ap/Spr 95, p. 305.
"Circa 1922." [AfAmRev] (29:1) Spr 95, p. 84-85.
"Domestic Work, 1937." [AnthNEW] (7) 95, p. 12.
"Gathering." [SouthernHR] (29:2) Spr 95, p. 156.
"Gesture of a Woman in Process" (from a photograph by Clifton Johnson, 1901). [AfAmRev] (29:1) Spr 95, p. 85-86.
"His Hands." [AfAmRev] (29:1) Spr 95, p. 83-84.
"Speculation, 1939." [GreensboroR] (58) Sum 95, p. 23.
6346. TRIBBLE, Jon
"A Careful Dissection." [SycamoreR] (7:1) Wint 95, p. 33-34.
"Nightwatchman." [Rosebud] (2:1) Spr 95, p. 100-101.

6347. TRIDLE, Chris
"Nortryptoline." [AnotherCM] (29) Spr 95, p. 177.
6348. TRILLIN, Calvin
"Adieu, Robert Packwood." [Nat] (261:10) 2 O 95, p. 338.
"The Admiral's Earthquake." [Nat] (258:6) 14 F 94, p. 186.
"Advice to Barney Frank Re Dick Armey's Slip of the Tongue." [Nat] (260:7) 20 F 95, p. 226.
"The Bigs." [Nat] (260:15) 17 Ap 95, p. 514.
"Bush, Backslid." [Nat] (260:22) 5 Je 95, p. 782.
"A Cheer for Republicans Willing to Compromise a Bit to Win With Powell." [Nat] (261:11) 9 O 95, p. 374.
"Clinton and Gingrich Play Chicken." [Nat] (261:19) 4 D 95, p. 695.
"Conflict." [Nat] (260:10) 13 Mr 95, p. 334.
"Corruption by Lyric." [Nat] (261:2) 10 Jl 95, p. 42.
"Dead Air." [Nat] (261:14) 30 O 95, p. 490.
"Defining Class Warfare." [Nat] (260:23) 12 Je 95, p. 818.
"Directional Advice for Robert Dole." [Nat] (260:18) 8 My 95, p. 622.
"Doing the White Male Kvetch" (A Pale Imitation of a Rag). [Nat] (260:14) 10 Ap 95, p. 478.
"The English, Again." [Nat] (258:5) 7 F 94, p. 149.
"An Explanation of Why Phil Gramm Is Not Doing Well in the Polls." [Nat] (261:3) 17-24 Jl 95, p. 79.
"The F.O.B. Lament: A Ditty, with Chorus, for Four Attorneys" (Sung in Dirge Time). [Nat] (258:16) 25 Ap 94, p. 546.
"Family Values Department (Republican Presidential Primaries Division)." [Nat] (260:21) 29 My 95, p. 746.
"Farewell, Governor Cuomo." [Nat] (260:3) 23 Ja 95, p. 82.
"Fresh Start." [Nat] (260:6) 13 F 95, p. 190.
"A Gangsta Rap by Robert Dole." [Nat] (260:25) 26 Je 95, p. 910.
"Grim Prospect." [Nat] (258:13) 4 Ap 94, p. 439.
"Labor Day Parade." [Nat] (261:8) 18 S 95, p. 261.
"Louis Farrakhan's Chastisement of Khalid Abdul Muhammad." [Nat] (258:8) 28 F 94, p. 258.
"McNamara's Book" (To be sung to the tune of "McNamara's Band," if at all). [Nat] (260:20) 22 My 95, p. 710.
"More Blues by Wanderin' Willie Clinton." [Nat] (261:18) 27 N 95, p. 655.
"NATO in the New World Order." [Nat] (258:3) 24 Ja 94, p. 77.
"New Bank Merger." [Nat] (261:9) 25 S 95, p. 302.
"New Threat." [Nat] (260:13) 3 Ap 95, p. 442.
"Newtness." [Nat] (260:5) 6 F 95, p. 155.
"Newt's Song." [Nat] (261:7) 11 S 95, p. 226.
"Nobody But Us Middle Class" (a song by the vaudeville team of Democrat & Republican). [Nat] (260:2) 9-16 Ja 95, p. 41.
"On Allegations From Arkansas State Troopers." [Nat] (258:2) 17 Ja 94, p. 41.
"On Brian (Kato) Kaelin." [Nat] (260:16) 24 Ap 95, p. 550.
"On Buffalo's Losing the Super Bowl." [Nat] (258:7) 21 F 94, p. 222.
"On Canada's Three Days of Fame." [Nat] (261:17) 20 N 95, p. 598.
"On Dick Cheney's Decision Not to Run for President." [Nat] (260:4) 30 Ja 95, p. 118.
"On Pete Wilson's Intentions." [Nat] (260:12) 27 Mr 95, p. 406.
"On the Candidacy of Lamar Alexander." [Nat] (260:11) 20 Mr 95, p. 370.
"On the Easing Aside of Newt Gingrich as Republican Spokesman on the Budget." [Nat] (261:22) 25 D 95, p. 815.
"On the First Casualty of Whitewater." [Nat] (258:12) 28 Mr 94, p. 402.
"On the Withdrawal of Pete Wilson." [Nat] (261:13) 13 O 95, p. 454.
"On Two White House Aides Becoming Heads of Organizations That Lobby." [Nat] (258:1) 3-10 Ja 94, p. 5.
"On Whitewater." [Nat] (258:4) 31 Ja 94, p. 114.
"One More Principled Personnel Change." [Nat] (260:1) 2 Ja 95, p. 6.
"Past Performances." [Nat] (258:15) 18 Ap 94, p. 510.
"Pete Wilson Prepares to Meet the Voters." [Nat] (261:1) 3 Jl 95, p. 6.
"Philosophic Differences." [Nat] (260:8) 27 F 95, p. 262.
"A Pol as Popular as Powell." [Nat] (261:6) 28 Ag-4 S 95, p. 190.
"Post-Election Coverage of Saddam Hussein's 100-0 Victory Over Nobody." [Nat] (261:15) 6 N 95, p. 526.
"Protection." [Nat] (261:4) 31 Jl-7 Ag 95, p. 117.

"Remarks on Air Force One." [Nat] (261:12) 16 O 95, p. 410.
"Repair." [Nat] (258:14) 11 Ap 94, p. 474.
"Replacing Dan." [Nat] (260:9) 6 Mr 95, p. 298.
"The Senator as Comedian." [Nat] (260:17) 1 My 95, p. 586.
"They Hope That Dole Will Soon Explode." [Nat] (261:5) 14-21 Ag 95, p. 154.
"Tonya's Kvetching" (A three-part round sung to the tune of "Scotland's Burning").
    [Nat] (258:11) 21 Mr 94, p. 366.
"The Troubles of Princess Di (Reprise)." [Nat] (261:21) 18 D 95, p. 775.
"Vengeance Opportunities." [Nat] (260:19) 15 My 95, p. 658.
"Welcome, Malcolm Forbes Jr." [Nat] (261:16) 13 N 95, p. 562.
"Win Some, Lose Some." [Nat] (261:20) 11 D 95, p. 735.
6349. TRINIDAD, David
    "Bewitched." [IllinoisR] (3:1/2) Fall 95-Spr 96, p. 37-39.
    "Cinnamon Toast" (for Tom Carey). [IllinoisR] (2:2) Spr 95, p. 21-25.
6350. TRIPLETT, Pimone
    "Manora." [QW] (41) Aut-Wint 95-96, p. 270-271.
6351. TRIVELPIECE, Laurel
    "Centered on the Swinging Earth." [ConnPR] (14:1) 95, p. 28.
    "Coping." [ConnPR] (14:1) 95, p. 29.
    "Dailiness." [Poetry] (166:1) Ap 95, p. 17.
    "Grieving." [ConnPR] (14:1) 95, p. 30.
    "In Remission." [Poetry] (166:1) Ap 95, p. 18.
    "Reaching for the Sun." [Poetry] (166:1) Ap 95, p. 16.
    "Safe in July." [ConnPR] (14:1) 95, p. 27.
6352. TROMBETTA, Lynn (Lynn Lyman)
    "Anniversary Poem." [ChironR] (43) Sum 95, p. 23.
    "The Bath." [Calyx] (16:1) Sum 95, p. 52-53.
    "The Turtle." [ChironR] (43) Sum 95, p. 23.
    "The Wild Turkey." [ChironR] (43) Sum 95, p. 23.
6353. TROMBLEY, Michael
    "Dance Card." [SpoonR] (20:1) Wint-Spr 95, p. 71-73.
    "Strand." [SpoonR] (20:1) Wint-Spr 95, p. 73.
6354. TROTZIG, Birgitta
    "A Death" (tr. by Rika Lesser). [ManhatR] (7:2) Wint 95, p. 30.
    "In a dark tree, a green caterpillar, creeping" (tr. by Rika Lesser). [ManhatR] (7:2)
        Wint 95, p. 33.
    "In Jerusalem's implacable bedrock Adam's bones are buried" (tr. by Rika Lesser).
        [ManhatR] (7:2) Wint 95, p. 31.
    "My Sister Life" (tr. by Rika Lesser). [ManhatR] (7:2) Wint 95, p. 32.
    "Snow: the old Jewish cemetery in Prague" (tr. by Rika Lesser). [ManhatR] (7:2)
        Wint 95, p. 29.
6355. TROUPE, Quincy
    "Back to the Dream Time: Miles Speaks from the Dead" (For Miles Dewey Davis,
        1926-1991). [Drumvoices] (5:1/2) Fall-Wint 95-96, p. 96.
    "Male Springtime Ritual" (For Hugh Masekela). [Drumvoices] (5:1/2) Fall-Wint 95-
        96, p. 97-98.
    "A Response to All You 'Angry White Males'." [Drumvoices] (5:1/2) Fall-Wint 95-
        96, p. 99-101.
    "River Town Packin House Blues." [RiverS] (42/43) 95, p. 11-14.
6356. TROUTNER, Jack
    "Crime and Catastrophe: Local Update of Richard Bosman's Painting, *11:05 to
        Chicago.*" [Vis] (47) 95, p. 38.
6357. TROWBRIDGE, William
    "Coat of Arms." [NewOR] (21:3/4) Fall-Wint 95, p. 92.
    "First Book of Shadow." [GeoR] (49:3) Fall 95, p. 632.
    "The Ghost." [MidwQ] (36:4) Sum 95, p. 450.
    "Gorgeous George." [Flyway] (1:1) Spr 95, p. 38.
    "Letter to Aethelred the Unready." [CharR] (21:1) Spr 95, p. 84.
    "Pale Riders." [NewL] (62:1) 96 (c1995), p. 114.
    "Walkers in the Mall." [Flyway] (1:1) Spr 95, p. 40.
6358. TRUMBORE, Anne
    "Rabbit." [NewYorkQ] (54) 95, p. 106.
TRUONG, Tran
    See TRAN, Truong
TSAI, Tsung
    See TSUNG, Tsai

TS'AN-LIAO, Tzu
  See TZU, Ts'an-liao
TSAOI, Máire Mhac an
  See Mhac an tSAOI, Máire
6359. TSENG, Jennifer
  "After the Funeral." [Calyx] (16:1) Sum 95, p. 62-63.
TSU, Chuang
  See CHUANG, Tsu
6360. TSUMURA, Masana
  "'The voices of Neptune' gradually die into a distance" (in Japanese and English, tr.
    by Jiro Nakano). [BambooR] (67/68) Sum-Fall 95, p. 93.
6361. TSUNG, Tsai
  "A thousand Pieces of Snow" (22 selections, tr. of Fung Hae Suh and Zhou Lu Jing,
    w. George Crane). [Archae] (5) Spr 95, p. 6-29.
6362. TSVETAEVA, Marina
  "I said, and another heard" (tr. by Nina Kossman). [GreenMR] (8:2) Fall-Wint 95-
    96, p. 140.
  "Nights Without a Loved One" (tr. by Nina Kossman). [ConnPR] (14:1) 95, p. 41.
  "No! Love's Hunger" (tr. by Nina Kossman). [ConnPR] (14:1) 95, p. 43.
  "Not wasting your words" (tr. by Nina Kossman). [GreenMR] (8:2) Fall-Wint 95-
    96, p. 140.
  "Where I dropped little tears" (tr. by Nina Kossman). [GreenMR] (8:2) Fall-Wint
    95-96, p. 141.
  "With the eyes of a spellbound witch" (tr. by Nina Kossman). [GreenMR] (8:2) Fall-
    Wint 95-96, p. 141.
  "With this hand, which seafarers" (tr. by Nina Kossman). [GreenMR] (8:2) Fall-
    Wint 95-96, p. 140.
  "Yes, the Mysterious, Improbable Friend" (tr. by Nina Kossman). [ConnPR] (14:1)
    95, p. 44.
6363. TU, Hoai Van
  "The Expatriate's Pain" (Excerpt, from *Poetic Feelings*). [AmerPoR] (24:1) Ja-F 95,
    p. 33.
6364. TU, Sikong
  "The Flowing Style" (tr. by Tony Barnstone and Chou Ping). [LitR] (38:3) Spr 95,
    p. 327.
  "The Graceful Style" (tr. by Tony Barnstone and Chou Ping). [LitR] (38:3) Spr 95,
    p. 326.
  "The Transcendent Style" (tr. by Tony Barnstone and Chou Ping). [LitR] (38:3) Spr
    95, p. 327.
  "The Vital Spirit Style" (tr. by Tony Barnstone and Chou Ping). [LitR] (38:3) Spr
    95, p. 326.
T'U, Ssu-k'ung
  See TU, Sikong
6365. TUCKER, Diane L.
  "Louise, Lost to Alzheimer's." [CanLit] (146) Aut 95, p. 86.
6366. TUCKER, Jennifer
  "Growing Up in America." [SinW] (56) Sum-Fall 95, p. 26-27.
6367. TUFTS, Carol
  "Black Hole." [CapeR] (30:1) Spr 95, p. 33.
6368. TUGWELL, Judith A.
  "Sun in My Second House." [WorldO] (27:2) Wint 95-96, p. 5.
6369. TULLOSS, Rod
  "The Murderer's House" (iv.4.86, Moyers, WV, for Stellie K.T. & Don Wagner).
    [US1] (30/31) 95, p. 22.
6370. TUMARKIN, Peter
  "Catenary." [SouthernHR] (29:2) Spr 95, p. 169.
6371. TURCO, Lewis
  "Blue Sun and Yellow Sky." [NewOR] (21:2) Sum 95, p. 92.
  "Ephraim Bourne" (1800-1836). [DefinedP] (2:1) Fall-Wint 93, p. 27-28.
  "Michael Pullen" (1861-1919). [DefinedP] (2:1) Fall-Wint 93, p. 26.
  "Villanelle of the First Day." [Elf] (5:3) Fall 95, p. 26.
6372. TURKKA, Sirkka
  "Deep in the forest, a big moose is asleep" (tr. by Sari Hantula). [InterPR] (21:2)
    Fall 95, p. 35.
  "Ilta on tullut. Kuin siipi." [InterPR] (21:2) Fall 95, p. 32.
  "Kärsimyksestä puhutaan paljon." [InterPR] (21:2) Fall 95, p. 36.

"Kirje Taivaasta: minun silmäni ovat vesissä." [InterPR] (21:2) Fall 95, p. 38.
"A letter from Heaven: my eyes are watering" (tr. by Sari Hantula). [InterPR] (21:2)
    Fall 95, p. 39.
"The night has come. As if a wing" (tr. by Sari Hantula). [InterPR] (21:2) Fall 95, p.
    33.
"People talk about suffering a lot" (tr. by Sari Hantula). [InterPR] (21:2) Fall 95, p.
    37.
"Syvällä metsässä nukkuu suuri hirvi." [InterPR] (21:2) Fall 95, p. 34.
6373. TURNER, Alison
    "Refugee Camp" (Second Place, Jacaranda Poetry Contest). [Jacaranda] (11) [95 or
        96?], p. 21.
6374. TURNER, Gordon
    "Hand." [CanLit] (144) Spr 95, p. 27-28.
6375. TURNER, Jack
    "TV Movie." [Poetry] (166:5) Ag 95, p. 273.
6376. TURNER, Ken
    "Hairpiece." [Footwork] (24/25) 95, p. 132.
    "Mary's Cats." [Footwork] (24/25) 95, p. 132.
    "Wise Use." [Footwork] (24/25) 95, p. 132.
6377. TUTHILL, Stacy
    "At Mammoth Cave" (Third Prize, First Annual Poetry Awards). [LiteralL] (2:1)
        Sum 95, p. 14.
6378. TUWIM, Julian
    "Housework" (tr. by Ed Cates). [Noctiluca] (2:1, #4) Spr 95, p. 5.
    "Quiet Storm" (tr. by Ed Cates). [Noctiluca] (2:1, #4) Spr 95, p. 6.
6379. TWICHELL, Chase
    "Aisle of Dogs." [Iowa] (25:1) Wint 95, p. 162-163.
    "Car Alarm." [Iowa] (25:1) Wint 95, p. 161.
    "Little Snowscape." [WillowS] (35) Ja 95, p. 50-51.
    "Silver Slur." [Iowa] (25:1) Wint 95, p. 160.
    "White Conclusion." [WillowS] (35) Ja 95, p. 52-53.
6380. TZU, Ts'an-liao
    "Summer Day in the Mountain" (tr. by Chris Laughrun). [LitR] (38:3) Spr 95, p.
        333.
6381. TZU, Yeh (4th c. CE)
    "Song: Winter skies are cold and low" (tr. by Sam Hamill). [PoetryE] (41) Aut 95, p.
        17.

6382. U, Sam Oeur
    "Bung Kriel (The Lake Where Cranes Mate)" (for Ginny Duncan, tr. by Ken
        McCullough). [Iowa] (25:3) Fall 95, p. 49-50.
    "The Elves Conceal My Buffalo and My Son: Phtdowl Concentration Camp, June
        1977" (for Ken McCullough, tr. by Ken McCullough). [Iowa] (25:3) Fall 95,
        p. 54-56.
    "The Loss of My Twins" (tr. by Ken McCullough). [Iowa] (25:3) Fall 95, p. 52-53.
    "The Moaning Nature of Cambodia" (for Carolyn Forché, tr. by Ken McCullough).
        [Iowa] (25:3) Fall 95, p. 56-57.
    "Oath of Allegiance (1952)" (tr. by Ken McCullough). [Iowa] (25:3) Fall 95, p. 50-
        52.
6383. UCHIDA, Eizo
    "Her burnt face swollen, a naked girl" (in Japanese and English, tr. by Jiro Nakano).
        [BambooR] (67/68) Sum-Fall 95, p. 94.
6384. UCHIDA, Kyoko
    "The Bordeaux Sequence" (Selections: 7 poems). [NowestR] (33:2) 95, p. 62-70.
    "Deadline." [NowestR] (33:2) 95, p. 64.
    "Habit." [NowestR] (33:2) 95, p. 70.
    "Medicine." [NowestR] (33:2) 95, p. 69.
    "Open Markets." [NowestR] (33:2) 95, p. 65.
    "Rehearsing." [NowestR] (33:2) 95, p. 66-67.
    "Television." [NowestR] (33:2) 95, p. 68.
    "Temporary." [NowestR] (33:2) 95, p. 63.
    "Warranty." [QW] (40) Spr-Sum 95, p. 67.
6385. UCHIKOSHI, Yoshiko
    "He led the free life, never doubting the war cause" (in Japanese and English, tr. by
        Jiro Nakano). [BambooR] (67/68) Sum-Fall 95, p. 95.

6386. UCHIMI, Kiyoko
"In this river, the silent voices of ten thousand and more" (in Japanese and English, tr. by Jiro Nakano). [BambooR] (67/68) Sum-Fall 95, p. 96.
6387. UDALL, Jay
"Birds, Water, Rock." [BellArk] (11:3) My-Je 95, p. 4.
"Lullaby." [BellArk] (11:6) N-D 95, p. 10.
"Naked Boy in DeVargas Park Fountain." [BellArk] (11:2) Mr-Ap 95, p. 13.
"Prayer." [BellArk] (11:2) Mr-Ap 95, p. 13.
"Returning." [Wind] (75) Spr 95, p. 26.
"A Way to Speak of Ordinary Love." [Pearl] (22) Fall-Wint 95, p. 21.
"Window Cleaning." [BellArk] (11:6) N-D 95, p. 10.
6388. UDOH, Evon
"Haiku" (2 poems). [Drumvoices] (5:1/2) Fall-Wint 95-96, p. 30.
6389. UGUAY, Marie
"Il Fut un Temps d'Attente" (tr. by Andrea Moorhead). [GrahamHR] (19) Wint 95-96, p. 71.
6390. ULISSE, Peter
"Pompeii" (from Memory Is an Illusive State). [AmerPoR] (24:4) Jl-Ag 95, p. 22.
6391. ULKU, A. K.
"Ars Poetica." [NowestR] (33:1) 95, p. 48.
6392. ULMER, James
"For Broadie." [IndR] (18:1) Spr 95, p. 133-134.
"For Chapman" (runner up, 1994 Borderlands Poetry Contest). [Border] (6) Spr-Sum 95, p. 67-68.
6393. UNDERWOOD, Robert
"I've Done Something Right." [Pearl] (22) Fall-Wint 95, p. 83.
"Tuned." [Pearl] (22) Fall-Wint 95, p. 83.
6394. UNGAR, Barbara Louise
"Narcissus." [MinnR] (43/44) 95, p. 41.
"The Only Woman I Know." [MinnR] (43/44) 95, p. 41.
6395. UNGER, Barbara
"The Refugee." [LitR] (38:3) Spr 95, p. 421.
6396. UPDIKE, John
"Epithalamium." [ParisR] (37:136) Fall 95, p. 73.
"Money." [LiteralL] (1:1) Je 94, p. 5.
"The Overhead Rack." [Harp] (291:1742) Jl 95, p. 27.
"The Overhead Rack." [OntR] (42) Spr-Sum 95, p. 92.
"Upon Winning One's Flight in the Senior Four-Ball." [NewYorker] (71:23) 7 Ag 95, p. 50.
6397. UPTON, Lee
"August Balcony." [RiverS] (41) 95, p. 48.
"Death of the Authors." [DenQ] (29:3) Wint 95, p. 34-39.
"First Vengeance." [Boulevard] (10:3, #30) Fall 95, p. 168.
"A Gardener's Library." [NewMyths] (2:2/3:1) 95, p. 154.
"Gertrude to Hamlet." [Iowa] (25:3) Fall 95, p. 79.
"Milk Glass Lamp in a Girl's Shape." [MassR] (36:2) Sum 95, p. 202.
"Ophelia's Descendants." [RiverS] (41) 95, p. 49.
"Possessive Case." [RiverS] (41) 95, p. 47.
"Provincial Love." [SycamoreR] (7:2) Sum 95, p. 68.
"The Root Cellar." [WilliamMR] (33) 95, p. 108.
"Seaweed Soup." [Boulevard] (10:3, #30) Fall 95, p. 169-170.
"The Virgin and Child with St. Anne and St. John the Baptist" (restored after 1987 shotgun blast). [MassR] (36:2) Sum 95, p. 200-201.
6398. URA, Kasu
"If you are armed, stop your foolishness" (in Japanese and English, tr. by Jiro Nakano). [BambooR] (67/68) Sum-Fall 95, p. 97.
6399. URDANG, Constance
"A Life You Might Say You Might Live." [RiverS] (42/43) 95, p. 122.
6400. URDANG, Elliott B.
"Bas Relief of Heroes" (tr. of Nichita Stanescu, w. Marguerite Dorian). [MidAR] (15:1/2) 95, p. 222-223.
URE, Alberto Jiménez
See JIMÉNEZ URE, Alberto
6401. UROSEVIC, Vlada
"Bad Dreams" (tr. by the author, w. B. R. Strahan). [Vis] (48) 95, p. 37.
"The End of the Tales" (tr. by Zoran Anchevski). [Vis] (48) 95, p. 36.

"Plastic Planet" (tr. by Bradley R. Strahan, w. the author). [Vis] (47) 95, p. 38.
"Truths" (tr. by Zoran Anchevski). [Vis] (48) 95, p. 37.
6402. URREA, Luis Alberto
    "Ghost Sickness." [ManyMM] [1:1] D 94, p. 11-27.
6403. URSU, Liliana
    "Above the Bridge" (tr. by Tess Gallagher and Adam Sorkin). [Kalliope] (17:3) 95,
        p. 19.
    "The Collector" (tr. of Grete Tartler, w. Adam J. Sorkin). [Vis] (48) 95, p. 46.
    "Mathematics" (tr. by Bruce Weigl). [KenR] (17:3/4) Sum-Fall 95, p. 117.
    "Really, Don't You Believe Me?" (tr. by Adam J. Sorkin and the author). [Vis] (48)
        95, p. 47.
    "The Russian Army in Moldova" (tr. by Bruce Weigl). [KenR] (17:3/4) Sum-Fall
        95, p. 117.
    "The Sacred and the Profane" (tr. by Adam J. Sorkin and the author). [Vis] (48) 95,
        p. 46.
    "Saint Anthony" (tr. by Bruce Weigl). [KenR] (17:3/4) Sum-Fall 95, p. 116.
    "Season's End" (for Mirela, tr. by Adam J. Sorkin, w. the poet). [SnailPR] (3:2) 95,
        p. 12-13.
6404. UTAH, Perry B.
    "Midnight." [ContextS] (4:2) 95, p. 3.

VACA, Gustavo Alberto Garcia
    See GARCIA VACA, Gustavo Alberto
6405. VAIL, Desire
    "The Managers Cocktail Party." [Rosebud] (2:2) Sum 95, p. 24-25.
6406. VAIRA, Ursula
    "Black Cipher, Immaculate Page." [WritersF] (21) 95, p. 188.
    "The Children Will Fall." [WritersF] (21) 95, p. 190.
    "I Meant to Say." [WritersF] (21) 95, p. 188.
    "Jessica and the Phosphorescent Sea." [WritersF] (21) 95, p. 189.
    "On the Snow Falls the Burden of Forgiveness." [WritersF] (21) 95, p. 191.
6407. VALENTE, Peter
    "Invisible Surfaces" (Selections). [Talisman] (15) Wint 95-96, p. 156-157.
6408. VALENTINE, Jean
    "The Baby Rabbits in the Garden." [Field] (53) Fall 95, p. 70.
    "Homesick." [AmerV] (38) 95, p. 19.
    "Soul (2)." [GlobalCR] (6) Fall 95, p. 21.
    "Tell Me, What Is the Soul" (Osip Mandelstam). [NewYorker] (71:13) 22 My 95, p.
        56.
6409. VALERIO, R. D.
    "To Ivory Forever." [Bogg] (67) 95, p. 25.
6410. VALERO, Roberto
    "Ventajas del Progreso." [LindLM] (14:1) Mr/Spr 95, p. 6.
6411. VALINOTTI, Nicholas
    "Census" (For Gail Esterman, my neighbor). [MinnR] (43/44) 95, p. 37.
    "For the American Dead" (one year after Kuwait). [MinnR] (43/44) 95, p. 38.
    "The Riots in L.A." [MinnR] (43/44) 95, p. 37.
6412. VALKEAPÄÄ, Nils-Aslak
    "The Sun My Father" (21 selections, tr. by Harald Gaski, Lars Nordstrom and Ralph
        Salisbury). [CharR] (21:1) Spr 95, p. 55-64.
    "The Sun, My Father" (Excerpt). [Nimrod] (38:2) Spr-Sum 95, p. 88.
VALLE, Lynda del
    See Del VALLE, Lynda
6413. VALLEJO, César
    "Agape" (tr. by Tony Barnstone and Willis Barnstone). [Jacaranda] (11) [95 or 96?],
        p. 70.
    "The Black Cup" (tr. by Tony Barnstone and Willis Barnstone). [Jacaranda] (11) [95
        or 96?], p. 71.
    "In That Corner Where We Slept Together" (tr. by Tony Barnstone and Willis
        Barnstone). [Jacaranda] (11) [95 or 96?], p. 68.
    "Masses" (tr. by Tony Barnstone and Willis Barnstone). [Jacaranda] (11) [95 or
        96?], p. 67.
    "Oh The Four Walls of The Cell" (tr. by Tony Barnstone and Willis Barnstone).
        [Jacaranda] (11) [95 or 96?], p. 69.

"There Exists a Man" (tr. by Clayton Eshleman and José Rubia Barcia). [RiverS] (42/43) 95, p. 6.
6414. VALLEJOS, Nelly Davis
"Fall" (tr. by Luciano P. Díaz). [Arc] (35) Aut 95, p. 38.
"Rain" (tr. by Luciano P. Díaz). [Arc] (35) Aut 95, p. 39.
"The Sad Grapes" (tr. by Luciano P. Díaz). [Arc] (35) Aut 95, p. 40.
6415. VALLONE, Antonio
"Camping Out in the Backyard." [LitR] (38:2) Wint 95, p. 285.
6416. VALLONE, Jessica
"Resistance." [AmerPoR] (24:3) My-Je 95, p. 16.
6417. VALVIS, James
"Accidents." [SlipS] (15) 95, p. 48.
"The Disease." [WormR] (35:1, #137) 95, p. 13.
"Just Your Average Guy." [WormR] (35:1, #137) 95, p. 13.
"Letter to the Editor." [WormR] (35:1, #137) 95, p. 12.
"Second Fiddle." [WormR] (35:1, #137) 95, p. 14.
"Song to Tonight." [Pearl] (22) Fall-Wint 95, p. 20.
Van ...
See also names beginning with "Van" without the following space, filed below in their alphabetic positions.
6418. Van BEEK, Edith
"Communion." [Nimrod] (38:2) Spr-Sum 95, p. 38.
"Pangnirtung on Baffin Island." [Nimrod] (38:2) Spr-Sum 95, p. 39.
"Sedna, Natar Ungalag." [Nimrod] (38:2) Spr-Sum 95, p. 37.
6419. Van DOREN, John
"Lions." [WillowR] (22) Spr 95, p. 23-24.
6420. Van DUYN, Mona
"At the New Orleans Zoo" (for Viktor Hamburger). [RiverS] (42/43) 95, p. 127-128.
6421. Van GERVEN, Claudia
"Get Plath Out of Your Poems!" (— Suzanne Juhasz). [Calyx] (16:2) Wint 95-96, p. 52.
"Sunbonnet Sue Signs on at Three Mile Island." [Calyx] (16:2) Wint 95-96, p. 50-51.
"Waiting for the Cyclamen to Bloom." [LullwaterR] (5:2) Fall-Wint 94, p. 102.
Van ITTERBEEK, Eugène
See ITTERBEEK, Eugène van
6422. Van OOY, Eldred
"Naming Things" (Toktok Nem Bilong Samting, from "Tok Pisin," tr. by Justin Spring). [Vis] (47) 95, p. 38.
6423. Van PEENEN, H. J.
"Wallowa Llamas." [BellArk] (11:4) Jl-Ag 95, p. 14.
6424. Van SPANCKEREN, Kathryn
"Columbus Ships in a Bottle." [Kalliope] (17:1) 95, p. 28.
6425. Van WALLEGHEN, Michael
"Shangri-la." [SouthernR] (31:2) Ap/Spr 95, p. 306-308.
6426. Van WERT, William (William F.)
"After Church." [LouisL] (12:1) Spr 95, p. 51-52.
"Flightless Bird." [WestB] (37) 95, p. 9.
"Playing with Fire." [PoetL] (90:1) Spr 95, p. 12-14.
6427. Van WINCKEL, Nance
"Black Jacket, Black Pants, Black Motorcycle." [Crazy] (48) Spr 95, p. 31.
"Cockadoodledo: Woman Selling Dogs in the Village." [DenQ] (30:2) Fall 95, p. 77-79.
"Every Good Thing" (Stela of Cheywath, 2250 B.C.). [ParisR] (37:137) Wint 95, p. 214.
"It." [IndR] (18:2) Fall 95, p. 76.
"No Blame." [IndR] (18:2) Fall 95, p. 75.
"Unfinished Canvas" (Flemish Peasant Family). [ParisR] (37:137) Wint 95, p. 212-213.
6428. Van ZANT, Frank
"If Walt Whitman Were Homeless Today." [SlipS] (15) 95, p. 60.
VanBEEK, Edith
See Van BEEK, Edith
6429. VANCIL, David
"Legend of Dracula." [FreeL] (15) Aut 95, p. 13.
"Two Sisters." [FreeL] (15) Aut 95, p. 12.

6430. Vande PLASSE, Kelly
"The Undressing." [NewYorkQ] (54) 95, p. 75.
6431. VANDENBURGH, Jane
"Friends of Dickens Who Knew Italian." [Thrpny] (61) Spr 95, p. 25.
6432. VanderMOLEN, Robert
"Making a Fire." [ArtfulD] (28/29) 95, p. 57.
"Rain." [ArtfulD] (28/29) 95, p. 56.
VanDOREN, John
See Van DOREN, John
VanDUYN, Mona
See Van DUYN, Mona
6433. VANG, Barbara
"On Waiting for a Poem to Come." [SantaBR] (3:2) Sum 95, p. 53.
"Remembering Dad." [SantaBR] (3:2) Sum 95, p. 53.
6434. VANOS, Tracey
"At Grandma's House." [Pearl] (22) Fall-Wint 95, p. 136.
VanPEENEN, H. J.
See Van PEENEN, H. J.
VanSPANCKEREN, Kathryn
See Van SPANCKEREN, Kathryn
VanWERT, William (William F.)
See Van WERT, William (William F.)
VanWINCKEL, Nance
See Van WINCKEL, Nance
VARELA, María Elena Cruz
See CRUZ VARELA, María Elena
6435. VARNER, William
"Craig." [PaintedB] (55/56) 95, p. 69-70.
6436. VARON, Jodi
"Love Song" (to the tune "Digging a Well in the Back Garden," tr. of Li He).
[YellowS] (12:4, #48) Sum 95, p. 12.
"Song: Sitting Through the Night" (tr. of Li He). [YellowS] (12:4, #48) Sum 95, p.
13.
6437. VARON, Susan
"It Was a Frightening Moment." [SnailPR] (3:2) 95, p. 11.
6438. VASILIU, Lucian
"Anima Mundi" (tr. by Adam J. Sorkin and Laurentiu Constantin). [Vis] (48) 95, p.
47-48.
"Field Blankets" (tr. by Adam J. Sorkin and Laurentiu Constantin). [Vis] (48) 95, p.
48.
6439. VAUGHAN, Rachael
"Foreign Devil." [Footwork] (24/25) 95, p. 84.
"Young, Fresh and Green." [Footwork] (24/25) 95, p. 84-85.
6440. VAUGHEN, Laurie Perry
"After Rape." [Kalliope] (17:2) 95, p. 36.
"Morning Walk" (First Place, 1995 James Dickey Poetry Contest). [LullwaterR]
(6:2) Fall-Wint 95, p. 46-47.
"Wild Flowers." [LullwaterR] (6:2) Fall-Wint 95, p. 48-49.
6441. VAZIRANI, Reetika
"August" (tr. of Paulo Colina, w. Phyllis Peres and Chi Lam). [Callaloo] (18:4) Fall
95, p. 734-735.
"Carnival" (tr. of Paulo Colina, w. Phyllis Peres, Jane Kamide and Chi Lam).
[Callaloo] (18:4) Fall 95, p. 736.
"Early Days in Patiala, 1959." [LitR] (38:3) Spr 95, p. 419.
"Ejo-Lorun" (tr. of Ricardo Aleixo, w. Phyllis Peres and Chi Lam). [Callaloo] (18:4)
Fall 95, p. 800.
"Great Mother" (tr. of Ricardo Aleixo, w. Phyllis Peres and Chi Lam). [Callaloo]
(18:4) Fall 95, p. 799.
"I Am" (tr. of Oliveira Silveira, w. Phyllis Peres and Chi Lam). [Callaloo] (18:4)
Fall 95, p. 813-814.
"Induca, Maria do Rosário" (tr. of Edimilson de Almeida Pereira, w. Phyllis Peres
and Chi Lam). [Callaloo] (18:4) Fall 95, p. 873.
"Letter to a Husband." [Callaloo] (18:2) Spr 95, p. 239-240.
"Man to the Apocryphal Power of Rouge: Part I of *Puya*" (tr. of Ronald Augusto).
[Callaloo] (18:4) Fall 95, p. 748-750.

"Mariana and the Word, Another Name" (tr. of Éle Semog, w. Phyllis Peres and Chi Lam). [Callaloo] (18:4) Fall 95, p. 755.
"The Mercator Projection" (for Charles Rowell). [InterQ] (2:1/2) 95, p. 126.
"Morning Prayer" (for Núbia Pereira, tr. of Edimilson de Almeida Pereira, w. Phyllis Peres and Chi Lam). [Callaloo] (18:4) Fall 95, p. 872.
"Mrs. Biswas's Career as a Painter." [PraS] (69:1) Spr 95, p. 111-112.
"Much to the Sea" (for a black woman, tr. of José Carlos Limeira, w. Phyllis Peres and Chi Lam). [Callaloo] (18:4) Fall 95, p. 818.
"Ouro Preto: Interpretation Itinerary" (tr. of Edimilson de Almeida Pereira, w. Phyllis Peres and Chi Lam). [Callaloo] (18:4) Fall 95, p. 874.
"Pieces of a Woman" (tr. of Ricardo Aleixo, w. Carolyn Richardson Durham and Chi Lam). [Callaloo] (18:4) Fall 95, p. 801.
"The Rajdhani Express." [PraS] (69:1) Spr 95, p. 113-114.
"Reading the Poem About the Yew Tree." [Callaloo] (18:2) Spr 95, p. 241.
"The Service." [InterQ] (2:1/2) 95, p. 127.
"This Is for You" (tr. of Éle Semog, w. Phyllis Peres and Chi Lam). [Callaloo] (18:4) Fall 95, p. 753.
"Women's College, 1955." [InterQ] (2:1/2) 95, p. 128.
6442. VEAZEY, Mary
"Mother Goose Loose." [Light] (15/16) Aut-Wint 95-96, p. 28.
6443. VECCHIONE, Glen
"Eclipse." [IndR] (18:2) Fall 95, p. 93-95.
6444. VEENENDAAL, Cornelia
"The Good Samaritan." [Comm] (122:15) 8 S 95, p. 12.
6445. VEGA, E. J.
"Penance." [RiverS] (44) 95, p. 50.
"Police Car" (one of two "Poems of New York"). [RiverS] (44) 95, p. 51.
"Trinity" (one of two "Poems of New York"). [RiverS] (44) 95, p. 51.
"Two Poems of New York." [RiverS] (44) 95, p. 51.
"Why Mother's Teeth Remained in Cuba." [RiverS] (44) 95, p. 49.
6446. VEGA, Janine Pommy
"Abuse" (for Kim Wozencraft). [HeavenB] (12) 95, p. 19.
"Plaza de Armas." [HeavenB] (12) 95, p. 19.
6447. VEGRI, Sasa
"Family (II)" (tr. by Dasha Culic Nisula). [Vis] (48) 95, p. 51.
6448. VEINBERG, Jon
"The Jogger." [Ploughs] (21:1) Spr 95, p. 9-11.
"Motel Drive." [Ploughs] (21:1) Spr 95, p. 12-13.
6449. VELADOTA, Christina
"Visiting My Dead Relatives." [GreensboroR] (59) Wint 95-96, p. 104-105.
VÉLEZ, Clemente Soto
     See SOTO VÉLEZ, Clemente
6450. VÉLEZ, Manuel
"Onion Fields" (para ti, Mamá). [ManyMM] (2:1) 95, p. 98-99.
6451. VENABLE, John R.
"Loggerheads." [TarRP] (34:2) Spr 95, p. 35.
6452. VENTURI, Robert
"Mals Mots: Aphorisms — Sweet and Sour — By an Anti-Hero Architect." [GrandS] (14:2, #54) Fall 95, p. 82-87.
6453. VERDICCHIO, Pasquale
"An Alphabet Elsewhere." [WestCL] (29:3, #18) Wint 95-96, p. 9.
"Relative Positions" (for Robin Blaser). [WestCL] (29:3, #18) Wint 95-96, p. 10.
"Twelve Tim." [WestCL] (29:3, #18) Wint 95-96, p. 8-9.
6454. VERDON, Robert
"Poor, 1958." [Footwork] (24/25) 95, p. 30.
6455. VERIGIN, Lisa
"The Anthropologist Recognizes an Ancient Symbol of Erotic Longing." [NewYorkQ] (55) 95, p. 97.
"Responding to Auden Responding to Brugel." [Plain] (16:1) Fall 95, p. 16.
6456. VERLAINE, Paul
"A la Promenade." [AntigR] (100) Wint 95, p. 100.
"L'Amour par Terre." [AntigR] (100) Wint 95, p. 102.
"Croquis Parisien." [AntigR] (100) Wint 95, p. 98.
"Dernier Espoir." [AntigR] (100) Wint 95, p. 106.
"L'Hiver A Cessé." [AntigR] (100) Wint 95, p. 104.
"Last Hope" (tr. by R. H. Morrison). [AntigR] (100) Wint 95, p. 107.

"Love Cast Down" (tr. by R. H. Morrison). [AntigR] (100) Wint 95, p. 103.
"On the Promenade" (tr. by R. H. Morrison). [AntigR] (100) Wint 95, p. 101.
"Parisian Sketch" (tr. by R. H. Morrison). [AntigR] (100) Wint 95, p. 99.
"The Winter's Past" (tr. by R. H. Morrison). [AntigR] (100) Wint 95, p. 105.
6457. VERMILYA, Miriam
    "Krogers, Four P.M." [NewRena] (9:2, #28) Spr 95, p. 110.
    "Reclamation." [NewRena] (9:2, #28) Spr 95, p. 109.
    "This Leg." [NewRena] (9:2, #28) Spr 95, p. 111.
6458. VERNON, William J.
    "May at St. Jude's Shelter." [DefinedP] (1:2) Spr-Sum 93, p. 31.
6459. VÉRTES, László
    "I Lock Myself In" (tr. of Sándor Csoóri, w. Len Roberts). [LitR] (38:3) Spr 95, p.
        450.
    "With a Hangover" (tr. of Sándor Csoóri, w. Len Roberts). [LitR] (38:3) Spr 95, p.
        449.
6460. VERTREACE, Martha (Martha M.)
    "Earthworks." [Kalliope] (17:1) 95, p. 36-37.
    "Evolution of Flight." [Kalliope] (17:1) 95, p. 40-41.
    "Philosopher's Stone." [SpoonR] (20:2) Sum-Fall 95, p. 54-55.
    "Scarification." [ChiR] (41:2/3) 95, p. 87-89.
    "Theatre of the Deaf" (for Paul Keeley). [Kalliope] (17:1) 95, p. 38-39.
    "Woman with Mirror // Maternity." [SpoonR] (20:2) Sum-Fall 95, p. 52-53.
6461. VESPER, Eric
    "Firewood." [PoetL] (90:3) Fall 95, p. 29.
    "The Search." [PoetL] (90:3) Fall 95, p. 28.
6462. VEST, D. C. Q.
    "The Quest of the Familiar." [HampSPR] Wint 95, p. 42-43.
    "Thorns and Roses." [HampSPR] Wint 95, p. 43.
6463. VETOCK, Jeff
    "Enough." [AxeF] (3) 90, p. 27.
    "Framework" (chapbook of poems). [AxeF] ([4]) 91, 24 p.
6464. VETTORI, Alessandro
    "Annunziata." [Chelsea] (59) 95, p. 40.
6465. VEVE, Michael
    "Service Economy Fantastique." [MassR] (36:4) Wint 95-96, p. 654.
6466. VIAN, Boris
    "If Poets Weren't So Stupid" (tr. by Julia Older). [ApalQ] (44/45) Fall 95-Wint 96,
        p. 45-46.
6467. VIANU, Lidia
    "The Great Blind Man" (tr. of Marin Sorescu, w. Adam J. Sorkin). [Vis] (48) 95, p.
        44.
    "Season" (tr. of Mircea Florin Sandru, w. Adam J. Sorkin). [Vis] (48) 95, p. 44.
    "Synchronization" (tr. of Marin Sorescu, w. Adam J. Sorkin). [Vis] (48) 95, p. 45.
6468. VICUÑA, Cecilia
    "Beloved Friend" (tr. by Suzanne Jill Levine). [AmerPoR] (24:3) My-Je 95, p. 18-
        19.
    "Mother & Daughter" (tr. by Suzanne Jill Levine). [AmerPoR] (24:3) My-Je 95, p.
        19.
    "Purmamarca" (in Spanish and English). [Chain] (2) Spr 95, p. 231-235.
6469. VIDLER, John
    "The Great Supermarket." [Bogg] (67) 95, p. 42.
6470. VIDYAPATI (14th c.)
    "First Love" (tr. by Sam Hamill). [PoetryE] (41) Aut 95, p. 27.
6471. VIERECK, Peter
    "Epic (4995 A.D.)." [PraS] (69:4) Wint 95, p. 67-68.
    "Goat Ode in Mid-Dive." [Boulevard] (10:3, #30) Fall 95, p. 117-133.
    "In Awe of Marriage." [NewRep] (212:5) 30 Ja 95, p. 38.
6472. VIGIL, Anthony R.
    "La Boda Chicana" (Globeville, ColorAztlán). [MidAR] (15:1/2) 95, p. 309-312.
6473. VIGIL, Mary Black
    "Augurs." [SoCoast] (19) 95, p. 33.
    "Pilgrimage." [SoCoast] (19) 95, p. 31-32.
    "Shapechanger: the Muse." [SoCoast] (19) 95, p. 35.
    "Till Death." [SoCoast] (19) 95, p. 34.
6474. VILEN, Anne
    "Taking the Cure in Reserve, Montana." [HighP] (10:3) Wint 95, p. 58-59.

6475. VILHJALMSDOTTIR, Linda
"Mona Lisa — Third Mosaic" (tr. by Sigurdur A. Magnússon). [Nimrod] (38:2) Spr-
Sum 95, p. 69.
"Nights" (tr. by Sigurdur A. Magnússon). [Nimrod] (38:2) Spr-Sum 95, p. 69.
6476. VILLANUEVA, Tino
"En el Claroscuro de los Años." [MassR] (36:4) Wint 95-96, p. 650.
"I Only Know that Now" (tr. by James Hoggard). [MassR] (36:4) Wint 95-96, p.
653.
"In the Chiaroscuro of the Years" (tr. by James Hoggard). [MassR] (36:4) Wint 95-
96, p. 651.
"Sólo Sé Que Ahora." [MassR] (36:4) Wint 95-96, p. 652.
6477. VILLAURRUTIA, Xavier (1903-1950)
"The Statue" (tr. by D. M. Stroud). [Noctiluca] (2:1, #4) Spr 95, p. 59.
6478. VINCENT, John
"Abandoned Warehouse in the Afternoon." [BelPoJ] (46:2) Wint 95-96, p. 22.
"Mr. Yuk." [Jacaranda] (11) [95 or 96?], p. 80.
"Never Strangers." [BelPoJ] (46:2) Wint 95-96, p. 23-24.
"Severed Hand." [Jacaranda] (11) [95 or 96?], p. 79.
6479. VINCENT, Paul
"Fairy Tale" (tr. of Tonnus Oosterhoff). [CimR] (112) Jl 95, p. 12.
VINCENZO, Jan di
See Di VINCENZO, Jan
6480. VINZ, Mark
"Amusing Myself." [MidwQ] (36:4) Sum 95, p. 451-452.
"Landscape with Hawk" (for John R. Milton). [SoDakR] (33:3/4) Fall-Wint 95, p.
209.
"Occupational Hazard." [NorthStoneR] (12) 95, p. 66.
6481. VIRGIL
"Aeneid" (Selection: Book II, Lines 268-297, tr. by Ian Ganassi). [NewEngR] (17:4)
Fall 95, p. 100-103.
6482. VISTE-ROSS, Louise
"A Triad with Red Poinsettias" (Nathan's 38th birthday eve poem, w. James Naiden
and Nathan Viste-Ross). [NorthStoneR] (12) 95, p. 205.
6483. VISTE-ROSS, Nathan
"Cubes" (first chapter of a book in progress, "Requiem: Missa Pro Vivus").
[NorthStoneR] (12) 95, p. 79-107.
"A Triad with Red Poinsettias" (Nathan's 38th birthday eve poem, w. James Naiden
and Louise Viste-Ross). [NorthStoneR] (12) 95, p. 205.
6484. VITALE, Carlos
"Más Allá" (Spanish tr. of the Italian of Benito La Mantia). [Luz] (8) Spr 95, p. 39-
40.
VITO, E. B. de
See De VITO, E. B.
6485. VLASOPOLOS, Anca
"August Voices." [SantaBR] (3:3) Fall-Wint 95, p. 68.
"Black Looks." [Vis] (47) 95, p. 23.
"Lasting Ivory." [SantaBR] (3:3) Fall-Wint 95, p. 67.
"Matinee, Cape Cod." [SantaBR] (3:3) Fall-Wint 95, p. 68.
6486. VOGEL, Erich
"Dear." [Parting] (8:1) Sum 95, p. 23.
"Thermia." [Parting] (8:1) Sum 95, p. 23.
6487. VOGEL, Frank
"A Lovely Warning." [Hellas] (6:2) Fall-Wint 95, p. 34.
6488. VOGELSANG, Arthur
"Bad Boy." [DenQ] (29:3) Wint 95, p. 40-41.
"Critical." [DenQ] (30:1) Sum 95, p. 98.
"The Lab." [DenQ] (30:1) Sum 95, p. 99.
"Liquids in Quantities." [DenQ] (30:1) Sum 95, p. 100-101.
"Lyric." [DenQ] (30:1) Sum 95, p. 102.
"The Umbrella." [DenQ] (30:1) Sum 95, p. 103-104.
6489. VOIGT, Ellen Bryant
"The Chosen." [SenR] (25:1) Spr 95, p. 64-66.
6490. VOISINE, Connie
"Blue Hat." [Calyx] (16:2) Wint 95-96, p. 67.
"Hum." [PoetryE] (41) Aut 95, p. 65.
"In English." [SenR] (25:2) Fall 95, p. 21-22.

6491. VOLDSETH, Beverly
"August." [MinnR] (43/44) 95, p. 40.
"Once in a Dream a Voice." [MinnR] (43/44) 95, p. 39.
"Wild Ricing at Deep Portage." [RagMag] (12:2) Spr 95, p. 110.
6492. VOLKMAN, Karen
"The Case." [ParisR] (37:135) Sum 95, p. 202.
"Chemistry." [Chelsea] (59) 95, p. 162.
"Chronicle." [ParisR] (37:135) Sum 95, p. 203-204.
"Infernal." [Chelsea] (59) 95, p. 163-164.
"Scarecrow." [HarvardR] (9) Fall 95, p. 95.
"Tulips." [PartR] (62:2) Spr 95, p. 296.
6493. VOLKMER, Jon
"Lines on a New Chivalry." [PaintedB] (55/56) 95, p. 83-84.
6494. VOLLMER, Judith
"The Approach." [WestB] (37) 95, p. 60-62.
"Asleep at the 2001 Club, Early Seventies." [ManyMM] (2:1) 95, p. 60-61.
Von GOETHE, Johann Wolfgang
See GOETHE, Johann Wolfgang von
Von TORNE, Volker
See TORNE, Volker von
VON WYSOCKI, Gisela
See WYSOCKI, Gisela von
6495. VONDRAK, Jayne R.
"In Search of Shallow Waters" (Literary Festival: Poetry: Honorable Mention).
[EngJ] (84:4) Ap 95, p. 41.
6496. VOSS, Fred
"Alchemy." [Pearl] (22) Fall-Wint 95, p. 66.
"Blessed" (to Joan Jobe Smith). [ChironR] (42) Spr 95, p. 8.
"Breaking the Ice." [Pearl] (22) Fall-Wint 95, p. 67.
"Caring." [ChironR] (44/45) Aut-Wint 95, p. 11.
"Don't Call Me Shakespeare." [Pearl] (22) Fall-Wint 95, p. 66.
"Finishing Touch" (for Robert Delaura). [Pearl] (22) Fall-Wint 95, p. 31.
"Getting the Most Out of Life." [ChironR] (42) Spr 95, p. 8.
"Goodstone University." [Pearl] (22) Fall-Wint 95, p. 68.
"Grateful." [ChironR] (42) Spr 95, p. 8.
"Lifeboat." [ChironR] (44/45) Aut-Wint 95, p. 11.
"Living Bible." [Pearl] (22) Fall-Wint 95, p. 67.
"Pure." [ChironR] (42) Spr 95, p. 8.
"Second Chance." [ChironR] (44/45) Aut-Wint 95, p. 11.
6497. VU, Cao
"The Bells" (tr. by Nguyen Ba Chung and Kevin Bowen). [Manoa] (7:2) Wint 95, p. 108.
6498. VU, Dung (grade 5, Bancroft Elementary, Washington, DC)
"On the Playground" (Poetry on the Metro Project). [WashR] (21:2) Ag-S 95, p. 15.

6499. W. T. K.
"Dark Side of the Dance." [InterPR] (21:1) Spr 95, p. 77.
"Fishing Lines." [InterPR] (21:1) Spr 95, p. 75.
"Wavering." [InterPR] (21:1) Spr 95, p. 76.
"What Happens to the Light." [InterPR] (21:1) Spr 95, p. 76.
6500. WAARD, Elly de
"70" (tr. by Wanda Boeke). [CimR] (112) Jl 95, p. 13.
6501. WACKER, Wendy
"Bebop in the '90s" (First Runner-Up, Poetry Award). [NewL] (62:1) 96 (c1995), p. 40-41.
"The Business" (First Runner-Up, Poetry Award). [NewL] (62:1) 96 (c1995), p. 35-37.
"Eating Bananas" (First Runner-Up, Poetry Award). [NewL] (62:1) 96 (c1995), p. 42-43.
"The End Times" (First Runner-Up, Poetry Award). [NewL] (62:1) 96 (c1995), p. 38-39.
6502. WADE, Cheryl Marie
"Reconciliation." [Kaleid] (30) Wint-Spr 95, p. 46.
6503. WADE, Cory
"The Ambition Bird." [Poetry] (165:4) Ja 95, p. 214.

6504. WADE, Michele
"Play Me Accordion Paper Dolls." [PaintedB] (55/56) 95, p. 109.
6505. WADE, Sidney
"Barn." [NewEngR] (17:4) Fall 95, p. 76.
"Byzantium." [NewEngR] (17:4) Fall 95, p. 74-75.
6506. WADSWORTH. CONNEMARA
"Whirlwind Child." [PoetL] (90:4) Wint 95-96, p. 57.
6507. WAGNER, Catherine
"Girl" (Finalist, 1995 Greg Grummer Award in Poetry). [Phoebe] (24:2) 95, p. 191-
193.
6508. WAGNER, Cathy
"Tongue." [ColR] (22:1) Spr 95, p. 45-46.
"Tongue Grimed the Things He Lay Upon." [ColR] (22:1) Spr 95, p. 47.
6509. WAGNER, Mark
"Lydia and the Animals." [HarvardR] (9) Fall 95, p. 100.
6510. WAGNER, Richard
"Back Then" (tr. by Rick Spuler). [PlumR] (9) [95 or 96], p. 3.
"Balladesque" (tr. by Mark Herman and Ronnie Apter). [GrahamHR] (19) Wint 95-
96, p. 68.
"Lili Marlene" (tr. by Mark Herman and Ronnie Apter). [GrahamHR] (19) Wint 95-
96, p. 67.
"Moment at the Supermarket" (tr. by Rick Spuler). [PlumR] (9) [95 or 96], p. 4.
"Remote Control" (tr. by Rick Spuler). [PlumR] (9) [95 or 96], p. 2.
"Slices" (tr. by Mark Herman and Ronnie Apter). [GrahamHR] (19) Wint 95-96, p.
66.
6511. WAGNER, Robert
"Vibrations." [SmPd] (32:1, #93) Wint 95, p. 9.
6512. WAGNER, Shari
"Convergences." [HopewellR] (7) 95, p. 116-117.
6513. WAGONER, David
"Bear." [NewEngR] (17:2) Spr 95, p. 7-8.
"By a River." [GettyR] (8:2) Spr 95, p. 310.
"Dead Letter from Out of Town." [Verse] (12:3) 95, p. 71.
"Elegy for the Nondescript." [SenR] (25:1) Spr 95, p. 20.
"For a Hedge of Wild Roses." [GettyR] (8:2) Spr 95, p. 311.
"For a Yong Shield Fern." [GettyR] (8:2) Spr 95, p. 312.
"In the Woods." [ColR] (22:2) Fall 95, p. 111-113.
"The Laughing Boy." [Nat] (260:6) 13 F 95, p. 215.
"My Father Laughing in the Chicago Theater." [Poetry] (166:3) Je 95, p. 138.
"My Passenger." [KenR] (17:3/4) Sum-Fall 95, p. 35-36.
"The Padded Cell." [Poetry] (166:5) Ag 95, p. 278.
"A Pair of Barn Owls, Hunting." [NewEngR] (17:2) Spr 95, p. 8.
"The Pink Boy." [Poetry] (166:3) Je 95, p. 139.
"The Rosebush" (A memory of Theodore Roethke). [KenR] (17:3/4) Sum-Fall 95, p.
34-35.
"Walking Around the Block with a Three-Year-Old." [VirQR] (71:2) Spr 95, p. 297.
"A Young Woman Trying on a Victorian Hat." [Nat] (260:8) 27 F 95, p. 288.
6514. WAIS, Roz
"Dusting Bimbos in a VW Diesel." [Ledge] (19) Wint 95, p. 123-124.
"Sinai, Second Month." [Ledge] (19) Wint 95, p. 125.
6515. WAITTS, Fileman
"The Beautiful Revolution." [HolCrit] (32:5) D 95, p. 20.
"Cacao Bay." [LullwaterR] (6:2) Fall-Wint 95, p. 86-87.
"Desolation." [PoetryE] (40) Spr 95, p. 125.
"Destruction." [PoetryE] (40) Spr 95, p. 126.
"Disaster." [PoetryE] (40) Spr 95, p. 127.
6516. WAKEFIELD, Kathleen
"After Looking at Bruegel." [Journal] (19:1) Spr-Sum 95, p. 56.
"Afterward." [Poetry] (166:4) Jl 95, p. 224.
"Book of Names." [Journal] (19:1) Spr-Sum 95, p. 57-58.
"The Rain Has No Edges." [Journal] (19:1) Spr-Sum 95, p. 59.
"Reconsidering the Rift." [Journal] (19:1) Spr-Sum 95, p. 55.
6517. WAKEMAN, Nancy
"Stages." [Vis] (49) 95, p. 15.
6518. WAKOSKI, Diane
"The Butcher's Apron." [ManyMM] [1:1] D 94, p. 111-113.

"The Emerald Book." [BelPoJ] (45:4) Chapbook 22, Sum 95, p. 73.
"Heavy." [RiverS] (44) 95, p. 29.
"Imagining Emily's Early Summer Garden." [RiverS] (42/43) 95, p. 170-171.
"Imagining Point Dume." [CarolQ] (48:1) Fall 95, p. 14-15.
"Losing Ground." [ManyMM] [1:1] D 94, p. 114-115.
"Malachite." [PlumR] (8) [95], p. 14-15.
"Queen Anne's Lace." [GreenMR] (8:1) Spr-Sum 95, p. 16-17.
"Roller Skate Jazz." [RiverS] (44) 95, p. 30-31.
"So Cold in Winter." [GreenMR] (8:1) Spr-Sum 95, p. 14-15.
"Violets." [ManyMM] [1:1] D 94, p. 116-117.
"Watching the Drinkers of Gran Marnier at the Peanut Barrel Bar in East Lansing."
    [RiverS] (44) 95, p. 32-33.
6519. WALCOTT, Derek
"XLII. Chicago's avenues, empty as Poland." [RiverS] (42/43) 95, p. 61.
6520. WALD, Elissa
"Prometheus and Hercules." [JamesWR] (12:3) Fall 95, p. 9.
6521. WALDEN, Gale
"My Mother's Voice." [SpoonR] (20:1) Wint-Spr 95, p. 92.
"Open Lands." [SpoonR] (20:1) Wint-Spr 95, p. 93.
6522. WALDEN, William
"Legacy." [FourQ] (9:1/2) Spr 95, p. 52.
6523. WALDIE, Donald J.
"You Are Always Somewhere: More Suburban Stories." [MassR] (36:2) Sum 95, p.
    325-328.
6524. WALDMAN, Anne
"Devil's Working Overtime" (from Iovis II). [HeavenB] (12) 95, p. 26-29.
"Do Comment." [Chain] (2) Spr 95, p. 236-237.
"Kalachakra Dream." [HeavenB] (12) 95, p. 6.
"Lacrimare, Lacrimatus." [Sulfur] (15:2, #37) Fall 95, p. 7-27.
"Nerves." [AmerPoR] (24:4) Jl-Ag 95, p. 8.
6525. WALDMAN, John
"The Heat." [LullwaterR] (5:1) 93-94, p. 32-33.
"Shaping." [SpoonR] (20:2) Sum-Fall 95, p. 88.
6526. WALDMAN, Ken
"Beneath Midwest Sky." [MidwQ] (37:1) Aut 95, p. 48-49.
"City Calendar." [Crucible] (31) Fall 95, p. 12.
"Class of '77." [Border] (6) Spr-Sum 95, p. 69.
"Into the White." [ArtfulD] (28/29) 95, p. 109.
"Lighthouse." [Wind] (75) Spr 95, p. 27-29.
"Muse." [DogRR] (14:1, #27) Sum 95, p. 17.
"Nome Post Office." [PoetL] (90:1) Spr 95, p. 45.
"Pipeline." [Elf] (5:3) Fall 95, p. 31.
"Salter's Funeral." [FreeL] (15) Aut 95, p. 32.
"Stutterer." [Flyway] (1:1) Spr 95, p. 52.
6527. WALDNER, Liz
"Birthday." [SycamoreR] (7:1) Wint 95, p. 27.
"A Gambol and Spring." [SycamoreR] (7:1) Wint 95, p. 26.
"Self Interrogation." [DenQ] (30:2) Fall 95, p. 80.
"A Very Big Wind." [Talisman] (15) Wint 95-96, p. 98.
6528. WALDROP, Keith
"Nocturne" (tr. of Johann Wolfgang von Goethe). [DefinedP] (2:1) Fall-Wint 93, p.
    7.
"The Silhouette of the Bridge (Memory Stand-Ins)" (Excerpts). [Avec] (10) 95, p.
    54-60.
6529. WALDROP, Rosmarie
"Adaptation." [OhioR] (54) 95, p. 72-73.
"The Allmar" (tr. of Jayne-Ann Igel). [ManhatR] (7:2) Wint 95, p. 72.
"Black / Red / Gold" (tr. of Gerhard Falkner). [ManhatR] (7:2) Wint 95, p. 64.
"Bright Pink." [OhioR] (54) 95, p. 74-75.
"Color." [Avec] (9) 95, p. 163.
"Composing Stick." [GrandS] (14:1, #53) Sum 95, p. 258-259.
"Constructive Procedure and Sweet Destiny" (tr. of Peter Waterhouse). [ManhatR]
    (7:2) Wint 95, p. 76.
"The Frog Prince." [NewAW] (13) Fall-Wint 95, p. 18.
"The Ice Is Broken" (tr. of Gerhard Falkner). [ManhatR] (7:2) Wint 95, p. 65.
"Identical." [Avec] (9) 95, p. 166.

"In a Flash" (for Cole Swensen). [Avec] (10) 95, p. 165-169.
"Latent Settlement." [ManhatR] (8:1) Fall 95, p. 71.
"Leaving the Identical" (tr. of Peter Waterhouse). [ManhatR] (7:2) Wint 95, p. 77.
"Like Many Others." [Avec] (9) 95, p. 162.
"The Matter of Light" (for Mei-mei Berssenbrugge). [ColR] (22:2) Fall 95, p. 137-138.
"Metamorphoses of the Leibniz Apple" (tr. of Peter Waterhouse). [ManhatR] (7:2) Wint 95, p. 75.
"Movie-Dad" (tr. of Gisela von Wysocki). [MichQR] (34:4) Fall 95, p. 548.
"Nightly Round" (tr. of Jayne-Ann Igel). [ManhatR] (7:2) Wint 95, p. 69.
"Not a Description." [NewAW] (13) Fall-Wint 95, p. 19.
"Of Solitude as the Space of Writing" (tr. of Edmond Jabès). [OhioR] (54) 95, p. 41-44.
"Outside Time, the Dream of the Book" (tr. of Edmond Jabès). [OhioR] (54) 95, p. 38-40.
"The Page as a Place to Subvert Both Whiteness and the Word" (tr. of Edmond Jabès). [OhioR] (54) 95, p. 36-37.
"The sex of houses gave birth to strange places" (tr. of Jayne-Ann Igel). [ManhatR] (7:2) Wint 95, p. 70.
"The Split" (tr. of Gerhard Falkner). [ManhatR] (7:2) Wint 95, p. 66.
"A Stranger and Early." [Avec] (9) 95, p. 164.
"Two to One" (tr. of Gerhard Falkner). [ManhatR] (7:2) Wint 95, p. 67.
"Unvoiced Sounds" (tr. of Jayne-Ann Igel). [ManhatR] (7:2) Wint 95, p. 71.
"Vesuvius" (tr. of Gerhard Falkner). [ManhatR] (7:2) Wint 95, p. 68.
"The Wall." [Avec] (9) 95, p. 165.
"The Widening of History" (tr. of Peter Waterhouse). [ManhatR] (7:2) Wint 95, p. 73-74.
"Working Out" (tr. of Elke Erb). [WorldL] (6) 95, p. 25.
6530. WALKER, Anne F.
"City of Recorded Space." [MalR] (110) Spr 95, p. 109.
"From the Last Letter." [SantaBR] (3:1) Spr 95, p. 117.
"Garden Grove, PCB Burial Grounds." [SantaBR] (3:1) Spr 95, p. 117.
6531. WALKER, Dara
"Babushka and Her Grandmother" (WritersCorps Program, Washington, DC). [WashR] (21:2) Ag-S 95, p. 6.
6532. WALKER, David
"Older Poet." [NewMyths] (2:2/3:1) 95, p. 234.
6533. WALKER, Jeanne Murray
"The Beetle Science Just Discovered." [WestB] (37) 95, p. 6.
"Centipede." [Nat] (260:9) 6 Mr 95, p. 323.
"Daddy Long Legs." [WestB] (37) 95, p. 7-8.
"Firefly." [Nat] (260:9) 6 Mr 95, p. 323.
"The Housefly." [WestB] (37) 95, p. 7.
"The New Physics." [Boulevard] (10:1/2, #28/29) Spr 95, p. 232-233.
"Pietá." [Shen] (45:2) Sum 95, p. 53.
"Ritual." [Shen] (45:2) Sum 95, p. 56.
"Saturday Morning at the Delaware River." [Shen] (45:2) Sum 95, p. 54-55.
"Science Teaches Us About Insects." [WestB] (37) 95, p. 5.
"Shopping for the Interview." [Shen] (45:2) Sum 95, p. 57.
"So Far, So Good." [Image] (11) Fall 95, p. 49.
"Water Strider." [WestB] (37) 95, p. 5-6.
"When the Lights Go Out." [Image] (11) Fall 95, p. 50.
6534. WALKER, Jim
"Firetruck." [PaintedB] (55/56) 95, p. 91-92.
"Lounge Acts." [PaintedB] (55/56) 95, p. 89-90.
6535. WALKER, Kevin
"Cats Would Dance." [PraS] (69:2) Sum 95, p. 103-104.
"Secretive." [PraS] (69:2) Sum 95, p. 105.
6536. WALKER, Sue
"Easter and All That Jazz." [SoCoast] (19) 95, p. 39-40.
"The Failure of Fantasy" (To Dr. B——y Regarding Our May 3 Appointment). [SoCoast] (19) 95, p. 38.
"Reasons to Find My Mother." [SoCoast] (19) 95, p. 36.
"Second-Hand Dealer." [SoCoast] (19) 95, p. 37.
6537. WALLACE, Anne C.
"Easter Hunt." [Footwork] (24/25) 95, p. 154.

"Trip to the Dentist 1945." [Footwork] (24/25) 95, p. 154-155.
6538. WALLACE, David
"Some Advice for Pilgrims Travelling with a Potato." [Grain] (23:2) Aut 95, p. 105.
6539. WALLACE, Mark
"The Necessity of Feet." [Avec] (9) 95, p. 102-111.
"Sonnets of a Penny-a-Liner" (9 selections). [Phoebe] (24:2) 95, p. 23-28.
6540. WALLACE, Robert
"The Good Night's Sleep." [Light] (13) Spr 95, p. 16.
6541. WALLACE, Ronald
"1957." [Crazy] (48) Spr 95, p. 64.
"1960." [Crazy] (48) Spr 95, p. 65.
"American Sonnet." [Vis] (47) 95, p. 7.
"Another Monday." [PoetryE] (41) Aut 95, p. 55.
"At the Vietnamese Restaurant." [PoetL] (90:1) Spr 95, p. 25.
"The Bad Sonnet." [CreamCR] (19:1) Spr 95, p. 144.
"Broken Sonnet." [Crazy] (48) Spr 95, p. 61.
"A Cat's Life." [Crazy] (48) Spr 95, p. 62.
"Chaos Theory." [Ploughs] (21:4) Wint 95-96, p. 169-171.
"Close-up." [ArtfulD] (28/29) 95, p. 64.
"Con Artist." [ArtfulD] (28/29) 95, p. 66.
"Decision Making." [TarRP] (34:2) Spr 95, p. 28.
"Fall Back." [Border] (7) Fall-Wint 96, p. 66.
"Found." [SycamoreR] (7:1) Wint 95, p. 54.
"Going Deaf." [Ascent] (19:3) Spr 95, p. 47.
"Guilty." [PoetL] (90:1) Spr 95, p. 24.
"Hair." [CreamCR] (19:1) Spr 95, p. 145.
"Land." [ArtfulD] (28/29) 95, p. 63.
"Living with Pain." [CreamCR] (19:1) Spr 95, p. 143.
"Lost." [SycamoreR] (7:1) Wint 95, p. 53.
"Man with Chain Saw." [FloridaR] (20:2) 95, p. 42-43.
"Memory's Daughter." [HiramPoR] (58/59) Spr 95-Wint 96, p. 76-77.
"Mermaids" (after a painting by Carl Marr). [LaurelR] (29:1) Wint 95, p. 17.
"The Moon in Broad Daylight." [GrahamHR] (19) Wint 95-96, p. 94.
"Morning." [ArtfulD] (28/29) 95, p. 65.
"Morning Glories." [Crazy] (48) Spr 95, p. 63.
"Mowing." [Vis] (47) 95, p. 7.
"Ode." [IllinoisR] (2:2) Spr 95, p. 12.
"Panties." [TarRP] (34:2) Spr 95, p. 29.
"The Pen is Mightier." [TarRP] (34:2) Spr 95, p. 29.
"Scrabble." [SycamoreR] (7:1) Wint 95, p. 52.
"Sea Changes." [Ascent] (19:3) Spr 95, p. 47.
"Sea Story." [IllinoisR] (2:2) Spr 95, p. 11.
"Serutan." [Border] (6) Spr-Sum 95, p. 70.
"Skin." [TarRP] (34:2) Spr 95, p. 28.
"Temps Perdu." [Hellas] (6:1) Spr-Sum 95, p. 31.
"Volleyball" (after Robert Frost." [PoetryE] (41) Aut 95, p. 54.
6542. WALLACE-CRABBE, Chris
"Florobiography." [Verse] (12:3) 95, p. 85.
"Glorying." [Verse] (12:2) 95, p. 140-141.
"The Swirling." [HarvardR] (8) Spr 95, p. 119.
"Yabbying." [Verse] (12:3) 95, p. 84.
WALLEGHEN, Michael van
See Van WALLEGHEN, Michael
6543. WALLENSTEIN, Barry
"Sleep." [GlobalCR] (6) Fall 95, p. 1.
6544. WALLS, Doyle Wesley
"Hits." [Spitball] (48) 95, p. 60-61.
6545. WALLS, Michael
"Mandelstam (1891-1938?)." [NewYorkQ] (54) 95, p. 99.
6546. WALSER, Robert
"The Murderess" (tr. by Annette Wiesner and Tom Whalen). [ProseP] (4) 95, p. 73-74.
6547. WALSH, Catherine
"Idír Eatoratha" (Excerpt). [WestCL] (29:2, #17) Fall 95, p. 102-107.
6548. WALSH, Joan
"In the Viewing Pavilion." [Confr] (56/57) Sum-Fall 95, p. 342.

6549. WALSH, Marty
"And Who's to Say It Wasn't Me." [Poem] (74) N 95, p. 8-9.
"April Fools." [Poem] (74) N 95, p. 10.
"Footloose." [Plain] (16:1) Fall 95, p. 4.
6550. WALSH, Timothy
"Leatherback." [ChironR] (44/45) Aut-Wint 95, p. 15.
6551. WALSH, William
"An Early Lunch." [NewRena] (9:2, #28) Spr 95, p. 68-69.
6552. WALTON, Rex
"An Edsoncise in Fruitility — Appearantly" [sic] (A Plainsongs Award Poem).
[Plain] (15:3) Spr 95, p. 20-21.
"In the Evening's Mist, Looking North toward Linoma." [Plain] (16:1) Fall 95, p.
10-11.
6553. WALTZ, William D.
"Behind the Wheel." [PoetryE] (39) Fall 94, p. 96-97.
"Collect Call Home." [PoetryE] (39) Fall 94, p. 99.
"Stopwatch." [PoetryE] (39) Fall 94, p. 98.
6554. WALZER, Kevin E.
"Churchyard Tree." [WestB] (37) 95, p. 70.
6555. WANEK, Connie
"Blue Moon" (for the sisters Jacobson). [Ascent] (19:3) Spr 95, p. 33.
"Daylilies." [PoetryE] (40) Spr 95, p. 128.
"Skim Milk." [Ascent] (19:3) Spr 95, p. 34.
6556. WANG, Christopher
"Sleaze." [SilverFR] (26) Wint 95, p. 45.
"Where Is Plato." [SilverFR] (26) Wint 95, p. 46-47.
6557. WANG, Jun
"Lumberman's Rattan Hat" (in Chinese and English, tr. from the Chinese by Jun
Wang). [NewRena] (9:2, #28) Spr 95, p. 128-131.
6558. WANG, Lenore Baeli
"Daddy Read Me Poetry." [US1] (30/31) 95, p. 19.
WANG, Ping
See PING, Wang
6559. WANG, Yun
"He Xin Lang (To the Bridegroom)" (tr. of Su Dong-Po). [WillowS] (36) Je 95, p.
97.
"Reading Mud in the Outhouse." [InterPR] (21:1) Spr 95, p. 81-82.
"The Small Mermaid." [InterPR] (21:1) Spr 95, p. 78-79.
"Threshold." [InterPR] (21:1) Spr 95, p. 80-81.
6560. WANIEK, Marilyn Nelson
"Abba Jacob in the Well." [KenR] (17:3/4) Sum-Fall 95, p. 80.
"Aches and Pains." [CrabOR] (1:1) Fall-Wint 95, p. 139.
"Calm, East of Landfall" (for John McWilliams). [CrabOR] (1:1) Fall-Wint 95, p.
137-138.
"Doubt." [AnthNEW] (7) 95, p. 8.
"Leaving the Hospice" (for Robert and Patrice Pfeffer). [CrabOR] (1:1) Fall-Wint
95, p. 140.
"Post-Prandial Conversation." [KenR] (17:3/4) Sum-Fall 95, p. 79-80.
"The Sorcerer's Apprentice." [SouthernR] (31:4) O/Aut 95, p. 946-947.
6561. WARD, B. J.
"Movement." [DefinedP] (1:2) Spr-Sum 93, p. 15.
6562. WARD, David Scott
"The Latest Season." [SouthernHR] (29:1) Wint 95, p. 49.
6563. WARD, Pam
"The Loser." [NewL] (62:1) 96 (c1995), p. 44-45.
6564. WARD, Robert
"Naughty." [Parting] (8:1) Sum 95, p. 30.
6565. WARD, Scott
"Drive Home." [TampaR] (11) Fall 95, p. 12.
6566. WARD, Thom
"Coasters." [FreeL] (14) Wint 95, p. 25.
"Comet." [PoetL] (90:1) Spr 95, p. 29.
"Hunting Skunk Cabbage." [TarRP] (34:2) Spr 95, p. 13.
"The Lullaby of John Philip Sousa." [Chelsea] (58) 95, p. 31-33.
"These Bears." [PoetryNW] (36:1) Spr 95, p. 26-28.
"Walking Down This Mountain." [YellowS] (12:4, #48) Sum 95, p. 22.

6567. WARDEN, Marine Robert
"At Least Orpheus." [Pearl] (22) Fall-Wint 95, p. 21.
6568. WAREHAM, Louise
"Compulsion." [Poetry] (165:5) F 95, p. 256.
"Object." [Poetry] (165:5) F 95, p. 255.
"Some Wrong." [Poetry] (165:5) F 95, p. 255.
6569. WARING, Belle
"The Brothers on the Trash Truck and My Near-Death Experience." [GreenMR]
(8:2) Fall-Wint 95-96, p. 42-43.
"Ending Green." [IndR] (18:1) Spr 95, p. 21-22.
"From the Diary of a Prisoner's Nurse, Mississippi, 1972." [GreenMR] (8:2) Fall-
Wint 95-96, p. 44-45.
"On Fever, Mood, and Crows." [IndR] (18:1) Spr 95, p. 19-20.
"So What Would You Have Done?" [IndR] (18:1) Spr 95, p. 17-18.
"Use the Following Construction in a Sentence." [AmerPoR] (24:5) S-O 95, p. 20.
6570. WARLAND, Betsy
"Cloudnotes." [CapilR] (2:16) Sum 95, p. 5-16.
6571. WARN, Emily
"The Fog." [PoetryE] (39) Fall 94, p. 100.
"Procession." [KenR] (17:3/4) Sum-Fall 95, p. 55.
"While the Secretaries Compose the Engineers' Torah." [KenR] (17:3/4) Sum-Fall
95, p. 54.
6572. WARNER, Al
"China Palace Imperial Garden." [Plain] (15:2) Wint 95, p. 6-7.
"Jacktown Cemetery." [ChironR] (43) Sum 95, p. 20.
6573. WARNER, Anne
"The Reporter." [CapeR] (30:2) Fall 95, p. 30-31.
6574. WARNER, Barrett
"Groundskeeper" (runner up, 1994 Borderlands Poetry Contest). [Border] (6) Spr-
Sum 95, p. 71.
"Logger." [BlackBR] (20) Spr-Sum 95, p. 29.
"Spilling Beans." [NortheastCor] (3) 95, p. 77.
6575. WARNER, Gale
"Near Mount Robson, Canada." [Blueline] (16) 95, p. 50-51.
6576. WARR, Michael
"Malcolm Is 'bout More Than Wearing a Cap." [RiverS] (44) 95, p. 54-55.
"Poem Inspired by a Crazed Negro Nazi Reciting Hitler's *Mein Kampf* to a 99.9
Percent African American Audience at Spice's Jazz Bar." [RiverS] (44) 95, p.
56-57.
"The Theory of Subtlety." [RiverS] (44) 95, p. 58-59.
6577. WARREN, Rosanna
"Country Music." [Verse] (12:2) 95, p. 142-143.
"Sea Gate and Goldenrod (Cranberry Island Elegy)" (for W.K.). [SenR] (25:1) Spr
95, p. 47-48.
"Turnus" (*Aeneid* XII, for Michael Putnam). [Arion] (3:2/3) Fall 95-Wint 96, p. 174.
6578. WARREN, Shirley
"After Seven Years a Jersey Girl Sends for Help from Someone Living on the
Outskirts of a Desert" (for Don). [Crucible] (30) Fall 94, p. 38.
6579. WARSH, Lewis
"Genuine Reasons." [RiverS] (44) 95, p. 3.
"Open All Night." [RiverS] (44) 95, p. 4-6.
6580. WARWICK, Ioanna-Veronika
"A Historical Parable Without a Clear Meaning." [LullwaterR] (5:1) 93-94, p. 64-
65.
"The Language Lesson." [OxfordM] (10:1) Wint 94-Spr 95, p. 64-66.
"My Father Preparing His Physics Lectures." [OxfordM] (10:1) Wint 94-Spr 95, p.
66.
"My Father's Dream." [OxfordM] (10:1) Wint 94-Spr 95, p. 64.
"Sex and the Gdansk Express." [SlipS] (15) 95, p. 49.
"Stages of Prayer." [TampaR] (10) Spr 95, p. 40-41.
"Third Language." [NewOR] (21:2) Sum 95, p. 82-83.
6581. WASHINGTON, James, Jr.
"County Fair." [AnthNEW] (7) 95, p. 41.
"Curbside." [LowellR] [1] Sum 94, p. 49.
"Reading Entrails." [LowellR] [1] Sum 94, p. 48.

474

WASHINGTON

6582. WASHINGTON, Romaine
"Drowning — Object Lesson #2." [LullwaterR] (6:1) Spr-Sum 95, p. 30-31.
6583. WASHINGTON, Shelly
"Alone Moves." [Footwork] (24/25) 95, p. 80.
"A Shadow in the Dark." [Footwork] (24/25) 95, p. 80.
6584. WATERHOUSE, Peter
"Constructive Procedure and Sweet Destiny" (tr. by Rosmarie Waldrop). [ManhatR] (7:2) Wint 95, p. 76.
"Leaving the Identical" (tr. by Rosmarie Waldrop). [ManhatR] (7:2) Wint 95, p. 77.
"Metamorphoses of the Leibniz Apple" (tr. by Rosmarie Waldrop). [ManhatR] (7:2) Wint 95, p. 75.
"The Widening of History" (tr. by Rosmarie Waldrop). [ManhatR] (7:2) Wint 95, p. 73-74.
6585. WATERHOUSE, Philip A.
"Salsa." [SantaBR] (3:2) Sum 95, p. 105.
6586. WATERS, Chris
"African Wrestling." [Parting] (8:2) Wint 95-96, p. 1.
"Quahogging." [Parting] (8:2) Wint 95-96, p. 28.
"Reticences." [HampSPR] Wint 95, p. 52.
"Rhus Radicans. Nahnosewak. Poison Ivy." [Parting] (8:2) Wint 95-96, p. 27.
6587. WATERS, Clay
"Returning to Lebenswelt." [PoetL] (90:3) Fall 95, p. 13-14.
6588. WATERS, Mary Ann
"The Flatteners." [FreeL] (14) Wint 95, p. 28-29.
6589. WATERS, Michael
"The Brooch." [Ploughs] (21:4) Wint 95-96, p. 172.
"Burning the Dolls." [SenR] (25:1) Spr 95, p. 62-63.
"Chrisoms" (early 19th C.). [Chelsea] (59) 95, p. 159.
"The Curiosities" (Medical Museum, Walter Reed Hospital). [MissR] (23:3) 95, p. 90-91.
"Parthenopi" (Ios). [GeoR] (49:2) Sum 95, p. 467.
"Pass-the-Plate." [CrabOR] (1:1) Fall-Wint 95, p. 141-142.
6590. WATERSON, Michael
"Elvis in Hell." [SantaBR] (3:1) Spr 95, p. 116.
"The 'h' in 'Pittsburgh'." [SantaBR] (3:1) Spr 95, p. 114.
"Mimosa." [SantaBR] (3:1) Spr 95, p. 113.
"Moon Walk." [SantaBR] (3:1) Spr 95, p. 115.
6591. WATKINS, Janiko J.
"Whole Note." [HangL] (67) 95, p. 99.
6592. WATKINS, William John
"Floral Arrangement" (for Wade 1963-1993). [Hellas] (6:2) Fall-Wint 95, p. 69.
"Ghost-Gathering." [Hellas] (6:2) Fall-Wint 95, p. 70.
"Great Petrarchan." [WindO] (60) Fall-Wint 95, p. 14.
"I Did Not Hug My Father at the End." [SoCaR] (28:1) Fall 95, p. 60.
"Inheritance." [Hellas] (6:2) Fall-Wint 95, p. 71.
"Jump Cut." [SoCaR] (28:1) Fall 95, p. 61.
"Lovers' Quarrels." [SoCaR] (28:1) Fall 95, p. 60-61.
"The Mad Professor Grades." [Hellas] (6:1) Spr-Sum 95, p. 28-29.
"The Mad Professor Sinks." [SoCaR] (28:1) Fall 95, p. 59.
"Old Wood Burns Best." [Bogg] (67) 95, p. 6.
"Your Mistress Is a Mouse with Pink Eyes." [Pearl] (22) Fall-Wint 95, p. 23.
6593. WATNIK, Harry
"He's a Good Boy." [Plain] (16:1) Fall 95, p. 6.
"Prisoner of the Bender." [RagMag] (12:2) Spr 95, p. 78.
"Tramping On." [SmPd] (32:1, #93) Wint 95, p. 37.
6594. WATSON, Anne
"Pride." [AnthNEW] (7) 95, p. 14.
6595. WATSON, Burton
"I came once to sit on Cold Mountain" (tr. of Han-shan, mid 7th c.). [Tricycle] (4:3, #15) Spr 95, p. 60.
"The Rabbit in the Moon" (tr. of Ryokan, Zen monk-poet, c. 1758-1831). [Tricycle] (4:4, #16) Sum 95, p. 56-57.
6596. WATSON, Craig
"Endurance" (For Michael Gizzi. Selections). [Avec] (9) 95, p. 50-60.

6597. WATSON, Ellen Doré
"E = MC^2." [Field] (53) Fall 95, p. 52.
"Funny How." [Field] (53) Fall 95, p. 50-51.
6598. WATSON, James
"Winter Sunset." [CarolQ] (48:1) Fall 95, p. 83.
6599. WATSON, Larry
"World Series." [NewEngR] (17:1) Wint 95, p. 125.
6600. WATSON, M. C.
"All That Was Said." [NewYorkQ] (54) 95, p. 82.
6601. WATSON, Miles
"Par Three with My Father." [QW] (41) Aut-Wint 95-96, p. 276.
6602. WATSON, Rebeccah (grade 4, Key Elementary, Washington, DC)
"Para Alguien" (tr. by Jacklyn W. Potter, Poetry on the Metro Project). [WashR]
(21:2) Ag-S 95, p. 15.
"To Someone" (Poetry on the Metro Project). [WashR] (21:2) Ag-S 95, p. 14.
6603. WATSON, Stephen
"//Kabbo's Request for Thread" (tr. of anonymous /Xam poem, w. W. H. Bleek and
Lucy Lloyd). [ColR] (22:1) Spr 95, p. 61.
"Our Blood Makes Smoke" (tr. of anonymous /Xam poem, w. W. H. Bleek and
Lucy Lloyd). [ColR] (22:1) Spr 95, p. 57.
"Song of the Broken String" (tr. of anonymous /Xam poem, w. W. H. Bleek and
Lucy Lloyd). [ColR] (22:1) Spr 95, p. 59-60.
"The Story of Ruyter" (tr. of anonymous /Xam poem, w. W. H. Bleek and Lucy
Lloyd). [ColR] (22:1) Spr 95, p. 58.
"The Wind Is One with the Man" (tr. of anonymous /Xam poem, w. W. H. Bleek
and Lucy Lloyd). [ColR] (22:1) Spr 95, p. 56.
6604. WATT, D.
"Oh Yeah?" [AxeF] (3) 90, p. 35.
6605. WATTERS, Samuel M.
"Coyote and White-Tailed Buck." [WeberS] (12:3) Fall 95, p. 82-83.
6606. WATTS, Koko
"Me and My Niggas" (WritersCorps Program, Washington, DC). [WashR] (21:2)
Ag-S 95, p. 11.
6607. WAYMAN, Tom
"The Burial of the Clown." [OntR] (43) Fall-Wint 95-96, p. 29-30.
"The Childhood of the Clown." [Event] (24:1) Spr 95, p. 45.
"The Death of the Clown." [OntR] (43) Fall-Wint 95-96, p. 27-28.
"The Monument to the Clown." [OntR] (43) Fall-Wint 95-96, p. 31-32.
"The Revenge of the Clown." [Event] (24:1) Spr 95, p. 46-47.
6608. WEATHERFORD, Carole Boston
"Sciatica." [Calyx] (16:1) Sum 95, p. 58-60.
6609. WEAVER, Margaret
"The Butterfly Effect." [PoetryNW] (36:2) Sum 95, p. 23.
"Escapes." [PoetryNW] (36:2) Sum 95, p. 22-23.
6610. WEAVER, Michael S.
"Enemies." [AfAmRev] (29:4) Wint 95, p. 623-624.
"The Southpaw." [AfAmRev] (29:4) Wint 95, p. 624-625.
6611. WEAVER, Roger
"The Man Who Wouldn't Fit In." [DogRR] (14:1, #27) Sum 95, p. 27.
6612. WEBB, Charles (Charles H., Charles Harper)
"20 Years Late to See *The Rocky Horror Picture Show.*" [MichQR] (34:4) Fall 95,
p. 516-517.
"At Supper Time." [ChironR] (43) Sum 95, p. 25.
"Bees." [LitR] (38:2) Wint 95, p. 289.
"Business As Usual." [Pearl] (22) Fall-Wint 95, p. 69.
"Buyer's Remorse." [QW] (40) Spr-Sum 95, p. 60.
"Le Comte de Weeb, Connoisseur of Fine Wine." [WormR] (35:2, #138) 95, p. 56-
57.
"Confession." [PoetL] (90:4) Wint 95-96, p. 16.
"The Crane Boy." [QW] (41) Aut-Wint 95-96, p. 148-149.
"Dandelions." [WormR] (35:2, #138) 95, p. 55-56.
"The Dead Run." [LaurelR] (29:1) Wint 95, p. 43.
"The Discovery of Poetry." [Pearl] (22) Fall-Wint 95, p. 71.
"Eating." [QW] (41) Aut-Wint 95-96, p. 150.
"Elephant Trunks." [SoCoast] (18) Ja 95, p. 59.

"Envying the President-Elect." [Pearl] (22) Fall-Wint 95, p. 70.
"Health." [PassN] (16:1) Sum 95, p. 3.
"Hollywood Confidential." [WormR] (35:2, #138) 95, p. 57.
"Marilyn's Machine." [ParisR] (37:135) Sum 95, p. 211.
"The Night My Father Died." [WormR] (35:1, #137) 95, p. 19.
"Not a *National Enquirer* Kind of Guy." [WormR] (35:2, #138) 95, p. 56.
"On the Efforts to Outlaw Sexual Relationships between Students and College
    Professors." [WormR] (35:1, #137) 95, p. 18.
"Parallel Lives." [WestB] (37) 95, p. 27.
"Prozac." [GreensboroR] (59) Wint 95-96, p. 119.
"A Refusal to Mourn a Bad Haircut." [WormR] (35:1, #137) 95, p. 17.
"The Shake and Bake Messiah." [ApalQ] (43) Spr 95, p. 71.
"She Drops into My Life." [SoCoast] (18) Ja 95, p. 21.
"Smoking." [NewYorkQ] (55) 95, p. 98.
"Sunglasses." [LaurelR] (29:1) Wint 95, p. 42.
"This Is Not a Song." [ChironR] (44/45) Aut-Wint 95, p. 18.
"Umbrellas." [HarvardR] (9) Fall 95, p. 99.
"Vandal Kills Vine Sculpture at Cal State Long Beach." [WormR] (35:2, #138) 95,
    p. 58.
"The Village Genius." [WestB] (37) 95, p. 26.
"The Way It Goes." [Jacaranda] (11) [95 or 96?], p. 86-87.
"Weeb Decides That, as a Child, Al Capone Must Have Decided to Skip Politics and
    Go Directly Into Crime." [ChironR] (42) Spr 95, p. 14.
"What the Poets Would Have Done for You." [PoetryE] (41) Aut 95, p. 52-53.
"With Head Held High." [WormR] (35:1, #137) 95, p. 17-18.
"Women's Beds." [Pearl] (22) Fall-Wint 95, p. 70.
6613. WEBB, Phyllis
"Three Anti Ghazals." [AntigR] (102/103) Sum-Aug 95, p. 227-229.
6614. WEBB, Robert
"Assessing the Blue Angel." [HampSPR] Wint 95, p. 17.
6615. WEBB, Sean
"Jot" (A sixties religious cartoon character with its own Sunday morning show).
    [OxfordM] (9:2) Fall-Wint 93, p. 8-9.
6616. WEBER, Diane E.
"White Crow." [Plain] (16:1) Fall 95, p. 38.
6617. WEBER, Elizabeth
"The Bull" (In memory of Isabel Weber, 1929-1992). [Verse] (12:3) 95, p. 53-55.
"January." [SycamoreR] (7:2) Sum 95, p. 21-22.
6618. WEBER, Mark
"And They Used to Call Faulkner in Oxford 'Count No Account'." [ChironR]
    (44/45) Aut-Wint 95, p. 27.
"A Drinking Buddy." [WormR] (35:2, #138) 95, p. 91.
"Etiquette." [WormR] (35:2, #138) 95, p. 90-91.
"Here Comes the Good Humor Man." [Pearl] (22) Fall-Wint 95, p. 82.
"Judsonian Therapy." [ChironR] (44/45) Aut-Wint 95, p. 27.
"Of Okies, Cheese, Chicken & Bread: Road Food." [WormR] (35:2, #138) 95, p. 90.
"Pensive." [WormR] (35:2, #138) 95, p. 92.
"She." [WormR] (35:2, #138) 95, p. 90.
"Superbowl Sunday Morning Comin' Down." [WormR] (35:2, #138) 95, p. 91.
"The Teapot Joan Scandal." [ChironR] (44/45) Aut-Wint 95, p. 27.
"Wino Wilderness." [Bogg] (67) 95, p. 21.
6619. WEBSTER, Catherine
"To the Fifty-Winged Egret Tree Along Moscher Slough." [BelPoJ] (46:2) Wint 95-
    96, p. 12.
6620. WEBSTER, Rachel J.
"A Mother's Death — the Soundings." [13thMoon] (13:1/2) 95, p. 45.
6621. WEBSTER, Rex
"Furnace." [PoetL] (90:3) Fall 95, p. 18.
"Stock Footage." [PoetL] (90:3) Fall 95, p. 19.
6622. WEE, Rebecca Liv
"Still Life." [Sonora] (30) Fall 95, p. 20.
6623. WEEKS, Robert Lewis
"Half-Way There." [HampSPR] Wint 95, p. 32.
"Harkening, Beyond Which Was Yesterday." [HampSPR] Wint 95, p. 33.
6624. WEEMS, Mary Elise
"Great Grandma Green (1882-1957)." [Pearl] (22) Fall-Wint 95, p. 144-145.

6625. WEHLE, Ellen
    "Elation." [PaintedB] (55/56) 95, p. 27.
    "Into the Well." [Plain] (15:2) Wint 95, p. 25.
    "Password." [Plain] (15:2) Wint 95, p. 24.
WEI, Guo
    See GUO, Wei
6626. WEI, Qingzhi (editor)
    "Poets' Jade Splinters" (Selections, tr. by Tony Barnstone and Chou Ping).
    [AmerPoR] (24:6) N-D 95, p. 41-50.
6627. WEIDMAN, Phil
    "6825." [WormR] (35:3, #139) 95, p. 135.
    "Addict." [WormR] (35:3, #139) 95, p. 126.
    "An Artist." [WormR] (35:3, #139) 95, p. 114.
    "At Norton Simon Museum." [WormR] (35:3, #139) 95, p. 112.
    "At the Controls." [WormR] (35:3, #139) 95, p. 104.
    "Backtrack" (with drawings by Rody Stains. 125 poems). [WormR] (35:3, #139) 95,
       p. 97-144.
    "Bad." [WormR] (35:3, #139) 95, p. 114.
    "Bait." [WormR] (35:3, #139) 95, p. 100.
    "Bank It." [WormR] (35:3, #139) 95, p. 130.
    "Bathtub Plug." [WormR] (35:3, #139) 95, p. 142.
    "Before It Gets Ugly." [WormR] (35:3, #139) 95, p. 134.
    "Before Me." [WormR] (35:3, #139) 95, p. 114.
    "Before the Wick Burns Out." [WormR] (35:3, #139) 95, p. 136.
    "Best Interests." [WormR] (35:3, #139) 95, p. 140.
    "Blue Sunday." [WormR] (35:3, #139) 95, p. 138.
    "Bubba." [WormR] (35:3, #139) 95, p. 113.
    "Bucking the Odds." [WormR] (35:3, #139) 95, p. 140.
    "Bypass." [WormR] (35:3, #139) 95, p. 130.
    "Call." [WormR] (35:3, #139) 95, p. 133.
    "Called." [WormR] (35:3, #139) 95, p. 132.
    "Child Proof." [WormR] (35:3, #139) 95, p. 108.
    "Circle." [WormR] (35:3, #139) 95, p. 124.
    "Clarity." [WormR] (35:3, #139) 95, p. 101.
    "Claude's Pin." [WormR] (35:3, #139) 95, p. 137.
    "Cleavage." [WormR] (35:3, #139) 95, p. 136.
    "Close to Home." [WormR] (35:3, #139) 95, p. 127.
    "Conversation." [WormR] (35:3, #139) 95, p. 142.
    "Correspondence." [WormR] (35:3, #139) 95, p. 102.
    "Couple." [WormR] (35:3, #139) 95, p. 124.
    "Cowboy Boots." [WormR] (35:3, #139) 95, p. 108.
    "Crack." [WormR] (35:3, #139) 95, p. 132.
    "Dad's Bow." [WormR] (35:3, #139) 95, p. 140.
    "December Visit to North Coast." [WormR] (35:3, #139) 95, p. 134.
    "Discount." [WormR] (35:3, #139) 95, p. 110.
    "Ernie's Wish." [WormR] (35:3, #139) 95, p. 126.
    "Even If It's Wrong." [WormR] (35:3, #139) 95, p. 138.
    "For the Teacher." [WormR] (35:3, #139) 95, p. 116.
    "Golden Eagle." [WormR] (35:3, #139) 95, p. 99.
    "Gordon's Blue Shoes." [WormR] (35:3, #139) 95, p. 118.
    "Guidance." [WormR] (35:3, #139) 95, p. 130.
    "Hard-Bound." [WormR] (35:3, #139) 95, p. 118.
    "Hard to Take." [WormR] (35:3, #139) 95, p. 100.
    "High." [WormR] (35:3, #139) 95, p. 139.
    "High Ground." [WormR] (35:3, #139) 95, p. 138.
    "Homesick." [WormR] (35:3, #139) 95, p. 98.
    "I Shut Off TV Talk." [WormR] (35:3, #139) 95, p. 100.
    "In Escrow." [WormR] (35:3, #139) 95, p. 124.
    "In the Mirror." [WormR] (35:3, #139) 95, p. 122.
    "Itch." [WormR] (35:3, #139) 95, p. 102.
    "Jump Start." [WormR] (35:3, #139) 95, p. 98.
    "Killing Time." [WormR] (35:3, #139) 95, p. 98.
    "Lesson in Aesthetics." [WormR] (35:3, #139) 95, p. 140.
    "Let It Ripen." [WormR] (35:3, #139) 95, p. 116.
    "Letters." [WormR] (35:3, #139) 95, p. 120.
    "Linked." [WormR] (35:3, #139) 95, p. 123.

"Little Glory." [WormR] (35:3, #139) 95, p. 143.
"Loser." [WormR] (35:3, #139) 95, p. 136.
"Loss." [WormR] (35:3, #139) 95, p. 106.
"Lost." [WormR] (35:3, #139) 95, p. 110.
"Lunch in Paradise." [WormR] (35:3, #139) 95, p. 110.
"Macho Side." [WormR] (35:3, #139) 95, p. 111.
"Made Up." [WormR] (35:3, #139) 95, p. 116.
"Magic Water Jar." [WormR] (35:3, #139) 95, p. 106.
"Mark." [WormR] (35:3, #139) 95, p. 132.
"Master." [WormR] (35:3, #139) 95, p. 134.
"Mementoes" [sic]. [WormR] (35:3, #139) 95, p. 112.
"Message: Drinking Diet Rite." [WormR] (35:3, #139) 95, p. 119.
"Message: When I had a studio." [WormR] (35:3, #139) 95, p. 112.
"Mom's Bell." [WormR] (35:3, #139) 95, p. 115.
"Mom's Dog Rule." [WormR] (35:3, #139) 95, p. 134.
"My Wobble." [WormR] (35:3, #139) 95, p. 100.
"Never Too Late to Score." [WormR] (35:3, #139) 95, p. 130.
"No Evil Could." [WormR] (35:3, #139) 95, p. 109.
"No Joke." [WormR] (35:3, #139) 95, p. 126.
"No Thanks." [WormR] (35:3, #139) 95, p. 122.
"Not So Old." [WormR] (35:3, #139) 95, p. 108.
"Old Topper." [WormR] (35:3, #139) 95, p. 126.
"Omen." [WormR] (35:3, #139) 95, p. 108.
"On Hands & Knees." [WormR] (35:3, #139) 95, p. 131.
"One-Way Conversation." [WormR] (35:3, #139) 95, p. 129.
"Parcel." [WormR] (35:3, #139) 95, p. 110.
"Pat's Dilemma." [WormR] (35:3, #139) 95, p. 118.
"The Perfect Time." [WormR] (35:3, #139) 95, p. 136.
"Potential." [WormR] (35:3, #139) 95, p. 138.
"Punctuation." [WormR] (35:3, #139) 95, p. 102.
"Ralph's Story." [WormR] (35:3, #139) 95, p. 132.
"Reading." [WormR] (35:3, #139) 95, p. 116.
"Right Mind." [WormR] (35:3, #139) 95, p. 104.
"Scouting High Sierra." [WormR] (35:3, #139) 95, p. 106.
"Scrutiny." [WormR] (35:3, #139) 95, p. 118.
"Search." [WormR] (35:3, #139) 95, p. 100.
"A Select Few." [WormR] (35:3, #139) 95, p. 128.
"Setting the World Right." [WormR] (35:3, #139) 95, p. 117.
"Shadow of Truth." [WormR] (35:3, #139) 95, p. 102.
"Shootings." [WormR] (35:3, #139) 95, p. 112.
"Small Summer Harvest." [WormR] (35:3, #139) 95, p. 142.
"A Sober Feast." [WormR] (35:3, #139) 95, p. 104.
"Some Friend." [WormR] (35:3, #139) 95, p. 121.
"Something for Nothing." [WormR] (35:3, #139) 95, p. 98.
"Splitting Fir Rounds." [WormR] (35:3, #139) 95, p. 107.
"Sponsor." [WormR] (35:3, #139) 95, p. 128.
"Squeeze." [WormR] (35:3, #139) 95, p. 116.
"Stop the Movie." [WormR] (35:3, #139) 95, p. 132.
"Strung Out." [WormR] (35:3, #139) 95, p. 106.
"Support." [WormR] (35:3, #139) 95, p. 108.
"There's a Limit." [WormR] (35:3, #139) 95, p. 122.
"These Occurrences." [WormR] (35:3, #139) 95, p. 114.
"Third Period." [WormR] (35:3, #139) 95, p. 103.
"Timing." [WormR] (35:3, #139) 95, p. 142.
"Too Late." [WormR] (35:3, #139) 95, p. 125.
"Two-Gallon Redwood." [WormR] (35:3, #139) 95, p. 136.
"Two of Me." [WormR] (35:3, #139) 95, p. 112.
"Unstable." [WormR] (35:3, #139) 95, p. 124.
"Visit with Alice." [WormR] (35:3, #139) 95, p. 105.
"Visual Learner." [WormR] (35:3, #139) 95, p. 128.
"Waiting for Marty." [WormR] (35:3, #139) 95, p. 128.
"Waitress." [WormR] (35:3, #139) 95, p. 130.
"Walking Mantra." [WormR] (35:3, #139) 95, p. 140.
"Wall." [WormR] (35:3, #139) 95, p. 98.
"A Warrior." [WormR] (35:3, #139) 95, p. 104.
"What It Used to Be Like." [WormR] (35:3, #139) 95, p. 104.

479

"Who Knows?" [WormR] (35:3, #139) 95, p. 138.
"Who's Craziest?" [WormR] (35:3, #139) 95, p. 142.
"Wishful Thinking." [WormR] (35:3, #139) 95, p. 110.
"Working Step Four." [WormR] (35:3, #139) 95, p. 141.
"You Guessed It." [WormR] (35:3, #139) 95, p. 122.
6628. WEIGEL, John A.
"Moonstruck." [Light] (13) Spr 95, p. 21.
6629. WEIGL, Bruce
"Color" (tr. of Nguyen Quyen, w. Nguyen Ba Chung). [Manoa] (7:2) Wint 95, p.
160.
"Mathematics" (tr. of Liliana Ursu). [KenR] (17:3/4) Sum-Fall 95, p. 117.
"The Russian Army in Moldova" (tr. of Liliana Ursu). [KenR] (17:3/4) Sum-Fall 95,
p. 117.
"Saint Anthony" (tr. of Liliana Ursu). [KenR] (17:3/4) Sum-Fall 95, p. 116.
6630. WEIL, Joe
"Elegy for Lady Clairol" (For my mother). [Footwork] (24/25) 95, p. 46.
"In My Universe There Is No Hope" (A Poem of Joy). [JINJPo] (17:2) Aut 95, p.
38-39.
"Ode to Elizabeth." [Footwork] (24/25) 95, p. 46-48.
"Upon Considering the Lust of Ken and Barbie." [JlNJPo] (17:2) Aut 95, p. 37.
6631. WEINBERGER, Florence
"God Let Moses See His Back" (based on a painting, *The Village of the Mermaids,*
by Paul Delvaux). [AnotherCM] (29) Spr 95, p. 186-187.
"Questions Regarding a Dream of Incompatible Fruit." [AnotherCM] (29) Spr 95, p.
188.
6632. WEINER, Estha
"In the Cemetery." [GlobalCR] (6) Fall 95, p. 98.
6633. WEINER, Hannah
"Ubliminal" [sic]. [Chain] (2) Spr 95, p. 238-239.
6634. WEINER, Jesse
"I Once Had a Friend." [NewYorkQ] (54) 95, p. 106.
6635. WEINER, Joshua
"The Dog State." [BostonR] (20:2) Ap-My 95, p. 17.
"Who They Were" (first appeared in *Threepenny Review,* Spring 1993). [BostonR]
(20:2) Ap-My 95, p. 17.
6636. WEINGARTEN, Roger
"Overwhelmed by Puberty, There Were." [GreenMR] (8:1) Spr-Sum 95, p. 99-101.
6637. WEINSTEIN, Debra
"In the Year of My Grandfather." [NewMyths] (2:2/3:1) 95, p. 70-71.
"The Story of Life." [AmerPoR] (24:3) My-Je 95, p. 5.
6638. WEINSTEIN, Muriel Harris
"Residents of the Margaret Tietz Nursing Home." [CapeR] (30:2) Fall 95, p. 11.
6639. WEINSTEIN, Norman
"Through a Blues Lens (Portrait of Arizona Dranes)." [RiverC] (15:2) Sum 95, p.
11.
"Through a Blues Lens (Portrait of Robert Pete Williams)." [RiverC] (15:2) Sum 95,
p. 10.
"Through a Blues Lens (Portrait of Thelonious Monk)." [RiverC] (15:2) Sum 95, p.
12.
6640. WEIR, Donna M.
"Baby Duppy" (An abortion poem or a response to *Beloved*). [CaribbeanW] (9) 95,
p. 21-22.
"Snapshots, Headlines and Clippings." [CaribbeanW] (9) 95, p. 17-20.
6641. WEISBERG, Barbara
"Tradition." [Bogg] (67) 95, p. 56.
6642. WEISS, David
"The Messenger of Space." [SenR] (25:1) Spr 95, p. 90.
"Wrist Watches." [TarRP] (35:1) Fall 95, p. 31.
6643. WEISS, Jason
"Crema Catalana" (tr. of Luisa Futoransky). [Sulfur] (15:2, #37) Fall 95, p. 132.
"She, the Fisherwoman" (tr. of Luisa Futoransky). [Sulfur] (15:2, #37) Fall 95, p.
133.
6644. WEISS, Mark
"Painted." [GrandS] (14:2, #54) Fall 95, p. 212-214.
6645. WEISSBORT, Daniel
"Between Scylla and Charybdis" (tr. of Yunna Morits). [InterQ] (2:1/2) 95, p. 77-78.

"Face" (tr. of Yunna Morits). [InterQ] (2:1/2) 95, p. 79.
"Line" (tr. of Yunna Morits). [InterQ] (2:1/2) 95, p. 76.
"Na ustvennom advige ushedshikh v sebya" (tr. of Yunna Morits, w. L. Medlin).
    [InterQ] (2:1/2) 95, p. 75.
6646. WEISSLITZ, E. F.
    "Amaryllis." [HolCrit] (32:1) F 95, p. 17.
    "Fugitive." [WindO] (59) Spr 95, p. 33.
6647. WEITZ, William
    "Crash." [Journal] (19:2) Fall-Wint 95, p. 56.
6648. WELCH, Don
    "The Funeral of Ice." [Nimrod] (39:1) Fall-Wint 95, p. 131.
    "Sarah." [PraS] (69:3) Fall 95, p. 143.
    "Scene I, Involving You and an Owl." [MidwQ] (36:4) Sum 95, p. 453-454.
    "Two Snails." [Nimrod] (39:1) Fall-Wint 95, p. 133.
6649. WELCH, Enid Santiago
    "Well-Fare with No Address." [MassR] (36:4) Wint 95-96, p. 655.
6650. WELCH, Lew
    "Memo Satori" (from Ring of Bone, 1973). [Tricycle] (5:1, #17) Fall 95, p. 79.
    "Step out onto the Planet" (from Ring of Bone, 1973). [Tricycle] (5:1, #17) Fall 95,
        p. 77.
6651. WELCH, Liliane
    "The Bookstore." [TickleAce] (27) Spr-Sum 94, p. 32.
    "The Cat." [TickleAce] (27) Spr-Sum 94, p. 33-34.
    "Nude with Head" (after a painting by Alberto Giacometti). [TickleAce] (27) Spr-
        Sum 94, p. 30.
    "Triptych." [TickleAce] (27) Spr-Sum 94, p. 31.
6652. WELISH, Marjorie
    "Collaborating with Materials." [Sulfur] (15:1, #36) Spr 95, p. 149-150.
    "Corresponding Saints." [Conjunc] (24) 95, p. 159.
    "New Preface by Author." [Sulfur] (15:1, #36) Spr 95, p. 148.
    "Preface." [Sulfur] (15:1, #36) Spr 95, p. 147.
6653. WELLER, Sonia Topper
    "It Was Always Your Voice." [WormR] (35:4, #140) 95, p. 151.
6654. WELLS, William
    "Tollbridge" (tr. of Salvatore Quasimodo). [OhioR] (54) 95, p. 31.
6655. WELSH, Lawrence
    "Black Lite." [ChironR] (43) Sum 95, p. 32.
    "Eastside Jazz." [WormR] (35:1, #137) 95, p. 14.
    "A True Profession." [WormR] (35:1, #137) 95, p. 15.
6656. WENDEROTH, Joe
    "Aesthetics of the Bases-Loaded Walk." [TriQ] (93) Spr-Sum 95, p. 100.
    "All the Hurry." [ConnPR] (14:1) 95, p. 21.
    "The Flat Road Runs Along Beside the Frozen River." [TriQ] (93) Spr-Sum 95, p.
        99.
    "Flowers Are a Tiresome Pastime" (— W. C. Williams). [TriQ] (93) Spr-Sum 95, p.
        101-102.
    "The half-want is all balance." [PraS] (69:3) Fall 95, p. 90.
    "In the Sentence of Sleep." [AmerPoR] (24:5) S-O 95, p. 16.
    "Like Blood from a Deep Cut." [PraS] (69:3) Fall 95, p. 90-91.
    "Morning Fiction." [AmerPoR] (24:5) S-O 95, p. 16.
    "New Dim." [ConnPR] (14:1) 95, p. 22-23.
    "Outside the Hospital." [AmerPoR] (24:5) S-O 95, p. 16.
    "The Senate." [PraS] (69:3) Fall 95, p. 91.
    "You." [AmerPoR] (24:5) S-O 95, p. 16.
6657. WENDT, Ingrid
    "At Fort Ebey State Park, Washington: September, 1990." [WeberS] (12:2) Spr-Sum
        95, p. 68-69.
    "Finnmark, an Idyll" (for Nils-Aslak Valkeapää). [Nimrod] (38:2) Spr-Sum 95, p.
        87.
    "Gas. 1940" (After a Painting by Edward Hopper). [WeberS] (12:2) Spr-Sum 95, p.
        67.
    "In This Columbus Year, I Look Back on My Life" (for Stephen Dow Beckham and
        Dell Hymes). [WeberS] (12:2) Spr-Sum 95, p. 68.
    "Jade Plant in Split Couplets." [ManyMM] (1:2) 95, p. 121.
    "Words of Our Time" (for Jorge Montealegre). [ManyMM] (1:2) 95, p. 119-120.

481

WHEELER

6658. WENTHE, William
"Along the C & O Right-of-Way." [Image] (10) Sum 95, p. 85-86.
"Story." [Image] (10) Sum 95, p. 86-87.
6659. WENTWORTH, Don
"Small Press Blues" (The Editor's Cut). [Bogg] (67) 95, p. 66.
6660. WERNER, Judith
"After the Fall." [Elf] (5:3) Fall 95, p. 33.
"Don't Worry, This Won't Be Graphic." [FourQ] (9:1/2) Spr 95, p. 63.
"Every Eskimo Is Someone's Aunt." [FourQ] (9:1/2) Spr 95, p. 62.
"In the Women's Spa." [Elf] (5:3) Fall 95, p. 32.
WERT, William (William F.) van
See VAN WERT, William (William F.)
6661. WESLOWSKI, Dieter
"Hands." [Os] (40) 95, p. 9.
"Once, I Sang the Wounds of Hernandez." [AxeF] (3) 90, p. 28.
"Once Upon a Time." [Os] (41) 95, p. 16.
"The Piano Notes Are Not." [AxeF] (3) 90, p. 28.
"Remembering Santander." [Os] (40) 95, p. 8.
"Terrible Angel." [PoetryE] (40) Spr 95, p. 129.
"Xavier." [NewOR] (21:3/4) Fall-Wint 95, p. 111.
6662. WEST, Alan
"The House of Wonders" (tr. by the author). [Noctiluca] (2:1, #4) Spr 95, p. 51-52.
6663. WEST, Marlys
"Bus Freaks" (runner up, 1994 Borderlands Poetry Contest). [Border] (6) Spr-Sum 95, p. 72-74.
6664. WEST, Richard M.
"The Aging Poet Is Apt to Play Hamlet Badly." [Bogg] (67) 95, p. 67.
"Losing It." [Pearl] (22) Fall-Wint 95, p. 12.
6665. WEST, Thomas A., Jr.
"Peace." [NewRena] (9:2, #28) Spr 95, p. 85.
6666. WESTERFIELD, Nancy G.
"Bible Study." [ChrC] (112:18) 24-31 My 95, p. 573.
"Drumming the Risen Lord." [ChrC] (112:12) 12 Ap 95, p. 389.
"Goes with the Territory." [Comm] (122:3) 10 F 95, p. 10.
"Jesus, His Winter." [ChrC] (112:4) 1-8 F 95, p. 114.
"Salad Ladies." [Comm] (122:2) 27 Ja 95, p. 14.
"Skeleton Staff." [ChrC] (112:34) 22-29 N 95, p. 1127.
6667. WESTERGAARD, Diane
"Elva." [CapeR] (30:1) Spr 95, p. 2-3.
6668. WETZSTEON, Rachel
"Surgical Moves." [PartR] (62:3) Sum 95, p. 452-453.
6669. WHALEN, John (John James)
"In My Sky." [YellowS] (12:4, #48) Sum 95, p. 40.
"Radio." [WillowS] (36) Je 95, p. 25.
6670. WHALEN, Tom
"Atonement." [ProseP] (4) 95, p. 75.
"The Murderess" (tr. of Robert Walser, w. Annette Wiesner). [ProseP] (4) 95, p. 73-74.
6671. WHALLEY, Karen
"Falling." [PassN] (16:2) Wint 95, p. 20-21.
"Love Must Be Actual." [PassN] (16:2) Wint 95, p. 22-23.
6672. WHEATLEY, Patience
"Annunciation to the Shepherds" (Cornelius Salteven 1607-1681). [Descant] (26:3, #90) Fall 95, p. 117.
"The Book" (From an Australian childhood). [Descant] (26:3, #90) Fall 95, p. 118.
"The Dedication: Talking Dirty" (To Louise, Barb, Ron, Judith and Kris). [Descant] (26:3, #90) Fall 95, p. 115-116.
6673. WHEDON, Tony
"Hornets." [HayF] (17) Fall-Wint 95, p. 68.
"Xinxiang Melons." [Confr] (56/57) Sum-Fall 95, p. 328.
6674. WHEELER, Charles B.
"Received at the Old Windmill" (winner, 1955 Winter Competition: Poetry). [Colum] (24/25) 95, p. 67-68.
"Supermarket" (corrected reprint from Fall 94 issue). [CumbPR] (14:2) Spr 95, p. 1-2.

WHEELER, Karen E. Brown
    See BROWN-WHEELER, Karen E.
6675. WHEELER, Sue
    "Blues Are So Hard." [Bogg] (67) 95, p. 18.
    "Everything Insists." [Event] (24:1) Spr 95, p. 49.
    "Not the Whole Story." [Quarry] (44:2) 95, p. 139-140.
    "Oaxaca. Renoir's 'Luncheon of the Boating Party'." [AntigR] (100) Wint 95, p. 162.
    "Season of Babies" (for Nigel, about-to-be-born). [Event] (24:1) Spr 95, p. 48.
6676. WHEELER, Susan
    "Alphabet's End." [ParisR] (37:135) Sum 95, p. 287-288.
    "Beavis' Day Off." [WestHR] (49:3) Fall 95, p. 255.
    "The Blanching Heart." [Chain] (2) Spr 95, p. 243-244.
    "Carnivorous Fowl, and Otherwise." [AmerLC] (7) 95, p. 97.
    "Ezra's Lament." [ColR] (22:2) Fall 95, p. 181-182.
    "Fractured Fairy Tale." [AmerLC] (7) 95, p. 98.
    "Knit in Your Will." [ParisR] (37:135) Sum 95, p. 287.
    "Landscaping for Privacy." [ParisR] (37:135) Sum 95, p. 285.
    "The Lip of the Snow in Lapland." [ColR] (22:2) Fall 95, p. 183.
    "Run on a Warehouse." [ParisR] (37:135) Sum 95, p. 286.
    "Sap Assured." [WestHR] (49:3) Fall 95, p. 254.
6677. WHINKLA, F. S.
    "Elegy, for Richard Brautigan." [DogRR] (14:1, #27) Sum 95, p. 3.
    "October 29, 1942." [DogRR] (14:1, #27) Sum 95, p. 25.
6678. WHITE, Anthony
    "Sestina for Six Surly Chefs and One Young Goat." [SouthernPR] (35:2) Wint 95, p.
        9-11.
6679. WHITE, Boyd
    "Cartography." [ManyMM] (2:1) 95, p. 45.
    "The Dark Country." [ManyMM] (2:1) 95, p. 47.
    "Gloaming." [ManyMM] (2:1) 95, p. 46.
6680. WHITE, Claire Nicolas
    "The Legend of Genoveva." [Prima] (18/19) 95, p. 41-49.
6681. WHITE, Danielle
    "Untitled: I know somebody that's fake, foggy and fresh" (WritersCorps Project,
        Washington, DC). [WashR] (21:2) Ag-S 95, p. 22.
6682. WHITE, Doris
    "Connecticut Night." [Footwork] (24/25) 95, p. 143.
    "Dream Dancing." [Footwork] (24/25) 95, p. 143.
6683. WHITE, Gail
    "Dead Armadillos." [ChironR] (44/45) Aut-Wint 95, p. 30.
    "The Intercessors." [ChironR] (44/45) Aut-Wint 95, p. 30.
    "Morton Arboretum." [MidwQ] (37:1) Aut 95, p. 50-51.
    "No Epitaphs, Please." [ChironR] (44/45) Aut-Wint 95, p. 30.
    "The Superior Nature of Animals." [ChironR] (44/45) Aut-Wint 95, p. 30.
    "The Virgin at Torcello." [Hellas] (6:1) Spr-Sum 95, p. 68.
6684. WHITE, J. D.
    "Erie Squall." [SewanR] (103:4) Fall 95, p. 505-506.
6685. WHITE, Jennifer
    "Pumpkin Woman's Grief." [WindO] (59) Spr 95, p. 35.
6686. WHITE, Julie Herrick
    "Hope College." [SycamoreR] (7:1) Wint 95, p. 32.
    "Naming the Buttons." [SoCaR] (28:1) Fall 95, p. 56-57.
6687. WHITE, Marian Frances
    "For Tommy (1957-1993)." [TickleAce] (27) Spr-Sum 94, p. 49-50.
    "March Wind Chimes" (a tribute to Cassie Brown 1919-1989). [TickleAce] (27)
        Spr-Sum 94, p. 51-52.
6688. WHITE, Michael
    "Bay of Naples." [Ploughs] (21:4) Wint 95-96, p. 175.
    "Ghost Pond." [Journal] (19:2) Fall-Wint 95, p. 13-14.
    "Here Below." [WestHR] (49:3) Fall 95, p. 222-223.
    "Palma Cathedral." [ColR] (22:1) Spr 95, p. 23-33.
    "Port Townsend." [Ploughs] (21:4) Wint 95-96, p. 173-174.
    "Promontory Point." [WestHR] (49:3) Fall 95, p. 224.
6689. WHITE, Mimi
    "Haareschneideraum: The Haircutting Room." [HarvardR] (8) Spr 95, p. 110-111.

6690. WHITE, Patti
"The Cipher." [HopewellR] (7) 95, p. 118-119.
6691. WHITE, Sharon
"Bone House." [Kalliope] (17:3) 95, p. 59-63.
6692. WHITE, Steven F.
"Circle" (tr. of Edimilson de Almeida Pereira). [Callaloo] (18:4) Fall 95, p. 714.
"The Dancer" (tr. of Edimilson de Almeida Pereira). [Callaloo] (18:4) Fall 95, p. 716.
"Fairy Tales for a Black Northeast" (tr. of Lepê Correia). [Callaloo] (18:4) Fall 95, p. 820.
"The Fruit" (tr. of Edimilson de Almeida Pereira). [Callaloo] (18:4) Fall 95, p. 715.
"Iron" (tr. of Edimilson de Almeida Pereira). [Callaloo] (18:4) Fall 95, p. 717.
"Meta-Score" (To D'Jesus Correia, tr. of Lepê Correia). [Callaloo] (18:4) Fall 95, p. 819.
"School" (tr. of Edimilson de Almeida Pereira). [Callaloo] (18:4) Fall 95, p. 713.
6693. WHITEBIRD, Joanie
"Afternoon at the Museum with Robert." [Vis] (49) 95, p. 16.
6694. WHITEHEAD, Catherine E.
"Atalanta." [CumbPR] (15:1) Fall 95, p. 62.
6695. WHITEHEAD, Gary J.
"Lazarus." [LowellR] [1] Sum 94, p. 55.
"Nocturne." [FreeL] (14) Wint 95, p. 18.
"Nor'easter." [FreeL] (14) Wint 95, p. 17.
"The Not So Latest Dance Craze." [LiteralL] (1:4) Ja-F 95, p. 21.
"Storm." [FreeL] (14) Wint 95, p. 16.
"Totem." [FreeL] (14) Wint 95, p. 17.
6696. WHITEHOUSE, Lisa
"Beginning" (for C.). [BellArk] (11:3) My-Je 95, p. 11.
WHITEMAN, Carol DuVal
See BLUE SPRUCE, Paula
6697. WHITLOW, Carolyn Beard
"Verily, Vérité." [KenR] (17:3/4) Sum-Fall 95, p. 155-159.
6698. WHITMAN, Ruth
"The Behavior of Birds." [YaleR] (83:4) O 95, p. 74.
"Vincent." [FreeL] (15) Aut 95, p. 11.
6699. WHITMAN, Walt (1819-1892)
"I Am He that Aches with Love." [PoetryE] (41) Aut 95, p. 35.
6700. WHITT, Laurie Anne
"Words for Relocation" (for Pauline Whitesinger). [Northeast] (5:12) Sum 95, p. 4-5.
6701. WHITTEMORE, Reed
"Ants." [Light] (13) Spr 95, p. 3.
"Ivies." [Light] (13) Spr 95, p. 5.
"A Late Bloomer" (reprinted from *The Faculty Voice,* University of Maryland). [Light] (13) Spr 95, p. 6.
"The Law of Inertia." [Light] (13) Spr 95, p. 5.
"Lear." [Light] (13) Spr 95, p. 6.
"Observations." [Light] (13) Spr 95, p. 3.
"On Writing." [Light] (13) Spr 95, p. 4.
"The Schools." [Light] (13) Spr 95, p. 5.
"A Swan There Was." [Light] (14) Sum 95, p. 10.
6702. WHITTEN, Les
"Half-Man." [Bogg] (67) 95, p. 3.
6703. WHITTER, Gail D.
"Memes." [Bogg] (67) 95, p. 37.
6704. WHITWORTH, Tom
"Suite: I Got You Me Us Them." [NewOR] (21:2) Sum 95, p. 51-54.
6705. WICKERS, Brian
"Moving Week" (2 selections). [MalR] (110) Spr 95, p. 110-111.
6706. WICKS, Susan
"A Disabled Toilet Is." [PoetryE] (39) Fall 94, p. 102.
"Weir." [CarolQ] (47:2) Wint 95, p. 33.
"When I Am Blind I Shall." [PoetryE] (39) Fall 94, p. 101.
6707. WIDERKEHR, Richard
"Moon Frogs." [WritersF] (21) 95, p. 162.
"Villanelle in Late-September." [HiramPoR] (58/59) Spr 95-Wint 96, p. 78.

6708. WIENEKE, Connie
"Coyote." [Stand] (36:2) Spr 95, p. 65-66.
6709. WIENER, Chet
"Non, Rien" (Excerpts, tr. of Agnès Rouzier). [Avec] (9) 95, p. 173-180.
6710. WIER, Dara
"5 1/2 Inch Lullaby." [Iowa] (25:1) Wint 95, p. 119.
"After the Birds Learned to Count to Eight." [BlackWR] (21:2) Spr-Sum 95, p. 52-53.
"Anything of Mine You Find Is Yours." [SouthernR] (31:1) Wint 95, p. 65.
"Company." [CrabOR] (1:1) Fall-Wint 95, p. 144-145.
"Interview." [HarvardR] (8) Spr 95, p. 107.
"Reflections Upon Sitting, Along with a Friend, for an Itinerant Painter, Manitoba, 1938." [BlackWR] (21:2) Spr-Sum 95, p. 54-55.
"Resolution." [CrabOR] (1:1) Fall-Wint 95, p. 143.
"A Secret Life." [Iowa] (25:1) Wint 95, p. 120-123.
6711. WIESE, Brooke
"Brooklyn Blues." [Ledge] (18) Sum 95, p. 53.
"Jazzed Up." [Ledge] (18) Sum 95, p. 54-56.
"Obsession Poem No. 7." [Plain] (15:3) Spr 95, p. 16-17.
"The Pier Was Dark and Slick and You Were Ash." [Flyway] (1:1) Spr 95, p. 14.
"Whose Perfume Am I Wearing Tonight, Writing." [LaurelR] (29:2) Sum 95, p. 86.
6712. WIESELTIER, Meir
"The Fowl of the Air" (tr. by Shirley Kaufman). [Field] (53) Fall 95, p. 72.
"Thin Livestock" (tr. by Shirley Kaufman). [Field] (53) Fall 95, p. 71.
"Window to the Future" (from "Windows near Mallarmé," tr. by Shirley Kaufman). [Field] (53) Fall 95, p. 73.
6713. WIESENTHAL, Chris
"Marionette Moves at the Salpêtrière Hospital for Hysterics, Paris, 1880" (for Greg Betts). [PottPort] (16:1) Fall 95, p. 14-16.
6714. WIESNER, Annette
"The Murderess" (tr. of Robert Walser, w. Tom Whalen). [ProseP] (4) 95, p. 73-74.
6715. WIGGINS, Dana (grade 9, Wilson High School, Washington, DC)
"Across from You" (Poetry on the Metro Project). [WashR] (21:2) Ag-S 95, p. 15.
WIGHTMAN, Ludmilla G. Popova
See POPOVA-WIGHTMAN, Ludmilla G.
6716. WILBUR, Frederick
"The Marbled Orb Weaver." [CumbPR] (14:2) Spr 95, p. 56.
"Under the Vulture Tree." [CumbPR] (14:2) Spr 95, p. 57.
6717. WILBUR, Richard
"Bone Key." [Atlantic] (276:3) S 95, p. 83.
"Compulsions." [Atlantic] (276:3) S 95, p. 83.
"Zea." [NewYorker] (71:10) 1 My 95, p. 67.
6718. WILD, Peter
"Beethoven." [OhioR] (53) 95, p. 130.
"Bringing Back the Buffalo." [PoetL] (90:2) Sum 95, p. 48.
"Educational Reform." [MidAR] (15:1/2) 95, p. 35-36.
"General Fu's Heavenly Chicken Balls." [TampaR] (10) Spr 95, p. 57.
"Martyrs." [WestHR] (49:1) Spr 95, p. 82.
"Petting Zoo." [TampaR] (10) Spr 95, p. 27.
"Pioneers." [WestHR] (49:1) Spr 95, p. 81.
"The Silent Dog Whistle." [OhioR] (53) 95, p. 131.
6719. WILDE-MENOZZI, Wallis
"As Light Pushed." [MissR] (23:3) 95, p. 93-94.
"Blanket." [MissR] (23:3) 95, p. 92.
"The Drops Make Noise." [MissR] (23:3) 95, p. 95-96.
6720. WILDER, Rex
"The Elk City, Oklahoma, Temporary Lake." [PoetL] (90:1) Spr 95, p. 31-32.
"Expecting You Home." [PoetL] (90:1) Spr 95, p. 30.
"The Last Ten Minutes." [ColR] (22:2) Fall 95, p. 184-185.
6721. WILDFONG, Rochelle
"On the Bus." [MassR] (36:2) Sum 95, p. 250-252.
6722. WILENSKY, Ben
"Coffee on the Morning Watch" (from *Psalms of a Sailor Jew: A Cycle of 18 Sea Poems*). [AmerPoR] (24:3) My-Je 95, p. 20.
"Injecting Poison." [Ledge] (19) Wint 95, p. 13-14.
"Order of the Day." [WritersF] (21) 95, p. 141.

"Widower." [Ledge] (19) Wint 95, p. 11-12.
6723. WILEY, J. B.
"I Dream." [SinW] (56) Sum-Fall 95, p. 20-21.
6724. WILK, Melvin Mordecai
"Things Are Looking Up." [MassR] (36:2) Sum 95, p. 300-301.
6725. WILKINS, Regina
"The Ammonia Stench of the Outhouse Hangs Thick" ("Ammonia" is spelled
       "Amonia" in poem). [Pembroke] (27) 95, p. 123.
"Where Is When." [PraS] (69:4) Wint 95, p. 143.
6726. WILKS, Jonathan
"While You Were Out." [AxeF] (3) 90, p. 26.
6727. WILLARD, Nancy
"Angel in a Window." [GettyR] (8:1) Wint 95, p. 141.
"The Garden of Stone Cabbages." [BelPoJ] (45:4) Chapbook 22, Sum 95, p. 74.
"Uninvited Houses." [BelPoJ] (45:4) Chapbook 22, Sum 95, p. 75.
"The Wisdom of the Jellyfish." [BelPoJ] (45:4) Chapbook 22, Sum 95, p. 76.
6728. WILLIAM (D.C. Center for Alcohol and Drug Abuse, Washington, DC)
"Ironing Boards" (WritersCorps Program). [WashR] (21:2) Ag-S 95, p. 5.
6729. WILLIAMS, Beverly J.
"Father." [Kaleid] (30) Wint-Spr 95, p. 42.
6730. WILLIAMS, C. K.
"Citadel" (tr. of Claire Malroux). [TriQ] (94) Fall 95, p. 191.
"Illumination" (tr. of Claire Malroux). [TriQ] (94) Fall 95, p. 193.
"Insight." [Thrpny] (63) Fall 95, p. 14.
"Prison for Stars" (tr. of Claire Malroux). [TriQ] (94) Fall 95, p. 192.
"Rough Being" (tr. of Claire Malroux). [TriQ] (94) Fall 95, p. 194.
6731. WILLIAMS, Darren
"My Morning" (WritersCorps Program, Washington, DC). [WashR] (21:2) Ag-S 95,
       p. 11.
"My Poem" (WritersCorps Program, Washington, DC). [WashR] (21:2) Ag-S 95, p.
       11.
6732. WILLIAMS, Hugo
"A Walking Gentleman." [Epoch] (44:3) 95, p. 296.
6733. WILLIAMS, James
"Arrival" (For Marina Pilar Gipps). [Poetry] (166:2) My 95, p. 103.
"Matriarchs." [WillowS] (36) Je 95, p. 11.
"Passage." [PoetL] (90:1) Spr 95, p. 21-22.
"Sleep." [WillowS] (36) Je 95, p. 10.
6734. WILLIAMS, John
"DOR: A Narrative Poem" (Excerpts). [AmerPoR] (24:2) Mr-Ap 95, p. 16.
6735. WILLIAMS, John (Washington, DC)
"What I Saw" (WritersCorps Project, Washington, DC). [WashR] (21:2) Ag-S 95, p.
       22.
6736. WILLIAMS, John A.
"Facing Jura: 50 Years After" (To Bill Robinson and Wendell J. Roye).
       [Drumvoices] (5:1/2) Fall-Wint 95-96, p. 105-106.
"Miami Red." [Drumvoices] (5:1/2) Fall-Wint 95-96, p. 103-104.
6737. WILLIAMS, Larry
"The Man Who Made His Anniversary Present" (WritersCorps Program,
       Washington, DC). [WashR] (21:2) Ag-S 95, p. 6.
6738. WILLIAMS, Marvin E.
"Freedom City, Homecoming." [CaribbeanW] (9) 95, p. 7-9.
"Long Bay (Beef Island)." [CaribbeanW] (9) 95, p. 10.
6739. WILLIAMS, Mary
"Inside Her Many-Hued Skins." [RiverS] (45) 95, p. 61-63.
6740. WILLIAMS, Melissa
"The Evidence of Clothes." [SpinningJ] (1) Fall 95-Wint 96, p. 6-7.
"Shhh" (for Andrew Cole). [SpinningJ] (1) Fall 95-Wint 96, p. 8.
6741. WILLIAMS, Miller
"Clutter of Silence" (Invention for Two Voices). [Hudson] (47:4) Wint 95, p. 583 -
       584.
"Holiday Inn: Surrounded by Someone Else's Reunion, He Comes to Terms" (for
       George Haley and the others). [KenR] (17:2) Spr 95, p. 144.
"Lay of the Badde Wyf." [Hudson] (47:4) Wint 95, p. 582-583.
"Living Will." [Hudson] (47:4) Wint 95, p. 586.
"On the Sacrifice of a Siamese Twin at Birth." [Hudson] (47:4) Wint 95, p. 586.

"A Tenth Anniversary Photograph, 1952." [Hudson] (47:4) Wint 95, p. 585.
6742. WILLIAMS, Norman
"Prayer for an Irish Father." [NewEngR] (17:1) Wint 95, p. 128.
"Taking Pan Fish" (Cedar Lake, Indiana). [NewEngR] (17:1) Wint 95, p. 127.
6743. WILLIAMS, Patricia C.
"I Be, Too." [Footwork] (24/25) 95, p. 159.
"Paterson Eyes." [Footwork] (24/25) 95, p. 159-160.
6744. WILLIAMS, Philip Lee
"Cinnamon Toast." [Poetry] (166:5) Ag 95, p. 264.
6745. WILLIAMS, Theresa A.
"She Lived in a Phantom World." [Footwork] (24/25) 95, p. 79.
6746. WILLIAMS, Thomas
"Afterthoughts of God in Absentia" (runner up, 1994 Borderlands Poetry Contest).
[Border] (6) Spr-Sum 95, p. 76.
"All the Way to Seaford" (runner up, 1994 Borderlands Poetry Contest). [Border]
(6) Spr-Sum 95, p. 75.
"A Tangle of Sparrows" (from *Alive Beyond Blue*). [AmerPoR] (24:1) Ja-F 95, p.
33.
6747. WILLIAMS, Tyrone
"How Like an Angel" (for Miles Davis, 1926-1991). [RiverS] (44) 95, p. 43-47.
"You Know What I'm Saying?" [RiverS] (44) 95, p. 48.
6748. WILLIAMSON, Alan
"Altamont." [Agni] (41) 95, p. 142-143.
"Dinosaurs" (after the PBS series). [VirQR] (71:3) Sum 95, p. 497-498.
"Enthusiasm." [VirQR] (71:3) Sum 95, p. 494-495.
"Letter to Santa Fe." [VirQR] (71:3) Sum 95, p. 495-496.
"Listening to Leonard Cohen" (Driving south from Charlottesville, January 1993).
[Agni] (41) 95, p. 139-141.
"The Moments." [NortheastCor] (3) 95, p. 107.
"Your Forest-Moonlight Picture." [NortheastCor] (3) 95, p. 106.
6749. WILLIAMSON, Greg
"Belvedere Marittimo." [SewanR] (103:2) Spr 95, p. 195.
"The Counterfeiter." [Poetry] (165:4) Ja 95, p. 195-196.
"A Dream Song." [PartR] (62:2) Spr 95, p. 302.
"The Field of Vision." [SewanR] (103:2) Spr 95, p. 197.
"Impression of Monet." [SewanR] (103:2) Spr 95, p. 196.
"The Mysterious Stranger." [Poetry] (165:4) Ja 95, p. 194.
"Up in the Air." [ParisR] (37:134) Spr 95, p. 36-37.
6750. WILLIAMSON, Stephen
"Finding the Airplane Too Late." [LiteralL] (1:4) Ja-F 95, p. 12.
"High Bridge above the Bronx River." [GreenHLL] (6) 95, p. 98-99.
6751. WILLIAMSON, Tharin
"Hosanna." [XavierR] (15:2) Fall 95, p. 38.
6752. WILLINGHAM, Sara
"Contact Print" (for Meg). [PoetryE] (41) Aut 95, p. 80-81.
"The Ledge." [PoetryE] (41) Aut 95, p. 79.
6753. WILLIS, Chinyere
"Daddy" (WritersCorps Project, Washington, DC). [WashR] (21:2) Ag-S 95, p. 22.
6754. WILLIS, Dawn Diez
"In the Photograph, a Boy." [WillowR] (22) Spr 95, p. 25.
6755. WILLIS, Omar
"The Willis Family" (WritersCorps Program, Washington, DC). [WashR] (21:2)
Ag-S 95, p. 6.
6756. WILLIS, Paul
"Cold Spring, East Fork." [SantaBR] (3:1) Spr 95, p. 84.
"Oso Creek." [SantaBR] (3:1) Spr 95, p. 83.
"Snake" (Matilija Wilderness). [SantaBR] (3:1) Spr 95, p. 83.
6757. WILLOUGHBY, N. C. Dylan
"At Carn Bugail, Gelligaer" (in memoriam for Vaughan). [GreenMR] (8:2) Fall-
Wint 95-96, p. 113.
6758. WILNER, Eleanor
"Abstraction." [BelPoJ] (45:4) Chapbook 22, Sum 95, p. 77-78.
"Facing into It." (for Larry Levis). [PraS] (69:1) Spr 95, p. 28-30.
"The Messenger" (for Marcia, and the man with orange hair). [PraS] (69:1) Spr 95,
p. 30-32.
"A Poem of Exile" (for Nell Altizer). [PraS] (69:1) Spr 95, p. 26-28.

"This Is Not the Truth." [NortheastCor] (3) 95, p. 37-38.
6759. WILOCH, Thomas
"Blessings." [Bogg] (67) 95, p. 57.
"Peter, Peter, Consumer of Vine-Grown Winter Squashes." [HawaiiR] (19:2) Fall 95, p. 96.
"Undersized Young Male Azure." [HawaiiR] (19:2) Fall 95, p. 97.
6760. WILSON, Charles A.
"The Love in Our Hearts" (WritersCorps Program, Washington, DC). [WashR] (21:2) Ag-S 95, p. 7.
6761. WILSON, David A.
"Alms for the Burned" (Tan Son Nhut, 1967). [War] (7:2) Fall-Wint 95, p. 51.
6762. WILSON, Dede
"Beside a Stone Lantern: Notes in a Japanese Journal." [PaintedB] (57) 95, p. 50.
"In Modern Japan, That Which Is Used Is Useless to Another, So I Imagine Him Burning His Boat Before He Leaves." [Flyway] (1:2) Fall 95, p. 32.
"Picture Shows." [HampSPR] Wint 95, p. 11.
"The Sun Rides on Its Own Melting." [HampSPR] Wint 95, p. 11.
"A World Begins to Speak." [Crucible] (31) Fall 95, p. 19.
WILSON, Fatima Lim
See LIM-WILSON, Fatima
6763. WILSON, Fiona
"Harp Music." [AntigR] (100) Wint 95, p. 62.
"Kelp." [GrandS] (13:3, #51) Wint 95, p. 137.
"Notes from Arizona." [Pequod] (39) 95, p. 89-94.
"Your Music." [AntigR] (100) Wint 95, p. 61.
6764. WILSON, Hannah
"The White Sweater." [Calyx] (16:1) Sum 95, p. 49.
"Widow's Walk." [Turnstile] (5:1) 95, p. 92-93.
6765. WILSON, John
"Birds." [LouisL] (12:1) Spr 95, p. 47.
"I Was." [LouisL] (12:1) Spr 95, p. 48.
6766. WILSON, Joyce
"The Burning Man." [HarvardR] (8) Spr 95, p. 111.
"There Are Days I Cannot Read" (Poem with Lines from Marianne Moore). [AntigR] (102/103) Sum-Aug 95, p. 182-183.
6767. WILSON, Leonore
"Almost Sonnet." [LaurelR] (29:2) Sum 95, p. 19.
6768. WILSON, Ralph
"Karl in Snow." [SenR] (25:2) Fall 95, p. 97.
"Leap or Become Invisible" (for James O'Ryan and Kevin Cantwell). [SenR] (25:2) Fall 95, p. 98-100.
6769. WILSON, Reed
"Aubade: The Gardens." [AntR] (53:2) Spr 95, p. 202.
"Edmund." [AntR] (53:2) Spr 95, p. 200-201.
6770. WILSON, Ronald
"Guide to Homes." [Poetry] (166:4) Jl 95, p. 197.
6771. WILSON, Steve
"Bearing Our Souls." [LitR] (38:2) Wint 95, p. 284.
"An Opening Volley Depicting the Matter of His Conceit." [MidwQ] (36:2) Wint 95, p. 166-167.
6772. WIMAN, Christian
"Elsewhere." [Poetry] (166:4) Jl 95, p. 192-193.
"Living Room" (For T. D. W., 1917-1974). [Poetry] (166:4) Jl 95, p. 193.
"The Long Home" (Excerpt). [PlumR] (8) [95], p. 61-65.
"The Long Home" (Excerpt). [Shen] (45:2) Sum 95, p. 5-14.
6773. WINAKUR, Jerald
"Are Butterflies Birds?" (Robert Penn Warren Poetry Prize: Second Prize). [CumbPR] (15:1) Fall 95, p. 63.
"A Denunciation of Quarks." [CumbPR] (15:1) Fall 95, p. 64.
6774. WINANS, A. D.
"Old Men." [ChironR] (44/45) Aut-Wint 95, p. 12.
"Reflections." [Footwork] (24/25) 95, p. 77.
"She Said." [ChironR] (44/45) Aut-Wint 95, p. 12.
"Tough Guy Poets." [ChironR] (44/45) Aut-Wint 95, p. 12.
6775. WINCH, Terence
"Angel Rush." [WestHR] (49:2) Sum 95, p. 121-122.

WINCKEL, Nance van
  See Van WINCKEL, Nance
6776. WIND, Chris
  "It's like a hunger strike, you assholes." [Bogg] (67) 95, p. 6.
6777. WINDAHL, Gibb
  "History." [PassN] (16:2) Wint 95, p. 32.
  "January." [GeoR] (49:4) Wint 95, p. 902-903.
  "Our Undoing." [PassN] (16:2) Wint 95, p. 33.
6778. WINDHAM, Carlos Kareem
  "I Want My MTV — a Poem." [ManyMM] (1:2) 95, p. 113-114.
6779. WINELAND, Jane A.
  "The Valley Revisited." [ChrC] (112:16) 10 My 95, p. 510.
6780. WINFIELD, Bill
  "Black Blood." [ManhatR] (8:1) Fall 95, p. 9.
  "Doll." [ManhatR] (8:1) Fall 95, p. 7.
  "Flying Object." [ManhatR] (8:1) Fall 95, p. 10.
  "Night Wind." [ManhatR] (8:1) Fall 95, p. 8.
6781. WINKLER, M.
  "The Minaret" (tr. by Bernhard Frank). [PoetryE] (40) Spr 95, p. 130.
6782. WINN, Steven
  "Phoebe Shops for Furniture." [Zyzzyva] (11:1, #41) Spr 95, p. 129.
6783. WINOGRAD, Kathryn
  "Blizzard." [WeberS] (12:2) Spr-Sum 95, p. 77-78.
  "How the Moon Saves Us from Chaotic Tilting." [PoetL] (90:2) Sum 95, p. 33-34.
  "Sleeping with Our Daughters." [DenQ] (30:2) Fall 95, p. 81-82.
  "The Weasel Sandman." [ManyMM] (1:3) 95, p. 24-25.
  "What Love Is." [WeberS] (12:2) Spr-Sum 95, p. 78-79.
WINTER, Corrine de
  See DeWINTER, Corrine
6784. WINTER, Jonah
  "Event Horizon in Bar Valhalla, New York." [Field] (52) Spr 95, p. 27-28.
6785. WINTER, Mary
  "The Sore on My Forehead's." [ApalQ] (44/45) Fall 95-Wint 96, p. 53-54.
6786. WINTER, Max
  "Sixteen Visions of the Immaculate Conception." [ParisR] (37:134) Spr 95, p. 163-165.
6787. WINTERER, Heather
  "Musing." [SpoonR] (20:2) Sum-Fall 95, p. 92-93.
6788. WINTERS, Bayla
  "Yes, Virginia, There Is a Forest Lawn." [FreeL] (15) Aut 95, p. 21.
6789. WINTERS, Mary
  "Diary." [Interim] (14:1) Spr-Sum 95, p. 25.
  "Difficult to Say." [PoetryE] (39) Fall 94, p. 103.
  "The Fleas' Tale." [WillowR] (22) Spr 95, p. 16.
  "Goodbye, Betty." [Parting] (8:2) Wint 95-96, p. 39.
  "Laughing at Another Person's Jokes." [PoetL] (90:2) Sum 95, p. 35.
  "Loser's Villanelle." [Border] (7) Fall-Wint 96, p. 67.
  "One Line from the Brothers Grimm." [ColEng] (57:2) F 95, p. 200.
  "Presentation Counts." [Comm] (122:20) 17 N 95, p. 16.
  "Robin Hood's Barn." [GreenHLL] (6) 95, p. 75.
  "Smoke." [ColEng] (57:2) F 95, p. 199.
  "Sort of a Ballad." [OxfordM] (10:1) Wint 94-Spr 95, p. 67.
  "Stuff." [GreenHLL] (6) 95, p. 76.
  "To a Dead House Fly." [SnailPR] (3:2) 95, p. 15.
  "Worth Saving." [Crucible] (31) Fall 95, p. 26.
  "You Forgot Your Glasses Today." [Interim] (14:1) Spr-Sum 95, p. 24.
6790. WINTERS, Paul-Victor
  "The Hyacinth" (for C. Salvatore). [Footwork] (24/25) 95, p. 207-208.
  "Poem in Three Parts for My Mother's Mother." [JlNJPo] (17:1) Spr 95, p. 32-35.
6791. WINWOOD, David
  "The Solution." [WritersF] (21) 95, p. 44.
6792. WIRTH-BROCK, Wendy
  "Docket #316" (Second Prize, The Pablo Neruda Prize for Poetry). [Nimrod] (39:1) Fall-Wint 95, p. 25-26.
  "Mary at Christmas" (Second Prize, The Pablo Neruda Prize for Poetry). [Nimrod] (39:1) Fall-Wint 95, p. 23.

"Night Vision" (Second Prize, The Pablo Neruda Prize for Poetry). [Nimrod] (39:1) Fall-Wint 95, p. 24.
6793. WISE, Eric
"Ka Knew." [AfAmRev] (29:3) Fall 95, p. 480.
6794. WITEK, Terri
"Baptismal Font." [SycamoreR] (7:2) Sum 95, p. 15.
"Errand." [OhioR] (53) 95, p. 125.
"The Hat." [SouthernR] (31:1) Wint 95, p. 66.
"Metallic." [SycamoreR] (7:2) Sum 95, p. 14.
"When Mother Was Famous." [NewRep] (213:20) 13 N 95, p. 49.
6795. WITHERS, Tamara
"Neighborhood" (WritersCorps Program, Washington, DC). [WashR] (21:2) Ag-S 95, p. 16.
6796. WITT, Harold
"About Robinson Jeffers" (one of three sonnets). [BellArk] (11:5) S-O 95, p. 31.
"At Dodd, Mead." [NewYorkQ] (54) 95, p. 104.
"At the Dilexi" (one of three sonnets). [BellArk] (11:5) S-O 95, p. 31.
"Biographies." [CharR] (21:1) Spr 95, p. 74.
"Los Comanches." [CharR] (21:1) Spr 95, p. 76.
"Drunk?" (one of three sonnets). [BellArk] (11:5) S-O 95, p. 31.
"Eros Denied." [Hellas] (6:1) Spr-Sum 95, p. 26.
"For Nothing." [CharR] (21:1) Spr 95, p. 75.
"A Hole in the World." [CharR] (21:1) Spr 95, p. 76.
"Homage to Ray Bradbury." [LitR] (38:3) Spr 95, p. 367-368.
"Jurassic Park." [CharR] (21:1) Spr 95, p. 74.
"Son of American Lit" (Selections: 2 poems). [BellArk] (11:1) Ja-F 95, p. 21.
"A Thousand Acres." [CharR] (21:1) Spr 95, p. 75.
6797. WITT, Sam
"Eclipse." [PoetryNW] (36:1) Spr 95, p. 24.
"Self-Portrait in a Dead Possum's Eye" (Honorable Mention, 1995 Editors' Prize). [SpoonR] (20:2) Sum-Fall 95, p. 46-47.
"Sunflower-Brother." [BlackWR] (21:2) Spr-Sum 95, p. 22-27.
"With Crickets." [GeoR] (49:2) Sum 95, p. 482-483.
WITT, Susan Kelly de
See KELLY-DeWITT, Susan
6798. WITTE, Francine
"Breath." [Ledge] (18) Sum 95, p. 21.
"First Rain." [Ledge] (18) Sum 95, p. 22.
6799. WITTE, George
"Halloween." [Flyway] (1:1) Spr 95, p. 100.
"Overlook." [Shen] (45:1) Spr 95, p. 24.
"Snapper." [Shen] (45:1) Spr 95, p. 25.
6800. WITTE, Phyllis
"To Grow Up in the Borough of Queens" (The 1994 Allen Ginsberg Poetry Awards: Honorable Mention). [Footwork] (24/25) 95, p. 205.
6801. WOESSNER, Warren
"Dead End." [MidwQ] (36:4) Sum 95, p. 456.
6802. WOHLFELD, Valerie
"The Creature of My Mother's Heart." [Epoch] (44:2) 95, p. 206.
"The Dreams of an Imaginary Woman." [Epoch] (44:2) 95, p. 205.
"In the Night Orchard." [Epoch] (44:2) 95, p. 208.
"The Two Necklaces." [Epoch] (44:2) 95, p. 207.
6803. WOJAHN, David
"After Wittgenstein." [TriQ] (95) Wint 95-96, p. 226-228.
"Allegorical Figure." [TriQ] (95) Wint 95-96, p. 232-233.
"Appetite: Black Paintings." [PoetryE] (41) Aut 95, p. 82-83.
"Dirge and Descent." [TriQ] (95) Wint 95-96, p. 238-239.
"Dirge Sung with Marianne Faithfull." [NoAmR] (280:5) S-O 95, p. 35.
"Excavation Photo." [GreenMR] (8:1) Spr-Sum 95, p. 18.
"Footage and Dirge." [PoetryE] (41) Aut 95, p. 84-85.
"Gallery IX: A Carved Bone Ring of Cormorants" (Edo Period, 1650). [PoetryNW] (36:3) Aut 95, p. 29-31.
"God of Journeys and Secret Tidings." [OhioR] (54) 95, p. 69.
"Hey, Joe." [TriQ] (95) Wint 95-96, p. 229-231.
"Lulu at Xanadu" (for Jon Anderson). [GreenMR] (8:1) Spr-Sum 95, p. 19-23.
"Oracle (after Plutarch)." [TriQ] (95) Wint 95-96, p. 235-237.

"Rajah in Babylon." [TriQ] (95) Wint 95-96, p. 223-225.
"Speech Grille." [TriQ] (95) Wint 95-96, p. 234.
"Stammer." [PoetryNW] (36:3) Aut 95, p. 28-29.
"Tractate for Doctor Tourette." [PoetryE] (41) Aut 95, p. 86-87.
6804. WOLBACH, Sarah
"On Reading Bishop's 'The Fish'" (runner up, 1994 Borderlands Poetry Contest).
[Border] (6) Spr-Sum 95, p. 77.
6805. WOLF, Edward
"I Do Not Drive." [Art&Und] (4:1, #14) Ja-F 95, p. 17.
6806. WOLF, Manfred
"The Art of Poetry" (tr. of Anna Enquist). [CimR] (112) Jl 95, p. 14.
"Harvest" (tr. of Anna Enquist). [CimR] (112) Jl 95, p. 14.
6807. WOLF, Michele
"Artificial Breathing" (Third Prize, 1995 Poetry Contest). [Ledge] (19) Wint 95, p.
86-87.
"Astigmatism" (Winner, Second Annual Chapbook Contest). [PaintedB] (57) 95, p.
52.
"The Diorama." [Hudson] (48:2) Sum 95, p. 276.
"Keep Going." [Hudson] (48:2) Sum 95, p. 275.
"Levitation" (Winner, Second Annual Chapbook Contest). [PaintedB] (57) 95, p.
53-54.
"Seizure." [Hudson] (48:2) Sum 95, p. 277.
"The Sleeping Gypsy" (Henri Rousseau, 1897). [Poetry] (166:5) Ag 95, p. 255.
6808. WOLFF, Rebecca
"Don't Know What to Call Him But He's Mighty Lak a Rose." [Iowa] (25:3) Fall 95,
p. 6.
"The Hite Report." [SouthernPR] (35:1) Sum 95, p. 34-35.
"Letters, Young and Old Poets." [GrandS] (14:2, #54) Fall 95, p. 249-251.
6809. WOLFSKILL, Jud
"What My Grandfather Whispered to Me on My Eighteenth Birthday."
[WilliamMR] (33) 95, p. 25.
6810. WOLMAN, Kenneth
"Glass Chorale" (after William Kennedy). [DefinedP] (3) 95, p. 41.
"Lilith." [JINJPo] (17:1) Spr 95, p. 9-11.
"Mark Antony, From Rome, to Cleopatra." [JINJPo] (17:1) Spr 95, p. 7-8.
"Why Husbands Don't Leave." [LowellR] (1) Sum 94, p. 73-74.
6811. WOLOCH, Cecilia
"Daddy's Tattoos" (First Prize, First Annual Poetry Awards). [LiteralL] (2:1) Sum
95, p. 13.
6812. WOLVERTON, Terry
"The Dead Stepfather." [Jacaranda] (11) [95 or 96?], p. 41.
"Legacy." [ManyMM] (2:1) 95, p. 63-69.
6813. WOMACK, Craig S.
"Apparitions." [JamesWR] (12:1) Wint 95, p. 16.
"Quilting." [JamesWR] (12:1) Wint 95, p. 13.
6814. WONG, Allegra
"The Hooked Rug." [Turnstile] (5:1) 95, p. 94.
6815. WOOD, Eben Y.
"Page of Cups." [PoetryE] (39) Fall 94, p. 104-105.
6816. WOOD, James
"Late Beauty." [VirQR] (71:3) Sum 95, p. 492-493.
"Sans Souci." [VirQR] (71:3) Sum 95, p. 493-494.
"Two Ponies." [VirQR] (71:3) Sum 95, p. 494.
6817. WOOD, John
"The Gates of the Elect Kingdom" (for Paul Zimmer. A New Orleans Review
Chapbook). [NewOR] (21:3/4) Fall-Wint 95, p. 53-78.
"Thinking of My Mother." [SouthernR] (31:1) Wint 95, p. 67-68.
6818. WOOD, Peter
"Looking Me Up in the Lexicon." [US1] (30/31) 95, p. 23.
6819. WOOD, Rebecca
"Broken English" (The 1994 Allen Ginsberg Poetry Awards: Honorable Mention).
[Footwork] (24/25) 95, p. 206.
6820. WOOD, Renate
"Black Hat." [TriQ] (94) Fall 95, p. 122-123.
"The Dump." [VirQR] (71:1) Wint 95, p. 104-105.
"Eurydice." [VirQR] (71:1) Wint 95, p. 105-106.

"If She Could Forget Her Mourning." [ManyMM] (2:1) 95, p. 24.
"My Mother's Hair." [ManyMM] (2:1) 95, p. 20-21.
"My Mother's Hand Thinks." [TriQ] (94) Fall 95, p. 124-125.
"Night Cows." [VirQR] (71:1) Wint 95, p. 106-107.
"The Nightgown." [TriQ] (94) Fall 95, p. 126.
"Season." [ManyMM] (2:1) 95, p. 19.
"Song of Forgetting." [ManyMM] (2:1) 95, p. 22.
"Still Life." [ManyMM] (2:1) 95, p. 23.
6821. WOODARD, Deborah
    "Beeman." [Thrpny] (62) Sum 95, p. 15.
6822. WOODHULL, Anne
    "The Priest." [MassR] (36:2) Sum 95, p. 234.
6823. WOODMAN, Christopher
    "Abstinence." [Vis] (49) 95, p. 31.
    "Offering." [Vis] (49) 95, p. 30-31.
6824. WOODRUFF, Elaine
    "Buried in Diamond Earrings" (Excerpt, from *Before the Burning*). [AmerPoR]
        (24:3) My-Je 95, p. 20.
6825. WOODRUFF, Keith
    "Delivery Driver." [TarRP] (34:2) Spr 95, p. 3.
6826. WOODRUFF, William
    "Amid tall grass palm." [WormR] (35:2, #138) 95, p. 62.
    "Fish swimming." [WormR] (35:2, #138) 95, p. 62.
    "Italian, Jewish." [WormR] (35:2, #138) 95, p. 62.
    "Kindling? no, the bats." [WormR] (35:2, #138) 95, p. 62.
    "Through Venice." [WormR] (35:2, #138) 95, p. 62.
    "A tossed-in rock." [WormR] (35:2, #138) 95, p. 62.
6827. WOODS, Christopher
    "Acolytes." [WeberS] (12:2) Spr-Sum 95, p. 109.
    "Beasts." [WeberS] (12:2) Spr-Sum 95, p. 109.
    "Blue." [WeberS] (12:2) Spr-Sum 95, p. 110.
    "The Fire That Night." [WeberS] (12:2) Spr-Sum 95, p. 110.
    "His Room in Arles." [GreenHLL] (6) 95, p. 33.
6828. WOODS, James
    "A Memorial Project." [ColR] (22:2) Fall 95, p. 161-162.
6829. WOODS, L. A. Ricci
    "My Nonna, Elvezia." [Footwork] (24/25) 95, p. 150.
6830. WOODSON, Michael
    "Boom Town" (runner up, 1994 Borderlands Poetry Contest). [Border] (6) Spr-Sum
        95, p. 78.
6831. WOODSUM, Douglas
    "Chocolate Covered Apricots." [MichQR] (34:2) Spr 95, p. 253-254.
6832. WOODWARD, Ann
    "As If Blind" (tr. of Dona Rosu). [Confr] (56/57) Sum-Fall 95, p. 335.
    "Your Name" (tr. of Dona Rosu). [Confr] (56/57) Sum-Fall 95, p. 335.
6833. WOOLF, Rafael
    "Not Goodbye." [DefinedP] (2:2) Spr-Sum 94, p. 33-34.
6834. WORFOLK, Dorothy
    "Witch's Brew." [BellArk] (11:5) S-O 95, p. 15.
6835. WORLEY, James
    "The Art of the Fugue." [ChrC] (112:26) 13-20 S 95, p. 851.
    "Mine Eyes Have Seen the Glory." [ChrC] (112:31) 1 N 95, p. 1020.
6836. WORLEY, Jeff
    "Breaking the Ice" (San Diego Sea World Bird Curator Uses Piped-in "Penguin
        Music" to Spur Mating.). [Wind] (76) Fall 95, p. 24.
    "Disappearance." [FloridaR] (21:1) 95, p. 26-27.
    "In Praise of the Armadillo." [TarRP] (35:1) Fall 95, p. 7.
    "Some Jumbled Philosophy: 3 A.M." [PraS] (69:3) Fall 95, p. 88-89.
    "Sunday Aubade." [LitR] (39:1) Fall 95, p. 38-39.
    "Team Photo, 1958." [LaurelR] (29:2) Sum 95, p. 107.
    "UFO Lands Near Beatrice, Nebraska. Dog Killed" (— *The Star*). [PraS] (69:3) Fall
        95, p. 87.
    "Valentine's Day." [LitR] (38:2) Wint 95, p. 240.
    "What You've Heard about Poets." [Boulevard] (10:1/2, #28/29) Spr 95, p. 235.
6837. WORMSER, Baron
    "1952." [ManhatR] (7:2) Wint 95, p. 24.

"Angel of Death." [ManhatR] (7:2) Wint 95, p. 28.
"Beethoven's Maid." [OntR] (42) Spr-Sum 95, p. 90-91.
"The Beltway." [VirQR] (71:2) Spr 95, p. 308-309.
"Children's Ward." [OntR] (42) Spr-Sum 95, p. 87.
"The Economy." [SouthwR] (80:4) Aut 95, p. 486-487.
"Environmental Fears." [RiverS] (44) 95, p. 8-9.
"Fast Food Incident." [ManhatR] (8:1) Fall 95, p. 49.
"For an Old Leftist." [RiverS] (44) 95, p. 10-11.
"Hymn to the Memory of D.H. Lawrence." [ManhatR] (7:2) Wint 95, p. 25-26.
"Ode for the American Comic, Lenny Bruce." [ManhatR] (8:1) Fall 95, p. 50-51.
"Palm Springs." [ManhatR] (7:2) Wint 95, p. 27.
"Psalm Reading in Fifth Grade, 1959." [VirQR] (71:2) Spr 95, p. 307.
"Rent." [OntR] (42) Spr-Sum 95, p. 89-90.
"Single Life Blues." [VirQR] (71:2) Spr 95, p. 308.
"Soup Kitchen (1991)." [OntR] (42) Spr-Sum 95, p. 88-89.
"Towards an Interstate Boddhisattva." [ManhatR] (8:1) Fall 95, p. 47-48.
"Urban Riot, 1992." [RiverS] (44) 95, p. 7.
"Who St. Augustine Was." [ManhatR] (8:1) Fall 95, p. 45-46.
6838. WOROZBYT, Theodore, Jr.
"Briefly Outside at the New Year's Eve Party, 1990." [SouthernPR] (35:1) Sum 95, p. 11-13.
"Especially at Midnight Leaving" (1994 Narrative Poetry Competition Prize Winner). [PoetL] (90:1) Spr 95, p. 6-8.
6839. WORTSMAN, Peter
"Painful Are the Inside Sounds." [ProseP] (4) 95, p. 76.
6840. WOUND, Lily
"Manlius, New York" (Second Prize). [HarvardA] Contest Issue, Spr 95, p. 17.
6841. WOZNIAK, Robert
"The Poem: I'm at it in candlelight." [CapeR] (30:1) Spr 95, p. 20.
"Public Radio." [CapeR] (30:1) Spr 95, p. 21.
6842. WREN, Andrea M.
"Her Rats" (re: rhonda manning's "dena and her rats, 1": a painting reproduced in *Literati Internazionale*). [Drumvoices] (5:1/2) Fall-Wint 95-96, p. 31.
"No Coal Hauling" (after "daughters of the dust"). [Drumvoices] (5:1/2) Fall-Wint 95-96, p. 32.
6843. WRIGHT, C. D.
"Because Fulfillment Awaits." [ColR] (22:2) Fall 95, p. 105.
"Like Horses." [ColR] (22:2) Fall 95, p. 107.
"Like Rocks." [ColR] (22:2) Fall 95, p. 106.
"The Shepherd of Resumed Desire." [ColR] (22:1) Spr 95, p. 38.
6844. WRIGHT, Carolyne
"Another Life" (tr. of Taslima Nasrin, w. Farida Sarkar). [GrandS] (14:1, #53) Sum 95, p. 172.
"Astrologer's Prediction" (tr. of Anuradha Mahapatra, w. Paramita Banerjee). [ManyMM] (1:3) 95, p. 158.
"Body Theory" (tr. of Taslima Nasrin, w. Mohammad Nurul Huda). [GrandS] (14:1, #53) Sum 95, p. 173-174.
"Broken Boat" (tr. of Rama Ghosh, w. Paramita Banerjee). [PoetryE] (39) Fall 94, p. 108.
"Conjugal Prayer" (tr. of Shamim Azad, w. Syed Manzoorul Islam and the author). [MidAR] (15:1/2) 95, p. 93.
"Eulene's *Noche Oscura*." [Iowa] (25:3) Fall 95, p. 160-161.
"Fantasy" (tr. of Ruby Rahman, w. Syed Manzoorul Islam and the author). [MidAR] (15:1/2) 95, p. 85-89.
"Guiltful" (tr. of Anuradha Mahapatra, w. Jyotirmoy Datta). [ManyMM] (1:3) 95, p. 159.
"I Go" (tr. of Rama Ghosh, w. Paramita Banerjee). [PoetryE] (39) Fall 94, p. 109.
"I Want to Pierce with the Arrows of My Voice" (tr. of Shamim Azad, w. Syed Manzoorul Islam and the author). [MidAR] (15:1/2) 95, p. 97, 99.
"Intraludus Euleneiae" (Benares, 5 a.m.). [InterQ] (2:3) 95, p. 109-110.
"It Goes Back with What Thoughts" (tr. of Vijaya Mukhopadhyay, w. Paramita Banerjee and the author). [MidAR] (15:1/2) 95, p. 65.
"Journal" (tr. of Ruby Rahman, w. Syed Manzoorul Islam and the author). [MidAR] (15:1/2) 95, p. 81, 83.
"Mahalaya" (tr. of Vijaya Mukhopadhyay, w. Paramita Banerjee and the author). [MidAR] (15:1/2) 95, p. 63.

"Martyrdom" (tr. of Yolanda Bedregal). [MidAR] (15:1/2) 95, p. 146.
"Moon-Struck" (tr. of Ruby Rahman, w. Syed Manzoorul Islam and the author).
    [MidAR] (15:1/2) 95, p. 77, 79.
"Night, I Know All About You" (tr. of Yolanda Bedregal). [MidAR] (15:1/2) 95, p.
    144-145.
"Nocturne of Hope" (tr. of Yolanda Bedregal). [MidAR] (15:1/2) 95, p. 143.
"Out-of-Order Remote-Control" (tr. of Shamim Azad, w. Syed Manzoorul Islam and
    the author). [MidAR] (15:1/2) 95, p. 95.
"Pointless Journey" (tr. of Yolanda Bedregal). [MidAR] (15:1/2) 95, p. 147-148.
"Primeval" (tr. of Anuradha Mahapatra, w. Jyotirmoy Datta). [ManyMM] (1:3) 95,
    p. 160.
"Sandhiprakash Raga" (tr. of Vijaya Mukhopadhyay, w. Paramita Banerjee and the
    author). [MidAR] (15:1/2) 95, p. 69.
"Sleep" (tr. of Anuradha Mahapatra, w. Jyotirmoy Datta). [ManyMM] (1:3) 95, p.
    161.
"Things Cheaply Had" (tr. of Taslima Nasrin, w. Mohammad Nurul Huda and the
    author). [NewYorker] (71:31) 9 O 95, p. 44.
"This Afternoon Knows" (tr. of Ruby Rahman, w. Syed Manzoorul Islam and the
    author). [MidAR] (15:1/2) 95, p. 73, 75.
"Twelve Fifty A.M." (tr. of Vijaya Mukhopadhyay, w. Paramita Banerjee and the
    author). [MidAR] (15:1/2) 95, p. 67.
"What Is There to Fear" (tr. of Rama Ghosh, w. Paramita Banerjee). [PoetryE] (39)
    Fall 94, p. 110.
"Wind" (tr. of Anuradha Mahapatra, w. Paramita Banerjee). [ManyMM] (1:3) 95, p.
    162.
6845. WRIGHT, Charles
    "Apologia Pro Vita Sua." [Poetry] (166:1) Ap 95, p. 1-4.
    "Apologia Pro Vita Sua III." [ParisR] (37:135) Sum 95, p. 33-36.
    "Christmas East of the Blue Ridge." [Ploughs] (21:4) Wint 95-96, p. 176.
    "Envoi." [Colum] (24/25) 95, p. 172-173.
    "A Journal of True Confessions" (Excerpt). [Verse] (12:2) 95, p. 144-145.
    "Lives of the Artists." [Field] (53) Fall 95, p. 90-94.
    "Lives of the Saints." [Poetry] (167:3) D 95, p. 125-129.
    "Looking Again at What I Looked at for Seventeen Years." [NewYorker] (71:3) 13
        Mr 95, p. 84.
    "Looking West from Laguna Beach at Night." [NewYorker] (71:3) 13 Mr 95, p. 82.
    "Meditation on Song and Structure." [NewRep] (213:12/13) 18-25 S 95, p. 54.
    "Meditation on Summer and Shapelessness." [ColR] (22:1) Spr 95, p. 16-18.
    "October II." [Ploughs] (21:4) Wint 95-96, p. 178.
    "Poem Almost Wholly in My Own Manner." [GettyR] (8:1) Wint 95, p. 22-24.
    "Slides of Verona." [SenR] (25:1) Spr 95, p. 17.
    "Umbrian Dreams." [Ploughs] (21:4) Wint 95-96, p. 177.
    "Venexia I." [Shen] (45:1) Spr 95, p. 105.
    "Venexia II." [Shen] (45:1) Spr 95, p. 106.
6846. WRIGHT, Charlotte M.
    "Pillows." [ChironR] (44/45) Aut-Wint 95, p. 21.
6847. WRIGHT, Elizabeth
    "She-Crab Soup." [13thMoon] (13:1/2) 95, p. 46-48.
6848. WRIGHT, Franz
    "Autobiography." [Field] (53) Fall 95, p. 57.
    "Child Rearing." [Field] (53) Fall 95, p. 56.
    "First Day on the Ward." [Field] (53) Fall 95, p. 59.
    "First Light." [Field] (53) Fall 95, p. 58.
6849. WRIGHT, G. T.
    "For Berryman, 1972." [NorthStoneR] (12) 95, p. 195.
6850. WRIGHT, Jeff
    "Easy Pickin's." [Talisman] (15) Wint 95-96, p. 137-139.
6851. WRIGHT, Katharine
    "In the Unit." [13thMoon] (13:1/2) 95, p. 49.
    "Knife Meditation." [13thMoon] (13:1/2) 95, p. 50.
    "Orthopedic." [NowestR] (33:1) 95, p. 49.
6852. WRIGHT, Kirby
    "Crab Newburg." [HawaiiR] (19:2) Fall 95, p. 159.
    "Dear Gordon." [HawaiiR] (19:2) Fall 95, p. 157.
    "Dream of a Ph.D." [HawaiiR] (19:2) Fall 95, p. 158.
    "Quake." [SlipS] (15) 95, p. 42.

6853. WRIGHT, Leilani
"Are You My Mother?" [LowellR] (2) c1996, p. 20.
6854. WRIGHT, Nancy Means
"Aunt Beulah Won't Take a Walk at Waterbury." [GreenMR] (8:2) Fall-Wint 95-96, p. 57.
"Recycling." [Kalliope] (17:3) 95, p. 51.
6855. WRIGLEY, Robert
"Flies." [BlackWR] (22:1) Fall-Wint 95, p. 87-88.
"Hoarfrost." [CrabOR] (1:1) Fall-Wint 95, p. 146.
"Part Elegy." [PoetryNW] (36:1) Spr 95, p. 17-19.
"Peace." [BlackWR] (22:1) Fall-Wint 95, p. 89-90.
6856. WROBLEWSKI, Michele
"Self-Portrait Found in the Iris of an Eye." [QW] (41) Aut-Wint 95-96, p. 277.
6857. WUNDERLICH, Mark
"All That, Stammering." [Chelsea] (59) 95, p. 108.
"The Bruise of This." [YaleR] (83:3) Jl 95, p. 19.
"Chapel of the Miraculous Medal." [Chelsea] (59) 95, p. 104.
"The Diagnosis." [GrahamHR] (19) Wint 95-96, p. 91.
"Fourteen Things We're Allowed to Bring to the Underworld." [Chelsea] (59) 95, p. 105.
"How I Was Told and Not Told." [YaleR] (83:3) Jl 95, p. 17-18.
"Hunt." [Agni] (41) 95, p. 101-102.
"In the Winter of This Climate." [Poetry] (167:3) D 95, p. 136.
"Letter Ending with a Verse by Karen Carpenter." [Chelsea] (59) 95, p. 106.
"No Place Like Home." [Chelsea] (59) 95, p. 107.
"On Opening." [Poetry] (167:3) D 95, p. 138.
"Pale Notion." [GrahamHR] (19) Wint 95-96, p. 93.
"Thirst." [GrahamHR] (19) Wint 95-96, p. 92.
"To Sleep in a New City." [Poetry] (167:3) D 95, p. 137.
"Unmade Bed." [Chelsea] (59) 95, p. 103.
6858. WYATT, Charles
"Distance." [SmPd] (32:1, #93) Wint 95, p. 8.
"Dreams." [WestB] (37) 95, p. 13.
"A Dromedary, c. 1633" (drawing, Rembrandt van Rijn). [CumbPR] (14:2) Spr 95, p. 14.
"Grasshoppers." [CumbPR] (15:1) Fall 95, p. 65-66.
"I Am Six Years Old." [Farm] (13:2 [i.e. 12:2]) Fall-Wint 95, p. 41.
"Lost child." [WestB] (37) 95, p. 12-13.
"Snake Spit." [Farm] (13:2 [i.e. 12:2]) Fall-Wint 95, p. 40.
"Study of a Pig, c. 1642-43" (drawing, Rembrandt van Rijn). [CumbPR] (14:2) Spr 95, p. 13.
"Woman with a Child Frightened by a Dog" (drawing, Rembrandt van Rijn). [FloridaR] (21:1) 95, p. 67.
6859. WYLAM, John
"The News at 3 A.M." [PoetL] (90:4) Wint 95-96, p. 55-56.
6860. WYMAN, Sarah
"Walls & Flowers." [Quarry] (43:4) 95, p. 111.
6861. WYNAND, Derk
"Voyage." [Event] (24:1) Spr 95, p. 50.
6862. WYREBEK, M.
"Unknowing." [BlackWR] (22:1) Fall-Wint 95, p. 125-126.
6863. WYSHYNSKI, James
"Commuting." [PaintedB] (57) 95, p. 42.
"Conceiving the Ukraine." [BelPoJ] (46:2) Wint 95-96, p. 32-34.
6864. WYSOCKI, Gisela von
"Movie-Dad" (tr. by Rosmarie Waldrop). [MichQR] (34:4) Fall 95, p. 548.
6865. WYTTENBERG, Victoria
"Moose." [PoetryNW] (36:1) Spr 95, p. 35-36.

XIAOLONG, Qiu
See QIU, Xiaolong
6866. XU, Juan
"Cover Girl" (tr. of Shu Ting). [AxeF] (3) 90, p. 46.
"Curves" (tr. of Gu Chen). [AxeF] (3) 90, p. 45.
"Far and Near" (tr. of Gu Chen). [AxeF] (3) 90, p. 45.

"In the Morning, It Has Just Rained" (tr. of Mang Ke). [AxeF] (3) 90, p. 44.
"New Bamboo." [AxeF] (3) 90, p. 43.
XUANJI, Yu
    See YU, Xuanji
6867. XUE, Chun-jian
    "Firefly" (tr. of Cai Qijiao, w. Edward Morin). [InterQ] (2:3) 95, p. 115.

6868. YAGUCHI, Yorifumi
    "Trash." [Noctiluca] (2:1, #4) Spr 95, p. 7.
YAKAMOCHI, Otomo no (718-785)
    See OTOMO no YAKAMOCHI (718-785)
6869. YALKUT, Carolyn
    "Etymology." [Confr] (56/57) Sum-Fall 95, p. 334-335.
6870. YAMAGUCHI, Tomiko
    "Her screams have ceased today" (in Japanese and English, tr. by Jiro Nakano).
        [BambooR] (67/68) Sum-Fall 95, p. 98.
6871. YAMANAKA, Lois-Ann
    "Prince PoPo, Prince JiJi." [Zyzzyva] (11:3/4, #43/44) 95, "The Best of Ten Years
        of ZYZZYVA," p. 125-127.
6872. YAMATO, Gloria
    "Trust." [SinW] (55) Spr-Sum 95, p. 44.
6873. YAMRUS, John
    "We Sat." [Bogg] (67) 95, p. 28.
YAN, Deng
    See DENG, Yan
6874. YARBROUGH, Anne
    "Fifty Prophets in a Cave, Hiding from Jezebel." [ChrC] (112:28) 11 O 95, p. 928.
6875. YARBROUGH, Ewa-Hryniewicz
    "All Souls' Day" (tr. of Krzysztof Lisowski). [LitR] (38:3) Spr 95, p. 356-357.
6876. YASIN, Mehmet
    "Our Cat's Tale" (tr. by Alev Reid, edited by Ruth Christie). [HarvardR] (8) Spr 95,
        p. 92.
6877. YASUDA, Hakutei
    "After the screaming, the scars, the scorched land" (in Japanese and English, tr. by
        Jiro Nakano). [BambooR] (67/68) Sum-Fall 95, p. 99.
6878. YASUI, Kaoru
    "The Atomic Bomb killed indiscriminately" (in Japanese and English, tr. by Jiro
        Nakano). [BambooR] (67/68) Sum-Fall 95, p. 100.
YASUSADA, Araki
    See ARAKI, Yasusada
6879. YATCHISIN, George
    "Evensong." [SantaBR] (3:2) Sum 95, p. 42.
    "Not Really North." [SantaBR] (3:2) Sum 95, p. 44.
    "A Reading." [SantaBR] (3:2) Sum 95, p. 43.
    "Stage Whisper." [AntR] (53:3) Sum 95, p. 323.
6880. YATES, Steve
    "Old Man Looking at a Highway." [XavierR] (15:1) Spr 95, p. 44.
6881. YATES, W. Ross
    "An Erratic." [Hellas] (6:1) Spr-Sum 95, p. 37.
6882. YAU, Emily
    "Saxman." [ConnPR] (14:1) 95, p. 13.
6883. YAU, John
    "Angel Atrapado XXIV." [NewAW] (13) Fall-Wint 95, p. 20-21.
    "Counterpoint." [CutB] (44) Sum 95, p. 86-87.
    "Days of 1975." [ProseP] (4) 95, p. 80.
    "In Between and Around." [PlumR] (8) [95], p. 18-22.
    "The Newly Renovated Opera House on Gilligan's Island." [ProseP] (4) 95, p. 77-
        79.
    "One More Excuse." [NewAW] (13) Fall-Wint 95, p. 22-24.
    "Peter Lorre Dreams He Is the Third Reincarnation of a Geisha." [Talisman] (15)
        Wint 95-96, p. 92-93.
6884. YAU, Julie
    "After a Number of Years I Read Lynne Savitt's Poems." [AxeF] (3) 90, p. 23.
6885. YBARRA, Ricardo Means
    "116th Medical Battalion." [PoetL] (90:3) Fall 95, p. 42.

"Su Yong Kim in Lynwood." [PoetL] (90:3) Fall 95, p. 43.
6886. YEAGER, Christopher M.
"I Don't Think It's a Nature Poem At All, Says My Wife." [SouthernPR] (35:1) Sum 95, p. 66-68.
6887. YEAGLEY, Joan
"The People of the Fire: Potawatomi." [MidwQ] (36:4) Sum 95, p. 458.
6888. YEARWOOD, Edwin
"A Voice in My Head." [ClockR] (10:1/2) 95-96, p. 37.
6889. YEATS, William Butler
"I Will Not in Grey Hours" (unpublished poem). [NewYRB] (42:13) 10 Ag 95, p. 14.
"The Magpie" (unpublished poem). [NewYRB] (42:13) 10 Ag 95, p. 14.
YEHUDA, Gil-Ohz Ben
   See BEN-YEHUDA, Gil-Ohz
6890. YÉPES AZPARREN, José Antonio
"Pajaro o Poema." [Luz] (8) Spr 95, p. 58.
6891. YESSON, Maximillian
"Recreational Metaphysics." [HawaiiR] (19:2) Fall 95, p. 36-37.
6892. YEZZI, David
"Sad Is Eros, Builder of Cities" (a wrecking site, Lower East Side). [SouthwR] (80:4) Aut 95, p. 443.
6893. YODER, Bart
"The Unconscious at Play in Dallas." [Pearl] (22) Fall-Wint 95, p. 27.
YORIKO, Ogihara
   See OGIHARA, Yoriko
6894. YOSANO, Akiko (1878-1942)
"The Day When Mountains Move" (tr. by Kenneth Rexroth and Ikuko Atsumi). [ManyMM] reprinted in every issue p. 2.
6895. YOSHIHARA, Sachiko
"Air Raid" (tr. by Naoshi Koriyama and Edward Lueders). [WeberS] (12:1) Wint 95, p. 52.
"An Epitaph" (tr. by Naoshi Koriyama and Edward Lueders). [WeberS] (12:1) Wint 95, p. 51-52.
"Low Tide" (tr. by Naoshi Koriyama and Edward Lueders). [WeberS] (12:1) Wint 95, p. 50-51.
"Of Bread and Roses" (tr. by Naoshi Koriyama and Edward Lueders). [WeberS] (12:1) Wint 95, p. 50.
"Quite Suddenly" (tr. by Naoshi Koriyama and Edward Lueders). [WeberS] (12:1) Wint 95, p. 51.
6896. YOUNG, Brian
"Lunar New Year." [OhioR] (53) 95, p. 33.
"Returning the Book of Common Prayer to the Library in Order to Check Out the Marquis de Sade." [GrandS] (14:1, #53) Sum 95, p. 229-230.
6897. YOUNG, C. Dale
"Art and the Rite of Confession." [NewDeltaR] (12:1) Fall-Wint 94, p. 78-79.
"Complaint of the Medical Illustrator." [SouthwR] (80:1) Wint 95, p. 135.
"Elegy." [CimR] (111) Ap 95, p. 76.
"Gross Anatomy." [NewEngR] (17:3) Sum 95, p. 181.
"The Hotel di L'Altissimo" (Montego Bay, Jamaica). [AntR] (53:3) Sum 95, p. 322.
"Vespers" (Clarendon, Jamaica). [SouthernR] (31:1) Wint 95, p. 69.
6898. YOUNG, David
"The Day of the Pollyanna" (tr. of Miroslav Holub, w. Dana Hábova). [GrandS] (13:4, #52) Spr 95, p. 58.
"Love Letter to Li Zi-An" (tr. of Xuanji Yu, w. Jiann L. Lin). [Field] (52) Spr 95, p. 57.
"Melancholy Thoughts" (tr. of Xuanji Yu, w. Jiann L. Lin). [Field] (52) Spr 95, p. 55.
"Metaphysics" (tr. of Miroslav Holub, w. the author). [GrandS] (13:4, #52) Spr 95, p. 60.
"Selling the Last Peonies" (tr. of Xuanji Yu, w. Jiann L. Lin). [Field] (52) Spr 95, p. 56.
"Sent to Secretary Liu" (tr. of Xuanji Yu, w. Jiann L. Lin). [Field] (52) Spr 95, p. 60.
"Tribute to a Master Alchemist" (tr. of Xuanji Yu, w. Jiann L. Lin). [Field] (52) Spr 95, p. 59.
"Visiting Master Zhao and Not Finding Him" (tr. of Xuanji Yu, w. Jiann L. Lin). [Field] (52) Spr 95, p. 58.

"Washing Yarn Temple" (tr. of Xuanji Yu, w. Jiann L. Lin). [Field] (52) Spr 95, p. 54.

"Whale Songs" (tr. of Miroslav Holub, w. the author). [GrandS] (13:4, #52) Spr 95, p. 59-60.

6899. YOUNG, Dean

"Clangor." [GettyR] (8:4) Aut 95, p. 610.

"Errata." [NewAW] (13) Fall-Wint 95, p. 86-87.

"Exquisite Corpse." [ColR] (22:1) Spr 95, p. 89-90.

"First You Must." [Sulfur] (15:2, #37) Fall 95, p. 145-146.

"Frottage." [GettyR] (8:4) Aut 95, p. 608-609.

"Inside the Bodies of the Broken-Hearted." [ChiR] (41:2/3) 95, p. 19.

"Instructions for Living." [ChiR] (41:2/3) 95, p. 20-22.

"One Story." [Thrpny] (61) Spr 95, p. 6.

"Roving Reporter." [PassN] (16:2) Wint 95, p. 26-27.

6900. YOUNG, Gary

"The chimes are silent, but spinning, catch the sun and startle me as I read." [SilverFR] (26) Wint 95, p. 24.

"Falling limbs have taken a piece of the house each of the last two storms." [SilverFR] (26) Wint 95, p. 23.

"Gene tells the story of a boy." [NewEngR] (17:1) Wint 95, p. 22.

"I was home from the hospital and not expected to survive." [DenQ] (29:4) Spr 95, p. 60.

"The light from her room was penetrating, otherworldly, blue." [DenQ] (29:4) Spr 95, p. 61.

"My father would say, you need a memory lesson, and he'd beat us." [NewEngR] (17:1) Wint 95, p. 22.

"My mother loved violets." [DenQ] (29:4) Spr 95, p. 60.

"We are less surrounded by water on this island than by air." [SilverFR] (26) Wint 95, p. 22.

6901. YOUNG, George

"A Chaos of Swallows." [CapeR] (30:2) Fall 95, p. 37.

"The Death of Shelley." [WritersF] (21) 95, p. 46.

"Garden of the Lost." [CapeR] (30:2) Fall 95, p. 36.

6902. YOUNG, Karl

"Variations on Lorca's 'Balanza'." [Noctiluca] (2:1, #4) Spr 95, p. 44.

6903. YOUNG, Kevin

"Belongings." [KenR] (17:1) Wint 95, p. 72-74.

"Tornado Weather." [SenR] (25:2) Fall 95, p. 23-30.

"Tuff Buddies" (for Robert Scott). [KenR] (17:1) Wint 95, p. 71-72.

6904. YOUNG, Linda

"Conversion of the Animals." [SpoonR] (20:2) Sum-Fall 95, p. 125-126.

"Snake in the Cinema." [SpoonR] (20:2) Sum-Fall 95, p. 127-128.

"Woman Falls from Burning Window." [NewYorkQ] (54) 95, p. 79.

6905. YOUNG, Patricia

"Annie Stays Out All Night with a Man Called Death." [Arc] (34) Spr 95, p. 43.

"In the Museum the Hominid Speaks to Her Lover." [MalR] (110) Spr 95, p. 120 - 122.

"On the Road to Prichard." [Arc] (34) Spr 95, p. 44-45.

"The Picnic." [MalR] (110) Spr 95, p. 116-117.

"Piece of Cake." [Event] (24:3) Wint 95-96, p. 70-71.

"Second-Hand Gloves." [Event] (24:3) Wint 95-96, p. 68-69.

"A Strange and Terrible Thing." [MalR] (110) Spr 95, p. 118-119.

"This Business of the Dresses." [Event] (24:3) Wint 95-96, p. 66-67.

"Three Days Before Christmas." [MalR] (113) Wint 95, p. 96-97.

"The Wall." [MalR] (113) Wint 95, p. 98-99.

6906. YOUNG, Robyn

"Draining Tinicum." [NortheastCor] (3) 95, p. 47.

6907. YOUNG, William Seth

"Nailing Down Words." [SouthernPR] (35:1) Sum 95, p. 45-46.

6908. YOUNG BEAR, Ray (Ray A.)

"The Crow-Children Walk My Circles in the Snow." [SenR] (25:1) Spr 95, p. 18-19.

6909. YOUNG-SADOWSKI, Jennifer

"Lot's Wife." [LullwaterR] (6:2) Fall-Wint 95, p. 52.

6910. YOUNGBERG, Gail

"Extension English." [Grain] (22:4) Spr 95, p. 134.

6911. YOUNGS, Anne Ohman
"Translating the Grass." [MidwQ] (36:2) Wint 95, p. 168-169.
6912. YOUSSEF, Sa'adi
"For Jamal Juma'a" (tr. by Khaled Mattawa). [ArtfulD] (28/29) 95, p. 12.
"On the Red Sea" (tr. by Khaled Mattawa). [WillowS] (36) Je 95, p. 104.
6913. YSKAMP, Amanda
"Automobile II." [LullwaterR] (5:1) 93-94, p. 12-13.
6914. YU, Charles
"Chinese Soap Opera." [PlumR] (9) [95 or 96], p. 12-13.
"His saw, my father's, moves much quicker." [PlumR] (9) [95 or 96], p. 16.
"One Theory of Garden Flowers." [PlumR] (9) [95 or 96], p. 14-15.
6915. YÜ, Seng
"To everything there is a season" (tr. by J. P. Seaton). [LitR] (38:3) Spr 95, p. 320.
6916. YU, Xuanji
"Love Letter to Li Zi-An" (tr. by David Young, w. Jiann L. Lin). [Field] (52) Spr 95,
p. 57.
"Melancholy Thoughts" (tr. by David Young, w. Jiann L. Lin). [Field] (52) Spr 95,
p. 55.
"Selling the Last Peonies" (tr. by David Young, w. Jiann L. Lin). [Field] (52) Spr
95, p. 56.
"Sent to Secretary Liu" (tr. by David Young, w. Jiann L. Lin). [Field] (52) Spr 95, p.
60.
"Tribute to a Master Alchemist" (tr. by David Young, w. Jiann L. Lin). [Field] (52)
Spr 95, p. 59.
"Visiting Master Zhao and Not Finding Him" (tr. by David Young, w. Jiann L. Lin).
[Field] (52) Spr 95, p. 58.
"Washing Yarn Temple" (tr. by David Young, w. Jiann L. Lin). [Field] (52) Spr 95,
p. 54.
6917. YUAN, Ch'iung-ch'iung
"Two Ballets" (tr. by Steve Bradbury). [HawaiiR] (19:2) Fall 95, p. 94-95.
6918. YUAN, Mei
"So Be It" (tr. by J. P. Seaton). [LitR] (38:3) Spr 95, p. 338.
6919. YUCE, Ali
"For the Road" (tr. by Sinan Toprak and Gerry LaFemina). [HayF] (16) Spr-Sum 95,
p. 61.
"To Blow Away the Darkness" (tr. by Sinan Toprak and Gerry LaFemina). [HayF]
(16) Spr-Sum 95, p. 60.
6920. YUE, An
"Homestead." [NewOR] (21:2) Sum 95, p. 20.
YUN, Ching
See CHING, Yun
YUN, Wang
See WANG, Yun
6921. YUN-KAI CHIH-PEN
"The Spring of the Year" (tr. by Chris Laughrun). [LitR] (38:3) Spr 95, p. 332.
YUNG, Liu (987-1053)
See LIU, Yung (987-1053)
6922. YURDANA, Matt
"A Gathering of Cardiovascular Surgeons." [CutB] (42) Sum 94, p. 12-14.
6923. YURMAN, R.
"Maiden Aunt." [Parting] (8:2) Wint 95-96, p. 38.
6924. YUZNA, Susan
"Positively Minneapolis." [LaurelR] (29:2) Sum 95, p. 61.
"Sleepless Everywhere." [CutB] (44) Sum 95, p. 25-27.
"There Are Pains Which Will Not Be Missed." [LaurelR] (29:2) Sum 95, p. 62-63.
"The Way of the Moth." [LaurelR] (29:2) Sum 95, p. 63-65.

6925. ZABOROWSKI, Karen
"Movers." [JINJPo] (17:1) Spr 95, p. 15.
6926. ZABUZHKO, Oksana
"As in a Rear-View Mirror" (tr. by Lisa Sapinkopf, w. the author). [MassR] (36:3)
Aut 95, p. 424.
"Conductor of Candles" (tr. by Lisa Sapinkopf and the author). [Ploughs] (21:4)
Wint 95-96, p. 180-181.

"Prypiat — Still Life" (tr. by Lisa Sapinkopf and the author). [Ploughs] (21:4) Wint 95-96, p. 179.
"Turn of the Century" (tr. by Lisa Sapinkopf, w. the author). [MassR] (36:3) Aut 95, p. 422-423.
6927. ZAHNISER, Edward
"Recipients." [DefinedP] (2:1) Fall-Wint 93, p. 33.
6928. ZALLER, Robert
"Excavations" (tr. of Lili Bita). [Footwork] (24/25) 95, p. 78.
"Theme with Shadows" (tr. of Lili Bita). [Footwork] (24/25) 95, p. 78.
6929. ZANDER, William
"Obsolete Technology." [Footwork] (24/25) 95, p. 42.
"Sailing to Kansas." [DefinedP] (3) 95, p. 61-62.
6930. ZANN, Erich
"Inception" (for Merriam Webster). [LiteralL] (1:3) N-D 94, p. 26.
ZANT, Frank Van
See Van ZANT, Frank
6931. ZAPOCAS, Andrés
"Andrés sin Tierra." [Americas] (23:3/4) Fall-Wint 95, p. 180.
"Bizco." [Americas] (23:3/4) Fall-Wint 95, p. 178.
"Constelación." [Americas] (23:3/4) Fall-Wint 95, p. 174.
"Gatuno." [Americas] (23:3/4) Fall-Wint 95, p. 176.
"Gaviota" (a A. Artorez). [Americas] (23:3/4) Fall-Wint 95, p. 176.
"Me-Nudo." [Americas] (23:3/4) Fall-Wint 95, p. 175.
"Neón" (para A. Artorez). [Americas] (23:3/4) Fall-Wint 95, p. 178.
"Nostalgia." [Americas] (23:3/4) Fall-Wint 95, p. 179.
"Querencia." [Americas] (23:3/4) Fall-Wint 95, p. 175.
"Under the Moon of Texas." [Americas] (23:3/4) Fall-Wint 95, p. 174.
6932. ZAWINSKI, Andrena
"Desperate Times." [Callaloo] (18:2) Spr 95, p. 386-387.
"Dinner Piece." [PoetL] (90:4) Wint 95-96, p. 27.
"You Get the Picture, America." [BlackBR] (20) Spr-Sum 95, p. 5-6.
6933. ZEALAND, Karen
"A Wife Reviews the Issues on Valentine's Day." [Kalliope] (17:1) 95, p. 5.
6934. ZEIGER, Gene
"The Piazza." [ProseP] (4) 95, p. 81.
6935. ZELCER, Brook
"Cloris." [Bogg] (67) 95, p. 22.
"Rufus." [Bogg] (67) 95, p. 23.
"Sharon's Favorite." [Bogg] (67) 95, p. 23.
"Why Marla Reads Tolstoy." [Bogg] (67) 95, p. 22.
6936. ZELLER, Ludwig
"Beatrifying the Syllables of the Game" (tr. by A. F. Moritz). [Arc] (35) Aut 95, p. 31.
"Body of Insomnia" (tr. by A. F. Moritz). [Arc] (35) Aut 95, p. 33.
"From One Scribe to Another" (for the poet John Robert Colombo, tr. by A. F. Moritz). [Arc] (35) Aut 95, p. 32.
"Woman Under the Lindens" (tr. by A. F. Moritz). [Arc] (35) Aut 95, p. 34.
6937. ZELTZER, Joel
"Casida of the Branches" (tr. of Federico García Lorca). [DefinedP] (1:2) Spr-Sum 93, p. 19.
"In a Different Style" (tr. of Federico García Lorca). [DefinedP] (1:2) Spr-Sum 93, p. 20.
"Interrupted Concert" (tr. of Federico García Lorca). [DefinedP] (1:2) Spr-Sum 93, p. 18.
6938. ZENAKOS, Augustin
"Draft for a Wake" (For Chris). [HarvardR] (8) Spr 95, p. 114.
6939. ZENITH, Richard
"The Gods Are Happy" (tr. of Fernando Pessoa). [PartR] (62:1) Wint 95, p. 107.
"I Got Off the Train" (tr. of Fernando Pessoa as Alvaro de Campos). [PartR] (62:1) Wint 95, p. 106.
6940. ZEPEDA, Rafael
"The Book Depository" (with Gerald Locklin, from "The Yellow Ford of Texas"). [Pearl] (22) Fall-Wint 95, p. 72-74.
"Lorraine Around?" [Pearl] (22) Fall-Wint 95, p. 76.
"The Wreckers." [Pearl] (22) Fall-Wint 95, p. 75.

6941. ZEPHANIAH, Benjamin
"Poor Millionaires." [RiverC] (15:2) Sum 95, p. 19.
"Something Blues." [RiverC] (15:2) Sum 95, p. 20.
6942. ZEPPER, Kevin
"Banquet." [BlackBR] (20) Spr-Sum 95, p. 28.
"The Observatory (Ennui)." [BlackBR] (21) Fall-Wint 95, p. 30.
6943. ZERFAS, Janice
"My Father Hates the Moon." [Footwork] (24/25) 95, p. 49.
6944. ZETZEL, Geraldine
"Take These." [CumbPR] (15:1) Fall 95, p. 67-68.
"What Comes." [CumbPR] (15:1) Fall 95, p. 69-70.
ZHAOMING, Qian
See QIAN, Zhaoming
6945. ZHITI, Visar
"I Am Setting the Alarm" (tr. by Ilir Ikonomi). [Vis] (48) 95, p. 7.
6946. ZHOU, Lu Jing
"A thousand Pieces of Snow" (w. Fung Hae Suh, 22 selections, tr. by Tsung Tsai
and George Crane). [Archae] (5) Spr 95, p. 6-29.
6947. ZIDE, Arlene
"A Pair of Glasses" (tr. of Savithri Rajeevan, w. Ayyappa Paniker). [ManyMM]
(1:3) 95, p. 152-153.
6948. ZIEROTH, David
"First Rain, Then Snow." [CanLit] (145) Sum 95, p. 105.
6949. ZIKA, B. Lynne
"Fried Chicken." [RagMag] (12:2) Spr 95, p. 106-107.
"Jacob." [RagMag] (12:2) Spr 95, p. 104-105.
6950. ZIMMER, Paul (Paul J.)
"Before the Moon Came Up Last Night." [GeoR] (49:4) Wint 95, p. 888.
"Blood Lock" (Operation Desert Rock, 1955). [LaurelR] (29:1) Wint 95, p. 108.
"Dear Mom." [GettyR] (8:3) Sum 95, p. 386.
"Divestment." [TarRP] (35:1) Fall 95, p. 2.
"The Example." [GettyR] (8:3) Sum 95, p. 387.
"How We Survive Childhood." [NewEngR] (17:1) Wint 95, p. 20.
"Love Poem." [LaurelR] (29:1) Wint 95, p. 109.
"Pearl-Handled Pistols." [TarRP] (35:1) Fall 95, p. 1.
"The Poetry of Aging Men." [TarRP] (35:1) Fall 95, p. 2.
6951. ZIMMERMAN, Irene
"Winter Pall Bearers." [ChrC] (112:10) 22-29 Mr 95, p. 318.
6952. ZIMMERMAN, Ruth
"Code Blue." [JINJPo] (17:2) Aut 95, p. 29.
"Last Communion." [JINJPo] (17:2) Aut 95, p. 28.
"Words Like Abandonment." [JINJPo] (17:2) Aut 95, p. 26-27.
6953. ZIMMERMANN, Rolf
"In Poland" (tr. by Anne Halley). [MassR] (36:3) Aut 95, p. 412-413.
6954. ZIRLIN, Larry
"Laundromat." [HangL] (66) 95, p. 77.
"On the F Line." [HangL] (66) 95, p. 77.
6955. ZISQUIT, Linda Stern
"Body Shop." [ParisR] (37:134) Spr 95, p. 222-223.
"Unopened Letters." [ParisR] (37:134) Spr 95, p. 222.
6956. ZIVAN, David
"Ragtime" (Sedalia, Missouri: Maple Leaf Club, Summer 1904). [TriQ] (95) Wint
95-96, p. 209-210.
6957. ZIYALAN, Mustafa
"Days" (tr. by Murat Nemet-Nejat). [Talisman] (14) Fall 95, p. 55.
ZOLA SANTIAGO, Rogério
See SANTIAGO, Rogério Zola
6958. ZOLLER, Ann
"Returning to the Sea." [Nimrod] (39:1) Fall-Wint 95, p. 132.
6959. ZORDANI, Bob
"The Philanderer's Rebuttal." [WillowR] (22) Spr 95, p. 11-12.
"Song for an Ex-Wife." [Poem] (74) N 95, p. 20-21.
"Song for an Ex-Wife." [SpoonR] (20:2) Sum-Fall 95, p. 137-138.
ZOTTE, Ann Claremont Le
See Le ZOTTE, Ann Claremont

6960. ZUBICK, Kelleen
"Late." [WillowS] (35) Ja 95, p. 42.
"Sergio's Bird." [ArtfulD] (28/29) 95, p. 141-142.
6961. ZUCKERMAN, Eric
"What All You Do Is Salmon." [Plain] (16:1) Fall 95, p. 33.
6962. ZWEIG, Ellen
"Critical Mass" (w. Meridel Rubenstein). [Conjunc] (24) 95, p. 165-187.
6963. ZWEIG, Martha
"Bestial." [GreenMR] (8:2) Fall-Wint 95-96, p. 52.
"Dictum." [GreenMR] (8:2) Fall-Wint 95-96, p. 54.
"Scarecrow." [SoCoast] (18) Ja 95, p. 4.
"Successor." [GreenMR] (8:2) Fall-Wint 95-96, p. 53.
6964. ZWICKY, Jan
"Beethoven: Adagio, Op. 127." [Descant] (26:1, #88) Spr 95, p. 110-111.
"Beethoven: Opus 95." [Descant] (26:1, #88) Spr 95, p. 105-109.
"Border Station." [MalR] (111) Sum 95, p. 68-69.
"Lilacs." [MalR] (111) Sum 95, p. 66-67.
"Small Song: Anger." [MalR] (113) Wint 95, p. 67.
"Small Song: Height of Summer." [MalR] (113) Wint 95, p. 71.
"Small Song: Mozart." [MalR] (113) Wint 95, p. 71.
"Small Song on Departures." [MalR] (113) Wint 95, p. 68.
"Small Song: Sandwiches." [MalR] (113) Wint 95, p. 67.
"Small Song: Up late listening to the rain." [MalR] (113) Wint 95, p. 69.
"Small Song: What are you thinking, little violin?" [MalR] (113) Wint 95, p. 70.
"Song: Wild Grape." [MalR] (113) Wint 95, p. 70.
"Unsong." [MalR] (113) Wint 95, p. 68.
"Unsong: August." [MalR] (113) Wint 95, p. 69.
6965. ZYDEK, Fredrick
"At Midnight." [Nimrod] (39:1) Fall-Wint 95, p. 134.
"Letter to Blain in Texas." [JamesWR] (12:2) Spr-Sum 95, p. 14.
"Letter to Kappel Contemplating Priesthood." [ChrC] (112:20) 21-28 Je 95, p. 640.
"The Miraculous Grove" (for Laura). [Nimrod] (39:1) Fall-Wint 95, p. 135.
"Praying All the Way." [ChrC] (112:25) 30 Ag-6 S 95, p. 804.
"Song of the Dreamer." [ChrC] (112:26) 13-20 S 95, p. 836.
"Thirty-third Meditation: Getting into the Psych Ward." [TampaR] (10) Spr 95, p. 58-59.
"Warehouse" (for Donald). [JamesWR] (12:2) Spr-Sum 95, p. 8.

Title Index

Titles are arranged alphanumerically, with numerals filed in numerical order before letters. Each title is followed by one or more author entry numbers, which refer to the numbered entries in the first part of the volume. Entry numbers are preceded by a space+colon+ space (:). Any numeral which preceeds the space+colon+space (:) is part of the title, not an entry number. Poems with "Untitled" in the title position are entered under "Untitled" followed by the first line of the poem and also directly under the first line. Numbered titles are entered under the number and also under the part following the number.

The Function of Shock : 2563.
Functional Through a Believing : 1156.
Fundraising : 5125.
Funeral : 4801.
Funeral Before My Dead Son's Third
  Birthday : 6298.
Funeral Before My Dead son's Third
  Birthday : 6298.
Funeral Cantata : 3497, 5280.
Funeral for a Tooth : 3545.
Funeral Forest : 5142.
Funeral March of Adolf Wolfli : 1481.
The Funeral of Ice : 6648.
Funereal : 2630.
Fungus : 771.
Funk : 1644.
Funny : 5577.
Funny How : 6597.
Furnace : 6621.
Furnished Rooms : 2999.
Further Revelations on the Planet Wokka :
  2586.
Further Triangulations : 2832.
The Fury Which Follows Small
  Disappointments : 1897.
Fusion Recipe : 321.
Future, Ancient, Fugitive: The First Seven
  Pages of an Adventure Novel : 877,
  6142.
The Future Folding into Itself : 1376.
The future weight of words unthought :
  463.
The Future's What We're Really After :
  794.
The Fuzzy Logic Series : 5344.

G T A : 1576.
Gagaku Dream : 1342.
Gagaku: He envies his demons : 5212.
Gagaku: No need to hear the words first :
  5212.
Gagaku: Now my girl in the kitchen hums
  to this gagaku music : 5212.
Gagaku: O I feel good : 5212.
Gagaku: Reading an old gagaku : 5212.
Gagaku: This just this : 5212.
Gagaku: While I boast here of my great
  love and happiness : 5212.
Gaia Spins : 514.
Gala Roses : 6230.
Gale and I in the Gazebo : 2370.
Galena Rose : 788.
Gallery IX: A Carved Bone Ring of
  Cormorants : 6803.
A Gambol and Spring : 6527.
The Game : 514.
Game 5 : 2122.
Game 10 : 2122.
The Gamekeeper : 5277.
The Games : 3479.
Gandhi and Poetry : 5490.
The Gang : 895.
A Gangsta Rap by Robert Dole : 6348.
Garage Meditation : 5865.
A Garden : 5013.

The Garden : 3768.
Garden Bouquet : 1548.
Garden Grove, PCB Burial Grounds : 6530.
Garden in Autumn : 4078, 5239.
Garden in the Field : 1901.
The garden insects : 2496, 3420.
Garden Justice : 385.
The Garden of Blood : 1680.
The Garden of Earthly Delights: Hell :
  2577, 4253.
Garden of Gethsemane : 806.
The Garden of Her Choosing : 1703.
The Garden of Sempervirons : 3997.
The Garden of Stone Cabbages : 6727.
Garden of the Lost : 6901.
Garden Party Invention : 2799.
The Garden Sibyl : 3565.
Garden Spider : 2524.
Garden Verses : 4889.
The Garden Walk : 6221.
Gardener : 2098.
The Gardener : 3856.
The Gardener's Last Instructions : 3975.
A Gardener's Library : 6397.
Gardening at Night : 4296.
Gardens for Carol : 2812.
A Gargoyle Warns a Sculptor in His Loft :
  4787.
Gas. 1940 : 6657.
Gas Giants : 2737.
Gas Stations : 2022.
Gaspé Homestead : 4175.
The Gate of Memory : 2730.
The Gatepost : 234, 2058.
The Gates of the Elect Kingdom : 6817.
Gathering : 461, 5257, 6345.
Gathering Altar Flowers: For Jim Neilson,
  Fall, 1993 : 4346.
Gathering at Nightfall : 2374.
Gathering Incense : 3475, 4628.
A Gathering of Cardiovascular Surgeons :
  6922.
A Gathering Place: 10 : 5712.
Gathering the Dear Sweet Dead : 1091.
Gatsby Quiz : 2483.
Gatuno : 6931.
Gaugin in Alaska : 5697.
Gauguin's New Life : 5716.
Gaviota : 6931.
Gazebo on Spruce Point : 1580.
Gedächtnisfeier : 2621.
Geese : 2051, 3303.
The Geese : 958, 5157.
Geminid Shower : 454.
Gender 101 : 5657.
Gendered Parts : 5907.
Gene tells the story of a boy : 6900.
Genealogia : 983.
Genealogies : 2450.
Genealogy : 983, 5439.
A Genealogy: a Borrowing : 2709.
The General Deals with the Separatists :
  1225.
General Fu's Heavenly Chicken Balls :
  6718.
Generation : 6018.

The Nausea in Shakespeare's *Othello* : 284.
Navajo? : 4316.
Navigation : 4969.
Nd' 'a Gente Ca Rirìte : 4939.
Ne jotka puhuvat, menettävät paljon sanoja
  : 4713.
Ne-m'oubliez-pas : 3271.
Near Avalon : 5604.
Near Drowning, Ihla Comprida, Brazil :
  4048.
Near McCracken's Pond : 514.
Near Mount Robson, Canada : 6575.
Near Phoenix : 992.
Near Silent Rhythm : 5505.
Near St. John's : 3877.
Near Stuart, Florida : 739.
Near the Grave of Amelia Earhart : 2428.
Near Wild Heaven : 5587.
Nearing the End of the Century : 4030.
The Necessary Angel : 2983.
Necessary Magic : 2430.
The Necessity of Feet : 6539.
Neckties : 972.
Nedwina Plough : 5215.
Need : 1953.
Needing 20 Windows and Looking for a
  Break, I Went to the Factory in Rocky
  Mount : 3912.
Needle and Spine : 3998.
Needle Park, Madison, Wisconsin : 1042.
Needle / Plow : 5585.
Needlework : 1788.
Neepawa : 675.
Negation of the Negation : 1026, 4192.
Negative Handprints at Gargas : 2090.
Nehemiah : 4505.
Neiges Fondantes : 2414.
Neighbor : 1917, 2379, 2679, 4091.
The Neighbor Ladies Gather at a Safe
  Distance : 1807.
Neighborhood : 1319, 3229, 6795.
The Neighborhood : 2630, 2958.
The Neighborhood, 1956 : 2257.
Neighborhood Poem : 3613.
Neighbors : 1921.
Nelijalkainen Me : 4145.
Nellie Fox Swings a Bat : 5220.
Nelson Algren's Bartender : 3764.
Nelson's Last Words, or, The Ballad of the
  Pair-Royal : 2074.
The Neo-Transcendentalist : 96.
Neón : 6931.
Neon Tetras : 2146.
Neptune : 1977.
Neptune Avenue : 4589.
Nerve : 2462.
Nerves : 6083, 6524.
Nesle Tower : 515, 3697.
The Nest : 3979.
The Net Prayer : 173.
Netherworlds : 3340.
Nets Thrown into the Sea : 2173.
Nettle : 1947.
Nettles : 1494, 2042.
Network : 3646.
Nevada, 1 : 3410, 4262.

Never Daytime : 5593.
Never Did Nothing Bad : 5121.
Never Make Dreams : 1652.
Never Make Unreasonable Demands :
  3686.
Never Shades of Gray : 339.
Never Strangers : 6478.
Never the Same Waters : 4560, 5640.
Never Too Late to Score : 6627.
Never Underestimate the Power of Soup :
  4146.
New Age Night at the Nuyorican : 691.
New Air : 259.
The New Asceticism : 2421.
New Bamboo : 6866.
New Bank Merger : 6348.
New Brunswick Station : 5178.
The New Dark : 2874.
New Dim : 6656.
New England, Early March : 3237.
New England Spring : 3975.
New Era : 1482, 6181.
A New Eve : 4504.
New Evidence of Love After Death : 4089.
New Hands : 1702.
New Home : 4251.
New Jersey Outdoors : 2707.
A New Metamorphose : 5401.
New Mexican Ridge-nosed Rattlesnake :
  2897.
New Mexico Solstice : 4485.
New Moon : 2222, 3349, 5029.
New Neighbor : 4545.
The New Order : 514.
New Orleans : 4995.
New Paths to Writer's Block (or, My
  Queendom for a Laser Printer) : 1627.
The New Physics : 6533.
New Poem : 3117.
New Preface by Author : 6652.
The New Road : 2487.
New Skin : 287.
New Students, Old Teacher : 1174, 4521.
New Threat : 6348.
New Time : 5504.
New Word Order : 6314.
New World Suite No. 3 : 737.
The New Year : 411, 1894.
New Year Triptych : 5453.
New Year's Eve : 1865.
New Years Eve, 1990 : 4871.
New Year's Fireworks : 669, 4519, 4520.
New York Sketches (P.S. # # in Staten
  Island) : 4771.
New York Sketches (Throgs Neck, Queens)
  : 4771.
New York Spontaneous : 1865.
New York Tenants : 1256.
Newborns : 2085.
The Newly Renovated Opera House on
  Gilligan's Island : 6883.
Newly-Weds at the Fair : 1076.
The News : 4261, 4682.
The News at 3 A.M. : 6859.
News from Home : 2257.
News from Mount Amiata : 2082, 4315.

On Natural Death : 6305.
On newspapers spread on depot platforms : 2948, 4461.
On Not Believing in Astrology : 656.
On Not Bothering to Apply to the Arts Council : 3975.
On Occasion : 1731.
On Opening : 6857.
On Palm Sunday : 2626.
On Passing Fifty : 2576.
On Pete Wilson's Intentions : 6348.
On Pike Street : 3247.
On Reading Bishop's 'The Fish' : 6804.
On Reading 'Days and Nights' by Kenneth Koch : 3954.
On Reading Descartes' Error : 6074.
On Reading of Wendell Willkie's Reception in China : 689, 2726.
On Saint Martinien's Day, July 2, 1993 : 3954.
On Sale This Week : 851.
On Saturday I Receive an Ad from Kmart : 3830.
On Seeing the Disney Version of The Little Mermaid : 379.
On Seeing the Place Where I First Made Love : 1824.
On Sharing Carvel with Aunt Roneta : 25.
On Shooting a Snake in My Front Yard : 1605.
On Skellig Michael : 1452.
On Stopping for Breakfast at the Mar-T Cafe, Great Bend Washington, of *Twin Peaks* Fame : 4900.
On such a day : 1491.
On Sunday Morning : 1980.
On the asphalt rests the bluejay : 2817.
On the banks of the fair Susquehannah : 909.
On the Beach : 1102, 2771.
On the Bias : 3697.
On the Block : 4160.
On the Blue Again : 3831.
On the Border of a Chill : 3915.
On the Brink of Leaving Holiday Town : 1726.
On the Bus : 6721.
On the Candidacy of Lamar Alexander : 6348.
On the Conditions *Presently* Needed : 5204.
On the Corner of Campbell and Kennedy Streets : 2389.
On the Day of Your Death : 2522.
On the Death Mask of Whitman : 6272.
On the Death of a Friend : 4143.
On the Death of Bukowski : 1170.
On the Djurgård Ferry : 234, 2058.
On the Easing Aside of Newt Gingrich as Republican Spokesman on the Budget : 6348.
On the Efforts to Outlaw Sexual Relationships between Students and College Professors : 6612.
On the Empty Shores of a Manmade Lake : 1925.
On the F Line : 6954.

On the Fall of a Tooth : 689, 2726.
On the First Casualty of Whitewater : 6348.
On the first few nights spent in Scotland : 1459.
On the Futility of Resisting the New Paradigm : 514.
On the Highway : 3340, 4521.
On the Home Front, 1917-1918 : 4019.
On the Hottest San Francisco Day in Recorded History He Plays Piano and She Listens : 358.
On the Inside of the Hot House : 259.
On the Inundated First Site of the Town of Greenville : 2586.
On the Island : 1348, 5942.
On the Last Day of This Year : 4710.
On the Nature of International Terrorism : 4294.
On the Playground : 6498.
On the Plaza Before the Basilica of the Virgin of Guadalupe : 3242.
On the Promenade : 4365, 6456.
On the Quay : 97.
On the Rappahannock : 1427.
On the Red Sea : 3946, 6912.
On the Road at Mandalay in Dallas : 5838.
On the Road to Prichard : 6905.
On the Road to Somewhere Else : 5738.
On the Run : 3601.
On the Sacrifice of a Siamese Twin at Birth : 6741.
On the Sagging Porch : 5738.
On the Screened Porch : 3767.
On the Shingle : 1900.
On the Shore : 4990.
On the Sidewalk : 4941.
On the Snow Falls the Burden of Forgiveness : 6406.
On the south side of Malta, where steep cliffs fall into the sea : 1436, 4159.
On the Subject of Boots : 3322.
On the Subway : 686.
On the Teaching of Prescriptive Grammar to a Young Inner City Boy : 2141.
On the temple bell : 2496, 3320.
On the Threshold : 2438, 2582.
On the Threshold of Silence : 4803.
On the train just before the doors open : 1633.
On the Use of Myth as Nostalgia for Universal Truth : 5425.
On the Vatican Steps : 5267.
On the verge of death : 3357.
On the Wards : 1399.
On the Way Home, a Woman : 2449.
On the Way to Southampton Town : 1574.
On the Way to the Meeting about Money at the Welfare Department : 2797.
On the Wheel of : 5380.
On the Withdrawal of Pete Wilson : 6348.
On the Word Reality : 601.
On Three Legs : 335.
On Top of the Empire State : 2214.
On Tuesday : 3585.
On Turning Forty : 5748.
On Two Gallon Men : 1942.

Quick Sell the Pig : 5306.
The Quickening : 1773.
Quiet Can Speak Audibly : 4243.
The Quiet Heart : 3683.
Quiet Potatoes : 259.
Quiet Storm : 984, 6378.
Quieted : 2705.
The Quilt : 3708.
Quilt Song : 2096.
Quilting : 6813.
Quinceañera : 2387.
Quinsy : 3316.
Quite Suddenly : 3352, 3736, 6895.
Quitting Time : 901.
Quod Erat Demonstrandum : 2756.

R A F Manoeuvre : 5393.
R. M. H. : 2555.
R.N., Women's Ward : 3520.
Rabbi qua Mystic : 1045.
Rabbit : 6358.
The Rabbit in the Moon : 5420, 6595.
The Raccoon : 2009.
Races : 1174.
Rachel's Tears : 357, 3235.
Radiation concealed : 2587, 4461.
Radio : 6669.
Radio Adventures, 1949 : 5956.
Radio Man : 4818.
Radio Waves : 4054.
Radiolaria : 6157.
Raeven : 6319.
RAF Manoeuvre : 5393.
Rage : 1570.
Ragga Ragga : 5140.
Raging : 4237.
Ragpickers : 6070.
Rags : 138.
Ragtime : 6956.
The Railroad Roundhouse : 6265.
Rails : 4514.
Rain : 1506, 3410, 4216, 4262, 4276, 4611,
    4770, 5550, 6414, 6432.
The Rain : 3112.
The Rain After Sunrise : 1897.
Rain Falls in Love with a Stream : 4069.
Rain for Nineteen Hours : 726.
The Rain Has No Edges : 6516.
(Rain in the Wind) : 5743.
The rain is falling on the white bones :
    3324, 4461.
The rain is slower at airports : 4870.
Rain of Shoes : 334.
Rain Trembles : 4817.
Raina : 4844.
The Rainbow : 838.
Rainbowy : 3496.
The Rain's Ability to Expose the Dual
    Nature of Existence : 1058.
Rainstorm, Coming Upon the Frogs : 5598.
Rainy-Day Ramble : 5767.
Rainy Night : 3065.
A Rainy Night and I Dream of Her Feet
    Again : 259.

The Rainy Season Arrives in Southern
    Kyushu : 4428.
Rainy Season / Whale Music : 1300.
Raise High the Glass : 11.
Raising Ali : 3662.
Raising the Mast : 4023.
Rajah in Babylon : 6803.
The Rajdhani Express : 6441.
Rake the Half-Hearted Fire : 1081.
Ralph and Alice : 4125.
Ralph Ellison : 3593.
Ralph's Story : 6627.
Ramadan : 4512.
Rambling in the Garden : 3124.
Rambling of the Poet : 906, 1506.
Rampion : 746.
Ramponio : 1865.
Rand McNally Says 378 Miles to the Coast
    : 5145.
The Ransom : 5786.
Raping a Woman : 108.
The Raptors : 1002.
Rapture : 1461.
Rapunzel in Thebes : 6201.
Raritan Valley : 600.
Raspberry : 2222.
Rat : 5180.
Rat Gives You His Free Hand : 664, 1784.
Rather Free, after Brecht : 3131, 3551.
The Rats of Hamelin : 1454.
A Rat's Tale : 4761.
Rattle and Roll : 2983.
Rattler : 4030.
Rattlesnake Glyph : 6154.
Rattletrap : 1548.
Rattus Norvegicus : 3867.
Die Räume : 4653.
Ravenous Flower : 2383.
Raving Sonnet : 4088.
Rawhide : 6206.
Ray : 2586.
Raymond of Penyafort : 3479.
The Razor : 4279, 5897.
Reach : 3603.
Reaching Bottom : 1895.
Reaching for the Sun : 6351.
A Reader's Deductions : 3455.
The Reader's Plaint : 6173.
Readiness : 4826.
The Readiness Is All, or The 1979 Death of
    Eula Love Is Still Unavailable on
    Videotape : 3454.
Reading : 1298, 5875, 6627.
A Reading : 6879.
Reading: A Memoir : 5408.
Reading Aloud to My Father : 3205.
Reading and Writing on the Farm : 5959.
Reading Chora? (A Condensed Duet) : 142.
Reading Cicero's *De Oratore* : 3485.
Reading Don Quixote Once More : 458.
Reading Dr. Nuland's Book : 601.
Reading Dr. Seuss to the Beautiful Children
    of Laurel Gardens : 307.
Reading Entrails : 6581.
Reading Late of the Death of Keats : 3205.
Reading List, 1950-1975 : 3848.

Two Poems of Accidental Pregnancy : 5142.
Two Poems of New York : 6445.
Two Poems with One Epigraph : 34.
Two Ponies : 6816.
Two randy men come to fuck Phyllis : 3906, 3948.
Two River Ledger : 3946.
Two Salutations : 2553.
Two score and more lines drawn to study the epicenter : 4461, 6199.
Two Sisters : 6429.
Two Snails : 6648.
Two Snakes : 2897.
Two Snowflakes : 603.
Two Songs For My Brother : 5164.
Two Stories : 4574, 4721.
The Two Syndrome : 1437.
Two to One : 1831, 6529.
Two Tragedies, with Preface : 1820.
Two Variations on a Theme by Papa, Leopold, Mozart : 1060.
Two Watchers : 5942.
A Two-Way Mirror : 1478.
Two Wills Contend : 3492.
The Two Women : 4666.
Two Women (La Muse) : 1707.
Two Worlds : 2235.
Tying Tin Cans to Tails : 3686.
Types of Life : 3115, 4873, 5730.
Tyttö on niin terve, että kuume : 5760.

U F O : 1501.
U F O Lands Near Beatrice, Nebraska. Dog Killed : 6836.
U. S. Grant in the Adirondacks : 3764.
Über der Tauben : 4653.
Ubliminal : 6633.
The Uele River : 3444.
UFO : 1501.
UFO Lands Near Beatrice, Nebraska. Dog Killed : 6836.
Ugly Ohio : 400.
Ugly, smiling Agnes with eight pearl buttons on her blouse : 4048.
Ukiyo-e : 838.
Ululu (A Page & Peephole Opera) : 1891.
Ulysses : 1500.
Ulysses in the Drug Store : 993.
Umbral de lo Abierto : 4957.
The Umbrella : 6488.
Umbrella Suite : 1794, 6084.
Umbrellas : 1378, 6612.
Umbrian Dreams : 6845.
The Umpire Refutes the Apotheosis of Hype : 630.
Unable to Find the Right Way : 657.
An Unbeaten Path : 367.
The Unbreakable Chain : 845.
The Uncertainty Principle : 3807.
Unchí na Miyé, na Oóyake Ota Kin: Grandma and I, and the Many Stories : 755.
Uncle Boyd : 2433.
Uncle Drunk : 4639.

Uncle Garland : 4024.
Uncle Isidoro : 6099.
Uncle Millet : 1597.
Uncle Patrick and the Doppelgangers : 2096.
Uncle Seagram : 759.
Unclean Poem : 417.
Uncles : 387.
The Unconscious at Play in Dallas : 6893.
Uncut and Crowded with Dandelions : 259.
Under a Spell : 2021, 3386.
Under Cygnus : 2245.
Under Glass in the Tropics of January : 2227.
Under God's Sidelong Shadow : 3920.
Under Stars : 1837.
Under the Apple Tree : 3578.
Under the Arbor : 4826.
Under the Big Top, My Swing Waits : 5759.
Under the City, Under the Sea : 644.
Under the Joshua Tree : 462.
Under the Moon of Texas : 6931.
Under the Perseids : 4759.
Under the Roof of Memory : 1414.
Under the Rug : 1292.
Under the summer sun : 4461, 4588.
Under the Tooth of Their Plow : 2349, 6216.
Under the Vulture Tree : 6716.
Under Treeline : 588.
Underground : 2941.
Underground Song : 1865.
The Underground Tunnel : 5045.
Underneath the Leaf : 664, 2990.
Underneathness : 5142.
Undersized Young Male Azure : 6759.
Understudy : 1971.
The Underworld : 2165.
Undestroyed but beautified, the *Genbaku* Dome : 4461, 6194.
Undoing the Misogynist : 2975.
The Undressing : 6430.
Undressing After a Funeral : 5995.
Undying Loyalty : 3627.
Unearned Chance : 5999.
Unearthed Gratitude : 5471.
The Unemployment Office : 4612.
Unexpected Places : 3912.
Unfashionable Admission : 1884.
Unfinished : 2510.
The Unfinished : 5659.
Unfinished Business : 4226.
Unfinished Canvas : 6427.
Unfinished Mural / Powder Room, Radio City Music Hall : 3707.
The Unfinished Room : 4817.
Unflagging Optimism : 4196.
Unfolded Maps : 6206.
The Unfolding, Coming Out : 4527.
Unfrozen : 1140.
Unglued : 665.
Unholy Sonnet 1 : 2987.
Unholy Sonnet 2 : 2987.
Unholy Sonnets : 2987.
The Uninhabited Angel : 2612.

The Voice of All Things, Singing : 4660.
The Voice of the Grackle : 4936.
Voices : 1092.
The Voices : 344.
Voices in the Dark Say 'Go On, Go On' :
    114.
Voices like Pulleys Rust Unused : 5693.
Voices: Mother and Daughter : 4654.
Voices of Children : 4328.
'The Voices of Neptune' gradually die into a
    distance : 4461.
'The voices of Neptune' gradually die into a
    distance : 6360.
Vol. XLIV, No. 3 : 4160.
Voladores : 2679.
The Volcano : 4168.
The Vole : 4382.
Volleyball : 6541.
The Volunteer : 2563.
Volunteer for Experiment : 3285.
Vortex of Indian Fevers : 3718.
Vow of Stability : 3655.
Vows : 6090.
Vox et Praeterea Nihil : 955.
Voy a Decirte Adiós : 4858.
Voyage : 2963, 6861.
Voyager : 2102.
Voyeur : 4319.
La Voz de los 80 : 920.
Vulnerable Bundles : 752.
Vultures at Kellogg Bay : 2985.
Vuorimiehenkatu. Helsinki : 2520, 2923.

W 50 : 4870.
W29 : 4870.
Waco : 2815.
The Wading Pool : 5763.
Wait : 5329.
Waiter, I Would Like a Dish of Feebly :
    4068.
Waiting : 2257, 2543.
The Waiting : 2185.
Waiting, and Things : 5155.
Waiting at the Beach : 5959.
The Waiting Ceremony : 228.
The Waiting Deputies : 3997.
Waiting for Angels : 864.
Waiting for Dark : 2597.
Waiting for Fever to Pass : 268.
Waiting for Marty : 6627.
Waiting for My Father : 5845.
Waiting for Persephone : 3578.
Waiting for Seven Birds to Fly in from
    Utica : 5006.
Waiting for the Boat : 2370.
Waiting for the Cyclamen to Bloom : 6421.
Waiting for the Woodsman : 2873.
Waiting for Winter in La Sardina Loca :
    3975.
Waiting on a Desperate Check : 3065.
Waiting on No Man : 5685.
The Waiting Room : 716.
Waiting Table : 1757.
Waitress : 6627.
The Waitress : 895, 4702.

The Wake : 2115, 6113.
Waked to Listen : 93.
The Wakeful : 753.
Waking : 2868.
The Waking : 5296.
Waking Among the Tibetans in McLeod
    Ganj : 60.
Waking on the Farm : 601.
Waking to a Stranger : 6342.
Waking Up : 3076.
Waking Up on a Sheep Island : 945.
The Walk : 2741, 3304.
Walk a Mile in My Shoes : 2026.
A Walk at First Light : 1104.
The Walk for Hunger : 2370.
Walk in Beauty : 1364.
Walkers in the Mall : 6357.
Walking Along Slate Creek Road,
    Wilderville, Oregon, 1991 : 299.
Walking Around the Block with a Three-
    Year-Old : 6513.
Walking Beans : 3277.
Walking Down Franklin Street : 1917.
Walking Down This Mountain : 6566.
A Walking Gentleman : 6732.
Walking Home : 5923.
Walking Home from a Bar Late at Night
    with an Old Friend, Feeling Our Age :
    629.
Walking Home in Igloolik : 2160.
Walking Mantra : 6627.
Walking on Fire : 5063.
Walking on the Beach : 3695.
Walking Song : 99.
Walking Stick : 4909.
Walking Through October : 194.
Walking to the Car : 1523.
Walking to Treatment : 5148.
The Walking Tour: Alexander Wilson in
    America : 3957.
Walking Toward Round Butte : 6339.
Walking with a Panther : 4369.
Walking with Margaret : 1940.
Walks : 6297.
The Walkways : 228.
Wall : 3590, 6627.
The Wall : 2980, 4594, 6529, 6905.
The Wall of a Museum : 2577, 4253.
Wallace P. Hipslit, Age Nine, Footloose
    and Fancy Free, Standing on a Swing,
    About to Break His Leg : 3698.
Wallet : 1988.
The Wallop : 4256.
Wallowa Llamas : 6423.
Wallpaper : 117.
Walls & Flowers : 6860.
La Wally : 5860.
Walt Disney World : 2572.
Walt Whitman Falls Asleep Over Florence
    Nightingale's *Notes on Nursing* :
    1334.
Walt Whitman, I Hear You Saying : 1329.
Walter Benjamin Leaves Paris (1940) :
    4738, 5988.
Walter Benjamin Se Va de París (1940) :
    4738.

About the Authors

RAFAEL CATALA (B.A., M.A., Ph.D., New York University) is president of The Ometeca Institute and editor-in-chief of *The Ometeca Journal*, both dedicated to the study and encouragement of relations between the sciences and the humanities. He was born in Las Tunas, Cuba, in 1942 and came to the United States in 1961. His books of poetry and literary criticism, as well as many essays and poems, have been published in the United States, Canada, Latin America, and Europe. He has taught Latin American Literature at NYU, Lafayette College, and Seton Hall University. In 1993-94 he was visiting professor at the University of Costa Rica. In 1995 and 1996 he held the Gates-Ferry Distinguished Lecturer Chair at Centenary College, where he led seminars on the creative process. Catalá is a major proponent and practitioner of *cienciapoesía* (sciencepoetry), an embodiment of the integration of aesthetics, ethics, and the sciences. A new book of critical essays about Catalá's poetry and literary work was published in 1994: *Rafael Catalá: del Círculo cuadrado a la cienciapoesía — Hacia una nueva poética latinoamericana* (Ed. by Luis A. Jiménez. Kent, WA: Ventura One). In 1997, Acropolis Press is publishing Catalá's *The Mysticism of Now*.

JAMES D. ANDERSON (B.A., Harvard College, M.S.L.S., D.L.S., Columbia University) is associate dean and professor of the School of Communication, Information, and Library Studies, at Rutgers the State University of New Jersey. His library career has included service at Sheldon Jackson College, Sitka, Alaska, and the Portland (Oregon) Public Library. He taught at Columbia, St. John's, and the City University of New York before coming to Rutgers in 1977, where he specializes in the design of textual databases for information retrieval. Major projects have included the international bibliography and database of the Modern Language Association of America and the bilingual (French and English) *Bibliography of the History of Art*, sponsored by the J. Paul Getty Trust and the French Centre National de la Recherche Scientifique in Paris. At Rutgers he also chairs the President's Select Committee for Lesbian and Gay Concerns, and for the Presbyterian Church (U.S.A.), he edits and publishes the monthly journal *More Light Update*, on lesbian and gay issues within that denomination.